All the writing resources you need . . . in P9-DHS-852 online

The Bedford Guide gives you all the tools you need to become a better writer. Complementing the text is a Web site, at **<bedfordstmartins.com/bedguide>**, that gives you help with every stage of the writing process and more.

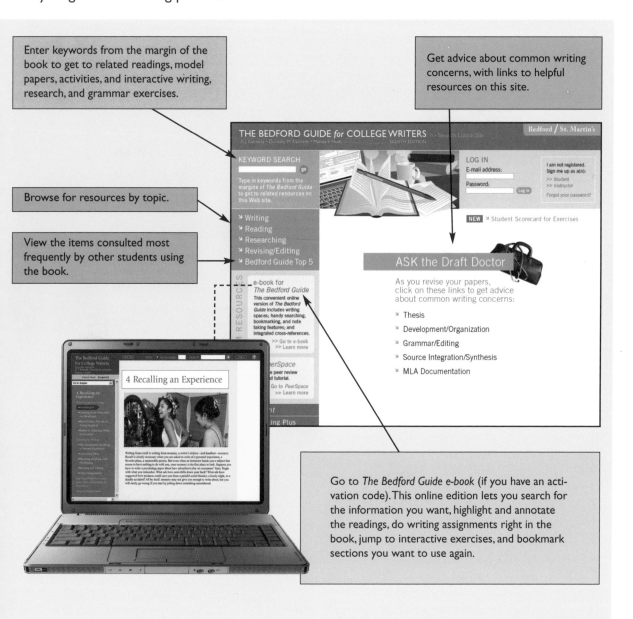

Enter keywords from the margin of the book to get to related readings, model papers, activities, and interactive writing, research, and grammar exercises.

Get advice about common writing concerns, with links to helpful resources on this site.

Browse for resources by topic.

View the items consulted most frequently by other students using the book.

Go to *The Bedford Guide* e-book (if you have an activation code). This online edition lets you search for the information you want, highlight and annotate the readings, do writing assignments right in the book, jump to interactive exercises, and bookmark sections you want to use again.

THE
BEDFORD
GUIDE
for COLLEGE WRITERS

X. J. KENNEDY ◆ DOROTHY M. KENNEDY

MARCIA F. MUTH

THE BEDFORD GUIDE
for COLLEGE WRITERS

EIGHTH EDITION

with Reader, Research Manual, and Handbook

BEDFORD / ST. MARTIN'S   Boston ◆ New York

FOR BEDFORD/ST. MARTIN'S

Developmental Editors: Beth Castrodale, Christina Gerogiannis
Senior Production Editor: Deborah Baker
Senior Production Supervisor: Joe Ford
Senior Marketing Manager: Karita dos Santos
Editorial Assistant: Stephanie Naudin
Copyeditor: Mary Lou Wilshaw-Watts
Text Design: Claire Seng-Niemoeller
Cover Design and Art: Hannus Design Associates
Composition: Monotype, LLC
Printing and Binding: R.R. Donnelley & Sons Company

President: Joan E. Feinberg
Editorial Director: Denise B. Wydra
Editor in Chief: Karen S. Henry
Director of Marketing: Karen Melton Soeltz
Director of Editing, Design, and Production: Marcia Cohen
Managing Editor: Elizabeth M. Schaaf

Library of Congress Control Number: 2007927473

Manufactured in the United States of America.

5   4   3   2   1   0
f   e   d   c   b   a

For information, write: Bedford/St. Martin's, 75 Arlington Street, Boston, MA 02116
(617-399-4000)

ISBN-10: 0-312-45279-9   ISBN-13: 978-0-312-45279-7 (Instructor's Annotated Edition)
ISBN-10: 0-312-66772-8   ISBN-13: 978-0-312-66772-6 (hardcover Student Edition)
ISBN-10: 0-312-45278-0   ISBN-13: 978-0-312-45278-0 (paperback Student Edition)

ACKNOWLEDGMENTS

Michael Abernethy, "Male Bashing on TV." First published on *PopMatters.com*, January 9, 2003. Copyright © 2003 by PopMatters.com. Reprinted with permission of PopMatters Media, Inc.

Russell Baker, "The Art of Eating Spaghetti" from pp. 186–89 of *Growing Up* by Russell Baker. Copyright © 1982 by Russell Baker. Published by Congdon and Weed/Contemporary Publishing. Reprinted by permission of Don Congdon Associates, Inc.

John Barbieri, "Save Hydrogen for Later; Ethanol Power is the Viable Option for Now" from the *Amherst Student*, April 19, 2006. Copyright © 2006. Reprinted with the permission of the *Amherst Student*.

Dave Barry, "From Now On, Let Women Kill Their Own Spiders." First published in the *Miami Herald*, February 12, 1999. Copyright © 1999 by Dave Barry. Reprinted with the permission of the author.

Sam Benen, "A Royal Mess: How Online Poker Has Enraptured Today's College Student" from *Business Today Online Journal*, November 13, 2006. Reprinted with the permission of the Federation for Student Communication.

Limm Bourgeau, from "Crucial Choices: Who Will Save the Wetlands if Everyone is at the Mall?" Reprinted with the permission of the author.

Judy Brady, "I Want a Wife." First published in *Ms.* Magazine, December 1971. Copyright © 1970 by Judy Brady. Reprinted with the permission of the author.

Suzanne Britt, "Neat People vs. Sloppy People" from *Show and Tell* (Raleigh, North Carolina: Morning Owl Press, 1982). Copyright © 1982 by Suzanne Britt. Reprinted with the permission of the author.

Acknowledgments and copyrights are continued at the back of the book on pages A-67–70, which constitute an extension of the copyright page. It is a violation of the law to reproduce these selections by any means whatsoever without the written permission of the copyright holder.

Preface: To the Instructor

When it was first published twenty years ago, *The Bedford Guide for College Writers* brought a lively and innovative approach to the teaching of writing. Since that time, authors X. J. and Dorothy M. Kennedy have won praise for their friendly, engaging writing style and their remarkable sense of what students need to know to succeed in the composition course. More recently, experienced teacher and writer Marcia F. Muth joined the author team, adding more practical advice to help all students, even those underprepared for college, become successful academic writers. The result is an unusually thorough and accessible book that continues to evolve to meet the needs of both students and instructors.

With its process-oriented rhetoric, provocative thematic reader, up-to-date research manual, and comprehensive handbook, *The Bedford Guide* gives students all the tools they need to succeed as writers. And now this new edition does even more to build essential academic writing skills, with expanded coverage of source-based writing, audience analysis, argumentation and reasoning, and more. Additionally, an expanded array of innovative student and instructor resources ensures that you and your students are supported every step of the way.

Everything You Need

The eighth edition of *The Bedford Guide for College Writers* continues to offer four coordinated composition books integrated into one convenient text — all of them now even better resources for students. *The Bedford Guide* is available in two other versions as well: as three books in one, without a handbook, and as two books in one, comprising a rhetoric and a reader. An e-book version is also available. (For more details on the e-book and other exciting new resources accompanying *The Bedford Guide*, see pp. xi–xiv.)

BOOK ONE: *A Writer's Guide*

This uniquely accessible — yet thorough — process-oriented rhetoric with readings helps students become better writers, regardless of their skill level. Addressing all the assignments and topics typically covered in the first-year writing course, it is divided into four parts.

Part One, "A College Writer's Processes," introduces students to the interconnected processes of writing (Chapter 1), reading (Chapter 2), and critical thinking (Chapter 3). In Chapter 3, coverage of logic and reasoning, expanded in this edition, helps students become better thinkers and writers.

In Part Two, "A Writer's Situations," nine core chapters—each including two sample readings (one by a student)—guide students step-by-step through a full range of common first-year writing assignments. If followed sequentially, these chapters lead students gradually into the rigorous analytical writing that will comprise most of their college writing. The rhetorical situations in Part Two include recalling an experience (Chapter 4), observing a scene (Chapter 5), interviewing a subject (Chapter 6), comparing and contrasting (Chapter 7), explaining causes and effects (Chapter 8), taking a stand (Chapter 9), proposing a solution (Chapter 10), evaluating (Chapter 11), and supporting a position with sources (Chapter 12). Chapter 12, new to this edition, helps students write position papers that draw on a few sources—an increasingly common academic writing assignment.

Part Three, "Special Writing Situations," offers helpful strategies and plenty of examples to support students' efforts in three additional situations: responding to literature (Chapter 13), writing in the workplace (Chapter 14), and writing for assessment (Chapter 15).

Part Four, "A Writer's Strategies," is a convenient resource for approaching all aspects of writing, and each chapter in this part has been updated with new examples. The first five chapters explain and illustrate the stages of the writing process: generating ideas (Chapter 16), stating a thesis and planning (Chapter 17), drafting (Chapter 18), developing (Chapter 19), and revising and editing (Chapter 20). Marginal annotations in the earlier parts of the book guide students to these chapters, which collectively serve as a writer's toolbox. Part Four also includes two chapters on using and analyzing visuals: "Strategies for Designing Your Document" (Chapter 21) and "Strategies for Understanding Visual Representations" (Chapter 22). Both chapters, which are the basis of the popular Bedford/St. Martin's supplement *Getting the Picture*, have been updated to include even more visuals.

BOOK TWO: *A Writer's Reader*

A Writer's Reader is a thematic reader, unique in a book of this kind. The reader offers 32 selections—19 of them new—arranged around five engaging themes that provide a meaningful context for students, giving them something to write about. The themes are families (Chapter 23), men and women (Chapter 24), popular culture (Chapter 25), electronic technology (Chapter 26), and education (Chapter 27). Electronic technology, a new chapter, was added in response to reviewer requests, and it explores possibilities and implications from online learning communities to free speech and privacy issues in the age of MySpace. Each reading is accompanied by apparatus that moves students smoothly from reading and thinking to writing. The selections are coordinated with *A Writer's Guide* and serve as models of the writing situations assigned there; a rhetorical table of contents (p. xl) helps students see these connections.

Each reading is introduced by a biographical headnote and a brief reading tip. Each is followed by questions on meaning, writing strategies, critical reading, vocabulary, and connections to other selections; journal prompts;

and suggested writing assignments, one personal and the other analytical. These questions move students from reading carefully for both thematic and rhetorical elements to applying new strategies and insights in their own writing.

BOOK THREE: *A Writer's Research Manual*

A Writer's Research Manual is a remarkably comprehensive guide to source-based writing, detailing all the essential steps for print, electronic, and field research. It covers planning and managing a research project (Chapter 28), working with sources (Chapter 29), finding sources (Chapter 30), evaluating sources (Chapter 31), integrating sources (Chapter 32), writing the research paper (Chapter 33), and documenting sources (Chapter 34). The chapter on working with sources is a new addition that focuses on the details of accurately drawing and recording information from sources. It offers detailed guidance on quoting, paraphrasing, and summarizing and on preparing a working bibliography (annotated and otherwise). Chapter 34 includes the most extensive coverage of MLA and APA documentation available in a book of this kind, with 82 MLA documentation models and 64 APA models — 25 percent more than in the previous edition. Additionally, the chapter includes a new MLA research paper and new selections from an APA paper.

All versions of the book also include a Quick Research Guide, which conveniently — and briefly — reviews how to find, evaluate, integrate, cite, and document sources.

BOOK FOUR: *A Writer's Handbook*

The most complete handbook of its kind, with superior ESL coverage (in ESL Guidelines), this useful reference includes clear explanations of grammar, style, and usage topics. It also includes nearly fifty exercise sets for practice in and out of class. Answers to half of the questions in each set are provided in the back of the book so that students can check their understanding. Additionally, frequent cross-references in the handbook refer students to additional practices on *Exercise Central*, the largest bank of online grammar exercises. These practices, written specifically for *The Bedford Guide*, include new ESL exercises to accompany all the ESL Guidelines in the book. Beyond the coverage in the handbook, a Quick Editing Guide — available with all versions of *The Bedford Guide* — gives special attention to the most troublesome grammar and editing problems.

New to the Eighth Edition

The revisions in this new edition reflect trends in composition courses and incorporate the suggestions of a host of reviewers. The changes have resulted in an even more practical book that helps students become better academic writers.

EXPANDED COVERAGE OF USING SOURCES

Reviewers have told us that, given the proliferation of sources (especially electronic ones, from which students can easily cut and paste), students need more help with incorporating sources effectively and ethically. Reviewers have also pointed out that while full research papers remain important components of the composition class, students increasingly are being asked to write papers that use a few sources, especially to support a position. We've responded to these trends with innovative new features.

A New Chapter on Position Papers (Chapter 12).   This chapter, focusing on position papers that draw on a few sources, shows students how to marshal evidence to support a stance while maintaining their own strong voice—a common academic writing challenge. It also shows, through text and graphics, how to cite and document this material fairly.

Information Captured from Your Source

Sample Working Thesis

A clear thesis statement establishes a framework for selecting source material as useful evidence and for explaining its relevance to readers.

> WORKING THESIS: In order to counter national and worldwide trends toward obesity, agricultural communities like Grand Junction need to apply their expertise as food producers to the promotion of healthy food products.

Quotation from an Indirect Source

A quotation from an indirect source captures the exact words of an author quoted within the source.

> An 1894 action by Congress created a holiday to recognize workers who "delved and carved" to produce what Americans enjoy (qtd. in Saletan).

If possible, go to the original source to be sure that the quotation is accurate and that you are using it appropriately. (See the bottom lefthand page.)

> Credit, though disputed, has gone to labor leader Peter McGuire for promoting the recognition of those who "delved and carved all the grandeur we behold" (US Dept. of Labor).

A New Chapter on Working with Sources (Chapter 29).   This chapter offers more-detailed advice on handling and documenting source material, with plenty of examples. It also features new **Source Navigators** (see p. ix), annotated facsimiles of original sources that show students where to find information needed to cite these sources in their notes and in their papers, following either MLA or APA style. Additionally, the chapter provides new coverage of annotated bibliographies.

A Practical Reorganization of MLA and APA Documentation.   The eighth edition arranges MLA and APA examples—print and electronic—under intuitive questions about author and genre that students can answer: *Who wrote it?* and *What type of source is it?* With its accessible language, this coverage serves as a bridge between how students think about sources and what they need to understand in order to document sources completely and correctly.

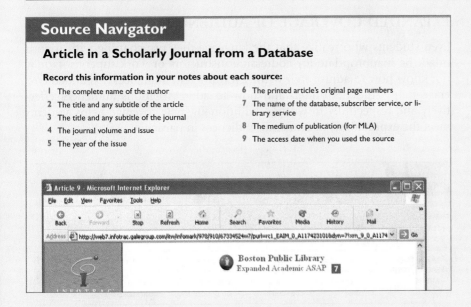

Source Navigator

Article in a Scholarly Journal from a Database

Record this information in your notes about each source:

1 The complete name of the author

2 The title and any subtitle of the article

3 The title and any subtitle of the journal

4 The journal volume and issue

5 The year of the issue

6 The printed article's original page numbers

7 The name of the database, subscriber service, or library service

8 The medium of publication (for MLA)

9 The access date when you used the source

UNIQUE SELF-ASSESSMENT CHARTS — DRAFT DOCTORS

These innovative charts are designed to make students stronger writers, regardless of their skill level. Specifically, the charts help students reflect on their own writing, identify its weaknesses, and then use relevant strategies for strengthening their papers. Draft Doctors address such important issues as supporting a stand, integrating sources, and strengthening thesis statements.

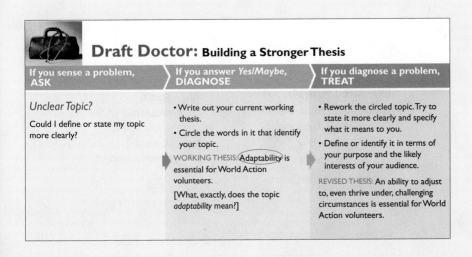

Draft Doctor: Building a Stronger Thesis

If you sense a problem, ASK	If you answer *Yes/Maybe,* DIAGNOSE	If you diagnose a problem, TREAT
Unclear Topic? Could I define or state my topic more clearly?	• Write out your current working thesis. • Circle the words in it that identify your topic. WORKING THESIS: (Adaptability) is essential for World Action volunteers. [What, exactly, does the topic *adaptability* mean?]	• Rework the circled topic. Try to state it more clearly and specify what it means to you. • Define or identify it in terms of your purpose and the likely interests of your audience. REVISED THESIS: An ability to adjust to, even thrive under, challenging circumstances is essential for World Action volunteers.

EXPANDED COVERAGE OF AUDIENCE

Even students who realize that the language they use chatting with friends might be inappropriate for addressing instructors or work supervisors may not know how to adjust their writing for different audiences. Expanded coverage helps students understand how to address various audiences effectively and respectfully in writing. Additionally, new coverage helps students meet the expectations of academic audiences in particular.

Audience Characteristics and Expectations	GENERAL AUDIENCE	COLLEGE INSTRUCTOR	WORK SUPERVISOR	CAMPUS FRIEND	PARENT OR GRANDPARENT
READER'S RELATIONSHIP TO YOU	Imagined but not known personally	Known briefly in a class context	Known for some time in a job context	Known in campus and social contexts	Known all of your life in family contexts
REASON FOR READING YOUR WRITING	Curious attitude and interest in your topic assumed	Professional responsibility for your knowledge and skills	Managerial interest in and reliance on your job performance	Personal interest based on shared circumstances	Family bond and lifelong concern about you
KNOWLEDGE ABOUT TOPIC	Level of awareness assumed and gaps addressed with logical presentation	Well informed about college topics but wants to see what you know	Informed about the business and expects reliable information from you	Friendly but may or may not be informed beyond social interests	Loving but may or may not be informed beyond family concerns

IMPROVED COVERAGE OF CRITICAL THINKING, REASONING, AND ARGUMENT

Chapter 3 ("Critical Thinking Processes") now provides advice on applying critical thinking to academic problems through analysis, synthesis, and evaluation. It also offers new coverage of inductive versus deductive reasoning

DEDUCTIVE PATTERN

FIRST: Broad generalization or conclusion. THEN: Details, examples, facts and supporting particulars

FIRST: Particulars, details, examples, facts all leading up to a generalization

INDUCTIVE PATTERN

and of sound versus weak reasoning. And Chapter 9 ("Taking a Stand") provides more support for making logical arguments, with new coverage of the Toulmin method, clearer advice on supporting claims effectively, and more.

AN IMPROVED SUITE OF ELECTRONIC RESOURCES

Never before have *Bedford Guide* users had access to a more extensive and innovative array of electronic resources, helping students with everything from planning and drafting to revising based on the comments of peers.

A Redesigned and Expanded Companion Web Site.   The companion Web site (at <bedfordstmartins.com/bedguide>) has a cleaner, less cluttered look while offering multiple routes of access to important information (by topic or keyword search). The site includes the following features:

- Interactive writing, research, and grammar practices, with new ESL exercises
- Readings and model papers
- New "Ask the Draft Doctor" feature: Students pick a writing concern they have and then get suggestions for improving their papers, as well as links to related resources on the Web site.
- New links for authors featured in *The Bedford Guide*
- Research and documentation advice
- New peer review worksheets
- Classroom activities, syllabi, and other instructor tools, including new PowerPoint presentations on writing, research, and grammar

Premium Web content (including an e-book and peer review resources) is also available. These resources are described in the following sections.

A New E-Book. The e-book offers the complete text of the print book, with state-of-the-art tools and multimedia from the book's Web site built in. Students can highlight and annotate the readings, respond to writing prompts directly in the book, jump to interactive exercises, and bookmark sections to be used for reference. Instructors can add their own materials — models, notes, assignments, course guidelines — and even reorganize chapters.

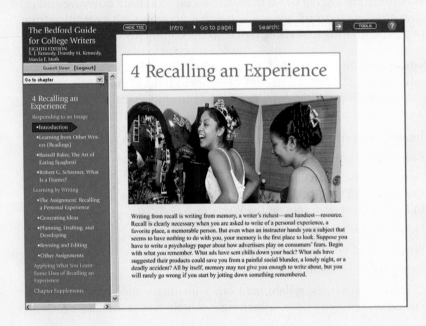

A New Peer Review Resource: *PeerSpace*. *PeerSpace* is a collection of confidence-building activities that teach best practices for peer review. Resources include an interactive simulation game, models, exercises, and assignments. When students are ready to put what they've learned into practice, there's *Comment* (see below), which is integrated into *PeerSpace*.

Other Electronic Resources

Comment for THE BEDFORD GUIDE FOR COLLEGE WRITERS (<comment.bedfordstmartins.com>). This Web-based peer-review software lets students share and comment on their writing. Instructors can create comments that link directly to specific passages in *The Bedford Guide e-Book*. Students who need more peer review help will find it in *PeerSpace*, integrated into *Comment*.

Re: Writing (at <bedfordstmartins.com/rewriting>). This free and open Web site collects Bedford/St. Martin's most popular and widely used online resources at a single address. It includes *Exercise Central* (more than 7,000 interactive online exercises), research and documentation advice, model documents, a tutorial on avoiding plagiarism, instructor resources, and more.

An Innovative New Online Course Space: *CompClass.*   This easy-to-use online course space integrates all the innovative media supporting *The Bedford Guide* — the e-book, *Comment*, the book companion site, and more — with course tools designed specifically for the reading, writing, practice, and discussion that writing instructors and students do. *CompClass* also lets you add spaces designed for writing — blogs, journals, and discussion forums — and mix in your own course materials, customizing the site so that it reflects the way you teach. *CompClass* is *your* composition course space — whether you teach online, face-to-face, or a little of each.

Exercise Central to Go.   This CD-ROM offers hundreds of practice items to improve students' writing and editing skills. Drawn from the popular *Exercise Central* Web site, the exercises cover a wide variety of topics, from identifying effective main points and support to integrating and documenting sources to fixing grammar errors. No Internet connection is necessary.

Testing Tool Kit: A Writing and Grammar Test Bank.   This CD-ROM allows instructors to create secure, customized tests and quizzes to assess students' writing and grammar competency and gauge their progress during the course. The CD includes nearly 2,000 test items on 47 writing and grammar topics, at two levels of difficulty. Also, ten pre-built diagnostic tests are included. Scoring is instantaneous when tests and quizzes are administered online.

Print Resources

Instructor's Annotated Edition of *The Bedford Guide for College Writers* puts information right where busy instructors need it: on the pages of the book itself. The marginal annotations offer teaching tips, analysis tips with readings, last-minute in-class activities, vocabulary glosses, additional assignments, and cross-references to other ancillaries.

Practical Suggestions for Teaching with *The Bedford Guide for College Writers*, by Dana Waters of Dodge City Community College, Shirley Morahan, and Sylvia A. Holladay, helps instructors plan and teach their composition course. This text includes practical advice on designing an effective course, sample syllabi, chapter-by-chapter support, and suggestions for using the electronic media package.

Teaching Composition: Background Readings, Third Edition, edited by T. R. Johnson of Tulane University, addresses the concerns of both first-year and veteran writing instructors. This collection includes thirty professional readings on composition and rhetoric written by leaders in the field. The selections are accompanied by helpful introductions, activities, and practical insights for inside and outside the classroom. The new edition offers up-to-date advice on avoiding plagiarism, classroom blogging, improving online instruction, and more.

Study Skills for College Writers, by Laurie Walker of Eastern Michigan University, is a handy booklet full of activities designed to help underprepared students improve their study skills. It offers many practical tips and strategies for managing time, taking notes, taking tests, and accessing college resources.

Ordering Information

To order any of the ancillaries, please contact your Bedford/St. Martin's sales representative, e-mail sales support at sales_support@bfwpub.com, or visit our Web site at <bedfordstmartins.com>. Note that activation codes are required for the e-book, *PeerSpace, Comment,* and *CompClass.* Codes can be purchased separately or packaged with the print book at a significant discount.

When ordering an access card for premium Web site content (the e-book and *PeerSpace*) packaged with the book, use these ISBNs:

- with Reader, Research Manual, and Handbook (hardcover):
  ISBN-13: 978-0-312-47756-1; ISBN-10: 0-312-47756-2
- with Reader, Research Manual, and Handbook (paperback):
  ISBN-13: 978-0-312-47759-2; ISBN-10: 0-312-47759-7
- with Reader and Research Manual (paperback only):
  ISBN-13: 978-0-312-47753-0; ISBN-10: 0-312-47753-8
- with Reader (paperback only): ISBN-13: 978-0-312-47744-8;
  ISBN-10: 0-312-47744-9

When ordering an access card for *Comment* packaged with the book, use these ISBNs:

- with Reader, Research Manual, and Handbook (hardcover):
  ISBN-13: 978-0-312-47755-4; ISBN-10: 0-312-47755-4
- with Reader, Research Manual, and Handbook (paperback):
  ISBN-13: 978-0-312-47758-5; ISBN-10: 0-312-47758-9
- with Reader and Research Manual (paperback only):
  ISBN-13: 978-0-312-47752-3; ISBN-10: 0-312-47752-X
- with Reader (paperback only): ISBN-13: 978-0-312-47743-1;
  ISBN-10: 0-312-47743-0

When ordering an access card for *CompClass* packaged with the book, use these ISBNs:

- with Reader, Research Manual, and Handbook (hardcover):
  ISBN-13: 978-0-312-47754-7; ISBN-10: 0-312-47754-6
- with Reader, Research Manual, and Handbook (paperback):
  ISBN-13: 978-0-312-47757-8; ISBN-10: 0-312-47757-0
- with Reader and Research Manual (paperback only):
  ISBN-13: 978-0-312-47751-6; ISBN-10: 0-312-47751-1
- with Reader (paperback only): ISBN-13: 978-0-312-47742-4;
  ISBN-10: 0-312-47742-2

When ordering *Study Skills for College Writers* packaged with your students' books, use these ISBNs:

- with Reader, Research Manual, and Handbook (hardcover):
  ISBN-13: 978-0-312-47696-0; ISBN-10: 0-312-47696-5

(continued)

Ordering Information (continued)

- with Reader, Research Manual, and Handbook (paperback): ISBN-13: 978-0-312-47691-5; ISBN-10: 0-312-47691-4
- with Reader and Research Manual (paperback only): ISBN-13: 978-0-312-47686-1; ISBN-10: 0-312-47686-8
- with Reader (paperback only): ISBN-13: 978-0-312-47680-9; ISBN-10: 0-312-47680-9

Thanks and Appreciation

Many individuals contributed significantly to the eighth edition of *The Bedford Guide for College Writers*, and we extend our sincerest thanks to all of them.

EDITORIAL ADVISORY BOARD

As we began to prepare the eighth edition, we assembled an Editorial Advisory Board to respond to the many significant changes we planned and to share ideas about how to make the book more useful to both students and teachers. These dedicated instructors responded thoroughly and insightfully to just about every new feature of the text, and we are extremely grateful to each and every one of them:

- Kathleen Beauchene, Community College of Rhode Island
- Jan Bone, Roosevelt University and Harper College
- Rita Buscher-Weeks, Spartanburg Technical College
- Helen Duclos, Arkansas State University
- Julie Freeman, Indiana University–Purdue University Indianapolis
- Leigh A. Martin, Community College of Rhode Island
- Terry Novak, Johnson & Wales University
- Brit Osgood-Treston, Riverside Community College
- Mark Reynolds, Jefferson Davis Community College
- Patrick Smith, Axia College of University of Phoenix
- Dana Waters, Dodge City Community College

OTHER COLLEAGUES

We also extend our gratitude to instructors across the country who took time and care to review this and previous editions, to participate in a focus group, and to send us their suggestions gleaned from experience with students. For this we thank Alice B. Adams, Prestonsburg Community College; Rosemary R. Adams, Eastern Connecticut State University; Ted Allder, University of Arkansas Community College at Batesville; Patricia Allen, Cape Cod Community College; Steve Amidon, University of Rhode Island; David Auchter, San Jacinto Junior College; Renee Bangerter, Fullerton College; Stuart Barbier, Delta College; Marci Bartolotta, Nova Southeastern University; Barry Batorsky, DeVry University; Shannon Beasley, Arkansas State University; Randolph A. Beckham, Germanna Community College; Pamela J. Behrens, Alabama A&M University; Carmine J. Bell, Pasco Hernando Community College; Kay Berg, Sinclair Community College; Tanya Boler, East Central Community College; Jeannie Boniecki, Naugatuck Valley Community College; Debbie Boyd, East Central Community College; Barbara Brown, San Jacinto College Central; Ty Buckman, Wittenberg University; Joan Campbell, Wellesley College; Tom Casey, El Paso Community College; Steve Cirrone, Tidewater Community College; Susan Romayne Clark, Central Michigan University; Ted Contreras, Long Beach City College; Nancy Cook, Sierra College; Jane Corbly, George Peabody College for Teachers; Monica Cox, Community College of Rhode Island; Carolyn Craft, Longwood College; Sheilah Craft, Marian College; Mary Cullen, Middlesex Community College; P. R. Dansby, San Jacinto Community College; Fred D'Astoli, Ventura College; Ed Davis, Sinclair Community College; Patricia Ann Delamar, University of Dayton; Irene Duprey-Gutierrez, University of Massachusetts, Dartmouth; Corinna Evett, Fullerton and Santa Ana Colleges; Carol Luers Eyman, St. Joseph School of Practical Nursing; Leora Freedman, Modesto Junior College; Sandy Fuhr, Gustavus Adolphus College; Jan Fulwiler, Lethbridge Community College; Pamela Garvey, St. Louis Community College–Meramec; Mary Ann Gauthier, St. Joseph College; Michael Gavin, Prince George's Community College; Olga Geissler, San Joaquin Delta College; Robert Gmerlin, Sierra College; Aaron Goldweber, Heald College; Daniel Gonzales, Louisiana State University; Sherry F. Gott, Danville Community College; Daniel V. Gribbin, University of Central Florida; Robert Grindy, Richland Community College; Joyce Hall, Border Institute of Technology; Jefferson Hancock, San Jose State University; Alyssa Harad, University of Texas at Austin; Johnnie Hargrove, Alabama A&M University; Judy Hatcher, San Jacinto College Central; Elaine Hays, University of Rhode Island; Diana Hicks, American River College; Marita Hinton, Alabama A&M University; Tom Hodges, Amarillo College; Jane Holwerda, Dodge City Community College; Patricia Hunt, Catonsville Community College; Elizabeth Jarok, Middlesex Community College; Barbara Jensen, Modesto Junior College; Greg Jewell, Madisonville Community College; Jean L. Johnson, University of North Alabama; Ted Johnston, El Paso Community College; Andrew Jones, University of California at Davis; Anne D. Jordan, Eastern Connecticut State University; M. L. Kayser, Heald College; Cynthia Kellogg, Yuba College; Dimitri Keriotis, Modesto Junior College; Kate Kiefer, Colorado State University; Yoon Sik Kim, Langston University; Kaye Kolkmann, Modesto Junior College; Fred A. Koslowski III, Delaware Valley College;

Brandy Kreisler, Axia College of University of Phoenix; Sandra Lakey, Pennsylvania College of Technology; Norman Lanquist, Eastern Arizona College; Colleen Lloyd, Cuyahoga Community College; Stephen Ma, University of Alberta; Susan Peck MacDonald, California State University at Long Beach; Jennifer Madej, Milwaukee Area Technical College; Janice Mandile, Front Range Community College; Phil Martin, Minneapolis Community and Technical College; Gerald McCarthy, San Antonio College; Miles S. McCrimmon, J. Sargeant Reynolds Community College; Jackie McGrath, College of DuPage; Jenna Merritt, Eastern Michigan University; Elizabeth Metzger, University of South Florida; Eric Meyer, St. Louis Community College–Meramec; Libby Miles, University of Rhode Island; Sandra Moore, Mississippi Delta Community College; Cleatta Morris, Louisiana State University at Shreveport; Robert Morse, Western International University; Sheryl A. Mylan, Stephen F. Austin State University; Clement Ndulute, Mississippi Valley State University; Jerry Nelson, Lincoln University; Peggy J. Oliver, San Jacinto College South; Laura Osborne, New River Community College; Mike Palmquist, Colorado State University; Geraldine C. Pelegano, Naugatuck Valley Community College; Laurel S. Peterson, Norwalk Community Technical College; Mary F. Pflugshaupt, Indiana State University; John F. Pleimann, Jefferson College; Kenneth E. Poitras, Antelope Valley College; Michael Punches, Oklahoma City Community College; Patrice Quarg, Cantonsville Community College; Jeanie Page Randall, Austin Peay State University; Betty Ray, Jones College; Joan Reteshka, Sewickley Academy; Kira Roark, University of Denver; Peggy Roche, California University of Pennsylvania; Dawn Rodrigues, University of Texas at Brownsville; Ann Westmoreland Runsick, Gateway Technical College; Karin Russell, Keiser University; Joyce Russo, Lakeland Community College; Wendy Schmidt, Axia College of University of Phoenix; Nancy J. Schneider, University of Maine at Augusta; Janis Schulte, Colby Community College; Susan Schurman, Ventura College; Patricia C. Schwindt, Mesa Community College; Herbert Shapiro, SUNY Empire State College; Andrea Shaw, Nova Southeastern University; Elizabeth Smart, Utah State University; Ognjen Smiljanic, Eastern Michigan University; Allison Smith, Middle Tennessee State University; David Sorrells, Lamar State College–Port Arthur; Ann Spencer-Livingstone, SUNY Morrisville Norwich Campus; Lori Spillane, Indiana University–Purdue University Indianapolis; Scott R. Stankey, Anoka-Ramsey Community College; Leroy Sterling, Alabama A&M University; Dean Stover, Gateway Community College; Ellen Straw, Mt. San Antonio College; Monnette Sturgill, Prestonsburg Community College; Ronald Sudol, Oakland University; Darlene Summers, Montgomery College; David Tammer, Eastern Arizona College; William G. Thomas, Saddleback College; Daphne Thompson, Johnson & Wales; Janice M. Vierk, Metropolitan Community College; Dave Waddell, California State University at Chico; Christopher Walker, Prince George's Community College; Laurie Walker, Eastern Michigan University; Carol Westcamp, University of Arkansas–Fort Smith; Patricia South White, Norwich University; Susan Whitlow, University of Arkansas–Fort Smith; Jim Wilcox, Southern

Nazarene University; Carmiele Wilkerson, Wittenberg University; Mary Zacharias, San Jacinto Community College Central; and Valerie P. Zimbaro, Valencia Community College.

CONTRIBUTORS

The eighth edition could not have been completed without the help of numerous individuals. Mark Gallaher wrote excellent apparatus for the new reading selections as well as tips for the *Instructor's Annotated Edition*. Tammy Sugarman (George State University) supplied numerous documentation examples for the book, building on her contributions to the research chapters of the previous edition. Julie Nichols (Okaloosa-Walton College) wrote engaging new ESL exercises for *Exercise Central*, all of them linked to the ESL Guidelines in *The Bedford Guide*. A special thanks to Dana Waters (Dodge City Community College) for once again revising *Practical Suggestions* and for suggesting many excellent student essays, some of which we have included in the book. Kathleen Beauchene (Community College of Rhode Island) also contributed to *Practical Suggestions*, adding advice on teaching with new reader selections. Once again, T. R. Johnson (Tulane University) edited *Teaching Composition: Background Readings* with energy and insight. Art researcher Linda Finigan helped us take the book in an even more visually rich direction, finding new photographs and other images. She also cleared permissions for the art, while Fred Courtright efficiently cleared text permissions under the able guidance of Sandy Schechter. Grace Talusan contributed engaging activities to *The Bedford Guide*'s companion Web site and also compiled links on authors featured in the reader. Jan Bone created PowerPoints for the book to spark class discussion and learning.

We are grateful as well for Mary Lou Wilshaw-Watts's thoughtful copyediting and, last but not least, for Claire Seng-Niemoeller's attractive and accessible designs of new visual elements.

STUDENT WRITERS

We offer sincere thanks to all the students who have challenged us over the years to find better ways to help them learn. In particular we would like to thank those who granted us permission to use their essays in the eighth edition. Focused as this textbook is on student writing, we consider it essential to provide effective model essays by students. The writings of Anne Cahill, Betsy Buffo, Jonathan Burns, Tim Chabot, Yun Yung Choi, David Ian Cohn, Michael Coil, Heather Colbenson, Geoffrey Fallon, Sarah Goers, Kelly Grecian, Heidi Kessler, Dawn Kortz, Lindsey Schendel, Robert G. Schreiner, Lillian Tsu, Donna Waite, and Carrie Williamson were included in earlier editions as well as this one. New to the eighth edition are the writings of John Barbieri, Sam Benen, Linn Bourgeau, Alan Espenlaub, Stephanie Hawkins, Cindy Keeler, Maegan Kinkelaar, Melissa Lamberth, Daniel Matthews, Angela Mendy, Susanna Olsen, Dennis O'Neil, and Ross Rocketto.

EDITORIAL

At Bedford/St. Martin's three individuals merit special recognition. President Joan E. Feinberg and Editorial Director Denise B. Wydra (also a former editor of *The Bedford Guide*) continue to contribute invaluable suggestions for improving the book for both students and instructors. We also greatly value the guidance of Editor in Chief Karen S. Henry, who has helped sustain the direction of the book throughout many editions and who has provided perceptive advice at crucial points in the development of the current edition.

The editorial effort behind this edition was truly a team endeavor. Marcia F. Muth assumed a major authorial role in the seventh edition, answering needs expressed by users with many exciting new features. She has continued in that role in the eighth edition, bringing innovation to every part of the book and making it an even stronger resource for all students, regardless of their skill level. Beth Castrodale skillfully managed all aspects of the eighth edition, keeping the team on track and on schedule. She once again brought to the project her sharp eye for textual and visual elements alike and her remarkable creative energy, cheerfully and patiently solving problems large and small. Karin Halbert, a gifted writer and editor, oversaw development of the book in its early stages and later helped with a variety of other tasks. This book could not have been completed without her. Christina Gerogiannis and Stephanie Naudin energetically developed *A Writer's Reader*, finding many excellent selections, and Christina helped with a host of other tasks as the development of this new edition got off the ground. Stephanie also took on many other responsibilities, from overseeing an extensive and ongoing review program to developing *Teaching Composition: Background Readings.* Kimberly White, succeeded by Daniel Cole, guided the development and production of the electronic resources, bringing incredible creativity and energy to the development of the e-book and other parts of the package. Anne Leung, a constant source of smart ideas, also helped develop the electronic resources, especially the book's companion Web site. Her insights and extensive contact with Web site users were invaluable in improving what was already a comprehensive resource. Other members of the Bedford/St. Martin's staff contributed greatly to the eighth edition. Many thanks and heartfelt appreciation go to Deborah Baker, whose exacting eye, careful hand, and great patience once again shepherded the book through production. We especially appreciate her care in overseeing the design updates and the production of the book's growing art program. Marcia Cohen, Elizabeth Schaaf, and John Amburg were immensely helpful in overseeing production. Donna Dennison and Billy Boardman oversaw the redesign of the book's cover, giving us a fresh look that still preserves the integrity of *The Bedford Guide.* Karita dos Santos skillfully coordinated the marketing of the book and offered much good advice based on feedback from the field. Karen Melton Soeltz and Jane Helms also offered valuable marketing advice. The book's promotion was ably handled by Shelby Disario and Pelle Cass, and Pelle created a colorful and appealing brochure.

Marcia Muth is especially grateful to the School of Education at the University of Colorado at Denver and Health Sciences Center for sponsoring her writing workshops. Finally, we once again thank our friends and families for their unwavering patience, understanding, and encouragement.

How to Use The Bedford Guide for College Writers

Just as you may be unsure of what to expect from your writing course, you may also be unsure of what to expect from your writing textbook. You may even be wondering how any textbook can improve your writing. In fact, a book alone can't make you a better writer, but practice can, and *The Bedford Guide for College Writers* guides your practice. This text offers help — easy to find and easy to use — for writing the essays most commonly assigned in the first-year composition course.

Underlying *The Bedford Guide* is the idea that writing is a necessary and useful skill in and beyond the writing course. For this reason, the book provides help with writing for other college courses, writing on the job, and writing as a member of a community. In other words, the skills you will learn throughout this book are transferable to other areas of your life, making *The Bedford Guide* both a time-saver and a money-saver.

The following sections describe how you can get the most out of this text. *The Bedford Guide* is designed so that you can move quickly and easily to the section you need. And once you are there, several key features can help you improve your writing by guiding your practice. Let us show you what we mean.

Finding Information in The Bedford Guide

It's easy to find what you need when you need it in *The Bedford Guide.* Each of the tools described here will direct you to useful information — fast.

Brief List of Contents.   Open the book to the inside front cover. At a glance you can see a list of the topics within *The Bedford Guide.* If you are looking for a specific chapter, this brief list of contents is the quickest way to find it.

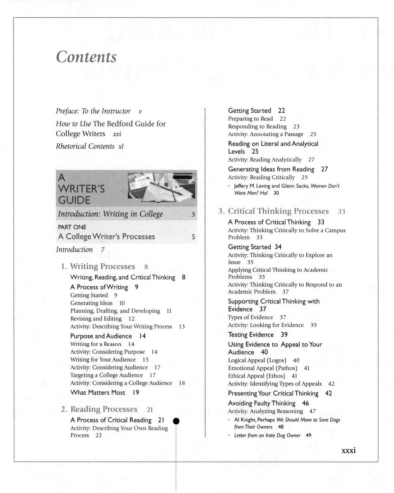

Detailed List of Contents.   Beginning on p. xxxi, the longer, more detailed list of contents breaks down the topics covered within each chapter of the book. Use this list to find a specific part of a chapter. For example, if you have been assigned to read Russell Baker's "The Art of Eating Spaghetti," a quick scan of the detailed contents will show you that it begins on page 56.

Rhetorical List of Contents.   This list, which begins on page xl, includes all of the readings in *The Bedford Guide*, organized by writing strategy. You can use this list to help you locate additional examples of a particular kind of writing such as comparing and contrasting or explaining causes and effects.

Resource Charts.   If you open the book to the inside back cover and its facing page, you'll find a chart showing where you can get help in the text or its companion Web site, no matter where you are in the writing process. If you find yourself stuck at a particular stage, consider turning here for help.

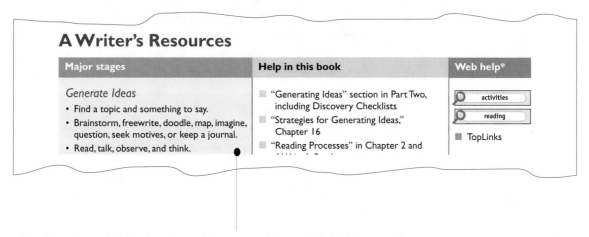

This chart is much like the three charts in Part One, which show you how to find resources specifically for writing (p. 20), reading (p. 32), and critical thinking (p. 50).

Index.   An index is a complete list of a book's contents in alphabetical order. Turn to page I-1 when you want to find all of the information available in the book for a particular topic. This example shows you all the places to look for help with your thesis.

List of Features for College Writers.   At the back of the book is a list of resources in *The Bedford Guide* that will help you become more adept at activities — such as thinking critically, supporting an argument or position, and using outside sources — that are essential for effective academic writing.

List of Visuals.   At the back of the book, you'll also find a list of different types of visuals in the book (organized by genre). Refer to this for ideas about how to use or analyze images effectively.

Guide to the Handbook.   Just before the resource chart in the back of the book, you'll find a guide that shows you at a glance the entire contents of *A Writer's Handbook*. Turn to this guide when you need help editing your essays. It gives exact page numbers for each handbook topic, such as "sentence fragments." If English is not your native language, turn to the page before this guide to find an index to the ESL Guidelines included in the handbook.

Marginal Cross-References.   You can find additional information quickly by using the references in the margins — notes on the sides of each page that tell you exactly where to turn in the book or on the Web site for more help or for other activities related to what you are reading. Many of the Web references include keywords. Simply type these words into a search box at <bedfordstmartins.com/bedguide> to get to the relevant information. Handbook pages also include definitions in the margins.

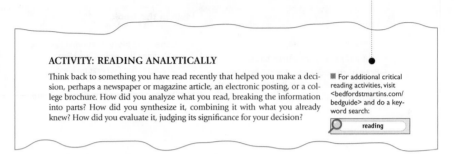

ACTIVITY: READING ANALYTICALLY

Think back to something you have read recently that helped you make a decision, perhaps a newspaper or magazine article, an electronic posting, or a college brochure. How did you analyze what you read, breaking the information into parts? How did you synthesize it, combining it with what you already knew? How did you evaluate it, judging its significance for your decision?

■ For additional critical reading activities, visit <bedfordstmartins.com/bedguide> and do a keyword search:

🔍 reading

Colored Edges.   If you need fast help with research, turn to the Quick Research Guide on the pages with the dark red edge. If you need help as you edit your essay, turn to the Quick Editing Guide on the pages with the dark blue edge. Frequent references in the margin note when you might want to turn to these resources.

If you are writing a research paper and are looking for guidelines for MLA documentation, check the pages with the brown edge. If you need to find APA guidelines, check the pages with the green edge.

Colored Tabs.   Your instructor may use correction symbols, such as "agr" for subject-verb agreement, to indicate areas in your draft that need editing. Blue tabs at the top of each page in *A Writer's Handbook* link these common correction symbols with explanations, examples, and exercises related to the particular editing problem. The example below shows a page from hand-book Chapter 35, section 4, on subject-verb agreement.

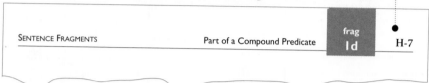

SENTENCE FRAGMENTS   Part of a Compound Predicate   **frag** **ld**   H-7

Answers to Exercises.   As you complete the exercises in the handbook, you will want to know if you're on track. Turn to pages A-61–A-66 in the back of the book to find the correct answers to the lettered exercises.

Becoming a Better Writer by Using The Bedford Guide

The Bedford Guide includes readings, checklists, tips for writing on a computer, and other help you can use to complete each writing assignment.

Model Readings.   *The Bedford Guide* is filled with examples of both professional and student essays to help you as you write your own. These essays are located on the blue-shaded pages in *A Writer's Guide* and in *A Writer's Reader*. All the essays in the book include informative notes about the author, helpful prereading questions, definitions of difficult words, questions for thinking more deeply about the reading, and suggestions for writing.

Reading Annotations.   The professional essays in *A Writer's Guide* begin with some annotations to point out notable features, such as the thesis and the first of the points supporting it. The student essays include a few intriguing questions in the margins to spark your imagination as you read.

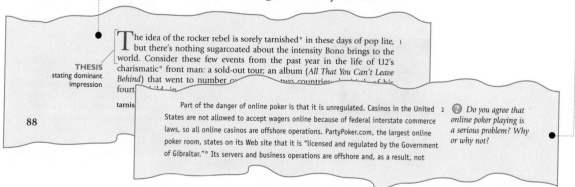

THESIS
stating dominant
impression

The idea of the rocker rebel is sorely tarnished° in these days of pop lite, but there's nothing sugarcoated about the intensity Bono brings to the world. Consider these few events from the past year in the life of U2's charismatic° front man: a sold-out tour; an album (*All That You Can't Leave Behind*) that went to number o~~ne~~ two countries; ~~~~ of his fourt~~~~ild in

tarnis~~~~

88

Part of the danger of online poker is that it is unregulated. Casinos in the United   2
States are not allowed to accept wagers online because of federal interstate commerce
laws, so all online casinos are offshore operations. PartyPoker.com, the largest online
poker room, states on its Web site that it is "licensed and regulated by the Government
of Gibraltar."° Its servers and business operations are offshore and, as a result, not

😊 *Do you agree that*
online poker playing is
a serious problem? Why
or why not?

Learning by Writing

THE ASSIGNMENT: WRITING AN EVALUATION

■ For writing activities for evaluating, visit <bedfordstmartins.com/bedguide> and do a keyword search:

activities

Pick a subject to evaluate — one you have personal experience with and feel competent to evaluate. This might be a movie, a TV program, a piece of music, an artwork, a new product, a government agency, a campus facility or policy, an essay or a reading, or anything else you can think of. Then in a thoughtful essay, analyze your subject and evaluate it. You will need to determine specific criteria for evaluation and make them clear to your readers. In writing your evaluation, you will have a twofold purpose: (1) to set forth your assessment of the quality of your subject and (2) to convince your readers that your judgment is reasonable.

Among the lively student-written evaluations we've seen are these:

A music major evaluated several works by American composer Aaron Copland, finding him trivial and imitative, "without a tenth of the talent or inventiveness that George Gershwin or Duke Ellington had in his little finger."

A student planning a career in business management evaluated a computer firm in which he had worked one summer. His criteria were efficiency, productivity, appeal to new customers, and employee satisfaction.

A student from Brazil, who had seen firsthand the effects of industrial development in the Amazon rain forest, evaluated the efforts of the U.S. government to protect forests and wetlands, comparing them with the efforts of environmentalists in her own country.

GENERATING IDEAS

Find Something to Evaluate.   Try using *brainstorming* or *mapping* to identify as many possible topics as you can think of. Select the ones with most potential — the ones that are most familiar or easiest to find out about. Spend enough time investigating these possibilities that you can comfortably choose one subject for your essay.

Consider Sources of Support.   You'll want to spend time finding material to help you develop a judgment. You may recall a program on television or hunt for an article to read. You might observe a performance or a sports team. An interview or conversation could reveal what others think. Perhaps you'll want to review several examples of your subject: watching several films, listening to several CDs, examining several works of art, or testing several

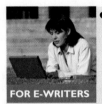
College production of *Romeo and Juliet*

Developing a Consensus
Meet with your writing group to discuss the subject you plan to evaluate, and see whether the group can help you arrive at a sound judgment. The others will need to see or hear your detailed report about what you're evaluating. If possible, pass around a product, show a photograph of artwork, play a song on a CD, or read aloud a short literary work or an idea expressed in a reading. Ask your listeners to explain the reasons for their own evaluations. Maybe they'll suggest criteria or evidence that hadn't occurred to you.

FOR GROUP LEARNING

products. You might also browse for information about your subject at several Web sites or attend a campus concert or play.

Establish Your Criteria.   Jot down criteria, standards to apply to your subject based on the features of the subject worth considering. How well, for example, does a popular entertainer score on musicianship, onstage manner, rapport with the audience, selection of material, originality? In evaluating the desirability of Portland as a home for a young careerist, you might ask: Does it provide an ample choice of decent-paying entry-level positions in growth firms? Any criterion you use to evaluate has to fit your subject, your audience, and your purpose. After all, ample entry-level jobs might not matter to an audience of retirees.

■ For more strategies for generating ideas, see Ch. 16.

Try Comparing and Contrasting.   Often you can readily size up the worth of a thing by setting it next to another of its kind. (When you *compare*, you point to similarities; when you *contrast*, you note differences.) To be comparable, of course, your two subjects need to have plenty in common. The quality of a Harley Davidson motorcycle might be judged by contrasting it with a Honda but not with a Hummer.

For example, if you are writing a paper for a film-history course, you might compare and contrast the classic German horror movie *The Cabinet of Dr. Caligari* with the classic Hollywood movie *Frankenstein*, concluding that *Caligari* is more artistic. In planning the paper, you might make two columns in which you list the characteristics of each film, point by point:

■ For more on comparing and contrasting, see Ch. 7.

	CALIGARI	FRANKENSTEIN
SETS	Dreamlike and impressionistic	Realistic, but with heavy Gothic atmosphere
	Sets deliberately angular and distorted	Gothic sets
LIGHTING	Deep shadows that throw figures into relief	Torches highlighting monster's face in night scene

---

Clear Assignments.   The "Learning by Writing" section in Chapters 4 to 12 presents the assignment for the chapter and guides you through the process of writing that type of essay. The "Facing the Challenge" box in each of these sections helps you through the most complicated step in the assignment.

Computer Advice.   Each "For E-Writers" box offers handy tips for using technology wisely as you write your paper.

Checking Your Source Citations

Use your software's search capacity to help you check your source credits. For example, search for all the quotation marks in your paper. As you find each one, make sure that it is one of a pair surrounding every quotation in your paper. Also check that the source and the page (or other location, if available) are identified for each quotation. Use color highlighting to help you spot and refine the details in your list of sources. For instance, if you tend to forget periods or other conventional punctuation after authors' names or titles, go through your list of sources, and highlight those marks in color, adding any that are missing. After all the entries are checked and corrected, restore the passage to the usual black color.

FOR E-WRITERS

Draft Doctors. In chapters 9, 12, 17, 32, and 34, and in the Quick Editing Guide, you'll find Draft Doctors to help you treat common writing problems. These special features help you figure out what you need to revise in a draft and then decide how to do so. You can also get help from the Draft Doctor on this book's companion Web site, at <bedfordstmartins.com/bedguide>.

Resources for Crediting Sources.   Source Navigators, on pp. 606–14, show you where to look in several major types of sources so that you can quickly find the details needed to credit these sources correctly.

In addition, each of the two major academic styles explained in this book has a directory to guide you to examples that show how to present source information correctly.

Citing and Listing Sources in MLA Style

Skim the following directory to find sample entries to guide you as you cite and list your sources. Notice that the examples are organized according to questions you might ask and that comparable print and electronic sources are grouped together. Also see pages 707–17 for a sample paper that illustrates MLA style.

CITING SOURCES IN MLA STYLE

Who Wrote It?

Individual Author Not Named in Sentence, 689

Individual Author Named in Sentence, 689

Two or Three Authors, 689

Four Authors or More, 689

Organization Author, 692

Author of an Essay from a Reader or Collection, 692

Unidentified Author, 692

What Type of Source Is It?

A Multivolume Work, 693

Indirect Source, 693

Visual Material, 693

How Are You Capturing the Source Material?

Overall Summary or Important Idea, 694

Specific Summary or Paraphrase, 694

Blended Paraphrase and Quotation, 694

Brief Quotation with Formal Launch Statement, 694

Useful Visuals.   Watch for images, figures, charts, tables, visual examples, and other graphics throughout the text. Although we hope that these visuals contribute to an attractive book, they have been selected or designed to help you learn more effectively. Some may suggest ideas for writing or expand your thinking about a topic; others present information so that it's easy to absorb.

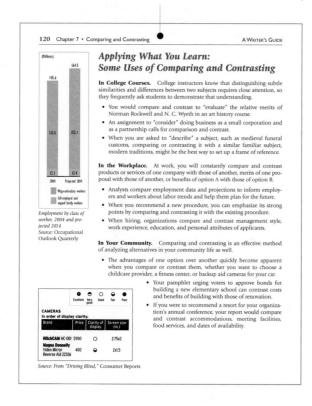

Helpful Checklists. Easy-to-use checklists help you to discover something to write about, get feedback from a peer, revise your draft, and edit using references to the Quick Editing Guide (the dark-blue-edged pages).

EDITING CHECKLIST

Common and Serious Problems in College Writing

▨ For more help, turn to the dark-blue-edged pages, and find the Quick Editing Guide sections noted there.

▨ For help documenting any sources in your paper, turn to the dark-red-edged pages, and find D6 and E1–E2 in the Quick Research Guide there.

Grammar Problems

___ Have you avoided writing sentence fragments?	A1
___ Have you avoided writing comma splices or fused sentences?	A2
___ Have you used the correct form for all verbs in the past tense?	A3
___ Do all verbs agree with their subjects?	A4
___ Have you used the correct case for all pronouns?	A5
___ Do all pronouns agree with their antecedents?	A6
___ Have you used adjectives and adverbs correctly?	A7

Sentence Problems

___ Does each modifier clearly modify the appropriate sentence element?	B1
___ Have you used parallel structure where necessary?	B2

Punctuation Problems

___ Have you used commas correctly?	C1
___ Have you used apostrophes correctly?	C2
___ Have you punctuated quotations correctly?	C3

Mechanics and Format Problems

___ Have you used capital letters correctly?	D1
___ Have you spelled all words correctly?	D2
___ Have you used correct manuscript form?	D3

Editing Advice. Editing advice in the Quick Editing Guide, Handbook, and Glossary helps you write correctly and concisely. The Handbook also includes ESL guidance.

Applying What You Learn. You can apply the writing skills that you learn using *The Bedford Guide* to writing in other college courses, at your job, in your community, and in your everyday life. The "Applying What You Learn" section that ends Chapters 4 through 12 shows how you might use different kinds of writing — for example, using observation to write a case study on the job or using evaluation to assess a public service in your community.

Contents

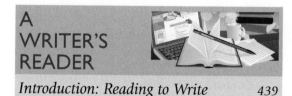

A
WRITER'S
READER

Introduction: Reading to Write   439

A WRITER'S RESEARCH MANUAL

Introduction: The Nature of Research 587

A
WRITER'S
HANDBOOK

Rhetorical Contents

(Essays listed in order of appearance)

A
Writer's
Guide

A Writer's Guide Contents

Introduction: Writing in College

As a college writer you probably wrestle with the question, What should I write? You may feel you have nothing to say or nothing worth saying. Sometimes your difficulty lies in understanding the requirements of your writing situation, sometimes in finding a topic, and sometimes in uncovering information about it. Perhaps you, like many other college writers, have convinced yourself that professional writers have some special way of discovering ideas for writing. But they have no magic. In reality, what they have is experience and confidence, the products of lots of practice writing.

In *The Bedford Guide for College Writers*, we want you to become a better writer by actually writing. To help you do so, we'll give you a lot of practice as well as useful advice about writing to help you build your skills and confidence. Because writing and learning to write are many-faceted tasks, each part of *A Writer's Guide* is devoted to a different aspect of writing.

Part One, "A College Writer's Processes." This part introduces writing, reading, and thinking critically — essential processes for meeting college expectations.

Part Two, "A Writer's Situations." The nine chapters in Part Two form the core of *The Bedford Guide*. Each presents a writing situation and then guides you as you write a paper in response. You'll develop skills in recalling, observing, interviewing, comparing and contrasting, explaining causes and effects, taking a stand, proposing a solution, evaluating, and supporting a position with sources.

Part Three, "Special Writing Situations." This part leads you through three special situations that most students encounter at some point — writing about literature, writing in the workplace, and writing for assessment.

Part Four, "A Writer's Strategies." Part Four is packed with tips and activities that you can use to generate ideas, plan, draft, develop, revise, and edit. You'll also find strategies for designing documents and analyzing images.

Together, these four parts contribute to a seamless whole, much like the writing process itself. Read them at a leisurely pace, study them for helpful information, browse through them for ideas, or turn to them in a pinch. They will guide you as you write — and as you become a more skillful and confident writer.

PART ONE

A
College Writer's
Processes

Introduction

Your composition course may be one of your first college classes. For this reason, the course will both introduce you to college expectations and equip you with the skills that you need to meet these expectations. You may already feel confident that your past education and experiences have prepared you well for higher education. On the other hand, like many students, you may feel worried about your skills or uncertain about what will be expected and how you will fare in the academic world. In either case, *The Bedford Guide for College Writers* will give you concrete advice to help you succeed.

You already know a good deal about what college instructors expect. Like other teachers you've had, they'll require you to come to class, contribute to discussions, and hand in assignments. But they hope and expect that you'll do far more than this — that you'll engage fully in what's sometimes called "the college experience." The richness of this experience depends on your active response to the intellectual exchanges, resources, and opportunities that surround you in college. Sometimes this environment seems intimidating, and you may feel that you are simply drifting with the current, passively absorbing ideas as they flow through your classrooms. But you can learn how to ask questions about your writing, reading, and thinking — and how to navigate your own voyage of discovery.

As you undertake the process of becoming a well-educated person, your college instructors will expect you to show how you have grown as a writer, a reader, and a thinker. More specifically, they will want you to write thoughtful, purposeful papers, appropriately directed to your audience. They will want you not only to rely on your own ideas but also to read the writings of others, to ask questions about what you read, and to conduct research in complex disciplines, sometimes using and documenting many sources. And they will expect you to think critically and to state your points clearly as you write, integrating and supporting your own ideas with those drawn from your reading. The first three chapters in this book briefly introduce the processes — writing, reading, and thinking critically — that will help you meet these essential academic expectations.

Chapter 1
Writing Processes

You are already a writer with long experience. In school you have taken notes, written book reports and term papers, answered exam questions, perhaps kept a journal. In community meetings you have recorded minutes, and on the job you've composed memos. You've sent e-mails or instant messages to friends, made shopping lists, maybe even tried your hand at writing songs or poetry. All this experience is about to pay off for you.

Unlike parachute jumping, writing in college is something you go ahead and try without first learning all there is to know. In truth, nothing anyone can tell you will help as much as learning by doing. In this book our purpose is to help you to write better, deeper, clearer, and more satisfying papers than you have ever written before and to learn to do so by actually writing. Throughout the book we'll give you a lot of practice — in writing processes, patterns, and strategies — to build confidence. And we'll pose various writing situations and say, "Go to it!"

Writing, Reading, and Critical Thinking

In college you will add new techniques and perform challenging tasks that expand what you already know about writing. You may be asked not only to recall an experience but also to reflect upon its significance. Or you may be asked to go beyond summarizing varied positions about an issue by presenting your own position or proposing a solution. Above all, you will be reading and thinking critically — not just stacking up facts but analyzing what you discover, deciding what it means, and weighing its value.

In your composition course, you can view each writing task as a problem to solve, often through careful reading and objective thinking. You will

For more on reading critically, see Ch. 2. For more on thinking critically, see Ch. 3.

need to read — and write — actively, engaging with the ideas of others. At the same time, you will need to think critically, analyzing and judging those ideas. To help you assess your own achievement, you will use criteria — models, conventions, principles, standards. As you write and rewrite, you can evaluate what you are doing by considering specific questions:

- Have you achieved your purpose?
- Have you considered your audience?
- Have you made your point clear by stating it as a thesis or unmistakably implying it?
- Have you supported your point with enough reliable evidence to persuade your audience?
- Have you arranged your ideas logically so that each follows from, supports, or adds to the one before it?
- Have you made the connections among ideas clear to a reader?
- Have you established an appropriate tone?

In large measure, learning to write well is learning what questions to ask as you write. Throughout *A Writer's Guide*, we include questions and suggestions designed to help you accomplish your writing tasks and reflect on your own processes as you write, read, and think critically.

A Process of Writing

Writing can seem at times an overwhelming drudgery, worse than scrubbing floors; at other moments, it's a sport full of thrills — like whizzing downhill on skis, not knowing what you'll meet around a bend. Surprising and unpredictable as the process may seem, nearly all writers do similar things:

- They generate ideas.
- They plan, draft, and develop their papers.
- They revise and edit.

These three activities form the basis of most effective writing processes, and they lie at the heart of each chapter in Part Two, "A Writer's Situations."

■ For more help with every stage of the writing process, visit <bedfordstmartins.com/ bedguide>.

GETTING STARTED

As you begin writing, two considerations — what you want to accomplish as a writer and how you want to appeal to your audience — will shape your direction. As you clarify your purpose and consider your audience, you are likely to gain confidence as a writer. Even so, your writing process may take you in unexpected directions. After all, your writing activities aren't lockstep stages: you don't always proceed in a straight line. You can skip around, taking up parts of the process in whatever order you like, work on several parts at a time, or circle back over what's already done. For example, while gathering material, you may feel an urge to play with a sentence until it clicks. Or while writing a draft, you may decide to look for more material. You may leap ahead, cross out, backtrack, adjust, question, test a fresh approach, tinker, polish — and then, at the end, spell-check the tricky words.

GENERATING IDEAS

 For strategies for generating ideas, see Ch. 16.

The first activity in writing — finding a topic and something to say about it — is often the most challenging and least predictable. Each chapter in Part Two includes a section called "Generating Ideas," which is filled with examples, questions, checklists, and visuals designed to trigger ideas and associations that will help you begin the chapter's writing assignment.

Discovering What to Write About.   Finding a topic is not always easy, but you may discover an idea while talking with friends, riding your bike, or staring out the window. Sometimes a topic lies near home, in a conversation or an everyday event you recall. Often, your reading will raise questions that call for investigation. Even if a particular writing assignment doesn't appeal to you, your challenge is to find a slant that does interest you. Find it, and words will flow — words that can engage readers as you accomplish your purpose.

Discovering Material.   You'll need information to shape and support your ideas — facts and figures, reports and opinions, examples and illustrations. How do you find supporting material that makes your slant on a topic clear and convincing to your audience? Luckily you have numerous sources at your fingertips. You can recall your experience and knowledge, observe things around you, converse with others who are knowledgeable, read enlightening materials that draw you to new approaches, and think critically about all these sources around you.

```
              ┌──────────────────────┐
        ┌─────→│  Discover topic idea │←─────┐
        │      └──────────────────────┘      │
        │                                     ↓
┌──────────────────────┐          ┌──────────────────────┐
│  Discover material    │          │  Discover material    │
│ to shape your topic   │          │ to develop your topic │
│        slant          │          │                       │
└──────────────────────┘          └──────────────────────┘
        ↑                                     │
        │      ┌──────────────────────┐      │
        └──────│ Discover topic slant │←─────┘
               └──────────────────────┘
```

PLANNING, DRAFTING, AND DEVELOPING

After discovering a topic and beginning to gather material about it, you will plan your paper, write a draft, and then develop your ideas further. Each chapter in Part Two has a section titled "Planning, Drafting, and Developing," designed to help you through these stages of the writing process for the assignment in that chapter.

Planning.   Having discovered a burning idea to write about (or at least a smoldering one) and some supporting material (but maybe not enough yet), you will sort out what matters most. If right away you see one main point, or thesis, for your paper, test various ways of stating it, given your purpose and audience:

MAYBE   Parking in the morning before class is annoying.

OR   Campus parking is a big problem.

Next arrange your ideas and material in a sensible order that will clarify your point. For example, you might group and label the ideas you have generated, make an outline, or analyze the main point, breaking it down into its parts:

> Parking on campus is a problem for students because of the long lines, inefficient entrances, and poorly marked spaces.

But if no clear thesis emerges quickly, don't worry. You may find one while you draft — that is, while you write an early version of your paper.

Drafting.   When your ideas first start to flow, you want to welcome them — lure them forth, not tear them apart — or they might go back into hiding. Don't be afraid to take risks at this stage: you'll probably be surprised and pleased at what happens, even though your first version will be rough. Writing takes time; a paper usually needs several drafts and may need a clearer introduction, stronger conclusion, more convincing evidence, or a revised plan. Especially when your subject is unfamiliar or complicated, you may throw out your first attempt and start over if a stronger idea hits you.

Developing.   As you draft, you'll weave in explanations, definitions, examples, details, and varied evidence to make your ideas clear and persuasive. For example, you may define an at-risk student, illustrate the problems faced by a single parent, or supply statistics about hit-and-run accidents. If you lack specific support for your main point, you can use strategies for developing ideas — or return to strategies for generating ideas. You'll keep gaining insights and drawing conclusions while you draft. By all means, welcome these ideas, and work them in if they fit.

For thesis and planning strategies, see Ch. 17.

For practice choosing a main point, visit <bedfordstmartins.com/bedguide> and do a keyword search:

thesis

For drafting strategies, see Ch. 18.

For strategies for developing ideas, see Ch. 19. For strategies for generating ideas, see Ch. 16. For advice on using a few sources, see the Quick Research Guide (the dark-red-edged pages).

Processes for Planning,
Drafting, and
Developing

REVISING AND EDITING

For revising and editing strategies, see Ch. 20.

You might want to relax once you have a draft, but for most writers, revising begins the work in earnest. Revising means both reseeing and rewriting, making major changes so that your paper accomplishes what you want it to. After you have a well-developed and well-organized revision, you are ready to edit: to correct errors and improve wording. Each chapter in Part Two has a "Revising and Editing" section where you will find revision and editing checklists with a suggestion for working with a peer.

Revising.   Revision is more than just changing words: in fact, you may revise what you know and what you think while you're writing or when you pause to reread. You can then reconsider your purpose and audience, rework your thesis, shift your plans, decide what to put in or leave out, rearrange for clarity, move sentences or paragraphs around, connect ideas differently, or express them better. Perhaps you'll add costs to a paper on parking problems or switch attention to fathers instead of mothers as you consider teen parenthood.

If you put aside your draft for a few hours or a day, you can reread it with fresh eyes and a clear mind. As humorist Leo Rosten has said, "You have to put yourself in the position of the negative reader, the resistant reader, the reader who doesn't surrender easily, the reader who is alien to you as a type, even the reader who doesn't like what you are writing." Other students can also help you — sometimes more than a textbook or an instructor can — by responding to your drafts as engaged readers.

Editing.   Editing means refining details and correcting flaws that may stand in the way of your readers' understanding and enjoyment. Don't edit too early, though, because you may waste time on some part that you later revise out. In editing, you usually make these repairs:

For editing advice, see the Quick Editing Guide (the dark-blue-edged pages).

- Get rid of unnecessary words.
- Choose livelier and more precise words.
- Replace incorrect or inappropriate wording.
- Rearrange words in a clearer, more emphatic order.
- Combine short, choppy sentences, or break up long, confusing sentences.
- Refine transitions for continuity of thought.
- Check grammar, usage, punctuation, and mechanics.

Proofreading.   Finally you'll proofread your paper, taking a last look, checking correctness, and catching doubtful spellings or word-processing errors.

For more on proofreading, see pp. 386–87.

REVISE	← PEER → RESPONSE	EDIT	→	PROOFREAD
• Purpose		• Grammar		• Spelling
• Thesis		• Sentences		• Incorrect words
• Audience		• Word choice		• Missing words
• Structure		• Punctuation		• Minor errors
• Support		• Mechanics		• Minor details
• Language		• Format for paper		

ACTIVITY: DESCRIBING YOUR WRITING PROCESS

Describe your writing process. How do you get started? How do you keep writing? What process do you go through to reach a final draft? Do your steps ever vary depending upon the type of writing you're doing? What step or strategy in your writing process would you most like to change?

Purpose and Audience

At any moment in the writing process, two questions are worth asking:

Why am I writing?   **Who is my audience?**

WRITING FOR A REASON

 For more on planning with your purpose in mind, see pp. 310–11. For more on revising for purpose, see pp. 372–73.

Like most college writing assignments, every assignment in this book asks you to write for a definite reason. For example, in Chapter 4 you'll be asked to recall a memorable experience in order to explain its importance for you; in Chapter 9, you'll take a stand on a controversy in order to convey your position and persuade readers to respect it. Be careful not to confuse the sources and strategies you are asked to apply in these assignments with your ultimate purpose for writing. "To compare and contrast two things" is not a very interesting purpose; "to compare and contrast two Web sites *in order to explain their differences*" implies a real reason for writing. In most college writing, your ultimate purpose will be to explain something to your readers or to convince them of something.

To sharpen your concentration on your purpose, ask yourself from the start: What do I want to do? And, in revising, Did I do what I meant to do? You'll find that these practical questions will help you slice out irrelevant information and remove other barriers to getting your paper where you want it to go.

ACTIVITY: CONSIDERING PURPOSE

Imagine that you are in the following writing situations. For each, write a sentence or two summing up your purpose as a writer.

1. The instructor in your introductory psychology course has assigned a paragraph about the meanings of three essential terms in your readings.
2. You're very upset about a change in financial-aid procedures and plan to write a letter asking the registrar to remedy the problem.
3. You're going to start a blog about your first year at college so that all of your extended family can envision the campus environment and share your experiences during the year.
4. Your supervisor wants you to write an article about the benefits of a new company service for the customer newsletter.
5. Your MySpace profile seemed appropriate when you were in high school, but you want to revise it now that you're attending college and have a job with future prospects.

WRITING FOR YOUR AUDIENCE

Your audience, or your readers, may or may not be defined in your assignment. Consider the following examples:

■ For more on planning for your readers, see pp. 310–11.

ASSIGNMENT 1   Discuss the advantages and disadvantages of homeschooling.

ASSIGNMENT 2   In a letter to parents of school-aged children, discuss the advantages and disadvantages of homeschooling.

If your assignment defines an audience, as the second example does, you will need to think about how to approach those readers and what to assume about their relationship to your topic. For example, what points would you include in a discussion aimed at parents? How would you organize your ideas? Would you discuss advantages or disadvantages first? On the other hand, how might your approach differ if the assignment read this way?

ASSIGNMENT 3   In a newsletter article for teachers, discuss the advantages and disadvantages of homeschooling.

Audiences may be identified by characteristics, such as occupation (teachers) or role (parents), that suggest values to which a writer might appeal. For example, most teachers and parents share the desire to help a student succeed. Even so, while a teacher might see a quiet classroom loner, a parent might see a shy animal lover who volunteers at the zoo. As the chart on page 16 suggests, you can analyze the preferences, biases, and concerns of your audience in order to engage and influence readers more successfully.

When you analyze what readers know, believe, and value, you can aim your writing toward them with a better chance of hitting your mark. Use these questions to help you write and revise for your audience:

AUDIENCE CHECKLIST

____ Who are your readers? What is their relationship to you?

____ What do your readers already know about this topic? What do you want them to learn?

____ How much detail will they want to read about this topic?

____ What objections are they likely to raise as they read? How can you anticipate and overcome their objections?

____ What's likely to convince them?

____ What's likely to offend them?

■ For more on revising for audience, see p. 374.

Audience Characteristics and Expectations	GENERAL AUDIENCE	COLLEGE INSTRUCTOR	WORK SUPERVISOR	CAMPUS FRIEND	PARENT OR GRANDPARENT
READER'S RELATIONSHIP TO YOU	Imagined but not known personally	Known briefly in a class context	Known for some time in a job context	Known in campus and social contexts	Known all of your life in family contexts
REASON FOR READING YOUR WRITING	Curious attitude and interest in your topic assumed	Professional responsibility for your knowledge and skills	Managerial interest in and reliance on your job performance	Personal interest based on shared circumstances	Family bond and lifelong concern about you
KNOWLEDGE ABOUT TOPIC	Level of awareness assumed and gaps addressed with logical presentation	Well informed about college topics but wants to see what you know	Informed about the business and expects reliable information from you	Friendly but may or may not be informed beyond social interests	Loving but may or may not be informed beyond family concerns
EXPECTED FORMS AND FORMATS	Essay, article, letter, report, or other format	Essay, report, or research paper using academic format	Memo, report, or letter using company format	Chats, notes, blog entries, sociable IMs, or other informal messages	Family e-mails, chats, letters, notes, or cards
EXPECTED LANGUAGE AND STYLE	Formal, using clear words and sentences	Formal, following academic conventions	Appropriate for advancing you and the company	Informal, using abbreviations, phrases, and slang	Informal, but showing your maturity
EXPECTED ATTITUDE AND TONE	Interested and thoughtful about the topic	Serious and thoughtful about the topic and course	Respectful, showing reliability and work ethic	Friendly and interested in shared experiences	Concerned about home and family despite new experiences
EXPECTED AMOUNT OF DETAIL	Sufficient detail to inform or persuade the reader envisioned	Enough sound or research-based evidence to support your thesis	General or technical information as needed	Much detail or little, depending on the topic	Enough to be reassured about your welfare and success

ACTIVITY: CONSIDERING AUDIENCE

Read the following renewal notices sent to subscribers of two magazines, *Zapped!* and the *Atlantic*. Examine the style, tone, language, sequence of topics, or other features of each letter. Write two short paragraphs — one about each letter — explaining what you can conclude about the letter's target audience and its appeal to that audience.

Zapped! misses you.

Dear Dan Morrison,

All last year, *Zapped!* magazine made the trek to 5 Snowden Lane and it was always a great experience. You took great care of *Zapped!*, and *Zapped!* gave you hours of entertainment, with news and interviews from the latest indie bands, honest-as-your-momma reviews of musical equipment, and your first glimpse of some of the finest graphic serials being published today.

But, Dan, we haven't heard from you and are starting to wonder what's up. Don't you miss *Zapped!*? One thing's for sure: *Zapped!* misses you.

We'd like to re-establish the relationship: if you renew your subscription by March 1, you'll get 20% off last year's subscription price. That's only $24 for another year of great entertainment. Just fill out the other side of this card and send it back to us; we'll bill you later.

Come on, Dan. Why wait?

Thanks,

Carly Bevins

Carly Bevins
Director of Sales

Figure 1.1   Letter from Zapped!

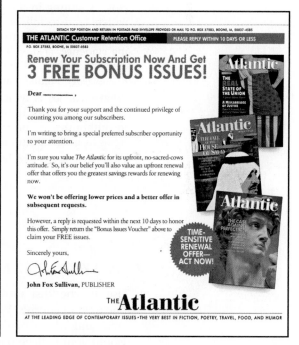

Figure 1.2   Letter from The Atlantic

TARGETING A COLLEGE AUDIENCE

In college, many of your assignments may resemble Assignment 1 on page 15. They may assume that you are addressing general college readers, represented by your instructor and possibly your classmates. Such readers typically expect clear, logical writing with lots of supporting evidence to explain or persuade. Of course, the format, approach, or evidence may differ by field. For example, biologists might expect the findings from your experiment while literature specialists might look for plenty of relevant quotations from the novel you're analyzing. Use these questions to help you pinpoint what your college audience expects:

COLLEGE AUDIENCE CHECKLIST

___ How has your instructor advised you to write for readers? What criteria related to audience will be used for grading your papers?

___ What do the assigned readings in your course assume about the expectations of an audience? Has your instructor recommended useful models or sample readings?

___ What topics and issues concern readers in the course area? What puzzles do they want to solve? How do they want to solve them?

___ How is writing in the course area commonly organized? For example, do writers tend to follow a persuasive pattern — introducing the issue, stating an assertion or a claim, backing the claim with logical points and supporting evidence, acknowledging other views, and concluding? Or do they use conventional headings — perhaps *Abstract, Introduction to the Problem, Methodology, Findings,* and *Discussion*?

___ What evidence is typically gathered to support ideas or interpretations — facts and statistics, quotations from texts, summaries of research, references to authorities or prior studies, results from experimental research, field notes from observations, or interviews?

___ What style, tone, and level of formality do writers in the course area tend to use?

ACTIVITY: CONSIDERING A COLLEGE AUDIENCE

1. Use the checklist above to examine reading or writing assignments for one of your courses. What are some prominent features of writing in the area, and which of these might be expected in student papers? How would your college paper differ from writing on the same topic for another audience (such as a letter to the editor, a newspaper article, a consumer brochure, an explanation for young students, or a Web page)?

2. Select a typical passage from a textbook or a reading assigned in a course. Rewrite the passage for a specific nonacademic audience (such as readers of a particular magazine or newspaper, visitors to a certain Web site, or amateurs interested in the area).

3. Find a nonacademic article, pamphlet, or Web page. Try your hand at rewriting a passage from it to present the material as a college textbook or reading in the field might. Then write an informal paragraph explaining why this task was easy, challenging, or impossible.

What Matters Most

Like a hard game of basketball, writing a college paper is strenuous. As the following chart shows, you can find help throughout the writing process in this book and on its Web site. Without getting in your way, we want to lend you all possible support and guidance. So, no doubt, does your instructor, someone closer to you than any textbook writers. Still, like even the best coaches, instructors and textbook writers can improve your game only so far. Advice on how to write won't make you a better writer. You'll learn more and have more fun when you take a few sentences to the hoop and make points yourself. After you sink a few baskets, you'll gain confidence in your ability and find the process of writing easier.

A Writer's Resources

Major stages	Help in this book	Web help*
Generate Ideas • Find a topic and something to say. • Brainstorm, freewrite, doodle, map, imagine, question, seek motives, or keep a journal. • Read, talk, observe, and think.	▪ "Generating Ideas" section in Part Two, including Discovery Checklists ▪ "Strategies for Generating Ideas," Chapter 16 ▪ "Reading Processes" in Chapter 2 and *A Writer's Reader*	activities reading ■ TopLinks
Plan • Think about your purpose and audience. • Convert a topic idea to a working thesis. • Organize by grouping or outlining.	▪ "Planning, Drafting, and Developing" sections in Part Two ▪ "Strategies for Stating a Thesis and Planning," Chapter 17	thesis organize
Draft • Start and restart. • Write paragraphs and topic sentences. • Write openings and conclusions. • Create coherence with transitions, repetitions, and pronouns.	▪ "Planning, Drafting, and Developing" sections in Part Two ▪ "Strategies for Drafting," Chapter 18 ▪ Advice on using graphics in Chapter 21	activities open_end coherence
Develop • Weave in supporting examples, details, and definitions. • Analyze, divide and classify, compare and contrast, or identify cause and effect. • Supply evidence—facts, statistics, expert testimony, and firsthand observation.	▪ "Planning, Drafting, and Developing" sections in Part Two ▪ "Strategies for Developing," Chapter 19 ▪ Advice on sources and citation style in Quick Research Guide	examples development support ■ Ask the Draft Doctor
Revise • Reconsider purpose, thesis, and audience. • Rework structure, support, and connections. • Stress what counts; whittle what doesn't. • Work with a peer editor.	▪ "Revising and Editing" sections in Part Two ▪ "Strategies for Revising and Editing," Chapter 20	process peer ■ Ask the Draft Doctor
Edit • Refine grammar, sentences, and word choice. • Correct punctuation and mechanics. • Check the paper's format.	▪ "Revising and Editing" sections in Part Two ▪ "Strategies for Revising and Editing," Chapter 20 ▪ Format for academic papers in Chapter 21 ▪ Quick Editing Guide	process ■ Exercise Centra ■ Ask the Draft Doctor
Proofread • Check for misspelled, incorrect, or missing words. • Check for minor errors and details.	▪ "Revising and Editing" sections in Part Two ▪ "Strategies for Revising and Editing," Chapter 20	process ■ Exercise Centra

*At <bedfordstmartins.com/bedguide>, use the search box shown to find writing resources or exercises by keyword.

Chapter 2
Reading Processes

What's so special about college reading? Don't you pick up the book, start on the first page, and keep going, just as you have ever since you met *The Cat in the Hat*? Reading from beginning to end works especially well when you are eager to find out what happens next, as in a thriller, or what to do next, as in a cookbook. On the other hand, much of what you read in college — textbooks, scholarly articles, research reports, or the papers of your peers — is complicated and challenging. Dense material like this often requires closer reading and deeper thinking — in short, a process for reading critically.

Reading critically is a useful skill. For assignments in this course alone, you will need to evaluate the strengths and weaknesses of essays by professionals and students. If you research any topic, you will need to figure out what your sources say, how you might use their information, and whether they are reliable. Critical reading is important in other courses, too. For example, you might analyze a sociology report on violent children for its assumptions and implications as well as the soundness of its argument. On the job, you may be required to verify that your product meets technical specifications, while in the community, you may want to respond to a proposal for a tax hike. Whenever your writing relies on critical reading, you need to explain what is going on in the text and then go further, making your own point based on what you have read.

A Process of Critical Reading

Reading critically means approaching whatever you read in an active, questioning manner. This essential college-level skill changes reading from a spectator sport to a contact sport. You no longer sit in the stands, watching graceful skaters glide by. Instead, you charge right into a rough-and-tumble hockey game, gripping your stick and watching out for your teeth.

For more on critical thinking, see Ch. 3.

Critical reading, like critical thinking, is not a specialized, isolated activity. It is a continuum of strategies that thoughtful people use every day to grapple with new information, to integrate it with existing knowledge, and to apply it to problems in daily life and in academic courses. Many readers do similar things:

- They get ready to do their reading.
- They respond as they read.
- They read on literal and analytical levels.

Building your critical reading skills can bring many benefits, especially if you aren't a regular reader. You'll open the door to new possibilities, information you've never encountered, and ideas unlikely to come up talking with friends. As you absorb and challenge what you read, you also deepen your resources as a writer.

ACTIVITY: DESCRIBING YOUR OWN READING PROCESS

How do you read a magazine, newspaper, or popular novel? What are your goals when you do this kind of reading? What's different about reading the material assigned in college? What techniques do you use for reading assignments? How might you read more effectively? Which of your strategies might help your classmates, especially in classes with a lot of reading?

Getting Started

College reading is active reading. Before you read, think ahead about how to approach the reading process — how to make the most of the time you spend reading.

PREPARING TO READ

Thinking about Your Purpose.   Naturally enough, your overall goal for doing most college reading is to be successful in your courses. When you begin to read, ask questions like these about your immediate purpose:

- What are you reading?
- Why are you reading?
- What do you want to do with the reading?
- What does your instructor expect you to learn from the reading?
- Do you need to memorize details, find main points, or connect ideas?
- How does this reading build on, add to, contrast with, or otherwise relate to other reading assignments in the course?

Planning Your Follow-Up.   When you are assigned a specific essay, chapter, or article or are required to choose a reading about a certain topic, ask yourself what your instructor probably expects to follow the reading:

- Do you need to be ready to discuss the reading during class?
- Will you need to mention it or analyze it during an examination?
- Will you need to write about it or its topic?
- Do you need to find its main points? Sum it up? Compare it? Question it? Spot its strengths and weaknesses? Draw useful details from it?

Skimming the Text.   Before you actively read a text, begin by skimming it — quickly reading only enough to introduce yourself to its content and organization. If the reading has a table of contents or subheadings, read those first to figure out what the material covers and how it is organized. Read the first paragraph and then the first (or first and last) sentence of each paragraph that follows. If the material has any illustrations or diagrams, read the captions.

RESPONDING TO READING

Reading Deeply.   The books, articles, and essays assigned in college often require more concentration from you as a reader than other readings do. Use the following questions to help you understand the complexities below the surface of a reading:

- Are difficult or technical terms defined in specific ways? How might you highlight, list, or record such terms so that you master them?
- How might you record or recall the details in the reading? How could you track or diagram interrelated ideas to grasp their connections?
- How do word choice, tone, and style alert you to the complex purpose of a reading that is layered or indirect rather than straightforward?
- How might you trace the progression of ideas in the reading? How do headings, previews of what's coming up, summaries of what's gone before, and transitions signal the organization?
- Does the reading include figurative or descriptive language, references to other works, or recurring themes? How do these elements enrich the reading?

For more on figurative language, see p. 248.

- Can you answer any reading questions supplied in your textbook, assignment, study guide, or syllabus? Can you restate headings in question form to create your own questions and then supply the answers? For example, change "Major Types of X" to "What are the major types of X?"

Keeping a Reading Journal.   A reading journal is an excellent place to record not just what you read but how you respond to it. It helps you read

For advice on keeping a writer's journal, see Ch. 16.

actively and build a reservoir of ideas for follow-up writing. You can use a special notebook or computer file to address questions like these:

- What is the subject of the reading? What is the writer's stand?
- What does the writer take for granted? What assumptions does he or she begin with? Where are these stated or suggested?
- What evidence supports the writer's main points?
- Do you agree with what the writer has said? Do his or her ideas clash with your ideas or question something you take for granted?
- Has the writer told you more than you wanted to know or failed to tell you something you wish you knew?
- What conclusions can you draw from the reading?
- Has the reading opened your eyes to new ways of viewing the subject?

For more on evaluating what you read, see section C in the Quick Research Guide (the dark-red-edged pages).

Annotating the Text.   Writing notes on the page (or on a photocopy if the material is not your own) is a useful way to trace the author's points, question them, and add your own comments as they pop up. You can underline key points, mark checks and stars by ideas when you agree or disagree, and jot questions in the margins.

The following passage ends the introduction of "The New Science of Siblings," written by Jeffrey Kluger (with reporting by Jessica Carsen, Wendy Cole, and Sonja Steptoe) and featured as the cover story in the July 10, 2006, *Time* (pp. 47–48). Notice how one writer annotated this passage:

For a Critical Reading Checklist, see pp. 28–29.

Key point — will this be a pain? Or a help?

Good quote — from UC Davis authority

Sums up past studies but new to me

Not exactly! My sister's definitely a striver, but I'm no rebel

Wow — global research!

Have to go for the drama — competition and favorites!!

Our spouses arrive comparatively late in our lives; our parents eventually leave us. Our siblings may be the only people we'll ever know who truly qualify as partners for life. "Siblings," says family sociologist Katherine Conger of the University of California, Davis, "are with us for the whole journey."

Within the scientific community, siblings have not been wholly ignored, but research has been limited mostly to discussions of birth order. Older sibs were said to be strivers; younger ones rebels; middle kids the lost souls. The stereotypes were broad, if not entirely untrue, and there the discussion mostly ended.

But all that's changing. At research centers in the United States, Canada, Europe, and elsewhere, investigators are launching a wealth of new studies into the sibling dynamic, looking at ways brothers and sisters steer one another into — or away from — risky behavior; how they form a protective buffer against family upheaval; how they educate one another about the opposite sex; how all siblings compete for family recognition and come to terms — or blows — over such impossibly charged issues as parental favoritism.

Scary - I never though my sis this wa

Cousins exampl pulled togeth when p ents sp

ACTIVITY: ANNOTATING A PASSAGE

Annotate the following passage on a recent trend.

For a sample annotated passage, see p. 24.

Every woman's dream is to find the perfect spouse and settle down for life, right? Although this may be the dream of some, it doesn't reflect reality, according to a recent analysis of census data. Based on this analysis, the *New York Times* reported that, for the first time in history, most U.S. women are single ("51% of Women Are Now Living without Spouse," 16 Jan. 2007; reported by Sam Roberts). Specifically, in 2005, 51 percent of women reported being unmarried, up from 49 percent in 2000 and 35 percent in 1950.

The *Times* and other media sources have pointed to several factors behind the shift, including the fact that women are waiting longer to get married. "We don't need men anymore," said twenty-nine-year-old New York City resident Jessica Cohen, in an interview with CBS News ("More Women Saying, 'I Don't,'" 16 Jan. 2007; reported by Kelly Wallace). As Cohen explained, "I mean, we want men, we want someone to share everything with, but I don't think we need to rush."

Other women are choosing to live with partners instead of marrying. Many divorced women are staying single or delaying remarriage. As divorced Baltimore attorney Catherine Flynn told MSNBC, "I get to make the choices myself about where I live, how I live, how I decorate my house" ("Watch Out, Men! More Women Opt to Live Alone," 16 Jan. 2007; reported by Dawn Fratangelo). And in another trend behind the shift, women are living longer as widows.

Social commentators who have studied marriage trends say that women today simply have more choices than were available in past generations. Many are financially independent and are even willing to raise children on their own. Freed from the need to find someone to support them as soon as possible, these women can take more time to find a partner with whom they are emotionally, intellectually, and spiritually compatible. But even then, they might not marry such a man, as the *Times* story shows.

Reading on Literal and Analytical Levels

Educational expert Benjamin S. Bloom identified six levels of cognitive activity: knowledge, comprehension, application, analysis, synthesis, and evaluation.[1] Each level acts as a foundation for the next. Each also becomes more complex and demands higher thinking skills than the previous one.

[1]Benjamin S. Bloom et al., *Taxonomy of Educational Objectives, Handbook 1: Cognitive Domain* (New York: McKay, 1956).

Experienced readers, however, jump among these levels, gathering information and insight as they occur. (See the reading skills figure below.)

The first three levels are literal skills. When you show that you know a fact, comprehend its meaning, and can apply it to a new situation, you demonstrate your mastery over the building blocks of thought. The last three levels — analysis, synthesis, and evaluation — are critical skills. These skills take you beyond the literal level: you break apart the building blocks to see how they work, recombine them in new and useful ways, and judge their worth or significance. To read critically, you must engage with a reading on both literal and analytical levels.

As you first tackle an unfamiliar reading, you may struggle simply to discover what — exactly — it presents to readers. For example, suppose you read in your history book a passage about Franklin Delano Roosevelt (FDR), the only American president elected to four consecutive terms of office.

Knowing.   Once you read the passage, even if you have little background in American history, you can decode and recall the information it presents about FDR and his four terms in office.

Comprehending.   To understand the passage, you need to know that a term for a U.S. president is four years and that *consecutive* means "continuous." Thus, FDR was elected to serve for sixteen years.

Applying.   To connect this knowledge to what you already know, you think of other presidents — George Washington, who served two terms; Grover Cleveland, who served two terms but not consecutively; Jimmy Carter, who served one term; and Bill Clinton, who served two terms. Then you realize that being elected to four terms is quite unusual. In fact, the Twenty-second Amendment to the Constitution, ratified in 1951, now limits a president to two terms.

Analyzing.   You can scrutinize FDR's four terms as president from various angles, selecting a principle for analysis that suits your purpose. Then you

Literal and Analytical Reading Skills
The information in this figure is adapted from Benjamin S. Bloom et al., Taxonomy of Educational Objectives, Handbook 1: Cognitive Domain *(New York: McKay, 1956).*

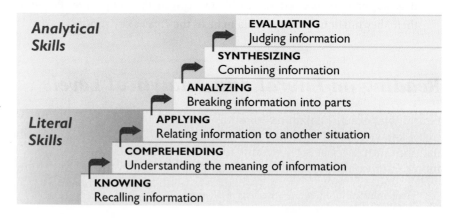

can use this principle to break the information into its components or parts. For example, you might analyze FDR's tenure in office in relation to the political longevity of other presidents. Why has FDR been the only president elected to serve four terms? What circumstances during his terms contributed to three reelections?

Synthesizing. To answer your questions, you may have to read more or review material you have read in the past. Then you begin synthesizing — recombining information, pulling together facts and opinions, identifying evidence accepted by all or most sources, examining any controversial evidence, and drawing whatever conclusions reliable evidence seems to support. For example, it would be logical to conclude that the special circumstances of the Great Depression and World War II contributed to FDR's four terms. On the other hand, it would not be logical to conclude that Americans reelected him out of pity because he had polio.

Evaluating. Finally, you evaluate your new knowledge to determine its significance, both to your understanding of Depression-era politics and to your assessment of your history book's approach. For instance, you might ask yourself, Why has the book's author chosen to make this point? How does it affect the rest of the discussion? Does this author seem reliable? And you may also have formed your own opinion about FDR's reelections, perhaps concluding that FDR's four-term presidency is understandable in light of the events of the 1930s and 1940s, that the author has mentioned this fact to highlight the unique political atmosphere of that era, and that, in your opinion, it is evidence neither for nor against FDR's excellence as a president.

ACTIVITY: READING ANALYTICALLY

Think back to something you have read recently that helped you make a decision, perhaps a newspaper or magazine article, an electronic posting, or a college brochure. How did you analyze what you read, breaking the information into parts? How did you synthesize it, combining it with what you already knew? How did you evaluate it, judging its significance for your decision?

■ For additional critical reading activities, visit <bedfordstmartins.com/bedguide> and do a keyword search:

reading

GENERATING IDEAS FROM READING

Like flints that strike each other and cause sparks, readers and writers provoke one another. For example, when your class discusses an essay, you may be surprised by the range of insights your classmates report. If you missed some of their insights during your reading, remember that they may be equally surprised by what you see.

■ For more on generating ideas, see Ch. 16.

Often you look to other writers — in books or magazines — to suggest a topic, provide information about it, or help you explain it or back it up with evidence. You may read because you want to understand ideas, test them, or debate with the writer, but reading is a dynamic process. It may change your ideas instead of support them. Here are suggestions for unlocking the potential hidden in a good text.

Looking for Meaty Pieces.   Spur your thinking about intriguing current topics by browsing through essay collections or magazines in the library or online. Try *Atlantic, Harper's, New Republic, Commentary,* or special-interest magazines such as *Architectural Digest* or *Scientific American.* Check the editorials and op-ed columns in your local newspaper, the *New York Times,* or the *Wall Street Journal.* Also search the Internet on interesting subjects that challenge you to think seriously (such as film classics or the effects of poverty on children). Look for articles that are meaty, not superficial, and that are written to inform and convince, not to entertain or amuse.

Logging Your Reading.   For several days keep a log of the articles that you find. Record the author, title, and source for each promising piece so that you can easily find it again. Briefly note the subject and point of view as well, so you identify a range of possibilities.

Recalling Something You Have Already Read.   What have you read lately that started you thinking? Return to a recent reading—a chapter in a humanities textbook, an article assigned in a sociology course, a research study for a biology course.

For more on paraphrase and summary, see Ch. 12 and D4–D5 in the Quick Research Guide (the dark-red-edged pages).

Capturing Complex Ideas.   When you find a challenging reading, do you sometimes feel too overwhelmed to develop ideas from it? If so, read slowly and carefully. Then consider two common methods of recording and integrating ideas from sources into papers. First try *paraphrasing:* restating an author's ideas fully but in your own words. Then try *summarizing:* reducing an author's main point to essentials. Accurately recording what a reading says can help you grasp its ideas, especially on literal levels. Once you understand what it says, you are equipped to agree, disagree, or raise questions.

Reading Critically.   Read a thought-provoking piece, slowly and carefully, both literally and analytically. Instead of just soaking up what the reading says, engage in a dialogue or conversation with the writer. Criticize. Wonder. Argue back. Demand convincing evidence. Use the following checklist to get you started as a critical reader:

CRITICAL READING CHECKLIST

___ What problems and issues does the author raise?

___ What is the author's purpose? Is it to explain or inform? To persuade? To amuse? In addition to this overall purpose, is the author trying to accomplish some other agenda?

___ How does the author appeal to you as a reader? Where do you agree, and where do you disagree? Where do you want to say "Yeah, right!" or "I don't think so!"?

___ How does this piece relate to your own experiences or thoughts? Have you encountered anything similar? Does the topic or approach intrigue you?

___ Are there any important words or ideas that you don't understand? If so, do you need to reread or turn to a dictionary or reference book?

___ What is the author's point of view? What does the author assume or take for granted? Where does the author reveal these assumptions? Do they make the selection seem weak or biased?

For more on facts and opinions, see pp. 37–38.

___ Which statements are facts that can be verified by observation, firsthand testimony, or research? Which are opinions? Does one or the other dominate the piece?

___ Is the writer's evidence accurate, relevant, and sufficient? Do you find it persuasive?

For more on evaluating evidence, see C1–C3 in the Quick Research Guide (the dark-red-edged pages).

Analyzing Writing Strategies.   Reading widely and deeply can reveal not only what others say but also how they shape it and state it. For some readings in this book, notes in the margin illustrate how to identify key features such as the introduction, thesis statement or main idea, major points, and supporting evidence. Ask questions such as these to help you identify writing strategies:

WRITING STRATEGIES CHECKLIST

___ How does the author introduce the reading and try to engage the audience?

___ Where does the author state or imply the main idea or thesis?

___ How is the text organized? What main points develop the thesis?

___ How does the author supply support — facts, data, statistics, expert opinions, personal experiences, observations, explanations, examples, or other information?

___ How does the author connect or emphasize ideas for readers?

___ How does the author conclude the reading?

___ What is the author's tone? How do the words and examples reveal the author's attitude, biases, or assumptions?

ACTIVITY: READING CRITICALLY

For a sample annotated passage, see p. 24.

Using the advice in this chapter, critically read the following essay from the *Chicago Tribune Online*. First, add your own notes and comments in the margin, responding on both literal and analytical levels. Second, add notes about the writer's writing strategies. (Sample annotations are supplied to help you get started.) Finally, write out your own well-reasoned conclusions about the reading.

For more practice reading critically, read and annotate "Guys Just Want to Have Fun" (pp. 482–84) or "Male Bashing on TV" (pp. 515–19) from *A Writer's Reader*.

Jeffery M. Leving and Glenn Sacks
Women Don't Want Men? Ha!

Writers quote from
media sources

The recent census data finding that for the first time the majority of 1
American women are unmarried is being greeted in a largely celebra-
tory tone. One newspaper explains, "Who needs a man? Not most women."
MSNBC warns, "Watch out, men! More women opt to live alone." CBS says,
"More women saying 'I don't.'" One newspaper cartoon depicts a happily divorced woman remembering her ex-husband bellowing, "Where's my dinner?! Iron my shirts!! Lose weight!!!" Several others depict women ponder-
ing the single life as their fat, lazy husbands drink beer and watch TV sports.
One female blogger summed up the female blogosphere's reaction — "Hur-
ray for all single women! You go girls!"

Writers sum up sources,
but not all women would
agree

The message is clear — men don't measure up and are no longer needed 2
nor often even wanted. Since women have careers now, we are told, men's
traditional contribution — financial support — has become largely irrelevant,
and men do not now nor did they ever contribute much more than that.

Thesis challenges
sources

In reality, men give a lot to their families — as much as women do. The 3
current trend away from marriage and toward divorce and/or remaining single
has more to do with overcritical women and their excessive expectations
than it does with unsuitable men.

Seems true in my family!

The most common charge leveled at men is that they don't hold up 4
their end in the home. Men do work, many critics say, but women work too,
and also do most of the childcare and housework — the "second shift."

Writers cite data

Research contradicts this. Census data show that only 40 percent of 5
married women with children under eighteen work full-time, and more
than a quarter do not hold a job outside the home. According to the Bureau
of Labor Statistics' 2004 Time Use Survey, men spend $1^1/_2$ times as many
hours working as women do, and full-time employed men still work signifi-
antly more hours than full-time employed women. When work outside the
home and inside the home are properly considered, it is clear that men do
at least as much as women. A 2002 University of Michigan Institute for Social Research survey found that women do eleven more hours of housework
a week than men, but men work at their jobs fourteen hours a week more
than women. According to the Bureau of Labor Statistics, men's total time at
leisure, sleeping, doing personal-care activities, or socializing is a statistically
meaningless 1 percent higher than women's. The Families and Work Institute in New York City found that fathers, despite their greater market labor
load, provide three-fourths as much childcare as mothers do. And these
studies do not account for the fact, strongly supported by federal Department of Labor data, that men's jobs tend to be more dangerous and physically straining than women's.

To what, then, do we attribute women's discontent with marriage and 6
relationships and the fact that they initiate the vast majority of divorces? A

new *Woman's Day* magazine poll found that 56 percent of married women would not or might not marry their husbands if they could choose again.

Nobody would dispute that, in selecting a mate, women are more discerning than men. This is an evolutionary necessity—a woman must carefully evaluate who is likely to remain loyal to her and protect and provide for her and her children. If a man and a woman go on a blind date and don't hit it off, the man will shrug and say "It went OK." The woman will give five reasons why he's not right for her.   7

A woman's discerning, critical nature doesn't disappear on her wedding day. Most marital problems and marriage counseling sessions revolve around why the wife is unhappy with her husband, even though they could just as easily be about why the husband is unhappy with the wife. In this common predivorce scenario there are only two possibilities—either she's a great wife and he's a lousy husband, or she's far more critical of him than he is of her. Usually it's the latter.   8

Despite last week's media homilies, it's doubtful that many men or women are truly happy alone. Much of women's cheerful "I don't need a man/I love my cats" reaction has a hollow ring to it and sounds a lot more like whistling in the dark than a celebration.   9

Yes, there are some men who make poor mates but not nearly enough to account for the divorce epidemic and the decline of marriage. While it's easy to blame men, many of the wounds women bear from failed relationships and loneliness are self-inflicted.   10

A Reader's Resources

Major stages	Help in this book	Web help*
Get Started • Prepare to read purposefully. • Plan your follow-up in discussions, exams, or essays. • Skim the text.	▪ Information about a writer's purposes in Chapters 1 and 17 ▪ Common academic and other writing situations in Parts Two and Three ▪ "Getting Started" as a reader (pp. 22–25) and "Getting Ready" as a writer (pp. 308–09)	reading examples ▪ TopLinks
Respond to Reading • Read deeply. • Keep a reading journal. • Annotate the text.	▪ Advice on journals in Chapter 16 ▪ Annotated readings in Part Two and *A Writer's Reader* ▪ Reading questions in Part Two and *A Writer's Reader*	reading ▪ TopLinks
Read on a Literal Level • Know and recall what you read. • Comprehend the information. • Apply the information to other situations.	▪ "Questions to Start You Thinking" about meaning after each reading ▪ "As You Read" questions before the readings in Part Two and *A Writer's Reader* ▪ "Responding to an Image" prompts in *A Writer's Reader* and "Observing the Characteristics of an Image" in Chapter 22 for advice about "reading" images	reading visual ▪ TopLinks
Read on an Analytical Level • Analyze by breaking into parts or components. • Synthesize by combining with other materials. • Evaluate and assess.	▪ "Questions to Start You Thinking" about reading critically and making connections after each reading in *A Writer's Reader* ▪ Advice in Chapters 12, 13, and 19 and the Quick Research Guide on summarizing, analyzing, and evaluating ▪ Advice on interpreting the meaning of an image in Chapter 22	reading evaluate visual ▪ TopLinks
Generate Ideas from Reading • Look for meaty pieces. • Log your reading. • Recall previous reading. • Capture complex ideas. • Read critically. • Analyze writing strategies.	▪ Advice on finding and evaluating sources in the Quick Research Guide ▪ Specialized advice about reading literature in Chapter 13 ▪ Paired and related readings in *A Writer's Reader* ▪ Sample annotations and reading questions in Part Two and *A Writer's Reader* ▪ "Questions to Start You Thinking" about writing strategies after each reading	reading evaluate ▪ TopLinks

*At <bedfordstmartins.com/bedguide>, use the search box shown to find writing resources or exercises by keyword.

Chapter 3
Critical Thinking Processes

*C*ritic, from the Greek word *kritikos*, means "one who can judge and discern" — in short, someone who thinks critically. College will have given you your money's worth if it leaves you better able to judge and discern — to determine what is more and less important, to make distinctions and recognize differences, to generalize from specifics, to draw conclusions from evidence, to grasp complex concepts, to choose wisely. The effective thinking that you will need in college, on the job, and in your daily life is active and purposeful, not passive and ambling. It is critical thinking.

A Process of Critical Thinking

You use critical thinking every day to solve problems and make decisions. Suppose you don't have enough money both to pay your tuition and to buy the car you need. First, you might pin down the causes of your financial problem. Next, you might examine your options to find the best solution, as shown in the graphic on page 34.

ACTIVITY: THINKING CRITICALLY TO SOLVE A CAMPUS PROBLEM

With classmates, identify a common problem for students at your college — juggling a busy schedule, parking on campus, making a class change, joining a social group, or some other issue. Working together, use critical thinking to explore the problem and identify possible solutions.

*Critical Thinking
Processes in Action*

? **Problem**
You can't afford both your college tuition and the car you need.

Solution

1 IDENTIFY CAUSES

Causes in your control:
Expensive vacation?
Credit-card debt?

Causes out of your control:
Medical emergency?
Job loss?
Tuition increase?
Financial aid policy change?

2 ANALYZE, SYNTHESIZE, AND EVALUATE OPTIONS

Do without a car	(*how?*)	• Get rides with family or friends? • Take public transportation?
Decrease your tuition	(*how?*)	• Take fewer courses?
Get more money	(*how?*)	• Get a loan from the bank? • Get a loan from the college? • Get a loan from a family member? • Get another job?

3 REACH A LOGICAL CONCLUSION
Apply for a short-term loan through the college for tuition.

Getting Started

■ For more on critical reading, see Ch. 2.

Using critical thinking, you can explore many problems step by step and reach reasonable solutions. Critical thinking, like critical reading, draws on a cluster of intellectual strategies and skills.

CRITICAL THINKING SKILL	DEFINITION	APPLICATIONS FOR READERS	APPLICATIONS FOR WRITERS
Analysis	Breaking down information into its parts and elements	Analyzing the information in articles, reports, and books to grasp the facts and concepts they contain	Analyzing events, ideas, processes, and structures to understand them and explain them to readers

(*continued on next page*)

CRITICAL THINKING SKILL	DEFINITION	APPLICATIONS FOR READERS	APPLICATIONS FOR WRITERS
Synthesis	Putting together elements and parts to form new wholes	Synthesizing information from several sources, examining implications, and drawing conclusions supported by reliable evidence	Synthesizing source materials with your own thoughts in order to convey the unique combination to others
Evaluation	Judging according to standards or criteria	Evaluating a reading by determining standards for judging, applying them to the reading, and arriving at a conclusion about its significance or value	Evaluating something in writing by convincing readers that your standards are reasonable and that the subject either does or does not meet those standards

These three activities — analysis, synthesis, and evaluation — are the core of critical thinking. They are not new to you, but applying them rigorously in college-level reading and writing may be. When you approach college reading and writing tasks, instructors will expect you (and you should expect yourself) to think, read, write, and think some more.

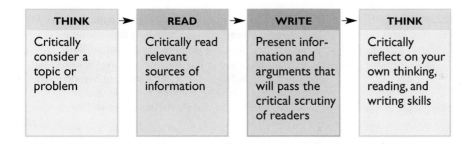

THINK	READ	WRITE	THINK
Critically consider a topic or problem	Critically read relevant sources of information	Present information and arguments that will pass the critical scrutiny of readers	Critically reflect on your own thinking, reading, and writing skills

ACTIVITY: THINKING CRITICALLY TO EXPLORE AN ISSUE

You have worked hard on a group presentation that will be a major part of your grade — and each member of the group will get the same grade. Two days before the project is due, you discover that one group member has plagiarized heavily from sources well known to your instructor. Working together with classmates, use critical thinking to explore your problem and determine what you might do.

APPLYING CRITICAL THINKING TO ACADEMIC PROBLEMS

As you write your college papers, you'll gain experience grappling with academic problems. You'll be expected to use your critical thinking skills — analyzing, synthesizing, and evaluating—as you read and write. Although you may simply dive in, using each skill as needed, sometimes the very wording of an assignment or examination question will alert you to a skill that your instructor expects you to use. What an instructor might expect is illustrated for the first sample assignment in each set in the chart below.

Using Critical Thinking for College Assignments	CRITICAL THINKING SKILL	SAMPLE COLLEGE WRITING ASSIGNMENTS
	Analysis: breaking into parts and elements based on a principle	• Describe the immediate causes of the 1929 stock market crash. (Analyze by using the principle of immediate causes to identify and explain the reasons for the 1929 crash.) • Trace the stages through which a bill becomes federal law. • Explain and illustrate the three dominant styles of parenting. • Define *romanticism,* identifying and illustrating its major characteristics.
	Synthesis: combining parts and elements to form new wholes	• Discuss the following statement: high-minded opposition to slavery was only one cause, and not a very important one, of the animosity between North and South that in 1861 escalated into civil war. (Synthesize by combining the causes or elements of the North-South animosity, going beyond the opposition to slavery, to form a new whole: your conclusion that accounts for the escalation into civil war.) • Imagine that you are a trial lawyer in 1921, charged with defending Nicola Sacco and Bartolomeo Vanzetti, two anarchists accused of murder. Argue for their acquittal on whatever grounds you can justify.
	Evaluation: judging according to standards or criteria	• Present and evaluate the most widely accepted theories that account for the disappearance of the dinosaurs. (Evaluate, based on standards such as scientific merit, the credibility of each theory.) • Defend or challenge the idea that houses and public buildings should be constructed to last no longer than twenty years. • Contrast the models of the solar system advanced by Copernicus and by Kepler, showing how the latter improved on the former.

ACTIVITY: THINKING CRITICALLY TO RESPOND TO AN ACADEMIC PROBLEM

Working with a classmate or a small group, select a sample assignment (not already explained) from the table on page 36 or from one of your classes. Explain how you would approach the assignment in order to demonstrate your critical thinking. Share your strategies for figuring out how to tackle college assignments.

Supporting Critical Thinking with Evidence

As you write a college paper, you try to figure out your purpose, the position you want to take, and ways to get readers to follow your logic and accept your points. Your challenge, of course, is not just to think clearly but to demonstrate your thinking to others, to persuade them to pay attention to what you say. And sound evidence is what critical readers want to see.

Sound evidence supports your main idea or thesis, substantiating your points for readers. It also bolsters your credibility as a writer, demonstrating the merit of your position. When you write, you need to marshal enough appropriate evidence to clarify, explain, and support your ideas. You need to weave claims, evidence, and your own interpretations together into a clearly reasoned explanation or argument. And as you do so, you need to select and test your evidence so that it will convince your readers.

> ■ For advice on using a few sources, see the Quick Research Guide (the dark-red-edged pages).

TYPES OF EVIDENCE

What is evidence? It is anything that demonstrates the soundness of a claim. Facts, statistics, firsthand observations, and expert testimony are four reliable forms of evidence. Other evidence might include examples, illustrations, details, and opinions. Depending on the purpose of your assignment, some kinds of evidence weigh more heavily than others. For example, readers might appreciate your memories of livestock care on the farm in an essay recalling your childhood summers. However, they would probably discount your memories in an argumentative paper about agricultural methods unless you could show that your memories are representative or that you are an expert on the subject. Personal experience may strengthen an argument but generally is not sufficient as its sole support. If you are in doubt about the type of evidence an assignment requires, ask your instructor whether you should use sources or rely on personal experience and examples.

> ■ For more on using evidence in a paper that takes a stand, see pp. 152–56.

Facts.   Facts are statements that can be verified objectively, by observation or by reading a reliable account. They are usually stated dispassionately: "If you pump the air out of a five-gallon varnish can, it will collapse." Of course, we accept many of our facts based on the testimony of others. For example, we believe that the Great Wall of China exists although we may never have seen it with our own eyes.

Sometimes people say facts are true statements, but truth and sound evidence may be confused. Consider the truth of these statements:

The tree in my yard is an oak.	*True* because it can be verified
A kilometer is 1,000 meters.	*True* using the metric system
The speed limit on the highway is 65 miles per hour.	*True* according to law
Fewer fatal highway accidents have occurred since the new exit ramp was built.	*True* according to research studies
My favorite food is pizza.	*True* as an opinion
More violent criminals should receive the death penalty.	*True* as a belief
Murder is wrong.	*True* as a value judgment

Some would claim that each statement is true, but when you think critically, you should avoid treating opinions, beliefs, judgments, or personal experience as true in the same sense that verifiable facts and events are true.

Statistics. Statistics are facts expressed in numbers. What portion of American children are poor? According to statistics from the U.S. Census Bureau, 13.4 million children (or 18.5 percent of all children) lived in poverty in 2005 compared with 11.7 million (or 16.3 percent) in 2001. Clear as such figures seem, they may raise complex questions. For example, how significant is the increase in the poverty rate over four years? What percentage of children were poor over longer terms such as ten years or twenty?

Most writers, without trying to be dishonest, interpret statistics to help their causes. The statement "Fifty percent of the populace have incomes above the poverty level" might substantiate the fine job done by the government of a developing nation. Putting the statement another way — "Fifty percent of the populace have incomes below the poverty level" — might use the same statistic to show the inadequacy of the government's efforts.

Even though a writer is free to interpret a statistic, statistics should not be used to mislead. On the wrapper of a peanut candy bar, we read that a one-ounce serving contains only 150 calories. The claim is true, but the bar weighs 1.6 ounces. Gobble it all — more likely than eating 62 percent of it — and you'll ingest 240 calories, a heftier snack than the innocent statistic on the wrapper suggests. Because abuses make some readers automatically distrustful, use figures fairly when you write, and make sure they are accurate. If you doubt a statistic, compare it with figures reported by several other sources. Distrust a statistical report that differs from every other report unless it is backed by further evidence.

Expert Testimony.   By "experts," we mean people with knowledge gained from study and experience of a particular field. The test of an expert is whether his or her expertise stands up to the scrutiny of others who are knowledgeable in that field. The views of Michael Jordan on how to play offense in basketball carry authority. So do the views of economist and former Federal Reserve chairman Alan Greenspan on what causes inflation. However, Jordan's take on the economy or Greenspan's thoughts on basketball might not be authoritative. Also consider whether the expert has any bias or special interest that would affect reliability. Statistics on cases of lung cancer attributed to smoking might be better taken from government sources than from the tobacco industry.

■ Should you want to contact a campus expert, turn to Ch. 6 for advice about interviews.

Firsthand Observation.   Firsthand observation is persuasive. It can add concrete reality to abstract or complex points. You might support the claim "The Meadowfield waste recycling plant fails to meet state guidelines" by recalling your own observations: "When I visited the plant last January, I was struck by the number of open waste canisters and by the lack of protective gear for the workers who handle these toxic materials daily."

■ For more on observation, see Ch. 5.

As readers, most of us tend to trust the writer who declares, "I was there. This is what I saw." Sometimes that trust is misplaced, however, so always be wary of a writer's claim to have seen something that no other evidence supports. Ask yourself, Is this writer biased? Might the writer have (intentionally or unintentionally) misinterpreted what he or she saw? Of course, your readers will scrutinize your firsthand observations, too; take care to reassure them that your observations are unbiased and accurate.

ACTIVITY: LOOKING FOR EVIDENCE

Using the issue you explored with classmates for the activity on page 33, what would you need to support your identification, explanation, or solution of the problem? Working with classmates, identify the kinds of evidence that would be most useful. Where or how might you find such evidence?

■ For more on selecting evidence to persuade readers, see pp. 155–156.

Testing Evidence

As both a reader and a writer, you should always critically test and question evidence to see whether it is strong enough to carry the weight of the writer's claims. Use these questions to determine whether evidence is useful and trustworthy:

■ For advice on evaluating sources of evidence, see C in the Quick Research Guide (the dark-red-edged pages).

EVIDENCE CHECKLIST

___ Is it accurate?
  • Do the facts and figures seem accurate based on what you have found in published sources, reports by others, or reference works?
  • Are figures or quoted facts copied correctly?

___ Is it reliable?
  • Is the source trustworthy and well regarded?
  • Does the source acknowledge any commercial, political, advocacy, or other bias that might affect the quality of its information?
  • Does the writer supplying the evidence have appropriate credentials or experience? Is the writer respected as an expert in the field?
  • Do other sources agree with the information?

___ Is it up-to-date?
  • Are facts and statistics — such as population figures — current?
  • Is the information from the latest sources?

___ Is it to the point?
  • Does the evidence back the exact claim made?
  • Is the evidence all pertinent? Does any of it drift from the point to interesting but irrelevant evidence?

___ Is it representative?
  • Are examples typical of all the things included in the writer's position?
  • Are examples balanced? Do they present the topic or issue fairly?
  • Are contrary examples acknowledged?

For information on mistakes in thinking, see pp. 46–47 and pp. 162–63.

___ Is it appropriately complex?
  • Is the evidence sufficient to account for the claim made?
  • Does it avoid treating complex things superficially?
  • Does it avoid needlessly complicating simple things?

___ Is it sufficient and strong enough to back the claim and persuade readers?
  • Are the amount and quality of the evidence appropriate for the claim and for the readers?
  • Is the evidence aligned with the existing knowledge of readers?
  • Does the evidence answer the questions readers are likely to ask?
  • Is the evidence vivid and significant?

Using Evidence to Appeal to Your Audience

For more on appeals, see pp. 157–58.

One way to select evidence and to judge whether it is appropriate and sufficient is to consider the types of appeal — logical, emotional, and ethical. Most effective arguments work on all three levels, using all three types of appeals with evidence that supports all three.

LOGICAL APPEAL (LOGOS)

When writers use a logical appeal (*logos* or "word" in Greek), they appeal to the reader's mind or intellect. This appeal relies on evidence that is factual, objective, clear, and relevant. Critical readers expect to find logical evidence that supports major claims and statements. For example, if a writer were arguing for term limits for legislators, she wouldn't want to base her argument on the evidence that some long-term legislators weren't reelected last term (irrelevant) or that the current system is unfair to young people who want to get into politics (not logical). Instead, she might argue that the absence of term limits encourages corruption, using evidence of legislators who repaid lobbyists for campaign contributions with key votes.

EMOTIONAL APPEAL (PATHOS)

When writers use an emotional appeal (*pathos* or "suffering" in Greek), they appeal to the reader's heart. They choose language, facts, quotations, examples, and images that evoke emotional responses. Of course, convincing writing does touch readers' hearts as well as their minds. Without this heartfelt tug, a strict logical appeal may seem cold and dehumanized. If a writer opposed hunting seals for their fur, he might combine statistics about the number of seals killed each year and the overall population decrease with a vivid description of baby seals being slaughtered. Some writers use emotional words and sentimental examples to manipulate readers — to arouse their sympathy, pity, or anger in order to convert them without much logical evidence — but dishonest emotional appeals may alienate readers. Instead of basing an argument against a political candidate on pitiful images of scrawny children living in roach-infested squalor, a good writer would report the candidate's voting record on issues that affect children.

ETHICAL APPEAL (ETHOS)

When writers use an ethical appeal (*ethos* or "character" in Greek), they call on the reader's sense of fairness and trust. They select and present evidence in a way that will make the audience trust them, respect their judgment, and believe what they have to say. The best logical argument in the world falls flat when readers don't take the writer seriously. How can you use an ethical appeal to establish your credibility as a writer? First you need to establish your credentials in the field through experience, reading, or interviews that helped you learn about the subject. If you are writing about environmental pollution, tell your readers that your allergies have been irritated by chemicals in the air. Identify medical or environmental experts you have contacted or whose publications you have read. Demonstrate your knowledge through the information you present, the experts and sources you cite, and the depth of understanding you convey. Establish a rapport with readers by indicating values and attitudes that you share with them and by responding seriously to opposing arguments. Finally, use language that is precise, clear, and appropriate in tone.

ACTIVITY: IDENTIFYING TYPES OF APPEALS

Bring to class the editorial or opinion page from a newspaper or news-magazine. Read some of the letters or articles. Identify the types of appeals used by each author to support his or her point.

Presenting Your Critical Thinking

For more on taking a stand, see Ch. 9; on proposals, see Ch. 10; on evaluation, see Ch. 11; and on supporting a position, see Ch. 12.

Why do you have to worry about critical thinking? Isn't it enough just to tell everybody else what you think? That tactic probably works fine when you casually debate with your friends. After all, they already know you, your opinions, and your typical ways of thinking. They may even find your occasional rant entertaining. Whether they agree or disagree, they probably tolerate your ideas because they are your friends.

When you write a paper in college, however, you face a different type of audience, one that expects you to explain what you assume, what you advocate, and why you hold that position. That audience also wants to learn the specifics — the reasons you find compelling, the evidence that supports your view, and the connections that relate each point to your position. Finally, your college audience expects reasoning, not emotional pleading or bullying or preaching.

How you reason and how you present your reasoning are important parts of gaining the confidence of college readers. College papers typically develop their points based on logic, not personal opinions or beliefs. Most are organized logically, often as a series of reasons, each making a claim, a statement, or an assertion that is backed up with persuasive supporting evidence. Your assignment or your instructor may recommend ways such as the following for showing your critical thinking.

For more about the statement-support pattern, see A3 in the Quick Research Guide (the dark-red-edged pages).

Reasoning Deductively or Inductively.   When you state a *generalization,* you present your broad, general point, viewpoint, or conclusion.

> The admissions requirements at Gerard College are unfair.

On the other hand, when you supply a *particular,* you present an instance, a detail, an example, an item, a case, or other specific evidence to demonstrate that a general statement is reasonable.

> A Gerard College application form shows the information collected by the admissions office. According to the admissions policies, standardized test scores are weighted more heavily than better predictors of performance, such as high school grades. Qualified students who do not test well often face a frustrating admissions process, as Irma Lang's situation illustrates.

Your particulars consist of details that back up your broader point; your generalizations connect the particulars so that you can move beyond isolated, individual cases.

Most college papers are organized *deductively.* They begin with a general statement (often a thesis) and then present particular cases to support or apply it. Readers like this pattern because it reduces mystery; they learn right away what the writer wants to show. Writers like this pattern because it helps them state up front what they want to accomplish (even if they have to figure some of that out as they write and state it more directly as they revise). Papers organized deductively sacrifice suspense but gain directness and clarity.

For more about thesis statements, see Ch. 17.

On the other hand, some papers are organized *inductively.* They begin with the particulars—a persuasive number of instances, examples, or details—and lead up to the larger generalization that they support. Because readers have to wait for the generalization, this pattern allows them time to adjust to an unexpected conclusion that they might initially reject. For this reason, writers favor this pattern when they anticipate resistance from their audience and want to move gradually toward the broader point.

For more on inductive and deductive reasoning, see pp. 357–59.

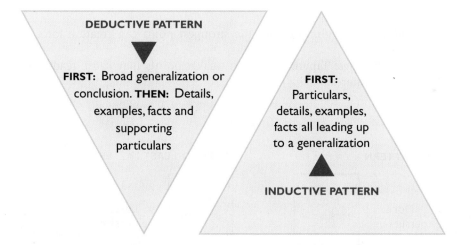

DEDUCTIVE PATTERN

FIRST: Broad generalization or conclusion. **THEN:** Details, examples, facts and supporting particulars

FIRST: Particulars, details, examples, facts all leading up to a generalization

INDUCTIVE PATTERN

Building Sequences and Scaffolds.   You may use several strategies for presenting your reasoning, depending on what you want to show and how you think you can show it most persuasively. You may develop a line of reasoning, a series of points and evidence, running one after another in a sequence or building on one another to support a persuasive scaffold (see p. 44).

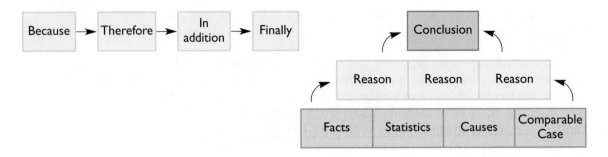

For more strategies for developing, see Ch. 19.

Developing Logical Patterns.   The following patterns are often used to organize reasoning in college papers. Although they can help you show relationships, they don't automatically prove them. In fact, each has advantages but may also have disadvantages, as the sample strengths and weaknesses illustrate.

Pattern: Least to Most
Advantage: Building up to the best points can produce a strong finish.
Disadvantage: Holding back on the strongest points makes readers wait.

Pattern: Most to Least
Advantage: Beginning with the strongest point can create a forceful opening.
Disadvantage: Tapering off with weaker points may cause readers to lose interest.

LEAST TO MOST PATTERN

| Least persuasive | More persuasive | Most persuasive |

MOST TO LEAST PATTERN

| Most persuasive | Less persuasive | Least persuasive |

For more on comparison and contrast, see Ch. 7.

Pattern: Comparison and Contrast
Advantage: Readers can easily relate comparable points about things of like kind.
Disadvantage: Some similarities or differences don't guarantee or prove others.

Pattern: Cause and Effect

Advantage: Tracing causes or effects can tightly relate and perhaps predict events.

Disadvantage: Weak links can call into question all relationships in a series of events.

▨ For more on cause and effect, see Ch. 8.

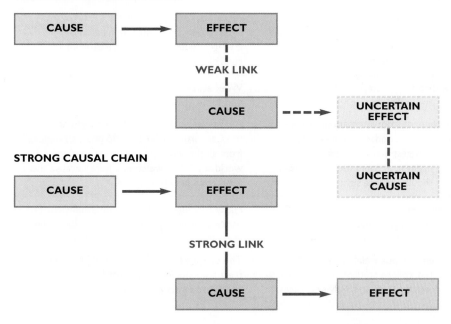

Avoiding Faulty Thinking

For specific logical fallacies, see pp. 162–63.

Common mistakes in thinking can distort evidence or lead to wrong conclusions. How can you avoid such mistakes as you write or spot them as you read? A good strategy is to look carefully at the ways in which you (or the author of a reading) describe events, relate ideas, identify reasons, supply evidence, and draw conclusions.

	SOUND REASONING	WEAK REASONING
Comparisons	Comparison that uses substantial likeness to project other similarities: Like the third graders in the innovative reading programs just described, the children in this town also could become better readers.	Inaccurate comparison that relies on slight or superficial likenesses to project other similarities: Like kittens eagerly stalking mice in the fields, young readers should gobble up the tasty tales that were the favorites of their grandparents.
Causes and Effects	Causal analysis that relies on well-substantiated connections relating events and outcomes: City water reserves have suffered from below-average rainfall, above-average heat, and steadily increasing consumer demand.	Faulty reasoning that oversimplifies causal relationships, confuses coincidences with causes, or assumes that a first event must cause a second: One cause—and one alone—accounts for the ten-year drought that has dried up local water supplies.
Reasons	Logical reasons that are supported by relevant evidence and presented with fair and thoughtful consideration: As the recent audit indicates, all campus groups that spend student activity fees should prepare budgets, keep clear financial records, and substantiate expenses.	Faulty reasons that rely on bias, emotion, or unrelated personal traits or that accuse, flatter, threaten, or inspire fear: All campus groups, especially the arrogant social groups, must stop ripping off the average student's fees and threatening to run college costs sky high.
Evidence	Evidence that is accurate, reliable, current, relevant, fair, and sufficient to persuade readers: Both the statistics from international agencies and the accounts of Sudanese refugees summarized earlier suggest that, while a fair immigration policy needs to account for many complexities, it should not lose sight of compassion.	Weak evidence that is insufficient, out of date, unreliable, slanted, or emotional: As five-year-old Lannie's frantic flight across the Canadian border in 1988 proves, refugees from all the war-torn regions around the world should be welcomed here because this is America, land of the free.
Conclusions	Solid conclusions that are based on factual evidence and recognize multiple options or complications: As the recent campus wellness study has demonstrated, college students need education about healthy food and activity choices.	Hasty conclusions that rely on insufficient evidence, assumptions, or simplistic two-option choices: The campus health facility should refuse to treat students who don't eat healthy foods and exercise daily.

Use the following questions to help you refine your reasoning as you plan, draft, or revise a college paper:

LOGICAL REASONING CHECKLIST

___ Have you reviewed your assignment or syllabus, looking for advice or requirements about the kind of reasoning or evidence expected?

___ Have you developed your reasoning on a solid foundation? Are your initial assumptions sound? Do you need to identify, explain, or justify them?

___ Is your thesis or position stated clearly? Are its terms explained or defined?

___ Have you presented your reasons for thinking that your thesis is sound? Have you arranged them in a sequence that will make sense to your audience? Have you used transitions to introduce and connect them so readers can't miss them?

___ Have you used evidence that your audience will respect to support each reason you present? Have you favored objective, research-based evidence (facts, statistics, and expert testimony that others can substantiate) rather than personal experiences or beliefs that others cannot or may not share?

___ Have you explained your evidence so that your audience can see how it supports your points and applies to your thesis? Have you used transitions to specify relationships for readers?

___ Have you enhanced your own credibility by acknowledging, rather than ignoring, other points of view? Have you integrated or countered these views?

___ Have you adjusted your tone and style so that you come across as reasonable and fair-minded? Have you avoided arrogant claims about proving (rather than showing) points?

___ If you have used any sources, have you credited them as expected by academic readers?

ACTIVITY: ANALYZING REASONING

Analyze the newspaper column and the letter on pages 48–49, looking for clear reasoning as well as flaws in logic. For each, identify its position, its sequence of reasons or points, its supporting evidence, and its methods of appealing to readers. The column by Al Knight appeared in the *Denver Post* on November 22, 2006.

Al Knight

Perhaps We Should Move to Save Dogs
from Their Owners

The election earlier this month settled a lot of the state's big issues, like who will sit in the governor's office, but there are plenty of little problems that were left for another day. One of them is whether Colorado should join a handful of other states and prohibit pickup owners from plying the state's major highways with one or several dogs loose in the truck bed. 1

Colorado is a big state with lots of open road. Anyone who has traveled those roads will have seen a truck owner speeding down the highway with his pet or pets running from side to side in the open bed, seemingly inches from certain disaster. There is, alas, more than the prospect of disaster. According to one estimate, 100,000 dogs are killed each year by either falling out of or being intentionally tossed out of careening pickup trucks. 2

Some states — including Virginia, Florida, New Hampshire, California, Rhode Island, Massachusetts, and Oregon — have passed legislation regulating the practice. Some localities and counties also have local ordinances on the subject. In all of these locations, proponents advanced arguments dealing with public as well as animal safety. A frolicking dog in the back of a pickup is an obvious distraction and hazard, not only for the truck owner and the dog but for anybody else on or near that road or highway. 3

As to animal safety, as far back as 1988, the Society for the Prevention of Cruelty to Animals did a study in Massachusetts that was based on interviews with 141 veterinarians. The organization found that those vets had treated 592 dogs that year for injuries received when tossed from the bed of a pickup. The Humane Society, in an article titled "Why Dogs and Pickup Trucks Don't Mix," stated the obvious quite nicely: "If your truck hits a bump, or if you step on the brakes suddenly or swerve to avoid an obstacle, your dog can easily be thrown from the truck bed and onto the road. Chances are, this will injure or kill your dog. But even if it doesn't, being struck by another vehicle probably will. Also, other drivers may cause an accident by swerving to avoid hitting your dog." 4

The question remains whether the plainly unwise practice of transporting loose dogs in pickup beds should be regulated. Would such a law, for example, interfere with the rights of farmers, ranchers, hunters, and others who might have a reason to transport dogs in this fashion? Well, the handful of states that have addressed that concern have carved out narrow exceptions to cover those situations. Oregon, for example, has an exception for ranching and farming which is limited to noninterstate highways and population centers with less than 5,000 people. In Tennessee, where a bill was considered and later defeated, the measure had a narrow exception for licensed hunters. In Texas, where there has been a petition drive urging the legislature to act, a proposed law has exceptions for hunters and ranchers. 5

These exceptions haven't satisfied everyone. During the Tennessee debate, one lawmaker complained that the proposed statute would "absolutely destroy the way people live with these animals."

Hysteria aside, there are good arguments to be made in favor of a state 6 statute requiring the use of carriers or restraints:

- The current system doesn't work. While many dogs can survive a ride in the back of a pickup, many will not.

- Public education doesn't seem to be a good option. The typical pickup/dog owner surely knows the risks but has chosen to ignore them. More education is unlikely to change that fact.

- Enforcement of a statute would be a breeze. The dog is typically in plain sight. A safety officer need not listen to the kind of stories offered when someone is stopped for speeding or a seat-belt violation. It would be hard for a driver to claim the officer was mistaken and that "the dog wasn't really in the bed of the pickup in the first place."

If one of the new legislators in Colorado wants to take on the task of 7 passing such a law, next year would be a good time to start.

Letter from an Irate Dog Owner

Dear Editor:

Even a city slicker should be able to see why dogs belong in pickup trucks. All dogs love riding out in the air. They need room to jump around. And you'd better just zip your lip if you see me driving down I-25 with my dog.

Who would want Colorado to turn into one of those wimpy states that amends its constitution whenever some bleeding heart starts feeling sorrowful about wolves or dolphins? Maybe we should bring fur coats back here instead of trying to force hard-working citizens to take their dogs out of their trucks. This whole issue stinks!

Dog owners have the right to do whatever they want with their animals. This is the kind of law that only busybodies would support. If you're thinking of supporting this issue, you'd better think again. Besides, if my dog had any complaints, he'd have to take them up with me!

An Irate Dog Owner

A Critical Thinker's Resources

Major stages	Help in this book	Web help*
Get Started • Analyze by breaking into parts or components. • Synthesize by combining with other materials. • Evaluate and assess.	▦ Summarizing, analyzing, synthesizing, and evaluating advice in Chapters 12 and 19 and the Quick Research Guide ▦ Criteria for evaluating sources in the Quick Research Guide ▦ Advice on interpreting images in Chapter 22	🔍 development 🔍 evaluate 🔍 visual
Apply Critical Thinking Skills • Think through topics, problems, and assignments. • Think critically as a reader. • Think critically as a writer.	▦ Logical thinking advice in Chapter 9, "Taking a Stand" ▦ A Writer's Reader and Part Two (for applying your critical thinking skills as a reader) ▦ Writing situations in Parts Two and Three (for applying your critical thinking skills)	🔍 reading 🔍 examples
Supply Evidence to Support Thinking • Find facts. • Add statistics. • Look for expert testimony. • Observe.	▦ Tips for finding and evaluating sources in the Quick Research Guide ▦ "Using Visuals to Reinforce Your Content" section in Chapter 21 ▦ Observing and interviewing advice in Chapters 5 and 6	🔍 support 🔍 visual 🔍 evaluate
Test Evidence • Read to confirm accuracy, reliability, and currency. • Select what is pertinent and representative. • Monitor complexity. • Supply enough strong evidence to persuade readers.	▦ Advice on critical reading in Chapter 2; questions and annotations with readings ▦ "Strategies for Developing," in Chapter 19 ▦ Critical thinking skills for researchers in the Quick Research Guide ▦ Part Two, especially Chapters 7 to 12 (for applying these skills)	🔍 reading 🔍 development 🔍 support
Use Evidence to Support Appeals • Appeal to logic. • Appeal to emotions. • Appeal to ethical issues of fairness and trust.	▦ Advice on making compelling appeals to readers in Chapters 9, 10, and 11 ▦ Advice on purpose and audience in Chapters 1 (pp. 14–19) and 17 (pp. 310–12)	🔍 support 🔍 examples
Present Your Critical Thinking • Develop logical reasoning. • Build sequences and scaffolds. • Watch out for faulty thinking.	▦ Advice on logical reasoning in Chapters 3, 9, 10, and 11 ▦ Advice on development in Chapter 19 ▦ Advice on avoiding faulty thinking (p. 46) and logical fallacies (pp. 162–63)	🔍 development

*At <bedfordstmartins.com/bedguide>, use the search box shown to find writing resources or exercises by keyword.

PART TWO

A Writer's Situations

Introduction

In Part Two, we present a sequence of writing situations that require you to use processes for writing, reading, and thinking critically. The nine writing assignments—recalling an experience, observing a scene, interviewing a subject, comparing and contrasting, explaining causes and effects, taking a stand, proposing a solution, evaluating, and supporting a position with sources—are arranged roughly in order of increasing complexity—that is, according to the level of critical reading and thinking required. Some require analysis—breaking something down into its components to understand it better. Others require synthesis—combining information from various sources with your own ideas in order to achieve a new perspective. Still others call for evaluation, using criteria to judge. Let's look at these writing situations in more detail.

Recalling an Experience.   Recalling an event depends on your richest resource as a writer—your memory. Chapter 4 guides you in focusing and shaping your writing from memory so that you can present recollections effectively and convey their importance to your readers.

Observing a Scene.   Observation relies on using your senses to see, hear, smell, touch, and taste what's around you. Chapter 5 helps you select and arrange compelling details in order to convey your insights about what you have observed.

Interviewing a Subject.   Interviewing adds to your writing the freshness of conversation and the liveliness of exchange with someone else. Chapter 6 encourages you to bring the subject of an interview to life as you distill the impression and information gained during your interview.

Comparing and Contrasting.   Comparing and contrasting focuses on the similarities and differences of two (or more) items or groups. Chapter 7 guides you first in analyzing each item and then in lining up the characteristics of each, side by side, to determine how they are alike and how they are different. Most important, because effective comparison and contrast has some significant purpose, you will convey your conclusion about how each alternative operates or which alternative is preferable.

Explaining Causes and Effects.   As you focus on an action, event, or situation, identifying causes means ferreting out roots and origins. Determining effects means figuring out results. Sometimes as you analyze, you will find a chain of causes and effects: a situation causes specific effects, which in turn cause other effects. Chapter 8 helps you to analyze and explain causes, effects, or both in order to support an overall point.

Taking a Stand.   When you take a stand, you argue for one side or another of an issue. Chapter 9 helps you develop your position in a controversy and present your opinion so that readers will respect it even if they do not agree with you. You may come to a debate with strong views or develop a position while looking into the matter. Once you reach a clear position, you will present your case persuasively to readers using solid, pertinent evidence — facts, statistics, expert opinion, and direct observation.

Proposing a Solution.   Proposing a solution requires not only taking a stand but also presenting a feasible solution to the problem at hand. Chapter 10 helps you identify a problem and then propose a convincing, workable solution. You will use two main methods of persuading readers to accept your recommendation: showing readers why the problem matters to them and supplying evidence to support your solution.

Evaluating.   Evaluating means judging: deciding whether an idea, a product, a work of art, or some other thing is good or bad, effective or ineffective. As Chapter 11 explains, you will identify specific criteria for judging your subject. Once your standards are clear, based on your personal preferences or the views of experts in the field, you can analyze your subject to see how well it meets your criteria. As you explain your judgment, you will also try to persuade readers that your view is reasonable.

Supporting a Position with Sources.   Especially in college papers, you often need to state and support a position with evidence from a few sources. Chapter 12 guides you through the process of reading a cluster of sources and capturing information from them in quotations, paraphrases, and summaries. You will launch such information with a suitable introduction, cite the source as you mention it, and list the source at the end of your paper. Finally, you will learn strategies for keeping sources in their proper supporting role by developing your own voice as a credible college writer.

Taken together, these nine chapters present many of the writing situations you will encounter in other college courses and in your career. Use the processes outlined in these chapters as resources when you meet unfamiliar writing situations or need to marshal appropriate evidence for essays.

Chapter 4
Recalling an Experience

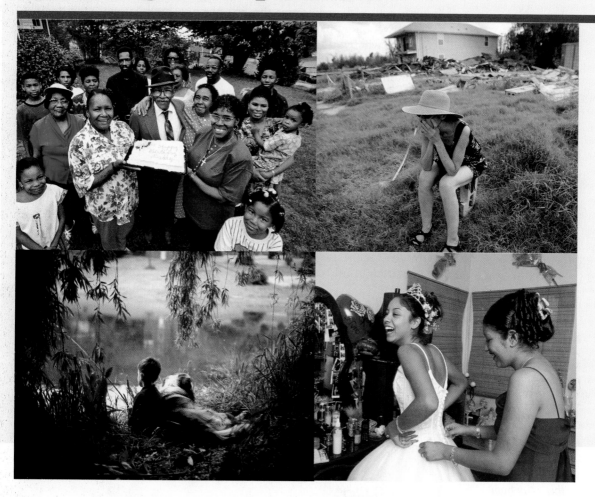

Responding to an Image

Look carefully at one of the photographs in the grid. In your view, when was this photograph taken? Who might the person or people be? Where are they, and why are they there? What are they doing? What relationships and emotions does the picture suggest with its focal point and arrangement? Write about an experience the image helps you recall or about a possible explanation of events in this picture. Use vivid detail to convey what happened to you or what might have happened to the people in the picture.

Writing from recall is writing from memory, a writer's richest—and handiest—resource. Recall is clearly necessary when you are asked to write of a personal experience, a favorite place, a memorable person. But even when an instructor hands you a subject that seems to have nothing to do with you, your memory is the first place to look. Suppose you have to write a psychology paper about how advertisers prey on consumers' fears. Begin with what you remember. What ads have sent chills down your back? What ads have suggested that their products could save you from a painful social blunder, a lonely night, or a deadly accident? All by itself, memory may not give you enough to write about, but you will rarely go wrong if you start by jotting down something remembered.

Learning from Other Writers

■ For more on thesis and support, see Chs. 17 and 19.

Here are two samples of good writing from recall—one by a professional writer, one by a college student. To help you begin to analyze the first reading, look for the notes in the margin. They identify features such as the main idea, or thesis, and the first of the main events that support it in a paper written from recall.

As You Read These Recollections

■ For more examples of writing from recall, visit <bedfordstmartins.com/bedguide> and do a keyword search:

As you read these essays, ask yourself the following questions:

1. Is the perspective of the essay primarily that of a child or an adult? Why do you think so?
2. What does the author realize after reflecting on the events recalled? Does the realization come soon after the experience or later, when the writer examines the events from a more mature perspective?
3. How does the realization change the individual?

In this essay from his autobiography Growing Up *(1982), columnist Russell Baker recalls being sixteen in urban Baltimore and wondering what to do with his life.*

Russell Baker
The Art of Eating Spaghetti

The only thing that truly interested me was writing, and I knew that sixteen-year-olds did not come out of high school and become writers. I thought of writing as something to be done only by the rich. It was so obviously not real work, not a job at which you could earn a living. Still, I had begun to think of myself as a writer. It was the only thing for which I seemed to have the smallest talent, and, silly though it sounded when I told people I'd like to be a writer, it gave me a way of thinking about myself which satisfied my need to have an identity.

Introduction

56

The notion of becoming a writer had flickered off and on in my head 2
since the Belleville days, but it wasn't until my third year in high school that **THESIS**
the possibility took hold. Until then I'd been bored by everything associated   stating main idea
with English courses. I found English grammar dull and baffling. I hated the
assignments to turn out "compositions," and went at them like heavy labor,
turning out leaden, lackluster paragraphs that were agonies for teachers to
read and for me to write. The classics thrust on me to read seemed as dead-
ening as chloroform.

Major event 1

When our class was assigned to Mr. Fleagle for third-year English I antici- 3
pated another grim year in that dreariest of subjects. Mr. Fleagle was notori-
ous among City students for dullness and inability to inspire. He was said to
be stuffy, dull, and hopelessly out of date. To me he looked to be sixty or seventy and prim to a fault. He wore primly severe eyeglasses, his wavy hair was
primly cut and primly combed. He wore prim vested suits with neckties
blocked primly against the collar buttons of his primly starched white shirts.
He had a primly pointed jaw, a primly straight nose, and a prim manner of
speaking that was so correct, so gentlemanly, that he seemed a comic antique.

I anticipated a listless,° unfruitful year with Mr. Fleagle and for a long 4
time was not disappointed. We read *Macbeth*. Mr. Fleagle loved *Macbeth* and
wanted us to love it too, but he lacked the gift of infecting others with his   Support for
own passion. He tried to convey the murderous ferocity of Lady Macbeth   major event 1
one day by reading aloud the passage that concludes

> . . . I have given suck, and know
> How tender 'tis to love the babe that milks me.
> I would, while it was smiling in my face,
> Have plucked my nipple from his boneless gums. . . .

The idea of prim Mr. Fleagle plucking his nipple from boneless gums was
too much for the class. We burst into gasps of irrepressible snickering. Mr.
Fleagle stopped.

"There is nothing funny, boys, about giving suck to a babe. It is the — 5
the very essence of motherhood, don't you see."

He constantly sprinkled his sentences with "don't you see." It wasn't a 6
question but an exclamation of mild surprise at our ignorance. "Your pronoun needs an antecedent, don't you see," he would say, very primly. "The
purpose of the Porter's scene, boys, is to provide comic relief from the horror, don't you see."

Late in the year we tackled the informal essay. "The essay, don't you see, 7
is the . . ." My mind went numb. Of all forms of writing, none seemed so
boring as the essay. Naturally we would have to write informal essays. Mr.
Fleagle distributed a homework sheet offering us a choice of topics. None
was quite so simpleminded as "What I Did on My Summer Vacation," but
most seemed to be almost as dull. I took the list home and dawdled until
the night before the essay was due. Sprawled on the sofa, I finally faced up

---

listless: Lacking energy or enthusiasm.

to the grim task, took the list out of my notebook, and scanned it. The topic on which my eye stopped was "The Art of Eating Spaghetti."

This title produced an extraordinary sequence of mental images. Surging   8
up out of the depths of memory came a vivid recollection of a night in Belleville when all of us were seated around the supper table — Uncle Allen, my mother, Uncle Charlie, Doris, Uncle Hal — and Aunt Pat served spaghetti for supper. Spaghetti was an exotic treat in those days. Neither Doris nor I had ever eaten spaghetti, and none of the adults had enough experience to be good at it. All the good humor of Uncle Allen's house reawoke in my mind as I recalled the laughing arguments we had that night about the socially respectable method for moving spaghetti from plate to mouth.

Suddenly I wanted to write about that, about the warmth and good feel-   9
ing of it, but I wanted to put it down simply for my own joy, not for Mr. Fleagle. It was a moment I wanted to recapture and hold for myself. I wanted to relive the pleasure of an evening at New Street. To write it as I wanted, however, would violate all the rules of formal composition I'd learned in school, and Mr. Fleagle would surely give it a failing grade. Never mind. I would write something else for Mr. Fleagle after I had written this thing for myself.

When I finished it the night was half gone and there was no time left to   10
compose a proper, respectable essay for Mr. Fleagle. There was no choice next morning but to turn in my private reminiscence° of Belleville. Two days passed before Mr. Fleagle returned the graded papers, and he returned everyone's but mine. I was bracing myself for a command to report to Mr. Fleagle immediately after school for discipline when I saw him lift my paper from his desk and rap for the class's attention.

"Now, boys," he said, "I want to read you an essay. This is titled 'The Art   11
of Eating Spaghetti.'"

And he started to read. My words! He was reading *my words* out loud to   12
the entire class. What's more, the entire class was listening. Listening attentively. Then somebody laughed, then the entire class was laughing, and not in contempt and ridicule, but with openhearted enjoyment. Even Mr. Fleagle stopped two or three times to repress a small prim smile.

I did my best to avoid showing pleasure, but what I was feeling was pure   13
ecstasy at this startling demonstration that my words had the power to make people laugh. In the eleventh grade, at the eleventh hour as it were, I had discovered a calling. It was the happiest moment of my entire school career. When Mr. Fleagle finished he put the final seal on my happiness by saying, "Now that, boys, is an essay, don't you see. It's — don't you see — it's of the very essence of the essay, don't you see. Congratulations, Mr. Baker."

Conclusion   For the first time, light shone on a possibility. It wasn't a very heartening   14
restating thesis   possibility, to be sure. Writing couldn't lead to a job after high school, and it was hardly honest work, but Mr. Fleagle had opened a door for me. After that I ranked Mr. Fleagle among the finest teachers in the school.

reminiscence: Memory.

Questions to Start You Thinking

Meaning

1. In your own words, state what Baker believes he learned in the eleventh grade about the art of writing. What incidents or statements help identify this lesson for readers? What lesson, if any, did you learn from the essay?

2. Why do you think Baker included this event in his autobiography?

3. Have you ever changed your mind about something you had to do, as Baker did about writing? Or about a person, as he did about Mr. Fleagle?

Writing Strategies

4. What is the effect, in paragraph 3, of Baker's repetitions of the words *prim* and *primly*? What other devices does he use to characterize Mr. Fleagle vividly? Why do you think Baker uses so much space to portray his teacher?

5. What does the quotation from *Macbeth* add to Baker's account? Had the quotation been omitted, what would have been lost?

6. How does Baker organize the essay? Why does he use this order?

STUDENT ESSAY

Robert G. Schreiner
What Is a Hunter?

What is a hunter? This is a simple question with a relatively straightforward answer. A hunter is, according to *Webster's New Collegiate Dictionary*, a person who hunts game (game being various types of animals hunted or pursued for various reasons). However, a second question is just as simple but without such a straightforward answer: What characteristics make up a hunter? As a child, I had always considered the most important aspect of the hunter's person to be his ability to use a rifle, bow, or whatever weapon was appropriate to the type of hunting being done. Having many relatives in rural areas of Virginia and Kansas, I had been exposed to rifles a great deal. I had done extensive target shooting and considered myself to be quite proficient in the use of firearms. I had never been hunting, but I had always thought that since I could fire a rifle accurately I would make a good hunter.

One Christmas holiday, while we were visiting our grandparents in Kansas, my grandfather asked me if I wanted to go jackrabbit hunting with him. I eagerly accepted, anxious to show off my prowess° with a rifle. A younger cousin of mine also wanted to come, so we all went out into the garage, loaded two .22 caliber rifles and a 20-gauge shotgun, hopped into the pickup truck, and drove out of town. It

In this college essay, Robert G. Schreiner uses vivid details to bring to life a significant childhood event.

1

2

prowess: Superior skill.

had snowed the night before, and to either side of the narrow road swept six-foot-deep powdery drifts. The wind twirled the fine crystalline snow into whirling vortexes° that bounced along the icy road and sprayed snow into the open windows of the pickup. As we drove, my grandfather gave us some pointers about both spotting and shooting jackrabbits. He told us that when it snows, jackrabbits like to dig out a hollow in the top of a snowdrift, usually near a fencepost, and lie there soaking up the sunshine. He told us that even though jackrabbits are a grayish brown, this coloration is excellent camouflage in the snow, for the curled-up rabbits resemble rocks. He then pointed out a few rabbits in such positions as we drove along, showing us how to distinguish them from exposed rocks and dirt. He then explained that the only way to be sure that we killed the rabbit was to shoot for the head and, in particular, the eye, for this was on a direct line with the rabbit's brain. Since we were using solid point bullets, which deform into a ball upon impact, a hit anywhere but the head would most likely only wound the rabbit.

How does the writer convey his grandfather's definition of hunting?

My grandfather then slowed down the pickup and told us to look out for the rabbits hidden in the snowdrifts. We eventually spotted one about thirty feet from the road in a snow-filled gully. My cousin wished to shoot the first one, so he hopped out of the truck, balanced the .22 on the hood, and fired. A spray of snow erupted about a foot to the left of the rabbit's hollow. My cousin fired again, and again, and again, the shots pockmarking the slope of the drift. He fired once more and the rabbit bounced out of its hollow, its head rocking from side to side. He was hit. My cousin eagerly gamboled into the snow to claim his quarry.° He brought it back holding it by the hind legs, proudly displaying it as would a warrior the severed head of his enemy. The bullet had entered the rabbit's right shoulder and exited through the neck. In both places a thin trickle of crimson marred the gray sheen of the rabbit's pelt. It quivered slightly and its rib cage pulsed with its labored breathing. My cousin was about to toss it into the back of the pickup when my grandfather pointed out that it would be cruel to allow the rabbit to bleed slowly to death and instructed my cousin to bang its head against the side of the pickup to kill it. My cousin then proceeded to bang the rabbit's head against the yellow metal. Thump, thump, thump, thump; after a minute or so my cousin loudly proclaimed that it was dead and hopped back into the truck.

3

Why do you think that the writer reacts as he does?

The whole episode sickened me to some degree, and at the time I did not know why. We continued to hunt throughout the afternoon, and feigning boredom, I allowed my cousin and grandfather to shoot all of the rabbits. Often, the shots didn't kill the rabbits outright so they had to be killed against the pickup. The thump, thump, thump of the rabbits' skulls against the metal began to irritate me, and I was

4

vortex: Rotation around an axis, as in a whirlwind.   **quarry:** Prey.

strangely glad when we turned around and headed back toward home. We were a few miles from the city limits when my grandfather slowed the truck to a stop, then backed up a few yards. My grandfather said he spotted two huge "jacks" sitting in the sun in a field just off the road. He pointed them out and handed me the .22, saying that if I didn't shoot something the whole afternoon would have been a wasted trip for me. I hesitated and then reluctantly accepted the rifle. I stepped out onto the road, my feet crunching on the ice. The two rabbits were about seventy feet away, both sitting upright in the sun. I cocked and leveled the rifle, my elbow held almost horizontal in the military fashion I had learned to employ. I brought the sights to bear on the right eye of the first rabbit, compensated° for distance, and fired. There was a harsh snap like the crack of a whip and a small jolt to my shoulder. The first rabbit was gone, presumably knocked over the side of the snowdrift. The second rabbit hadn't moved a muscle; it just sat there staring with that black eye. I cocked the rifle once more and sighted a second time, the bead of the rifle just barely above the glassy black orb that regarded me so passively. I squeezed the trigger. Again the crack, again the jolt, and again the rabbit disappeared over the top of the drift. I handed the rifle to my cousin and began making my way toward the rabbits. I sank into powdery snow up to my waist as I clambered to the top of the drift and looked over.

On the other side of the drift was a sight that I doubt I will ever forget. There   5
was a shallow, snow-covered ditch on the leeward side of the drift and it was into this ditch that the rabbits had fallen, at least what was left of the rabbits. The entire ditch, in an area about ten feet wide, was spattered with splashes of crimson blood, pink gobbets of brain, and splintered fragments of bone. The twisted corpses of the rabbits lay in the bottom of the ditch in small pools of streaming blood. Of both the rabbits, only the bodies remained, the heads being completely gone. Stumps of vertebrae protruded obscenely from the mangled bodies, and one rabbit's hind legs twitched spasmodically. I realized that my cousin must have made a mistake and loaded the rifle with hollowpoint explosive bullets instead of solid ones.

I shouted back to the pickup, explaining the situation, and asked if I should   6
bring them back anyway. My grandfather shouted back, "No, don't worry about it, just leave them there. I'm gonna toss these jacks by the side of the road anyway; jackrabbits aren't any good for eatin'."

Looking at the dead, twitching bodies I thought only of the incredible waste of   7
life that the afternoon had been, and I realized that there was much more to being a hunter than knowing how to use a rifle. I turned and walked back to the pickup, riding the rest of the way home in silence.

Why do you think the writer returns in silence?

compensate: Counterbalance.

Questions to Start You Thinking

Meaning

1. Where in the essay do you first begin to suspect the writer's feelings about hunting? What in the essay or in your experience led you to this perception?
2. How would you characterize the writer's grandfather? How would you characterize his cousin?
3. How did the writer's understanding of himself change as a result of this hunting experience?

Writing Strategies

4. How might the essay be strengthened or weakened if the opening paragraph were cut out? Without this paragraph, how would your understanding of the author and his change be different?
5. Would Schreiner's essay be more or less effective if he explained in the last paragraph what he means by "much more to being a hunter"?
6. What are some of Schreiner's memorable images?
7. Using highlighters or marginal notes, identify the essay's introduction, thesis, major events, support for each event, and conclusion. How effective is the organization of this essay?

Learning by Writing

THE ASSIGNMENT: RECALLING A PERSONAL EXPERIENCE

■ For writing activities for recalling an experience, visit <bedfordstmartins.com/bedguide> and do a keyword search:

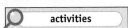

Write about one specific experience that changed how you acted, thought, or felt. Use your experience as a springboard for reflection. Your purpose is not merely to tell an interesting story but to show your readers — your instructor and your classmates — the importance of that experience for you.

We suggest you pick an event that is not too personal or too subjective. Something that happened to you or that you observed, an encounter with a person who greatly influenced you, a decision that you made, or a challenge or an obstacle that you faced will be easier to recall (and to make vivid for your readers) than an interior experience like a religious conversion or falling in love.

Memorable student papers have recalled experiences heavy and light:

One writer recalled guitar lessons with a teacher who at first seemed harsh but who turned out to be a true friend.

Another student recalled a childhood trip when everything went wrong and she discovered the complexities of change.

Another recalled competing with a classmate who taught him a deeper understanding of success.

Facing the Challenge: Writing from Recall

The major challenge writers confront when writing from recall is to focus their essays on a main idea. When writing about a familiar—and often powerful—experience, it is tempting to include every detail that comes to mind and equally easy to overlook familiar details that would make the story's relevance clearer to the reader.

Once you are certain of your *purpose* in writing about a particular event—what you want to show readers about your experience—you can transform a laundry list of details into a narrative that connects events clearly around a main idea. You can select details that work together to convey the significance of your experience. To help you decide what to show your readers, respond to each of the following questions in a few sentences:

- What was important to you about the experience?
- What did you learn from it?
- How did it change you?
- How would you reply to a reader who asked "So what?"

Once you have decided on your main point about the experience, you should select the details that best illustrate that point and show readers why the experience was important to you.

GENERATING IDEAS

You may find that the minute you are asked to write about a significant experience, the very incident will flash to mind. Most writers, though, will need a little time for their memories to surface. Often, when you are busy doing something else—observing the scene around you, talking with someone, reading about someone else's experience—the activity can trigger a recollection. When a promising one emerges, write it down. Perhaps, like Russell Baker, you found success when you ignored what you thought you were supposed to do in favor of what you really wanted to do. Perhaps, like Robert Schreiner, you learned from a painful experience.

For more strategies for generating ideas, see Ch. 16.

Try Brainstorming.   When you brainstorm, you just jot down as many ideas as you can. You can start with a suggestive idea—*disobedience, painful lesson, childhood, peer pressure*—and list under it whatever occurs through free association. You can also use the questions in the following checklist:

For more on brainstorming, see pp. 296–98.

DISCOVERY CHECKLIST

— Did you ever break an important rule or rebel against authority? Did you learn anything from your actions?

— Did you ever succumb to peer pressure? What were the results of going along with the crowd? What did you learn?

___ Did you ever regard a person in a certain way and then have to change your opinion of him or her?

___ Did you ever have to choose between two equally attractive alternatives? How might your life have been different if you had chosen differently?

___ Have you ever been appalled by witnessing an act of prejudice or insensitivity? What did you do? Do you wish you had done something different?

For more on freewriting, see pp. 298–99.

Try Freewriting.   Devote ten minutes to freewriting — simply writing without stopping. If you get stuck, write "I have nothing to say" over and over, until ideas come. They will come. After you finish, you can circle or draw lines between related items, considering what main idea connects events.

For more on doodling or sketching, see pp. 299–300.

Try Doodling or Sketching.   As you remember an experience such as breaking your arm during a soccer tournament, try sketching or doodling whatever helps you recollect the event and its significance. Begin turning your doodles into words by adding comments on main events, notable details, and their impact on you.

For more on mapping, see p. 301.

Try Mapping Your Recollections.   Identify a specific time period such as your birthday last year, the week when you decided to enroll in college, or a time when you changed in some way. On a blank page, on movable sticky notes, or in a computer file, record all the details you can recall about that time — people, statements, events, locations, and related physical descriptions.

For more on using a reporter's questions, see pp. 303–04.

Try a Reporter's Questions.   Once you recall an experience you want to write about, ask "the five *W*'s and an *H*" that journalists find useful.

- Who was involved?
- What happened?
- Where did it take place?
- When did it happen?
- Why did it happen?
- How did the events unfold?

FOR E-WRITERS

Creating Your Writing Space

As you keyboard words onto a screen and use the Edit menu to copy, cut, or paste, you can manipulate your writing to answer the writing task. You may start generating ideas by brainstorming, freewriting, answering reporter's questions, outlining a chronology, or writing directly about the experience you recall. Some students write out notes or guidelines in bold type to remind themselves about their tasks and their assignment's challenges. As you find and develop your own writing processes, you should actively create your own electronic writing space to support these processes.

Any question might lead to further questions — and to further discovery.

- **Who** was involved? → What did the others look like?
  → What did they say or do?
  → Would their words supply any lively quotations?

- **What** happened? → What did you think as the event unfolded?
  → When did you see the importance of the experience?

Consider Sources of Support. Because your memory drops as well as retains, you may want to check your recollections against those of a friend or family member who was there. Did you keep a journal at the time? Was the experience a turning point (big game, graduation) that your family would have documented with photos? Was it sufficiently public (such as a demonstration) or universal (such as a campus orientation) to have been recorded in a newspaper? If so, these resources can refresh your memory so that you rediscover forgotten details or angles.

Family photograph

PLANNING, DRAFTING, AND DEVELOPING

Now, how will you tell your story? If the experience is still fresh in your mind, you may be able simply to write a draft, following the order of events and shaping your story as you go along. If you want to plan before you write, here are some suggestions.

■ For more strategies for planning, drafting, and developing papers, see Chs. 17, 18, and 19.

Start with a Main Idea, or Thesis. As you think about the experience, jot down a few words that identify it and express its importance to you. Next, begin to shape these words into a sentence that states the significance of the experience — the main idea that you want to convey to a reader. If you aren't certain yet about what that idea is or how to put it into words, just begin writing. You can work again on your thesis as you revise.

■ For more on stating a thesis, see pp. 312–19.

■ For exercises on choosing effective thesis statements, visit <bedfordstmartins.com/bedguide> and do a keyword search:

| TOPIC IDEA + SLANT | reunion in Georgia + really liked meeting family |
| WORKING THESIS | When I went to Georgia for a family reunion, I enjoyed meeting many relatives. |

Establish a Chronology. Retelling an experience is called *narration,* and the simplest way to organize is chronologically — relating the essential

■ For examples of time markers and other transitions, see pp. 346–49.

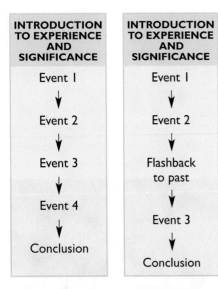

events in the order in which they occurred. On the other hand, sometimes you can start an account of an experience in the middle and then, through *flashback*, fill in whatever background a reader needs to know.

Richard Rodriguez, for instance, begins *Hunger of Memory* (Boston: David R. Godine, 1982), a memoir of his bilingual childhood, with an arresting sentence:

> I remember, to start with, that day in Sacramento, in a California now nearly thirty years past — when I first entered a classroom, able to understand about fifty stray English words.

The opening hooks our attention. In the rest of his essay, Rodriguez fills us in on his family history, on the gulf he came to perceive between the public language (English) and the language of his home (Spanish).

▧ For more on providing details, see pp. 353–55.

■ For exercises on supporting a thesis, visit <bedfordstmartins.com/bedguide> and do a keyword search:

▧ For more on the placement of visuals, see pp. 410–16.

Show Your Audience What Happened.   How can you make your recollections come alive for your readers? Look again at Russell Baker's account of Mr. Fleagle teaching *Macbeth* and at the way Robert G. Schreiner depicts his cousin putting the wounded rabbits out of their misery. These two writers have not merely told us what happened; they have *shown* us, by creating scenes that we can see in our mind's eye.

As you tell your story, zoom in on at least two or three such specific scenes. Show your readers exactly what happened, where it occurred, what was said, who said it. Use details and words that appeal to all five senses — sight, sound, touch, taste, and smell. Because photographs and illustrations can clarify visual details for readers, carefully position any images you decide to include. (Be sure that your instructor approves such additions.)

REVISING AND EDITING

▧ For more revising and editing strategies, see Ch. 20.

After you have written an early draft, put it aside for a day or two — or a few hours if your deadline is looming. Then read it over carefully. Try to see it through the eyes of one of your readers, noting both the pleasing parts and the confusing spots. Revise to ensure that you've expressed your thoughts and feelings clearly and strongly in a way that will reach your readers; edit to repair any distracting weaknesses in grammar or expression.

Focus on a Main Idea, or Thesis.   As you read over the essay, return to your purpose: What was so important about this experience? Why is it so memorable? Will readers be able to see why this experience was a crucial one in your life? Will they understand how your life has been different ever since? Be sure that you specify a genuine difference, reflecting the incident's

Learning to Be a Peer Editor

To practice peer response before trying your skills on a classmate's paper, select any student-written paper from this book's table of contents. Write a short but detailed letter to the student writer. Tell the writer what is effective and ineffective about the essay, and explain why. Compare comments with others in your class who chose the same paper. What did you notice in the essay? Is its main idea or thesis clear to you? What did you miss that others noticed? As you will see, several people can notice far more than one individual can.

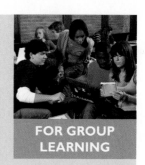

FOR GROUP LEARNING

real impact on you. In other words, revise to keep your essay focused on a single main idea or thesis.

> WORKING THESIS   When I went to Georgia for a family reunion, I enjoyed meeting many relatives.

> REVISED THESIS   Meeting my Georgia relatives showed me how powerfully two values — generosity and resilience — unite my family.

For more on stating a thesis, see pp. 312–19.

Add Concrete Detail.   Ask whether you have made events come alive for your audience by recalling them in sufficient concrete detail. Be specific enough that your readers can see, smell, taste, hear, and feel what you experienced. Make sure that all your details support your main idea or thesis. Notice again Robert Schreiner's focus in his second paragraph on the world outside his own skin: his close recall of the snow, of his grandfather's pointers about the habits of jackrabbits and the way to shoot them. As you revise, you may well recall more vivid details to include.

For more about providing details, see pp. 353–55.

Follow a Clear Sequence.   Reconsider the order of events in terms of your audience, looking for changes that might make your essay easier for readers to follow. For example, if a classmate seems puzzled about the sequence of your draft, you might make a rough outline or list of the main events to check the clarity of your arrangement. Or you might add more transitions to connect events so that readers can tell exactly where your account is going.

For more on outlining, see pp. 325–33.

For more on transitions, see pp. 346–49.

Revise and rewrite until you've related your experience and its impact as well as you can. Here are some useful questions about revising your paper:

REVISION CHECKLIST

___ Where have you shown why this experience was important and how it changed your life?

___ How have you engaged readers so that they will want to keep reading? Will they find your paper dramatic, instructive, or revealing? Will they see and feel what you experienced?

___ Why do you begin your narration as you do? Is there another place in the draft that would make a better beginning?

___ If the events are not in chronological order, how have you made the organization easy for readers to follow?

___ In what ways does the ending provide a sense of finality?

___ Do you stick to a point? Is everything relevant to your main idea or thesis?

___ If you portray any people, how have you made their importance clear? Which details make them seem real, not just shadowy figures?

___ Does any dialogue have the ring of real speech? Read it aloud. Try it on a friend.

For more editing and proofreading strategies, see pp. 384–87.

After you have revised your recall essay, edit and proofread it. Carefully check the grammar, word choice, punctuation, and mechanics — and then correct any problems you find. Here are some questions to get you started:

EDITING CHECKLIST

For more help, turn to the dark-blue-edged pages, and find the sections of the Quick Editing Guide noted here.

___ Is your sentence structure correct? Have you avoided writing fragments, comma splices, or fused sentences?	A1, A2
___ Have you used correct verb tenses and forms throughout? When you present a sequence of past events, is it clear what happened first and what happened next?	A3
___ When you use transitions and other introductory elements to connect events, have you placed any needed commas after them?	C1
___ In your dialogue, have you placed commas and periods before (inside) the closing quotation mark?	C3
___ Have you spelled everything correctly, especially the names of people and places? Have you capitalized names correctly?	D1, D2

When you have made all the changes you need to make, save your file, print out a clean copy of your paper — and hand it in.

OTHER ASSIGNMENTS

1. Choose a person outside your immediate family who had a marked effect on your life, either good or bad. Jot down ten details that might help a reader understand what that person was like. Consider the person's physical appearance, way of talking, and habits as well as any memorable incidents. When your list is finished, look back at "The Art of Eating Spaghetti" to identify the kinds of detail Baker uses in his portrait of Mr. Fleagle, noting any you might add to your list. Then write a paper in which you portray that person, including details to help your audience understand his or her impact on you.

2. Recall a place you were once fond of — your grandmother's kitchen, a tree house, a library, a locker room, a vacation retreat. If you have a pho-

Have a classmate or friend read your draft and suggest how you might present the main idea about your experience more clearly and vividly. Ask your peer editor questions such as these about writing from recall:

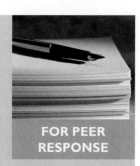

FOR PEER RESPONSE

- What do you think the writer's main idea or thesis is? Where is it stated or clearly implied? Why was this experience significant?

- What emotions do the people in the essay feel? How did *you* feel while reading the essay?

- Where does the essay come alive? Underline images, descriptions, and dialogue that seem especially vivid.

- If this were your paper, what is the one thing you would be sure to work on before handing it in?

For general questions for a peer editor, see p. 377.

tograph of the place, looking at it may help to jog your memory. Write a paper that explains to your audience why this place was memorable. What made it different from other places? Why was it important to you? What do you feel when you remember it?

3. Write a paper or the text for a podcast in which you recall some familiar ceremony, ritual, or observation. Such a tradition can pertain to a holiday, a rite of passage (confirmation, bar or bat mitzvah, college orientation, graduation), a sporting event, a family custom. Explain to your audience the importance of the tradition to you, using whatever information you recall. How did the tradition originate? Who takes part? How has it changed through the years? What does it add to the lives of those who observe it?

Applying What You Learn: Some Uses of Recalling Experience

In College Courses.   Virtually every paper, no matter what it sets out to accomplish, can benefit from vivid examples that you recall.

- Recalling a relevant personal experience can engage your readers' interest and provide a springboard for your investigation, analysis, explanation, or argument. For example, your recollections of visiting or living in another country might introduce a sociology paper on cultural differences.

- Your recollection of events may provide the foundation for the reflective journal you keep during an internship or clinical experience.

- Your personal experience can add authority to the judgments and conclusions you offer in your academic writing assignments. In a paper for an anthropology course, you might recall your impressions of visiting the Anasazi ruins at Mesa Verde.

In the Workplace.   Recall is useful as you write on the job.

- Recalling your past jobs and workplace skills might help you identify opportunities at the next campus career day.
- Detailed data that help you recall past successes, failures, or customer comments can provide compelling reasons for adopting your proposals for changing a product or service.
- Recalling past contacts with customers or clients can remind them of your company's valuable product or service and help to personalize your letters, e-mail messages, or other contacts with them.

Career day, Iowa State University

Reunion Memories

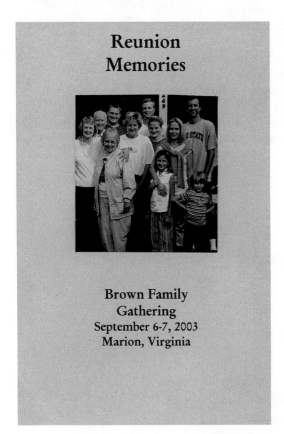

**Brown Family
Gathering**
September 6-7, 2003
Marion, Virginia

In Your Community.   In your private life, your memory is a source not only for personal journals, diaries, or correspondence, but also for your writing as an involved member of your community.

- Your personal experiences can lend enormous impact to an appeal for changes in city plans, school policies, or government funding. If your child has been upset by her school's use of standardized tests, recalling her frustration could alert the school board to problems with the testing policies.
- Recalling and recording how you have organized or implemented plans can save time and improve an event the next time around.
- Recalling events from your childhood or from your happiest or most difficult days with your family can make your next reunion or holiday gathering even more meaningful for you.

Chapter 5
Observing a Scene

Responding to an Image

A scene like this one might look and feel very different to different observers, depending on their vantage points, emotions, background, and experience. In this image, what prominent element attracts your attention? Who is the observer? What details might be important for this observer? Although visual details are obviously central, feel free to describe sound, smell, and touch, as well as any emotions that might come into play. Next, identify a second person who might be observing this scene. Which details might matter most to this other observer? In what ways are your two lists of details similar or different?

Most writers begin to write by recalling what they know. Then they look around and add what they observe. Some writing consists almost entirely of observation — a reporter's eyewitness account of a fire, an anthropologist's field notes, a clinical report by a nurse detailing a patient's condition, a scientist's account of a laboratory experiment. So does any writing that describes a person, place, or thing. In other instances, observation provides support, details to make a point clear or convincing.

If you need more to write about, open your eyes — and your other senses. Take in not only what you can see but also what you can hear, smell, touch, and taste. Then when you write, report your observations in concrete detail. Of course, you can't record everything your senses bring you. You must be selective based on what's important and relevant for your purpose and your audience. To make a football game come alive for readers of your college newspaper, you might mention the overcast cold weather and the buttery smell of popcorn. But if your purpose is primarily to explain which team won and why, you might stress the muddy playing field, the most spectacular plays, and the players who scored.

Learning from Other Writers

■ For more on thesis and support, see Chs. 17 and 19.

Here are two essays by writers who observe their surroundings and reflect on their observations. As you begin to analyze the first reading, look for the notes in the margin. They identify features such as the main impression created in the observation and stated in the thesis, the first of the locations observed, and the supporting details that describe the location.

■ For more examples of writing from observation, visit <bedfordstmartins.com/ bedguide> and do a keyword search:

examples

As You Read These Observations

As you read these essays, ask yourself the following questions:

1. Specifically, what does the writer observe? Places? People? Behavior? Nature? Things?

2. What senses does the writer rely on? What sensory images does each writer develop? Find some striking passages in which the writer reports his or her observations. What makes these passages memorable to you?

3. Why does the writer use observation? What conclusion does the writer draw from reflecting on the observations?

Eric Liu

The Chinatown Idea

In this selection from The Accidental Asian (1998), Eric Liu describes a childhood visit to Chinatown in New York City.

Another family outing, one of our occasional excursions to the city. It was a Saturday. I was twelve. I remember only vaguely what we did during the day — Fifth Avenue, perhaps, the museums, Central Park, Carnegie Hall. But I recall with precision going to Chinatown as night fell.

— Introduction

We parked on a side street, a dim, winding way cluttered with Chinese placards° and congested with slumbering Buicks and Chevys. The license

— Vantage point I

plates — NEW YORK, EMPIRE STATE — seemed incongruous here, foreign. We walked a few blocks to East Broadway. Soon we were wading through thick crowds on the sidewalk, passing through belts of aroma: sweat and breath, old perfume, spareribs. It was late autumn and chilly enough to numb my cheeks, but the bustle all around gave the place an electric warmth. Though it was evening, the scene was lit like a stage, thanks to the aluminum lamps hanging from every produce stand. Peddlers lined the street, selling steamed buns and chicken feet and imitation Gucci bags. Some shoppers moved along slowly. Others stopped at each stall, inspecting the greens, negotiating the price of fish, talking loudly. I strained to make sense of the chopped-off twangs of Cantonese coming from every direction, but there were more tones than I knew: my ear was inadequate; nothing was intelligible.

— Supporting detail

This was the first time I had been in Chinatown after dark. Mom held Andrea's hand as we walked and asked me to stay close. People bumped us, brushed past, as if we were invisible. I felt on guard, alert. I craned my neck as we walked past a kiosk° carrying a Chinese edition of *Playboy*. I glanced sidelong at the teenage ruffians on the corner. They affected an air of menace with their smokes and leather jackets, but their feathery almost-mustaches and overpermed hair made them look a bit ridiculous. Nevertheless, I kept my distance. I kept an eye on the sidewalk, too, so that I wouldn't soil my shoes in the streams of putrid° water that trickled down from the alleyways and into the parapet° of trash bags piled up on the curb.

I remember going into two stores that night. One was the Far Eastern Bookstore. It was on the second floor of an old building. As we entered, the sounds of the street fell away. The room was spare and fluorescent. It looked like an earnest community library, crowded with rows of chest-high shelves. In the narrow aisles between shelves, patrons sat cross-legged on the floor, reading intently. If they spoke at all it was in a murmur. Mom and Dad each found an absorbing book. They read standing up. My sister and I, meanwhile, wandered restlessly through the stacks, scanning the spines for stray English words or Chinese phrases we might recognize. I ended up in children's books and leafed through an illustrated story about the three tigers. I couldn't read it. Before long, I was tugging on Dad's coat to take us somewhere else.

---

placards: Posters, signs.   **kiosk:** Booth.   **putrid:** Rotten; decaying.   **parapet:** Wall; suggesting a castle.

73

The other shop, a market called Golden Gate, I liked much more. It was 5
noisy. The shoppers swarmed about in a frenzy. On the ground level was an
emporium° of Chinese nonperishables: dried mushrooms, spiced beef, sea-
weed, shredded pork. Open crates of hoisin sauce° and sesame chili paste.
Sweets, like milky White Rabbit chews, coconut candies, rolls of sour "haw
flakes." Bags of Chinese peanuts, watermelon seeds. Down a narrow flight of
stairs was a storehouse of rice cookers, ivory chopsticks, crockery, woks that
hung from the wall. My mother carefully picked out a set of rice bowls and
serving platters. I followed her to the long checkout line, carrying a basket
full of groceries we wouldn't find in Poughkeepsie. I watched with wonder
as the cashier tallied up totals with an abacus.

THESIS —
stating main impression

We had come to this store, and to Chinatown itself, to replenish our 6
supply of things Chinese: food and wares, and something else as well. We
had ventured here from the colorless outer suburbs to touch the source, to
dip into a pool of undiluted Chineseness. It was easier for my parents, of
course, since they could decode the signs and communicate. But even I,
whose bond to his ancestral culture had frayed down to the inner cord of
appetite — even I could feel somehow fortified by a trip to Chinatown.

Yet we knew that we couldn't stay long — and that we didn't really want 7
to. We were Chinese, but we were still outsiders. When any peddler addressed us in Cantonese, that became obvious enough. They seemed so familiar and so different, these Chinatown Chinese. Like a reflection distorted

Conclusion drawn
from observation

just so. Their faces were another brand of Chinese, rougher-hewn. I was fascinated by them. I liked being connected to them. But was it because of
what we shared — or what we did not? I began that night to distinguish between my world and theirs.

It was that night, too, as we were making our way down East Broadway, 8
that out of the blur of Chinese faces emerged one that we knew. It was Po-
Po's° face. We saw her just an instant before she saw us. There was surprise
in her eyes, then hurt, when she peered up from her parka. Everyone hugged
and smiled, but this was embarrassing. Mom began to explain: we'd been
uptown, had come to Chinatown on a whim, hadn't wanted to barge in on
her unannounced. Po-Po nodded. We made some small talk. But the realization that her daily routine was our tourist's jaunt,° that there was more
than just a hundred miles between us, consumed the backs of our minds
like a flame to paper. We lingered for a minute, standing still as the human
current flowed past, and then we went our separate ways.

Afterward, during the endless drive home, we didn't talk about bump- 9
ing into Po-Po. We didn't talk about much of anything. I looked intently
through the window as we drove out of Chinatown and sped up the FDR
Drive, then over the bridge. Manhattan turned into the Bronx, the Bronx
into Yonkers, and the seams of the parkway clicked along in soothing intervals as we cruised northward to Dutchess County. I slipped into a deep,

emporium: Marketplace.   **hoisin sauce:** A sweet brown sauce that is a popular Chinese condiment.   **Po-Po:** The narrator's grandmother.   **jaunt:** trip, outing.

open-mouthed slumber, not awakening until we were back in Merrywood, our development, our own safe enclave. I remember the comforting sensation of being home: the sky was clear and starry, the lawn a moon-bathed carpet. We pulled into our smooth blacktop driveway. Silence. It was late, perhaps later than I'd ever stayed up. Still, before I went to bed, I made myself take a shower.

Questions to Start You Thinking

Meaning

1. Why do Liu and his family go to Chinatown?

2. How do Liu and his family feel when they encounter Po-Po? What observations and descriptions lead you to that conclusion?

3. What is the significance of the last sentence? How does it capture the essence of Liu's Chinatown experience?

Writing Strategies

4. In which paragraphs or sections does the writer's use of sensory details capture the look, feel, or smell of Chinatown? In general, how successfully has Liu included various types of observations and details?

5. How does Liu organize his observations? Is this organization effective? Why or why not?

6. Which of the observations and events in this essay most clearly reveal that Liu considers himself to be a "tourist"?

STUDENT ESSAY

Michael Coil
Communications

Walking into the county government building, a visitor would not imagine what goes on in the basement twenty-four hours a day, seven days a week. The building is so quiet, and nobody is in sight. I make my way down the stairs and into the basement. A long hallway and an inconspicuous,° unmarked brown wooden door lead me to the communications center, where the radio traffic for all of Dodge City and Ford County is handled. Nothing along the way even hints at the amount of emotion that is felt in this small space.

For his first-year composition class, Michael Coil took a fresh look at a familiar location.

What kinds of places does this building bring to mind?

Inside the center a kitchen is connected to a workspace with a large glass window that looks in on the main room. An office for the supervisor sits closed and locked, and a bathroom hides around the corner. The smell of constantly brewing coffee is thick, as though permanently tattooed on the air. I step through the

inconspicuous: Not noticeable.

❓ *When have you had a similar change in perception?*

kitchen and past the long window into the Dispatch Room. As a police officer for the city, I have been in the Dispatch Room many times, but I have never sat and thought of everything that goes on there. I begin to see things through new eyes.

The first thing to attract my attention is the number of computers at the work- 3 stations. I see three individual stations, each with a tall leather chair and a computer keyboard. At each station is a line of computer screens of various shapes and sizes, all brightly lit and streaming with information. A large green digital clock on the wall keeps the time, and a stack of printers taller than I am decorates the wall beside me. I notice a quiet hum from the many hard drives and printer fans. It is cold outside, but still the heat of the machines makes it necessary to run the air conditioner.

A television hangs from the ceiling in the corner. I can tell it's muted because 4 it makes no sound though lines streaming with information slide off the screen. The reporters on the screen appear to be talking about Iraq. The anchorman looks angry, but nobody in the room pays him any attention. The only real noise is from the three 911 dispatchers talking happily. The mood is light, and conversation seems to come very easily.

A phone rings, and one of the dispatchers answers. She enters something on her 5 screen and then hangs up. She tells me that the hospital was calling to ask them to page one of the on-call doctors. The dispatchers resume their conversation. They are casual and friendly, and their conversation ranges from what they ate today to the personalities of their dogs at home. I find it easy to talk with them, and I can tell that spending so much time side by side in this room brings the three dispatchers together like close friends.

After a few minutes the phone rings again. The situation is different this time. 6 The first phone that rang was a normal ring without unusual volume or tone, but this one makes my blood churn. It is loud, obnoxious,° and ugly. It's like combining the screech of a vulture and the wail of a dying animal. The air becomes thick and tense. The conversation stops in mid-sentence, and I can feel all of the dispatchers tense up in anticipation of what they are about to hear. The three of them pick up the phone, and one begins to talk. Another begins to type on the computer screen, and the third gets on the radio and dispatches the call to the police. From where I am sitting at the rear of the workspace, I can hear the woman on the phone screaming. I can't quite decipher° what she is saying, but by the dispatcher's rising tone, I can tell it is not good. Repeatedly the caller is told to calm down and tell what's going on. With each command the dispatcher's voice gets more edgy. Hearts are racing now, and the room fills with dread. "Somebody is breaking into my house," the voice on the line finally pushes out. I read the screen and see that she lives not far from

❓ *How can a ring be "obnoxious"?*

obnoxious: Offensive, intolerable.   decipher: Interpret.

where we are sitting. It only takes a minute or two for the first unit to arrive, but sitting and listening to that poor woman's plea for help makes that short time feel like an eternity. The officers inform the dispatcher that they are in front of the house, and they don't see anybody. The person must have left just moments before they got there. The dispatcher speaking with the woman leans back slowly in her chair, causing it to groan softly. She rubs her hands on her face as though she were sweating and suddenly goes back into her casual mode. She politely tells the woman to answer the door because the police are standing out front, then pauses a moment and says goodbye.

How have you responded to the sounds that the writer has described?

Several minutes pass before I can collect myself and begin to process everything I just saw and heard. I feel as though I had been sitting in the house with that distraught woman watching helplessly. I feel suddenly tired, stressed, and still my nerves are shaking from the adrenaline. The dispatchers, however, return to their conversation without missing a beat. The tension filters silently away, and the mood becomes friendly again. Only a unique and brave person could willingly face challenges like that one on a day-to-day basis.

7

As I walk out of the communications room, I see multiple cartoons cut out of the newspaper and taped to the doorway. I think to myself, What a difficult task it must be to come back down after eight hours on the emotional rollercoaster. It would be so easy for the dispatchers to become bitter, angry people, but they are quite the opposite. They are inviting and friendly, and though they will always deny it, they are modern-day heroes waiting to come to our rescue. Day and night they sit, behind the brown unmarked wooden door, at the end of the long marble hallway, always ready to help.

8

Questions to Start You Thinking

Meaning

1. Is the Dispatch Room as "quiet" as Coil originally suspects as he enters the building? Which paragraph best supports your answer?
2. In paragraph 8, Coil uses the term "modern-day heroes" to describe the dispatchers. What details in his account support that description?
3. What does Coil learn about himself from his visit to the Dispatch Room?

Writing Strategies

4. How does comparing and contrasting the dispatchers' behavior before a call and during a call help Coil create a vivid impression of the room?
5. Which sense does Coil use most effectively? Point to a few examples that support your choice.
6. Paragraph 6 includes the only dialogue in the essay. What is its effect?

7. Using highlighters or marginal notes, identify the essay's introduction, thesis, major vantage points for observation, details supporting each part of the observation, and conclusion. How effective is this organization?

Learning by Writing

THE ASSIGNMENT: OBSERVING A SCENE

■ For writing activities for observing a scene, visit <bedfordstmartins.com/bedguide> and do a keyword search:

Observe a place near your campus, home, or job and the people who frequent this place. Then write a paper in which you describe the place, the people, and their actions so as to convey the spirit of the place and offer some insight into the impact of the place on the people.

This assignment is meant to start you observing closely enough that you go beyond the obvious. Go somewhere nearby, and station yourself where you can mingle with the people there. Open your senses—all of them, so that you see, smell, taste, hear, and feel. Jot down what you immediately notice, especially the atmosphere and its effect on the people there. Take notes describing the location, people, and actions and events you see. Then use your observations to convey the spirit of the scene. What is your main impression of the place? Of the people there? Of the relationship between the people and

---

Facing the Challenge: Observing a Scene

The major challenge writers face when writing from observation is to select compelling details that fully convey an engaging main impression of a scene. As we experience the world, we are bombarded by sensory details, but our task as writers is to choose those that bring a subject alive for readers. For example, describing an oak as "a big tree with green leaves" is too vague to help readers envision the tree or grasp what is unique about it. Use these questions to help you notice sensory details:

- What colors, shapes, and sizes do you see?
- What tones, pitches, and rhythms do you hear?
- What textures, grains, and physical features do you feel?
- What fragrances and odors do you smell?
- What sweet, spicy, or other flavors do you taste?

After recording the details that define the scene, ask two more questions:

- What overall main impression do these details establish?
- Which specific details will best show the spirit of this scene to a reader?

Your answers will help you decide which details to include in your paper and which to leave out.

the place? Remember, your purpose is not only to describe the scene but also to express thoughts and feelings connected with what you observe.

Three student writers wrote about these observations:

One student, who works nights in the emergency room, observed the scene and the community that abruptly forms when an accident victim arrives: doctors, nurses, orderlies, the patient, and friends or relatives.

Another observed a bar mitzvah celebration that reunited a family for the first time in many years.

Another observed the activity in the bleachers in a baseball stadium before, during, and after a game.

GENERATING IDEAS

Although setting down observations might seem a cut-and-dried task, to many writers it is true discovery. Here are some ways to generate such observations.

Brainstorm. First, you need to find a scene to observe. What places interest you? Which are memorable? Start brainstorming—listing rapidly any ideas that come to mind. Here are a few questions to help you start your list:

For more strategies for generating ideas, see Ch. 16.

For more on brainstorming, see pp. 296–97.

DISCOVERY CHECKLIST

— Where do people gather for some event or performance (a stadium, a church, a theater, an auditorium)?

— Where do people get together for some activity (a gym, a classroom)?

— Where do crowds form while people are getting things or services (a shopping mall, a dining hall or student union, a dentist's waiting room)?

— Where do people go for recreation or relaxation (an arcade, a ballpark)?

— Where do people gather (a fire, a party, a wedding, a graduation)?

Get Out and Look. If nothing on your list strikes you as compelling, plunge into the world to see what you see. Visit a city street or a country hillside, a campus building or a practice field, a lively scene— a mall, an airport, a fast-food restaurant, a student hangout—or one with only a few people sunbathing, walking dogs, or tossing Frisbees. Stand off in a corner for a while, and then mix with the group to gain different views of the scene.

Band practice at University of California, Berkeley

Record Your Observations. Michael Coil's essay "Communications" began with

■ For more on journal keeping, see pp. 306–07.

some notes Coil made about his county communications center and the phone traffic it receives. He was able to mine those notes for details to bring his subject to life.

Your notes on a subject — or tentative subject — can be taken in any old order or methodically. To draw up an "observation sheet," fold a sheet of paper in half lengthwise. Label the left column "Objective," and impartially list what you see, like a zoologist looking at a new species of moth. Label the right column "Subjective," and list your thoughts and feelings about what you observe. If possible, keep looking at your subject while you write.

Objective	Subjective
The ticket holders form a line outside the old brick hall, standing two or three deep all the way down the block.	This place has seen concerts of all kinds — you can feel the history as you wait, as if the hall protects the crowds and the music.
Groups of friends talk, a few couples hug, and some guys laugh as they tell jokes.	The crowd seems relaxed and friendly, all waiting to hear their favorite group.
Everyone shuffles forward when the doors finally open, looking around at the crowd and edging toward the entrance.	The excitement and energy grow with the wait, but it's just the concert ritual — the prelude to a perfect night.

The quality of your paper will depend in large part on the truthfulness and accuracy of your observations. Your objective notes on an observation sheet will trigger more subjective notes. As your list grows, write on one side of your paper only: later you can spread out your notes and look at them all at once. Even in the sample observation sheet made at the concert venue, a main impression is starting to take shape. The old hall shelters concertgoers and musicians alike, channeling their enthusiasm into the music.

Include a Range of Images.   Have you captured not just sights but sounds, touches, odors? Have you observed from several vantage points or on several occasions to deepen your impressions? Have you added sketches or doodles to your notes, perhaps drawing the features or mapping the shape of the place? Can you begin writing as you continue to observe your subject? Have you noticed how other writers use *images*, evoking sensory experience, to record what they sense? In the memoir *Northern Farm* (New York: Rinehart, 1948), naturalist Henry Beston describes a remarkable sound: "the voice of ice," the midwinter sound of a whole frozen pond settling and expanding in its bed.

Sometimes there was a sort of hollow oboe sound, and sometimes a groan with a delicate undertone of thunder.... Just as I turned to go, there came from below one curious and sinister crack which ran off into a sound like the whine of a giant whip of steel lashed through the moonlit air.

PLANNING, DRAFTING, AND DEVELOPING

After recording your observations, look over your notes or your observation sheet, circling whatever looks useful. Maybe you can rewrite your notes into a draft, throwing out details that don't matter, leaving those that do. Maybe you'll need a plan to help you organize all the observations, laying them out graphically or in a simple scratch outline.

> For more strategies for planning, drafting, and developing, see Chs. 17, 18, and 19.

Start with a Main Impression or Thesis.   What main insight or impression do you want to get across? Answering this question will help you decide which details to include and which to omit. It will also help you avoid a dry recitation of observed facts.

> For more on stating a thesis, see pp. 312–19.

> For exercises on choosing effective thesis statements, visit <bedfordstmartins.com/bedguide> and do a keyword search:

thesis

PLACE OBSERVED   Smalley Green after lunch

MAIN IMPRESSION   relaxing activity is good after a morning of classes

WORKING THESIS   After their morning classes, students have fun relaxing on Smalley Green with their dogs and Frisbees.

Organize to Show Your Audience Your Point.   How do you map out a series of observations? Your choice will depend on your purpose in writing and the main impression that you want to create. Whatever your choice, be sure to add transitions — words or phrases that guide the reader from one vantage point, location, or idea to the next. Experiment with options such as the ones at the top of the next page.

> For more organization strategies, see pp. 319–33.

As you create your "picture," you bring a place to life using the details that capture its spirit. If your instructor approves, consider whether adding a photograph, sketch, diagram, or other illustration would enhance your written observation.

> For transitions that mark place or direction, see p. 347.

REVISING AND EDITING

Your revising, editing, and proofreading will all be easier if you have taken accurate notes on your observations. But what if, when you look over your draft, you find that you don't have enough detail? If you have any doubts, go back to the scene, and take more notes to flesh out your draft.

> For more revising and editing strategies, see Ch. 20.

Focus on a Main Impression or Thesis.   As you begin to revise, ask a friend to read your observation, or read it yourself as if you had never visited the place you observed. While reading, you might notice gaps that would

Sequential Organization

SPATIAL MOVEMENT	top → bottom	left → right	near → far	center → edge

PROMINENT FEATURES	*least:* Sunday suit, light blue blouse, dramatic flowered hat ↓ *most:* Grandma's sharp eyes, spotting the best in others

SPECIFIC DETAILS TO GENERAL IMPRESSION	souvenir sellers calling, small waves slapping tour boats, and pungent fish frying on Fisherman's Wharf ↓ In all this commotion, a visitor sees the wharf's vitality.

COMMON AND ORDINARY TO UNUSUAL FEATURES	mounds of bright leaves, crisp fall air, children bouncing ↓ the sheer joy of every moment at the playground across from the pediatric cancer center

puzzle a reader or decide that the spirit of the place seems understated. Consider whether the main impression you want to convey would be clearer if you sharpened its description in your thesis.

■ For more on stating a thesis, see pp. 312–19.

WORKING THESIS   After their morning classes, students have fun relaxing on Smalley Green with their dogs and Frisbees.

REVISED THESIS   When students, dogs, and Frisbees accumulate on Smalley Green after lunch, they show how much campus learning takes place outside of class.

■ For exercises on supporting a thesis, visit <bedfordstmartins.com/bedguide> and do a keyword search:

Add Relevant and Powerful Details.   Next, check your selection of details. Does each detail contribute to your main impression? Should any details be dropped or added? Should any be rearranged so that your organization, moving from point to point, is clearer? Could any observations be described more vividly or powerfully? Could more precise or more concrete wording strengthen the way you present the details?

Let a classmate or friend respond to your draft, suggesting how to use detail to convey your main impression more powerfully. Ask your peer editor to answer questions such as these about writing from observation:

- What is the main insight or impression you carry away from this writing?

- Which sense does the writer use particularly well? Are any senses neglected that could be used?

- Can you see and feel what the writer experienced? Would more details make this writing more compelling? Put check marks wherever you want more detail.

- How well has the writer used evidence from the senses to build a main impression? Which sensory impressions contribute most strongly to the overall picture? Which seem superfluous?

- If this were your paper, what is the one thing you would be sure to work on before handing it in?

FOR PEER RESPONSE

For general questions for a peer editor, see p. 377.

To see where your draft could need work, you might consider these questions:

REVISION CHECKLIST

___ Have you accomplished your purpose — to convey to readers your overall impression of your subject and to share some telling insight about it?

___ What can you assume your readers know? What do they need to be told?

___ Have you gathered enough observations to describe your subject? Have you observed with *all* your senses when possible — even smell and taste?

___ Have you been selective, including details that effectively support your overall impression?

___ Which observations might need to be checked for accuracy? Which might need to be checked for richness or fullness?

___ Is your organizational pattern the most effective for your subject? Is it easy for readers to follow? Would another pattern work better?

After you have revised your observation essay, edit and proofread it. Carefully check the grammar, word choice, punctuation, and mechanics — and then correct any problems you find. If you have added more details while revising, consider whether they have been sufficiently blended with the ideas already there.

Here are some questions to get you started when editing and proofreading your observation paper:

For more editing and proofreading strategies, see pp. 384–87.

▨ For more help, turn to the dark-blue-edged pages, and find the sections of the Quick Editing Guide noted here.

EDITING CHECKLIST

___ Is your sentence structure correct? Have you avoided writing fragments, comma splices, and fused sentences?   A1, A2

___ Have you used an adjective whenever describing a noun or pronoun? Have you used an adverb whenever describing a verb, adjective, or adverb? Have you used the correct form when comparing two or more things?   A7

___ Is it clear what each modifier in a sentence modifies? Have you created any dangling or misplaced modifiers?   B1

___ Have you used parallel structure wherever needed, especially in lists or comparisons?   B2

FOR GROUP LEARNING

Reading Your Writing Aloud

Try reading your draft aloud to your group. Rehearse your reading beforehand, and deliver it with feeling. Ask your audience to stop you when something isn't clear. Have a pencil in hand to mark such problems, or ask someone else to note them for you. After you've finished reading aloud, ask for reactions. (Or ask your listeners any of the questions in the peer response checklist on page 83.) Have someone record the most vital suggestions and reactions that your draft provokes. If possible, audiotape your reading and the reactions. Review both the notes and the tape when you revise.

FOR E-WRITERS

Strengthening Descriptive Words

When you write an observation, you will use modifiers (adjectives or adverbs) to qualify other words so that your observations are clear. However, adverbs like *very* and *really* or adjectives like *beautiful* and *great* are vague rather than concrete and precise. Read your draft aloud, and note any vague or imprecise modifiers. Then, use the Find function in your word processor's Edit menu to help you locate each place in your paper where you have used *really*, for example, or another vague modifier. As you find each modifier, ask, "Is it specific enough?" "Will it guide my reader through my way of seeing?" Delete any weak modifiers, or replace them with more specific words.

OTHER ASSIGNMENTS

1. To develop your powers of observation, go for a walk, recording your observations in two or three detailed paragraphs. Let your walk take you through either an unfamiliar scene or a familiar scene worth a closer look than you normally give it (such as a supermarket, a city street, an

open field). Avoid a subject so familiar that you would struggle to see it from a fresh perspective (such as a dormitory corridor or a parking lot). Sum up your impression of the place, including any opinion you form through your close observations.

2. Try this short, spontaneous writing exercise. Begin the assignment immediately after class, and turn it in the same afternoon.

> Go to a nearby public place — a café, library, copy center, art gallery — and select a person who catches your eye, who somehow intrigues you. Try to choose someone who looks as if she or he will stay put for a while. Settle yourself where you can observe your subject unobtrusively. Take notes, if you can do so without being observed.
>
> Now, carefully and tactfully (we don't want any fistfights or lawsuits) notice everything you can about this person. Start with physical characteristics, but focus on other things too. How does the person talk? Move? What does the person's body language tell you?
>
> Write a paragraph describing the person. Pretend that the person is going to hold up a bank ten minutes from now, and the police will expect you to supply a full and accurate description.

3. The perspective of a tourist, an outsider alert to details, often reveals the distinctive character of places and people. Think of some place you have visited as an outsider in the past year, and jot down any notable details you recall. Or spend a few minutes as a tourist right now. Go to a busy spot on or off campus, and record your observations of anything you find amusing, surprising, puzzling, or intriguing. Then write an essay on the unique character of the place.

Applying What You Learn: Some Uses of Observing a Scene

In College Courses.   Observing and accurately recording observations are critical to your success in many courses besides English, especially those with labs, field trips, or practica that prepare you for your career.

- Students in the social sciences — sociology, criminal justice, psychology, anthropology — often take field trips requiring them to observe behavior closely and report their observations. Similarly, students in the humanities or fine arts may be expected to observe and record their impressions of a play, a concert, an exhibit, or a historical site.

- Classes in health, education, or other professional fields may include clinical or field observations.

- Science classes — biology, anatomy, physics, or chemistry — may call for lab reports, recording observations of experiments, or field reports on animal life within a habitat.

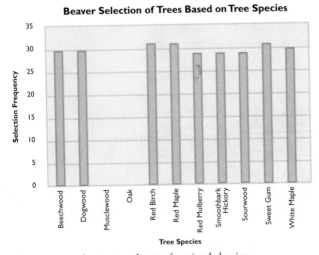

From a research report on beaver foraging behavior

In the Workplace. In many careers and professions, observation and analysis provide valuable information and lend credibility to your writing.

- If you choose a career in nursing, teaching, or social work, you will probably write case studies based on observation, sometimes for publication, sometimes for reference.

- Journalists draw on what they observe to report news events or write feature articles. During interviews, body language, tone of voice, and surroundings may be as revealing as a subject's words.

- Many careers will require you to make field observations and report your findings to your superiors. Architects and engineers observe at a building site; biologists and conservationists observe animals in the wild; astronomers observe movement in the night sky.

In Your Community.   Observation is a primary resource for your writing as an active member of your community.

- Vivid observations in an editorial or proposal calling for resolution of a neighborhood problem—a dangerous intersection, a poorly lighted park, a run-down building—will make the hazards real for readers.

- Joining the planning group for a community project, such as a sports arena or a performing arts center, may require you to observe facilities in other communities and report your findings. Observing another community's festival also can provide ideas and identify logistical details for planning an event in your own community.

- You may need to report to authorities and to insurance agents what you've observed at the site of an accident, a natural disaster, or a crime. Photos of the scene can be useful support.

A fraternity house destroyed during a three-day party

Chapter 6
Interviewing a Subject

Responding to an Image

Suppose that you had an opportunity to interview media personality Oprah Winfrey, President Barack Obama, figure skater Michelle Kwan, or musician and advocate Bono. What two or three questions would you most like to ask the interviewee? Based on the person's public image and his or her personality as revealed in these photos, what kind of response would you expect to receive? How do you think the photographer has tried to bring the person to life or suggest something about the person?

Don't know what to write about? Go talk with someone. Meet for half an hour with an anthropology professor, and you probably will have plenty of material for a paper. Just as likely, you can get a paper's worth of information from a ten-minute exchange with a mechanic who relines brakes. Both the mechanic and the professor are experts. But even people who aren't usually considered experts may tell you things you didn't know and provide you with material.

As this chapter suggests, you can direct a conversation by asking questions to elicit what you want to find out. You do so in an *interview* — a special kind of conversation with a purpose — usually to help you understand the other person or to find out what that person knows.

Learning from Other Writers

For more on thesis and support, see Chs. 17 and 19.

Here are two essays whose writers talked to someone and reported the conversations, using direct quotations and telling details to reveal engaging personalities. To help you begin to analyze the first reading, look for the notes in the margin. They identify features such as the main idea, or thesis, and the quotations providing support.

For more examples of writing based on interviews, visit <bedfordstmartins.com/bedguide> and do a keyword search:

examples

As You Read These Interview Essays

As you read these essays, ask yourself the following questions:

1. Was the conversation reported from an informal discussion or planned as an interview? Does the writer report the conversation directly or indirectly?

2. What does the interview show about the character and personality of the individual speaking? What does it show about the author who is listening?

3. Why do you think the writer draws on conversation?

Elaina Richardson interviewed Bono, lead singer of the rock band U2, for this article, which was originally published in O, The Oprah Magazine, *in February 2002.*

THESIS
stating dominant impression

Elaina Richardson

Bono-Fire: U2's Brilliant Front Man Rocks Convention

The idea of the rocker rebel is sorely tarnished° in these days of pop lite, but there's nothing sugarcoated about the intensity Bono brings to the world. Consider these few events from the past year in the life of U2's charismatic° front man: a sold-out tour; an album (*All That You Can't Leave Behind*) that went to number one in thirty-two countries; the birth of his fourth child in May; talks with the leaders of the world's strongest

tarnished: Dulled, diminished.   **charismatic:** Powerfully appealing.

economies — the G8 — in Genoa, Italy, in July; the death of his father in
August; countless one-on-ones about AIDS relief and trade with cabinet officials from Colin Powell° to Condoleezza Rice.° Where does his stamina°
come from? "God made me stubborn," Bono says with a throaty laugh that
tells you something about the state of his vocal cords. . . . "Stubbornness
and Catholic guilt," he continues. "That'll work for you every time. And I've
had the best life that a man's ever had: I don't just mean with U2, I mean
with my family and even my father, whose loss I feel every day, he lived a
long and colorful life, and he left me with a sense of moral outrage."

Elaboration of dominant impression

Quotations showing subject's personality

Description added to bring subject to life

This is how Bono talks, long strings of run-on sentences that can encom- 2
pass° pub life, the AIDS pandemic° in Africa, blues guitar, and a healthy
dose of self-deprecation.° The bottom line of all this speechifying° is that
it's time for a major initiative that would combine debt cancellation for the
world's poorest nations with trade reform and a commitment from phar-
maceutical companies to give free HIV drugs to African countries. Bono
spouts numbers effortlessly and accurately, noting that sub-Saharan Africa°
spends around $13.5 billion a year repaying debts to rich countries, which
is more than double what it spends on health care.

His charm lies in the fact that, whether he's at an audience with Pope 3
John Paul II or singing "Beautiful Day" for 20,000, his need to communicate is palpable.° There was a time when Bono harangued° the world — "Am
I bugging you?" he would spit at U2 fans, all the while making it clear that
he didn't give a damn if he was. A decade later he has learned a more effective path: "Sometimes instead of climbing over the barricades you've got to
walk around them, and sometimes you discover that the real enemy is not
what you think it is," he says. That attitude has led to some strange-seeming
bedfellows,° chief among them Senator Jesse Helms, the eighty-year-old
archconservative° from North Carolina, who became Bono's champion in
the struggle to get a debt-relief plan through Congress. According to Bono,
"When I first started going to Washington for meetings on Capitol Hill, I'm
sure I looked like a very exotic creature, but eventually they didn't see me,
they just saw the argument. And the thing about the pictures of me the rock
star with, say, Jesse Helms the politican is — it's really unhip for both of us,
you know, it's a bad look for the two of us!"

While the other guys in U2 may find it incredibly unsexy to have the 4
likes of Orrin Hatch° or Paul Volcker° hanging backstage, Bono knows that

Colin Powell: Former secretary of state under President George W. Bush.   **Condoleezza
Rice:** National Security advisor and then secretary of state under President George W.
Bush.   **stamina:** Endurance.   **encompass:** Include.   **pandemic:** Illness   affecting
many people across a large geographic area.   **self-deprecation:** Playing down one's own
accomplishments.   **speechifying:** Speechlike talk.   **sub-Saharan Africa:** The part of
Africa south of the Sahara Desert.   **palpable:** Obvious.   **harangued:** Lectured; taunted.
bedfellows: Friends or allies.   **archconservative:** Someone who is very conservative.
Orrin Hatch: Republican senator from Utah.   **Paul Volcker:** Former chairman of the
Federal Reserve, the central U.S. banking system.

Quotation from another
person providing insight

power is not always pretty. ("Just the sight of Orrin Hatch in the mosh pit°
. . . it's exciting," Bono says, and you can't tell if he means it or not.) "I think
that politicians are attracted at first by the celebrity," says Harvard economics professor Jeffrey Sachs, "but once they meet him they find that he is out-
standingly capable." Along with producer Bobby Shriver, Sachs became part
of Bono's American kitchen cabinet in 1999 in the quest to get debt relief
on the agenda. In his Class Day address at Harvard in June, Bono summed
up the trio: "Sachs and I, with Bobby Shriver, hit the road like some kind of
surreal° crossover act.° A Rock Star, a Kennedy, and a Noted Economist
crisscrossing the globe like the Partridge family° on psychotropic° drugs."

The results have already been impressive: in November of 2000, Congress 5
passed legislation authorizing $435 million in debt relief. Last July President
Bush and the G8 countries focused the debate on issuing grants rather than
loans to developing nations, and Bono is sure a lot more is about to happen.

Provocative quotation

"I'm confident that President Bush has a real feeling for the AIDS pandemic.
Essentially, what we're asking for is a kind of Marshall Plan° for Africa. A few
months ago that didn't look like a possibility, but post–September 11 the
comparisons are striking. When you have nothing, you are easy prey to
terrorists and to groups who keep alive the lie that the West is not interested
in your calamity.° We've just seen what happens when one country,
Afghanistan, implodes.° God knows what will happen if the entire continent
of Africa is left on its current trajectory,° which is disaster."

Background and influences

Born in Ballymun, Dublin, in 1960 (he was Paul Hewson then) to a 6
Protestant mother and a Catholic father, Bono is no stranger to the links between economic depression, bigotry, and terrorism. But he has an idealist's
faith that all three can be overcome. The Sandinistas° and the Troubles° in
Ireland were Bono's issues when the band came on the scene in 1978, and
by 1983 U2 had released the first of many anthems° in "Sunday, Bloody
Sunday": "I can't believe the news today, I can't close my eyes and make it
go away." Bono was married by the time this record came out, to his high
school girlfriend, Ali Stewart, and neither one of them was interested in
closing their eyes. Bob Geldof's Live Aid° work "woke them up to what was
happening in Africa," and, Bono recalls, "Ali and I got quite caught up in it.
We went to work in Ethiopia for a month. We worked in an orphanage, in
one of those awful camps, and we'd wake up in the morning to the sight of

mosh pit: Place in front of rock or punk performers where people jump around or slam
into each other.   surreal: Strange or dreamlike.   crossover act: Something that appeals to diverse audiences (for example, both jazz and rock fans).   Partridge family: A
fictional family rock band from a 1970s sitcom of the same name.   psychotropic: Affecting the mind.   Marshall Plan: A post–World War II program to rebuild European
countries.   calamity: Catastrophe or disaster.   implodes: Breaks down.   trajectory:
Course; path.   Sandinistas: Left-wing group that led a 1979 revolution in Nicaragua.
the Troubles: The violent struggles from 1968 to 1998 between Catholic and Protestant
factions in Northern Ireland.   anthems: Songs with special political or cultural significance.   Live Aid: A series of concerts in 1985 to raise money for famine relief in
Ethiopia.

thousands of people walking through the mist in the hopes of getting some food. My experience there was very hard to forget. . . . We went back to our daily life in Ireland and me being in a band, but we'd always hoped we might be able to look at the structure of the problem. There's a certain kind of poverty that is structural, not just misfortune, and so when I heard about this plan to use the millennium as an opportunity to give the poorest countries a chance to start again, I thought, 'This is major, and it's the right thing to do.' "

Four children and twenty-one years into life with Bono, Ali hasn't lost 7 any of her ability to roll up her sleeves either. She is deeply involved with the Chernobyl° Children's Project (one of six campaigns highlighted on U2's Web site and on their albums), even getting behind the wheel of a truck to drive from Dublin to Belarus° with food and emergency supplies. "Irish women are very informed and very vocal," Bono says, before releasing his chesty laugh again. "And I should know because I'm living with one, and it's hard to keep up."

Yeats° has a famous line about the sound and fury of politics: "The best 8 lack all conviction, while the worst / Are full of passionate intensity." But Bono, the self-conscious rebel-rocker, with his mop of lank° hair and his sunglasses and his tireless talk, gives that line the lie, transforming passionate intensity into action that just might change the world.

Literary quotation and observation lead into restatement of thesis

Questions to Start You Thinking

Meaning

1. What makes Bono a "rocker rebel," according to Richardson? What evidence does she use to support this view?

2. In paragraph 2, Bono outlines changes that are needed to solve serious world problems. What are these changes? What results have been achieved?

3. Over the years, how has Bono changed the ways in which he communicates his views to people?

Writing Strategies

4. Richardson gives some of Bono's personal history in paragraph 6. How does this add to the article and the impression of Bono?

5. What seem to be Richardson's feelings about her dominant impression of Bono? What observations and details does she include to affect your impression of him?

6. Throughout this essay, Richardson uses quotations from Bono to reveal his personality and philosophy. Would this essay be as effective if she paraphrased rather than quoted? Why or why not?

Chernobyl: Ukrainian city that was the site of a 1986 nuclear disaster. **Belarus:** Eastern European nation that borders Ukraine, where the 1986 Chernobyl nuclear disaster occurred. **Yeats:** Irish poet and dramatist William Butler Yeats (1865–1939). **lank:** Straight.

STUDENT ESSAY

Dawn Kortz
Listen

Dawn Kortz, who wrote this as a student at Dodge City Community College, creates a lively portrait of an elderly man.

Mic-Leo's Café—named after the two sisters that own it, Mickey and Lee—is   1
tucked into a corner of the Eckles Building, a former department store located in
downtown Dodge City, Kansas. The first time I saw the café, I fell in love. It is
decorated in warm tones of green and burgundy, with plants in almost every corner.
The tables are of every shape, size, and color imaginable, giving the room a cozy,
comfortable feeling. Warm sunlight wafts through the café during business hours
from the large plate windows that make up the front of the café. The people that
come to Mic-Leo's Café are, for the most part, regulars—folks we all know by name.
In the mornings the local businessmen and farmers can be seen gathering around
the tables, drinking coffee, and sharing stories of grandchildren, politics, and golf.
Among these regulars is Emmett Sherwood, who taught me how to appreciate the past.

Can you identify with Kortz's relationship with Emmett? In what way?

I first met Emmett when I began working at Mic-Leo's Café as a part-time wait-   2
ress trying to earn some extra money for college. Emmett, a grandfatherly man, has a
gift for making everyone around him laugh with his colorful personality and stories.
Interested in Emmett and how much of Dodge City's history he has lived through, I
arrange to meet with him at the café early one afternoon. As we settle ourselves
into a quiet corner, I take notice of the deliberate, professional way that Emmett is
dressed. It is obvious from his clothing that he is from another generation. Unlike
my generation, which believes comfort is the most important quality in clothing,
Emmett dresses for style. Today, like every other day, he is wearing dress slacks and
a starched white shirt and tie. When I ask him about his clothing and why he wears
a tie every day, he replies, "Going to town requires dignity." The only casual thing
Emmett is wearing is his signature bright red beret. The red color matches Emmett's
bright personality. Everyone who knows Emmett recognizes him by his hat.

I can tell that Emmett is excited to have a captive audience listen to his stories   3
by the eagerness with which he accepts my invitation for this interview. As we begin
to talk, I notice the far-off look in his eyes, as if he is trying to remember the old
days, his youth, and how the city he loves looked when he first arrived. After each
of us is served a cup of steaming coffee, Emmett begins by telling me he was born in
Oklahoma but grew up in St. Johns, Kansas. As a young man of fourteen, he became
attracted to the big city and in 1920 moved to Dodge City, Kansas, where he was
married, raised a family, and continues to live.

Emmett points out the window and shows me where, on Saturdays, the farmers   4
would come to town and set up open-air markets for the town folks to trade for

baked goods, produce, and eggs. "For me," he says, "going shopping at Wal-Mart can't compare to the feeling I got when I dressed up to go to town, see friendly folks, and help my neighbor." Emmett fondly remembers the 1920s as a time of growth for the nation and for Dodge City and as a happy, carefree time. With a smile and a mischievous twinkle, Emmett remembers the saloons and harlot houses--and especially the popular Harvey House restaurant where the waitresses wore black and white outfits which "sported the shortest skirts anyone in Dodge had seen until then." He blushes and his voice drops to a hush as he recalls this detail. He recovers and goes on to describe Front Street, the only street at the time to be paved with the distinctive red brick that now covers most of downtown. Front Street was the center of business for Dodge City; the Eckles Building, too, is located here. Emmett explains that all of the most prominent establishments were located in the downtown square, including the famous O'Neal Hotel. Emmett glows as he remembers the dances and shows he saw there, but his eyes glaze over as he recounts the fire that destroyed the beautiful, majestic building.

I ask Emmett what Dodge City was like during the Great Depression. Emmett recalls with sadness families and children that he knew then. Many went hungry while the men went to look for jobs, sometimes even leaving the state in search of an opportunity. Other men, who before the Depression worked in stores, were forced to work fields for local farmers for enough food to feed their families. "I am lucky to have always had a decent job and a place to sleep," Emmett says reflectively. "People these days think they need so much; they're wrong." Emmett's words are especially meaningful in today's material world. 5

How are Emmett's words "especially meaningful" today?

The time after World War II was important for Dodge City. Emmett remembers it as a period of economic boom when everyone had a renewed sense of pride in the United States. After the war ended, the communities came together to celebrate the return of their fathers, sons, and husbands. For the first time in history, it was common for women to work outside of the home, and Emmett remarks, "We never could get them back home!" I know he is teasing by his smile. 6

As we wind down our interview, coffee cups sitting cold and empty, I thank Emmett for taking the time to talk. The café has emptied, and the sun has started going down—leaving a chill in the air. As Emmett slowly rises to leave, stretching his weak back from the long period of inactivity, I appreciate his age for the first time. As he walks down the sidewalk toward his car, he turns and with a tip of his head waves good-bye. 7

Today, when I look around the city in which I live, I realize that what I see is not what Dodge City has always been. Emmett has given me a new appreciation of the past. He has instilled in me the importance of history—my family history, my town's history, my country's history, and my world's history. Every day when he 8

Do you agree with Kortz's conclusion about the importance of history?

comes into Mic-Leo's and I serve him coffee, I remember our talk, and I can only hope that there are others like Emmett sharing their life stories with people of another generation. I also hope that there are more people of my generation willing to take the time to listen.

Questions to Start You Thinking

Meaning

1. What is the main point of Kortz's essay?
2. What kind of man is Emmett Sherwood? How does Kortz feel about him?
3. How is Emmett's history the history of Dodge City? Is an interview an effective method of relating the history of a place? Why or why not?

Writing Strategies

4. Why does Kortz begin her essay with a description of Mic-Leo's Café? What sensory details does she use to create the scene for a reader? How does Kortz's description serve as a frame for her conversation with Emmett?
5. What details does Kortz use to describe Emmett? What senses does she draw on? Does she provide enough detail for you to form a clear image of him?
6. How much of what Emmett says does Kortz quote directly? Why does she choose to quote directly rather than paraphrase in these places? Would her essay be stronger if she used more of Emmett's own words?
7. Using highlighters or marginal notes, identify the essay's introduction, thesis, major emphases, supporting quotation and description for each emphasis, and conclusion. How effective is the organization of this essay?

Learning by Writing

THE ASSIGNMENT: INTERVIEWING

■ For writing activities for interview-based writing, visit <bedfordstmartins.com/ bedguide> and do a keyword search:

Write a paper about someone who interests you and base the paper primarily on a conversation with that person. Select any acquaintance, friend, relative, or person you have heard about whose traits, interests, activities, background, or outlook on life might intrigue your readers. Your purpose is to show this person's character and personality—to bring your subject to life for your readers—through his or her conversation.

Notable student papers from a similar assignment included these:

One student wrote about a high school science teacher who had quit teaching for a higher-paying job in the computer industry, only to return three years later to the classroom.

■ To interview someone for information about something, see Other Assignments on p. 102.

One writer recorded the thoughts and feelings of a discouraged farmer she had known since childhood.

Another learned about adjustment to life in a new country by talking to his neighbor from Somalia.

GENERATING IDEAS

If an image of the perfect subject has flashed into your mind, consider yourself lucky, and set up an appointment with that person at once. If you have drawn a blank, you'll need to cast about for a likely interview subject.

For strategies for generating ideas, see Ch. 16.

Brainstorm for Possible Subjects. Try brainstorming for a few minutes, seeing what pops into mind. Your subject need not be spectacular or unusual; ordinary lives can make fascinating reading. As you begin examining the possibilities, you may find the following questions helpful:

For more on brainstorming, see pp. 296–97.

DISCOVERY CHECKLIST

___ Are you acquainted with anyone whose life has been unusually eventful, stressful, or successful?

___ Are you curious about why someone you know made a certain decision or how that person got to his or her current point in life?

___ Is there an expert or a leader whom you admire or are puzzled by?

___ Do you know someone whose job or hobby interests you?

___ What older person could tell you about life thirty or even fifty years ago?

___ Who has passionate convictions about society, politics, sex, or childrearing?

___ Whose background and life history would you like to know more about?

___ Whose lifestyle, values, or attitudes are utterly different from your own and from those of most people you know?

Tap Local Interview Resources. Investigate campus resources such as the directory, student guide, Web page, departmental faculty lists, student activity officers and sponsors, recent yearbook photographs, stories from the newspaper archives, or facilities such as the theater, media, or sports centers. Look for students, staff, or faculty with intriguing backgrounds or experiences. Campuses and libraries often maintain lists or databases of local authorities, researchers, and authors available for press contacts or expert advice. Identify several prospects in case your first choice isn't available.

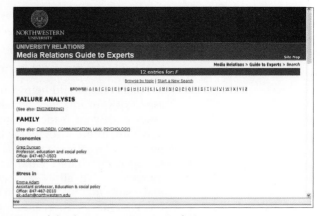

Experts' database on a university Web site

Set Up an Interview.   Find out whether your prospect will grant an interview, talk at length — an hour, say — and agree to appear in your paper. If you sense reluctance, your wisest course is to find another subject.

Don't be timid about asking for an interview. After all, your request is flattering, acknowledging that person as someone with valuable things to say. Try to schedule the interview on your subject's own ground — his or her home or workplace. The details you observe in those surroundings can make your essay more vivid.

For more on asking a reporter's questions, see pp. 303–04.

Prepare Questions.   The interview will go better if you have prepared questions in advance. Ask about the person's background, everyday tasks, favorite activities, and hopes to encourage your subject to open up. Asking for a little imagining may elicit a revealing response. (If your house were on fire, what would you try to save? If you had your life to live over, what would you do differently?)

You can't find out everything about someone, but you can focus on whatever aspects best reveal his or her personality. Good questions will help

---

Facing the Challenge: Writing from an Interview

The major challenge writers face when writing from an interview is to find a clear focus for the paper. They must first sift through the huge amount of information generated in an interview and then decide what dominant impression of the subject to present in an essay. Distilling the material you have gathered into a focused, overall impression may seem overwhelming. As a writer, however, you have the responsibility to select and organize your material for your readers, not simply transcribe your notes.

To identify possible angles, jot down answers to these questions:

• What did you find most interesting about the interview?

• What topics did your subject talk about the most?

• What did he or she become most excited or animated about?

• What topics generated the most interesting quotations?

Your answers should help you to determine a dominant impression — the aspect of your interviewee's character or personality that you want to emphasize for your readers. Once you have this focus, you can pick the details and direct quotations from the interview that best illustrate the points you want to make. Use direct quotations strategically and sparingly to reveal the character traits that you wish to emphasize. Select colorful quotations that allow readers to "hear" your subject's distinctive voice. Make sure that all quotations — long or short — are accurate. To capture the dynamic of conversation, include your own observations as well as actual quotations.

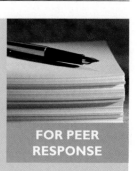

Ask a classmate to read the questions you plan to use in your interview and then to respond to the following:

- Are the questions appropriate for the person who will be interviewed?
- Will the questions help gather the information you are seeking?
- Are any of the questions unclear? How could you rephrase them?
- Do any of the questions seem redundant? Irrelevant?
- What additional questions might you ask?

FOR PEER RESPONSE

you lead the conversation where you want it to go, get it back on track when it strays, and avoid awkward silences. For example, to interview someone with an unusual job or hobby, you might ask questions like these:

- How long have you been a park ranger?
- How did you get involved in this work?
- How have you learned about the physical features and ecological balance in your park?
- What happens in a typical day on the job?
- Has this job changed your life or your concerns in any way?
- What are your plans and hopes for the future?

One good question can get some people talking for hours, and four or five may be enough for any interview, but it's better to prepare too many than too few. You can easily skip any that seem irrelevant during the interview.

Be Flexible and Observant.　　Sometimes a question won't interest your subject as much as you'd hoped it would. Or the person may seem reluctant to answer, especially if you're unwittingly trespassing into private territory, such as someone's love life. Don't badger. If you wait silently for a bit, you might be rewarded. But if the silence persists, just go on to the next question. Anytime the conversation heads toward a dead end, you can always steer it back: "But to get back to what you were saying about . . ."

Sometimes the most rewarding question simply grows out of what the subject says or an item you note in the environment. Observing your subject's clothing, expressions, mannerisms, and equipment may also suggest unexpected facets of personality. For example, Kortz describes both the café and Emmett's clothing as she introduces his character.

For more on using observation, see Ch. 5.

Decide How to Record the Interview.　　Many interviewers use only paper and pen or pencil to take notes unobtrusively. Even though they can't write down everything the person says, they want to look the subject in the eye

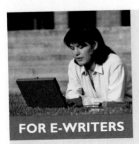

FOR E-WRITERS

Transcribing Your Interview Notes

After your interview, follow the lead of reporters who routinely transcribe conversations into computer files. Try to type in the exact conversation from your tape or as much of the interview as possible from your notes. If you have used both tape and notes, combine them in a single computer file, but use bold to distinguish your notes. Save the complete, unedited conversation transcript and original notes with a descriptive name.

Open a new file to begin your draft. As you quote and summarize your subject's ideas, you can return to your transcript and notes to copy or check the wording. In this way you can refine your draft while preserving your original research in the first file. Use the menu in your word processor to go back and forth between the two files as you copy and paste quotations into your draft. Add quotation marks to show exact words from the interview.

and keep the conversation lively. As you take notes, be sure to record or sketch details on the scene—names and dates, numbers, addresses, surroundings, physical appearance. Also jot down memorable words just as the speaker says them. Put quotation marks around them so that when you transcribe your notes later, you will know that they are quoted directly.

A telephone or an e-mail interview sounds easy but lacks the lively interplay you can achieve face-to-face. You'll miss observing the subject's possessions and environment, which so often reveal personality, or seeing your subject's smiles, frowns, or other body language. Meet with your subject if possible.

Many professionals advise against using a tape recorder because it may inhibit the subject and make the interviewer lazy about concentrating on the subject's responses. Too often, the objections go, it tempts the interviewer simply to quote the rambling conversation from the tape without shaping it into good writing. If you do bring a tape recorder to your interview, be sure that the person you're talking with has no objections. Arm yourself with a pad of paper and a pen or pencil just in case the recorder malfunctions. Perhaps the best practice is to tape-record the interview but at the same time take notes. Write down the main points, and use your tape as a backup to check for accuracy or to expand an idea or a quotation.

As soon as the interview ends, rush to the nearest desk, and write down everything you remember but couldn't record. The questions you prepared for the interview will guide your memory, as will notes you took while talking.

PLANNING, DRAFTING, AND DEVELOPING

■ For more strategies for planning, drafting, and developing, see Chs. 17, 18, and 19.

After your interview, you may have a good notion of what to include in your first draft, what to emphasize, what to quote directly, what to summarize. But if your notes seem a confused jumble, what should you do?

Evaluate Your Material.   Remember that your purpose in this assignment is to reveal your subject's character and personality through his or her conversation. Start by listing the details you're already likely to include. As you sift your material, you may find these questions useful:

For strategies for using examples and details, see Ch. 19.

> What part of the conversation gave you the most insight into your subject's character and circumstances?
>
> Which direct quotations reveal the most about your subject? Which are the most amusing, pithy, witty, surprising, or outrageous?
>
> Which objects in the subject's environment provide you with valuable clues about his or her interests?
>
> What, if anything, did your subject's body language reveal? Did it suggest discomfort, pride, self-confidence, shyness, pomposity?
>
> What did tone or gestures tell you about the person's state of mind?
>
> How can you summarize your subject's character or personality?
>
> Does one theme run through your material? If so, what is it?

Photographs, sketches, or your own doodles also may help you clarify the dominant impression and main emphases for your paper.

Focus Your Thesis on a Dominant Impression.   Most successful portraits focus on a single dominant impression of the interview subject. How would you characterize your subject in one sentence? Try to state a single main impression that you want to convey about your subject. Then eliminate anything that doesn't contribute to this view.

For more on stating a thesis, see pp. 312–19.

For exercises on choosing effective thesis statements, visit <bedfordstmartins.com/bedguide> and do a keyword search:

thesis

| DOMINANT IMPRESSION | Del talked a lot about the freedom of the press. |
| WORKING THESIS | Del Sampat is a true believer in the freedom of the press. |

If you have lots of material and if, as often happens, your conversation rambled, you may want to develop the dominant impression by emphasizing just a few things about your subject—personality traits, views on particular topics, or shaping influences. To find such a focus, try grouping your details in three layers of notes, following the pattern in the graphic below.

For more on grouping ideas, see Ch. 17.

1. Dominant Impression   ☐
2. Main Emphases   ☐   ☐
      points about traits, views, influences
3. Supporting Details   ☐   ☐   ☐   ☐   ☐
      quotations, reported words, description

Bring Your Subject to Life for Your Audience.   At the beginning of your paper, can you immediately frame the person you interviewed? A quotation, a bit of physical description, a portrait of your subject at home or at work

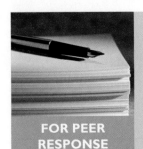

FOR PEER RESPONSE

For general questions for a peer editor, see p. 377. For peer response worksheets, visit <bedfordstmartins.com/bedguide> and do a keyword search:

peer

Have a classmate or friend read your draft and suggest how to make the portrait more vivid, complete, and clear. Ask your peer editor to answer questions such as these about writing from an interview:

- Does the essay opening make you want to know the person portrayed? If so, how has the writer interested you? If not, what gets in your way?

- What seems to make the person interviewed interesting to the writer?

- What is the writer's dominant impression of the person interviewed?

- Does the writer include any details that contradict or are unrelated to the dominant impression or insight?

- Do the quoted words or reported speech "sound" real to you? Do any quotations seem at odds with the dominant impression of the person?

- Would you leave out any of the conversation the writer used? Mark anything you would omit.

- Do you have questions about the subject that aren't answered?

- If this were your paper, what is the one thing you would be sure to work on before handing it in?

can bring the person instantly to life in your reader's mind. If your instructor approves adding an image, consider where to place it so that it supplements your text but does not overshadow your essay.

When you quote directly, be as accurate as possible, and don't put into quotation marks anything your subject didn't say. Sometimes you may want to quote a whole sentence or more, sometimes just a phrase. Keep evaluating your quotations until they all convey the essence of your subject.

■ For more on using visuals, see p. 410–16.

■ For more on selecting and presenting quotations, see D3 and D6 in the Quick Research Guide (the dark-red-edged pages). For more on punctuating quotations, see C3 in the Quick Editing Guide (the dark-blue-edged pages).

Double-Check Important Information.   You may find that you can't read your hasty handwriting or that some crucial bit of information escaped when you were taking notes. In such a case, telephone the person you interviewed to ask specific questions so that you will not take much time. You may also want to read back to your subject any direct quotations you intend to use, so that he or she can confirm their accuracy.

REVISING AND EDITING

■ For more revising and editing strategies, see Ch. 20.

As you read over your first draft, keep in mind that your purpose was to make the person you interviewed come alive for your reader.

Conducting a Collective Interview

With your whole class or your writing group, interview someone with special knowledge or expertise. Public figures often visit schools and are used to facing class questions. Or someone on campus might visit to discuss a problem that interests your group. Plan the interview in advance:

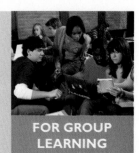

FOR GROUP LEARNING

- What do you want to find out?
- What lines of questioning will you pursue?
- What topic will each student ask about?
- How much time will each group member have to ask a series of questions?
- Who will take notes?

Preview each other's questions to avoid duplication. Ask open-ended, rather than yes/no, questions to encourage discussion. Your group's product can be many individual papers or one collaborative paper.

Focus on Your Main Idea or Thesis.   Once you have finished a draft, you may realize that you still feel swamped by too much information. Will your readers feel that your essay is overloaded? Will they understand the dominant impression you want to convey about the person you have interviewed? To be certain that they will, first polish and refine your thesis.

For more on stating a thesis, see pp. 312–19.

WORKING THESIS   Del Sampat is a true believer in the freedom of the press.

REVISED THESIS   Del Sampat, news editor for the *Campus Times,* sees every story he writes as an opportunity to exercise and defend the freedom of the press.

Screen Your Details.   Using your revised thesis as a guide, look again at the quotations and other details you have included. Will readers see how each of these strengthens the dominant impression expressed in your thesis? Keep only those that support your thesis and enhance the dominant impression. Drop all the others, even if they are vivid or catchy.

For exercises on supporting a thesis, visit <bedfordstmartins.com/bedguide> and do a keyword search:

support

Remember, readers will be interested in your observations and insights. This checklist may help you revise your work to strengthen them:

REVISION CHECKLIST

____ Are the details focused on a dominant impression you want to emphasize? Are all of them relevant? How do you convey the impression to readers?

____ How do the parts of the conversation you've reported reveal the subject's unique personality, character, mood, or concerns?

— Should your paper have a stronger beginning? Is your ending satisfactory?

— Should some quotations be summarized or indirectly quoted? Should some explanation be enlivened by adding specific quotations?

— When the direct quotations are read out loud, do they sound as if they're from the mouth of the person you're portraying?

— Where might you need to add revealing details about the person's surroundings, personal appearance, or mannerisms?

— Have you included your own pertinent observations and insights?

— Does any of your material strike you now as irrelevant or dull?

For more editing and proofreading strategies, see pp. 384–87.

After you have revised your essay, edit and proofread it. Carefully check the grammar, word choice, punctuation, and mechanics — and then correct any problems you find. Here are some questions to get you started when editing and proofreading your paper:

EDITING CHECKLIST

For more help, turn to the dark-blue-edged pages, and find the sections of the Quick Editing Guide noted here.

— Is it clear what each pronoun refers to so that the *he*'s and *she*'s are not confusing? Does each pronoun agree with (match) its antecedent?   A6

— Have you used the correct case (*he* or *him*) for all your pronouns?   A5

— Is your sentence structure correct? Have you avoided writing fragments, comma splices, or fused sentences?   A1, A2

— Have you used quotation marks, ellipses (to show the omission of words), and other punctuation correctly in all your quotations?   C3

OTHER ASSIGNMENTS

1. Interview someone from whom you can learn, possibly someone whose profession interests you or whose advice can help you solve a problem or make a decision. Your purpose will be to communicate what you have learned, not to characterize the person you interview.

2. Write a paper based on an interview with at least two members of your extended family about some incident that is part of your family lore. Direct your paper to younger relatives. If accounts of the event don't always agree, combine them into one vivid account, noting that some details may be more trustworthy than others. Give credit to your sources.

3. After briefly talking with fifteen or twenty students on your campus to find out what careers they are preparing for, write a short essay summing up what you find out. What are their reasons for their choices? Are most intent on earning money or on other pursuits? How many have to pay back college loans? Provide some quotations to flesh out your survey. From the information you have gathered, characterize your classmates. Are they materialists? Idealists? Practical people?

Applying What You Learn:
Some Uses of Writing from an Interview

In College Courses.   Often you will find yourself interviewing people who can contribute valuable insights into what you are studying.

- In a human development course, you might interview people at various stages of the life cycle — asking about the transition from student life to the working world, about parenthood, or about widowhood or retirement.

- History students may interview people who have firsthand knowledge of an event or era they are studying — a veteran of the Vietnam War, a farmer who remembers a major drought, a woman who participated in the famous Selma to Montgomery civil rights march.

- Education students may interview classroom teachers to gain an understanding of the demands and rewards of teaching.

In the Workplace.   Interviewing is a useful tool, too, for writing on the job.

- Journalists interview "informed sources" to give readers the complete story; conversely, political figures, authors, or actors often use interviews to air their opinions.

- Businesses interview customers to gain feedback on a product or service so they can meet consumer demands.

- Professional investigators conduct interviews to gather evidence — insurance adjusters settling a claim, lawyers preparing a case, medical researchers tracking a disease.

In Your Community.   As a citizen of the larger community, you will find conversation can provide the support you need in many writing tasks.

- Interviewing experts can help you make informed evaluations of community proposals. If county commissioners propose raising taxes to build a new sewage treatment center, you might talk to a waste water management expert about the merits of the plan.

- Information from experts or citizens can support your position on civic issues, such as the need for a traffic light or more transit police.

- Interviewing the missionary group speaking at your church is a good way to create a flyer or pamphlet seeking support for the group's work.

Survey about an issue

Chapter 7
Comparing and Contrasting

Responding to an Image

Examine the buildings in this photograph. List some of the ways that they are similar and different. What do their similarities and differences suggest to you? Although the residents and neighbors of these buildings are not visible in the photograph, what do you suppose the similarities and differences mean to them? What broader issues and changes might these buildings suggest or represent? Why do you suppose that the photographer shot the photograph from the location and angle that he did?

W hich city—Dallas or Atlanta—has more advantages and more draw-backs for a young single person thinking of settling down to a career? As singers and songwriters, how are Beyoncé Knowles and Shakira similar and dissimilar? Such questions invite answers that set two subjects side by side.

When you compare, you point out similarities; when you contrast, you discuss differences. When you write about two complicated subjects, usually you will need to do both. Considering Mozart and Bach, you might find that each has traits the other has—or lacks. Instead of concluding that one is great and the other inferior, you might conclude that they're two distinct composers, each with an individual style. On the other hand, if your main purpose is to judge between two subjects (as when you'd recommend moving either to Dallas or to Atlanta), you would look especially for positive and negative features, weigh the attractions and faults of each city, and then stick your neck out and make your choice.

Learning from Other Writers

In this chapter you will be asked to write a paper setting two subjects side by side, comparing and contrasting them. Let's see how two other writers have used these familiar habits of thought in writing. To help you begin to analyze the first reading, look for the notes in the margin. They identify features such as the thesis, or main idea, the sequence of the broad subjects considered, and the specific points of comparison and contrast.

■ For more on thesis and support, see Chs. 17 and 19.

As You Read These Comparisons and Contrasts

As you read these essays, ask yourself the following questions:

1. What two (or more) items are compared and contrasted? Does the writer use comparison only? Contrast only? A combination of the two? Why?
2. What is the purpose of the comparison and contrast? What idea does the information support or refute?
3. How does the writer organize the essay? Why?

■ For more examples of writing based on comparing and contrasting, visit <bedfordstmartins.com/bedguide> and do a keyword search:

examples

Suzanne Britt takes a lighthearted look at neat and sloppy people in this selection from her essay collection Show and Tell *(1983).*

Suzanne Britt
Neat People vs. Sloppy People

I 've finally figured out the difference between neat people and sloppy people. The distinction is, as always, moral. Neat people are lazier and meaner than sloppy people.

Sloppy people, you see, are not really sloppy. Their sloppiness is merely the unfortunate consequence of their extreme moral rectitude.° Sloppy people

rectitude: Correctness, decency.

[margin notes:]
1 —Introduction
—THESIS
Setting up subjects
2 —Subject A

Point 1— carry in their mind's eye a heavenly vision, a precise plan, that is so stupendous, so perfect, it can't be achieved in this world or the next.

Point 2— Sloppy people live in Never-Never Land. Someday is their métier.° 3
Someday they are planning to alphabetize all their books and set up home catalogs. Someday they will go through their wardrobes and mark certain items for tentative mending and certain items for passing on to relatives of similar shape and size. Someday sloppy people will make family scrapbooks into which they will put newspaper clippings, postcards, locks of hair, and the dried corsage from their senior prom. Someday they will file everything on the surface of their desks, including the cash receipts from coffee purchases at the snack shop. Someday they will sit down and read all the back issues of *The New Yorker*.

For all these noble reasons and more, sloppy people never get neat. They 4 aim too high and wide. They save everything, planning someday to file, order, and straighten out the world. But while these ambitious plans take clearer and clearer shape in their heads, the books spill from the shelves onto the floor, the clothes pile up in the hamper and closet, the family mementos accumulate in every drawer, the surface of the desk is buried under mounds of paper, and the unread magazines threaten to reach the ceiling.

Sloppy people can't bear to part with anything. They give loving atten- 5 tion to every detail. When sloppy people say they're going to tackle the surface of a desk, they really mean it. Not a paper will go unturned; not a rubber band will go unboxed. Four hours or two weeks into the excavation, the desk looks exactly the same, primarily because the sloppy person is meticulously creating new piles of papers with new headings and scrupulously stopping to read all the old book catalogs before he throws them away. A neat person would just bulldoze the desk.

Exaggeration to make a point and add humor

Neat people are bums and clods at heart. They have cavalier° attitudes 6 toward possessions, including family heirlooms. Everything is just another dust-catcher to them. If anything collects dust, it's got to go and that's that. Neat people will toy with the idea of throwing the children out of the house just to cut down on the clutter.

Neat people don't care about process. They like results. What they want 7 to do is get the whole thing over with so they can sit down and watch the rasslin' on TV. Neat people operate on two unvarying principles: Never handle any item twice, and throw everything away.

The only thing messy in a neat person's house is the trash can. The 8 minute something comes to a neat person's hand, he will look at it, try to decide if it has immediate use and, finding none, throw it in the trash.

Neat people are especially vicious with mail. They never go through 9 their mail unless they are standing directly over a trash can. If the trash can is beside the mailbox, even better. All ads, catalogs, pleas for charitable contributions, church bulletins, and money-saving coupons go straight into the trash can without being opened. All letters from home, postcards from

métier: Trade, specialty. **cavalier:** Dismissive.

Europe, bills, and paychecks are opened, immediately responded to, then dropped in the trash can. Neat people keep their receipts only for tax purposes. That's it. No sentimental salvaging of birthday cards or the last letter a dying relative ever wrote. Into the trash it goes.

Neat people place neatness above everything, even economics. They are 10 incredibly wasteful. Neat people throw away several toys every time they walk through the den. I knew a neat person once who threw away a perfectly good dish drainer because it had mold on it. The drainer was too much trouble to wash. And neat people sell their furniture when they move. They will sell a La-Z-Boy recliner while you are reclining in it. ————— Another exaggeration for effect

Neat people are no good to borrow from. Neat people buy everything in 11 expensive little single portions. They get their flour and sugar in two-pound bags. They wouldn't consider clipping a coupon, saving a leftover, reusing plastic nondairy whipped cream containers, or rinsing off tin foil and draping it over the unmoldy dish drainer. You can never borrow a neat person's newspaper to see what's playing at the movies. Neat people have the paper all wadded up and in the trash by 7:05 A.M.

Neat people cut a clean swath° through the organic as well as the inor- 12 ganic world. People, animals, and things are all one to them. They are so insensitive. After they've finished with the pantry, the medicine cabinet, and the attic, they will throw out the red geranium (too many leaves), sell the dog (too many fleas), and send the children off to boarding school (too many scuff marks on the hardwood floors). — Concluding exaggeration for effect

Questions to Start You Thinking

Meaning

1. Does Britt favor one group over the other? Which details or statements support your response?

2. Based on the details presented here, to which group do you belong? What specific details describe you most accurately?

3. What is Britt's purpose in contrasting neat people and sloppy people? Is her goal to explain or to convince? Or is it something else?

Writing Strategies

4. In the introductory paragraph, Britt jumps right into the essay. Is that technique effective? How else might she have begun her essay?

5. Which method of organization does Britt use to arrange her essay? How effectively does she switch between her two subjects of "sloppy" and "neat"?

6. From reading this essay, are readers to assume that "sloppy" and "neat" people have nothing in common? Why?

swath: Path.

STUDENT ESSAY

Tim Chabot
Take Me Out to the Ball Game, but Which One?

Student Tim Chabot compares and contrasts baseball and basketball, asking which deserves the title of America's national pastime.

For much of the twentieth century, baseball has been considered the   1
national pastime of the United States. Hank Aaron, home runs, and hot dogs
seem as American as Thanksgiving. Many American presidents, from Eisenhower
to Bush, have participated in the tradition of a celebrity throwing out the first
ball on opening day of a new baseball season. But beginning in the 1990s,
baseball stars were being eclipsed by the stars of another game invented in
America—basketball. Some argue that Michael Jordan and Shaquille O'Neal,
basketball greats and household names, are more famous than any current
pitcher or home run king. This shift has raised a question in the minds of
many: Should baseball continue to be considered our national pastime, or
should basketball take its place?

❓ Why do you think the writer raises this question here?

Both sports are very popular with American sports fans. In addition, both   2
games attract fans of all races—white, African American, Asian American,
Hispanic—and all classes, rich and poor, educated and uneducated. Baseball has
become a national treasure through its appeal to a wide, wide audience. At a
Saturday afternoon game, men, women, grandparents, and kids of all ages wait to
catch a fly ball. The appeal of basketball is growing, the sport having become
popular in urban and rural areas, on high school and college campuses. Both
sports are played in quite a variety of locations. Baseball games occur on neighborhood sandlots as well as official diamonds. Basketball requires little space and
equipment, so pickup basketball games occur in almost every neighborhood park
and virtually anywhere that a hoop can be rigged up.

Although both sports are popular with American fans, attending a baseball game   3
is quite different from attending a basketball game. Baseball is a family-oriented
spectator sport. Because of the widely diverse baseball fans with varied attention
spans, attending a baseball game is like going to an open-air carnival, and the game
itself is only one of the many spectacles. If fans are bored with the game, they can
listen to the vendors hawking ice cream, watch a fight brewing in the bleacher
seats, stand in line to buy peanuts or hot dogs, participate in "the wave," or just
bask in the sun. Only diehard fans keep a constant eye on the game itself because
there are frequent breaks in the play.

❓ Do you agree with the analogy between baseball and an "open-air carnival"?

In contrast, the central spectacle of any basketball arena is definitely the game   4
itself. Few distractions to entertain a casual fan occur, except for cheerleaders for
college teams. Basketball arenas are always indoors, and the games are usually at
night, creating an atmosphere that is urban and adult. The constant motion of the

sport rivets° attention to the game itself. Attending a basketball game can be compared to an exciting night on the town, while watching a baseball game is like relaxing with the family in the backyard.

*What other differ-
ences in attending the
games come to mind?*

The pace of the two games is also quite different. The leisurely pace of a base-   5
ball game contributes to its popularity because it offers relaxation to harried Americans. Each batter may spend several minutes at the plate, hit a few foul balls, and
reach a full count of three balls and two strikes before getting on base, hitting a
routine pop fly, or striking out. While batters slow things down by stepping out of
the box to practice their swing, pitchers stall the play by "holding the runners on"
to prevent stolen bases. The substitution of relief pitchers suspends the game and
gives spectators an opportunity to purchase junk food or memorabilia. In games in
which star pitchers duel, the audience may see only a few men on base in nine in-
nings and a very low score. Also, the tradition of the seventh-inning stretch under-
scores baseball's appeal to a person who wants to take it easy and relax.

On the other hand, the quick pace of basketball has contributed to its popular-   6
ity in our fast-paced society. Players run down the court at sometimes exhausting
speed for a "fast break," successful baskets can occur merely seconds apart, each
team may score as many as one hundred points a game, and the ball changes sides
hundreds of times, as opposed to every half-inning in baseball. Games can be won or
lost in the few seconds before the final buzzer. Basketball players are always in motion, much like American society. The pounding excitement of basketball appeals to
people who play hard as well as work hard.

These two sports require different athletic abilities from the players. Although   7
baseball games are slow-paced, the sport places a premium on athletic precision and
therefore showcases strategy and skill rather than brute physical strength. The
choice of a pitch, the decision to bunt or to steal a base, and the order of batters
are all careful strategic moves that could affect the outcome of the whole game.
Baseball has been called the "thinking person's game" because of its emphasis on
statistics and probabilities. Although mental strategy and dexterity° are emphasized,
physical strength is important, too. A strong arm obviously increases the power of a
player's throw or of his swing, and speed is essential in running bases. But intimidating physical ability is not necessarily a required element to become a major
league player, and even out-of-shape players can become stars if their bats are hot.
The importance of skill over brawn has contributed to baseball's popularity not
merely as a spectator sport but also as a sport in which millions of Americans participate, from Little League to neighborhood leagues for adults.

*Do you agree
that baseball requires
"skill" and basketball
"brawn"?*

Unlike baseball, basketball emphasizes physical power, stamina, and size since   8
jumping high, running fast, and just being tall with long legs and big hands usually

rivets: Commands or fixes attention to.   **dexterity:** Skill in using the hands or body.

contribute to a player's success. Skill and dexterity are certainly necessary in executing a slam dunk or dribbling past a double team, but these skills are usually combined with physical strength. In order to be a successful rebounder, a player needs to be extremely aggressive and occasionally commit fouls. Many more injuries occur on basketball courts than on baseball fields. Perhaps the physical power and intimidation required in basketball have led to the media's focus on individual players' star qualities. Magic, Bird, Jordan, Shaq, and Le Bron James are icons° who have taken the place of baseball stars of previous generations like Joe DiMaggio, Ted Williams, and Babe Ruth. Furthermore, in the international arena of the Olympics, basketball came to be seen as a symbol of American strength and power, as the 1992 Dream Team demolished all of its opponents.

If the rest of the world now equates basketball with America, should we consider it to be our true national pastime? The increasing popularity of basketball seems to reflect the change in American society in the past few decades, a change to a more fast-paced and aggressive culture. But basketball doesn't yet appeal to as diverse an audience as does baseball, and thus it doesn't seem to deserve to be called a national phenomenon—yet. Until kids, women, and grandparents are as prevalent at a Lakers game as are young males, baseball will retain its title as the national pastime. But the exciting speed of basketball may soon have more appeal than the leisurely pace of baseball.

Why do you agree or disagree with this conclusion?

9

Questions to Start You Thinking

Meaning

1. In what specific ways does Chabot claim that baseball and basketball are similar? In what ways are these two sports different? Do the similarities outweigh the differences, or vice versa?

2. Can you think of other ways these two sports are similar and different?

3. Would you nominate another sport, say soccer or ice hockey, for the national pastime? If so, why?

Writing Strategies

4. Is Chabot's support for his comparison and contrast sufficient and balanced? Explain.

5. What transitional devices does Chabot use to indicate when he is comparing and when he is contrasting?

6. What is Chabot's thesis? Why does Chabot state it where he does?

7. Using highlighters or marginal notes, identify the essay's introduction, thesis, contrasting subjects, points of comparison and contrast, and conclusion. How effective is the organization of this essay?

icons: Images or symbols.

Learning by Writing

THE ASSIGNMENT: COMPARING AND CONTRASTING

Write a paper in which you compare and contrast two items to enlighten readers about both subjects. The specific points of similarity and difference will be important, but you will go beyond them to draw a conclusion from your analysis. This conclusion, your thesis, needs to be more than "point A is different from point B" or "I prefer subject B to subject A." You will need to explain why you have drawn your conclusion. You'll also need to provide specific supporting evidence to explain your position and to convince your readers of its soundness. You may choose two people, two kinds of people, two places, two objects, two activities, or two ideas, but be sure to choose two you care about. You might write an impartial paper that distinctly portrays both subjects, or you might show why you favor one over the other.

Engaging student papers from similar assignments include these:

An American student compared and contrasted her home life with that of her roommate, a student from Nigeria. Her goal was to deepen her understanding of Nigerian society and her own.

A student who was interested in history compared and contrasted civilian responses to the Vietnam and Iraq wars, considering how popular attitudes about military service had changed.

Another writer compared and contrasted conditions at two city facilities, making a case for a revised funding formula.

■ For writing activities for comparing and contrasting, visit <bedfordstmartins.com/bedguide> and do a keyword search:

activities

GENERATING IDEAS

Find Two Subjects.   Pick subjects you can compare and contrast purposefully. An examination question may give them to you, ready-made: "Compare and contrast ancient Roman sculpture with that of the ancient Greeks." But suppose you have to find your subjects for yourself. You'll need to choose things that have a sensible basis for comparison, a common element.

■ For strategies for generating ideas, see Ch. 16.

moon rocks + stars = no common element

Dallas + Atlanta = cities to consider settling in

Montel Williams + Oprah Winfrey = television talk-show hosts

Besides having a common element, the subjects should have enough in common to compare but differ enough to throw each other into sharp relief.

sports cars + racing cars = common element + telling differences

sports cars + oil tankers = limited common element + unpromising differences

Try generating a list or brainstorming. Recall what you've recently read, discussed, or spotted on the Web. Let your mind skitter around in search of pairs that go together, or play the game of *free association*, jotting down a

■ For more on brainstorming, see pp. 296–97.

word and whatever it brings to mind: *Democrats? Republicans. New York? Los Angeles. MySpace? Friendster.* Or try the following questions:

DISCOVERY CHECKLIST

___ Do you know two people who are strikingly different in attitude or behavior (perhaps your parents or two brothers, two friends, two teachers)?

___ Can you think of two groups of people who are both alike and different (perhaps two teams or two clubs)?

___ Have you taken two courses that were quite different but both valuable?

___ Do you prefer one of two places where you have lived or visited?

___ Can you recall two events in your life that shared similar aspects but turned out to be quite different (perhaps two sporting events or two romances or the births of two children)?

___ Can you compare and contrast two holidays or two family customs?

___ Are you familiar with two writers, two artists, or two musicians who seem to have similar goals but quite different accomplishments?

Once you have a list of pairs, put a star by those that seem promising. Ask yourself what similarities immediately come to mind. What differences? Can you jot down several of each? Are these striking, significant similarities and differences? If not, move on until you discover a workable pair.

Limit the Scope of Your Paper.   If you propose to compare and contrast Japanese literature and American literature in 750 words, your task is probably impossible. But to cut down the size of this subject, you might compare and

---

Facing the Challenge: Comparing and Contrasting

The major challenge that writers face when comparing and contrasting two subjects is to determine their purpose. Writers who skip this step run the risk of having readers ask, "So, what's the point?" Suppose you develop brilliant points of similarity and difference between the films of Oliver Stone and those of Stanley Kubrick. Do you want to argue that one director is more skilled than the other? Or perhaps you want to show how they treat love or war differently in their films? Consider the following questions as you determine your primary purpose for comparing and contrasting:

• Do you want to inform your readers about these two subjects in order to provide a better understanding of the two?

• Do you want to persuade your readers that one of the two subjects is preferable to the other?

Asking what you want to demonstrate, discover, or prove *before* you begin to draft will help you to write a more effective comparison-and-contrast essay.

Making a Comparison-and-Contrast Table

After deciding what to compare, open a file and record what you know about subject A and then subject B. (Separate them with a page break if you wish.) Next, use your word processor menu to create a table with three columns (up and down) and at least half a dozen rows (across). Use the first row to label the columns: Categories (left), subject A (middle), and subject B (right).

FOR E-WRITERS

Now read over your notes on subject A. When you spot related details, identify a logical category that encompasses them. Enter the category name in the left column of the second row of your table, and copy the related details for subject A into the middle column. Repeat this process, labeling more rows as categories and moving corresponding details into the subject A column for each row. (Insert new rows at the end of your table as needed.)

■ For more on tables, see pp. 414–15.

Next review your notes on subject B. If some details fall into categories already listed in your table, copy those details into the subject B column for each category. If new categories emerge, add them in new rows along with the subject B details. After you finish categorizing your notes, round out the table — adding details to fill in empty cells, combining similar categories, or adding entirely new categories. Select the most promising categories from your table as common features for logical comparison and contrast in your essay.

contrast, say, a haiku of Bashō about a snake with a short poem about a snake by Emily Dickinson. This topic you could cover adequately in 750 words.

Explore Each Member of Your Pair to Build Support.   As you examine your two subjects, your goal is twofold. You want to analyze each using a similar approach so that you have a reasonable basis for comparison and contrast. You also want to find the details and examples that you'll need to support your points. Consider these sources of support:

• Two events, processes, procedures	Ask a reporter's questions — 5 W's (who, what, where, when, why) and an H (how).
• Two events from the past	Using the same questions, interview someone present at each event, or read news or other accounts.
• Two perceptions (public and private)	Interview someone behind the scenes; read or listen to contrasting views.
• Two approaches or viewpoints	Browse online for Web sites or pages that supply different examples.
• Two subject ideas	Read a few articles for options.
• Two policies or options	Look for studies or government statistics like those on page 113.

■ For more on using a reporter's questions, see pp. 303–05.

■ For more on interviewing, see Ch. 6.

■ For advice on finding a few useful sources, turn to B1–B2 in the Quick Research Guide (the dark-red-edged pages). For more on using sources for support, see Ch. 12.

Per Capita Personal Income in
Great Lakes States, 2005
Sources: Personal income data from U.S. Bu-
reau of Economic Analysis <www.bea.gov>
and population data from U.S. Census Bureau
<www.census.gov>.

State	2005 Personal Income (in millions)	2005 Population (in thousands)	2005 Per Capita Personal Income
Illinois	$462,857	12,763	$36,266
Indiana	$195,372	6,272	$31,150
Michigan	$331,304	10,121	$32,734
Ohio	$365,319	11,464	$31,867
Wisconsin	$184,087	5,536	$33,253

PLANNING, DRAFTING, AND DEVELOPING

As you start planning your paper, be prepared to cover both subjects in a similar fashion. If you use two columns (one for each subject), a table, or a scratch outline to record ideas, you can easily identify promising points of comparison or contrast, consolidate supporting details, and spot gaps in your information. Remind yourself of your goal in comparing and contrasting the two subjects. What is it you want to show, argue, or find out?

For more on planning, drafting, and developing, see Chs. 17, 18, and 19. For more on outlines, see pp. 325–33.

For more on stating a thesis, see pp. 312–19.

State Your Purpose in a Thesis.   You need a reason to place two subjects side by side — a reason that you and your audience will find compelling and worthwhile. Ask yourself if you prefer one subject in the pair over the other. What reasons can you give for your preference? It's also all right not to have a preference; you can try instead to understand both subjects more clearly, making a point about each or both. Comparing and contrasting need not be a meaningless exercise. Try instead to think clearly and pointedly in order to explain an idea about which you care.

For exercises on choosing effective thesis statements, visit <bedfordstmartins.com/bedguide> and do a keyword search:

thesis

TWO SUBJECTS	two teaching styles in required biology courses
REASON	to show why one is better
WORKING THESIS	Although students learn a lot in both of the required introductory biology courses, one class teaches information and the other teaches how to be a good learner.

For exercises on supporting a thesis, visit <bedfordstmartins.com/bedguide> and do a keyword search:

support

Select a Pattern to Help Your Audience Follow Your Evidence.   Besides understanding your purpose and thesis, readers also need to follow your supporting evidence — the clusters of details that reveal the nature of each subject you consider. They're likely to expect you to follow one of two ways to organize a comparison-and-contrast essay.

OPPOSING PATTERN, SUBJECT BY SUBJECT

Subject A
    Point 1
    Point 2
    Point 3

ALTERNATING PATTERN, POINT BY POINT

Point 1
    Subject A
    Subject B

Point 2
        Subject A
Subject B   Subject B
Point 1   Point 3
Point 2   Subject A
Point 3   Subject B

Although both patterns present the same information, each has its own advantages and disadvantages.

Use the Opposing Pattern of Organization.   When you use the *opposing pattern* of *subject by subject,* you state all your observations about subject A and then do the same for subject B. In the following paragraph from *Whole Brain Thinking* (New York: William Morrow, 1984), Jacquelyn Wonder and Priscilla Donovan, management consultants, use the opposing pattern of organization to explain the differences in the brains of females and males.

For other examples, see pp. 367–68.

At birth there are basic differences between male and female brains. The female cortex is more fully developed. The sound of the human voice elicits more left-brain activity in infant girls than in infant boys, accounting in part for the earlier development in females of language. Baby girls have larger connectors between the brain's hemispheres and thus integrate information more skillfully. This flexibility bestows greater verbal and intuitive skills. Male infants lack this ready communication between the brain's lobes; therefore, messages are routed and rerouted to the right brain, producing larger right hemispheres. The size advantage accounts for males having greater spatial and physical abilities and explains why they may become more highly lateralized and skilled in specific areas.

Subject A: Female brain

Point 1: Development

Point 2: Consequences
Shift to subject B: Male brain
Point 1: Development
Point 2: Consequences

For a single paragraph or a short essay, the opposing pattern can effectively unify all the details about each subject, like neat versus sloppy people in Suzanne Britt's essay. For a long essay or a complicated subject, it has a drawback: readers might find it difficult to remember all the separate information about subject A while reading about subject B.

Use the Alternating Pattern of Organization.   There's a better way to organize most longer papers: the *alternating pattern* of *point by point.* Using this method, you take up one point at a time, applying it first to one subject and then the other. If your paper will have headings, you can use them to identify these points as well, thus helping readers preview the structure at a glance and anticipate what's covered in each section. Tim Chabot uses this pattern to lead the reader along clearly and carefully, looking at each subject before moving on to the next point. His outline might have looked like this:

For more on headings, see pp. 405–09.

THESIS: The exciting speed of basketball may soon have more appeal than the leisurely pace of baseball.

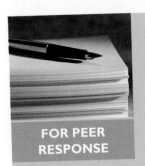

FOR PEER RESPONSE

For general questions for a peer editor, see p. 377.

You may want a classmate or friend to respond to your draft, suggesting how to present your two subjects more clearly. Ask your peer editor to answer questions like these about comparison and contrast:

- How does the introduction motivate you to read the entire essay?
- What is the point of the comparison and contrast of the two subjects? Is the thesis stated in the essay, or is it implied?
- Is the essay organized by the opposing pattern or by the alternating pattern? Is the pattern appropriate, or would the other one work better?
- Are the same categories discussed for each item? If not, should they be?
- Are there enough details for you to understand the comparison and contrast? Put a check where more details or examples would be useful.
- If this were your paper, what is the one thing you would be sure to work on before handing it in?

I. Similarities of fans
   A. Appeal to diverse groups
      1. Baseball
      2. Basketball
   B. Varied locations
      1. Baseball
      2. Basketball

II. Difference in atmosphere at game
   A. Baseball as a diverse family-oriented spectator sport
      1. Many distractions
      2. Frequent breaks in play
   B. Basketball as game-focused sport
      1. Few distractions
      2. Constant game activity

III. Difference in pace of game
   A. Leisurely pace of baseball
      1. Slow batters
      2. Stalling pitchers
      3. Substitution of relief pitchers
      4. Low score
      5. Seventh-inning stretch
   B. Quick pace of basketball
      1. Fast players
      2. High scores
      3. Frequent changes of sides
      4. Constant motion

Comparing and Contrasting Yourself with a Partner

Using assignment 3 on page 119 as a guide, compare and contrast yourself with a classmate in a collaborative essay. Decide together what your focus will be: Your backgrounds? Your hobbies? Your career goals? Your study habits? Your taste in music or clothes? Your politics? Then each partner should work alone on a detailed analysis of himself or herself, given this focus. Together again, compare your analyses, decide how to shape the essay, and draft, revise, and edit the paper. If your instructor approves, consider a mixed-media presentation.

FOR GROUP LEARNING

IV. Different athletic abilities of players
    A. Baseball as a mental game
        1. Emphasis on athletic precision
            a. Strategy
            b. Skill
            c. Decision making
        2. Physical strength less important
    B. Basketball as a physical game
        1. Emphasis on physical power
            a. Jumping high
            b. Running fast
            c. Being tall and big
            d. Being aggressive
        2. Importance of skill and dexterity

For more on outlines, see pp. 325–33. For Tim Chabot's full paper, see pp. 108–10.

Add Transitions.   Once your essay is organized, you can bring cohesion to it through effective transitional words and phrases — *on the other hand, in contrast, also, both, yet, although, finally, unlike.* Your choice of wording will depend on the content, but keep it varied and smooth. Jarring, choppy transitions distract attention instead of contributing to a unified essay, each part working to support a meaningful thesis.

For more on transitions, see pp. 346–49.

REVISING AND EDITING

Focus on Your Thesis.   Reconsider your purpose when you review your draft. If your purpose is to illuminate two subjects impartially, ask whether you have given readers a balanced view. Obviously it would be unfair to set forth all the advantages of Oklahoma City and all the disadvantages of Honolulu and then conclude that Oklahoma City is superior on every count.

    Of course, if you love Oklahoma City and can't stand Honolulu, or vice versa, go ahead: don't be balanced; take a stand. Even so, you will want to include the same points about each city and to admit, in all honesty, that Oklahoma City has its faults. One useful way to check for balance or thoroughness is to outline your draft and give the outline a critical look.

For more on revising and editing strategies, see Ch. 20.

For more on outlines, see pp. 325–33.

■ For more on stating a
thesis, see pp. 312–19.

If classmates have made suggestions, perhaps about clearer wording to
sharpen distinctions, use their ideas as you rework your thesis.

WORKING THESIS   Although students learn a lot in both of the required introductory biology courses, one class teaches information
and the other teaches how to be a good learner.

REVISED THESIS   Although students learn the basics of biology in both of
the required introductory courses, one class teaches how
to memorize information and the other teaches an invaluable lesson: how to be an active learner.

Vary Your Wording.   Make sure, as you go over your draft, that you have escaped a monotonous drone: A does this, B does that; A has these advantages,
B has those. Comparison and contrast needn't result in a paper as symmetrical
■ For strategies for in-
creasing coherence, see
pp. 346–49.
as a pair of sneakers. Revising and editing give you a chance to add lively details, transitions, dashes of color, and especially variety:

The menu is another major difference between the Cozy Cafe and the Wilton

Inn. For lunch, the Cozy Cafe offers sandwiches, hamburgers, and chili. For lunch, *at*

features
the Wilton Inn offers dishes such as fajitas, shrimp salads, and onion soup topped

with Swiss cheese. For dinner, the Cozy Cafe continues to serve the lunch menu and
adding
adds home-style comfort foods such as meatloaf, stew, macaroni and cheese, and
after five o'clock
barbecued ribs. By dinner, the Wilton's specialties for the day are posted--perhaps

marinated buffalo steak or orange-pecan salmon.

In critiquing your draft as you rewrite, this checklist may prove handy:

REVISION CHECKLIST

___ Does your introduction present your topic and main point clearly? Is it interesting enough to make a reader want to read the whole essay?

___ Is your reason for doing all the comparing and contrasting unmistakably
clear? What do you want to demonstrate, argue for, or find out? Do you
need to reexamine your goal?

___ Have you used the same categories for each item so that you treat them
fairly? In discussing each feature, do you always look at the same thing?

___ What have you concluded about the two? Do you prefer one to the other? If
so, is this preference (and your rationale for it) clear?

___ Does your draft look thin at any point for lack of evidence? If so, how
might you develop your ideas?

___ Are there any spots where you need to revise a boringly mechanical, monotonous style ("On one hand, . . . now on the other hand")?

After you have revised your comparison-and-contrast essay, edit and proofread it. Carefully check the grammar, word choice, punctuation, and mechanics — and then correct any problems you may find. Here are some questions to get you started editing and proofreading your paper:

■ For more editing and proofreading strategies, see pp. 384–87.

EDITING CHECKLIST

___	Have you used the correct comparative forms (for two things) and superlative forms (for three or more) for adjectives and adverbs?	A7
___	Is your sentence structure correct? Have you avoided writing fragments, comma splices, or fused sentences?	A1, A2
___	Have you used parallel structure in your comparisons and contrasts? Are your sentences as balanced as your ideas?	B2
___	Have you used commas correctly after introductory phrases and other transitions?	C1

■ For more help, turn to the dark-blue-edged pages and find the sections of the Quick Editing Guide noted here.

OTHER ASSIGNMENTS

1. Listen to two different recordings of the same piece of music as performed by two different groups, orchestras, or singers. What elements of the music does each stress? What contrasting attitudes toward the music do you detect? In an essay, compare and contrast these versions.

2. Write an essay in which you compare and contrast the subjects in any of the following pairs for the purpose of throwing light on both. In a short paper, you can trace only a few similarities and differences, but don't hesitate to observe, go to the library, or interview a friendly expert.

■ For more on using sources to support a position, see Ch. 12 and the Quick Research Guide (the dark-red-edged pages).

> Women and men as single parents
> Living at home and living away from home
> The coverage of a world event on television and in a newspaper
> The experience of watching a film on a DVD and in a theater
> The styles of two athletes playing in the same position (two pitchers, two quarterbacks, two goalies)
> English and another language
> Your college and a rival college
> Two differing views of a current controversy
> Northern and southern California (or two other regions)
> Two similar works of architecture (two churches, two skyscrapers, two city halls, two museums, two campus buildings)
> Two articles, essays, or Web sites about the same topic

3. In a serious or nonserious way, introduce yourself to your class by comparing and contrasting yourself with someone else. You might choose either a real person or a character in a film, a TV series, a novel, or a comic strip, but you and this other person should have much in common. Choose a few points of comparison (an attitude, a habit, or a way of life), and deal with each in an essay or, if your instructor approves, a mixed-media format.

(Millions)

164.5

145.6

133.5   152.1

12.1   12.4

2004   Projected 2014

■ Wage-and-salary workers
■ Self-employed and
  unpaid family workers

Employment by class of worker, 2004 and projected 2014
Source: Occupational Outlook Quarterly

Applying What You Learn: Some Uses of Comparing and Contrasting

In College Courses.   College instructors know that distinguishing subtle similarities and differences between two subjects requires close attention, so they frequently ask students to demonstrate that understanding.

- You would compare and contrast to "evaluate" the relative merits of Norman Rockwell and N. C. Wyeth in an art history course.
- An assignment to "consider" doing business as a small corporation and as a partnership calls for comparison and contrast.
- When you are asked to "describe" a subject, such as medieval funeral customs, comparing or contrasting it with a similar familiar subject, modern traditions, might be the best way to set up a frame of reference.

In the Workplace.   At work, you will constantly compare and contrast products or services of one company with those of another, merits of one proposal with those of another, or benefits of option A with those of option B.

- Analysts compare employment data and projections to inform employers and workers about labor trends and help them plan for the future.
- When you recommend a new procedure, you can emphasize its strong points by comparing and contrasting it with the existing procedure.
- When hiring, organizations compare and contrast management style, work experience, education, and personal attributes of applicants.

In Your Community.   Comparing and contrasting is an effective method of analyzing alternatives in your community life as well.

- The advantages of one option over another quickly become apparent when you compare or contrast them, whether you want to choose a childcare provider, a fitness center, or backup aid cameras for your car.
- Your pamphlet urging voters to approve bonds for building a new elementary school can contrast costs and benefits of building with those of renovation.
- If you were to recommend a resort for your organization's annual conference, your report would compare and contrast accommodations, meeting facilities, food services, and dates of availability.

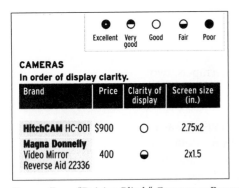

	●	◐	○	◑	●
	Excellent	Very good	Good	Fair	Poor

CAMERAS
In order of display clarity.

Brand	Price	Clarity of display	Screen size (in.)
HitchCAM HC-001	$900	○	2.75x2
Magna Donnelly Video Mirror Reverse Aid 22336	400	◑	2x1.5

Source: From "Driving Blind," Consumer Reports

Chapter 8
Explaining Causes and Effects

Responding to an Image

This image shows both causes and effects. What causes can you identify? What effects? Also consider artistic choice—the selection of the scene and the vantage point from which it was photographed. What mood does the photograph create? How does it affect you personally?

When a house burns down, an insurance company assigns a claims adjuster to look into the disaster and ask, Why? He or she investigates to find the answer—the *cause* of the fire, whether lightning, a cooking mishap, or a match that someone deliberately struck—and presents it in a written report. The adjuster also details the *effects* of the fire—what was destroyed or damaged, what repairs will be needed, how much they will cost.

Often in college you are asked to investigate and think like the insurance adjuster, tracing causes or identifying effects. To do so, you have to gather information to marshal evidence. Effects, by the way, are usually easier to identify than causes. Results of a fire are apparent to an onlooker the next day, although its cause may be obscure. For this reason, seeking causes and effects may be an uncertain pursuit, and you are unlikely to set forth definitive explanations with absolute certainty.

Learning from Other Writers

For more on thesis and support, see Chs. 17 and 19.

The following essays explore causes and effects, each examining a different environment. To help you begin to analyze the first reading, look for the notes in the margin. They identify features such as the thesis, or main idea, and the first of the causes or effects that develop it in a paper analyzing cause and effect.

For more examples of writing that explains causes and effects, visit <bedfordstmartins.com/bedguide> and do a keyword search:

examples

As You Read These Cause-and-Effect Essays

As you read these essays, ask yourself the following questions:

1. Does the writer explain causes? Or effects? Or both? Why?

2. Does the writer perceive and explain a chain or series of causal relationships? If so, how are the various causes and effects connected?

3. What evidence does the writer supply? Is the evidence sufficient to clarify the causal relationships and to provide credibility to the essay?

William Severini Kowinski examines some of the underlying reasons for "mall culture" in this excerpt from his book The Malling of America *(1985).*

Quotation used to preview writer's focus

William Severini Kowinski
Kids in the Mall: Growing Up Controlled

Butch heaved himself up and loomed over the group. "Like it was different for me," he piped. "My folks used to drop me off at the shopping mall every morning and leave me all day. It was like a big free baby-sitter, you know? One night they never came back for me. Maybe they moved away. Maybe there's some kind of a Bureau of Missing Parents I could check with."
–Richard Peck, *Secrets of the Shopping Mall*, a novel for teenagers

From his sister at Swarthmore, I'd heard about a kid in Florida whose | 1
mother picked him up after school every day, drove him straight to the
mall, and left him there until it closed — all at his insistence. I'd heard about
a boy in Washington who, when his family moved from one suburb to another, pedaled his bicycle five miles every day to get back to his old mall,
where he once belonged.

— Introduction

Their stories aren't unusual. The mall is a common experience for the | 2
majority of American youth; they have probably been going there all their
lives. Some ran within their first large open space, saw their first fountain,
bought their first toy, and read their first book in a mall. They may have
smoked their first cigarette or first joint or turned them down, had their first
kiss or lost their virginity in the mall parking lot. Teenagers in America now
spend more time in the mall than anywhere else but home and school.
Mostly it is their choice, but some of that mall time is put in as the result of
two-paycheck and single-parent households, and the lack of other viable°
alternatives. But are these kids being harmed by the mall?

— Situation described in transitional paragraph

— Question raised about effects

I wondered first of all what difference it makes for adolescents to experi- 3
ence so many important moments in the mall. They are, after all, at play in
the fields of its little world and they learn its ways; they adapt to it and make
it adapt to them. It's here that these kids get their street sense, only it's mall
sense. They are learning the ways of a large-scale artificial environment: its
subtleties and flexibilities, its particular pleasures and resonances,° and the
attitudes it fosters.

— **THESIS**
specifying effects

The presence of so many teenagers for so much time was not something 4
mall developers planned on. In fact, it came as a big surprise. But kids became
a fact of mall life very early, and the International Council of Shopping Centers
found it necessary to commission a study, which they published along with a
guide to mall managers on how to handle the teenage incursion.°

The study found that "teenagers in suburban centers are bored and 5
come to the shopping centers mainly as a place to go. Teenagers in suburban centers spent more time fighting, drinking, littering, and walking than
did their urban counterparts, but presented fewer overall problems." The report observed that "adolescents congregated in groups of two to four and
predominantly at locations selected by them rather than management." This
probably had something to do with the decision to install game arcades,
which allow management to channel these restless adolescents into naturally contained areas away from major traffic points of adult shoppers.

The guide concluded that mall management should tolerate and even 6
encourage the teenage presence because, in the words of the report, "The
vast majority support the same set of values as does shopping center management." *The same set of values* means simply that mall kids are already pre-
programmed to be consumers and that the mall can put the finishing

viable: Effective or practical.   **resonances:** Profound and lasting impacts.   **incursion:**
Invasion.

touches to them as hard-core, lifelong shoppers just like everybody else. That, after all, is what the mall is about. So it shouldn't be surprising that in spending a lot of time there, adolescents find little that challenges the assumption that the goal of life is to make money and buy products, or that just about everything else in life is to be used to serve those ends.

Growing up in a high-consumption society already adds inestimable 7 pressure to kids' lives. Clothes consciousness has invaded the grade schools, and popularity is linked with having the best, newest clothes in the currently acceptable styles. Even what they read has been affected. "Miss [Nancy] Drew wasn't obsessed with her wardrobe," noted the *Wall Street Journal*. "But today the mystery in teen fiction for girls is what outfit the heroine will wear next." Shopping has become a survival skill and there is certainly no better place to learn it than the mall, where its importance is powerfully reinforced and certainly never questioned.

Use of contrast —

The mall as a university of suburban materialism, where Valley Girls 8 and Boys from coast to coast are educated in consumption, has its other lessons in this era of change in family life and sexual mores° and their economic and social ramifications.° The plethora° of products in the mall, plus the pressure on teens to buy them, may contribute to the phenomenon that psychologist David Elkind calls "the hurried child": kids who are exposed to too much of the adult world too quickly, and must respond with a sophistication that belies their still-tender emotional development. Certainly the adult products marketed for children — form-fitting designer jeans, sexy tops for preteen girls — add to the social pressure to look like an adult, along with the home-grown need to understand adult finances (why mothers must work) and adult emotions (when parents divorce).

Education comparison:
negative

Kids spend so much time at the mall partly because their parents allow 9 it and even encourage it. The mall is safe, it doesn't seem to harbor any unsavory activities, and there is adult supervision; it is, after all, a controlled environment. So the temptation, especially for working parents, is to let the mall be their babysitter. At least the kids aren't watching TV. But the mall's role as a surrogate mother may be more extensive and more profound.

Karen Lansky, a writer living in Los Angeles, has looked into the subject 10 and she told me some of her conclusions about the effects on its teenaged denizens of the mall's controlled and controlling environment. "Structure is the dominant idea, since true 'mall rats' lack just that in their homelives," she said, "and adolescents about to make the big leap into growing up crave more structure than our modern society cares to acknowledge." Karen pointed out some of the elements malls supply that kids used to get from their families, like warmth (Strawberry Shortcake dolls and similar cute and cuddly merchandise), old-fashioned mothering ("We do it all for you," the fast-food slogan), and even home cooking (the "homemade" treats at the food court).

mores: Moral principles or codes of conduct.   **ramifications:** Consequences stemming from an initial plan, act, or process.   **plethora:** Abundance.

The problem in all this, as Karen Lansky sees it, is that while families 11
nurture children by encouraging growth through the assumption of responsibility and then by letting them rest in the bosom of the family from the
rigors° of growing up, the mall as a structural mother encourages passivity
and consumption, as long as the kid doesn't make trouble. Therefore all
they learn about becoming adults is how to act and how to consume.

Kids are in the mall not only in the passive role of shoppers — they also 12
work there, especially as fast-food outlets infiltrate the mall's enclosure. There
they learn how to hold a job and take responsibility, but still within the same
value context. When *CBS Reports* went to Oak Park Mall in suburban Kansas
City, Kansas, to tape part of their hour-long consideration of malls, "After the
Dream Comes True," they interviewed a teenaged girl who worked in a fast-
food outlet there. In a sequence that didn't make the final program, she described the major goal of her present life, which was to perfect the curl on
top of the ice-cream cones that were her store's specialty. If she could do that,
she would be moved from the lowly soft-drink dispenser to the more prestigious ice-cream division, the curl on top of the status ladder at her restaurant.
These are the achievements that are important at the mall.

Other benefits of such jobs may also be overrated, according to Lau- 13
rence D. Steinberg of the University of California at Irvine's social ecology
department, who did a study on teenage employment. Their jobs, he found,
are generally simple, mindlessly repetitive, and boring. They don't really
learn anything, and the jobs don't lead anywhere. Teenagers also work primarily with other teenagers; even their supervisors are often just a little
older than they are. "Kids need to spend time with adults," Steinberg told
me. "Although they get benefits from peer relationships, without parents
and other adults it's one-sided socialization. They hang out with each other,
have age-segregated jobs, and watch TV."

Perhaps much of this is not so terrible or even so terribly different. Now 14
that they have so much more to contend with in their lives, adolescents
probably need more time to spend with other adolescents without adult im-
positions, just to sort things out. Though it is more concentrated in the mall
(and therefore perhaps a clearer target), the value system there is really the
dominant one of the whole society. Attitudes about curiosity, initiative, self-
expression, empathy, and disinterested learning aren't necessarily made in
the mall; they are mirrored there, perhaps a bit more intensely — as through
a glass brightly.

Besides, the mall is not without its educational opportunities. There are 15
bookstores, where there is at least a short shelf of classics at great prices, and
other books from which it is possible to learn more than how to do sit-ups.
There are tools, from hammers to VCRs, and products, from clothes to
records, that can help the young find and express themselves. There are
older people with stories, and places to be alone or to talk one-on-one with
a kindred spirit. And there is always the passing show.

Education comparison: positive

rigors: Harsh difficulties.

The mall itself may very well be an education about the future. I was 16 struck with the realization, as early as my first forays into Greengate,[1] that the mall is only one of a number of enclosed and controlled environments that are part of the lives of today's young. The mall is just an extension, say, of those large suburban schools — only there's Karmelkorn instead of chem lab, the ice rink instead of the gym: It's high school without the impertinence of classes.

Growing up, moving from home to school to the mall — from enclosure 17 to enclosure, transported in cars — is a curiously continuous process, without much in the way of contrast or contact with unenclosed reality. Places must tend to blur into one another. But whatever differences and dangers there are in this, the skills these adolescents are learning may turn out to be useful in their later lives. For we seem to be moving inexorably° into an age of preplanned and regulated environments, and this is the world they will inherit.

Still, it might be better if they had more of a choice. One teenaged girl 18 confessed to *CBS Reports* that she sometimes felt she was missing something by hanging out at the mall so much. "But I'm here," she said, "and this is what I have."

Conclusion; writer ends with another quotation

Questions to Start You Thinking

Meaning

1. According to Kowinski, what do teenagers seek at the mall?

2. In paragraph 6, Kowinski quotes a study concluding that mall management and teens share "the same set of values." What are the values they share? What is the effect of these values on teenagers?

3. How do mall experiences shape the kinds of adults these teens become?

4. Kowinski compares the mall experience to high school. In what ways is it similar to high school? How is it different?

Writing Strategies

5. Kowinski examines both negative and positive effects of mall life on teens. In which paragraphs do you find negative effects? Where does he include positive effects? How well does this organization work?

6. Does Kowinski's essay deal predominantly with causes or effects? Where and to what degree does he examine each of these? How would his essay change if he limited his focus to only causes or only effects?

7. Kowinski begins his essay with a quotation from Richard Peck's *Secrets of the Shopping Mall.* Is this an effective beginning? Why or why not? In what other ways might he have begun his essay?

inexorably: Incapable of being stopped or deterred.

[1] Greengate Mall in Greensburg, Pennsylvania, where Kowinski began his research on malls. [Eds.]

STUDENT ESSAY

Yun Yung Choi
Invisible Women

Yun Yung Choi examines the adoption of a new state religion in her native Korea and the effects of that adoption on Korean women.

For me, growing up in a small suburb on the outskirts of Seoul, the adults' preference for boys seemed quite natural. All the important people that I knew—doctors, lawyers, policemen, and soldiers—were men. On the other hand, most of the women that I knew were either housekeepers or housewives whose duty seemed to be to obey and please the men of the family. When my teachers at school asked me what I wanted to be when I grew up, I would answer, "I want to be the wife of the president." Because all women must become wives and mothers, I thought, becoming the wife of the president would be the highest achievement for a woman. I knew that the birth of a boy was a greatly desired and celebrated event, whereas the birth of a girl was a disappointing one, accompanied by the frequent words of consolation for the sad parents: "A daughter is her mother's chief help in keeping house."

❓ How would you have answered this question?

These attitudes toward women, widely considered the continuation of an unbroken chain of tradition, are, in fact, only a few hundred years old, a relatively short period considering Korea's long history. During the first half of the Yi dynasty, which lasted from 1392 to 1910, and during the Koryo period, which preceded the Yi dynasty, women were treated almost as equals with many privileges that were denied them during the latter half of the Yi dynasty. This turnabout in women's place in Korean society was brought about by one of the greatest influences that shaped the government, literature, and thoughts of the Korean people—Confucianism.°

Throughout the Koryo period, which lasted from 918 to 1392, and throughout the first half of the Yi dynasty, according to Laurel Kendall in her book *View from the Inner Room*, women were important and contributing members of the society and not marginal and dependent as they later became. Women were, to a large extent, in command of their own lives. They were permitted to own property and receive inheritances from their fathers. Wedding ceremonies were held in the bride's house, where the couple lived, and the wife retained her surname. Women were also allowed freedom of movement—that is, they were able to go outside the house without any feelings of shame or embarrassment.

With the introduction of Confucianism, however, the rights and privileges that women enjoyed were confiscated. The government of the Yi dynasty made great efforts to incorporate into society the Confucian ideologies, including the principle of *agnation*. This principle, according to Kendall, made men the important members of

Confucianism: Ethical system based on the teachings of Chinese philosopher Confucius (551–479 B.C.).

How do you respond to this historical background?

society and relegated° women to a dependent position. The government succeeded in Confucianizing the country and encouraging the acceptance of Confucian proverbs such as the following: "Men are honored, but women are abased." "A daughter is a 'robber woman' who carries household wealth away when she marries."

The unfortunate effects of this Confucianization in the lives of women were numerous. The most noticeable was the virtual confinement of women. They were forced to remain unseen in the *anbang*, the inner room of the house. This room was the women's domain, or, rather, the women's prison. Outside, a woman was carried through the streets in a closed sedan chair. Walking outside, she had to wear a veil that covered her face and could travel abroad only after nightfall. Thus, it is no wonder that Westerners traveling through Korea in the late nineteenth century expressed surprise at the apparent absence of women in the country.   5

Women received no formal education. Their only schooling came from government textbooks. By giving instruction on the virtuous° conduct of women, these books attempted to fit women into the Confucian stereotype—meek, quiet, and obedient. Thus, this Confucian society acclaimed particular women not for their talent or achievement but for the degree of perfection with which they were able to mimic the stereotype.   6

A woman even lost her identity in such a society. Once married, she became a stranger to her natal° family, becoming a member of her husband's family. Her name was omitted from the family *chokpo*, or genealogy book, and was entered in the *chokpo* of her in-laws as a mere "wife" next to her husband's name.   7

Even a desirable marriage, the ultimate hope for a woman, failed to provide financial and emotional security for her. Failure to produce a son was legal grounds for sending the wife back to her natal home, thereby subjecting the woman to the greatest humiliation and to a life of continued shame. And because the Confucian ideology stressed a wife's devotion to her husband as the greatest of womanly virtues, widows were forced to avoid social disgrace by remaining faithfully unmarried, no matter how young they were. As women lost their rights to own or inherit property, these widows, with no means to support themselves, suffered great hardships. Thus, as Sandra Martielle says in *Virtues in Conflict*, what the government considered "the ugly custom of remarriage" was slowly eliminated at the expense of women's happiness.   8

This male-dominated system of Confucianism is one of the surviving traditions from the Yi dynasty. Although the Constitution of the Republic of Korea proclaimed on July 17, 1948, guarantees individual freedom and sexual equality, these ideals failed to have any immediate effect on the Korean mentality that stubbornly adheres   9

---

relegated: Reduced to a less important position.   **virtuous:** Moral, honorable.   **natal:** Relating to one's birth.

to its belief in the superiority of men. Women still regard marriage as their prime objective in life, and little girls still wish to become the doctor's wife, the lawyer's wife, and even the president's wife. But as the system of Confucianism is slowly being forced out of existence by new legal and social standards, perhaps a day will come, after all, when a little girl will stand up in class and answer, "I want to be the president."

> *Why do you think the writer ends with this quotation?*

Questions to Start You Thinking

Meaning

1. What effect does Choi observe? What cause does she attribute it to?
2. What specific changes in Korean culture does Choi attribute to the introduction of Confucianism?
3. What evidence do you find of the writer's critically rethinking an earlier belief and then revising it? What do you think may have influenced her to change her belief?

Writing Strategies

4. What does Choi gain by beginning and ending with her personal experience?
5. Where does Choi use the strategy of comparing and contrasting? Do you think this is effective?
6. How does Choi consider readers for whom her culture might be foreign?
7. Using highlighters or marginal notes, identify the essay's introduction, thesis, major causes or effects, supporting explanations and details for each of these, and conclusion. How effective is the organization of this essay?

Learning by Writing

THE ASSIGNMENT: EXPLAINING CAUSES AND EFFECTS

Pick a disturbing fact or situation that you have observed, and seek out the causes and effects to help you and your readers understand the issue better. You may limit your essay to the causes *or* the effects, or you may include both but emphasize one more than the other. Yun Yung Choi uses the last approach when she briefly identifies the cause of the status of Korean women (Confucianism) but spends most of her essay detailing effects of this cause.

The situation you choose may have affected you and people you know well, such as student loan policies, the difficulty of working while going to school, or divorce in the family. It might have affected people in your city or region — a small voter turnout in an election, decaying bridge supports, or

> ■ For writing activities for cause and effect, visit <bedfordstmartins.com/bedguide> and do a keyword search:
>
>
> activities

pet owners not using pooper-scoopers. It may affect society at large — identity theft, immigration laws, or the high cost of health care. It might be gender or racial stereotypes on television, binge drinking at parties, spouse abuse, teenage suicide, global warming, student debt, or the use of dragnets for ocean fishing. Don't think you must choose an earthshaking topic to write a good paper. On the contrary, you will do a better job if you are personally familiar with the situation you choose.

Papers written in response to this assignment have included the following:

One student cited her observations of the hardships faced by Indians in rural Mexico as one cause of the recent rebellions there.

Another analyzed the negative attitudes of men toward women at her workplace and the resulting tension, inefficiency, and low production.

A third contended that buildings in Miami are not constructed to withstand hurricanes due, for one reason, to an inadequate inspection system.

GENERATING IDEAS

■ For more strategies for generating ideas, see Ch. 16.

Find a Topic.   What familiar situation would be informative or instructive to explore? This assignment leaves you the option of writing from personal experience, from what you know, what you can find out, or a combination of the two. Begin by letting your thoughts wander over the results of an undesirable situation. Has the situation always been this way? Or has it changed in the last few years? Have things gotten better or worse?

The ideas in the following list may help you search your memory:

DISCOVERY CHECKLIST

___ Has a difficult situation resulted from a change in your life (a new job; a fluctuation in income; personal or family upheaval following death, divorce, accident, illness, or good fortune; a new school)?

___ Has the environment changed (due to air pollution, a flood or a storm, a new industry, the failure of an old industry)?

___ Has a disturbing situation been caused by an invention (the computer, the DVD player, the television, the ATM, the cell phone)?

___ Do certain employment trends cause you concern (for women in management, for blacks in the military, for white males in nursing)?

___ Is a situation on campus or in your neighborhood, city, or state causing problems for you (traffic, housing costs, population, health care)?

■ For more on brainstorming, see pp. 296–97.

When your thoughts begin to percolate, jot down likely topics. Then choose the idea that you care most about and that promises to be neither too large nor too small. A paper confined to the causes of a family's move from New Jersey to Montana might be only one sentence long: "My father's company transferred him." But the subsequent effects of the move on the family might become an interesting essay. On the other hand, you might need hundreds of pages to study all the effects of gangs in urban high schools. Instead, you might consider just one unusual effect, such as gang members staking out territory in the parking lot of a local school.

List Causes and Effects.   Your choice tentatively made, write for ten or fifteen minutes, identifying likely causes and effects. After noting those you see, consider which are immediate (evident and close at hand), which are remote (underlying, more basic, or earlier), and how you might arrange them in a logical sequence or causal chain.

FOCUS ON CAUSAL CHAIN

Remote Causes	→	Immediate Causes	→	**SITUATION**		→ Immediate Effects	→ Remote Effects
Foreign competition	→	Sales, profits drop	→	**Clothing factory closing**	→	Jobs vanish	→ Town flounders

---

Once you have figured out the basic causal relationships, focus on complexities or implications. Probe more deeply for contributing, related, or even hidden factors. When you begin to draft your paper, these ideas will be a rich resource, allowing you to concentrate on the causes or effects you find most important and skip any that are minor.

For more on thinking critically, see Ch. 3.

FOCUS ON IMMEDIATE EFFECTS			**FOCUS ON REMOTE EFFECTS**
Factory workers lose jobs	→	Households curtail spending	Town economy undermined
Grocery and other stores suffer	→	Businesses fold	Food pantry, social services overwhelmed
Workers lose health coverage	→	Health needs ignored	Hospital limits services and doctors leave
Retirees fear benefits lost	→	Confidence erodes	Unemployed and young people leave

---

Try Mapping the Situation.   If a visual technique might help you analyze the situation, try mapping. Using a blank page, movable sticky notes, or a computer file, identify and position causes and effects in order to show their relationships or relative importance.

For more on mapping, see p. 301.

Consider Sources of Support.   After identifying causes and effects, note your evidence next to each item. You can then see at a glance exactly where you need more material. Star or underline any causes and effects that stand

For advice on finding a few pertinent sources, turn to the Quick Research Guide (the dark-red-edged pages).

Facing the Challenge: Causes and Effects

The major challenge writers face when exploring causal relationships is how to limit the subject. When you explore a given phenomenon—from teenage drug use to the success of your favorite band—devoting equal space to all possible causes and effects will either overwhelm your readers or put them to sleep. Instead, you need to decide what you want to show your readers—and then emphasize the causal relationships that help achieve this purpose.

Rely on your purpose to help you decide which part of the relationship—cause or effect—to stress and how to limit your ideas to strengthen your overall point. If you are writing about your parents' divorce, for example, you may be tempted to discuss all the possible *causes* for their separation and then analyze all the *effects* it has had on you. Your readers, however, won't want to know about every single argument your parents had. Both you and your readers will have a much easier time if you make some decisions about your focus:

- Do you want to concentrate on *causes* or *effects*?
- Which of your explanations are most and least effective?
- How can you emphasize the points that are most important to you?
- Which relatively insignificant or irrelevant ideas can you omit?

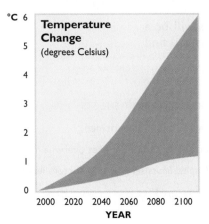

Projected global temperature change. Source: Intergovernmental Panel on Climate Change.

◼ For Choi's complete essay, see pp. 127–29.

out as major ones. A way to rate the items on your list is to ask, How significant is this cause? Would the situation not exist without it? (This major cause deserves a big star.) Or would the situation have arisen without it, for some other reason? (This minor cause might still matter but be less important.) Has this effect had a resounding impact? Is it necessary to explain the results adequately?

As you set priorities—identifying major causes or effects and noting missing information—you may wish to talk with others, use a search engine, or browse the library Web site for sources of supporting ideas, concrete details, and reliable statistics. For example, you might look for illustrations of the problem, accounts of comparable situations, or charts showing current data and projections.

PLANNING, DRAFTING, AND DEVELOPING

Start with a Scratch Outline and Thesis.   Yun Yung Choi's "Invisible Women" follows a clear plan. The essay was written from a brief scratch outline that simply lists the effects of the change:

Intro—Personal anecdote

—Tie with Korean history

—Then add working thesis: The turnabout for women resulted from the in-
fluence of Confucianism in all aspects of society.

Comparison and contrast of status of women before and after Confucianism

Effects of Confucianism on women

1. *Confinement*
2. *Little education*
3. *Loss of identity in marriage*
4. *No property rights*

Conclusion: Impact still evident in Korea today but some hints of change

■ For more about
informal outlines, see
pp. 326–28.

■ For exercises on
choosing effective thesis
statements, visit
<bedfordstmartins.com/
bedguide> and do a key-
word search:

        The paper makes its point: it identifies Confucianism as the reason for
the status of Korean women and details four specific effects of Confucianism
on women in Korean society. And it shows that cause and effect are closely
related: Confucianism is the cause of the change in the status of Korean
women, and Confucianism has had specific effects on Korean women.

■ For more about stating
your main point in a
thesis, see pp. 312–19.

Organize to Show Causes and Effects to Your Audience.   The main
part of your paper — showing how the situation came about (the causes) or
what followed as a result (the effects) or both — more than likely will follow
one of these patterns:

I. The situation	I. The situation	I. The situation
II. Its causes	II. Its effects	II. Its causes
		III. Its effects

        You can begin planning your paper by grouping the causes and effects
and then classifying them as major or minor. If, for example, you are writing
about the reasons more college students accumulate credit-card debt now
than they did a generation ago, you might list the following:

■ For more planning
strategies, see Ch. 17.

1. easy credit
2. high credit limits
3. compulsive buying

On reflection you might decide that compulsive buying — especially of CDs,
DVDs, games, and electronic equipment — is a major cause and that the
availability of credit actually is a minor one. You could then organize the
causes from least to most important, giving the major one more space and
the final place in your essay. When your plan seems logical to you, discuss it
or share your draft with a classmate, a friend, or your instructor. Ask whether
your organization will make sense to someone else.

Introduce the Situation.   When you draft the first part of your paper,
describe the situation you want to explain in no more than two or three
paragraphs. Make clear to your readers your task — explaining causes,

explaining effects, or explaining both. Instead of doing this in a flat, mechanical fashion ("Now I am going to explain the causes"), announce your task casually, naturally, as if you were talking to someone: "At first, I didn't realize that keeping six pet cheetahs in our backyard would bother the neighbors." Or, tantalize your readers as one writer did in a paper about her father's sudden move to a Trappist monastery: "The real reason for Father's decision didn't become clear to me for a long while."

■ For more on using sources for support, see Ch. 12 or the Quick Research Guide (the dark-red-edged pages).
■ For exercises on supporting a thesis, visit <bedfordstmartins.com/bedguide> and do a keyword search:

Work in Your Evidence.   Some writers want to rough out a cause-and-effect draft, positioning all the major points first and then circling back to pull in supporting explanations and details. Others want to plunge deeply into each section — stating the main point, elaborating, and working in the evidence all at once. Tables, charts, and graphs can often consolidate information that substantiates or illustrates causes or effects. If such additions would strengthen your essay, place your graphics near the related text discussion, supporting but not duplicating it.

■ For more revising and editing strategies, see Ch. 20.

■ For more on stating a thesis, see pp. 312–19.

REVISING AND EDITING

Because explaining causes and effects takes hard thought, set aside plenty of time for rewriting. As Yun Yung Choi approached her paper's final version, she wanted to rework her thesis with greater precision and more detail.

WORKING THESIS   The turnabout for women resulted from the influence of Confucianism in all aspects of society.

REVISED THESIS   This turnabout in women's place in Korean society was brought about by one of the greatest influences that shaped the government, literature, and thoughts of the Korean people — Confucianism.

She also faced a problem pointed out by classmates who had read her draft: how to make a smooth transition from recalling her own experience to probing causes.

, a relatively short time, considering Korea's long history

(emphasize that everyone thinks that) ——➤ widely

These attitudes toward women, ~~which I once~~ believed to be the continuation of an unbroken chain of tradition, are, in fact, only a few hundred years old. During the

[tell when]

first half of the Yi dynasty, which lasted from 1392 to 1910, and during [the Koryo period,] women were treated almost as equals, with many privileges that were denied them during the latter half of the Yi dynasty. This upheaval in women's place in Korean society was brought about by one of the greatest influences that shaped the government, literature, and thoughts of the Korean people: Confucianism. Because of

Confucianism, my birth was not greeted with joy and celebration but rather with

these words of consolation: "A daughter is her mother's chief help in keeping house."

(Belongs in opening paragraph)

In revising a paper that traces causes, effects, or both, you might consider questions like these:

REVISION CHECKLIST

___ Have you shown your readers your purpose in presenting causes or effects?

___ Is your explanation thoughtful, searching, and reasonable?

___ Where might you need to reorganize or add transitions so your paper is easy for readers to follow?

If you are tracing causes,

___ Have you made it clear that you are explaining causes?

___ Do you need to add any significant causes?

___ At what points might you need to add more evidence to convince readers that the causal relationships are valid, not just guesses?

___ Do you need to drop any remote causes you can't begin to prove? Or any assertions made without proof?

___ Have you oversimplified by assuming only one small cause accounts for a large phenomenon or that one thing caused another just because the one preceded the other?

For more on evidence, see pp. 37–42. For more on mistakes in thinking called logical fallacies, see pp. 162–63.

If you are determining effects,

___ Have you made it clear that you are explaining effects?

___ What possible effects have you left out? Are any of them worth adding?

___ At what points might you need to supply more evidence that these effects have occurred?

___ Could any effect have resulted not from the cause you describe but from some other cause?

Making a Cause-and-Effect Table

Use the Table menu in your word processor to help you assess the importance of causes and effects. Set up a table with four columns; label them "Major Cause," "Minor Cause," "Major Effect," and "Minor Effect." Divide up your causes and effects accordingly, making entries under each heading. Refine your table as you relate, order, or limit your points.

FOR E-WRITERS

■ For more editing and proofreading strategies, see pp. 384–87.

After you have revised your cause-and-effect essay, edit and proofread it. Carefully check the grammar, word choice, punctuation, and mechanics — and then correct any problems you find. Here are some questions to get you started when editing and proofreading your paper:

■ For more help, turn to the dark-blue-edged pages and find the sections of the Quick Editing Guide noted here.

EDITING CHECKLIST

____ Have you used correct verb tenses and forms throughout? When you describe events in the past, is it clear what happened first and what happened next?   **A3**

____ Have you avoided creating fragments when adding causes or effects? (Check revisions carefully, especially those beginning *"Because . . ."* or *"Causing . . . ."*) Have you avoided comma splices or fused sentences when trying to integrate ideas smoothly?   **A1, A2**

____ Do your transitions and other introductory elements have commas after them, if these are needed?   **C1**

FOR PEER RESPONSE

■ For general questions for a peer editor, see p. 377. For peer response worksheets, visit <bedfordstmartins.com/ bedguide> and do a keyword search:

🔍 ____peer____

■ For more on evidence, see pp. 37–42. For mistakes in thinking called logical fallacies, see pp. 162–63.

Let a classmate or friend read your draft, considering how you've analyzed causes or effects. Ask your peer editor to answer questions such as the following: If the writer explains causes,

• Does the writer explain, rather than merely list, causes?

• Do the causes seem logical and possible?

• Are there other causes that the writer might consider? If so, list them.

If the writer explains effects,

• Do all the effects seem to be results of the situation the writer describes?

• Are there other effects that the writer might consider? If so, list them.

For all cause-and-effect papers,

• What is the writer's thesis? Does the explanation of causes or effects help the writer accomplish the purpose of the essay?

• Is the order of supporting ideas clear? Can you suggest a better organization?

• Are you convinced by the writer's logic? Do you see any logical fallacies?

• Are any causes or effects hard to accept?

• Do the writer's evidence and detail convince you? Put stars where more or better evidence is needed.

• If this were your paper, what is the one thing you would be sure to work on before handing it in?

Explaining the News

In class or in your writing group, tell aloud a two-minute story that you invent to explain the causes behind any surprising event in the morning's news. Either realistic explanations or tall tales are acceptable. Prepare some brief notes about your story in advance. Invite the others to comment on it, and, with their reactions in mind, write it down to turn in at the next class, embellished and improved as you wish. If your group wants to tape or podcast its version of the news, select an anchor, decide on the order of your stories, and rehearse first. Invite your class to enjoy and evaluate your presentation.

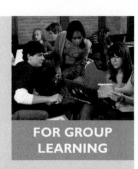

FOR GROUP LEARNING

OTHER ASSIGNMENTS

1. Pick a change that has taken place during your lifetime — a noticeable, lasting transformation produced by an event or a series of events. Explore its causes and effects to help you and your audience understand that change better. The change might have affected only you, such as a move, a decision, or an alteration in a strong personal opinion or belief. It might have also affected others in your community (a new zoning law), in a region (the growth of a new industry), or in society at large (general access to the Internet). Or it might be a new invention, medical breakthrough, or deep-down shift in the structure or attitudes of society.
2. Explore your own motives and explain your reasons for taking some step or for doing something in a routine way.
3. Read a newspaper or magazine article that probes the causes of some contemporary problem: the shortage of certain types of jobs, for instance, or tuition increases in your state. Can you suggest causes that the article writer ignored? Write an essay in which you argue that the author has or has not done a good job of explaining the causes of this problem.

For more on supporting a position with sources, see Ch. 12.

Applying What You Learn: Some Uses of Explaining Causes and Effects

In College Courses.   Both writing assignments and examination questions often pose problems in causality.

- One or two paragraphs that explore the causes of a phenomenon or its effects might add depth to a paper on almost any subject — a sociology paper about teenage parenthood or a literature paper on romanticism in American fiction.

- Exam questions may call for you to identify causes ("Trace the causes of the decline of automobile sales in America") or survey effects ("What economic effects were immediately evident when Prohibition was repealed in 1933?").

- Instructors in many courses will ask you to write about causal relationships. In a speech pathology course, you might investigate effects of head trauma, fetal alcohol syndrome, or learning disabilities.

In the Workplace. Understanding causal relationships, often driving issues of the workplace, can make the difference between success or failure.

- Advertising agencies and marketing departments examine causes and effects to determine how to convince consumers to buy.

- State Department officials and military officers analyze international relations and issue reports — the possible consequences of an impending war between Pakistan and India, the effects of instability in the Middle East, or the causes of genocide in Darfur.

- Economic analysts look at circumstances that will produce changes in the workforce.

In Your Community. Understanding why a problem exists or what might result from a proposed action allows you to add your voice to those who favor the status quo or who support change.

- Your professional or civic organization may outline likely consequences of a proposed practice, making clear the group's stance.

- Images of the long-term effects of dumping in your city's landfill can help build a persuasive poster campaign for recycling.

- A letter sharing evidence of the effects of a dress code on student behavior in other schools can assist school-board members in making a decision beneficial to your child.

Data on workforce changes. Source: Business 2.0

Chapter 9
Taking a Stand

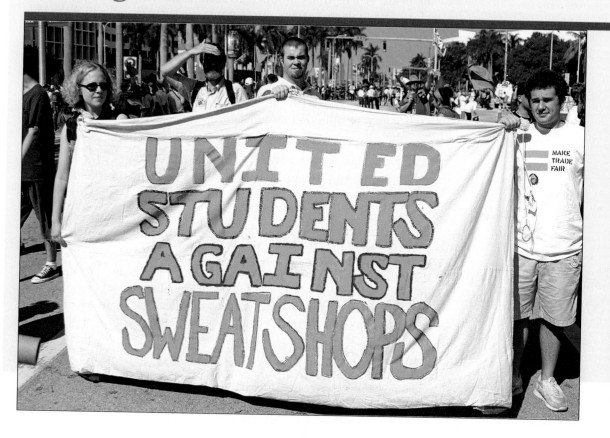

Responding to an Image

The banner in this image identifies a group and its position. What is the stance being taken? What issues and concerns might have led to this position? Based on the image, what event do you think it portrays? What might the photographer have wanted to convey?

Both in and outside of class, you'll hear controversial issues discussed — immigration policy, the use of standardized testing, disaster preparedness, global outsourcing of jobs, copyright issues, health care. Even in academic fields, experts don't always agree, and issues may remain controversies for years. Taking a stand in response to such issues will help you understand the controversy and clarify what you believe.

Writing of this kind has a twofold purpose — to state an opinion and to win your readers' respect for it. What you say might or might not change a reader's opinion. But if you fulfill your purpose, a reader at least will see good reasons for your views. In taking a stand, you do these things:

- You state your opinion or stand.
- You give reasons with evidence to support your position.
- You enlist your readers' trust.
- You consider and respect what your readers probably think and feel.

Learning from Other Writers

For more on thesis and support, see Chs. 17 and 19.

In the following two essays, the writers take a stand on issues of importance to them. To help you begin to analyze the first reading, look for the notes in the margin. They identify features such as the thesis, or main idea, and the first of the points that support it in a paper that takes a stand.

For more such writings, visit <bedfordstmartins.com/bedguide> and do a keyword search:

 examples

As You Read These Essays That Take a Stand

As you read these essays, ask yourself the following questions:

1. What stand does the writer take? Is it a popular opinion, or does it break from commonly accepted beliefs?
2. How does the writer appeal to readers?
3. How does the writer support his or her position? Is the evidence sufficient to gain your respect? Why or why not?

As a result of persuasive efforts such as Suzan Shown Harjo's essay, the Native American Graves Protection and Repatriation Act was passed in 1990.

Introduction appeals to readers

Suzan Shown Harjo

Last Rites for Indian Dead

What if museums, universities, and government agencies could put 1 your dead relatives on display or keep them in boxes to be cut up and otherwise studied? What if you believed that the spirits of the dead could not rest until their human remains were placed in a sacred area?

THESIS — The ordinary American would say there ought to be a law — and there 2 is, for ordinary Americans. The problem for American Indians is that there

140

are too many laws of the kind that make us the archaeological property of the United States and too few of the kind that protect us from such insults.

THESIS
taking a stand
Point 1

Some of my own Cheyenne relatives' skulls are in the Smithsonian Institution today, along with those of at least 4,500 other Indian people who were violated in the 1800s by the U.S. Army for an "Indian Crania Study." It wasn't enough that these unarmed Cheyenne people were mowed down by the cavalry at the infamous Sand Creek massacre; many were decapitated and their heads shipped to Washington as freight. (The Army Medical Museum's collection is now in the Smithsonian.) Some had been exhumed° only hours after being buried. Imagine their grieving families' reaction on finding their loved ones disinterred° and headless.

3

Some targets of the army's study were killed in noncombat situations and beheaded immediately. The officer's account of the decapitation of the Apache chief Mangas Coloradas in 1863 shows the pseudoscientific nature of the exercise. "I weighed the brain and measured the skull," the good doctor wrote, "and found that while the skull was smaller, the brain was larger than that of Daniel Webster."

4

Supporting evidence

These journal accounts exist in excruciating detail, yet missing are any records of overall comparisons, conclusions, or final reports of the army study. Since it is unlike the army not to leave a paper trail, one must wonder about the motive for its collection.

5

The total Indian body count in the Smithsonian collection is more than 19,000, and it is not the largest in the country. It is not inconceivable that the 1.5 million of us living today are outnumbered by our dead stored in museums, educational institutions, federal agencies, state historical societies, and private collections. The Indian people are further dehumanized by being exhibited alongside the mastodons and dinosaurs and other extinct creatures.

6

Where we have buried our dead in peace, more often than not the sites have been desecrated. For more than two hundred years, relic-hunting has been a popular pursuit. Lately, the market in Indian artifacts has brought this abhorrent activity to a fever pitch in some areas. And when scavengers come upon Indian burial sites, everything found becomes fair game, including sacred burial offerings, teeth, and skeletal remains.

7

One unusually well-publicized example of Indian grave desecration occurred two years ago in a western Kentucky field known as Slack Farm, the site of an Indian village five centuries ago. Ten men — one with a business card stating "Have Shovel, Will Travel" — paid the landowner $10,000 to lease digging rights between planting seasons. They dug extensively on the forty-acre farm, rummaging through an estimated 650 graves, collecting burial goods, tools, and ceremonial items. Skeletons were strewn about like litter.

8

What motivates people to do something like this? Financial gain is the first answer. Indian relic-collecting has become a multimillion-dollar industry. The price tag on a bead necklace can easily top $1,000; rare pieces fetch tens of thousands.

9

Question used as transition

---

exhumed: Dug up out of the earth.   **disinterred:** Taken out of a place of burial.

And it is not just collectors of the macabre° who pay for skeletal re- 10
mains. Scientists say that these deceased Indians are needed for research that
someday could benefit the health and welfare of living Indians. But just how
many dead Indians must they examine? Nineteen thousand?

There is doubt as to whether permanent curation of our dead really 11
benefits Indians. Dr. Emery A. Johnson, former assistant Surgeon General,
recently observed, "I am not aware of any current medical diagnostic or
treatment procedure that has been derived from research on such skeletal remains. Nor am I aware of any during the thirty-four years that I have been
involved in American Indian . . . health care."

Indian remains are still being collected for racial biological studies. 12
While the intentions may be honorable, the ethics of using human remains
this way without the full consent of relatives must be questioned.

Some relief for Indian people has come on the state level. Almost half 13
of the states, including California, have passed laws protecting Indian burial
sites and restricting the sale of Indian bones, burial offerings, and other sacred items. Representative Charles E. Bennett (D-Fla.) and Senator John
McCain (R-Ariz.) have introduced bills that are a good start in invoking the
federal government's protection. However, no legislation has attacked the
problem head-on by imposing stiff penalties at the marketplace, or by
changing laws that make dead Indians the nation's property.

Some universities — notably Stanford, Nebraska, Minnesota, and Seattle — 14
have returned, or agreed to return, Indian human remains; it is fitting that
institutions of higher education should lead the way.

Congress is now deciding what to do with the government's extensive 15
collection of Indian human remains and associated funerary objects. The secretary of the Smithsonian, Robert McC. Adams, has been valiantly° attempting to apply modern ethics to yesterday's excesses. This week, he announced
that the Smithsonian would conduct an inventory and return all Indian
skeletal remains that could be identified with specific tribes or living kin.

Transition to concluding proposal

But there remains a reluctance generally among collectors of Indian re- 16
mains to take action of a scope that would have a quantitative impact and a
healing quality. If they will not act on their own — and it is highly unlikely
that they will — then Congress must act.

Conclusion proposes action

The country must recognize that the bodies of dead American Indian 17
people are not artifacts to be bought and sold as collector's items. It is not
appropriate to store tens of thousands of our ancestors for possible future
research. They are our family. They deserve to be returned to their sacred
burial grounds and given a chance to rest.

The plunder of our people's graves has gone on too long. Let us rebury 18
our dead and remove this shameful past from America's future.

---

macabre: Gruesome, ghastly.   **valiantly:** Bravely.

Questions to Start You Thinking

Meaning

1. What is the issue Harjo identifies? How extensive does she show it to be?
2. What is Harjo's position on this issue? Where does she first state it?
3. What evidence does Harjo present to refute the claim that housing skeletal remains of Native Americans in museums is necessary for medical research and may benefit living Indians?

Writing Strategies

4. What assumptions do you think Harjo makes about her audience?
5. What types of evidence does Harjo use to support her argument? How convincing is the evidence to you?
6. How does Harjo use her status as a Native American to enhance her position? Would her argument be as credible if it were written by someone of another background?
7. How does she appeal to the emotions of the readers in the essay? In what ways do these strategies strengthen or detract from her logical reasons?
8. Why does Harjo discuss what legislatures and universities are doing in response to the situation?

STUDENT ESSAY

Sam Benen
A Royal Mess

The poker boom has come home to roost. Once an edgy and provocative novelty,° televised poker is now the norm. Go to any college campus at any time and you can find a group of guys playing a no-limit Texas hold'em° game. On the one hand, reasonable people ought not to be alarmed by poker on TV and $20 games amongst friends. On the other hand, a shocking state of affairs has arisen among college students who play online poker. As someone who is highly familiar with the online poker scene at college, I posit° that there are serious hazards associated with college students gambling online.

Part of the danger of online poker is that it is unregulated. Casinos in the United States are not allowed to accept wagers online because of federal interstate commerce laws, so all online casinos are offshore operations. PartyPoker.com, the largest online poker room, states on its Web site that it is "licensed and regulated by the Government of Gibraltar."° Its servers and business operations are offshore and, as a result, not

Sam Benen's opinion piece originally appeared in Business Today, *an online student journal at Princeton University.*

Do you agree that online poker playing is a serious problem? Why or why not?

---

novelty: Something new and exciting.   **Texas hold'em:** A popular variety of poker. **posit:** State an opinion.   **Gibraltar:** A British colony on a landmass connected to Spain.

subject to any United States laws or taxes. Online poker is also unregulated in the sense that one can play poker online 24 hours a day, 7 days a week, 365 days a year, without exception, and there is no restriction on the amount of money a player can win or lose in a given session. That means a college student could stay up all night and gamble away thousands of dollars. I recall two specific instances on this campus when people I know suffered five-digit losses in online poker. Some time ago, I was talking to a Princeton student (I choose to keep him anonymous) who had recently lost $15,000 in a night. When I asked him how he intended to cope with such a striking down-swing, I recall him saying very stoically,° "Yeah, I should probably cool it for a while and focus on other things in life." There is no reason to believe that such horror stories are restricted to Princeton or the Ivy League. Based on the inherent° lack of regulation in online poker, it is easy to imagine students across the nation doing the same.

Since online gambling remains unchecked by our government, a glaring question   3
is whether online poker is legal. The PartyPoker.com "Terms and Conditions of Use" state that you may only play real money games (as opposed to playing money games also offered that do not involve betting of real money) if you are at least eighteen years of age "or such other minimum legal age in the jurisdiction° where you are connecting." The agreement, which one must acknowledge and sign before activating a real money account, also states that it is the player's sole responsibility to abide by° "the laws that apply in the jurisdiction from where you are connecting." In other words, if you are situated somewhere where gambling is illegal, then you are not allowed to play online poker. Even if gambling is legal in your state, you still need to be at least twenty-one to gamble just about everywhere in the United States. If you are gambling online and are underage, then you are breaking the law; not to mention you have falsely signed a contractual agreement stating that you are legally allowed to play (I won't even touch upon kids under eighteen who are playing online poker).

Why is it, then, that so many underage college students play online poker? Part   4
of it is the same reason that so many drink underage: because seemingly everyone does so, and the punishment for getting caught is a slap on the wrists. There is such a low risk of getting caught, and the penalties are lenient° enough that there are ef-fectively no legal ramifications.° [Making it harder to buy] into online poker games is not a significant deterrent to students, either. Despite a recent initiative in which the lion's share° of banks that issue credit and debit cards blocked all online gaming transactions, depositing into online poker is remarkably hassle free. In order to buy in, one can set up an account with a foreign online cash intermediary,° i.e. an equivalent of PayPal operated outside of the United States (the most common are

---

stoically: Without emotion.   inherent: Part of something's nature.   jurisdiction: A territory or an area of control.   abide by: Follow.   lenient: Mild or forgiving.   ramifications: Consequences.   lion's share: Greatest share; majority.   intermediary: Someone or something that comes between (and may aid interaction between) two people or entities.

Firepay.com and Neteller.com), and then use this middleman to channel in the funds. PartyPoker offers an even easier method of depositing, where a player can costlessly write electronic checks from his checking account just by supplying his account number and ABA° routing number. In either case, a player has 24/7/365 real-time access to every dollar in his or her checking account. So much for the idea that it's somehow difficult or complicated to start playing for real, big money online.

Moreover, using a combination of basic poker strategy, common sense, and discipline, a student can earn thousands of dollars a year playing poker online (compare that to a campus job that pays under $10 an hour). Indeed the house always makes money, but an online poker player is not playing against the casino. Rather, players wager against other players who are simultaneously° logged into the game interface° through the server, and the house takes a small percentage of all the money in play as a fee for hosting the game. Most people who play online are impulsive,° irrational,° and sometimes plain stupid; it is very easy for a savvy° individual to capitalize on the weaknesses of others and make money. Many college students who play semiprofessionally try to compute their hourly rate (and other personal statistics), as though playing poker online were some kind of job with a predictable wage over time. With the kind of morons on the Internet throwing away their money the way they do, thinking of poker as a job in which one methodically takes money from less intelligent people is not all that far-fetched.

Because it can be fun and easy to make money playing poker online, students often overlook one of the main hazards associated with playing—how to legally handle all the money they make. To clarify, "making money" by playing poker online involves a few steps. Once your account is funded, it functions as a poker wallet where you keep a virtual bankroll. You take money from this wallet to buy chips for the various games. All gains (and losses) from the games are credited to (or deducted from) your account. If the amount of money in your account increases because you win at the tables, you must withdraw against the virtual dollars in your poker wallet if you want to realize the gains. The money flows out of the poker account via the same financial intermediary through which you funded the account, and the profit appears on your bank statement within a few business days. Now, the quagmire:° every citizen is bound to report all sources of income to the IRS, but how would a college student claim online poker gains? If you are nineteen years old, then you don't want to admit that you made the money gambling underage, but the only alternative is to defraud the IRS. The people I know who make a substantial amount of money gambling online are split down the middle between those who don't claim it at

5

6 *Do colleges have any responsibility to address student gambling? If so, what actions might they take?*

ABA: American Bankers Association.   **simultaneously:** At the same time.   **interface:** Means of accessing a computer program or Web site.   **impulsive:** Acting with little or no thought or reflection.   **irrational:** Without reason or logic.   **savvy:** Knowledgeable. **quagmire:** A messy situation (literally, a swamp).

all (which, to my mind, is a blatant° evasion of income tax) and those who claim it as miscellaneous income. I wonder what an IRS agent would think if he were auditing someone who had $10,000 in "miscellaneous income" at age nineteen. By the way, in the event of an audit, all poker cash-outs are completely traceable.

Do you agree that online casinos should take more responsibility for screening users? Why or why not?

It strikes me as particularly scary that so much of online poker playing by   7
college students is illegal. It also disturbs me that online casinos do not perform any kind of background check on the accounts they are opening to see whether the players are underage in their jurisdiction. I won't even expound° upon the addictive element of online poker that is potentially destructive to a student's grades and social life. Nevertheless, there is something intrinsically° wrong with college students having access to unlimited gambling for unlimited amounts of money. In reality, thankfully, most students I know who play poker online play for low stakes and treat it as an innocent waste of time. I don't find any fault with students who keep up to a few hundred dollars in their poker account to play an occasional game. But even if online poker is a relatively harmless vice° most of the time, it has the capacity, albeit° seldom, to devastate a student. Even if a student is profiting financially, there is the murky° issue of income tax. From personal experience, I can say that online poker is a lot of fun and potentially very profitable with proper play, but the whole world of online poker is laden with legal risks, gray areas, and very real detriments.°

Questions to Start You Thinking

Meaning

1. What points does Benen make to support his position that online poker playing among students has serious consequences?
2. Why, according to Benen, do so many students play online poker despite the risks?
3. What kind of gambling, according to the author, is not a cause for concern?

Writing Strategies

4. What kind of support does Benen use to back up his claims about the dangers of online poker? Do you find his argument effective? Why or why not?
5. To what extent does Benen account for other points of view? How does the inclusion (or absence) of opposing views affect your opinion on the issue?
6. This article was written for a student business journal. How might Benen change the article if he were writing for a parenting magazine?
7. Using highlighters or marginal notes, identify the essay's introduction, thesis, major points or reasons, supporting evidence for each point, and conclusion. How effective is the organization of this essay?

blatant: Clear or obvious.   **expound:** To state in detail.   **intrinsically:** By nature.
vice: An immoral deed or activity.   **albeit:** Although.   **murky:** Unclear or uncertain.
detriments: Negative consequences.

Learning by Writing

THE ASSIGNMENT: TAKING A STAND

Find a controversy that rouses your interest. It might be a current issue, a long-standing one, or a matter of personal concern: military benefits for national guard troops sent to war zones, the contribution of sports to a school's educational mission, or the need for menu changes at the cafeteria to accommodate ethnic, religious, and personal preferences. Your purpose isn't to solve a social or moral problem but to make clear exactly where you stand on an issue and to persuade your readers to respect your position, perhaps even to accept it. As you reflect on your topic, you may change your position, but don't shift positions in the middle of your essay.

Assume that your readers are people who may or may not be familiar with the controversy, so provide some background or an overview to help them understand the situation. Furthermore, your readers may not have taken sides yet or may hold a position different from yours. You'll need to consider their views and choose strategies that will enlist their support.

Here are brief summaries of a few good papers that take a stand:

A writer who pays her own college costs disputed the opinion that working during the school year provides a student with valuable knowledge. Citing

■ For writing activities for taking a stand, visit <bedfordstmartins.com/ bedguide> and do a keyword search:

activities

Facing the Challenge: Taking a Stand

The major challenge writers face when taking a stand is to gather enough relevant evidence to support their position. Without such evidence, you'll convince only those who agreed with you in the first place. You also won't persuade readers by ranting emotionally about an issue or insulting as ignorant those who hold different opinions. Moreover, few readers respect an evasive writer who avoids taking a stand.

What does work is respect — yours for the views of readers who will, in turn, respect your opinion, even if they don't agree with it. You convey — and gain — respect when you anticipate readers' objections or counterarguments, demonstrate knowledge of these alternate views, and present evidence that addresses others' concerns as it strengthens your argument.

To anticipate and find evidence that acknowledges other views, list groups that might have strong opinions on your topic. Then try putting yourself in the shoes of a member of each group by writing a paragraph on the issue from *her* point of view.

- What would her opinion be?
- On what grounds might she object to your argument?
- How can you best address her concerns and overcome her objections?

Your paragraph will suggest additional evidence to support your claims.

her painful experience, she maintained that devoting full time to studies is far better than juggling school and work.

Another writer challenged his history textbook's portrayal of Joan of Arc as "an ignorant farm girl subject to religious hysteria."

A member of the wrestling team argued that the number of weight categories in wrestling should be increased because athletes who overtrain to qualify for the existing categories often damage their health.

GENERATING IDEAS

For more strategies for generating ideas, see Ch. 16.

For this assignment, you will need to select an issue, take a stand, develop a clear position, and assemble evidence that supports your view.

For more on brainstorming, see pp. 296–97. For more on keeping a journal, see pp. 306–07.

Find an Issue.   The topic for this paper should be an issue or controversy that interests both you and your audience. Try brainstorming a list of possible topics. To get started, look at the headlines of a newspaper or newsmagazine, review the letters to the editor, check the political cartoons on the opinion page, or watch for stories or photos on civic demonstrations or protests. You might also consult the indexes to *CQ Researcher* or *Opposing Viewpoints* in the library, watch a news broadcast, use a search engine to browse news or opinion Web sites, talk with friends, or consider topics raised in class. If you keep a journal, look over your entries to see what has perplexed or angered you. If you need to understand the issue better or aren't sure you want to take a stand on it, investigate by freewriting, reading, or turning to other sources.

Student war protest

Once you have a list of possible topics, drop those that seem too broad or complex or that you don't know much about. Weed out anything that might not hold your interest or that of your readers. From your new, shorter list, pick the issue or controversy for which you can make the strongest argument.

For advice on finding a few sources, see B1–B2 in the Quick Research Guide (the dark-red-edged pages).

Start with a Question and a Thesis.   At this stage, many writers find it useful to pose the issue as a question — a question that will be answered through the position they take. Skip vague questions that most readers wouldn't debate or convert them to questions that allow different stands.

VAGUE QUESTION   Is stereotyping bad?

CLEARLY DEBATABLE   Should we fight gender stereotypes in advertising?

You can help focus your position by stating it in a sentence — a thesis, or statement of your stand. Your statement can answer your question:

WORKING THESIS   We should expect advertisers to fight rather than rein-force gender stereotypes.

OR   Most people who object to gender stereotypes in adver-tising need to get a sense of humor.

For more on stating a thesis, see pp. 312–19.

Your thesis should invite continued debate, not state a fact, by taking a strong position that could be argued.

FACT   Hispanics constitute 16 percent of the community but only 3 percent of our school population.

WORKING THESIS   Our school should increase its outreach to the Hispanic community, which is underrepresented on campus.

Use Formal Reasoning to Refine Your Position.   When you take a posi-tion about a debatable matter, you are likely to use reasoning as well as spe-cific evidence to support your position. A *syllogism* is a series of statements, or premises, used in traditional formal logic to lead deductively to a logical conclusion.

MAJOR STATEMENT   All students must pay tuition.

MINOR STATEMENT   You are a student.

CONCLUSION   Therefore, you must pay tuition.

For a syllogism to be logical, ensuring that its conclusion always applies, its major and minor statements must be true, its definitions of terms must re-main stable, and its classification of specific persons or items must be accu-rate. In real-life arguments, such tidiness may be hard to achieve.

For example, maybe we all agree with the major statement on page 149: all students must pay tuition. However, some students owe tuition, but it is paid for them through a loan or scholarship. Others are admitted under special programs, such as a free-tuition benefit for families of college employees or a back-to-college program for retirees. Further, the word *student* is general; it might apply to students at public high schools who pay no tuition. Next, everyone might agree that you are a student, but maybe you haven't completed registration or the computer has mysteriously dropped you from the class list. Such complications can threaten the success of your conclusion, especially if your audience doesn't accept it. In fact, many civic and social arguments revolve around questions such as these: What — exactly — is the category or group affected? Is its definition or consequence stable — or does it vary? Who falls in or out of the category?

Use Informal Toulmin Reasoning to Refine Your Position.   A contemporary approach to logic is presented by the philosopher Stephen Toulmin in *The Uses of Argument*. He describes an informal way of arguing that acknowledges the power of assumptions in our day-to-day reasoning. This approach starts with a concise statement — the essence of an argument — that makes a claim and supplies a reason to support it.

——————————————— CLAIM ——————————————— ┐ ┌————— REASON —————

Students should boycott the campus cafeteria because the food costs too much.

You develop a claim by supporting your reasons with evidence — your *data* or grounds. For example, your evidence might include facts about the cost of lunches on campus, especially in contrast to local fast-food options, and statistics about the limited resources of most students enrolled at your campus.

However, most practical arguments rely on a *warrant*, your thinking about the connection or relationship between your claim and your supporting data. Because you accept this connection and assume that it applies, you generally assume that others also take it for granted. For instance, nearly all students probably would accept your assumption that a campus cafeteria should serve the needs of its customers. Many might also agree that students should take action rather than allow a campus cafeteria to take advantage of them by charging high prices. Even so, you could state your warrant directly if you thought that your readers would not see the same connection that you do. You also could back up your warrant, if necessary, in various ways:

- using facts, perhaps based on quality and cost comparisons with food service operations on other campuses

- using logic, perhaps based on research findings about the relationship between cost and nutrition for institutional food as well as the importance of good nutrition for brain function and learning

■ For more on appeals, see pp. 40–41.

- making emotional appeals, perhaps based on happy memories of the cafeteria or irritation with its options

- making ethical appeals, perhaps based on the college mission statement or other expressions of the school's commitment to students

As you develop your reasoning, you might adjust your claim or your data to suit your audience, your issue, or your refined thinking. For instance, you might *qualify* your argument (perhaps limiting your objections to most, but not all, of the cafeteria prices). You might also add a *rebuttal* by identifying an *exception* to it (perhaps excluding the fortunate, but few, students without financial worries due to good jobs or family support). Or you might simply reconsider your claim, concluding that the campus cafeteria is, after all, convenient for students and that the manager might be willing to offer more inexpensive options without a student boycott.

—————————— REVISED CLAIM —————————— ┐┌— REASON —

The campus cafeteria should offer less expensive options because most

students can't afford a well-rounded meal at current prices.

Toulmin reasoning is especially effective for making claims like these:

- Fact—*Loss of polar ice can accelerate ocean warming.*

- Cause—*The software company went bankrupt because of its excessive borrowing and poor management.*

- Value—*Cell phone plan A is a better deal than cell phone plan B.*

- Policy—*Admissions policies at Triborough University should be less restrictive.*

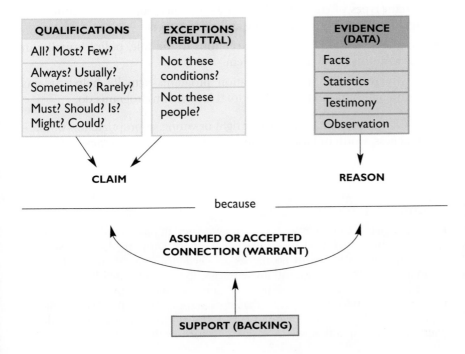

Use these questions to develop or clarify your reasoning as you take a stand:

DISCOVERY CHECKLIST

___ What issue or controversy concerns you? What current debate engages you?

___ What position do you want to take? How can you state your stand? What evidence might you need to support it?

___ How might you refine your working thesis? How could you make your statements more accurate, your definitions clearer, or your categories more exact?

___ What assumptions are you making? What clarification of or support for these assumptions might your audience need?

___ How might you qualify your thesis? What exceptions should you note? What other views might you want to recognize?

Select Evidence to Support Your Position.   As you begin to look for evidence to support your position or claim, consider the issue in terms of the three general types of claims — claims that require substantiation, claims that provide evaluation, and claims that endorse policy.

1. Claims of substantiation require examining and interpreting information in order to resolve disputes about facts, circumstances, causes or effects, definitions, or the extent of a problem, as in these examples:

- Certain types of cigarette ads, such as the once-popular Joe Camel ads, significantly encourage smoking among teenagers.

- Despite a few well-publicized exceptions to the rule, police brutality in this country is not a major problem.

- On the whole, bilingual education programs actually help students learn English more quickly than total immersion programs do.

2. Claims of evaluation consider right or wrong, appropriateness or inappropriateness, worth or lack of worth involved in issues, as in these instances:

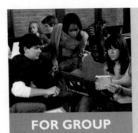

FOR GROUP LEARNING

Making a Claim

Have each member of your writing group write out, in one complete sentence, the core claim or position he or she will support. Drop all these "position statements" into a hat, with no names attached. Then, draw and read each aloud in turn. For each position, invite the group to suggest useful supporting evidence, counterevidence, and possible sources for both. Ask the group's recorder to list suggestions on a separate page for each claim. Finally, match up writers with claims, and share reactions. If this activity causes you to alter your stand, be thankful: it will be easier to revise now than later.

- Research using fetal tissue is unethical in a civilized society.
- English-only legislation promotes cultural intolerance in our society.
- Keeping children in foster care for years, instead of releasing them for adoption, is wrong.

3. Claims of policy challenge or defend approaches for achieving generally accepted goals, as in the following:

- The federal government should support the distribution of clean needles to reduce the rate of HIV infection among intravenous drug users.
- Denying illegal immigrant children enrollment in public schools will reduce the problem of illegal immigration.
- All teenagers accused of murder should be tried as adults.

To help you decide how to support your claim, try to reduce it to its core question. Then brainstorm or use other planning strategies to figure out what reliable and persuasive evidence might answer the question.

For more on planning, see Ch. 17.

TYPE OF CLAIM	CORE QUESTION	POSSIBLE SUPPORTING EVIDENCE
Substantiation	What happened?	• Facts and information (parties involved, dates, times, places) and clear definitions of terms (such as *police brutality* or *total immersion*)
		• Logical, well-supported reasoning patterns such as comparison and contrast (using statistics to contrast "a few well-publicized exceptions" with a majority of instances that are "not a problem") or cause-and-effect analysis (using information from authorities or investigative reports to demonstrate how actions of tobacco companies "significantly encourage smoking" or bilingual programs "help students learn English faster")
Evaluation	What is right?	• Explanations or definitions of appropriate criteria for judging or assessing (deciding what's "unethical in a civilized society")
		• Corresponding details and reasons showing how the topic does or does not meet the criteria (details or applications of English-only legislation that meet the criteria for "cultural intolerance" or reasons with supporting details that show why years of foster care meet the criteria for being "wrong")
Policy	What should be done?	• Explanations and definition of the policy goal (assuming that most in your audience agree that it is desirable to reduce "the rate of HIV infection" or "the problem of illegal immigration" or to try murderers in the same way regardless of age)
		• Corresponding details and reasons showing how your policy recommendation would meet the goal (such as results of "clean needle" trials or examples of crime statistics and cases involving teen murderers) and, if needed, explanations or definitions of the policy's limits or applications (such as why some teens should not be tried as adults because of their situations)

Consider Your Audience as You Develop Your Claim. The nature of your audience might influence the type of claim you choose to make. For example, suppose you wish to promote the distribution of free condoms in high school. The following table illustrates how the responses of your audience might vary with your claim.

These three types of claims may also be used as support for a position. Stating supporting claims as supporting points can provide topic sentences to help your reader follow your reasoning. Each topic sentence can establish one of your points as it introduces supporting examples, statistics, or other evidence.

For more about forms of evidence, see pp. 37–42.

For more about using sources, see Ch. 12 and the Quick Research Guide (the dark-red-edged pages).

Assemble Supporting Evidence. Your claim stated, you'll need evidence to support it. What is evidence? It is anything that demonstrates the soundness of your position and the points you make in your argument—facts, statistics, observations, expert testimony, illustrations, examples, and case studies.

The three most important sources of evidence are these:

1. *Facts, including statistics.* Facts are statements that can be verified by objective means; statistics are facts expressed in numbers. Facts usually form the basis of a successful argument.
2. *Expert testimony.* Experts are people with knowledge of a particular field gained from study and experience.
3. *Firsthand observation.* Your own observations can be persuasive if you can assure your readers that your account is accurate.

AUDIENCE	TYPE OF CLAIM	POSSIBLE EFFECT ON AUDIENCE
Conservative parents who believe that free condoms would promote immoral sexual behavior	*Evaluation:* In order to save lives and prevent unwanted pregnancies, distributing free condoms in high school is our moral duty.	Counterproductive if the parents feel that you are accusing them of immorality for not agreeing with you
Conservative parents who believe that free condoms would promote immoral sexual behavior	*Substantiation:* Distributing free condoms in high school can effectively reduce pregnancy rates and the spread of STDs, especially AIDS, without substantially increasing the rate of sexual activity among teenagers.	Possibly persuasive, based on effectiveness, if parents feel that you recognize their desire to protect their children from harm, no matter what, and your evidence deflates their main fear (promoting sexual activity)
School administrators who want to do what's right but don't want hordes of angry parents pounding down the school doors	*Policy:* Distributing free condoms in high school to prevent unwanted pregnancies and the spread of STDs, including AIDS, is best accomplished as part of a voluntary sex education program that strongly emphasizes abstinence as the primary preventative.	Possibly persuasive if administrators see that you address health and pregnancy issues without setting off parental outrage (by proposing a voluntary program that would promote abstinence, thus addressing a primary concern of parents)

Of course, evidence must be used carefully to avoid defending logical fallacies—common mistakes in thinking—and making statements that lead to wrong conclusions. Examples are easy to misuse (claiming proof by example or using too few examples). Because two professors you know are dissatisfied with state-mandated testing programs, you can't claim that all or even most professors are. Even if you surveyed more professors at your school, you could speak only generally of "many professors." To claim more, you might need to conduct scientific surveys, access reliable statistics in the library or on the Internet, or solicit the views of a respected expert in the area.

For more on logical fallacies, see pp. 162–63.

Record Evidence.   For this assignment, you will need to record your evidence in written form. Take notes in a notebook, on index cards, or in a computer file. Be sure to note exactly where each piece of information comes from. Keep the form of your notes flexible so that you can easily rearrange them as you plan your draft.

Test and Select Evidence to Persuade Your Audience.   Now that you've collected some evidence, you need to sift through it to decide which pieces of information to use. Evidence is useful and trustworthy when it is accurate, reliable, up-to-date, to the point, representative, appropriately complex, and sufficient and strong enough to back the claim and persuade your readers. You may find that your evidence supports a stand different from the one you intended to take. Might you find some facts, testimony, and observations that would support your original position after all? Or should you rethink your position? If so, revise your working thesis. Does your evidence cluster around several points or reasons? If so, use your evidence to help plan the sequence of your essay.

For more on testing evidence, see pp. 39–40.

In addition, consider whether information presented visually would strengthen your case or make your evidence easier for readers to grasp. For example, graphs can effectively show facts or figures, tables can convey terms or comparisons, and photographs or other illustrations can substantiate situations. Test each visual as you would test other evidence for accuracy, reliability, and relevance. Mention each visual in your text, and place the visual close to that reference. Cite the source of any visual you use and of any data you consolidate in your own graph or table.

For more on the use of visuals and their placement, see pp. 410–16.

Most effective arguments take opposing viewpoints into consideration whenever possible. Use these questions to help you assess your evidence from this standpoint.

ANALYZE YOUR READERS' POINTS OF VIEW

- What are their attitudes? Interests? Priorities?
- What do they already know about the issue?
- What do they expect you to say?
- Do you have enough appropriate evidence that they'll find convincing?

FOCUS ON THOSE WITH DIFFERENT OR OPPOSING OPINIONS
- What are their opinions or claims?
- What is their evidence?
- Who supports their positions?
- Do you have enough appropriate evidence to show why their claims are weak, only partially true, misguided, or just plain wrong?

ACKNOWLEDGE AND REBUT THE COUNTERARGUMENTS
- What are the strengths of other positions? What might you want to concede or grant to be accurate or relevant?
- What are the limitations of other positions? What might you want to question or challenge?
- What facts, statistics, testimony, observations, or other evidence would support questioning, qualifying, challenging, or countering other views?

PLANNING, DRAFTING, AND DEVELOPING

For more on stating a thesis, see pp. 312–19.

Reassess Your Position and Your Thesis.   Now that you have looked into the issue, what is your current position? If necessary, revise the thesis that you formulated earlier. Then summarize your reasons for holding this view, and list your supporting evidence.

For exercises on choosing effective thesis statements, visit <bedfordstmartins.com/bedguide> and do a keyword search:

thesis

WORKING THESIS	We should expect advertisers to fight rather than reinforce gender stereotypes.
REFINED THESIS	Consumers should spend their shopping dollars thoughtfully in order to hold advertisers accountable for reinforcing rather than resisting gender stereotypes.

Organize Your Material to Persuade Your Audience.   Arrange your notes into the order you think you'll follow, perhaps making an outline. One useful pattern is the classical form of argument:

For more on outlines, see pp. 325–33.

1. Introduce the subject to gain the readers' interest.
2. State your main point or thesis.
3. If useful, supply the historical background or an overview of the situation.
4. Present your points or reasons and provide evidence to support them.
5. Refute the opposition.
6. Reaffirm your main point.

For exercises on supporting a thesis, visit <bedfordstmartins.com/bedguide> and do a keyword search:

support

Especially when you expect readers to be hostile to your position, you may want to take the opposite approach: refute the opposition first, then replace those views by building a logical chain of evidence that leads to your main point, and finally state your position. If you state your position too early, you might alienate resistant readers or make them defensive. Of course, you can always try both approaches to see which one works better. Note also that some papers will be mostly based on refutation (countering

Making Columns of Appeals

Try making three columns to write about your logical, emotional, and ethical appeals. Using the Format menu, select "Columns," and click on the number "3." Label the first column "Logical Appeals." Here write the claims and support that rely on reasoning and sound evidence. Create the next column, generally by going to the Insert menu, clicking on "Break," selecting "Column break," and clicking "OK." Label your second column "Emotional Appeals," and note the claims and support that may affect readers' emotions. Now create a third column, headed "Ethical Appeals." Record here your claims and support based on values and your understanding of the values of opposing points of view. To move back and forth between columns, simply move your cursor. As you reread each column, consider how to relate your claims and support across columns, how to organize your ideas persuasively, and how best to merge or separate your logical, emotional, and ethical appeals. Try color coding if you want to identify related ideas.

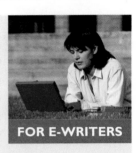

FOR E-WRITERS

opposing views) and some mostly on confirmation (directly supporting your position). Others might even alternate refutation and confirmation rather than separate them.

Define Your Terms.   To prevent misunderstanding, make clear any unfamiliar or questionable terms used in your thesis. If your position is "Humanists are dangerous," give a short definition of what you mean by *humanists* and by *dangerous* early in the paper.

Attend to Logical, Emotional, and Ethical Appeals.   The logical appeal engages readers' intellect; the emotional appeal touches their hearts; the ethical appeal draws on their sense of fairness and reasonableness. A persuasive argument usually operates on all three levels. For example, you might use all three appeals to support a thesis about the need to curb accidental gunshot deaths, as the following table illustrates.

For more on appeals, see pp. 40–41.

TYPE OF APPEAL	WAYS OF MAKING THE APPEAL	POSSIBLE SUPPORTING EVIDENCE
Logical (logos)	• Rely on clear reasoning and sound evidence to influence a reader's thinking. • Demonstrate what you claim, and don't claim what you can't demonstrate. • Test and select your evidence.	• Supply current and reliable statistics about gun ownership and accidental shootings. • Prepare a bar graph that shows the number of incidents each year in Lion Valley during the past ten years, using data from the county records. • Describe the immediate and long-term consequences of a typical shooting accident.

(*continued on next page*)

TYPE OF APPEAL	WAYS OF MAKING THE APPEAL	POSSIBLE SUPPORTING EVIDENCE
Emotional (pathos)	• Choose examples and language that will influence a reader's feelings. • Include effective images, but don't overdo them. • Complement logical appeals, but don't replace them.	• Describe the wrenching scenario of a father whose college-age son unexpectedly returns home at 3 A.M. The father mistakes his son for an intruder and shoots him, throwing the family into turmoil. • Use quotations and descriptions from newspaper accounts to show reactions of family members and neighbors.
Ethical (ethos)	• Use a tone and approach that appeal to your reader's sense of fairness and reasonableness. • Spell out your values and beliefs, and acknowledge values and beliefs of others with different opinions. • Establish your credentials, if any, and the credentials of experts you cite. • Instill confidence in your readers so that they see you as a caring, trustworthy person with reliable views.	• Establish your reasonable approach by acknowledging the views of hunters and others who store guns at home and follow recommended safety procedures. • Supply the credentials or affiliation of experts ("Raymond Fontaine, public safety director for the town of Lion Valley"). • Note ways in which experts have established their authority ("During my interview with Ms. Dutton, she related recent incidents involving gun accidents in the home, testifying to her extensive knowledge of this issue in our community.")

For pointers on integrating and documenting sources, see Ch. 12 and D6 and E1–E2 in the Quick Research Guide (the dark-red-edged pages).

For more revising and editing strategies, see Ch. 20.

Credit Your Sources.   As you write, make your sources of evidence clear. One simple way to do so is to incorporate your source into the text: "According to an article in the October 15, 2007, issue of *Time*" or "According to my history professor, Dr. Harry Cleghorn..."

REVISING AND EDITING

When you're writing a paper taking a stand, you may be tempted to fall in love with the evidence you've gone to such trouble to collect. Taking out information is hard to do, but if it is irrelevant, redundant, or weak, the evidence won't help your case. Play the crusty critic as you reread your paper. Consider outlining what it actually includes so that you can check for missing or unnecessary points or evidence. Pay special attention to the suggestions of friends or classmates who read your draft for you. Apply their advice by ruthlessly cutting unneeded material, as in the following passage:

The school boundary system requires children who are homeless or whose families move frequently to change schools repeatedly. ~~They often lack clean clothes, winter coats, and required school supplies.~~ As a result, these children

Enlist several other students to read your draft critically and tell you whether they accept your arguments. For a paper in which you take a stand, ask your peer editors to answer questions such as these:

- Can you state the writer's claim?

- Do you have any problems following or accepting the reasons for the writer's position? Would you make any changes in the reasoning?

- How persuasive is the writer's evidence? What questions do you have about it? Can you suggest good evidence the writer has overlooked?

- Has the writer provided enough transitions to guide you through the argument?

- Has the writer made a strong case? Are you persuaded to his or her point of view? If not, is there any point or objection that the writer could address to make the argument more compelling?

- If this were your paper, what is the one thing you would be sure to work on before handing it in?

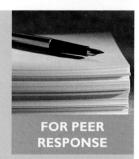

FOR PEER RESPONSE

For general questions for a peer editor, see pp. 377.

struggle to establish strong relationships with teachers, to find caring advocates at school, and even to make friends to join for recess or lunch.

Use the Draft Doctor (pp. 160–61) to help you figure out how to improve your draft. Skim down the left column to identify questions you might ask about problems in your draft. When you answer a question with "Yes" or "Maybe," move straight across the row to the Diagnose column next to that question. Use the diagnostic activities to identify gaps or weaknesses, and then move across the row again to the Treat column on the right. Use the advice that suits your problem as you revise.

As you continue to revise, here are some questions to consider:

For online help from the Draft Doctor, visit <bedfordstmartins.com/ bedguide>.

REVISION CHECKLIST

___ Is your main point, or thesis, clear? Do you stick to it rather than drifting into contradictions?

___ Where might you need better reasons or more evidence?

___ Have you tried to keep in mind your readers and what would appeal to them? Where have you answered their likely objections?

___ Have you defined all necessary terms and explained your points clearly?

___ Is your tone suitable for your readers? Are you likely at any places to alienate them, or, at the other extreme, to sound weak or apologetic?

___ Might your points seem stronger if arranged in a different sequence?

___ Have you unfairly omitted any evidence that would hurt your case?

___ In rereading your paper, do you have any excellent, fresh thoughts? If so, where might you make room for them?

Draft Doctor: Strengthening Support for a Stand

If you sense a problem, ASK	If you answer *Yes/Maybe*, DIAGNOSE	If you diagnose a problem, TREAT
Missing Points? Did I leave out some of the main points that I planned to include or that I promised in my thesis?	• List the main points you meant to include. • List the main points that your thesis states or suggests. • Check both lists against your draft by highlighting each point in your draft.	• Add any missing point. • Express any assumptions—points, main ideas, reasons—that are in your head but not in your draft. • Revise your thesis, adding or dropping points, until it makes a promise you can deliver to readers.
Missing Supporting Evidence? Did I leave out evidence—facts, statistics, expert testimony, firsthand observations, details, or examples—needed to support my points?	• Highlight or color code each bit of supporting evidence in your draft. • Put a check by any passages that lack supporting evidence. • Jot reminders to yourself about where to add more evidence.	• Add any missing evidence that you meant to include. • For each checked passage, brainstorm or ask questions (who, what, where, when, why, how) to decide what support readers might expect. • Add the facts, statistics, expert testimony, observations, details, or examples needed to support each main point.
Vague Support? Would any of the support in my draft seem unclear to my audience?	• Read your draft aloud, listening to it as a reader would. • Mark any vague or imprecise patches. **Draft:** A new student parking lot should be constructed now because delaying is *a bad idea*. [What is "a bad idea"?]	• State each point plainly and directly enough that it will be clear to your audience. • Use simple, direct words to replace any vague language. **Revision:** A new student parking lot should be constructed now because any delay will frustrate current students and might reduce future enrollment.
Inappropriate Support? Would my instructor (or others) find any of my supporting evidence unsuitable for this type of paper?	• Reread the assignment (or the criteria in your syllabus) to figure out what support is expected. • Mark any support that might not meet expectations.	• Drop anything that ignores what's required. For example, if you are asked to explain the point made in a reading, don't tell a personal story instead.

If you sense a problem, ASK	If you answer *Yes/Maybe*, DIAGNOSE	If you diagnose a problem, TREAT
Irrelevant Support? Would readers find any of my support unrelated or off-topic?	• Reread your thesis statement. Use an X to mark anything that doesn't directly support it.	• Return to each mark, and rework or drop any supporting evidence that strays from your thesis, or revise your thesis to align it accurately with your support. • Decide whether you need to add more relevant information.
Disconnected Support? Does my support seem disconnected from the sequence of my draft? Does my draft seem to jump from point to point?	• Underline your thesis for easy reference. • Place a check by any support that isn't clearly connected to your thesis in your draft, not just in your mind. • Highlight your transitions so you can see where they are sparse or missing.	• Connect your thesis and your support by previewing or explaining how they relate (*The primary reasons why ...,The four stages ..., Several traditional explanations ..., This event triggered ...*). • Add transitions to show the sequence of ideas (*first, second, next, then, finally*) or set priorities (*a minor point, despite, most importantly*).
One-Sided Support? Have I skipped mentioning opposing or alternative perspectives? Have I mentioned them but treated them disrespectfully?	• Highlight passages in which you recognize other points of view (or copy them into a separate file) so that you can look at them on their own. • Read these passages to see whether they sound fair.	• Identify other points of view if they are expected and you have left them out. • Acknowledge credible alternative views, agreeing or explaining your differences. • Reasonably challenge or counter questionable views. • Edit your wording so your tone is respectful of others.
Any Other Weak Support? After a final look at the supporting points and evidence in my draft, should I revise anything else?	• Read your draft out loud, marking any support that sounds weak or awkward. • Ask your peer editors how to improve support for your stand.	• Return to each mark to add facts, statistics, expert testimony, observations, or examples. • Consider the useful suggestions of your peers. • Revise until your draft does what you want it to do.

For more editing and proofreading strategies, see pp. 384–87.

After you have revised your argument, edit and proofread it. Carefully check the grammar, word choice, punctuation, and mechanics—and then correct any problems you find. Wherever you have given facts and figures as evidence, check for errors in names and numbers. Here are some questions to get you started editing and proofreading:

EDITING CHECKLIST

For more help, turn to the dark-blue-edged pages and find the sections of the Quick Editing Guide noted here.

___ Is it clear what each pronoun refers to? Does each pronoun agree with (match) its antecedent? Do pronouns used as subjects agree with their verbs? Carefully check sentences making broad claims about *everyone, no one, some, a few,* or some other group identified by an indefinite pronoun.   A6

___ Have you used an adjective whenever describing a noun or pronoun? Have you used an adverb whenever describing a verb, adjective, or adverb? Have you used the correct form when comparing two or more things?   A7

___ Have you set off your transitions, other introductory elements, and interrupters with commas, if these are needed?   C1

___ Have you spelled and capitalized everything correctly, especially names of people and organizations?   D1, D2

___ Have you correctly punctuated quotations from sources and experts?   C3

RECOGNIZING LOGICAL FALLACIES

For more on faulty thinking, see pp. 46–47.

Logical fallacies are common mistakes in thinking that may lead to wrong conclusions or distort evidence. Here are a few familiar logical fallacies.

TERM	EXPLANATION	EXAMPLE
Non Sequitur	Stating a claim that doesn't follow from your first premise or statement; Latin for "It does not follow"	Jenn should marry Mateo. In college he got all A's.
Oversimplification	Offering easy solutions for complicated problems	If we want to end substance abuse, let's send every drug user to prison for life. (Even aspirin users?)
Post Hoc Ergo Propter Hoc	Assuming a cause-and-effect relationship where none exists even though one event preceded another; Latin for "after this, therefore because of this"	After Jenny's black cat crossed my path, everything went wrong, and I failed my midterm.

(continued on next page)

TERM	EXPLANATION	EXAMPLE
Allness	Stating or implying that something is true of an entire class of things, often using *all, everyone, no one, always,* or *never*	Students enjoy studying. (All students? All subjects? All the time?)
Proof by Example or Too Few Examples	Presenting an example as proof rather than as illustration or clarification; overgeneralizing (the basis of much prejudice)	Armenians are great chefs. My neighbor is Armenian, and can he cook!
Begging the Question	Proving a statement already taken for granted, often by repeating it in different words or by defining a word in terms of itself	Rapists are dangerous because they are menaces. Happiness is the state of being happy.
Circular Reasoning	Supporting a statement with itself; a form of begging the question	He is a liar because he simply isn't telling the truth.
Either/Or Reasoning	Oversimplifying by assuming that an issue has only two sides, a statement must be true or false, a question demands a yes or no answer, or a problem has only two possible solutions (and one that's acceptable)	What are we going to do about global warming? Either we stop using all of the energy-consuming vehicles and products that cause it, or we just learn to live with it.
Argument from Dubious Authority	Using an unidentified authority to shore up a weak argument or an authority whose expertise lies outside the issue, such as a television personality selling insurance	According to some of the most knowing scientists in America, smoking two packs a day is as harmless as eating oatmeal cookies.
Argument *ad Hominem*	Attacking an individual's opinion by attacking his or her character, thus deflecting attention from the merit of a proposal; Latin for "against the man"	Diaz may argue that we need to save the whales, but he's the type who gets emotional over nothing.
Argument from Ignorance	Maintaining that a claim has to be accepted because it hasn't been disproved or that it has to be rejected because it has not been proved	Despite years of effort, no one has proved that ghosts don't exist; therefore, we should expect to see them at any time. No one has ever shown that life exists on any other planet; clearly the notion of other living things in the universe is absurd.
Argument by Analogy	Treating an extended comparison between familiar and unfamiliar items, based on similarities and ignoring differences, as evidence rather than as a useful way of explaining	People were born free as the birds; it's cruel to expect them to work.
Bandwagon Argument	Suggesting that everyone is joining the group and readers who don't may miss out on happiness, success, or a reward	Purchasing the new Swallowtail admits you to the nation's most elite group of drivers.

OTHER ASSIGNMENTS

1. Write a letter to the editor of your newspaper or a newsmagazine in which you agree or disagree with the publication's editorial stand on a current question or with the recent words or actions of some public figure. Make clear your reasons for holding your view.
2. Write one claim each of substantiation, of evaluation, and of policy for or against censoring pornographic Web sites. Indicate an audience each claim might address effectively. Then list reasons and types of evidence you might need to support one of these claims. Finally, for the same claim, indicate what opposing viewpoints you would need to consider and how you could best do so.
3. Write a short paper, blog entry, or class posting expressing your view on one of these topics or another that comes to mind. Make clear your reasons for believing as you do.

For more on supporting a position with sources, see Ch. 12.

Bilingual education	Raising the minimum wage
Nonsmokers' rights	Protecting the rain forests
Dealing with date rape	Controlling terrorism
Salaries of professional athletes	Prayer in public schools

Applying What You Learn: Some Uses of Taking a Stand

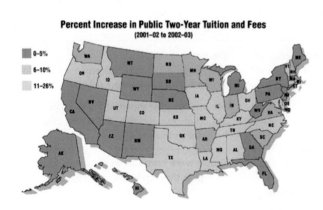

Percent Increase in Public Two-Year Tuition and Fees
(2001–02 to 2002–03)

0–5%
6–10%
11–26%

In College Courses.   When assignments and examination questions ask you to take a stand on a controversy, your responses indicate clearly to your instructor how firmly you grasp the material.

- In a health-care course, you might be asked to criticize this statement: "There's too much science and not enough caring in modern medicine."

- In a criminal justice course, you might be asked to state and defend your opinion on juvenile sentencing.

- In your research paper for an economics course, you might be asked to take a stand on the state budget allocations in terms of their effects on college tuition.

In the Workplace.   In nearly every professional position — lawyer, teacher, nurse, business manager, journalist — you will be invited to state and support your views for others in your profession or the public.

- Scientists must persuade the scientific community that their research findings are valid, publishing their work in journals for evaluation by their peers.

- Social workers write documents to persuade courts and other agencies that certain actions or services are best for the welfare of their clients.

- Facing fierce competition, executives must convince their CEO that their ideas will result in impressive benefits for the company.

In Your Community.   As an active citizen, you may feel compelled to inform and influence the public on matters of concern to all.

- You may want to write a letter to the editor of your newspaper or to your political representative about a controversial issue faced by your community — controlling violence in your schools, funding a new drainage system, enforcing the leash law.

- You may represent the tenants in your apartment building by writing a letter of protest to a landlord who wants to raise rents.

- You may write a letter and design a poster to protest a company's operating and marketing policies.

Chapter 10
Proposing a Solution

If you polluted the air in the 80's,
here's your chance to redeem yourself

Riders wanted.

Responding to an Image

This advertisement appeared as a "spoof ad" on Adbusters, a Web site that advocates a critical eye toward advertisements of all kinds (<www.adbusters.org>). What is the problem posed by the ad? What techniques are used to help viewers understand the problem? What solution does the ad propose? Is this solution realistic and workable? What is the significance of the "Riders wanted" logo, and how does it affect the credibility of the ad's message? Compare this ad to the Volkswagen ad that appears on page 425, noting the similarities and differences between the two images. How does awareness of Volkswagen's advertising help to make this a more effective spoof?

Sometimes when you learn of a problem such as the destruction of the rain forest, homelessness, or famine, you say to yourself, "Something should be done about that." You can do something constructive yourself — through the powerful and persuasive activity of writing.

Your purpose in such writing, as political leaders and advertisers well know, is to rouse your audience to action. Even in your daily life at college, you can write a letter to your college newspaper or to someone in authority and try to stir your readers to action. Does some college policy irk you? Would you urge students to attend a rally for a cause or a charity?

The uses of such writing go far beyond these immediate applications. In Chapter 9, you took a stand and backed it up with evidence. Now go a step further, writing a *proposal* — a recommendation for taking action. If, for instance, you have made the claim "Our national parks are in sorry condition," you might urge readers to act — to write to their representatives in Congress or to visit a national park and pick up trash. On the other hand, you might suggest that the Department of the Interior be given a budget increase to hire more park rangers, purchase additional park land to accommodate more visitors, and buy more cleanup equipment. You might also suggest that the department could raise funds through sales of park DVDs as well as increased revenues from visitors attracted by the DVDs. The first paper would be a call to immediate action on the part of your readers; the second, an attempt to forge a consensus about what needs to be done.

Learning from Other Writers

The writers of the following two essays propose sensible solutions for pressing problems. To help you begin to analyze the first reading, look for the notes in the margin. They identify features such as the introduction of the problem, the thesis, or main idea, and the introduction of the proposed solution.

■ For more on thesis and support, see Chs. 17 and 19.

As You Read These Proposals

As you read these essays, ask yourself the following questions:

1. What problem does the writer identify? Does the writer rouse you to want to do something about the problem?
2. What solution does the writer propose? What evidence supports the solution? Does the writer convince you to agree with this solution?
3. How is the writer qualified to write on this subject?

■ For more examples of writing that proposes a solution, visit <bedfordstmartins.com/bedguide> and do a keyword search:

examples

Wilbert Rideau, editor of the Angolite, *the Louisiana State Penitentiary newsmagazine, offers a voice seldom heard in the debate over crime control — that of the criminal.*

Wilbert Rideau

Why Prisons Don't Work

I was among thirty-one murderers sent to the Louisiana State Penitentiary 1 in 1962 to be executed or imprisoned for life. We weren't much different from those we found here, or those who had preceded us. We were unskilled, impulsive, and uneducated misfits, mostly black, who had done dumb, impulsive things — failures, rejects from the larger society. Now a generation has come of age and gone since I've been here, and everything is much the same as I found it. The faces of the prisoners are different, but behind them are the same impulsive, uneducated, unskilled minds that made dumb, impulsive choices that got them into more trouble than they ever thought existed. The vast majority of us are consigned to suffer and die here so politicians can sell the illusion that permanently exiling people to prison will make society safe.

Getting tough has always been a "silver bullet," a quick fix for the crime 2 and violence that society fears. Each year in Louisiana — where excess is a way of life — lawmakers have tried to outdo each other in legislating harsher mandatory penalties and in reducing avenues of release. The only thing to do with criminals, they say, is get tougher. They have. In the process, the purpose of prison began to change. The state boasts one of the highest lockup rates in the country, imposes the most severe penalties in the nation, and vies to execute more criminals per capita than anywhere else. This state is so tough that last year, when prison authorities here wanted to punish an inmate in solitary confinement for an infraction,° the most they could inflict on him was to deprive him of his underwear. It was all he had left.

If getting tough resulted in public safety, Louisiana citizens would be 3 the safest in the nation. They're not. Louisiana has the highest murder rate among states. Prison, like the police and the courts, has a minimal impact on crime because it is a response after the fact, a mop-up operation. It doesn't work. The idea of punishing the few to deter the many is counterfeit because potential criminals either think they're not going to get caught or they're so emotionally desperate or psychologically distressed that they don't care about the consequences of their actions. The threatened punishment, regardless of its severity, is never a factor in the equation. But society, like the incorrigible° criminal it abhors, is unable to learn from its mistakes.

Prison has a role in public safety, but it is not a cure-all. Its value is lim- 4 ited, and its use should also be limited to what it does best: isolating young criminals long enough to give them a chance to grow up and get a grip on their impulses. It is a traumatic experience, certainly, but it should be only a temporary one, not a way of life. Prisoners kept too long tend to embrace the criminal culture, its distorted values and beliefs; they have little choice — prison is their life. There are some prisoners who cannot be returned to society — serial killers, serial rapists, professional hit men, and the like — but

---

infraction: Violation.   **incorrigible:** Incapable of reform.

the monsters who need to die in prison are rare exceptions in the criminal landscape.

Crime is a young man's game. Most of the nation's random violence is ⁵ committed by young urban terrorists. But because of long, mandatory sentences, most prisoners here are much older, having spent fifteen, twenty, thirty, or more years behind bars, long past necessity. Rather than pay for new prisons, society would be well served by releasing some of its older prisoners who pose no threat and using the money to catch young street thugs. Warden John Whitley agrees that many older prisoners here could be freed tomorrow with little or no danger to society. Release, however, is governed by law or by politicians, not by penal professionals. Even murderers, those most feared by society, pose little risk. Historically, for example, the domestic staff at Louisiana's Governor's mansion has been made up of murderers, hand-picked to work among the chief-of-state and his family. Penologists° have long known that murder is almost always a once-in-a-lifetime act. The most dangerous criminal is the one who has not yet killed but has a history of escalating offenses. He's the one to watch.

Transitions (underlined) for coherence

Rehabilitation can work. Everyone changes in time. The trick is to influ- ⁶ ence the direction that change takes. The problem with prisons is that they don't do more to rehabilitate those confined in them. The convict who enters prison illiterate will probably leave the same way. Most convicts want to be better than they are, but education is not a priority. This prison houses 4,600 men and offers academic training to 240, vocational training to a like number. Perhaps it doesn't matter. About 90 percent of the men here may never leave this prison alive.

The only effective way to curb crime is for society to work to prevent the ⁷ criminal act in the first place, to come between the perpetrator° and crime. Our youngsters must be taught to respect the humanity of others and to handle disputes without violence. It is essential to educate and equip them with the skills to pursue their life ambitions in a meaningful way. As a community, we must address the adverse life circumstances that spawn criminality. These things are not quick, and they're not easy, but they're effective. Politicians think that's too hard a sell. They want to be on record for doing something now, something they can point to at reelection time. So the drumbeat goes on for more police, more prisons, more of the same failed policies.

Conclusion summing up solution

Ever see a dog chase its tail? ⁸

Questions to Start You Thinking

Meaning

1. Does Rideau convince you that the belief that "permanently exiling people to prison will make society safe" is an "illusion" (paragraph 1)?

2. According to Rideau, why don't prisons work?

3. What does he propose as solutions to the problem of escalating crime? What other solutions can you think of?

Penologists: Those who study prison management and criminal justice.   **perpetrator:** One who is responsible for an action or a crime.

Writing Strategies

4. What justifications, if any, for the prison system has Rideau left out of his essay? Do these omissions help or hurt his essay? Why or why not?

5. What evidence does the author provide to support his assertion that Louisiana's "getting tough" policy has not worked? Does he provide sufficient evidence to convince you? Does he persuade you that action is necessary?

6. What would make Rideau's argument for his proposals more persuasive?

7. Other than himself, what authorities does Rideau cite? Why do you think he does this?

8. Does the fact that the author is a convicted criminal strengthen or weaken his argument? Why do you think he mentions this in his first sentence?

9. How do you interpret the last line, "Ever see a dog chase its tail?" Is this line an effective way for Rideau to end his essay? Explain.

STUDENT ESSAY

John Barbieri's opinion piece appeared in the Amherst Student, *the newspaper of Amherst College, in April 2006.*

⟨?⟩ *Do you have any experience with, or views about, alternative energy?*

John Barbieri

Save Hydrogen for Later; Ethanol Power Is the Viable Option for Now

Face it. Hydrogen power is not going to happen anytime soon. It's too costly   1
and underdeveloped to provide a replacement for gasoline-powered cars. And even if the costly infrastructure° and technology needed for hydrogen cars are developed, hydrogen cars will have a negligible° impact on the environment because hydrogen is produced using electricity, and in the United States, electricity is produced primarily by fossil fuels. As a result, switching over to hydrogen cars will not actually reduce greenhouse emissions;° it will only shift where they are produced. It's time to stop waiting for a solution that isn't going to help or happen and implement° one that already is here. It's time to look toward ethanol.

Ethanol is an alternative fuel option that can be made by fermenting° and   2
distilling° starch that has been converted into simple sugars. Anything from corn and wheat to biomass, which is basically waste plant material, can be used to produce ethanol. Since ethanol can be produced entirely from plant sources, it is a renewable energy source. Ethanol can also be combined with gasoline to make E85,

infrastructure: Physical foundation or resources needed for a system to work.   negligible: Small.   greenhouse emissions: Pollutants, including carbon dioxide, that trap heat in the atmosphere, much as a greenhouse holds heat. Fossil fuels like gasoline are a major source of greenhouse-gas emissions.   implement: Carry out; put into place.   fermenting: Using enzymes to turn complex organic substances into their component parts.   distilling: Extracting the essence from something; concentrating.

which is 85 percent ethanol, or E95, which is 95 percent ethanol. Both of these fuels are considered to be alternative fuels under the Energy Policy Act of 1992.

Ethanol-powered vehicles have many advantages over gasoline-powered vehicles. Since ethanol has a higher hydrogen-to-carbon ratio than gasoline, it produces fewer greenhouse gases than gasoline. Furthermore, where gasoline must for the most part be imported from abroad, ethanol can be produced from corn and biomass, which are abundant in the United States. As a result, by switching over to ethanol the United States can finally reduce its dependence on overseas oil. Between 1978 and 2005, Brazil was able to reduce its dependence on oil from about 85 percent to nearly 0 percent by switching over to ethanol-powered vehicles, according to Brazilian officials. Following the precedent set by Brazil, the United States could easily reduce its oil consumption and finally become energy independent. Ethanol costs about the same amount as gasoline per gallon, and as gasoline prices continue to rise, ethanol could soon become cheaper than gasoline.

3

Why is dependence on foreign oil a problem?

Ethanol offers many distinct advantages over hydrogen power as well. First, the production of ethanol creates much less pollution than the production of hydrogen in a country where a large percentage of power is produced by fossil fuels. In the United States, nearly 90 percent of electricity is produced by fossil-fuel-burning power plants. Furthermore, many of the nuclear power plants in the United States will soon be out of commission; as a result, it is likely that the reliance on fossil fuels in the United States will increase even further. Making ethanol from plant sources creates about 200 times less pollution than producing an equivalent amount of electricity in a fossil-fuel power plant. Moreover, the production of hydrogen using electricity is only 70 percent efficient. As a result, in the United States making ethanol creates much less pollution as a by-product than making hydrogen. While ethanol may not be a perfectly "clean" energy source, it certainly creates less pollution than either gasoline or hydrogen would, given our current electricity production capacities.

4

Second, Ethanol can be stored and transported much more efficiently than hydrogen. Ethanol exists naturally as a liquid, while hydrogen exists naturally as a gas. Consequently, more ethanol can be stored in a smaller space than hydrogen. In fact, trying to store hydrogen effectively has been a significant hurdle for those trying to develop hydrogen cars. Even those who have tried to store hydrogen as a compressed gas, metal hydride, have had limited success. This problem does not exist for ethanol-powered cars because ethanol can be stored in the exact same way as gasoline. Unlike hydrogen, which would most likely need to be produced on site due to its lack of transportability, ethanol could be mass produced at another site more efficiently and then be transported to fuel stations.

5

Third, it is less costly to implement ethanol as an alternative power source than it would be to implement hydrogen power. To create a hydrogen economy, hydrogen cars would have to be researched further, hydrogen fuel stations and production

6

plants would have to be built, and more effective hydrogen storage systems would have to be created. All of this infrastructure would cost billions of dollars and would take a significant amount of time to implement. Current gas stations could easily be converted to supply ethanol or could supply ethanol in addition to gasoline just as many gas stations have diesel pumps along with gasoline pumps. There are also already many "flex-fuel" cars on the road that can run on either gasoline or ethanol. GM and Ford have been producing these cars since the 1980s to get a government subsidy° but have not advertised the flex-fuel capability because they did not believe it would affect consumer decisions on whether or not to buy the cars. Today, there are over 1.5 million flex-fuel cars on the road, and GM and Ford have plants that could easily produce more if the demand for flex-fuel cars increased.

What images or messages might ads for flex-fuel cars include?

Ethanol is an excellent alternative energy source for the United States to look toward in the coming years. It is cleaner than gasoline and costs the same amount per gallon. Ethanol can be produced from corn and biomass produced in the United States and can consequently reduce American dependence on foreign oil for energy. Less pollution is created producing ethanol than producing hydrogen, given the high percentage of electricity produced by fossil fuels in the United States. Furthermore, an ethanol infrastructure would be much easier to implement than a hydrogen one, especially as GM and Ford have already produced millions of flex-fuel cars that can run on either ethanol or gasoline and could easily produce many more. And ethanol doesn't just have to power our cars. It can heat our homes, power our lights, and much more. Hydrogen may be the alternative fuel of the future, but ethanol is the alternative fuel of today.

7

Questions to Start You Thinking

Meaning

1. What problem would the use of ethanol address? Does Barbieri provide enough background on this problem?

2. How is ethanol produced, and what is the benefit of this means of production?

3. In what ways, according to Barbieri, is ethanol superior to gasoline and hydrogen as a fuel source? Do you find these arguments convincing? Why or why not?

Writing Strategies

4. What kinds of transitions does Barbieri use to lead readers through his points? How effective do you find them?

5. Is Barbieri's evidence specific and sufficient? Explain.

6. Do you find Barbieri's conclusion to be effective? Why or why not?

7. Using highlighters or marginal notes, identify the essay's introduction, explanation of the problem, thesis, proposal to solve the problem, and conclusion. How effective is the organization of this essay?

subsidy: Monetary support or assistance.

Learning by Writing

THE ASSIGNMENT: PROPOSING A SOLUTION

In this essay you'll first carefully analyze and explain a specific social, eco-nomic, political, civic, or environmental problem—a problem you care about and strongly wish to see resolved. The problem may be large or small, but it shouldn't be trivial. It may affect the whole country or mainly people in your city, campus, or classroom. Show your readers that this problem really exists and that it matters to you and to them. After setting forth the problem, you also may want to explain why it exists. Write for an audience who, once aware of the problem, may be expected to help do something about it.

 For writing activi-ties for proposing a solution, visit <bedfordstmartins.com/bedguide> and do a key-word search:

activities

The second thing you are to accomplish in the essay is to propose one or more ways to solve the problem or at least alleviate it. In making a proposal, you urge action by using words like *should, ought,* and *must*: "This city ought to have a Bureau of Missing Persons"; "Small private aircraft should be banned from flying close to a major commercial airport." Lay out the reasons why your proposal deserves to be implemented; supply evidence that your solution is reasonable and can work. Remember that your purpose is to con-vince readers that something should be done about the problem.

Students cogently argued for action in the following papers:

Based on research studies and statistics, one student argued that using stan-dardized test scores from the SAT or the ACT as criteria for college admis-sions is a problem because it favors aggressive students from affluent fami-lies. His proposal was to abolish this use of the scores.

Another argued that one solution to vacation frustration is to turn every-thing—planning, choosing a location, arranging transportation, reserving lodging—over to a travel agent.

A third argued that the best solution to the problem of her children's poor education is homeschooling.

GENERATING IDEAS

Identify a Problem.   Brainstorm by writ-ing down all the possible topics that come to mind. Observe events around you to identify irritating campus or community problems you would like to solve. Watch for ideas as you read the newspaper or listen to the news. Browse through issue-oriented Web sites. Look for sites sponsored by large nonprofit foundations that accept grant pro-posals and fund innovative solutions to so-cietal issues. Then star the ideas that seem to have the most potential. Here are a few questions to help ideas start flowing:

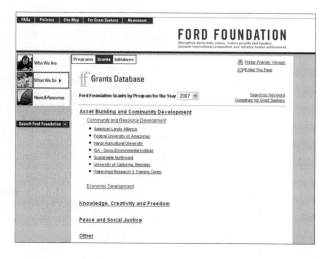

DISCOVERY CHECKLIST

____ Can you recall any problem that needs a solution? What problems do you meet every day or occasionally? What problems concern people near you?

____ What conditions in need of improvement have you observed on television or in your daily activities? What action is called for?

____ What problems have been discussed recently on campus or in class?

____ What problems are discussed in blogs, chat rooms, newspapers, or newsmagazines such as *Time, Newsweek,* or *U.S. News & World Report*?

Consider Your Audience.   Readers need to believe that your problem is real and your solution is feasible. If you are addressing your classmates, maybe they haven't thought about the problem before. Try to discover ways to make it personal for them, to show that it affects them and deserves their attention. Here are some questions to ask yourself about your readers:

• Who are your readers? How would you describe them?

• Why should your readers care about this problem? Does it affect their health, welfare, conscience, or pocketbook?

• Have they ever expressed any interest in the problem? If so, what has triggered their interest?

• Do they belong to any organization or segment of society that makes them especially susceptible to — or uninterested in — this problem?

Facing the Challenge: Proposing a Solution

The major challenge writers face when writing a proposal is to develop a detailed and convincing solution. Finding solutions is much harder than finding problems. Convincing readers that you have found a reasonable, workable solution is harder still. For example, suppose you propose the combination of a rigorous exercise program and a low-fat diet as a solution for obesity. While these solutions seem reasonable and workable to you, readers who have lost weight and then gained it back might point out that their main problem is not losing weight but maintaining weight loss over time. To account for their concerns and enhance your credibility, you might revise your solution to focus on realistic long-term goals and strategies for sticking to an exercise program. For instance, you might recommend that friends walk together two or three times a week or that employees lobby for a fitness center at work.

To develop a realistic solution that fully addresses a problem and satisfies the concerns of readers, consider questions such as these:

• How might the problem affect different groups of people?

• What range of concerns are your readers likely to have?

• What realistic solution addresses the concerns of readers about *all* aspects of the problem?

- What attitudes about the problem do you share with your readers? Which of their assumptions or values that differ from yours will affect how they view your proposal?

Think about Solutions.   Once you've chosen a problem, brainstorm — alone or with classmates — for possible solutions, or use your imagination. Some problems, such as reducing international tensions, present no easy solutions. Still, give some thought to any problem that seriously concerns you, even if it has thwarted teams of experts. Sometimes a solution will reveal itself to a novice thinker, and even a small contribution to a partial solution is worth offering. You can use several strategies to think about problems and solutions:

For more on brainstorming, see pp. 296–97. For more on imagining, see pp. 302–03.

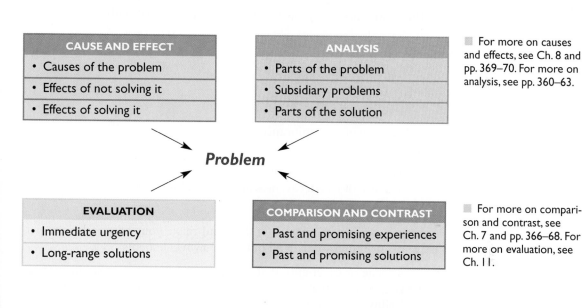

For more on causes and effects, see Ch. 8 and pp. 369–70. For more on analysis, see pp. 360–63.

For more on comparison and contrast, see Ch. 7 and pp. 366–68. For more on evaluation, see Ch. 11.

Consider Sources of Support.   To show that the problem really exists, you'll need evidence and examples. If you feel that further research in the library will help you know more about the problem, now is the time to do it. In addition, previous efforts to solve the problem may help you develop your solution. Consider whether local history archives, past newspaper stories or photographs, accounts of public meetings, interviews with others, or Web sites sponsored by interested organizations might identify concerns of readers or practical limitations of solutions.

For more on evidence, see Ch. 3. For more on using evidence to support an argument, see pp. 152–56.

For advice on finding a few sources, see A and B in the Quick Research Guide (the dark-red-edged pages).

PLANNING, DRAFTING, AND DEVELOPING

Start with Your Proposal and Your Thesis.   A basic approach is to state your proposal in a sentence that can act as your thesis.

■ For more on stating a thesis, see pp. 312–19. For strategies for planning, drafting, and developing, see Chs. 17, 18, and 19.

■ For exercises on choosing effective thesis statements, visit <bedfordstmartins.com/bedguide> and do a keyword search:

thesis

■ For more on outlines, see pp. 325–33.

PROPOSAL   Let people get divorced without going to court.

WORKING THESIS   The legislature should pass a law allowing couples to divorce without having to go to court.

From such a statement, the rest of the argument may start to unfold, often falling naturally into a simple two-part shape:

1. *A claim that a problem exists.* This part explains the problem and supplies evidence of its significance — for example, the costs, adversarial process, and stress of divorce court for a couple and their family.
2. *A claim that something ought to be done about it.* This part proposes a solution to the problem — for example, legislative action to authorize other options such as mediation.

These two parts can grow naturally into an informal outline.

1. Introduction
   Overview of the situation
   Working thesis stating your proposal
2. Problem
   Explanation of its nature
   Evidence of its significance
3. Solution
   Explanation of its nature
   Evidence of its effectiveness and practicality
4. Conclusion

You can then expand your outline and make your proposal more persuasive by including some or all of the following elements:

- Knowledge or experience that qualifies you to propose a solution (your experience as a player or a coach, for example, that establishes your credibility as an authority on Little League)
- Values, beliefs, or assumptions that have caused you to feel strongly about the need for action
- An estimate of the resources — money, people, skills, material — and the time required to implement the solution (perhaps including what is available now and what needs to be obtained)
- Step-by-step actions needed to achieve your solution
- Controls or quality checks to monitor implementation
- Possible obstacles or difficulties that may need to be overcome
- Reasons your solution is better than others proposed or tried already
- Any other evidence that shows that your suggestion is practical, reasonable in cost, and likely to be effective

■ For exercises on supporting a thesis, visit <bedfordstmartins.com/bedguide> and do a keyword search:

support

Making Problem-Solution Columns

To propose a solution persuasively, you must show that you understand a problem well enough to suggest solutions while addressing specific audience needs. Considering these ideas in columns can help you see them differently than you do as you write. After drafting your ideas in one file, open a new file, go to the Format menu and choose "Columns," and then click on "3." Label the first column "Problems," the second "Solutions," and the third "Readers' Objections." Use your draft file to copy and paste your ideas into the appropriate column in your new file. Add points as needed so that you move logically from problem to solution and answer readers' objections point by point.

FOR E-WRITERS

Imagine Possible Objections of Your Audience.   You can increase the likelihood that readers will accept your proposal in two ways. First, start your proposal by showing that a problem exists. Then, when you turn to your claim that something should be done, begin with a simple and inviting suggestion. For example, a claim that national parks need better care might begin by suggesting that readers head for such a park and personally size up the situation. Besides drawing readers into the problem and the solution, you may think of objections they might raise — reservations about the high cost, the complexity, or the workability of your plan, for instance. You can persuade your readers by anticipating an objection that might occur to them and laying it to rest.

Cite Sources Carefully.   When you collect ideas and evidence from outside sources, you need to document your evidence — that is, tell where you found everything. Check with your instructor on the documentation method he or she wants to use. You may also want to identify sources as you introduce them to assure a reader that they are authoritative.

■ For pointers on integrating and documenting sources, see Ch. 12 and D6 and E1–E2 in the Quick Research Guide (the dark-red-edged pages).

According to *Newsweek* correspondent Josie Fair, . . .

In his biography *FDR: The New Deal Years*, Davis reports . . .

While working as a Senate page in the summer of 2007, I observed . . .

You can introduce a table, graph, drawing, map, photograph, or other visual evidence in much the same way.

■ For more advice about integrating visuals, see pp. 410–16.

As the 2000 census figures in Table 1 indicate, . . .

The photograph illustrating the run-down condition of the dog park (see Fig. 2) . . .

REVISING AND EDITING

■ For more revising and editing strategies, see Ch. 20.

As you revise, concentrate on a clear explanation of the problem and solid supporting evidence for the solution. Make your essay coherent and its parts clear to help achieve your purpose of convincing your readers.

Clarify Your Thesis.   Your readers are likely to rely on your thesis to identify the problem and possibly to preview your solution. Look again at your thesis from a reader's point of view.

WORKING THESIS   The legislature should pass a law allowing couples to divorce without having to go to court.

REVISED THESIS   Because divorce court can be expensive, adversarial, and stressful, passing a law that allows couples to divorce without a trip to court would encourage simpler and more harmonious ways of ending a marriage.

Reorganize for Unity and Coherence.   When Heather Colbenson revised her first draft, she wanted to clarify the presentation of her problem.

Why would high schools in farming communities drop agriculture classes and the

The main reason that   *is that*

FFA programs? Small schools are cutting ag programs because the state has not pro-

vided significant funding for the schools to operate. The small schools have to make

Move main reason last for emphasis

cuts, and some small schools are deciding that the agriculture classes are not as im-

portant as other courses. Some small schools are consolidating to receive more aid.

Why did I put a solution here? Move to end!

Many of these schools have been able to save their ag programs.

One reason is that m

Rewrite this! Not really college require-ments but college-prep courses vs. others when budget is tight

Many colleges are demanding that students have two years of foreign language.

In small schools, like my own, the students could take either foreign language or ag

classes. Therefore, students choose language classes to fill the college requirement.

When the students leave the ag classes to take foreign language, the number of stu-

dents declines, which makes it easier for school administrators to cut ag classes.

■ For strategies for achieving coherence see pp. 346–49.

Her revised paper was more forcefully organized and more coherent, making it easier for readers to follow. The bridges between ideas were now on paper, not just in her mind.

■ For more on errors in reasoning, see pp. 46–47 and 162–63.

Be Reasonable.   Exaggerated claims for your solution will not persuade your readers. Neither will oversimplifying the problem so that the solution

Exchanging Written Reactions

Exchange proposals with another student, and read each other's draft. Then take turns sharing first reactions — positive as well as negative. After this exchange, take your partner's draft home for a day or two. Before your next meeting, write a review letter to your partner in which you thoughtfully critique the draft and suggest revisions. (To help the writer, mark the draft as you comment on the organization, thesis, support, and so forth.) Exchange letters during your next meeting, and discuss your experiences. What did you learn about proposing solutions? About writing? About peer editing?

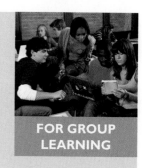

FOR GROUP LEARNING

seems more likely to apply. Don't be afraid to express your own reasonable doubts about the completeness of your solution. If necessary, rethink both the problem and the solution.

In looking back over your draft once more, consider these questions:

REVISION CHECKLIST

—— Does your introduction invite the reader into the discussion?

—— Is your problem clear? How have you made it relevant to readers?

—— Have you clearly outlined the steps necessary to solve the problem?

—— Where have you demonstrated the benefits of your solution?

—— Have you considered other solutions before rejecting them for your own?

—— Have you anticipated the doubts readers may have about your solution?

—— Do you come across as a well-meaning, reasonable writer willing to admit that you don't know everything? If you sound preachy, have you overused *should* and *must*?

—— Have you avoided promising that your solution will do more than it can possibly do? Have you made believable predictions for its success?

After you have revised your proposal, edit and proofread it. Carefully check the grammar, word choice, punctuation, and mechanics — and then correct any problems you find. If you have used sources, be sure that you have cited them correctly in your text and added a list of works cited.

Make sure your sentence structure helps you make your points clearly and directly. Don't let yourself slip into the passive voice, a grammatical construction that represents things as happening without any obvious agent: "The problem should be remedied by spending more money on prevention." Instead, every sentence should specify who should take action: "The dean of students should remedy the problem by spending more money on prevention."

For more editing and proofreading strategies, see pp. 348–87. For more on documenting sources, see E1–E2 in the Quick Research Guide (the dark-red-edged pages).

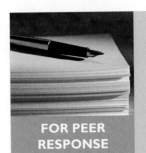

FOR PEER RESPONSE

For general questions for a peer editor, see p. 377. For peer response worksheets, visit <bedfordstmartins.com/ bedguide> and do a keyword search:

peer

Ask several classmates or friends to review your proposal and solution, answering questions such as these:

- What is your overall reaction to this proposal? Does it make you want to go out and do something about the problem?
- Are you convinced that the problem is of concern to you? If not, why not?
- Are you persuaded that the writer's solution is workable?
- Has the writer paid enough attention to readers and their concerns?
- Restate what you understand to be the proposal's major points:
  - Problem
  - Explanation of problem and why it matters
  - Proposed solution
  - Explanation of proposal and its practicality
  - Reasons and procedure to implement proposal
  - Proposal's advantages, disadvantages, and responses to other solutions
  - Final recommendation
- If this were your paper, what is the one thing you would be sure to work on before handing it in?

Here are some questions to get you started editing and proofreading:

EDITING CHECKLIST

For more help, turn to the dark-blue-edged pages, and find the sections of the Quick Editing Guide noted here.

___ Is it clear what each pronoun refers to? Is any *this* or *that* ambiguous? Does each pronoun agree with (match) its antecedent?	A6
___ Is your sentence structure correct? Have you avoided writing fragments, comma splices, or fused sentences?	A1, A2
___ Do your transitions and other introductory elements have commas after them, if these are needed?	C1
___ Have you spelled and capitalized everything correctly, especially names of people and organizations?	D1, D2

OTHER ASSIGNMENTS

1. If you followed the assignment in Chapter 9 and took a stand, now write a few paragraphs extending that paper to propose a solution that argues for action. To gather ideas, brainstorm with classmates first.
2. Write a memo to your supervisor at work in which you propose an innovation (related to procedures, schedules, policies, or similar matters) that could benefit your department or company.

3. Choose from the following list a practice that you find inefficient, unethical, unfair, or morally wrong as a solution to a problem. In a few paragraphs, give reasons for your objections. Then propose a better solution in an essay, letter to the editor, blog entry, or class posting.

Censorship   Genetic engineering
Corporal punishment for children   Outsourcing jobs
Laboratory experiments on animals   Dumping wastes in the ocean

Applying What You Learn: Some Uses of Proposals

In College Courses.   Many courses will require writing a proposal, often a plan to be approved before implementation.

- Students embarking on a research project may be required to submit to an adviser or a committee a proposal that sets forth what they will investigate and how they will conduct their study.

- In social science courses, you may examine a current issue and propose a solution to the disclosure of adoption records, the rising costs of prescription drugs, prison overcrowding, or racial profiling.

- Students who object to a grade can file a grievance proposing a grade change. Like writers of persuasive essays, they state a claim and supply evidence in support of it.

In the Workplace.   Proposals often suggest new projects, recommend purchases or changes in procedure, and solve personnel problems.

- After gathering comments from workers and financial analyses, the human resources office prepares proposals outlining benefits such as medical and dental insurance.

- When a company builds or renovates a building, the architect submits a proposal outlining the plans, and then contractors submit bids, proposing to complete the work for a certain cost.

- Every job application is a proposal. Applicants propose that an employer hire them and support that proposal by selecting the best evidence for their résumés and letters or applications.

In Your Community.   Every day we encounter proposals for solutions—in editorials, in books, in public-service announcements, in political debate.

- You might write to the board proposing that your congregation begin a building fund to expand your overcrowded fellowship hall. Your proposal would include evidence of the need for more space, the cost of the addition, ways of raising the money, and a time frame for completion.
- In a speech to your local service club, you might inform them about the drop-out rate at your local high school and propose that members donate their time to work with at-risk teens.
- Alarmed by the low literacy rate of many adults in your community, you propose a tutoring program to the library and design posters to promote it.

Chapter 11
Evaluating

Responding to an Image

This image originally appeared on the cover of an issue of *Utne,* next to these lines promoting a featured article: "Clear your head. Too many choices? How to make up your mind without losing it." What does this image suggest about decision making, a critical step in evaluation? How does the image guide a viewer's eye to its focal point? What details contribute to the overall impression it conveys? In what ways does it reflect the feelings of writers and others who must repeatedly make and present thoughtful choices? In your journal, notebook, or laptop, record your responses—as a writer—to this image.

Evaluating means judging. You do it when you decide what candidate to vote for, pick which camera to buy, or recommend a new restaurant to your friends. All of us pass judgments—often snap judgments—as we move through a day's routine. A friend asks, "How was that movie you saw last night?" and you reply, "Terrific—don't miss it" or maybe "Pretty good, but it had too much blood and gore for me."

But to *write* an evaluation calls for you to think more critically. As a writer you first decide on *criteria*, or standards for judging, and then come up with evidence to back up your judgment. Your evaluation zeroes in on a definite subject that you inspect carefully in order to reach a considered opinion. The subject might be a film, a book, a sports team, a group of performers, a product, a body of research: the possibilities are endless.

Learning from Other Writers

■ For more on thesis and support, see Chs. 17 and 19.

Here are evaluations by a professional writer and by a student. To help you begin to analyze the first reading, look for the notes in the margin. They identify features such as the thesis, or main idea, the criteria for evaluation, and the evidence supporting the writer's judgment, all typical of essays that evaluate.

As You Read These Evaluations

■ For more examples of evaluative writing, visit <bedfordstmartins.com/bedguide> and do a keyword search:

examples

As you read these essays, ask yourself the following questions:

1. Do you consider the writer qualified to evaluate the subject he or she chose? What biases and prejudices might the writer bring to the evaluation?
2. What criteria for evaluation does the writer establish? Are these reasonable standards for evaluating the subject?
3. What is the writer's assessment of the subject? Does the writer provide sufficient evidence to convince you of his or her evaluation?

Seth Stevenson regularly evaluates advertising for Slate.com. In this particular Ad Report Card, published in May 2006, Stevenson discusses a startling television spot for the Volkswagen Jetta.

Seth Stevenson

Wham! Bam! Buy a VW, Ma'am!

The spot: Four young people are riding in a Volkswagen Jetta. They're engaged in some lighthearted banter° when BLAM! An SUV runs a red light and smashes into their driver's side door. Air bags deploy. Glass shatters. We fade out, and then fade back in on the Jetta's passengers, unharmed,

banter: Casual talk; chitchat.

standing next to the badly damaged car as police sirens wail. "Holy sh-," says one of the passengers, with the profanity° cut off before she can finish pronouncing it. "Safe happens," reads the on-screen slogan,° and then some text tells us that the Jetta has received the "highest government side impact rating."

This Volkswagen spot—along with another one just like it—has prompted massive amounts of reader mail. Some of you are terrified, some of you are appalled,° and some of you think the ads are absolutely brilliant. Personally, I don't find these to be works of surpassing° genius, but I do think they're pretty sharp.

> **THESIS**
> presenting judgment

For one, the execution° is remarkable. I'm not sure I've seen a more realistic depiction of a car crash. The spots capture that out-of-nowhere moment at the heart of all accidents, when everyday mundanity° flashes into a hyperintense freak-out explosion. The ads also hint at an accident's aftermath: hours of jittery° detachment.° Anyone who's been in a car crash will recognize this mood triptych.°

> Introduction to first criterion: execution

Visually, I love that they've avoided clichéd° slow-mo° footage of headlights exploding, glass shards floating through the crisp night air, and so forth. This choice reminds me of my other favorite car-crash scene, from Steven Soderbergh's *Erin Brockovich:* in a single, unadorned, middle-distance shot (with no foreshadowing° whatsoever), we see Julia Roberts's car get violently crunched as it rolls through an intersection. The Volkswagen spot is similarly stripped-down. It's a brutally frank look at the physical chaos° that results when an SUV enters your sedan without an invitation.

> Supporting evidence

So, the execution is fantastic, but what about the concept? Why a campaign that centers on safety? It seems particularly odd given that a recent VW campaign was all about aggressive, high-speed driving, and finding your inner "fast." Now we're asked to contemplate° air bags and government safety ratings? Granted, the "Make Friends with Your Fast" campaign was for the pocket-rocket GTI, while this "Safe Happens" campaign is for the slightly more grown-up Jetta. But still, I'm feeling some . . . whiplash.

> Introduction to second criterion: concept

According to Kurt Schneider, general manager for creative content at Volkswagen, the idea was to find a fresh way to pitch safety. "Safety has mostly been portrayed in a more rational, family-oriented way," he says. "This was an attempt to reach eighteen- to thirty-four-year-olds [the target market for the Jetta] by presenting safety in a more emotional and dramatic light. We show young people out with friends, and the message is about protecting the people who are close to you."

> Supporting evidence

profanity: Swearword.   **slogan:** Headline; advertising claim.   **appalled:** Shocked. **surpassing:** Exceptional; extraordinary.   **execution:** The way in which something is carried out or achieved.   **mundanity:** Ordinariness.   **jittery:** Nervous.   **detachment:** Lack of emotional involvement.   **triptych:** Series of three.   **clichéd:** Something that has been repeated so often that it is no longer fresh.   **slow-mo:** Slow motion.   **foreshadowing:** Hinting at what is to come.   **chaos:** Disorder; disarray.   **contemplate:** To think about or seriously consider.

I like this argument. But there's a reason that safety traditionally gets 7 pitched at families and not at the childless. Most parents are obsessively fixated° on their kids' well-being, while most fancy-free° young folks don't give safety much thought. In urging young people to take heed,° Volkswagen seems to be fighting human nature.

Supporting evidence — (continued)

Their plan, obviously, is to get us totally freaked about car crashes. And, 8 judging by the posttraumatic° e-mails I'm getting from readers, that plan appears to be working. Since these spots are filmed mostly from inside the cars and feature likable, attractive but not-too-attractive characters, the viewer is led to feel like part of the gang. When the accidents hit, we feel like victims, too. If being drawn into these violent clips doesn't get you thinking about auto fatalities, nothing will.

The question is whether this will translate into Volkswagen sales. Will 9 young people (1) actually start prioritizing° safety in their car shopping, and (2) if so, will those people looking for safety now decide that VW is the answer? I've always found safety an oddly slippery brand attribute. Every carmaker throws its safety claims out there, and they all seem to wash right over me. Blah blah front-impact blah blah stars blah side curtain blah government rating. Volvo has its safety rep all sewn up, but I've no idea whether Volvos are in fact any safer than other cars. And, despite these ads, I've no idea whether Volkswagens are, either.

Conclusion underscoring — thesis, with a final grade

Grade: B. I'm not sure Jetta's target demo° can be convinced to care 10 about safety. But I'm thoroughly convinced that these ads will haunt their dreams and keep the Volkswagen brand at the front of their thoughts. That's half the battle.

As for the appropriateness of the ads and all the outraged reaction: they 11 don't really bother me much. Volkswagen says it's trying to keep the spots from airing before 9 P.M., so little kids are less likely to see them. And part of me thinks it's healthy for us to contemplate our mortality° during the breaks in our sitcoms.°

Questions to Start You Thinking

Meaning

1. Why, based on Stevenson's description, might viewers find the Jetta ads shocking?

---

fixated: Focused.   **fancy-free:** Without cares or concerns.   **take heed:** Pay attention to.   **posttraumatic:** A reference to posttraumatic stress disorder, in which a past trauma haunts the victim over an extended period.   **prioritizing:** In this sense, giving a high rank or importance to something.   **demo:** Short for *demographic*, the age group that Volkswagen is aiming for with the Jetta ads (eighteen- to thirty-four-year-olds).   **mortality:** Death.   **sitcoms:** Short for *situation comedies*, television comedies that take place in certain situations or settings.

2. Why, according to the author, do car advertisers tend to direct claims about safety to parents more than to young people? Why did Volkswagen do the reverse with the Jetta ad?

3. What is Stevenson's personal view of ads that make claims about safety?

Writing Strategies

4. What is Stevenson's overall judgment of the Jetta ads, and what criteria does he use to make this judgment?

5. In your view, how well does he support his judgment? Point to some specific examples in making your case.

6. Stevenson quotes an ad executive at Volkswagen in paragraph 6. How does this quotation contribute to Stevenson's evaluation? What other outside sources might Stevenson have included to enhance his points?

7. How would you describe Stevenson's tone, the quality of his writing that reveals his attitude toward his topic and his readers? What specific words, phrases, or sentences contribute to his tone? Does the tone seem appropriate for his purpose and audience?

STUDENT ESSAY

Dennis O'Neil

Katrina Documentary Gives Voice to Survivors

Dennis O'Neil wrote this review of Spike Lee's documentary on Hurricane Katrina for the Louisville Cardinal, the newspaper of the University of Louisville. The review was published in September 2006.

Spike Lee's film *When the Levees° Broke: A Requiem° in Four Acts* cuts straight to the heart of the Hurricane Katrina tragedy and gives voice to the New Orleans survivors in an unprecedented° way. The epic,° 256-minute documentary provides a multitude° of different perspectives on the disaster and demonstrates the tragic effect that the disaster has had on New Orleans and its citizens.

"It is very important, not just here in the United States but all over the world, that people hear the stories from these individuals, these witnesses, who saw the horror of what happened in New Orleans," Lee said in a recent interview with HBO. The film is Lee's third collaboration with HBO (after the Oscar-nominated *4 Little Girls* as well as *Jim Brown: All American*), which wanted Lee to craft the "documentary of record" about the tragedy. Three months after Katrina hit, Lee and a small crew made the first of eight trips to New Orleans to shoot raw footage of the disaster and gather subjects for interviews. Ultimately,° close to one hundred subjects appear in

Levees: Walls or embankments that hold back water to prevent flooding.   **Requiem:** A solemn chant, song, or other work of art that honors the dead.   **unprecedented:** New; never achieved before.   **epic:** Large in scope.   **a multitude:** Many.   **Ultimately:** Finally; in the end.

the film, all from various walks of life, including academics, military personnel, politicians, celebrities, activists, and residents of New Orleans who were the most affected by the tragedy.

The film is divided into four one-hour acts with acts 1 and 2 encompassing° the   3
period of time between the earliest threats of Katrina to the point where survivors were finally beginning to be evacuated five days after the storm hit. Many of the interview subjects offer strong evidence that the flood of New Orleans was not caused entirely by Katrina but because the city's levee system was not structurally adequate, as it was not strong enough to withstand even a category-three° storm.

What images or voices from the Katrina disaster persist in your memory?

The film offers harrowing° and graphic° images of the disaster while it was in   4
progress, as well as of the aftermath in which the survivors fled their flooded homes for various sanctuaries° around the city. Lee shows the roof on the New Orleans Superdome slowly turning to rust as the storm progresses and how federal aid, which was so quick to assist the tsunami victims in Asia,° didn't arrive until long after the worst had already occurred.

"It was absolutely horrific° conditions," said survivor Fred Johnson to Lee.   5
"It was like being in the middle of a war and all you could do was stand there and feel helpless."

Many of the personal tragedies experienced by the survivors are addressed in the   6
film, such as that of Herbert Freeman Jr., a resident of the Lower Ninth Ward neighborhood of New Orleans, whose mother passed away during the disaster. Freeman was forced to leave her dead body sitting in the Superdome with a note attached to her because she couldn't be airlifted out and Freeman couldn't take her with him. She sat there for days before someone noticed her.

Acts 3 and 4 of the film heavily depict° the aftermath of the tragedy, as the   7
survivors were shepherded° to various areas of the country to restart their lives. Many of them recount° the various hardships of being separated from family members, looking for new homes, fighting with insurance companies, and experiencing the heartache of losing the only home many of them have ever known.

What does "home" mean to you? What do you value in it?

"Thanksgiving was a heart-wrenching situation," said Pastor James Pullings to   8
Lee. "It broke my heart to hear people saying, 'I want to go home, but I have no home to go to.'"

---

encompassing: Covering; consisting of.   **category-three:** A storm characterized by 111- to 130-mph winds and 9- to 12-foot storm surges. Hurricane Katrina made landfall as a category-four storm, with wind speeds up to 140 mph.   **harrowing:** Upsetting. **graphic:** Vivid, often in a disturbing way.   **sanctuaries:** Places of safety.   **tsunami victims in Asia:** A reference to the post-earthquake tidal wave that killed more than 200,000 people in 2004.   **horrific:** Horrifying; terrible.   **depict:** Show or portray.   **shepherded:** Led.   **recount:** Recall; describe.

Many of the film's most poignant° moments involve survivors returning to New   9
Orleans and being confronted by the devastation that has occurred there. In one
scene, the elderly Wilhelmina Blanchard returns to her home and breaks into uncon-
trollable sobs as she sees the horrific state that it is now in. "I had heard of the
devastation," she says through tears, "but I didn't know it was this bad."

"You walk through your old neighborhood," says actor Wendell Pierce, "and you   10
see a house with the number two on the door, and you realize, 'Man, two people died
in that house.' And it's just so deafeningly quiet."

But Lee's ultimate victory with the film is that he doesn't allow the silence to   11
drown out the heart of New Orleans that still beats underneath it. The film's most
moving moment occurs when Terence Blanchard, who composed the film's mournful,
elegiac° score, walks the ghostly silent streets of New Orleans and plays on his
trumpet a soulful jazz lullaby, as if humming a crippled giant to sleep.

"One of the things that I hope this documentary does is remind America that   12
New Orleans is not over with," added Lee. "It's not done."

*What does "It's
not done" suggest to
you?*

Questions to Start You Thinking

Meaning

1. Why did Spike Lee make the documentary described in the essay?

2. What content (visual, testimonial, and so on) did Lee include to make his
   point about the effects of Hurricane Katrina on its survivors and on New
   Orleans?

3. What is the "ultimate victory" of the film, according to O'Neil?

Writing Strategies

4. What criteria does O'Neil use to judge Lee's documentary? To what extent
   has the film met these criteria, according to O'Neil?

5. Does O'Neil provide enough evidence to support his judgment? Why or
   why not?

6. O'Neil makes extensive use of quotations. Do you find the quotations effective or overdone?

7. Using highlighters or marginal notes, identify the essay's introduction, thesis, criteria for evaluation, supporting evidence, and conclusion. How effective is the organization of the essay?

---

poignant: Touching or moving.   **elegiac:** Sorrowful.

Learning by Writing

THE ASSIGNMENT: WRITING AN EVALUATION

■ For writing activities for evaluating, visit <bedfordstmartins.com/ bedguide> and do a key-word search:

activities

Pick a subject to evaluate — one you have personal experience with and feel competent to evaluate. This might be a movie, a TV program, a piece of music, an artwork, a new product, a government agency, a campus facility or policy, an essay or a reading, or anything else you can think of. Then in a thoughtful essay, analyze your subject and evaluate it. You will need to determine specific criteria for evaluation and make them clear to your readers. In writing your evaluation, you will have a twofold purpose: (1) to set forth your assessment of the quality of your subject and (2) to convince your readers that your judgment is reasonable.

Among the lively student-written evaluations we've seen are these:

A music major evaluated several works by American composer Aaron Copland, finding him trivial and imitative, "without a tenth of the talent or inventiveness that George Gershwin or Duke Ellington had in his little finger."

A student planning a career in business management evaluated a computer firm in which he had worked one summer. His criteria were efficiency, productivity, appeal to new customers, and employee satisfaction.

A student from Brazil, who had seen firsthand the effects of industrial development in the Amazon rain forest, evaluated the efforts of the U.S. government to protect forests and wetlands, comparing them with the efforts of environmentalists in her own country.

GENERATING IDEAS

College production of Romeo and Juliet

Find Something to Evaluate.   Try using *brainstorming* or *mapping* to identify as many possible topics as you can think of. Select the ones with most potential — the ones that are most familiar or easiest to find out about. Spend enough time investigating these possibilities that you can comfortably choose one subject for your essay.

Consider Sources of Support.   You'll want to spend time finding material to help you develop a judgment. You may recall a program on television or hunt for an article to read. You might observe a performance or a sports team. An interview or conversation could reveal what others think. Perhaps you'll want to review several examples of your subject: watching several films, listening to several CDs, examining several works of art, or testing several

Developing a Consensus

Meet with your writing group to discuss the subject you plan to evaluate, and see whether the group can help you arrive at a sound judgment. The others will need to see or hear your detailed report about what you're evaluating. If possible, pass around a product, show a photograph of artwork, play a song on a CD, or read aloud a short literary work or an idea expressed in a reading. Ask your listeners to explain the reasons for their own evaluations. Maybe they'll suggest criteria or evidence that hadn't occurred to you.

FOR GROUP LEARNING

products. You might also browse for information about your subject at several Web sites or attend a campus concert or play.

Establish Your Criteria.   Jot down criteria, standards to apply to your subject based on the features of the subject worth considering. How well, for example, does a popular entertainer score on musicianship, onstage manner, rapport with the audience, selection of material, originality? In evaluating the desirability of Portland as a home for a young careerist, you might ask: Does it provide an ample choice of decent-paying entry-level positions in growth firms? Any criterion you use to evaluate has to fit your subject, your audience, and your purpose. After all, ample entry-level jobs might not matter to an audience of retirees.

■ For more strategies for generating ideas, see Ch. 16.

Try Comparing and Contrasting.   Often you can readily size up the worth of a thing by setting it next to another of its kind. (When you *compare*, you point to similarities; when you *contrast*, you note differences.) To be comparable, of course, your two subjects need to have plenty in common. The quality of a Harley Davidson motorcycle might be judged by contrasting it with a Honda but not with a Hummer.

■ For more on comparing and contrasting, see Ch. 7.

For example, if you are writing a paper for a film-history course, you might compare and contrast the classic German horror movie *The Cabinet of Dr. Caligari* with the classic Hollywood movie *Frankenstein*, concluding that *Caligari* is more artistic. In planning the paper, you might make two columns in which you list the characteristics of each film, point by point:

	CALIGARI	*FRANKENSTEIN*
SETS	Dreamlike and impressionistic	Realistic, but with heavy Gothic atmosphere
	Sets deliberately angular and distorted	Gothic sets
LIGHTING	Deep shadows that throw figures into relief	Torches highlighting monster's face in night scene

By jotting down each point and each bit of evidence side by side, you can outline your comparison and contrast with great efficiency. Once you have listed them, decide on a possible order for the points.

■ For more on defining, see pp. 356–57.

Try Defining Your Subject.   Another technique for evaluating is to define your subject, indicating its nature so clearly that your readers can easily distinguish it from others of its kind. In defining, you help your readers understand your subject — its structure, its habitat, its functions. In evaluating a classic television show such as *Roseanne* or *The Mary Tyler Moore Show,* you might want to do some *extended* defining, discussing the nature of sitcoms over the years, their techniques, their views of women, their effects on the audience. Unlike a *short definition,* as in a dictionary, an extended definition is intended not simply to explain but to judge: What is the nature of my subject? What qualities make my subject unique, unlike others of its sort?

Develop a Judgment That You Can Explain to Your Audience.   In the end, you will have to come to a decision: Is your subject good, worthwhile, significant, exemplary, preferable — or not? Most writers come to a judgment gradually as they explore their subjects and develop criteria.

Facing the Challenge: Evaluating

The major challenge writers face when writing evaluations is to make clear to their readers the criteria they have used to arrive at their opinion. While you may not be an expert in any field, you should never underestimate your powers of discrimination. When reviewing a movie, for example, you may begin by simply summarizing the story of the film and saying whether you like it or not. However, for readers who are wondering whether to see the movie, you need to go beyond these comments. For example, you might find a movie's special effects, exotic sets, and unpredictable plot effective but wish that the characters had seemed more believable. Based on these criteria, you might come up with the thesis that the movie may not be realistic but is extremely entertaining and well worth seeing.

Once you've chosen a topic, use the following questions to help you clarify and apply standards for evaluating it:

• What features or standards do you plan to use as criteria for evaluating your topic?

• How could you briefly explain each of the criteria for a reader?

• What judgment or evaluation about your topic do these criteria support?

After identifying your criteria, you can examine each in turn. Explaining your criteria will ensure that you move beyond a summary to an opinion or judgment that you can justify to your readers.

To close in on a promising subject, ask yourself a few questions:

DISCOVERY CHECKLIST

___ What criteria do you plan to use in making your evaluation? Are they clear and reasonably easy to apply?

___ What evidence can back up your judgments?

___ Would comparing or contrasting help in evaluating your subject? If so, with what might you compare or contrast your subject?

___ What specific qualities define your subject, setting it apart from all the rest of its class?

PLANNING, DRAFTING, AND DEVELOPING

Start with a Thesis.   Reflect a moment: What is your purpose in this evaluation? What main point do you wish to make? Try writing a paragraph that sums up the purpose of your evaluation, or work on stating a thesis that summarizes your main point.

TOPIC + JUDGMENT	campus performance of *Lobby Hero* — liked the seniors featured in it plus the problems the play raised
WORKING THESIS	Chosen to showcase the achievements of graduating seniors, the play *Lobby Hero* also brings up ethical problems.

Consider Your Criteria.   Many writers find that a list of specific criteria gives them confidence and provokes ideas. Consider filling in a chart with three columns — criteria, evidence, judgment — to help focus your thinking.

Develop an Organization.   You may want to begin with a direct statement of your judgment: Based on durability, cost, and comfort, the Classic 7 is an ideal campus backpack. On the other hand, you may want to reserve judgment by opening with a question about your subject: How good a film is *The Departed*? Each approach suggests a different organization:

Thesis or main point	→	Supporting evidence	→	Return to thesis
Opening question	→	Supporting evidence	→	Overall judgment

In either case, you'll supply plenty of evidence — details, examples, possibly comparisons or contrasts — so that readers find your case compelling. You'll also cluster your evidence around your points or criteria for judgment so that readers know how and why you have reached your judgment. You might try both patterns of organization (or a different one altogether) and see which works better for your subject and purpose.

■ For more on stating a thesis, see pp. 312–19.

■ For exercises on choosing effective thesis statements, visit <bedfordstmartins.com/bedguide> and do a keyword search:

thesis

■ For more on outlining, see pp. 325–33.

■ For exercises on supporting a thesis, visit <bedfordstmartins.com/bedguide> and do a keyword search:

support

FOR PEER RESPONSE

For general questions for a peer editor, see p. 377. For peer response worksheets, visit <bedfordstmartins.com/bedguide> and do a keyword search:

🔍 peer

Enlist the advice of a classmate or friend as you determine your criteria for evaluation and your judgment. Ask your peer editor to answer questions like these about your evaluation:

- What is your overall reaction to this essay? Does the writer persuade you to agree with his or her evaluation?
- When you finish the essay, can you tell exactly what the writer thinks of the subject? Where does the writer express this opinion?
- How do you know what criteria the writer is using for evaluation?
- Does the writer give you sufficient evidence for his or her judgment? Put stars wherever more or better evidence is needed.
- What audience does the writer seem to have in mind?
- Would you recommend any changes in the essay's organization?
- If this were your paper, what is the one thing you would be sure to work on before handing it in?

Most writers find that an outline — even a rough list — helps them keep track of points to make. If you intend to compare and contrast your subject with something else, one way to arrange the points is *subject by subject*: discuss subject A, and then discuss subject B. For a longer comparison, a better way to organize is *point by point*, applying each point first to one subject and then to the other. If appropriate and approved by your instructor, you also might plan to include a sketch, photograph, or other illustration of your subject or develop a comparative table summarizing the features of similar items you have compared.

REVISING AND EDITING

For more on stating a thesis, see pp. 315–18. For more revising and editing strategies, see Ch. 20.

Focus on Your Thesis.   As you begin to revise, make your thesis as precise and clear as possible.

WORKING THESIS   Chosen to showcase the graduating seniors, the play *Lobby Hero* also brings up ethical problems.

REVISED THESIS   This year's senior showcase play, *Lobby Hero* by Kenneth Lonergan, spotlights outstanding performers and raises timely ethical issues.

Be Fair.   Make your judgments reasonable, not extreme. A reviewer can find fault with a film and still conclude that it is worth seeing. There's nothing wrong, of course, with a fervent judgment ("This is the trashiest excuse for a play I have ever suffered through"), but consider your readers and their

Supporting Judgments

After you have written a draft of your evaluative essay, you will need to consider how well you have linked specific support to your judgments. Scroll through the draft, and highlight each judgment or opinion with color. (Look under "Format" to find "font" choices, including color.) Then go back to the beginning, and this time highlight all facts and evidence with a different color. Are your judgments followed by or related to the evidence to support your claims? Do you need to modify your judgments or revise your support? Do you need to add more support at any points or move sentences around so that your support is more closely linked to your judgments? Connecting your claims with your evidence makes your evaluation persuasive and interesting.

FOR E-WRITERS

likely reactions. Read some reviews in your local newspaper or watch some movie critics on television to see how they balance their judgments. Because readers will have more confidence in your opinions if you seem fair and reasonable, revise your tone and your wording where needed. For example, one writer revised his opening after he realized that he was evaluating the audience rather than the performance.

> The most recent performance by a favorite campus group--Rock Mountain--
> *disappointing concert   Although t*
> was an ~~incredibly revolting~~ experience. ~~T~~he ~~outlandish~~ crowd ignored the DJ who
>   *people*
> introduced the group, and a few ~~nameless members of one social group spent~~
>   *ed*
> ~~their time~~ tossing around trash cans in front of the stage, *the opening number*
>
> *still announced the group's powerful musical presence.*

Use this handy checklist as you think critically about your draft:

REVISION CHECKLIST

— Is the judgment you pass on your subject unmistakably clear?

— Have you given your readers evidence to support each point you make?

— Have you been fair? If you are championing something, have you deliberately skipped over any of its disadvantages or faults? If you are condemning your subject, have you omitted any of its admirable traits?

— Have you anticipated and answered readers' possible objections?

— If you compare one thing with another, do you look consistently at the same points in both?

For more on comparison and contrast, see Ch. 7 and pp. 366–68.

■ For more editing and
proofreading strategies,
see pp. 384–87.

After you have revised your evaluation, edit and proofread it. Carefully
check grammar, word choice, punctuation, and mechanics—and then correct any problems you find. Make sentences in which you describe the subject of your evaluation as precise and useful as possible. If you have used
comparisons or contrasts, make sure these are clear: don't lose your readers
in a fog of vague pronouns or confusing references.

Here are some questions to help you start editing and proofreading:

EDITING CHECKLIST

■ For more help turn
to the dark-blue-edged
pages and find the sec-
tions in the Quick Editing
Guide noted here.

___ Is the reference of each pronoun clear? Does each pronoun agree   A6
with (match) its antecedent?

___ Is it clear what each modifier in a sentence modifies? Have you   B1
created any dangling or misplaced modifiers, especially in descriptions
of your subject?

___ Have you used parallel structure wherever needed, especially in lists   B2
or comparisons?

OTHER ASSIGNMENTS

1. Write an evaluation of a college course you have taken or are now taking. Analyze its strengths and weaknesses. Does the instructor present
the material clearly, understandably, and interestingly? Can you confer
with the instructor if you need to? Are the assignments pointed and purposeful? Is the textbook helpful, readable, and easy to use? Does this
course give you your money's worth?

■ For more on respond-
ing to literature, see
Ch. 13.

2. Read these two poems on a similar theme critically, and decide which
seems to you the better poem. Then, in a brief essay, set forth your
evaluation. Some criteria to apply might be the poet's choice of concrete, specific words that appeal to the senses and his awareness of his
audience.

Putting in the Seed
ROBERT FROST (1874–1963)

You come to fetch me from my work tonight
When supper's on the table, and we'll see

If I can leave off burying the white
Soft petals fallen from the apple tree
(Soft petals, yes, but not so barren quite,
Mingled with these, smooth bean and wrinkled pea),
And go along with you ere you lose sight
Of what you came for and become like me,
Slave to a springtime passion for the earth.
How Love burns through the Putting in the Seed
On through the watching for that early birth

When, just as the soil tarnishes with weed,
The sturdy seedling with arched body comes
Shouldering its way and shedding the earth crumbs.

Between Our Folding Lips
T. E. BROWN (1830–1897)

Between our folding lips
God slips
An embryon life, and goes;
And this becomes your rose.
We love, God makes: in our sweet mirth
God spies occasion for a birth.
Then is it His, or is it ours?
I know not — He is fond of flowers.

3. Visit a restaurant, a museum, or a tourist attraction, and write an evaluation of it for others who might consider a visit. Or evaluate an unfamiliar magazine, an essay in this textbook, a proposal under consideration
at work, or a source you have read for a college class. Be sure to specify
your criteria for evaluation.

Applying What You Learn:
Some Uses of Evaluating

In College Courses.   In writing assignments and on exams, you'll be
asked over and over to evaluate. Evaluation demonstrates to your instructor
your sound understanding and considered opinion of a topic.

- Speech pathology students might be asked to consider the long-standing
  controversy that rages in education for the deaf by describing and then
  evaluating three currently disputed teaching methods — oral/aural, sign-
  ing, and a combination of the two.

- Students of language and linguistics might be asked to evaluate Skin-
  ner's behaviorist theory of articulation therapy.

- Students often are asked to evaluate their instructors and courses; outside class, students on some campuses are invited to evaluate their campus facilities or student services.

In the Workplace.   Every executive or professional needs to evaluate people,
projects, goals, and results.

- Political commentators and newspaper editors evaluate the state of the
  economy, the actions of the administration or Congress, the decisions
  of the Supreme Court, and the merits of proposed legislation.

Career Services
UNIVERSITY

Evaluating Job Offers

- To evaluate all the factors associated with the position offered and the organization, ask for sufficient time to consider the offer. Sufficient time will depend on your needs and the needs of the organization. The amount of time you need may be different from what the company needs. You may be asked to give your decision sooner than you wish. If, at the end of that time, you have not been able to make a decision, ask for an extension, which may or may not be granted.

- Consider the position, the goals established for the position, the company's track record, what is projected for the company's future, opportunity for promotion, personalities of supervisor and coworkers, management style, and corporate culture.

- Follow up with other organizations that are considering you for employment in which you still have interest. Explain that you have received another offer, but because of your interest in their organization/position, you are following up with them to learn the status of your candidacy.

Web page from George Mason University Career Services

Ratings for video games get more specific

The rating board for the video game industry announced a new age category to fill the gap between "E" for everyone and "T" for teen.

New rating category
E10+ (Everyone 10 and older)
▶ Ages 10 and up
▶ May contain more cartoon, fantasy or mild violence, mild profanity and/or minimally suggestive themes

Existing rating categories

	EC (Early Childhood)	E (Everyone)	T (Teen)	M (Mature)	AO (Adults Only)
Ages	3+	6+	13+	17+	18+
May contain	No material parents would find inappropriate	Minimal cartoon, fantasy or mild violence and/or infrequent use of mild language	Violence, suggestive themes, crude humor, minimal blood and/or infrequent use of strong language	Mature sexual themes, more intense violence and/or strong language	Graphic depictions of sex and/ or violence

SOURCE: Entertainment Software Rating Board

Ratings for video games

- Agencies such as police departments, civil defense units, rescue squads, or the Red Cross evaluate their performance in crisis situations to refine their responses.

- Every job applicant is evaluated by the employer — and every job applicant also evaluates the employer, the workplace, and the job offer.

In Your Community.   Written evaluation is common in our daily lives.

- In a posting to an online discussion group, you might explain your evaluation of the topic or of comments of others in the group.

- Friends, peers, or co-workers may ask you to write a letter of recommendation for a job or a commendation for an award. In either case, you'll evaluate relevant characteristics of performance or merit.

- Parents may evaluate the suitability of video games for their children based on industry ratings.

Chapter 12
Supporting a Position with Sources

 Electronic Resources

Search databases listed by subject:

Architecture	General
Art	Genealogy
Biography	Government
Business	Health
Education	History
Encyclopedia	Images

Responding to an Image

These images show activities that might help a student gather evidence from sources to support a position in a college paper. What does each image suggest about possible sources? What do the images suggest about the process of inquiry? Which activities look most intriguing? What other activities might have appeared in images on this page?

Suppose you conducted a survey at your school, asking a random group of students nearing graduation to describe a typical college writing assignment. The odds are good that the typical assignment might boil down to reading a few texts and writing a paper about them. Simple as this description sounds, it does suggest what you probably expect from a college education: an opportunity to absorb and think seriously about provocative ideas. It also suggests the values that lie behind many college expectations—a deep respect for the process of inquiry (the academic method of asking and investigating intriguing questions) and for the products of disciplined inquiry (the analyses, interpretations, and studies that are well regarded in each academic field).

When you first tackle such assignments, you may wonder "How do I figure out what my instructor really wants?" or "How could I possibly do that?" In response, you may turn to peripheral questions such as "How long does my paper have to be?" or "How many sources do I have to use?" instead of facing the central question: "How can I learn the skills I need to use a few sources to develop and support a position in a college paper?" Unlike a presidential debate or a Super Bowl game, a paper that takes a position generally doesn't have two distinct sides or a single winner. Instead of pitting either/or alternatives against each other, the writer of a typical college paper makes a point by joining the ongoing exchange of ideas about a topic that intrigues or challenges others in the field. Each paper builds on and responds to the exchanges of the past—the articles, essays, reports, books, and other texts that convey the perspectives, research findings, and conclusions of others. Although reading such sources may seem daunting, it is a reassuring expectation. After all, you are not expected to know everything yourself but simply to work conscientiously at learning what others know. Your paper, in turn, advances or redirects the exchange in order to convey your well-grounded point of view or to defend your well-reasoned interpretation.

Learning from Other Writers

■ For more on thesis and support, see Chs. 17 and 19.

■ For more such writings, visit <bedfordstmartins.com/bedguide> and do a keyword search:

examples

The selections here illustrate how two different writers draw on evidence from sources to substantiate their points. The notes in the margin of the first reading will help you begin to analyze features such as the thesis, or main idea, and the variety of methods used to introduce and integrate information from sources.

As You Read These Essays That Support a Position with Sources

As you read these essays, ask yourself the following questions:

1. What thesis, or main idea, expresses the position supported by the essay? How does the writer try to help readers appreciate the importance of this position?

2. In what ways does the writer use information from sources to develop and support a thesis? Do you find this information relevant and persuasive?

3. How does the writer vary the way each source is introduced and the way information is drawn from it?

This excerpt comes from David Callahan's book The Cheating Culture: Why More Americans Are Doing Wrong to Get Ahead *(2004). This selection illustrates the use of MLA style to cite and list sources.*

David Callahan
A Question of Character

Opinion surveys confirm an explosion of material° desires over the past two decades, along with a growing focus on financial success and the increasing linkage in people's minds between meeting these goals and achieving happiness. For example, in 1975, less than 20 percent of Americans surveyed identified a vacation home as being part of the "good life." By the early 1990s, that number had jumped to 35 percent. Less than 15 percent of people put a swimming pool in their dream scenario° in 1975; in 1991, nearly a third of people did. A second car and a second color television became far more important during this period as well, as did travel abroad° and having fashionable clothes.

Financial goals also began pushing aside other aspirations.° The number of Americans who saw the good life as hinging on "a lot of money" and "a job that pays more than average" jumped substantially in the 1980s, rising from a minority of Americans who emphasized these two goals to a majority. As Americans expanded the list of material possessions that they saw as central to the good life, they de-emphasized the importance of other aspects° of life. Even as more people admitted hankering after° swimming pools and vacation homes, they also reported a declining focus on having a happy marriage or an interesting job (Ladd and Bowman 51).

The shifting values and priorities of Americans over the past two decades have been especially evident among young people. Since 1966, the Cooperation Institutional Research Program has tracked the attitudes and demographic° characteristics of college freshman (Astin et al.). Over 700 campuses participate in the surveys every year. In all, more than nine million students have been surveyed. The trends among freshmen perfectly illustrate the rise of the money obsession and the sidelining of less materialistic goals.

In the first years of the survey, during the late 1960s, less than 50 percent of college freshman saw the goal of being well-off financially as either essential or very important, and just over half said the chief benefit of a college education is that it increased their earning potential. The shift toward materialism° among

1 THESIS
Presenting position

Point 1: goal shifts in general population

2
Supporting evidence, including facts, statistics, and examples to demonstrate a change

Paraphrase (see pp. 218–19)
Source authors and page in parentheses

3 Point 2: goal shifts among young people

Et al. ("and others") used for source with more than three authors

Author's position based on sources cited in next paragraphs

4

---

material: Concerning monetary, as opposed to spiritual, value; concerning physical possessions.   **scenario:** Situation.   **abroad:** Outside of one's country.   **aspirations:** Dreams; goals.   **aspects:** Parts.   **hankering after:** Desiring.   **demographic:** Referring to the characteristics of certain populations.   **materialism:** A concern with physical or material security or possessions rather than intellectual or spiritual pursuits.

young people began in the mid-1970s, as the idealism° of the 1960s faded and harsh new economic times arrived. For example, the number of students who said they went to college to "make more money" climbed ten percentage points in just three years, beginning in 1976. By the mid-1980s, three-quarters of college students stressed the goal of being well-off financially, a ratio that held through the 1990s. Today, this goal remains one of two or three of the highest-rated objectives of college freshman, along with the status-oriented goal of becoming "an authority in my field" (Astin et al. 46–47).

Paraphrase
(see pp. 218–19)

Direct quotation
(see pp. 214–15)
Source author and
page numbers cited in
parentheses.

By 1986, more than a quarter of college freshman reported that they 5
planned to go into business, a career choice that trumped° the closest rival by nearly three to one. This was also the year in which 40 percent of Yale's graduating class of 1,300 applied for a job at one investment bank alone, First Boston. Economics courses were oversubscribed° at Yale and other top universities as students hurried to qualify themselves to join the gold rush on Wall Street. The promise of vast riches had an intoxicating° appeal and was not illusory.° "Never before have so many unskilled twenty-four-year-olds made so much money in so little time as did in this decade," wrote Yale graduate Michael Lewis, who joined Salomon Brothers.° (This statement, of course, would be dated by the dot-com era° [Lewis, *Liar's* 24, 9].)

Short version of title
used because two works
by Michael Lewis are
cited (see para. 7)

As making money moved front and center, young people stopped caring 6
about other things. In the late 1960s, believe it or not, the most important goal of college freshman was "developing a meaningful philosophy of life," cited by over 80 percent of entering students. The centrality of this goal waned° steadily over the next twenty years, reaching an all-time low of 39 percent in 1987, at the height of the '80s boom. Interest in keeping up with politics and cleaning up the environment also markedly — and permanently — declined during the 1980s. The outlook among America's young was epitomized° by Alex Keaton, the teenage star of the hit television show *Family Ties*. Alex was a briefcase-toting° microyuppie,° played brilliantly by Michael J. Fox. To the horror of his bohemian° parents, he was all business and money, brandishing° an inch-thick résumé in one episode. Alex never doubted that kids like him were the wave of the future.

Author continues
statement-support pattern

He was right. While young people's interest in mainstream business ca- 7
reers dipped sharply after the crash of 1987,° the money obsession morphed° into a new kind of market populism° by the late 1990s. Making money was

Transition from previous
point

---

idelism: A concern with high-minded, as opposed to practical, goals.   **trumped:** Defeated.   **oversubscribed:** Overenrolled.   **intoxicating:** Creating enthusiasm; having an effect like alcohol.   **illusory:** Imaginary.   **Salomon Brothers:** An investment bank. **dot-com era:** The period, roughly 1997–2001, when many Internet businesses saw sharp increases in their stock values and received large amounts of investor funds.   **waned:** Declined.   **epitomized:** Clearly illustrated.   **briefcase-toting:** Briefcase-carrying. **microyuppie:** Small, referring to Fox's short stature, young urban professional.   **bohemian:** Artistic or unconventional.   **brandishing:** Shaking or waving.   **crash of 1987:** A record-breaking plunge in the Dow Jones Industrial Average, a measure of stock-market value.   **morphed:** Changed.   **populism:** A concern with the interests of the average person.

way cool, and you didn't need a suit to do it. Teenagers swapped stock tips and traded over the Internet during lunch breaks. One fifteen-year-old in New Jersey amassed° a nearly million-dollar fortune by masquerading° as multiple people on Yahoo! and hyping° low-priced stocks. The money was rolling in until SEC° investigators arrived at his door (Lewis, "Jonathan" 26). Other teenagers built technology companies in their refinished basements, imagining themselves as the next Steve Jobs.° If Alex Keaton came back to the future° of the late 1990s, he would have staged an IPO° from his bedroom.

For young people, though, the biggest social-health story of the 1990s was **8** the onslaught° of a virulent° new strain of consumerism. The disease begins earlier and earlier with children these days, and it just gets worse. Parents complain endlessly about pressures from their kids to keep up with the Johnnies at the locker next door — with expensive video games, designer-label clothing, digital music players (to play pirated music), home computers, and cell phones. "Over the past ten years, more people have come to think of themselves as having their identities shaped by their consumer goods," commented Alissa Quart, author of *Branded*, a book about consumerism among teenagers. "But teens and tweens° are more vulnerable° and more open to a warped° relationship that the brands are selling to them. It's an emptied-out relationship where they pour themselves into a brand and see themselves through objects, rather than through people or ideas" (qtd. in Holstein). Quart's book is filled with stories about sixth graders lusting after $500 Kate Spade bags and startling statistics, like how kids spend $600 billion a year of their parents' money and advertisers spend $12 billion a year to influence those buying decisions. She also shows the way in which movies and television programs about teenagers now emphasize an amazingly opulent° lifestyle in places like Beverly Hills.°

A bit of competitive spending might be fine if it weren't so hard to keep **9** up with those who set today's standards of material well-being. As Juliet Schor has documented in *The Overspent American*, nobody actually compares themselves anymore to the Joneses of yesteryear — that is, the next-door neighbor in a similar income group. We are now likely to compare ourselves with "reference groups" who make much more money than we do. If you're rich, you compare yourself to the superrich. You don't want a "McMansion,"° you want a real mansion — like the one you saw lovingly

Marginal notes:

Short title added to identify which work by Lewis

Synthesis and application of ideas (see p. 224)

Point 3: shift toward consumerism

Source quoted in another source, no page needed for one-page article

Summary of information (see p. 220)

---

amassed: Collected; accumulated.   **masquerading:** Playing the role of; acting as. **hyping:** Speaking with excessive enthusiasm about something.   **SEC:** Securities and Exchange Commission, the U.S. government body that investigates misdeeds related to stock trading.   **Steve Jobs:** Cofounder and chief executive officer of Apple Computer. **back to the future:** Reference to the title of the 1985 film in which the main character, played by Michael J. Fox, travels back in time, where he puts his future existence at risk. **IPO:** Initial public offering, a company's first sale of stock on the public market.   **onslaught:** Attack.   **virulent:** Dangerously potent.   **tweens:** Young people *between* childhood and their teenage years.   **vulnerable:** Susceptible to; available to.   **warped:** Distorted.   **opulent:** Luxurious.   **Beverly Hills:** A wealthy part of Los Angeles. **"McMansion":** A large home that, like McDonald's hamburgers, is mass-produced and appeals to many people.

described in a rerun of *Lifestyles of the Rich and Famous*. If you're upper middle class, you compare yourself to the rich. If you're middle class or lower class, you might compare yourself to both the upper middle class and the rich (Schor). . . .

Conclusion underscoring position

With pressures like these, it's no surprise that many Americans believe 10 that more money would make them happier. And yet, like a mirage,° people's definition of enough money keeps flitting° farther into the distance. Between 1987 and 1996, a period of only modest income gains for most households, the estimate among Americans as to how much annual income they needed to live in "reasonable comfort" increased by 30 percent, while the amount of money they felt they would need to fulfill all their dreams nearly doubled, from $50,000 to $90,000. According to one survey conducted in the early '90s, 85 percent of American households aspired° to have a lifestyle associated with those in the top fifth of the income ladder. Only 15 percent said they would be satisfied ending up as middle class or just "living a comfortable life." A majority of Americans consistently report that they don't have enough income to live the life they want. Gaps between financial dreams and realities are hardly new in America. Some might even say that these gaps are what America is all about and that they are a good thing, keeping people on their toes and the economy humming. Yet there's a fine line between aspiration and envy, and between a healthy desire to get ahead and a relentless° struggle to keep up. Judging by poll data, America crossed that line quite a while ago (Schor 13; Ladd and Bowman 95).

Each source cited in Callahan's essay listed alphabetically by author, with full publication information; first line of entry at left margin; subsequent lines indented ½"

Section and page both supplied for a newspaper article

Author's name listed only once for two works by the same author

Works Cited

Astin, Alexander W., et al. *The American Freshman: Thirty-Year Trends*. Los Angeles: Higher Education Research Institute, 1997. Print.

Holstein, William. "Marketers Crank It Up for a New Generation." *New York Times* 26 Jan. 2003: III6. Print.

Ladd, Everett Carll, and Karlyn H. Bowman. *Attitudes toward Economic Inequality*. Washington: AEI, 1988. Print.

Lewis, Michael. "Jonathan Lebed's Extracurricular Activities." *New York Times Magazine* 25 Feb. 2001: 26+. Print.

---. *Liar's Poker*. New York: Penguin, 1989. Print.

Quart, Alissa. *Branded: The Buying and Selling of Teenagers*. New York: Perseus, 2003. Print.

Schor, Juliet. *The Overspent American: Upscaling, Downshifting, and the New Consumer*. New York: Basic, 1998. Print.

Questions to Start You Thinking

Meaning

1. What position does Callahan take in this essay?

2. What age group particularly concerns Callahan? What has changed about this age group since the mid-1970s?

mirage: A shimmering illusion of water that appears in hot, dry places, like deserts.
flitting: Moving or shifting.   **aspired:** Hoped.   **relentless:** Never-ending.

3. In paragraph 9, Callahan refers to "competitive spending." What does he mean by this, and what has changed about such spending?

4. How has Callahan arranged the main points in his essay? How do these points develop his thesis (stated in paragraph 1) and lead up to paragraph 10?

Writing Strategies

5. What types of evidence does Callahan use to support his position? How convincing is this evidence to you?

6. Callahan states most source information in his own words rather than quoting sources directly. What seem to be the advantages and disadvantages of these two approaches?

7. How would you describe Callahan's tone, the quality of his writing that reveals his attitude toward his topic and his readers? What specific words, phrases, or sentences contribute to his tone? Does the tone seem appropriate for his purpose and audience?

8. Compare this selection, excerpted from a book, with an article written for a newspaper (see, for example, "Katrina Documentary Gives Voice to Survivors," p. 187). What differences in formatting, style, and presentation do you notice between the two selections?

STUDENT ESSAY

Melissa Lamberth

Overworked!

In the song "Nine to Five," Dolly Parton speaks for the overworked employee whose life is drained away by the clock. The amount of time Americans are working is on the increase, and Americans are growing weary.° Shorter workdays or more opportunities to take time off need to be available in order to provide a safer, happier, and more energetic workplace.

In her book *The Overworked American*, Schor writes, "The rise of work time was unexpected. For nearly a hundred years, hours had been declining. When this decline abruptly° ended in the late 1940s, it marked the beginning of a new era in work time" (1). Schor explains how this surprising increase has grown during recent years: "Each year, the change is small, amounting to about nine hours, or slightly more than one additional day of work. In any given year, such a small increment° has probably been imperceptible,° but the accumulated increase over two decades is substantial" (2). If Americans are gaining a little over a day of work each year, that is over ten days in a decade! This does not leave much time for family responsibilities or, much less, for leisure time.

1

2

Melissa Lamberth wrote this essay for a composition course at Riverside Community College. She used MLA style to cite and list sources. For more on this citation style, see E1–E2 in the Quick Research Guide (the dark-red-edged pages).

❓ *Do you feel overworked? Why or why not?*

weary: Tired.   **abruptly:** Suddenly.   **increment:** Unit (of growth, in this case). **imperceptible:** Not noticeable.

Overworked employees may present a problem not only in the household but   3
also in the workplace and even on the road. In his essay "Four Weeks Vacation,"
Robinson writes, "The health implications° of sleep-deprived° motorists weaving
their way to the office or operating machinery on the job are self-evident" (481). An
employee may work a couple of hours of overtime, drive home in traffic for half an
hour or an hour, cook or eat dinner with the family, and then clean up after dinner.
On top of that, there are errands to run and bills to pay. How much time does that
leave the individual to rest? This schedule easily could lead to a "sleep-deprived mo-
torist" or an injured machine operator.

The toll that overworked employees take on the family is also evident. In recent   4
years, it has become more and more common for both parents to go to work to support the family. Time is a very important factor in keeping relationships in the
household healthy. If both parents are spending a majority of their time working, it
may be very difficult to find time to raise the kids and keep a marriage intact. In an
article titled "Just What the Worker Needs — Longer Days, No Overtime," Eisenbrey
writes, "Women are working many more weeks per year and hours per week, on average, than they did 30 or even 10 years ago. Middle-class married couples with children and a head of household between the ages of 25 and 54 now work an average
of 98 weeks a year, compared with 78 weeks in 1969. Overtime for either spouse —
but especially the mother — can have serious effects on a family."

*What do you
think of these ideas?
Are they practical?*

All these added stresses, caused by overworking, are carried straight back to the   5
workplace the next morning. Negative attitudes set in. Employees start to hate work.
As a result, morale goes down in the workplace. It is a vicious° cycle that Americans
are stuck in. How can this cycle be stopped? Overtime, for one thing, should not be
required but only allowed as an option. If employees have too much extra work to do,
employers should consider giving the work to someone else. This could mean hiring
another employee or dividing the extra work among employees who are not as busy.

Employees also need to have more opportunities to take time off. If the employee   6
can't take desired time off due to a heavy workload, which is common in the workplace, employers need to consider hiring temporary employees or going through a
temp agency to find employees who will work during the regular employee's time off.
This work relief will make for a happier, less stressed employee. In an SFGate.com
article titled "You Deserve a Month Off," columnist Mark Morford wrote, "We need more
time off. A lot more time. Longer vacations. Extended breaks. Chunks of contiguous°
time which you can roll around on the tongue of your id° and feel all swoony° and

---

implications: Consequences.   **sleep-deprived:** Lacking restorative slumber.   **vicious:**
Harmful; nasty.   **contiguous:** Uninterrupted.   **id:** The part of the personality concerned with instincts and basic needs.   **swoony:** Given to fainting (in this case, out of
happiness).

blissed.° When's the last time you saw an unhappy Aussie°? Exactly." Morford is implying that employees need more time off in order to be happier. He went on to say,
"It prevents burnouts and ameliorates° loathings° and lightens the spirit and lets
the psyche° breathe. . . ."

Some employers may claim that hiring temporary employees so that an   7
employee can have time off would not be cost-effective. However, good employees
are valuable. With that value in mind, hiring someone for a couple of weeks would
be worthwhile so that the regular employee could come back to work rested, re-
freshed, and more productive than ever!

Employers may believe that family- and life-related programs that teach employ-   8
ees how to manage stress and time are the answers to stress in the workplace. That
notion may lead some employees to question "Where are we going to get the time
for such programs?!?" They have their kids' soccer and softball games, meetings with
teachers, dinner to cook, and laundry to do. Employees simply have no time to be
involved in those programs.

An October 11, 2005, press release from an organization named Take Back Your   9
Time announced the sixty-fifth anniversary of the forty-hour workweek (Burger). In
its honor, this group declared October 24th Take Back Your Time Day. In the press release, John de Graaf, Take Back Your Time's national coordinator, stated, "It's 65
years later, productivity is quadruple what it was then, and still most Americans are
working more than 40 hours a week. If 40 hours was enough to support a family   *If you had more
then, it should take even less work time now. We need to start by getting the work-   time, what would you
week back down to 40 hours." The organization is fighting for protected 40-hour   do with it?*
workweeks and for higher wages so that Americans don't have to work more than 40
hours to support a family above the poverty line. They are also fighting for salaried
workers who work long hours to be given comp time° for time required of them by
their employers that goes over the 40-hour workweek and for time-and-a-half overtime premiums° to be protected and strengthened.

These goals are positive stepping stones that will lead to a more positive work-   10
place. There should be no need for more than 40 hours of work each week when Americans didn't need to work this much 65 years ago. Technology has radically increased
productivity. Employers need to embrace this and "let their people go!" Let them take
an extra week off! Let them opt out of overtime! Let them get off work a couple of
hours early! In the long run, employees won't be let go, in the literal° sense, because
they will be more productive and punctual.° And that is well worth it.

---

blissed: Happy.   **Aussie:** Australian.   **ameliorates:** Makes better.   **loathings:** Ha-
treds.   **psyche:** Mind.   **comp time:** Compensatory time—time off given for extra
time worked.   **premiums:** Extra payments.   **literal:** Referring to the exact meaning of
a word or expression.   **punctual:** On time.

Works Cited

Burger, Gretchen. "Take Back Your Time." *Take Back Your Time*. CRESP at Cornell U, 11
Oct. 2005. Web. 15 Oct. 2005.

Eisenbrey, Ross. "Just What the Worker Needs--Longer Days, No Overtime."
Los Angeles Times. Los Angeles Times, 14 Feb. 2003. Web. 16 Oct. 2005.

Morford, Mark. "You Deserve a Month Off." *SFGate*. Hearst Communications, 19 Apr.
2002. Web. 12 Oct. 2005.

Robinson, Joe. "Four Weeks Vacation." *The Bedford Guide for College Writers*. 7th ed.
Ed. X. J. Kennedy, Dorothy M. Kennedy, Sylvia A. Holladay, and Marcia F. Muth.
Boston: Bedford, 2005. 479–84. Print.

Schor, Juliet B. *The Overworked American: The Unexpected Decline of Leisure*. New
York: Basic, 1992. Print.

Questions to Start You Thinking

Meaning

1. What position does Lamberth support in this essay?

2. According to Lamberth, what difficulties and risks do overworked people
face inside and outside of work?

3. What responsibilities do employers have to improve the lives of overworked
employees, according to the author?

Writing Strategies

4. What types of evidence does Lamberth use to support her position? How
convincing is this evidence to you?

5. Has Lamberth considered alternative views? How does the inclusion (or
lack) of these views contribute to or detract from the essay?

6. Exclamation points are used in several places. Do you find this to be an effective or ineffective stylistic choice?

7. Using highlighters or marginal notes, identify the essay's introduction, thesis, major points, supporting evidence for each point, and conclusion. How
effective is the organization of this essay?

Learning by Writing

■ For writing activities
on supporting a position
with sources, visit
<bedfordstmartins.com/
bedguide> and do a
keyword search:

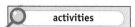
activities

THE ASSIGNMENT: SUPPORTING A POSITION WITH SOURCES

Identify a cluster of readings about a topic that interests you. For example,
choose some related readings from one of the thematic groups in *A Writer's
Reader*, select several related essays from different thematic groups there, or
draw on a group of related readings assigned in your class. If your topic is

assigned and you don't begin with any particular interest in it, develop your intellectual curiosity by looking for an angle, an implication, or a vantage point that will engage you or relate in some way to your own experience. Read (or reread) the selections, allowing your curiosity to stimulate your thinking as you consider how each supports, challenges, or deepens your understanding of the topic.

Based on the information in your cluster of readings, develop an enlightening position about the topic that you'd like to share with an audience of college readers. Support this position — your working thesis — using quotations, paraphrases, summaries, and syntheses of the information in the readings as evidence. As you write your paper, be careful to present your information from sources clearly and to credit your sources appropriately.

■ See the contents of *A Writer's Reader* on p. 438.

Papers written in response to this type of assignment encompass great variety:

> One student examined local language usage that combined words from English and Spanish, drawing on essays about language diversity to analyze the patterns and implications of such usage.

> Another writer used a cluster of readings about technology to evaluate the looming privacy issues on a popular Web site for student profiles.

> Yet another, based on personal experience with a blended family and several essays about families, investigated and challenged misconceptions about family units today.

GENERATING IDEAS

Pin Down Your Working Topic and Your Cluster of Readings.   Try to specify what you're going to work on. This task is relatively easy if your instructor has assigned the topic and the required set of readings. If not, figure out what limits your instructor has set and which decisions are yours. Carefully follow any directions about the number or types of sources that you are expected to use. Instead of hunting only for sources that share your initial views about the topic, look for a variety of reliable and relevant sources so that you can broaden, even challenge, your perspective.

■ For more strategies for generating ideas, see Ch. 16.

Consider Your Audience.   You are writing for an audience of college readers intrigued by your topic (unless your instructor specifies some other group). In addition, your instructor probably holds several expectations. One is a broad goal, making sure that you are prepared to succeed when you take on future college writing assignments, including full research papers. For this reason, you'll be expected to quote, paraphrase, and summarize information from sources. Each time you use such material, you'll also need to introduce — or launch — it and credit its source, thus demonstrating essential skills for source-based writing.

■ For advice about finding and evaluating academic sources, turn to B and C in the Quick Research Guide (the dark-red-edged pages).

In addition, your instructor will want to see your own position emerge from the swamp of information that you are reading. Even if you feel that

One Student Thinking through a Topic
General Subject: Men and Women (Ch. 24)
Assigned topic: State and support a position about differences in the behavior of men and women.

What do I know about?

What do I care about?

RECALL PERSONAL EXPERIENCES: Friends at school? Competition for jobs? Pressure on parents to be good role models?

CONSIDER READINGS: Barry? Ehrenreich? Brady? Perrin? Staples? Jensen?

- *Stereotypes of women—emotional and caring*
- *Stereotypes of men—tough and agressive*
- *What about me? I'm a woman in training to be a police officer—and I'm a mother. I'm emotional, caring, aggressive, and tough.*

I bet that men and women are more alike than different. What do the readings say? What evidence do they present?

- **RETURN TO THE READINGS.**
- **TEST AND REFINE YOUR WORKING THESIS.**
- **LOOK FOR EVIDENCE.**

your ideas are like a prehistoric creature, dripping as it struggles out of the swamp onto solid ground, encourage your creature to reach dry land. Jot down your own ideas whenever they pop into mind. Highlight them in color on the page or on the screen. Store them in your writing notebook or in a special file so that you can find them, watch them accumulate, and give them well-deserved prominence in your paper.

■ For more on generating ideas, see Ch. 16.

Take an Academic Approach.   As a writer, you'll find that your experience and imagination remain your own deep well, an endless reservoir from which you can draw ideas whenever you need them. When you write an academic paper, this deep well may help you identify an intriguing topic, raise a compelling question about it, or pursue an unusual slant. For example, you might recall talking with your grandmother about the high cost of her prescriptions and decide to investigate the controversy about importing low-cost prescription medications from other countries.

■ For more on reading critically, see Ch. 2.

Besides drawing on your personal reserves, you'll also be expected to investigate your topic using authoritative sources. These sources—articles,

Facing the Challenge: Finding Your Voice

The major challenge that writers face when using sources to support a position is finding their own voices. You create your voice as a college writer through your choice of language, choice of words, and angle of vision. You probably want to present yourself as a reasonable writer with credible and engaging insights, a thoughtful person a reader will want to hear from. Finding your own voice may be especially difficult because of the complicated process of writing a source-based paper. After all, you need to read carefully to identify information that might strengthen or deepen your discussion. You need to select and capture that information by quoting, paraphrasing, or summarizing. You need to find a place for it in your draft, introduce it, feed it in, and, of course, credit it. By the time you've done all of this, you'll probably feel that your sources have taken over your paper. You may feel that there's no room left for your own voice and, even if there were, it's too soft or shy to jostle past the powerful words of your sources. That, however, is your challenge.

As you develop your voice as a college writer and use it to guide your readers' understanding, you'll restrict your sources to their proper role, acting as supporting evidence. Don't let them get pushy or dominate your writing. Use these questions to help you strengthen your voice:

For more on evidence, see pp. 37–42 and pp. 152–56.

- Can you write out a list or informal passage explaining what you'd like readers to hear from your voice? Where could you add more of this in your draft?

- Have you used your own voice, not quotations or paraphrases from sources, to introduce your topic, state your thesis, and draw your conclusions?

- Have you generally relied on your own voice to open and conclude your paragraphs and to reinforce your main ideas in every passage?

- Have you alternated between your voice and the voices of your sources? Can you strengthen your voice if it gets trampled by a herd of sources?

- Have you used your voice to identify and introduce source material before you present it? Have you used your voice to explain or interpret source material after you include it?

- Have you used your voice to tell readers why your sources are relevant, how they support your points, and what their limits might be?

- Have you carefully created your voice as a college writer, balancing passion and personality with rock-solid reasoning?

Whenever you are uncertain about the answers to these questions, make an electronic copy of your file or print it out. Highlight all of the wording in your own voice in a bright, visible color. Check for the presence and prominence of this highlighting, and then revise the white patches (the material drawn from sources) as needed to strengthen your voice.

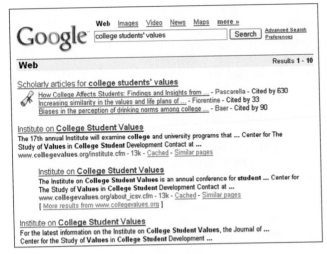

Web search

essays, reports, books, Web pages, and other reliable materials — are your second deep well. When one well runs dry for the moment, start pumping the other. As you use your critical reading skills to tap your second reservoir, you join the academic exchange. This exchange is the flow of knowledge from one credible source to the next as writers and researchers raise questions, seek answers, evaluate information, and advance knowledge. As you inquire about your topic, you'll move from what you already know to deeper knowledge and a more complex appreciation of varied perspectives on the topic. Welcome sources that shed light on your inquiry rather than simply agree with a view you already hold.

Skim Your Sources.   When you work with a cluster of readings, you'll need to read them carefully and probably repeatedly. Start out, however, by skimming — quickly reading only enough to find out how the reading is organized and what direction it takes. First, leaf through the reading, glancing at any headings or figure labels. Return to the first paragraph, read it in full, but then read only the first sentence of each subsequent paragraph. At the end, read the final paragraph in full. Then stop to consider what you've already learned about the reading. Do the same with your other selections, classifying or comparing them as you begin to think about what they might contribute to your paper.

Here are a few questions to help you begin the process of juggling your ideas, your sources, and your instructor's expectations:

DISCOVERY CHECKLIST

___ What topic have you been assigned or are you considering? What ideas about it can you generate using brainstorming, freewriting, or another strategy for generating ideas?

___ What cluster of readings will you begin with? What do you already know about these readings? What have you learned about them simply by skimming them?

___ What purpose would you like to achieve in your paper? Who is your primary audience? What will your instructor expect you to accomplish?

___ What clues about how to proceed can you draw from the two sample essays in this chapter or from other readings that your instructor has identified as useful models?

Evaluating Reliable Sources

When you select your own sources, you'll need to evaluate them to be certain that they are reliable choices that your audience will respect. When your sources are identified in your assignment, you'll still need to know their strengths, weaknesses, and limitations so that you introduce and use them effectively. Bring your articles, essays, and other sources to a small-group evaluation session. Using the guidelines in C3 in the Quick Research Guide (the dark-red-edged pages), discuss your common sources or a key source selected by each writer in the group. Look for aspects that you might mention in a paper to bolster a source's credibility with readers (for example, the author's professional affiliation) as well as for limitations that might restrict what the sources can substantiate.

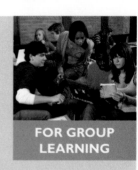

FOR GROUP LEARNING

PLANNING, DRAFTING, AND DEVELOPING

Start with a Working Thesis. Sometimes you start reading for a source-based paper with a clear position in mind; other times, you begin simply with your initial response to your cluster of sources. Either way, try to state your main idea as a working thesis even if you expect to rewrite it — or even replace it — later on. Once your thesis takes shape in words, you can assess the richness and relevance of your reading based on a clear main idea.

■ For more on stating a thesis, see pp. 312–19.

■ For exercises on choosing effective thesis statements, visit <bedfordstmartins.com/ bedguide> and do a keyword search:

thesis

FIRST RESPONSE TO SOURCES	Joe Robinson, author of "Four Weeks Vacation," and others say that workers need more vacation time, but I can't see my boss agreeing to this.
WORKING THESIS	Although most workers would like longer vacations, many employers do not believe that they would benefit, too.

Read Each Source Thoughtfully. Before you begin copying quotations from a source, read it through, slowly and carefully, in order to understand what it says. During this reading, don't scribble notes or vigorously highlight. Simply read. After you have figured out what the source says and how it develops its ideas, you are ready to decide how you might use its information to support your own ideas. Read again, this time sifting and selecting as you try to discover what's relevant to your thesis. Think also about the contribution of each source to the academic exchange.

- How does the source use its own sources to support its position?
- Does it review major sources chronologically (by date), thematically (by topic), or by some other method?
- Does it use sources to supply background for its own position? Does it compare its position or research findings with those of other studies?
- What audience does the source address? What was its author's purpose?
- How might you want to use the source as you contribute to the exchange?

Join the Academic Exchange.   When you find a well-researched article that follows academic conventions, it identifies its sources for several reasons. First, it gives honest credit to the work on which it relies — work done by other researchers and writers. They deserve this credit because they have provided useful information that has contributed to the article's credibility and substantiated its points. In addition, the article informs you about its sources so that you, or any other reader, could find them yourself.

The visual on pages 216–17 illustrates how this exchange of ideas and information works and how you, from the moment you begin to use sources in your college writing, join this exchange. The middle of the visual shows the opening of a sample article about a global health problem: obesity. Because this article appears online, it credits its sources by providing a link to each one. A comparable printed article might identify its sources by supplying brief in-text citations (in parentheses in MLA style and APA style), footnotes, numbers keyed to its references, or source identifications in the text itself. To the left of and below the source article are several of its sources. (They, in turn, also supply information about their sources.) The column to the right of the source article illustrates ways that you might capture information from the source.

For more on plagiarism, see D1 in the Quick Research Guide (the dark red-edged pages).

For an avoiding-plagiarism tutorial, visit <bedfordstmartins.com/rewriting>.

For more on critical reading, see Ch. 2.

For more on citing and listing sources, see E1 and E2 in the Quick Research Guide (the dark-red-edged pages).

Capture Information and Record Source Details.   Consider how you might eventually want to capture each significant passage or point from a source in your paper — by quoting the exact words of the source, by paraphrasing its ideas in your own words, or by summarizing its essential point. Keeping accurate notes and records as you work with your sources will help you avoid accidental plagiarism (using someone else's words or ideas without giving the credit due). Accurate notes also help to reduce errors or missing information when you add the source material to your draft.

As you capture information, also plan ahead so that you can acknowledge each source following academic conventions. Record the details about the source necessary to identify it in your discussion and to list it with other sources at the end of your paper. Using examples for a paper that relates land use and threats to wildlife, like the tortoise, the next sections illustrate how to capture and credit your sources. Compare the examples with the original passage from the source.

Identify Significant Quotations.   When an author expresses an idea so memorably that you want to reproduce those words exactly, quote them word for word. Direct quotations can add life, color, and authority to your paper. On the other hand, too many quotations can drown your voice and overshadow your point.

ORIGINAL   The tortoise is a creature that has survived virtually unchanged
              since it first appeared in the geologic record more than 150 mil-
              lion years ago. The species became threatened, however, when

ranchers began driving their herds onto Mojave Desert lands for
spring grazing, at the very time that the tortoise awakens from
hibernation and emerges from its burrows to graze on the greening desert shrubs and grasses. As livestock trampled the burrows
and monopolized the scarce desert vegetation, tortoise populations plummeted. (page 152)

Babbitt, Bruce. *Cities in the Wilderness: A New Vision of Land Use
    in America*. Washington: Island Press-Shearwater Books, 2005.
    Print.

TOO MUCH QUOTATION   When "tortoise populations plummeted," a species "that has
survived virtually unchanged since it first appeared in the geologic record more than 150 million years ago" (Babbitt 152) had
losses that helped to justify setting workable boundaries for the
future expansion of Las Vegas.

MEMORABLE QUOTATION   When "tortoise populations plummeted" (Babbitt 152), an
unlikely species that has endured for millions of years helped to establish workable boundaries for the future expansion of Las Vegas.

Most writers begin by highlighting or copying too many quotations,
often because they are still struggling to master the ideas in the source. The
better you understand both the reading and your own thesis, the more effectively you'll choose quotations. After all, a quotation in itself is not necessarily effective evidence, and too many quotations will suggest that your writing is padded or lacks original thought.

HOW TO QUOTE

- Select a quotation that is both notable and pertinent to your thesis.
- Record it accurately, writing out exactly what it says. Include its punctuation
  and capitalization. Avoid abbreviations that might later be ambiguous.
- Mark both its beginning and ending with quotation marks.
- Note the page or other location (such as an electronic paragraph) where
  the quotation appears. If the quotation begins on one page but ends on
  another, mark where the switch occurs so that the credit in your draft will
  be accurate no matter how much of the quotation you eventually use.
- Double-check the accuracy of each quotation as you record it.

For more on quota-
tions, see D3 in the Quick
Research Guide (the
dark-red-edged pages).

Use an ellipsis mark — three spaced dots (. . .) within a sentence or four dots
(. . . .), a period and three spaced dots, concluding a sentence — to show
where you leave out any original wording. You may omit wording that doesn't
relate to your point, but don't distort the original meaning. For example, if a
reviewer calls a movie "a perfect example of poor directing and inept acting,"
don't quote this comment as "perfect . . . directing and . . . acting."

For more on punctuat-
ing quotations and using
ellipsis marks, see C3 in
the Quick Editing Guide
(the dark-blue-edged
pages).

THE ACADEMIC EXCHANGE

Suppose that you used the center article to support a position. The various ways you might use this source are shown on the right-hand page. In turn, your source drew on other writings, some of which are shown to the left of and below the center article.

Sources Cited in Your Source

Source: U.S. Department of Agriculture

<www.usda.gov>

AREI Chapter 3.5: Global Resources and Productivity

Keith Wiebe

Abstract—*Global food production has grown faster than population in recent decades, due largely to improved seeds and increased use of fertilizer and irrigation. Soil degradation which has slowed yield growth in some areas, depends on farmers' incentives to adopt conservation practices, but does not threaten food security at the global level.*

Introduction

Increased resource use and improvements in technology and efficiency have increased global food production more rapidly than population in recent decades, but 800 million people remain food insecure (fig. 3.5.1). . . .

Source: World Bank

<web.worldbank.org>

Poverty Analysis: Overview

Trends in poverty over time: Living Standards have improved...

Living standards have risen dramatically over the last decades. The proportion of the developing world's population living in extreme economic poverty -- defined as living on less than $1 per day ($1.08 in 1993 dollars, adjusted to account for differences in purchasing power across countries) -- has fallen from 28 percent in 1990 to 21 percent in 2001.

Substantial improvements in social indicators have accompanied growth in average incomes. Infant mortality rates in low- and middle-income countries have fallen from 86 per 1,000 live births in 1980 to 60 in 2002. Life expectancy in these countries has risen from 60 to 65 between 1980 and 2002. For more health, nutrition and population statistics, see the HNPStats database. . . .

Your Source <www.slate.com>

Please Do Not Feed the Humans

THE GLOBAL EXPLOSION OF FAT.
By William Saletan
Posted Saturday, Sept. 2, 2006, at 8:22 AM ET

In 1894, Congress established Labor Day to honor those who "from rude nature have delved and carved all the grandeur we behold." In the century since, the grandeur of human achievement has multiplied. Over the past four decades, global population has doubled, but food output, driven by increases in productivity, has outpaced it. Poverty, infant mortality, and hunger are receding. For the first time in our planet's history, a species no longer lives at the mercy of scarcity. We have learned to feed ourselves.

We've learned so well, in fact, that we're getting fat. Not just the United States or Europe, but the whole world. Egyptian, Mexican, and South African women are now as fat as Americans. Far more Filipino adults are now overweight than underweight. In China, one in five adults is too heavy, and the rate of overweight in children is 28 times higher than it was two decades ago. In Thailand, Kuwait, and Tunisia, obesity, diabetes, and heart disease are soaring.

Hunger is far from conquered. But since 1990, the global rate of malnutrition has declined an average of 1.7 percent a year. Based on data from the World Health Organization and the U.N. Food and Agriculture Organization, for every two people who are malnourished, three are now overweight or obese. Among women, even in most African countries, overweight has surpassed underweight. The balance of peril is shifting.

Indirect Source: U.S. Department of Labor

<www.dol.gov/opa/aboutdol/laborday.htm>

The History of Labor Day

Labor Day: How it Came About; What it Means

"Labor Day differs in every essential way from the other holidays of the year in any country," said Samuel Gompers, founder and longtime president of the American Federation of Labor. "All other holidays are in a more or less degree connected with conflicts and battles of man's prowess over man, of strife and discord for greed and power, of glories achieved by one nation over another. Labor Day...is devoted to no man, living or dead, to no sect, race, or nation."

Labor Day, the first Monday in September, is a creation of the labor movement and is dedicated to the social and economic achievements of American workers. It constitutes a yearly national tribute to the contributions workers have made to the strength, prosperity, and well-being of our country.

Founder of Labor Day

More than 100 years after the first Labor Day observance, there is still some doubt as to who first proposed the holiday for workers.

Some records show that Peter J. McGuire, general secretary of the Brotherhood of Carpenters and Joiners and a cofounder of the American Federation of Labor, was first in suggesting a day to honor those "who from rude nature have delved and carved all the grandeur we behold."

Information Captured from Your Source

Sample Working Thesis

A clear thesis statement establishes a framework for selecting source material as useful evidence and for explaining its relevance to readers.

> **WORKING THESIS:** In order to counter national and worldwide trends toward obesity, agricultural communities like Grand Junction need to apply their expertise as food producers to the promotion of healthy food products.

Quotation from an Indirect Source

A quotation from an indirect source captures the exact words of an author quoted within the source.

> An 1894 action by Congress created a holiday to recognize workers who "delved and carved" to produce what Americans enjoy (qtd. in Saletan).

If possible, go to the original source to be sure that the quotation is accurate and that you are using it appropriately. (See the bottom lefthand page.)

> Credit, though disputed, has gone to labor leader Peter McGuire for promoting the recognition of those who "delved and carved all the grandeur we behold" (US Dept. of Labor).

Quotation from a Source

A quotation captures the author's exact words directly from the source.

> As Saletan observes, "We have learned to feed ourselves," but the success of agricultural enterprise and technology does not guarantee that well-fed people are healthy.

Paraphrase of a Source

A paraphrase restates an author's specific ideas fully and accurately, using your own words and sentences.

> Though the number of hungry people drops nearly 2 percent annually, more people, including African women, are now overfed by a ratio of 3 to 2 and thus have traded the health risks of malnutrition for those of obesity (Saletan).

Summary of a Source

A summary reduces an author's main point to essentials, using your own words and sentences.

> Given that a worldwide shift in food security has led to an obesity epidemic (Saletan), consumers need lighter, healthier food options, a goal that the Grand Junction agricultural community can actively support.

MLA Works Cited Entry

Author's Name   Title of Article   Title of Magazine Sponsor/Publisher

Saletan, William. "Please Do Not Feed the Humans: The Global Explosion of Fat." *Slate*. Washington Post. Newsweek Interactive, 2 Sept. 2006. Web. 28 Sept. 2006.

Publication Date   Medium   Access Date

Paraphrase Specific Information.   The technique of paraphrasing involves restating an author's ideas in your own language. A paraphrase is generally about the same length as the original. Because it conveys the ideas and emphasis of the original but uses your words and sentences, it helps bring your own voice to the fore. A fresh and creative paraphrase expresses your style without awkwardly jumping between it and your source's style. Be sure to name the source, however, so that your reader knows exactly where you move from one to the other.

Here, again, is the original passage by Bruce Babbitt, followed by a sloppy paraphrase. The paraphrase suffers from a common fault, slipping in too many of the words from the original source. (These borrowed words are underlined in the paraphrase.) Those words need to be expressed in the writer's own language or identified as direct quotations with quotation marks.

ORIGINAL   The tortoise is a creature that has survived virtually unchanged since it first appeared in the geologic record more than 150 million years ago. The species became threatened, however, when ranchers began driving their herds onto Mojave Desert lands for spring grazing, at the very time that the tortoise awakens from hibernation and emerges from its burrows to graze on the greening desert shrubs and grasses. As livestock trampled the burrows and monopolized the scarce desert vegetation, tortoise populations plummeted. (page 152)

Babbitt, Bruce. *Cities in the Wilderness: A New Vision of Land Use in America*. Washington: Island Press-Shearwater Books, 2005. Print.

SLOPPY PARAPHRASE   Babbitt says that the tortoise is a creature in the Mojave that is virtually unchanged over 150 million years. Over the millennia, the tortoise would awaken from hibernation just in time for spring grazing on the new growth of the region's shrubs and grasses. In recent years the species became threatened. When cattle started to compete for the same food, the livestock trampled the tortoise burrows and monopolized the desert vegetation while the tortoise populations plummeted (152).

To avoid picking up language from the original as you paraphrase, state each sentence afresh instead of just changing a few words in the original. If possible, take a short break, and then check each sentence against the original. Highlight any identical words or sentence patterns, and then rework your paraphrase again. Proper nouns or exact terms for the topic (such as *tortoise*) do not need to be rephrased.

The next example avoids parroting the original by making different word choices while reversing or varying sentence patterns.

> PARAPHRASE   As Babbitt explains, a tenacious survivor in the Mojave is the
>   150-million-year-old desert tortoise. Over the millennia, the hi-
>   bernating tortoise would rouse itself each spring just in time to
>   enjoy the new growth of the limited regional plants. In recent
>   years, when cattle began competing for the same territory, the
>   larger animals destroyed tortoise homes, ate tortoise food, and
>   thus eliminated many of the tortoises themselves (152).

A common option is to blend paraphrase with brief quotation, carefully using quotation marks to identify any exact words drawn from the source.

> BLENDED   Babbitt describes a tenacious survivor in the Mojave, the
>   150-million-year-old desert tortoise. Over the millennia, the
>   hibernating tortoise would rouse itself each spring just in time to
>   munch on the new growth of the sparse regional plants. When cattle
>   started to compete for the same food supply and destroyed the
>   tortoise homes and food, the "tortoise populations plummeted" (152).

In a brief paraphrase, be just as careful to avoid slipping in the author's words or closely shadowing the original sentence structure. If a source says, "President Bush called an emergency meeting of his cabinet to discuss the new crisis," and you write, "The president called his cabinet to hold an emergency meeting to discuss the new crisis," your words are too close to those of the source. One option is to quote the original, though it doesn't seem worth quoting word for word. Or, better, you could write, "Summoning his cabinet to an emergency session, Bush laid out the challenge before them."

HOW TO PARAPHRASE

- Select a passage with detailed information relevant to your thesis.
- Reword the passage, representing it accurately but using your own language.
- Change both its words and its sentence patterns to your own. Replace its words with different expressions. Begin and end sentences differently, simplify long sentences, and reorder information.
- Note the page or other location (such as an electronic paragraph) where the original appears in your source. If the passage runs from one page onto the next, record where the page changes so that your credit will be accurate no matter how much of the paraphrase you use.
- After a break, recheck your paraphrase against the original to be certain that it does not repeat the same words or merely replace a few with synonyms. Revise as needed, placing fresh words in fresh arrangements.

For more on paraphrases, see D4 in the Quick Research Guide (the dark-red-edged pages).

For advice on writing a synopsis of a literary work, see pp. 256–58.

Summarize an Overall Point.   Summarizing is a useful way of incorporating the general point of a whole paragraph or section of a work. You briefly state the main sense of the original in your own words and identify the source of the ideas or information. Like a paraphrase, a summary uses your own language and thus increases the prominence of your voice. A summary is generally much shorter than the original; it expresses only the most important ideas — the essence — of the original. The following example summarizes the section of Babbitt's book containing the passage quoted on pages 214–15 and 218.

SUMMARY   According to Bruce Babbitt, former Secretary of the Interior and governor of Arizona, the isolated federal land in the West traditionally has been open to cattle and sheep ranching. These animals have damaged the arid land by grazing too aggressively, and the ranchers have battled wildlife grazers and predators alike to reduce competition with their stock. Protecting species such as the gray wolf and the desert tortoise has meant limiting grazing, an action supported by the public in order to conserve the character and beauty of the public land.

HOW TO SUMMARIZE

For more on summaries, see D5 in the Quick Research Guide (the dark-red-edged pages).

• Select a passage, an article, a chapter, or an entire book whose main idea bears on your thesis.

• Read the selection carefully until you have mastered its overall point.

• Write a sentence or a series of sentences that states its essence in your own words.

• Revise your summary until it is as concise, clear, and accurate as possible. Replace any vague generalizations with precise words.

• Name your source as you begin your summary, or identify it in parentheses.

For more on plagiarism, see D1 in the Quick Research Guide (the dark-red-edged pages).

For an avoiding plagiarism tutorial, visit <bedfordstmartins.com/rewriting>.

For sample source citations and lists, see the readings on pp. 201–08 and the MLA and APA examples in E in the Quick Research Guide (the dark-red-edged pages).

Credit Your Sources Fairly.   As you quote, paraphrase, or summarize, be certain to note which source you are using and exactly where the material appears in the original. Carefully citing and listing your sources will give credit where it's due as it enhances your credibility as a careful writer.

Although academic fields prefer particular formats for their papers, MLA style is widely used in composition, English, and other humanities courses. In MLA style, you credit your source twice. First, briefly note the author's last name (and the page number in the original) in the text as you quote, paraphrase, summarize, or refer to the source. You may wish to mention the author's name (or a short version of the title if the author is not identified) as you introduce the information from the source. If not, note it and the page number of the original in parentheses after you present the

Methods of Capturing Information from Sources	QUOTATION	PARAPHRASE	SUMMARY
FORMAT FOR WORDING	Use exact words from the source, and identify any additions, deletions, or other changes	Use your words and sentence structures, translating the content of the original passage	Use your words and sentence structures, reducing the original passage to its core
COMMON USE	Capture lively and authoritative wording	Capture specific information while conserving its detail	Capture the overall essence of a source or a passage in brief form
ADVANTAGES	Catch a reader's attention; emphasize the authority of the source	Treat specifics fully without shifting from your voice to the source's	Concentrate on a broad but clear point without shifting from your voice to the source's
COMMON PROBLEMS	Quoting too much Quoting inaccurately	Slipping in the original wording Following the original sentence patterns too closely	Losing impact by bogging down in too much detail Drifting into vague generalities
MARKERS	Add quotation marks to show the source's exact words Use ellipses and brackets to mark any changes Identify source in launch statement or text citation and in list of sources	Identify source in launch statement or text citation and in final list of sources	Identify source in launch statement or text citation and in final list of sources

material. Next, fully identify the source in an alphabetical list at the end of your paper.

Let Your Draft Evolve.   No matter how many quotations, paraphrases, and summaries you assemble, chunks of evidence captured from sources do not — on their own — constitute a solid paper. You need to interpret and explain that evidence for your readers, helping them to see exactly why, how, and to what extent it supports your position.

To develop a solid draft, you may want to start with your evidence, using one of these methods to arrange your quotations, paraphrases, and summaries in a logical and compelling order.

■ For exercises on supporting a thesis, visit <bedfordstmartins.com/bedguide> and do a keyword search:

support

- Cut and paste the chunks of evidence, moving them around in a file until they fall into a logical order.
- Print each chunk on a separate page, and arrange the pages on a flat surface like a table, floor, or bed until you reach a workable sequence.
- Label each chunk with a key word, and use the key words to work out an informal outline.

Once your evidence is organized logically, add the commentary needed to connect the chunks for your readers: introduce, conclude, and connect your pieces of evidence with your own explanations and interpretations. (Feel free to ignore any leftovers from your sources unless they cover key points that you still need to integrate.) Let your draft expand as you alternate evidence and interpretation.

 For more on planning and drafting, see Chs. 17 and 18.

An alternative is to start with your position or your conclusion, focusing on how you want your paper to present it. You can state your case directly, explaining your thesis and supporting points in your own words, or you can write out directions, telling yourself what to do in each part of a draft (in preparation for actually doing it). Either way, use this working structure to identify where to embed the evidence from your sources. Let your draft grow as you pull in your sources and expand your comments.

DEVELOPMENT CHECKLIST

For sample quotations, paraphrases, and summaries, see D3, D4, and D5 in the Quick Research Guide (the dark-red-edged pages).

— Have you quoted only notable passages that add support and authority to your discussion?

— Have you checked your quotations for accuracy and marked where each begins and ends with quotation marks?

— Have you paraphrased accurately, reflecting both the main points and the supporting details in the original?

— Does each paraphrase use your own words without repeating or echoing the words or the sentence structure of the original?

— Have you briefly stated any supporting ideas that you wish to summarize, sticking to the overall point without bogging down in details or examples?

— Has each summary remained respectful of the ideas and opinions of others, even if you disagree with them?

—— Have you identified the source of every quotation, paraphrase, summary, or source reference by noting in parentheses the last name of the writer and the page number (if available) where the passage appears in the source?

—— Have you ordered your evidence logically and effectively?

—— Have you interpreted and explained your evidence from sources with your own comments?

For more on finding your voice, see Facing the Challenge on p. 211.

REVISING AND EDITING

As you read over the draft of your paper, remember what you wanted to accomplish: to develop an enlightening position about your topic and to share this position with a college audience, using sources to support your ideas.

For more on reviewing and editing strategies, see Ch. 20.

Strengthen Your Thesis.   As you begin revising, you may decide that your working thesis is ambiguous, poorly worded, hard to support, or simply off the mark. Revise it so that it clearly alerts readers to your main idea.

For more on stating a thesis, see pp. 312–19.

WORKING THESIS   Although most workers would like longer vacations, most employers do not believe that they would benefit, too.

REVISED THESIS   Despite assumptions to the contrary, employers who increase vacation time for workers also are likely to increase creativity, productivity, and the bottom line.

Launch Each Source.   Whenever you quote, paraphrase, summarize, or refer to a source, launch it with a suitable introduction. An effective launch sets the scene for your source material, prepares your reader to accept it, and marks the transition from your words and ideas to those of the source.

For more about launching sources, see D6 in the Quick Research Guide (the dark-red-edged pages).

As you create a launch statement, often you will first identify the source — by the author's last name or by a short version of the title when the author isn't named — in your introductory sentence or in parentheses. Then try to suggest why you've selected this source and mentioned it at this point, perhaps noting its contribution to your discussion, its credibility, its vantage point, or its relationship to other sources. Vary your launch statements to avoid tedium and to add emphasis. Boost your credibility as a writer by establishing the credibility of your sources.

Here are some typical patterns for launch statements:

As Yung demonstrates, . . .

Although Zeffir maintains . . . , Matson suggests . . .

Many schools educated the young but also unified the community (Hill 22). . . .

In *Forward March*, Smith's study of the children of military personnel, . . .

Another common recommendation is . . . ("Safety Manual").

Based on years of experience as a travel consultant, Lee explains . . .

■ These examples follow
MLA style. See D6 and E1
in the Quick Research
Guide (the dark-red-
edged pages) for more
about how to capture,
launch, and cite sources in
your text using either
MLA or APA style.

When you quote or paraphrase information from a specific page (or other location, such as a paragraph on a Web page), also include that exact location.

The classic definition of . . . (Bagette 18).

Benton distinguishes four typical steps in this process (248–51).

Synthesize Several Sources.   Often you will compare, contrast, or relate two or three sources to deepen your discussion or to illustrate a range of views. When you synthesize, you pull together several sources in the same passage to build a new interpretation or reach a new conclusion. You go beyond the separate contributions of the individual sources to relate the sources to each other and to connect them to your thesis. A synthesis should be easy to follow and use your own wording.

HOW TO SYNTHESIZE

- Summarize (see p. 220) each of the sources you want to synthesize. Boil down each summary to its essence.

- Write a few sentences that state in your own words how the sources are related. For example, are they similar, different, or related? Do they share assumptions and conclusions, or do they represent alternatives, opposites, or opponents? Do they speak to chronology, influence, logical progression, or diversity of opinion?

- Write a few more sentences stating what their relationships mean for your thesis and the position developed in your paper.

- Refine your synthesis statements until they are as clear and illuminating as possible. Embed them as you move from one source summary to the next and as you reach new interpretations or conclusions that go beyond the separate sources.

Use Your Own Voice to Interpret and Connect.   By the time your draft is finished, you may feel that you have found relevant evidence in your sources but that they now dominate your draft. As you reread, you may discover passages that simply string together ideas from sources.

DRAFT

Whole passage repeats "says"

Repeats sentence pattern opening with author

Jumps from one source to the next without transitions

Easterbrook says in "In Search of the Cause of Autism: How about Television?" that television may injure children who are susceptible to autism. The Centers for Disease Control and Prevention says that autism trails only mental retardation among disabilities that affect children's development. The Kaiser Family Foundation study says that parents use television and other electronic entertainment "to help them manage their household and keep their kids

entertained" (Rideout, Hamel, and Kaiser Family Foundation 4).

When your sources overshadow your thesis, your explanations, and your writing style, revise to restore balance. Try strategies such as these to regain control of your draft:

- Add your explanation and interpretation of the source information so that your ideas are clear.
- Add transitions, and state the connections that you assume are obvious.
- Arrange information in a logical sequence, not in the order in which you read it.
- Clarify definitions, justify a topic's importance, and recognize alternative views to help your audience appreciate your position.
- Reword to vary your sentence openings, and avoid repetitive wording.

Your thoughtful revision can help your audience understand what you want to say, why you have included each source, and how you think that it supports your thesis.

REVISION

Two recent studies take very different looks at the development of children in *Connects two sources*

our society. First, a research study sponsored by the Kaiser Family Foundation

examines how parents use television and other electronic options "to help them *Adds transitions*

manage their household and keep their kids entertained" (Rideout, Hamel, and

Kaiser Family Foundation 4). Next, based on statistics about how often major

developmental disabilities occur in children, the Centers for Disease Control and

Prevention reports that autism currently trails only mental retardation among

disabilities that affect children's development. Journalist and book author Gregg *Identifies author's experience to add credibility*

Easterbrook pulls together these two views, using the title of his article to raise his

unusual question: "In Search of the Cause of Autism: How about Television?" He urges

study of his speculation that television may injure children who are vulnerable to *Defines issue and justifies concern*

autism and joins an ongoing debate about what causes autism, a challenging disability

that interferes with children's ability to communicate and interact with other people.

■ For examples of sources cited in the text and listed in MLA or APA style, see E in the Quick Research Guide (the dark-red-edged pages).

List Your Sources as College Readers Expect.   When you use sources in a college paper, you'll be expected to identify them twice: briefly when you draw information from them and fully when you list them at the end of your paper, following a conventional system. The list of sources for the draft and revision in the preceding section would include the following entries.

Centers for Disease Control and Prevention. "Frequently Asked Questions—Prevalence." *Autism Information Center.* CDC, 30 Jan. 2006. Web. 12 Sept. 2006.

Easterbrook, Gregg. "In Search of the Cause of Autism: How about Television?" *Slate.*
Washington Post.Newsweek Interactive, 5 Sept. 2006. Web. 12 Sept. 2006.

Rideout, Victoria, Elizabeth Hamel, and Kaiser Family Foundation. *The Media Family:
Electronic Media in the Lives of Infants, Toddlers, Preschoolers and Their Parents.*
Menlo Park, CA: Henry J. Kaiser Family Foundation, May 2006. *Kaiser
Family Foundation.* Web. 12 Sept. 2006.

■ To get online help from the Draft Doctor, visit <bedfordstmartins.com/bedguide>.

Use the Draft Doctor (pp. 228–30) to help you figure out how to improve your draft. Skim down the left column to identify questions you might ask about problems in your draft. When you answer a question with "Yes" or "Maybe," move straight across the row to the Diagnose column next to that question. Use the diagnostic activities to identify gaps or weaknesses, and then move straight across the row to the Treat column on the right. Use the advice that suits your problem as you revise.

FOR E-WRITERS

Checking Your Source Citations

Use your software's search capacity to help you check your source credits. For example, search for all the quotation marks in your paper. As you find each one, make sure that it is one of a pair surrounding every quotation in your paper. Also check that the source and the page (or other location, if available) are identified for each quotation. Use color highlighting to help you spot and refine the details in your list of sources. For instance, if you tend to forget periods or other conventional punctuation after authors' names or titles, go through your list of sources, and highlight those marks in color, adding any that are missing. After all the entries are checked and corrected, restore the passage to the usual black color.

Have several classmates read your draft critically, considering how effectively you have used your sources to support a position. Ask your peer editors to answer questions such as these:

- Can you state the writer's position on the topic?

- Do you have any trouble seeing how the writer's points and the supporting evidence from sources connect? How might the writer make the connections clearer?

- How effectively does the writer capture the information from sources? Would you recommend that any of the quotations, paraphrases, or summaries be presented differently?

- Are any of the source citations unclear? Can you tell where source information came from and where quotations and paraphrases appear in a source?

- Is the writer's voice clear? Do the sources overshadow the writer's voice in any spots?

- If this were your paper, what is the one thing you would be sure to work on before handing it in?

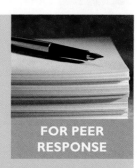

FOR PEER RESPONSE

For general questions for a peer editor, see p. 377. For peer response worksheets, visit <bedfordstmartins.com/bedguide> and do a keyword search:

peer

REVISION CHECKLIST

—— Is your thesis, or main idea, clear? Is it distinguished from the points made by your sources?

—— Do you speak in your own voice, interpreting and explaining your sources instead of allowing them to dominate your draft?

—— Have you moved smoothly back and forth between your explanations and your source material?

—— Have you credited every source in the text and in a list at the end of your paper? Have you carefully included each detail expected in the format for crediting sources?

—— Have you been careful to quote, paraphrase, summarize, and credit your sources accurately and ethically? Have you hunted up any missing information, double-checked all quotations, and rechecked the accuracy of anything prepared hastily?

For more on strengthening your voice, see Facing the Challenge on p. 21.

After you have revised your paper, edit and proofread it. Carefully check the grammar, word choice, punctuation, and mechanics — and then correct any problems you find. Be certain to check the punctuation with your quotations, making sure that each quotation mark is correctly placed and that you have used other punctuation, such as commas, correctly. See page 231 for some questions to get you started editing and proofreading.

Draft Doctor: Integrating Source Information Effectively

If you sense a problem, ASK	If you answer *Yes/Maybe*, DIAGNOSE	If you diagnose a problem, TREAT
Too Many Quotations? Have I strung together too many quotations?	• Highlight the words in your draft directly quoted from sources. • Identify any large colored patches where you probably quote too much. • Circle the striking or powerful words, if any, in each clump.	• Reduce your quotations to significant words, presented in a passage or blended with your words. Either way, always set off each quotation with a pair of quotation marks. • Delete the rest, or restate it in your own words. • Clearly identify the source of the quoted or restated material in the style expected.
Too Many Long Quotations? Have I dropped too many long quoted passages into my draft?	• Draw a vertical line in the margin to show the length of each quoted passage. • Check the length and frequency of these lines, looking for any longer than an inch or two. • Read each long quotation critically to master its meaning. Highlight its most significant wording.	• Quote only compelling words; paraphrase, sum up, or delete the rest. • If the significant words are long enough for a block quotation, follow the format for indenting and citing the source in MLA or another style. • Edit each quotation to be sure that you stick to one system at a time: quotation marks for the exact words in a short quotation; indentation without quotation marks for a long quotation.
Too Little Voice? Have I lost my own voice and allowed my sources to take over my draft?	• Highlight the material from sources in one color and your own commentary in another. • Check the color balance in each paragraph. If the source color dominates, consider strengthening your own voice.	• Restore your voice by adding a topic sentence to link each paragraph to your thesis and a concluding sentence to sum up its point. • Add your own transitions (*further, most importantly*) and explanations when you advance from point to point or source to source. • Weave in your ideas until they, not your sources, control your draft.

228

If you sense a problem, ASK	If you answer *Yes/Maybe,* DIAGNOSE	If you diagnose a problem, TREAT
Weak Launch Statements? Have I tossed source material into my draft without preparing my audience for it?	• Underline each sentence or part of a sentence that introduces source information. • Check each launch statement to see whether it assures a reader that the information is credible, relevant, and logically related to your thesis. (See D6 in the Quick Research Guide.)	• Improve each launch statement by relating the source material to your thesis. • Launch a quotation, paraphrase, or summary by telling readers why they should confidently accept the material. • Note an author's credentials or affiliations significant to readers. • Identify historical or current contributions of a source, or relate it to other sources.
Too Few Source Credits? Have I identified a source only once or twice even though I use its material throughout a passage or paragraph?	• Select a passage that relies heavily on a main source. Use one color to highlight your ideas and different colors to mark material from other sources. • Draw a slash mark at each point in the passage where you make a switch from your ideas to a source (or vice versa) or from source to source. **Draft:** Smith points out X, and Y remains unsolved. [Who says Y is unsolved? Smith? You? Somebody else?]	• At each slash marking a switch between sources, add a launch statement to identify the second source. • At each slash marking a switch to your ideas (or when your color begins), phrase your comment so that it does not sound like more of the source. **Revision:** Although Smith points out X, she discusses but does not solve Y. (Smith says it all.) **Revision:** Although Smith points out X, she does not discuss Y [switch to you] which Wheeler investigates [switch to Wheeler]. • At each slash marking a switch from your ideas (or when your color ends), identify your source again. • When you quote and then continue with material from the same source, identify it again to avoid confusion.

If you sense a problem, ASK	If you answer *Yes/Maybe*, DIAGNOSE	If you diagnose a problem, TREAT
Too Much Repetition? Do I repeat the same words in my launch statements or transitions?	• Identify words (such as *says*) or transitions (such as *also*) that you might overuse. • Search for oft-used words, or highlight them, to see how many times you repeat them.	• Edit your wording for variety and precision. Instead of *says*, try *emphasizes, suggests, reviews, presents,* or *explains*. For *also*, try *in addition, furthermore,* or *similarly.* • Do the same for your own favorite expressions.
Problems with Citation Style? Have I skipped over or confused any details of the formats for crediting sources in my paper? (Make sure you know the style—MLA, APA, or another—expected by your instructor.)	• Go through your draft line by line, marking where you mention and should cite each source in your sentence or in parentheses. • Check that a matching full entry for each source is listed in the correct format in the Works Cited, References, or other bibliography that ends your paper. • Refer to the style examples as you cite and list each source.	• Include the author's name or a short version of the title (if the author is not named) in your sentence or in parentheses. Add the page, line, or other location (if available) for every quotation and paraphrase. Add anything else required. • Make your full entry for each source listed at the end match the pattern expected in the style you are using. Edit the indentation, sequence of details, capitalization, and punctuation.
Any Other Source Problems? After a final look at the sources in my draft, should I revise anything else?	• Read your draft out loud, marking any weak spots in your introduction, use, or citation of sources. • Ask your peer editors how you might improve your use of sources.	• Return to each mark to strengthen your presentation of sources. • Consider the useful suggestions of your peers. • Revise until your draft accomplishes what you want it to do.

EDITING CHECKLIST	

— Do all the verbs agree with their subjects, especially when you switch from your words to those of a source?　　　　　　　A4

— Do all the pronouns agree with their antecedents, especially when you use your words with a quotation from a source?　　A6

— Have you used commas correctly, especially where you integrate material from sources?　　　　　　　　　　　　　　C1

— Have you punctuated all your quotations correctly?　　　　C3

■ For more more help, turn to the Quick Editing guide (the dark-blue-edged pages), to the sections noted here.

OTHER ASSIGNMENTS

1. Create a concise Web site that addresses a question of interest to you. Select and read a few reliable sources about that question, and then create several screens or short pages to explain what you have learned. For example, you might want to define or explain aspects of the question, justify the conclusion you have reached, or evaluate alternative answers as well as your own. Identify all of your sources, and supply links when appropriate.

2. Read several sources about the same topic. Instead of using those sources as evidence to support your own position about the topic, analyze how well they function as sources. State your thesis about them, and analyze their strengths and weaknesses using clear criteria. (See, for example, the criteria for evaluating sources in C in the Quick Research Guide, the dark-red-edged pages.)

3. Locate several different accounts of a notable event in newspapers, magazines, published letters or journals, books, blogs, or other sources, depending on the time when the event occurred. State and support a thesis that explains and accounts for the differences among the accounts. Use the accounts as evidence to support your position.

Applying What You Learn: Some Uses of Position Papers Supported by Sources

In College Courses.　　In most courses, especially in the humanities and social sciences, you'll be expected to use sources to support a position.

• After reading a short story, poem, or play, students in a literature course might read several critical essays about it and then write essays supporting their own conclusions.

• Students in a sociology course might be asked to read several articles about families and then write a paper reviewing the viewpoints of the articles and supporting a conclusion about them.

- Students in a history course might be asked to read a first-person account, a contemporary secondhand article or report, and a later critical examination of an event or situation in order to develop and support their own thesis about it.

In the Workplace.   Many jobs require reading several reports, technical documents, or other papers and preparing an explanation of the matter, with conclusions that the materials support.

- Newspaper reporters draw on multiple sources to develop a consolidated account of an event or explanation of a situation.

- Organizations such as police departments, fire departments, and social-service agencies assemble multiple accounts and records in order to explain and draw conclusions about something that has happened.

- Employees often must unify reports from different sources in order to make and support a recommendation about how to solve a problem.

Workplace reports

In Your Community.   Partisans, activists, and concerned citizens all gather source materials about issues of concern, consolidating them to persuade others to support and implement their views.

- You might write a letter to the editor, supporting an opinion with information from several respected sources.

- Your civic group might want to raise money for a diabetes clinic, developing a position paper supported by sources to substantiate the need and the possible community benefits.

- Your child's school invites parents to contribute to a grant proposal that includes sources to document a local problem and propose solutions implemented elsewhere.

PART THREE

Special Writing Situations

Introduction

Much of your writing during college will fall into one of the categories covered in Part Two. However, three common situations that you're likely to encounter will call for specialized forms of writing — writing about literature, writing for the workplace, and writing for assessment.

In college English and humanities classes, you'll write papers about literature. You may need to write a personal response, a synopsis, a paraphrase, a review, a comparison and contrast, or — most common in college — a literary analysis. Chapter 13 concentrates on the literary analysis, explaining how to analyze a piece of literature, how to develop a coherent interpretation, and how to present it persuasively. It also provides brief advice on writing a synopsis or a paraphrase of a literary work.

Whether you are working while you attend college or looking forward to a career once you finish, you'll need to use your writing skills in the workplace. As a consumer, a client, or an employee, you may need to write a business letter to straighten out a bill or lodge a complaint. You may need to write memos and e-mail messages as part of your current job. In addition, when you apply for a new position, you may need to write a résumé and letter of application. To simplify such tasks, Chapter 14 offers recommendations and samples for workplace writing.

Finally, as a student you'll face testing situations in which you must demonstrate your knowledge of a subject as well as your proficiency in writing, often constrained by a time limit. Writing essay examinations, short-answer quizzes, impromptu essays, and portfolio entries requires you to use special skills — reading carefully, planning globally, composing quickly, and proofreading independently. Chapter 15 gives valuable tips on how not only to survive but also to thrive in such situations.

Chapter 13

Responding to Literature

As countless readers know, reading fiction gives pleasure and delight. Whether you are reading Stephen King or Stephen Crane, you can be swept up into an imaginative world where you journey to distant lands and meet exotic people. You may also meet characters like yourself and encounter familiar as well as new ways of viewing life. By sharing the experiences of literary characters, you gain insight into your own problems and tolerance of others.

More often than not, a writing assignment in a literature or humanities course will require you first to read closely a literary work (short story, novel, play, or poem) and then to divide it into its elements, explain its meaning, and support your interpretation with evidence from the work. Such analysis is not an end in itself; its purpose is to illuminate the meaning of the work, to help you and others understand it better.

There are certain basic ways of writing about literature, each with its own purpose. We emphasize the *literary analysis*, which requires you to analyze, interpret, and evaluate what you read (pp. 250–56). We also introduce the synopsis, a summary of the events in a narrative, and the paraphrase, an expression of the content of a work in your own words (pp. 256–58). Because literary analysis has its own vocabulary—as do fields as diverse as scuba diving, gourmet cooking, and engineering—we also supply a handy glossary of terms used to discuss the elements of fiction, poetry, and drama (see pp. 248–49).

Literary Analysis

LEARNING FROM OTHER WRITERS

In a composition course, Jonathan Burns was given an assignment to write a literary analysis of "The Lottery," a provocative short story by Shirley Jackson. Read this story yourself to understand its meaning. Then read on to see what Jonathan Burns made of it.

Shirley Jackson
The Lottery

The morning of June 27th was clear and sunny, with the fresh warmth of 1 a full-summer day; the flowers were blossoming profusely and the grass was richly green. The people of the village began to gather in the square, between the post office and the bank, around ten o'clock; in some towns there were so many people that the lottery took two days and had to be started on June 26th, but in this village, where there were only about three hundred people, the whole lottery took less than two hours, so it could begin at ten o'clock in the morning and still be through in time to allow the villagers to get home for noon dinner.

The children assembled first, of course. School was recently over for the 2 summer, and the feeling of liberty sat uneasily on most of them; they tended to gather together quietly for a while before they broke into boisterous play, and their talk was still of the classroom and the teacher, of books and reprimands. Bobby Martin had already stuffed his pockets full of stones, and the other boys soon followed his example, selecting the smoothest and roundest stones; Bobby and Harry Jones and Dickie Delacroix—the villagers pronounced his name "Dellacroy"—eventually made a great pile of stones in one corner of the square and guarded it against the raids of the other boys. The girls stood aside, talking among themselves, looking over their shoulders at the boys, and the very small children rolled in the dust or clung to the hands of their older brothers or sisters.

Soon the men began to gather, surveying their own children, speaking 3 of planting and rain, tractors and taxes. They stood together, away from the pile of stones in the corner, and their jokes were quiet and they smiled rather than laughed. The women, wearing faded house dresses and sweaters, came shortly after their menfolk. They greeted one another and exchanged bits of gossip as they went to join their husbands. Soon the women, standing by their husbands, began to call to their children, and the children came reluctantly, having to be called four or five times. Bobby Martin ducked under his mother's grasping hand and ran, laughing, back to the pile of stones. His father spoke up sharply, and Bobby came quickly and took his place between his father and his oldest brother.

The lottery was conducted—as were the square dances, the teenage 4 club, the Halloween program—by Mr. Summers, who had time and energy to devote to civic activities. He was a round-faced, jovial man and he ran the coal business, and people were sorry for him, because he had no children and his wife was a scold. When he arrived in the square, carrying the black wooden box, there was a murmur of conversation among the villagers, and he waved and called, "Little late today, folks." The postmaster, Mr. Graves, followed him, carrying a three-legged stool, and the stool was put in the center of the square and Mr. Summers set the black box down on it. The villagers kept their distance, leaving a space between themselves and the stool, and when Mr. Summers said, "Some of you fellows want to give me a hand?" there was a hesitation before two men, Mr. Martin and his oldest son, Baxter, came forward to hold the box steady on the stool while Mr. Summers stirred up the papers inside it.

The original paraphernalia for the lottery had been lost long ago, and 5 the black box now resting on the stool had been put into use even before Old Man Warner, the oldest man in town, was born. Mr. Summers spoke frequently to the villagers about making a new box, but no one liked to upset even as much tradition as was represented by the black box. There was a story that the present box had been made with some pieces of the box that had preceded it, the one that had been constructed when the first people settled down to make a village here. Every year, after the lottery, Mr. Summers began talking again about a new box, but every year the subject was allowed to fade off without anything's being done. The black box grew shabbier each year; by now it was no longer completely black but splintered badly along one side to show the original wood color, and in some places faded or stained.

Mr. Martin and his oldest son, Baxter, held the black box securely on the 6 stool until Mr. Summers had stirred the papers thoroughly with his hand. Because so much of the ritual had been forgotten or discarded, Mr. Summers had been successful in having slips of paper substituted for the chips of wood that had been used for generations. Chips of wood, Mr. Summers had argued, had been all very well when the village was tiny, but now that the population was more than three hundred and likely to keep on growing, it was necessary to use something that would fit more easily into the black box. The night before the lottery, Mr. Summers and Mr. Graves made up the slips of paper and put them in the box, and it was then taken to the safe of Mr. Summers's coal company and locked up until Mr. Summers was ready to take it to the square next morning. The rest of the year, the box was put away, sometimes one place, sometimes another; it had spent one year in Mr. Graves's barn and another year underfoot in the post office, and sometimes it was set on a shelf in the Martin grocery and left there.

There was a great deal of fussing to be done before Mr. Summers de- 7 clared the lottery open. There were the lists to make up — of heads of families, heads of households in each family, members of each household in each family. There was the proper swearing-in of Mr. Summers by the postmaster, as the official of the lottery; at one time, some people remembered, there had been a recital of some sort, performed by the official of the lottery, a perfunctory, tuneless chant that had been rattled off duly each year; some people believed that the official of the lottery used to stand just so when he said or sang it, others believed that he was supposed to walk among the people, but years and years ago this part of the ritual had been allowed to lapse. There had been, also, a ritual salute, which the official of the lottery had had to use in addressing each person who came up to draw from the box, but this also had changed with time, until now it was felt necessary only for the official to speak to each person approaching. Mr. Summers was very good at all this; in his clean white shirt and blue jeans, with one hand resting carelessly on the black box, he seemed very proper and important as he talked interminably to Mr. Graves and the Martins.

Just as Mr. Summers finally left off talking and turned to the assembled villagers, Mrs. Hutchinson came hurriedly along the path to the square, her sweater thrown over her shoulders, and slid into place in the back of the crowd. "Clean forgot what day it was," she said to Mrs. Delacroix, who stood next to her, and they both laughed softly. "Thought my old man was out back stacking wood," Mrs. Hutchinson went on, "and then I looked out the window and the kids was gone, and then I remembered it was the twenty-seventh and came a-running." She dried her hands on her apron, and Mrs. Delacroix said, "You're in time, though. They're still talking away up there." 8

Mrs. Hutchinson craned her neck to see through the crowd and found her husband and children standing near the front. She tapped Mrs. Delacroix on the arm as a farewell and began to make her way through the crowd. The people separated good-humoredly to let her through; two or three people said, in voices just loud enough to be heard across the crowd, "Here comes your Missus, Hutchinson," and "Bill, she made it after all." Mrs. Hutchinson reached her husband, and Mr. Summers, who had been waiting, said cheerfully, "Thought we were going to have to get on without you, Tessie." Mrs. Hutchinson said, grinning, "Wouldn't have me leave m'dishes in the sink, now, would you, Joe?" and soft laughter ran through the crowd as the people stirred back into position after Mrs. Hutchinson's arrival. 9

"Well, now," Mr. Summers said soberly, "guess we better get started, get this over with, so's we can go back to work. Anybody ain't here?" 10

"Dunbar," several people said. "Dunbar, Dunbar." 11

Mr. Summers consulted his list. "Clyde Dunbar," he said. "That's right. He's broke his leg, hasn't he? Who's drawing for him?" 12

"Me, I guess," a woman said, and Mr. Summers turned to look at her. "Wife draws for her husband," Mr. Summers said. "Don't you have a grown boy to do it for you, Janey?" Although Mr. Summers and everyone else in the village knew the answer perfectly well, it was the business of the official of the lottery to ask such questions formally. Mr. Summers waited with an expression of polite interest while Mrs. Dunbar answered. 13

"Horace's not but sixteen yet," Mrs. Dunbar said regretfully. "Guess I gotta fill in for the old man this year." 14

"Right," Mr. Summers said. He made a note on the list he was holding. Then he asked, "Watson boy drawing this year?" 15

A tall boy in the crowd raised his hand. "Here," he said. "I'm drawing for m'mother and me." He blinked his eyes nervously and ducked his head as several voices in the crowd said things like "Good fellow, Jack," and "Glad to see your mother's got a man to do it." 16

"Well," Mr. Summers said, "guess that's everyone. Old Man Warner make it?" 17

"Here," a voice said, and Mr. Summers nodded.   18

A sudden hush fell on the crowd as Mr. Summers cleared his throat and   19
looked at the list. "All ready?" he called. "Now, I'll read the names — heads
of families first — and the men come up and take a paper out of the box.
Keep the paper folded in your hand without looking at it until everyone has
had a turn. Everything clear?"

The people had done it so many times that they only half listened to the   20
directions; most of them were quiet, wetting their lips, not looking around.
Then Mr. Summers raised one hand high and said, "Adams." A man disen-
gaged himself from the crowd and came forward. "Hi, Steve," Mr. Summers
said, and Mr. Adams said, "Hi, Joe." They grinned at one another humor-
lessly and nervously. Then Mr. Adams reached into the black box and took
out a folded paper. He held it firmly by one corner as he turned and went
hastily back to his place in the crowd, where he stood a little apart from his
family, not looking down at his hand.

"Allen," Mr. Summers said. "Anderson. . . . Bentham."   21

"Seems like there's no time at all between lotteries anymore," Mrs.   22
Delacroix said to Mrs. Graves in the back row. "Seems like we got through
with the last one only last week."

"Time sure goes fast," Mrs. Graves said.   23

"Clark. . . . Delacroix."   24

"There goes my old man," Mrs. Delacroix said. She held her breath   25
while her husband went forward.

"Dunbar," Mr. Summers said, and Mrs. Dunbar went steadily to the box   26
while one of the women said, "Go on, Janey," and another said, "There she
goes."

"We're next," Mrs. Graves said. She watched while Mr. Graves came   27
around from the side of the box, greeted Mr. Summers gravely, and selected
a slip of paper from the box. By now, all through the crowd there were men
holding the small folded papers in their large hands, turning them over and
over nervously. Mrs. Dunbar and her two sons stood together, Mrs. Dunbar
holding the slip of paper.

"Harburt. . . . Hutchinson."   28

"Get up there, Bill," Mrs. Hutchinson said, and the people near her   29
laughed.

"Jones."   30

"They do say," Mr. Adams said to Old Man Warner, who stood next to   31
him, "that over in the north village they're talking of giving up the lottery."

Old Man Warner snorted. "Pack of crazy fools," he said. "Listening to   32
the young folks, nothing's good enough for *them*. Next thing you know,
they'll be wanting to go back to living in caves, nobody work anymore, live
that way for a while. Used to be a saying about 'Lottery in June, corn be
heavy soon.' First thing you know, we'd all be eating stewed chickweed and
acorns. There's *always* been a lottery," he added petulantly. "Bad enough to
see young Joe Summers up there joking with everybody."

"Some places have already quit lotteries," Mrs. Adams said.   33

"Nothing but trouble in *that*," Old Man Warner said stoutly. "Pack of   34
young fools."

"Martin." And Bobby Martin watched his father go forward. "Over-   35
dyke. . . . Percy."

"I wish they'd hurry," Mrs. Dunbar said to her older son. "I wish they'd   36
hurry."

"They're almost through," her son said.   37

"You get ready to run tell Dad," Mrs. Dunbar said.   38

Mr. Summers called his own name and then stepped forward precisely   39
and selected a slip from the box. Then he called, "Warner."

"Seventy-seventh year I been in the lottery," Old Man Warner said as he   40
went through the crowd. "Seventy-seventh time."

"Watson." The tall boy came awkwardly through the crowd. Someone   41
said, "Don't be nervous, Jack," and Mr. Summers said, "Take your time, son."

"Zanini."   42

After that, there was a long pause, a breathless pause, until Mr. Sum-   43
mers, holding his slip of paper in the air, said, "All right, fellows." For a
minute, no one moved, and then all the slips of paper were opened. Suddenly, all the women began to speak at once, saying, "Who is it?" "Who's
got it?" "Is it the Dunbars?" "Is it the Watsons?" Then the voices began to
say, "It's Hutchinson. It's Bill." "Bill Hutchinson's got it."

"Go tell your father," Mrs. Dunbar said to her older son.   44

People began to look around to see the Hutchinsons. Bill Hutchinson   45
was standing quiet, staring down at the paper in his hand. Suddenly, Tessie
Hutchinson shouted to Mr. Summers, "You didn't give him time enough to
take any paper he wanted. I saw you. It wasn't fair!"

"Be a good sport, Tessie," Mrs. Delacroix called, and Mrs. Graves said,   46
"All of us took the same chance."

"Shut up, Tessie," Bill Hutchinson said.   47

"Well, everyone," Mr. Summers said, "that was done pretty fast, and   48
now we've got to be hurrying a little more to get done in time." He consulted his next list. "Bill," he said, "you draw for the Hutchinson family. You
got any other households in the Hutchinsons?"

"There's Don and Eva," Mrs. Hutchinson yelled. "Make *them* take their   49
chance!"

"Daughters draw with their husbands' families, Tessie," Mr. Summers   50
said gently. "You know that as well as anyone else."

"It wasn't *fair*," Tessie said.   51

"I guess not, Joe," Bill Hutchinson said regretfully. "My daughter draws   52
with her husband's family, that's only fair. And I've got no other family except the kids."

"Then, as far as drawing for families is concerned, it's you," Mr. Sum-   53
mers said in explanation, "and as far as drawing for households is concerned, that's you, too. Right?"

"Right," Bill Hutchinson said.   54

"How many kids, Bill?" Mr. Summers asked formally.   55

"Three," Bill Hutchinson said. "There's Bill, Jr., and Nancy, and little   56
Dave. And Tessie and me."

"All right, then," Mr. Summers said. "Harry, you got their tickets back?"   57

Mr. Graves nodded and held up the slips of paper. "Put them in the box,   58
then," Mr. Summers directed. "Take Bill's and put it in."

"I think we ought to start over," Mrs. Hutchinson said, as quietly as she   59
could. "I tell you it wasn't *fair*. You didn't give him time enough to choose.
*Every*body saw that."

Mr. Graves had selected the five slips and put them in the box, and he   60
dropped all the papers but those onto the ground, where the breeze caught
them and lifted them off.

"Listen, everybody," Mrs. Hutchinson was saying to the people around   61
her.

"Ready, Bill?" Mr. Summers asked, and Bill Hutchinson, with one quick   62
glance around at his wife and children, nodded.

"Remember," Mr. Summers said, "take the slips and keep them folded   63
until each person has taken one. Harry, you help little Dave." Mr. Graves
took the hand of the little boy, who came willingly with him up to the box.
"Take a paper out of the box, Davy," Mr. Summers said. Davy put his hand
into the box and laughed. "Take just *one* paper," Mr. Summers said. "Harry,
you hold it for him." Mr. Graves took the child's hand and removed the
folded paper from the tight fist and held it while little Dave stood next to
him and looked up at him wonderingly.

"Nancy next," Mr. Summers said. Nancy was twelve, and her school   64
friends breathed heavily as she went forward, switching her skirt, and took a
slip daintily from the box. "Bill, Jr.," Mr. Summers said, and Billy, his face
red and his feet overlarge, nearly knocked the box over as he got a paper out.
"Tessie," Mr. Summers said. She hesitated for a minute, looking around defi-
antly, and then set her lips and went up to the box. She snatched a paper
out and held it behind her.

"Bill," Mr. Summers said, and Bill Hutchinson reached into the box and   65
felt around, bringing his hand out at last with the slip of paper in it.

The crowd was quiet. A girl whispered, "I hope it's not Nancy," and the   66
sound of the whisper reached the edges of the crowd.

"It's not the way it used to be," Old Man Warner said clearly. "People   67
ain't the way they used to be."

"All right," Mr. Summers said. "Open the papers. Harry, you open little   68
Dave's."

Mr. Graves opened the slip of paper and there was a general sigh   69
through the crowd as he held it up and everyone could see that it was blank.
Nancy and Bill, Jr., opened theirs at the same time, and both beamed and
laughed, turning around to the crowd and holding their slips of paper above
their heads.

"Tessie," Mr. Summers said. There was a pause, and then Mr. Summers 70 looked at Bill Hutchinson, and Bill unfolded his paper and showed it. It was blank.

"It's Tessie," Mr. Summers said, and his voice was hushed. "Show us her 71 paper, Bill."

Bill Hutchinson went over to his wife and forced the slip of paper out of 72 her hand. It had a black spot on it, the black spot Mr. Summers had made the night before with the heavy pencil in the coal-company office. Bill Hutchinson held it up, and there was a stir in the crowd.

"All right, folks," Mr. Summers said. "Let's finish quickly." 73

Although the villagers had forgotten the ritual and lost the original 74 black box, they still remembered to use stones. The pile of stones the boys had made earlier was ready; there were stones on the ground with the blowing scraps of paper that had come out of the box. Mrs. Delacroix selected a stone so large she had to pick it up with both hands and turned to Mrs. Dunbar. "Come on," she said. "Hurry up."

Mrs. Dunbar had small stones in both hands, and she said, gasping for 75 breath, "I can't run at all. You'll have to go ahead and I'll catch up with you."

The children had stones already, and someone gave little Davy Hutchin- 76 son a few pebbles.

Tessie Hutchinson was in the center of a cleared space by now, and she 77 held her hands out desperately as the villagers moved in on her. "It isn't fair," she said. A stone hit her on the side of the head.

Old Man Warner was saying, "Come on, come on, everyone." Steve 78 Adams was in the front of the crowd of villagers, with Mrs. Graves beside him.

"It isn't fair, it isn't right," Mrs. Hutchinson screamed, and then they 79 were upon her.

Questions to Start You Thinking

Meaning

1. Where does this story take place? When?
2. How does this lottery differ from what we usually think of as a lottery? Why would people conduct a lottery such as this?
3. What does this story mean to you?

Writing Strategies

4. Can you see and hear the people in the story? Do they seem to be real or based on fantasy? Who is the most memorable character to you?
5. Are the events believable? Does the ending shock you? Is it believable?
6. Is this story realistic, or is Jackson using these events to represent something else?

For Burns's synopsis of "The Lottery," see pp. 257–58. For more on writing a summary, see D5 and D6 in the Quick Research Guide (the dark-red-edged pages).

For examples of annotated passages, see p. 24 and p. 30.

Read Closely.   As Jonathan Burns read "The Lottery," he was carried along quickly to the startling ending. After the immediate impact of the story wore off, Burns reread it, savoring some of the details he had missed during his first reading. Then he wrote a summary or *synopsis* of "The Lottery" to get a clear fix on the literal events in the story.

But Burns knew that he could not write a good essay without reading the story closely, marking key points in the text. By rereading *at least* three times, he could check his interpretations and be sure that evidence from the story supported his claims. When you analyze a complex work of literature, allow time for several close readings, each for a different reason.

For more on literal and critical reading, see Ch. 2.

READING CHECKLIST

Reading to Comprehend

___ What is the literal meaning? Write a few sentences explaining the overall situation — what happens to whom, where, when, why, and how.

___ What are the facts of the situation — the events of the plot, the aspects of the setting, and the major attributes, words, and actions of the characters?

___ What does all the vocabulary mean, especially in titles and in poems? Look up any unfamiliar words or words whose familiar meanings don't seem to fit the context.

Reading to Analyze

___ What are the main parts or elements of the work? Read, read aloud, mark, or make notes on such elements as theme, character, language, style, symbol, or form.

___ What does the literary work mean? What does it imply?

___ What does it suggest about the human condition? How does it expand your understanding? What insights can you apply to your own life?

Reading to Evaluate

___ How do you assess the soundness and plausibility of what the author says?

___ Are the words and tone appropriate for the purpose and audience?

___ Does the author achieve his or her purpose? Is it a worthwhile purpose?

Plan and Organize an Analysis.   Jonathan Burns knew he had to analyze the important elements — such as setting, character, and tone — in "The Lottery" to understand the story well enough to write about it. He immediately thought of the story's undertone of violence but decided that it was so subtle that writing about it would be difficult. Then he considered the especially memorable characters, Mr. Summers and Old Man Warner.

And of course there was Tessie Hutchinson; he could hear her screams as the stones hit her. But he could not think of much to say except the vague statement that they were memorable. All of a sudden, he hit on the surprise ending. How did Jackson manipulate all the details to generate such a shock?

To begin to focus his thinking, he brainstormed for possible essay titles having to do with the ending, some serious, others less so: Death Comes as a Surprise, The Unsuspected Finish, Patience of the Devil. He chose the straightforward title "The Hidden Truth." After reviewing his notes, Burns realized that Jackson uses characterization, symbolism, and ambiguous description to build up to the ending. He listed details from the story under those three headings to make an informal plan for his paper:

For more on brainstorming, see pp. 296–97. For more on seeking motives of characters, see pp. 305–06.

Title: The Hidden Truth
Working Thesis: In "The Lottery" Jackson effectively crafts a shock ending.
1. Characterization that contributes to the shock ending
   –The children of the village
   –The adults of the village
   –Conversations among the villagers
2. Symbols that contribute to the shock ending
   –The stones
   –The black box
3. Ambiguous description that contributes to the shock ending
   –The word "lottery"
   –Comments
     –"clean forgot"
     –"wish they'd hurry"
     –"It isn't fair."
   –Actions
   –Relief
   –Suspense

For more on stating a thesis, see pp. 312–19. For more on organizing ideas and outlining, see pp. 319–33.

Then he drafted the following introduction:

For more on introductions, see pp. 340–42.

Unsuspecting, the reader follows Shirley Jackson's softly flowing tale of a rural community's timeless ritual, the lottery. Awareness of what is at stake—the savage murder of one random member—comes slowly. No sooner does the realization set in than the story is over. It is a shock ending.

What creates the shock that the reader experiences reading "The Lottery"? Shirley Jackson takes great care in producing this effect, using elements such as language, symbolism, and characterization to lure the reader into not anticipating what is to come.

With his synopsis, his plan, his copy of the story, and this beginning of a draft, Burns revised the introduction and wrote the following essay.

STUDENT ESSAY

Jonathan Burns

The Hidden Truth: An Analysis of Shirley Jackson's "The Lottery"

It is as if the first stone thrown strikes the reader as well as Mrs. Hutchinson.   1
And even though there were signs of the stoning to come, somehow the reader is
taken by surprise at Tessie's violent death. What factors contribute to the shock
ending to "The Lottery"? On closer examination of the story, the reader finds that
through all the events leading up to the ending, Shirley Jackson has used
unsuspicious characterizations, unobtrusive symbolism, and ambiguous descriptions
to achieve so sudden an impact.

By all appearances, the village is a normal place with normal people. Children   2
arrive at the scene first, with school just over for the summer, talking of teachers
and books, not of the fact that someone will die today (237). And as the adults
show up, their actions are just as stereotypical: the men talk of farming and taxes,
while the women gossip (237). The scene conveys no trace of hostility, no sense of
dread in anyone: death seems very far away here.

The conversations between the villagers are no more ominous. As the husbands   3
draw slips of paper for their families, the villagers make apparently everyday
comments about the seemingly ordinary event of the lottery. Mr. Summers is regarded
as a competent and respected figure, despite the fact that his wife is "a scold" (237).
Old Man Warner brags about how many lotteries he's seen and rambles on criticizing
other towns that have given up the tradition (240–41). The characters' comments
show the crowd to be more a closely knit community than a murderous mob.

The symbols of "The Lottery" seem equally ordinary. The stones collected by the   4
boys (237) are unnoticed by the adults and thus seem a trivial detail. The reader
thinks of the "great pile" (237) as children's entertainment, like a stack of imaginary
coins, rather than an arsenal. Ironically, no stones are ever thrown during the
children's play, and no violence is seen in the pile of stones.

Similarly, Jackson describes the box and its history in great detail, but nothing   5
seems unusual about it. It is just another everyday object, stored away in the post
office or on a shelf in the grocery (238). Every other day of the year, the box is in
plain view but goes virtually unnoticed. The only indication that the box has lethal
consequences is that it is painted black (238), yet this is an ambiguous detail, as
a black box can also signify mystery or magic, mystical forces that are sometimes
thought to exist in any lottery.

In her ambiguous descriptions, Jackson refers regularly to the village's lottery   6
and emphasizes it as a central ritual for the people. The word *lottery* itself is ironic,
as it typically implies a winning of some kind, like a raffle or sweepstakes. It is

The numbers in parentheses are page-number citations following MLA style. For more advice on citing and listing sources, see D6 and E in the Quick Research Guide (the dark-red-edged pages).

paralleled to square dances and to the teenage club, all under the direction of Mr. Summers (237), activities people look forward to. There is no implied difference between the occurrences of this day and the festivities of Halloween: according to Jackson, they are all merely "civic activities" (237). Equally ambiguous are the people's emotions: some of the villagers are casual, such as Mrs. Hutchinson, who arrives late because she "'[c]lean forgot'" what day it is (239), and some are anxious, such as Mrs. Dunbar, who repeats to her son, "'I wish they'd hurry,'" without any sign of the cause of her anxiety (241). With these descriptive details, the reader finds no threat or malice in the villagers, only vague expectation and congeniality.

Even when it becomes clear that the lottery is something no one wants to win,   7
Jackson presents only a vague sense of sadness and mild protest. The crowd is relieved that the youngest of the Hutchinsons, Davy, doesn't draw the fatal slip of paper (242). One girl whispers that she hopes it isn't Nancy (242), and when the Hutchinson children discover they aren't the winners, they beam with joy and proudly display their blank slips (242). Suspense and excitement grow only when the victim is close to being identified. And when Tessie is revealed as the winner of the lottery (243), she merely holds her hands out "desperately" and repeats, "'It isn't fair'" (243).

With a blend of character, symbolism, and description, Jackson paints an overall   8
portrait of a gentle-seeming rural community, apparently no different from any other. The tragic end is sudden only because there is no recognition of violence beforehand, despite the fact that Jackson has provided the reader with plenty of clues in the ample details about the lottery and the people. It is a haunting discovery that the story ends in death, even though such is the truth in the everyday life of all people.

Questions to Start You Thinking

Meaning

1. What is Burns's thesis?
2. What major points does he use to support the interpretation stated in his thesis? What specific elements of the story does he include as evidence?

Writing Strategies

3. How does this essay differ from a synopsis, a summary of the events of the plot? (For a synopsis of "The Lottery," see pp. 257–58.)
4. Does Burns focus on the technique of the short story or on its theme?
5. Is his introduction effective? Compare and contrast it with his first draft (p. 245). What did he change? Which version do you prefer?
6. Why does he explain characterization first, symbolism second, and description last? How effective is this organization? Would discussing these elements in a different order have made much difference?
7. Is his conclusion effective?
8. How does he tie his ideas together as he moves from paragraph to paragraph? How does he keep the focus on ideas and technique instead of plot?

A Glossary of Terms for Literary Analysis

Characters. Characters are imagined people. The author shows you what they are like through their actions, speech, thoughts, attitudes, and background. Sometimes a writer also includes physical characteristics or names or relationships with other people. For example, in "The Lottery," the description of Mr. Summers introduces the lottery official as someone with civic interests who wants to avoid slip-ups (paragraphs 4, 9, and 10).

Figures of Speech. Figures of speech are lively or fresh expressions that vary the expected sequence or sense of words. Some common types of figurative language are the *simile,* a comparison using *like* or *as;* the *metaphor,* an implied comparison; and *personification,* the attribution of human qualities to inanimate or nonhuman creatures or things. In "The Lottery," three boys *guard* their pile of stones "against the *raids*" of others (paragraph 2).

Imagery. Images are words or groups of words that refer to any sense experience: seeing, hearing, smelling, tasting, touching, or feeling. The images in "The Lottery" help readers envision the "richly green" grass (paragraph 1), the smooth and round stones the children gather (paragraph 2), the "hush" that comes over the crowd (paragraph 19), and Mrs. Dunbar "gasping for breath" (paragraph 75).

Irony. Irony results from readers' sense of discrepancy. A simple kind of irony, *sarcasm,* occurs when you say one thing but mean the opposite: "I just love scrubbing the floor." In literature, an *ironic situation* sets up a contrast or incongruity. In "The Lottery," cruel and horrifying actions take place on a sunny June day in an ordinary village. *Ironic dialogue* occurs when a character says one thing, but the audience or reader is aware of another meaning. When Old Man Warner reacts to giving up the lottery as "wanting to go back to living in caves" (paragraph 32), he implies that such a change would return the villages to a more primitive life. His comment is ironic because the reader is aware that this lottery is a primitive ritual. A story has an *ironic point of view* when readers sense a difference between the author and the narrator or the character who perceives the story; Jackson, for instance, clearly does not condone the actions of the villagers.

Plot. Plot is the arrangement of the events of the story — what happens to whom, where, when, and why. If the events follow each other logically and are in keeping with the characters, the plot is *plausible,* or believable. Although the ending of "The Lottery" at first may shock readers, the author uses *foreshadowing,* hints or clues such as the villagers' nervousness about the lottery, to help readers understand future events or twists in the plot.

Most plots place the *protagonist,* or main character, in a *conflict* with the *antagonist,* some other person or group. In "The Lottery," a reader might see Tessie as the protagonist and the villagers as the antagonist. *Conflict* consists of two forces trying to conquer each other or resist being conquered —

not merely vaguely defined turmoil. *External conflicts* occur outside an individual — between two people, a person and a group (Tessie versus the villagers), two groups (lottery supporters and opponents), or even a character and the environment. *Internal conflicts* between two opposing forces or desires occur within an individual (such as fear versus hope as the lottery slips are drawn). The *central conflict* is the primary conflict for the protagonist that propels the action of the story. Events of the plot *complicate* the conflict (Tessie arrives late, Bill draws the slip) and lead to the *climax*, the moment when the outcome is inevitable (Tessie draws the black dot). This outcome is the *resolution*, or conclusion (the villagers stone Tessie). Some stories let events unfold without any apparent plot — action and change occur inside the characters.

Point of View. The point of view, the angle from which a story is told, might be the author's or a character's. The *narrator* is the one who tells the story and perceives the events, perhaps with limited knowledge or a part to play. Three common points of view are those of a *first-person narrator* (*I*), the *speaker* who tells the story; a *third-person narrator* (*he* or *she*) who participates in the action (often as the protagonist); and a *third-person narrator* who simply observes. The point of view may be *omniscient* (told through several characters' eyes); *limited omniscient* (told through one character's eyes); or *objective* (not told through any character's eyes). In "The Lottery," a third-person objective narrator seemingly looks on and reports what occurs without knowing what the characters think.

Setting. Setting refers to the time and place of events and may include the season, the weather, and the people in the background. The setting often helps establish a literary work's *mood* or *atmosphere*, the emotional climate that a reader senses. For example, the first sentence of "The Lottery" establishes its setting (paragraph 1).

Symbols. Symbols are tangible objects, visible actions, or characters that hint at meanings beyond themselves. In "The Lottery," the black box suggests outdated tradition, resistance to change, evil, cruelty, and more.

Theme. A theme is a work's main idea or insight — the author's observation about life, society, or human nature. Sometimes you can sum up a theme in a sentence ("Human beings cannot live without illusion"); other times, a theme may be implied, hard to discern, or one of several in a work.

To state a theme, go beyond a work's topic or subject by asking yourself, What does the author say about this subject? Details from the story should support your statement of theme, and your theme should account for the details. "The Lottery" treats subjects such as the unexpected, scapegoating, outmoded rituals, and violence; one of its themes might be stated as "People are selfish, always looking out for number one."

LEARNING BY WRITING

The Assignment: Analyzing a Literary Work.   For this assignment, you are to be a literary critic — analyzing, interpreting, and evaluating a literary selection for your classmates. Your purpose is to deepen their understanding because you will have devoted time and effort to digging out the meaning and testing it with evidence from the work itself. Even if they too have studied the work carefully, you will try to convince them that your interpretation is valid.

Write an essay interpreting a literary work that intrigues you or expresses a worthwhile meaning. Your instructor may want to approve your selection. After careful analysis of the work, you will become the expert critic, explaining the meaning you discern, supporting your interpretation with evidence from the work, and evaluating the effectiveness of literary elements used by the author and the significance of the theme.

You cannot include everything about the work in your paper, so you should focus on one element (such as character, setting, or theme) or the interrelationship of two or three elements (as Jonathan Burns did when he analyzed characterization, symbolism, and description in his interpretation of "The Lottery"). Although a summary, or *synopsis*, of the plot is a good beginning point, retelling the story is not a satisfactory literary analysis.

These college writers successfully responded to such an assignment:

One showed how the rhythm, rhymes, and images of Adrienne Rich's poem "Aunt Jennifer's Tigers" mesh to convey the poem's theme of tension between a woman's artistic urge and societal constraints.

Another writer who was a musician analyzed the credibility of Sonny as a musician in James Baldwin's "Sonny's Blues" — his attitudes, actions, struggles, relationship with his instrument and with other musicians — and concluded that Sonny is a believable character.

A psychology major concluded that the relationship between Hamlet and Claudius in Shakespeare's *Hamlet* represents in many ways the tension, jealousy, and misunderstanding between stepsons and stepfathers.

Find a Subject.   Read several literary works to find two or three you like. You might start with a favorite author or a favorite short story among those read for this course. Next, reread the works that interest you, and select one to concentrate on. Choose the one that strikes you as especially significant — realistic or universal, moving or disturbing, believable or shocking — with a meaning that you wish to share with your classmates.

For more on analysis, see pp. 360–63.

Generate Ideas.   Analyzing a literary work is the first step in interpreting meaning and evaluating literary quality. As you read the work, identify its elements and analyze them as Jonathan Burns did for "The Lottery." Then focus on *one* significant element or a cluster of related elements. When you write your interpretation, restrict your discussion to that focus.

We provide three checklists to guide you in analyzing different types of literature. Each of these is an aid to understanding, *not* an organizational outline for writing about literature. The first checklist focuses on short stories and novels, but some of its questions can help you analyze setting, character, theme, or your reactions as a reader for almost any kind of literary work.

DISCOVERY CHECKLIST

Analyzing a Short Story or a Novel

___ What is your reaction to the story? Jot it down.

___ Who is the *narrator* — not the author, but the one who tells the story?

___ What is the *point of view?*

___ What is the *setting* (time and place)? What is the *atmosphere* or *mood?*

___ How does the *plot* unfold? Write a synopsis, or summary, of the events in time order, including relationships among those events.

___ What are the *characters* like? Describe their personalities, traits, and motivations based on their actions, speech, habits, and so on. What strategies does the author use to develop the characters? Who is the *protagonist?* The *antagonist?* Do any characters change? Are the changes believable?

___ How would you describe the story's *style,* or use of language? Is it informal, conversational, or formal? Does the story use dialect or foreign words?

___ What are the *external conflicts* and the *internal conflicts?* What is the *central conflict?* Express the conflicts using the word *versus,* such as "dreams versus reality" or "the individual versus society."

___ What is the *climax* of the story? Is there any *resolution?*

___ Are there important *symbols?* What might they mean?

___ What does the *title* of the story mean?

___ What are the *themes* of the story? Are they universal (applicable to all people everywhere at all times)? Write down your interpretation of the main theme. How is this theme related to your own life?

___ What other literary works or experiences from life does the story make you think of? Write them down.

■ For a glossary of literary terms, see pp. 248–49.

■ For more on writing a synopsis, see p. 258.

When looking at a poem, consider the elements specific to poetry and those shared with other genres, as the following checklist suggests.

DISCOVERY CHECKLIST

Analyzing a Poem

___ What is your reaction to the poem? Jot it down.

___ Who is the *speaker* — not the author, but the one who narrates?

___ Is there a *setting?* How does it relate to the meaning of the poem? What *mood* or emotional *atmosphere* does it suggest?

___ Can you put the poem into your own words — paraphrase it?

___ What is striking about the poem's language? Is it informal or formal? Does it use irony or figurative language: *imagery, metaphor, personification?* Identify repetition or words that are unusual, used in an unusual way, or *archaic* (no longer commonly used). Consider *connotations,* the suggestions conjured by the words: *house* versus *home,* though both refer to the same place.

___ Is the poem *lyric* (expressing emotion) or *narrative* (telling a story)?

___ How is the poem structured or divided? Does it use *couplets* (two consecutive rhyming lines), *quatrains* (units of four lines), or other units? How do the beginning and end relate to each other and to the poem as a whole?

___ Does the poem use *rhyme* (words that sound alike)? If so, how does the rhyme contribute to the meaning?

___ Does the poem have *rhythm* (regular meter or beat, patterns of accented and unaccented syllables)? How does the rhythm contribute to the meaning?

___ What does the *title* of the poem mean?

___ What is the major *theme* of the poem? How does this underlying idea unify the poem? How is it related to your own life?

___ What other literary works or experiences from life does the poem make you think of? Write them down.

A play is written to be seen and heard, not read. You may analyze what kind it is and how it would appear onstage, as this checklist suggests.

DISCOVERY CHECKLIST

Analyzing a Play

___ What is your reaction to the play? Jot it down.

___ Is the play a serious *tragedy* (which arouses pity and fear in the audience and usually ends unhappily with the death or downfall of the *tragic hero*)? Or is it a *comedy* (which aims to amuse and usually ends happily)?

___ What is the *setting* of the play? What is its *mood?*

___ In brief, what happens? Summarize each act of the play.

___ What are the characters like? Who is the *protagonist?* Who is the *antagonist?* Are there *foil characters* who contrast with the main character and reveal his or her traits? Which characters are in conflict? Which change?

___ Which speeches seem especially significant?

___ What is the plot? Identify the *exposition* or background information needed to understand the story. Determine the main *external* and *internal* conflicts. What is the *central conflict?* What events *complicate* the central conflict? How are these elements of the plot spread throughout the play?

___ What is the *climax* of the play? Is there a *resolution* to the action?

___ What does the *title* mean?

___ Can you identify any *dramatic irony,* words or actions of a character that carry meaning unperceived by the character but evident to the audience?

—— What is the major *theme* of the play? Is it a universal idea? How is it related to your own life?

—— What other literary works or experiences from life does the play make you think of? Write them down.

Consider Your Audience.   When you write your analysis, your purpose is to explain the work's deeper meaning. Don't try to impress readers with your brilliance. Instead, regard them as friends in whose company you are discussing something familiar to all, though they may not have studied the work as carefully as you have. This assumption will help you decide how much evidence from the work to include and will reduce summarizing.

Identify Your Support.   After you have determined the major element or cluster of elements that you intend to focus on, go through the work again to find all the passages that relate to your main point. Mark them as you find them, or put them on note cards or in a computer file, along with the page references. If you use any quotations, quote exactly.

For more on planning, drafting, and developing, see Chs. 17, 18, and 19.

Develop Your Main Idea or Thesis.   Begin by trying to express your point in a thesis statement that identifies the literary work and the author. Suppose you start with a working thesis on the theme of "The Lottery":

For more on stating a thesis, see pp. 312–19.

WORKING THESIS   In "The Lottery," Shirley Jackson reveals the theme.

But this statement is too vague, so you rewrite it to be more precise:

IMPROVED   In "The Lottery" by Shirley Jackson, the theme is tradition.

This thesis is better but still doesn't state the theme clearly or precisely. You try other ways of expressing what Jackson implies about tradition:

IMPROVED   In "The Lottery" by Shirley Jackson, one of the major themes is that outmoded traditions can be harmful.

Adding *one of* shows that this is not the story's only theme, but the rest is vague. What does *outmoded* mean? How are traditions harmful?

MORE PRECISE   In "The Lottery" by Shirley Jackson, one of the major themes is that traditions that have lost their meaning can still move people to act abnormally without thinking.

This thesis is better but may change as you write the analysis. For instance, you might go beyond interpretation of Jackson's ideas by adding *tragic* to convey your evaluation of her observation of the human condition:

EVALUATION   In "The Lottery," Shirley Jackson reveals the tragic theme that
ADDED   traditions that have lost their meaning can still move people
                to abnormal and thoughtless action.

Or you might say this, alerting readers to your main points:

PREVIEW
ADDED
In "The Lottery," Shirley Jackson effectively uses symbolism and irony to reveal the theme that traditions that have lost their meaning can still move people to abnormal and thoughtless action.

■ For a story that shows character change, see "The Story of an Hour," pp. 259–60.

When planning your essay, focus on analyzing ideas, not retelling events. One way to maintain that focus is to analyze your thesis, dividing it into parts and then developing each part in turn in your essay. The thesis just presented could be divided into (1) use of symbolism to reveal theme and (2) use of irony to reveal theme. Similarly, you might divide a thesis about character change into the character's original traits or attitudes, the events that cause change, and the character's new traits or attitudes.

Introduce Your Essay.   Tie your beginning to your main idea, or thesis. If you are uncertain how to begin, try one of these openings:

- Focus on a character's universality (pointing out that most people might feel as Tessie in "The Lottery" did if their names were drawn).
- Focus on a theme's universality (discussing briefly how traditions seem to be losing their meaning in modern society).

FOR PEER RESPONSE

Ask one of your classmates to read your draft, considering how effectively you have analyzed the literary work and presented your analysis. Ask your peer editor to answer specific questions such as these:

- What is your first reaction to the literary analysis?
- In what ways does the analysis add to your understanding of the literary work? In what ways does it add to your insights into life?
- Does the introduction make you want to read the rest of the analysis? What changes would you suggest to strengthen the opening?
- Is the main idea clear? Is there sufficient relevant evidence from the work to support that point? Put stars wherever additional evidence is needed. Put a check mark by any irrelevant information.
- Does the writer go beyond plot summary to analyze elements, interpret meaning, and evaluate literary merit? If not, how might the writer revise?
- Is the analysis organized by ideas instead of events? What changes in organization would you suggest?
- Do the transitions guide you smoothly from one point to the next? Do the transitions focus on ideas, not on time or position in the story? Note any places where the writer might add transitions.
- If this were your paper, what is the one thing you would be sure to work on before handing it in?

For general questions for a peer editor, see p. 377. For peer response worksheets, visit <bedfordstmartins.com/ bedguide> and do a keyword search:

peer

- Quote a striking line from the work ("and then they were upon her" or "'Lottery in June, corn be heavy soon'").

- Start with a statement of what the work is about, with your reaction to the work when you read it, with a parallel personal experience, or with a comment about a technique that the writer uses.

- Ask a "Have you ever?" question to draw readers into your interpretation.

For more on introductions, see pp. 340–42.

Support Your Interpretation.   As you develop your analysis, include supporting evidence — descriptions of setting and character, summaries of events, quotations of dialogue, and other specifics. Cite page numbers (for prose) or line numbers (for poetry) where the details can be found in the work. Integrate evidence from the story with your comments and ideas.

Keep the focus on ideas, not events, by using transition markers that refer to character traits and personality change, not to time. Say "Although Mr. Summers was . . ." instead of "At the beginning of the story Mr. Summers was . . . ." Write "Tessie became . . ." instead of "After that Tessie was . . ." State "The villagers in 'The Lottery' changed . . . ," not "On the next page . . . ."

For more on citing and listing literary works, see MLA style in E in the Quick Research Guide (the dark-red-edged pages).

For a list of transitions showing logical connections, see p. 347.

Conclude Your Essay.   When you reach the end, don't just stop writing. Use the same techniques you use for introductions — personal experience, comment on technique, quotation — to provide a sense of finality and closing for your readers. Refer to or reaffirm your thesis. Often an effective conclusion ties in directly with the introduction.

For more on conclusions, see pp. 343–44.

Revise and Edit.   Consider these questions as you shape your draft:

For more revising and editing strategies, see Ch. 20.

REVISION CHECKLIST

___ Have you clearly identified the literary work and the author near the beginning of the analysis?

___ Is your main idea or thesis clear? Does everything else relate to it?

___ Have you focused on one element or a cluster of related elements in your analysis? Have you organized around these ideas rather than events?

___ Do your transitions focus on ideas, not on plot or time sequence? Do they guide readers easily from one section or sentence to the next?

___ Are your interpretations supported by evidence from the literary work? Do you need to add examples of dialogue, action, or description? Have you selected details relevant to the points of analysis, not interesting sidelights?

___ Have you woven the details from the work smoothly into your text? Have you cited their correct page or line numbers? Have you quoted and cited carefully instead of lifting language without proper attribution?

___ Do you understand all the words and literary terms you use?

___ Have you tried to share your insights into the meaning of the work with your readers, or have you slipped into trying to impress them?

For more editing and proofreading strategies, see pp. 384–87.

After you have revised your literary analysis, check the grammar, word choice, punctuation, and mechanics — and then correct any problems you find. Make sure that you smoothly introduce all of your quotations and references to the work and weave them into your own discussion. Here are some questions to get you started editing and proofreading your paper:

EDITING CHECKLIST

For more help, turn to the dark-blue-edged pages, and find the Quick Editing Guide sections noted here.

___ Have you used the present tense for events in the literary work and for comments about the author's presentation?	A3
___ Have you used quotation marks correctly whenever you give the exact words of the literary work?	C3
___ Have you used correct manuscript format for your paper?	D3

Strategies for Writing about Literature: Synopsis and Paraphrase

LEARNING FROM OTHER WRITERS: SYNOPSIS

In your literature courses you will often be asked to write synopses of short stories and novels and to paraphrase poems. Both skills are valuable because they help you get the chronology straight, pick out the significant events and details, and relate the parts of a work to each other and to the themes of the work.

For more on summarizing and paraphrasing, see Ch. 12 and D in the Quick Research Guide on the dark-red-edged pages.

A *synopsis* is a summary of the plot of a narrative — a short story, a novel, a play, or a narrative poem. It describes the literal meaning, condensing the story to the major events and the most significant details. You do not include your interpretation, but you summarize the work in your own words, taking care not to lift language or sentence structure from the work itself. Like a synopsis, a *paraphrase* conveys the meaning of the original piece of literature and the relationships of its parts in your own words. A paraphrase, however, converts the original poetry to your own prose or the original prose to your own words in a passage about as long as the original.

For "The Lottery," see pp. 237–43.

In preparation for writing his literary analysis of "The Lottery" — to make sure he had the sequence of events clear — Jonathan Burns wrote the following synopsis of the story.

STUDENT EXAMPLE

Jonathan Burns
A Synopsis of "The Lottery"

Around ten o'clock on a sunny June 27, the villagers gathered in the square for   1
a lottery, expecting to be home in time for lunch. The children came first, glad that
school was out for the summer. The boys romped and gathered stones, the girls
talked quietly in small groups, and the little ones hovered near their brothers and
sisters. Then the men came, followed by the women. When parents called, the
children came reluctantly.

Mr. Summers, who always conducted the town lottery, arrived with the black   2
wooden box and set it on the three-legged stool that Mr. Graves had brought out.
The villagers remained at a distance from these men and didn't respond when Mr.
Summers asked for help. Finally, Mr. Martin and his son held the shabby black box as
Mr. Summers mixed the papers in it. Although the townspeople had talked about
replacing the box, they never had, but they had substituted paper slips for the
original wooden chips. To prepare for the drawing, they listed the members of every
household and swore in Mr. Summers. Although they had dropped many aspects of
the original ritual, the official still greeted each person individually.

Tessie Hutchinson rushed into the square, telling her friend Mrs. Delacroix she   3
had almost forgotten what day it was. Then she joined her husband and children.

When Mr. Summers asked if everyone was present, he was told that Clyde Dunbar   4
was absent because of a broken leg but that his wife would draw for the family.
Summers noted that the Watson boy was drawing for his mother and checked to
see if Old Man Warner was present.

The crowd got quiet. Mr. Summers reminded everybody of what they were to   5
do and began to call the names in alphabetical order. People in the group joked
nervously as the names were called. Mrs. Delacroix and Mrs. Graves commented on
how fast time had passed since the last lottery, and Old Man Warner talked about
how important the lottery was to the villagers. When Mr. Summers finished calling
the roll, there was a pause before the heads of households opened their slips.
Everybody wondered who had the special slip of paper, who had won the lottery.
They discovered it was Bill Hutchinson. When Tessie complained that the drawing
hadn't been done fairly, the others told her to "Be a good sport" (241).

Mr. Graves put five slips into the box, one for each member of Bill Hutchinson's   6
family. Tessie kept charging unfairness. The children drew first, then Tessie, then
Bill. The children opened their slips, smiled broadly, and held blank pieces of paper
over their heads. Bill opened his, and it was blank too. Tessie wouldn't open hers;
Bill had to do it for her. Hers had a black spot on it.

Mr. Summers urged the villagers to complete the process quickly. They picked up   7
stones, even little Davy Hutchinson, and started throwing them at Tessie, as she
kept screaming, "It isn't fair, it isn't right" (243). Then they stoned her.

Questions to Start You Thinking

Meaning

1. In what ways does this synopsis help you understand the story better?
2. Why isn't a synopsis as interesting as a short story?
3. Can you tell from this synopsis whether Burns understands Jackson's story beyond the literal level? How can you tell?

Writing Strategies

4. Does Burns retell the story accurately and clearly? Does he get the events in correct time order? How does he show the relationships of the events to each other and to the whole?
5. Does Burns select the details necessary to indicate what happened in "The Lottery"? Why do you think he omits certain details?
6. Are there any details, comments, or events that you would add to his synopsis? Why or why not?
7. How does this synopsis differ from Burns's literary analysis (pp. 246–47)?

LEARNING BY WRITING: SYNOPSIS

The Assignment: Writing a Synopsis of a Story by Kate Chopin.
Whenever you have trouble understanding a story or have a lot of stories to read, writing a synopsis can help you easily review a story's specifics. Keep your synopsis of the plot true to the original, noting accurate details in time order. Condensing a story to a few hundred words forces you to focus on the most important details and the sequence of events, often leading to a statement of theme.

Kate Chopin was a nineteenth-century American writer whose female characters search for their own identity and for freedom from oppression. For practice, write a synopsis of two to three hundred words of Chopin's "The Story of an Hour." Use these questions to help you get started:

DISCOVERY CHECKLIST

___ What are the major events and details of the story?
___ In what time order do events take place?
___ How are the parts of the story related (without adding your interpretations)?
___ Which of the author's words might you want to quote?

Kate Chopin

The Story of an Hour

Knowing that Mrs. Mallard was afflicted with a heart trouble, great care was taken to break to her as gently as possible the news of her husband's death. 1

It was her sister Josephine who told her, in broken sentences, veiled hints that revealed in half concealing. Her husband's friend Richards was there, too, near her. It was he who had been in the newspaper office when intelligence of the railroad disaster was received, with Brently Mallard's name leading the list of "killed." He had only taken the time to assure himself of its truth by a second telegram, and had hastened to forestall any less careful, less tender friend in bearing the sad message. 2

She did not hear the story as many women have heard the same, with a paralyzed inability to accept its significance. She wept at once, with sudden, wild abandonment, in her sister's arms. When the storm of grief had spent itself she went away to her room alone. She would have no one follow her. 3

There stood, facing the open window, a comfortable, roomy armchair. Into this she sank, pressed down by a physical exhaustion that haunted her body and seemed to reach into her soul. 4

She could see in the open square before her house the tops of trees that were all aquiver with the new spring life. The delicious breath of rain was in the air. In the street below a peddler was crying his wares. The notes of a distant song which someone was singing reached her faintly, and countless sparrows were twittering in the eaves. 5

There were patches of blue sky showing here and there through the clouds that had met and piled one above the other in the west facing her window. 6

She sat with her head thrown back upon the cushion of the chair, quite motionless, except when a sob came up into her throat and shook her, as a child who has cried itself to sleep continues to sob in its dreams. 7

She was young, with a fair, calm face, whose lines bespoke repression and even a certain strength. But now there was a dull stare in her eyes, whose gaze was fixed away off yonder on one of those patches of blue sky. It was not a glance of reflection, but rather indicated a suspension of intelligent thought. 8

There was something coming to her and she was waiting for it, fearfully. What was it? She did not know; it was too subtle and elusive to name. But she felt it, creeping out of the sky, reaching toward her through the sounds, the scents, the color that filled the air. 9

Now her bosom rose and fell tumultuously. She was beginning to recognize this thing that was approaching to possess her, and she was striving to beat it back with her will—as powerless as her two white slender hands would have been. 10

When she abandoned herself a little whispered word escaped her slightly parted lips. She said it over and over under her breath: "Free, free, 11 free!" The vacant stare and the look of terror that had followed it went from her eyes. They stayed keen and bright. Her pulses beat fast, and the coursing blood warmed and relaxed every inch of her body.

She did not stop to ask if it were not a monstrous joy that held her. A 12 clear and exalted perception enabled her to dismiss the suggestion as trivial.

She knew that she would weep again when she saw the kind, tender 13 hands folded in death; the face that had never looked save with love upon her, fixed and gray and dead. But she saw beyond that bitter moment a long procession of years to come that would belong to her absolutely. And she opened and spread her arms out to them in welcome.

There would be no one to live for during those coming years; she would 14 live for herself. There would be no powerful will bending her in that blind persistence with which men and women believe they have a right to impose a private will upon a fellow creature. A kind intention or a cruel intention made the act seem no less a crime as she looked upon it in that brief moment of illumination.

And yet she had loved him — sometimes. Often she had not. What did 15 it matter! What could love, the unsolved mystery, count for in face of this possession of self-assertion which she suddenly recognized as the strongest impulse of her being.

"Free! Body and soul free!" she kept whispering.   16

Josephine was kneeling before the closed door with her lips to the 17 keyhole, imploring for admission. "Louise, open the door! I beg; open the door — you will make yourself ill. What are you doing, Louise? For heaven's sake open the door."

"Go away. I am not making myself ill." No; she was drinking in a very 18 elixir of life through that open window.

Her fancy was running riot along those days ahead of her. Spring days, 19 and summer days, and all sorts of days that would be her own. She breathed a quick prayer that life might be long. It was only yesterday she had thought with a shudder that life might be long.

She arose at length and opened the door to her sister's importunities. 20 There was a feverish triumph in her eyes, and she carried herself unwittingly like a goddess of Victory. She clasped her sister's waist, and together they descended the stairs. Richards stood waiting for them at the bottom.

Someone was opening the front door with a latchkey. It was Brently 21 Mallard who entered, a little travel-stained, composedly carrying his gripsack and umbrella. He had been far from the scene of the accident, and did not even know there had been one. He stood amazed at Josephine's piercing cry; at Richards's quick motion to screen him from the view of his wife.

But Richards was too late.   22

When the doctors came they said she had died of heart disease — of joy 23 that kills.

LEARNING BY WRITING: PARAPHRASE

The Assignment: Writing a Paraphrase of a Poem.   When you study poetry, you can benefit from paraphrasing—expressing the content of a poem in your own words without adding your opinions or interpretations. Writing a paraphrase forces you to divide the poem into logical sections, to figure out what the poet says in each section, and to discern how the parts relate. After paraphrasing a poem, you should find it easier to state its theme—its main idea or insight—in a sentence or two. Use these questions to get started:

■ For more on paraphrasing, see Ch. 12 and D4 and D6 in the Quick Research Guide (the dark-red-edged pages).

■ See pp. 196–97 and the Other Assignments section below for poems you might paraphrase.

DISCOVERY CHECKLIST

___ What are the poem's major sections? What does the poet say in each one?

___ How are the sections of the poem related?

___ Are any words unfamiliar or used in a special sense, different from the usual meanings? What do those words mean in the context of the poem?

___ Does the poet use images to create sensory pictures or figurative language to create comparisons? How do these contribute to the meaning?

■ For more on figures of speech or imagery, see p. 248.

Other Assignments for Writing about Literature

1. Use a poem, a play, or a novel instead of a short story to write the literary analysis assigned in this chapter (p. 250).
2. Write an essay comparing and contrasting a literary element in two or three short stories or poems.
3. Read the poem below by Robert Frost (1874–1963). Write an essay using a paraphrase of the poem as a springboard for your thoughts on a fork in the road of your life—a decision that made a difference for you.

■ For more on writing a comparison and contrast essay, see Ch. 7.

■ For another poem by Robert Frost, see pp. 196–97.

The Road Not Taken

Two roads diverged in a yellow wood,
And sorry I could not travel both
And be one traveler, long I stood
And looked down one as far as I could
To where it bent in the undergrowth;

Then took the other, as just as fair,
And having perhaps the better claim,
Because it was grassy and wanted wear;
Though as for that the passing there
Had worn them really about the same,

And both that morning equally lay
In leaves no step had trodden black.
Oh, I kept the first for another day!
Yet knowing how way leads on to way,
I doubted if I should ever come back.

I shall be telling this with a sigh
Somewhere ages and ages hence:
Two roads diverged in a wood, and I —
I took the one less traveled by,
And that has made all the difference.

For more on writing a comparison and contrast essay, see Ch. 7.

4. Read the poem below by Edwin Arlington Robinson (1869–1935). Have you known and envied someone similar to Richard Cory, a person everyone thought had it all? What happened to him or her? What did you discover about your impression of this person? Write a personal response essay to compare and contrast the person you knew with Richard Cory. Be sure to analyze the poem and draw on your own experience.

Richard Cory

Whenever Richard Cory went down town,
We people on the pavement looked at him:
He was a gentleman from sole to crown,
Clean favored, and imperially slim.

And he was always quietly arrayed,
And he was always human when he talked;
But still he fluttered pulses when he said,
"Good-morning," and he glittered when he walked.

And he was rich — yes, richer than a king —
And admirably schooled in every grace:
In fine, we thought that he was everything
To make us wish that we were in his place.

So on we worked, and waited for the light,
And went without the meat, and cursed the bread;
And Richard Cory, one calm summer night,
Went home and put a bullet through his head.

For more about analyzing visuals, see Ch. 22. For more on analysis in general, see pp. 360–63.

5. Write a critical analysis of a song, a movie, or a television program. Be sure to hear or view the work several times to pull out the specific evidence necessary to support your interpretation. If your instructor approves, present your analysis in a podcast, a multimedia format, or a series of Web pages.

Chapter 14
Writing in the Workplace

M ost of the world's workplace communication takes place in writing. Although a conversation or voice mail may be forgotten or ignored, a letter, memorandum (memo), or e-mail provides a permanent record of business exchanges, often calling for action.

Personnel managers, the people who do the hiring in large corporations, tend to be keenly interested in applicants who can write clearly, accurately, and effectively. A survey conducted at Cornell University asked executives to rate in importance the qualities they would like employees to possess. Skill in writing was ranked in fourth place, ahead of both managerial and analytical skills, suggesting the practical value of a writing course.

In this chapter, we first outline some general guidelines for workplace writing and then show you four kinds likely to prove useful in your career — letters, memoranda, e-mail, and résumés.

EFFECTIVE
WORKPLACE
WRITING

Respectful tone

Clear purpose

Concise, clear, well-organized presentation

Reader's point of view

Guidelines for Writing in the Workplace

Good workplace writing succeeds in achieving a clear purpose. When you write to a business, your writing represents you; when you write as part of your job, your writing represents your company as well.

263

KNOW YOUR PURPOSE

Your purpose, or reason for writing, helps you select and arrange information; it gives you a standard against which to measure your final draft. Most likely, you will want to create a certain response in your readers, informing them about something or motivating them to take a specific action.

DISCOVERY CHECKLIST

___ Do you want to inform—announce something, update others, explain some specialized knowledge, or reply to a request?

___ Do you want to motivate some action—get a question answered, a wrong corrected, a decision made, or a personnel director to hire you?

___ When your readers are finished reading what you've written, what do you want them to think? What do you want them to do?

KEEP YOUR AUDIENCE IN MIND

Consider everything in your workplace writing from your audience's point of view. After all, your purpose is not to express your ideas but to have readers act on them, even if the action is simply to notice your grasp of the situation. If you don't know the person to whom you are writing, make educated guesses based on what you know about the position or company.

Especially when your purpose is to motivate, focus on how "you, the reader" will benefit instead of what "I, the writer" would like.

"I" ATTITUDE   Please send me the form so that I can process your order.

"YOU" ATTITUDE   To make sure that you receive your shipment promptly, please send me the order form.

DISCOVERY CHECKLIST

___ What do your readers already know about the subject? Are they experts in the field? Have they been kept up to date on the situation?

___ What do your readers need to know? What information do they expect you to provide? What information do they need before they can take action?

___ What can you assume about your readers' priorities and expectations? Are they busy executives, deluged with reports and messages? Are they conscientious administrators who will appreciate your attention to detail?

___ What is most likely to motivate your readers to take the action you want?

USE AN APPROPRIATE TONE

Tone is the quality of writing that reveals your attitude toward your topic and your readers. If you show readers that you respect them, their intelligence, and their feelings, they are far more likely to view you and your message favorably. Most workplace writing today ranges from the informal to the slightly formal. Gone are extremely formal phrases such as *enclosed herewith, be advised that,* or *pursuant to the stated request.* At the other extreme, slang, overfriendliness, and a too casual style might cast doubts on your seriousness or credibility. Strive for a relaxed and conversational style, using simple sentences, familiar words, and the active voice.

TOO CASUAL	I hear that thing with the new lackey is a definite go.
TOO FORMAL	This office stands informed that the administration's request for supplementary personnel has been honored.
APPROPRIATE	I understand that a new office assistant has been hired.

In all your business writing, be courteous and considerate. If you are writing to complain, remember that your reader may not be the one who caused the problem — and you are more likely to win your case with courtesy than with sarcasm or insults. When delivering bad news, remember that your reader may interpret a bureaucratic response as cold and unsympathetic. And if you have made a mistake, acknowledge it.

REVISION CHECKLIST

___ Have you avoided slang terms and extremely casual language?

___ Have you avoided unnecessarily formal or sophisticated words?

___ Are your sentences of a manageable length?

___ Have you used the active voice ("I am sending it") rather than the passive voice ("It is being sent")?

___ Does anything you've written sound blaming or accusatory?

___ Do you hear a friendly, considerate, competent person behind your words?

___ Have you asked someone else to read your writing to check for tone?

PRESENT INFORMATION CAREFULLY

In business, time is money: time wasted reading irrelevant, poorly written material is money wasted. To be effective, your business writing should be concise, clear, and well organized.

For advice on document design, see Ch. 21.

Concise writing shows that you respect your readers' time. In most cases, if a letter, memo, or résumé is longer than a page or two, it's too long. You might need to find a better way to present the material, or you might need to cut unneeded information or details.

For sample business documents, see the figures later in this chapter.

Clear writing ensures that the information you convey is accurate, complete, and unambiguous. Put what's most important in a prominent spot (usually at the beginning). Let your readers know exactly what you want them to do — politely, of course. If you have a question, ask it. If you want something, request it.

Clear presentation and organization are also important for PowerPoint slides and Web sites. For examples, see p. 404, p. 407, and p. 411.

Well-organized writing helps readers move through it quickly and easily. Write every piece of business correspondence so that it can be skimmed. Make the topic absolutely clear from the beginning, usually the first paragraph of a letter or the subject line of a memo or e-mail message. Use a conventional format that your readers will expect (see Figures 14.1 and 14.3 later in this chapter). Break information into easily processed chunks; order these chunks logically and consistently. Finally, use topic sentences and headings (when appropriate) to label each chunk of information and to give your readers an overview of your document.

REVISION CHECKLIST

For more revising and editing strategies, see Ch. 20.

___ Have you kept your letter, memo, or résumé to a page or two?

___ Have you cut all unnecessary or wordy explanations?

___ Have you scrutinized every word to ensure that it can't be misinterpreted? Have you supplied all the background information readers need?

___ Have you emphasized the most important part of your message? Will readers know what you want them to do?

___ Have you followed a consistent, logical order and a conventional format?

___ If appropriate, have you included labels and headings?

Business Letters

For advice on job application letters, see pp. 275–76.

To correspond with outside parties, either individual people or other groups, organizations use business letters to request and provide information, motivate action, respond to requests, and sell goods and services. Because letters become part of the permanent record, they can be checked later to determine exactly who said what and when. You should keep a copy of every letter you write, a printout as well as a backup on disk or network.

A good business letter is brief — limited to one page if possible. It supplies whatever information the reader needs, no more. A letter of inquiry might simply request a booklet, a sample, or some promotional material. For a special request, however, you might add why you are writing, what you need, and when you need it. On the other hand, a letter of complaint focuses on your problem — what product is involved, when and where you purchased it, exactly why you are unhappy, and how you'd like the problem solved. Include specifics such as product numbers and dates, and maintain a courteous tone. Because they are so brief, business letters are often judged on details—grammar, punctuation, format, appearance, openings, and closings.

FORMAT FOR BUSINESS LETTERS

The format of business letters (see Figure 14.1) is well established by convention. Remember that the physical appearance of a letter is very important.

■ For another sample letter, see p. 276.

- Use 8½-by-11-inch bond paper, with matching envelopes. Write on only one side of the page.
- Single-space and use an extra line of space to separate paragraphs and the different elements of the letter. In very short letters, it's acceptable to leave additional space before the inside address.

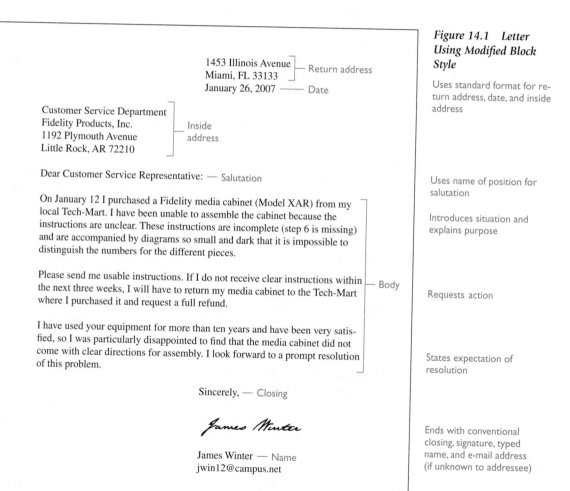

Figure 14.1   Letter Using Modified Block Style

1453 Illinois Avenue — Return address
Miami, FL 33133
January 26, 2007 —— Date

Customer Service Department
Fidelity Products, Inc. — Inside address
1192 Plymouth Avenue
Little Rock, AR 72210

Dear Customer Service Representative: — Salutation

On January 12 I purchased a Fidelity media cabinet (Model XAR) from my local Tech-Mart. I have been unable to assemble the cabinet because the instructions are unclear. These instructions are incomplete (step 6 is missing) and are accompanied by diagrams so small and dark that it is impossible to distinguish the numbers for the different pieces.

Please send me usable instructions. If I do not receive clear instructions within the next three weeks, I will have to return my media cabinet to the Tech-Mart where I purchased it and request a full refund. — Body

I have used your equipment for more than ten years and have been very satisfied, so I was particularly disappointed to find that the media cabinet did not come with clear directions for assembly. I look forward to a prompt resolution of this problem.

Sincerely, — Closing

James Winter

James Winter — Name
jwin12@campus.net

Uses standard format for return address, date, and inside address

Uses name of position for salutation

Introduces situation and explains purpose

Requests action

States expectation of resolution

Ends with conventional closing, signature, typed name, and e-mail address (if unknown to addressee)

- Leave margins of at least one inch on both sides; try to make the top and bottom margins fairly even, although you may have a larger bottom margin if your letter is very short.
- Pay attention to grammar, punctuation, and mechanics. Your readers will.

Return Address.   This is your address or the address of the company for which you are writing. Abbreviate only the state using its two-letter postal abbreviation. Omit a return address on preprinted letterhead stationery that already provides this information.

Date.   Supply this on the line right after the return address. Spell out the month; follow it by the day, a comma, and the year.

Inside Address.   This is the address of the person to whom you are writing. Begin with the person's full name and title (*Mr., Ms., Dr., Professor*); when addressing a woman without a professional title, use *Ms.* unless you know that she prefers *Miss* or *Mrs.* The second line should identify the position the person holds (if any), and the third line should name the organization (if you are writing to one). If you don't know who will read your letter, you may start with the name of the position, department, or organization. Avoid abbreviations in the address except for the state.

Salutation.   Skip a line, and then type *Dear* followed by the person's title, last name, and a colon. If you don't know the name of the person who will read your letter, you can use the position that person holds (*Dear Editor*) or the name of the organization (*Dear Angell's Bakery*) in place of a name.

Body.   This is your message. Leave one line of space between paragraphs, and begin each paragraph even with the left margin (no indentations). Paragraphs should generally be no longer than seven or eight typed lines.

Closing.   Leave one line of space after the last paragraph, and then use a conventional closing followed by a comma: *Sincerely, Sincerely yours, Respectfully yours, Yours truly.*

Typed Name with Position.   Leave four lines of space after the closing, and type your name in full, even if you will sign only your first name. Do not include a title before your name. If you are writing on behalf of an organization, you can include your position on the next line. You also may add your e-mail address or telephone number here unless supplied on your stationery or in your message.

Signature.   Print the letter, and sign your name in the space above the typed name. Unless you have a personal relationship with the recipient, use both your first and last names. Do not include a title before your name.

Abbreviations at End.   Leave at least two lines of extra space between your typed name and any abbreviations used to communicate more information about the letter. Put each abbreviation on a separate line. If you send a copy to someone other than the recipient, use *cc:* followed by the name of the person or organization receiving a copy. If the letter is accompanied by another document in the same envelope, use *Enc.* or *Enclosure.* If the letter has been typed by someone other than the person who wrote and signed it, the writer's initials are given in capital letters, followed by a slash and the initials of the typist in lowercase letters: *VW/dbw.*

Modified and Full Block Style.   Two standard formats specify the placement of the elements on the page. To align a letter using *modified block style* (see Figure 14.1), you need to imagine a line running down the center of the page from top to bottom. Place the return address, date, closing, signature, and typed name so that the left side of each aligns with this center line. The *full block style* is generally used only on letterhead stationery with the name and address of the organization. Omit typing the return address, and align all the elements at the left margin.

Envelope Formats.   The U.S. Postal Service recommends a format that uses all capital letters, standard abbreviations, and no punctuation; this style makes the information on the envelope easier for the Postal Service to scan and process. However, the conventional envelope format (see Figure 14.2) may be preferred and is always safe to use.

Figure 14.2
Envelope Formats

U.S. Postal Service format

Conventional format

Memoranda

A *memorandum* (*memo* for short) is a form of communication used within a company to request or exchange information, to make announcements, and to confirm conversations. Memos are frequently used to convey information to large groups — an entire team, department, or organization. Generally, the topic of a memo is quite narrow and should be apparent to the reader at a glance. Memos tend to be written in the first person (*I* or *we*) and can range from the very informal (if written to a peer) to the extremely formal (if written to a high-ranking superior on an important matter). Most are short, but the memo format can be used to convey proposals and reports; long memos freely use headings, subheadings, lists, and other features that are easy to scan. (For a sample, see Figure 14.3.)

FORMAT FOR MEMORANDA

Although every organization has its own format for memos, the heading generally consists of a series of lines with clear labels (followed by colons).

Date:	(date on which memo is sent)
To:	(person or persons to whom it is primarily addressed)
cc:	(names of anyone else who receives a copy)
From:	(name of the writer)
Subject: *or* Re:	(concise, accurate statement of the memo's topic)

The subject line often determines whether a memo is read. (The old-fashioned abbreviation *Re:* for *regarding* is still used, but we recommend the more common *Subject*.) Accurately sum up the topic in a few words ("Agenda for 12/10 meeting," "Sales estimates for new product line").

E-Mail

E-mail is popular because it is easy, speedy, and convenient, combining immediacy with the permanence of letters and memos, whether within organizations or between organizations and outside parties. However, letters and memos are often still preferred for formal, official correspondence.

Because it seems so conversational, e-mail may not be polished as other written messages are. People who correspond regularly through e-mail tend to overlook one another's quirks; however, your e-mail messages are a part of the official record and have no guarantee of privacy. Your confidential chat with a friend or colleague can be intercepted, recorded on other computers, and distributed in print or over a network.

INTERLINK SYSTEMS, INC.

To: All Employees
From: Erica Xiang **EX**
Subject: Changes in employee benefits
Date: October 26, 2006

Each fall the Human Resources group looks closely at the company's health insurance benefits to make certain that we are providing an excellent level of coverage in a way that makes economic sense. To that end, we have made some changes to our plan, effective January 1, 2007. Let me outline the three major changes.

1. We are pleased to be able to offer employees the opportunity, through a **Flexible Spending Account**, to pay for dependent care and unreimbursed health expenses on a pre-tax basis, a feature that can result in considerable savings. I have attached a summary and will provide more information on this benefit at our staff meeting tomorrow, October 27, at 10:30 A.M. I will be available immediately after the meeting to answer any specific questions.

2. Those of you who have taken advantage of our **vision care benefit** in the past know that it offers significant help in paying for eye exams, eyeglasses, and contact lenses. The current plan will change slightly on January 1. Employees and covered dependents will be eligible to receive up to $50 each year toward the cost of a routine eye exam and up to $100 every two years toward the cost of eyeglasses or contact lenses. If you see a provider within our health insurance network, you will pay only $10 per office visit.

3. We at Interlink Systems feel strongly that our health insurance benefits are excellent, but as you know, the cost of such plans continues to rise every year. In the interest of maintaining excellent coverage for our employees, we will raise our **employee contribution**. Starting January 1, we are asking employees with single coverage to contribute $12.50 more per pay period toward the cost of medical insurance, and employees who cover dependents to contribute $40 more per pay period. Even with this increase, the amount the company asks its employees to contribute towards the premiums (about 8%) is significantly less than the nationwide average of 30%.

Please contact me if you have questions or concerns about the changes that I have outlined in this memo. You can reach me at x462 or at exiang@interlink.net.

Enclosure

Figure 14.3
Memorandum

Uses standard format to identify readers, writer, topic, and date

Explains purpose, noting reader's priorities

Previews clear organization in blocks

Uses friendly tone to note new benefit for employees

Offers assistance

Introduces benefit change with positive background

Presents increased cost carefully, noting coverage quality and high employer contribution

Offers more help and supplies contact information

Notes enclosure

FORMAT FOR E-MAIL

Although e-mail is flexible, its headings are predetermined by your mail system and almost universally follow a memo format: *To:*, *cc:*, *Subject:*, and an automatic *From:* line with your name as sender. Write messages that your audience will find helpful, efficient, and courteous.

- Use a clear subject line to simplify replying and archiving.
- Move promptly to your purpose: state what you need and when.
- Be concise, adding headings and space between sections if needed.
- Follow company practice as you include or delete a trail of message replies.
- Observe company etiquette in copying messages to others.
- Avoid personal statements, humor, or informality that might undermine your professional credibility.

Résumés and Application Letters

The most important business correspondence you write may be the résumé and letter you use to apply for a job. Direct, persuasive, correct prose can help you stand out from the crowd.

RÉSUMÉS

In a résumé, you present yourself as someone who has the qualifications to excel at a job and to be an asset to the organization. Job seekers often have copies of a single résumé on hand, but you may want to customize your résumé for each application if you can easily print attractive copies.

Although a résumé is highly formatted, it also allows a wide variety of decisions about style, organization, and appearance. In this section, we describe a typical résumé, but many formats are acceptable. Unless you have a great deal of relevant work experience, your résumé should be no longer than one page. The standard résumé consists of a heading and labeled sections that detail your experience and qualifications. Within each section, use brief, pointed phrases and clauses rather than complete sentences. Use action verbs (*supervised*, *ordered*, *maintained*) and the active voice whenever possible. Highlight labels with underlining, boldface, or a larger type size. Arrange information on the page so that it is pleasing to the eye; use the best paper and clearest printer you can. (For an example, see Figure 14.4.)

For more on document design, see Ch. 21.

If you submit electronic applications, you may need to prepare your résumé in several different forms: a text file that you can attach to an e-mail message, an electronically readable version that a company can scan into its database, or a Web version that you can post on your site or a job site (see Figure 14.5). For all these versions, format carefully so that recipients can

Figure 14.4
Conventional Résumé

Anne Cahill
402 Pigeon Hill Road
Windsor, CT 06095
(860) 555-5763
acahill783@yahoo.com

Centers heading with
contact information

Labels sections

Objective   Position as Registered Nurse in pediatric hospital setting

Education   **University of Connecticut**, Storrs, CT. Bachelor of Science,
                       Major in nursing, May 2007. GPA: 3.5; licensed as Registered
                       Nurse by the State of Connecticut in June 2007

Specifies background
and experience

                       Manchester Community Technical College, Manchester, CT.
                       Associate degree in occupational therapy, May 2001. GPA: 3.3.

Work Experience
9/02–present   **Certified Occupational Therapy Assistant**, Johnson
                       Memorial Hospital, Stafford Springs, CT
                       • Assist children with delayed motor development and cerebral
                         palsy to develop skills for the activities of daily life

9/00–9/02   **Nursing Assistant**, Woodlake Healthcare Center, Tolland, CT
                       • Helped geriatric residents with activities of daily living
                       • Assisted nursing staff in treating acute care patients

Places current information
first

9/98–9/00   **Cashier**, Stop and Shop Supermarket, Vernon, CT
                       • Trained newly hired cashiers

Clinical Internships   **St. Francis Hospital**, Hartford, CT
                       • Student Nurse, Maternity and Postpartum, spring 2007

                       Hartford Hospital, Hartford, CT
                       • Student Nurse, Pediatrics, fall 2006

                       Visiting Nurse and Community Health, Mansfield, CT
                       • Student Nurse, Community, spring 2006

                       Manchester General Hospital, Manchester, CT
                       • Student Nurse, Medical-Surgical, fall 2005

Computer Skills   • Proficient with Microsoft Office, Database, and Windows
                         applications
                       • Experienced with Internet research

Adds relevant skills for
health-care record keeping

Activities   • Student Union Board of Governors, University of Connecticut,
                         class representative
                       • Intramural soccer

References   Available upon request

Figure 14.5
Résumé for the Web

Uses clear and direct heading

Organizes menu of available information

Creates professional Web design using bullets, color, and white space

Anne Cahill

Objective: **Position as a Registered Nurse in pediatric hospital setting**

- Education

- Experience

- Other Activities

- References

- Contact Me

Profile

New nursing graduate combines proficiency in the latest nursing techniques with significant clinical experience

- Experienced in providing professional, compassionate health-care services to children, others

- Able to work proficiently and productively in hospital settings

- Accustomed to working in a team with a broad range of health professionals and administrators

- Proficient with Microsoft Office, Database, and Windows applications and with Internet research

easily read what you supply. Turn to your campus career center for résumé samples and advice about using alternate formats to your advantage.

Heading.   The heading is generally centered (or otherwise pleasingly aligned) on the page with separate lines for your name; street address, city, state, and zip code; phone number; and e-mail address.

Employment Objective.   This optional section allows personnel officers to see at a glance your priorities and goals. Try to sound confident and eager but not pompous or presumptuous.

Education.   This section is almost always included, often first. Specify each postsecondary school you've attended, your major, your date of graduation (or expected graduation), and your grade point average (if it reflects well on you). You can also add any awards, honors, or relevant course work.

Experience.   In this key section, list each job with the most recent one first. You can include both full-time and part-time jobs. For each, give the name of the organization, your position, your responsibilities, and the dates you held the job. Describe your involvement in any unusual projects or responsibility for any important developments. Highlight details that show relevant work experience and leadership ability. Minimize information unconnected to the job for which you're applying.

Skills.   List any special skills (data processing, technical drawing, multiple languages) that aren't obvious from your education and work experience.

Activities.   You can specify either professional interests and activities (*Member of Birmingham Bricklayers Association*) or personal pursuits (*skiing, hiking, needlepoint*) showing that you are dedicated and well-rounded.

References.   If a job advertisement requests references, provide them. Always contact your references in advance to make sure they are willing to give you a good recommendation. For each person, list the name, his or her organization and position, and the organization's address and phone number. If references have not been requested, you can simply note "Available on request."

APPLICATION LETTERS

When writing a letter applying for a job, you should follow all the guidelines for other business letters. Remember that your immediate objective is to obtain an interview. As you compete against other candidates, your letter and résumé are all the employer has to judge you on. If you're responding to an advertisement, read it critically.

For general guidelines for business letters, see pp. 267–69.

- What qualifications are listed? Ideally, you should have all the required qualifications, but if you lack one, try to find something in your background that compensates, some similar experience in a different form.

- What else can you tell about the organization or position from the ad? How does the organization represent itself? If you're unfamiliar with the organization and you can't glean much about it from the ad, check the company's Web site.

- How does the ad describe the ideal candidate? As a team player? A dynamic individual? If you feel that you are the person this organization is looking for, you'll want to portray yourself this way in your letter.

In your letter, you want to spark your readers' interest, convince them that you're a qualified and attractive candidate, and motivate them to interview you. Whenever possible, address your letter to the person responsible for screening applicants and setting up interviews; you may need to call the organization to find out this person's name. In the first paragraph, identify the job, indicate how you heard about it, and summarize your qualifications. In the second paragraph, expand on your qualifications, highlighting key information on your résumé. Supplement it with additional details if necessary to show your readers that you're a better candidate than the other applicants. In the third paragraph, restate your interest in the job, ask for an interview, and let your prospective employer know how to reach you. (For a sample application letter, see Figure 14.6 below.) If you get an interview, follow up with a thank-you note. The note may reemphasize your qualifications and strong interest in the position.

Figure 14.6
Application Letter

Follows standard letter format

Addresses specific person

Identifies job sought and describes interest

Explains qualifications

Confirms interest and supplies contact information

Encloses résumé and proof of certification

402 Pigeon Hill Road
Windsor, CT 06095
July 8, 2007

Sheryl Sullivan
Director of Nursing
Center for Children's Health and Development
St. Francis Hospital and Medical Center
114 Woodland Street
Hartford, CT 06105

Dear Ms. Sullivan:

I am writing to apply for the full-time position as a pediatric nurse at the Center for Children's Health and Development at St. Francis Hospital, which was advertised on the Eastern Connecticut Health Network Web site. I feel that my varied clinical experiences and my desire to work with children ideally suit me for the job. In addition, I am highly motivated to grow and succeed in the field of health care.

For the past five years, I have worked as a certified occupational therapy assistant. In this capacity, I help children with delayed motor function acquire the skills necessary to achieve as high a level of independence as possible. While working as a COTA, I attended nursing school with the ultimate goal of becoming a pediatric nurse. My varied clinical experiences as a student nurse and my previous experience as a nurse's aide in a geriatric center have exposed me to many types of care. I feel that these experiences have helped me to become a well-rounded caregiver; they also, however, have reinforced my belief that my skills and talents are best suited to working with children.

I believe that I would be a strong addition to the medical team at the Children's Center. My clinical experiences have prepared me to deal with a wide range of situations. In addition, I am dedicated to maintaining and enhancing the well-being of children. I am enclosing proof of my recent certification as a Registered Nurse in the state of Connecticut. Please write to me at the address above, e-mail me at acahill783@yahoo.com, or call me at (860) 555-5763. Thank you for your consideration. I look forward to hearing from you.

Sincerely,

Anne Cahill

Anne Cahill

Enclosures

Chapter 15
Writing for Assessment

Most college writing is done for assessment—that is, most of the papers you hand in are eventually evaluated and graded. But some college writing tasks exist *only* as methods of assessment: they are designed not to help you expand your writing skills (or content knowledge) but to allow you to demonstrate that you have mastered them. You often need to do such writing on the spot—a quiz to finish in twenty minutes, a final exam to complete in a few hours, an impromptu essay to dash off in one class period. How do you discover and shape your ideas in a limited time?

In this chapter we provide tips for three types of in-class writing that are commonly used for assessment—the essay exam, the short-answer exam, and the timed writing assignment. We also discuss the writing portfolio, a collection of writing samples that demonstrates your strengths as a writer.

Essay Examinations

In many courses an essay exam is the most important kind of in-class writing. Instructors believe that such writing shows that you haven't just memorized a batch of material but that you have examined it critically and can clearly communicate your thoughts about it to someone else.

For more on critical thinking and college assignments, see pp. 35–36.

PREPARING FOR THE EXAM

Some instructors favor open-book exams, in which you bring your books and perhaps your notes to class for reference. In an open-book exam, ability to memorize and recall is less important than ability to reason and to select what matters. On the other hand—if the exam will be closed book—it's a good idea to fix in your memory vital names, dates, and definitions.

A good way to prepare for any exam, whether the books are closed or open, is to imagine likely questions and then plan answers. If your instructor has supplied sample questions, pattern new ones after them. To study with a textbook, look for the main ideas in relevant chapters. Then ask yourself: What do these ideas have to do with each other? How might they be combined? What conclusions can I draw?

LEARNING FROM ANOTHER WRITER

To look at techniques for answering *any* exam question, let's take one example. A final exam in developmental psychology posed this question:

> What evidence indicates innate factors in perceptual organization? You might find it useful to recall any research that shows how infants perceive depth and forms.

In response, David Ian Cohn sat back in his chair for a few minutes and thought over the reading he'd done for the course. What perception research had used babies for subjects? He jotted down ideas, crossed out a couple of weak ones, and drew lines linking ideas that went together. Then he took a deep breath and wrote this straightforward answer:

For an illustration of linking, see pp. 322–23.

> Research on infants is probably the best way to demonstrate that some factors in perceptual organization are innate. As the cliff box experiment shows, an infant will avoid what looks like a drop-off, even though its mother calls it and even though it can feel glass covering the drop-off area. The same infant will crawl to the other end of the box, which appears (and is) safe. Apparently, infants do not have to be taught what a cliff looks like.
>
> Psychologists have also observed that infants are aware of size constancy. They recognize a difference in size between a 10 cm box at a distance of one meter and a 20 cm box at a distance of two meters. If this phenomenon is not innate, it is at least learned early, for the subjects of the experiment were infants of sixteen to eighteen months.
>
> When shown various patterns, infants tend to respond more noticeably to patterns that resemble the human face than to those that appear random. This seemingly innate recognition helps the infant identify people (such as its mother) from less important inanimate objects.
>
> Infants also seem to have an innate ability to match sight with sound. When simultaneously shown two television screens, each depicting a different subject, while being played a tape that sometimes matched one screen and sometimes the other, infants looked at whichever screen matched what they heard—not always, but at least twice as often.

Questions to Start You Thinking

Meaning

1. What is the main idea of Cohn's answer?

2. If you were the psychology instructor, how could you immediately see that Cohn had thoroughly dealt with the question and only with the question?

Writing Strategies

3. In what places is Cohn's answer concrete and specific, not vague and general?

4. Suppose Cohn had tacked on a concluding sentence: "Thus I have conclusively proved that there are innate factors in perceptual organization, by citing much evidence showing that infants definitely can perceive depth and forms." Would that sentence strengthen his answer? Why or why not?

GENERATING IDEAS

When the clock on the wall is ticking away, generating ideas right on the exam sheet will save time. First read over all the questions on the exam carefully. If you don't understand what a question calls for, ask your instructor right away. If you are offered a choice, just cross out questions you are *not* going to answer so you don't waste time on them by mistake. Annotate questions, underline important points, and scribble short definitions. Write reminders that you will notice while you work: TWO PARTS! or GET IN EXAMPLE OF ABORIGINES.

Plan a Concrete Answer.   Few people can dash off an excellent essay exam answer without first taking time to plan. Instructors prefer answers that are concrete and specific rather than those that wander in the clouds of generality. David Cohn's answer to the psychology question cites evidence all the way through — particular experiments in which infants were subjects. Try writing a brief, informal outline like David Cohn's:

> *Thesis: Research on infants is probably the best way to demonstrate that some*
>   *factors in perceptual organization are innate.*
> *Cliff box — kid fears drop despite glass, mother; knows shallow side safe*
> *Size constancy — learned early if not intrinsic*
> *Shapes — infants respond more/better to face shape than nonformed*
> *Match sound w/ sight — 2 TVs, look twice as much at right one*

■ For David Cohn's complete answer, see p. 278.

Focus on the Question.   Instructors also prefer answers that are organized and coherent rather than rambling. Often a question will contain directive words that help you define your task: *evaluate, compare, discuss, explain, describe, summarize, trace the development of.* You can put yourself on the right track if you incorporate a form of such a word in your first sentence.

■ For more on critical thinking and college assignments, see pp. 34–37.

QUESTION   Define socialism, and give examples of its main varieties.

ANSWER   Socialism is defined as . . .

ANSWER   Socialism is an economic and political concept, difficult to define because it takes many forms. It . . .

PLANNING FOR TYPICAL EXAM QUESTIONS

For examples of many methods of development, see Ch. 19.

Most exam questions fall into types. If you can recognize them, you will know how to organize and begin to write. Here are examples.

For more on explaining cause and effect, see Ch. 8 and pp. 369–70.

The Cause and Effect Question.   These questions usually mention *causes, effects,* or both.

What were the immediate causes of the Dust Bowl in the 1930s?

Describe the main economic effects of a low prime interest rate.

For more on comparing and contrasting, see Ch. 7 and pp. 366–69.

The Compare or Contrast Question.   This popular type of question asks you to point out similarities (comparing), discuss differences (contrasting), or do both. In the process you explain not one subject but two, paralleling the points you make about each, giving both equal space.

Compare and contrast *iconic memory* and *eidetic imagery,* defining the terms and indicating the ways in which they differ and are related or alike.

After supplying a one-sentence definition of each term, a student proceeded first to contrast and then to compare, for full credit.

> Iconic memory is a picturelike impression that lasts for only a fraction of a second in short-term memory. Eidetic imagery is the ability to take a mental photograph, exact in detail, as though its subject were still present. But iconic memory soon disappears. Unlike an eidetic image, it does not last long enough to enter long-term memory. IM is common; EI is unusual: very few people have it. Both iconic memory and eidetic imagery are similar, however: both record visual images, and every sighted person of normal intelligence has both abilities to some degree.

A question of this kind doesn't always use the words *compare* and *contrast.* Directions to *show similarities* or *identify likenesses* ask for comparisons, while those to *distinguish, differentiate,* or *show differences* ask for contrasts, perhaps to evaluate in what respects one thing is better than the other.

For more on definition, see pp. 356–57.

The Definition Question.   A brief definition may set the stage for answering another question; an extended definition with an illustration or multiple definitions of related terms may stand alone.

Explain three common approaches to parenting—*permissive, authoritarian-restrictive,* and *authoritative.* [Supply a trio of definitions.]

Define the Stanislavsky method of acting, citing outstanding actors who have followed it. [Explain a single method and give examples.]

The Demonstration Question.   This kind of question supplies a statement and asks you to back it up.

> Demonstrate the truth of Freud's contention that laughter may contain elements of aggression.

In other words, you need to explain Freud's claim and then supply evidence to support it. You might refer to crowd scenes you have experienced, analyze a joke or a scene in a film, or use examples from your reading.

The Discussion Question.   A discussion question may tempt the unwary to shoot the breeze.

> Discuss three events that precipitated Lyndon B. Johnson's withdrawal from the 1968 presidential race.

This question looks like an open invitation to ramble about Johnson and the war in Vietnam, but it isn't. Try rewording the question to help you focus your discussion: "Why did President Johnson decide not to seek another term? Analyze the causes and briefly explain each."

Sometimes a discussion question won't announce itself with the word *discuss,* but uses *describe* or *explain* or *explore.*

> Describe the national experience following passage of the Eighteenth Amendment. What did most Americans learn from it?

Provided you know that this amendment banned the sale, manufacture, and transportation of alcoholic drinks and that it was finally repealed, you can discuss its effects — or perhaps the reasons for its repeal.

The Divide or Classify Question.   Sometimes you are asked to slice the subject into sections, sort things into kinds, or break the idea, place, person, or process into its parts.

> ▓ For more on division and classification, see pp. 364–66.

> Identify the ways in which each resident of the United States uses, on average, 1,595 gallons of water a day. How and to what degree might a person reduce this amount?

For a start, you would divide up water use into several parts — drinking, cooking, bathing, washing cars, and so on. Then, after that division, you would give tips for water conservation and tell how effective each is.

> What different genres of film did Robert Altman direct? Name at least one outstanding example of each kind.

This classification question asks you to sort films into categories — possibly comedy, war, drama, mystery, western.

The Evaluation Question.   This favorite calls on you to think critically and to present an argument.

> ▓ For more on evaluating, see Chs. 9 and 11.

> Evaluate this suggestion, giving reasons for your judgments: cities should stop building highways to the suburbs and instead build public lightrail systems.

Other argument questions might begin "Defend the idea of ..." or "Show weaknesses in the concept of ..." or otherwise call on you to take a stand.

For more on process analysis, see pp. 362–64.

The Process Analysis Question.   Often you can spot this kind of question by the word *trace*:

> Trace the stages through which a bill becomes a state law.
>
> Trace the development of the medieval Italian city-state.

Both questions ask you to tell how something occurs or occurred. In brief, you divide the process into steps and detail each step. The next question calls for the other type of process analysis, the "how-to" variety:

> An employee has been consistently late for work, varying from fifteen minutes to a half hour daily. This employee has been on the job only five months but shows promise of learning skills that your firm needs badly. How would you deal with this situation?

The Response Question.   A question might supply a statement, a comment, or a quotation for close reading, asking you to test the writer's opinion against what you know. Carefully read the statement a few times, and then jot down contrary or supporting evidence.

> Was the following passage written by Gertrude Stein, Kate Chopin, or Tillie Olsen? On what evidence do you base your answer?
>
>> She waited for the material pictures which she thought would gather and blaze before her imagination. She waited in vain. She saw no pictures of solitude, of hope, of longing, or of despair. But the very passions themselves were aroused within her soul, swaying it, lashing it, as the waves daily beat upon her splendid body. She trembled, she was choking, and the tears blinded her.

If you were familiar with the stories of Kate Chopin, who specializes in physical and emotional descriptions of impassioned women, you would point to language (*swaying, lashing*) that marks the passage as hers.

DRAFTING: THE ONLY VERSION

When you have two or more essay questions to answer, block out your time roughly based on the points or minutes your instructor allots to each. Give extra minutes to a complicated question with several parts. Then pace yourself as you write. For example, wrap up question 2 at 10:30 and move on.

As you draft, give yourself room for second thoughts by writing on only one side of the page in your exam booklet and skipping every other line. Should you wish to add material later, you can do so with ease.

Begin with the Easy Questions.   Many students find that it boosts their morale to start with the question they feel best able to answer. Unless your instructor specifies otherwise, why not skip around? Clearly number or label each answer as your instructor does. Then begin in such a way that the instructor will immediately recognize which question you're answering. If the task is "Compare and contrast the depression of the 1930s with the recession of 2001," you might begin in this way:

> *Compared to the paralyzing depression that began in 1929, the recession of 2001 seems like a bad case of measles.*

Try Stating Your Thesis at the Start.   Making your opening sentence a thesis statement — a sentence that immediately makes clear the main point — often makes good sense. Then the rest of your answer can back up that statement. An easy way to get started is to turn the question into a statement and use it to begin an answer.

For more on thesis statements, see pp. 312–19. For David Cohn's thesis and complete answer, see p. 278 and 279.

QUESTION
What reasons for leasing cars and office equipment, instead of purchasing them, can be cited for a two-person partnership?

ANSWER
I can cite at least four reasons for a two-person partnership to lease cars and office equipment. For one thing, under present tax laws, the entire cost of a regular payment under a leasing agreement may be deducted. . . .

Stick to the Question.   You may be tempted to throw into your answer everything you have learned in the course. But to do so defeats the purpose of the examination — to use your knowledge, not to parade it. Answer by selecting and shaping *what matters*. On the other hand, if a question has two parts, answer both.

Name three styles of contemporary architecture and evaluate one of them.

Stay Specific.   Pressed for time, some exam takers think, "I haven't got time to get specific here. I'll just sum this up in general." That's a mistake. Every time you throw in a broad statement ("The Industrial Revolution was beneficial for the peasant"), take time to add specific examples ("In Dusseldorf, as Taine tells us, deaths from starvation among displaced Prussian farmworkers dropped from a peak of almost 10 percent a year").

REVISING: REREADING AND PROOFING

If you have paced yourself, you'll have at least a few minutes left to look over your work. Check that your ideas are clear and hang together. Add sentences wherever new ones are needed. If you recall a key point, add a paragraph on a blank left-hand page. Just draw an arrow to show where it goes.

Naturally, errors occur more often when you write under pressure than when you have time to proofread carefully. On an exam, what you say and how forcefully you say it matter most. Still, no instructor will object to careful corrections. You can add words with carets (∧) or neatly strike them out.

When your paper or blue book is returned, consider these questions as you look it over so that you improve your essay-exam skills:

ESSAY EXAM CHECKLIST

___ Did you answer the whole question, not just part of it?

___ Did you stick to the point, not throw in unrequested information?

___ Did you make your general statements clear by citing evidence or examples?

___ Did you proofread for omissions and lack of clarity?

___ On what questions do you feel you did a good job, whatever your grade?

___ If you had to write this exam over again, how would you now go about it?

Short-Answer Examinations

The *short-answer exam* may call on you to identify names or phrases from your reading, in a sentence or a few words.

> Identify the following: Clemenceau, Treaty of Versailles, Maginot line.

> *Georges Clemenceau — This French premier, nicknamed The Tiger, headed a popular coalition cabinet during World War I and at the Paris Peace Conference demanded stronger penalties against Germany.*

For more about writing definitions, see pp. 356–57.
Writing a short identification is much like writing a short definition. Mention the general class to which a thing belongs to make clear its nature.

> *Treaty of Versailles — pact between Germany and the Allies that . . .*
> *Maginot line — fortifications that . . .*

Timed Writings

Many composition instructors give you experience in writing on demand by assigning impromptu in-class essays. Their purpose is to test your writing skills, not your recall. For such writings, your time is limited, the setting is controlled (usually you're at a desk without a dictionary or a spell checker), and you can't choose your subject. Even so, your usual methods of writing, used in a hurry, can still serve you well.

Budget Your Time.   For an in-class essay, if you have forty-five minutes to write, a good rule of thumb is to spend ten minutes preparing, thirty minutes writing, and five minutes rereading and making last-minute changes. Plan quickly to avoid rushing to get your ideas on paper in an essay — the part you will be graded on.

Consider Types of Topics.   Often you can expect the same types of questions for in-class writings as for essay exams. Do what the key words say.

For common types of exam questions, see pp. 279–82.

What were the *causes* of World War I?

Compare and contrast the theories of capitalism and socialism.

Define civil rights.

Add your personal twist to a general subject, but note the key words.

Analyze a problem in education that is *difficult to solve*.

Discuss ways to cope with stress.

Standardized tests often ask you to respond to a short passage, testing not only your writing ability but also your reading comprehension.

Thomas Jefferson stated, "If a nation expects to be ignorant and free, in a state of civilization, it expects what never was and never will be." *How* is his comment *relevant* to education today?

Choose Your Topic Wisely.   For on-the-spot writing, the trick is to make the topic your own. If you have a choice, pick the one you know most about, not the one you think will impress your readers. They'll be most impressed by logical argument and solid evidence. If you have to write on a broad subject, bring it down to something you have observed or experienced. Have you witnessed traffic jams, brownouts, or condos ruining beaches? Then write about increased population, using these examples.

Think before You Write.   Despite your limited time, read the instructions or questions carefully, restrict your topic to something you know about, focus on a main idea, and jot down main points for development. If a good hook to open or conclude occurs to you, use it, too.

Thinking Fast

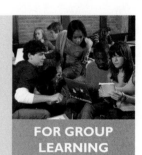

FOR GROUP LEARNING

To practice planning quickly for timed writing or tests, brainstorm as a class to explore approaches to sample topics provided in this chapter. Select one class member (or three, in turn) to record ideas on the board. Devote exactly ten minutes of discussion per topic to these key parts of a successful response:

• possible thesis sentences

• possible patterns of organization

• possible kinds and sources of evidence

Expect a wide range of ideas. Spend the last part of class evaluating them.

Don't Try to Be Perfect.   No one expects in-class essays to read as smoothly as reports written over several weeks. You can't polish every sentence or remember the exact word for every spot. And never waste time recopying. Devote your time to the more important parts of writing.

For more on making corrections, see the Quick Editing Guide (the dark-blue-edged pages).

Save Time to Proofread.   The last few minutes when you read over your work and correct glaring errors may be the best-spent minutes of all. Cross out errors and make corrections neatly using asterisks (*), arrows, and carets (^). Especially check for the following:

- letters omitted (-*ed* or -*s*), added (develop*e*), or inverted (rec*ie*ve)
- wrong punctuation (a comma instead of a period)
- omitted apostrophes (*dont* instead of *don't*)
- omitted words ("She going" instead of "She *is* going")
- wrong (*except* instead of *accept*) or misspelled words (*mispelled*)

Writing for Portfolio Assessment

The writing portfolio is a popular method of assessment for college classes. It is a printed or electronic collection of pieces of writing that represent the writer's best work. Compiled over time and across projects, a portfolio showcases a writer's talent, hard work, and ability to make thoughtful choices about content and presentation. For a single course, the portfolio is usually due at the end of the term and includes pieces you have written and revised for that course. Most portfolios need some kind of introduction (usually a self-assessment or rationale) addressed to readers, who might be teachers, supervisors, evaluators, parents, or classmates.

Portfolio courses typically emphasize revision and reflection — the ability to identify and discuss your choices, strengths, or learning processes. In such a course, you'll need to save all your drafts and notes, keep track of your choices and changes, and near the end of the term select and submit your best writing.

UNDERSTANDING PORTFOLIO ASSESSMENT

The portfolio is a method of evaluation and teaching that shapes the whole course from beginning to end. For example, your portfolio course will probably emphasize responses to your writing — from your classmates and your instructor — but not necessarily grades on your separate papers. The portfolio method attempts to shift attention to the writing process itself — to discovery, planning, drafting, peer response, revision, editing — allowing time for your skills to develop before the writing "counts" and the portfolio is graded.

The portfolio method is flexible, but you need to read your instructor's syllabus and assignment sheets carefully and listen well in class to determine what kind of portfolio you'll be expected to keep. Below are a few typical types, and more than one might be used in a course.

A Writing Folder.   Students are asked to submit all drafts, notes, outlines, scribbles, doodles, and messy pages — in short, all writing done for the course, whether finished or unfinished. Students may also be asked to revise two or three of their most promising pieces for a "presentation portfolio." The folder is usually not accompanied by a reflective cover letter.

A Learning (or Open) Portfolio.   Students are free to submit a variety of materials that have contributed to their learning. They may even be free to determine the contents, organization, and presentation of the portfolio. A learning portfolio for a composition class might include photos or other nonprint objects collected to demonstrate learning.

A Closed Portfolio.   Students must turn in assignments that are specified by the instructor, or their options for what to include may be limited.

A Midterm Portfolio.   The portfolio is given a trial run at midterm, or the midterm grade is determined by one or two papers that are submitted for evaluation, perhaps accompanied by a brief self-assessment.

A Final or Presentation Portfolio.   The portfolio is evaluated at the end of the course after being revised, edited, and polished for presentation.

A Modified or Combination Portfolio.   The student has some, but not unlimited, choice in what to include. For example, the instructor may ask for three entries that show certain features or parts of the course.

Find out what kind of portfolio your instructor has in mind. Here's one likely scenario. You are required to submit a modified or combination portfolio — one that contains, for example, three revised papers (out of the five or six drafts required). You decide, late in the term, which three to re-vise and edit. You also may be asked to reflect on what those choices say about you as a writer, to show your learning in the course, or to explain your decisions while writing a paper. Here are some typical questions your instructor, syllabus, or assignment sheets may answer:

- How many papers should you include in the portfolio?
- Do all these papers need to be revised? If so, what level of revision is expected? What criteria will be used to assess them?
- How much of the course grade is determined by the portfolio grade? Are the portfolio entries graded separately, or does the entire portfolio receive one grade?
- May you include papers written for other courses or entries other than texts — such as photos, videos, maps, Web pages, or other visuals?

- Should you preface the portfolio with an introduction or a cover letter? What is expected in this piece: Description? Explanation? Exploration? Application? Reflection? Self-assessment?
- Does each entry need a separate cover sheet? Should descriptions of your processes or choices appear before or after each entry?

TIPS FOR KEEPING A PORTFOLIO

Keep Everything, and Stay Organized.   Don't throw anything away! Keep all your notes, lists, drafts, outlines, clusters, responses from readers, photocopied articles, and references for works cited. If you have your own computer, *back up everything* to a disk. (Better yet, use a jump drive or zip drive, both of which are sturdier than disks.) If you use the computer lab, save your work to a disk, and keep an extra blank disk in your backpack. Use a system to organize everything. For example, invest in a good folder with pockets, and label their contents as you store the drafts, notes, outlines, and peer review forms for each assignment.

Manage Your Time.   The portfolio isn't due until the end of the course (or at midterm), but planning ahead will save you time and frustration. For example, as your instructor returns each assignment with comments, make changes in response while the ideas are fresh. If you don't understand or know how to approach your instructor's comments, ask right away — at the end of class or during office hours that week. Make notes about what you want to do. Then, even if you want to let a paper simmer, you will have both a plan and some fresh insight when you work on it again.

For more help with self-assessment see the For Peer Response questions, the Revision Checklists, and the Draft Doctors throughout *The Bedford Guide*. Also, see "Ask the Draft Doctor" at <bedfordstmartins.com/ bedguide>.

Practice Self-Assessment.   For complex activities, it's important to your improvement to step back and evaluate your own performance. Maybe you have great ideas but find it hard to organize them. Maybe you write powerful thesis statements but run out of ideas to support them. Don't wait until the portfolio cover letter is due to begin tracking your learning or assessing your strengths, weaknesses, or preferences.

You can practice self-assessment from the first day of class. For example, after reviewing the syllabus, write one or two paragraphs about how you think you will do in this course. What do you expect to do well on, and why? What may be hard for you, and why? For each paper you share with peers or hand in, write a journal entry about what the paper does well and what it still needs. Keep track, in a log or journal, of your process to plan, re-search, or draft each paper — where you get stuck and where things click.

For more on keeping a journal, see pp. 306–07.

Choose the Entries Carefully.   If you can select what to include, consider the course emphasis. Of course, you want to select pieces your evaluator will think are "the best," but also consider which show the most promise or po-tential. Which drafts show creativity, insight, or an unusual approach to the assignment? Which show variety — different purposes, audiences, or voices?

Which show depth — your ability to do thorough research or stay with a topic for several weeks? Also consider the order of the entries — which piece might work best first or last, and how each placement affects the whole.

Write a Strong Reflective Introduction or Cover Letter.   Your introduction — usually a self-assessment in the form of a cover letter, a statement, or a description for each of your entries — could be the most important text you write all semester. Besides introducing readers to your collection and portraying you as a writer, it explains your choices in putting the portfolio together and demonstrates that you can evaluate your work and your writing process. For many portfolio-based courses, the reflective introduction or cover letter is the "final exam," testing what you've learned about good writing, readers' needs, and the details of a careful self-presentation.

Ask these questions about writing a reflective introduction or cover letter:

DISCOVERY CHECKLIST

___ Who will read this reflection?
___ What qualities of writing will your reader value?
___ Will the reader suggest changes or evaluate your work?
___ What will the outcome of the reading be? How much can you influence it?
___ What do you want to emphasize about your writing? What are you proud of? What have you learned? What did you have trouble with?
___ How can you present your writing ability in the best light?

If your reader or evaluator is your instructor, look back over responses on your returned papers, and review the course syllabus and assignment sheets. What patterns do you see in your instructor's concerns or directions? What could you tell a friend about this reader's expectations — or pet peeves? Use what you've learned about his or her values as a reader to compose a convincing, well-developed introduction or cover letter.

If your readers or evaluators are unknown, ask your instructor for as much information as possible so you can decide which logical, ethical, or emotional appeals might be most effective. Although you won't know your readers personally, it's safe to assume that they will be trained in portfolio assessment and will share many of your instructor's ideas about good writing. If your college writing program has guidelines, consult them, too. For more on appeals, see pp. 40–41.

How long should your introduction or cover letter be? Check with your instructor, but regardless of length, develop your ideas or support your claims as in any effective writing. If you are asked to write a letter, follow the format for a business letter: include the date, a salutation, and a closing.

In the reflective introduction, you might try some of the following (but don't try to use all of them):

- Discuss your best entry and why it is your best.
- Detail your revisions — the improvements you want readers to notice.
- Review everything included, touching on the strengths of each.
- Outline your writing and revising process for one or more entries.
- State what the portfolio illustrates about you as a writer, student, researcher, or critical thinker.
- Acknowledge your weaknesses, but show how you've worked to overcome them.
- Acknowledge the influence of your readers on your entries.
- Reflect on what you've learned about writing and reading.
- Lay the groundwork for a positive evaluation of your work.

Polishing the Final Portfolio.   From the first page to the last, your portfolio should be ready for public presentation, a product you can take pride in or show to others. Think about creative ways to give your portfolio a final distinctive feature, such as having it bound at your local copy shop, adding a colorful cover or illustrations, or including a table of contents or a running head. Although a cheerful cover will not make up for weak writing or careless editing, readers will value your extra effort.

PART FOUR

A Writer's Strategies

Introduction

The following seven chapters constitute a manual offering in-depth advice on writing strategies. The word *strategy* may remind you of warfare: in the original Greek sense of the word, it is a way to win a battle. Writing a college paper, you'll probably agree, is a battle of a kind. In this manual you'll find an array of small weapons to use — and perhaps some heavy artillery.

Here are techniques you can learn, methods you can follow, good practices you can observe. The first five chapters offer a wealth of suggestions for approaching each of the stages of the writing process: generating ideas, planning, drafting, developing, and revising and editing. In Part Two, each stage was covered for each assignment, and relevant strategies were mentioned briefly. Here, each stage of the writing process gets a full chapter, and the strategies for each are explained and illustrated more fully. The last two chapters here offer advice on strategies of increasing importance — designing your own documents and understanding visual representations.

No strategy will appeal to every writer, and no writer uses every one for every writing task. Consider this part of the book a reference guide or instruction manual. Turn to it when you need more help, when you're curious, or when you'd like to enlarge your repertoire of writing skills. We can't tell you which of the ideas and techniques covered in these pages will work for you, but we can promise that if you try some of them, you'll be rewarded.

Chapter 16
Strategies for Generating Ideas

For most writers, the hardest part of writing comes first — confronting a blank page. Fortunately, you can prepare for that moment, both for finding ideas and for getting ready to write. All of the tested techniques that follow have worked for some writers — both professionals and students — and some may work for you.

Finding Ideas

When you begin to write, you need to start the ideas flowing. Sometimes ideas appear effortlessly on the paper or screen, perhaps triggered by the opportunities and resources around you — something you read, see, hear, discuss, or think about. (See the top half of the graphic on p. 295.) But at other times you need an arsenal of idea generators, strategies you can use at any point in the writing process — whenever your ideas dry up or you need more examples or evidence. If one strategy doesn't work for a particular writing task, try another. (See the strategies presented in the lower half of the graphic, all detailed in the following pages.)

BUILDING FROM YOUR ASSIGNMENT

Learning to write is learning what questions to ask yourself. Sometimes your assignment triggers this process by raising some questions and answering others. For example, Ben Tran jotted his notes in his book as his instructor and classmates discussed the first assignment for his composition class — recalling a personal experience.

The assignment clarified what audience to address and what purpose to try to accomplish in the paper. It also raised three big questions for Ben:

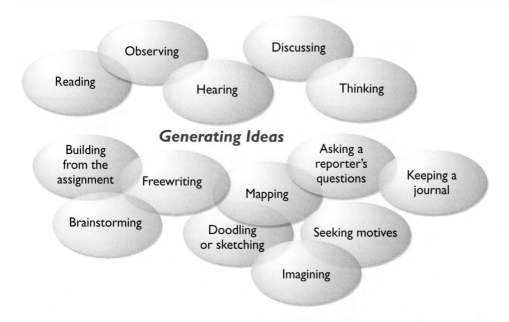

Which experience should I pick? How did it change me? Why was it so important for me? His classmates asked their instructor other questions about the length, format, and due date for the essay. As class ended, Ben didn't know what he'd write about, but he had figured out the questions to tackle first, using other strategies for generating ideas.

■ For more detail about this assignment, turn to p. 62 in Ch. 4.

Need to pick one event with consequences

Write about one specific experience that changed how you acted, thought, or felt. Use your experience as a springboard for reflection. Your purpose is not merely to tell an interesting story but to show your readers—your instructor and your classmates—the importance of that experience for you.

What readers?
class + prof.

What purpose? 2 parts! Tell the story but do more—reflect & show importance

Sometimes an assignment will assume that you already understand something critical—how to address a particular audience, for example, or what to include in a certain type of writing. When Amalia Blackhawk read her argument assignment, she jotted down several questions about its assumptions to ask her instructor.

nything OK?
only
wspaper type
issue?

Select a campus or local issue that matters to you, and write a letter to the editor about it. Be certain to tell readers what the issue is, why it is important, and how you propose to address it. Assume that your letter will appear in a special opinion feature that allows letters longer than the usual word-count limits.

itor of
at?

at's my purpose?
rsuading readers
respect my view or to agree?

My classmates? The publication's readers?

How long is the usual letter? How long should mine be? Anything else letters like this should do?

Try these steps as you examine an assignment:

1. *Read through the assignment once* simply to discover its overall direction.
2. *Read it again,* this time marking any information that answers questions about your situation as a writer. Does the assignment identify or suggest your audience, your purpose in writing, the type of paper expected, the parts typical of that kind of writing, or the format required?
3. *List the questions that the assignment raises for you.* Figure out exactly what you need to decide—the type of topic to pick, the focus to develop, the issues or aspects to consider, or other guidelines to follow.
4. *Finally, list any questions that the assignment doesn't answer or ask you to answer.* Ask your instructor about these questions during or after class.

■ Activity: Building from Your Assignment

Select an assignment from this book, another textbook, or another class, and make some notes about it. What questions does the assignment answer for you? Which questions or decisions does it direct to you? What other questions might you want to ask your instructor? When you finish your notes, exchange assignments with a classmate, and make notes about that assignment, too. Working with your partner, compare your responses to both assignments.

BRAINSTORMING

A *brainstorm* is a sudden insight or inspiration. As a writing strategy, brainstorming uses free association to stimulate a chain of ideas, often to personalize a topic and break it down into specifics. When you brainstorm, you start with a word or phrase and spend a set period of time simply scribbling a list of ideas as rapidly as possible, writing down whatever comes to mind with no editing or going back.

Brainstorming can be a group activity. In the workplace, it is commonly used to fill a specific need—finding a name for a product, a corporate emblem, a slogan for an advertising campaign. In college, you can try group brainstorming with a few other students or your entire class. Members of the group sit facing one another. They designate one person to record on paper, screen, or chalkboard whatever the others suggest or the best idea in the air at a busy moment. After several minutes of calling out ideas, the group can look over the recorder's list to identify useful results. Online a group might toss out ideas during a chat or post them for all to consider.

On your own, you might brainstorm to define a topic, generate an example while writing, or come up with a title for a finished paper. Angie Ortiz brainstormed after her instructor assigned a paper ("Demonstrate from your own experience how electronic technology is changing our lives"). First, she wrote *electronic technology* at the top of the page and set her alarm for fifteen minutes. Then she began to scribble words and phrases.

Group Brainstorming

Working with a small group of classmates — or the entire class — choose one subject from the list on page 298 that each person knows about. Brainstorm about it individually for ten minutes. Then compare and contrast by exchanging or posting the brainstorming lists of all in the group. Although the group began with the same subject, each writer's treatment will be unique because of differences in experience and perspective. What does this exercise tell you about group brainstorming as a strategy for generating topics?

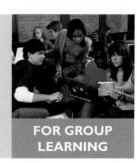

FOR GROUP LEARNING

Electronic technology
Electronic stuff — iPod, cell phone, laptop, Blackberry. Then there's TV, cable, DVDs. Too much?!
Always on call — at home, in car, at school. Always something playing.
Spend so much time in electronic world — phone calls, I Ming, listening to tunes.
Cuts into time really hanging with friends — face-to-face time.
Less aware of my surroundings outside of the electronic world?

When her alarm went off, Ortiz took a break. After returning to her list, she crossed out ideas that did not interest her and circled her final promising question. From her rough list, a focus began to emerge: the capacity of the electronic world to expand information but reduce awareness.

When you want to brainstorm, try this advice:

1. *Start with a key word or phrase* — one that will launch your thoughts in a productive direction. If you need a topic, begin with a general word or phrase (for example, *computer*); if you need an example for a paragraph in progress, use a specific word or phrase (for example, *financial errors computers make*).
2. *Set a time limit.* Ten to fifteen minutes is long enough for strenuous thinking.
3. *Rapidly list brief items.* Stick to words, phrases, or short sentences that you can quickly scan later.
4. *Don't stop.* Don't worry about spelling, repetition, absurdity, or relevance. Don't judge, and don't arrange: just produce. Record whatever comes into your head, as fast as your fingers can type or your pen can fly. If your mind goes blank, keep moving, even if you only repeat what you've just written.

When you finish, circle or check anything that suggests a provocative direction. Scratch out whatever looks useless or dull. Then try some conscious organizing: Are any thoughts related? Can you group them? If so, does the group suggest a topic?

■ **Activity:** Brainstorming

From the following list, choose a subject that interests you, that you know some-thing about, and that you'd like to learn more about — in other words, that you might like to write on. Then brainstorm for ten minutes.

travel	fear	exercise
dieting	dreams	automobiles
family	technology	sports
advertisements	animals	education

Now look over your brainstorming list, and circle any potential topic for a paper. How well did this brainstorming exercise work for you? Can you think of any variations that would make it more useful?

FREEWRITING

To tap your unconscious by *freewriting*, simply write a series of sentences without stopping for fifteen or twenty minutes. The sentences don't have to be grammatical or coherent or stylish; just keep them flowing to unlock an idea's potential.

■ For Ortiz's brain-storming, see pp. 296–97.

Generally, freewriting is most productive if it has an aim — for example, finding a topic, a purpose, or a question you want to answer. Angie Ortiz wrote her topic at the top of a page — and then explored her rough ideas.

> *Electronic devices — do they isolate us? I chat all day on computers and phones, but that's quick communication, not in-depth conversation. I don't really spend much time hanging with friends and getting to know what's going on in their lives. I love listening to my iPod on campus, but maybe I'm not as aware of my surroundings as I could be. I miss seeing things, like the new art gallery that I walk by every day. I didn't even notice the new sculpture park in front! Then, at night, I do assignments on my computer, browse the Web, and watch some cable. I'm in my own little electronic world most of the time. I love technology, but what else am I missing?*

The result, as you can see, wasn't polished prose. Still, in twenty minutes she produced a paragraph to serve as a springboard for her finished essay.

If you want to try freewriting, here's what you do:

1. *Write a sentence or two at the top of your page or computer screen* — the idea you plan to develop by freewriting.
2. *Write steadily without stopping for at least ten minutes.* Express whatever comes to mind, even "My mind is blank," until some new thought floats into view.
3. *Don't censor yourself.* Don't cross out false starts or grammar errors. Don't worry about connecting ideas or finding perfect words.
4. *Feel free to explore.* Your initial sentences can serve as a rough guide, but they shouldn't be a straitjacket. If you find yourself straying from your original idea, a change in direction may be valuable.

Trying Invisible Writing

Invisible writing is a kind of freewriting done on a word processor. After typing your topic at the beginning of a file, darken or turn off your monitor so that you cannot read what's on the screen. Then freewrite. If you feel uneasy, try to relax and concentrate on the ideas. After ten minutes, turn the monitor back on, scroll to the beginning, and read what you have written.

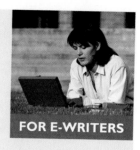

FOR E-WRITERS

5. *Prepare yourself*—if you want to. While you wait for your pencil to start racing, you may want to ask yourself some of these questions:

What interests you about the topic? What aspects do you care most about?

What do you recall about this topic from your own experience? What do you know about it that the next person doesn't?

What have you read about the topic? Observed or heard about it?

How might you feel about this topic if you were someone else (a parent, an instructor, a person from another country)?

6. *Repeat the process, looping back to expand a good idea if you wish.* Poke at the most interesting parts to see if they will further unfold:

What does that mean? If that's true, what then? So what?

What other examples or evidence does this statement call to mind?

What objections might a reader raise? How might you answer them?

■ Activity: Freewriting

Select an idea from your current thinking or from a brainstorming list. Write it at the top of a page or screen. Freewrite about it for fifteen minutes. Share your freewriting with your classmates. If you wish, repeat this process, looping back to explore a provocative idea from your freewriting.

DOODLING OR SKETCHING

If you fill the margins of your notebooks with doodles, harness this artistic energy to generate ideas for writing. Elena Lopez began to sketch her collision with a teammate during a soccer tournament (Figure 16.1). She added stick figures, notes, symbols, and color as she outlined a series of events and their consequences.

Figure 16.1 Doodling or
Sketching to Generate
Ideas

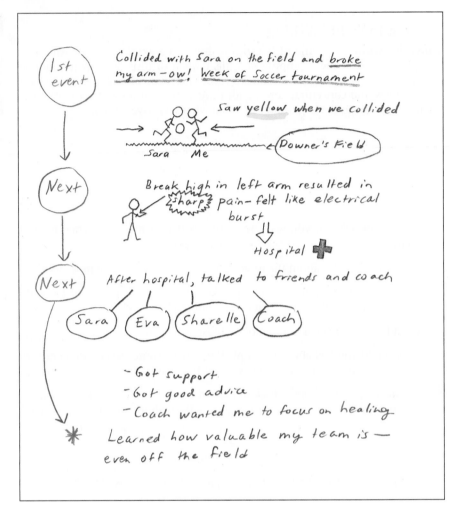

Try this advice as you develop ideas by doodling or sketching:

1. *Give your ideas room to grow.* Open a new file using a drawing program, doodle in pencil on a blank page, or sketch on a series of pages to capture a sequence of events.
2. *Concentrate on your topic, but welcome new ideas.* Begin with a key visual in the center or at the top of a page. Add sketches or doodles as they occur to you; they may embellish, expand, define, or redirect your topic.
3. *Add icons, symbols, colors, figures, labels, notes, or questions.* Freely mix visuals and text, recording ideas without stopping to refine them.
4. *Follow up on your discoveries.* After a break, return to your pages to see how your ideas have evolved. Add notes to make connections, identify sequences, or convert visual concepts into descriptive sentences.

■ See Ch. 21 for ways to add effective visuals to your writing.

■ **Activity:** Doodling or Sketching

Start with a doodle or sketch that illustrates your topic. Add related events, ideas, or details to develop your topic visually. Share your material with classmates, and then use their observations or questions to help you refine your direction as a writer.

MAPPING

Mapping taps your visual and spatial creativity as you generate ideas. When you use mapping, you position ideas on the page or in a file to show their relationships or relative importance — radiating outward from a key term in the center, dropping down from a key word at the top, sprouting upward from a root idea, branching out from a trunk, flowing across the page or screen in a chronological or causal sequence, or following a circular, spiral, sequential, or other familiar form.

Andrew Choi used mapping to gather ideas for his proposal for revitalizing the campus radio station (Figure 16.2). He noted ideas on colored sticky notes — blue for problems, yellow for solutions, and pink for implementation details. Then he moved the sticky notes around on a blank page, arranging them as he connected ideas.

Here are some suggestions for mapping:

1. *Allow space for your map to develop.* Open a computer file, find some posterboard for arranging sticky notes or cards, or use a large page for notes.
2. *Begin with your topic or a key idea.* Drawing on your imagination, memory, class notes, or reading, place a key word at the center or top of a page or screen.
3. *Add related ideas, examples, issues, or questions.* Quickly and spontaneously place these points above, below, or beside your key word.
4. *Refine the connections.* As your map evolves, use lines, arrows, or loops to connect ideas; box or circle them to focus attention; add colors to relate points or to distinguish source materials from your own ideas.

After a break, continue mapping to probe one part more deeply, refine the structure, add detail, or build an alternate map from a different viewpoint. Because mapping is so versatile, use it also to develop graphics that present ideas in visual form.

See Ch. 21 for ways to add effective visuals to your writing. See also pp. 323–24 on clustering.

■ **Activity:** Mapping

Start with a key word or idea that you know about. Map related ideas, using visual elements to show how they connect. Share your map with classmates, and then use their questions or comments to refine your mapping.

Figure 16.2 Mapping to Generate Ideas

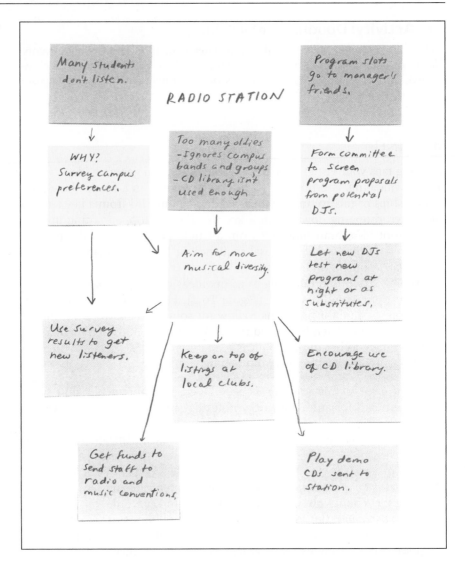

IMAGINING

Your imagination is a valuable resource for exploring possibilities — analyzing an option, evaluating an alternative, or solving a problem. Through imagination, you can discover surprising ideas, original examples, striking expressions, and unexpected relationships.

Suppose that you asked, "What if the average North American life span were more than a century?" No doubt a longer life span would mean that more people would be old. How would that shift affect doctors and nurses, hospitals, and other medical facilities? How might city planners respond to

Group Mapping

Working with a group of three to five classmates, write on a notecard the word or phrase your instructor assigns to the entire class—for example, *campus dining* or *balancing work and college.* Then spend ten or fifteen minutes writing other ideas on new note cards and arranging them around the central card. Move the cards around, and draw connecting lines or arrows if that helps to relate your ideas. Share each group's ideas with the entire class.

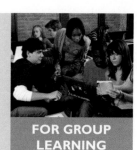

FOR GROUP LEARNING

the needs of so many more old people? What would the change mean for shopping centers? For television programming? For leisure activities? For the social security system? For taxes?

Use some of the following strategies to unleash your imagination:

1. *Speculate about changes, alternatives, and options.* What common assumption—something most people take for granted—might you question or deny? What problem or deplorable condition would you like to remedy? What changes in policy, practice, or attitude might avoid problems you foresee for the future? What different paths in life—each with challenges and successes—might you take?
2. *Shift perspective.* Experiment by taking a point of view other than your usual one. How would someone on the opposite side of an issue respond? How would a plant, an animal, or a Martian? Try shifting the debate (to whether people over sixty-five, not teenagers, should be allowed to drink) or the time frame (from present to past or future).
3. *Envision what might be.* Join the many other writers who have imagined a utopia (an ideal state) or an anti-utopia. By envisioning, you can conceive of possible alternatives—a better way of treating illness, electing a president, or finding meaningful order in a chaotic jumble.
4. *Synthesize.* Synthesizing (generating new ideas by combining previously separate ideas) is the opposite of analyzing (breaking ideas down into component parts). Synthesize to make fresh connections, fusing materials—perhaps old or familiar—into something new.

For more about analysis and synthesis, see pp. 34–36.

■ Activity: Imagining

Begin with a problem that cries out for a solution, a condition that requires a remedy, or a situation that calls for change. Ask "What if?" or start with "Suppose that" to trigger your imagination. Speculate about what might be, record your ideas, and share them with your classmates.

ASKING A REPORTER'S QUESTIONS

Journalists, assembling facts to write a news story, ask themselves six simple questions—the five *W*'s and an *H*:

Who?   Where?   Why?
What?   When?   How?

In the *lead*, or opening paragraph, of a good news story, the writer tries to condense the whole story into a sentence or two, answering all six questions.

> A giant homemade fire balloon [*what*] startled residents of Costa Mesa [*where*] last night [*when*] as Ambrose Barker, 79, [*who*] zigzagged across the sky at nearly 300 miles per hour [*how*] in an attempt to set a new altitude record [*why*].

Later in the news story, the reporter will add details, using the six basic questions to generate more about what happened and why.

For your college writing you can use these six helpful questions to generate specific details for your essays. The questions can help you explore the significance of a childhood experience, analyze what happened at some moment in history, or investigate a campus problem. Their purpose is to help you gather ideas. Don't worry if some of them go nowhere or lead to repetitious answers. Later you'll weed out irrelevant points, keeping only those that look promising for your topic.

For a topic that is not based on your personal experience, you may need to do reading or interviewing to answer some of the questions. Take, for example, the topic of the assassination of President John F. Kennedy, and notice how each question can lead to further questions.

- *Who* was John F. Kennedy? What was his background? What kind of person was he? What kind of president? Who was with him when he was killed? Who was nearby? Who do most people believe shot him?

- *What* happened to Kennedy—exactly? What events led up to the assassination? What happened during the assassination? What did the people around him do? What did the media do? What did everyone across the country do? Ask someone who remembers this event what he or she did on hearing about it.

- *Where* was Kennedy assassinated? The city? The street? Where was he going? What was he riding in? Where was he sitting? Where did the shots likely come from? Where did the shots hit him? Where did he die?

- *When* was he assassinated—the day, month, year, time? When did Kennedy decide to go to this city? When—precisely—were the shots fired? When did he die? When was a suspect arrested?

- *Why* was Kennedy assassinated? What are some of the theories of the assassination? What solid evidence is available to explain it? Why has this event caused so much controversy?

- *How* was Kennedy assassinated? What kind of weapon was used? How many shots were fired? Specifically what caused his death? How can we get at the truth of this event?

■ **Activity:** Asking a Reporter's Questions

Choose one of the following topics, or use one of your own:

  A memorable event in history or in your life
  A concert or other performance that you have attended
  An accomplishment on campus
  An occurrence in your city
  An important speech
  A proposal for change
  A questionable stand someone has taken

Answer the six reporter's questions about the topic. Then write a sentence or two synthesizing the answers to the six questions. Incorporate that sentence into an introductory paragraph for an essay that you might write later.

SEEKING MOTIVES

In a surprisingly large part of your college writing, you will try to explain the motives behind human behavior. In a history paper, you might consider how George Washington's conduct shaped the presidency. In a psychology report, you might try to explain the behavior of participants in an experiment. In a literature essay, you might analyze the motives of Hester Prynne in *The Scarlet Letter*. Because people, including characters in fiction, are so complex, this task is challenging.

■ For more on writing about literature, see Ch. 13.

If you want to understand any human act, according to philosopher–critic Kenneth Burke, you can break it down into a set of five basic components, a *pentad*, and ask questions about each one. While covering much the same ground as the reporter's questions, Burke's pentad differs in that it can show how the components of a human act affect one another. This line of thought can take you deeper into the motives for human behavior than most reporters' investigations ever go.

Suppose that you are preparing to write a political-science paper on President Lyndon Baines Johnson, known as LBJ. Right after President Kennedy's assassination in 1963, Vice President Johnson was sworn in as president. A year later, in 1964, he was elected to the post by a landslide. By 1968, however, Johnson had decided not to run for a second term. You decide to use Burke's pentad to investigate why he made this decision.

1. *The act:* What was done?

      Announcing the decision to leave office without standing for reelection.

2. *The actor:* Who did it?

      President Johnson.

3. *The agency:* What means did the person use to make it happen?

      A televised address to the nation.

4. *The scene:* Where, when, and under what circumstances did the act happen?

Washington, D.C., March 31, 1968. Protesters against the Vietnam War were gaining numbers and influence. The press was increasingly critical of the escalating war. Senator Eugene McCarthy, an antiwar candidate for president, had made a strong showing against LBJ in the New Hampshire primary election.

5. *The purpose or motive for acting:* What could have made the person do it?

LBJ's motives might have included avoiding a probable defeat, escaping further personal attacks, sparing his family, making it easier for his successor to pull the country out of the war, and easing bitter dissent among Americans.

To carry Burke's method further, you can pair the five components and begin fruitful lines of inquiry by asking questions, as illustrated below, about the pairs:

actor to act	act to scene	scene to agency
actor to scene	act to agency	scene to purpose
actor to purpose	act to purpose	agency to purpose

PAIR   actor to agency

QUESTION   What did LBJ [actor] have to do with his televised address [agency]?

ANSWER   Commanding the attention of a vast audience, LBJ must have felt he was in control — even though his ability to control the situation in Vietnam was slipping.

Not all the paired questions will prove fruitful; some may not even apply. But one or two might reveal valuable connections and start you writing.

■ Activity: Seeking Motives

Choose an action that puzzles you — perhaps something you, a family member, or a friend has done; a decision of a historical or current political figure; or something in a movie, television program, or literary selection. Then apply Burke's pentad to try to determine the motives for the action. If you wish, you can also pair up the components to perceive deeper relationships. When you believe you understand the individual's motivation, write a paragraph explaining the action, and share it with your classmates.

KEEPING A JOURNAL

For ideas about keeping a reading journal, see pp. 23–24.

Journal writing richly rewards anyone who engages in it every day or several times a week. You can write anywhere or anytime: all you need is a notebook, a writing implement, and a few minutes to record an entry. To keep a valuable journal, you need only the honesty and willingness to set down what you genuinely think and feel.

Your journal will become a mine studded with priceless nuggets — thoughts and observations, reactions and revelations that are yours for the taking. When you write, you can rifle your well-stocked journal freely—not only for writing topics, but for insights, examples, and other material.

Reflective Journal Writing.   What do you write in your journal? When you make an entry, put less emphasis on recording what happened, as you would in a diary, than on *reflecting* about what you do or see, hear or read, learn or believe. An entry can be a list or an outline, a paragraph or an essay, a poem or a letter you don't intend to send, even a page of doodling. Describe a person or a place, set down a conversation, or record insights into your actions or those of others. Consider your pet peeves, fears, dreams, treasures, convictions or moral dilemmas, or the fate of the world—or the country—if you were in charge. Use your challenges and successes as a writer to nourish and inspire your writing, recording what worked, what didn't, and how you reacted to each.

Responsive Journal Writing.   Sometimes you *respond* to something in particular—to your reading for an assignment, to classroom discussions, to a movie, to a conversation or an observation. This type of journal entry is more focused than the reflective entry. Faced with a long paper to write, you might assign *yourself* a response journal. Then when the time comes to draft your paper, you will have plenty of material to use.

For more on responding to reading, see Ch. 2.

For responsive journal prompts, see the end of each selection in *A Writer's Reader.*

Warm-Up Journal Writing.   To prepare for an assignment, you can group ideas, scribble outlines, sketch beginnings, capture stray thoughts, record relevant material. Of course, what starts as a quick comment on an essay (or a responsive journal entry) may turn into the draft of a paper. In other words, don't let the categories here straitjacket you. A journal can be what you want it to be, and the best journal is the one that's useful to *you.*

■ Activity: Keeping a Journal

Keep a journal for at least a week. Each day record your thoughts, feelings, observations, and reactions. Reflect on what happens, and respond to what you read. Try at least one of the responsive prompts following a selection in *A Writer's Reader.* At the end of the week, bring your journal to class, and read aloud to your classmates the entry you like best.

Keeping an E-Journal

Keeping an e-journal is as simple as creating a file and making entries by date or subject. Record ideas, feelings, images, memories, quotations, and any other writing you wish. You will quickly notice how easy it is to copy and paste inspiring e-mail, quotations from Web pages, or digitized images and sounds into your e-journal. Always identify the source of copied material so that you won't later confuse it with your original writing. As your e-journal grows, you will develop a ready supply of "seeds" and support for writing.

FOR E-WRITERS

Getting Ready

Once you have generated a suitable topic and some ideas related to that topic, you are ready to get down to the job of actually writing.

SETTING UP CIRCUMSTANCES

If you can write only with your shoes off or with a can of soda nearby, set yourself up that way. Some writers need to hear blaring rap music; others need quiet. Create an environment that puts you in the mood for writing.

Devote One Special Place to Writing.   Your place should have good lighting and space to spread out. It may be a desk in your bedroom, the dining room table, or a quiet library cubicle — someplace where no one will bother you and where your mind and body will be ready to settle in for work. Try to make it a place where you can leave your projects and keep handy your pens, paper, computer, dictionary, and reference materials.

Establish a Ritual.   Some writers find that a ritual relaxes them and helps them get started. You might open a soda, straighten your desk, turn music on (or off), and create a new file on the computer.

Relocate.   If you're not getting anywhere with your writing, try moving from the college library to home or from the kitchen to your bedroom. Try an unfamiliar place — a bowling alley, a restaurant, an airport.

Reduce Distractions.   Most of us can't prevent interruptions, but we can reduce them. If you are expecting your boyfriend to call, call him before you start writing. If you have small children, write when they are asleep or at school. Let your voice mail take calls. Block out the noises around you, and concentrate hard on your writing. Let others know you are serious about writing, and allow yourself to give your full attention to it.

Exhaust Your Excuses.   If you, like many writers, are an expert procrastinator, help yourself run out of reasons not to write. Is your room annoyingly jumbled? Straighten it. Sharpen those pencils, throw out that trash, and make that phone call. Then, with your room, your desk, and your mind swept clean, sit down and write.

Write at the Time Best for You.   Some people think best early in the morning, while others favor the small hours when the world is still and their stern self-critic might be asleep, too. Writing at dawn or in the wee hours also reduces distractions from other people.

Write on a Schedule.   Many writers find that it helps to write at a predictable time of day. This method worked marvels for English novelist

Anthony Trollope, who would start at 5:30 A.M., write 2,500 words before 8:30 A.M., and then go to his job at the post office. (He wrote more than sixty books.) Even if you can't set aside the same time every day, it may help to decide, "Today from four to five, I'll sit down and write."

PREPARING YOUR MIND

Sometimes ideas, images, or powerful urges to write will arrive like sudden miracles. When they come, even if you are taking a shower or getting ready to go to a movie, yield to impulse and write. Your words probably will flow with little exertion. Encourage such moments by opening your mind to inspiration.

Talk about Your Writing. Discuss your ideas with a classmate or friend, encouraging questions, comments, and suggestions. Talk in person, by phone, or through e-mail. Or talk to yourself, using a voice-activated tape recorder, while you sit through traffic jams, walk your dog, or ride your bike.

Lay Out Your Plans. Tell any nearby listener — student down the hall, spouse, parent, friend — why you want to write this particular paper, what material you'll put into it, how you're going to lay it out. If the other person says, "That sounds good," you'll be encouraged. Even if the reaction is a yawn, you'll have set your own thinking in motion.

Keep a Notebook or Journal Handy. Always keep some paper in your pocket or backpack or on the night table to write down good ideas that pop into your mind. Imagination may strike in the grocery checkout line, in the doctor's waiting room, or during a lull on the job.

For advice about journals, see pp. 306–07.

Read. The step from reading to writing is a short one. Even when you're just reading for fun, you start to involve yourself with words. Who knows? You might also hit on something useful for your paper. Or read purposefully: Set out to read and take notes.

Use the following questions to help you get ready to write:

DISCOVERY CHECKLIST

___ Is your environment organized for writing? What changes might help you reduce distractions and procrastination?

___ Have you scheduled enough time to get ready to write? How might you adjust your schedule or your expectations to encourage productivity?

___ Is your assignment clear? What additional questions might you want to ask about what you are expected to do?

___ Have you generated enough ideas that interest you? What other strategies for generating ideas might help you expand, focus, or deepen your ideas?

Chapter 17
Strategies for Stating a Thesis and Planning

Starting to write often seems a chaotic activity, but you can use the strategies in this chapter to help create order. For most papers, you will first want to consider your purpose and audience and then focus on a central point by discovering, stating, and improving a thesis. To help you sensibly arrange your material, the chapter also includes advice on grouping ideas and on outlining.

Shaping Your Topic for Your Purpose and Your Audience

■ For critical questions about audience and more about purpose, see p. 311. For more about both, see pp. 14–18.

As you work on your college papers, you may feel as if you're juggling—selecting weighty points and lively details, tossing them into the air, catching each one as it falls, keeping them all moving in sequence. Busy as you are simply juggling, however, your performance almost always draws a crowd—

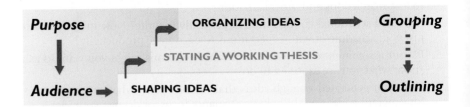

your instructor, your classmates, or other readers. They'll expect you to attend to their concerns as you try to achieve your purpose — probably informing, explaining, or persuading.

Thinking carefully about your audience and purpose can help you plan a paper more effectively. If you want to show your classmates and instructor the importance of an event, you'll need to decide how much detail about the event those readers need. If most of them have gotten speeding tickets, for instance, they'll need less information about that experience than bus riders or other city commuters might. However, to achieve your purpose, you'll need to go beyond what happened to why the event mattered to you. No matter how many tickets your readers have gotten, they won't know exactly how that experience changed you unless you share that information effectively. In fact, they may incorrectly assume that you were worrying about being late to class or paying higher insurance rates when, in fact, you had suddenly realized how narrowly you had escaped an accident like your cousin's and how that recognition motivated you to change your driving habits.

Similarly, if you want to persuade county officials to adopt your proposal for changing the way absentee ballots are distributed to college students, you'll need to support your idea with reasons and evidence — drawing on the state election laws and legal precedents familiar to these readers as well as the experiences of student voters. In fact, you may need to show not only how your proposal would solve existing problems but also why it would improve the situation more effectively than other proposals.

Although your assignment may help you to define your purpose and audience, you can refine your understanding using questions such as these:

- *What is your general purpose?* What specifically would you like to accomplish in your paper? How would you like your readers to react to your paper? Do you want them to smile, think, or agree? To understand, learn, accept, respect, care, change, or reply? How might you plan your writing to accomplish your aims?

- *Who are your readers?* If they are not clearly identified in your assignment or by your situation, what do you assume about them? What do they know or want to know? What opinions do they hold? What do they find informative or persuasive? How might you appeal effectively to them?

- *How might you narrow and focus your ideas about the topic,* given what you know or assume about your purpose and audience? Which slant would best accomplish your purpose? What points would appeal most strongly to your readers? What details would engage or persuade them?

- *What qualities of good writing have been discussed in your class,* explained in your syllabus, or identified in assigned readings? What criteria for college writing have emerged from exchanges of drafts with classmates or comments from your instructor? How might you shape your writing to demonstrate desirable qualities to your readers?

■ **Activity:** Considering Purpose and Audience

Think back to a recent writing task—a college essay, a job application, a report or memo at work, a message to a relative, a letter to a campus office, or some other piece. Write a brief description of your situation as a writer at that time. What was your purpose? Who—exactly—were your readers? How did you account for both as you planned your writing? How might you have made your writing more effective?

Stating and Using a Thesis

Most pieces of effective writing are unified around one main point. That is, all the subpoints and supporting details are relevant to that point. Generally, after you have read an essay, you can sum up the writer's main point in a sentence, even if the author has not stated it explicitly. We call this summary statement a *thesis.*

Often a thesis will be *explicit,* plainly stated, in the piece of writing itself. In "The Myth of the Latin Woman: I Just Met a Girl Named María" from *The Latin Deli* (Athens: University of Georgia Press, 1993), Judith Ortiz Cofer states her thesis in the last sentence of the first paragraph—"You can leave the Island, master the English language, and travel as far as you can, but if you are a Latina, especially one like me who so obviously belongs to Rita Moreno's gene pool, the Island travels with you." This clear statement, strategically placed, helps readers see her main point.

Sometimes a thesis is *implicit,* indirectly suggested rather than directly stated. In "The Niceness Solution," a selection from Bruce Bawer's *Beyond Queer* (New York: Free Press, 1996), Paul Varnell describes an ordinance "banning rude behavior, including rude speech," passed in Raritan, New Jersey. After discussing a 1580 code of conduct, he identifies four objections to such attempts to limit free speech. He concludes with this sentence: "Sensibly, Raritan Police Chief Joseph Sferro said he would not enforce the new ordinance." Although Varnell does not state his main point in one concise sentence, readers know that he opposes the Raritan law and any other attempts to legislate "niceness."

The purpose of most academic and workplace writing is to inform, to explain, or to convince. To achieve any of these purposes, you must make your main point crystal clear. A thesis sentence helps you clarify that idea in your own mind and stay on track as you write. It also helps your readers readily see your point and follow your discussion. Sometimes you may want to imply your thesis, but if you state it explicitly, you ensure that readers cannot miss it.

HOW TO DISCOVER A WORKING THESIS

It's rare for a writer to develop a perfect thesis statement early in the writing process and then to write an effective essay that fits it exactly. What you should aim for is a *working thesis* — a statement that can guide you but that you will ultimately refine. Ideas for a working thesis are probably all around you.

▨ Look for specific advice under headings that mention a thesis in Chs. 4–12. Watch for the red labels that identify thesis examples.

Your topic identifies the area you want to explore. To convert a topic to a thesis, you need to add your own slant, attitude, or point. A useful thesis contains not only the key words that identify your *topic* but also the *point* you want to make or the *attitude* you intend to express.

Topic   +   Slant or Attitude or Point   =   Working Thesis

Suppose you want to identify and write about a specific societal change. After listening to discussion in class and thinking about the topic, you decide to focus on changes in formal courtesy.

TOPIC IDEA   Old-fashioned formal courtesy

Now you experiment, auditioning ideas to make the topic your own.

AUDITION   Old-fashioned formal courtesy is a thing of the past.

Identifying Theses

Working in a small group, select five essays from Part Two of this book to read carefully (or your instructor may choose the essays for your group). Then, individually, write out the thesis for each essay. Some thesis sentences are stated outright (explicit), but others are indirect (implicit). Compare and contrast the thesis statements that you identified with those your classmates found, and discuss the similarities and differences. How can you account for the differences? Try to agree on a thesis statement for each essay.

FOR GROUP LEARNING

Although your audition sentence emphasizes change, it's still a circular statement, repeating rather than advancing a workable point. It doesn't say anything new about old-fashioned formal courtesy; it simply offers a definition of *old-fashioned*. You still need to find and state your own slant—maybe examining why things have changed.

TOPIC IDEA + SLANT   old-fashioned formal courtesy + its decline as gender roles have changed

WORKING THESIS   As the roles of men and women have changed in our society, old-fashioned formal courtesy has declined.

For advice about revising a thesis, see pp. 372–73.

Beginning with this working thesis, you could focus on how changing societal attitudes toward gender roles have caused changes in courtesy. Later, when you revise, you may refine your thesis further—perhaps restricting it to courtesy toward the elderly, toward women, or, despite stereotypes, toward men. The chart on page 315 suggests ways to develop a working thesis.

Once you have a working thesis, be sure its point accomplishes the purpose of your assignment. For example, suppose your assignment asks you to compare and contrast two local newspapers' coverage of a Senate election. Ask yourself what the point of that comparison and contrast is. Simply noting a difference won't be enough to satisfy most readers.

NO SPECIFIC POINT   The *Herald's* coverage of the Senate elections was different from the *Courier's*.

WORKING THESIS   The *Herald's* coverage of the Senate elections was more thorough than the *Courier's*.

■ Activity: Discovering a Thesis

Write a sentence, a working thesis, that unifies each of the following groups of details. Then compare and contrast your theses with those of your classmates. What other information would you need to write a good paper on each topic? How might the thesis statement change as you write the paper?

1. Cigarettes are expensive.
   Cigarettes can cause fires.
   Cigarettes cause unpleasant odors.
   Cigarettes can cause health problems for smokers.
   Secondhand smoke from cigarettes can cause health problems.

2. Clinger College has a highly qualified faculty.
   Clinger College has an excellent curriculum in my field.
   Clinger College has a beautiful campus.
   Clinger College is expensive.
   Clinger College has offered me a scholarship.

3. Crisis centers report that date rape is increasing.
   Most date rape is not reported to the police.
   Often the victim of date rape is not believed.
   Sometimes the victim of date rape is blamed or blames herself.
   The effects of date rape stay with a woman for years.

HOW TO STATE A THESIS

Once you have a notion of your topic and main point, these four suggestions may help you state or improve a thesis to guide your planning and drafting.

- *State the thesis sentence exactly.* Replace vague or general wording with concise, detailed, and down-to-earth language.

  TOO GENERAL   There are a lot of troubles with chemical wastes.

  Are you going to deal with all chemical wastes, throughout all of history, all over the world? Will you list all the troubles they can cause?

  MORE SPECIFIC   Careless dumping of leftover paint is to blame for a recent outbreak of skin rashes in Atlanta.

  If you are writing an argument, you need to take a stand on an issue that is debatable and thus would allow others to take different positions. State yours exactly.

  SPECIFIC STAND   The recent health consequences of carelessly dumped leftover paint require Atlanta officials both to regulate and to educate.

- *State just one central idea in the thesis sentence.* If your paper is to focus on one point, your thesis should state only one main idea.

  TOO MANY IDEAS   Careless dumping of leftover paint has caused a serious problem in Atlanta, and a new kind of biodegradable paint has been developed, and it offers a promising solution to one chemical waste dilemma.

  ONE CENTRAL IDEA   Careless dumping of leftover paint has caused a serious problem in Atlanta.

  OR   A new kind of biodegradable paint offers a promising solution to one chemical waste dilemma.

- *State your thesis positively.* You can usually find evidence to support a positive statement, but you'd have to rule out every possible exception in order to prove a negative one. Negative statements also may sound halfhearted and seem to lead nowhere.

  NEGATIVE   Medical researchers do not know what causes breast cancer.

  POSITIVE   The causes of breast cancer remain a challenge for medical researchers.

  Presenting the topic positively as a "challenge" might lead to a paper about an exciting quest. Besides, to show that researchers are working on the problem would be relatively easy, given an hour of online research.

- *Limit your thesis to a statement that you can demonstrate.* A workable thesis is limited so that you can support it with sufficient convincing evidence. It should stake out just the territory that you can cover thoroughly within the length assigned and the time available, and no more. The shorter the essay, the less development your thesis should promise or require. Likewise, the longer the essay, the more development and complexity your thesis should suggest.

DIFFICULT TO SHOW   For centuries, popular music has announced vital trends in Western society.

DIFFICULT TO SHOW   My favorite piece of music is Beethoven's Fifth Symphony.

The first thesis above could inform a whole encyclopedia of music; the second would require that you explain why that symphony is your favorite, contrasting it with all the other musical compositions you know. The following thesis sounds far more workable for a brief essay.

POSSIBLE TO SHOW   In the past two years, a rise in the number of pre-teenagers has resulted in a comeback for heavy metal on the local concert scene.

Unlike a vague statement or a broad, unrestricted claim, a limited thesis statement narrows and refines your topic, thus restricting your essay to a reasonable scope.

TOO VAGUE   Native American blankets are very beautiful.

TOO BROAD   Native Americans have adapted to many cultural shifts.

POSSIBLE TO SHOW   For some members of the Apache tribe, working in high-rise construction has allowed both economic stability and cultural integrity.

If the suggestions in this chapter have helped you draft a working thesis — even an awkward or a feeble one — you'll find plenty of advice about improving it in the next few pages and more later about revising it. But what if you're freezing up because your thesis simply won't take shape? First, relax. Your thesis will emerge later on — as your thinking matures and you figure out your paper's true direction, as peer readers spot the idea in your paper you're too close to see, as you talk with your instructor and suddenly grasp how to take your paper where you want it to go. In the meantime, plan and write so that you create a rich environment that will encourage your thesis to emerge.

For more on revising a thesis, see pp. 372–73.

■ **Activity:** Examining Thesis Statements

Discuss each of the following thesis sentences with your classmates. Answer these questions for each:

Is the thesis stated exactly?
Does the thesis state just one idea?
Is the thesis stated positively?
Is the thesis sufficiently limited for a short essay?
How might the thesis be improved?

1. Teenagers should not get married.
2. Cutting classes is like a disease.
3. Students have developed a variety of techniques to conceal inadequate study from their instructors.

■ For exercises on choosing effective thesis statements, visit <bedfordstmartins.com/bedguide> and do a keyword search:

thesis

4. Older people often imitate teenagers.

5. Violence on television can be harmful to children.

6. I don't know how to change the oil in my car.

HOW TO IMPROVE A THESIS

■ To get online help from the Draft Doctor, visit <bedfordstmartins.com/bedguide>.

Simply knowing what a solid working thesis *should* do may not help you improve your thesis. Whether yours is a first effort or a refined version, turn to the Draft Doctor (pp. 320–21) to help you figure out ways to strengthen your thesis. Skim down the left column to identify questions you might ask about your thesis. When you answer a question with "Yes" or "Maybe," move straight across the row to the Diagnose column next to that question. Use the diagnostic activities to identify gaps or weaknesses, and then move straight across the row again to the Treat column on the right. Use the advice that suits your thesis as you rework it.

HOW TO USE A THESIS TO ORGANIZE

■ For more on using a thesis to develop an outline, see pp. 325–27.

Often a good, clear thesis will suggest an organization for your ideas.

WORKING THESIS	Despite the disadvantages of living in a downtown business district, I wouldn't live anywhere else.
FIRST ¶S	Disadvantages of living in the business district
NEXT ¶S	Advantages of living there
LAST ¶	Affirmation of your fondness for downtown city life

A clear thesis helps to organize you, keeping you on track as you write. Just putting your working thesis into words can stake out your territory. Your thesis can then direct you as you select details and connect sections of the essay. Its purpose is to guide you on a quest, not to limit your ideas.

■ For more on key terms in college assignments, see p. 36 and pp. 280–83.

In addition, your thesis can prepare your readers for the pattern of development or sequence of ideas that you plan to present. As a writer, you look for key words (such as *compare*, *propose*, or *evaluate*) when you size up an assignment. Such words alert you to what's expected. When you write or revise your thesis, you can use such terms or their equivalents (such as *benefit* or *consequence* instead of *effect*) to preview for readers the likely direction of your paper. Then they, too, will know what to expect.

WORKING THESIS	Expanding the campus program for energy conservation would bring welcome financial and environmental benefits.
FIRST ¶S	Explanation of the campus energy situation and the need for the proposed program expansion
NEXT ¶S	Financial benefits for the college and students
NEXT ¶S	Environmental benefits for the region and beyond
LAST ¶	Concluding assertion of the value of the program

As you write, however, you don't have to cling to a thesis for dear life. If further investigation changes your thinking, you can change your thesis.

WORKING THESIS   Because wolves are a menace to people and farm animals, they ought to be exterminated.

REVISED THESIS   The wolf, a relatively peaceful animal useful in nature's scheme of things, ought to be protected.

You can restate your thesis at any time: as you write, as you revise, as you revise again.

■ Activity: Using a Thesis to Preview Organization

Each of the following thesis statements is from a student paper in a different field of study. Discuss them with your classmates, considering how each one previews the essay to come and how you would expect the essay to be organized into sections.

1. Although the intent of inclusion is to provide the best care for all children by treating both special- and general-education students equally, some people in the field believe that the full inclusion of disabled children in mainstream classrooms may not be in the best interest of either type of student. (From "Is Inclusion the Answer?" by Sarah E. Goers)

2. With ancient Asian roots and contemporary European influences, the Japanese language has continued to change and to reflect cultural change as well. (From "Japanese: Linguistic Diversity" by Stephanie Hawkins)

3. *Manifest destiny* was an expression by leaders and politicians in the 1840s to clarify continental extension and expansion and in a sense revitalize the mission and national destiny for Americans. (From ethnic studies examination answer by Angela Mendy)

4. By comparing the *Aeneid* with *Troilus and Criseyde,* one can easily see the effects of the code of courtly love on literature. (From "The Effect of the Code of Courtly Love: A Comparison of Virgil's *Aeneid* and Chaucer's *Troilus and Criseyde*" by Cindy Keeler)

5. The effects of pollutants on the endangered Least Tern entering the Upper Newport Bay should be quantified so that necessary action can be taken to further protect and encourage the species. (From "Contaminant Residues in Least Tern [*Sterna antillarum*] Eggs Nesting in Upper Newport Bay" by Susanna Olsen)

Organizing Your Ideas

When you organize an essay, you select an order for the parts that makes sense and shows your readers how the ideas are connected. Often your organization will not only help a reader follow your points but also reinforce

Draft Doctor: Building a Stronger Thesis

If you sense a problem, ASK	If you answer Yes/Maybe, DIAGNOSE	If you diagnose a problem, TREAT
Unclear Topic? Could I define or state my topic more clearly?	• Write out your current working thesis. • Circle the words in it that identify your topic. WORKING THESIS: (Adaptability) is essential for World Action volunteers. [What, exactly, does the topic *adaptability* mean?]	• Rework the circled topic. Try to state it more clearly and specify what it means to you. • Define or identify it in terms of your purpose and the likely interests of your audience. REVISED THESIS: An ability to adjust to, even thrive under, challenging circumstances is essential for World Action volunteers.
Unclear Slant? Could I define or state my slant more clearly?	• Write out your current working thesis. • Underline the words that state your slant, attitude, or point about your topic. WORKING THESIS: Volunteering is an invaluable experience. [Why or in what ways is volunteering invaluable?]	• Rework your underlined slant. Jot down possibilities that might sharpen it and express an engaging approach to your topic. • Refine it to address more effectively your purpose as a writer and your audience's interests, concerns, or values. REVISED THESIS: Volunteering builds practical skills while connecting volunteers more fully to their communities.
Broad Thesis? Could I limit my thesis to make sure that I can successfully develop it?	• Write out your current working thesis. • Decide whether it establishes a task that you could accomplish given the time available and the length expected. WORKING THESIS: Rock and roll has evolved dramatically since the 1950s. [Tracing this history in a few pages would be impossible.]	• Restrict your thesis to a slice of the pie, not the whole pie. Focus on one part or element, not several. Break it apart, and pick only a chunk. • Limit its scope by reducing multiple ideas to one point or converting a negative statement to a positive one. REVISED THESIS: The music of the alternative-rock band Wilco continues to evolve as members experiment with vocal moods and instrumentation.

If you sense a problem, ASK	If you answer *Yes/Maybe*, DIAGNOSE	If you diagnose a problem, TREAT
Boring Thesis? Could I make my thesis more interesting for me and for my audience?	• Write out your current working thesis. • Brainstorm about angles or ways to refine it so that you will want to write about it and your audience will want to read about it. WORKING THESIS: Across cultures, weddings include traditions that wish the couple well.	• Reword your thesis until it presents something you'd like to probe, investigate, or show. • Adjust its angle until it expresses the right hold on the topic— seizing the topic from an engaging direction, grasping it securely so it can't slip away, turning it over to reveal the unexpected. REVISED THESIS: From the red clothes and decorations in Chinese weddings to the sugar sprinkled over Iranian brides and grooms, weddings in nearly every culture include traditions aimed at bringing happiness, luck, or fertility to the couple.
Thesis without a Preview? Should I revise my thesis so that it previews the plan for my paper and alerts my audience about what to expect?	• Write out your current working thesis. • List the points about it that you might want to explain and illustrate. • Group your points—first, next, and last—as you might present them to develop your thesis. WORKING THESIS: Raising tuition at Bradley State is counterproductive.	• Rework your thesis to indicate the direction in which your paper goes. • State your preview or prediction clearly in order to prepare readers for the points you raise. REVISED THESIS: Raising tuition at Bradley State is counterproductive because this change would jeopardize both enrollments and income without solving the current financial dilemma.
Any Other Thesis Refinements? After a final look at the refined thesis for my draft, can I improve it further?	• Read your current working thesis out loud to yourself, marking any rough spots. • Ask your peer editors how you might improve the statement and development of your thesis. • Follow any advice about your thesis from your instructor.	• Improve your thesis as needed; for example, smooth out its wording, adjust its slant, reduce its scope, or reverse it. • If your thesis seems entirely misguided or unworkable, toss it out. Make a fresh start. • Consider the useful suggestions of your peers. • Revise until your thesis does what you want it to do.

your emphases by moving from beginning to end or from least to most significant, as the table below illustrates.

GROUPING YOUR IDEAS

While exploring a topic, you will usually find a few ideas that seem to belong together — two facts on New York traffic jams, four actions of New York drivers, three problems with New York streets. But similar ideas seldom appear together in your notes because you did not discover them all at the same time. To identify an effective order for your ideas, you'll need to sort them into groups and arrange them in sequences. Here are five common ways to work:

1. *Rainbow connections.* List all the main points you're going to express. Don't recopy the rest of your material. Use highlighters or colored pencils to mark points that go together with the same color. When you write, follow the color code, and deal with related ideas at the same time.
2. *Linking.* Make a list of major points, and then draw lines (in color if you wish) to link related ideas. Number each linked group to identify a sequence for discussing the ideas. Figure 17.1 illustrates a linked list for an essay on Manhattan driving. The writer has connected related points and supplied each linked group with a heading. Each heading will probably

ORGANIZATION	MOVEMENT	TYPICAL USE	EXAMPLE
Spatial	Left to right, right to left, bottom to top, top to bottom, front to back, outside to inside	• Describing a place, a scene, or an environment • Describing a person's physical appearance	You might describe an ocean vista, moving from the tidepools on the rocky beach to the plastic buoys floating offshore to the sparkling water meeting the sunset sky.
Chronological	What happens first, second, and next, continuing until the end	• Narrating an event • Explaining steps in a procedure • Explaining the development of an idea, a school of thought, or a trend	You might narrate the events that led up to an accident: leaving home late, stopping for an errand, rushing along the highway, racing up to the intersection.
Logical	General to specific, specific to general, least important to most important, cause to effect, problem to solution	• Explaining an idea • Persuading readers to accept a stand, a proposal, or an evaluation	You might analyze the effects of last year's storms by selecting four major consequences, placing the most important one last for emphasis.

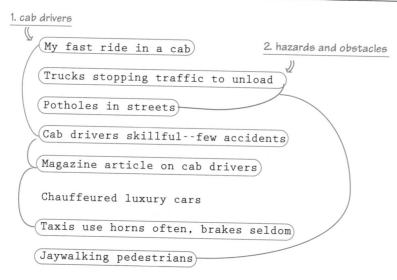

1. cab drivers

My fast ride in a cab

2. hazards and obstacles

Trucks stopping traffic to unload

Potholes in streets

Cab drivers skillful--few accidents

Magazine article on cab drivers

Chauffeured luxury cars

Taxis use horns often, brakes seldom

Jaywalking pedestrians

Figure 17.1 The Linking Method for Grouping Ideas

inspire a topic sentence to introduce each major division of the essay. Because one point, chauffeured luxury cars, failed to relate to any other, the writer has a choice: drop the point or develop ideas about it.

3. *Solitaire.* Collect notes and ideas on roomy (5-by-8-inch) file cards. To organize, spread out the cards; arrange and rearrange them, as in a game of solitaire. When each idea seems to lead to the next, gather all the cards into a deck in this order. As you write, deal yourself a card at a time and translate its contents into sentences. This technique is particularly helpful when you write about literature or from research.

4. *Slide show.* If you are familiar with presentation software such as Power-Point, write your notes and ideas on "slides" (the software equivalent of blank sheets). When you're done, the program gives you the option of viewing your slides one by one or viewing the entire collection. In PowerPoint, choose View and then Slide Sorter. Shuffle and reshuffle your slides into the most promising order.

5. *Clustering.* Like mapping, clustering is a visual method useful for generating as well as grouping ideas. In the middle of a piece of paper, write your topic in a word or a phrase. Then think of the major divisions into which this topic might be organized. For an essay on Manhattan drivers, the major divisions might be the *types* of drivers: (1) taxi drivers, (2) bus drivers, (3) truck drivers, (4) New York drivers of private cars, and (5) out-of-town drivers of private cars. Arrange these divisions around your topic, and circle them too. Draw lines out from the major topic to the subdivisions. You now have a rough plan for an essay. (See Figure 17.2.)

■ For more about mapping, see pp. 301–02.

Figure 17.2 The Clustering Method for Grouping Ideas

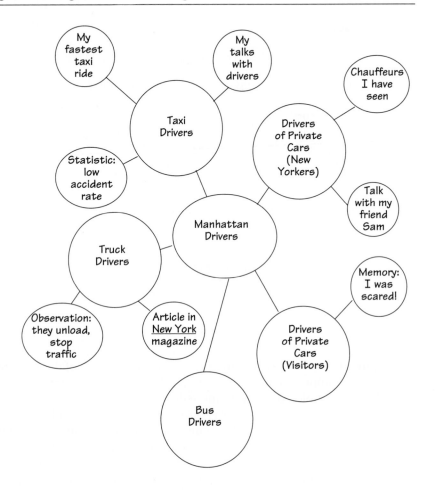

Around each division, make another cluster of details you might include—examples, illustrations, facts, statistics, bits of evidence, opinions. Circle each specific item, and connect it to the appropriate type of driver. When you write your paper, you can expand the details into one paragraph for each type of driver.

This technique lets you know where you have enough specific information to make your paper clear and interesting—and where you don't. If one subtopic has no small circles around it (such as "bus drivers" in Figure 17.2), you should either think of some specifics to expand it or drop it.

■ Activity: Clustering

Generate clusters for three of the following topics. With your classmates, discuss which one of the three would probably help you write the best paper.

teachers	fast food	civil rights
Internet sites	leisure activities	substance abuse
my favorite restaurants	musicians	technology

OUTLINING

A familiar way to organize is to outline. A written outline, whether brief or detailed, acts as a map that you make before a journey. It shows where to leave from, where to stop along the way, and where to arrive. If you forget where you are going or what you want to say, you can consult your written outline to get back on track. When you turn in your essay, your instructor may request an outline as both a map for readers and a skeletal summary of your material.

How can you arrive at a useful outline? Some writers like to begin with a working thesis. If it's clear, it may suggest how to develop or expand an outline, allowing the plan for the paper to grow naturally from the idea behind it. Others prefer to start with a loose informal outline — perhaps just a list of points to make. If readers find your papers mechanical, such an outline may free up your writing. Still others, especially for research papers or complicated arguments, like to lay out a complex job very carefully in a detailed formal outline. If readers find your writing disorganized and hard to follow, this more detailed plan might be especially useful. In any case, your thesis can be a good guide for planning.

For more on thesis statements, see pp. 312–19.

For more on using outlining for revision, see p. 375.

Thesis-Guided Outlines.   Your working thesis may identify points that you can use to organize your paper. (Of course, if it doesn't, you may want to revise your thesis and then return to your outline or vice versa.) For example, suppose that you are assigned an anthropology paper on the people of Melanesia. You decide to focus on the following idea:

> *Working Thesis: Although the Melanesian pattern of family life may look strange to Westerners, it fosters a degree of independence that rivals our own.*

Emphasizing Ideas

Here are some of the easy computer tools you can use to highlight, categorize, and shape your thinking by distinguishing your points on a screen.

Highlighting

Boxing

Showing color

Using **bold**, *italics,* underlining

- Adding bullets

1. Numbering

Changing fonts

Varying print sizes

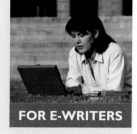

FOR E-WRITERS

To use these features, click on their icons on your toolbar, or use your menu. You can also see your experiments with organization by using an option like Track Changes or by creating a table or column of ideas in a separate window to the left of your text.

Laying out ideas in the same order that they follow in the two parts of this thesis statement, you might make a simple outline like this:

1. *Features that appear strange to Westerners*
   —A woman supported by her brother, not her husband
   —Trial marriages common
   — Divorce from her children possible for any mother

2. *Admirable results of system*
   —Wives not dependent on husbands for support
   —Divorce between mates uncommon
   —Greater freedom for parents and children

This informal outline suggests an essay that naturally falls into two parts — features that seem strange and admirable results of the system. When you are creating a thesis-guided outline, look for the key element of your working thesis that can suggest a useful organization, as the table on page 327 illustrates.

Informal Outlines.   For in-class writing, brief essays, and familiar topics, a short or informal outline, also called a *scratch outline*, may serve your needs. Jot down a list of points in the order you plan to make them. Use this outline, for your eyes only, to help you get organized, stick to the point, and remember ideas under pressure. The following example outlines a short paper explaining how outdoor enthusiasts can avoid illnesses carried by unsafe drinking water. It simply lists each of the methods for treating potentially unsafe water that the writer plans to explain.

Working Thesis: Campers and hikers need to ensure the safety of the water that they drink from rivers or streams.

Introduction: Treatments for potentially unsafe drinking water

1. *Small commercial filter*
   —Remove bacteria and protozoa including salmonella and E. coli
   —Use brands convenient for campers and hikers

2. *Chemicals*
   —Use bleach, chlorine, or iodine
   —Follow general rule: 12 drops per gallon of water

3. *Boiling*
   —Boil for 5 minutes (Red Cross) to 15 minutes (National Safety Council)
   —Store in a clean, covered container

Conclusion: Using one of three methods of treating water, campers and hikers can enjoy safe water from natural sources.

KEY ELEMENT OF THESIS	EXAMPLES OF KEY ELEMENT	SAMPLE THESIS STATEMENT	QUESTION YOU MIGHT ASK	POSSIBLE ORGANIZATION OF OUTLINE
Plural word	Words such as *benefits, advantages, teenagers,* or *reasons*	A varied personal exercise program has four main *advantages.*	What are the types, kinds, or examples of this word?	List outline headings based on the categories or cases you identify.
Key word identifying an approach or vantage point	Words such as *claim, argument, position, interpretation,* or *point of view*	Wylie's *interpretation* of Van Gogh's last paintings unifies aesthetic and psychological considerations.	What are the parts, aspects, or elements of this approach?	List outline headings based on the components that you identify.
Key word identifying an activity	Words such as *preparing, harming,* or *improving*	*Preparing* a pasta dinner for surprise guests can be an easy process.	How is this activity accomplished, or how does it happen?	Supply a heading for each step, stage, or element that the activity involves.
One part of the sentence subordinate to another	Sentence part beginning with a qualification such as *despite, because, since,* or *although*	*Although* the new wetland preserve will protect only some wildlife, it will bring several long-term benefits to the region.	What does the qualification include, and what does the main statement include?	Use a major heading for the qualification and another for the main statement.
General evaluation that assigns a quality or value to someone or something	Evaluative words such as *typical, unusual, valuable, notable,* or other specific qualities	When other parents meet Sandie Burns on the soccer field sidelines, they may be surprised to see her wheelchair, but they soon discover that she is a *typical* soccer mom.	What examples, illustrations, or clusters of details will show this quality?	Add a heading for each extended example or each group of examples or details you want to use.
Claim or argument advocating a certain decision, action, or solution	Words such as *should, could, might, ought to, need to,* or *must*	In spite of these tough economic times, the student senate *should* strongly recommend extended hours for the library computer lab.	Which reasons and evidence will justify this opinion? Which will counter the opinions of others who disagree with it?	Provide a heading for each major justification or defensive point; add headings for countering reasons.

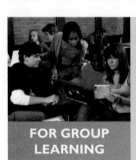

Outlining

Discuss the formal topic outline on pages 330–31 with some of your class-mates or the entire class, considering the following questions:

- Would this outline be useful in organizing an essay?
- How is the organization logical? Is it easy to follow? What are other possible arrangements for the ideas?
- Is this outline sufficiently detailed for a paper? Can you spot any gaps?
- What possible pitfalls would the writer using this outline need to avoid?

This simple outline could easily fall into a five-paragraph essay or grow to eight paragraphs — introduction, conclusion, and three pairs of paragraphs in between. You probably won't know until you write the paper exactly how many paragraphs you'll need.

An informal outline can be even briefer than the preceding one. To answer an exam question or prepare a very short paper, your outline might be no more than an *outer plan* — three or four phrases jotted in a list:

> *Isolation of region*
> *Tradition of family businesses*
> *Growth of electronic commuting*

The process of making an informal outline can help you figure out how to develop your ideas. Say you plan a "how-to" essay analyzing the process of buying a used car, beginning with this thesis:

> *Working Thesis: Despite traps that await the unwary, preparing yourself before you shop can help you find a good used car.*

The key word in this thesis is *preparing*. When you ask yourself *how* the buyer should prepare before shopping for a used car, you're likely to outline several ideas:

> –*Read car blogs, car magazines, and Consumer Reports.*
> –*Check craigslist, dealer sites, and classified ads.*
> –*Make phone calls to several dealers.*
> –*Talk to friends who have bought used cars.*
> –*Know what to look and listen for when you test-drive.*
> –*Have a mechanic check out any car before you buy it.*

After starting your paper with some horror stories about people who got taken by car sharks, you can discuss, point by point, your bits of advice. Of course, you can always change the sequence, add or drop an idea, or revise your thesis as you go along.

■ **Activity:** Moving from Outline to Thesis

Write a possible thesis statement based on each of the following informal outlines. Be certain that your thesis expresses a possible slant, attitude, or point (even if you don't know enough about the topic to be sure that the position is entirely defensible). Share and compare thesis statements with your classmates. What similarities and differences do you find? How do you account for these?

1. Cell Phones
   Get the financial and service plans of various cell-phone companies.
   Read the cell-phone contracts as well as the promotional offers.
   Look for the time period, flexibility, and cancellation provisions.
   Check the day and evening calling times, total minutes, and other extra charges.
   Find out about the availability and costs for extended calling locations (international, national, and regional calls).

2. Popular Mystery Novels
   Both Tony Hillerman and Margaret Coel write mysteries with Native American characters and settings.
   Hillerman's novels feature members of the Navajo Tribal Police.
   Coel's novels feature a female attorney who is an Arapaho and a Jesuit priest at the reservation mission who grew up in Boston.
   Hillerman's stories take place mostly on the extensive Navajo Reservation in Arizona, New Mexico, and Utah.
   Coel's stories are set mostly on the large Wind River Reservation in Wyoming.
   Hillerman and Coel try to convey tribal culture accurately although their mysteries involve different tribes.
   Both also explore similarities, differences, and conflicts between white and Native American cultures.

3. Downtown Playspace
   The Downtown Playspace project has financial and volunteer support but needs more.
   Statistics indicate the need for a regional facility to expand options for children.
   The Downtown Playspace will be available to visitors of the Children's Museum and to local children in Headstart, preschool, and elementary schools.
   It will combine a state-of-the-art outdoor playground with an indoor technology space.
   Land and a building are available, but both require renovation.

Formal Outlines. A *formal outline* is an elaborate guide, built with time and care, for a long, complex paper. Because major reports, research papers, and senior theses require so much work, some professors and departments ask a writer to submit a formal outline at an early stage and to include one in the final draft. A formal outline shows how ideas relate one to another — which ones are equal and important (*coordinate*) and which are less important (*subordinate*). It clearly and logically spells out where you are going. If

■ For sample formal outlines, see pp. 330–33.

you outline again after writing a draft, you can use the revised outline to check your logic then as well, perhaps revealing where to revise.

When you make a full formal outline, follow these steps:

- Place your thesis statement at the beginning.
- List the major points that support and develop your thesis, labeling them with roman numerals (I, II, III).
- Break down the major points into divisions with capital letters (A, B, C), subdivide those using arabic numerals (1, 2, 3), and subdivide those using small letters (a, b, c). Continue until your outline is fully developed. If a very complex project requires further subdivision, use arabic numerals and small letters in parentheses.
- Indent each level of division in turn: the deeper the indentation, the more specific the ideas. Align like-numbered or -lettered headings under one another.

For more on parallelism, see B2 in the Quick Editing Guide (the dark-blue-edged pages).

- Cast all headings in parallel grammatical form: phrases or sentences, but not both in the same outline.

For more on analysis and division, see pp. 360–66.

CAUTION: Because an outline divides or analyzes ideas, some readers and instructors disapprove of categories with only one subpoint, reasoning that you can't divide anything into one part. Let's say that your outline on earthquakes lists a 1 without a 2:

> D. Probable results of an earthquake include structural damage.
>   1. House foundations crack.

Logically, if you are going to discuss the *probable results* of an earthquake, you need to include more than one result:

> D. Probable results of an earthquake include structural damage.
>   1. House foundations crack.
>   2. Road surfaces are damaged.
>   3. Water mains break.

Not only have you now come up with more points, but you have also emphasized the one placed last.

A *formal topic outline* for a long paper might include several levels of ideas, as this outline for Linn Bourgeau's research paper illustrates. Such an outline can help you work out both a persuasive sequence for the parts of a paper and a logical order for any information from sources.

Crucial Choices: Who Will Save the Wetlands If Everyone Is at the Mall?

Working Thesis: Federal regulations need to foster state laws and educational requirements that will help protect the few wetlands that are left, restore as many as possible of those that have been destroyed, and take measures to improve the damage from overdevelopment.

I.   Illinois wetlands

   A. Loss for nature and humans

      1. More flooding and poorer water quality

      2. Lost ability to prevent floods, clean water, and store water

   B. Need for protection of humankind

II. Dramatic floods

   A. Cost in dollars and lives

      1. Thirteen deaths between 1988 and 1998

      2. Cost about $39 million a year

   B. Great Midwestern Flood of 1993

      1. Disregard for wetlands-flood control correlation

      2. Disregard for preventive role of wetlands

III. Education deficits

   A. Inadequately informed legislators

      1 No "isolated wetland"

      2. Interconnections in natural water systems

      3. Ramifications beyond local area

   B. Uninformed students

      1. High school science courses often electives

      2. College students without knowledge of water systems

IV. Changes in laws

   A. Possible transfer of wetlands responsibility from federal government to states

      1. Too much room for interest groups to take over

      2. Need for federal oversight

   B. Perseverance needed (Citizens for Conservation and Deer Point Homes)

   C. New laws for well-researched proposals

      1. Costs of water quality and flooding crises

      2. Misinterpreted or ignored wetlands

      3. Preservation unless no other choice

V.   Need to save wetlands

   A. New federal definition including all the varieties and watersheds

      1. Concept of interconnectedness, now missing, through re-education

      2. No isolated issue or wetlands

   B. Choices in schools, legislature, and people's daily lives

A topic outline may help you work out a clear sequence of ideas but may not elaborate or connect them. Although you may not be sure how everything will fit together until you write a draft, you may find that a *formal sentence outline* clarifies what you want to say. It also moves you a step closer to drafting topic sentences and paragraphs even though you would still need to add detailed information. Notice how this sentence outline for Linn Bourgeau's research paper expands her ideas.

Crucial Choices: Who Will Save the Wetlands If Everyone Is at the Mall?

Working Thesis: Federal regulations need to foster state laws and educational requirements that will help protect the few wetlands that are left, restore as many as possible of those that have been destroyed, and take measures to improve the damage from overdevelopment.

I. Over the past 288 years, the people of Illinois have chosen to legislate and drain away 90 percent of the wetlands once abundant across the state.

    A. The degradation of wetlands is a loss for both nature and humans in Illinois.

       1. Destroying wetlands creates more flooding and poorer water quality.

       2. The wetlands have the ability to stave off floods, to clean the water supply, and to add to the aquifers that store water.

    B. The wetlands need to be protected because they protect and serve humankind.

II. Floods are dramatic and visible consequences of not protecting wetlands.

    A. The cost of flooding can be tallied in dollars spent and in lives lost.

       1. Thirteen people died in floods between 1988 and 1998.

       2. Flooding consistently costs about $39 million a year.

    B. The Great Midwestern Flood of 1993 could have been avoided.

       1. Illinois and other states did not heed the correlation between wetlands and flood control.

       2. Preventing floods is a valuable role of wetlands, whose plants and soil manage excess water.

III. Education deficits affect both legislators and students.

    A. Legislators are not adequately informed about ecological concepts.

       1. Legislators need to know that an "isolated wetland" simply does not exist.

       2. The law needs to consider interconnections in natural water systems.

       3. People can't escape the ramifications well beyond their local area.

    B. Most students are not informed either.

       1. Science courses often are electives in secondary education.

       2. College students lack knowledge of how water systems work.

IV. Change must begin with laws.

A. Because federal laws fail to protect wetlands, this task might go to the states.

   1. However, state control leaves too much room for interest groups to take over.

   2. State governments need the guidance of federal oversight.

B. Perseverance is needed to get politicians to see the value of wetlands, as two cases—Citizens for Conservation and Deer Point Homes—show.

C. New federal laws should implement well-researched proposals.

   1. Water quality and flooding crises deplete funds and natural resources.

   2. Wetlands have largely been misinterpreted or ignored in the laws.

   3. Wetlands should be preserved unless there is no other choice.

V. Who will save the wetlands if everyone is at the mall?

A. The federal definition of wetlands should include all the varieties, including watersheds.

   1. The vital concept of interconnectedness, now missing from wetland laws, means a re-education of everyone from legislators to fourth graders.

   2. The value of wetlands is not an isolated issue any more than wetlands are isolated from one another.

B. The choices made in the schools, the legislature, and people's daily lives will determine the future of water quality and flooding.

■ Activity: Outlining

1. Using one of your groups of ideas from the activities in Chapter 16, construct a formal topic outline that might serve as a guide for an essay.

2. Now turn that topic outline into a formal sentence outline.

3. Discuss both outlines with your classmates and your instructor, bringing up any difficulties you encountered. If you get any better notions for organizing your ideas, change the outline.

4. Write an essay based on your outline.

■ For exercises on organizing support effectively, visit <bedfordstmartins.com/bedguide> and do a keyword search:

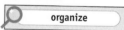

organize

Chapter 18
Strategies for Drafting

Learning to write well involves learning what key questions to ask yourself: How can I begin this draft? What should I do if I get stuck? How can I flesh out the bones of my paper? How can I end effectively? How can I keep my readers with me? In this chapter we offer advice to get you going and keep you going, drafting the first paragraph to the last.

Making a Start Enjoyable

A playful start may get you hard at work before you know it.

- **Time Yourself.** Set your watch, alarm, or egg timer, and vow to draft a page before the buzzer sounds. Don't stop for anything. If you're writing nonsense, just push on. You can cross out later.

- **Slow to a Crawl.** If speed quotas don't work, time yourself to write with exaggerated laziness, maybe a sentence every fifteen minutes.

- **Scribble on a Scrap.** If you dread the blank sheet of paper or screen, try starting on scrap paper, the back of a list, or a small notebook page.

- **Begin Writing the Part You Find Most Appetizing.** Start in the middle or at the end, wherever the thoughts come easily to mind. As novelist Bill Downey observes, "Writers are allowed to have their dessert first."

- **State Your Purpose.** Set forth what you want to achieve: To tell a story? To explain something? To win a reader over to your way of thinking?

- **Slip into a Reader's Shoes.** Put yourself in your reader's place. Start writing what you'd like to find out from the paper.

For more about purpose and audience, see pp. 14–18 and pp. 310–12.

- **Nutshell It.**   Summarize the paper you want to write. Condense your ideas into one small, tight paragraph. Later you can expand each sentence until the meaning is clear and all points are adequately supported.

- **Shrink Your Immediate Job.**   Break the writing task into smaller parts, and do only the first one. Turn out, say, just the first two paragraphs.

- **Seek a Provocative Title.**   Write down a dozen possible titles for your paper. If one sounds strikingly good, don't let it go to waste!

- **Record Yourself.**   Talk a first draft into a tape recorder or your voice mail. Play it back. Then write. Even if it is hard to transcribe your spoken words, this technique may set your mind in motion.

- **Speak Up.**   On your feet, before an imaginary cheering crowd, spontaneously utter a first paragraph. Then — quick! — tape it or write it out.

- **Take Short Breaks.**   Even if you don't feel tired, take a break every half hour or so. Get up, walk around the room, stretch, or get a drink of water. Two or three minutes should be enough to refresh your mind.

Restarting

When you have to write a long or demanding essay that you can't finish in one sitting, you may return to it only to find yourself stalled. You tromp your starter and nothing happens. Your engine seems reluctant to turn over. Try the following suggestions for getting back on the road.

Formatting and Organizing Your Drafts

Use your word processor menu to set the margin widths, line spacing, print size, and other aspects of your paper's format and layout. If your instructor has not specified formatting, customize your files to produce pages with one-inch margins and double spacing, using 12-point type.

FOR E-WRITERS

Next, whether you store your work on disks or on the hard drive of your own computer, figure out a simple file-naming and folder system to make it easy for you to keep track of your work. Some students prefer file names that identify the course, term, assignment, and draft number, while others note the paper topic or activity with the draft number — Eng101F2007-1-1 or Recall-1. When you revise a draft, duplicate and rename the file — Eng101F2007-1-2 or Recall-2 — instead of simply rewriting the original file. Then all the versions of your paper will be available in case you want to retrieve writing from an early draft or your instructor wants to review the stages of your writing process. Use the menu or the help screen to create a folder for each course; store all your drafts for the class there.

■ For more advice on document design, see Ch. 21.

- **Leave Hints for How to Continue.**   If you're ready to quit, jot down any remaining ideas. Tell yourself what you think might come next, or write the first sentence of the next section. When you come back to work, you will face not a blank wall but rich and suggestive graffiti.

- **Pause in Midstream.**   End a writing session by breaking off in midsentence or midparagraph. Just leave a sentence trailing off into space, even if you know what its closing words should be. When you return to your task, you can start writing again immediately.

- **Repeat.**   If the next sentence refuses to appear, simply recopy the last one until that shy creature emerges on the page.

- **Reread.**   When you return to work, spend a few minutes rereading what you have already written or what you have planned.

- **Switch Instruments.**   Do you compose on the computer? Try writing in longhand. Or drop your pen to type. Try writing on note cards or colored paper.

- **Change Activities.**   When words won't come, turn to something quite different. Run, walk your dog, cook a favorite meal, or nap. Or reward yourself — after you reach a certain point in your labors — with a trip to the vending machine, a call to a friend, or a TV show. All the while, your unconscious mind will be working on your writing task.

Paragraphing

For more on developing ideas within paragraphs, see Ch. 19.

An essay is written not in large, indigestible lumps but in *paragraphs* — small units, each more or less self-contained, each contributing some new idea in support of the thesis or main point of the essay. Writers dwell on one idea at a time, stating it, developing it, illustrating it with examples or a few facts — *showing* readers, with plenty of detailed evidence, exactly what they mean.

Paragraphs can be as short as one sentence or as long as a page. Sometimes the length is governed by the audience, the purpose of the writing, or the medium in which it appears. Journalists expect newspaper readers to gobble up facts like popcorn, quickly skimming articles with short one- or two-sentence paragraphs. College writers, in contrast, should assume their readers' willingness to read through well-developed paragraphs.

When readers see a paragraph indentation, they interpret it as a pause, a chance for a deep breath. After that signpost, they expect you to concentrate on a new aspect of your thesis for the rest of that paragraph. The following sections in this chapter give you advice on guiding readers through your writing — using opening paragraphs to draw them in, topic sentences to focus and control body paragraphs within an essay, and concluding paragraphs to wrap up the discussion.

Using Topic Sentences

A *topic sentence* spells out the main idea of a paragraph in the body of an essay. It guides you as you write, and it hooks your readers as they discover what to expect and how to interpret the paragraph. As the topic sentence establishes the focus of the paragraph, it also relates the paragraph to the thesis of the essay, supporting the topic and main point of the essay as a whole. (For this reason, much of the advice on topic sentences for paragraphs also extends to thesis statements for essays.) To convert an idea to a topic sentence, you need to add your own slant, attitude, or point.

■ For more on thesis statements, see pp. 312–21.

> Main Idea   +   Slant or Attitude or Point   =   Topic Sentence

How can you write a good topic sentence? Make it interesting, accurate, and limited. The more pointed and lively your topic sentence, the more it will interest your readers. Even a dull and vague start can be enlivened once you zero in on a specific point.

MAIN IDEA + SLANT	television + everything that's wrong with it
DULL START	There are many things wrong with television.
POINTED TOPIC SENTENCE	Of all the disappointing television programming, what I dislike most is melodramatic news.
¶ PLAN	Illustrate the point with two or three melodramatic news stories.

A topic sentence also should be an accurate guide to the rest of the paragraph so that readers expect just what the paragraph delivers.

INACCURATE GUIDE	All types of household emergencies can catch people off guard. [The paragraph covers steps for emergency preparedness — not the variety of emergencies.]
ACCURATE TOPIC SENTENCE	Although an emergency may not be a common event, emergency preparedness should be routine at every home.

¶ PLAN	Explain how a household can prepare for an emergency with a medical kit, a well-stocked pantry, and a communication plan.

Finally, a topic sentence should be limited so you don't mislead or frustrate readers about what the paragraph covers.

MISLEADING	Seven factors have contributed to the increasing obesity of the average American. [The paragraph discusses only one — portion size.]
LIMITED TOPIC SENTENCE	Portion size is a major factor that contributes to the increasing obesity of average Americans.
¶ PLAN	Define healthy portion sizes, contrasting them with the large portions common in restaurants and packaged foods.

Open with a Topic Sentence.   Usually the topic sentence appears first in the paragraph, followed by sentences that clarify, illustrate, and support what it says. It is typically a statement but can sometimes be a question, alerting the reader to the topic without giving away the punchline. The following example comes from "The Virtues of the Quiet Hero," Senator John McCain's essay about "honor, faith, and service," presented on October 17, 2005, as part of the "This I Believe" series on National Public Radio's *All Things Considered*. Here, as in all the following examples, we have put the topic sentence in *italics*.

> *Years later, I saw an example of honor in the most surprising of places.* As a scared American prisoner of war in Vietnam, I was tied in torture ropes by my tormentors and left alone in an empty room to suffer through the night. Later in the evening, a guard I had never spoken to entered the room and silently loosened the ropes to relieve my suffering. Just before morning, that same guard came back and retightened the ropes before his less humanitarian comrades returned. He never said a word to me. Some months later on a Christmas morning, as I stood alone in the prison courtyard, that same guard walked up to me and stood next to me for a few moments. Then with his sandal, the guard drew a cross in the dirt. We stood wordlessly there for a minute or two, venerating the cross, until the guard rubbed it out and walked away.

This paragraph moves from a general statement to specific examples. The topic sentence clearly states at the outset what the paragraph is about. The second sentence introduces the situation that McCain is recalling. Then the next half-dozen sentences supply two concrete, yet concise, illustrations of his central point.

Place a Topic Sentence near the Beginning.   Sometimes the first sentence of a paragraph acts as a transition, linking what is to come with what has gone before. Then the *second* sentence might be the topic sentence. This pattern is illustrated in the following paragraph from "You Wanna Take This

Online?" by Jeff Chu (*Time,* 8 Aug. 2005). The paragraph before this one recounts thirteen-year-old Taylor Hern's discovery of her name on an online "List of Hos" and ends with her question: "'Who would actually make time in their schedule to do something like that?'"

> Turns out, many of her peers would. *Technology has transformed the lives of teens, including the ways they pick on one another.* If parents and teachers think it's hard to control mean girls and bullying boys in school, they haven't reckoned with cyberspace. Cyberbullying can mean anything from posting pejorative items like the List of Hos to spreading rumors by e-mail to harassing by instant message. It was experienced in the preceding two months by 18 percent of 3,700 middle schoolers surveyed by researchers at Clemson University. Their study is scheduled to be presented at this month's American Psychological Association meeting. The phenomenon peaks at about age thirteen; 21 percent of eighth graders surveyed reported being cyberbullied recently. And incidents of online bullying are like roaches: for every one that's reported, many more go unrecorded. "Our statistics are conservative," says Clemson psychologist Robin Kowalski. "Part of the problem is kids not recognizing that what's happening is a form of bullying."

End with a Topic Sentence.   Occasionally a writer, especially one trying to persuade the reader to agree, piles detail on detail. Then, with a dramatic flourish, the writer *concludes* with the topic sentence, as student Heidi Kessler does.

> A fourteen-year-old writes to an advice columnist in my hometown newspaper that she has "done it" lots of times and sex is "no big deal." At the neighborhood clinic where my aunt works, a hardened sixteen-year-old requests her third abortion. A girl-child I know has two children of her own, but no husband. A college student in my dorm now finds herself sterile from a "social disease" picked up during casual sexual encounters. Multiply these examples by thousands. *It seems clear to me that women, who fought so hard for sexual freedom equal to that of men, have emerged from the battle not as joyous free spirits but as the sexual revolution's walking wounded.*

This paragraph moves from the particular to the general — from four examples about individuals to one large statement about American women at the end. By the time you come to the end of the paragraph, you might be ready to accept the conclusion in the topic sentence.

Imply a Topic Sentence.   It is also possible to find a perfectly unified, well-organized paragraph that has no topic sentence at all, like the following from "New York" (*Esquire,* July 1960) by Gay Talese:

> Each afternoon in New York a rather seedy saxophone player, his cheeks blown out like a spinnaker, stands on the sidewalk playing "Danny Boy" in such a sad, sensitive way that he soon has half the neighborhood peeking out of windows tossing nickels, dimes, and quarters at his feet. Some of the

coins roll under parked cars, but most of them are caught in his out-stretched hand. The saxophone player is a street musician named Joe Gabler; for the past thirty years he has serenaded every block in New York and has sometimes been tossed as much as $100 a day in coins. He is also hit with buckets of water, empty beer cans and eggs, and chased by wild dogs. He is believed to be the last of New York's ancient street musicians.

No one sentence neatly sums up the writer's idea. Like most effective para-graphs that do not state a topic sentence, this one contains something just as good — a *topic idea*. The author doesn't allow his paragraph to wander aimlessly. He knows exactly what he wants to achieve — a description of how Joe Gabler, a famous New York street musician, plies his trade. Because Talese keeps this purpose firmly in mind, the main point — that Gabler meets both reward and abuse — is clear to the reader as well.

■ Activity: Shaping Topic Sentences

Discuss each of the following topic sentences with your peer group, answering these questions:

> Will it catch readers' attention?
> Is it accurate?
> Is it limited?
> How might you develop the idea in the rest of the paragraph?
> Can you improve it?

1. Television commercials stereotype people.
2. Living away from home for the first time is hard.
3. It's good for a child to have a pet.
4. A flea market is a good place to buy jewelry.
5. Pollution should be controlled.
6. Everybody should recycle wastes.

Writing an Opening

Even writers with something to say may find it hard to begin. Often they are so intent on writing a brilliant opening that they freeze, unable to write at all. They forget even the essentials — setting up the topic, sticking to what's relevant, and establishing a thesis. If you feel like a deer paralyzed by headlights when you face your first page, try these ways of tackling the opening:

- Start with your thesis statement, with or without a full opening para-graph. Fill in the rest later.

- Write your thesis statement—the one you planned or one you'd now like to develop—in the middle of a page. Go back to the top of the page, and concisely add the background a reader needs to appreciate where you're going.

- Write a long beginning for your first draft; then cut it down to the most dramatic, exciting, or interesting essentials.

- Simply set down words—any words—on paper, without trying to write an arresting opening. Rewrite later.

- Write the first paragraph last, after you know exactly where your essay goes.

- Move your conclusion to the beginning, and write a new ending.

- Write a summary for yourself and your readers.

Your opening paragraph should intrigue readers—engaging their minds and hearts, exciting their curiosity, drawing them away from their preoccupations into the world set forth in your writing. Use this checklist as you hunt for an effective opening that fits your paper. Then read the sample opening paragraphs that follow.

DISCOVERY CHECKLIST

___ What vital background might readers need?
___ What general situation might help you narrow down to your point?
___ What facts or statistics might make your issue compelling?
___ What powerful anecdote or incident might introduce your point?
___ What striking example or comparison would engage a reader?
___ What question will your thesis—and your essay—answer?
___ What lively quotation would set the scene for your essay?
___ What assertion or claim might be the necessary prelude for your essay?
___ What points should you preview to prepare a reader for what will come?
___ What would compel someone to keep on reading?

Begin with a Story.   Often a simple anecdote can capture your readers' interest and thus serve as a good beginning. Here is how Nicholas Kulish opens his essay "Guy Walks into a Bar" (*New York Times,* 5 Feb. 2006):

> Recently my friend Brandon and I walked along Atlantic Avenue in Brooklyn looking for a place to watch a football game and to quench our thirst for a cold brew. I pushed open the door and we were headed for a pair of empty stools when we both stopped cold. The bar was packed with under-age patrons.

Most of us, after an anecdote, want to read on. What will the writer say next? What has the anecdote to do with the essay as a whole? In this case, Kulish's opening anecdote sets the stage for his objections to parents bringing their babies and toddlers to bars.

Comment on a Topic or Position.   Sometimes a writer expands on a topic, bringing in vital details, as David Morris does to open his article "Rootlessness" (*Utne Reader*, May/June 1990):

> Americans are a rootless people. Each year one in six of us changes residences; one in four changes jobs. We see nothing troubling in these statistics. For most of us, they merely reflect the restless energy that made America great. A nation of immigrants, unsurprisingly, celebrates those willing to pick up stakes and move on: the frontiersman, the cowboy, the entrepreneur, the corporate raider.

After stating his point baldly, Morris supplies statistics to support his contention and briefly explains the phenomenon. This same strategy can be used to present a controversial opinion, then back it up with examples.

Ask a Question.   An essay can begin with a question and answer, as James H. Austin begins "Four Kinds of Chance," in *Chase, Chance, and Creativity: The Lucky Art of Novelty* (New York: Columbia UP, 1978):

> What is chance? Dictionaries define it as something fortuitous that happens unpredictably without discernible human intention. Chance is unintentional and capricious, but we needn't conclude that chance is immune from human intervention. Indeed, chance plays several distinct roles when humans react creatively with one another and with their environment.

Beginning to answer the question in the first paragraph leads readers to expect the rest of the essay to continue the answer.

For more on thesis statements, see pp. 312–21.

End with the Thesis Statement.   Opening paragraphs often end by stating the essay's main point. After capturing readers' attention with an anecdote, gripping details, or pertinent examples, you lead readers in exactly the direction your essay goes. In his response to the question "Should Washington stem the tide of both legal and illegal immigration?" ("Symposium," *Insight on the News*, 11 Mar., 2002), Daniel T. Griswold uses this strategy to begin his answer:

> Immigration always has been controversial in the United States. More than two centuries ago, Benjamin Franklin worried that too many German immigrants would swamp America's predominantly British culture. In the mid-1800s, Irish immigrants were scorned as lazy drunks, not to mention Roman Catholics. At the turn of the century a wave of "new immigrants" — Poles, Italians, Russian Jews — were believed to be too different ever to assimilate into American life. *Today the same fears are raised about immigrants from Latin America and Asia, but current critics of immigration are as wrong as their counterparts were in previous eras.*

Writing a Conclusion

The final paragraphs of an essay linger longest in readers' minds, as does E. B. White's conclusion to "Once More to the Lake" (p. 463). In the essay, White describes his return with his young son to a vacation spot he had loved as a child. As the essay ends in an unforgettable image, he recalls how old he really is and realizes the inevitable passing of generations.

> When the others went swimming my son said he was going in, too. He pulled his dripping trunks from the line where they had hung all through the shower and wrung them out. Languidly, and with no thought of going in, I watched him, his hard little body, skinny and bare, saw him wince slightly as he pulled up around his vitals the small, soggy, icy garment. As he buckled the swollen belt, suddenly my groin felt the chill of death.

White's classic ending opens with a sentence that points back to the previous paragraph as it also looks ahead. Then White leads us quickly to his final, chilling insight. And then he stops.

It's easy to say what *not* to do at the end of an essay: don't leave your readers half expecting you to go on. Don't restate everything you've already said. Don't introduce a brand-new topic that leads away from your point. And don't signal that the end is near with an obvious phrase like "As I have said."

"How *do* you write an ending, then?" you might well ask. Use this checklist as you tackle your conclusion. Then read the sample concluding paragraphs that follow.

DISCOVERY CHECKLIST

—— What restatement of your thesis would give readers a satisfying sense of closure?

—— What provocative implications of your thesis might answer "What now?" or "What's the significance of what I've said?"

—— What snappy quotation or statement would wrap up your point?

—— What closing facts or statistics might confirm the merit of your point?

—— What final anecdote, incident, or example might round out your ideas?

—— What question has your essay answered?

—— What assertion or claim might you want to restate?

—— What summary might help a reader pull together what you've said?

—— What would make a reader sorry to finish such a satisfying essay?

End with a Quotation.   An apt quotation can neatly round out an essay, as literary critic Malcolm Cowley shows in *The View from Eighty* (New York: Viking, 1980), his discussion of the pitfalls and compensations of old age.

> "Eighty years old!" the great Catholic poet Paul Claudel wrote in his journal. "No eyes left, no ears, no teeth, no legs, no wind! And when all is said and done, how astonishingly well one does without them!"

State or Restate Your Thesis.   In a sharp criticism of American schools, humorist Russell Baker in "School vs. Education" ends by stating his main point, that schools do not educate.

> Afterward, the former student's destiny fulfilled, his life rich with Oriental carpets, rare porcelain, and full bank accounts, he may one day find himself with the leisure and the inclination to open a book with a curious mind, and start to become educated.

End with a Brief Emphatic Sentence.   For an essay that traces causes or effects, evaluates, or argues, a pointed concluding thought can reinforce your main idea. In "Don't Mess with Mother" (*Newsweek,* 19 Sept. 2005), Anna Quindlen ends her essay about the environmental challenges posed by post-Katrina New Orleans this way:

> New Orleans will be rebuilt, but rebuilt how? In the heedless, grasping fashion in which so much of this country has been built over the past fifty years, which has led to a continuous loop of floods, fires and filth in the air and water? Or could the new New Orleans be the first city of a new era, in which the demands of development and commerce are carefully balanced against the good of the land and, in the long run, the good of its people? We have been crummy stewards of the Earth, with a sense of knee-jerk entitlement that tells us there is always more where this came from.
>   There isn't.

Stop When the Story Is Over.   Even a quiet ending can be effective, as long as it signals clearly that the essay is finished. Journalist Martin Gansberg simply stops when the story is over in his true account of the fatal stabbing of a young woman, Kitty Genovese, in full view of residents of a Queens, New York, apartment house. The residents, unwilling to become involved, did nothing to interfere. Here is the last paragraph of his account, "Thirty-eight Who Saw Murder Didn't Call Police" (*New York Times,* 17 Mar. 1964):

> It was 4:25 A.M. when the ambulance arrived to take the body of Miss Genovese. It drove off. "Then," a solemn police detective said, "the people came out."

■ For more exercises on openings and conclusions, visit <bedfordstmartins.com/bedguide> and do a keyword search:

open_end

■ **Activity:** Opening and Concluding

Openings and conclusions frame an essay, contributing to the unity of the whole. The opening sets up the topic and main idea; the conclusion reaffirms the thesis and rounds off the ideas. Discuss the following with your classmates.

1. Here are two possible opening paragraphs from a student essay on the importance of teaching children how to swim.

    A. Humans inhabit a world made up of over 70 percent water. In addition to these great bodies of water, we have built millions of swimming pools for sports and leisure activities. At one time or another most people will be faced with either the danger of drowning or the challenge of aquatic recreation. For these reasons, it is essential that we learn to swim. Being a competitive swimmer and a swimming instructor, I fully realize the importance of knowing how to swim.

B. Four-year-old Carl, curious like most children, last spring ventured out onto his pool patio. He fell into the pool and, not knowing how to swim, helplessly sank to the bottom. Minutes later his uncle found the child and brought him to the surface. Because Carl had no pulse, his uncle administered CPR until the paramedics arrived. Eventually the child was revived. During his stay in the hospital, his mother signed him up for beginning swimming classes. Carl was a lucky one. Unlike thousands of other children and adults, he got a second chance.

1. Which introduction is more effective? Why?
2. What would the body of this essay consist of? What kinds of evidence would be included?
3. Write a suitable conclusion for this essay.

2. If you were to read each of the following introductions from professional essays, would you want to read the entire essay? Why?

A. During my ninth hour underground, as I scrambled up a slanting tunnel through the powdered gypsum, Rick Bridges turned to me and said, "You know, this whole area was just discovered Tuesday." (David Roberts, "Caving Comes into Its Golden Age: A New Mexico Marvel," *Smithsonian* Nov. 1988: 52)

B. From the batting average on the back of a George Brett baseball card to the interest rate fluctuations that determine whether the economy grows or stagnates, Americans are fascinated by statistics. (Stephen E. Nordlinger, "By the Numbers," *St. Petersburg Times* 6 Nov. 1988: 11)

C. "What does it look like under there?"
    It was always this question back then, always the same pattern of hello and what's your name, what happened to your eye and what's under there. (Natalie Kusz, "Waiting for a Glass Eye," *Road Song* [New York: Farrar, 1990], rpt. in *Harper's* Nov. 1990)

3. How effective are these introductions and conclusions from student essays? Could they be improved? If so, how? If they are satisfactory, explain why. What would be a catchy yet informative title for each essay?

A. Recently a friend down from New York astonished me with stories of several people infected — some with AIDS — by stepping on needles washed up on the New Jersey beaches. This is just one incident of pollution, a devastating problem in our society today. Pollution is increasing in our world because of greed, apathy, and Congress's inability to control this problem. . . .
    Wouldn't it be nice to have a pollution-free world without medical wastes floating in the water and washing up on our beaches? Without cars and power plants spewing greenhouse gases? With every corporation abiding by the laws set by Congress? In the future we can have a pollution-free world, but it is going to take the cooperation of everyone, including Congress, to ensure our survival on this Planet Earth.

B. The divorce rate has risen 700 percent in this century and continues to rise. More than one out of every two couples who are married end up divorcing. Over one million children a year are affected by divorce in the family. From these statistics it is clear that one of the greatest problems concerning the family today is divorce and the adverse effects it has on our society. . . .

Divorce causes problems that change people for life. The number of divorces will continue to exceed the 700 percent figure unless married couples learn to communicate, to accept their mates unconditionally, and to sacrificially give of themselves.

4. Choose one of the topics that you generated in Chapter 16, and write at least three different introductions with conclusions. Ask your classmates which is the most effective.

Achieving Coherence

Effective writing proceeds in some sensible order, each sentence following naturally from the one before it. Yet even well-organized prose can be hard to read unless it is *coherent* and effectively integrates its elements. To make your writing coherent, you can use various devices to tie together words in a sentence, sentences in a paragraph, paragraphs in an essay.

Add Transitional Words and Sentences.   You use transitions every day to help your readers and listeners follow your train of thought. For example, you might say to a friend, "Well, *on the one hand,* a second job would help me save money for tuition. *On the other hand,* I'd have less time to study." But some writers rush through, omitting links between thoughts or mistakenly assuming that connections they see will automatically be clear to readers. Often just a word, phrase, or sentence of transition inserted in the right place will transform a disconnected passage into a coherent one.

Many words and phrases specify connections between or within sentences. In the chart on page 347, *transitional markers* are grouped by purpose or the kind of relation or connection they establish.

Occasionally a whole sentence serves as a transition. For example, the first sentence of a new paragraph may hark back to the previous paragraph while simultaneously revealing a new or narrower direction. The following excerpt comes from "Preservation Basics: Why Preserve Film," a page on the Web site of the National Film Preservation Foundation (NFPF) at <http://www.filmpreservation.org/sm_index.html>. The first paragraph introduces the organization's mission; the next two each open with transitional sentences that introduce major challenges to that mission. We have italicized the transitional sentences.

Since Thomas Edison's invention of the kinetoscope in 1893, Americans have traveled the world using motion pictures to tell stories, document traditions, and capture current events. Their work stands as the collective memory of the first century witnessed by the moving image. By saving and sharing these motion pictures, we can illuminate our common heritage with a power and immediacy unique to film.

COMMON TRANSITIONS	
TO MARK TIME	then, soon, first, second, next, recently, the following day, in a little while, meanwhile, after, later, in the past, finally
TO MARK PLACE OR DIRECTION	in the distance, close by, near, far away, above, below, to the right, on the other side, opposite, to the west, next door
TO SUMMARIZE OR RESTATE	in other words, to put it another way, in brief, in simpler terms, on the whole, in fact, in a word, to sum up, in short, in conclusion, to conclude, therefore
TO RELATE CAUSE AND EFFECT OR RESULT	therefore, accordingly, hence, thus, for, so, consequently, as a result, because of, due to, eventually, inevitably
TO ADD OR AMPLIFY OR LIST	and, also, too, besides, as well, moreover, in addition, furthermore, in effect, second, in the second place, again, next
TO COMPARE	similarly, likewise, in like manner, in the same way
TO CONCEDE	whereas, on the other hand, with that in mind, still, and yet, even so, in spite of, despite, at least, of course, no doubt, even though
TO CONTRAST	on the other hand, but, or, however, unlike, nevertheless, on the contrary, conversely, in contrast, instead, counter to
TO INDICATE PURPOSE	to this end, for this purpose, with this aim
TO EXPRESS CONDITION	although, though
TO GIVE EXAMPLES OR SPECIFY	for example, for instance, in this case, in particular, to illustrate
TO QUALIFY	for the most part, by and large, with few exceptions, mainly, in most cases, generally, some, sometimes, typically, frequently, rarely
TO EMPHASIZE	it is true, truly, indeed, of course, to be sure, obviously, without doubt, evidently, clearly, understandably

Preservationists are working against the clock. Made on perishable plastic, film decays within years if not properly stored.

Already the losses are high. The Library of Congress has documented that fewer than 20 percent of U.S. feature films from the 1920s survive in complete form in American archives; of the American features produced before 1950, only half still exist. For shorts, documentaries, and independently produced works, we have no way of knowing how much has been lost.

The first paragraph establishes the value of "saving and sharing" the American film legacy. The next two paragraphs use key words related to preservation and its absence (*perishable, decays, losses, lost*) to clarify that what follows builds on what has gone before. Each also opens with a short, dramatic transition to one of the major problems: time and existing loss.

Supply Transition Paragraphs.   Transitions may be even longer than sentences. In a long and complicated essay, moving clearly from one idea to the next will sometimes require a short paragraph of transition.

> So far, the physical and psychological effects of driving nonstop for hundreds of miles seem clear. The next consideration is why drivers do this. What causes people to become addicted to their steering wheels?

Use a transition paragraph only when you sense that your readers might get lost if you don't patiently lead them by the hand. If your essay is short, one question or statement beginning a new paragraph will be enough.

Besides guiding readers through the structure of your essay, a transition paragraph can aid your movement between one branch of argument and your main trunk or between a digression and your main direction. In this excerpt from *The Film Preservation Guide: The Basics for Archives, Libraries, and Museums* (San Francisco: NFPF, 2004; <http://www.filmpreservation.org/preservation/fpg.pdf>), the writer introduces the importance of inspecting a film and then devotes the next paragraph to a digression — referring readers to an inspection sheet in the appendix.

> Inspection is the single most important way to date a film, identify its technical characteristics, and detect damage and decay. Much can be learned by examining your film carefully, from start to finish.
>
> A standardized inspection work sheet (see appendix B) lists things to check and helps organize notes. This type of written report is the foundation for future preservation actions. Collecting the information during inspection will help you make informed decisions and enable you to document any changes in film condition over time.
>
> Signs of decay and damage may vary across the length of the film. . . .

The second paragraph acts as a transition, guiding readers to specialized information in the appendix and drawing readers back to the overall purpose of inspection, assessing the extent of damage to a film. Then the passage continues with the main point: how to learn about a film through an inspection.

Select Repetition.   Another way to clarify the relationship between two sentences, paragraphs, or ideas is to repeat a key word or phrase. Such purposeful repetition almost guarantees that readers will understand how all the parts of a passage fit together. Note the repetition of the word *anger* in the following paragraph (italics ours) from *Of Woman Born* (New York: Norton, 1976) by poet Adrienne Rich. In this complex paragraph, the writer explores her relationship with her mother. The repetition holds all the parts together and makes clear the unity and coherence of the paragraph's ideas.

And I know there must be deep reservoirs of *anger* in her; every mother has known overwhelming, unacceptable *anger* at her children. When I think of the conditions under which my mother became a mother, the impossible expectations, my father's distaste for pregnant women, his hatred of all that he could not control, my *anger* at her dissolves into grief and *anger* for her, and then dissolves back again into *anger* at her: the ancient, unpurged *anger* of the child.

Strengthen Pronouns.   Because they always refer back to nouns or other pronouns, pronouns serve as transitions by making readers refer back as well. Note how certain pronouns (in italics) hold together the following paragraph from "Misunderstood Michelle" by columnist Ellen Goodman in *At Large* (New York: Summit Books, 1981):

> I have two friends who moved in together many years ago. *He* looked upon this step as a trial marriage. *She* looked upon it as, well, moving in together. *He* was sure that in a matter of time, after *they* had built up trust and confidence, *she* would agree that marriage was the next logical step. *She*, on the other hand, was thrilled that here at last was a man *who* would never push *her* back to the altar.

The paragraph contains other transitions, too: time markers like *many years ago, in a matter of time,* and *after; on the other hand,* which indicates a contrast; and repetition of words related to marriage like *trial marriage, marriage,* and *the altar.* All serve the main purpose of transitions — keeping readers on track.

■ Activity: Identifying Transitions

Go over one of the papers you have already written for this course, and circle all the transitional devices you can detect. Then share your paper with a classmate. Can the classmate find additional transitions? Does the classmate think you need transitions where you don't have any?

■ For more exercises on transitions, visit <bedfordstmartins.com/bedguide> and do a keyword search:

coherence

Chapter 19

Strategies for Developing

■ For examples of development strategies, visit <bedfordstmartins.com/bedguide> and do a keyword search:

 development

How can you spice up your general ideas with the stuff of real life? How can you tug your readers deeper and deeper into your essays until they say, "I see just what you mean"? Well-developed essays have such power because they back up general points with evidence that comes alive for readers. In this chapter we cover nine indispensable methods of development—giving examples, providing details, defining, reasoning inductively and deductively, analyzing a subject, analyzing a process, dividing and classifying, comparing and contrasting, and showing causes and effects. Although you may choose to use only one method within a single paragraph, a strong essay almost always requires a combination of developmental strategies.

Whenever you develop a piece of writing or return to it to revise, you face a challenge: How do you figure out what to do? Sometimes you may suspect that you've wandered into the Writer's Grill, a local hang-out offering a huge buffet lunch. You watch others load their plates, but you still hesitate. Which foods will taste best? Which will be healthy choices? Which will make your meal a relaxing experience? How much will fit on your plate? For you as a writer, the answers to such questions are all individual. They depend on your situation, the clarity of your main idea or thesis, and the state of your draft, as the following checklist suggests.

DISCOVERY CHECKLIST

Purpose

___ Does your assignment recommend or require specific methods of development?

___ Which methods might be most useful to explain, inform, or persuade?

___ What type of development might best achieve your specific purpose?

Audience

___ Which developmental strategies would best clarify your topic for readers?

___ Which would best demonstrate your thesis to your readers?

___ What kinds of evidence will your specific readers prefer? Which strategies might develop this evidence most effectively?

Thesis

___ What development does your thesis promise or imply that you will supply?

___ What sequence of developmental strategies would best support your thesis?

Essay Development

___ Has a reader or peer editor pointed out any ideas in your draft that need fuller or more effective development?

___ Where might your readers have trouble following or understanding without more or better development?

Paragraph Development

___ Should any paragraphs with one or two sentences be developed more fully?

___ Should any long paragraphs with generalizations, repetition, and wordy phrasing be developed differently so that they are richer and deeper?

Giving Examples

An example — the word comes from the Latin *exemplum,* "one thing chosen from among many" — is a typical instance that illustrates a whole type or kind. Giving examples to support a generalization is probably the most often used means of development. This example, from *In Search of Excellence* (New York: Harper and Row, 1982) by Thomas J. Peters and Robert H. Waterman Jr., explains the success of America's top corporations:

> Although he's not a company, our favorite illustration of closeness to the customer is car salesman Joe Girard. He sold more new cars and trucks, each year, for eleven years running, than any other human being. In fact, in a typical year, Joe sold more than twice as many units as whoever was in second place. In explaining his secret of success, Joe said: "I sent out over thirteen thousand cards every month."
>
> Why start with Joe? Because his magic is the magic of IBM and many of the rest of the excellent companies. It is simply service, overpowering service, especially after-sales service. Joe noted, "There's one thing that I do that a lot of salesmen don't, and that's believe the sale really begins *after* the sale — not before. . . . The customer ain't out the door, and my son has made up a thank-you note." Joe would intercede personally, a year later, with the service manager on behalf of his customer. Meanwhile he would keep the communications flowing.

Notice how Peters and Waterman focus on the specific, Joe Girard. They don't write *corporation employees* or even *car salespeople.* Instead, they zero in on one particular man to make the point come alive.

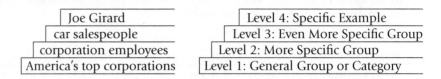

Joe Girard	Level 4: Specific Example
car salespeople	Level 3: Even More Specific Group
corporation employees	Level 2: More Specific Group
America's top corporations	Level 1: General Group or Category

This ladder of abstraction moves from the general — America's top corporations — to a specific person — Joe Girard. The specific example of Joe Girard makes closeness to the customer *concrete* to readers: he is someone readers can relate to. To check the level of specificity in a paragraph or an outline, draw a ladder of abstraction for it. Do the same to restrict a broad subject to a topic manageable in a short essay. If you haven't climbed to the fourth or fifth level, you are probably being too general and need to add specifics.

An example doesn't always have to be a specific individual. Sometimes you can create a picture of something readers have never encountered or give an abstraction a recognizable personality and identity. Using this strategy, Jonathan Kozol makes real the plight of illiterate people in our health-care system in this paragraph from *Prisoners of Silence: Breaking the Bonds of Adult Illiteracy in the United States* (New York: Continuum, 1980):

> Illiterates live, in more than literal ways, an uninsured existence. They cannot understand the written details on a health insurance form. They cannot read waivers that they sign preceding surgical procedures. Several women I have known in Boston have entered a slum hospital with the intention of obtaining a tubal ligation and have emerged a few days later after having been subjected to a hysterectomy. Unaware of their rights, incognizant of jargon, intimidated by the unfamiliar air of fear and atmosphere of ether that so many of us find oppressive in the confines even of the most attractive and expensive medical facilities, they have signed their names to documents they could not read and which nobody, in the hectic situation that prevails so often in those overcrowded hospitals that serve the urban poor, had ever bothered to explain.

Examples aren't trivial doodads you add to a paragraph for decoration; they are what holds your readers' attention and shows them that your writing makes sense. By using examples, you make your ideas more concrete and tangible. To give plenty of examples is one of the writer's chief tasks. When you need more, you can generate them at any point in the writing process. Begin with your own experience, even with a topic about which you know little, or try conversing with others, reading, digging in the library, or browsing on the Web.

■ For ways to generate ideas, see Ch. 16.

Consider these questions when you use examples in your writing:

____ Are your examples relevant to your main idea or thesis?

____ Are your examples the best ones you can think of? Will readers find them strong and appropriate?

____ Are your examples really specific? Or do they just repeat generalities?

____ From each paragraph, can you draw a ladder of abstraction to at least the fourth level?

■ Activity: Giving Examples

To help you get in the habit of thinking specifically, fill in a ladder of abstraction for five of the following general subjects. Then share your ladders with classmates, and compare and contrast your specifics with theirs.

Examples:

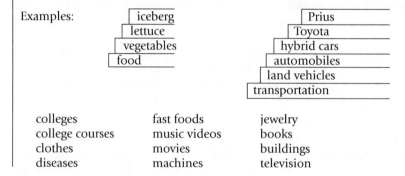

| iceberg |
| lettuce |
| vegetables |
| food |

| Prius |
| Toyota |
| hybrid cars |
| automobiles |
| land vehicles |
| transportation |

colleges	fast foods	jewelry
college courses	music videos	books
clothes	movies	buildings
diseases	machines	television

Providing Details

A *detail* is any specific, concrete piece of information — a fact, a bit of the historical record, your own observation. Details make scenes and images more realistic and vivid for readers. They also back up generalizations, convincing readers that the writer can make broad assertions with authority.

Mary Harris "Mother" Jones told the story of her life as a labor organizer in *The Autobiography of Mother Jones* (1925; Chicago: Kerr, 1980). She lends conviction to her general statement about a coal miner's lot at the end of the nineteenth century with ample evidence from her own experience and observations.

> Mining at its best is wretched work, and the life and surroundings of the miner are hard and ugly. His work is down in the black depths of the earth. He works alone in a drift. There can be little friendly companionship as there is in the factory; as there is among men who build bridges and houses, working together in groups. The work is dirty. Coal dust grinds itself into the skin, never to be removed. The miner must stoop as he works in the drift. He becomes bent like a gnome.

His work is utterly fatiguing. Muscles and bones ache. His lungs breathe coal dust and the strange, damp air of places that are never filled with sunlight. His house is a poor makeshift and there is little to encourage him to make it attractive. The company owns the ground it stands on, and the miner feels the precariousness of his hold. Around his house is mud and slush. Great mounds of culm [the refuse left after coal is screened], black and sullen, surround him. His children are perpetually grimy from playing on the culm mounds. The wife struggles with dirt, with inadequate water supply, with small wages, with overcrowded shacks.

Although Mother Jones, not a learned writer, relies on short, simple sentences, her writing is clear and powerful because of the specific details she uses. Her opening makes two general statements: (1) "Mining . . . is wretched work," and (2) the miner's "life and surroundings" are "hard and ugly." She supports these generalizations with a barrage of factual evidence and detail, including well-chosen verbs: "Coal dust *grinds* itself into the skin." The result is a moving, convincingly detailed portrait of the miner and his family.

In *Lipstick Jihad: A Memoir of Growing Up Iranian in America and American in Iran* (New York: Public Affairs, 2005), Azadeh Moaveni uses details to evoke the "drama and magic" she experienced during a childhood visit to Iran.

To my five-year-old suburban American sensibilities, exposed to nothing more mystical than the Smurfs, Iran was suffused with drama and magic. After Friday lunch at my grandfather's, once the last plates of sliced cantaloupe were cleared away, everyone retired to the bedrooms to nap. Inevitably there was a willing aunt or cousin on hand to scratch my back as I fell asleep. Unused to the siesta ritual, I woke up after half an hour to find the bed I was sharing with my cousin swathed in a tower of creamy gauze that stretched high up to the ceiling. "Wake up," I nudged him, "we're surrounded!" "It's for the mosquitoes, *khareh*, ass, go back to sleep." To me it was like a fairy tale, and I peered through the netting to the living room, to the table heaped with plump dates and the dense, aromatic baklava we would nibble on later with tea. The day before I had helped my grandmother, Razi joon, make ash-e gooshvareh, "earring stew"; we made hoops out of the fresh pasta, and dropped them into the vat of simmering herbs and lamb. Here even the ordinary had charm, even the names of stews.

For more on transitions, see pp. 346–49.

To guide readers through her details, Moaveni uses transitions — chronological (*After Friday lunch, after half an hour, The day before*), spatial (*through the netting to the living room*), and thematic (*To me it was like a fairy tale*).

Quite different from Moaveni's personal, descriptive details are Guy Garcia's objective facts in "Influencing America" (*Time*, 13 Aug. 2005). Garcia heaps up statistical details to substantiate his claim that Hispanics are "helping to define" mainstream America even though they face "prejudice and enormous social and economic hurdles."

Nearly a quarter of all Latinos live in poverty; the high school drop out rate for Latino youths between the ages of sixteen and nineteen is 21 percent — more than triple that of non-Hispanic whites. Neo-nativists like Pat Buchanan and Samuel Huntington still argue that the "tsunami" of non–English speakers from Latin America will destroy everything that America stands for. Never mind that most Hispanics are religious, family-centric, enterprising, and patriotic. In the *Time* poll, 72 percent said they considered moral issues such as abortion and issues of faith important or very important. This year the government announced that undocumented workers were pouring billions into Social Security and Medicare for benefits that they would never be allowed to claim. Of the 27,000 troops serving in the U.S. armed forces who are not U.S. citizens, a large percentage are from Mexico and the rest of Latin America.

Providing details is one of the simplest yet most effective ways of developing ideas. All it takes on your part is close attention and precise wording to communicate details to readers. If readers were on the scene, what would they see, hear, smell, or feel? Which small details from your reading are most meaningful to you? Would a bit of research turn up just the right fact or statistic? Remember that effective details have a specific purpose: they must help make your images more evocative or your point more convincing. Every detail should support — in some way — your main idea.

Here are some questions to consider when you use details:

DISCOVERY CHECKLIST

___ Do all your details support your point of view, main idea, or thesis?
___ Do you have details of sights? Sounds? Tastes? Touch? Smells?
___ Have you included enough details to make your writing clear and interesting?
___ Have you arranged your details in an order that is easy to follow?

■ Activity: Providing Details

To practice using specific details, brainstorm with classmates or alone on one of the following subjects. Include details that appeal to all five senses. Group the details in your list (see pp. 322–24), and write a paragraph or two using your specific details. Begin by stating a main idea that conveys an engaging impression of your subject (not "My grandmother's house was in Topeka, Kansas" but "My grandmother's house was my childhood haven").

For more on brainstorming, see pp. 296–98.

For more exercises on supporting details, visit <bedfordstmartins.com/bedguide> and do a keyword search:

the things in my room	a memorable event	my job
my grandmother's home	an unusual person	a classroom
a haunted house	my favorite pet	the cafeteria
my old car	a hospital room	an incident

Defining

Define, from the Latin, means "to set bounds to." You define a thing, a word, or a concept by describing it so that it is distinguished from all similar things. If people don't agree on the meaning of a word or an idea, they can't share knowledge about it. Scientists in particular take special care to define their terms precisely. In his article "A Chemist's Definition of pH" from *The Condensed Chemical Dictionary* (New York: Reinhold, 1981), Gessner G. Hawley begins with a brief definition:

> pH is a value taken to represent the acidity or alkalinity of an aqueous solution; it is defined as the logarithm of the reciprocal of the hydrogen-ion concentration of a solution:
>
> $$pH = \ln \frac{1}{[H^+]}$$

If you use a word in a special sense or invent a word, you have to explain it or your readers will be lost. In "The Futile Pursuit of Happiness" (*New York Times*, 7 Sept. 2003), Jon Gertner reports on "affective forecasting," an intriguing area of study by economists and psychologists such as Professors Daniel Gilbert of Harvard and Tim Wilson of the University of Virginia. These researchers are exploring what people expect will bring them happiness and how their expectations pan out. Not surprisingly, this new area of study has generated new terms, as the following paragraph explains.

> Gilbert and his collaborator Tim Wilson call the gap between what we predict and what we ultimately experience the *impact bias* — *impact* meaning the errors we make in estimating both the intensity and duration of our emotions and *bias* our tendency to err. The phrase characterizes how we experience the dimming excitement over not just a BMW but also over any object or event that we presume will make us happy. Would a 20 percent raise or winning the lottery result in a contented life? You may predict it will, but almost surely it won't turn out that way. And a new plasma television? You may have high hopes, but the impact bias suggests that it will almost certainly be less cool, and in a shorter time, than you imagine. Worse, Gilbert has noted that these mistakes of expectation can lead directly to mistakes in choosing what we think will give us pleasure. He calls this *miswanting*.

Sometimes you will define an unfamiliar word to save your readers a trip to the dictionary or a familiar but often misunderstood concept to clarify the meaning you intend. For example, what would you mean by *guerilla, liberal,* or *minimum wage*? The more complex or ambiguous an idea, a thing, a movement, a phenomenon, or an organization, the longer the definition you will need to clarify the term for your readers.

Here are some questions to consider when you use definitions:

___ Have you used definitions to help your readers understand the subject matter, not to show off your knowledge?

___ Have you tailored your definition to the needs of your audience?

___ Is your definition specific, clear, and accurate?

___ Would your definition benefit from an example or from details?

■ Activity: Defining

Write an extended definition (a paragraph or so) of one of the following words. Begin with a one-sentence definition of the word. Then, instead of getting most of your definition from a dictionary or textbook, expand and clarify your ideas using some of the strategies in this chapter — examples, details, induction or deduction, analysis (subject, process, causal), division, classification, comparison, contrast. You may also use *negation* (explaining what something is by stating what it is not). Share your definition with your classmates.

education	abuse	exercise	literacy
privacy	jazz	dieting	success
taboo	hip-hop	gossip	fear
prejudice	flu	security	gender

Reasoning Inductively and Deductively

As you develop a typical paragraph in a paper, you are likely to rely on both generalizations and particulars. A *generalization* is a broad statement that establishes the point you want to make, the viewpoint you hold, or the conclusion you have reached. A *particular* is an instance, a detail, or an example — some specific that supplies evidence that a general statement is reasonable. Your particulars support your generalizations; by presenting compelling instances, details, and examples, you back up your broader point. At the same time, your generalizations pull together your particulars, identifying patterns or connections that relate individual cases.

To relate particulars and generalizations, you can use an inductive or deductive process. An *inductive process* begins with the particulars — a convincing number of instances, examples, tests, or experiments. Taken together, these particulars substantiate a larger generalization. In this way a number of long-term studies of weight loss can eventually lead to a consensus about the benefits of walking, eating vegetables, or some other variable. Less formal inductive reasoning is common as people *infer* or conclude that particulars do or do not support a generalization. For example, if your sister ate strawberries three times and got a rash each time, she might infer that she is allergic to strawberries. Induction breaks down when the particulars are too weak or too few to support a generalization: for example, not enough weight-loss studies have

■ For more on reasoning, see Chs. 3 and 9.

■ For more on the statement-support pattern, see A3 in the Quick Research Guide (the dark-red-edged pages).

■ For more on induction and deduction, see Ch. 3.

comparable results or not enough clear instances occur when strawberries — and nothing else — trigger a reaction.

A *deductive process* begins with a generalization and applies it to another case. When your sister says no to a piece of strawberry pie, she does so because, based on her assumptions, she *deduces* that it, too, will trigger a rash. Deduction breaks down when the initial generalization is flawed or when a particular case doesn't fit the generalization. For instance, suppose that each time your sister ate strawberries she drizzled them with lemon juice, the real culprit. Or suppose that the various weight-loss studies defined low-fat food so differently that no one could determine how their findings might be related.

Once you have reached your conclusions as a writer — either by using particulars to support generalizations or by applying reliable generalizations to other particulars — you still need to decide how to present your reasoning to your readers. Do you want your readers to follow your own process, perhaps examining numerous cases before reaching a conclusion about them? Or do you want them to learn what you've concluded first and then review the evidence? Because academic audiences tend to expect conclusions first, many writers begin essays with thesis statements and paragraphs with topic sentences. On the other hand, if your readers are likely to reject an unexpected thesis initially, you may need to show them the evidence first and then lead them gently but purposefully to your point.

In "The Good Heart" (*Newsweek*, 3 Oct. 2005), Anne Underwood opens with a paragraph organized inductively: she describes a particular situation that has helped substantiate the broad, even surprising, generalization with which she concludes the paragraph.

> You can call it the Northridge Effect, after the powerful earthquake that struck near Los Angeles at 4:30 on a January morning in 1994. Within an hour, and for the rest of the day, medics responding to people crushed or trapped inside buildings faced a second wave of deaths from heart attacks among people who had survived the tremor unscathed. In the months that followed, researchers at two universities examined coroners' records from Los Angeles County and found an astonishing jump in cardiovascular deaths, from 15.6 on an average day to 51 on the day of the quake itself. Most of these people turned out to have a history of coronary disease or risk factors such as high blood pressure. But those who died were not involved in rescue efforts or trying to dig themselves out of the rubble. Why did they die? In the understated language of the *New England Journal of Medicine*, "emotional stress may precipitate cardiac events in people who are predisposed to such events." To put it simply, they were scared to death.

Underwood goes on to review the impact on heart attack patients of various factors such as anxiety, depression, and childhood trauma. Then, in the following passage, she first states and supports a generalization about the effects of common stresses in adult life, citing the results of an inductive study. In the second paragraph, she deductively applies the generalization to a particular case.

> And if stress in childhood can lead to heart disease, what about current stressors — longer work hours, threats of layoffs, collapsing pension funds?

A study last year in the *Lancet* examined more than 11,000 heart-attack sufferers from 52 countries and found that in the year before their heart attacks, patients had been under significantly more strains—from work, family, financial troubles, depression, and other causes—than some 13,000 healthy control subjects. "Each of these factors individually was associated with increased risk," says Dr. Salim Yusuf, professor of medicine at Canada's McMaster University and senior investigator on the study. "Together, they accounted for 30 percent of overall heart-attack risk." But people respond differently to high-pressure work situations. The key to whether it produces a coronary seems to be whether you have a sense of control over life, or live at the mercy of circumstances and superiors.

That was the experience of John O'Connell, a Rockford, Illinois, laboratory manager who suffered his first heart attack in 1996, at the age of 56. In the two years before, his mother and two of his children had suffered serious illnesses, and his job had been changed in a reorganization. "My life seemed completely out of control," he says. "I had no idea where I would end up." He ended up on a gurney with a clot blocking his left anterior descending artery—the classic "widowmaker." Two months later he had triple bypass surgery. A second heart attack when he was 58 left his cardiologist shaking his head. There's nothing more we can do for you, doctors told him.

Use these questions to help you present your reasoning clearly and persuasively:

DISCOVERY CHECKLIST

____ Do your generalizations follow logically from your particulars? Can you substantiate what and how much you claim?

____ Are your particulars typical, numerous, and relevant enough to support your generalizations? Are your particulars substantial enough to warrant the conclusion you have drawn?

____ Are both your generalizations and your particulars presented clearly? Have you identified your assumptions for your readers?

____ How do you expect your reasoning patterns to affect your readers? What are your reasons for opening with generalizations or reserving them until the end of a paragraph or passage?

____ Is your reasoning in an explanatory paper clear and logical? Is your reasoning in an argumentative paper rigorous enough to withstand the scrutiny of readers? Have you avoided generalizing too broadly or illogically connecting generalizations and particulars?

■ Activity: Reasoning Inductively and Deductively

Look through a recent magazine for an article that explores a health, an environmental, or an economic issue. Read the article, looking for paragraphs organized inductively and deductively. Why do you think the writer chose one pattern or the other in the various sections of the article? How well do those patterns work from a reader's point of view?

Analyzing a Subject

When you *analyze* a subject, you divide it into its parts and then examine one part at a time. If you have taken any chemistry, you probably analyzed water: you separated it into hydrogen and oxygen, its two elements. You've heard many a commentator or blogger analyze the news, telling us what made up an event—who participated, where it occurred, what happened. Analyzing a news event may produce results less certain and clear-cut than analyzing a chemical compound, but the principle is similar—to take something apart for the purpose of understanding it better.

■ For more on division and classification, see pp. 364–66. For more on process analysis, see pp. 362–64. For more on cause and effect, see pp. 369–70.

Analysis helps readers grasp something complex: they can more readily take in the subject in a series of bites than in one gulp. For this reason, college textbooks do a lot of analyzing: an economics book divides a labor union into its component parts, an anatomy text divides the hand into its bones, muscles, and ligaments. In your college papers, you might analyze and explain to readers anything from a contemporary subculture (What social groups make up the homeless population of Los Angeles?) to an ecosystem (What animals, plants, and minerals coexist in a rain forest?). Analysis is so useful that you can apply it in many situations: breaking down the components of a subject to classify them, separating the stages in a process to see how it works, or identifying the possible results of an event to project consequences.

In *Cultural Anthropology: A Perspective on the Human Condition* (St. Paul: West, 1987), Emily A. Schultz and Robert H. Lavenda briefly but effectively demonstrate by analysis how a metaphor like "the Lord is my shepherd" makes a difficult concept ("the Lord") easy to understand.

> The first part of a metaphor, the metaphorical subject, indicates the domain of experience that needs to be clarified (e.g., "the Lord"). The second part of a metaphor, the metaphorical predicate, suggests a domain of experience which is familiar (e.g., sheep-herding) and which may help us understand what "the Lord" is all about.

In much the same way, Lillian Tsu, a government major at Cornell University, uses analysis in her essay "A Woman in the White House" to identify major difficulties faced by female politicians in the United States.

Although traditionally paternalistic societies like the Philippines and Pakistan and socially conservative states like Great Britain have elected female leaders, particular characteristics of the United States' own electoral system have complicated efforts to elect a female president. Despite social modernization and the progress of the women's movement, the voters of the United States have lagged far behind those of other nations in their willingness to trust in the leadership of a female executive. While the women's movement succeeded in changing Americans' attitudes as to what roles are socially acceptable for women, female candidates have faced a more difficult task in U.S. elections than their male counterparts have. Three factors have been responsible for this situation—political socialization, lack of experience, and open discrimination.

Next, Tsu treats these three factors in turn, beginning each section with a transition that emphasizes the difficulties faced: "One obstacle," "A second obstacle," "A third obstacle." The opening list and the transitions direct readers through a complicated essay, moving from the explanation of the three factors to the final section on implications.

When you plan an analysis, you might label slices in a pielike circle or arrange subdivisions in a list running from smallest to largest or from least to most important. Make sure that your analysis has a purpose—that it will demonstrate something about your subject or tell your readers something they didn't know before. For example, to show the ethnic composition of New York City, you might divide the city geographically into neighborhoods— Harlem, Spanish Harlem, Yorkville, Chinatown, Little Italy. To explain New York's social classes, however, you might start with homeless people and work up to the wealthy elite. The way you slice your subject into pieces will depend in part on the point you want to make about it—and the point you end up making will depend in part on how you've sliced it up. As you develop your ideas, you may also find that you have a stronger point to make—that New York City's social hierarchy is oppressive and unstable, for example.

How can you help your readers follow your analysis? Some writers begin by identifying the subdivisions into which they are going to slice their subject ("The federal government has three branches"). If you name or label each part you mention, define the terms you use, and clarify with examples, you will also help distinguish each part from the others. Finally, using transitions, leading readers from one part to the next, helps make your essay readable.

For more on transitions, see pp. 346–49.

Here are some questions to consider when you use analysis:

DISCOVERY CHECKLIST

___ Exactly what will you try to achieve in your analysis?

___ How does your analysis support your main idea or thesis?

___ How will you break your subject into parts?

___ How can you make each part clear to your readers?

___ What definitions, details, and examples would help clarify each part?

___ What transitions would clarify your movement from part to part?

■ Activity: Analyzing a Subject

Analyze one of the following subjects by making a list of its basic parts or elements. Then use your list as the basis for a paragraph or short essay explaining each part. Be sure to identify the purpose or point of your analysis. Compare your analysis with those of others in your class who chose the same subject.

a college	a choir, orchestra, or other musical group
a news source	a computer or other technological device
a reality TV show	a basketball, baseball, hockey, or other team
effective teaching	a family
a healthy lifestyle	leadership, heroism, or service

Analyzing a Process

Analyzing a process means telling step by step how something is, was, or could be done. You can analyze an action or a phenomenon — how a skyscraper is built, how a revolution begins, how sunspots form, how to make chili. This strategy can also explain large, long-ago events that a writer couldn't possibly have witnessed or complex technical processes that a writer couldn't personally duplicate. Here, for instance, is a paragraph from "The Case for Cloning" (*Time* 9 Feb. 1998) in which Madeleine Nash describes the process of cloning cells. Her *informative* process analysis sets forth how something happens.

> Cloning individual human cells . . . is another matter. Biologists are already talking about harnessing for medical purposes the technique that produced the sheep called Dolly. They might, for example, obtain healthy cells from a patient with leukemia or a burn victim and then transfer the nucleus of each cell into an unfertilized egg from which the nucleus has been removed. Coddled in culture dishes, these embryonic clones — each genetically identical to the patient from which the nuclei came — would begin to divide. The cells would not have to grow into a fetus, however. The addition of powerful growth factors could ensure that the clones develop only into specialized cells and tissue. For the leukemia patient, for example, the cloned cells could provide an infusion of fresh bone marrow, and for the burn victim, grafts of brand-new skin. Unlike cells from an unrelated donor, these cloned cells would incur no danger of rejection; patients would be spared the need to take powerful drugs to suppress the immune system.

In contrast, the *directive* or "how-to" process analysis tells readers how to do something (how to box, invest for retirement, clean a painting) or how to make something (how to draw a map, blaze a trail, set up a computer). Especially on Web sites, directions may consist of simple step-by-step lists designed for browsers who want quick advice. In essays and articles, however, the basics may be supplemented with advice, encouragement, or relevant experience. In the following example from "How to Catch More Trout" (*Outdoor Life* May 2006), Joe Brooks identifies the critical stages in the process in his first paragraph:

> Every move you make in trout fishing counts for or against you. The way you approach a pool, how you retrieve, how you strike, how you play the fish, how you land him — all are important factors. If you plan your tactics according to the demands of each situation, you'll catch a lot more trout over a season.

Then Brooks introduces the first stage:

> The first thing you should do is stand by the pool and study it awhile before you fish. Locate the trout that are rising consistently. Choose one (the lowest in the pool, preferably), and work on him. If you rush right in and start casting, you'll probably put down several fish that you haven't seen. And you can scare still more fish by false-casting all over the place. A dozen fish you might have caught with a more careful approach may see the line and go down before you even drop the fly on the surface.

He continues with stages and advice until he reaches the last step:

> The safest way to land a fish is to beach it. If no low bank is handy, you can fight a fish until he is tired and then pull his head against a bank or an up-jutting rock and pick him up. Hold him gently. The tighter your grip, the more likely he is to spurt from your fingers, break your leader tippet, and escape. Even if you intend to put him back, you want to feel that he is really yours — a trout you have cast and caught and released because you planned it that way.

Throughout the article, Brooks skillfully addresses his audience — readers of *Outdoor Life*, people who probably already know how to fish, hunt, and enjoy outdoor recreation. As his title indicates, Brooks isn't explaining how to catch trout but how to catch *more* trout. For this reason, he skips topics for beginners (such as how to cast) and instead urges readers to plan and implement more sophisticated tactics to increase their catch.

Process analysis can also be turned to humorous ends, as illustrated in this paragraph from "How to Heal a Broken Heart (in One Day)" by student Lindsey Schendel.

> To begin your first day of mourning, you will wake up at 11 a.m., thus banishing any feelings of fatigue. Forget eating a healthy breakfast; toast two waffles, and plaster them with chocolate syrup instead of maple. Then make sure you have a room of serenity so you may cry in peace. It is important that you go through the necessary phases of denial and depression. Call up a friend or family member while you are still in your serious, somber mood. Explain to that person the hardships you are facing and how you don't know if you can go on. Immediately afterwards, turn on any empowering music, get up, and dance.

Like more serious process directions, this paragraph includes steps or stages (sleeping late, eating breakfast, crying and calling, and getting up and dancing). They are arranged in chronological order with transitions marking the movement from one to the other (*To begin, then, while, immediately afterwards*).

For more on transitions, see pp. 346–49.

Process analyses are wonderful ways to show your readers the inside workings of events or systems, but they can be difficult to follow. Be sure to divide the process into logical steps or stages and to put the steps in a sensible chronological order. Add details or examples wherever your description might be ambiguous or abstract; use transitions to mark the end of one step and the beginning of the next.

Here are some questions to consider when you use process analysis:

___ Do you thoroughly understand the process you are analyzing?

___ Do you have a good reason to analyze a process at this point in your writing? How does your analysis support your main idea or thesis?

___ Have you broken the process into logical and useful steps? Have you adjusted your explanation of the steps for your audience?

___ Is the order in which you present these steps the best one possible?

___ Have you used transitions to guide readers from one step to the next?

■ Activity: Analyzing a Process

Analyze one of the following processes or procedures as the basis of a paragraph or short essay. Then share your process analysis with classmates. Can they follow your analysis easily? Do they spot anything you left out?

registering for college classes	falling in love
studying for a test	buying a used car
having the flu (or another illness)	moving

Dividing and Classifying

■ For more on analyzing a subject, see pp. 360–61.

To divide is to break something down, identifying or analyzing its components. It's far easier to take in a subject, especially a complex one, a piece at a time. The thing divided may be as concrete as a medical center (which a writer might divide into specialty units) or as abstract as a person's knowledge of art (which the writer might divide into knowledge of sculpture, painting, drawing, and other forms). To classify is to make sense of a complicated and potentially bewildering array of things — works of literature, this year's movies — by sorting them into categories (*types* or *classes*) that you can deal with one at a time. Literature is customarily arranged by genre — novels, stories, poems, plays. Movies might be sorted by audience (movies for children, teenagers, or mature audiences).

Dividing and classifying are like two sides of the same coin. In theory, any broad subject can be *divided* into components, which can then be *classified* into categories. In practice, it's often difficult to tell where division stops and classification begins.

In the following paragraph from his college textbook *Wildlife Management* (San Francisco: Freeman, 1978), Robert H. Giles Jr. uses division to simplify an especially large, abstract subject: the management of forest wildlife in America. To explain which environmentalists assume which duties and responsibilities, Giles divides forest wildlife management into six levels or areas of concern, arranged roughly from large to small, all neatly explained in fewer than two hundred words.

> There are six scales of forest wildlife management: (1) national, (2) regional, (3) state or industrial, (4) county or parish, (5) intra-state region, management unit, or watershed, and (6) forest. Each is different. At the national and regional levels, management includes decisions on timber harvest quotas, grazing policy in forested lands, official stance on forest taxation bills, cutting policy relative to threatened and endangered species, management coordination of migratory species, and research fund allocation. At the state or industrial level, decision types include land acquisition, sale, or trade; season setting; and permit systems and fees. At the county level, plans are made, seasons set, and special fees levied. At the intra-state level, decisions include what seasons to recommend, what stances to take on bills not affecting local conditions, the sequence in which to attempt land acquisition, and the placement of facilities. At the forest level, decisions may include some of those of the larger management unit but typically are those of maintenance schedules, planting stock, cutting rotations, personnel employment and supervision, road closures, equipment use, practices to be attempted or used, and boundaries to be marked.

In a textbook lesson on how babies develop, Kurt W. Fischer and Arlyne Lazerson, writing in *Human Development* (New York: Freeman, 1984), describe a research project that classified individual babies into three types according to temperament.

> The researchers also found that certain of these temperamental qualities tended to occur together. These clusters of characteristics generally fell into three types — the easy baby, the difficult baby, and the baby who was slow to warm up. The *easy infant* has regular patterns of eating and sleeping, readily approaches new objects and people, adapts easily to changes in the environment, generally reacts with low or moderate intensity, and typically is in a cheerful mood. The *difficult infant* usually shows irregular patterns of eating and sleeping, withdraws from new objects or people, adapts slowly to changes, reacts with great intensity, and is frequently cranky. The *slow-to-warm-up infant* typically has a low activity level, tends to withdraw when presented with an unfamiliar object, reacts with a low level of intensity, and adapts slowly to changes in the environment. Fortunately for parents, most healthy infants — 40 percent or more — have an easy temperament. Only about 10 percent have a difficult temperament, and about 15 percent are slow to warm up. The remaining 35 percent do not easily fit one of the three types but show some other pattern.

When you divide and classify, your point is to make order out of a complex or overwhelming jumble.

- Make sure the components and categories you identify are sensible, given your purpose, and follow the same principle of classification or analysis for all categories. For example, if you're trying to discuss campus relations, it makes sense to divide the school population into *instructors, students,* and *support staff;* it would make less sense to divide it into *people from the South, people from the other states,* and *people from overseas.*

- Try to group apples with apples, not with oranges, so that all the components or categories are roughly equivalent. For example, if you're classifying television shows and you've come up with *reality shows, dramas, talk shows, children's shows, news,* and *cartoons,* then you've got a problem: the last category is probably part of *children's shows.*
- Check that your final system is simple and easy for your readers to understand. Most people can handle only about seven things at once. If you've got more than five or six components or categories, perhaps you need to combine or eliminate some.

Consider these questions when you use division or classification:

DISCOVERY CHECKLIST

___ How does your division or classification support your main idea or thesis?
___ Do you use the most logical principle to divide or classify for your purpose?
___ Do you stick to one principle throughout?
___ Have you identified components or categories that are comparable?
___ Have you arranged your components or categories in the best order?
___ Have you given specific examples for each component or category?
___ Have you made a complex subject more accessible to your readers?

■ **Activity:** Dividing and Classifying

For more on brainstorming, see pp. 296–98.

To practice dividing and classifying, choose one or two of the following subjects. Brainstorm for five minutes on each, trying to come up with as many components as you can. With your classmates, create one large list by combining items from all who chose each subject. Working together, take the largest list and try to classify the items on it into logical categories. Feel free to add or change components or categories if you've overlooked something.

| students | customers | sports | families |
| teachers | Web sites | vacations | drivers |

Comparing and Contrasting

For advice on writing a comparison and contrast essay, see Ch. 7.

Often you can develop ideas by setting a pair of subjects side by side, comparing and contrasting them. When you compare, you point out similarities; when you contrast, you discuss differences. In daily life, we compare and contrast to decide which menu item to choose, which car (or other product) to buy, which college course to sign up for. A comparison and contrast can lead to a final evaluation and a decision about which thing is better, but it doesn't have to.

Working together, these twin strategies use one subject to clarify another. The dual method works well for a pair similar in nature — two cities, two films, two economic theories. Because this method shows that you have observed and understood both subjects, college instructors will often ask you to compare and contrast on exams ("Discuss the chief similarities and differences between nineteenth-century French and English colonial policies in West Africa").

You can use two basic methods of organization for comparison and contrast — the opposing pattern and the alternating pattern. Using the *opposing pattern*, you discuss all the characteristics or subdivisions of the first subject in the first half of the paragraph or essay and then discuss all the characteristics of the other subject. Using the *alternating pattern*, you move back and forth between the two subjects. This pattern places the specifics close together for immediate comparison and contrast. Whichever pattern you choose, be sure to cover the same subpoints for each subject and to follow the same order in each part, as illustrated for a comparison and contrast of two brothers.

For more on these organizing patterns, see pp. 114–17.

OPPOSING PATTERN, SUBJECT BY SUBJECT	ALTERNATING PATTERN, POINT BY POINT
Subject A: Jim	Point 1: Appearance
Point 1: Appearance	Subject A: Jim
Point 2: Personality	Subject B: Jack
Point 3: Interests	Point 2: Personality
Subject B: Jack	Subject A: Jim
Point 1: Appearance	Subject B: Jack
Point 2: Personality	Point 3: Interests
Point 3: Interests	Subject A: Jim
	Subject B: Jack

When you compare and contrast, think carefully about why you are doing so. Compare Jack and Jim to do more than point out lanky or curly hair. Instead, use their differences to highlight their powerful bond as brothers or their similarities to support a generalization about a family strength.

The following selection opens Chapter One of *Rousseau's Dog* by David Edmonds and John Eidinow (New York: HarperCollins, 2006). The book tells the story of the bitterness that grew between David Hume and Jean-Jacques Rousseau, two eighteenth-century philosophers with very different views and styles.

On the evening of January 10, 1766, the weather in the English Channel was foul — stormy, wet, and cold. That night, after being held in harbor by unfavorable winds, a packet boat beat its way, rolling and plunging, from Calais to Dover. Among the passengers were two men who had met for the first time some three weeks earlier in Paris, a British diplomat and a Swiss refugee. The refugee was accompanied by his beloved dog, Sultan, small and brown with a curly tail. The diplomat stayed below, tormented by sea-sickness. The refugee remained on deck all night; the frozen sailors marveled at his hardiness.

If the ship had foundered, she would have carried to the bottom of the Channel two of the most influential thinkers of the eighteenth century.

The diplomat was David Hume. His contributions to philosophy on induction, causation, necessity, personal identity, morality, and theism are of such enduring importance that his name belongs in the league of the most elite philosophers, the league that would also include Plato, Aristotle, Descartes, Kant, and Wittgenstein. A contemporary and friend of Adam Smith's, he paved the way to modern economics; he also modernized historiography.

The refugee was Jean-Jacques Rousseau. His intellectual range and achievements were equally staggering. He made epochal contributions to political theory, literature, and education. His autobiography, *The Confessions,* was a stunningly original work, one that has spawned countless successors but still sets the standard for a narrative of self-revelation and artistic development. *Émile,* his educational tract, transformed the debate about the upbringing of children and was instrumental in altering our perceptions of childhood. *On the Social Contract,* his most significant political publication, has been cited as an inspiration for generations of revolutionaries. More fundamentally, Rousseau altered the way we view ourselves, our emotions, and our relationship to society and to the natural world.

■ For a sample paper and outline using the alternating pattern, see pp. 108–10 and pp. 115–17.

■ For another example using the opposing pattern, see p. 105.

In the first paragraph of this selection, the authors use a short form of the alternating pattern to introduce the two men — moving briefly from diplomat to refugee, diplomat to refugee. The next paragraph asserts their significance, providing a transition to the third and fourth paragraphs, which use the opposing pattern to introduce the contributions, stature, and legacy of the two. As the first chapter continues comparing and contrasting, the difference between the temperaments of the two men — and the potential for deep conflict — grows increasingly clear to readers.

Consider these questions when you use comparison and contrast:

DISCOVERY CHECKLIST

___ Is your reason for comparing and contrasting unmistakably clear? Does it support or develop your main idea or thesis?

___ Have you chosen to write about the *major* similarities and differences?

___ Have you compared or contrasted like things? Have you discussed the same categories or features for each item?

___ Have you selected points of comparison and supporting details that will intrigue, enlighten, and persuade your audience?

___ Have you used the best possible arrangement, given your subject and the point you're trying to make?

___ If you are making a judgment, have you treated both subjects fairly?

___ Have you avoided moving mechanically from "On the one hand" to "On the other hand"?

■ **Activity: Comparing and Contrasting**

Write a paragraph or two in which you compare and contrast the subjects in one of the following pairs:

baseball and football (or two other sports)
living in an apartment (or dorm) and living in a house
two cities or towns you are familiar with
two musicians
communicating by phone and e-mail
watching a sports event on television and in person

Identifying Causes and Effects

From the time we are children, we ask why. Why can't I go out and play? Why is the sky blue? Why did my goldfish die? Seeking causes and effects continues into adulthood, so it's natural that explaining causal relationships is a common method of development. To use this method successfully, you must think about the subject critically, gather evidence, draw judicious conclusions, and clarify relationships.

■ For advice on writing a cause and effect essay, see Ch. 8.

In the following paragraph from "What Pop Lyrics Say to Us" (*New York Times*, 24 Feb. 1985), Robert Palmer speculates on the causes that led young people to turn to rock music for inspiration as well as the effects of their expectations on the musicians of the time.

> By the late '60s, the peace and civil rights movement were beginning to splinter. The assassinations of the Kennedys and Martin Luther King had robbed a generation of its heroes, the Vietnam War was escalating despite the protests, and at home, violence was on the rise. Young people turned to rock, expecting it to ask the right questions and come up with answers, hoping that the music's most visionary artists could somehow make sense of things. But rock's most influential artists—Bob Dylan, the Beatles, the Rolling Stones—were finding that serving as the conscience of a generation exacted a heavy toll. Mr. Dylan, for one, felt the pressures becoming unbearable, and wrote about his predicament in songs like "All Along the Watchtower."

Instead of focusing on causes *or* effects, often writers trace a *chain* of cause and effect relationships, as Charles C. Mann and Mark L. Plummer do in "The Butterfly Problem" (*Atlantic Monthly* Jan. 1992).

> More generally, the web of species around us helps generate soil, regulate freshwater supplies, dispose of waste, and maintain the quality of the atmosphere. Pillaging nature to the point where it cannot perform these functions is dangerously foolish. Simple self-protection is thus a second motive for preserving biodiversity. When DDT was sprayed in Borneo, the biologists Paul and Anne Ehrlich relate in their book *Extinction* (1981), it killed all the houseflies. The gecko lizards that preyed on the flies ate their pesticide-filled corpses and died. House cats consumed the dying lizards; they died

too. Rats descended on the villages, bringing bubonic plague. Incredibly, the housefly in this case was part of an intricate system that controlled human disease. To make up for its absence, the government was forced to parachute cats into the area.

Consider these questions when you identify causes and effects:

DISCOVERY CHECKLIST

___ Is your use of cause and effect clearly tied to your main idea or thesis?

___ Have you identified actual causes? Have you supplied persuasive evidence to support them?

___ Have you identified actual effects, or are they conjecture? If conjecture, are they logical possibilities? Can you find persuasive evidence to support them?

___ Have you judiciously drawn conclusions about causes and effects? Have you avoided faulty thinking and logical fallacies?

___ Have you presented your points clearly and logically so that your readers can follow them easily?

___ Have you considered other causes or effects, immediate or long-term, that readers might find relevant?

For more on faulty thinking and logical fallacies, see pp. 46–47 and pp. 162–63.

■ Activity: Identifying Causes and Effects

1. Identify some of the *causes* of *five* of the following. Then discuss possible causes with your classmates.

failing an exam	stage fright	losing a job
an automobile accident	losing/winning a game	losing weight
poor health	stress	going to college
good health	getting a job	getting a scholarship

2. Identify some of the *effects* of *five* of the following. Then discuss possible effects with your classmates.

an insult	dieting	divorce
a compliment	speeding	traveling to another country
learning to read	winning the lottery	drinking while driving

3. Identify some of the *causes and effects* of *one* of the following. You may need to do a little research to identify the chain of causes and effects for the event. How might you use what you have discovered as part of an essay? Discuss your findings with your classmates.

the online shopping boom	the bird flu
the Vietnam War	recycling
the attacks of September 11, 2001	a gay-marriage court case
the discovery of atomic energy	the uses of solar energy
a major U.S. Supreme	global climate change
Court decision	racial tension

Chapter 20
Strategies for Revising and Editing

Good writing is rewriting. When Ernest Hemingway was asked what made him rewrite the last page of the novel *A Farewell to Arms* thirty-nine times, he replied, "Getting the words right." His comment reflects the care that serious writers take in revising their work. In this chapter we provide strategies for revising and editing — ways to rethink muddy ideas and emphasize important ones, to rephrase obscure passages and restructure

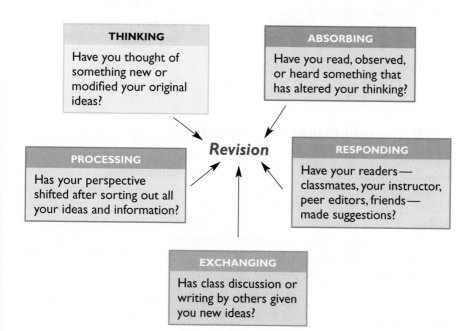

THINKING
Have you thought of something new or modified your original ideas?

ABSORBING
Have you read, observed, or heard something that has altered your thinking?

PROCESSING
Has your perspective shifted after sorting out all your ideas and information?

Revision

RESPONDING
Have your readers — classmates, your instructor, peer editors, friends — made suggestions?

EXCHANGING
Has class discussion or writing by others given you new ideas?

garbled sentences. Our advice applies not only to rewriting whole essays but also to rewriting sentences and paragraphs. In addition, we give you tips for editing and proofreading grammar, spelling, punctuation, and mechanics.

Re-viewing and Revising

Revision means "seeing again" — discovering again, conceiving again, shaping again. As an integral aspect of the total writing process, it may occur at any and all stages of the process, and most writers do a lot of it. *Macro revising* is making large, global, or fundamental changes that affect the overall direction or impact of writing — its purpose, organization, or audience. Its companion is *micro revising*, paying attention to the details of language. It involves sentences, words, punctuation, and grammar — including ways to create emphasis and eliminate wordiness.

MACRO REVISING	MICRO REVISING
• **PURPOSE:** Have you refined what you want to accomplish?	• **EMPHASIS:** Can you position your ideas more effectively?
• **THESIS:** Could you state your main point more accurately?	• **CONCISENESS:** Can you spot extra words that you might cut?
• **AUDIENCE:** Should you address your readers differently?	• **CLARITY:** Can you make any sentences and words clearer?
• **STRUCTURE:** Should you reorganize any part of your writing?	
• **SUPPORT:** Do you need to add, drop, or rework your support?	

REVISING FOR PURPOSE AND THESIS

When you revise for purpose, you make sure that your writing accomplishes what you want it to do. If your goal is to create an interesting profile of a person, have you done so? If you want to persuade your readers to take a certain course of action, have you succeeded? Of course, if your project has evolved or your assignment is now clearer to you, the purpose of your final essay may differ from your purpose when you began. To revise for purpose, try to step back and see your writing as other readers will. Concentrate on what's actually in your paper, not what you assume is there.

At this point you'll probably want to revise your working thesis statement (if you've developed one) or create a thesis sentence (if you haven't). First scrutinize your working thesis. Reconsider how it is worded:

■ For more on stating and improving a working thesis, see pp. 312–18.

- Is it stated exactly in concise yet detailed language?
- Is it focused on only one main idea?
- Is it stated positively rather than negatively?
- Is it limited to a demonstrable statement?

Then consider how accurately your thesis now represents your main idea and your draft as a whole:

- Does each part of your essay directly relate to your thesis?
- Does each part of your essay develop and support your thesis?
- Does your essay deliver everything your thesis promises?

If you find unrelated or contradictory passages, you have several options: re-vise the thesis, revise the essay, or revise both.

You may find that your ideas have deepened, your topic has become more complex, or your essay has developed along new lines during the process of writing. If so, you may want to refine or expand your thesis statement so that it accurately represents this evolution.

WORKING THESIS The *Herald*'s coverage of the Senate elections was more thorough than the *Courier*'s.

REVISED THESIS The *Herald*'s coverage of the Senate elections was less timely but more thorough and more impartial than the *Courier*'s.

WORKING THESIS As the roles of men and women have changed in our society, old-fashioned formal courtesy has declined.

REVISED THESIS As the roles of men and women have changed in our society, old-fashioned formal courtesy has declined not only toward women but also toward men.

Here are helpful questions about revising for purpose and thesis:

REVISION CHECKLIST

___ Do you know exactly what you want your essay to accomplish? Can you put it in one sentence: "In this paper I want to . . ."?

___ Is your thesis stated outright in the essay? If not, have you provided clues so that your readers will know precisely what it is?

___ Does every part of the essay work to achieve the same goal?

___ Have you tried to do too much? Does your coverage of your topic seem too thin? If so, how might you reduce the scope of your thesis and essay?

___ Does your essay say all that needs to be said? Is everything—ideas, connec-tions, supporting evidence—on paper, not just in your head?

___ In writing the essay, have you changed your mind, rethought your assump-tions, made a discovery? Does anything now need to be recast?

___ Do you have enough evidence? Is every point developed fully enough to be clear? To be convincing?

■ To see one student's revising and editing process, visit <bedfordstmartins.com/bedguide> and do a keyword search:

process

REVISING FOR AUDIENCE

An essay is successful only if it succeeds with its particular audience, and what works with one audience can fall flat with another. Visualize one of your readers poring over the essay, sentence by sentence, reacting to what you have written. What expressions do you see on that reader's face? Where does he or she have trouble understanding? Where have you hit the mark? Your organization, your selection of details, your word choice, and your tone all affect your readers, so pay special attention to these aspects.

Here are some helpful questions about revising for your audience:

REVISION CHECKLIST

___ Who will read this essay?

___ Does the essay tell your readers what they want to know rather than what they probably know already?

___ Are there any places where readers might fall asleep? If so, can you shorten, delete, or liven up such passages?

___ Does the opening of the essay mislead your readers by promising something that the essay never delivers?

___ Do you unfold each idea in enough detail to make it both clear and interesting? Would readers appreciate more detailed evidence?

___ Have you anticipated questions your audience might ask?

___ Where might readers raise serious objections? How might you anticipate their objections and answer them?

___ Have you used any specialized or technical language that your readers might not understand? If so, have you worked in brief definitions?

___ What is your attitude toward your audience? Are you chummy, angry, superior, apologetic, condescending, preachy? Should you revise to improve your attitude? Ask your peers for an opinion.

___ Will your readers think you have told them something worth knowing?

REVISING FOR STRUCTURE AND SUPPORT

When you revise for structure and support, you make sure that the order of your ideas, your selection of supporting material, and its arrangement are as effective as possible. You may have all the ingredients of a successful essay — but they may be a confusing mess.

■ For more on paragraphs, topic sentences, and transitions, see Ch. 18.

In a well-structured essay, each paragraph, sentence, and phrase serves a clear function. Are your opening and closing paragraphs relevant, concise, and interesting? Is everything in each paragraph on the same topic? Are all ideas adequately developed? Are the paragraphs arranged in the best possible order? Finally, review each place where you lead readers from one idea to the next to be certain that the transition is clear and painless.

An outline can be useful for discovering what you've succeeded in getting on paper. Start by finding the topic sentence of each paragraph in your draft (or creating one, if necessary) and listing them in order. Label the sentences *I., II., A., B.,* and so on to indicate the logical relationships of ideas in your essay. Do the same with the supporting details under each topic sentence, labeling them also with letters and numbers and indenting appropriately. Now look at the outline. Does it make sense on its own, without the essay to explain it? Would a different order or arrangement be more effective? Do any sections look thin and need more evidence? Are the connections between parts in your head but not on paper? Maybe too many ideas are jammed into too few paragraphs. Maybe you don't include as many specific details and examples as you need — or maybe you need stronger ones. Work on the outline until you get it into strong shape, and then rewrite the essay to follow it.

For more on using outlining for planning, see pp. 325–33.

Try these helpful questions about revising for structure and support:

REVISION CHECKLIST

—— Does your introduction set up the whole essay? Does it both grab readers' attention and hint at what is to follow?

—— Does the essay fulfill all that you promise in your opening?

—— Would any later passage make a better beginning?

—— Is your thesis clear early in the essay? If explicit, is it positioned prominently?

—— Do the paragraph breaks seem logical?

—— Is the main idea of each paragraph clear? Have you used a topic sentence in every paragraph?

—— Is the main idea of each paragraph fully developed? Where might you need more details or better evidence to be convincing?

—— Within each paragraph, is each detail or piece of evidence relevant to the topic sentence? If you find a stray bit, should you omit it or move it to another paragraph?

—— Are all the ideas directly relevant to the main point of the essay?

—— Would any paragraphs make more sense in a different order?

—— Does everything follow clearly? Does one point smoothly lead to the next? Would transitions help make the connections clearer?

—— Does the conclusion follow from what has gone before, or does it seem arbitrarily tacked on?

■ Activity: Tackling Macro Revision

Even if you don't know exactly what needs to be changed in a draft, this activity will help you get started making productive changes. Select a draft that would benefit from revision. Then, based on your sense of the draft's greatest need, choose one of the revision checklists, and use it to guide a first revision. Let the draft sit for a few hours or a day or so. Then consider what else you'd like to improve, and select one of the remaining checklists to work with.

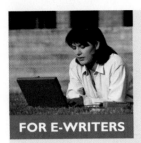

FOR E-WRITERS

Exchanging Drafts

E-mail can be an efficient way for writers and readers to exchange drafts. You can either copy and paste a document into the e-mail message or attach a document. Copying the draft into the message may remove some formatting, such as italics or bold but usually works well and avoids spreading computer viruses. If you want to preserve the formatting and believe your reader has compatible software, you may attach the document instead. If you use the Save As option, probably under the File menu, you can create a duplicate version of your file in another format such as Rich Text Format (rtf) which can be opened in any word-processing software.

WORKING WITH A PEER EDITOR

Of course, there's no substitute for having someone else go over your writing. Many college assignments ask you to write for an audience of classmates, but even if your essay is written for a different group (the town council or readers of *Newsweek,* for example), having a classmate read your essay is a worthwhile revision strategy. To gain all you can as a writer from a peer review, you need to play an active part in the discussion of your work:

- Ask your reader questions. (If this prospect seems difficult, write a "Dear Editor" letter or memo ahead of time, and bring it to your meeting.)
- Be open to new ideas — for focus, organization, or details.
- Use what's helpful, but trust yourself as the writer.

To be a helpful, supportive peer editor, try to offer honest, intelligent feedback, not judgment.

- Look at the big picture: purpose, focus, clarity, coherence, organization, support.
- When you spot strengths or weaknesses, be specific: note examples.
- Answer the writer's questions, and also use the questions supplied throughout this book to concentrate on essentials, not details.

See specific checklists in the "Revising and Editing" sections in Chs. 4 to 12.

As a writer, you can ask your peer editor to begin with your specific questions or use applicable questions from the general checklist on page 377.

Revising for Emphasis, Conciseness, and Clarity

After you've revised for the large issues in your draft — purpose, thesis, audience, structure, and support — you're ready to turn your attention to micro revising. Now is the time to look at your language, to emphasize what matters most, and to communicate it concisely and clearly.

Questions for a Peer Editor

FIRST QUESTIONS FOR A PEER EDITOR

What is your first reaction to this paper?

What is this writer trying to tell you?

What are this paper's greatest strengths?

Does it have any major weaknesses?

What one change would most improve the paper?

QUESTIONS ON MEANING

Do you understand everything? Is the draft missing any information that you need to know?

Does this paper tell you anything you didn't know before?

Is the writer trying to cover too much territory? Too little?

Does any point need to be more fully explained or illustrated?

When you come to the end, has the paper delivered what it promised?

Could this paper use a down-to-the-ground revision?

QUESTIONS ON ORGANIZATION

Has the writer begun in a way that grabs your interest and quickly draws you into the paper's main idea? Or can you find a better beginning at some later point?

Does the paper have one main idea, or does it juggle more than one?

Would the main idea stand out better if anything were removed or added?

Might the ideas in the paper be more effectively arranged? Do any ideas belong together that now seem too far apart?

Can you follow the ideas easily? Are transitions needed? If so, where?

Does the writer keep to one point of view — one angle of seeing?

Does the ending seem deliberate, as if the writer meant to conclude, not just run out of gas? How might the writer strengthen the conclusion?

QUESTIONS ON WRITING STRATEGIES

Do you feel that this paper addresses you personally?

Do you dislike or object to any statement the writer makes or any wording the writer uses? Is the problem word choice, tone, or inadequate support to convince you? Should the writer keep or change this part?

Does the draft contain anything that distracts you or seems unnecessary?

Do you get bored at any point? How might the writer keep you reading?

Is the language of this paper too lofty and abstract? If so, where does the writer need to come down to earth and get specific?

Do you understand all the words used? Do any specialized words need clearer definitions?

■ For online peer response worksheets, visit <bedfordstmartins.com/bedguide> and do a keyword search:

peer

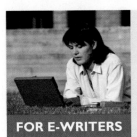

Tracking Comments and Exchanges

A simple way to work with a peer editor's help is to start by saving your file with a new title. Add a "+" and your peer's initials to the file name to keep track of different drafts. When you and your peer exchange texts, you may each want to use all capitals for your comments in each other's drafts. The capitalized comments will be easy to distinguish from the original.

Some word processors also offer editing systems, such as Track Changes in the Tools menu. This resource allows peer editors to highlight possible changes in your draft using underlining, color differences, and strikeouts. You can easily see suggestions, even from several readers.

STRESSING WHAT COUNTS

An ineffective writer treats all ideas as equals. An effective writer decides what matters most and shines a bright light on it. You can't emphasize merely by *italicizing*, putting things in "quotation marks," or throwing them into CAPITALS. Such devices grow monotonous, stressing nothing at all. Instead, emphasize things that count using the most emphatic positions in an essay, a paragraph, or a sentence — the beginning and the end.

Stating It First.   In an essay, you might start with what matters most. For an economics paper on import quotas (such as the number of foreign cars allowed into a country), student Donna Waite summed up her conclusion.

> Although an import quota has many effects, both for the nation imposing the quota and for the nation whose industries must suffer from it, I believe that the most important effect is generally felt at home. A native industry gains a chance to thrive in a marketplace of lessened competition.

A paper that takes a stand or makes a proposal might open with the writer's position.

> Our state's antiquated system of justices of the peace is inefficient.

> The United States should orbit a human observer around Mars.

In a single sentence, as in an essay, you can stress things at the start. Consider the following unemphatic sentence:

> When Congress debates the Hall-Hayes Act removing existing protections for endangered species, as now seems likely to occur on May 12, it will be a considerable misfortune if this bill should pass, since the extinction of many rare birds and animals would certainly result.

The debate and its probable timing consume the start of the sentence. Here's a better use of this emphatic position:

> The extinction of many rare birds and animals would certainly follow passage of the Hall-Hayes Act.

Now the writer stresses what he most fears — the dire consequences of the act. (A later sentence might add the date and his opinion about passage.)

Stating It Last.   To place an idea last can throw weight on it. Emphatic order, proceeding from least important to most, is dramatic: it builds up and up. In a paper on import quotas, however, a dramatic buildup might look contrived. Still, in an essay on how city parks lure visitors to the city, the thesis sentence — summing up the point of the essay — might stand at the very end: "For the urban core, improved parks could bring about a new era of prosperity." Giving the evidence first and leading up to the thesis at the end is particularly effective in editorials and informal persuasive essays.

A sentence that uses climactic order, suspending its point until the end, is a *periodic* sentence. Notice how novelist Julian Green builds to his point of emphasis.

> Amid chaos of illusions into which we are cast headlong, there is one thing that stands out as true, and that is — love.

CUTTING AND WHITTLING

Like pea pickers who throw out dirt and pebbles, good writers remove needless words that clog their prose. One of the chief joys of revising is to watch 200 paunchy words shrink to a svelte 150. To see how saving words helps, let's first look at some wordiness. In what she imagined to be a gracious style, a New York socialite once sent this dinner invitation to Hu Shi, the Chinese ambassador:

> O learned sage and distinguished representative of the numerous Chinese nation, pray deign to honor my humble abode with your noble presence at a pouring of libations, to be followed by a modest evening repast, on the forthcoming Friday, June Eighteenth, in this Year of the Pig, at the approximate hour of eight o'clock, Eastern Standard Time. Kindly be assured furthermore, O most illustrious sire, that a favorable reply at your earliest convenience will be received most humbly and gratefully by the undersigned unworthy suppliant.

In reply, the witty diplomat sent this telegram:

> CAN DO. HU SHI.

Hu Shi's reply disputes a common assumption — that the more words an idea takes, the more impressive it will seem. Most good contemporary writers know that the more succinctly they can state an idea, the clearer and more forceful it will be.

▥ For more on transi-
tions, see pp. 346–49.

Cut the Fanfare.   Why bother to announce that you're going to say something? Cut the fanfare. We aren't, by the way, attacking the usefulness of
transitions that lead readers along.

WORDY   As far as getting ready for winter is concerned, I put antifreeze in
            my car.

REVISED   To get ready for winter, I put antifreeze in my car.

WORDY   The point should be made that . . .
            Let me make it perfectly clear that . . .
            In this paper I intend to . . .
            In conclusion I would like to say that . . .

Use Strong Verbs.   Forms of the verb *be* (*am, is, are, was, were*) followed
by a noun or an adjective can make a statement wordy, as can *There is* or
There are. Such weak verbs can almost always be replaced by active verbs.

WORDY   The Akron game was a disappointment to the fans.

REVISED   The Akron game disappointed the fans.

WORDY   There are many people who dislike flying.

REVISED   Many people dislike flying.

Use Relative Pronouns with Caution.   When a clause begins with a relative pronoun (*who, which, that*), you often can whittle it to a phrase.

WORDY   Venus, which is the second planet of the solar system, is called the
            evening star.

REVISED   Venus, the second planet of the solar system, is called the evening
            star.

Cut Out Deadwood.   The more you revise, the more shortcuts you'll discover. Phrases such as *on the subject of, in regard to, in terms of,* and *as far as . . .
is concerned* often simply fill space. Try reading the sentences below without
the words in *italics*.

Howell spoke for the sophomores, and Janet *also* spoke for the seniors.

He is *something of* a clown but *sort of the* lovable *type*.

As a major in *the field of* economics, I plan to concentrate on *the area of*
international banking.

The decision *as to* whether *or not* to go is up to you.

Cut Descriptors.   Adjectives and adverbs are often dispensable. Contrast
these two versions:

WORDY   Johnson's extremely significant research led to highly important
            major discoveries.

REVISED   Johnson's research led to major discoveries.

Be Short, Not Long.   While a long word may convey a shade of meaning that a shorter synonym doesn't, in general favor short words over long ones. Instead of *the remainder*, write *the rest*; instead of *activate, start* or *begin*; instead of *adequate* or *sufficient, enough*. Look for the right word—one that wraps an idea in a smaller package.

> WORDY   Andy has a left fist that has a lot of power in it.
>
> REVISED   Andy has a potent left.

By the way, it pays to read. From reading, you absorb words like *potent* and set them to work for you.

KEEPING IT CLEAR

Recall what you want to achieve—clear communication with your readers using specific, unambiguous words arranged in logical order. Aim for direct, forceful expression.

> WORDY   He is more or less a pretty outstanding person in regard to good looks.
>
> REVISED   He is strikingly handsome.

Try to read your draft as a brand-new reader would. Be sure to return, after a break, to passages that you have struggled to write; heal any battle scars by focusing on clarity.

> UNCLEAR   Thus, after a lot of thought, it should be approved by the board even though the federal funding for all the cow-tagging may not be approved yet because it has wide support from local cattle ranchers.
>
> CLEAR   In anticipation of federal funding, the Livestock Board should approve the cow-tagging proposal widely supported by local cattle ranchers.

Here is a list of questions to use in slimming and clarifying your writing:

MICRO REVISION CHECKLIST

—— Have you positioned what counts at the beginning or the end?

—— Are you direct, straightforward, and clear?

—— Do you announce an idea before you utter it? If so, consider chopping out the announcement.

—— Can you substitute an active verb wherever you use a form of the verb *be* (*is, was, were*)?

—— Can you recast any sentence that begins *There is* or *There are*?

—— Can you reduce to a phrase any clause beginning with *which, who,* or *that*?

—— Have you added deadwood or too many adjectives and adverbs?

—— Do you see any long words where short words would do?

—— Have you kept your writing clear?

■ Activity: Tackling Micro Revision

Think back over the revisions you've already made to your draft and the advice you've received from peer editors or other readers. Is your paper more likely to seem bland (because it lacks emphasis), wordy (because it needs a good trimming), or foggy (because it needs to be more clear, direct, and logical)? Pick one issue as your focus for the moment, and concentrate on adding emphasis, cutting extra words, or expressing ideas clearly.

For his composition class, Daniel Matthews was assigned a paper using a few sources. He was to write about an "urban legend," a widely accepted and emotionally appealing — but untrue — tale about events. The following selection from his paper, "The Truth about 'Taps,'" introduces his topic and briefly explains both the legend and the true story about it. The first draft illustrates macro revisions (highlighted in the margin) and micro revisions (marked in the text). Following the draft is the clear and concise final version.

FIRST DRAFT

Avoid "you" in case readers have not shared this experience.

Anyone who has ever
~~As you know, whenever you have~~ attended the funeral services for a fallen

has
veteran of the United States of America, ~~you have~~ stood fast as a lone bugler filled the

nation
air with the mournful ~~and sullenly appropriate~~ last tribute to a defender of the ~~United~~

T
~~States of America.~~ ~~As most of us know,~~ the name of the bugle call is "Taps," and the

legend   has   ed   has
~~story~~ behind its origin ~~is one that is~~ gaining ~~a~~ popularity ~~of its own~~ as it ~~is more and~~

Rework paragraph to summarize legend when first mentioned.

~~more frequently being~~ circulated in this time of war on terror. Although ~~it is~~

~~clear that~~ this tale ~~of the origin~~ of a beautiful ode to a fallen warrior is heartfelt ~~and~~

As such, i
~~full of purposeful intent,~~ it is an "urban legend." ~~I~~t fails to provide due justice to the

memories of the men responsible for the true origin of "Taps."

INSERT:
According to this story, Union Captain Robert Ellicombe discovered that a Confederate casualty was, in fact, his son, a music student in the South. The father found "Taps" in his son's pocket, and the tune was first played at a military burial as his son was laid to rest (Coulter).

true
General Daniel Butterfield is the originator of the bugle call "Taps," ~~formerly~~

⊙
~~known as "Lights Out."~~ Butterfield served ~~as a general~~ in the Union army during the

Civil War and was awarded the Medal of Honor for actions during that time. One of

his most endearing claims to fame is the bugle call "Taps," which he composed at

Harrison's Landing in 1862 (Warner 167). ~~The bugle call~~ "Taps" originates from another call named "Lights Out"~~; this call was~~ used by the Army to signal the end of the day,

Group all the discussion of the versions in one place.

Butterfield, wanting a new and original call unique to his command, summoned

bugler Oliver Willcox Norton to his tent one night. ~~and~~ rather than compose an altogether

Divide long sentence to keep it clear.

new tune, he instead modified the notes to the call "Lights Out" (US Military District of

Shortly thereafter

Washington). ~~Then~~ this call could be heard ~~being used~~ up and down the Union lines as

the other commanders ~~who had~~ heard the call ~~liked it~~ and adapted it for their own use.

Strengthen paragraph conclusion by sticking to its focus.

and itself   *"Tattoo," a*

~~This call, the modified version of "Lights Out" is~~ also ~~in a way~~ a derivative of ~~the~~ British

bugle call ~~"Tattoo" which is very~~ similar in both sound and purpose ~~to "Lights Out,"~~

(Villanueva)~~. notes this as well in his paper "24 Notes That Tap Deep Emotion."~~

REVISED DRAFT

Anyone who has ever attended the funeral services for a fallen veteran of the United States of America has stood fast as a lone bugler filled the air with a mournful last tribute to a defender of the nation. The name of the bugle call is "Taps," and the legend behind its origin has gained popularity as it has circulated in this time of war on terror. According to this story, Union Captain Robert Ellicombe discovered that a Confederate casualty was, in fact, his son, a music student in the South. The father found "Taps" in his son's pocket, and the tune was first played at a military burial as his son was laid to rest (Coulter). Although this tale of a beautiful ode to a fallen warrior is heartfelt, it is an "urban legend." As such, it fails to provide due justice to the memories of the men responsible for the true origin of "Taps."

General Daniel Butterfield is the true originator of the bugle call "Taps." Butterfield served in the Union army during the Civil War and was awarded the Medal of Honor for actions during that time. One of his most endearing claims to fame is the bugle call "Taps," which he composed at Harrison's Landing in 1862 (Warner

167). "Taps" originates from another call named "Lights Out," used by the army to signal the end of the day and itself a derivative of "Tattoo," a British bugle call similar in both sound and purpose (Villanueva). Butterfield, wanting a new and original call unique to his command, summoned bugler Oliver Willcox Norton to his tent one night. Rather than compose an altogether new tune, he instead modified the notes to the call "Lights Out" (US Military District of Washington). Shortly thereafter this call could be heard up and down the Union lines as other commanders heard the call and adapted it for their own use.

Editing and Proofreading

Editing means correcting and refining grammar, punctuation, and mechanics. Proofreading means taking a final look at your paper to check correctness and to catch spelling or word-processing errors. Don't edit and proofread too soon. In your early drafting, don't fret over the correct spelling of an unfamiliar word; it may be revised out in a later version. If the word stays in, you'll

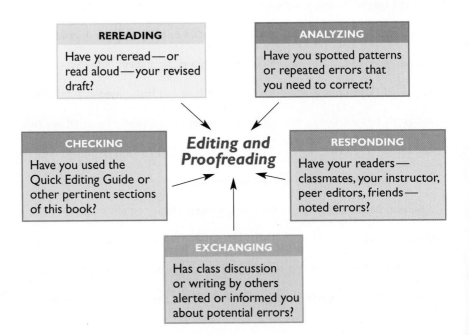

REREADING
Have you reread—or read aloud—your revised draft?

ANALYZING
Have you spotted patterns or repeated errors that you need to correct?

CHECKING
Have you used the Quick Editing Guide or other pertinent sections of this book?

Editing and Proofreading

RESPONDING
Have your readers—classmates, your instructor, peer editors, friends—noted errors?

EXCHANGING
Has class discussion or writing by others alerted or informed you about potential errors?

have time to check it later. After you have revised, however, you are ready to refine and correct. In college, good editing and proofreading can make the difference between a C and an A. On the job, it may help you get a promotion. Readers, teachers, and bosses like careful writers who take time to edit and proofread.

EDITING

As you edit, whenever you doubt whether a word or construction is correct, consult a good reference handbook. Learn the grammar conventions you don't understand so you can spot and eliminate problems in your own writing. Practice until you easily recognize major errors such as fragments and comma splices. Ask for assistance from a peer editor or a tutor in the writing center if your campus has one.

EDITING	**PROOFREADING**
• **GRAMMAR:** Are your sentences and their parts correct?	• **SPELLING:** Have you spell-checked and reread attentively?
• **SENTENCES:** Are your sentences clear and effective?	• **INCORRECT WORDS:** Have you mistakenly picked any wrong words?
• **WORD CHOICE:** Are your words correct and well selected?	• **MISSING WORDS:** Have you left out any words?
• **PUNCTUATION:** Do you need to add, correct, or drop any marks?	• **MINOR ERRORS:** Can you see any small mistakes?
• **MECHANICS:** Do you need to correct capitals, italics, or other matters?	• **MINOR DETAILS:** Do you need to correct any details?
• **FORMAT:** Do you need to adjust margins, spacing, or headings?	

Use the "Quick Editing Guide" at the end of this book to get you started (look for the pages with dark blue edges). It briefly reviews grammar, style, punctuation, and mechanics problems typically found in college writing and supplies definitions, examples, and a checklist to help you tackle each one. Here is an editing checklist for the problems explained there, along with the section letter and number:

EDITING CHECKLIST

Common and Serious Problems in College Writing

For more help, turn to the dark-blue-edged pages, and find the Quick Editing Guide sections noted there.

For help documenting any sources in your paper, turn to the dark-red-edged pages, and find D6 and E1–E2 in the Quick Research Guide there.

Grammar Problems

___ Have you avoided writing sentence fragments?	A1
___ Have you avoided writing comma splices or fused sentences?	A2
___ Have you used the correct form for all verbs in the past tense?	A3
___ Do all verbs agree with their subjects?	A4
___ Have you used the correct case for all pronouns?	A5
___ Do all pronouns agree with their antecedents?	A6
___ Have you used adjectives and adverbs correctly?	A7

Sentence Problems

___ Does each modifier clearly modify the appropriate sentence element?	B1
___ Have you used parallel structure where necessary?	B2

Punctuation Problems

___ Have you used commas correctly?	C1
___ Have you used apostrophes correctly?	C2
___ Have you punctuated quotations correctly?	C3

Mechanics and Format Problems

___ Have you used capital letters correctly?	D1
___ Have you spelled all words correctly?	D2
___ Have you used correct manuscript form?	D3

PROOFREADING

All writers make mistakes as they put ideas on paper. Because the mind works faster than the pencil (or the word processor), when you are distracted by someone talking or your cell phone ringing, you may omit a word or put in the wrong punctuation. A moment's break in concentration can lead to errors. Making such mistakes isn't bad — you simply need to take the

FOR E-WRITERS

Understanding Checkers and Their Limits

Spell checkers are handy tools, but they aren't foolproof. They can't tell you that you've used *their* when you meant *there, affect* when you meant *effect,* or *won* when you meant *own.* Grammar checkers also can alert you to many types of sentence problems, but you have to reason through the suggestions carefully. A checker may question long sentences and unusual constructions that are perfectly correct. As the writer, you, not the software, should always have the final word. (See also p. A-1.)

Proofreading in Pairs

Select a passage, from this textbook or elsewhere, that is about one hundred words long. Type up the passage, intentionally adding ten errors in grammar, spelling, punctuation, or capitalization. Swap passages with a classmate; proofread, then check each other's work against the originals. Share your proofreading strategies.

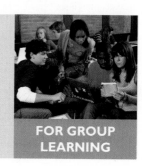

FOR GROUP LEARNING

time to find and correct them. Proofreading does take patience but is a skill you can develop. For instance, when you simply glance at the spelling of *environment,* you may miss the second *n.* When you read normally, you usually see only the shells of words — the first and last letters. You fix your eyes on the print only three or four times per line or less. When you proofread, try to create a situation that will help you concentrate on detail.

- Let a paper sit several days, overnight, or at least a few hours before proofreading so that you allow time to gain perspective.
- Budget enough time to proofread thoroughly. For a long essay or complex research paper with a list of sources, schedule several sessions.
- Ask someone else to read your paper and tell you if it is free of errors. But take pride in your own work. *Don't* let someone else do it for you.
- Use a dictionary or a spell checker whenever you can.
- Keep a list of your habitual errors, especially those your instructor has already pointed out. Double-check for these errors (such as leaving off *-s* or *-ed* endings or putting in unnecessary commas).

To proofread effectively, you should try to look at the letters in each word and the punctuation marks between words without sliding over these symbols. Use the following questions to help you slow down and concentrate:

PROOFREADING CHECKLIST

— Have you read what you have written very slowly, looking at every word and letter? Have you tried to see what you have actually written, not what you think is there?

— Have you read your paper aloud? Have you used speaking to slow yourself down so you can see and hear mistakes?

— Have you read the essay backward so that you look at each word instead of getting caught up in the flow of ideas?

— Have you read your essay several times, focusing each time on a specific area of difficulty? (For example, read once for spelling, once for punctuation, and once for a problem that recurs in your writing.)

■ Activity: Editing and Proofreading

■ For editing exercises, visit Exercise Central at <bedfordstmartins.com/ bedguide>.

Read the following passage carefully. Assume that the organization of the paragraph is satisfactory, but find and correct fifteen errors in sentence structure, grammar, spelling, punctuation, and capitalization. After you have corrected the passage, discuss with your classmates the changes you have made and your reasons for making those changes.

Robert Frost, one of the most poplar American poets. He was born in San Francisco in 1874, and died in Boston in 1963. His family moved to new England when his father died in 1885. There he completed highschool and attended colledge but never graduate. Poverty and problems filled his life. He worked in a woll mill, on a newspaper, and at varous odd jobs. Because of ill health he settled on a farm and began to teach school to support his wife and children. Throughout his life he dedicated himself to writing poetry, by 1915 he was in demand for public readings and speaking engagements. He was awarded the Pulitzer Prize for poetry four times—in 1924, 1931, 1937, and 1943. The popularity of his poetry rests in his use of common themes and images. everyone can relate to his universal poems, such as "Birches" and "Stopping by Woods on a Snowy Evening." Students read his poetry in school from seventh grade through graduate school, so almost everyone recognize lines from his best-loved poems. America is proud of it's son, the homespun poet Robert Frost.

Chapter 21

Strategies for Designing Your Document

Whether the document you prepare is an essay, a research paper, or a business letter, creating an effective design for it helps you achieve your purpose and meet the expectations of your audience. Through your own reading, you may have noticed that you respond differently to documents depending upon their appearance. For example, look quickly at Figure 21.1. Which of the two newspapers there seems more appealing to you?

If you prefer *USA Today,* you're like many Americans — you like the look of a colorful, casual newspaper and may even consider it easier to read. But if someone asked which of the two newspapers seems more credible or trustworthy, many would say the *Wall Street Journal.* Its closely typed text, narrow columns, and limited use of color create a look more "respectable" than that of the open, friendly *USA Today* with its abundant pictures, more colorful design, and playful tone. As you can see, the same features that make the *Wall Street Journal* seem more credible than *USA Today* may also make it less inviting to read. Like other newspapers, however, the *Wall Street Journal* freely uses headlines, short paragraphs, column dividers, white space, page numbers, and other visual markers that help the reader grasp the structure of the text at a glance and decide where to plunge in. Without such visual markers, the pages of the *Wall Street Journal* would provide the reader few pathways into its content.

Occasionally, college students are assigned a composition that looks and reads like a newspaper. But most of the papers you will write are not as visually complex as the *Wall Street Journal* or *USA Today.* Instead of calling for multiple columns, headlines, and graphics, your teacher will most likely expect to see double spacing, one-inch margins, numbered pages, and indented block quotations — visual markers typical of college compositions. Figure 21.2 shows two pages — the first page and the list of sources — of a typical college composition that follows the guidelines of the Modern Language Association (MLA).

For more on manu-script format, turn to D3 in the Quick Editing Guide (the dark-blue-edged pages).

389

Figure 21.1
Front Pages of USA Today *and the* Wall Street Journal *(with common features labeled)*

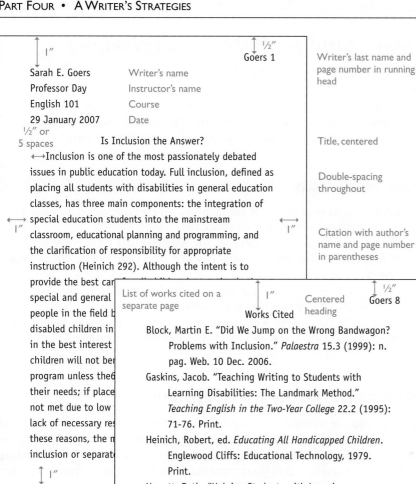

Goers 1

Sarah E. Goers — Writer's name

Professor Day — Instructor's name

English 101 — Course

29 January 2007 — Date

½" or 5 spaces

Is Inclusion the Answer? — Title, centered

Inclusion is one of the most passionately debated issues in public education today. Full inclusion, defined as placing all students with disabilities in general education classes, has three main components: the integration of special education students into the mainstream classroom, educational planning and programming, and the clarification of responsibility for appropriate instruction (Heinich 292). Although the intent is to provide the best car...

special and general ...

people in the field b...

disabled children in ...

in the best interest ...

children will not be...

program unless the6...

their needs; if place...

not met due to low...

lack of necessary res...

these reasons, the n...

inclusion or separat...

1"

Writer's last name and page number in running head

Title, centered

Double-spacing throughout

Citation with author's name and page number in parentheses

List of works cited on a separate page

Goers 8

Works Cited — Centered heading

Block, Martin E. "Did We Jump on the Wrong Bandwagon? Problems with Inclusion." *Palaestra* 15.3 (1999): n. pag. Web. 10 Dec. 2006.

Gaskins, Jacob. "Teaching Writing to Students with Learning Disabilities: The Landmark Method." *Teaching English in the Two-Year College* 22.2 (1995): 71-76. Print.

Heinich, Robert, ed. *Educating All Handicapped Children*. Englewood Cliffs: Educational Technology, 1979. Print.

Hewett, Beth. "Helping Students with Learning Disabilities: Collaboration between Writing Centers and Special Services." *Writing Lab* 25.3 (2000): 1-4. Print.

Jacobson, Linda. "Disabled Kids Moving into Regular Classrooms." *Atlanta Journal* 5 May 1994: C1. Print.

Maushard, Mary. "Special Schools Fall Victim to 'Inclusion.'" *Sun* [Baltimore] 13 June 1993: B1. *NewsBank*. ½" Web. 21 Dec. 2006.

Radebaugh, Barbara. "NEA vs. AFT." William Rainey Harper Coll., Palatine, IL. 21 Jan. 1999. Lecture.

Rios, Denise A. "Special Students Joining Regular Classrooms." *Orange County Register* 9 June 1994: A24. *NewsBank*. Web. 11 Dec. 2006.

List alphabetized by author's last name

First line of entry at left margin

Subsequent lines indented ½" or 5 spaces

Figure 21.2
The First Page and Works Cited Page of a Student Research Paper in MLA Format

Understanding Four Basic Principles of Document Design

■ For more advice on designing documents, visit <bedfordstmartins.com/ bedguide> and do a keyword search:

Four key principles of document design will help you to produce effective documents in and out of the classroom. Use these questions based on the principles to help you design college papers or other documents:

DISCOVERY CHECKLIST

___ Who are your readers? What are their key concerns? How might your document design acknowledge their concerns?

___ What form or genre do readers expect? What features do they see as typical of that form? What visual evidence would they expect or accept as appropriate?

___ What problems or constraints will your readers face? How can your document design help to address these constraints?

___ What is the purpose of your document? How can its design help achieve this purpose? How can it enhance your credibility as a writer?

PRINCIPLE 1: KNOW YOUR AUDIENCE

Whether you are writing an essay for class or preparing a different type of document, identifying your audience is a good first step toward creating an effective design. For most papers for a composition course, your primary reader is your teacher and your secondary readers include your peers. For some assignments, you might include other readers as well.

■ For more on purpose and audience, see pp. 14–18 and pp. 310–12.

Suppose you've written a paper explaining the benefits of a longer school year to a real-world audience. An audience of parents would have different concerns than an audience of community leaders or of school officials or teachers. Teachers, for example, would need to be assured that their paychecks would keep pace with the longer work year. The school board would need to be convinced that the increased costs for salaries, building operations, and transportation would pay off in higher student achievement. And other civic leaders might want to know the effects on community safety, traffic congestion, and seasonal employment rates.

In deciding how to design your document, you might consider ways to acknowledge, even highlight, the concerns of your particular audience, perhaps using headings, white space, and variations in type style. You might also consider whether your audience is likely to read every word of your argument or to skim it for key points. Perhaps tables, graphs, or diagrams would make information more accessible. Thinking about such issues means you'll have a better chance of reaching your audience.

PRINCIPLE 2: SATISFY YOUR AUDIENCE'S EXPECTATIONS

When you think about a newspaper, a particular type of publication comes to mind because the newspaper is a familiar *genre*, or form. As Figure 21.1 shows, almost all newspapers share a set of defined features: a masthead, headlines, pictures with captions, graphics, and articles arranged in columns of text. Even if details of the form vary, newspapers are still recognized as newspapers. Similarly, *Utne Reader* and *Parenting* both belong to the genre of the magazine: both feature articles arranged in columns, notable quotations set in larger type, and photographs. Despite significantly different content, magazines share a common genre identification, as Figure 21.3 illustrates.

For samples of workplace genres, see Ch. 14.

Like the newspaper and the magazine, the college paper can be thought of as a genre. Readers, including your teacher and your peers, have expectations about what topics are appropriate for such documents, how they should be written, and how they should look. Readers also have expectations about visual evidence such as graphs, tables, photographs, or other illustrations, depending on the field and the assignment. Check your syllabus to see if a specific document design is required.

For advice about a general format for papers, see D3 in the Quick Editing Guide (the dark-blue-edged pages).

Usually your readers expect your paper to be word processed, double-spaced with numbered pages. Some teachers want a cover page with your name, the title of your paper, your course number and section, the date, and perhaps other information. Others prefer that you follow the MLA paper format, simply supplying a four-line identifier and a centered title on the first page (see Figure 21.2). Some will ask you to include your last

Creating a Template

Unless your teacher encourages unusual or creative formatting, don't experiment too much with the appearance of a college paper. In fact, you can easily apply expected features to your papers by creating a template for papers with the same specifications. First, format your paper the way you want it to look. Then, create a document template that you can use any time you begin a new paper:

FOR E-WRITERS

1. Create a duplicate copy of your formatted file.
2. Delete all of the text in the document.
3. Use the Save As feature to save the file as a document template.
4. Give the template a name, such as "English paper" or "Paper form."
5. When you create a new file, choose this template from the options in your template folder. (Use the Help box for more on templates.)

Figure 21.3
Common Features in
Magazine Design: Page
Spread from Utne Reader,
November–December
2006 (top) and Parenting,
June/July 2003 (bottom)

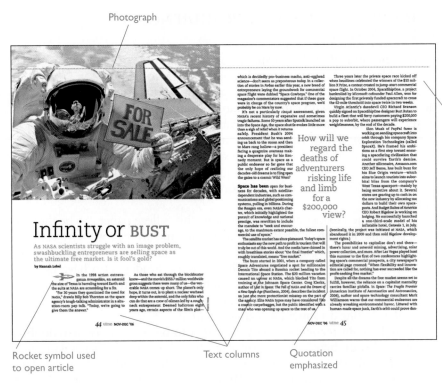

Photograph

Rocket symbol used
to open article

Text columns

Quotation
emphasized

Image
text u
and fr
by do
line

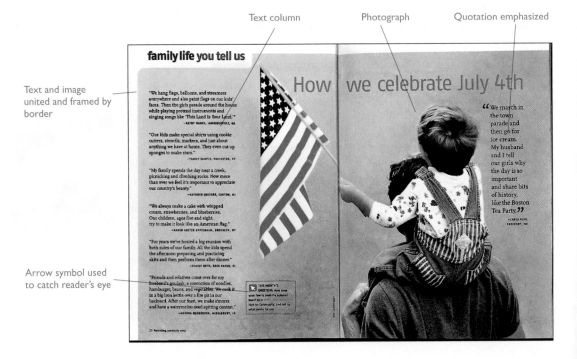

Text column

Photograph

Quotation emphasized

Text and image
united and framed by
border

Arrow symbol used
to catch reader's eye

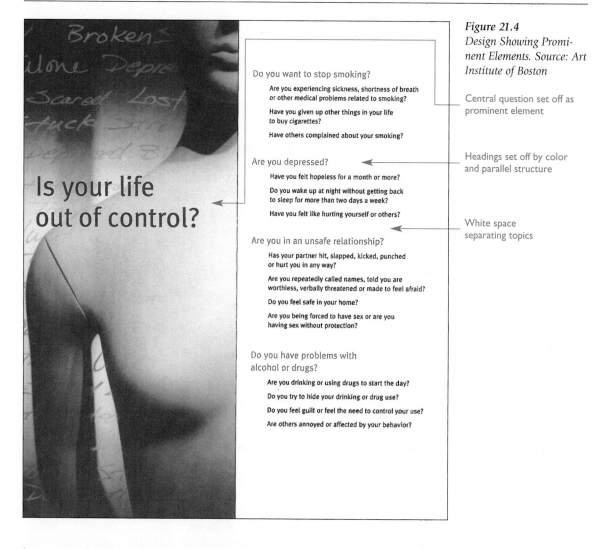

Figure 21.4
Design Showing Promi-
nent Elements. Source: Art
Institute of Boston

Central question set off as
prominent element

Headings set off by color
and parallel structure

White space
separating topics

Is your life
out of control?

Do you want to stop smoking?

Are you experiencing sickness, shortness of breath
or other medical problems related to smoking?

Have you given up other things in your life
to buy cigarettes?

Have others complained about your smoking?

Are you depressed?

Have you felt hopeless for a month or more?

Do you wake up at night without getting back
to sleep for more than two days a week?

Have you felt like hurting yourself or others?

Are you in an unsafe relationship?

Has your partner hit, slapped, kicked, punched
or hurt you in any way?

Are you repeatedly called names, told you are
worthless, verbally threatened or made to feel afraid?

Do you feel safe in your home?

Are you being forced to have sex or are you
having sex without protection?

Do you have problems with
alcohol or drugs?

Are you drinking or using drugs to start the day?

Do you try to hide your drinking or drug use?

Do you feel guilt or feel the need to control your use?

Are others annoyed or affected by your behavior?

in a 12-point size, sometimes you may need to use larger type for signs, posters, and visuals (such as PowerPoint slides) for oral presentations. Test such materials for readability by printing samples in various type sizes and standing back from them at the distance of your intended audience.

■ For examples of PowerPoint slides, see p. 404.

Figure 21.5 shows the same sentence written in four different 12-point fonts: Times New Roman, Courier New, Arial, and Comic Sans MS. Although the examples are all written in the standard 12-point size, the typefaces occupy different amounts of horizontal space on the page.

Serif or Sans Serif Fonts.   Times New Roman and Courier New are called *serif* fonts. A serif font has small tails, or serifs, at the ends of the letters. Arial and Comic Sans MS are *sans serif* — without serifs — and thus have

Times New Roman	An estimated 40 percent of young children have an imaginary friend.
Courier New	An estimated 40 percent of young children have an imaginary friend.
Arial	An estimated 40 percent of young children have an imaginary friend.
Comic Sans MS	An estimated 40 percent of young children have an imaginary friend.

solid, straight lines and no tails at the tips of the letters, as these examples show:

Times New Roman (serif) K k P p   Arial (sans serif) K k P p

Sans serif fonts have a clean look but are less readable than serif fonts, especially in long passages. If you look over your local newspaper, you may see both serif and sans serif fonts. Typically, sans serif fonts are used for headlines and other display type, such as advertisements and "pull quotes" (interesting quotations "pulled out" of an article and printed in larger type to catch the reader's eye). On the other hand, most newspapers choose serif fonts for their article (or "body") text. In fact, Times New Roman, the default font on many word processors, was developed for the *Times* newspaper in London for its own use. Other common serif fonts include Palatino and New Century Schoolbook. A combination of fonts can provide maximum readability and emphasis, as Figure 21.6 shows.

If you decide to combine two different fonts, keep these points in mind:

- Serif and sans serif fonts can be combined in the same document, though document designers recommend using only one of each.
- For further emphasis, you may vary the type size or type style, such as italics or bold, for each font.

Novelty Fonts.   For most college and professional writing, novelty fonts — those that are unusual or decorative — are inappropriate. **Comic Sans MS** is a novelty font, as are *Brush Script* and **Tempus Sans**. While these casual, playful typefaces may suit some writing situations, novelty fonts can set the wrong tone for your paper, especially if your subject is technical or serious.

For example, if you are writing a paper about civil liberties, Comic Sans MS might suggest that readers don't need to take your arguments seriously

Watching TV with a Critical Eye By second grade, kids have figured out, often from personal experience, that the toys they see in commercials don't always measure up in real life. Children this age are old enough to get into more sophisticated discussions about fact and opinion.

Figure 21.6
Sans Serif Heading Used with Serif Body Font.
Source: Kiplinger's, *February 2000*

or that you lack respect for a serious subject. Figure 21.7 shows two versions of the same text — one set in Times New Roman, which is appropriate for an academic setting, and the other set in Comic Sans MS, which generally is not. In academic or other serious writing, stick with standard fonts that are familiar to readers and that set a professional tone.

For more on typefaces in visuals, see pp. 426–27.

Italics.   When you *italicize* words, you call the reader's attention to them.

- Use italics for book, film, magazine, or electronic database titles.
     My favorite novel is *Wuthering Heights.*
- Use italics for foreign words.
     My Finnish grandmother called me *Kultani* ("my golden one").

Times New Roman	*Comic Sans MS*

Does Heightened Surveillance Make Us More or Less Secure?
 	
    Since the terrorist attacks of September 11, 2001, a wide-ranging debate has ensued over whether face-recognition systems and other surveillance tools should be used to identify potential terrorists. While proponents see these tools as an essential defense when loosely organized terrorist "cells" might strike at any time, opponents say these systems are flawed at best and jeopardize the civil liberties of all citizens.
	Does Heightened Surveillance Make Us More or Less Secure?
	
	    Since the terrorist attacks of September 11, 2001, a wide-ranging debate has ensued over whether face-recognition systems and other surveillance tools should be used to identify potential terrorists. While proponents see these tools as an essential defense when loosely organized terrorist "cells" might strike at any time, opponents say these systems are flawed at best and jeopardize the civil liberties of all citizens.

Figure 21.7   *Identical Text Set in Two Fonts. Sources: See Figure 21.9*

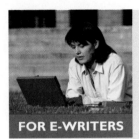

FOR E-WRITERS

Changing Your Type Style

Your word-processing program is likely to supply several ways of changing type style. When you look at the screen, your toolbar probably includes boxes that identify the font you are using (such as Times New Roman) and the point size of the characters (such as 12). Nearby you may spot other small boxes or icons that, with a click, shift what you type to bold, italics, or underlined text — all necessary in academic papers if only for the various styles of documenting sources. You can also use your mouse to highlight sections of text and then click on these icons to change the text style for that passage. Clicking on the Format menu and then on Font generally supplies a menu of design options, such as shadows or small capitals.

- Use italics for your first use of a technical or scientific term, and provide a definition for the reader. After that, use regular type without emphasis.

    AIDS patients monitor their levels of *helper T-cells* because these cells detect antigens in the body and activate other cells to fight the antigens. Because HIV destroys helper T-cells, this information indicates the status of a patient's immune system.

  Italicized words appear lighter in weight than nonitalicized words. This lightness, coupled with the slant of the letters, makes italics unsuitable for sustained reading. Use italics for emphasis, not for large blocks of text.

■ For examples of bold-
face type in résumés, see
p. 273.

Boldface.   Boldface type is suitable for emphasis only. Too much produces the "raisin bread" effect, a random scattering of dark spots across a light page, illustrated in Figure 21.8. Because this scattering encourages the reader to "hear" the words as emphasized, it creates a choppy, unnatural rhythm.

Many teachers expect you to choose emphatic words, not to rely on boldface type for emphasis in academic papers. In other documents, use boldface selectively, highlighting only words that you want the reader to see or "hear" with emphasis added. In general, reserve boldface type primarily for headings, key points in a list of factors, or similar uses.

Longevity.   People are living longer today, so Social Security funds need to stretch to accommodate these longer lives.

Inflation.   Dollars paid into the system in 1980 are worth less today, and interest on the fund has not kept pace with the need for the dollars.

Figure 21.8
The Raisin-Bread Effect
Produced by Too Much
Boldface

Treating Carpal Tunnel Syndrome

Physicians **generally** suggest one of **three** methods of treating patients with carpal tunnel syndrome. **First,** reducing the amount of repeated **wrist** movement **can** allow the median nerve to heal. **This** can be accomplished by changing habits or **positions** or by using a wrist **splint**. . . .

PREPARING LISTS

The organization or placement of material on a page — its layout — can make information more accessible for readers. For example, lists are easier to read when they are displayed rather than integrated.

INTEGRATED LIST   Movies are rated by the film-rating board of the Classification and Rating Administration (CARA) based on several criteria, including these: overall theme, use of language, presence of violence, presence of nudity and sexual content, and combined use of these elements in the context of an individual film.

DISPLAYED LIST   Movies are rated by the film-rating board of the Classification and Rating Administration (CARA) based on several criteria, including these:
- overall theme
- use of language
- presence of violence
- presence of nudity and sexual content
- combined use of these elements in the context of an individual film

Bulleted List.   One type of displayed list uses a mark called a *bullet* to set off a bit of information. The most common bullet is the small round one often available in a word processor's bulleted list function (•). Bulleted lists are common in business and other documents but not necessarily in academic papers.

Use a bulleted list to enumerate steps, reasons, or items, especially when the order isn't significant, as in this example:

Controversy surrounding the 2000 presidential election climaxed in Florida, where several balloting issues converged.

- A controversial Palm Beach County ballot was blamed for several thousand votes possibly cast in error for a third-party candidate, Pat Buchanan.

Creating Lists

Your toolbar may show small icons or boxes for developing bulleted or numbered lists. If so, one click on an icon adds a number or bullet to your text, while a second click removes it from a passage. When you type a return at the end of one listed item, the next bullet or number appears. Your Insert menu probably includes a Symbol option. Click here for alternative symbols — for example, square bullets or different sizes of round bullets. Generally, a click on the selected item (perhaps with an Insert command) adds it to your text. For academic papers, use such devices conservatively, always following any specific directions from your instructor or from the style guide preferred by the field. In APA style, for instance, simply type out a list within a sentence, placing letters inside pairs of parentheses: (a), (b), and (c).

FOR E-WRITERS

- A Florida law triggered a statewide ballot recount when the votes for the two main candidates were separated by less than 1 percent.

- Outstanding absentee ballots had to be counted to determine which candidate had received the most votes.

For examples of the use of bullets in résumés, see p. 273.

Bullets — perhaps combined with headings, white space, and boldface type — can highlight skills or titles in a résumé, making it easier for readers to spot a job applicant's relevant experience. Web résumés, like other Web pages, divide information to fit the screen. They may use design devices to emphasize links and categories, such as education and experience.

Numbered List.   Another type of displayed list, the numbered list, can emphasize important sequences, especially in activity plans, how-to advice, instructional writing, or other process descriptions. Here is a simplified sequence of activities for making an article of clothing:

1. Select your pattern and fabric.
2. Lay out the pattern and pin it to the fabric, paying careful attention to the arrows and grain lines.
3. Cut out the fabric pieces following the outline of the pattern.
4. Sew the garment together using the pattern's step-by-step instructions.

USING WHITE SPACE STRATEGICALLY

For examples of the use of white space in print and Web résumés, see p. 273 and p. 274. For more about white space in visuals, see pp. 424–25.

White space is just that: space within a document that is free of text. Blank space gives the eye a rest and can frame important information, increasing emphasis as you guide the reader through your document.

College Papers.   When you write college papers, you use white space to assist your readers. For example, one-inch margins and double-spacing provide some respite for the reader's eyes. Adding extra white space to indent the first line of your paragraphs helps the reader immediately differentiate one paragraph from the next. In addition, indenting an extended "block" quotation sets it off as a special kind of text.

For sample pages from an academic paper, see p. 391. For advice on the format for a college paper, see D3 in the Quick Editing Guide (the dark-blue-edged pages).

As you can see in Figure 21.9, white space is crucial to the appearance of your papers. Were this example single-spaced, its closely spaced lines would be much too cramped, interfering with readers' ability to keep their place in the text and possibly intimidating them. When text elements are close together and look fairly uniform, readers may feel as if they are trying to merge onto a congested freeway. Some may give up if they don't see openings where they can easily jump in and begin to navigate the text.

However, if you separate sections of your paper by hitting the enter key an extra time or two — especially if your paper is double-spaced — you will trap too much white space between sections. This extra space may create a gap that prevents the reader's eye from making natural connections within the text and seeing your paper as a cohesive unit.

Centered title with
space on both sides

Does Heightened Surveillance
Make Us More or Less Secure?

Indented
paragraph

Since the terrorist attacks of September 11, 2001, a wide-ranging debate has ensued over whether face-recognition systems and other surveillance tools should be used to identify potential terrorists. While proponents see these tools as an essential defense when loosely organized terrorist "cells" might strike at any time, opponents say these systems are flawed at best and jeopardize the civil liberties of all citizens.

Barry Steinhardt, director of the Technology and Liberty Program of the American Civil Liberties Union, sees a clear threat to personal freedom:

> Many people still do not grasp that Big Brother surveillance is no longer the stuff of books and movies.... Given the capabilities of today's technology, the only thing protecting us from a full-fledged surveillance society are the legal and political institutions we have inherited as Americans. Unfortunately, the September 11 attacks have led some to embrace the fallacy that weakening the Constitution will strengthen America. ("'Big Brother'")

Extended
quotation
indented as
a block

However, others argue that technology can make us safer — and, in fact, already has. Video monitoring systems using closed-circuit televisions have been in use for years in such places as the United Kingdom, where officials say that crime has declined significantly as a result ("Law, Order, and Terrorism").

Figure 21.9
Text Using White Space. Sources: "'Big Brother' Is No Longer a Fiction, ACLU Warns in New Report." American Civil Liberties Union. ACLU, 15 Jan. 2003. Web. 23 June 2003. "Law, Order, and Terrorism: Other Nations' Remedies," Dahlia Lithwick. Slate. Washington Post.Newsweek Interactive, 5 Oct. 2001. Web. 23 June 2003.

Readable double-spaced lines

Text framed
by margins

Visuals.   Effective use of space is important in visuals — such as transparencies or PowerPoint slides — for presentations. Providing ample space and limiting the text on each slide helps readers absorb your major points. For example, the slide in Figure 21.10 contains too much text, making it hard to read and potentially distracting for the audience. In contrast, Figure 21.11 contains less text and more open space, making each point easier to read. It also uses bullets effectively to highlight the main points. These points are meant only to summarize major issues and themes, not to detail all of them; you can flesh out your main points during your talk. Though the slides have been reduced to fit in this book, the original type sizes were large

Figure 21.10
PowerPoint Slide with Too
Much Text and Too Little
Space

Service Learning Components

- Training workshops--2 a week for the first 2 weeks of the semester
- After-school tutoring--3 two-hour sessions per week at designated school
- Journal-keeping--1 entry per session
- Submission of journal and final report-- report should describe 3 most important things you learned and should be 5-10 pages

Figure 21.11
PowerPoint Slide with
Brief Text and Effective
Use of Space

Service Learning Components

- Training workshops
- After-school tutoring
- Journal-keeping
- Submission of journal and final report

enough to be viewed by the presenter's classmates: 44 points for the heading and 32 points for the body.

Finally, as you can see, the "white space" without text in these slides is actually blue. Some public-speaking experts believe that black type on a white background can be too stark for a slide; instead, they recommend a dark blue background with yellow or white type. However, others believe that black on white is fine and may in fact be what the audience is accustomed to. Presentation software like PowerPoint makes it easy for you to experiment with these options.

USING HEADINGS AND ALIGNMENT

Readers look for cues about what's most important and about how components are related to one another. Effective document design provides just such cues through features like headings and subheadings. Clear headings help your readers navigate by showing a document's hierarchy of ideas. Appropriately aligned headings guide the reader's eye.

Heading Levels.   The relative size and prominence of the section headings indicate how a document is structured and which sections are most important. Headings also name the sections so that readers know where they are and where they are going. Though headings are often unnecessary in short essays, they can focus the attention of readers while providing a useful pathway through complex documents such as research papers, lab reports, business proposals, and Web-based documents.

Use typographical elements to distinguish clearly between levels of headings and subheadings within your document. Once you decide what a major section (or *level-one*) heading should look like — boldfaced and italicized, for example — be consistent with comparable headings. Treat minor headings consistently as well. In this book, you'll notice that all of the major headings within a chapter are set like this:

Level-One Heading   [17-point, boldfaced, italicized, in color]

Level-two and level-three headings are set like this:

LEVEL-TWO HEADING   [12-point, capitalized, boldfaced]

Level-Three Heading   [10-point, boldfaced]

Each of these styles is used consistently in order to give readers visual cues to both content and organization. The headings differ from each other and from the main text in size, style, and color. Differentiating headings in such ways makes your text easier to read and easier to use whether your reader is scrutinizing every word or scanning only key points.

If your instructor asks you to follow the guidelines of a particular style, you may have less flexibility in formatting headings. For example, the American Psychological Association (APA) illustrates five levels of headings, all in the same regular font style and size as the body text but varying capitalization, placement (centered or left), and underlining to distinguish the levels. MLA, however, does not recommend headings or discuss their design.

Heading Consistency.   The headings in your document should be brief, clear, and informative. The four most common styles of headings are *-ing*

■ For more on MLA and APA style, see E1–E2 in the Quick Research Guide (the dark-red-edged pages). For even more MLA help, consult the *MLA Handbook for Writers of Research Papers*, or go to <www.mla.org/style>. For even more APA help, consult the *Publication Manual of the American Psychological Association* or <www.apastyle.org>.

■ For more on parallel structure, see B2 in the Quick Editing Guide (the dark-blue-edged pages).

(gerund) phrases, noun phrases, questions, and imperative sentences. Effective writers use consistent parallel phrasing, whatever the style they choose. In other words, if you write a level-one heading as an *-ing* phrase, make sure that all of the level-one headings that follow are also *-ing* phrases.

Here are some examples of each style of heading:

-ING PHRASES
Using the College Catalog
Choosing Courses
Declaring a Major

NOUN PHRASES
The Benefits of Electronic Commerce
The Challenges of Electronic Commerce
The Characteristics of the Online Shopper

QUESTIONS
What Is Hepatitis C?
Who Is at Risk?
How Is Hepatitis C Treated?

IMPERATIVE SENTENCES
Initiate Your IRA Rollover
Learn Your Distribution Options
Select New Investments

■ For more information on Web design, visit the Web Style Guide at <www.webstyleguide .com>.

In general, Web pages—especially home pages and site guides—tend to have more headings than other types of documents because they are designed to help readers find information quickly, within a small viewing frame. If you are designing a Web page, consider what different users might want to find on your site. Then clearly connect your headings and content to users' needs.

The Web page shown in Figure 21.12 organizes links under three major categories—Connecting, Organizing, and Sponsoring. All three are identified by *-ing* words that suggest action in progress. Under these broad headings are links to other content on the site, most identified by nouns and noun phrases (such as Member Benefits or Summer Institutes). However, two links that urge action by the viewer—Join and Update—both begin with verbs. Such headings use parallel structure to identify and group topics and also to accomplish a purpose, here to encourage participation in service learning.

Heading Alignment. Besides being consistently styled and phrased, headings should also be consistently placed, or aligned, along the same vertical line. Figure 21.13 illustrates confusing alignment, mixing left-aligned, right-aligned, and fully justified text running out to both the left and right margins. Because your title is generally centered, you might be tempted to center all of your headings, but doing so may introduce nonfunctional white space that detracts from the design of your paper. Instead, rely on the graphic designer's principle of alignment: each element should be aligned with at least one other item, rather than having an alignment all its own.

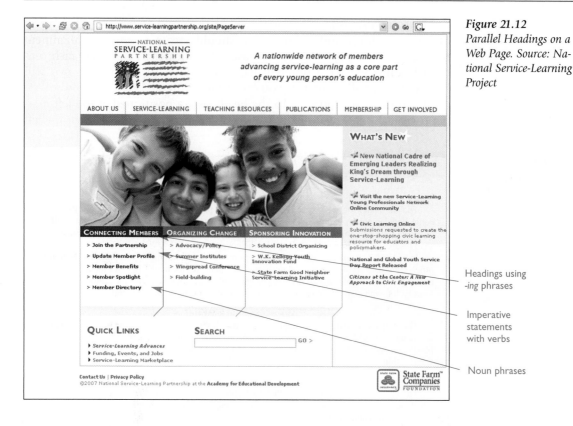

Figure 21.12
Parallel Headings on a Web Page. Source: National Service-Learning Project

Headings using -ing phrases

Imperative statements with verbs

Noun phrases

The Progressive Party Platform of 1912

Centered title

The Rule of the People

The National Progressive party, committed to the principles of government by a self-controlled democracy expressing its will through representatives of the people, pledges itself to secure such alterations in the fundamental law of the several States and the United States as shall insure the representative character of the government.

Left-aligned text

In particular, the party declares for direct primaries for the nomination of State and National officers; for nationwide preferential primaries for candidates for presidency; for the direct election of the United States Senators by the people; and we urge on the States the policy of the short ballot, with responsibility to the people secured by the initiative, referendum and recall.

Amendment of Constitution

The Progressive party, believing that a free people should have the power from time to time to amend their fundamental law so as to adapt it progressively to the changing needs of the people, pledges itself to provide a more easy and expeditious method of amending the Federal Constitution. . . .

Equal Suffrage

The Progressive party, believing that no people can justly claim to be a true democracy which denies political rights on account of sex, pledges itself to the task of securing equal suffrage to men and women alike.

Fully justified text, aligned at left and right

Right-aligned text

Figure 21.13
Centered Title over Text with Varying Alignments. Source: "The Progressive Party Platform of 1912." From National Party Platforms 1840–1964. *Kirk H. Porter and Donald Bruce Johnson, comps. U of Illinois P., 1966, 175–78.*

But centering *is* an alignment, you might protest. Indeed, centering all of your headings and subheadings should create a uniform alignment throughout your paper. Except in cases of coincidence, however, each centered heading will be a different length and thus, to the reader's eye, will have a different alignment, as you can see in Figure 21.14.

In contrast, in Figure 21.15 the headings are positioned at the left margin (or "flush left," as designers call it) to create a strong line down the left

Figure 21.14
Centered Headings
(no strong alignment).
Source: See Figure 21.13

The Progressive Party Platform of 1912

The Rule of the People

The National Progressive party, committed to the principles of government by a self-controlled democracy expressing its will through representatives of the people, pledges itself to secure such alterations in the fundamental law of the several States and the United States as shall insure the representative character of the government.

In particular, the party declares for direct primaries for the nomination of State and National officers; for nationwide preferential primaries for candidates for presidency; for the direct election of the United States Senators by the people; and we urge on the States the policy of the short ballot, with responsibility to the people secured by the initiative, referendum and recall.

Amendment of Constitution

The Progressive party, believing that a free people should have the power from time to time to amend their fundamental law so as to adapt it progressively to the changing needs of the people, pledges itself to provide a more easy and expeditious method of amending the Federal Constitution. . . .

Equal Suffrage

The Progressive party, believing that no people can justly claim to be a true democracy which denies political rights on account of sex, pledges itself to the task of securing equal suffrage to men and women alike.

Figure 21.15
Left-aligned Title, Headings, and Text (strong alignment). Source: See Figure 21.13

The Progressive Party Platform of 1912

The Rule of the People

The National Progressive party, committed to the principles of government by a self-controlled democracy expressing its will through representatives of the people, pledges itself to secure such alterations in the fundamental law of the several States and the United States as shall insure the representative character of the government.

In particular, the party declares for direct primaries for the nomination of State and National officers; for nationwide preferential primaries for candidates for presidency; for the direct election of the United States Senators by the people; and we urge on the States the policy of the short ballot, with responsibility to the people secured by the initiative, referendum and recall.

Amendment of Constitution

The Progressive party, believing that a free people should have the power from time to time to amend their fundamental law so as to adapt it progressively to the changing needs of the people, pledges itself to provide a more easy and expeditious method of amending the Federal Constitution. . . .

Equal Suffrage

The Progressive party, believing that no people can justly claim to be a true democracy which denies political rights on account of sex, pledges itself to the task of securing equal suffrage to men and women alike.

side of the page. This line helps keep the reader's eye moving downward and forward through the paper. The indented paragraphs also line up with each other, creating another strong alignment on the page. The text itself lines up along the left margin. The Web page in Figure 21.12 also groups and aligns the headings.

Much of the time you will use both left-aligned text and left-aligned headings in your document. Right-aligned text is rare in a college paper, except for special elements such as running headers and footers (discussed below). Some people like the tidy look of fully justified text, even on both sides, but you should use it with caution. The computer justifies text by adding extra white space between words and by hyphenating words that don't fit on a line; both techniques make text harder to read. Many teachers prefer left alignment only and no automatic hyphenation, as the MLA and APA guidelines advise.

USING REPETITION PURPOSEFULLY

Though common in poetry and in technical writing, too much verbal repetition may be frowned upon in academic writing. *Visual* repetition, however, can assist a reader. If you were driving along a freeway and the familiar navigation signs — the green and white rectangles — suddenly changed to purple triangles, you might wonder whether you had strayed into a different country. Similarly, if the font or alignment suddenly changes in a paper, the reader immediately asks: What is this new navigational cue? What am I expected to do now?

To avoid disorienting readers, repeat one or two fonts throughout your paper to sustain a clean, uncluttered look. Consistent headings and subheadings also serve as a kind of road map to guide the readers' progress. Another simple design strategy is the use of running, or repeated, headers and footers. A *running header* is a line of information that appears consistently at the top of each page of your document, while a *running footer* appears consistently at the bottom of pages. Check the top of this page and the few after or before it to figure out the pattern for this book's running headers. As part of the header or the footer, writers sometimes include information such as the document title, its file name, or a distinctive graphic. Once you create a header or footer, your word processor can automatically insert it on each page with the page number, if you've selected that option, or with the date. Figure 21.16 illustrates the type of header required in MLA style.

Fallon 2

Claremont's third message is that activism is needed to combat this

terrorism and hatred, and he provides clear models for activism. . . .

Figure 21.16
Sample Header (running header) in MLA Style, from Geoffrey Fallon's "Hatred within an Illustrated Medium: Those Uncanny X-Men"

FOR E-WRITERS

Adding Running Heads

Most word-processing programs can add running heads to your papers, auto-matically supplying your last name and the page number (or other informa-tion) at the top of each page. Check the View or Format menu for a Header or Footer option. In the Header box, use the tab key or your mouse to move to the header location you desire — generally the far right side for an academic paper. Type the header information — such as your last name (in MLA style), a key word from your title (in APA style), or your own identifier for a draft — and then click on the Page Number option or icon. Each page will be correctly numbered in sequence even if you delete or add passages.

USING COLOR EFFECTIVELY

Until recently, college papers typically have not included much color. How-ever, word-processing software and other programs now make it possible to include color graphics, photographs, and other images in papers. Make sure that color serves a purpose — for instance, to highlight key information — instead of being used merely as decoration. For example, a good use of color would be to distinguish the slices in a pie chart (see p. 414).

If you are creating documents beyond college papers, you may have even more opportunities to use color. For example, on a Web page you can use color to highlight headings and key information, as in Figure 21.17, or to emphasize a theme such as the patriotic nature of service learning, as in Figure 21.12. On any given page, avoid using too many colors because they can overload readers and defeat the purpose of helping them find important information. Also, choose your colors carefully. For example, although yel-low is an attention-getting color, as school buses and traffic signs illustrate, words written in yellow on a white background are hard to read.

Using Visuals to Reinforce Your Content

Some of your documents may benefit from the addition of graphs, dia-grams, maps, photographs, or other materials that add visual interest, con-vey information, and reinforce your text. You might prepare these yourself or incorporate such materials from other sources, giving credit and request-ing permission, if needed (see p. 415). In either case, visual materials should suit your purpose and your audience, not be used as decoration. Check your software for tools for creating graphics like pie charts, bar charts, and tables. If you are unfamiliar with these functions, ask for advice at the computer lab.

ADDING VISUALS

When could your document benefit from visuals? To answer this question, think about the ways in which visual material can support your point.

- To discuss a conflict in a certain geographical area, supply a map.
- To illustrate an autobiographical essay, scan an image of yourself as a baby or at some important moment in your life.
- To clarify the stages or steps in a process, a procedure, or a set of directions, include a diagram.
- To present statistical information, add graphs, charts, or tables.

Process Diagrams and Illustrations.   A paper explaining a process such as wastewater treatment in King County, Washington, might include a diagram, as in Figure 21.18. On the other hand, Figure 21.19 shows another way to illustrate a process. Notice how the drawings and descriptions work together to provide an overview of the tasks at an archaeological site.

Colorful images draw the eye
and point out key events
and resources

Additional color
images illustrate links

Green headers indicate
online sources at the
Smithsonian

Blue headers indicate
links to various
museums

Figure 21.17
Use of Color on a Web Page. Source: The Smithsonian Institution

Figure 21.18
A Diagram Showing the
Process of Wastewater
Treatment in King County,
Washington. Source: King
County, Washington,
Department of Natural
Resources Wastewater
Treatment Division

Figure 21.19
Illustration of Work at an
Archaeological Dig.
Source: Dorling Kindersley,
Children's Illustrated
Encyclopedia

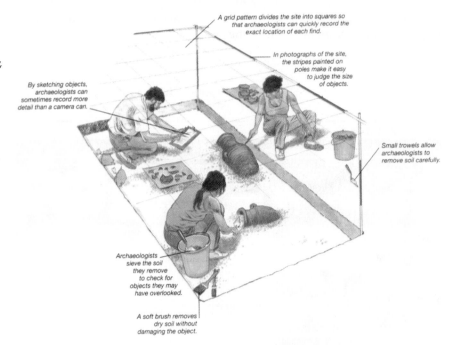

■ For more advice on
preparing graphs and
charts, visit
<bedfordstmartins.com/
bedguide> and do a key-
word search:

Comparative Graphs and Charts.   Graphics in college papers, magazines, Web sites, and other publications also consolidate information —
both numerical and verbal — in visual form. As the following examples
show, the various types of graphics convey information through visual elements such as size, shape, direction, and color.

- To illustrate a trend, a relationship, a comparison, or a contrast — the
  number of children who use the Internet or the ratio of men to women

Adding Visuals to Your Text

How can you add visuals to your paper? In a few cases—such as using material from a print source with a deadline only hours away—your simplest method may be the old-fashioned one: add an extra page break in your text where you want to place the material, print the final version of your file, and then use the numbered blank page to photocopy or present the material in your paper. Much of the time, however, you can create your own material right in your text file. To prepare a table, use the Insert or the Table menu. Simply add page breaks before and after it if you wish to present it on its own page, as some instructors and academic style manuals prefer.

FOR E-WRITERS

Other options for adding boxes, graphs, pie charts, bar charts, or art may be available through the Insert menu, a Drawing or Clip Art option, or related spreadsheet or presentation software. Use a scanner to integrate printed material, or try an image editor to scan photographs or add digital photos. Turn to your computer lab for help in using or accessing sophisticated software applications or equipment more advanced than your own. For a complex project, get help well ahead of your deadline, and allow plenty of time to learn new techniques for integrating visuals. Be sure to request permission to use images when needed, and acknowledge visual sources as carefully as textual sources.

at your college—create a graph in a spreadsheet. For example, Figure 21.20 compares trends in album sales for two years.

- To illustrate percentages or shares of a whole, add a pie chart, such as those in Figure 21.21. These charts indicate how much of the complete (100%) market for albums (total and current month) is controlled by various distributors.

Weekly Album Sales

Figure 21.20
A Graph Comparing Album Sales in 2005 and 2006 (Months—January to January). Source: Billboard, week ending November 29, 2006

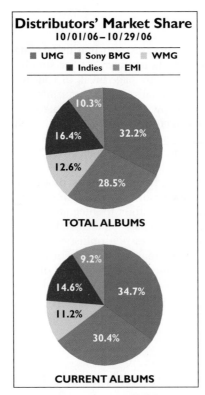

Figure 21.21   *Pie Charts Showing Album Distributors' Market Share. Source:* Billboard, *week ending October 29, 2006*

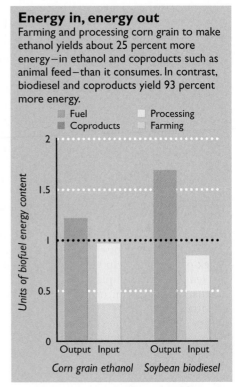

Figure 21.22   *A Bar Chart Presenting Numerical Comparisons. Source:* Technology Review, *September/October 2006; Jason Hill, University of Minnesota,* Proceedings of the National Academy of Sciences.

- To compare various values or amounts, provide a bar chart like the one in Figure 21.22. This chart illustrates an advantage of soybean-based biodiesel over corn-based ethanol by contrasting the energy required to produce each alternative fuel.

Comparative Tables.   Consider using a table to organize textual information for easier reading. Typically, tables have columns (running up and down) and rows (running across). Tables are common in academic and workplace writing but are also used in popular magazines, as Figure 21.23 shows. The information in this table could have been explained in a paragraph, but a block of text would have been less accessible for readers — and far less visually interesting. Notice how the little photographs of the various objects described bring the design to life.

how much is a serving? a 21st-century guide

STANDARD FOOD SERVING guidelines—like figuring a serving of meat for a cassette tape—are so last century. Since debit cards and personal digital assistants (PDAS) have replaced checkbooks and date books in your purse, here's a modern way to spot serving sizes:

FOOD ITEM	MODERN EQUIVALENT
a medium potato	the mini (6 oz.) soda can
3 ounces of meat	floppy disk
one scoop of ice cream	a round iMac mouse
3 ounces of grilled fish	PDA
1 ounce of cheese	pager
1 tablespoon of olive oil (or other cooking oil)	an individual eye-shadow compact
a serving of pretzels or other snack food	a coffee mug's full

Figure 21.23
A Table Organizing Textual Data.
Source: Health, *May 2002, page 35*

CREDITING SOURCES

If you include visual materials from another source, printed or electronic, credit that source in your essay. Be sure to ask permission, if required, to use an image so that you don't risk violating the copyright. If you download an image from the Web, check the site for its guidelines for the use of images. Follow these guidelines, asking permission if necessary and giving credit to the owner of the copyright. If you are uncertain about whether you can use an image from a source, check with your teacher.

For more on the MLA and APA documentation styles, see E1–E2 in the Quick Research Guide (the dark-red-edged pages).

ARRANGING VISUALS AND TEXT IN YOUR DOCUMENT

Using visuals can create problems in *layout,* the arrangement of text and graphics on a page. Here are some guidelines for ensuring that your layout is effective and appropriate for your purpose and audience.

Integration of Visuals and Text.   Because you are including the visual to support an idea in your text, your reader will make better sense of the graph, chart, diagram, or photograph if you provide a context for it. In an introductory sentence, you should give your reader this information:

- The number or letter of the visual (for example, Figure 6)
- Its location (on page 9, in section 3)
- Its content
- The point that it helps you to make

Also supply a label with your visual to identify its topic and number.

Placement and Alignment of Visuals.   Placing a visual close to the related discussion will make your document easy for readers to follow. Readers may get distracted if they must flip from the body of the text to an appendix, for example. In addition, when your headings and text are aligned at the left margin to sustain a strong forward flow through the document, you may not want to disrupt the flow by centering your visuals. Let your eye be the judge.

Balance between Visuals and Text.   The visuals should support, not overshadow, the content of your paper. Try to strike a balance between the size of any single graphic or image and the related chunks of text. Though a reader's eye should be drawn to the visual, try to give it an appropriate — rather than excessive — share of the page layout.

Consider the following questions as you design your document:

DOCUMENT DESIGN CHECKLIST

___ Does your document design meet your readers' expectations and acknowledge their constraints?

___ Does your document design help to achieve your purpose? Does it help emphasize your key points and clear organization?

___ Have you used appropriate fonts, or typefaces, in your document? Do you use boldface and italic type sparingly for emphasis? Have you used bulleted or numbered lists when appropriate to call out information?

___ Do you use white space strategically, calling attention to or linking portions of text rather than creating gaps between textual elements?

___ Do your headings, subheadings, and alignment provide readers with clear and purposeful navigational cues?

___ Have you used repeated elements, such as running headers or footers, that increase visual coherence?

___ Do your diagrams, photographs, or other illustrations clarify your content? Do your graphs, charts, or tables present numerical or textual information "at a glance"?

___ Have you used color effectively to highlight, distinguish, or organize information?

___ Does your layout integrate the visuals using appropriate placement, size, and alignment?

___ Have you secured any permission needed to use copyrighted material? Have you credited the source of each visual?

■ Activities and Assignments

1. Experiment with the fonts available on your computer. Using a paragraph or two from a recent paper, go through the font list to see how your sentences look in various fonts. Test different sizes as well as the bold and italic versions. How readable is each font?

2. Look at a bulletin board, literature rack, magazine shelf, or other location that displays different examples of printed material. Identify different uses of fonts to establish a mood or convey a message. Select one example that you find particularly effective, and briefly explain how the font helps to convey the desired mood or message to the audience. If possible, include a copy of the example with your paper.

3. Using your favorite search engine (Google or Yahoo!, for example), locate an online example of a research paper or report. (The keywords "research paper" or "research report" should return several examples.) Or find a technical or government report online or in the library. Read the abstract or introduction to get an idea of the author's topic. Then quickly skim the report in order to answer the following questions:

   a. What is the purpose of the report?

   b. Who is the intended audience? How can you tell?

   c. In what ways does the writer use document design to address readers' needs and constraints?

   d. How does the writer use document design to help make his or her point?

   e. What design revisions would you recommend to the writer? How might these changes improve the audience's reading experience?

   Write a brief essay presenting your findings.

4. FOR GROUP WORK: Assemble several different documents that you are reading or might read — perhaps a textbook, a newspaper, a magazine, an online article, a brochure, a catalog, or a campus publication. Examine each document carefully, considering which aspects of the design seem effective or ineffective in achieving the writer's purpose and meeting the reader's needs. Then, bring your documents and notes to class. In groups of three to five students, share your findings.

5. FOR GROUP WORK: In a small group, examine several different documents — one supplied by each group member or one or two of the sets prepared for activity 4. For each document, consider what other design choices might have made the visual presentation more effective. When you've finished your analysis, share your findings with the class.

Chapter 22
Strategies for Understanding Visual Representations

On a street-corner billboard, a man is biting into a jelly doughnut while driving, a look of horror on his face. He's horrified because a big blob of purple jelly (captured in midair) is about to land in the middle of his white dress shirt. The only other picture on the billboard is a detergent manufacturer's logo.

Other billboards on this corner advertise such diverse commodities as fast food, cell-phone services, and the radiology department at a local hospital. Thousands of drivers pause at this intersection to wait out a red light — a captive audience for aggressive and compelling visual representations. It's a good location for the detergent ad: drivers who pass the billboard, especially those who are eating in their cars, will relate to the problem of food spills on nice clothes. Obviously, the company that sponsored the ad hopes these people will remember its brand — the one that can tackle even the worst stains on the whitest shirts — the next time they buy laundry detergent.

The specific images on these billboards change with time, but images are a constant and persistent presence in our lives. The sign atop a taxi invites us to try the new ride at a local tourist attraction. A celebrity sporting a milk moustache smiles from the side of a city bus, accompanied by the familiar question, "Got milk?" The lettering on a pickup truck urges us to call for a free landscaping estimate. On television, video, and the Web, advertising images surround us, trying to shape our opinions about everything from personal hygiene products to snack foods to political candidates.

Advertisements are not the only visual representations that affect us. Cartoons, photographs, drawings, paintings, logos, graphics, and other two-dimensional media originate from a variety of sources with a variety of purposes — and all work to evoke responses. The critical skills you develop for analyzing these still images also apply to other types of visual representations, including television commercials, films, and stage productions. We can't help but notice visual images, and whether we respond with a smile or a frown, one thing is certain: visuals help to structure our views of reality.

Using Strategies for Visual Analysis

Begin a visual analysis by conducting a *close reading* of the image. Like a literal and critical reading of a written text, a close reading of an image involves careful, in-depth examination of the advertisement, photograph, cartoon, artwork, or other visual representation. Your close reading should focus on the following three levels of questions:

■ For a model visual analysis and visual-analysis activity, visit <bedfordstmartins.com/bedguide> and do a keyword search:

- **What is the big picture?** What is the source of the image? What is its purpose? What audience does it address? What prominent element in the image stands out? What focal point draws the eye?

- **What characteristics of the image can you observe?** What story does the image tell? What people or animals appear in the image? What are the major elements of the image? How are they arranged?

- **How can you interpret what the image suggests?** What feeling or mood does it create? What is its cultural meaning? What are the roles of any signs, symbols, or language that it includes? What is the image about?

The rest of the chapter explains these three levels of visual analysis in more detail. You may discover that your classmates respond differently to some images than you do. Your personal cultural background and your experiences may influence how you interpret the meaning of an image. If you plan

■ For more on literal and critical reading of texts, see Ch. 2. For a checklist for analyzing images, see pp. 433–34.

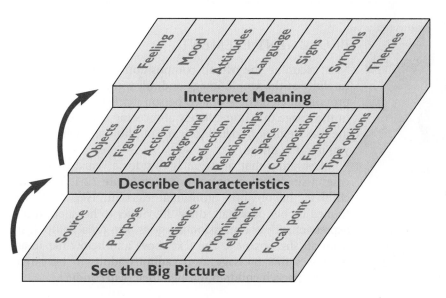

to write about the image you analyze, take notes or use your journal to record your observations and interpretations. Be sure to include a copy of the image, if one is available, when you solicit peer review of your essay or submit it to your teacher.

Level One: Seeing the Big Picture

> For more on crediting sources of visuals, see p. 415.

Begin your close reading of an image by discovering what you can about its source and overall composition. If you include the image in a paper, you will need to cite the source and its "author" or artist, just as you would if you were including text from a reading, an article, or a literary work.

PURPOSE AND AUDIENCE

> For more on purpose and audience, see pp. 14–18 and pp. 310–12.

Identifying the purpose and intended audience for an image is sometimes complicated. For example, an image may appear in its original context or in a different situation, used seriously, humorously, or allusively. Use these questions to help you explore the purpose of and audience for the image:

DISCOVERY CHECKLIST

Figure 22.1
Public-Service Advertise-ment with One Prominent Element. Source: Act Against Violence.org/Ad Council

____ What is the context for the image? For example, if it is an advertisement, when and where did it run? If it is a photograph, painting, or other work of art, who is the artist? Where has it been published or exhibited?

____ What is the purpose of the image?

____ What audience does the image aim to attract?

PROMINENT ELEMENT

Next, examine the overall composition of the image. Look carefully at the whole image and ask yourself, "Is there one prominent element — object, person, background, writing — in the image that immediately attracts my attention?" Examine that element in detail to figure out how and why it draws you into the image.

Answering that question is easy for a visual that show-cases a single object or person, as in Figure 22.1. There, the child is the obvious prominent element. Her dark eyes, framed by her dark hair, draw the viewer to her alert, intent expression. That expression suggests her capacity to learn from all she observes. The text above and below her image reinforces this message as it cautions adults to be careful what they teach children through their own conduct.

Identifying the prominent element can be more complicated for a visual with several characters. For example, consider which form draws your eye in Figure 22.2. Many people would first notice the dark-haired Caucasian girl. Her prominence in the picture can be explained in part by her position at the left side of the photograph, framed by the white porch railing. People who read from left to right and top to bottom — including most Americans and Europeans — also typically read photographs in the same way, which means that the viewer's eye is likely to be drawn into the photograph at the upper left corner. For this reason, artists and photographers often position key elements — those they want viewers to see right away — somewhere in the upper left quadrant of the image. (See Figure 22.3.)

FOCAL POINT

There is another reason the reader's eye might be drawn first to the girl on the left: notice that all of the other children are turned slightly toward her, straining to see the pages of the magazine she is holding. Not only is she positioned so as to provide a focal point for the viewer, but she is also the focal point of action within the photograph.

Now, take a look at the child on the right side of the picture. You may have noticed her first. Or, once you did notice her, you may have been surprised that she didn't attract your attention right away. After all, she provides some contrast within the photograph because she sits apart from the other girls, seems to be a little younger, and does not appear to be included in their little group. What's more, she's not wearing any clothes. Still, most people won't notice her first because of the path the eye typically travels within a photograph. Because of the left-to-right and top-to-bottom reading pattern that Americans and Europeans take for granted, most of us view photographs in a Z pattern, as depicted in Figure 22.4. Even though most viewers would notice the child on the far right last, they would still pause to look at her. Thus, the bottom right corner of an image is a second very important position that a skilled photographer can use to retain the viewers' attention. When you look at the "big picture" in this way, you can see the overall composition of the image, identify its prominent element, and determine its focal point.

Level Two: Observing the Characteristics of an Image

As you concentrate on the literal reading of a written text, you become aware of the information it presents, you comprehend what it means, and you are able to apply it in relation to other situations. Similarly, your close reading of an image includes observing its *denotative* or literal characteristics. At this stage, you focus on exactly what the image depicts — observing it objectively — rather than probing what it means or signifies.

For more about reading on a literal level, see pp. 25–29. For a checklist for analyzing images, see pp. 433–34.

Figure 22.2 (top)
Photograph of Four Children, Kodak Picture of the Day, October 22, 2000

Figure 22.3 (above left)
Photograph Divided into Quarters

Figure 22.4 (above right)
Z Pattern Often Used to Read Images

Figure 22.5 (right)
Close-Up Detail of Photograph

CAST OF CHARACTERS

Objects.   Examine the condition, colors, sizes, functions, and positions of the objects included in the image. In Figure 22.2, for example, only one object is depicted in the image: a large magazine. Everything else in the image is either a figure or part of the background.

Figures.   Look closely at any figures (men, women, children, animals) in the image. Consider their facial expressions, poses, hairstyles and colors, ages, sexes, ethnicity, possible education, suggested occupations, apparent relationships to each other, and so on.

Figure 22.2 shows four girls, three about eight or nine years old and the fourth a few years younger. Three of the girls are Caucasian, and one is African American. The dark-haired Caucasian girl is wearing a colorful bathing suit as is the African American girl. Between them sits a light-haired Caucasian girl, wearing shorts and a short-sleeved blue and white flowered T-shirt. All three appear to be dressed appropriately for the weather. The three girls pore over the magazine held by the dark-haired Caucasian girl. Judging from their facial expressions, they are totally engrossed in the magazine, as well as a little puzzled. The girls seem to be looking at a picture; the magazine is turned sideways with the spine at the bottom.

The fourth child, the youngest in the photograph, sits slightly apart from the others. Her light hair appears damp—possibly from swimming, we might conclude, because two of the other girls are attired in swimsuits. We can see that her skin is tanned and that she has several small bruises on her legs, probably acquired during play. Her right leg is crossed over her left, causing her body to turn slightly away from the other girls. Her face is turned toward them, however, and she seems to be trying to see what they are looking at. Her hands are raised, her eyes are bright, and she's smiling at whatever she is able to see of the magazine.

STORY OF THE IMAGE

Action.   The action shown in an image suggests its "plot" or story, the events surrounding the moment captured in the image. In Figure 22.2, four children are seated on the steps of a house looking at a magazine on a summer day. Because no adults appear in the picture and the children look puzzled, we might assume that they are looking at something they don't understand, possibly something adults might frown on. On the other hand, they are not being secretive, so this impression may not be accurate.

Background.   The background in an image shows where and when the action takes place. In Figure 22.2, the children are seated on the wooden steps of a blue house. We might conclude that the steps are part of a back porch rather than a front porch because the porch is relatively small and the steps begin immediately: there is no deck and consequently nowhere to sit except on the steps themselves. The top step is painted blue, and the railing is painted white to match the white metal door and window frames. In a few places the paint is chipped or worn away. But these signs of disrepair simply seem to indicate that the house is lived in and comfortable; they are not severe enough to suggest that the occupants are poor. In the windows next to the steps and on the door, we can see the reflections of trees. The children's clothes identify the season as summer.

DESIGN AND ARRANGEMENT

Selection of Elements.   When you look at the design of an image, you might reflect on both the elements within the image and their organization.

- What are the major colors and shapes?
- How are they arranged?
- Does the image appear balanced? Are light and dark areas arranged symmetrically?
- Does the image appear organized or chaotic?
- Is one area of the picture darker (heavier) or brighter (lighter) than other areas?
- What does the design make you think of—does it evoke a particular emotion, historical period, or memory?

In Figure 22.2, the most prominent shape is the white porch railing that frames the children and draws the viewer's eye in toward the action. The image appears balanced, in that the white door provides the backdrop for the youngest child, while the blue siding and white porch railing frame the other girls. Therefore, the image is split down the center, both by the separation of the figures and by the shapes that make up the background. The brightly colored summer clothing worn by the girls on the left side also accentuates the youngest child's monochromatic nakedness.

Relationship of Elements.   Visual elements may be related to one another or to written material that appears with them. As you notice such relationships, consider what they tell you. In Figure 22.2, for instance, the three older girls are grouped together around the magazine, and the youngest child is clearly not part of their group. She is separated physically from the others by a bit of space and by the vertical line formed by the doorframe, which splits the background in two. Moreover, her body is turned slightly away from them, and she is not clothed. However, her gaze, like the other girls', is on the magazine that they are scrutinizing; this element of the picture connects all of the children.

For more information on white space in document design, see pp. 402–04.

Use of Space.   An image may be surrounded by a lot of "white space" — empty space without text or graphics — or it may be "busy," filled with visual and written elements. White space is effective when it provides relief from an otherwise busy layout or when it directs the reader's eye to key elements of the image. The image in Figure 22.2 does not include any empty space; its shapes and colors guide the viewer's eye.

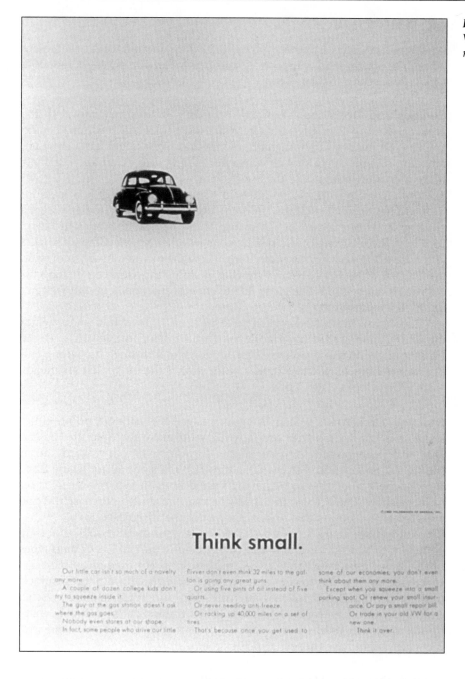

Figure 22.6
Volkswagen Advertise-
ment, about 1959

In contrast, look at the image in Figure 22.6. It specifically uses white space to call attention to the Volkswagen's small size. When this advertisement was produced back in 1959, many American cars were large and heavy. The VW, a German import, provided consumers with an alternative type of vehicle, and the advertising emphasized this contrast.

ARTISTIC CHOICES

Whether an image is a photograph, a drawing, or another form of representation, the person who composes it considers its artistic effect, its function, and its connection to related text.

Composition Decisions.   Aesthetic or artistic choices may vary with the preferences of the designer and the characteristics of the medium. For example, if an image is a photograph, the photographer might use a close-up, medium, or wide-angle shot to compose it — and also determine the angle of the shot, the lighting, and the use of color.

The picture of the four children in Figure 22.2 (p. 422) is a medium shot and has been taken at the children's eye level. If the photograph were a close-up, only one aspect of the image would be visible. Notice in Figure 22.5 how the meaning of the picture changes when we view the girls' faces as a close-up. We have no way of telling where the picture was taken or what the girls are doing; moreover, by moving in closer, this view completely cuts out the youngest child. The girls' attentiveness is still apparent, but we can't quite tell what its object is.

In contrast, in the Volkswagen ad (Figure 22.6), the white space creates the effect of a long shot taken from below with a telephoto lens. We see the car as it might appear if we were looking down at it through the wrong end of a pair of binoculars. This vantage point shrinks the car so that an already small vehicle looks even smaller.

■ For more about the ways visuals support content, see pp. 410–14.

Function Decisions.   When using an image to illustrate a point, either alone or in connection with text, a writer must make sure that the illustration serves the overall purpose of the document. In other words, form should follow function. For example, the 1959 Oldsmobile ad, Figure 22.7, shows people who seem to be having a good time; in fact, one scene is set near the shore. These illustrations suggest that those who purchase the cars will enjoy life, a notion that undoubtedly suits the advertiser's goals.

■ For a sample pie chart, see Figure 21.21, p. 414. For sample photographs, turn to the images opening Chs. 4 to 12 and 23 to 27.

Writers have many choices available to them for illustrations — not only photographs and drawings but also charts, graphs, and tables. Certain types of visuals are especially suited to certain functions. For example, a pie chart is perhaps the best way to convey parts of a whole visually. A photograph effectively captures the drama and intensity of the moment — a child's rescue, a family's grief, or an earthquake's toll. When you look at newspapers, magazines, and other publications, consider how the visuals function and why the writer might have chosen to include them.

■ For more on typefaces, see pp. 396–400.

Typeface Options.   Many images, especially advertisements, combine image and text, using the typeface to set a particular mood and convey a particular impression. For example, Times New Roman is a common typeface, easy to read and somewhat conservative, whereas Comic Sans MS is considered informal — almost playful — and looks handwritten. Any printed element included in an image may be trendy or conservative, large or small, in rela-

Figure 22.7
Oldsmobile Advertisement,
1959

tion to the image as a whole. Further, it may be meant to inform, evoke emotion, or decorate the page.

Look back at Figure 22.6 (p. 425), the 1959 Volkswagen ad. The words "Think small" are printed in a sans serif typeface—spare and unadorned, just like the VW itself. The ad also includes a significant amount of text across the bottom of the page. While this text is difficult to read in the

For a definition and example of sans serif type, see pp. 397–98.

Figure 22.8 *Stairway.*
Source: Design for Communication: Conceptual Graphic Design Basics

Figure 22.9 *Type as Cultural Cliché.*
Source: Publication Design

reproduction in this book, it humorously points out the benefits of driving a small imported vehicle instead of one of the many large, roomy cars common at the time.

In contrast to the VW ad campaign, the 1959 Oldsmobile marketing strategy promoted a big vehicle, not a small one, as Figure 22.7 illustrates. Here the cars are shown in medium to close-up view to call attention to their length. Happy human figures positioned in and beside the cars emphasize their size, and the cars are painted in bright colors, unlike the VW's serviceable black. The type in the ad, like the other visual elements, reflects and promotes the Oldsmobile's size. The primary text in the center of the page is large enough to be read in the reproduction here. It introduces the brand name by opening the first sentence with the Oldsmobile '59 logo and praises the cars' expansive size, space, power, and other features. Near the bottom of each car image, however, are a few lines of "fine print" that are difficult to read in the reproduction—brief notes about other features of the car.

Other images besides advertisements use type to set a mood or convey feelings and ideas. Figure 22.8 is a design student's response to an assignment that called for using letters to create an image. The student used a simple typeface and a stairlike arrangement to help viewers "experience" the word *stairway*. Figure 22.9 illustrates how certain typefaces have become associated with particular countries—even to the point of becoming clichés. In fact, designers of travel posters, travel brochures, and other such publications often draw on predictable typographical choices like these to suggest a feeling or mood—for example, boldness, tradition, adventure, history.

Just as type can establish a mood or tone, the absence of any written language in an image can also affect how we view that image. Recall Figure 22.2 (p. 422), the photograph of the children sitting on the porch looking at a magazine. Because we can't see the magazine's title, we are left to wonder — perhaps with amusement — about what has so engrossed the children. If the title of the magazine — *Sports Illustrated, Wired, People* — were revealed to us, the photograph might seem less intriguing. By leaving us to speculate about the identity of the magazine, the photographer may keep us looking longer and harder at the image.

Level Three: Interpreting the Meaning of an Image

When you read a written text on an analytical level, you engage actively with the text. You analyze its parts from different angles, synthesize the material by combining it with related information, and finally evaluate or judge its significance. When you interpret an image, you do much the same, actively questioning and examining what the image *connotes* or suggests, speculating about what it signifies.

For more on reading analytically, see pp. 25–29. For a checklist for analyzing images, see pp. 433–34.

Because interpretation is more personal than observation, this process can reveal deep-seated individual and cultural values. In fact, interpreting an image is sometimes emotional or difficult because it may require you to examine beliefs that you are unaware of holding. You may even become impatient with visual analysis, perhaps feeling that too much is being read into the image. Like learning to read critically, however, learning to interpret images is a valuable skill. When you see an image that attracts you, chances are good that you like it because it upholds strong cultural beliefs. Through close reading of images, you can examine how image makers are able to perpetuate such cultural values and speculate about why — perhaps analyzing an artist's political motivations or an advertiser's economic motivations. When you interpret an image, you go beyond literal observation to examine what the image suggests and what it may mean.

GENERAL FEELING OR MOOD

To begin interpreting an image, consider what feeling or mood it creates and how it does so. If you are a woman, you probably recall huddling, around age eight or nine, with a couple of "best friends" as the girls do in Figure 22.2. As a result, the interaction in this photograph may seem very familiar and may evoke fond memories. If you are a man, this photograph may call up somewhat different memories. Although eight-year-old boys also cluster in small groups, their motivations may differ from those behind little girls' huddles. Moreover, anyone who was ignored or excluded at a young age

Figure 22.10
Photograph Conveying a
Mood. Source: Jonathan
Nourok, PhotoEdit

may feel a rush of sympathy for the youngest child; her separation from the older children may dredge up age-old hurt feelings.

For many viewers, the image may also suggest a mood associated with summer: sitting on the back porch after a trip to the swimming pool, spending a carefree day with friends. This "summer" mood is a particular cultural association related to the summers of childhood. By the time we reach college, summer no longer has the same feeling. Work, summer school, separations, and family responsibilities—maybe even for children like those in the picture—obliterate the freedoms of childhood summer vacations. However, another image might capture or represent a different version of this feeling or mood. As Figure 22.10 illustrates, an adult version of the "summer mood" might use similar colors and bright light to evoke a similar feeling. In this image, the cluster of childhood friends has been replaced by a solitary, reflective person, tapping the beauty of a summer scene through the creative experience of painting.

SOCIOLOGICAL, POLITICAL, ECONOMIC, OR CULTURAL ATTITUDES

On the surface, the Volkswagen ad in Figure 22.6 (p. 425) is simply an attempt to sell a car. But its message might be interpreted to mean "scale down"—lead a less consumer-oriented lifestyle. If Volkswagen had distributed this ad in the 1970s, it would have been unremarkable—faced with the first energy crisis that adversely affected American gasoline prices, many advertisers used ecological consciousness to sell cars. In 1959, however, energy conservation was not really a concern. Contrasted with other automobile ads of its time, the Volkswagen ad seems somewhat eccentric, making the novel suggestion that larger cars are excessively extravagant.

Figure 22.11
Photograph Using a Missing
Element to Convey a Mes-
sage. Source: Public Service
Announcement, Americans
for National Parks

Whereas the Volkswagen ad suggests that "small" refers both to size and affordability, the Oldsmobile ad in Figure 22.7 (p. 427) depicts a large vehicle and implies a large price tag. By emphasizing the Vista-Panoramic view and increased luggage space and by portraying the car near a seashore, the ad leads viewers to think about going on vacation. It thus implies luxury and exclusivity—not everyone can afford this car or the activities it suggests.

Sometimes what is missing from an image is as important as what is included. For instance, Figure 22.11 deliberately contrasts presence and absence, projecting a possible future scene—without the bear—to bring home its message about the need to protect and preserve our national parks and their residents. What's missing also may be more subtle, especially for viewers who wear the blinders of their own times, circumstances, or expecta-

Here today...

tions. For example, viewers of today might readily notice the absence of people of color in the 1959 Oldsmobile ad, An interesting study might investigate what types of magazines originally carried this ad, whether their readers recognized what was missing, and whether (and if so, how) Oldsmobiles were also advertised in publications aimed at Asian, African, or Spanish-speaking Americans.

LANGUAGE

Just as you would examine figures, colors, and shapes when you observe the literal characteristics of an image, so you need to examine its words, phrases, and sentences when you interpret what it suggests. Does its language provide information, generate an emotional response, or do both? Do its words repeat a sound or concept, signal a comparison (such as a "new, improved" product), carry sexual overtones, issue a challenge, or offer a definition or philosophy of life? The words in the center of the Oldsmobile ad in Figure 22.7, for instance, are calculated to associate the car with a leisurely, affluent lifestyle. On the other hand, VW's "Think small" ad in Figure 22.6 turns compactness into a goal, a quality to be desired in a car and, by extension, in life.

Frequently advertisements employ wordplay — lighthearted or serious — to get their messages across. Consider, for example, the public-service advertisement in Figure 22.12, which was created by a graphic-design student. This ad features a play on the word *tolerance*, which is scrambled on the chalkboard so that the letters in the center read *learn*. The chalkboard, a typical feature of the classroom, suggests that tolerance is a basic lesson to be learned. Also, the definition of tolerance at the bottom of the ad is much like other definitions students might look up in a dictionary. (It reads, "The capacity for, or practice of, recognizing or respecting the behavior, beliefs, opinions, practices, or rights of others, whether agreeing with them or not.")

Wordplay can also challenge viewers' preconceptions about a visual image. The billboard in Figure 22.13 shows a romantic — indeed, seductive — scene. The sophisticated couple gaze deeply into each other's eyes as the man kisses the woman's hand. However, the verbal exchange undermines that intimate scene and viewers' expectations about what happens next. Instead of a similar compliment in response to "Your scent is intoxicating," the billboard makes plain its antismoking position with the reply: "Yours is carcinogenic." In just seven words, the billboard counters the suave, romantic image of smoking with the reality of smelly, cancer-causing tobacco smoke.

Figure 22.12
Public-Service Advertisement Showing Wordplay.
Source: Design for Communication: Conceptual Graphic Design Basics

Figure 22.13
Billboard Showing Wordplay.
Source: Photograph by Bill
Aron, PhotoEdit

SIGNS AND SYMBOLS

Signs and symbols, such as product logos, are images or words that communicate key messages. In the Oldsmobile ad in Figure 22.7 (p. 427), the product logo doubles as the phrase that introduces the description of the 1959 model. Sometimes a product logo alone may be enough, as in the Hershey chocolate company's holiday ads that include little more than a single Hershey's Kiss. The shape of the Kiss serves as a logo or symbol for the company.

If you look back at the second magazine spread in Figure 21.3 (see p. 394), you'll see a prominent cultural symbol — the U.S. flag. The flag is held by a little boy who is sitting on a man's shoulders, presumably his father's. In this spread, the flag is associated not only with the Fourth of July, the article's subject, but also with a family's values. Even without the headings and quotations, the symbolism comes across clearly.

Figure 22.14 also combines a widely recognizable symbol — the bars and locked door of a jail cell — with the image of a child. This child, however, is not riding securely on dad's shoulders while celebrating a patriotic holiday. Instead, the child is confined in what looks like a bedroom scattered with toys. This public-service announcement turns around the usual message of the cell-door symbol, applying it not only to the potential offender but also to that person's family. The surprising image of the young child behind bars suggests the complex and potentially long-lasting effects of a prison sentence on families and relatives.

THEMES

The theme of an image is not the same as its plot. When you identify the plot, you identify the story that is told by the image. When you identify the theme, on the other hand, you explain what the image is about. An ad for a diamond ring may tell the story of a man surprising his wife with a ring on their twenty-fifth wedding anniversary, but the advertisement's theme could be sex, romance, commitment, or some other concept. Similarly, the theme of a soft-drink ad might be competition, community, compassion, or individualism. A painting of the ocean might be about cheerfulness, fear, or loneliness.

Through a close reading, you can unearth clues and details to support your interpretation of the theme and convince others of its merit. For example, when you first glance at the image in Figure 22.15, it appears to illus-

Figure 22.14
Public-Service Advertisement Using Symbolism.
Source: Project Safe Neighborhoods/Ad Council

trate a recipe for a tasty margarita. As you read the list of ingredients, you find that they suggest a tale of too many drinks and a drunk-driving accident after running a red light. Instead of promoting an alcoholic beverage or promising relaxing fun, this public-service announcement challenges the assumption that risky behavior won't carry consequences. Its text counters its suggestive image and reminds viewers of its theme—that well-being comes not from alcohol-fueled confidence but from responsible choices.

Ask the following questions as you analyze an image, such as a chapter opener in this book or an example in this chapter, or as you prepare to present your analysis in an essay:

Figure 22.15
Poster Conveying a Theme. Source: U.S. Department of Transportation/Ad Council

VISUAL ANALYSIS CHIECKLIST

Seeing the Big Picture

What is the source of the image? What is its purpose and audience?

What prominent element in the image immediately attracts your attention? How and why does it draw you into the image?

—— What is the focal point of the image? How does the image direct your attention to this point? What path does your eye follow as you observe the image?

Observing the Characteristics of an Image

—— What objects are included in the image?

—— What figures (people or animals) appear in the image?

—— What action takes place in the image? What is its "plot" or story?

—— What is in the background of the image? Where does the action of the image take place? What kind of place is it?

—— What elements contribute to the design of the image? What colors and shapes does the image include? How are they arranged or balanced? What feeling, memory, or association does the design evoke?

—— How are the pictorial elements related to one another? How are they related to any written material? What do these relationships tell you as a viewer?

—— How does the image use space? Does it include a lot of white space, or does it seem cluttered and busy?

—— What composition decisions has the designer or artist made? What type of shot, shot angle, lighting, or color is used?

—— What is the function of the image? How does form support function?

—— What typefaces are used? What impressions do they convey?

Interpreting the Meaning of an Image

—— What general feeling do you get from looking at the image? What mood does it create? How does it create this mood?

___ What sociological, political, economic, or cultural attitudes are reflected in the image?

___ What language is included in the image? How does the language function?

___ What signs and symbols can you identify? What role do these play?

___ What theme or themes can you identify in the image?

■ Activities and Assignments

1. Find a print ad that evokes a strong emotional response. Study the ad closely, observing its characteristics and interpreting its meaning. Write an essay in which you explain the techniques by which the ad evokes your emotional response. Include a copy of the ad with your essay, and consult others to determine whether they have the same response to the ad.

2. Volkswagen continues to produce thought-provoking advertisements like the one shown in Figure 22.6 on page 425. Video clips of some of the company's recent television ads can be found on its Web site at <www.vw.com/vwlife/commercial.html>. View one or two of these advertisements, considering such features as their stories or "plots"; the choice of figures, settings, and images; the angles from which subjects are filmed; and any text messages included. Based on your analysis of the ads, decide what message you think that the company wants to communicate about its cars. In an essay, describe this message and the audience that Volkswagen seems to be aiming for, and discuss how the artistic choices in the ads might appeal to this audience.

3. Compile a design notebook. Over several weeks, collect ten or twelve images that appeal to you. You may wish to choose examples of a particular genre, or your teacher may assign a genre or theme. For example, you might select advertisements, portraits, or photographs of campus landmarks. You might choose landscape paintings by different artists or snack food advertisements from magazines aimed at different audiences. On the other hand, your collection might revolve around a theme, such as friendship, competition, community, or romance. As you collect these images, "read" each one closely, and write short responses explaining your reactions to the images. At the end of the collection period, choose two or three images. Write an essay in which you compare or contrast them, analyzing how they illustrate the same genre, convey a theme, or appeal to different audiences.

4. Visit a music store, and find a CD cover whose design interests you. Make notes about design choices such as its prominent element and focal point, the use of color and imagery, and the use of typography. Based on the design, try to predict what kind of music is on the CD. If the store has CD-listening stations, try to listen to a track or two. Did the music match your expectations based on the CD design? If you were the CD designer, would you have made any different artistic choices? Write a brief essay discussing your observations, and attach a copy of the CD cover, if possible. (You might be able to print it out from the Web.) As an alternative assignment, listen to some music that's new to you, and design a CD cover for it, applying the elements described in this chapter. Describe in a brief paper the

■ For a sample analysis of a Volkswagen ad, see "Wham! Bam! Buy a VW, Ma'am!" (p. 184).

visual elements you would include on your CD cover. If you wish, sketch your design for the cover, using colored pencils or markers or pasting in images or type from print sources, such as magazines or newspapers.

5. **FOR GROUP WORK:**   Select some type of image (for example, an advertisement; a visual from a magazine or image database; a CD, DVD, or video-cassette cover) and, on your own, make notes on its "literal" characteristics. (For guidance, see "Observing the Characteristics of an Image," pp. 421–29.) Then, bring your image and notes to class. In small groups of three to five students, share your images and discuss your literal readings.

6. **FOR GROUP WORK:**   In a small group, pick one or two of the images that the group members analyzed for activity 5. Ask each group member, in turn, to suggest possible interpretations of the images. (For guidance, see "Interpreting the Meaning of an Image," pp. 429–33.) What different interpretations do group members suggest? How do you account for their differences? Share your findings with the rest of the class.

A
Writer's
Reader

A Writer's Reader Contents

Introduction: Reading to Write **439**

Introduction:
Reading to Write

A *Writer's Reader* is a collection of thirty-two carefully selected professional essays. We hope, first of all, that you will read these pieces simply for the sake of reading—enjoying and responding to the ideas presented. Good writers read widely, and in doing so, they increase their knowledge of the craft of writing. Second, we hope that you will actively study these essays as solid examples of the situations and strategies explored in *A Writer's Guide.* The authors represented in this reader, experts from varied fields, have faced the same problems and choices you do when you write. You can learn from studying their decisions, structures, and techniques. Finally, we hope that you will find the content of the essays intriguing—and that the essays, along with the questions posed after each one, will give you ideas to write about.

Each chapter in *A Writer's Reader* concentrates on a familiar broad theme—families, men and women, popular culture, electronic technology, and education. In some essays the writers focus on the inner world and write personal experience and opinion papers. In others the authors turn their attention to the outer world and write informational and persuasive essays. Within each chapter, the last two selections are a pair of essays on the same subject. We've provided these pairs so that you can see how different writers use different strategies to address similar issues.

Each chapter in the reader begins with an image, a visual activity, and a Web search activity, all intended to stimulate your thinking and writing. Each reading selection is preceded by biographical information about the author, placing him or her—and the piece itself—into a cultural and informational context. Next a reading note, As You Read, suggests a way to consider the selection. Following each reading are five Questions to Start You Thinking that consistently cover the same ground: meaning, writing strategies, critical thinking, vocabulary, and connections with one or more of the other selections in *A Writer's Reader.* Each paired essay is also followed by a question that asks you about a link between the essays. After these questions come a couple of journal prompts designed to get your writing juices flowing. Finally, two possible assignments make specific suggestions for writing. The first assignment is directed toward your inner world, asking you to draw generally on your personal experience and your understanding of the essay. The second is outer directed, asking you to look outside yourself and write an evaluative or argumentative paper, one that may require further reading or research.

For more on journal writing, see pp. 306–07.

439

Chapter 23
Families

Responding to an Image

Carefully examine this family photograph, making thorough notes about the
clothing, positions, facial expressions, posture, race, gender, and other attributes
of the people. Also, make notes about the surroundings. What might these attributes and surroundings indicate about the occasion? What kind of family does
this photograph portray? Does this family portrait remind you of any others
you've seen?

Search the Library of Congress online archive called American Memory <http://memory.loc.gov/ammem/> by entering a subject related to your family's history, such as a state or city where your ancestors or family have lived, an industry a relative has worked in, or a historical event or natural disaster that affected your family in some way. Locate and study a specific photograph or document on this subject. Imagine that your family has a direct connection to the photo or document you have found. Write an imaginary narrative about one or more members of your family based on your finding.

■ For reading activities linked to this chapter, visit <bedfordstmartins.com/ bedguide> and do a keyword search:

reading

Christy De'on Miller
Give Me Five More Minutes

Christy De'on Miller *was born in 1955 and grew up in Texas and New Mexico. After serving in the military and working secretarial jobs, she earned a BA in English from Texas Tech University in 2003. Four months after she graduated, her son, Lance Corporal Aaron C. Austin, was killed in Iraq during his second tour of duty as a marine. Miller is currently working with journalist Steve Ramos on a book about Aaron. The following selection, published on Salon.com in 2006, is Miller's moving account of learning the news that her son was killed. A longer version of the essay first appeared in* Operation Homecoming: Iraq, Afghanistan, and the Home Front, in the Words of U.S. Troops and Their Families *(2006), a compilation of writings that soldiers and their loved ones submitted to a project funded by the National Endowment for the Arts.*

AS YOU READ: *Identify the objects Miller uses to help her recall her son.*

■ For more about Christy De'on Miller, visit <bedfordstmartins.com/ bedguide> and do a keyword search:

author

On April 26, 2004, I woke up around 4:00 in the morning and turned on   1
the television in my bedroom. At least 12 marines had been injured, and by 6:00 A.M., reporters were saying that one had died. I typed Aaron a letter, as I'd been doing daily for several weeks, trying to sound positive. Outside of mentioning that we had one marine down, I avoided the hard news of the day.

It was around 4:00 or 5:00 P.M. when the two marines drove up to my   2
house. The noncommissioned officer began to approach me. It seemed to take an eternity for him to cross my lawn — I think I must have walked some, gone to meet him halfway.

He began, "Ma'am, are you Christy Miller? Can we go inside? We need   3
to talk to you." His wasn't an easy job.

"No, we've got to do this outside." Mine, still the harder.   4

The other marine, the officer, said, "Ma'am, your son was killed in ac-   5
tion today in Al Anbar Province."

I said, "My son was killed in the firefight that's on the television right   6
now. He was killed in Fallujah. There's been one marine killed today."

There, in that moment, the tiniest and longest length of time, there 7
must've been a mechanical failure, an embodiment of someone's (it couldn't
have been mine) heart and brain colliding.

"Mine," I finished. Yes, the marine was mine. 8

My son, Lance Corporal Aaron C. Austin, United States Marine Corps 9
machine gunner, team leader Echo Company, Second Battalion, First Marine
Regiment, First Marine Division was killed in action on April 26, 2004, in
Fallujah, Iraq. He was born on July 1, 1982, at 8:53 P.M. central daylight savings time in Amherst, Texas. Circumcised and sent home on the Fourth of
July, he was my breast-fed, blanket-sucking baby boy, a little Linus° look-
alike. He threw his blanket away when he was ten. God, how I wish for that
blanket now. It surely would carry some scent.

Aaron's company commander, Captain Zembiec, wrote me right after it 10
happened. He wrote,

> Your son was killed in action today. He was conducting a security patrol
> with his company this morning, in enemy territory. His company had
> halted in two buildings, strongpointing them and looking for insurgents. A
> large number of enemy personnel attacked Aaron and his platoon at
> around 1100. Despite intense enemy machine gun and rocket propelled
> grenade fire, your son fought like a lion. He remained in his fighting posi-
> tion until all his wounded comrades could be evacuated from the rooftop
> they were defending. . . . We held a memorial service this afternoon in
> honor of your son. With the exception of the marines on security, every
> man in the company attended the service. Aaron was respected and admired
> by every marine in his company. His death brought tears to my eyes, tears
> that fell in front of my marines. I am unashamed of that fact.

From the men who first told me the news, who had stood outside my 11
home, compassionate marines in dress blues, to those who entered my living room and placed before me the one remaining box of my son's life, and
then, on bent knee, took out a smaller box from within the larger, and
handed over to me Aaron's watch, the one removed from his body at the
time of death — it is to these men that I owe so much.

I began to wear Aaron's watch, which was still on Baghdad time. His 12
watch became my watch. His alarm would go off at 3:28:24. Then again at
3:33:20. Aaron always said, "Give me five more minutes, Mom." This early
alarm, its hidden meaning, meant only for him, for duty on a rooftop possibly,
is 5:30 P.M. (the evening before) my time.

When the battery goes dead on a digital watch — it's gone. Blank. Not 13
even a zero. Aaron's watch stopped somewhere between late afternoon on
the twenty-eighth of November and noon on the thirtieth. Since then, I've
experienced the first Mother's Day without my son, his twenty-second birthday, and the homecoming of his unit. More of the "firsts" will soon be behind me. I don't know if the seconds, thirds, and fourths get any better.

At times I believe I can learn to live a life without my son. After all, I 14
must. There are other mothers who have lost their boys — car accidents, war,

Linus: Character who carries a security blanket in the *Peanuts* comic strip .

illness—who can shop for dinner at the local grocer's without the macaroni-and-cheese boxes suddenly causing them grief. But the memory of him is planted in everything around me. Inside of me. So much of him has been lost, is fading, breaking down. His blanket, his watch, his uniform.

The military uses commercial washers to clean personal items before 15 they are handed over to the families. Understandable, but it leaves a synthetic laundry smell. Aaron's scent is gone. These are the realizations, the moments I've most dreaded. And they come out of nowhere.

I went through several rounds of "looking for him." Articles, pictures, 16 his voice, things like that. He used to chew on the caps of pens, his dog tags, everything, so I saved a few things I found like that. You're not ever preparing for this day, so everything had pretty much been washed, given away, or thrown out when Aaron deployed.° I did find his voice on a couple of tapes, including when he was in the third grade, and he was studying for a spelling test, spelling dinosaur words over and over. Then his voice for a few minutes back in '98, I think, and then, after his first trip to Iraq when a news station interviewed him. Each and every new little discovery is uplifting for a while, it lends hope, and then you remember why you're doing it.

Then one day, I was in a closet, and I looked down and saw a pair of 17 Aaron's house shoes, lizard-striped ones. The shoes brought a smile and tears and when I grabbed them up, and noticed a kind of grimy stain in the bottom, I sniffed, over and over. I cried, of course, but I was still so happy. It was the smell of his feet. No one ever expects that kind of smell to be a gift, but to me, that day, it was. Still, every once in a while, I go and get them out of his room. Now they sit by his bed, close to our two pairs of boots: jungle boots I wore in Panama and his pair, from Iraq.

The days have become different. Sorrow is a tile in the mosaic° and 18 flashes of grief still come. But I believe that time does heal. I think it teaches. The moments pass. I can't say how. It's not of my doing. Sometimes I question. Why has God taken the only child that remained? Left me with no hope for a grandchild? I'm certain there can be no more. No more children.

And yet I have no particular animosity° for my son's killer. He's a name- 19 less and faceless combatant to me. Should I ever have the opportunity to meet him, I hope that I'd forgive him. To me, the buck° stops with the Father. His power stings at times. But He's listened to me; perhaps He's even cried with me. And yes, I do know what I'm talking about here. It's a belief, man. Aaron's words. You either believe in God or you don't. Yes, I'd forgive. I do forgive. There is absolutely nothing I'd do to keep myself from spending eternity with God and Aaron.

The words *forever* and *eternity* mean something to me now. Before, I 20 wouldn't concentrate on their true definition, on their essence. I thought they were for later. Now, I have an aching need to know that forever and

deployed: Traveled with other military personnel to the site of battle.   **mosaic:** A pattern created through the arrangement of small tiles.   **animosity:** Ill-will, hostility. **the buck:** A reference to the saying, "The buck stops here," meaning that responsibility for a problem or situation ultimately rests at this point.

eternity started long before my time—way before Aaron, before the marines came to my home that day.

Questions to Start You Thinking

1. CONSIDERING MEANING: Where in the essay does Miller refer to its title? What is her point in doing so? What other meaning might the essay's title have for Miller?

2. IDENTIFYING WRITING STRATEGIES: Miller uses recall to open her essay with a powerful anecdote (paragraphs 1–8). Why do you think she chose this strategy? How do you respond to this opening, and how effective do you find it?

3. READING CRITICALLY: How would you describe Miller's tone in her essay? How does she avoid bitterness in writing about the circumstances of her son's death?

4. EXPANDING VOCABULARY: In paragraphs 2, 19, and 20, Miller uses the word *eternity*. What does she mean by *eternity*? What subtle differences can you detect in her three uses of the word?

5. MAKING CONNECTIONS: Both Miller and E. B. White in "Once More to the Lake" (pp. 463–68) write about their relationships with their sons, as well as the need to hold on to memories. What similarities can you find in the ideas presented by these two writers? In the tone of their writing? What are some differences? (Consider, in particular, the final paragraph of each essay.)

Journal Prompts

1. Miller seems almost obsessed with recapturing her son's scent. Why do you think smells have the power to call up vivid memories? Write about a time or two when you responded nostalgically to a smell.

2. Respond to the saying, "Children should not die before their parents do." Why do you think it is considered more difficult for a parent to lose a child than for a child to lose a parent?

Suggestions for Writing

1. Recall a time when you lost someone for whom you cared a great deal—perhaps due to death, a breakup, a move, a family change, or some other circumstance. Write an essay in which you describe how you responded to this loss. Like Miller, you might use examples and description to bring your recollections to life. As you draft, consider how your tone could help you convey your feelings through the words you choose.

2. The war in which Miller's son died has sparked considerable controversy. Write an essay exploring your responses to the war in Iraq. If they have changed over time, then detail those changes. Why do you think ending the conflict in Iraq has proved more difficult than originally anticipated? To prepare for this essay, you may want to do some brief research to help you recall the sequence of events leading up to or following the invasion of Iraq.

Amy Tan
Mother Tongue

Amy Tan was born in 1952 in Oakland, California, a few years after her parents immigrated to the United States from China. After receiving a BA in English and linguistics and an MA in linguistics from San Jose State University, Tan worked as a specialist in language development before becoming a freelance business writer in 1981. Tan's first short story (1985) became the basis for her first novel, The Joy Luck Club *(1990), which was a phenomenal best-seller and was made into a movie. Tan's second novel,* The Kitchen God's Wife *(1991), was equally popular. She has also written children's books,* The Moon Lady *(1992) and* The Chinese Siamese Cat *(1994). With her next novels,* The Hundred Secret Senses *(1995) and* The Bonesetter's Daughter *(2001), Tan returned to themes of family relationships, loyalty, and ways of reconciling the past with the present. Most recently she published* The Opposite of Fate *(2003), a book of autobiographical essays, and* Saving Fish from Drowning *(2005), a novel. "Mother Tongue" first appeared in* Threepenny Review *in 1990; in this essay, Tan explores the effect of her mother's "broken" English — the language Tan grew up with — on her life and writing.*

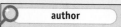

■ For more about
Amy Tan, visit
<bedfordstmartins.com/
bedguide> and do a key-
word search:

    author

AS YOU READ: *Identify the difficulties Tan says exist for a child growing up in a family that speaks nonstandard English.*

I am not a scholar of English or literature. I cannot give you much more 1 than personal opinions on the English language and its variations in this country or others.

I am a writer. And by that definition, I am someone who has always 2 loved language. I am fascinated by language in daily life. I spend a great deal of my time thinking about the power of language — the way it can evoke an emotion, a visual image, a complex idea, or a simple truth. Language is the tool of my trade. And I use them all — all the Englishes I grew up with.

Recently, I was made keenly aware of the different Englishes I do use. I 3 was giving a talk to a large group of people, the same talk I had already given to half a dozen other groups. The nature of the talk was about my writing, my life, and my book, *The Joy Luck Club*. The talk was going along well enough, until I remembered one major difference that made the whole talk sound wrong. My mother was in the room. And it was perhaps the first time she had heard me give a lengthy speech, using the kind of English I have never used with her. I was saying things like, "The intersection of memory upon imagination" and "There is an aspect of my fiction that relates to thus-and-thus" — a speech filled with carefully wrought° grammatical phrases, burdened, it suddenly seemed to me, with nominalized° forms,

wrought: Crafted.   **nominalized:** Made into a noun from a verb.

445

past perfect tenses, conditional phrases, all the forms of Standard English that I had learned in school and through books, the forms of English I did not use at home with my mother.

Just last week, I was walking down the street with my mother, and I again found myself conscious of the English I was using, and the English I do use with her. We were talking about the price of new and used furniture and I heard myself saying this: "Not waste money that way." My husband was with us as well, and he didn't notice any switch in my English. And then I realized why. It's because over the twenty years we've been together I've often used that same kind of English with him, and sometimes he even uses it with me. It has become our language of intimacy, a different sort of English that relates to family talk, the language I grew up with.

So you'll have some idea of what this family talk I heard sounds like, I'll quote what my mother said during a recent conversation which I video-taped and then transcribed.° During this conversation, my mother was talk-ing about a political gangster in Shanghai who had the same last name as her family's, Du, and how the gangster in his early years wanted to be adopted by her family, which was rich by comparison. Later, the gangster became more powerful, far richer than my mother's family, and one day showed up at my mother's wedding to pay his respects. Here's what she said in part:

"Du Yusong having business like fruit stand. Like off the street kind. He is like Du Zong — but not Tsung-ming Island people. The local people call putong, the river east side, he belong to that side local people. That man want to ask Du Zong father take him in like become own family. Du Zong father wasn't look down on him, but didn't take seriously, until that man big like become a mafia. Now important person, very hard to inviting him. Chinese way, came only to show respect, don't stay for dinner. Respect for making big celebration, he shows up. Mean gives lots of respect. Chinese custom. Chinese social life that way. If too important won't have to stay too long. He come to my wedding. I didn't see, I heard it. I gone to boy's side, they have YMCA dinner. Chinese age I was nineteen."

You should know that my mother's expressive command of English be-lies° how much she actually understands. She reads the *Forbes* report, listens to *Wall Street Week*, converses daily with her stockbroker, reads all of Shirley MacLaine's books with ease — all kinds of things I can't begin to under-stand. Yet some of my friends tell me they understand fifty percent of what my mother says. Some say they understand eighty to ninety percent. Some say they understand none of it, as if she were speaking pure Chinese. But to me, my mother's English is perfectly clear, perfectly natural. It's my mother tongue. Her language, as I hear it, is vivid, direct, full of observation and im-agery. That was the language that helped shape the way I saw things, ex-pressed things, made sense of the world.

transcribed: Made a written copy of what was said.   **belies:** Shows to be false.

Lately, I've been giving more thought to the kind of English my mother 8
speaks. Like others, I have described it to people as "broken" or "fractured"
English. But I wince when I say that. It has always bothered me that I can
think of no way to describe it other than "broken," as if it were damaged
and needed to be fixed, as if it lacked a certain wholeness and soundness.
I've heard other terms used, "limited English," for example. But they seem
just as bad, as if everything is limited, including people's perceptions of the
limited English speaker.

I know this for a fact, because when I was growing up, my mother's 9
"limited" English limited *my* perception of her. I was ashamed of her English. I believed that her English reflected the quality of what she had to say.
That is, because she expressed them imperfectly her thoughts were imperfect. And I had plenty of empirical evidence to support me: the fact that
people in department stores, at banks, and at restaurants did not take her
seriously, did not give her good service, pretended not to understand her, or
even acted as if they did not hear her.

My mother has long realized the limitations of her English as well. 10
When I was fifteen, she used to have me call people on the phone to pretend I was she. In this guise, I was forced to ask for information or even to
complain and yell at people who had been rude to her. One time it was a
call to her stockbroker in New York. She had cashed out her small portfolio
and it just so happened we were going to go to New York the next week, our
very first trip outside California. I had to get on the phone and say in an
adolescent voice that was not very convincing, "This is Mrs. Tan."

And my mother was standing in the back whispering loudly, "Why he 11
don't send me check, already two weeks late. So mad he lie to me, losing me
money."

And then I said in perfect English, "Yes, I'm getting rather concerned. 12
You had agreed to send the check two weeks ago, but it hasn't arrived."

Then she began to talk more loudly. "What he want, I come to New 13
York tell him front of his boss, you cheating me?" And I was trying to
calm her down, make her be quiet, while telling the stockbroker, "I can't
tolerate any more excuses. If I don't receive the check immediately, I am
going to have to speak to your manager when I'm in New York next week."
And sure enough, the following week there we were in front of this astonished stockbroker, and I was sitting there red-faced and quiet, and my
mother, the real Mrs. Tan, was shouting at his boss in her impeccable broken English.

We used a similar routine just five days ago, for a situation that was far 14
less humorous. My mother had gone to the hospital for an appointment, to
find out about a benign brain tumor a CAT scan had revealed a month ago.
She said she had spoken very good English, her best English, no mistakes.
Still, she said, the hospital did not apologize when they said they had lost
the CAT scan and she had come for nothing. She said they did not seem to
have any sympathy when she told them she was anxious to know the exact
diagnosis, since her husband and son had both died of brain tumors. She

said they would not give her any more information until the next time and she would have to make another appointment for that. So she said she would not leave until the doctor called her daughter. She wouldn't budge. And when the doctor finally called her daughter, me, who spoke in perfect English—lo and behold—we had assurances the CAT scan would be found, promises that a conference call on Monday would be held, and apologies for any suffering my mother had gone through for a most regrettable mistake.

I think my mother's English almost had an effect on limiting my possi- 15 bilities in life as well. Sociologists and linguists probably will tell you that a person's developing language skills are more influenced by peers. But I think that the language spoken in the family, especially in immigrant families which are more insular, plays a large role in shaping the language of the child. And I believe that it affected my results on achievement tests, IQ tests, and the SAT. While my English skills were never judged as poor, compared to math, English could not be considered my strong suit. In grade school I did moderately well, getting perhaps B's, sometimes B-pluses, in English and scoring perhaps in the sixtieth or seventieth percentile on achievement tests. But those scores were not good enough to override the opinion that my true abilities lay in math and science, because in those areas I achieved A's and scored in the ninetieth percentile or higher.

This was understandable. Math is precise; there is only one correct an- 16 swer. Whereas, for me at least, the answers on English tests were always a judgment call, a matter of opinion and personal experience. Those tests were constructed around items like fill-in-the-blank sentence completion, such as, "Even though Tom was _____ , Mary thought he was _____ ." And the correct answer always seemed to be the most bland combinations of thoughts, for example, "Even though Tom was shy, Mary thought he was charming," with the grammatical structure "even though" limiting the correct answer to some sort of semantic° opposites, so you wouldn't get answers like, "Even though Tom was foolish, Mary thought he was ridiculous." Well, according to my mother, there were very few limitations as to what Tom could have been and what Mary might have thought of him. So I never did well on tests like that.

The same was true with word analogies, pairs of words in which you 17 were supposed to find some sort of logical, semantic relationship—for example, "*Sunset* is to *nightfall* as _____ is to _____ ." And here you would be presented with a list of four possible pairs, one of which showed the same kind of relationship: *red* is to *stoplight, bus* is to *arrival, chills* is to *fever, yawn* is to *boring*. Well, I could never think that way. I knew what the tests were asking, but I could not block out of my mind the images already created by the first pair, "*sunset* is to *nightfall*"—and I would see a burst of colors against a darkening sky, the moon rising, the lowering of a curtain of stars. And all the other pairs of words—*red, bus, stoplight, boring*—just threw up a

semantic: Relating to the meaning of language.

mass of confusing images, making it impossible for me to sort out something as logical as saying: "A sunset precedes nightfall" is the same as "a chill
precedes a fever." The only way I would have gotten that answer right would
have been to imagine an associative situation, for example, my being dis-
obedient and staying out past sunset, catching a chill at night, which turns
into feverish pneumonia as punishment, which indeed did happen to me.

I have been thinking about all this lately, about my mother's English,   18
about achievement tests. Because lately I've been asked, as a writer, why
there are not more Asian Americans enrolled in creative writing programs.
Why do so many Chinese students go into engineering? Well, these are
broad sociological questions I can't begin to answer. But I have noticed in
surveys — in fact, just last week — that Asian students, as a whole, always do
significantly better on math achievement tests than in English. And this
makes me think that there are other Asian American students whose English
spoken in the home might also be described as "broken" or "limited." And
perhaps they also have teachers who are steering them away from writing
and into math and science, which is what happened to me.

Fortunately, I happen to be rebellious in nature and enjoy the challenge   19
of disproving assumptions made about me. I became an English major my
first year in college, after being enrolled as pre-med. I started writing non-
fiction as a freelancer the week after I was told by my former boss that
writing was my worst skill and I should hone my talents toward account
management.

But it wasn't until 1985 that I finally began to write fiction. And at first I   20
wrote using what I thought to be wittily crafted sentences, sentences that
would finally prove I had mastery over the English language. Here's an example from the first draft of a story that later made its way into *The Joy Luck
Club*, but without this line: "That was my mental quandary in its nascent°
state." A terrible line, which I can barely pronounce.

Fortunately, for reasons I won't get into today, I later decided I should   21
envision a reader for the stories I would write. And the reader I decided
upon was my mother, because these were stories about mothers. So with
this reader in mind — and in fact she did read my early drafts — I began to
write stories using all the Englishes I grew up with: the English I spoke to
my mother, which for lack of a better term might be described as "simple";
the English she used with me, which for lack of a better term might be described as "broken"; my translation of her Chinese, which could certainly be
described as "watered down"; and what I imagined to be her translation of
her Chinese if she could speak in perfect English, her internal language, and
for that I sought to preserve the essence, but neither an English nor a Chinese structure. I wanted to capture what language ability tests can never reveal: her intent, her passion, her imagery, the rhythms of her speech, and
the nature of her thoughts.

nascent: Beginning; only partly formed.

Apart from what any critic had to say about my writing, I knew I had   22
succeeded where it counted when my mother finished reading my book and
gave me her verdict: "So easy to read."

Questions to Start You Thinking

1. CONSIDERING MEANING: What are the Englishes that Tan grew up with?
   What other Englishes has she used in her life? What does each English have
   that gives it an advantage over the other Englishes in certain situations?

2. IDENTIFYING WRITING STRATEGIES: What examples does Tan use to analyze
   the various Englishes she uses? How has Tan been able to synthesize her
   Englishes successfully into her present style of writing fiction?

3. READING CRITICALLY: Although Tan explains that she writes using "all the
   Englishes" she has known throughout her life (paragraph 21), she doesn't
   do that in this essay. What are the differences between the English Tan uses
   in this essay and the kinds she says she uses in her fiction? How does the
   language she uses here fit the purpose of her essay?

4. EXPANDING VOCABULARY: In paragraph 9, Tan writes that she had "plenty of
   empirical evidence" that her mother's "limited" English meant that her
   mother's thoughts were "imperfect" as well. Define *empirical*. What does
   Tan's use of this word tell us about her present attitude toward the way she
   judged her mother when she was growing up?

5. MAKING CONNECTIONS: Tan and Richard Rodriguez ("Public and Private
   Language," pp. 571–76) recount learning English as they grew up in homes
   where English was a second language. What similarities do you find in
   their experiences and the obstacles they faced? How did learning English
   affect their self-images? How did it influence their relationships with their
   families?

Journal Prompts

1. Describe one of the Englishes you use to communicate. When do you use it,
   and when do you avoid using it?

2. In what ways are you a "translator," if not of language, then of current
   events and fashions, for your parents or other members of your family?

Suggestions for Writing

1. In a personal essay explain an important event in your family's history,
   using your family's various Englishes or other languages.

2. Take note of and, if possible, transcribe one conversation you have had with
   a parent or other family member, one with a teacher, and one with a close
   friend. Write an essay comparing and contrasting the "languages" of the
   three conversations. How do the languages differ? How do you account for
   these differences? What do you think would happen if someone used
   "teacher language" to talk to a friend or used "friend language" in a class
   discussion or paper?

Anna Quindlen
Evan's Two Moms

Anna Quindlen *was born in 1953 in Philadelphia. After graduating from Barnard College in 1974, she worked briefly as a reporter for the* New York Post *before moving to the* New York Times. *There she wrote the "About New York" column and then two syndicated columns: "Life in the 30s," which drew on her experiences with her family and neighborhood, and until 1994, when she left the* Times, *"Public and Private," which explored political issues. She is currently a contributing editor and columnist for* Newsweek. *Quindlen won the Pulitzer Prize for Commentary in 1992, and many of her columns have been collected in the books* Living Out Loud *(1986),* Thinking Out Loud *(1993), and* Loud and Clear *(2005). Quindlen also has written five novels—* Object Lessons *(1991),* One True Thing *(1994),* Black and Blue *(1998),* Blessings *(2002), and* Rise and Shine *(2007)—as well as the advice books* A Short Guide to a Happy Life *(2000) and* Being Perfect *(2005). In "Evan's Two Moms," written in 1992, Quindlen emphatically argues that gay marriage should be legalized.*

■ For more about Anna Quindlen, visit <bedfordstmartins.com/bedguide> and do a keyword search:

author

AS YOU READ: *Identify the main points Quindlen uses to support her position.*

Evan has two moms. This is no big thing. Evan has always had two moms—in his school file, on his emergency forms, with his friends. "Ooooh, Evan, you're lucky," they sometimes say. "You have two moms." It sounds like a sitcom, but until last week it was emotional truth without legal bulwark.° That was when a judge in New York approved the adoption of a six-year-old boy by his biological mother's lesbian partner. Evan. Evan's mom. Evan's other mom. A kid, a psychologist, a pediatrician. A family.

The matter of Evan's two moms is one in a series of events over the last year that lead to certain conclusions. A Minnesota appeals court granted guardianship of a woman left a quadriplegic in a car accident to her lesbian lover, the culmination of a seven-year battle in which the injured woman's parents did everything possible to negate the partnership between the two. A lawyer in Georgia had her job offer withdrawn after the state attorney general found out that she and her lesbian lover were planning a marriage ceremony; she's brought suit. The computer company Lotus announced that the gay partners of employees would be eligible for the same benefits as spouses.

Add to these public events the private struggles, the couples who go from lawyer to lawyer to approximate legal protections their straight counterparts take for granted, the AIDS survivors who find themselves shut out of their partners' dying days by biological family members and shut out of

bulwark: Strong support.

451

their apartments by leases with a single name on the dotted line, and one solution is obvious.

Gay marriage is a radical notion for straight people and a conservative   4
notion for gay ones. After years of being sledgehammered by society, some gay men and lesbian women are deeply suspicious of participating in an institution that seems to have "straight world" written all over it.

But the rads of twenty years ago, straight and gay alike, have other   5
things on their minds today. Family is one, and the linchpin of family has commonly been a loving commitment between two adults. When same-sex couples set out to make that commitment, they discover that they are at a disadvantage: No joint tax returns. No health insurance coverage for an uninsured partner. No survivor's benefits from Social Security. None of the automatic rights, privileges, and responsibilities society attaches to a marriage contract. In Madison, Wisconsin, a couple who applied at the Y with their kids for a family membership were turned down because both were women. It's one of those small things that can make you feel small.

Some took marriage statutes that refer to "two persons" at their word   6
and applied for a license. The results were court decisions that quoted the Bible and embraced circular argument: marriage is by definition the union of a man and a woman because that is how we've defined it.

No religion should be forced to marry anyone in violation of its tenets,°   7
although ironically it is now only in religious ceremonies that gay people can marry, performed by clergy who find the blessing of two who love each other no sin. But there is no secular° reason that we should take a patchwork approach of corporate, governmental, and legal steps to guarantee what can be done simply, economically, conclusively, and inclusively with the words "I do."

"Fran and I chose to get married for the same reasons that any two   8
people do," said the lawyer who was fired in Georgia. "We fell in love; we wanted to spend our lives together." Pretty simple.

Consider the case of *Loving v. Virginia*, aptly named. At the time, sixteen   9
states had laws that barred interracial marriage, relying on natural law, that amorphous° grab bag for justifying prejudice. Sounding a little like God throwing Adam and Eve out of paradise, the trial judge suspended the one-year sentence of Richard Loving, who was white, and his wife, Mildred, who was black, provided they got out of the State of Virginia.

In 1967 the Supreme Court found such laws to be unconstitutional.   10
Only twenty-five years ago and it was a crime for a black woman to marry a white man. Perhaps twenty-five years from now we will find it just as incredible that two people of the same sex were not entitled to legally commit themselves to each other. Love and commitment are rare enough; it seems absurd to thwart them in any guise.

---

tenets: Principles.   **secular:** Relating to nonreligious matters.   **amorphous:** Having no specific shape.

Questions to Start You Thinking

1. CONSIDERING MEANING: According to Quindlen, what is unjust about not allowing gay men and lesbians to marry *legally*?

2. IDENTIFYING WRITING STRATEGIES: Quindlen ends her essay with a comparison of gay marriage and interracial marriage (paragraphs 9 and 10). How does she use this comparison to support her argument? Do you think it is a valid comparison? Why or why not?

3. READING CRITICALLY: What kinds of appeals does Quindlen use in her essay? How are they appropriate or inappropriate for addressing her opponents' arguments? (See pp. 40–41 for an explanation of kinds of appeals.)

4. EXPANDING VOCABULARY: Define *marriage* as Quindlen would define it. How does her definition of the term differ from the one in the dictionary?

5. MAKING CONNECTIONS: What privileges of the majority culture are gay families and immigrant families (Tan, "Mother Tongue," pp. 445–50) sometimes denied?

Journal Prompts

1. In your opinion, is the dictionary definition of *marriage* inadequate? If so, how do you think it should be revised? If you think the dictionary definition is fine, defend it against attack.

2. Imagine that you have the power to design and create the perfect parents. What would they be like? What criteria would they have to meet to live up to your vision of ideal parents?

Suggestions for Writing

1. Describe the most unconventional family you know. How is this family different from other families? How is it the same?

2. In your opinion, would two parents of the same gender help or hurt a child's development? Write an essay comparing and contrasting the possible benefits and disadvantages of this type of family. Use specific examples—hypothetical or gathered from your own observation or reading—to illustrate your argument.

Anjula Razdan
What's Love Got to Do with It?

Anjula Razdan *was a senior editor of the* Utne Reader, *where she wrote on topics ranging from international politics to pop culture. The daughter of Indian immigrants whose marriage was arranged, Razdan grew up in Illinois and currently works as a freelance writer and editor in Washington, D.C. In this selection, which appeared in the* Utne Reader *in 2003, Razdan asks her readers to consider whether arranging marriages might more effectively create lasting relationships*

■ For more about Anjula Razdan, visit <bedfordstmartins.com/bedguide> and do a keyword search:

author

than choosing mates based on romantic attraction. To explore this question, she draws on her own experiences and observations as well as the testimony of experts.

AS YOU READ: *Look for Razdan's account of both the benefits and the drawbacks of arranged marriages.*

One of the greatest pleasures of my teen years was sitting down with a   1
bag of cinnamon Red Hots and a new LaVyrle Spencer romance, immersing myself in another tale of star-crossed lovers drawn together by the heart's mysterious alchemy.° My mother didn't get it. "Why are you reading that?" she would ask, her voice tinged with both amusement and horror. Everything in her background told her that romance was a waste of time.

Born and raised in Illinois by parents who emigrated from India thirty-   2
five years ago, I am the product of an arranged marriage, and yet I grew up under the spell of Western romantic love — first comes love, *then* comes marriage — which both puzzled and dismayed my parents. Their relationship was set up over tea and samosas° by their grandfathers, and they were already engaged when they went on their first date, a chaperoned trip to the movies. My mom and dad still barely knew each other on their wedding day — and they certainly hadn't fallen in love. Yet both were confident that their shared values, beliefs, and family background would form a strong bond that, over time, would develop into love.

"But, what could they possibly know of *real love*?" I would ask myself   3
petulantly° after each standoff with my parents over whether or not I could date in high school (I couldn't) and whether I would allow them to arrange my marriage (I wouldn't). The very idea of an arranged marriage offended my ideas of both love and liberty — to me, the act of choosing whom to love represented the very essence of freedom. To take away that choice seemed like an attack not just on my autonomy as a person, but on democracy itself.

And, yet, even in the supposedly liberated West, the notion of choosing   4
your mate is a relatively recent one. Until the nineteenth century, writes historian E. J. Graff in *What Is Marriage For? The Strange Social History of Our Most Intimate Institution* (Boston: Beacon Press, 1999), arranged marriages were quite common in Europe as a way of forging alliances, ensuring inheritances, and stitching together the social, political, and religious needs of a community. Love had nothing to do with it.

Fast forward a couple hundred years to twenty-first-century America,   5
and you see a modern, progressive society where people are free to choose their mates, for the most part, based on love instead of social or economic gain. But for many people, a quiet voice from within wonders: Are we really better off? Who hasn't at some point in their life — at the end of an ill-fated

---

alchemy: A medieval predecessor of chemistry that aimed to turn base metals into gold.   **samosas:** Small, fried Indian pastries filled with seasoned vegetables or meat.   **petulantly:** Irritably.

relationship or midway through dinner with the third "date-from-hell" this month — longed for a matchmaker to find the right partner? No hassles. No effort. No personal ads or blind dates.

The point of the Western romantic ideal is to live "happily ever after," 6 yet nearly half of all marriages in this country end in divorce, and the number of never-married adults grows each year. Boundless choice notwithstanding, what does it mean when the marital success rate is the statistical equivalent of a coin toss?

"People don't really know how to choose a long-term partner," offers 7 Dr. Alvin Cooper, the director of the San Jose Marital Services and Sexuality Centre and a staff psychologist at Stanford University. "The major reasons that people find and get involved with somebody else are proximity and physical attraction. And both of these factors are terrible predictors of long-term happiness in a relationship."

At the moment we pick a mate, Cooper says, we are often blinded by 8 passion and therefore virtually incapable of making a sound decision.

Psychology Today editor Robert Epstein agrees. "[It's] like getting drunk 9 and marrying someone in Las Vegas," he quips. A former director of the Cambridge Center for Behavioral Studies, Epstein holds a decidedly unromantic view of courtship and love. Indeed, he argues it is our myths of "love at first sight" and "a knight in a shining Porsche" that get so many of us into trouble. When the heat of passion wears off — and it always does, he says — you can be left with virtually nothing "except lawyer's bills."

Epstein points out that many arranged marriages result in an enduring 10 love because they promote compatibility and rational deliberation ahead of passionate impulse. Epstein himself is undertaking a bold step to prove his theory that love can be learned. He wrote an editorial in *Psychology Today* last year seeking women to participate in the experiment with him. He proposed to choose one of the "applicants," and together they would attempt to fall in love — consciously and deliberately. After receiving more than 1,000 responses, none of which seemed right, Epstein yielded just a little to impulse, asking Gabriela, an intriguing Venezuelan woman he met on a plane, to join him in the project. After an understandable bout of cold feet, she eventually agreed.

In a "love contract" the two signed on Valentine's Day this year to seal 11 the deal, Epstein stipulates that he and Gabriela must undergo intensive counseling to learn how to communicate effectively and participate in a variety of exercises designed to foster mutual love. To help oversee and guide the project, Epstein has even formed an advisory board made up of high-profile relationship experts, most notably Dr. John Gray, who wrote the best-selling *Men Are from Mars, Women Are from Venus.* If the experiment pans out, the two will have learned to love each other within a year's time.

It may strike some as anathema° to be so premeditated about the 12 process of falling in love, but to hear Epstein tell it, most unions fail exactly

anathema: An abomination; blasphemy.

because they aren't intentional enough; they're based on a roll of the dice and a determination to stake everything on love. What this means, Epstein says, is that most people lack basic relationship skills, and, as a result, most relationships lack emotional and psychological intimacy.

A divorced father of four, Epstein himself married for passion — "just 13 like I was told to do by the fairy tales and by the movies" — but eventually came to regret it. "I had the experience that so many people have now," he says, "which is basically looking at your partner and going, 'Who are you?' " Although Epstein acknowledges the non-Western tradition of arranged marriage is a complex, somewhat flawed institution, he thinks we can "distill key elements of [it] to help us learn how to create a new, more stable institution in the West."

Judging from the phenomenon of reality-TV shows like *Married by* 14 *America* and *Meet My Folks* and the recent increase in the number of professional matchmakers, the idea of arranging marriages (even if in nontraditional ways) seems to be taking hold in this country — perhaps nowhere more powerfully than in cyberspace. Online dating services attracted some twenty million people last year (roughly one-fifth of all singles — and growing), who used sites like Match.com and Yahoo Personals to hook up with potentially compatible partners. Web sites' search engines play the role of patriarchal grandfathers, searching for good matches based on any number of criteria that you select.

Cooper, the Stanford psychologist and author of *Sex and the Internet: A* 15 *Guidebook for Clinicians* (Brunner-Routledge, 2002) — and an expert in the field of online sexuality — says that because online interaction tends to downplay proximity, physical attraction, and face-to-face interaction, people are more likely to take risks and disclose significant things about themselves. The result is that they attain a higher level of psychological and emotional intimacy than if they dated right away or hopped in the sack. Indeed, online dating represents a return to what University of Chicago Humanities Professor Amy Kass calls the "distanced nearness" of old-style courtship, an intimate and protected (cyber)space that encourages self-revelation while maintaining personal boundaries.

And whether looking for a fellow scientist, someone else who's HIV- 16 positive, or a B-movie film buff, an online dater has a much higher likelihood of finding "the one" due to the computer's capacity to sort through thousands of potential mates. "That's what computers are all about — efficiency and sorting," says Cooper, who believes that online dating has the potential to lower the nation's 50 percent divorce rate. There is no magic or "chemistry" involved in love, Cooper insists. "It's specific, operationalizable factors."

Love's mystery solved by "operationalizable factors"! Why does that 17 sound a little less than inspiring? Sure, for many people the Internet can efficiently facilitate love and help to nudge fate along. But, for the diehard romantic who trusts in surprise, coincidence, and fate, the cyber-solution to love lacks heart. "To the romantic," observes English writer Blake Morrison in *The Guardian*, "every marriage is an arranged marriage — arranged by fate, that is, which gives us no choice."

More than a century ago, Emily Dickinson mocked those who would 18 dissect birds to find the mechanics of song:

> *Split the Lark — and you'll find the Music*
> *Bulb after Bulb, in Silver rolled —*
> *Scantily dealt to the Summer Morning*
> *Saved for your Ear when Lutes be old.*
>
> *Loose the Flood — you shall find it patent —*
> *Gush after Gush, reserved for you —*
> *Scarlet Experiment! Skeptic Thomas!*
> *Now, do you doubt that your Bird was true?*

In other words, writes Deborah Blum in her book, *Sex on the Brain* (Pen- 19 guin, 1997), "kill the bird and [you] silence the melody." For some, nurturing the ideal of romantic love may be more important than the goal of love itself. Making a more conscious choice in mating may help partners handle the complex personal ties and obligations of marriage; but romantic love, infused as it is with myth and projection and doomed passion, is a way to live *outside* of life's obligations, outside of time itself — if only for a brief, bright moment. Choosing love by rational means might not be worth it for those souls who'd rather roll the dice and risk the possibility of ending up with nothing but tragic nobility and the bittersweet tang of regret.

In the end, who really wants to examine love too closely? I'd rather curl 20 up with a LaVyrle Spencer novel or dream up the French movie version of my life than live in a world where the mechanics of love — and its giddy, mysterious buzz — are laid bare. After all, to actually unravel love's mystery is, perhaps, to miss the point of it all.

Questions to Start You Thinking

1. CONSIDERING MEANING: According to the experts whom Razdan quotes, why is cyberspace an ideal venue for facilitating relationships?

2. IDENTIFYING WRITING STRATEGIES: How does Razdan use cause and effect to explain the high divorce rate in the United States?

3. READING CRITICALLY: What type of evidence does Razdan use to explore whether arranged marriages are more successful than relationships based on romantic attraction? Do you think the evidence is relevant, credible, and sufficient? Why, or why not? What other type of evidence might she have used?

4. EXPANDING VOCABULARY: In commenting on her parents' arranged marriage, Razdan asks in paragraph 3, "But, what could they possibly know of *real love*?" How do you define *real love*? Do you think that Razdan would agree with your definition?

5. MAKING CONNECTIONS: The statement that "nearly half of all marriages in this country end in divorce" (paragraph 6) applies to Noel Perrin's marriage ("A Part-Time Marriage," pp. 494–96). Given his experiences, how do you think he would respond to Razdan's essay? Would he be in favor of arranged marriages?

Journal Prompts

1. Write a brief personal ad for a mate, using the writing style associated with personals. Keep in mind that the words you choose and the way you organize your ad reveal something about your personality.

2. One of the experts whom Razdan quotes mentions the myth of "love at first sight" (paragraph 9). Write about a time when you fell in love at first sight or present your opinion on whether such a thing exists.

Suggestions for Writing

1. Write an essay that uses your personal experiences and observations to develop a specific idea presented in Razdan's essay. For example, you might recall your own "date-from-hell" (paragraph 5), a friend's experience with an online dating service, or a matchmaker friend's success rate. Based on your experiences and observations, you might write about current dating practices or about "relationship skills" needed for a successful marriage.

2. Drawing examples from this reading and your own observations, write an essay arguing for or against arranged marriages. You might also do some research to find additional support for your argument.

Danzy Senna
The Color of Love

■ For more about Danzy Senna, visit <bedfordstmartins.com/ bedguide> and do a keyword search:

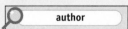

Danzy Senna, *born in 1970 in Boston, earned her BA at Stanford University and her MFA from the University of California, Irvine. Senna's essays and short stories have been widely anthologized, and her journalistic writing has appeared in such publications as the* Nation, *the* Utne Reader, *and* Newsweek. *Her best-selling novel* Caucasia *(1988) won several awards, and in 2002 she received a prestigious Whiting Award, given each year to ten writers of exceptional ability and promise. Her most recent book is the psychological thriller* Symptomatic *(2004). Senna recently moved from Massachusetts to Los Angeles and is currently working on a screenplay and on a nonfiction book about her father's life. In "The Color of Love," Senna, the daughter of a white mother and a black father, explores the complexities — racial and otherwise — of her relationship with her grandmother. The essay originally appeared in* O: The Oprah Magazine *in 2000.*

AS YOU READ: *Consider how her grandmother displays both love for Senna and prejudice toward her. How does Senna respond?*

W e had this much in common: We were both women, and we were 1
    both writers. But we were as different as two people can be and still
exist in the same family. She was ancient — as white and dusty as chalk —
and spent her days seated in a velvet armchair, passing judgments on the
world below. She still believed in noble bloodlines; my blood had been
mixed at conception. I believed there was no such thing as nobility or class
or lineage, only systems designed to keep some people up in the big house
and others outside, in the cold.

    She was my grandmother. She was Irish but from that country's Protes- 2
tant elite, which meant she seemed more British than anything. She was an
actress, a writer of plays and novels, and still unmarried in her thirties when
she came to America to visit. One night while in Boston, she went to a dinner party, where she was seated next to a young lawyer with blood as blue as
the ocean. Her pearl earring fell in his oyster soup — or so the story goes —
and they fell in love. My grandmother married that lawyer and left her native Ireland for New England.

    How she came to have black grandchildren is a story of opposites. It 3
was 1968 in Boston when her daughter — my mother — a small, blonde
Wasp° poet, married my father, a tall and handsome black intellectual, in
an act that was as rebellious as it was hopeful. The products of that unlikely
union — my older sister, my younger brother, and I — grew up in urban
chaos, in a home filled with artists and political activists. The old lady across
the river in Cambridge seemed to me an endangered species. Her walls were
covered with portraits of my ancestors, the pale and dead men who had
conquered Africa and built Boston long before my time. When I visited,
their eyes followed me from room to room with what I imagined to be an
expression of scorn. Among the portraits sat my grandmother, a bird who
had flown in to remind us all that there had indeed been a time when lineage and caste° meant something. To me, young and dark and full of energy,
she was the missing link between the living and the dead.

    But her blood flowed through me, whether I liked it or not. I grew up to 4
be a writer, just like her. And as I struggled to tell my own stories — about
race and class and post–civil rights America — I wondered who my grandmother had been before, in Dublin, when she was friend and confidante to
literary giants such as William Butler Yeats and Samuel Beckett. Once, while
snooping in her bedroom, I discovered her novels, the ones that had been
published in Ireland when she was my age. I stared at her photograph on
the jacket and wondered about the young woman who wore a mischievous
smile. Had she ever worried about becoming so powerful that no man would
want her? Did she now feel that she had sacrificed her career and wild Irish-
woman dreams to become a wife and mother and proper Bostonian?

    I longed to know her — to love her. But the differences between us were 5
real and alive, and they threatened to squelch our fragile connection. She

---

Wasp: An acronym (for White Anglo-Saxon Protestant) referring to a member of the
prevailing American social class.   **caste:** Class or social group.

was an alcoholic. In the evening, after a few glasses of gin, she could turn vicious. Though she held antiquated racist views, my grandmother would still have preferred to see my mother married and was saddened when my parents split in the seventies. She believed that a woman without a man was pitiable. The first question she always asked me when she saw me: "Do you have a man?" The second question: "What is he?" That was her way of finding out his race and background. She looked visibly pleased if he was a Wasp, neutral if he was Jewish, and disappointed if he was black.

My mother ignored her hurtful comments but felt them just the same.   6
She spent her visits to my grandmother's house slamming dishes in the kitchen, hissing her anger just out of hearing range, then raving, on the drive home, about what awful thing her mother had said this time. Like my mother, I knew the rule: I was not to disrespect elders. She was old and gray and would soon be gone. But I had inherited my grandmother's short temper. When I got angry, even as a child, I felt as if blood were rushing around in my head, red waves battering the shore. Words spilled from my mouth — cutting, vicious words that I regretted.

One autumn day in Cambridge, at my grandmother's place, I lost my   7
temper. I was home from college for the holidays, staying in her guest room. I woke from a nap to the sound of her enraged voice shouting at what I could only imagine was the television.

"Idiot! You damn fool!" she bellowed. "You stupid, stupid woman!" It   8
has to be *Jeopardy!*, I thought. She must be yelling at those tiny contestants on the screen. She knows the answers to those questions better than they do. But when the shouting went on for a beat too long, I went to the top of the stairs and looked down into the living room. She was speaking to a real person: her cleaning lady, a Greek woman named Mary, who was on her hands and knees, nervously gathering the shards of a broken vase. My grandmother stood over her, hands on hips, cursing.

"You fool," my grandmother repeated. "How in bloody hell could you   9
have done something so stupid?"

"Grandma." I didn't shout her name but said it loudly enough that she,   10
though hard of hearing, glanced up.

"Oh, darling!" she piped, suddenly cheerful. "Would you like a cup of   11
tea? You must be dreadfully tired."

Mary was on her feet again. She smiled nervously at me, then rushed   12
into the kitchen with the pieces of the broken vase.

I told myself to be a good girl, to be polite. But something snapped. I   13
marched down the stairs, and even she noticed something on my face that made her sit in her velvet chair.

"Don't you ever talk to her that way," I shouted. "Where do you think   14
you are? Slavery was abolished long ago."

I stood over her, tall and long-limbed, daring her to speak. My grand-   15
mother shook her head. "It's about race, isn't it?"

"Race?" I said, baffled. "Mary's white. This is about respect — treating   16
other human beings with respect."

She wasn't hearing me. All she saw was color. "The tragedy about you," 17
she said soberly, "is that you are mixed." I felt those waves in my head:
"Your tragedy is that you're old and ignorant," I spat. "You don't know the
first thing about me."

She cried into her hands. She seemed diminished, a little old woman. 18
She looked up only to say, "You are a cruel girl."

I left her apartment trembling yet feeling exhilarated by what I had 19
done. But my elation soon turned to shame. I had taken on an old lady. And
for what? Her intolerance was, at her age, deeply entrenched. My rebuttals
couldn't change her.

Yet that fight marked the beginning of our relationship. I've since de- 20
cided that when you cease to express anger toward those who have hurt you,
you are essentially giving up on them. They are dead to you. But when you
express anger, it is a sign that they still matter, that they are worth the fight.

After that argument, my grandmother and I began a conversation. She 21
seemed to see me clearly for the first time, or perhaps she, a "cruel girl" herself, had simply met her match. And I no longer felt she was a relic. She was
a living, breathing human being who deserved to be spoken to as an equal.

I began visiting her more. I would drive to Cambridge and sit with 22
her, eating mixed nuts and sipping ginger ale, regaling° her with tales of my
latest love drama or writing project. In her presence, I was proudly black and
young and political, and she was who she was: subtly racist, terribly elitist,
and awfully funny. She still said things that angered me: She bemoaned my
mother's marriage to my father, she said that I should marry not for love but
for money, and she told me that I needn't identify as black, since I didn't
look it. I snapped back at her. But she, with senility creeping in, didn't seem
to hear me; each time I came, she said the same things.

Last summer I went into hiding to work on my second novel at a writ- 23
ers' retreat in New Hampshire. The place was a kind of paradise for creative
souls, a hideaway where every writer had his or her own cabin in the woods
with no phone or television—no distractions to speak of. But I was miser-
able. I could not write. Even the flies outside my window seemed to whisper,
"Go out and play. Forget the novel. Leave it till tomorrow."

I woke one morning at four, the light outside my window still blue. I 24
felt panic and sadness, though I didn't know why. I got up, dressed, and
went outside for a walk through the forest. But the panic persisted, and I
began to cry. I assumed that my writer's block had seized me suddenly.

That night I ate dinner in the main house and received a call on the pay 25
phone from my mother. She told me my grandmother had fallen and broken her leg. But that wasn't all; she had subsequently suffered a heart attack.
Her other organs were failing. I had to hurry if I wanted to say good-bye.

I drove to Boston that night, not believing that we could be losing her. 26
She would make it. I was certain. Sure, she was ninety-two, frail, unable to
walk steadily. But she was lucid,° and her tongue was as sharp as ever.

---

regaling: Entertaining.   **lucid:** Mentally sound.

Somehow I had imagined her as indestructible, made immortal by power and cruelty and wit.

The woman I found in the hospital bed was barely recognizable. My 27 grandmother had always been fussy about her appearance. She never showed her face without makeup. Even in the day, when it was just she and the cleaning lady, she dressed as if she were ready for a cocktail party. At night she usually had cocktail parties; doddering° old men hovered around her, sipping Scotch and bantering about theater and politics.

My grandmother's face had swollen to twice its normal size, and tubes 28 came out of her nose. She had struggled so hard to pull them out that the nurses had tied her wrists to the bed rails. Her hair was gray and thin. Her body was withered and bruised, barely covered by the green hospital gown.

Her hazel eyes were all that was still recognizable, but the expression in 29 them was different from any I had ever seen on her—terror. She was terrified to die. She tried to rise when she saw me, and her eyes pleaded with me to help her, to save her, to get her out of this mess. I stood over her, and I felt only one thing: overwhelming love. Not a trace of anger. That dark gray rage I'd felt toward her was gone as I stroked her forehead and told her she would be okay, even knowing she would not.

For two days, my mother, her sisters, and I stood beside my grand- 30 mother, singing Irish ballads and reading passages to her from the works of her favorite novelist, James Joyce. For the first time, she could not talk. At one point, she gestured wildly for pen and paper. I brought her the pen and the paper and held them up for her, but she was too weak for even that. What came out was only a faint, incomprehensible line.

In death we are each reduced to our essence: the spirit we are when we 31 are born. The trappings we hold on to our whole lives—our race, our money, our sex, our age, our politics—become irrelevant. My grandmother became a child in that hospital bed, a spirit about to embark on an un- known journey, terrified and alone, no matter how many of us were crowded around her. In the final hours, even her skin seemed to lose its wrinkles and take on a waxy glow. Then, finally, the machines around us went silent as she left us behind to squabble in the purgatory of the flesh.

Questions to Start You Thinking

1. CONSIDERING MEANING: What are the similarities and differences between Senna and her grandmother? How do the differences result in conflict?

2. IDENTIFYING WRITING STRATEGIES: Identify some ways Senna makes her grand- mother come alive for readers. Where is her description vivid enough for you to see her as Senna does? Which details are particularly effective? Why?

3. READING CRITICALLY: How would you describe the tone of the essay? Sup- port your opinion with specific passages.

doddering: Feeble.

4. EXPANDING VOCABULARY: In describing her grandmother, Senna explains, "I had imagined her as indestructible, made immortal by power and cruelty and wit" (paragraph 26). In your own words, define *immortal*. How can "power and cruelty and wit" make someone immortal?

5. MAKING CONNECTIONS: In "Evan's Two Moms" (pp. 451–52), Anna Quindlen makes a comparison between gay marriage and interracial marriage. How is Senna's situation both similar to and different from that of a child of same-sex parents? What advice might Senna give about the prejudice that such a child might encounter?

Journal Prompts

1. Recall a time when you or someone you know was verbally abused. How did you respond?

2. At the end of her life, Senna's grandmother "gestured wildly for pen and paper" (paragraph 30), but she was unable to write. If she had been able to write a sentence or two, what might she have written to Senna?

Suggestions for Writing

1. Senna notes that "when you cease to express anger toward those who have hurt you, you are essentially giving up on them" (paragraph 20). Write an essay about a time when expressing anger had a positive effect on a relationship. Be sure to recall the events leading up to the confrontation as well as the resolution to the problem.

2. Senna suggests that her grandmother's prejudice is a result of age and ignorance. What other factors might contribute to an individual's prejudices? Write an essay presenting your views about how prejudice develops and what can be done to prevent it.

E. B. White
Once More to the Lake

E. B. (Elwyn Brooks) White *(1899–1985) was born in Mount Vernon, New York. After serving in the army, he graduated from Cornell University and moved to Seattle to work as a reporter. His career led him back to the East Coast, where he joined the staff of the recently established* New Yorker *magazine in 1927. For half a century, his satires, poems, and essays helped define that magazine's distinctive style of elegant wit and social comment. He moved to Maine in 1933, and his widely read books for children,* Stuart Little *(1945),* Charlotte's Web *(1952), and* The Trumpet of the Swan *(1970), draw on his familiarity with the country to celebrate life's blend of sadness, happiness, love, and loss. In the following essay, first published in* Harper's *magazine in 1941, White reflects on the experience of returning with his son to a favorite scene from his own childhood. In the paired selection*

■ For more about E. B. White, visit <bedfordstmartins.com/ bedguide> and do a keyword search:

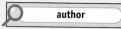
author

that follows (pp. 470–72), Nancy Gibbs offers a different view of summer vacations, proposing that parents relax summer rules and schedules so their children can enjoy memorable experiences like the one that White describes.

AS YOU READ: *Notice what, according to White, changes a person's perspective from childhood to adulthood.*

August 1941

One summer, along about 1904, my father rented a camp on a lake in 1 Maine and took us all there for the month of August. We all got ringworm from some kittens and had to rub Pond's Extract on our arms and legs night and morning, and my father rolled over in a canoe with all his clothes on; but outside of that the vacation was a success and from then on none of us ever thought there was any place in the world like that lake in Maine. We returned summer after summer — always on August 1 for one month. I have since become a salt-water man, but sometimes in summer there are days when the restlessness of the tides and the fearful cold of the sea water and the incessant wind that blows across the afternoon and into the evening make me wish for the placidity of a lake in the woods. A few weeks ago this feeling got so strong I bought myself a couple of bass hooks and a spinner and returned to the lake where we used to go, for a week's fishing and to revisit old haunts.

I took along my son, who had never had any fresh water up his nose and 2 who had seen lily pads only from train windows. On the journey over to the lake I began to wonder what it would be like. I wondered how time would have marred this unique, this holy spot — the coves and streams, the hills that the sun set behind, the camps and the paths behind the camps. I was sure that the tarred road would have found it out, and I wondered in what other ways it would be desolated. It is strange how much you can remember about places like that once you allow your mind to return into the grooves that lead back. You remember one thing, and that suddenly reminds you of another thing. I guess I remembered clearest of all the early mornings, when the lake was cool and motionless, remembered how the bedroom smelled of the lumber it was made of and of the wet woods whose scent entered through the screen. The partitions in the camp were thin and did not extend clear to the top of the rooms, and as I was always the first up I would dress softly so as not to wake the others, and sneak out into the sweet outdoors and start out in the canoe, keeping close along the shore in the long shadows of the pines. I remembered being very careful never to rub my paddle against the gunwale° for fear of disturbing the stillness of the cathedral.

The lake had never been what you would call a wild lake. There were 3 cottages sprinkled around the shores, and it was in farming country al-

gunwale: Upper edge of the side of a boat.

though the shores of the lake were quite heavily wooded. Some of the cottages were owned by nearby farmers, and you would live at the shore and eat your meals at the farmhouse. That's what our family did. But although it wasn't wild, it was a fairly large and undisturbed lake and there were places in it that, to a child at least, seemed infinitely remote and primeval.

I was right about the tar: it led to within half a mile of the shore. But when I got back there, with my boy, and we settled into a camp near a farmhouse and into the kind of summertime I had known, I could tell that it was going to be pretty much the same as it had been before — I knew it, lying in bed the first morning smelling the bedroom and hearing the boy sneak quietly out and go off along the shore in a boat. I began to sustain the illusion that he was I, and therefore, by simple transposition, that I was my father. This sensation persisted, kept cropping up all the time we were there. It was not an entirely new feeling, but in this setting it grew much stronger. I seemed to be living a dual existence. I would be in the middle of some simple act, I would be picking up a bait box or laying down a table fork, or I would be saying something and suddenly it would be not I but my father who was saying the words or making the gesture. It gave me a creepy sensation.

We went fishing the first morning. I felt the same damp moss covering the worms in the bait can, and saw the dragonfly alight on the tip of my rod as it hovered a few inches from the surface of the water. It was the arrival of this fly that convinced me beyond any doubt that everything was as it always had been, that the years were a mirage, and that there had been no years. The small waves were the same, chucking the rowboat under the chin as we fished at anchor, and the boat was the same boat, the same color green and the ribs broken in the same places, and under the floorboards the same fresh water leavings and debris — the dead hellgrammite, the wisps of moss, the rusty discarded fishhook, the dried blood from yesterday's catch. We stared silently at the tips of our rods, at the dragonflies that came and went. I lowered the tip of mine into the water, tentatively, pensively dislodging the fly, which darted two feet away, poised, darted two feet back, and came to rest again a little farther up the rod. There had been no years between the ducking of this dragonfly and the other one — the one that was part of memory. I looked at the boy, who was silently watching his fly, and it was my hands that held his rod, my eyes watching. I felt dizzy and didn't know which rod I was at the end of.

We caught two bass, hauling them in briskly as though they were mackerel, pulling them over the side of the boat in a businesslike manner without any landing net, and stunning them with a blow on the back of the head. When we got back for a swim before lunch, the lake was exactly where we had left it, the same number of inches from the dock, and there was only the merest suggestion of a breeze. This seemed an utterly enchanted sea, this lake you could leave to its own devices for a few hours and come back to, and find that it had not stirred, this constant and trustworthy body of water. In the shallows, the dark, water-soaked sticks and twigs, smooth and old, were undulating in clusters on the bottom against the clean ribbed sand,

and the track of the mussel was plain. A school of minnows swam by, each minnow with its small individual shadow, doubling the attendance, so clear and sharp in the sunlight. Some of the other campers were in swimming, along the shore, one of them with a cake of soap, and the water felt thin and clear and unsubstantial. Over the years there had been this person with the cake of soap, this cultist, and here he was. There had been no years.

Up to the farmhouse to dinner through the teeming dusty field, the road under our sneakers was only a two-track road. The middle track was missing, the one with the marks of the hooves and the splotches of dried, flaky manure. There had always been three tracks to choose from in choosing which track to walk in; now the choice was narrowed down to two. For a moment I missed terribly the middle alternative. But the way led past the tennis court, and something about the way it lay there in the sun reassured me; the tape had loosened along the backline, the alleys were green with plantains° and other weeds, and the net (installed in June and removed in September) sagged in the dry noon, and the whole place steamed with midday heat and hunger and emptiness. There was a choice of pie for dessert, and one was blueberry and one was apple, and the waitresses were the same country girls, there having been no passage of time, only the illusion of it as in a dropped curtain — the waitresses were still fifteen; their hair had been washed, that was the only difference — they had been to the movies and seen the pretty girls with the clean hair.

Summertime, oh, summertime, pattern of life indelible° with fade-proof lake, the wood unshatterable, the pasture with the sweetfern and the juniper forever and ever, summer without end; this was the background, and the life along the shore was the design, the cottages with their innocent and tranquil design, their tiny docks with the flagpole and the American flag floating against the white clouds in the blue sky, the little paths over the roots of the trees leading from camp to camp and the paths leading back to the outhouses and the can of lime for sprinkling, and at the souvenir counters at the store the miniature birchbark canoes and the postcards that showed things looking a little better than they looked. This was the American family at play, escaping the city heat, wondering whether the newcomers in the camp at the head of the cove were "common" or "nice," wondering whether it was true that the people who drove up for Sunday dinner at the farmhouse were turned away because there wasn't enough chicken.

It seemed to me, as I kept remembering all this, that those times and those summers had been infinitely precious and worth saving. There had been jollity and peace and goodness. The arriving (at the beginning of August) had been so big a business in itself, at the railway station the farm wagon drawn up, the first smell of the pine-laden air, the first glimpse of the smiling farmer, and the great importance of the trunks and your father's enormous authority in such matters, and the feel of the wagon under you for the long ten-mile haul, and at the top of the last long hill catching the

---

plantains: Common wild plants.   **indelible:** Unable to be removed.

first view of the lake after eleven months of not seeing this cherished body of water. The shouts and cries of the other campers when they saw you, and the trunks to be unpacked, to give up their rich burden. (Arriving was less exciting nowadays, when you sneaked up in your car and parked it under a tree near the camp and took out the bags and in five minutes it was all over, no fuss, no loud wonderful fuss about trunks.)

Peace and goodness and jollity. The only thing that was wrong now, really, was the sound of the place, an unfamiliar nervous sound of the outboard motors. This was the note that jarred, the one thing that would sometimes break the illusion and set the years moving. In those other summertimes all motors were inboard; and when they were at a little distance, the noise they made was a sedative, an ingredient of summer sleep. They were one-cylinder and two-cylinder engines, and some were make-and-break and some were jump-spark, but they all made a sleepy sound across the lake. The one-lungers throbbed and fluttered, and the twin-cylinder ones purred and purred, and that was a quiet sound, too. But now the campers all had outboards. In the daytime, in the hot mornings, these motors made a petulant, irritable sound; at night in the still evening when the afterglow lit the water, they whined about one's ears like mosquitoes. My boy loved our rented outboard, and his great desire was to achieve single-handed mastery over it, and authority, and he soon learned the trick of choking it a little (but not too much), and the adjustment of the needle valve. Watching him I would remember the things you could do with the old one-cylinder engine with the heavy flywheel,° how you could have it eating out of your hand if you got really close to it spiritually. Motorboats in those days didn't have clutches, and you would make a landing by shutting off the motor at the proper time and coasting in with a dead rudder. But there was a way of reversing them, if you learned the trick, by cutting the switch and putting it on again exactly on the final dying revolution of the flywheel, so that it would kick back against compression and begin reversing. Approaching a dock in a strong following breeze, it was difficult to slow up sufficiently by the ordinary coasting method, and if a boy felt he had complete mastery over his motor, he was tempted to keep it running beyond its time and then reverse it a few feet from the dock. It took a cool nerve, because if you threw the switch a twentieth of a second too soon you would catch the flywheel when it still had speed enough to go up past center, and the boat would leap ahead, charging bull-fashion at the dock.

We had a good week at the camp. The bass were biting well and the sun shone endlessly, day after day. We would be tired at night and lie down in the accumulated heat of the little bedrooms after the long hot day and the breeze would stir almost imperceptibly outside and the smell of the swamp drift in through the rusty screens. Sleep would come easily and in the morning the red squirrel would be on the roof, tapping out his gay routine. I kept remembering everything, lying in bed in the mornings—the

flywheel: A heavy wheel revolving on a shaft to regulate machinery.

small steamboat that had a long rounded stern like the lip of a Ubangi,° and how quietly she ran on the moonlight sails, when the older boys played their mandolins° and the girls sang and we ate doughnuts dipped in sugar, and how sweet the music was on the water in the shining night, and what it had felt like to think about girls then. After breakfast we would go up to the store and the things were in the same place — the minnows in a bottle, the plugs and spinners disarranged and pawed over by the youngsters from the boys' camp, the Fig Newtons and the Beeman's gum. Outside, the road was tarred and cars stood in front of the store. Inside, all was just as it had always been, except there was more Coca-Cola and not so much Moxie and root beer and birch beer and sarsaparilla. We would walk out with the bottle of pop apiece and sometimes the pop would backfire up our noses and hurt. We explored the streams, quietly, where the turtles slid off the sunny logs and dug their way into the soft bottom; and we lay on the town wharf and fed worms to the tame bass. Everywhere we went I had trouble making out which was I, the one walking at my side, the one walking in my pants.

One afternoon while we were at that lake a thunderstorm came up. It was the revival of an old melodrama that I had seen long ago with childish awe. The second-act climax of the drama of the electrical disturbance over a lake in America had not changed in any important respect. This was the big scene. The whole thing was so familiar, the first feeling of oppression and heat and a general air around camp of not wanting to go very far away. In midafternoon (it was all the same) a curious darkening of the sky, and a lull in everything that had made life tick; and then the way the boats suddenly swung the other way at their moorings with the coming of a breeze out of the new quarter, and the premonitory° rumble. Then the kettle drum, then the snare, then the bass drum and cymbals, then crackling light against the dark, and the gods grinning and licking their chops in the hills. Afterward the calm, the rain steadily rustling in the calm lake, the return of light and hope and spirits, and the campers running out in joy and relief to go swimming in the rain, their bright cries perpetuating the deathless joke about how they were getting simply drenched, and the children screaming with delight at the new sensation of bathing in the rain, and the joke about getting drenched linking the generations in a strong indestructible chain. And the comedian who waded in carrying an umbrella.

When the others went swimming my son said he was going in, too. He pulled his dripping trunks from the line where they had hung all through the shower and wrung them out. Languidly, and with no thought of going in, I watched him, his hard little body, skinny and bare, saw him wince slightly as he pulled up around his vitals the small, soggy, icy garment. As he buckled the swollen belt, suddenly my groin felt the chill of death.

Ubangi: People who live near the Ubangi River in the Central African Republic and Zaire. The women traditionally pierce and stretch their lips around flat wooden disks. **mandolins:** Small stringed instruments often used in ballads and folk music. **premonitory:** Warning.

Questions to Start You Thinking

1. CONSIDERING MEANING: How have the lake and the surrounding community, as White depicts them, changed since he was a boy?

2. IDENTIFYING WRITING STRATEGIES: Notice the details White uses to describe life at the lake. How many different sensory experiences do his images evoke? Identify and then analyze at least four memorable images from the essay, explaining what makes each memorable.

3. READING CRITICALLY: White compares the past with the present to show that "there had been no years" since his childhood at the lake (paragraph 5). How does this comparison shape the tone of White's essay? How does the tone change at the end? What is the effect of this sudden change?

4. EXPANDING VOCABULARY: Define *primeval* (paragraph 3), *transposition* (paragraph 4), *hellgrammite* (paragraph 5), *undulating, cultist* (paragraph 6), and *petulant* (paragraph 10). What is White's purpose in using adult words rather than a child's words to look back on his childhood experience?

5. MAKING CONNECTIONS: Both White and Danzy Senna ("The Color of Love," pp. 458–62) write about a relationship with a close family member. While they both use narration to reveal the intricacies of these relationships, Senna adds dialogue to her narration. As a reader, are you affected more by one approach than the other? Which approach do you find more successful? Or do you find each effective in its own way?

Link to the Paired Essay

While White and Nancy Gibbs ("Free the Children," pp. 470–72) both address childhood summers, their essays have very different purposes. How would you define each writer's purpose? How do the strategies they use in developing their essays differ? Are they similar in any ways?

Journal Prompts

1. Describe a place that has special meaning for you. Why is it special?

2. Use White's description of a thunderstorm (paragraph 12) as a model to describe a natural event that you have witnessed.

Suggestions for Writing

1. Think of a place you knew as a child and then visited again as an adult. Write an essay explaining how the place had changed and not changed. Use observation and recall to make the place as memorable for your readers as it was for you.

2. How do you think nostalgia — the desire to return to an important and pleasant time in the past — influences the way we remember our own experiences? Use examples from White's essay and from your experience to illustrate your explanation.

Nancy Gibbs
Free the Children

 For more about Nancy Gibbs, visit <bedfordstmartins.com/bedguide> **and do a keyword search:**

`🔍 author`

Nancy Gibbs *was born in New York, received a BA in history from Yale University, and then studied politics and philosophy at Oxford University. Gibbs joined* Time *magazine in 1985 as a reporter for the International section and is currently editor-at-large. She has written over one hundred cover stories on topics including the September 11 terrorist attacks, the war in Iraq, Hurricane Katrina, and stem-cell research. Gibbs is also a visiting professor of journalism at Princeton University, where she teaches a seminar about the divided political culture of the United States. She lives near New York City with her husband and two daughters. In "Free the Children," which first appeared in* Time *in 2003, Gibbs voices her concern over modern parents' tendency to overprotect their children. Both she and E. B. White ("Once More to the Lake," pp. 464–68) idealize summer as a time for exploration, a time for kids simply to enjoy their freedom with, as Gibbs puts it, "no one keeping score."*

AS YOU READ: *Note some of the specific things Gibbs suggests allowing children to do when they are out of school for the summer. How do you respond to her suggestions?*

My daughters are upstairs shrieking. And thumping. Nothing sounds broken, so I am leaving them alone to savor the outlaw feeling of playing hooky from the afternoon session of camp. They know absences don't count against them on some Permanent Record somewhere.

I long for them to have a whole summer that doesn't matter. When they can read for fun, even books that don't appear on the officially sanctioned summer reading list. When even the outfielders get to play first base sometimes because the game doesn't count. When they can ruin their brand-new sneakers because they found a great new creek. When a rule can be bent, if only to test its strength, and they can play all they want, without playing for keeps.

I want summer not to count because what happens as a result counts for so much. Maybe we adults idealize our own red-rover° days, the hot afternoons spent playing games that required no coaches, eating foods that involved no nutrition, getting dirty in whole new ways and rarely glancing in the direction of a screen of any kind. Ask friends about the people and places that shaped them, and summer springs up quickly when they tell their story: their first kiss, first beer, first job that changed everything. The best summer moments were stretchy enough to carry us all through the year, which is why it's worth listening to all the warnings from social scientists about our Hurried Children who for the rest of the year wear their schedules like clothes that are too tight.

red-rover: An outdoor children's game.

The experts have long charted the growing stress and disappearing 4 downtime of modern children; now they say the trend extends across class and region. The combination of double shifts, shrinking vacations, fear of boredom, and competitive instincts conspires to clog our kids' summer just as much as the rest of the year. Even camp isn't likely to be about s'mores and spud° anymore: there is math camp and weight camp and leadership camp, as though summer were about perfecting ourselves, when in fact the opposite may be true.

That's because summer should be a season of grace — not of excuses but 5 of exceptions, ice cream an hour before dinner just because it's so hot out, bedtimes missed in honor of meteor showers, weekdays and weekends that melt together because nothing feels like work. It's not just about relaxing; it's about rehearsing. All our efforts to guard and guide our children may just get in the way of the one thing they need most from us: to be deeply loved yet left alone so they can try a new skill, new slang, new style, new flip-flops. So they can trip a few times, make mistakes, cross them out, try again, with no one keeping score.

This may require some reeducation, a kind of summer school of play 6 that teaches kids not to expect to be entertained every moment, to adjust to days measured out not in periods of practices but in large clumps of opportunity called Morning and Afternoon. Go build a fort. Use every single art supply in the house to make something big. Be bored and see where it takes you, because the imagination's dusty wilderness is worth crossing if you want to sculpt your soul.

Giving children some summer privacy and freedom takes nerve, and not 7 just because this is also precious time to be together as a family. Last summer, the Amber Alert° summer, who could take their eyes off their kids in the front yard? When my seven-year-old was half an hour late coming home one afternoon and the lifeguards and counselors starting asking me what she looked like, what she was wearing, I couldn't get enough air in my lungs to tell them, the fear was so strangling.

But when we finally found her, happily engrossed near Dead Man's 8 Cave catching frogs with a friend, I had to take a deep breath and remember that maybe I had neglected to teach her to call home if she was going to be late, because I had never needed to. She is shuttled from school to playdate to soccer to chess, and only in the summer does she control her own time and whereabouts at all. Do I punish her for savoring liberty the first time she ever tasted it? So we had a long talk while sitting under a tree before I grounded her for a day.

We are bombarded with reasons to stay inside: we're afraid of mosquitoes 9 because of West Nile° and grass because of pesticides and sun because of cancer and sunscreen because of vitamin-D deficiency. Ours is the generation that knows too much, including what other kids are doing in the summer to get a

spud: Another children's game.   Amber Alert: A missing-child bulletin issued by law enforcement agencies.   West Nile: A virus spread by infected mosquitoes.

head start in the marathon that ends with a fat envelope from a top school. So apart from the challenge of trusting our kids, there is the challenge of trusting ourselves, steering by the stars of instinct and memory rather than parent peer pressure or all those guidebooks on how to raise a Successful Child.

I send my girls out to play in the hope that by summer's end I will see   10 the gifts that freedom brings. Kids seem four inches taller in September than in June, whether they've grown any or not. And the measuring stick is marked off in bruises healed and flags captured, friends lost and found, goals achieved without anyone's help. I hope for the discipline not to discipline them too much because that's how I will learn how strong they have become.

Questions to Start You Thinking

1. CONSIDERING MEANING: According to Gibbs, what are some of the benefits of allowing children unsupervised free time during the summer?

2. IDENTIFYING WRITING STRATEGIES: In paragraphs 7 and 8, Gibbs uses recall to share a specific experience involving one of her daughters. What is her point in including this anecdote? What does it contribute to the essay as a whole?

3. READING CRITICALLY: In paragraph 3, Gibbs refers to "all the warnings from social scientists about our Hurried Children," and in the next paragraph she mentions "experts" who have "charted the growing stress and disappearing downtime of modern children." Is this evidence sufficient to establish that a problem exists? Why or why not? What do these brief references suggest about Gibbs's intended audience?

4. EXPANDING VOCABULARY: Reread paragraph 5, in which Gibbs writes that summer is "not just about relaxing; it's about rehearsing." What does she mean by *rehearsing* in this context, and why is the word important to her point?

5. MAKING CONNECTIONS: In "They've Got to Be Carefully Taught" (pp. 564–66), Susan Brady Konig argues that our educational system forces ideas on children rather than allowing them to develop more naturally, as Gibbs feels they should. How do you think that freedom and structure affect the development of children?

Link to the Paired Essay

In "Once More to the Lake" (pp. 464–68), E. B. White writes about a summer vacation that he and his son spend at a rustic fishing camp. How might Gibbs respond to White's vacation with his son? Does White allow his son the "summer privacy and freedom" that Gibbs advocates (paragraph 7)? What might White think of the world of children today?

Journal Prompts

1. Do you agree with Gibbs that children today experience significant stress and a lack of downtime? Why or why not?

2. How closely supervised was your free time when you were a child? If you have children, how closely do you supervise their free time? Do you think that Gibbs diminishes the benefits of parental supervision? Why or why not?

Suggestions for Writing

1. In a personal essay, write about a special experience you had as a child during a summer break. In what ways does your experience support or counter Gibbs's point about the importance of allowing children unsupervised free time?

2. Write an essay, addressed to parents of children under the age of twelve, proposing what you see as the ideal way to treat their children's summer break. What sorts of activities should be available to them? What should parents participate in, and when should they leave their children alone? Develop your ideas as specifically as possible.

Chapter 24
Men and Women

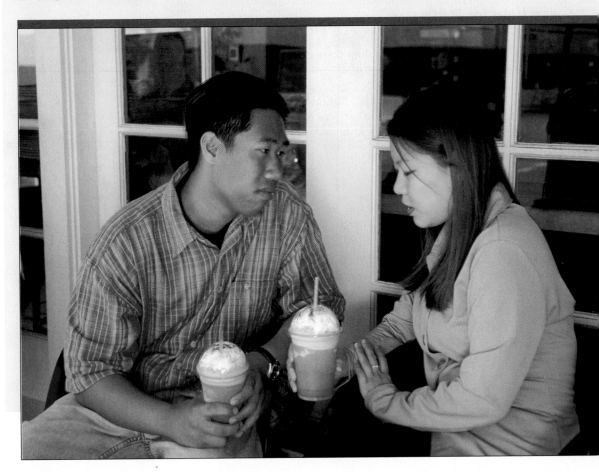

Responding to an Image

Examine this photograph, including the setting and the body language of the man and woman. What similarities and differences do you note? What emotions are apparent? If you were to add dialogue to this picture, what might the man and woman be saying or thinking? Based on your analysis, what general point does the photograph make about relationships? (You also might want to compare and contrast this image with the one on p. 529.)

■ For reading activities linked to this chapter, visit <bedfordstmartins.com/bedguide> and do a keyword search:

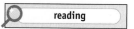
reading

Web Search

Use a search engine such as Yahoo! or InfoSeek that locates Web sites rather than specific pages to find one Web source or publication marketed for women and one marketed for men. Read a few pages of each, and compare and contrast the content. How are they similar? How are they different? Do you think they stereotype women and men? How, and for what reasons?

■ For more about Robert Jensen, visit <bedfordstmartins.com/bedguide> and do a keyword search:

author

Robert Jensen
The High Cost of Manliness

Robert Jensen *was born in 1958 and grew up in Fargo, North Dakota. After earning a BA in social studies and secondary education from Moorhead State University and graduate degrees in journalism from American University and the University of Minnesota, Jensen started his career as a newspaper journalist. He is now a professor of journalism at the University of Texas at Austin, where he teaches courses on media law, ethics, and politics and also regularly contributes to a variety of publications. His scholarly books include* Pornography: The Production and Consumption of Inequality *(1998),* Writing Dissent: Taking Radical Ideas from the Margins to the Mainstream *(2001),* Citizens of the Empire: The Struggle to Claim Our Humanity *(2004), and* The Heart of Whiteness: Confronting Race, Racism, and White Privilege *(2005). An outspoken critic of current U.S. foreign policy, Jensen gained widespread attention over his series of controversial opinion pieces in the* Houston Chronicle *soon after the September 11 terrorist attacks. In the following essay, which first appeared on* Alternet.org *in September 2006, Jensen calls for abandoning the prevailing definition of masculinity, arguing that it is "toxic" to both men and women.*

AS YOU READ: *Identify what Jensen sees as the dominant conception of masculinity in contemporary culture. What does he think of this conception?*

It's hard to be a man; hard to live up to the demands that come with the dominant conception of masculinity, of the tough guy.

So, guys, I have an idea — maybe it's time we stop trying. Maybe this masculinity thing is a bad deal, not just for women but for us.

We need to get rid of the whole idea of masculinity. It's time to abandon the claim that there are certain psychological or social traits that inherently come with being biologically male. If we can get past that, we have a chance to create a better world for men and women.

The dominant conception of masculinity in U.S. culture is easily summarized: men are assumed to be naturally competitive and aggressive, and being a real man is therefore marked by the struggle for control, conquest, and domination. A man looks at the world, sees what he wants, and takes it. Men who don't measure up are wimps, sissies, fags, girls. The worst insult one man can

475

hurl at another—whether it's boys on the playground or CEOs in the board-room—is the accusation that a man is like a woman. Although the culture ac-knowledges that men can in some situations have traits traditionally associated with women (caring, compassion, tenderness), in the end it is men's strength-expressed-as-toughness that defines us and must trump any femalelike softness. Those aspects of masculinity must prevail for a man to be a "real man."

That's not to suggest, of course, that every man adopts that view of mas-   5
culinity. But it is endorsed in key institutions and activities—most notably in business, the military, and athletics—and is reinforced through the mass media. It is particularly expressed in the way men—straight and gay alike—talk about sexuality and act sexually. And our culture's male heroes reflect those characteristics: they most often are men who take charge rather than seek consensus, seize power rather than look for ways to share it, and are willing to be violent to achieve their goals.

That view of masculinity is dangerous for women. It leads men to seek   6
to control "their" women and define their own pleasure in that control, which leads to epidemic levels of rape and battery. But this view of mas-culinity is toxic for men as well.

If masculinity is defined as conquest, it means that men will always struggle   7
with each other for dominance. In a system premised on hierarchy° and power, there can be only one king of the hill. Every other man must in some way be subordinated to the king, and the king has to always be nervous about who is coming up that hill to get him. A friend who once worked on Wall Street—one of the preeminent° sites of masculine competition—described coming to work as like walking into a knife fight when all the good spots along the wall were taken. Masculinity like this is life lived as endless competition and threat.

No one man created this system, and perhaps none of us, if given a choice,   8
would choose it. But we live our lives in that system, and it deforms men, nar-rowing our emotional range and depth. It keeps us from the rich connections with others—not just with women and children, but other men—that make life meaningful but require vulnerability.

This doesn't mean that the negative consequences of this toxic masculinity   9
are equally dangerous for men and women. As feminists have long pointed out, there's a big difference between women dealing with the possibility of being raped, beaten, and killed by the men in their lives and men not being able to cry. But we can see that the short-term material gains that men get are not adequate compensation for what we men give up in the long haul—which is to surrender part of our humanity to the project of dominance.

Of course there are obvious physical differences between men and   10
women—average body size, hormones, reproductive organs. There may be other differences rooted in our biology that we don't yet understand. Yet it's also true that men and women are more similar than we are different, and that given the pernicious° effects of centuries of patriarchy° and its re-

hierarchy: A grouping based on relative rank.   preeminent: Most important.   pernicious: Destructive.   patriarchy: Social organization in which the father is supreme;
male control of most of the power in a society.

lentless devaluing of things female, we should be skeptical of the perceived differences.

What we know is simple: in any human population, there is wide indi-   11
vidual variation. While there's no doubt that a large part of our behavior is rooted in our DNA, there's also no doubt that our genetic endowment is highly influenced by culture. Beyond that, it's difficult to say much with any certainty. It's true that only women can bear children and breast-feed. That fact likely has some bearing on aspects of men's and women's personalities. But we don't know much about what the effect is, and given the limits of our tools to understand human behavior, it's possible we may never know much.

At the moment, the culture seems obsessed with gender differences, in the   12
context of a recurring intellectual fad (called "evolutionary psychology" this time around, and "sociobiology" in a previous incarnation) that wants to explain all complex behaviors as simple evolutionary adaptations — if a pattern of human behavior exists, it must be because it's adaptive in some ways. In the long run, that's true by definition. But in the short term it's hardly a convincing argument to say, "Look at how men and women behave so differently; it must be because men and women are fundamentally different" when a political system has been creating differences between men and women.

From there, the argument that we need to scrap masculinity is fairly   13
simple. To illustrate it, remember back to right after 9/11. A number of commentators argued that criticisms of masculinity should be rethought. Cannot we now see — recognizing that male firefighters raced into burning buildings, risking and sometimes sacrificing their lives to save others — that masculinity can encompass a kind of strength that is rooted in caring and sacrifice? Of course men often exhibit such strength, just as do women. So, the obvious question arises: What makes these distinctly masculine characteristics? Are they not simply human characteristics?

We identify masculine tendencies toward competition, domination, and   14
violence because we see patterns of differential behavior; men are more prone to such behavior in our culture. We can go on to observe and analyze the ways in which men are socialized to behave in those ways, toward the goal of changing those destructive behaviors. That analysis is different than saying that admirable human qualities present in both men and women are somehow primarily the domain of one gender. To assign them to a gender is misguided and demeaning to the gender that is then assumed not to possess them to the same degree. Once we start saying "strength and courage are masculine traits," it leads to the conclusion that woman are not as strong or courageous.

Of course, if we are going to jettison° masculinity, we have to scrap fem-   15
ininity along with it. We have to stop trying to define what men and women are going to be in the world based on extrapolations° from physical sex differences. That doesn't mean we ignore those differences when they matter, but we have to stop assuming they matter everywhere.

---

jettison: Throw out.   **extrapolations:** Predictions.

I don't think the planet can long survive if the current conception of ¹⁶
masculinity endures. We face political and ecological challenges that can't
be met with this old model of what it means to be a man. At the more intimate level, the stakes are just as high. For those of us who are biologically
male, we have a simple choice: we men can settle for being men, or we can
strive to be human beings.

Questions to Start You Thinking

1. CONSIDERING MEANING: What does Jensen see as the negative consequences
   of the commonly held idea of masculinity?
2. IDENTIFYING WRITING STRATEGIES: Where in the essay does Jensen use comparison and contrast in writing about men and women? What is his point
   in doing so?
3. READING CRITICALLY: In paragraph 5, Jensen admits that not all men conceive
   of masculinity in terms of competition and aggression. Do you think he goes
   on to provide enough evidence to support his claim that this view of masculinity is dominant in U.S. culture? Why or why not?
4. EXPANDING VOCABULARY: In paragraph 12, Jensen refers to the current obsession with gender differences in the United States as a "recurring intellectual
   fad." What does he mean by this phrase, and what does it contribute to his
   argument?
5. MAKING CONNECTIONS: In "Guys Just Want to Have Fun" (pp. 482–84),
   Barbara Ehrenreich also writes about views of men and women in contemporary U.S. culture. In what ways do her observations correspond with
   Jensen's? In what ways do they differ?

Journal Prompts

1. Do you agree, as Jensen puts it, that the "worst insult one man can hurl at
   another . . . is the accusation that a man is like a woman" (paragraph 4)?
   What do you think about insults that liken a woman to a man?
2. In the essay's final paragraph, Jensen writes that he doesn't think "the
   planet can long survive if the current conception of masculinity endures."
   How do you respond to this statement?

Suggestions for Writing

1. Jensen writes in paragraph 13 about the idea of strength. In an essay, discuss how you define *human strength*, considering the physical, the intellectual, and the emotional.
2. Jensen acknowledges that gender differences are in some part determined
   by biological factors. However, he is more concerned about the influence of
   social conditioning. Write an essay analyzing how a particular social force
   does or does not contribute to stereotypes of masculinity and femininity.
   For example, you might consider the influence of some aspect of popular
   culture, education, sports, or children's toys. Use examples from your experience as well as other evidence to support your point.

Brent Staples
Black Men and Public Space

Brent Staples *was born in 1951 in Chester, Pennsylvania, and earned a PhD in psychology from the University of Chicago. He wrote for the* Chicago Sun-Times *and* Down Beat *magazine before joining the* New York Times *in 1985, where he moved from metropolitan news to the* New York Times Book Review. *Since 1990, Staples has been a member of the* Times *editorial board, writing regular columns on politics and culture. His work also has appeared in such magazines as* New York Woman, Ms., *and* Harper's, *and he is the author of the memoir* Parallel Time: Growing Up in Black and White *(1994). In the following essay, published in a slightly different version in* Ms. *magazine in September 1986, Staples considers how his presence affects other pedestrians at night.*

■ For more about Brent Staples, visit <bedfordstmartins.com/bedguide> and do a key-word search:

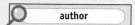
author

AS YOU READ: *Identify why other pedestrians respond to Staples with anxiety.*

My first victim was a woman — white, well dressed, probably in her late twenties. I came upon her late one evening on a deserted street in Hyde Park, a relatively affluent neighborhood in an otherwise mean, impoverished section of Chicago. As I swung onto the avenue behind her, there seemed to be a discreet, uninflammatory distance between us. Not so. She cast back a worried glance. To her, the youngish black man — a broad six feet two inches with a beard and billowing hair, both hands shoved into the pockets of a bulky military jacket — seemed menacingly close. After a few more quick glimpses, she picked up her pace and was soon running in earnest. Within seconds, she disappeared into a cross street.

That was more than a decade ago. I was twenty-one years old, a graduate student newly arrived at the University of Chicago. It was in the echo of that terrified woman's footfalls that I first began to know the unwieldy inheritance I'd come into — the ability to alter public space in ugly ways. It was clear that she thought herself the quarry of a mugger, a rapist, or worse. Suffering a bout of insomnia, however, I was stalking sleep, not defenseless wayfarers. As a softy who is scarcely able to take a knife to a raw chicken — let alone hold one to a person's throat — I was surprised, embarrassed, and dismayed all at once. Her flight made me feel like an accomplice in tyranny. It also made it clear that I was indistinguishable from the muggers who occasionally seeped into the area from the surrounding ghetto. The first encounter, and those that followed, signified that a vast, unnerving gulf lay between nighttime pedestrians — particularly women — and me. And I soon gathered that being perceived as dangerous is a hazard in itself. I only needed to turn a corner into a dicey situation, or crowd some frightened, armed person in a foyer somewhere, or make an errant move after being pulled over by a policeman. Where fear and weapons meet — and they often do in urban America — there is always the possibility of death.

479

In that first year, my first away from my hometown, I was to become 3
thoroughly familiar with the language of fear. At dark, shadowy intersections,
I could cross in front of a car stopped at a traffic light and elicit the *thunk,*
thunk, thunk, thunk of the driver — black, white, male, or female — hammer-
ing down the door locks. On less traveled streets after dark, I grew accustomed to but never comfortable with people crossing to the other side of
the street rather than pass me. Then there were the standard unpleasantries
with policemen, doormen, bouncers, cabdrivers, and others whose business
it is to screen out troublesome individuals *before* there is any nastiness.

I moved to New York nearly two years ago and I have remained an avid 4
night walker. In central Manhattan, the near-constant crowd cover mini-
mizes tense one-on-one street encounters. Elsewhere — in SoHo, for example,
where sidewalks are narrow and tightly spaced buildings shut out the
sky — things can get very taut indeed.

After dark, on the warrenlike° streets of Brooklyn where I live, I often see 5
women who fear the worst from me. They seem to have set their faces on neutral, and with their purse straps strung across their chests bandolier-style, they
forge ahead as though bracing themselves against being tackled. I understand,
of course, that the danger they perceive is not a hallucination. Women are particularly vulnerable to street violence, and young black males are drastically
overrepresented among the perpetrators of that violence. Yet these truths are
no solace against the kind of alienation that comes of being ever the suspect, a
fearsome entity with whom pedestrians avoid making eye contact.

It is not altogether clear to me how I reached the ripe old age of twenty- 6
two without being conscious of the lethality nighttime pedestrians attributed to me. Perhaps it was because in Chester, Pennsylvania, the small,
angry industrial town where I came of age in the 1960s, I was scarcely noticeable against a backdrop of gang warfare, street knifings, and murders. I
grew up one of the good boys, had perhaps a half-dozen fistfights. In retro-
spect, my shyness of combat has clear sources.

As a boy, I saw countless tough guys locked away; I have since buried 7
several, too. They were babies, really — a teenage cousin, a brother of twenty-
two, a childhood friend in his mid-twenties — all gone down in episodes of
bravado played out in the streets. I came to doubt the virtues of intimidation early on. I chose, perhaps unconsciously, to remain a shadow — timid,
but a survivor.

The fearsomeness mistakenly attributed to me in public places often has 8
a perilous flavor. The most frightening of these confusions occurred in the
late 1970s and early 1980s, when I worked as a journalist in Chicago. One
day, rushing into the office of a magazine I was writing for with a deadline
story in hand, I was mistaken for a burglar. The office manager called security and, with an ad hoc° posse, pursued me through the labyrinthine halls,
nearly to my editor's door. I had no way of proving who I was. I could only
move briskly toward the company of someone who knew me.

---

warrenlike: Like a maze.   **ad hoc:** Spur of the moment.

Another time I was on assignment for a local paper and killing time be- 9
fore an interview. I entered a jewelry store on the city's affluent Near North
Side. The proprietor excused herself and returned with an enormous red
Doberman pinscher straining at the end of a leash. She stood, the dog extended toward me, silent to my questions, her eyes bulging nearly out of her
head. I took a cursory look around, nodded, and bade her good night.

Relatively speaking, however, I never fared as badly as another black 10
male journalist. He went to nearby Waukegan, Illinois, a couple of summers
ago to work on a story about a murderer who was born there. Mistaking the
reporter for the killer, police officers hauled him from his car at gunpoint
and but for his press credentials would probably have tried to book him.
Such episodes are not uncommon. Black men trade tales like this all the time.

Over the years, I learned to smother the rage I felt at so often being taken 11
for a criminal. Not to do so would surely have led to madness. I now take
precautions to make myself less threatening. I move about with care, particularly late in the evening. I give a wide berth° to nervous people on subway
platforms during the wee hours, particularly when I have exchanged business
clothes for jeans. If I happen to be entering a building behind some people
who appear skittish, I may walk by, letting them clear the lobby before I return, so as not to seem to be following them. I have been calm and extremely
congenial on those rare occasions when I've been pulled over by the police.

And on late-evening constitutionals I employ what has proved to be an 12
excellent tension-reducing measure: I whistle melodies from Beethoven and
Vivaldi and the more popular classical composers. Even steely New Yorkers
hunching toward nighttime destinations seem to relax, and occasionally
they even join in the tune. Virtually everybody seems to sense that a mugger
wouldn't be warbling bright, sunny selections from Vivaldi's *Four Seasons*. It
is my equivalent of the cowbell that hikers wear when they know they are in
bear country.

Questions to Start You Thinking

1. CONSIDERING MEANING: What misconceptions do people have about
   Staples because he is a young black man? What does he feel causes such
   misconceptions?

2. IDENTIFYING WRITING STRATEGIES: At the end of the essay, how does Staples
   use comparison to explain his behavior?

3. READING CRITICALLY: What kinds of appeals — emotional, logical, ethical —
   does Staples use? Are his appeals appropriate for the purpose of his essay?
   Why or why not? (For an explanation of kinds of appeals, see pp. 40–41.)

4. EXPANDING VOCABULARY: Define *affluent, uninflammatory* (paragraph 1), *unwieldy, quarry, errant* (paragraph 2), *bandolier, solace* (paragraph 5), *lethality*
   (paragraph 6), and *bravado* (paragraph 7). Why do you think Staples uses
   such formal language in this essay?

berth: Space.

5. MAKING CONNECTIONS: In "The Color of Love" (pp. 458–62), Danzy Senna writes about being the daughter of a black father and a white mother and, in particular, about her relationship with her prejudiced white grandmother. How might Senna and Staples respond to one another's experiences?

Journal Prompts

1. Are stereotypes ever useful? Why or why not?

2. Have you or someone you know ever been wrongfully stereotyped or pre-judged? How did you react?

Suggestions for Writing

1. Staples describes his feelings about being the object of racial fear. Have you or someone you know ever been the object of such a fear or of other misconceptions based on prejudice or stereotyping? Write a short personal essay discussing the causes and effects of the experience. What preconceptions were you or your acquaintance the victim of? How did you or your acquaintance respond?

2. What do you think causes the stereotype of African American men that Staples is addressing? Write an essay that analyzes this stereotype, drawing on several outside sources to support your analysis.

Barbara Ehrenreich
Guys Just Want to Have Fun

■ For more about Barbara Ehrenreich, visit <bedfordstmartins.com/bedguide> and do a key-word search:

author

Barbara Ehrenreich, *born in 1941, holds a BA from Reed College and a PhD from Rockefeller University. A writer and social activist, her critiques of such issues as health-care policy and workplace rights have appeared in publications including* Ms., Mother Jones, Nation, New Republic, *and* Time, *and she currently writes a regular column for the* Progressive. *She is also the author of several books, including* Fear of Falling: The Inner Life of the Middle Class *(1988),* Snarling Citizen: Essays *(1995),* Blood Rites: Origins and History of the Passion of War *(1997),* Bait and Switch: The (Futile) Pursuit of the American Dream *(2006), and* Dancing in the Streets: A History of Collective Joy *(2007). To write the best-selling* Nickel and Dimed: On (Not) Getting by in America *(2001), in which she explores the harsh realities of surviving on a wage of six to seven dollars an hour, Ehrenreich spent two years waiting tables, cleaning houses, and performing other low-wage jobs. In "Guys Just Want to Have Fun," from* Time *magazine in 2006, Ehrenreich examines evolving gender roles in education and the workplace. Although women are now more likely than men to earn a college degree, she argues that a shift in corporate culture is continuing to favor men in the business world.*

AS YOU READ: *Identify what you see as Ehrenreich's underlying purpose in writing this essay. What point does she want to impress on readers?*

When I was in college, I followed a simple strategy: go where the boys 1
are. Sure, that led me into many settings where inebriants° flowed,
but my reasoning was strictly practical. Men ruled the world, as anyone
could see, so the trick was to do as they did. No girlie major like art history
or French lit for me. I started in chemistry and then proceeded up the gender gradient to physics, finally achieving in Classical Mechanics the exalted
status of only girl in the class.

But that was an era when the cool kids smoked Gauloises° and argued 2
about Kierkegaard° and Trotsky.° Today, as two recent reports have revealed,
it's the girls who achieve and the boys who coast along on gut courses congenial to hangovers. Boys are less likely to go to college in the first place
(only 45 percent of college students under twenty-five are male) and are less
likely to graduate as well. If I tried to follow my original strategy now, I
would probably end up with an MA in *Madden*, the football video game,
and a postgraduate stay in rehab.

The trend has occasioned some predictions of a coming matriarchy in 3
which high-achieving women will rule over a nation of slacker guys. We've
all seen the movie, an endless loop culminating most recently in *You, Me
and Dupree.*° That little girls' T-shirt slogan — GIRLS RULE, BOYS DROOL — is
beginning to look less like a slur and more like an empirical° observation.

But it may be that the boys still know what they're doing. Among other 4
things that have changed since the '60s is the corporate culture, which once
valued literacy, numeracy, high GPAs and the ability to construct a simple
sentence. No doubt there are still workplaces where such achievements are
valued, but when I set out as an undercover journalist seeking a white-collar
corporate job for my book *Bait and Switch*, I was shocked to find the emphasis entirely on such elusive qualities as "personality," "attitude," and "lika-
bility." Play down the smarts, the career coaches and self-help books advised, cull° the experience and exude a "positive attitude."

In a June article on corporate personality testing, the *Washington Post* re- 5
ported on a woman who passed the skills test for a customer-care job but
wasn't hired because she failed the personality test. Those tests, including
the ubiquitous Myers-Briggs test, have no scientific credibility or predictive
value, as Annie Murphy Paul showed in her 2004 book, *Cult of Personality.*
You can have one Myers-Briggs personality on Tuesday and another when
you retake the test on Thursday. Their chief function, as far as I could tell
when I took them, was to weed out the introverts. When asked whether
you'd rather be the life of the party or curl up with a book, the correct answer is always "Party!"

---

inebriants: Substances that make one drunk.   **Gauloises:** A brand of French cigarettes.   **Kierkegaard:** Søren Kierkegaard (1813–1855), a nineteenth-century Danish
philosopher.   **Trotsky:** Leon Trotsky (1879–1940), leader of the Communist revolution
in Russia.   ***You, Me and Dupree:*** A 2006 comic film about a lazy, immature male character.   **empirical:** Based on evidence.   **cull:** Remove inferior parts from.

So the best preparation for that all-important personality test may well 6 be a college career spent playing poker and doing tequila shots. An Atlanta woman I interviewed, a skilled Web-site writer, was fired without explanation after a few weeks at a job. "I tried to fit in," she told me. "I went to lunch with the guys, but all they talked about was sports, which I know nothing about, and they all seemed to know each other from college." Poor thing, she had probably wasted her college years in the library.

The business world isn't totally hostile to higher education — an MBA 7 still counts for something. But as G. J. Meyer wrote in his classic 1995 book, *Executive Blues: Down and Out in Corporate America*, a higher degree in something other than business or law — or, worse, a stint of college teaching — can impart a deadly "academic stench" to one's résumé. And what are we to make of the growing corporate defiance of elementary grammar? At a job fair I attended, AT&T Wireless solicited sales reps with the question, if it was a question, "Are you ready to put your skills to work. Like the way you're a quick study. How you're good at finding solutions." Take that, you irritating, irrelevant English 101 professors!

Maybe we need a return to gender-segregated higher education, with 8 the academic equivalent of Pinocchio's Pleasure Island for boys, where they can hone their "people skills" at keg parties. But we will need those high-achieving girls more than ever. Someone, after all, is going to have to figure out how to make an economy run by superannuated° slacker boys competitive again in a world filled with Chinese and Indian brainiacs. I'd still major in physics if I were doing it again, just because there ought to be at least a few Americans, of whatever gender, who know something beyond the technology of beer bongs.

Questions to Start You Thinking

1. CONSIDERING MEANING: According to Ehrenreich, what are the general differences between today's male and female college students? In general, what character traits does Ehrenreich think are most valued in today's business world, and which gender is more likely to hold these qualities?

2. IDENTIFYING WRITING STRATEGIES: Where in the essay does Ehrenreich discuss causes and effects? How does this strategy contribute to her purpose?

3. READING CRITICALLY: What point is Ehrenreich making in her final paragraph? How convincing do you find her argument here?

4. EXPANDING VOCABULARY: In paragraph 3, what does Ehrenreich mean by "a coming matriarchy"? Discuss whether she is using the term *matriarchy* literally or in a special sense here

5. MAKING CONNECTIONS: In "Why Not a Dollar?" (pp. 488–93), Evelyn F. Murphy writes about the increasing wage gap between men and women in the U.S. workforce. How might Ehrenreich explain that gap?

superannuated: Advancing in age.

Journal Prompts

1. Does your experience bear out what Ehrenreich says about the differences between male and female college students? If so, how do you explain these differences? If not, how would you describe the work habits of male and female students?

2. What do you think are the most important qualities employers should seek in potential employees? To what extent are these qualities shared equally by women and men?

Suggestions for Writing

1. Analyze the employee characteristics and work ethic valued by your current or recent employer. Then write an essay that agrees with, disagrees with, or qualifies Ehrenreich's position, using that recent experience to support your view.

2. In the final paragraph of this selection, Ehrenreich refers to "gender-segregated higher education." Do some research about current views on this topic. Then write an essay either summarizing the arguments on both sides or taking a stand of your own on the topic.

Dave Barry

From Now On, Let Women Kill Their Own Spiders

Dave Barry *was born in 1947 in Armonk, New York. According to his own biographical statement, he has been "steadily growing older ever since without ever actually reaching maturity." He attended Haverford College and started his career in journalism at the* Daily Local News *in West Chester, Pennsylvania. As a syndicated writer for the* Miami Herald *from 1983 to 2005, Barry's humorous columns appeared in hundreds of newspapers, and he won the Pulitzer Prize for Commentary in 1988. Barry is the author of numerous books, which include* Babies and Other Hazards of Sex *(1984),* Dave Barry's Complete Guide to Guys *(1995),* Dave Barry Is from Mars and Venus *(1997),* Boogers Are My Beat *(2003), and his recent* Dave Barry's Money Secrets *(2006) and* The Shepherd, the Angel, and Walter the Christmas Miracle Dog *(2006). The article "From Now On, Let Women Kill Their Own Spiders" first appeared in the* Miami Herald. *In this piece, Barry pokes fun at miscommunication between men and women. Identifying with both, he laughs at how the sexes inevitably bewilder and infuriate each other.*

■ For more about
Dave Barry, visit
<bedfordstmartins.com/
bedguide> and do a keyword search:

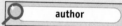

AS YOU READ: *Try to discover what Barry is really criticizing.*

From time to time I receive letters from a certain group of individuals that   1
I will describe, for want of a better term, as "women." I have such a letter
here, from a Susie Walker of North Augusta, S.C., who asks the following

question: "Why do men open a drawer and say, 'Where is the spatula?' instead of, you know, looking for it?"

This question expresses a commonly held (by women) negative stereotype   2
about guys of the male gender, which is that they cannot find things around
the house, especially things in the kitchen. Many women believe that if you
want to hide something from a man, all you have to do is put it in plain sight
in the refrigerator, and he will never, ever find it, as evidenced by the fact that a
man can open a refrigerator containing 463 pounds of assorted meats, poultry,
cold cuts, condiments, vegetables, frozen dinners, snack foods, desserts, etc.,
and ask, with no irony whatsoever, "Do we have anything to eat?"

Now I could respond to this stereotype in a snide° manner by making   3
generalizations about women. I could ask, for example, how come your average woman prepares for virtually every upcoming event in her life, including dental appointments, by buying new shoes, even if she already owns as
many pairs as the entire Riverdance troupe. I could point out that, if there
were no women, there would be no such thing as Leonardo DiCaprio. I
could ask why a woman would walk up to a perfectly innocent man who is
minding his own business watching basketball and demand to know if a
certain pair of pants makes her butt look too big, and then, no matter what
he answers, get mad at him. I could ask why, according to the best scientific
estimates, 93 percent of the nation's severely limited bathroom-storage
space is taken up by decades-old, mostly empty tubes labeled "moisturizer."
I could point out that, to judge from the covers of countless women's magazines, the two topics most interesting to women are (1) Why men are all
disgusting pigs, and (2) How to attract men.

Yes, I could raise these issues in response to the question asked by Susie   4
Walker of North Augusta, S.C., regarding the man who was asking where the
spatula was. I could even ask WHY this particular man might be looking for the
spatula. Could it be that he needs a spatula to kill a spider, because, while he
was innocently watching basketball and minding his own business, a member
of another major gender — a gender that refuses to personally kill spiders but
wants them all dead — DEMANDED that he kill the spider, which nine times
out of ten turns out to be a male spider that was minding its own business? Do
you realize how many men arrive in hospital emergency rooms every year,
sometimes still gripping their spatulas, suffering from painful spider-inflicted
injuries? I don't have the exact statistics right here, but I bet they are chilling.

As I say, I could raise these issues and resort to the kind of negativity in-   5
dulged in by Susie Walker of North Augusta, S.C. But I choose not to. I
choose, instead, to address her question seriously, in hopes that, by improving the communication between the genders, all human beings — both men
and women, together — will come to a better understanding of how dense°
women can be sometimes.

I say this because there is an excellent reason why a man would open   6
the spatula drawer and, without looking for the spatula, ask where the spat-

snide: Sarcastic, especially in a nasty manner.   **dense:** Slow-witted.

ula is: the man does not have TIME to look for the spatula. Why? Because he is busy thinking. Men are almost always thinking. When you look at a man who appears to be merely scratching himself, rest assured that inside his head, his brain is humming like a high-powered computer, processing millions of pieces of information and producing important insights such as, "This feels good!"

We should be grateful that men think so much, because over the years 7 they have thought up countless inventions that have made life better for all people, everywhere. The shot clock in basketball is one example. Another one is underwear-eating bacteria. I found out about this thanks to the many alert readers who sent me an article from *New Scientist* magazine stating that Russian scientists — and you KNOW these are guy scientists — are trying to solve the problem of waste disposal aboard spacecraft, by "designing a cocktail of bacteria to digest astronauts' cotton and paper underpants." Is that great, or what? I am picturing a utopian future wherein, when a man's briefs get dirty, they will simply dissolve from his body, thereby freeing him from the chore of dealing with his soiled underwear via the labor-intensive, time-consuming method he now uses, namely, dropping them on the floor.

I'm not saying that guys have solved all the world's problems. I'm just 8 saying that there ARE solutions out there, and if, instead of harping endlessly about spatulas, we allow guys to use their mental talents to look for these solutions, in time, they will find them. Unless they are in the refrigerator.

Questions to Start You Thinking

1. CONSIDERING MEANING: What is Barry satirizing in his essay?

2. IDENTIFYING WRITING STRATEGIES: Barry's essay is filled with rhetorical questions. Locate some of these, and consider how he answers them. What evidence does he provide to support his answers? How does this evidence affect his tone? How does it affect meaning?

3. READING CRITICALLY: What generalizations about women does Barry make in paragraph 3? How do these serve to support his main point?

4. EXPANDING VOCABULARY: Define *utopian* (paragraph 7). According to Barry, how would underwear-eating bacteria contribute to a utopian future?

5. MAKING CONNECTIONS: Both Barry and Judy Brady ("I Want a Wife," pp. 497–99) use satire, humorously attacking human mistakes and shortcomings in their essays. Compare and contrast their use of satire.

Journal Prompts

1. Put your imagination to work to suggest other inventions — besides underwear-eating bacteria — that would benefit man- (or woman-) kind. Follow Barry's model and have fun.

2. Discuss a conversation you've heard that involved man or woman bashing. What was the tone of the conversation? How serious were the participants? What are the effects of such remarks?

Suggestions for Writing

1. Stereotypes can be useful in literature and film, but in real life they may be damaging. Write an essay in which you examine real-life stereotypes, recalling behavior you have observed and experienced.

2. Using Barry's essay as a model, write an essay satirizing an issue you find unfair, irritating, or just amusing.

Evelyn F. Murphy
Why Not a Dollar?

 For more about Evelyn F. Murphy, visit <bedfordstmartins.com/ bedguide> and do a keyword search:

[🔍   author]

Evelyn F. Murphy was born in Panama in 1940, where her father was stationed during World War II. She and her family moved from one army base to the next throughout her childhood. She received a bachelor's degree and a PhD from Duke University and a master's degree from Columbia University. Using her education in mathematics and economics initially as an economist, she began her public career in the late 1970s as secretary of environmental affairs for Massachusetts and later served as the state's secretary of economic affairs. In 1986, she was elected lieutenant governor of Massachusetts, becoming the first woman in the state's history to hold constitutional office. She is now president of The WAGE Project, Inc., a nonprofit group that aims to end wage discrimination against working women. The following selection is a chapter from Murphy's Getting Even: Why Women Don't Get Paid Like Men — and What to Do about It *(2005), cowritten with E. J. Graff. Murphy uses sources to show that women's earnings aren't catching up to men's; in fact, she argues, the gender wage gap is actually widening.*

AS YOU READ: *Pay attention to Murphy's use of statistics. To what extent does she rely on statistics to make her point?*

Sometimes I ask people, "What should women be earning today compared with men?" I don't ask what women *are* earning, which hardly anyone can answer with certainty, but what women *should* be earning. Most people shrug and say they have no idea, or guess that it should be about eighty cents to a man's dollar.

No one says "One dollar." That is the correct answer. There should be no gender wage gap at all.

Is that an exaggeration? Statisticians point out that women do not yet have quite as many years' experience in the workforce as men have. It's true that for the generation that began working in the 1960s, fewer women than men have a steady forty or fifty years of on-the-job experience. So maybe there should be a gap of a few pennies — at most! — to reflect that slight disadvantage. But not 23 cents' worth. Social scientists hedge° their conclusions about what causes that broad gap with disclaimers. They acknowledge

hedge: Make excuses for.

that biases exist in their measurements. They admit that they cannot say for sure that differences between women and men in what's called "merit" — education, experience, and other personal capital — add up to 23 cents. But despite the absence of rock-hard proof, this explanation has been accepted. Instead of demanding an immediate end to the wage gap, most Americans believe that it's closing slowly, at an evolutionary pace, moving women penny by penny toward equality.

But that's just not so. If the explanations heard forty years ago were 4 correct — if the reason for the wage gap was indeed that there was a "merit gap" and that in 1965 women had inferior qualifications, little experience, and less career commitment — that gap would have disappeared by now. The wage gap should have closed more than a decade ago. Instead, for several years during the 1990s, it actually widened.[1] It should have disappeared at every rung, from entry level to executive suite. Women have closed the education, career time, and commitment gap. So why hasn't the wage gap closed as well?

Some commentators answer this question by pulling out little slivers of 5 data — comparing, say, male and female engineering graduates' starting salaries in a particular year — to announce that women are already even. Their claim is that young women and young men (in that job category, at least, for that year) made just about the same amount when they got their first jobs. Therefore, the claim goes, the gender wage gap is over: the very newest generation of adults has gotten even.

But that's just plain wrong. The only way to reach such a conclusion is 6 to cherry-pick the most equal job category during its most equal year (ignoring the vast majority of working women, who are far from equal) — and then to ignore how those young women fare as the years go by. Otherwise, here's what you find: women start out behind, and the longer they work, the further behind they fall. One former bank clerk (now an administrator) told me that when she and her husband entered the job market in the 1970s, doing the same work, they "started off at the same range of pay and he just completely left me behind. His salary just kept going up and up every year, and mine just went up incrementally."

That experience has continued for every generation since. We have heard 7 in recent years that young women have caught up within high school and college, matching or surpassing young men as valedictorians, school newspaper editors, and the like. But that's no longer true once women and men start competing not for grades and accolades but for dollars. No matter how *nearly* equal some are at that first job, the wage gap between men and women in their age group keeps widening throughout their lives.

Take those new graduates just entering the job market, the data sliver 8 sometimes held up as proof of emerging equality. For a brief shining moment in 1991, young women and young men in their first postcollege jobs did get much closer to even: the women earned $20,556 while the men earned $22,479, just (just!), a 9 percent difference. That sounds terrific: 9 percent, when only thirty years before it had been 41 percent. Had that apparent trend continued, women and men might be even by now. But it did not—not for that generation of women, who rapidly fell farther behind, and not for their little sisters, for whom even the *entering* wage gap widened. The young women and men who entered the job market in 2003 were actually *farther* apart than their counterparts in 1991.[2] When these women started working, they earned 16 percent less than young men college grads. So much for the optimistic belief that the gender wage gap is steadily declining with each successive generation of workers.

Why have so many of us held that belief? Because most people thought   9
that the wage gap was narrowing over the last forty years because women were catching up on "merit." A close analysis of the data proves that it's not so. The largest drop in the wage gap—a hefty 8 cents during the 1980s— came not because women were catching up, but because men's real wages were declining, as manufacturing left the United States. Women caught up at men's expense. That's much of the story in the post–World War II American economy: in bad economic times, men's wages flatten, even decline; women catch up only by comparison, not because they're actually gaining more equal treatment on the job. Look at that unpleasant *increase* in the starting wage gap between female and male college graduates in 1991 and 2003. American women's hard work, increasing skills, and improving qualifications do *not* put us on an inevitable course toward equal pay.

If You Graduated in 1991, Your Raises Have Not Kept Pace with Men's

Let's illustrate that more fully by looking at what's happened to a single gen- 10
eration of women and men—a generation whose mothers worked, whose entire lives had been spent under the assumption that they could and would be equal on the job.

What happened to your wages if you graduated from college and en- 11
tered the job market in 1991? Over the decade, *their raises did not keep pace with men's.* At the beginning of the decade, they were making 91 cents to a man's dollar. By the end of the decade, these very same women were making only 89 cents to a man's dollar. These women fell behind. They lost money. Their wage gap widened.

Let me repeat that: their wage gap expanded during the nation's biggest 12
economic expansion since the 1950s. It expanded for the generation of women and men *most equally prepared* for the job market in history. The wage gap widened. In 2003, the twenty-five-to-thirty-four-year-old women who had graduated from college were making, on average, $47,364—and the men who had graduated alongside them were making, on average, $53,271. Women's real wages had grown by 130 percent—while men's real wages had grown by 137 percent.

Remember, these are no longer baby boomers, the ones who were just 13
breaking open the doors to women's employment, fighting male chauvinist attitudes and general social resistance, and who may have aimed too low, considering that often their mothers didn't work. These young adults grew up with mothers who were just as educated, qualified, employed, and employable as

their fathers. These young men and women didn't simply grow up believing that women *could* work, if given the chance; they actually knew women who were bus drivers and doctors, heavy-metal guitarists and helicopter pilots, corporate managers and professional tennis players, state senators and Supreme Court justices. These aren't the trailblazers. These are the trail followers.

Remember, too, that most of these college-educated women could not afford to drop out of work for a couple of years to be stay-at-home moms. These women took their maternity leave (and some husbands even took paternity leave) to have a child — and then had to go right back to full-time work. Those families needed both paychecks — the wife's *and* the husband's — just to keep up their standard of living.[3]   14

These full-time, year-round working women hadn't even hit their thirty-fifth birthdays, and they were already behind by $6,000 a year — when they had started only $2,000 a year behind. That's a lot of tamales, diapers, or movies. Add that up for a few years, and that's a Ford F150 SuperCrew instead of a Chevy Cavalier. That's a renovated kitchen, a year's college tuition, a time-share in Florida, a significant retirement fund contribution.   15

Young women with only a high school diploma fell even further behind during these years. When between the ages of eighteen to twenty-four these women entered the job market in 1991, working year-round and full-time, they were earning an average of $13,558 — while men with their age, education, and experience earned $16,559. That was a nasty 18 percent gap.[4] By 2003, these women earned 22 cents less for every dollar their male counterparts took home. Having started out earning $3,000 a year less than their male peers, these women were now earning $7,000 a year less — an enormous bite out of a low-wage paycheck.   16

Women who graduated from professional schools and started their working careers in 1991 fared a little better than these other working women. When between the ages of twenty-five and thirty-four these women entered the job market, working year-round and full-time, they were earning an average of $43,429 — while men with their age, credentials, and experience earned $61,038. That was a nasty 29 percent gap for a group of people with the same qualifications. By the year 2003, female JDs, MBAs, and MDs between the ages of thirty-five and forty-four were making an average of $97,756 each year while men their age, with the same credentials, made $113,805, outearning them by only — *only!* — 14 percent.   17

Except for that small number of high-earning women with professional degrees, this recent generation of women starting their working careers followed that same old trend: the longer they worked, the more they fell behind.   18

Women Fall Farther Behind Men over a Lifetime

The wage gap is an expanding bullet in a woman's finances, tearing away at her checkbook more and more each year. Perhaps that's why, for so many women, the creeping suspicion that things are unfair transforms into a smoldering sense of outrage somewhere between the ages of thirty-five and forty-five. Having expected that by working hard they would earn the appropriate   19 rewards, they look around in some shock — and reluctantly realize that the men they graduated with or were hired alongside are farther along in their finances and careers. They come to the distressing conclusion that either they've utterly bungled their careers — or they've been cheated out of their rightful earnings.

Heidi Hartmann, president of the Institute for Women's Policy Research, who's been tracking the shifts in men's and women's wages for decades, says that when times are good, men advance more than women do. Nobody knows why. But understanding why is important. For that brief moment between 1993 and 2000, women should have gotten even. These were the most promising set of circumstances since the mid-1960s, which saw the Equal Pay Act passed in 1963; Title VII of the Civil Rights Acts, which banned gender discrimination at work, passed in 1964; and an Executive Order banning discrimination by federal employees and federal contractors, issued in 1965. That's when we as a nation started paying attention to the idea that women deserve equal pay. [20]

In the 1990s, more than a generation later, women were as qualified as men in just about every particular. This was the decade in which the economy's transformation from brawn to brains, from a manufacturing to a service- and information-based economy, seemed complete. And that's where women are just as well equipped as men: in human relations, in verbal and numeric skills (if you look at the SATs or GREs), in solving problems and creating ideas. America's commitment to reaching wage equality for women — and all that meant for women and men becoming socially equal as well — had failed. [21]

If women's earnings could not catch up to men's in a time of nearly unreal prosperity, at a time when women's qualifications had caught up, what was holding them back? [22]

The answer is simple: discrimination. [23]

Notes

1. Policy analysts pinned the explanation of why the gender wage gap widened in the mid-1990s on "welfare reform." Their theory: since almost all — 90 percent — of welfare recipients were women, when these low-skilled, untrained mothers lost their welfare support and were forced to join the full-time workforce in low-paying jobs, their wages dragged the average of women's overall wages down. That explanation sounds plausible. But it's wrong. Women's average wages dropped between 1993 and 1996 — *before* Congress passed the welfare reform law in 1996. A number of states experimented with reforming welfare before national legislation took effect. In these states, some welfare recipients did trickle into minimum-wage work before national welfare reform passed — but not enough of them to drag down the overall average of women's wages. Even in August 1996, when welfare reform passed, welfare recipients still had more time before they had to seek work. Not until 1997, 1998, and 1999 did large numbers of former welfare recipients start working in low-paying jobs. And in those years, contrary to welfare reform theories, average women's wages *increased* — and the wage gap narrowed.
2. Table P-32, "Educational Attainment — Full-Time, Year-Round Workers 18 Years Old and Over, by Mean Earnings, Age, and Sex: 1991 to 2003," U.S. Census Bureau, *Historical Income Tables — People*, Washington, D.C., 2005.
3. Lawrence Michel, Jared Berstein, John Schmitt, *State of Working America 1998–99*, Economic Policy Institute, Washington, D.C., Chapter 1: Family Income.

4. "Educational Attainment—People 25 Years Old and Over by Median Income and Sex: 1991 to 2001," in U.S. Census Bureau, *Historical Income Tables—People,* Washington, D.C.

Questions to Start You Thinking

1. CONSIDERING MEANING: Why, according to Murphy, should the wage gap between women and men have disappeared for people who entered the workforce since the early 1990s? Why does she think it has not?

2. IDENTIFYING WRITING STRATEGIES: Consider Murphy's use of italics throughout the essay. What is the effect of the italicized words and phrases? What do they contribute to Murphy's tone?

3. READING CRITICALLY: How convincing do you find Murphy's explanation for the wage gap between women and men? Can you think of other possible reasons why women, on average, earn less than men?

4. EXPANDING VOCABULARY: In paragraph 13, Murphy refers to "male chauvinist attitudes." What does the term *chauvinist* mean in this context, and what is its origin? Why do you think it is less commonly used today than in the 1960s and 1970s?

5. MAKING CONNECTIONS: Tamara Draut's "What's a Diploma Worth, Anyway?" (pp. 561–63) focuses on declining wages for both males and females entering the workforce since 2000. How do the statistics Draut offers affect your view of Murphy's argument?

Journal Prompts

1. How do you respond to Murphy's argument? Are you surprised to learn of the wage gap between women and men? What do you think of Murphy's comment in paragraph 1 that many people she questioned believed a woman should earn "about eighty cents to a man's dollar"?

2. In paragraph 13, Murphy refers to "young adults [who] grew up with mothers who were just as educated, qualified, employed, and employable as their fathers . . . [who] actually knew women who were bus drivers and doctors, heavy-metal guitarists and helicopter pilots, corporate managers and professional tennis players, state senators and Supreme Court justices." Do you feel women have achieved equality with men? Why or why not?

Suggestions for Writing

1. In the selection's final paragraph, Murphy claims that what has kept the gender wage gap from closing is discrimination. How would you define *discrimination*? In what ways might different groups be discriminated against? As you plan your essay, consider examples from your own experience, the experience of friends, and your reading.

2. Write an essay about another controversial workplace issue. For example, you might explore one of these questions: Should employers be allowed to monitor employees' electronic communications? Is drug testing in the workplace an invasion of privacy? Why are women underrepresented in certain careers? Support your conclusions with evidence from sources, as Murphy does.

Noel Perrin
A Part-Time Marriage

■ For more about
Noel Perrin, visit
<bedfordstmartins.com/
bedguide> and do a key-
word search:

 author

Noel Perrin *(1927–2004) was born in New York City. He earned degrees at Williams College, Duke University, and Cambridge University and for over forty years taught English and environmental studies at Dartmouth College. For all his academic credentials, much of his fame as a writer comes from three volumes of essays on part-time farming —* Second Person Rural *(1980),* Third Person Rural *(1983), and* Last Person Rural *(1991). After his death in 2004, some of his finest essays from these books were collected in* Best Person Rural *(2006). Perrin's* A Child's Delight *(1997) is a collection of essays celebrating some of his favorite but underappreciated children's books. In the following essay, first published in the* New York Times Magazine *on September 9, 1984, Perrin satirizes the postdivorce behavior of many middle-class couples and proposes a somewhat unusual remedy for the problems that plague modern marriages. In the paired selection that follows (pp. 497–99), Judy Brady also satirizes marital roles, but with a very different purpose.*

AS YOU READ: *Identify the problems with marriage that Perrin addresses.*

When my wife told me she wanted a divorce, I responded like any nor- 1
mal college professor. I hurried to the college library. I wanted to get hold of some books on divorce and find out what was happening to me.

Over the next week (my wife meanwhile having left), I read or skimmed 2
about twenty. Nineteen of them were no help at all. They offered advice on financial settlements. They told me my wife and I should have been in counseling. A bit late for *that* advice.

What I sought was insight. I especially wanted to understand what was 3
wrong with me that my wife had left, and not even for someone else, but just to be rid of *me*. College professors think they can learn that sort of thing from books.

As it turned out, I could. Or at least I got a start. The twentieth book was 4
a collection of essays by various sociologists, and one of the pieces took my breath away. It was like reading my own horoscope.

The two authors had studied a large group of divorced people much like 5
my wife and me. That is, they focused on middle-class Americans of the straight-arrow persuasion. Serious types, believers in marriage for life. Likely to be parents — and, on the whole, good parents. Likely to have pillar-of-the-community potential. But, nevertheless, all divorced.

Naturally there were many different reasons why all these people had 6
divorced, and many different ways they behaved after the divorce. But there was a dominant pattern, and I instantly recognized myself in it. Recognized my wife, too. Reading the essay told me not only what was wrong with me, but also with her. It was the same flaw in both of us. It even gave me a hint as to what my postdivorce behavior was likely to be, and how I might find happiness in the future.

494

This is the story the essay told me. Or, rather, this is the story the essay 7
hinted at, and that I have since pieced together with much observation, a
number of embarrassingly personal questions put to divorced friends, and
to some extent from my own life.

Somewhere in some suburb or small city, a middle-class couple separate. 8
They are probably between thirty and forty years old. They own a house and
have children. The conscious or official reason for their separation is quite
different from what it would have been in their parents' generation. Then, it
would have been a man leaving his wife for another, and usually younger,
woman. Now it's a woman leaving her husband in order to find herself.

When they separate, the wife normally stays in the house they occupied 9
as a married couple. Neither wants to uproot the children. The husband
moves to an apartment, which is nearly always going to be closer to his
place of employment than his house was. The ex-wife will almost certainly
never see that apartment. The husband, however, sees his former house all
the time. Not only is he coming by to pick up the children for visits; if he
and his ex-wife are on reasonably good terms, he is apt to visit them right
there, while she makes use of the time to do errands or to see a friend.

Back when these two were married, they had an informal labor division. 10
She did inside work, he did outside. Naturally there were exceptions: she
gardened, and he did his share of the dishes, maybe even baked bread. But
mostly he mowed the lawn and fixed the lawn mower; she put up any new
curtains, often enough ones she had made herself.

One Saturday, six months or a year after they separated, he comes to see 11
the kids. He plans also to mow the lawn. Before she leaves, she says, "That
damn overhead garage door you got is off the track again. Do you think
you'd have time to fix it?" Apartment life makes him restless. He jumps at
the chance.

She, just as honorable and straight-arrow as he, has no idea of asking 12
for this as a favor. She invites him to stay for an early dinner. She may put
it indirectly — "Michael and Sally want their daddy to have supper with
them" — but he is clear that the invitation also proceeds from her.

Provided neither of them has met a really attractive other person yet, 13
they now move into a routine. He comes regularly to do the outside chores,
and always stays for dinner. If the children are young enough, he may read
to them before bedtime. She may wash his shirts.

One such evening, they both happen to be stirred not only by physical 14
desire but by loneliness. "Oh, you might as well come upstairs," she says
with a certain self-contempt. He needs no second invitation; they are upstairs
in a flash. It is a delightful end to the evening. More delightful than anything
they remember from their marriage, or at least from the later part of it.

That, too, now becomes part of the pattern. He never stays the full 15
night, because, good parents that they are, they don't want the children to
get any false hopes up — as they would, seeing their father at breakfast.

Such a relationship may go on for several years, may even be inter- 16
rupted by a romance on one side or the other and then resume. It may even

grow to the point where she's mending as well as washing his shirts, and he is advising her on her tax returns and fixing her car.

What they have achieved postdivorce is what their marriage should have   17 been like in the first place. Part-time. Seven days a week of marriage was too much. One afternoon and two evenings is just right.

Although our society is even now witnessing de facto part-time arrange-   18 ments, such as the couple who work in different cities and meet only on weekends, we have no theory of part-time marriage, at least no theory that has reached the general public. The romantic notion still dominates that if you love someone, you obviously want to be with them all the time.

To me it's clear we need such a theory. There are certainly people who   19 thrive on seven-day-a-week marriages. They have a high level of intimacy and they may be better, warmer people than the rest of us. But there are millions and millions of us with medium or low levels of intimacy. We find full-time family memberships a strain. If we could enter marriage with more realistic expectations of what closeness means for us, I suspect the divorce rate might permanently turn downward. It's too bad there isn't a sort of glucose tolerance test for intimacy.

As for me personally, I still do want to get married again. About four   20 days a week.

Questions to Start You Thinking

1. CONSIDERING MEANING: How did Perrin's divorce affect him?
2. IDENTIFYING WRITING STRATEGIES: How does Perrin use cause and effect to support the solution he proposes?
3. READING CRITICALLY: What is Perrin's purpose in writing this essay? Do you think he is serious about his proposal for a part-time marriage? What evidence in his essay leads you to your conclusion?
4. EXPANDING VOCABULARY: Notice Perrin's use of the words *straight-arrow*, *pillar-of-the-community* (paragraph 5), *dominant* (paragraph 6), *self-contempt* (paragraph 14), *de facto* (paragraph 18), and *glucose tolerance test* (paragraph 19). How does Perrin's vocabulary fit or challenge your expectations of how a college professor writes? Find other examples to support your answer.
5. MAKING CONNECTIONS: How might Perrin respond to Dave Barry's more comic view of relations between men and women in "From Now On, Let Women Kill Their Own Spiders" (pp. 485–87)? What do these two essays suggest about the roles taken on by wives and husbands? Do they reflect the kinds of roles you are familiar with?

■ For useful links to Web sources on topics including *families*, visit <bedfordstmartins.com/ toplinks>.

Link to the Paired Essay

How might Perrin react to Judy Brady's point of view in "I Want a Wife" (pp. 497–99)? By reading Brady's essay, might Perrin have a better understanding of why his wife left him to "find herself"? Would he appreciate Brady's satire?

Journal Prompts

1. Would you prefer a full- or part-time marriage? Why?

2. Sketch out a theory or a plan for part-time marriage. What elements or rules would be needed to make it successful?

Suggestions for Writing

1. Write an essay explaining how divorce has affected you or those around you.

2. Take a stand on the solution Perrin proposes. In a short essay, agree or disagree with the idea of part-time marriage. Is it a constructive response to problems of marital incompatibility? Why or why not?

Judy Brady
I Want a Wife

Judy Brady *was born in 1937 in San Francisco, where she now makes her home. A graduate of the University of Iowa, Brady has contributed to various publications and has traveled to Cuba to study class relationships and education. She edited the book* 1 in 3: Women with Cancer Confront an Epidemic *(1991), drawing on her own struggle with the disease, and she continues to write and speak about cancer and its possible environmental causes. In the following piece, which has been reprinted frequently since its appearance in* Ms. *magazine in December 1971, Brady considers the role of the American housewife. While she has said that she is "not a 'writer,'" this essay shows Brady to be a satirist adept at taking a stand and provoking attention.*

■ For more about Judy Brady, visit <bedfordstmartins.com/ bedguide> and do a keyword search:

🔍 **author**

AS YOU READ: *Ask yourself why Brady says she wants a wife rather than a husband.*

I belong to that classification of people known as wives. I am A Wife. And, 1 not altogether incidentally, I am a mother.

Not too long ago a male friend of mine appeared on the scene fresh 2 from a recent divorce. He had one child, who is, of course, with his ex-wife. He is looking for another wife. As I thought about him while I was ironing one evening, it suddenly occurred to me that I, too, would like to have a wife. Why do I want a wife?

I would like to go back to school so that I can become economically 3 independent, support myself, and, if need be, support those dependent upon me. I want a wife who will work and send me to school. And while I am going to school I want a wife to take care of my children. I want a wife to keep track of the children's doctor and dentist appointments. And to keep track of mine, too. I want a wife to make sure my children eat properly and are kept clean. I want a wife who will wash the children's clothes and keep them mended. I want a wife who is a good nurturant° attendant to my children, who arranges for their schooling, makes sure that they have an adequate social life with their peers, takes them to the park, the zoo, etc. I want a wife who takes care of the children when they are sick, a wife who arranges to be around when the children need special care, because, of course, I cannot miss classes at school. My wife must arrange to lose time at work and not lose the job. It may mean a small cut in my wife's income from time to time, but I guess I can tolerate that. Needless to say, my wife will arrange and pay for the care of the children while my wife is working.

I want a wife who will take care of *my* physical needs. I want a wife who   4 will keep my house clean. A wife who will pick up after my children, a wife who will pick up after me. I want a wife who will keep my clothes clean, ironed, mended, replaced when need be, and who will see to it that my personal things are kept in their proper place so that I can find what I need the minute I need it. I want a wife who cooks the meals, a wife who is a *good* cook. I want a wife who will plan the menus, do the necessary grocery shopping, prepare the meals, serve them pleasantly, and then do the cleaning up while I do my studying. I want a wife who will care for me when I am sick and sympathize with my pain and loss of time from school. I want a wife to go along when our family takes a vacation so that someone can continue to care for me and my children when I need a rest and change of scene.

I want a wife who will not bother me with rambling complaints about   5 a wife's duties. But I want a wife who will listen to me when I feel the need to explain a rather difficult point I have come across in my course of studies.

I want a wife who will take care of the details of my social life. When   6 my wife and I are invited out by my friends, I want a wife who will take care of the babysitting arrangements. When I meet people at school that I like and want to entertain, I want a wife who will have the house clean, will prepare a special meal, serve it to me and my friends, and not interrupt when I talk about things that interest me and my friends. I want a wife who will have arranged that the children are fed and ready for bed before my guests arrive so that the children do not bother us. I want a wife who takes care of the needs of my guests so that they feel comfortable, who makes sure that they have an ashtray, that they are passed the hors d'oeuvres, that they are offered a second helping of the food, that their wine glasses are replenished when necessary, that their coffee is served to them as they like it. And I want a wife who knows that sometimes I need a night out by myself.

I want a wife who is sensitive to my sexual needs, a wife who makes   7 love passionately and eagerly when I feel like it, a wife who makes sure that I am satisfied. And, of course, I want a wife who will not demand sexual

nurturant: Kind, loving, nourishing.

attention when I am not in the mood for it. I want a wife who assumes the complete responsibility for birth control, because I do not want more children. I want a wife who will remain sexually faithful to me so that I do not have to clutter up my intellectual life with jealousies. And I want a wife who understands that *my* sexual needs may entail more than strict adherence to monogamy. I must, after all, be able to relate to people as fully as possible.

If, by chance, I find another person more suitable as a wife than the wife   8
I already have, I want the liberty to replace my present wife with another one. Naturally, I will expect a fresh, new life; my wife will take the children and be solely responsible for them so that I am left free.

When I am through with school and have a job, I want my wife to quit   9
working and remain at home so that my wife can more fully and completely take care of a wife's duties.

My God, who *wouldn't* want a wife?   10

Questions to Start You Thinking

1. CONSIDERING MEANING: How does Brady define the traditional role of the wife? Does she think that a wife should perform all of the duties she outlines? How can you tell?

2. IDENTIFYING WRITING STRATEGIES: How does Brady use observation to support her stand? What other approaches does she use?

3. READING CRITICALLY: What is the tone of this essay? How does Brady establish it? Considering that she was writing for a predominantly female — and feminist — audience, do you think Brady's tone is appropriate?

4. EXPANDING VOCABULARY: Why does Brady use such simple language in this essay? What is the effect of her use of such phrases as *of course* (paragraph 2), *Needless to say* (paragraph 3), and *Naturally* (paragraph 8)?

5. MAKING CONNECTIONS: In "Why Not a Dollar?" (pp. 488–92), Evelyn F. Murphy writes about the wage gap between women and men in the workplace. How might the traditional role assigned to women that Brady describes contribute to women on average getting paid less than men?

Link to the Paired Essay

Does Noel Perrin's presentation of himself as a husband in "A Part-Time Marriage" (pp. 494–96) strike you as similar to or different from the kind of husband suggested by Brady in "I Want a Wife"? Point to specific passages in Perrin's essay to support your answer. Given Brady's purpose in her essay, what do you think she might have to say to Perrin about his proposed "solution" to the problems of modern marriages?

Journal Prompts

1. Exert your wishful thinking — describe your ideal mate.
2. Begin with a stereotype of a husband, wife, boyfriend, girlfriend, father, or mother, and write a satirical description of that stereotype.

Suggestions for Writing

1. In a short personal essay, explain what you want or expect in a wife, husband, or life partner. Do your hopes and expectations differ from social and cultural norms? If so, in what way(s)? How has your parents' relationship shaped your attitudes and ideals?

2. How has the role of a wife changed since this essay was written? Write an essay comparing and contrasting the post-2000 wife with the kind of wife Judy Brady claims she wants.

Chapter 25
Popular Culture

Responding to an Image

Read this comic strip frame by frame, and summarize its basic story. What is the significance of its title? Overall, what is the comic strip's purpose? How does it combine text and visual images to comment on our ability to counter the effects of advertising? Why do you think the writer/artist chose to convey her message through a comic strip?

Web Search

For reading activities linked to this chapter, visit <bedfordstmartins.com/bedguide> and do a key-word search:

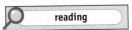
reading

Visit adflip <www.adflip.com/>, a site that archives both classic and modern print advertisements. Click on "Current Ads," and choose one that interests you. Then search one of the site's classic-ad collections, looking for a similar product from a different decade. Compare and contrast the two ads. How do their visual and written components differ? What techniques or appeals do the advertisers use to sell the products? What does each ad reveal about the culture of its decade or about its intended audience? Write an essay using specific details from the ads to support your thesis or main idea about the pair.

Tara Parker-Pope
Custom-Made

For more about Tara Parker-Pope, visit <bedfordstmartins.com/bedguide> and do a key-word search:

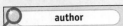
author

Tara Parker-Pope is the author of the weekly Health Journal column for the Wall Street Journal, *where she enjoys "taking this really technical, complicated stuff and distilling it down into something that people can understand and use to make decisions about their health." After graduating from the University of Texas with an MA in sociology, she went on to work as a political and government reporter for the* Houston Chronicle *and the* Austin-American Statesman. *She joined the* Wall Street Journal *in 1993, where she wrote about consumer products, marketing, and advertising before starting the Health Journal column in 2000. She is the author of* Cigarettes: Anatomy of an Industry from Seed to Smoke *(2001) and* The Hormone Decision *(2007). "Custom-Made" was first published in the* Wall Street Journal Europe *in 1996. Using numerous examples, Parker-Pope illustrates how global brands such as Domino's, McDonald's, and Heinz adapt their products and marketing tactics to appeal to local tastes.*

AS YOU READ: *Notice the many different countries Parker-Pope writes about. What do you learn about the tastes and lifestyles of people in these different countries?*

Pity the poor Domino's Pizza Inc. delivery man.   1

In Britain, customers don't like the idea of him knocking on their 2 doors—they think it's rude. In Japan, houses aren't numbered sequentially—finding an address means searching among rows of houses numbered willy-nilly.° And in Kuwait, pizza is more likely to be delivered to a waiting limousine than to someone's front door.

"We honestly believe we have the best pizza-delivery system in the 3 world," says Gary McCausland, managing director of Domino's international division. "But delivering pizza isn't the same all over the world."

And neither is making cars, selling soap, or packaging toilet paper. Inter- 4 national marketers have found that just because a product plays in Peoria, that doesn't mean it will be a hit in Helsinki.

willy-nilly: Without a particular order.

To satisfy local tastes, products ranging from Heinz ketchup to Cheetos   5
chips are tweaked, reformulated, and reflavored. Fast-food companies such
as McDonald's Corporation, popular for the "sameness" they offer all over
the world, have discovered that to succeed, they also need to offer some
local appeal — selling beer in Germany and adding British Cadbury chocolate sticks to their ice-cream cones in England.

The result is a delicate balancing act for international marketers: How   6
does a company exploit the economies of scale° that can be gained by
global marketing while at the same time making its products appeal to local
tastes?

The answer: be flexible, even when it means changing a tried-and-true   7
recipe, even when consumer preferences, like Häagen-Dazs green tea ice
cream, sound awful to the Western palate.

"It's a dilemma we all live with every day," says Nick Harding, H. J.   8
Heinz Company's managing director for northern Europe. Heinz varies the
recipe of its famous ketchup in different markets, selling a less-sweet version
in Belgium and Holland, for instance, because consumers there use ketchup
as a pasta sauce (and mayonnaise on french fries). "We're looking for the
economies from globalizing our ideas, but we want to maintain the differences necessary for local markets," says Mr. Harding.

For those who don't heed such advice, the costs are high. U.S. auto   9
makers, for instance, have done poorly in Japan, at least in part because they
failed to adapt. Until recently, most didn't bother even to put steering
wheels on the right, as is the standard in Japan. While some American makers are beginning to conform, European companies such as Volkswagen AG,
Daimler-Benz AG, and Bayerische Motoren Werke AG did it much sooner,
and have done far better in the Japanese market as a result.

For Domino's, the balancing act has meant maintaining the same basic   10
pizza-delivery system worldwide — and then teaming up with local franchisers
to tailor the system to each country's needs. In Japan, detailed wall maps,
three times larger than those used in its stores elsewhere, help delivery
people find the proper address despite the odd street-numbering system.

In Iceland, where much of the population doesn't have phone service,   11
Domino's has teamed with a Reykjavik drive-in movie theater to gain access
to consumers. Customers craving a reindeer-sausage pizza (a popular flavor
there) flash their turn signal, and a theater employee brings them a cellular
phone to order a pizza, which is then delivered to the car.

Local Domino's managers have developed new pizza flavors, including   12
mayo jaga (mayonnaise and potato) in Tokyo and pickled ginger in India.
The company, which now has 1,160 stores in 46 countries, is currently trying to develop a nonbeef pepperoni topping for its stores in India.

When Pillsbury Company, a unit of Britain's Grand Metropolitan PLC,   13
wanted to begin marketing its Green Giant brand vegetables outside the United
States, it decided to start with canned sweet corn, a basic product unlikely to

economies of scale: A decrease in the average per unit cost of production that occurs
with an increase in the number of units produced.

require any flavor changes across international markets. But to Pillsbury's surprise, the product still was subject to local influences. Instead of being eaten as a hot side dish, the French add it to salad and eat it cold. In Britain, corn is used as a sandwich and pizza topping. In Japan, school children gobble down canned corn as an after-school treat. And in Korea, the sweet corn is sprinkled over ice cream. . . .

The drive for localization has been taken to extremes in some cases: 14 Cheetos, the bright orange and cheesy-tasting chip brand of PepsiCo Inc.'s Frito-Lay unit, are cheeseless in China. The reason? Chinese consumers generally don't like cheese, in part because many of them are lactose intolerant. So Cheetos tested such flavors as Peking duck, fried egg, and even dog to tempt the palates of Chinese.

Ultimately, says Tom Kuthy, vice president of marketing for PepsiCo 15 Foods International's Asia-Pacific operations, the company picked a butter flavor, called American cream, and an Asianized barbecue flavor called Japanese steak. Last year, Frito rolled out its third flavor, seafood.

In addition to changing the taste, the company also packaged Cheetos 16 in a 15-gram size priced at one yuan, about 12 cents, so that even kids with little spending money can afford them.

The bottom line: these efforts to adapt to the local market have paid off. 17 Mr. Kuthy estimates that close to 300 million packages of Cheetos have been sold since they were introduced two years ago in Guangzhou. Cheetos are now available in Shanghai and Beijing as well.

Frito isn't through trying to adapt. Now the company is introducing a 18 33-gram pack for two yuan. Mr. Kuthy also is considering more flavors, but dog won't be one of them. "Yes, we tested the concept, but it was never made into a product," he says. "Its performance was mediocre."

Other PepsiCo units have followed with their own flavor variations. In 19 Thailand, Pizza Hut has a tom yam-flavored pizza based on the spices of the traditional Thai soup. In Singapore, you can get a KFC Zinger chicken burger that is hot and spicy with Asia's ubiquitous chili. The Singaporean pizza at Pizza Hut comes with ground beef, green peppers, and chili. Elsewhere in Asia, pizzas come in flavors such as Mongolian, with pork, chili, and garlic; salmon, with a creamy lobster sauce; and Satay, with grilled chicken and beef.

Coming up with the right flavor combinations for international con- 20 sumers isn't easy. Part of the challenge is building relationships with customers in far-flung markets. For years, the founders of Ben & Jerry's Home-made Inc. had relied on friends, co-workers, and their own taste buds to concoct such unusual ice-cream flavors as Chunky Monkey and Cherry Garcia.

But introducing their ice cream abroad, by definition, meant losing that 21 close connection with their customers that made them successful. "For Ben and me, since we've grown up in the United States, our customers were people like us, and the flavors we made appealed to us," says cofounder Jerry Greenfield, scooping ice cream at a media event in the Royal Albert Hall in London. "I don't think we have the same seat-of-the-pants feel for places like England. It's a different culture."

As a result, one of the company's most popular flavors in the United 22
States, Chocolate Chip Cookie Dough, flopped in Britain. The nostalgia
quotient of the ice cream, vanilla-flavored with chunks of raw cookie dough,
was simply lost on the Brits, who historically haven't eaten chocolate-chip
cookies. "People didn't grow up in this country sneaking raw cookie-dough
batter from Mom," says Mr. Greenfield.

The solution? Hold a contest to concoct a quintessential British ice cream. 23
After reviewing hundreds of entries, including Choc Ness Monster and Cream
Victoria, the company in July introduced Cool Britannia, a combination of
vanilla ice cream, strawberries, and chocolate-covered Scottish shortbread.
(The company plans to sell Cool Britannia in the United States eventually.)

And in a stab at building a quirky relationship with Brits, the duo opted 24
for a publicity stunt when Britain's beef crisis° meant farmers were left with
herds of cattle that couldn't be sold at market. Ben & Jerry's creative solution: use the cows to advertise. The company's logo was draped across the
backs of grazing cattle, and the stunt made the front page of major London
newspapers.

The company has just begun selling ice cream in France but isn't sure 25
whether the company will try contests for a French flavor in that market.
One reason: it's unclear whether Ben & Jerry's wry humor, amusing to the
Brits, will be understood by the laconic° French. "We're going to try to get
more in touch, more comfortable with the feel of the French market first,"
says Mr. Greenfield.

But for every success story, there have been a slew of global marketing 26
mistakes. In Japan, consumer-products marketer Procter & Gamble Company
made several stumbles when it first entered the market in the early 1970s.

The company thought its thicker, more-absorbent Pampers diapers in 27
big packs like those favored in America would be big sellers in Japan. But
Japanese women change their babies twice as often as Americans and prefer
thin diapers. Moreover, they often have tiny apartments and no room to
store huge diaper packs.

The company adapted by making thinner diapers packaged in smaller bags. 28
Because the company shifted gears quickly, Procter & Gamble is now one of the
largest and most successful consumer-goods companies in Japan, with more
than $1 billion in annual sales and market leadership in several categories.

Questions to Start You Thinking

1. CONSIDERING MEANING: Why is it important that U.S. companies learn to
   adapt their product lines for different international markets?

2. IDENTIFYING WRITING STRATEGIES: Which examples do you find particularly
   effective in illustrating Parker-Pope's point about product adaptation? Why
   do you suppose she included so many examples? What is their effect?

---

beef crisis: A reference to mad cow disease, which infected many British cattle and pre-
vented their consumption as meat.   **laconic:** Marked by using few words.

3. **READING CRITICALLY:** Throughout the essay, Parker-Pope includes quotations from executives of U.S. companies. Is this strategy effective for the point she is trying to make? Why or why not?

4. **EXPANDING VOCABULARY:** Consider Parker-Pope's title for the essay. In what sense does "Custom-Made" have a double meaning?

5. **MAKING CONNECTIONS:** In "Latino Style Is Cool. Oh, All Right: It's Hot" (below), Ruth La Ferla examines how young Hispanics have adopted fashions that reflect their heritage. How might U.S. product manufacturers adapt themselves to this Latino market? Have you noticed any examples of companies doing so in their advertising, for example?

Journal Prompts

1. Which of the product adaptations that Parker-Pope writes about sound appealing to you? Which sound like something you wouldn't want to try? What do you suppose contributes to your response?

2. Think of a snack you enjoy eating. Then be creative and come up with ways you might adapt its flavor for alternative versions that could broaden its share of the market.

Suggestions for Writing

1. Choose a type of consumer product that inspires intense competition among different companies — soft drinks, for example, or running shoes or toothpaste or cellular phone service. Then analyze some print and television ads for different brands of the product, considering how they appeal to you or might appeal to others. In an essay, compare and contrast each brand's advertising, and make some conjectures about the target audience in each case.

■ For more advice on evaluating, see Ch. 11.

2. Pick a type of product (jeans, shoes, fast food, cars), and list at least three criteria that you think are essential for it. For example, for jeans, you might select good fit, stylishness, and a price below fifty dollars. Then evaluate two or three different examples of this product based on how well they meet your criteria. What suggestions might you make to the manufacturers to improve their products?

Ruth La Ferla

Latino Style Is Cool. Oh, All Right: It's Hot

■ For more about Ruth La Ferla, visit <bedfordstmartins.com/bedguide> and do a keyword search:

Ruth La Ferla was born in 1936, in Munich, Germany, and moved to Chicago, Illinois, with her family in 1939. She earned a bachelor's degree from Knox College and a master's degree in German literature from the University of Illinois. From 1985 to 1991, she wrote for the New York Times Sunday Magazine *and then went on to work for* Elle. *In 2000, she returned to the* New York Times *as a*

fashion writer, publishing articles in the Thursday Styles pages and in the Sunday Lifestyle section. She has also worked as a fashion editor for Women's Wear Daily *and* Avenue. *"Latino Style Is Cool. Oh, All Right: It's Hot" first appeared in the* New York Times *on April 15, 2001, around the time that Jennifer Lopez introduced her new clothing line, JLo. La Ferla wanted to explore the rise of Latino stars in the media and how their visibility might affect the fashion industry. During her investigation, she discovered Latino culture's proud expression of heritage through fashion.*

AS YOU READ: *Identify the primary characteristics of the Latino style that La Ferla describes.*

On a recent Friday afternoon, Lisa Forero, her dark, shoulder-length   1
hair parted in the center, stalked the corridors of La Guardia High School of Performing Arts in Manhattan, perched on four-inch platform boots. Ms. Forero, a drama major, played up her curves in a form-fitting gray spandex dress and wore outsize gold hoops on her ears. Her fingertips were airbrushed in tints of pink and cream.

Did she fret that her image — that of a saucy bombshell — bordered on   2
self-parody? Not a bit. Dressing up as a familiar stereotype is Ms. Forero's pointedly aggressive way of claiming her Latino heritage, she says. Ms. Forero, seventeen, acknowledged that she had not always been so bold. "Two or three years ago, I didn't usually wear gold," she said, "and I usually wouldn't get my nails done. But as I've gotten older, I've needed to identify more with my cultural background."

Her sandy-haired classmate Kenneth Lamadrid, seventeen, is just as   3
brash. "Because of the way I look and because my parents called me Ken, a lot of people don't know that I'm Cuban," he said. But Mr. Lamadrid takes pains to set them straight. That afternoon, he was wearing a souvenir from a recent family reunion, a snug T-shirt emblazoned with the names of all of his relatives who have emigrated to the United States from Cuba. "I'm wearing my family history," he said. "You have to be proud of who you are."

Ms. Forero and Mr. Lamadrid are members of a population that, accord-   4
ing to the 2000 census, seems on the verge of becoming America's largest minority group. Wildly heterogeneous,° its members come from more than twenty countries and represent a mixture of races, backgrounds, and even religions. What Latinos share, as Ms. Forero well knows, is a common language — Spanish — and rapidly expanding cultural clout.°

"Hispanic is hip," she observed dryly. "Right now, it's the thing to be."   5
Indeed, in the last couple of years Latinos have been surprised and flattered to find themselves courted as voters, consumers, workers, and entertainers. And now many are bemused to discover that, like hip-hop–influenced African Americans before them, they are admired as avatars° of urban chic.

---

heterogeneous: From diverse sources.   **clout:** Power.   **avatars:** Perfect representations of.

"There is an emerging Latino style, and I think it appeals to more than 6
just Latinos," said Clara Rodriguez, a professor of sociology at Fordham
University in Manhattan and the author of *Latin Looks: Images of Latinas and
Latinos in the U.S. Media* (Westview Press, 1997). Dr. Rodriguez made a
point of distinguishing between pervasive archetypes — the smoldering
vamp, the brilliantined° Lothario° — and the fashion personas adopted by
young urban Hispanics, which allude to those types without aping them.
These Latin Gen X-ers are rediscovering their roots and flaunting them, she
said, while communicating solidarity by the way they dress.

Rodrigo Salazar, the editor of *Urban Latino*, a general-interest magazine for 7
young Hispanics, expressed a similar view. "As we stake our claim in the culture, we are starting to take control of our own images," Mr. Salazar said.
Young, trend-conscious Latinos do that in part, he said, by experimenting with
fashion and cultivating a street-smart style that is more overtly sensual than
hip-hop and is at the same time heavily steeped in Hispanic iconography.°

Flounces, ruffles, and ear hoops are among the generic, ostentatiously° 8
Hispanic symbols being tossed into a pan-Latino° blender these days. Even
crosses are part of the mix, not as a symbol of faith but as a hip accessory. Mr.
Salazar conceded that such items lend themselves to ethnic stereotyping but ar-
gued that perhaps that is all the more reason to flaunt them. For many young
Hispanics, he said, they are a visual shorthand that signals their identity.

Latino style also incorporates the provocative cropped T-shirts, low- 9
slung chinos, stacked heels, and chains that are the fashion insignia of cho-
los, members of Latin street gangs. And it incorporates components of a
style adopted by young Puerto Rican New Yorkers in the late 1970s: fitted
shirts in phantasmagorical° patterns, hip-riding denims, cropped halters,
blouses tied at the midriff, navel-baring T-shirts, and platform shoes. Similar
regalia survives as the style uniform of pop icons like Ricky Martin and Jennifer Lopez.

But the look is also indebted to the traditional garb favored by an earlier 10
generation of Latino immigrants. On some days, for example, Mr. Lamadrid,
the drama student, wears a guayabera, a loose multipocket shirt like the
ones his Cuban grandfather used to wear. Nowadays, the shirts, worn by
many young Hispanics as a badge of their heritage, have been appropriated
by non-Hispanics as well.

"We take our lead from the things we've seen our parents wear and the 11
things we've seen in movies," Mr. Salazar said, "but our style is evolving as
our influence is growing. We're seeing ourselves in the street, and we're following the cues of our friends and celebrities who are Latino."

Mr. Salazar was describing a cultural pastiche° that has become increas- 12
ingly identifiable — and some maintain, consummately marketable. Its po-

---

brilliantined: Hair slicked back with a shiny pomade.   **Lothario:** A man known for
seducing women.   **iconography:** Symbolism.   **ostentatiously:** Marked by showi-
ness.   **pan-Latino:** Across Latino culture.   **phantasmagorical:** Fantastic, as related to
what is not real.   **pastiche:** Mixture.

tential mass appeal is surely not lost on Ms. Lopez, the singer and actress, who is negotiating with Andy Hilfiger, Tommy's younger brother, to market her own brand of Latina glam in a fashion line.

At the same time, Latina chic is being packaged for mass consumption by 13 some leading apparel makers. In the last several months, Ralph Lauren, Nike, Tommy Hilfiger, and the Gap have played to the current fascination with Latina exoticism in advertisements featuring variations on the full-lipped, south-of-the-border sexpot. Ralph Lauren's campaign showcases the Spanish film star Penélope Cruz in a snug top and a swirling skirt, performing what looks like flamenco. Both Guess and Sergio Valente display ads in which halter tops and rump-clutching denims encase Brazilian brunettes. And Vertigo, a midprice sportswear company, is showing its scarlet trouser suit on a raven-haired vamp, a ringer — it can't be coincidence — for a young Bianca Jagger.

"Our industry has become enamored with the dark, mysterious confidence 14 that these women portray," said Steven Miska, the president of Sergio Valente.

Magazine editors, too, find the Latin look compelling. The March issue 15 of Italian *Vogue*, the fashionista's bible, has a feature in which young Latino-Americans model the season's key looks.

Is the industry trying to market Latinness as a commodity? "Definitely," 16 said Sam Shahid, the president and creative director of Shahid, a New York advertising agency with fashion clients. Mr. Shahid employed Hispanic models for the latest Abercrombie & Fitch catalog. "No one moves as freely," he said, then added: "Selling a Latin look doesn't mean it has to be a Carmen Miranda,° cha-cha type thing. 'Latin' can simply be a sultry sex appeal."

Should Mr. Hilfiger and Ms. Lopez reach an agreement, industry insid- 17 ers speculate that the collection will draw heavily on Ms. Lopez's Puerto Rican heritage. "Her flash look, the stacked heels, the low-rise jeans — these things are already being emulated by people well outside the Hispanic community," said Tom Julian, a trend analyst for Fallon Worldwide, a Minneapolis branding company.

Deliberately packaging an urban Hispanic look for mass consumption 18 makes sense to Mr. Julian. "Ethnicity is good in today's marketplace," he said. "All of a sudden you are talking about hair, makeup, clothing, and accessories that are part of a lifestyle that is distinctive, that has a point of view." Noting that so-called urban apparel — the streetwise casual wear favored by young blacks and Hispanics — is a $5 billion-a-year business, he ventured that a Latino subgenre could generate at least half that amount.

Some Hispanics bristle at the reduction of their identity to a handful of 19 styling cues, which might then be peddled as Latin chic. They are uneasy about being lumped by outsiders into an undifferentiated cultural mass. "I think the world would often like to describe us as a bunch of hot tamales," said Betty Cortina, the editorial director of *Latina*, a lifestyle magazine for

---

Carmen Miranda: Brazilian singer, actress, and star of 1940s American movie musicals, noted for her outrageous costumes (including headdresses made from fruit) and thick, comic accent.

young women. "That happens to be the way many Latinas see themselves," she conceded, "but if our cultural identity is all wrapped up in a sexy sense of style, then we have a lot of work to do."

Others maintain that a degree of cultural stereotyping is inevitable and [20] may not be all bad. "It's important for people to understand that within the Latin community there is range," said Elisa Jimenez, a New York fashion designer and performance artist of part-Mexican descent. At the same time, an attraction to certain cultural stereotypes can be positive, she asserted, if "it inspires us to be happier, more expressive — any or all of those things that we want to be more of."

Latino-influenced apparel and grooming are seductive to many non- [21] Latins intent on borrowing elements of a culture that they perceive as more authentic, spontaneous, and alluring than their own. "Latin equals sexy," said Kim Hastreiter, the editor of *Paper*, a magazine that features a generous sampling of Latino artists, models, fashion, film and pop stars in its April issue. "It's heat and a certain aliveness."

Ms. Hastreiter might have been describing Cindy Green, a New York [22] performance artist and the graphic design director of the DKNY fashion house. Ms. Green flaunts acrylic-tipped nails airbrushed in hot pink and silver, a hyperfeminine look copied from the young Latina women she sees on her way to work. "I'm completely obsessed with my nails," she said, adding that she is just as much taken with the tight ponytails, dark lip liner, and extreme makeup worn by many young Hispanic women. "I come from Ohio," she said, "and all this is very exotic to me."

Danielle Levitt, a New York City fashion photographer, is equally besot- [23] ted. "I can't explain my attraction to things that are Latin," she said. "I think it's the glamour." Ms. Levitt likes to pile on Latina-style gold bangles and heart-shaped pendants. At her throat she wears an elaborate gold nameplate, similar to those worn on the air by the stars of *Sex and the City*, a show that is arguably influenced by Latina style.

Ms. Jimenez had never designed clothes that were identifiably Latin [24] until Kbond, a vanguard Los Angeles clothing store, asked her recently for a look that was patently Hispanic. She responded by lopping the sleeves off a series of ruffled men's tuxedo shirts — "tricking them out," as she put it, into "sexy little halters" for women.

At the moment she is selling a line of sportswear steeped in Latin kitsch [25] — "La Vida Loca" T-shirts, for example, printed with the characteristically Mexican images of a rose, a pair of dice, and a skull. "It's time to get our heritage out there," Ms. Jimenez declared with mingled defiance and mirth. She envisions her designs teamed with uptight little handbags and immaculate white jeans.

Who's going to wear them? [26]

"Are you kidding?" she said. "They're going to be the height of Upper [27] East Side° chic."

Upper East Side: An upper-class neighborhood in New York City.

Questions to Start You Thinking

1. CONSIDERING MEANING: What are some of the reasons La Ferla gives for young Latino women and men adopting exotic styles associated with traditional Hispanic culture?

2. IDENTIFYING WRITING STRATEGIES: How does La Ferla use cause and effect in this essay? Why is this strategy particularly appropriate to her purpose?

3. READING CRITICALLY: Skim through the essay again, paying particular attention to the quotations La Ferla includes — from teenage Latinos and Latinas, a sociology professor, fashion editors and designers, and advertising and marketing experts. Why do you think she chose to interview this wide variety of people? What is the effect of the many quotations?

4. EXPANDING VOCABULARY: Define *allude, aping, flaunting,* and *solidarity* (paragraph 6). How do these words help readers understand the sources of contemporary Latino style?

5. MAKING CONNECTIONS: In "They've Got to Be Carefully Taught" (pp. 564–66), Susan Brady Konig writes somewhat critically about her daughter's preschool teacher requiring the young students in her class to identify with their cultural background and heritage. In contrast, the teenagers quoted in the beginning of La Ferla's essay enthusiastically present theirs. To what extent might aggressively asserting one's heritage be a positive thing? To what extent might it be a negative thing?

Journal Prompts

1. What do you identify as your cultural or ethnic heritage? How does this identification contribute to your personal style? (Keep in mind that your personal style may be a reaction against your family heritage.)

2. How fashion conscious are you? Do you follow the latest trends, intentionally buck them, or just ignore them altogether? Why do you feel about fashion as you do?

Suggestions for Writing

1. Take some time to observe the different fashion choices (clothing, hairstyles, accessories, and so forth) that characterize various groups in your community. You might, for example, choose to observe people on your campus, at a shopping mall or supermarket, or, if you live in a city, simply on the street. Make notes on your observations, and then write an essay in which you classify the various styles you observed.

2. In paragraph 4, La Ferla refers to the fact that 2000 census data suggest that Hispanic residents are "on the verge of becoming America's largest minority group." Do some research about the causes of this boom in the Hispanic population and the kinds of responses it has generated among both non-Hispanics and Hispanics. Then write an essay explaining these causes and effects.

Stephen King
Why We Crave Horror Movies

 For more about
Stephen King, visit
<bedfordstmartins.com/
bedguide> and do a key-
word search:

author

Stephen King was born in 1947 in Portland, Maine, and attended the University of Maine at Orono. He now lives in Bangor, Maine, where he writes his best-selling horror novels, many of which have been made into popular movies. The prolific King is also the author of screenplays, teleplays, short fiction, essays, e-books, and (under the pseudonym Richard Bachman) novels. His well-known horror novels include Carrie *(1974),* Firestarter *(1980),* Pet Sematary *(1983),* Misery *(1987),* The Green Mile *(1996),* Wizard and Glass *(1997), and* Hearts in Atlantis *(1999). His most recent books include* On Writing: A Memoir of the Craft *(2000), the novels* Cell *(2006) and* Lisey's Story *(2006), and the final installments of his epic fantasy series* The Dark Tower, *which he is currently adapting into a comic-book series for Marvel. Since 2003, King has also written a regular column on pop culture for* Entertainment Weekly. *In the following essay, first published in* Playboy *in December 1981, King draws on his extensive experience with horror to explain the human craving to be frightened.*

AS YOU READ: *Identify the needs that King says horror movies fulfill for viewers.*

I think that we're all mentally ill; those of us outside the asylums only hide it a little better — and maybe not all that much better, after all. We've all known people who talk to themselves, people who sometimes squinch their faces into horrible grimaces when they believe no one is watching, people who have some hysterical fear — of snakes, the dark, the tight place, the long drop . . . and, of course, those final worms and grubs that are waiting so patiently underground.

When we pay our four or five bucks and seat ourselves at tenth-row center in a theater showing a horror movie, we are daring the nightmare.

Why? Some of the reasons are simple and obvious. To show that we can, that we are not afraid, that we can ride this roller coaster. Which is not to say that a really good horror movie may not surprise a scream out of us at some point, the way we may scream when the roller coaster twists through a complete 360 or plows through a lake at the bottom of the drop. And horror movies, like roller coasters, have always been the special province° of the young; by the time one turns forty or fifty, one's appetite for double twists or 360-degree loops may be considerably depleted.

We also go to reestablish our feelings of essential normality; the horror movie is innately conservative, even reactionary. Freda Jackson as the horrible melting woman in *Die, Monster, Die!* confirms for us that no matter how far we may be removed from the beauty of a Robert Redford or a Diana Ross, we are still light-years from true ugliness.

province: Area.

512

And we go to have fun.   5

Ah, but this is where the ground starts to slope away, isn't it? Because   6
this is a very peculiar sort of fun indeed. The fun comes from seeing others
menaced — sometimes killed. One critic suggested that if pro football has
become the voyeur's° version of combat, then the horror film has become
the modern version of the public lynching.

It is true that the mythic, "fairy-tale" horror film intends to take away   7
the shades of gray. . . . It urges us to put away our more civilized and adult
penchant° for analysis and to become children again, seeing things in pure
blacks and whites. It may be that horror movies provide psychic relief on
this level because this invitation to lapse into simplicity, irrationality, and
even outright madness is extended so rarely. We are told we may allow our
emotions a free rein . . . or no rein at all.

If we are all insane, then sanity becomes a matter of degree. If your in-   8
sanity leads you to carve up women like Jack the Ripper or the Cleveland
Torso Murderer, we clap you away in the funny farm (but neither of those
two amateur-night surgeons was ever caught, heh-heh-heh); if, on the other
hand, your insanity leads you only to talk to yourself when you're under
stress or to pick your nose on your morning bus, then you are left alone to
go about your business . . . though it is doubtful that you will ever be invited to the best parties.

The potential lyncher is in almost all of us (excluding saints, past and   9
present; but then, most saints have been crazy in their own ways), and every
now and then, he has to be let loose to scream and roll around in the grass.
Our emotions and our fears form their own body, and we recognize that
it demands its own exercise to maintain proper muscle tone. Certain of
these emotional muscles are accepted — even exalted — in civilized society;
they are, of course, the emotions that tend to maintain the status quo° of
civilization itself. Love, friendship, loyalty, kindness — these are all the emotions that we applaud, emotions that have been immortalized in the couplets of Hallmark cards and in the verses (I don't dare call it poetry) of
Leonard Nimoy.

When we exhibit these emotions, society showers us with positive rein-   10
forcement; we learn this even before we get out of diapers. When, as children, we hug our rotten little puke of a sister and give her a kiss, all the
aunts and uncles smile and twit and cry, "Isn't he the sweetest little thing?"
Such coveted treats as chocolate-covered graham crackers often follow. But if
we deliberately slam the rotten little puke of a sister's fingers in the door,
sanctions follow — angry remonstrance° from parents, aunts, and uncles; instead of a chocolate-covered graham cracker, a spanking.

But anticivilization emotions don't go away, and they demand periodic   11
exercise. We have such "sick" jokes as "What's the difference between a

---

voyeur: One who takes inordinate pleasure in the act of watching.   **penchant:** Strong
inclination.   **status quo:** Existing state of affairs.   **remonstrance:** Objection.

truckload of bowling balls and a truckload of dead babies?" (You can't un-load the truckload of bowling balls with a pitchfork . . . a joke, by the way, that I heard originally from a ten-year-old.) Such a joke may surprise a laugh or a grin out of us even as we recoil, a possibility that confirms the thesis: if we share a brotherhood of man, then we also share an insanity of man. None of which is intended as a defense of either the sick joke or insanity but merely as an explanation of [how] the best horror films, like the best fairy tales, manage to be reactionary, anarchistic, and revolutionary all at the same time.

The mythic horror movie, like the sick joke, has a dirty job to do. It delib- 12
erately appeals to all that is worst in us. It is morbidity unchained, our most base instincts let free, our nastiest fantasies realized . . . and it all happens, fit-tingly enough, in the dark. For those reasons, good liberals often shy away from horror films. For myself, I like to see the most aggressive of them — *Dawn of the Dead*, for instance — as lifting a trapdoor in the civilized fore-brain and throwing a basket of raw meat to the hungry alligators swimming around in that subterranean river beneath.

Why bother? Because it keeps them from getting out, man, it keeps 13
them down there and me up here. It was Lennon and McCartney who said that all you need is love, and I would agree with that.

As long as you keep the gators fed. 14

Questions to Start You Thinking

1. CONSIDERING MEANING: What does King mean when he says that "we're all mentally ill" (paragraph 1)? Is this a serious statement? Why or why not?

2. IDENTIFYING WRITING STRATEGIES: How does King use analysis, breaking a complex topic into parts, to support his argument?

3. READING CRITICALLY: Why do you think King uses the inclusive pronoun *we* so frequently throughout his essay? What effect does the use of this pro-noun have on your response to his argument?

4. EXPANDING VOCABULARY: Define *innately* (paragraph 4). What does King mean when he says horror movies are "innately conservative"? Does he contradict himself when he says they are also "reactionary, anarchistic, and revolutionary" (paragraph 11)? Why or why not?

5. MAKING CONNECTIONS: How do King's reasons for our craving for horror movies relate to James Poniewozik's reasons for the popularity of reality television ("Why Reality TV Is Good for Us," pp. 520–24)? In what ways do the two writers agree or disagree about viewers' needs and about the ca-pacity of movies or television to address those needs?

Journal Prompts

1. What is your response to "sick" jokes? Why?

2. Recall a movie that exercised your "anticivilization emotions" (paragraph 11). Describe your state of mind before, during, and after the movie.

Suggestions for Writing

1. What genre of movie do you prefer to watch, and why? What cravings does this type of movie satisfy?

2. Do you agree that "the horror film has become the modern version of the public lynching" (paragraph 6)? Write an argument in which you defend or refute this suggestion, citing examples from King's essay and from your own moviegoing experience to support your position.

Michael Abernethy
Male Bashing on TV

Michael Abernethy *was born in Bristol, Tennessee, in 1960. He holds a BA from Baylor University and an MA from the University of North Texas. He currently teaches communication studies and writing at Indiana State University, and he is also a film and television critic for PopMatters.com. Before becoming a full-time writer and educator, Abernethy worked in hotel and restaurant management. "Male Bashing on TV," first published on PopMatters.com in 2003, takes on an issue that some may find trivial. To Abernethy, however, the increasingly negative portrayal of men on sitcoms and commercials is no laughing matter.*

AS YOU READ: *Why, according to Abernethy, is male bashing on television a serious problem?*

■ For more about Michael Abernethy, visit <bedfordstmartins.com/bedguide> and do a keyword search:

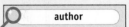
author

Warning for our male readers: the following article contains big words 1 and complex sentences. It might be a good idea to have a woman nearby to explain it to you.

It's been a hard day. Your assistant at work is out with the flu and there 2 is another deadline fast approaching. Your wife is at a business conference, so you have to pick up your son at daycare, make dinner, clean the kitchen, do a load of laundry, and get Junior to bed before you can settle down on the sofa with those reports you still need to go over.

Perhaps a little comedy will make the work more bearable, you think, 3 so you turn on CBS's Monday night comedies: *King of Queens, Yes, Dear, Everybody Loves Raymond,* and *Still Standing.* Over the next two hours, you see four male lead characters who are nothing like you. These men are selfish and lazy, inconsiderate husbands and poor parents.

And the commercials in between aren't any better. Among them: A fem- 4 inine hygiene ad: two women are traveling down a lovely country road, laughing and having a great time. But wait. One of them needs to check the freshness of her minipad, and, apparently, the next rest area is six states away. A woman's voice-over interjects, "It's obvious that the interstate system was designed by men."

A digital camera ad: a young husband walks through a grocery store, try- 5
ing to match photos in his hand with items on the shelves. Cut to his wife
in the kitchen, snapping digital pictures of all the items in the pantry so that
hubby won't screw up the shopping.

A family game ad: a dorky guy and beautiful woman are playing Trivial 6
Pursuit. He asks her, "How much does the average man's brain weigh?" Her
answer: "Not much."

A wine ad: a group of women are sitting around the patio of a beach 7
house, drinking a blush wine. Their boyfriends approach, but are denied re-
freshment until they have "earned" it by building a sand statue of David.

Welcome to the new comic image of men on TV: incompetence at its 8
worst. Where television used to feature wise and wonderful fathers and husbands, today's comedies and ads often feature bumbling husbands and
inept, uninvolved fathers. On *Still Standing*, Bill (Mark Addy) embarrasses
his wife Judy (Jamie Gertz) so badly in front of her reading group that she
is dropped from the group. On *Everybody Loves Raymond*, Raymond (Ray
Romano) must choose between bathing the twin boys or helping his daughter with her homework. He begrudgingly agrees to assist his daughter, for
whom he is no help whatsoever.

CBS is not the only guilty party. ABC's *My Wife and Kids* and *According to* 9
Jim, Fox's *The Bernie Mac Show*, *The Simpsons*, *Malcolm in the Middle*, and (the
recently cancelled) *Titus* and the WB's *Reba* also feature women who are better organized and possess better relational skills than their male counterparts. While most television dramas tend to avoid gender stereotypes, as
these undermine "realism," comic portrayals of men have become increasingly negative. The trend is so noticeable that it has been criticized by men's
rights groups and some television critics.

It has also been studied by academicians Dr. Katherine Young and Paul 10
Nathanson in their book, *Spreading Misandry°: The Teaching of Contempt for
Men in Popular Culture*. Young and Nathanson argue that in addition to
being portrayed as generally unintelligent, men are ridiculed, rejected, and
physically abused in the media. Such behavior, they suggest, "would never
be acceptable if directed at women." Evidence of this pattern is found in a
2001 survey of one thousand adults conducted by the Advertising Standards
Association in Great Britain, which found two-thirds of respondents thought
that women featured in advertisements were "intelligent, assertive, and caring," while the men were "pathetic and silly." The number of respondents
who thought men were depicted as "intelligent" was a paltry° 14 percent.
(While these figures apply to the United Kingdom, comparable advertisements air in the United States.)

Some feminists might argue that, for decades, women on TV looked 11
mindless, and that turnabout is fair play. True, many women characters

misandry: Hatred of men.   **paltry:** Trivial; small.

through the years have had little more to do than look after their families. From the prim housewife whose only means of control over her children was, "Wait till your father gets home!" to the dutiful housewife whose husband declares "My wife: I think I'll keep her," women in the '50s and '60s were often subservient. (This generalization leaves out the unusual someone like Donna Reed, who produced her own show, on which she was not subservient.)

Then, during the "sexual revolution," TV began to feature independent 12 women who could take care of themselves (Mary and Rhoda on *The Mary Tyler Moore Show, Julia,* Alice and Flo on *Alice,* Louise and Florence on *The Jeffersons*). So now, thirty years later, you'd think that maybe we'd have come to some parity.° Not even.

Granted, men still dominate television, from the newsroom to prime- 13 time. And men do plenty on their own to perpetuate the image of the immature male, from Comedy Central's *The Man Show* to the hordes of drunken college boys who show up every year on MTV's Spring Break. What's the problem with a few jokes about how dumb men can be? C'mon, can't we take a few jokes?

If only it was just a few. The jokes have become standard fare. Looking 14 at a handful of sitcoms makes the situation seem relatively insignificant, but when those sitcoms are combined with dozens of negative ads which repeat frequently, then a poor image of men is created in the minds of viewers.

According to *Gender Issues in Advertising Language,* television portrayals 15 that help create or reinforce negative stereotypes can lead to problems with self-image, self-concept, and personal aspirations. Young men learn that they are expected to screw up, that women will have the brains to their brawn, and that childcare is over their heads. And it isn't just men who suffer from this constant parade of dumb men on TV. Children Now reports a new study that found that two-thirds of children they surveyed describe men on TV as angry and only one-third report ever seeing a man on television performing domestic chores, such as cooking or cleaning. There are far too few positive role models for young boys on television.

Moreover, stereotypical male-bashing portrayals undermine the core 16 belief of the feminist movement: equality. Just think. What if the butt of all the jokes took on another identity? Consider the following fictional exchanges:

> "It is so hard to get decent employees."
> "That's because you keep hiring blacks."
>
> "I just don't understand this project at all."
> "Well, a woman explained it to you, so what did you expect?"

parity: Equality.

"I can't believe he is going out again tonight."

"Oh please, all Hispanics care about is sex."

All of these statements are offensive, and would rightfully be objected to by advocates of fair representation in the media. However, put the word "man" or "men" in place of "blacks," "woman," and "Hispanics" in the above sentences and they're deemed humorous. Are men who ask to be treated civilly overly sensitive or are we as justified in our objections as members of NOW,° the NAACP,° GLAAD,° and other groups which protest demeaning television portrayals, whether those portrayals are on sitcoms, dramas, advertisements, or moronic TV like *The Man Show*?

Most of the shows I'm talking about are popular. Maybe that means that   17
I am being too sensitive. Yet, many U.S. viewers didn't have a problem with *Amos and Andy* or *I Dream of Jeannie*, both famous for their offensive stereotypes. These shows enjoyed good ratings, but neither concept is likely to be revived anytime soon, as "society" has realized their inappropriateness.

All this is not to say buffoonery — male or female — isn't a comic staple.   18
Barney on *The Andy Griffith Show*, Ted on *The Mary Tyler Moore Show*, and Kramer on *Seinfeld* were all vital characters, but the shows also featured intelligent males. And these clowns were amusing because they were eccentric personalities, not because they were men. The same could be said of many female characters on TV, like *Alice*'s Flo, *Friends'* Phoebe, or Karen on *Will & Grace*. Good comedy stems from creative writing and imaginative characterizations, not from degrading stereotypes.

Fortunately, some people are working to change the way television   19
portrays men. J. C. Penney recently ran an ad for a One Day sale, with a father at the breakfast table, with his infant crying and throwing things. The father asks the child when his mother will be home. Lana Whited of the *Roanoke Times*, syndicated columnist Dirk Lammers, and the National Men's Resource Center were just a few who objected to this image of an apparently incompetent and uncaring father, one who would let his child cry without making any attempt to calm him. Penney's got the message; their recent holiday ad featured a father, mother, and son all happily shopping together.

Few men I know want a return to the "good ole days." Those generaliza-   20
tions were as unrealistic as the idea that all men are big slobbering goofballs. Hope lies beyond such simplistic oppositions, in shows like *The Cosby Show* or *Mad about You*, which placed their protagonists on level playing fields. Paul Reiser and Cosby did, on occasion, do moronic things, but so did Helen Hunt and Phylicia Rashad. People — because they are people, not just gendered people — are prone to fall on their faces occasionally.

Undoubtedly, there are men out there who are clones of Ward Cleaver,   21
just as there are men who resemble Al Bundy. But the majority is some-

---

NOW: National Organization for Women.   **NAACP:** National Association for the Advancement of Colored People.   **GLAAD:** Gay and Lesbian Alliance Against Defamation.

where in between. We're trying to deal the best we can with the kids, the spouse, the job, the bills, the household chores, and the countless crises that pop up unexpectedly. After all that, when we do get the chance to sit down and relax, it would be nice to turn on the TV and not see ourselves reflected as idiots.

Questions to Start You Thinking

1. CONSIDERING MEANING: In Abernethy's opinion, what generates the best kind of comedy?

2. IDENTIFYING WRITING STRATEGIES: What strategies does Abernethy use to help readers understand the complexity and extent of male bashing on television?

3. READING CRITICALLY: Abernethy states that jokes about men's incompetence have become "standard fare" on television (paragraph 14). Does he provide sufficient relevant evidence to support this statement? Which of his examples are particularly striking?

4. EXPANDING VOCABULARY: In paragraph 10, Abernethy cites a study in which only 14 percent of respondents thought that men on television were depicted as "intelligent." How do you define *intelligent*? What kind of intelligence do you think Abernethy would like to see male sitcom characters display?

5. MAKING CONNECTIONS: In paragraph 18, Abernethy declares, "Good comedy stems from creative writing and imaginative characterizations, not from degrading stereotypes." How might Dave Barry ("From Now On, Let Women Kill Their Own Spiders," pp. 485–87) respond to this statement?

Journal Prompts

1. As Abernethy points out in paragraph 11, "Some feminists might argue that, for decades, women on TV looked mindless, and that turnabout is fair play." Do you agree or disagree with this attitude? Why?

2. How do you define *good comedy*? In your opinion, does stereotyping add to or detract from humor?

Suggestions for Writing

1. Is Abernethy overreacting? Using additional examples from television shows or commercials that you have seen, write an essay responding to his point of view.

2. Select a magazine geared to women and one geared to men, and then thumb through the advertisements. How are males portrayed in each magazine's ads? Does the treatment differ between the two magazines? In what ways does it support or refute Abernethy's point? Present your analysis in a comparison-and-contrast essay.

James Poniewozik
Why Reality TV Is Good for Us*

 For more about
James Poniewozik, visit
<bedfordstmartins.com/
bedguide> and do a key-
word search:

author

James Poniewozik, *a native of Monroe, Michigan, is a graduate of the Univer-*
sity of Michigan and New York University. Since 1999 he has been the media and
television critic for Time *magazine, writing on subjects ranging from the television*
series The Sopranos *to the effects of September 11 on popular culture. Before join-*
ing the staff of Time, *Poniewozik served as the media critic and Media section edi-*
tor for Salon.com. *He also has written for such publications as* Fortune, Rolling
Stone, New York, *the* New York Times Book Review, *and* Talk *and regularly*
contributes to NPR's On the Media *and* All Things Considered. *With a viewpoint*
markedly different from that of Terry Golway ("A Nation of Idol-Worshipers," pp.
525–27), Poniewozik extols the virtues of the often criticized but hugely popular
genre of reality television in the following selection from a 2003 issue of Time.

AS YOU READ: *Determine why Poniewozik suggests that reality-television characters*
set a good example for viewers.

For eight single professional women gathered in Dallas, it is holy 1
Wednesday — the night each week that they gather in one of their
homes for the Traveling *Bachelorette* Party. Munching snacks and passing a
bottle of wine, they cheer, cry, and cackle as their spiritual leader, Trista
Rehn, braves heartache, indecision, and the occasional recitation of bad poetry to choose from among her twenty-five swains.° Yet something is unsettling Leah Hudson's stomach, and it's not just the wine. "I hate that we've
been sucked into the Hoover vac of reality TV," says Hudson, thirty. "Do we
not have anything better to do than to live vicariously through a bunch of
fifteen-minute-fame seekers?"

There you have the essence of reality TV's success: it is the one mass- 2
entertainment category that thrives because of its audience's contempt for it.
It makes us feel tawdry, dirty, cheap — if it didn't, we probably wouldn't
bother tuning in. And in this, for once, the audience and critics agree. Just
listen to the raves for America's hottest TV genre.

"The country is gripped by misanthropy!"° — New York *Observer* 3

"Ridiculous and pernicious!° Many kinds of cruelty are passed off as enter- 4
tainment!" — Washington *Post*

"So-called reality television just may be killing the medium!" — San Fran- 5
cisco *Chronicle*

O.K., we added the exclamation points, but you get the idea. Yes, view- 6
ers are tuning in to *Joe Millionaire, The Bachelorette,* and *American Idol* by the
tens of millions. Yet, to paraphrase Winston Churchill,° never have so many
watched so much TV with so little good to say about it.

* Reported by *Time*'s Amy Lennard Goehner, Jeanne McDowell, and Adam Pitluk.

swains: Admirers.   **misanthropy:** Hatred of humanity.   **pernicious:** Cruel.   **Winston Churchill:** British prime minister during World War II.

Well, that ends here. It may ruin reality producers' marketing plans for a   7
TV critic to say it, but reality TV is, in fact, the best thing to happen to television in several years. It has given the networks water-cooler buzz again; it
has reminded viewers jaded by sitcoms and dramas why TV can be exciting;
and at its best, it is teaching TV a new way to tell involving human stories.

A few concessions up front. First, yes, we all know that there's little real-   8
ity in reality TV: those "intimate" dates, for instance, are staged in front of
banks of cameras and sweltering floodlights. But it's the only phrase we've
got, and I'm sticking with it. Second, I don't pretend to defend the indefen-
sible: *Are You Hot? The Search for America's Sexiest People* isn't getting any
help from me. And finally, I realize that comparing even a well-made reality
show with, say, *The Simpsons* is not merely comparing apples with oranges;
it's comparing onions with washing machines — no reality show can match
the intelligence and layers of well-constructed fiction.

On a sheer ratings level, the latest wave of reality hits has worked a sea   9
change for the networks. And it has put them back on the pop-cultural map,
after losing the buzz war to cable for years. Reality shows don't just reach
tens of millions of viewers but leave them feeling part of a communal experience — what network TV does best, but sitcoms and dramas haven't done
since *Seinfeld* and *Twin Peaks.* (When was the last time *CSI* made you call
your best friend or holler back at your TV?) "Reality has proven that network
television is still relevant," says Mike Fleiss, creator of the *Bachelor* franchise.

This has sitcom and drama writers praying for the reality bust. "The   10
networks only have so much time and resources," says Amy Sherman-
Palladino, creator of *Gilmore Girls.* "Rather than solely focusing on convincing the Olsen twins to allow themselves to be eaten by bears in prime time,
I wish they would focus on coming up with something that would really
last." TV does seem to be in overkill mode, as the networks have signed up
dozens of dating shows, talent searches, and other voyeurfests. And like an
overheated NASDAQ, the reality market is bound to correct. But unlike earlier TV reality booms, this one is supported by a large, young audience that
grew up on MTV's *The Real World* and considers reality as legitimate as dramas and sitcoms — and that, for now, prefers it.

And why not? It would be easier to bemoan reality shows' crowding out   11
sitcoms and dramas if the latter weren't in such a rut. But the new network
shows of fall 2002 were a creatively timid mass of remakes, bland family
comedies, and derivative° cop dramas. Network executives dubbed them
"comfort" — i.e., familiar and boring — TV. Whereas reality TV — call it "dis-
comfort TV" — lives to rattle viewers' cages. It provokes. It offends. But at
least it's trying to do something besides help you get to sleep. Some upcoming reality concepts are idealistic, like FX's *American Candidate,* which aims
to field a "people's candidate" for president in 2004. Others are lowbrow,
like ABC's *The Will* (relatives battle for an inheritance), Fox's *Married by
America* (viewers vote to help pair up a bride and groom), and NBC's *Around
the World in 80 Dates* (American bachelor seeks mates around the world;

derivative: Unoriginal.

after all, how better to improve America's image then to send a stud to other countries to defile their women?). But all of them make you sit up and pay attention. "I like to make a show where people say, 'You can't put that on TV,' " says Fleiss. "Then I put it on TV."

By and large, reality shows aren't supplanting° creative successes like *24* 12 or *Scrubs;* they're filling in for duds like *Presidio Med* and *MDs.* As NBC reality chief Jeff Gaspin says, "There is a little survival-of-the-fittest thing this ends up creating." When sitcoms started cloning goofy suburban dads and quirky, pretty yuppies, we got *The Osbournes.* And now reality TV is becoming our source for involved stories about personal relationships. This used to be the stuff of dramas like the canceled *Once and Again,* until programmers began concentrating on series like *CSI* and *Law & Order,* which have characters as detailed and individuated as checkers pieces. By the time *Survivor* ends, you know its players better than you know *Law & Order*'s Detective Briscoe after eleven years. Likewise, the WB's *High School Reunion,* which brings together classmates after ten years, is really asking whether you're doomed to live out your high school role — "the jock," "the nerd," or whatnot — for life. Last fall two scripted shows, *That Was Then* and *Do Over,* asked the same questions but with cardboard characters and silly premises involving time travel. They got canceled. *High School Reunion* got a second season.

In Britain, where reality has ruled Britannia's (air)waves for years, TV 13 writers are starting to learn from reality's success. The sitcom *The Office* uses reality-TV techniques (jerky, handheld camera work, "confessional" interviews) to explore the petty politics of white-collar workers. Now airing on BBC America, it's the best comedy to debut here this season, because its characters are the kind of hard-to-pigeonhole folks you find in life — or on reality TV. On *Survivor* and *The Amazing Race,* the gay men don't drop Judy Garland references in every scene. MTV's *Making the Band 2* — a kind of hip-hop *American Idol* — gave center stage to inner-city kids who would be portrayed as perps or victims on a cop drama.

But aesthetics° aside, the case against reality TV is mainly moral — and 14 there's a point to it. It's hard to defend the deception of *Joe Millionaire* — which set up twenty women to court construction worker Evan Marriott by telling them he was a multimillionaire — as hilarious as its fool's-gold chase can be. Even the show's Potemkin° Croesus° contends that producers hid the show's premise from him until the last minute. "The day before I left for France, I signed confidentiality papers which said what the show was about," Marriott tells *Time.* "At that point, could I really back out?" Others are concerned about the message of meanness. "There's a premium on the lowest common denominator of human relationships," James Steyer, author

supplanting: Replacing.   **aesthetics:** Artistic beauty and taste.   **Potemkin:** Something that appears impressive on the surface but is shabby underneath, referring to Grigori Aleksandrovich Potemkin's construction of fake villages for Catherine the Great's tours of the Ukraine and the Crimea.   **Croesus:** A very wealthy man, referring to a king of Lydia who was renowned for his riches.

of *The Other Parent: The Inside Story of the Media's Effect on Our Children.* "It's often women degrading themselves. I don't want my nine-year-old thinking that's the way girls should behave."

So *The Bachelorette* is not morally instructive for grade-schoolers. But   15
wallowing in the weaknesses and failings of humanity is a trademark of satire — people accused Jonathan Swift and Mark Twain of being misanthropes too — and much reality TV is really satire boiled down to one extreme gesture. A great reality-TV concept takes some commonplace piety of polite society and gives it a wedgie. Companies value team spirit; *Survivor* says the team will screw you in the end. The cult of self-esteem says everybody is talented; *American Idol*'s Simon Cowell says to sit down and shut your pie hole. Romance and feminism says a man's money shouldn't matter; *Joe Millionaire* wagers $50 million that they're wrong.

The social criticisms of reality TV rest on two assumptions: that millions   16
of other people are being taken in by reality TV's deceptions (which the critic himself — or herself — is able to see through) or are being led astray by its unsavory messages (to which the critic is immune). When a reality show depicts bad behavior, it's immoral, misanthropic, sexist, or sick. When *The Sopranos* does the same thing, it's nuanced storytelling. We assume that viewers can empathize with Tony Soprano without wanting to be him; we assume they can maintain critical distance and perceive ironies between his words and the truth. Why? Because we assume that people who like *The Sopranos* are smarter, more mature — better — than people who like *The Bachelorette.*

And aren't they? Isn't there something simply wrong with people who   17
enjoy entertainment that depends on ordinary people getting their heart broken, being told they can't sing, or getting played for fools? That's the question behind the protests of CBS's plans to make a real-life version of *The Beverly Hillbillies* with a poor rural family. Says Dee Davis, president of the Center for Rural Strategies, "If somebody had proposed, 'Let's go into the barrio° in L.A. and find a family of immigrants and put them in a mansion, and won't it be funny when they interview maids?' then people could see that's a step too far." It's hard to either defend or attack a show that doesn't exist yet, but it's also true that the original sitcom was far harder on Mr. Drysdale than the Clampetts. And on *The Osbournes,* Ozzy — another Beverly Hills fish out of water — was "humiliated" into becoming the most beloved dad in America.

Indeed, for all the talk about "humiliation TV," what's striking about   18
most reality shows is how good humored and resilient most of the participants are: the *American Idol* rejectees stubbornly convinced of their own talent, the *Fear Factor* players walking away from vats of insects like Olympic champions. What finally bothers their detractors is, perhaps, not that these people are humiliated but that they are not. Embarrassment, these shows demonstrate, is survivable, even ignorable, and ignoring embarrassment is a skill we all could use. It is what you risk — like injury in a sport — in order

barrio: Spanish-speaking neighborhood in the United States.

to triumph. "What people are really responding to on these shows is people pursuing their dreams," says *American Candidate* producer R. J. Cutler. A reality show with all humiliation and no triumph would be boring.

And at their best, the shows offer something else entirely. One of the 19 most arresting moments this TV season came on *American Idol,* when a single mom and professional boxer from Detroit flunked her audition. The show went with her backstage, with her adorable young son, as she told her life story. Her husband, a corrections officer, was murdered a few years before. She had taken up boxing — her ring name is "Lady Tiger" — because you can't raise a kid on waitress money. Her monologue went from defiance ("You'll see my album. Lady Tiger don't stop") to despair ("You ain't going nowhere in Detroit. Nowhere") to dignified resolve for her son's sake ("We're never going to quit, are we, angel?"). It was a haunting slice of life, more authentic than any *ER* subplot.

Was Lady Tiger setting a bad example for her son on national TV? 20 Or setting a good example by dreaming, persevering and being proud? *American Idol* didn't say. It didn't nudge us to laugh at her or prod us to cry for her. In about two minutes, it just told a quintessentially° American story of ambition and desperation and shrinking options, and it left the judgment to us. That's unsettling. That's heartbreaking. And the reality is, that's great TV.

Questions to Start You Thinking

1. CONSIDERING MEANING: According to Poniewozik, what are the main reasons that "reality TV is . . . the best thing to happen to television in several years" (paragraph 7)?

2. IDENTIFYING WRITING STRATEGIES: What criteria does Poniewozik use to evaluate reality television? In his opinion, how do traditional sitcoms and dramas fare when judged according to the same criteria?

3. READING CRITICALLY: Where does Poniewozik address arguments against reality television? Does he present sufficient evidence to support his evaluation in the face of these opposing viewpoints?

4. EXPANDING VOCABULARY: Define *individuated* (paragraph 12). What does Poniewozik mean when he finds today's fictional television characters "as detailed and individuated as checkers pieces"? Does the comparison work?

5. MAKING CONNECTIONS: How do reality shows like *The Bachelor* or *Beauty and the Geek* relate to or differ from the institution of arranged marriage that Anjula Razdan analyzes ("What's Love Got to Do with It?" pp. 453–57)?

Link to the Paired Essay

■ For useful links to Web sources on topics including *popular culture,* visit <bedfordstmartins.com/toplinks>.

Compare and contrast Poniewozik's essay with Terry Golway's "A Nation of Idol-Worshipers" (pp. 525–27) in terms of each writer's purpose, intended audience, use of evidence, and tone. Which argument do you find more convincing, and why?

quintessentially: Most representative; classic.

Journal Prompts

1. Are you offended by reality television or entertained? Explain why.

2. Would you like to participate in a reality television show? Why, or why not? Which program would you like to be on, if any?

Suggestions for Writing

1. Imagine that you have the opportunity to create a reality television show. Write an essay in which you pitch the show to a television producer. Describe your show's premise, purpose, intended audience, and participants' characteristics. Include a paragraph that convinces the producer that your show, sure to be a blockbuster, is a must-have for the next television season.

2. Do additional research on the factors that have led to the success or failure of a specific reality television show. Based on what you learn from your research and from this reading, develop criteria for evaluating reality television programs. Using your criteria, write an essay that reviews, either negatively or positively, a reality television show.

Terry Golway
A Nation of Idol-Worshipers

Terry Golway, *born in 1955, is a freelance writer based in New Jersey, where he is currently curator of the John Kean Center for American History at Kean University. A veteran journalist, Golway is also the author or coauthor of several books on Irish and Irish American history, including* Irish Rebel: John Devoy and America's Fight for Ireland's Freedom *(1998),* For the Cause of Liberty: A Thousand Years of Ireland's Heroes *(2000), and* The Irish in America *(1997), a companion volume to the PBS television series* Long Journey Home: The Irish in America. *In one of his most recent books,* So Others Might Live: A History of New York's Bravest *(2003), Golway—whose father, father-in-law, godfather, and uncles were all firefighters—traces the history of the New York City Fire Department from its beginnings as a volunteer force in the 1700s to its tragic losses on September 11, 2001. In "A Nation of Idol-Worshipers," first published in* America *on July 31, 2006, Golway laments America's obsession with the cult of celebrity, which is fueled in large part by shows like* American Idol.

■ For more about Terry Golway, visit <bedfordstmartins.com/ bedguide> and do a keyword search:

 author

AS YOU READ: *Think about why Golway might have written this essay. What effect do you suppose he hoped it would have on his readers?*

The columnist Russell Baker once wrote a piece about the discovery he made one evening after he retired to his basement and, with nothing else to do, turned on the television set. All sorts of new and alien life forms invaded the basement. There was, he would write, a country living in his cellar—a country with which he was not particularly acquainted.

That's how I felt several months ago when I found myself in the pres- 2
ence of actual grown-ups, who were parsing° the results of a television show
called *American Idol*. In addition to being unaware that so-called talent
shows had been a staple of broadcasting since Guglielmo Marconi° figured
out wireless communications, these grown-ups admitted that their children
were hooked on the show. One grown-up announced that his teenage
daughter, who likes to sing in the shower, has decided that one day she will
be an "American Idol."

When I suggested that there were other avenues to "idolhood," like 3
medicine, social work, engineering, or teaching, my friend laughed. Apparently he thought I was kidding. I wasn't. Was I being a killjoy? Yes. Snob-
bish? Perhaps. But kidding? Not a chance.

The startling popularity of *American Idol* and its knockoffs provides fur- 4
ther proof that America is, in the words of writer Neil Postman, amusing itself to death. As never before, young people are being taught to believe that
genuine American idols sing and dance and look beautiful in front of a television camera, that pop culture is the only culture that matters, and that
achievement that doesn't bring the dubious° reward of fame is hardly worth
the effort.

One of the new *Idol* knockoffs is called *America's Got Talent*. The title 5
suggests that television executives were stunned to learn about this surfeit°
of American talent, but given their line of work, their surprise is understandable. As talented as America may be, however, the country doesn't have
enough engineers, mathematicians, scientists, and systems analysts. The culture no longer recognizes this kind of work as worthy of aspiration.

That's absurd, and most of us know that. Surely the people who put on 6
these awful shows know they're selling dubious goods. After all, many of
them are products of America's finest universities. (That thought alone
ought to tell us something about our society.) They are familiar, presumably,
with the work of genuine American idols — people who have actually contributed to society rather than merely distracted it.

For the men and women who are the "brains" behind shows like *Ameri-* 7
can Idol and its imitators, all of this is an exercise in postmodern irony.° But
for the kids who watch, and even for some of the grown-ups, it is completely serious. And that's the frightening part.

At the risk of sounding like a middle-aged crank, I remember when chil- 8
dren aspired to be astronauts, rocket scientists, cancer-conquering doctors,
firefighters, clergy and religious and, yes, even political leaders. Not every aspiring president made it to the Oval Office. And not every would-be fire-
fighter passed the physical. But at least those dreams were born of a society
that valued service and citizenship. Today's "Idol-worshipers" are the products of a society that values extreme narcissism and shallow fame.

Parsing: Analyzing.   **Guglielmo Marconi:** Inventor of the radio.   **dubious:** Doubtful.   **surfeit:** Overabundance.   **irony:** Referring to something that is deliberately
contrary to what one would expect, often in an amusing way.

That's not to say that serious people cannot spend a few frivolous mo-   9
ments watching a silly show just for fun. I've spent more than a few hours
this summer following the exploits of the golfer Phil Mickelson. This curious pastime could be regarded as an even more serious sign of American decline than the popularity of *American Idol*. But then again, at least Phil Mickelson is not hostage to the whims of a snooty British judge.

I realize that actors and singers have long been regarded as secular°   10
gods — this did not start with *American Idol*. The cult of celebrity and fame
has been around for generations. Kids in the 1960s worshiped the Beatles,
so I am told. Bobby-soxers° fainted at the sight of the young Frank Sinatra.
Young men fell in love with the likes of Elizabeth Taylor and Betty Grable.
Movie fan magazines have been chronicling the lives of the famous since
the Roaring Twenties.

Still, it seems clear to me that today's Americans devote more time,   11
money, and energy in pursuit of trivial pop culture than ever before. Entire
television channels are devoted to one of my favorite oxymorons,° "entertainment news." A word from a single talk-show host can and does inspire
millions of people to buy a book that most of them probably will never
read. Serious magazines struggle to find new readers, but magazines devoted
to the lives of movie stars make their owners rich, if not famous.

And, of course, there is this business of what makes an "American Idol."   12
In the aftermath of 9/11, we swore that we were changed people, that we
would forever honor the sacrifices of society's true heroes. We claimed that
we understood how we had let trivia consume our lives.

For a while our idols were people who gave of themselves, who put   13
their own lives at risk for the sake of others. Fame and glamour were put in
their rightful place. Eternal values reasserted themselves. We saw the difference between reality and fantasy.

Today, less than five years after that life-altering outrage, we debate the   14
merits of singers who wish to be seen as an American idol. We encourage
our children to worship these idols, to go forth and do likewise.

We really haven't learned much, have we?   15

Questions to Start You Thinking

1. CONSIDERING MEANING: What does Golway see as the negative effects of the
   American obsession with a "cult of celebrity and fame" (paragraph 10)?
   What does he think society should value more highly than celebrity?

2. IDENTIFYING WRITING STRATEGIES: Where in the essay does Golway suggest
   that the issue he is writing about is not completely one-sided? Why do you
   suppose he does so? How does he then go about picking up the thread of
   his own argument?

---

secular: Not pertaining to religion.   **Bobby-soxers:** Teenage girls in the 1940s.
oxymorons: Contradictions in terms.

3. READING CRITICALLY: Golway presents little hard evidence to back up his claims about the "cult of celebrity and fame"; for example, he might have cited the ratings for *American Idol* or compared the readership of celebrity-centered magazines with more serious publications. What does the fact that he didn't do so suggest to you about his intended audience and his thoughts about the "cult of celebrity" more generally?

4. EXPANDING VOCABULARY: In paragraph 8, Golway refers to the United States as "a society that values extreme narcissism." Define *narcissism*. To what extent do you feel that shows such as *American Idol* celebrate this concept?

5. MAKING CONNECTIONS: How might Golway's views relate to Barbara Ehrenreich's point in "Guys Just Want to Have Fun" (pp. 482–84) that employers increasingly value personality over education and demonstrated competence when hiring and promoting employees? What do both writers' observations suggest about contemporary society?

Link to the Paired Essay

James Poniewozik ("Why Reality TV Is Good for Us," pp. 520–24) offers a much more positive take on *American Idol* than does Golway. What do the two writers see differently about the program? To what extent might the fact that Poniewozik is a television critic, someone who watches a considerable amount of television, as opposed to Golway, who seems not to watch much television at all, contribute to their differing opinions?

Journal Prompts

1. What is your attitude toward shows like *American Idol*? Are you a big fan, an occasional viewer, or an active avoider of such television fare? Explain why.

2. How do you account for the popularity of *American Idol* and other programs that are essentially talent contests, whether for amateurs or for celebrities competing in an activity for which they are not known, such as *Dancing with the Stars*?

Suggestions for Writing

1. As this essay illustrates, reality television shows can provide a glimpse into our society, mirroring our values, desires, and way of life. What Golway sees in shows like *American Idol* is a self-absorbed society obsessed with shallow fame. To what extent do you agree or disagree with Golway's view? Write an essay in which you analyze one or more of these shows, explaining what *you* think they reveal about American society.

2. Do some research about the most highly rated programs on television, in both primetime and daytime, on the networks and on cable. Be sure to consider as well what programs appeal to various age groups. Then write an essay in which you explore what seems to appeal to the majority of Americans and why.

Chapter 26
E-Technology

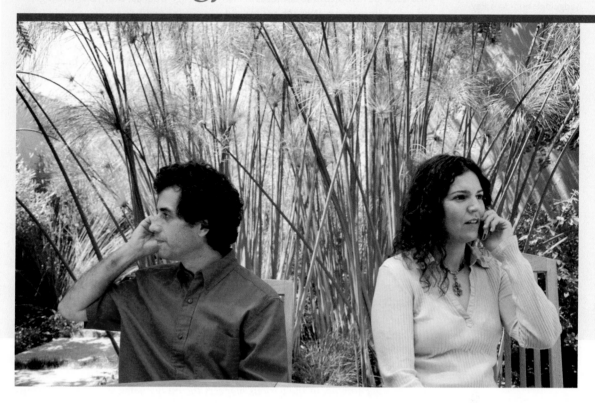

Responding to an Image

At first glance, how would you describe the overall feeling conveyed by this image? What is significant about the directions in which the man and woman are facing and about what they are doing? How does the background contribute to the mood of the picture? What point does the image seem to be making about the impact of communication technology? Translate that point into a caption for the illustration or into a thesis for an essay. (You also might want to compare and contrast this image with the one on p. 474.)

For reading activities linked to this chapter, visit <bedfordstmartins.com/bedguide> and do a keyword search:

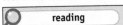

Web Search

Think of a topic of great personal interest to you—a hobby, a political or social issue, a subject of study, something you know a lot about. Then look for varied Web sites devoted to this topic, especially message boards, chat rooms, blogs, and other interactive sites where individuals come together to share their thoughts on and experiences with the topic. As you browse through such sites, think about the kinds of communities the Web creates. How do people relate to one another online? What do they learn from one another, and where do they fail to connect? Ultimately, do you think of the Internet as a unifying force—bringing together people who would not normally come into contact? Or do you view the Internet as an isolating force—allowing people to remain anonymous and to avoid direct human contact?

Harvard Magazine
Creating Community, Online and Off

Harvard Magazine *was founded in 1898 by alumni of Harvard University. Published bimonthly, it covers campus news as well as current social and political issues. Although affiliated with Harvard University, the magazine is independently edited to maintain an objective viewpoint. According to its Web site, the magazine's mission is "keeping alumni of Harvard University connected to the university and to each other." The following article, from the January–February 2004 issue of the magazine, discusses the popularity of blogging, examining its benefits and drawbacks as well as its capacity for building community among students and faculty at a campus.*

AS YOU READ: *Think about the various bloggers the essay quotes. How are they similar, and how are they different?*

The weeks leading up to Thanksgiving were especially busy for Harvard bloggers.

Robert John Bennett '68, who's writing a novel online, posted chapters 4 through 12 of part V ("Harvard—The Fourth Year") on his blog—short for Weblog, or online journal. Another blogger, Cynthia Rockwell, a sociology department staff member and freelance movie reviewer, debated the value of scholarly film criticism: "Does this kind of criticism illuminate, or does it bleach raw? I don't know. Do artists need critics? I don't know." Harvard Law School (HLS) librarian Vernica Downey used her blog to remind readers about National Children's Book Week ("The theme this year is 'Free to Read'"). And in his blog, Nathan Paxton cheered that month's landmark state-court decision lifting the ban on same-sex marriages. "This is great," the PhD candidate in government wrote. "The issue of the place of gays in our society is going to be the hot-button culture-wars issue of 2004."

530

Meanwhile, one particularly prolific commentator, known online only   3
as The Redhead, waxed wistful about single life. "How is it that some people
find their soulmates (if there is such a thing) at sixteen?" she mused one
bleak November afternoon. "Where are all the beautiful souls in this city
(they're too young, or they're married, or they're smokers, or they're in love
with someone else)? There's no justice in the universe."

Welcome to Weblogs at Harvard Law, an experimental community where   4
more than 350 students, faculty and staff members, and alumni have signed
up to publicly express their thoughts about everything from social issues to
software, from literature to love. Based at the Berkman Center for Internet
and Society, the initiative is free and available to anyone with a Harvard.edu
e-mail address. And except for a few private blogs limited to specific classes,
all Harvard-hosted blogs can be read by anybody on the Web.

Harvard's blogging project stems from a November 2002 conference,   5
sponsored by the Berkman Center, to examine the university's "digital identity." Provost Steven E. Hyman challenged those present to use the Internet
to unify their famously decentralized° institution, building bridges among
isolated departments and schools. "The question became how we could set
up the different parts of Harvard to talk to each other better," says center director John Palfrey '94, JD '01. Participants also hoped to create exciting new
online communities and fresh ways to use technology in teaching.

With their grassroots appeal, blogs seemed like a good first step. Shortly   6
after the conference, the center recruited a new fellow, blogging pioneer
Dave Winer, to spearhead the online community. Winer's own tech-talk
journal, DaveNet, was among the Internet's first blogs; founded in 1994, it
predated the term identifying it by several years. "I found this way of telling
stories that didn't have a filter, and it worked," says Winer, who went on to
found UserLand Software Inc. of Los Altos, California, which makes Web-
publishing products, and to launch an even better-known blog, Scripting
News. After arriving at Harvard in early 2003, Winer quickly adapted his
blogging software, Manila, for the university's Weblog community and
launched the program in March.

Blogs are public online journals, written in reverse chronological order,   7
with the most recent entries at the top. Unlike most graphic-rich Web sites,
they consist primarily of unadorned text and links to other sites, although
serious bloggers also upload photographs, audio, and video. Blogs usually
present a single author's voice, but increasingly groups and organizations
are using the format as well: the law school's LLM class of '04, the library at
Harvard's Rowland Institute, and the Berkman Center itself, among others,
maintain Weblogs.

All are part of a fast-growing worldwide community dubbed the "blogo-   8
sphere." About five million blogs now exist, according to Perseus Development Corporation; the Braintree, Massachusetts–based market-research firm
expects that number to double before 2005.

---

decentralized: Lacking a central point of focus.

What draws people to blogging? First, of course, they have something to   9
say. "I blog to talk, to let it out, to experiment with words, to Be Heard," The
Redhead writes. "I miss standing onstage in plays I believed in; I miss projecting my voice across a thousand seats. I'm loud for a reason. I have a lot
to say, and a strong set of lungs, and passion. And maybe out there, someone's got a question I can help answer."

In addition, blogging is refreshingly simple, requiring virtually no tech-   10
nical design know-how, or special software. Harvard users simply go to the
project's Web site (http://blogs.law.harvard.edu), where they can create a
blog in two or three minutes by following the instructions. From there, they
can post text, links, and photographs as easily as they send e-mail messages.

Blogging is also a cheap — or, in the Berkman Center's case, free — form   11
of publishing using existing space on university computers. And from a
user's perspective, it's wonderfully liberated from editorial interference. "You
know that old saying that freedom of the press belongs to whoever has the
press?" Winer asks. "Now *everybody* has the press."

As Harvard's diverse blogger population illustrates, "everybody" isn't the   12
stereotypical bored, barely literate teenager. Today lawyers, librarians, and
researchers use online journals for networking and sharing information; en-
trepreneurs use them for marketing and customer service; college professors
and students use them to extend in-class discussion. They're increasingly
popular among journalists, too. Several correspondents (and at least one
Iraqi citizen) maintained high-profile blogs at the height of last year's war in
Iraq, and Harvard's Nieman Foundation for Journalism devoted a chunk of
the fall 2003 issue of its quarterly magazine to examining the role of blogs
in newsrooms. Politicians are adopting blogs as well. By late 2003, nearly
every presidential candidate had one, though most real blogging was being
done by campaign staff members.

At Harvard, as elsewhere, blog styles are as different as the people behind   13
them. Many are online diaries, often featuring an online persona or alter ego.
The Redhead — who by mid November hadn't missed a single day of blogging
since the project's launch — writes about anything on her mind: her job, a
class, a party, a conversation, an observation. "I let myself have fun, but I try to
make sure there's a point," she says. Sometimes she prepares a single long
entry first thing in the morning or late at night; sometimes she writes several
and posts quick-hit entries — one or two sentences on a single topic, written as
rapidly as an e-mail message — throughout her day. (Fortunately, The Redhead, a.k.a. Wendy Koslow, is program coordinator for the Berkman Center,
where occasional on-the-job blogging is not only permitted, but encouraged.)

Many Harvard bloggers specialize. Vernica Downey, the HLS librarian,   14
writes primarily about research, rare books, and children's literature. Her
blog, titled "Thinking While Typing," draws a small but loyal audience of
regular readers. "I'm very popular among German librarians, for some reason," says Downey, who writes primarily outside work. HLS fellow Christopher Lydon, a former public-radio talk-show host, uses his site to explore

the social and cultural effects of blogging. He posts extensive text and audio interviews with leading bloggers, including some of those managing the on-line presidential campaigns.

Some educators use blogs as teaching tools. John Palfrey, a lecturer at   15
both HLS and the Extension School, posts syllabi, reading materials, and lectures on class blogs; he encourages, but doesn't require, students to use them. He views the technology as a way to extend the classroom experience, and to provide a new forum for people who might be too shy to speak up in person. "This helps us explore how people express themselves," says Palfrey, who also maintains an HLS blog on legal issues.

One Harvard staff member blogs to support a blossoming stage career.   16
Erin Judge, an assistant to two HLS professors by day, does stand-up comedy in Boston-area clubs at night. Her blog, "On Being (un)Funny," prompts some people to see her shows, she says. Its real strength, though, is as a test-ing ground for new material. "When I go onstage, I have five to seven min-utes. There's no room to try out something you're taking a risk on — cer-tainly not at first," she says. "So I find it very valuable to have this forum. I try to write something of length three times a week." Then she collects feed-back from regular readers — friends, fellow comics, other bloggers, her mother in Texas — and revises her routines before performing them.

Like other communities, Harvard's Weblog project relies on rules. Users   17
can't run businesses or political campaigns using the university's technology, and they can't imply that Harvard endorses anything they write. At the same time, the project's coordinators — who believe the experiment will work only if bloggers know they can publish freely — never censor content. That is a critical factor for participants, who tend to become passionate about free speech. "I feel like I can say whatever I want," Judge says. "If anybody else I know had a blog at the place where they work, they wouldn't feel comfort-able posting certain things."

Asked how coordinators would handle, for instance, a blog containing   18
hate speech, Palfrey says that hasn't been a problem — yet. "The community is self-policed, and that works remarkably well."

Until late October, the university hadn't interfered, either. But then col-   19
lege junior Derek Slater posted internal memos from Diebold Election Sys-tems, an electronic voting-machine manufacturer, on his blog. The docu-ments, which described possible security flaws in the company's equipment, had already been widely circulated online. After Slater posted them, Diebold complained to Harvard, arguing that Slater — and Harvard, as host — had vi-olated U.S. copyright law. Initially, Harvard told Slater to "cease and desist" and warned him that, in keeping with school policy, he would be banned from University computer systems for a year if it happened again. Slater, backed by the Berkman Center, argued that posting the memos fell within the copyright law's "fair use" provision. In November, Harvard's general counsel agreed, saying the university no longer considered the matter a vio-lation. Diebold later dropped the complaint.

Despite blogging's popularity, it has some drawbacks. The biggest prob- 20
lem: many blogs are downright boring. The worst offenders take the most
mundane material imaginable and share it with the world. One typical example, from a Harvard-hosted blog: "After approximately twenty years of
use, my GE toaster oven broke last night. Today I went to Target to buy a
new one. . . . They had a very nice Black & Decker toaster oven for $29.99
and I purchased it. My mother purchased a toaster oven for less about a year
ago. However, hers does not work. But she won't admit it."

Another pitfall: abandonment. Perseus, the market-research company, 21
says two-thirds of all blogs languish° unattended (which researchers define
as having no posts for two months), while one-quarter are "one-day wonders," created and then forgotten. Not surprisingly, the Harvard project's directory is littered with apparently abandoned blogs. In one case, an incoming freshman kept a detailed diary of his first few days on campus this past
fall, even creating Dickens-style headings for his chapters ("In Which I Do
Something Entirely Unexpected"). By the following week, though, he'd apparently lost interest; he never blogged again.

Because the Web is a public medium, bloggers occasionally attract un- 22
wanted attention. Koslow's high-spirited site briefly attracted a male fan
whose constant e-mail messages made her uncomfortable. "I e-mailed him
and said, 'Please don't contact me anymore,'" says Koslow, who doesn't
know whether the man was part of the Harvard community. "The second
time I did that, it worked." The experience made her more cautious about
posting personal information: she took her work e-mail address off the blog
and now uses nicknames or initials when referring to friends and colleagues.

Despite the growing pains, most bloggers remain true believers in their 23
medium's value and promise. Downey, for instance, feels guilty if she gets so
busy she goes several days without blogging. When that happens, she says,
she posts a message letting readers know "I'm still here; this Weblog hasn't
been abandoned." Once she decided to take a break from blogging, perhaps
permanently — but she missed it so much she found herself back online
within a week.

Coordinators can't yet say whether Harvard's blog project is, in fact, 24
building intellectual bridges on campus. "It's way too early to declare victory," Palfrey says. But it *is* building community. Some participants have become fast friends off-line, gathering for weekly meetings at the law school.
In October, many attended the HLS-sponsored BloggerCon, a conference
that attracted 150 participants from as far away as Japan. Meanwhile, Palfrey
says, Stanford Law School expects to offer Weblogs to all its students, beginning this fall.

Online, many Harvardians faithfully stop by fellow participants' blogs to 25
read and comment on each other's posting. "I feel like my blog has a little
neighborhood," says Koslow. Dave Winer, project coordinator and medium

languish: Lie idle.

pioneer, skims maybe a dozen blogs daily. "Every one of them is a teacher of mine," he says, "and they teach me something new every day."

Questions to Start You Thinking

1. CONSIDERING MEANING: What are some of the reasons that blogging has become so popular? What are some of the drawbacks to blogging?

2. IDENTIFYING WRITING STRATEGIES: This essay is clearly organized into specific sections. What is the focus of each section, and where does each begin and end? How are the transitions between the sections signaled?

3 READING CRITICALLY: Who seems to be the intended audience for this essay? What do you think is the writer's intended purpose? How well do you think this purpose is achieved?

4. EXPANDING VOCABULARY: Paragraph 6 refers to the "grassroots appeal" of blogs. What is the meaning of this phrase, and how does it relate to the point of the essay?

5. MAKING CONNECTIONS: In "How Computers Change the Way We Think" (pp. 552–58), Sherry Turkle argues that blogging and other online technologies have affected the way we view privacy. Do the people interviewed for this essay seem to have concerns about privacy issues? Should they?

Journal Prompts

1. What kinds of communication do you participate in online? What do you see as the positive and negative aspects of electronic communication?

2. If you were to start your own blog, what would you write about? Your daily life? A hobby? An issue you feel passionate about? Explain why you would choose this topic. If you already have a blog, what do you write about? What have you gained from the experience?

Suggestions for Writing

1. In the conclusion of the essay, the author makes the point that Harvard's blog project is "building community." Write an essay about a community that you are a part of—your family, a church or other religious organization, a school, a sports team, a club, or some other group. Discuss how this group could (or already does) use the Internet to foster a greater sense of community.

2. Spend some time reading a variety of blogs, either at the Harvard Web site (see paragraph 10) or elsewhere on the Internet. You might start at *Technorati* <http://technorati.com>, where you can see a list of the most popular blogs and do a keyword search of blog postings. Make notes about the kinds of things bloggers write about. Then write an essay classifying the different kinds of blogs you encountered. Be sure to use plenty of examples as support.

David Gelernter

Computers Cannot Teach Children Basic Skills

David Gelernter *was born in 1955. Although his undergraduate degree from Yale University is in classical Hebrew literature, he went on to receive a PhD in computer science from the State University of New York at Stony Brook. Gelernter has been a professor of computer science at Yale since 1983, and his writings and theories on technology have been highly influential. He is also a painter and an art critic, and he serves on the National Council for the Arts. In 1993, he lost part of his right hand and the sight in one eye after opening a mail bomb sent by Theodore Kaczynski, the "Unabomber" terrorist opposed to the advancement of technology, who targeted prominent professors and business executives. Gelernter chronicled his recovery in the memoir* Drawing Life: Surviving the Unabomber *(1997). His other books include* Mirror Worlds *(1991),* The Muse in the Machine: Computerizing the Poetry of Human Thought *(1994),* 1939: The Lost World of the Fair *(1995), and* Machine Beauty *(1998). He has written for such publications as* Commentary, *the* New York Times, *the* Wall Street Journal, *the* Washington Post, *the* National Review, *and* Time. *In "Computers Cannot Teach Children Basic Skills," first published in* New Republic *in 1994, Gelernter challenges the widely held view that computers are always a "godsend" in the classroom.*

AS YOU READ: *Identify the solution Gelernter proposes for making effective use of computers in the classroom.*

Over the last decade an estimated $2 billion has been spent on more than 1 2 million computers for America's classrooms. That's not surprising. We constantly hear from Washington that the schools are in trouble and that computers are a godsend. Within the education establishment, in poor as well as rich schools, the machines are awaited with nearly religious awe. An inner-city principal bragged to a teacher friend of mine recently that his school "has a computer in every classroom . . . despite being in a bad neighborhood!"

Computers Teach Some Things Well

Computers should be in the schools. They have the potential to accomplish 2 great things. With the right software, they could help make science tangible or teach neglected topics like art and music. They could help students form a concrete idea of society by displaying on-screen a version of the city in which they live — a picture that tracks real life moment by moment.

In practice, however, computers make our worst educational nightmares 3 come true. While we bemoan the decline of literacy, computers discount words in favor of pictures and pictures in favor of video. While we fret about the decreasing cogency° of public debate, computers dismiss linear argu-

cogency: Logic, persuasiveness.

ment and promote fast, shallow romps across the information landscape. While we worry about basic skills, we allow into the classroom software that will do a student's arithmetic or correct his spelling.

Computers Lower Reading Skills

Take multimedia. The idea of multimedia is to combine text, sound, and 4 pictures in a single package that you browse on-screen. You don't just *read* Shakespeare; you watch actors performing, listen to songs, view Elizabethan buildings. What's wrong with that? By offering children candy-coated books, multimedia is guaranteed to sour them on unsweetened reading. It makes the printed page look even more boring than it used to look. Sure, books will be available in the classroom, too — but they'll have all the appeal of a dusty piano to a teen who has a Walkman handy.

So what if the little nippers don't read? If they're watching Olivier° in- 5 stead, what do they lose? The text, the written word along with all of its at- tendant pleasures. Besides, a book is more portable than a computer, has a higher-resolution display, can be written on and dog-eared, and is compara- tively dirt cheap.

Hypermedia, multimedia's comrade in the struggle for a brave new 6 classroom,° is just as troubling. It's a way of presenting documents on- screen without imposing a linear start-to-finish order. Disembodied para- graphs are linked by theme; after reading one about the First World War, for example, you might be able to choose another about the technology of bat- tleships, or the life of Woodrow Wilson, or hemlines in the '20s. This is an- other cute idea that is good in minor ways and terrible in major ones. Teach- ing children to understand the orderly unfolding of a plot or a logical argument is a crucial part of education. Authors don't merely agglomerate° paragraphs; they work hard to make the narrative read a certain way, prove a particular point. To turn a book or a document into hypertext is to invite readers to ignore exactly what counts — the story.

The real problem, again, is the accentuation° of already bad habits. Dy- 7 namiting documents into disjointed paragraphs is one more expression of the sorry fact that sustained argument is not our style. If you're a newspaper or magazine editor and your readership is dwindling, what's the solution? Shorter pieces. If you're a politician and you want to get elected, what do you need? Tasty sound bites. Logical presentation be damned.

Another software species, "allow me" programs, is not much better. 8 These programs correct spelling and, by applying canned grammatical and stylistic rules, fix prose. In terms of promoting basic skills, though, they have all the virtues of a pocket calculator.

Olivier: Lawrence Olivier, a British actor noted for his Shakespearean performances. **brave new classroom:** Reference to the Aldous Huxley novel *Brave New World,* in which technology makes life happy but empty.   **agglomerate:** Jumble together.   **accentua- tion:** Making more intense.

In Kentucky, as the *Wall Street Journal* reported, students in grades K–3   9
are mixed together regardless of age in a relaxed environment. It works
great, the *Journal* says. Yes, scores on computation tests have dropped 10 percent at one school, but not to worry: "Drilling addition and subtraction in
an age of calculators is a waste of time," the principal reassures us. Meanwhile, a Japanese educator informs University of Wisconsin mathematician
Richard Akey that in his country, "calculators are not used in elementary or
junior high school because the primary emphasis is on helping students develop their mental abilities." No wonder Japanese kids blow the pants off
American kids in math. Do we really think "drilling addition and subtraction in an age of calculators is a waste of time"? If we do, then "drilling
reading in an age of multimedia is a waste of time" can't be far behind.

Prose-correcting programs are also a little ghoulish, like asking a com-   10
puter for tips on improving your personality. On the other hand, I ran this
viewpoint through a spell checker, so how can I ban the use of such programs in schools? Because to misspell is human; to have no idea of correct
spelling is to be semiliterate.

Conditions on the Use of Computers

There's no denying that computers have the potential to perform inspiring   11
feats in the classroom. If we are ever to see that potential realized, however,
we ought to agree on three conditions. First, there should be a completely
new crop of children's software. Most of today's offerings show no imagination. There are hundreds of similar reading and geography and arithmetic
programs, but almost nothing on electricity or physics or architecture. Also,
they abuse the technical capacities of new media to glitz up old forms instead of creating new ones. Why not build a time-travel program that gives
kids a feel for how history is structured by zooming you backward? A spec-
trum program that lets users twirl a frequency knob to see what happens?

Second, computers should be used only during recess or relaxation peri-   12
ods. Treat them as fillips,° not as surrogate teachers. When I was in school
in the '60s, we all loved educational films. When we saw a movie in class,
everybody won: teachers didn't have to teach, and pupils didn't have to
learn. I suspect that classroom computers are popular today for the same
reasons.

Most important, educators should learn what parents and most teachers   13
already know: you cannot teach a child anything unless you look him in the
face. We should not forget what computers are. Like books — better in some
ways, worse in others — they are devices that help children mobilize their
own resources and learn for themselves. The computer's potential to do
good is modestly greater than a book's in some areas. Its potential to do
harm is vastly greater, across the board.

---

fillips: Things that are added for excitement but are not essential.

Questions to Start You Thinking

1. CONSIDERING MEANING: What are the primary shortcomings Gelernter believes computers have as educational tools?

2. IDENTIFYING WRITING STRATEGIES: Where in the essay does Gelernter present his solution as to how computers should be used in the classroom? Do you find this placement effective? Why or why not?

3. READING CRITICALLY: In several places in the essay, Gelernter compares computers with books. Review what he has to say about computers and books. Do you think he makes an effective argument here? Why or why not?

4. EXPANDING VOCABULARY: Define *bemoan, literacy, fret, linear,* and *romps* (paragraph 3). Then, in your own words, summarize Gelernter's point in paragraph 3. What does his word choice suggest about his intended audience?

5. MAKING CONNECTIONS: What might Gelernter have to say about the kind of education Annie Dillard describes in the selection from her autobiography on pages 577–79? Could she have learned the same thing by simply using a computer? Why or why not?

Journal Prompts

1. What kind of learning have you done on computers? How effective do you find such learning?

2. In the essay's final paragraph, Gelernter writes that "you cannot teach a child anything unless you look him in the face." What does he mean? Do you agree?

Suggestions for Writing

1. To what extent do you agree or disagree with Gelernter's position? Write an essay in which you take a stand about the value of computers in the classroom. Focus, in particular, on the basic skills of reading, writing, and mathematics, but feel free to consider other areas in which computers may or may not be effective teaching tools.

2. Gelernter wrote this essay in 1994. Do some research on how computers have come to be used in classrooms since then. For example, what kinds of software have been developed for educational purposes? How much time does the average student spend using a computer in the classroom? Are computers being used to teach basic skills? Write an essay in which you use your findings to support your position about how Gelernter would feel about the use of computers in education today.

Steven Levy
From *The Perfect Thing*

Steven Levy, *senior editor of* Newsweek *and author of the magazine's "The Technologist" column, is one of America's most acclaimed technology writers. Born in 1951, Levy grew up in Philadelphia and earned his undergraduate degree from Temple University. He then received an MA in literature from Pennsylvania State University. He began his journalism career covering everything from sports to rock music to wedding announcements before joining* Newsweek *in 1995. Levy's work also has appeared in such publications as the* New Yorker, *the* New York Times Magazine, Harper's, *and* Premiere, *and he is a regular contributor to* Wired *magazine. Levy's six books include* Hackers: Heroes of the Computer Revolution *(1984), which brought the word* hacker *into people's daily vocabulary and was named by* PC Magazine *as the best sci-tech book written in the last twenty years, and* Crypto: How the Code Rebels Beat the Government — Saving Privacy in the Digital Age *(2001), winner of the grand eBook prize at the 2001 Frankfurt Book festival. The following selection is from his latest book,* The Perfect Thing: How the iPod Shuffles Commerce, Culture, and Coolness *(2006). In this excerpt, Levy questions the social impact of the groundbreaking device: "Has the iPod destroyed the social fabric? Has it transmogrified us into a zombie culture?"*

AS YOU READ: *Think about how Levy describes iPod users. How does he characterize them?*

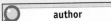

■ For more about Steven Levy, visit <bedfordstmartins.com/ bedguide> and do a keyword search:

author

I n February 2005, the writer Andrew Sullivan visited New York City and 1 became severely discombobulated. The energizing, cacophonous° racket he had associated with New York had fallen silent. Even more disconcerting,° the city's formerly boisterous° population had apparently been mind-jacked by some alien force. Staring at the suddenly quiescent street life, he fingered the culprit. It was the Gizmo That Stole Gotham:

> There were little white wires hanging down from their ears, or tucked into pockets, purses, or jackets. The eyes were a little vacant. Each was in his or her own musical world, walking to their soundtrack, stars in their own music video, almost oblivious to the world around them. These are the iPod people. Even without the white wires you can tell who they are. They walk down the street in their own MP3 cocoon, bumping into others, deaf to small social cues, shutting out anyone not in their bubble.

Even Sullivan's own status as an iPod owner — "I joined the cult a few 2 years ago; the sect of the little white box worshipers," he confessed — did not mitigate his sorrow at what had been lost. "Walk through any airport in the United States these days and you will see person after person gliding through the social ether as if on autopilot," he wrote. "Get on a subway and

cacophonous: Noisy.   disconcerting: Disturbing.   boisterous: Noisily enthusiastic.

you're surrounded by a bunch of Stepford° commuters staring into mid-space as if anaesthetized by technology. Don't ask, don't tell, don't overhear, don't observe. Just tune in and tune out."

Has the iPod destroyed the social fabric? Has it transmogrified us into a zombie culture? Has love of our own tunes lured us into aural narcissism,° locking us in a cycle of self-love, from our hand-picked music library straight to our brains, via earbuds? It's something an unplugged observer might well ask. In certain places — the gym, the subway, the airplane, the schoolyard — it may seem that the immediate environment, and the people in it, gets less attention than the increasingly inevitable iPod.

Outsiders are getting frustrated at the party they haven't been invited to. To those who depend on making cold connections, it's beyond frustration. Pity the poor beggars and street musicians who must now compete with the personal concerts buzzing in the heads of potential donors. For politicians seeking to press voter flesh, it's a nightmare. "This is a whole new hazard in campaigning!" Gifford Miller, striving to be New York City's mayor in 2005, told *New York* magazine, "We have to come up with something to jam the iPods!" (Miller, of course, lost the primary.)

And it's not just mendicants,° pols,° and social critics who worry about the effect; even some enthusiastic iPod owners are concerned about the impact on the social dynamic. Wayne Coyne, the singer and guitarist for the Flaming Lips, for instance, loves the access to his music that the iPod gives him but admits, "There's an insulation that happens. I can see space is at a premium in a community like Manhattan, but in a way it's saying, 'I'm with you people, but I don't want to deal with you.' I don't really like that some-times — I like the idea of 'Let's deal with each other, why not?'"

Coyne's lament is typical of this form of social criticism. But it's misguided. Think of your experiences in the subway and gym before the iPod became standard issue and supposedly made everyone into an extra from *The Village of the Damned*. Did people in those pre-'pod environments spontaneously break out into chatter, exchange intimacies, and otherwise "deal with each other"? No. They avoided eye contact and counted the minutes until the torturous boredom of those social hells might end. Now people happily listen to their favorite music, marvel at how their personal soundscapes enliven their surroundings, and appreciate the cozy (albeit virtual) protective covering that their iPods provide them. Amazingly, *that* seems to make observers crazy.

Questions to Start You Thinking

1. CONSIDERING MEANING: According to Levy, what concerns do critics have about the popularity of iPods?
2. IDENTIFYING WRITING STRATEGIES: In paragraphs 1 and 2, Levy quotes Andrew Sullivan quite extensively. What is the effect of these quotations?

Stepford: Robotic, zombielike. The word originates from *The Stepford Wives*, a 1972 novel in which the men of the fictional town of Stepford replace their wives with robots. **narcissism:** Self-love.   **mendicants:** Beggars.   **pols:** Politicians.

3. READING CRITICALLY: Levy devotes most of this selection to laying out various criticisms of iPods. Where does he begin to counter these concerns? Do you find his defense of iPods sufficient to counteract these criticisms?

4. EXPANDING VOCABULARY: Define *discombobulated* (paragraph 1) and *transmogrified* (paragraph 3). Why might Levy have chosen to use these words rather than simpler synonyms?

5. MAKING CONNECTIONS: The *Harvard Magazine* essay "Creating Community, Online and Off" (pp. 530–35) discusses how modern technology can bring people together. Levy, on the other hand, reminds readers how it can push people apart. What do you think is the main effect of personal technologies — portable music players, cell phones, laptop computers, and so on? What examples support your opinion?

Journal Prompts

1. What is your opinion of iPods? How do you respond to the criticisms that Levy mentions?

2. If you could create a "personal soundtrack," what would it consist of? What kind of music would you use to characterize your daily life?

Suggestions for Writing

1. Consider another electronic device that some people criticize and others embrace — cell phones, for example, or video games or even television. Write an essay in which you evaluate both the pros and the cons of your subject.

2. One issue related to the use of iPods and other such devices is that of copyright infringement when music is downloaded without specific permission. Do some research about the arguments on both sides of this issue, and then write an essay in which you take a stand for or against greater enforcement of copyright protection.

Merrill Markoe
Who Am I?

 For more about Merrill Markoe, visit <bedfordstmartins.com/bedguide> and do a keyword search:

author

Merrill Markoe *was born in New York City in 1951. After earning an MFA from the University of California at Berkeley and spending a year as an art instructor, she left teaching to try her hand at comedy writing. Markoe says that "nobody was more surprised" than she when her first script landed her a job as a writer for the television program* Laugh In 2. *She went on to become the Emmy-winning cocreator and original head writer of* Late Night with David Letterman. *After leaving the show in 1988, Markoe worked as a television news correspondent and freelance writer for such shows as* Newhart, Moonlighting, *and* Sex and the City. *Markoe now spends much of her time writing books, including the humorous essay collections* What the Dogs Have Taught Me and Other Amazing Things I've Learned *(1992),* How to Be Hap-Hap-Happy Like Me *(1994), and* Merrill Markoe's

Guide to Love *(1997). She also has published two novels,* It's My F —— ing Birthday *(2002) and* Walking in Circles Before Lying Down *(2006), and has written for such publications as* Rolling Stone, Time, New York Woman, *the* New York Times, *and the* Los Angeles Times. *In this essay, first published in* ON *Magazine in March 2001, Markoe offers a humorous take on online personality quizzes.*

AS YOU READ: *Note the different results of each personality quiz that Markoe takes. Do the quizzes help her answer the question in the essay's title?*

Having spent a fair amount of time and money in therapy, debating my 1
every move with a licensed and supposedly caring professional, I was under the impression that I had a pretty good idea of what I was all about. At least until I started taking personality quizzes on the Internet. As any reader of cheesy women's magazines will tell you, this quiz-taking business can be both time-consuming and pointless in terms of gaining meaningful advice. But it can also be as utterly seductive as the horoscope pages. For about a minute and a half, the quiz glistens like a beacon of knowledge before you, offering answers to all the important questions in life. Five minutes later, awash in self-loathing, you can't even remember what it said or why you ever buy that magazine.

As it turns out, the Internet is so full of this kind of self-improvement 2
quiz that it could be argued that the only thing that separates the Net from an average issue of *Cosmopolitan* is that *Cosmo* offers only one quiz at a time. And the Internet seems to have fewer ads for panty liners.

I came to know of this one day when, quite by accident, I encountered a 3
quiz at a handy site called QuizBox.com that promised to tell me how "attractive" I was. I guess I needed a little reassurance (with emphasis on the word *little* — if the quiz couldn't see me, how reassuring could it be?). I willingly submitted to seemingly irrelevant questions like "Which city would you like to visit?" (I chose Paris over Tokyo or Beijing because, in the montage° in my imagination, I thought I looked more attractive in Paris.) I also selected a peck over a big kiss as my first-date kissing style because a rash of unappealing recent first dates was still fresh in my mind, and this quiz didn't specify whether the guy I was allegedly going on this first date with had any sex appeal.

After my scores were tallied, the quiz passed judgment. It said, in no un- 4
certain terms, that I needed to improve my personality. I also needed to be more optimistic and smile more. I could be attractive if I would try, it sighed, but clearly it didn't think I was trying hard enough.

So there I was, alone in my house and suddenly a lot less attractive than 5
I had been a few minutes earlier. I wasn't going to take this lying down. To recoup my losses, like a woman feverishly playing the slot machines, I continued to take more quizzes.

Instantly I was able to wrest myself from the jaws of low self-esteem via 6
the "What kind of personality do you have?" quiz. This time, when asked to answer the question "If you could wish for anything what would it be?" I

montage: A series of images.

chose "Become a beauty queen." (After all, my health was already pretty good, my eyes are already pretty nice, and being clever was apparently getting me nowhere.) Much to my delight, the quiz was favorably impressed. "People with your kind of character are few and far between," it informed me. "Everybody likes to be around people with your personality."

Feeling a bit more confident, I was also getting genuinely curious about the possibility of learning something new about myself this way. So I went on taking quizzes. Which is how I came to find out that every single thing I did defined my personality.   7

There was an egg test that revealed that because I eat fried eggs white-part first, instead of yolk first, I am "logical, smart, and inventive . . . though sometimes too cold and selfish." That I only eat egg whites, period, didn't seem to factor in one way or another.   8

Next, by picking toilet stall No. 2 out of a drawing of three empty stalls ("The Toilet Test"), I learned I was "an efficient person" yet also "a romantic person" who can be "too hasty making decisions in love." I guess it serves me right for being so cavalier° about my toilet-stall selections.   9

On "The Eating Test," I made the mistake of picking eggs and toast over cereal for breakfast, while also admitting to sometimes skipping lunch entirely because of worry about my weight. Now I had inadvertently shown myself to be "jealous of people who are smarter and better looking" than I am. A harsh evaluation, I felt, for someone "with my kind of character."   10

So I left QuizBox.com's petty judgments behind and typed "personality quiz" into the Yahoo! search engine. This led me to "The Ultimate Personality Test." Three cups of coffee later (and still in my pajamas at one in the afternoon), I was saddened to learn that I was a "secret agent" who "professionally, likes to work in a cubicle and eat lunch at the desk."   11

But my mood improved considerably once I clicked on the next test I could find, and my choice of an abstract pattern from an assortment of designs offered me a complete reevaluation. Now, thank heavens, I was "dynamic, active, extroverted" and "willing to accept certain risks and to make a strong commitment in exchange for interesting and varied work."   12

So which was it? Was I a cubicle worker or a risk taker? Hoping to get off this emotional roller coaster, I wandered over to TheSpark.com, where yet another personality test branded me "an accountant. Reserved. Meticulous. Dependable." And this despite the fact that on the very same page "The Sexy Test" said I was 75 percent sexier than their average quiz taker! Because this puzzling new image of "sexy accountant" didn't provide me with anything except an idea for a horrible new sitcom, I took a deep, cleansing breath and dived into the elaborate "How Others See You" quiz, where I emerged "extroverted, agreeable but neurotic and not very conscientious." I found this confusing because a quiz at a women's financial site insisted that I was "thorough, meticulous, and calm" only a few minutes later.   13

By the end of a long day, I also learned that my taste in room decor is "middle class" ("What Class Are You?"), despite the fact that my "plant per-   14

cavalier: Arrogant; disdainful.

sonality" is "woodland natural." My "workout personality" is "40% inspirational, 30% spontaneous, and 30% analytical (sailing, training for a triathlon, and softball recommended)." And my religious beliefs are Unitarian Universalist, neopagan, or Malayan Buddhist.

Although the Ayurvedic Foundation's site tells me I have a Pitta consti- 15 tution, meaning I am "hot, sharp, liquid, and oily," an insurance company's longevity quiz says that I will live to be ninety-five.

So there it is: I am extroverted and reserved, passive and active, risk tak- 16 ing and afraid of change. I am also calm, neurotic, and meticulous, dependable and not very conscientious. So what if my workout program of alternating the gym with yoga does not fit my personality? Who cares if I should belong to a religion I have never heard of? All things considered, I have to say that it feels great to really get to know myself at last.

Questions to Start You Thinking

1. CONSIDERING MEANING: How do you interpret Markoe's final sentence in this selection?

2. IDENTIFYING WRITING STRATEGIES: In paragraph 4, Markoe writes about the first quiz as if it were an actual person criticizing her. How does she do this? What is the effect?

3. READING CRITICALLY: What is Markoe's purpose in writing this essay? How do you think she wants readers to respond? Do all the quizzes she quotes from seem to be real? Why or why not?

4. EXPANDING VOCABULARY: Define the adjectives Markoe uses to describe herself in the first two sentences of paragraph 16. How do these words contribute to the point she is making in the essay as a whole?

5. MAKING CONNECTIONS: In "What's Love Got to Do with It?" (pp. 453–57), Anjula Razdan discusses online dating services, which often use personality questionnaires to match up potential mates. Razdan quotes several experts on Internet dating, including one who says, "That's what computers are all about — efficiency and sorting" (paragraph 16). How might Markoe respond to this statement? How do you think she might feel about online dating services?

Journal Prompts

1. Find a personality quiz, either online or in a popular magazine, and answer the questions as honestly as you can. To what extent do the quiz results match the personality you see yourself as having?

2. Do you ever feel that you or others you know spend too much time online? Explain why you think Internet surfing can become addictive.

Suggestions for Writing

1. Spend an hour or so taking as many different online personality quizzes as you can. Then, like Markoe, write an essay in which you use examples to share your results with readers. Your tone will depend on how seriously you take those results.

2. Markoe makes the point in paragraph 1 that quiz taking can be "as utterly seductive as the horoscope pages." Write an essay in which you analyze what lies behind the appeal of quizzes, horoscopes, and other tools that claim to reveal people's personalities. What is it that people are looking for when they seek out these guides?

Alex Koppelman

MySpace or OurSpace?

 For more about Alex Koppelman, visit <bedfordstmartins.com/bedguide> and do a keyword search:

author

Alex Koppelman *was born in 1982 in Baltimore, Maryland. He graduated from the University of Pennsylvania in 2005 and is currently a staff writer for* Salon.com, *where he covers news and politics. Before joining* Salon, *he helped found the online magazine* Dragonfire, *serving as the Arts and Entertainment editor and media critic, and he also has written for the* Huffington Post *blog. In addition to writing for* Salon, *he is currently a contributing editor for* SMITH *Magazine, a new interactive magazine that aims to publish "the best in personal media . . . blogs, memoirs, diaries, viral videos, social networking, the mash-up between the professional and the amateur." In this article, first published on* Salon.com *in June 2006, Koppelman reports on privacy concerns raised by cases in which students have been suspended from school or arrested based on their postings to social-networking sites. In the paired essay that follows, Sherry Turkle also takes a close look at how social-networking sites — among other computer technologies — are affecting the ways people think and behave.*

AS YOU READ: *Consider how school authorities and law-enforcement agents have responded to teenagers' postings on MySpace. What are the primary concerns of people on both sides of the issue — those who support such monitoring and those who criticize it?*

In October, seventeen-year-old Dimitri Arethas posted a doctored photo on his MySpace page depicting his public high school's black vice principal as RoboCop. Arethas said he found the photo, which had a racial slur scrawled on it, on another student's Web site, and that he posted it to his own MySpace page thinking it was funny. Arethas, of Charlotte, North Carolina, claims he didn't mean the post to be racist and says that most of his fellow students thought the post was funny too.

But one anonymous student didn't, and brought it to the attention of 2 school administrators. As a result, Arethas says principal Joel Ritchie, who did not respond to a request for comment, suspended Arethas for ten days.

Arethas, who says he apologized and removed the photo when he was 3 initially confronted, was incensed° by the suspension, and contacted his local paper, the *Charlotte Observer*, and the American Civil Liberties Union.

incensed: Angered.

With the help of ACLU lawyers, Arethas was able to convince the school to end the suspension. He returned after two days.

"Maybe what I did was wrong, morally," Arethas said in a recent e-mail, 4 "but I had every right to express myself. I just chose to do it as a picture, instead of rambling down the hallways yelling, 'Man! This school sucks.'"

Arethas isn't the only student to be disciplined for what he posted to his 5 MySpace profile. The past few years have seen an explosion in the number of schools taking to the Web to find out what students are saying and doing. And punishment has followed, from a Pennsylvania school that suspended one student for creating a parody MySpace profile of his principal to a California school that suspended twenty students simply for viewing one student's MySpace profile, which contained threats against another student. And some public school systems, like Illinois's Community High School District 128, are even taking steps to monitor everything their students say on sites like MySpace. According to the *Chicago Tribune*, under new guidelines, students who participate in extracurricular activities will need to sign a pledge in which they agree that the school can discipline them if it finds evidence that they have posted any "illegal or inappropriate" material online. Even some police are beginning to patrol MySpace, seeing the site as an effective tool for catching teenage criminals.

All of this new scrutiny poses a vital question for MySpace, which claims 6 76 million users and is now the largest of all the Web's social-networking sites: What will happen to the site if and when users no longer feel safe expressing themselves there? And in an age where teenagers are accustomed to living their lives online, what will happen when they learn that what they thought was private is, in fact, public, and not without consequence?

"I never thought [this] would happen," Arethas says of his suspension. 7 "I figured only my friends would see my profile page."

Most large online social-networking services have undergone similar 8 challenges as they've grown, with users feeling safe in the widely held though mistaken perception that what they posted was private, or at least that it would only be seen by a select group of people. Other sites have also, like MySpace, dealt with users who have preyed on other more gullible° ones, as with the recent high-profile arrests of men who used MySpace to lure young girls. But few sites have grown as large, and as quickly, as MySpace, which was acquired in July 2005 by Rupert Murdoch's News Corporation for $580 million. And few have specialized so effectively in encouraging kids to get comfortable and open up.

As with all forms of electronic media, people still have a hard time 9 wrapping their minds around the fact that little online is truly private. A sampling of MySpace's offerings reveals the evidence: posts explore almost every aspect of users' personal lives, from typical teenage angst about acne and unrequited° crushes to more incriminating fare — sexually suggestive images and photos of drinking and drug use — as well as professions of love, anger, and every emotion in between.

gullible: Easily fooled.   **unrequited:** Not returned.

"MySpace has encouraged its users to be aware that what they post on   10
their MySpace profile is available for the public to see," says MySpace
spokesman Matthew Grossman, adding that "part of why MySpace has been
so successful is because people can share their feelings." While Grossman
stresses that MySpace does not spy on its users, or share their information,
the site will work with law enforcement "if they [law enforcement] go
through the proper legal channels," such as a subpoena or warrant. The
site's privacy statement makes that caveat° explicit. But many users haven't
heeded those warnings. They do so now at their peril, because more and
more, they are being watched.

"We patrol the Internet like we patrol the streets," Officer James McNamee,   11
a member of the Barrington, Illinois, police department's Special Crimes
Unit, says. "We'll go in on a MySpace or a Xanga, we'll pick out our area,
and we'll just start surfing it, checking it, seeing what's going on."

McNamee says the fact that police have only recently realized what a   12
powerful tool social-networking sites can be for investigative purposes may
be what makes MySpace users feel the site is their own private realm.

"We're still playing catch-up," McNamee says. "I wouldn't say we're   13
super far behind, but we're learning as we go and I think that's the reason
some [teens] feel like, 'Oh, this is an invasion of our privacy.' Well, no, it's
not, it's just that we were behind on learning that we should have been paying attention to this, and now we're paying attention."

McNamee says they've found pictures of graffiti, with the artists stand-   14
ing next to it, "smiling, all happy about their activity," they've found evidence of drug dealing — "where they could hook up, who was dealing drugs
. . . photos of their money . . . photos of their drugs" — they've even found a
"We Hate Barrington Police Department" blog. ("We don't care," McNamee
says of the blog. "It's kind of funny to us; we'll let them vent that way.")

The question of what public-school students have the right to say, and   15
where they have the right to say it, remains murky, with little in the way of
definitive jurisprudence to guide schools and courts. Indeed, just about the
only thing experts on the topic seem to agree on is that no one really knows
what the law is.

"There have been some court decisions, and in all honesty they've been a   16
little bit confused," says Mark Goodman, the executive director of the Student Press Law Center. "And it really isn't just Internet-based speech, but actually any kind of expression by students outside of school. There really have
been relatively few cases going to court on this issue, so it's understandable
[to a certain extent] why there would be some confusion surrounding it."

Goodman, for his part, believes that the law is on the students' side.   17

> In a public school, I believe the law's pretty clear that the school does not
> have the authority to punish students for expression they engage in outside
> of school. There are really important fundamental reasons for that. At the
> very least, it's a major usurpation° of parental authority. Outside of school,

caveat: Warning.   usurpation: Wrongful taking away.

parents have the authority to discipline their children. . . . I think the problem is a lot of people simply presume that the Internet in effect becomes school expression, and I simply don't believe it does. I think there are legally important distinctions, and very good policy reasons why the school shouldn't have that authority.

Marc Rotenberg, who teaches information privacy law at the George- 18 town University Law Center and is the executive director of the Electronic Privacy Information Center, believes the issue is not so clear-cut.

"The key point is whatever is publicly accessible," Rotenberg says. "If a 19 student writes an article in the town paper that defames one of the teachers, the fact that it didn't happen in a school publication really is irrelevant. The school will still act on that information if it's public and available to the community. . . . The courts have not, particularly in the last few years, been sympathetic to student privacy claims, and I don't think there's any reason to think it would be otherwise when the conduct is posted to publicly available Web sites. . . . The critical point here is that yes, I think students should have the freedom to express their views, and I don't think there should be any type of prior restraint on publication, whether it's in print or online media. But that doesn't mean what you say may not have some repercussions."

There are no such questions about whether the police have a right to pa- 20 trol MySpace.

"If it is a public forum that is accessible to others, then presumably the 21 police are welcome to participate, as they would be welcome to enter a shopping mall or something like that," Rotenberg says.

Kurt Opsahl, a staff lawyer with the Electronic Frontier Foundation, a non- 22 profit organization whose mission is to defend Internet free speech, agrees.

"You have of course a constitutional right not to incriminate yourself, 23 but you have to exercise that right by not incriminating yourself," Opsahl says. "If you post a photo of yourself engaged in apparently illegal activity with text confirming what you're doing, that can be used against you. Anything you say can and will be used against you, as they say in the Miranda warnings."

But according to James McNamee, MySpace's younger users, or at least 24 the ones he sees in his virtual patrols, haven't yet caught on to that.

"Some people criticize MySpace, and there's no reason to criticize it," he 25 says. "It's a social-networking Internet site that's doing a great function, in my view. The problem is young people aren't sure how to handle it yet. They're not understanding that it's the World Wide Web, they don't get that concept. They think only their friends are looking at it."

Eight MySpace users in Wilkes-Barre, Pennsylvania, learned the hard 26 way that the people visiting their MySpace profiles were not just friends. Wilkes-Barre police, stumped by a rash of graffiti in the downtown area, turned to MySpace to seek suspects.

"The police dug very deep to find me," says one of those arrested in the 27 case, who asked to remain anonymous because of ongoing legal proceedings, and who would communicate only through MySpace. "I didn't have my name, phone number, or any info on me online. I've never used my real name, I've never had my own Internet connection (always another person's name), and I never had my address or name at all posted or registered online."

That user, who denies any involvement in the graffiti, says he was aware 28 of the public nature of the site — "I always think that people are looking," he says — but that some of his friends were not, and that he thinks the police overstepped their bounds.

"I feel that police shouldn't lie and disguise their identity to gain friend- 29 ship with people they can't see, or ever meet without [informants]."

Dimitri Arethas also feels his rights were violated. "A home page is basi- 30 cally as private as it gets," he told the *Observer* at the time of his suspension.

When asked recently if he still felt that way, his answer was much the 31 same.

"Private like exclusive to only your friends? No, not that kind of pri- 32 vate," he said. "[But] someone has to personally seek out your name and find you in order to view your MySpace, which is what stirs me up. That's where I got some sense of privacy. I could have never imagined someone printing out my profile page and then turning it in."

Mark Goodman worries about the lessons students like Arethas will 33 learn as more face consequences for what they post to sites like MySpace.

> What I would hate to see happen, and I think it has happened in some communities at least, is students deciding they can't publish unpopular or controversial viewpoints on their MySpace page or an independent Web site because they're afraid school officials will punish them for it. That, I think, is very disturbing, and those are the young people who, as adults, are going to believe the government should be regulating what the public says. It has very troubling implications for their appreciation of the First Amendment in the world outside of school.

Arethas says that he has become more cautious about what he posts. 34 "Gotta play the political game now," he says. He took his MySpace profile down for a week after the incident, but decided to put it back up — without the offending photo — when he realized, he says, that he "could pretty much get away with it," and that he "had won the case" by being reinstated to school. He still believes the school was wrong to suspend him.

Goodman thinks, though, that few students would act as Arethas did. He 35 points to a study on high school students' attitudes toward the First Amendment, conducted by researchers at the University of Connecticut. Released early last year, the study found that 49 percent of students thought that newspapers should need government approval for their stories, 75 percent didn't realize flag burning was legal, and more than a third thought the First Amendment went too far. Half believed the government could censor the Internet.

"I think the point of it, ultimately, is how can we expect anything differ- 36 ent [than the survey results]," Goodman says. "A direct result of these actions is young people's dismissiveness of the fundamental values of free expression that we as a nation supposedly hold dear."

The MySpace user arrested in the Wilkes-Barre case agrees.   37

> I think that MySpace is the epitome° of free speech, and censorship, all
> rolled in one. And I think that America with[out] free speech is not free at
> all. Just think about the people that have been censored. Go to another
> country, like Denmark and there is no censorship at all, and the kids grow-
> ing up there don't look at it as dirty, just as life. When we make things ille-
> gal, or "dirty to look at" we create the feeling that it's bad.

Questions to Start You Thinking

1. CONSIDERING MEANING: Why are some people concerned about school and
   other authorities policing teenagers' Web postings? How can this issue be
   seen as involving freedom of speech?

2. IDENTIFYING WRITING STRATEGIES: Consider Koppelman's use of quotations
   in this selection. How do the quotations help him to develop his point?
   Why do you think he chose to quote his sources so extensively?

3. READING CRITICALLY: Does Koppelman present a balanced view of his topic?
   Or does he seem to lean toward one side of the issue — either in favor of or
   opposed to the policing of students' Web postings? Explain what you see as
   his purpose in writing the selection.

4. EXPANDING VOCABULARY: Define *murky, definitive,* and *jurisprudence* (paragraph 15). What point is Koppelman making in this paragraph?

5. MAKING CONNECTIONS: The essay from *Harvard Magazine,* "Creating Community, Online and Off" (pp. 530–35), mentions that the Harvard blogs
   are not censored. Do you feel that schools should have the right to censor
   content on blog sites that they provide to students? Why or why not?

Link to the Paired Essay

In the essay that follows ("How Computers Change the Way We Think,"
pp. 552–58), Sherry Turkle writes that "in a democracy, privacy is a right, not
merely a privilege" (paragraph 11). Of the people whom Koppelman quotes in
his essay, which do you think would agree with Turkle's statement? Which
would disagree? Explain your reasoning, as well as where you stand on the
issue.

Journal Prompts

1. Write about the kinds of personal information you share online. How safe
   do you feel providing this information? Did Koppelman's essay change the
   way you feel about your online privacy?

2. What is your response to Dimitri Arethas's case? Explain why you think his
   suspension was fair or unfair. Would your response be different if the photograph had not contained a racial slur?

---

epitome: Most perfect example.

Suggestions for Writing

1. Why do you think young people are so eager to create pages on sites such as MySpace, to share photographs and information about their personal lives with anyone who happens upon the page? Write an essay in which you explain some reasons for the phenomenal popularity of MySpace and other sites like it.

2. Write an essay in which you take a stand on students' freedom of speech. For example, should schools be able to discipline students for what they post to Web sites? Should administrators have a say in what students can publish in school newspapers or in letters to community newspapers? What about messages written on students' clothing? Support your position by citing examples from Koppelman's essay as well as from additional research.

Sherry Turkle
How Computers Change the Way We Think

For more about Sherry Turkle, visit <bedfordstmartins.com/ bedguide> and do a keyword search:

author

Sherry Turkle was born in 1948 in New York City. A graduate of Radcliffe College, the University of Chicago, and Harvard University, she is a clinical psychologist and a professor of sociology at the Massachusetts Institute of Technology. She also founded and directs the MIT Initiative on Technology and Self, a research center devoted to "the social and psychological dimensions of technological change." Turkle's teaching and writing, which focus on people's relationship with technology, have earned her the nickname cybershrink. Her books include Psychoanalytic Politics: Jacques Lacan and Freud's French Revolution *(1978, revised 1992);* The Second Self: Computers and the Human Spirit *(1984, revised 2005); and* Life on the Screen: Identity in the Age of the Internet *(1995). She is currently writing a book on how technology — rapidly evolving to become more humanlike — is changing what it means to be human. In the following essay, first published in* the Chronicle of Higher Education *in 2004, Turkle explores how technologies such as online chat, PowerPoint, word processors, and simulation games are radically affecting our "habits of mind."*

AS YOU READ: *Identify the areas in which Turkle sees computers changing the way people think. Does she present her opinions on whether these changes are good or bad?*

The tools we use to think change the ways in which we think. The invention of written language brought about a radical shift in how we process, organize, store, and transmit representations of the world. Although writing remains our primary information technology, today when we think about the impact of technology on our habits of mind, we think primarily of the computer.

My first encounters with how computers change the way we think came soon after I joined the faculty at the Massachusetts Institute of Technology in the late 1970s, at the end of the era of the slide rule and the beginning of the era of the personal computer. At a lunch for new faculty members, sev-

eral senior professors in engineering complained that the transition from
slide rules to calculators had affected their students' ability to deal with issues of scale. When students used slide rules, they had to insert decimal
points themselves. The professors insisted that that required students to
maintain a mental sense of scale, whereas those who relied on calculators
made frequent errors in orders of magnitude. Additionally, the students with
calculators had lost their ability to do "back of the envelope" calculations,
and with that, an intuitive feel for the material.

That same semester, I taught a course in the history of psychology. There, 3
I experienced the impact of computational objects on students' ideas about
their emotional lives. My class had read Freud's essay on slips of the tongue,
with its famous first example: the chairman of a parliamentary session opens
a meeting by declaring it closed. The students discussed how Freud interpreted such errors as revealing a person's mixed emotions. A computer-science
major disagreed with Freud's approach. The mind, she argued, is a computer.
And in a computational dictionary—like we have in the human mind—
"closed" and "open" are designated by the same symbol, separated by a sign
for opposition. "Closed" equals "minus open." To substitute "closed" for
"open" does not require the notion of ambivalence or conflict.

"When the chairman made that substitution," she declared, "a bit was 4
dropped; a minus sign was lost. There was a power surge. No problem."

The young woman turned a Freudian slip into an information-processing 5
error. An explanation in terms of meaning had become an explanation in
terms of mechanism.

Such encounters turned me to the study of both the instrumental and 6
the subjective sides of the nascent° computer culture. As an ethnographer
and psychologist, I began to study not only what the computer was doing
for us, but what it was doing *to* us, including how it was changing the way
we see ourselves, our sense of human identity.

In the 1980s, I surveyed the psychological effects of computational ob- 7
jects in everyday life—largely the unintended side effects of people's tendency to project thoughts and feelings onto their machines. In the twenty
years since, computational objects have become more explicitly designed to
have emotional and cognitive effects. And those "effects by design" will become even stronger in the decade to come. Machines are being designed to
serve explicitly as companions, pets, and tutors. And they are introduced in
school settings for the youngest children.

Today, starting in elementary school, students use e-mail, word process- 8
ing, computer simulations, virtual communities, and PowerPoint software.
In the process, they are absorbing more than the content of what appears on
their screens. They are learning new ways to think about what it means to
know and understand.

What follows is a short and certainly not comprehensive list of areas 9
where I see information technology encouraging changes in thinking. There

nascent: Just being born.

can be no simple way of cataloging whether any particular change is good
or bad. That is contested terrain. At every step we have to ask, as educators
and citizens, whether current technology is leading us in directions that
serve our human purposes. Such questions are not technical; they are social,
moral, and political. For me, addressing that subjective side of computation
is one of the more significant challenges for the next decade of information
technology in higher education. Technology does not determine change, but
it encourages us to take certain directions. If we make those directions clear,
we can more easily exert human choice.

Thinking about Privacy

Today's college students are habituated to a world of online blogging, in-   10
stant messaging, and Web browsing that leaves electronic traces. Yet they
have had little experience with the right to privacy. Unlike past generations
of Americans, who grew up with the notion that the privacy of their mail
was sacrosanct,° our children are accustomed to electronic surveillance as
part of their daily lives.

I have colleagues who feel that the increased incursions on privacy have   11
put the topic more in the news, and that this is a positive change. But middle-
school and high-school students tend to be willing to provide personal
information online with no safeguards, and college students seem uninterested in violations of privacy and in increased governmental and commercial surveillance. Professors find that students do not understand that in a
democracy, privacy is a right, not merely a privilege. In ten years, ideas about
the relationship of privacy and government will require even more active
pedagogy.° (One might also hope that increased education about the kinds
of silent surveillance that technology makes possible may inspire more active political engagement with the issue.)

Avatars° or a Self?

Chat rooms, role-playing games, and other technological venues offer us   12
many different contexts for presenting ourselves online. Those possibilities
are particularly important for adolescents because they offer what Erik Erik-
son described as a moratorium, a time out or safe space for the personal ex-
perimentation that is so crucial for adolescent development. Our dangerous
world — with crime, terrorism, drugs, and AIDS — offers little in the way of
safe spaces. Online worlds can provide valuable spaces for identity play.

But some people who gain fluency in expressing multiple aspects of self   13
may find it harder to develop authentic selves. Some children who write nar-
ratives for their screen avatars may grow up with too little experience of how
to share their real feelings with other people. For those who are lonely yet
afraid of intimacy, information technology has made it possible to have the
illusion of companionship without the demands of friendship.

sacrosanct: Most sacred or holy.   **pedagogy:** Teaching.   **avatars:** Graphic representations of people in a virtual reality environment such as the Internet.

From Powerful Ideas to PowerPoint

In the 1970s and early 1980s, some educators wanted to make programming 14 part of the regular curriculum for K–12 education. They argued that because information technology carries ideas, it might as well carry the most powerful ideas that computer science has to offer. It is ironic that in most elementary schools today, the ideas being carried by information technology are not ideas from computer science like procedural thinking, but more likely to be those embedded in productivity tools like PowerPoint presentation software.

PowerPoint does more than provide a way of transmitting content. It 15 carries its own way of thinking, its own aesthetic° — which not surprisingly shows up in the aesthetic of college freshmen. In that aesthetic, presentation becomes its own powerful idea.

To be sure, the software cannot be blamed for lower intellectual standards. 16 Misuse of the former is as much a symptom as a cause of the latter. Indeed, the culture in which our children are raised is increasingly a culture of presentation, a corporate culture in which appearance is often more important than reality. In contemporary political discourse, the bar has also been lowered. Use of rhetorical devices at the expense of cogent° argument regularly goes without notice. But it is precisely because standards of intellectual rigor outside the educational sphere have fallen that educators must attend to how we use, and when we introduce, software that has been designed to simplify the organization and processing of information.

In *The Cognitive Style of PowerPoint* (Graphics Press, 2003), Edward R. 17 Tufte suggests that PowerPoint equates bulleting with clear thinking. It does not teach students to begin a discussion or construct a narrative. It encourages presentation, not conversation. Of course, in the hands of a master teacher, a PowerPoint presentation with few words and powerful images can serve as the jumping-off point for a brilliant lecture. But in the hands of elementary-school students, often introduced to PowerPoint in the third grade, and often infatuated with its swooshing sounds, animated icons, and flashing text, a slide show is more likely to close down debate than open it up.

Developed to serve the needs of the corporate boardroom, the software 18 is designed to convey absolute authority. Teachers used to tell students that clear exposition depended on clear outlining, but presentation software has fetishized° the outline at the expense of the content.

Narrative, the exposition of content, takes time. PowerPoint, like so 19 much in the computer culture, speeds up the pace.

Word Processing versus Thinking

The catalog for the Vermont Country Store advertises a manual typewriter, 20 which the advertising copy says "moves at a pace that allows time to compose your thoughts." As many of us know, it is possible to manipulate text on

aesthetic: Conception of beauty.   **cogent:** Logical.   **fetishized:** Turned into an object of irrational devotion.

a computer screen and see how it looks faster than we can think about what the words mean.

Word processing has its own complex psychology. From a pedagogical 21 point of view, it can make dedicated students into better writers because it allows them to revise text, rearrange paragraphs, and experiment with the tone and shape of an essay. Few professional writers would part with their computers; some claim that they simply cannot think without their hands on the keyboard. Yet the ability to quickly fill the page, to see it before you can think it, can make bad writers even worse.

A seventh grader once told me that the typewriter she found in her 22 mother's attic is "cool because you have to type each letter by itself. You have to know what you are doing in advance or it comes out a mess." The idea of thinking ahead has become exotic.

Taking Things at Interface Value

We expect software to be easy to use, and we assume that we don't have to 23 know how a computer works. In the early 1980s, most computer users who spoke of transparency meant that, as with any other machine, you could "open the hood" and poke around. But only a few years later, Macintosh users began to use the term when they talked about seeing their documents and programs represented by attractive and easy-to-interpret icons. They were referring to an ability to make things work without needing to go below the screen surface. Paradoxically, it was the screen's opacity that permitted that kind of transparency. Today, when people say that something is transparent, they mean that they can see how to make it work, not that they know how it works. In other words, transparency means epistemic opacity.

The people who built or bought the first generation of personal computers 24 understood them down to the bits and bytes. The next generation of operating systems were more complex, but they still invited that old-time reductive understanding. Contemporary information technology encourages different habits of mind. Today's college students are already used to taking things at (inter)face value; their successors in 2014 will be even less accustomed to probing below the surface.

Simulation and Its Discontents

Some thinkers argue that the new opacity is empowering, enabling anyone 25 to use the most sophisticated technological tools and to experiment with simulation in complex and creative ways. But it is also true that our tools carry the message that they are beyond our understanding. It is possible that in daily life, epistemic opacity can lead to passivity.

I first became aware of that possibility in the early 1990s, when the first 26 generation of complex simulation games were introduced and immediately became popular for home as well as school use. SimLife teaches the principles of evolution by getting children involved in the development of complex ecosystems; in that sense it is an extraordinary learning tool. During one session in which I played SimLife with Tim, a thirteen-year-old, the screen before us flashed a message: "Your orgot is being eaten up." "What's an orgot?" I asked. Tim didn't know. "I just ignore that," he said confidently. "You don't need to know that kind of stuff to play."

For me, that story serves as a cautionary tale. Computer simulations en- 27 able their users to think about complex phenomena as dynamic, evolving systems. But they also accustom us to manipulating systems whose core assumptions we may not understand and that may not be true.

We live in a culture of simulation. Our games, our economic and politi- 28 cal systems, and the ways architects design buildings, chemists envisage molecules, and surgeons perform operations all use simulation technology. In ten years the degree to which simulations are embedded in every area of life will have increased exponentially. We need to develop a new form of media literacy: readership skills for the culture of simulation.

We come to written text with habits of readership based on centuries of 29 civilization. At the very least, we have learned to begin with the journalist's traditional questions: who, what, when, where, why, and how. Who wrote these words, what is their message, why were they written, and how are they situated in time and place, politically and socially? A central project for higher education during the next ten years should be creating programs in information-technology literacy, with the goal of teaching students to interrogate simulations in much the same spirit, challenging their built-in assumptions.

Despite the ever-increasing complexity of software, most computer envi- 30 ronments put users in worlds based on constrained choices. In other words, immersion in programmed worlds puts us in reassuring environments where the rules are clear. For example, when you play a video game, you often go through a series of frightening situations that you escape by mastering the rules—you experience life as a reassuring dichotomy° of scary and safe. Children grow up in a culture of video games, action films, fantasy epics, and computer programs that all rely on that familiar scenario of almost losing but then regaining total mastery: there is danger. It is mastered. A still-more-powerful monster appears. It is subdued. Scary. Safe.

Yet in the real world, we have never had a greater need to work our way 31 out of binary° assumptions. In the decade ahead, we need to rebuild the culture around information technology. In that new sociotechnical culture, assumptions about the nature of mastery would be less absolute. The new culture would make it easier, not more difficult, to consider life in shades of gray, to see moral dilemmas in terms other than a battle between Good and Evil. For never has our world been more complex, hybridized, and global. Never have we so needed to have many contradictory thoughts and feelings at the same time. Our tools must help us accomplish that, not fight against us.

Information technology is identity technology. Embedding it in a cul- 32 ture that supports democracy, freedom of expression, tolerance, diversity,

---

dichotomy: Division into two opposite groups.   **binary:** Marked by two parts.

and complexity of opinion is one of the next decade's greatest challenges. We cannot afford to fail.

When I first began studying the computer culture, a small breed of 33 highly trained technologists thought of themselves as "computer people." That is no longer the case. If we take the computer as a carrier of a way of knowing, a way of seeing the world and our place in it, we are all computer people now.

Questions to Start You Thinking

1. CONSIDERING MEANING: In your own words, explain the six major ways in which Turkle says that computers are changing the way people think. Why does she think it is important that we pay attention to these changes?

2. IDENTIFYING WRITING STRATEGIES: Why do you think Turkle presents the six areas of change in the order that she does? Does there seem to be a logic behind this order?

3. READING CRITICALLY: How clearly does Turkle establish causes and effects in this selection? Do you find her arguments convincing? Why or why not?

4. EXPANDING VOCABULARY: Reread paragraph 23, in which Turkle writes about the fact that most computer users have little understanding of how computers work. Define *transparency*, *epistemic*, and *opacity*, and explain what Turkle means at the end of this paragraph when she says that "transparency means epistemic opacity."

5. MAKING CONNECTIONS: How might Turkle respond to David Gelernter's arguments in "Computers Cannot Teach Children Basic Skills" (pp. 536–38)? How might Gelernter respond to Turkle? Explain whether the two are basically in agreement or disagreement.

Link to the Paired Essay

In paragraph 32, Turkle writes, "Information technology is identity technology. Embedding it in a culture that supports democracy, freedom of expression, tolerance, diversity, and complexity of opinion is one of the next decade's greatest challenges." In "MySpace or OurSpace?" (pp. 546–51), Alex Koppelman deals with a similar theme. Nevertheless, these essays differ in many ways. Compare and contrast the two writers' purposes, audiences, and writing styles, pointing to specific passages in each essay to support your opinion.

Journal Prompts

1. Choose one of the changes Turkle writes about here, and explore your own thoughts about it. Do you essentially agree with Turkle? Why or why not?

2. To what extent do you rely on computers in your daily life? How would your life be different without computers?

Suggestions for Writing

1. What are some possible negative effects of people's reliance on computers? Drawing on your own observations, write an essay in which you explore a cause-and-effect relationship between computer use and some particular human behavior or ways of thinking.

2. In paragraph 31, Turkle writes, "Never has our world been more complex, hybridized, and global. Never have we so needed to have many contradictory thoughts and feelings at the same time." What would you point to as some of the important challenges the world faces over, say, the next fifty years? Write an essay in which you identify several challenges and discuss the extent to which computer technology might contribute to solving them or to making them worse. Consult outside sources to support your position.

For more on supporting a position with sources, see Ch. 12. For more on finding and documenting sources, see the Quick Research Guide (the dark-red-edged pages).

Chapter 27
Education

Responding to an Image

At first glance, this cartoon may appear to be about nothing more than a school basketball game. However, a closer look reveals a deeper message. Why does the scene include two scoreboards? How does the composition of the image guide a viewer's eye to them? What does the cartoon suggest about the role of sports in today's schools, the relationship between sports and academics, or the standards for evaluating athletes and other students? Could the cartoon also be making a comment about standardized testing? Write a brief editorial that might accompany this cartoon.

Web Search

The educational system is facing many challenges, two of which are highlighted in this cartoon — the role of sports in education and standardized testing. Conduct your own investigation into these and other challenges by visiting Education Week on the Web <www.edweek.org/context/topics/> or the National Education Association home page . Which of the issues highlighted on these Web sites do you consider the most important and deserving of immediate attention? Why? Use the Internet to find at least one other reliable source of information on this topic. Be able to explain how you found your source and which criteria you used to evaluate its reliability and usefulness.

■ For Web reading activities linked to this chapter, visit <bedfordstmartins.com/bedguide> and do a key-word search:

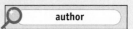
reading

Tamara Draut

What's a Diploma Worth, Anyway?

Tamara Draut *holds an MPA from Columbia University and a BSJ from Ohio University. As the director of the Economic Opportunity Program at Demos, a policy-research organization in New York City, Draut is currently studying the challenges faced by low- and middle-income households struggling to pay off debt and work their way into the middle class. She is the coauthor of several Demos reports, including "Millions to the Middle: Three Strategies to Grow the Middle Class," "Retiring in the Red: The Growth of Debt among Older Americans," and "Borrowing to Make Ends Meet: The Growth of Credit Card Debt in the '90s." She recently published the book* Strapped: Why America's 20- and 30-Somethings Can't Get Ahead *(2006). Draut's research has been cited in many newspapers and magazines, and she has appeared as a commentator on television news shows. "What's a Diploma Worth, Anyway?" first appeared on the Web site TomPaine.com on September 5, 2006, and it was later reposted on Alternet.org. In this piece, Draut offers a dismal answer to the question that she poses in the essay's title. In today's economy, she claims, a bachelor's degree doesn't mean what it used to.*

AS YOU READ: *Identify Draut's three main concerns regarding the economic situation of college graduates today.*

■ For more about Tamara Draut, visit <bedfordstmartins.com/bedguide> and do a key-word search:

author

Go to college. Work hard. Save money. For the baby-boom generation, this mantra was considered the tried-and-true recipe for getting ahead in America. If you're a parent of a twenty-something today, chances are you gave this advice to your own kids as they emerged from teen-hood into adulthood.

And indeed, a generation ago, most people found that if they followed these three rules, they'd earn a spot under the security blanket of America's middle class. But as one famous boomer said so eloquently, "the times, they are a-changin'."

The recently released *2006 Economic Report of the President* reported that ₃ earnings for workers with college degrees declined between 2000 and 2004 — yet another thread of evidence in a growing mound that for those just starting out, the golden rules are no longer so golden.

Getting a bachelor's degree is the required ticket for entry into the ₄ middle class today, but the security once implied in that status is gone. In addition to the exigencies° now felt by middle-class Americans of all ages — rising health-care costs, soaring home prices, and flat or falling incomes — today's new generation of college grads bear an added vulnerability of massive debt.

"Middle class" for a college-educated twenty- or thirty-something today ₅ means carrying five-figure student-loan debt. Two-thirds of college graduates borrow money to help pay for school, putting them $20,000 in the red on average. At current interest rates for federal student loans of 6.8 percent, that amounts to a $230 monthly payment for the next ten years. And for those trying to buy more security with an advanced degree — just try getting ahead without one — leaves today's aspiring professionals with a combined student loan debt of $46,900 on average.

So, what about hard work? Surely young workers who put their nose to ₆ the grindstone can earn enough to pay off those debts and earn their way to economic security. They are certainly trying. According to one study, Generation X — those now twenty-five to forty years old, work nearly three hours more per week than did young baby boomers in 1977. But those extra work hours aren't adding up to enough additional earnings to counter the effect of student-loan debts. Compared to 1980, the median earnings for a young worker aged twenty-five to thirty-four with a bachelor's degree or higher were only 6.6 percent higher in 2004. During the same time period, student-loan debt has more than doubled.

Even if student-loan debt hadn't risen, young workers would still find ₇ getting ahead to be harder today than it was for the previous generation. Remember that the bulk of today's under-thirty-four crowd entered the labor force during the 1990s — the culmination of America's post-industrial transition. By the beginning of the 1990s, the rules of the game had been totally rewritten. Wall Street investors pushed short-term profits over long-term stability. Global competition created new pressures for companies to cut costs. The new economy had found its sea legs. Gen Xers became the first group of young adults faced with building their lives in this volatile° new economy.

A generation ago, the labor market was like an escalator: productivity ₈ went up and so did wages. So young workers back then experienced a steady and swift progression in earnings. Today's labor market is like an automated airport walkway: the economy grows faster, but wages remain flat.

Now, the hardest nut for Americans of all ages: savings. Over the last ₉ twenty years, our nation's personal saving rate has plummeted from about 8

---

exigencies: Urgent demands.   **volatile:** Characterized by unexpected change.

percent through the 1980s and early 1990s to zero (actually negative) today. These figures are just for run-of-mill savings. How are young people doing with other types of saving, like retirement? Forty percent of people under age thirty-five had a retirement account in 2004, with $11,000 in holdings on average.

The living standards of America's college graduates, particularly those 10 under thirty-five, are declining. Of course, lesser-educated Americans experienced this painful reality much sooner, and much more dramatically. But now that all three main pillars of American success — education, hard work, and savings — show signs of serious weakness, we're running out of options. Young people are enrolling in college in record numbers, working longer hours, and doing their best to save for retirement. Yet, in all likelihood, this will be the first generation to not surpass their parents' standard of living.

America's declining economic future didn't just happen. Like global 11 warming, we've arrived at this point because for too long our leaders refused to acknowledge the problem, or made policy decisions that helped get us here. Recognizing this is now our only option.

Questions to Start You Thinking

1. CONSIDERING MEANING: According to Draut, why are today's college graduates less well-off than previous generations?

2. IDENTIFYING WRITING STRATEGIES: How does Draut's opening paragraph forecast the organization of her essay? What are the essay's three main parts? Where does each begin, and how does Draut signal the beginning of each section? Do you find her organization effective?

3. READING CRITICALLY: In paragraph 10, Draut writes that the "living standards of America's college graduates, particularly those under thirty-five, are declining." Has she presented enough evidence to convince you of this? Why or why not?

4. EXPANDING VOCABULARY: In paragraph 1, Draut refers to the "baby-boom generation." What is this generation, and how did it get its name?

5. MAKING CONNECTIONS: In "The Right to Fail" (pp. 567–70), first published in 1970, William Zinsser offers a different take on the relative value of a college education. How do his views differ from Draut's, and what might account for these differences? What do you suppose Draut would think of Zinsser's argument?

Journal Prompts

1. What are your reasons for being in college? How do your criteria for evaluating the value of your education resemble or differ from Draut's?

2. Where do you see yourself after you finish your college degree? Describe what you hope your life will be like five to ten years from now.

Suggestions for Writing

1. Write an essay of your own titled "What's a Diploma Worth, Anyway?" Drawing on your own experience, explain what a college diploma means to you.

2. Do some research about the baby-boom generation and Generation X. Drawing on outside sources as well as interviews with people you know, write an essay in which you compare and contrast the two generations in terms of their general values, goals, economic and social situations, and any other characteristics that interest you.

Susan Brady Konig
They've Got to Be Carefully Taught

■ For more about Susan Brady Konig, visit <bedfordstmartins.com/ bedguide> and do a keyword search:

 author

Susan Brady Konig *was born in 1951 in Paris, France, and grew up in New York City, where she now lives with her husband and four children. After graduating from Georgetown University, Konig worked at the* Washington Post *as an assistant to the Style section's fashion editor. She later became an editor for* Seventeen *magazine and a regular columnist for the* New York Post. *Konig currently writes about everything from pop culture to parenting to politics for* National Review Online *and* Catholic Digest, *and her writing also has appeared in such publications as* Ladies' Home Journal, Travel & Leisure, Us, *and* Parade. *Her first book,* Why Animals Sleep So Close to the Road (and Other Lies I Tell My Children), *was published in 2005. In "They've Got to Be Carefully Taught," an event at her daughter's preschool prompts Konig to question the emphasis that many schools place on teaching cultural diversity. The essay originally appeared in the* National Review *in 1997.*

AS YOU READ: *Note how the preschoolers respond to the cultural diversity activities that Konig describes.*

At my daughter's preschool it's time for all the children to learn that they 1 are different from one another. Even though these kids are at that remarkable age when they are thoroughly color blind, their teachers are spending a month emphasizing race, color, and background. The little tots are being taught in no uncertain terms that their hair is different, their skin is different, and their parents come from different places. It's Cultural Diversity Month.

I hadn't really given much thought to the ethnic and national back- 2 grounds of Sarah's classmates. I can guarantee that Sarah, being two and a half, gave the subject absolutely no thought. Her teachers, however, had apparently given it quite a lot of thought. They sent a letter asking each parent to contribute to the cultural-awareness effort by "providing any information and/or material regarding your family's cultural background. For example:

favorite recipe or song." All well and good, unless your culture isn't diverse enough.

The next day I take Sarah to school and her teacher, Miss Laura, anxious 3
to get this Cultural Diversity show on the road, begins the interrogation.

"Where are you and your husband from?" she cheerily demands.   4

"We're Americans," I reply — less, I must confess, out of patriotism than 5
from sheer lack of coffee. It was barely 9:00 A.M.

"Yes, of course, but where are you from?" I'm beginning to feel like a 6
nightclub patron being badgered by a no-talent stand-up comic.

"We're native New Yorkers."   7

"But where are your people from?"   8

"Well," I dive in with a sigh, "my family is originally Irish on both sides. 9
My husband's father was from Czechoslovakia and his mother is from the
Bronx, but her grandparents were from the Ukraine."

"Can you cook Irish?"   10

"I could bring in potatoes and beer for the whole class."   11

Miss Laura doesn't get it.   12

"Look," I say, "we're Americans. Our kids are Americans. We tell them 13
about American history and George Washington and apple pie and all that
stuff. If you want me to do something American, I can do that."

She is decidedly unexcited.   14

A few days later, she tells me that she was trying to explain to Sarah that 15
her dad is from Ireland.

"Wrong," I say, "but go on."   16

"He's not from Ireland?"   17

"No," I sigh. "He's from Queens. I'm from Ireland. I mean I'm Irish — 18
that is, my great-grandparents were. Don't get me wrong, I'm proud of my
heritage — but that's entirely beside the point. I told you we tell Sarah she's
American."

"Well, anyway," she smiles, "Sarah thinks her Daddy's from *Iceland!* Isn't 19
that cute?"

Later in the month, Miss Laura admits that her class is not quite getting 20
the whole skin-color thing. "I tried to show them how we all have different
skin," she chuckled. Apparently, little Henry is the only one who successfully grasped the concept. He now runs around the classroom announcing
to anyone who'll listen, "I'm white!" Miss Laura asked the children what
color her own skin was. (She is a light-skinned Hispanic, which would make
her skin color . . . what? Caramel? Mochaccino?) The kids opted for purple
or orange. "They looked at me like I was crazy!" Miss Laura said. I just smile.

The culmination of Cultural Diversity Month, the day when the parents 21
come into class and join their children in a glorious celebration of multicul-
tural disparity,° has arrived. As I arrive I see a large collage on the wall depicting the earth, with all the children's names placed next to the country they
are from. Next to my daughter's name it says "Ireland." I politely remind

disparity: Difference.

Miss Laura that Sarah is, in fact, from America and suggest that, by insisting otherwise, she is confusing my daughter. She reluctantly changes Sarah's affiliation to USA. It will be the only one of its kind on the wall.

The mom from Brazil brings in a bunch of great music, and the whole 22 class is doing the samba and running around in a conga line. It's very cute. Then I get up to teach the children an indigenous folk tune from the culture of Sarah's people, passed down through the generations from her grandparents to her parents and now to Sarah—a song called "Take Me Out to the Ballgame." First I explain to the kids that Sarah was born right here in New York—and that's in what country, Sarah? Sarah looks at me and says, "France." I look at Miss Laura, who just shrugs.

I stand there in my baseball cap and sing my song. The teacher tries to 23 rush me off. I say, "Don't you want them to learn it?" They took long enough learning to samba! I am granted permission to sing it one more time. The kids join in on the "root, root, root" and the "1, 2, 3 strikes you're out," but they can see their teacher isn't enthusiastic.

So now these sweet, innocent babies who thought they were all the 24 same are becoming culturally aware. Two little girls are touching each other's hair and saying, "Your hair is blonde, just like mine." Off to one side a little dark-haired girl stands alone, excluded. She looks confused as to what to do next. She knows she's not blonde. Sure, all children notice these things eventually, but, thanks to the concerted efforts of their teachers, these two- and three-year-olds are talking about things that separate rather than connect.

And Sarah only knows what she has been taught: Little Henry is white, 25 her daddy's from Iceland, and New York's in France.

Questions to Start You Thinking

1. CONSIDERING MEANING: What does Konig suggest are the consequences of introducing ideas of race, color, and national background to young children?

2. IDENTIFYING WRITING STRATEGIES: How does Konig go about drawing Miss Laura as a character? What impression does she create of her?

3. READING CRITICALLY: This essay originally appeared in the *National Review,* a politically conservative magazine of news and commentary. How do you think the majority of the magazine's readers would have responded to the essay?

4. EXPANDING VOCABULARY: Define *indigenous.* In paragraph 22, Konig writes about teaching the children "an indigenous folk tune," which turns out to be "Take Me Out to the Ballgame." In what sense is her use of the word *indigenous* ironic?

5. MAKING CONNECTIONS: Amy Tan ("Mother Tongue," pp. 445–50) and Richard Rodriguez ("Public and Private Language," pp. 571–76) also write about issues of ethnicity and education. How might Konig react to their observations? How might students be introduced to matters of cultural difference without contributing to a sense of separateness?

Journal Prompts

1. How was the subject of cultural diversity treated in your early education? How did you respond?

2. Konig writes in the first paragraph that young children are "color blind." Later in the essay, she says that "all children notice [differences in race and so forth] eventually" (paragraph 24). What are your earliest memories of recognizing racial and ethnic differences?

Suggestions for Writing

1. Write an essay recalling a classroom experience that you feel had more negative results than positive ones for you and your classmates. Like Konig, be sure to bring the classroom experience to life with specific details.

2. Konig makes a point of referring to her family as "Americans." Is there a difference in being "American" and in being "Hispanic American" or "Asian American" or "African American" or "Native American"? Write an essay in which you explore your own responses to such labels. Why might some ethnic Americans prefer simply to be called "Americans"? Conversely, why might some prefer the more specific term that indicates their heritage? What do you see as positive and negative consequences of such labeling?

William Zinsser
The Right to Fail

William Zinsser *was born in New York City in 1922. After receiving his BA from Princeton University in 1944, he worked as a feature writer for the* New York Herald Tribune *and later became the newspaper's drama and film critic. Zinsser has written numerous books and contributed articles to magazines including* Life, *the* New Yorker, *and the* Atlantic. *Although he has covered subjects ranging from American landmarks to jazz, he is probably best known for his classic guides to writing:* On Writing Well *(1976),* Writing with a Word Processor *(1983),* Inventing the Truth *(1987),* Writing to Learn *(1988), and* Writing about Your Life *(2004). Zinsser has taught humor and nonfiction writing at Yale University, and he currently teaches at the New School University and the Columbia University Graduate School of Journalism in New York City. In "The Right to Fail," an excerpt from* The Lunacy Boom *(1970), Zinsser makes the case that failure is an important aspect of human experience.*

AS YOU READ: *Identify the benefits of failure that Zinsser presents.*

■ For more about William Zinsser, visit <bedfordstmartins.com/bedguide> and do a keyword search:

author

I like "dropout" as an addition to the American language because it's brief and it's clear. What I don't like is that we use it almost entirely as a dirty word.

We only apply it to people under twenty-one. Yet an adult who spends 2
his days and nights watching mindless TV programs is more of a dropout
than an eighteen-year-old who quits college, with its frequently mindless
courses, to become, say, a VISTA volunteer. For the young, dropping out is
often a way of dropping in.

To hold this opinion, however, is little short of treason in America. A boy 3
or girl who leaves college is branded a failure — and the right to fail is one of
the few freedoms that this country does not grant its citizens. The American
dream is a dream of "getting ahead," painted in strokes of gold wherever we
look. Our advertisements and TV commercials are a hymn to material success, our magazine articles a toast to people who made it to the top. Smoke
the right cigarette or drive the right car — so the ads imply — and girls will be
swooning into your deodorized arms or caressing your expensive lapels. Happiness goes to the man who has the sweet smell of achievement. He is our
national idol, and everybody else is our national fink.°

I want to put in a word for the fink, especially the teen-age fink, because 4
if we give him time to get through his finkdom — if we release him from the
pressure of attaining certain goals by a certain age — he has a good chance of
becoming our national idol, a Jefferson° or a Thoreau,° a Buckminster
Fuller° or an Adlai Stevenson,° a man with a mind of his own. We need
mavericks° and dissenters and dreamers far more than we need junior vice
presidents, but we paralyze them by insisting that every step be a step up to
the next rung of the ladder. Yet in the fluid years of youth, the only way for
boys and girls to find their proper road is often to take a hundred side trips,
poking out in different directions, faltering, drawing back, and starting again.

"But what if we fail?" they ask, whispering the dreadful word across the 5
Generation Gap to their parents, who are back home at the Establishment,
nursing their "middle-class values" and cultivating their "goal-oriented society." The parents whisper back: "Don't!"

What they should say is "Don't be afraid to fail!" Failure isn't fatal. 6
Countless people have had a bout with it and come out stronger as a result.
Many have even come out famous. History is strewn with eminent dropouts,
"loners" who followed their own trail, not worrying about its odd twists and
turns because they had faith in their own sense of direction. To read their bi-
ographies is always exhilarating, not only because they beat the system, but
because their system was better than the one that they beat.

Luckily, such rebels still turn up often enough to prove that individual- 7
ism, though badly threatened, is not extinct. Much has been written, for in-

fink: Tattletale or other contemptible person.   Jefferson: Thomas Jefferson
(1743–1826), the third president of the United States and the main author of the Decla-
ration of Independence.   Thoreau: Henry David Thoreau (1817–1862), an American
writer and naturalist.   Buckminster Fuller: American inventor, architect, and engineer
(1895–1983) who dropped out of Harvard to work on solving global resource and environmental problems.   Adlai Stevenson: American politician (1900–1965) who was
greatly admired for championing liberal causes but badly lost two presidential elections.
mavericks: Nonconformists.

stance, about the fitful scholastic career of Thomas P. F. Hoving, New York's former Parks Commissioner and now director of the Metropolitan Museum of Art. Hoving was a dropout's dropout, entering and leaving schools as if they were motels, often at the request of the management. Still, he must have learned something during those unorthodox years, for he dropped in again at the top of his profession.

His case reminds me of another boyhood — that of Holden Caulfield in   8
J. D. Salinger's *The Catcher in the Rye*, the most popular literary hero of the postwar period. There is nothing accidental about the grip that this dropout continues to hold on the affections of an entire American generation. Nobody else, real or invented, has made such an engaging shambles of our "goal-oriented society," so gratified our secret belief that the "phonies" are in power and the good guys up the creek. Whether Holden has also reached the top of his chosen field today is one of those speculations that delight fanciers of good fiction. I speculate that he has. Holden Caulfield, incidentally, is now thirty-six.

I'm not urging everyone to go out and fail just for the sheer therapy   9
of it, or to quit college just to coddle° some vague discontent. Obviously it's better to succeed than to flop, and in general a long education is more helpful than a short one. (Thanks to my own education, for example, I can tell George Eliot from T. S. Eliot. I can handle the pluperfect tense in French, and I know that Caesar beat the Helvetii because he had enough frumentum.°) I only mean that failure isn't bad in itself, or success automatically good.

Fred Zinnemann, who has directed some of Hollywood's most honored   10
movies, was asked by a reporter, when *A Man for All Seasons* won every prize, about his previous film *Behold a Pale Horse*, which was a box-office disaster. "I don't feel any obligation to be successful," Zinnemann replied. "Success can be dangerous — you feel you know it all. I've learned a great deal from my failures." A similar point was made by Richard Brooks about his ambitious money loser, *Lord Jim*. Recalling the three years of his life that went into it, talking almost with elation about the troubles that befell his unit in Cambodia, Brooks told me that he learned more about his craft from this considerable failure than from his many earlier hits.

It's a point, of course, that applies throughout the arts. Writers, play-   11
wrights, painters, and composers work in the expectation of periodic defeat, but they wouldn't keep going back into the arena if they thought it was the end of the world. It isn't the end of the world. For an artist — and perhaps for anybody — it is the only way to grow.

Today's younger generation seems to know that this is true, seems will-   12
ing to take the risks in life that artists take in art. "Society," needless to say, still has the upper hand — it sets the goals and condemns as a failure everybody who won't play. But the dropouts and the hippies are not as afraid of failure as their parents and grandparents. This could mean, as their elders

---

coddle: Indulge; satisfy.   **frumentum:** Latin word for corn or grain.

might say, that they are just plumb lazy, secure in the comforts of an affluent state. It could also mean, however, that they just don't buy the old standards of success and are rapidly writing new ones.

Recently it was announced, for instance, that more than two hundred   13
thousand Americans have inquired about service in VISTA (the domestic
Peace Corps) and that, according to a Gallup survey, "more than three million American college students would serve VISTA in some capacity if given
the opportunity." This is hardly the road to riches or to an executive suite.
Yet I have met many of these young volunteers, and they are not pining
for traditional success. On the contrary, they appear more fulfilled than the
average vice president with a swimming pool.

Who is to say, then, if there is any right path to the top, or even to say   14
what the top consists of? Obviously the colleges don't have more than a partial answer — otherwise the young would not be so disaffected with an education that they consider vapid.° Obviously business does not have the
answer — otherwise the young would not be so scornful of its call to be an
organization man.

The fact is, nobody has the answer, and the dawning awareness of this   15
fact seems to me one of the best things happening in America today. Success
and failure are again becoming individual visions, as they were when the
country was younger, not rigid categories. Maybe we are learning again to
cherish this right of every person to succeed on his own terms and to fail as
often as necessary along the way.

Questions to Start You Thinking

1. CONSIDERING MEANING: What does Zinsser mean when he says that "dropping out is often a way of dropping in" (paragraph 2)? Why is this especially true for young adults?

2. IDENTIFYING WRITING STRATEGIES: Identify some of the concrete examples
   that Zinsser uses to illustrate his points. Are his examples extensive and varied enough to be convincing? Why or why not?

3. READING CRITICALLY: Zinsser is savvy enough to admit that his position is
   "little short of treason in America" (paragraph 3). Where else does he acknowledge that his advice might seem outlandish? How does he counter
   the opposition?

4. EXPANDING VOCABULARY: In paragraph 3, Zinsser writes, "Our advertisements and TV commercials are a hymn to material success." Define *hymn*.
   What does the word suggest about the American attitude toward material
   success? How does Zinsser feel about the American dream?

5. MAKING CONNECTIONS: If Carl T. Rowan ("Unforgettable Miss Bessie,"
   pp. 580–83) were to write a journal response to Zinsser's essay, what do you
   think he would write? How, suggests Rowan, is school success important in
   ways perhaps not considered by Zinsser?

vapid: Dull.

Journal Prompts

1. What is your definition of the "American dream" (paragraph 3)?

2. Who would you like to share Zinsser's essay with in order to open up that person's mind about failure? Why?

Suggestions for Writing

1. In paragraph 10, Zinsser offers the following quote from a movie director: "Success can be dangerous — you feel you know it all. I've learned a great deal from my failures." Write an essay in which you recall a personal experience that illustrates this statement.

2. Originally written in 1970, Zinsser's essay includes some examples that may not be familiar to you. Write an essay that supports and updates Zinsser's position by drawing on more current examples from history, literature, sports, current events, or popular culture. Imagine a specific audience for your essay (perhaps a sibling, a friend, or a high school class), and be sure that your examples will have an impact on those readers.

Richard Rodriguez
Public and Private Language

Richard Rodriguez, *the son of Spanish-speaking Mexican American parents, was born in 1944 and grew up in San Francisco, where he currently lives. He earned a BA at Stanford University and received graduate degrees in English from Columbia University and the University of California at Berkeley. A full-time writer and lecturer, Rodriguez is an editor at Pacific News Service and has served as a contributing editor for* Harper's Magazine, U.S. News & World Report, *and the Sunday "Opinion" section of the* Los Angeles Times. *His work has appeared in numerous publications including the* New York Times, *the* Wall Street Journal, *the* American Scholar, Time, Mother Jones, *and the* New Republic, *and he is a regular contributor to PBS's* News Hour with Jim Lehrer. *His books, which often draw on autobiography to explore race and ethnicity in American society, include* Hunger of Memory *(1982), from which the following selection is drawn,* Days of Obligation: An Argument with My Mexican Father *(1992), and* Brown: The Last Discovery of America *(2002). In "Public and Private Language," he recounts the origin of his complex views of bilingual education.*

AS YOU READ: *Discover the ways in which learning English changed Rodriguez's life and his relationship with his family.*

For more about Richard Rodriguez, visit <bedfordstmartins.com/ bedguide> and do a keyword search:

🔍 **author**

S upporters of bilingual education today imply that students like me miss ı
a great deal by not being taught in their family's language. What they seem not to recognize is that, as a socially disadvantaged child, I considered

Spanish to be a private language. What I needed to learn in school was that I had the right — and the obligation — to speak the public language of *los gringos.*° The odd truth is that my first-grade classmates could have become bilingual, in the conventional sense of that word, more easily than I. Had they been taught (as upper-middle-class children are often taught early) a second language like Spanish or French, they could have regarded it simply as that: another public language. In my case such bilingualism could not have been so quickly achieved. What I did not believe was that I could speak a single public language.

Without question, it would have pleased me to hear my teachers address me in Spanish when I entered the classroom. I would have felt much less afraid. I would have trusted them and responded with ease. But I would have delayed — for how long postponed? — having to learn the language of public society. I would have evaded — and for how long could I have afforded to delay? — learning the great lesson of school, that I had a public identity.

Fortunately, my teachers were unsentimental about their responsibility. What they understood was that I needed to speak a public language. So their voices would search me out, asking me questions. Each time I'd hear them, I'd look up in surprise to see a nun's face frowning at me. I'd mumble, not really meaning to answer. The nun would persist, "Richard, stand up. Don't look at the floor. Speak up. Speak to the entire class, not just to me!" but I couldn't believe that the English language was mine to use. (In part, I did not want to believe it.) I continued to mumble. I resisted the teacher's demands. (Did I somehow suspect that once I learned public language my pleasing family life would be changed?) Silent, waiting for the bell to sound, I remained dazed, diffident,° afraid.

Because I wrongly imagined that English was intrinsically° a public language and Spanish an intrinsically private one, I easily noticed the difference between classroom language and the language of home. At school, words were directed to a general audience of listeners. ("Boys and girls. . . .") Words were meaningfully ordered. And the point was not self-expression alone but to make oneself understood by many others. The teacher quizzed: "Boys and girls, why do we use that word in this sentence? Could we think of a better word to use there? Would the sentence change its meaning if the words were differently arranged? And wasn't there a better way of saying much the same thing?" (I couldn't say. I wouldn't try to say.)

Three months. Five. Half a year passed. Unsmiling, ever watchful, my teachers noted my silence. They began to connect my behavior with the difficult progress my older sister and brother were making. Until one Saturday morning three nuns arrived at the house to talk to our parents. Stiffly, they sat on the blue living room sofa. From the doorway of another room, spying

---

los gringos: Spanish for "foreigner," often used as a derogatory term for English-speaking Americans.   **diffident:** Shy.   **intrinsically:** Essentially; inherently.

the visitors, I noted the incongruity° — the clash of two worlds, the faces and voices of school intruding upon the familiar setting of home. I overheard one voice gently wondering, "Do your children speak only Spanish at home, Mrs. Rodriguez?" While another voice added, "That Richard especially seems so timid and shy."

That Rich-heard!   6

With great tact the visitors continued, "Is it possible for you and your 7 husband to encourage your children to practice their English when they are home?" Of course, my parents complied. What would they not do for their children's well-being? And how could they have questioned the Church's authority which those women represented? In an instant, they agreed to give up the language (the sounds) that had revealed and accentuated our family's closeness. The moment after the visitors left, the change was observed. *"Ahora,°* speak to us *en inglés,"°* my father and mother united to tell us.

At first, it seemed a kind of game. After dinner each night, the family 8 gathered to practice "our" English. (It was still then *inglés,* a language foreign to us, so we felt drawn as strangers to it.) Laughing, we would try to define words we could not pronounce. We played with strange English sounds, often overanglicizing our pronunciations. And we filled the smiling gaps of our sentences with familiar Spanish sounds. But that was cheating, somebody shouted. Everyone laughed. In school, meanwhile, like my brother and sister, I was required to attend a daily tutoring session. I needed a full year of special attention. I also needed my teachers to keep my attention from straying in class by calling out, *Rich-heard* — their English voices slowly prying loose my ties to my other name, its three notes, *Ri-car-do.* Most of all I needed to hear my mother and father speak to me in a moment of seriousness in broken — suddenly heartbreaking — English. The scene was inevitable: one Saturday morning I entered the kitchen where my parents were talking in Spanish. I did not realize that they were talking in Spanish however until, at the moment they saw me, I heard their voices change to speak English. Those *gringo* sounds they uttered startled me. Pushed me away. In that moment of trivial misunderstanding and profound insight, I felt my throat twisted by unsounded grief. I turned quickly and left the room. But I had no place to escape to with Spanish. (The spell was broken.) My brother and sisters were speaking English in another part of the house.

Again and again in the days following, increasingly angry, I was obliged 9 to hear my mother and father: "Speak to us *en inglés."* (*Speak.*) Only then did I determine to learn classroom English. Weeks after, it happened: one day in school I had my hand raised to volunteer an answer. I spoke out in a loud voice. And I did not think it remarkable when the entire class understood. That day, I moved very far from the disadvantaged child I had been only days earlier. The belief, that calming assurance that I belonged in public, had at last taken hold.

---

incongruity: Lack of harmony or appropriateness.   ***Ahora:*** Spanish for "now."
en inglés: Spanish for "in English."

Shortly after, I stopped hearing the high and loud sounds of *los gringos*. 10
A more and more confident speaker of English, I didn't trouble to listen to
how strangers sounded, speaking to me. And there simply were too many
English-speaking people in my day for me to hear American accents anymore. Conversations quickened. Listening to persons whose voices sounded
eccentrically pitched, I usually noted their sounds for an initial few seconds
before I concentrated on *what* they were saying. Conversations became
content-full. Transparent. Hearing someone's *tone* of voice — angry or questioning or sarcastic or happy or sad — I didn't distinguish it from the words
it expressed. Sound and word were thus tightly wedded. At the end of a day,
I was often bemused, always relieved, to realize how "silent," though
crowded with words, my day in public had been. (This public silence measured and quickened the change in my life.)

At last, seven years old, I came to believe what had been technically true 11
since my birth: I was an American citizen.

But the special feeling of closeness at home was diminished by then. 12
Gone was the desperate, urgent, intense feeling of being at home; rare was
the experience of feeling myself individualized by family intimates. We remained a loving family, but one greatly changed. No longer so close; no
longer bound tight by the pleasing and troubling knowledge of our public
separateness. Neither my older brother nor sister rushed home after school
anymore. Nor did I. When I arrived home there would often be neighborhood kids in the house. Or the house would be empty of sounds.

Following the dramatic Americanization of their children, even my par- 13
ents grew more publicly confident. Especially my mother. She learned the
names of all the people on our block. And she decided we needed to have a
telephone installed in the house. My father continued to use the word *gringo*.
But it was no longer charged with the old bitterness or distrust. (Stripped of
any emotional content, the word simply became a name for those Americans not of Hispanic descent.) Hearing him, sometimes, I wasn't sure if he
was pronouncing the Spanish word *gringo* or saying gringo in English.

Matching the silence I started hearing in public was a new quiet at 14
home. The family's quiet was partly due to the fact that, as we children
learned more and more English, we shared fewer and fewer words with our
parents. Sentences needed to be spoken slowly when a child addressed his
mother or father. (Often the parent wouldn't understand.) The child would
need to repeat himself. (Still the parent misunderstood.) The young voice,
frustrated, would end up saying, "Never mind" — the subject was closed.
Dinners would be noisy with the clinking of knives and forks against dishes.
My mother would smile softly between her remarks; my father at the other
end of the table would chew and chew at his food, while he stared over the
heads of his children.

My *mother!* My *father!* After English became my primary language, I no 15
longer knew what words to use in addressing my parents. The old Spanish
words (those tender accents of sound) I had used earlier — *mamá* and *papá* —
I couldn't use anymore. They would have been all-too-painful reminders of

how much had changed in my life. On the other hand, the words I heard neighborhood kids call *their* parents seemed equally unsatisfactory. *Mother* and *Father; Ma, Papa, Pa, Dad, Pop* (how I hated the all-American sound of that last word especially) — all these terms I felt were unsuitable, not really terms of address for *my* parents. As a result, I never used them at home. Whenever I'd speak to my parents, I would try to get their attention with eye contact alone. In public conversations, I'd refer to "my parents" or "my mother and father."

My mother and father, for their part, responded differently, as their chil- 16
dren spoke to them less and less. My mother grew restless, seemed troubled and anxious at the scarcity of words exchanged in the house. It was she who would question me about my day when I came home from school. She smiled at the small talk. She pried at the edges of my sentences to get me to say something more. (What?) She'd join conversations she overheard, but her intrusions often stopped her children's talking. By contrast, my father seemed reconciled to the new quiet. Though his English improved some-what, he retired into silence. At dinner he spoke very little. One night his children and even his wife helplessly giggled at his garbled English pronun-ciation of the Catholic Grace before Meals. Thereafter he made his wife recite the prayer at the start of each meal, even on formal occasions, when there were guests in the house. Hers became the public voice of the family. On official business, it was she, not my father, one would usually hear on the phone or in stores, talking to strangers. His children grew so accustomed to his silence that, years later, they would speak routinely of his shyness. (My mother would often try to explain: both his parents died when he was eight. He was raised by an uncle who treated him like little more than a menial servant. He was never encouraged to speak. He grew up alone. A man of few words.) But my father was not shy, I realized, when I'd watch him speaking Spanish with relatives. Using Spanish, he was quickly effusive.° Es-pecially when talking with other men, his voice would spark, flicker, flare alive with sounds. In Spanish, he expressed ideas and feelings he rarely re-vealed in English. With firm Spanish sounds, he conveyed confidence and authority English would never allow him.

The silence at home, however, was finally more than a literal silence. 17
Fewer words passed between parent and child, but more profound was the silence that resulted from my inattention to sounds. At about the time I no longer bothered to listen with care to the sounds of English in public, I grew careless about listening to the sounds family members made when they spoke. Most of the time I heard someone speaking at home and didn't dis-tinguish his sounds from the words people uttered in public. I didn't even pay much attention to my parents' accented and ungrammatical speech. At least not at home. Only when I was with them in public would I grow alert to their accents. Though, even then, their sounds caused me less and less concern. For I was increasingly confident of my own public identity.

effusive: Talkative; unreserved.

Today I hear bilingual educators say that children lose a degree of "indi- 18
viduality" by becoming assimilated into public society. (Bilingual schooling
was popularized in the seventies, that decade when middle-class ethnics
began to resist the process of assimilation — the American melting pot.) But
the bilingualists simplistically scorn the value and necessity of assimilation.
They do not seem to realize that there are *two* ways a person is individualized. So they do not realize that while one suffers a diminished sense of *private* individuality by becoming assimilated into public society, such assimilation makes possible the achievement of *public* individuality.

Questions to Start You Thinking

1. CONSIDERING MEANING: What created the new "silence" in the Rodriguez
   household? Explain why.
2. IDENTIFYING WRITING STRATEGIES: How does Rodriguez use comparison and
   contrast to convey his experience learning English?
3. READING CRITICALLY: How does Rodriguez use dialogue to make the experience he recalls more vivid for his readers? Is this strategy effective in helping
   him achieve his purpose? Why or why not?
4. EXPANDING VOCABULARY: Rodriguez uses the terms *private* and *public*. What
   do these words mean when used as adjectives to describe "language" and
   "identity"?
5. MAKING CONNECTIONS: Both Rodriguez and Amy Tan ("Mother Tongue,"
   pp. 445–50) are from homes in which English was spoken as a second language. Compare and contrast how each writer's mastery of English affected
   his or her mother.

Journal Prompts

1. Recall a time when your public identity was at odds with your private self.
2. Has an accomplishment that you are proud of ever had a negative effect on
   another aspect of your life or on other people around you?

Suggestions for Writing

1. If you speak a second language, write an essay recalling your experience
   learning it. What were some of your struggles? Can you relate to Rodriguez's
   experience? How do you use that language today? If you do not know a second language, write an essay in which you analyze the possible benefits of
   learning one. What language would you like to learn? Why?
2. According to Rodriguez, "Supporters of bilingual education today imply
   that students like me miss a great deal by not being taught in their family's
   language" (paragraph 1). Rodriguez counters this assumption by showing
   how his immersion in English allowed him to develop a public identity that
   ultimately led to his success. At the same time, however, his English-only
   immersion hurt his family life. Write an essay in which you take a stand on
   the complex topic of bilingual education, using further reading and research
   to support your position about how it does or does not benefit students.

Annie Dillard
From *An American Childhood*

Annie Dillard, *born in 1945 in Pittsburgh, Pennsylvania, is an acclaimed poet and essayist known for her nature and spiritual writing. After graduating from Hollins College in Virginia, Dillard settled in the Blue Ridge Mountains to write her first volume of poetry,* Tickets for a Prayer Wheel *(1974). Her second book, a collection of essays titled* Pilgrim at Tinker Creek *(1974), won a Pulitzer Prize. Since then, Dillard has published numerous books including* Holy the Firm *(1978), a prose poem;* Living by Fiction *(1982), a book of literary criticism;* Teaching a Stone to Talk *(1982), a collection of essays;* An American Childhood *(1987), a memoir; and* The Writing Life *(1989), a volume of short meditations on the writing process. Her most recent books include* For the Time Being *(1999) and* The Maytrees: A Novel *(2007). Dillard is currently professor emeritus at Wesleyan University. In this selection from* An American Childhood, *Dillard vividly describes how viewing an amoeba through a microscope leads to a sudden epiphany that would guide her throughout her education.*

■ For more about Annie Dillard, visit \<bedfordstmartins.com/bedguide\> and do a keyword search:

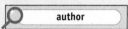

AS YOU READ: *Think about what Dillard was like as a child. What words would you use to describe her?*

After I read *The Field Book of Ponds and Streams* several times, I longed for a microscope. Everybody needed a microscope. Detectives used microscopes, both for the FBI and at Scotland Yard. Although usually I had to save my tiny allowance for things I wanted, that year for Christmas my parents gave me a microscope kit.

In a dark basement corner, on a white enamel table, I set up the microscope kit. I supplied a chair, a lamp, a batch of jars, a candle, and a pile of library books. The microscope kit supplied a blunt black three-speed microscope, a booklet, a scalpel, a dropper, an ingenious device for cutting thin segments of fragile tissue, a pile of clean slides and cover slips, and a dandy array of corked test tubes.

One of the test tubes contained "hay infusion." Hay infusion was a wee brown chip of grass blade. You added water to it, and after a week it became a jungle in a drop, full of one-celled animals. This did not work for me. All I saw in the microscope after a week was a wet chip of dried grass, much enlarged.

Another test tube contained "diatomaceous earth." This was, I believed, an actual pinch of the white cliffs of Dover.° On my palm it was an airy, friable chalk. The booklet said it was composed of the siliceous bodies of diatoms — one-celled creatures that lived in, as it were, small glass jewelry boxes with fitted lids. Diatoms, I read, come in a variety of transparent geometrical shapes. Broken and dead and dug out of geological deposits, they made chalk, and a fine abrasive used in silver polish and toothpaste. What I

white cliffs of Dover: A famous British geological landmark.

577

saw in the microscope must have been the fine abrasive — grit enlarged. It was years before I saw a recognizable, whole diatom. The kit's diatomaceous earth was a bust.

All that winter I played with the microscope. I prepared slides from things 5 at hand, as the books suggested. I looked at the transparent membrane inside an onion's skin and saw the cell. I looked at a section of cork and saw the cells, and at scrapings from the inside of my cheek, ditto. I looked at my blood and saw not much; I looked at my urine and saw a long iridescent crystal, for the drop had dried.

All this was very well, but I wanted to see the wildlife I had read about. I 6 wanted especially to see the famous amoeba, who had eluded me. He was supposed to live in the hay infusion, but I hadn't found him there. He lived outside in warm ponds and streams, too, but I lived in Pittsburgh, and it had been a cold winter.

Finally late that spring I saw an amoeba. The week before, I had gath- 7 ered puddle water from Frick Park; it had been festering in a jar in the basement. This June night after dinner I figured I had waited long enough. In the basement at my microscope table I spread a scummy drop of Frick Park puddle water on a slide, peeked in, and lo, there was the famous amoeba. He was as blobby and grainy as his picture; I would have known him anywhere.

Before I had watched him at all, I ran upstairs. My parents were still at 8 the table, drinking coffee. They, too, could see the famous amoeba. I told them, bursting, that he was all set up, that they should hurry before his water dried. It was the chance of a lifetime.

Father had stretched out his long legs and was tilting back in his chair. 9 Mother sat with her knees crossed, in blue slacks, smoking a Chesterfield. The dessert dishes were still on the table. My sisters were nowhere in evidence. It was a warm evening; the big dining-room windows gave onto blooming rhododendrons.

Mother regarded me warmly. She gave me to understand that she was 10 glad I had found what I had been looking for, but that she and Father were happy to sit with their coffee, and would not be coming down.

She did not say, but I understood at once, that they had their pursuits 11 (coffee?) and I had mine. She did not say, but I began to understand then, that you do what you do out of your private passion for the thing itself.

I had essentially been handed my own life. In subsequent years my par- 12 ents would praise my drawings and poems, and supply me with books, art supplies, and sports equipment, and listen to my troubles and enthusiasms, and supervise my hours, and discuss and inform, but they would not get involved with my detective work, nor hear about my reading, nor inquire about my homework or term papers or exams, nor visit the salamanders I caught, nor listen to me play the piano, nor attend my field hockey games, nor fuss over my insect collection with me, or my poetry collection or stamp collection or rock collection. My days and nights were my own to plan and fill.

When I left the dining room that evening and started down the dark 13
basement stairs, I had a life. I sat down to my wonderful amoeba, and there
he was, rolling his grains more slowly now, extending an arc of his edge for
a foot and drawing himself along by that foot, and absorbing it again and
rolling on. I gave him some more pond water.

I had hit pay dirt. For all I knew, there were paramecia, too, in that 14
pond water, or daphniae, or stentors, or any of the many other creatures I
had read about and never seen: volvox, the spherical algal colony; euglena
with its one red eye; the elusive, glassy diatom; hydra, rotifers, water bears,
worms. Anything was possible. The sky was the limit.

Questions to Start You Thinking

1. CONSIDERING MEANING: Why was Dillard's discovery of the amoeba so important to her childhood development? How did her parents respond to
   her excitement? What did this experience help her to learn?

2. IDENTIFYING WRITING STRATEGIES: Where in the essay does Dillard use specific descriptive details to help readers see what she sees? How effective do
   you find her use of such details?

3. READING CRITICALLY: How does Dillard go about communicating to readers
   her excitement over discovering the amoeba? What sort of picture does she
   paint of herself as a girl, and how do you think she expects readers to respond?

4. EXPANDING VOCABULARY: Define *friable* and *siliceous* (paragraph 4). Why do
   you suppose Dillard chose to use this sophisticated vocabulary in this paragraph? Also consider the scientific vocabulary she uses in her final paragraph. Do you think she expects readers to be familiar with these terms?

5. MAKING CONNECTIONS: In "Public and Private Language" (pp. 571–76),
   Richard Rodriguez also writes about discovering a life independent of his parents. What do he and Dillard have in common, and how are they different?

Link to the Paired Essay

In "Unforgettable Miss Bessie" (pp. 580–83), Carl T. Rowan also writes of
struggling to achieve educational goals. Despite their many differences, what
attitudes do Dillard and Rowan share?

Journal Prompts

1. What activities did you enjoy pursuing by yourself as a child? Recall a specific
   time when you pursued one of these activities on your own and reflect on
   what you learned from the experience.

2. Think about something, like Dillard's microscope, that you wanted very
   badly when you were young. If you finally received it as a gift or were able
   to buy it for yourself, what was your response? Did it meet your expectations, or did it disappoint you in any way? How long did it continue to occupy you? If you didn't receive it, write about how the disappointment affected you.

Suggestions for Writing

1. Recall a time when you struggled to accomplish something important to you, as Dillard struggled to see the amoeba. Write an essay in which you relate your struggle, your triumph (or failure), and the effects of the experience. Be sure that readers understand why the goal meant so much to you.

2. In paragraph 12, Dillard writes, "I had essentially been handed my own life. . . . My days and nights were my own to plan and fill." Through her story of discovering the amoeba on her own, Dillard makes the implicit point that children should be allowed the freedom to explore and learn and grow without their parents watching over their every move. Write an essay that supports Dillard's position by drawing on examples from your own experience and from the essays in this book.

Carl T. Rowan
Unforgettable Miss Bessie

■ For more about Carl T. Rowan, visit <bedfordstmartins.com/ bedguide> and do a keyword search:

author

Journalist and political figure **Carl T. Rowan** *(1925–2000) was born in Ravenscroft, Tennessee. After graduating from Oberlin College, he received a master's degree in journalism from the University of Minnesota. Rowan then wrote for the Minneapolis Tribune before becoming deputy secretary of state under President John F. Kennedy. He later served as a delegate to the United Nations and as U.S. ambasdor to Finland. Rowan eventually returned to journalism, writing a syndicated column for the* Chicago Sun-Times *until 1998. In 1987, he founded Project Excellence, a scholarship program for African American high school students. His several books include* Just Between Us Blacks *(1974),* Breaking Barriers: A Memoir *(1991), and* The Coming Race War in America: A Wake-Up Call *(1996). In the following essay, published in* Reader's Digest *in 1985, Rowan tells the story of a teacher who had a lasting impact on his life and on his view of himself.*

AS YOU READ: *Note how Miss Bessie affected the author as a young man.*

She was only about five feet tall and probably never weighed more than 1 110 pounds, but Miss Bessie was a towering presence in the classroom. She was the only woman tough enough to make me read *Beowulf*° and think for a few foolish days that I liked it. From 1938 to 1942, when I attended Bernard High School in McMinnville, Tennessee, she taught me English, history, civics — and a lot more than I realized.

I shall never forget the day she scolded me into reading *Beowulf*.   2

"But Miss Bessie," I complained, "I ain't much interested in it."   3

Her large brown eyes became daggerish slits. "Boy," she said, "how dare 4 you say 'ain't' to me! I've taught you better than that."

"Miss Bessie," I pleaded, "I'm trying to make first-string end on the foot- 5 ball team, and if I go around saying 'it isn't' and 'they aren't,' the guys are gonna laugh me off the squad."

Beowulf: A long story in poetic form, written in the eighth century in Old English.

"Boy," she responded, "you'll play football because you have guts. But   6
do you know what *really* takes guts? Refusing to lower your standards to
those of the crowd. It takes guts to say you've got to live and be somebody
fifty years after all the football games are over."

I started saying "it isn't" and "they aren't," and I still made first-string   7
end — and class valedictorian — without losing my buddies' respect.

During her remarkable 44-year-career, Mrs. Bessie Taylor Gwynn   8
taught hundreds of economically deprived black youngsters — including
my mother, my brother, my sisters, and me. I remember her now with
gratitude and affection — especially in this era when Americans are so
wrought-up° about a "rising tide of mediocrity"° in public education and
the problems of finding competent, caring teachers. Miss Bessie was an
example of an informed, dedicated teacher, a blessing to children, and an
asset to the nation.

Born in 1895, in poverty, she grew up in Athens, Alabama, where there   9
was no public school for blacks. She attended Trinity School, a private institution for blacks run by the American Missionary Association, and in 1911
graduated from the Normal School (a "super" high school) at Fisk University in Nashville. Mrs. Gwynn, the essence of pride and privacy, never talked
about her years in Athens; only in the months before her death did she reveal that she had never attended Fisk University itself because she could not
afford the four-year course.

At Normal School she learned a lot about Shakespeare, but most of all   10
about the profound importance of education — especially, for a people
trying to move up from slavery. "What you put in your head, boy," she
once said, "can never be pulled out by the Ku Klux Klan,° the Congress,
or anybody."

Miss Bessie's bearing of dignity told anyone who met her that she was   11
"educated" in the best sense of the word. There was never a discipline problem in her classes. We didn't dare mess with a woman who knew about the
Battle of Hastings, the Magna Carta, and the Bill of Rights — and who could
also play the piano.

This frail-looking woman could make sense of Shakespeare, Milton,   12
Voltaire, and bring to life Booker T. Washington and W. E. B. DuBois. Believing that it was important to know who the officials were that spent taxpay-
ers' money and made public policy, she made us memorize the names of
everyone on the Supreme Court and in the President's Cabinet. It could be
embarrassing to be unprepared when Miss Bessie said, "Get up and tell the
class who Frances Perkins° is and what you think about her."

---

wrought-up: Worked up; upset.   **"rising tide of mediocrity":** A reference, from a 1983
report from the National Commission on Excellence in Education, to sinking standards
said to be threatening the U.S. educational system.   **Ku Klux Klan:** The collective name
of several organizations that have persecuted African Americans and other groups since
the 1860s.   **Frances Perkins:** Secretary of labor under U.S. President Franklin D. Roosevelt and the first woman to hold a cabinet post.

Miss Bessie knew that my family, like so many others during the Depres- 13
sion,° couldn't afford to subscribe to a newspaper. She knew we didn't even
own a radio. Still, she prodded me to "look out for your future and find
some way to keep up with what's going on in the world." So I became a delivery boy for the Chattanooga *Times*. I rarely made a dollar a week, but I got
to read a newspaper every day.

Miss Bessie noticed things that had nothing to do with schoolwork, but 14
were vital to a youngster's development. Once a few classmates made fun of
my frayed, hand-me-down overcoat, calling me "Strings." As I was leaving
school, Miss Bessie patted me on the back of that old overcoat and said,
"Carl, never fret about what you *don't* have. Just make the most of what you
do have — a brain."

Among the things that I did not have was electricity in the little frame 15
house that my father had built for $400 with his World War I bonus. But be-
cause of her inspiration, I spent many hours squinting beside a kerosene
lamp reading Shakespeare and Thoreau, Samuel Pepys and William Cullen
Bryant.

No one in my family had ever graduated from high school, so there was 16
no tradition of commitment to learning for me to lean on. Like millions of
youngsters in today's ghettos and barrios, I needed the push and stimulation
of a teacher who truly cared. Miss Bessie gave plenty of both, as she im-
mersed me in a wonderful world of similes, metaphors, and even ono-
matopoeia. She led me to believe that I could write sonnets as well as
Shakespeare, or iambic-pentameter verse to put Alexander Pope to shame.

In those days the McMinnville school system was rigidly "Jim Crow,"° 17
and poor black children had to struggle to put anything in their heads. Our
high school was only slightly larger than the once-typical little red school-
house, and its library was outrageously inadequate — so small, I like to say,
that if two students were in it and one wanted to turn a page, the other one
had to step outside.

Negroes, as we were called then, were not allowed in the town library, 18
except to mop floors or dust tables. But through one of those secret Old
South arrangements between whites of conscience and blacks of stature,
Miss Bessie kept getting books smuggled out of the white library. That is
how she introduced me to the Brontës, Byron, Coleridge, Keats, and Ten-
nyson. "If you don't read, you can't write, and if you can't write, you might
as well stop dreaming," Miss Bessie once told me.

So I read whatever Miss Bessie told me to, and tried to remember the 19
things she insisted that I store away. Forty-five years later, I can still recite her
"truths to live by," such as Henry Wadsworth Longfellow's lines from "The
Ladder of St. Augustine":

Depression: Severe economic downturn lasting from the stock market crash of 1929
until the start of World War II.   **"Jim Crow":** Segregation of African Americans under
discriminatory laws and customs.

The heights by great men reached and kept
Were not attained by sudden flight.
But they, while their companions slept,
Were toiling upward in the night.

Years later, her inspiration, prodding, anger, cajoling, and almost os- 20
motic° infusion of learning finally led to that lovely day when Miss Bessie
dropped me a note saying, "I'm so proud to read your column in the
Nashville *Tennessean.*"

Miss Bessie was a spry 80 when I went back to McMinnville and visited 21
her in a senior citizens' apartment building. Pointing out proudly that her
building was racially integrated, she reached for two glasses and a pint of
bourbon. I was momentarily shocked, because it would have been scan-
dalous in the 1930s and '40s for word to get out that a teacher drank, and
nobody had ever raised a rumor that Miss Bessie did.

I felt a new sense of equality as she lifted her glass to mine. Then she re- 22
vealed a softness and compassion that I had never known as a student.

"I've never forgotten that examination day," she said, "when Buster Mar- 23
tin held up seven fingers, obviously asking you for help with question number seven, 'Name a common carrier.'° I can still picture you looking at your
exam paper and humming a few bars of 'Chattanooga Choo Choo.' I was so
tickled, I couldn't punish either of you."

Miss Bessie was telling me, with bourbon-laced grace, that I never 24
fooled her for a moment.

When Miss Bessie died in 1980, at age 85, hundreds of her former stu- 25
dents mourned. They knew the measure of a great teacher: love and motivation. Her wisdom and influence had rippled out across generations.

Some of her students who might normally have been doomed to 26
poverty went on to become doctors, dentists, and college professors. Many,
guided by Miss Bessie's example, became public-school teachers.

"The memory of Miss Bessie and how she conducted her classroom did 27
more for me than anything I learned in college," recalls Gladys Wood of
Knoxville, Tennessee, a highly respected English teacher who spent 43 years
in the state's school system. "So many times, when I faced a difficult classroom problem, I asked myself, *How would Miss Bessie deal with this?* And I'd
remember that she would handle it with laughter and love."

No child can get all the necessary support at home, and millions of 28
poor children get *no* support at all. This is what makes a wise, educated,
warm-hearted teacher like Miss Bessie so vital to the minds, hearts, and
souls of this country's children.

---

osmotic: Like the transfer of substances through a cell membrane (osmosis).   **common
carrier:** A public transportation system, such as a railway or airline.

Questions to Start You Thinking

1. CONSIDERING MEANING: Why did Rowan look up to Miss Bessie? How did she influence him?

2. IDENTIFYING WRITING STRATEGIES: How does Rowan use both recall and cause and effect to illustrate the power of a caring teacher? Which details and bits of dialogue seem especially engaging? How does he organize them in a logical sequence?

3. READING CRITICALLY: What is Rowan's purpose in this essay? How does his selection of details and dialogue work toward achieving this purpose?

4. EXPANDING VOCABULARY: Define *dignity.* How does Rowan apply this word to Miss Bessie, and how could it also apply to him?

5. MAKING CONNECTIONS: In "Public and Private Language" (pp. 571–76), Richard Rodriguez refers to the "private language" of his Spanish-speaking home as opposed to the "public language" of school. In what way might the type of speech criticized by Miss Bessie in paragraph 4 be considered a form of "private language"? What larger point is she making about such language, and how might Rodriguez respond?

Link to the Paired Essay

Taken together, Rowan's essay and Annie Dillard's excerpt from *An American Childhood* (pp. 577–79) suggest that a person's motivation to become educated can come from both internal and external sources. To what extent, and in what ways, were Rowan and Dillard internally and externally motivated?

Journal Prompts

1. Write about an accomplishment that you are proud of.

2. Rowan describes delivering the newspaper so that he would be able to read it. Write about a time when you made an extra effort to better yourself.

Suggestions for Writing

1. Write about a time when a teacher, a work supervisor, or some other influential person took a special interest in helping you to succeed. Recall how this person influenced you and how he or she changed your life. Include plenty of detail to bring that person to life.

2. Rowan writes that Miss Bessie contributed to the success of "students who might normally have been doomed to poverty." Write an essay in which you argue that education is the key to success. Use the readings in this text and your own experiences and observations to support your point.

A Writer's Research Manual

A Writer's Research Manual Contents

Introduction:
The Nature of Research

Does cell phone use cause brain tumors?

What steps can law enforcement take to help prevent domestic violence?

How do strict death penalty laws affect crime rates?

Is it true that about a million children in the United States are homeless?

Why is baseball exempt from antitrust laws?

You may have asked yourself questions like these. Perhaps you discussed them with friends, asked a teacher about the subject, or read an article about the issue. In doing so, you were conducting informal research to satisfy your curiosity.

In your day-to-day life, you also conduct practical research to help you solve problems and make decisions. You may want to buy a digital camera, consider an innovative medical procedure, or plan a vacation. To become better informed, you may talk with friends, search the Internet, request product information from sales personnel, compare prices, read articles in relevant publications, and check advertising. You pull together and weigh as much information as you can, preparing yourself to make a well-informed decision.

When one of your college professors assigns a research paper due in a month or two, you won't be expected to discover the secrets of the human brain or to solve the problem of world hunger. On the other hand, you will find that research isn't merely pasting together information and opinions from other people. Instead, the excitement lies in using research to draw conclusions and arrive at your own fresh view. The key is to start your investigation as professional researchers do — with a research question that you truly want to learn more about. Like a detective, you will need to plan your work but remain flexible, backtracking or jumping ahead if it makes sense to do so. If you meet an insurmountable obstacle, you must turn around, go sideways, or set out in another direction altogether.

Whenever you use research to come to a conclusion based on facts and expert opinions — whether in your personal life, for a college class, or on the job — this research manual will provide you with effective, efficient strategies and procedures.

Chapter 28, "Planning and Managing Your Research Project." This chapter introduces the basics for completing a research assignment, from generating ideas and developing your research question through managing your project with a realistic schedule, a system for taking notes, and a research archive.

Chapter 29, "Working with Sources."   This chapter offers advice on keeping a working bibliography; capturing information in quotations, paraphrases, and summaries; and developing an annotated bibliography.

Chapter 30, "Finding Sources in the Library, on the Internet, and in the Field."   What resources are available to answer your research question? The useful tips in this chapter suggest the best ways to locate promising sources.

Chapter 31, "Evaluating Sources."   This chapter discusses the critical process of evaluating, or judging, the information you gather in order to select the best evidence for your paper. It provides questions you can use to evaluate library, Internet, and field resources as you conduct your research.

Chapter 32, "Integrating Sources."   This chapter explains how to use sources ethically and avoid plagiarism. It illustrates how to incorporate source material — quoting, summarizing, and paraphrasing — using launch statements and source citations.

Chapter 33, "Writing Your Research Paper."   Here you will learn how to pull together, or synthesize, the information from your sources so that you answer your research question in a readable, trustworthy paper.

Chapter 34, "Documenting Sources."   This chapter explains when and how to cite your sources, illustrating MLA and APA documentation styles. Here you will find a sample student research paper in MLA style that integrates a variety of sources and selections from a research paper in APA style.

Chapter 28

Planning and Managing Your Research Project

Writing a research paper is a useful skill, essential not only in an academic community but also in the workplace. Engineers rely on research studies when they write feasibility reports. Health-care workers synthesize research findings to help them decide how to treat patients. Businesses depend on market research to sell their products.

Although research writing is a practical skill — and one you'll draw on for the rest of your life — learning to conduct research efficiently and effectively can be daunting. The Internet, television, books, newspapers, and magazines shower us with facts and figures, statements and reports, views and opinions — some of them half-baked, some revealing and trustworthy. College research requires you to sort through this mass of words, distinguishing fact from opinion, off-the-wall claims from expert interpretations.

As you investigate a topic and write a paper based on your findings, you will build valuable skills such as these:

- You'll learn how to find a topic and develop it into a focused and answerable research question.

- You'll manage your schedule, keep records, and gather materials in an archive.

- You'll capture information from sources by quoting, paraphrasing, and summarizing.

- You'll draw from a wide range of sources, using library, Internet, and field research techniques to complement one another.

- You'll integrate evidence from your sources to support your own ideas, rather than simply repeat what they say.

- You'll think critically — by evaluating, analyzing, and synthesizing.

- You'll learn to cite and list your sources in a form that scholars and professionals follow in writing research reports and articles.

This chapter will help you plan and manage your research project by creating a research schedule and building a research archive. Armed with these skills and tools, you will find yourself prepared to accomplish even the most formidable research task.

Beginning Your Inquiry

A research paper is often the most engaging and complex assignment in a course. You may already have learned how to take research notes or how to make a working bibliography, but as we guide you through the research process, we'll pause to explain these special skills. Mastering them, if you haven't done so already, will speed you on your way to completing your assignment and becoming an accomplished research writer.

THE ASSIGNMENT: WRITING FROM SOURCES

Find a topic that intrigues you, and develop a focused research question about it. Answering the question will probably require you to return to writing situations you addressed in Part Two of this book, such as comparing and contrasting, explaining causes and effects, taking a stand, proposing a solution, or evaluating. After conducting whatever research is necessary, synthesize the information you assemble to develop your own reasonable answer to the research question. Then write a paper, persuasively using a variety of source material to convey your conclusions.

Having a real audience can help you select what to include or exclude as you write your report. If possible, try to use your paper to benefit your campus administration, your employer, or a particular cause or nonprofit group on campus or in your local community. Because your final paper answers your research question, it will be more than a stack of facts. Reading and digesting the ideas of others is just the first step. During the research process, you'll also bring your own intelligence to bear on what you have discovered.

For advice on scheduling your research project, see pp. 599–600.

Generating Ideas and Asking a Research Question

What most effectively helps members of the military return to civilian life after a stressful tour of duty?

How accurately do standardized tests measure learning?

What can be done to assist homeless families in your community?

The Research Process

Choose a general topic that interests you, following your assignment (see p. 590).

Set your goals, choose your territory, and specify the aspect of the topic that intrigues you (see pp. 590–93).

State your research question (see pp. 593–95).

Manage your project (see pp. 598–602).

- Create a schedule and plan a method of recording notes.
- Organize a research archive, and draw the details from sources.

Begin working with your sources (see Ch. 29).

- Start a working bibliography.
- Quote, paraphrase, and summarize to capture information in your notes (see pp. 615–23).

Search for and evaluate reliable sources that might help to answer your research question (see Chs. 30 and 31).

- Use the library catalog, databases, and reference materials.
- Search carefully on the Internet.
- Interview, observe, or conduct other field research.

Integrate reliable information and evidence to support your answer to your research question.

- Use sources ethically to avoid plagiarism (see Chs. 29 and 32).
- Quote, paraphrase, and summarize to capture source materials in your paper (see Chs. 29 and 32).
- Clarify the thesis that answers your question, and support it as you write your paper (see Ch. 33).
- Cite and list your sources (see pp. 606–14 and Ch. 34).

To define a narrow research question, start with your own interests and research goals.

CHOOSING YOUR TERRITORY

To explore, you need a territory—a research topic that stimulates your curiosity. If you need ideas, listen to the academic exchanges around you. Perhaps the reading, writing, or discussion in a course intrigues you. For example, your geography course might alert you to the global threats to forests. To target your research from the beginning, try to narrow "global threats to forests," maybe to "farming practices that threaten rain forests." As you learn more, you can continue to narrow your topic and the question you ask about it.

Here are a few questions to help you find a research topic:

DISCOVERY CHECKLIST

___ Can you recall an experience that raises interesting questions or creates unusual associations in your mind?

___ What have you observed recently—at school or work, online, or on television today—that you could more thoroughly investigate?

___ What new perspectives on issues or events have friends, classmates, commentators, bloggers, or others offered?

___ What problem would you like to solve?

___ What have you read about lately that you'd like to pursue further?

TAKING AN OVERVIEW

Before launching an expedition into a little-known territory, a smart explorer first makes a reconnaissance flight to take an overview of the terrain. The explorer then chooses the very spot to set up camp—the point on the map that looks most promising. Research writers do something like that, too. They first get a broad overview to see what parts of the territory look promising and then zero in on one small area. As you explore the terrain in your territory, pay attention to a range of viewpoints and consider changes and trends. Figure out which narrow focus will best hold your interest and most effectively take shape in your paper.

For charts detailing the information you can get from print and electronic sources, see pp. 596–97.

Begin in the Library.   How do you take an overview? Say you are looking for preliminary information on the sociology of the family or, more specifically, on "blended families." Your college library probably subscribes to many specialized databases (like *Sociological Abstracts, PsycINFO, Medline, ERIC,* and the *MLA Bibliography*). You often can familiarize yourself with your topic and the broad range of available sources by beginning your overview here.

For more on electronic searches, see pp. 637–43 and Ch. 30.

Go Online.   You can also browse on the Internet, visiting Web sites and reading blogs or messages posted to discussion forums. Search engines—

such as Google, and Yahoo! — can lead you to a wide range of Web pages (see p. 642 for URLs). Google (<http://groups.google.com>) also can help you locate groups and mailing lists related to your topic such as support groups for blended families or exchanges on family law.

Talk with Experts.   If you're curious about America's fascination with the automobile, consider meeting with a professor, such as a sociologist or a journalist, who specializes in the area. Or talk with friends or acquaintances who are particularly passionate about their cars. Or spend time at an auto show, carefully observing and talking with the people who attend.

For more on interviewing, see pp. 644–45 and Ch. 6.

Revisit Your Purpose and Audience.   If necessary, refine the purpose of your research and your analysis of your audience in light of what you have discovered thus far. Consider what goal or goals you'd like your research to accomplish — whether in your personal life, for a college class, or on the job.

For more on purpose and audience, see pp. 14–18 and 310–12.

Satisfy curiosity	Analyze a situation
Take a new perspective	Substantiate a conclusion
Make a decision	Support a position
Solve a problem	Advocate for change

For example, suppose your overview of campus programs has led you to a proposal by the International Students Office for matching first-year students with host families during holidays. You'd like to find out what such programs cost, how they work, what they offer both foreign students and host families. At first, you thought that your purpose would be to persuade community members to participate. As you learned more, however, you decided that the real challenge was to persuade the director of student activities to support the project.

TURNING A TOPIC INTO A QUESTION

Once you have staked out an area to explore, you can move from the broad to the specific by asking more precise questions. Ask exactly what you want to find out, and your task will leap into focus.

BROAD OVERVIEW	Family structures
TOPIC	Blended families
SPECIFIC QUESTION	How do blended families today differ from those a century ago?
BROAD OVERVIEW	Contemporary architecture
TOPIC	Landscape architecture
SPECIFIC QUESTION	In what ways have the principles of landscape architecture shaped urban renewal in this city?

Generate Ideas.   You might start by freewriting, mapping, or brainstorming, jotting down whatever questions come to mind. Then, select one that appears promising. Your instructor also may have some suggestions, but you will probably be more motivated investigating a question you select.

For more on generating ideas, see Ch. 16.

Size Up Your Question.   Ask these questions as you test for a workable research question:

- Is your question debatable? Does it allow for a range of opinions so that you can support your own view rather than explain something that's generally known and accepted?
- Is it interesting to you? Will your discoveries interest your readers?
- Is it narrow enough to allow for a productive investigation in the few weeks you have? Does it stick to a single focus?

BROAD QUESTION	How is the climate of the earth changing?
NARROWER QUESTION	How will El Niño affect global climate changes in the next decade?
BROAD QUESTION	Who are the world's best living storytellers?
NARROWER QUESTION	How is Irish step dancing a form of storytelling?
BROAD QUESTION	Why is there poverty?
NARROWER QUESTION	What notable welfare-to-work programs exist in the southeastern United States?

Although you should restrict your topic, a question can be too narrow or too insignificant. If so, it may be impossible to find relevant sources.

TOO NARROW	How did John F. Kennedy's maternal grandfather influence the decisions he made during his first month as president?

A question may also be so narrow that it's uninteresting. Avoid questions that can be answered with a simple yes or no or with a few statistics.

TOO NARROW	Are there more black students or white students in the entering class this year?
BETTER	How does the ratio of black students to white students affect campus relations at our school?

Instead, ask a question that will lead you into the heart of a lively controversy. The best research questions ask about issues that others take seriously and debate, issues likely to be of real interest to you and your readers.

Hone Your Question.   Make the wording of your question specific and simple: identify one thing to find out, not several. The very phrasing of a well-crafted question can suggest keywords for searching databases, the library catalog, or the Web.

QUESTION	What has caused a shortage of affordable housing in northeastern cities?
POSSIBLE SEARCH TERMS	Housing shortage, affordable urban housing

If your question doesn't suggest such leads, try more concrete wording.

Refine Your Question.   Until you start your research, you can't know how fruitful your research question will be. If it doesn't lead you to definite facts or reliable opinions, if it doesn't start you thinking critically, you'll need to reword it or throw it out and ask a new question. But at the very least, your first question can establish a definite direction in which to start looking.

After tentatively stating a research question, use these questions to refine it:

RESEARCH CHECKLIST

Questioning Your Question

___ Is the scope of your question appropriate — not too immense and not too narrow? Will you be able to answer it given the time you have and the length limits for your paper?

___ Can you find enough current information about your question?

___ Have you worded your question concretely and specifically, so that it states exactly what you are looking for?

___ Does your question probe an issue that engages you personally?

Predict an Answer in a Working Thesis.   Some writers find a research project easier to tackle if they have not only a question but also an answer in mind. At this stage, however, you need to be flexible, ready to change your answer or even your question if your research turns up something unexpected.

You can state a proposed answer as a working thesis.

For more on stating and using a thesis, see pp. 312–19.

RESEARCH QUESTION   How does a school dress code benefit students?

WORKING THESIS   Instituting a school dress code decreases the incidence of school violence.

Explore Your Working Thesis to Guide Your Research.   Even though you may revise or replace your working thesis before your paper is finished, you can let it guide you now. For example, examine your thesis to identify terms that you will need to define or subtopics that you will want to explore. Make a list or rough outline of the sequence of points that you are likely to develop. Note the major alternative or opposing views that are likely to emerge. This early exploration will help you to pursue the sources and information you need and to avoid chasing after the wild hares that may dart out to distract you.

Remember that a working thesis is meant to guide your research, not hinder it. If all you find is support for what you already think, then your working thesis may be too dominant, and you may no longer be conducting true research. To avoid this possibility, some writers delay formulating a working thesis until they've already done substantial research or even begun drafting. Your approach will depend on your assignment, your instructor's expectations, and your own work style.

SURVEYING YOUR RESOURCES

You can quickly test whether your question is likely to lead to an ample research paper by spending an hour or so conducting a fast search at the library or its Web site. You'll want to learn whether you'll find enough ideas, opinions, facts, statistics, and expert testimony to address your question. If your survey turns up a skimpy list of sources or, more likely, hundreds of sources, consider refining your question. Try to pick a question that is the focus of a dozen or twenty available sources. If you need help conducting a reliable search, ask a librarian for advice.

Finding Evidence and Opinions in Print Sources	Source for Facts and Statistics	Source for Expert Testimony	Source for Opinions
Scholarly Book	Extensive facts and data on book's topic reported from reliable sources or original study	Written by expert scholars, researchers, or professionals	Book presents author's point of view supported by own and other scholarly research
Popular Nonfiction Book	Facts and data may or may not be included	Written by experts, professionals, practitioners, journalists, or informed writers	Book presents author's point of view or experience with or without support from research
Scholarly Journal	Facts and data on article's topic reported from reliable sources or original study	Written by expert scholars, researchers, or professionals	Articles present authors' points of view supported by their own and other scholarly research; letters or responses to articles express views of readers
News Magazine	Facts, data, and quotations in text, graphics, or sidebars may be attributed to persons interviewed, published reports, or unidentified sources	Written by freelance and staff journalists who may quote experts, participants, or observers	Articles may reflect magazine's focus or point of view; opinion features—columns, pro-con articles, and letters from readers—may represent varied views
Popular Magazine	Facts and data included in popular or catchy form may not be attributed to original source	Written by staff and freelance writers who may quote others, including popular experts	Articles may reflect magazine's focus or area of interest; columns and letters from readers may present varied views
Newspaper	Facts, data, and quotations in text, graphics, or sidebars may be attributed to persons interviewed, published reports, or unidentified sources	Written by local and wire-service journalists, columnists, and others who may quote participants, observers, or experts	Extensive opinion features include editorials (views of paper's editors), letters to the editor (views of readers), and featured columns (views of columnists)
Pamphlet or Booklet	Facts and data may or may not be included	Written by experts, professionals, researchers, or interested individuals	Contents may reflect opinions and point of view of writer or sponsor
Reference Work	Extensive facts and explanations cited from reliable sources or supplied by expert authors of entries	Written by scholars, specialists, and staff experts in subject	Articles may review several or present one of the alternative approaches or views of a topic

Finding Evidence and Opinions in Electronic Sources	Source for Facts and Statistics	Source for Expert Testimony	Source for Opinions
Online Reference Site	List of topics or links may lead to specialized facts or statistics	Expert academic sources available	Academic links to varied approaches and views on re-search topics
Gateway Site for a Topic or Field	Site pages with facts or links, such as *Polling Report* at <www.pollingreport.com>	Expert academic and field sources available	Topic links; opinion sites, such as *Public Agenda* at <www.publicagenda.com>
Online Document Collection	Documents posted on site with facts or statistics	Expert and well-regarded authors and documents available	Texts that present arguments or express opinions
Professional Web Site	Reports, newsletters, and surveys, such as MetLife Foundation's "Survey of the American Teacher" at <www.metlife.com>	Expert and professional views available, promoting sponsor or sponsor's interests	Materials, advice, and sponsored reports that support interests or views of organization
Academic Web Site	Library links to facts or statistics, such as "Community Information by Zip Code" at <http://library.csun.edu/mfinley/zipstats.html>	Department or library links and lists of campus experts to interview or e-mail may be available	Possible links to campus or local newspaper with editorials and letters on current issues
Government Web Site	Agency studies and reports with extensive statistics and other facts, such as *The World Factbook* at <www.cia.gov/library/publications/the-world-factbook>	Expert analysis of research studies, policy options, and consumer topics available	Reports or pages that reflect specific mission or objectives of agency
Online Newspaper or News Service	Reports and boxes with facts or statistics to develop news cover-age or provide background	Quotations and background from participants, observers, and analysts may be available	Editorials, letters to editor, regu-lar or featured columnists, polls of site visitors
Interest-Group or Personal Web Site	Facts and statistics that support or promote group interests	Range available from expert to partisan to oddball views	Opinions, advocacy, and personal views that shape site content

In addition, decide which types of sources to concentrate on. Some research questions require a wide range of sources. Others are better suited to a narrower range, perhaps restricted by date or discipline. Target those most likely to yield the best information to answer your question. Understanding the types of information available in various print and electronic sources can help you plan your research. See the charts on pp. 596 and 597 and on pp. 658–61.

■ For more character-istics of the sources described in the chart above, see pp. 658–61.

■ To review the types of evidence, see pp. 40–41.

USING KEYWORDS AND LINKS

Keywords are terms or phrases that identify the topics discussed in a research source. When you enter the keywords into an electronic search engine (whether in a library catalog or database, or on the Web), the engine will return to you a list of all the sources it can find with that keyword.

■ To practice using key-
words, visit the Bedford
Research Room Web site
at <bedfordstmartins/
researchroom.com>.

■ For advanced search
strategies, see p. 641.
For a list of search
engines, see p. 642.

■ For advice on creating
a working bibliography,
see pp. 603–15.

Finding the best keywords for a particular topic and search engine is essential. Start by using the main terms in your research question. As you survey possible sources, write down or print out the keywords you use, noting whether they produce too few or too many results. Some keywords will work better than others, and certain combinations of keywords may produce the best results.

As your keywords lead you to Web sites compiled by specialists or people who share an interest, you can browse through the information and resources gathered there. These sites often contain *links* — lists of related sites — also relevant to your research project. These links, in turn, often contain their own lists of related Web pages. By following these connections systematically, you can benefit from the work of others and rapidly expand your own knowledge. Be careful, however, not to look only for information that supports a preconceived notion. Research should be an opportunity to learn more about a topic to answer an authentic question, not simply to collect evidence that supports what you already think.

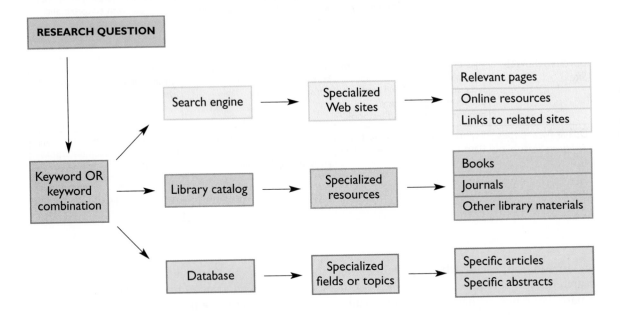

Managing Your Project

No matter what your question or where you plan to look for material, you will want to manage your project wisely. You will need a schedule to use your time efficiently, a plan for recording and organizing information, and a working bibliography to keep track of where you've been and where you need to go.

CREATING A SCHEDULE

If your instructor doesn't assign a series of deadlines, set some for yourself. You can be sure that a research paper will take longer than you expect. If you procrastinate and try to toss everything together in a desperate all-night siege, you will not be satisfied with the result. Instead, start with a clear-cut schedule that breaks your project into a series of small tasks.

■ For downloadable sample schedules (and research checklists), visit <bedfordstmartins.com/bedguide> and do a keyword search:

schedules

SAMPLE SCHEDULE

- *Week One:* If you are not assigned a topic, start thinking about your interests. Take an overview by searching through your library or on the Internet.

- *Week Two:* Begin narrowing your topic to a workable research question. Survey the available resources, and start your working bibliography and your research archive. Annotate possible sources when useful.

Collaborative Research

Research groups, in class or at work, require cooperative effort but can reward all concerned with deeper and more creative outcomes than one individual could achieve. Your team might consolidate all its work or share the research but produce separate papers, presentation pages, or Web pages. With your instructor's approval, divide up the tasks so that all members are responsible for their own portions of the work. Then agree on your due dates and group meetings as illustrated by the following schedule, which describes a process for producing a single paper collaboratively.

FOR GROUP LEARNING

- *Week One:* Meet to get acquainted and to select someone to act as an organizer, e-mailing or calling to make sure things progress as planned; individually investigate interests and options for a project topic.

- *Week Two:* Meet again to select a topic, narrow it, and turn it into a research question that your instructor approves.

- *Week Three:* Individually survey available resources and contribute entries and annotations to a collaborative working bibliography. Meet to agree on assigned tasks, and then individually gather material for the group's research archive.

For details on research archives, see pp. 601–02.

- *Weeks Four and Five:* Continue to find sources, read and evaluate them, and record source notes.

- *Week Six:* Meet to evaluate the sources and information everyone has found and decide what is missing or weak. Draft a working thesis, and create a working outline for presenting what everyone has learned.

For advice on working and annotated bibliographies, see pp. 603–15 and pp. 621–23.

- *Week Seven:* Guided by the group's plan, individually draft assigned sections. Swap drafts, read them over, and respond with suggestions.

- *Week Eight:* Work together to consolidate the revised draft, read it carefully, and agree on final changes. Appoint one member to prepare a polished copy and one or two others to act as final editors and proofreaders.

- *Week Three:* Begin your research in earnest. Locate and evaluate your most promising sources. Take notes, and build your archive.
- *Week Four:* Continue narrowing your research, identifying promising sources, evaluating them as you go along, and taking efficient notes.
- *Week Five:* State your working thesis, and begin planning or outlining your paper. Continue to update your bibliography and research archive, putting your sources in the order in which you think you might use them. Target any gaps in your information.
- *Week Six:* Refine your thesis statement. Start your first draft, noting where you draw on your sources.
- *Week Seven:* Complete your first draft. Begin thinking about ways to revise and improve it. Seek feedback from a peer editor.
- *Week Eight:* Revise and edit your draft. Check that you have correctly presented and credited all quotations, paraphrases, and summaries from your sources. Finally, proofread the entire paper, checking for any errors.

Each week you can make up a more detailed schedule, identifying tasks by the day or by the type to increase your efficiency while varying your activities.

DAILY SCHEDULE
Monday — finish library catalog search
Tuesday — start article indexes
Thursday — read e-mails and printouts from databases
Sunday night — organize files and add notes

ACTIVITY SCHEDULE
library search — EBSCOHost and InfoTrac
Web search — government sites
reading — new printouts and e-mails from databases
writing — revised research question — thesis?

RECORDING INFORMATION

Plan ahead so that your system for recording information produces what you need: relevant evidence from reliable sources to develop and support your answer to your research question. Avoid two extremes — collecting everything or counting only on memory.

■ For advice on working with sources, see Ch. 29; for advice on integrating sources, see Ch. 32.

Use Time-Honored Methods for Depth.   Remember this trusty advice: copy judiciously and take notes. Selectively copying (either photocopying or saving to a computer file) will help you accumulate material, but copying whatever you find will waste your money and time. Instead, try taking notes, annotating, highlighting, quoting, paraphrasing, and summarizing — all time-honored methods for absorbing, evaluating, and selecting information from a source. Such methods not only identify potentially useful materials, they also prepare them for their smooth transfer and integration into a paper.

Innovate for Efficiency.   As practice improves your time-honored skills, increase your efficiency by developing techniques such as these:

- Write a summary on the first page of a printout or photocopy.
- Add a paraphrase in the margin next to a key section of a printout.
- Identify a lively or concrete quotation with a highlighter.
- E-mail information from a library database to yourself so that it is easy to move into an electronic folder or file.
- Record key quotations (including sources and page numbers) in a computer file so that you can easily reorganize them to find an effective sequence.
- Record summaries of sources on sticky notes or print them out on cards so that you can quickly rearrange them in various orders.
- Use a graphics program or a big sheet of poster board to sketch out a "storyboard" for the main "events" that you want to cover in your paper.

Many college researchers use note cards (with one note on each) or word-processing files (with clearly separated entries). Both are more flexible than taking notes on sheets of notebook paper. When the time comes to organize the material, it's easy to reshuffle cards or move around electronic notes to arrive at a logical order.

Take Accurate and Thorough Notes.   Read the entire article or section of a book before beginning to take notes. This method will help you decide what — and how much — to record so that you dig out the useful nuggets without distorting the meaning. Double-check all statistics and lists. Make your notes and citations full enough that, once they're written, you are totally independent of the source from which they came.

Read as a Critic.   If you're tired or distracted, it's easy to stop thinking while you're recording notes. Instead, try to read and write as a skeptical critic. Distinguish what's significant for answering your research question and what's only slightly related. If you wish, add your own ratings (*, +, !! or – , ??) at the top or in the margin. When you feel that you're rereading what you have already learned from authoritative sources, you may be ready to stop reading, start shaping your paper, and begin identifying information gaps yet to fill.

For more on critical reading, see Ch. 2.

STARTING A RESEARCH ARCHIVE

You can organize the information you accumulate from library, Internet, and field sources by creating a research archive. An *archive* is a place where information is systematically stored for later use. If you have ever found yourself staring at a pile of books, photocopies, and printouts, wondering which one contained the fact or quotation that you wanted to use, you know the importance of organizing. Consider several techniques for creating a research archive.

File Paper Copies.   To use this method, try to get all important sources in a paper format: photocopy book passages and periodical articles, print out electronic sources (with your date of access), and keep questionnaires and other field material. Then put these pages in a separate file folder for each source, labeled with title or subject and author. Attach sticky notes next to key passages, or highlight them so you can locate them quickly. Make sure the author (or short title) and page number are identified on your copy so that you can connect them to a corresponding entry with the details needed to credit your source. If necessary, write that information on the photocopy.

For advice on a working bibliography, see pp. 603–15.

Save Computer Files.   You can save Web pages, e-mail messages, posts to newsgroups and mailing lists, transcripts of chats, and records from databases to a disk, a jump drive, a hard drive, or a network drive. Be certain that you carefully save or note URLs or search paths, your dates of access, and similar details for these electronic sources. Give each file a descriptive name so that you can find the information quickly later on. Clearly distinguish the sources you save from your own notes about sources. You can also organize the files in different electronic folders or directories, also named so you can easily tell what each contains. Be sure to back up all of your electronic records.

Save Favorites and Bookmarks.   You can save the locations of Web sites in your browser so that you can easily return to them. Microsoft Internet Explorer calls these saved locations *favorites*, while Mozilla Firefox and Netscape Navigator call them *bookmarks*. You can annotate these locations and organize them into folders, much as you organize computer files.

Save Search Results.   If a database or Internet search was very productive but you don't have time to locate each relevant source at that moment, note where you searched and what keywords you used. Then you can easily repeat the search at a later date. You can also print out the search results or save them to a computer file so you don't need to rerun the search.

Use the following questions to organize as a researcher:

RESEARCH CHECKLIST

Getting Organized

___ Have you identified and stated an intriguing research question?

___ What has your quick survey of available library and online sources revealed? Do you expect to find enough information — but not too much — to answer your research question?

___ Which types of sources might be best for beginning your research?

___ Have you created a realistic research schedule based on your assigned deadlines? Have you reworked it to allow plenty of time for your research while meeting your other responsibilities?

___ Have you decided how you want to record research information? Have you taken a few notes to test whether your method will be easy to keep up and will help you compile useful and accurate information?

___ Have you begun organizing your research archive — for example, by opening files and setting up folders on the computer or buying file folders for paper copies?

Chapter 29

Working with Sources

Besides actively managing your research project, you will want to develop your skills as you work with sources. You'll need to gather two different kinds of information about each source that you use.

- First, in a source entry, you will record the details that identify the source so that you can find it and correctly credit it in your paper. These source entries form a working bibliography, discussed in the first part of this chapter.

- Second, in source notes, you will capture information of value to your inquiry as quotations, paraphrases, or summaries ready for possible use in your paper. These methods of capturing information are discussed in the second part of the chapter.

■ For more on how to quote, paraphrase, and summarize, see pp. 214–21 and 615–20. See also Ch. 32 on integrating sources.

The chapter concludes with advice on developing an annotated bibliography, which combines a source entry with a summary in order to inform readers about the scope and thrust of your research.

Starting a Working Bibliography

Your working bibliography is a detailed list of the books, articles, Web sites, and other resources that you either plan to consult or have consulted. It has two purposes:

> It guides your research by recording which sources you've examined and which you intend to examine.

> It helps you document or identify the sources you have used by recording detailed information about each source.

Each entry in your working bibliography eventually needs to follow the format or style required for your paper, generally MLA (Modern Language Association) style or possibly APA (American Psychological Association) style. Ask your instructor which style you are expected to use.

Choose a Method for Compiling Your Working Bibliography.   Pick the method that suits you best, the one that you can use most easily and efficiently during the course of your research. Here are some options:

- Note cards, recording one source per card
- Small notebook
- Word-processing program
- Computer database
- Hand-held electronic storage tool

Keep Careful Records.   Whatever your method, the more carefully you record your tentative sources, the more time you'll save later when you list the works you actually used and cited. At that point, you'll be grateful to find all the necessary titles, authors, dates, page numbers, and URLs (Internet addresses) at your fingertips — and you'll avoid a frantic, last-minute database search or time-consuming trip to the library.

Start a bibliographic entry for each source you intend to consult. At this point, your information may be incomplete: "Dr. Edward Denu — cardiologist — interview about drug treatments." Later, once you locate the source or conduct field research, you'll be able to fill in the complete information.

For examples of MLA and APA documentation forms see Ch. 34.

Record What You Will Need.   What should each source entry in your working bibliography contain? Eventually it should include everything necessary to find the source as well as to write the final list of sources to be placed at the end of your paper. Although the formats for entries in MLA and APA style differ in the arrangement and presentation of the details, both require recording much the same information. Learning to record this information when it's readily apparent (and to hunt for it when it's not) is a valuable skill that will save you time and improve the accuracy of your research writing.

The chart on page 605 summarizes what you'll need to record as you begin to gather sources, both the basics — the details nearly always required to identify each type of source — and the common additions or complications likely to crop up in varied sources. When in doubt, record more than you think you'll need so you don't have to return to the source later on.

Drawing the Details from Your Sources

For more examples of MLA and APA style, see Ch. 34.

The Source Navigators on pages 606–14 show how to find identifying information in several types of sources that you are likely to use as a college researcher. Each sample source is keyed to a menu illustrating where to look for the details you'll need to record. Each sample source is accompanied first by a source note or card following MLA style with an entry ready to be copied directly from a working bibliography to a list of works cited for the final paper. Below that example, the entry also appears in a source note or card in APA style. Stick to the style your instructor expects you to use.

Type of Information to Record	THE BASICS	COMMON ADDITIONS
NAMES	• Complete name of the author, as supplied in the source, unless not identified	• Names of coauthors, in the order listed in the source • Names of any editor, compiler, translator, contributor, or editor of a special journal issue
TITLES	• Title and any subtitle of an article, Web page, or posting (placed in quotation marks in MLA) • Title and any subtitle of a journal, magazine, newspaper, book, or Web site (italicized in MLA and APA)	• Title of a special issue of a journal • Title of a series of books or pamphlets and any item number
PUBLICATION DETAILS FOR PERIODICALS	• Volume and issue numbers for a journal (or a magazine in APA) • Section number for a newspaper	• Any edition of a newspaper
PUBLICATION DETAILS FOR BOOKS	• Place of publication, using the first city listed • Name of the publisher	• Edition number (4th) or description (revised) • Volume number and total volumes, if more than one • Names and locations of copublishers • Publisher's imprint
PUBLICATION DETAILS FOR ELECTRONIC SOURCES	• Name of the database, subscriber service, or library service (italicized in MLA) • Name of any site sponsor or publisher	• Details of any original or alternate print publication • Document numbers
DATES	• Year of publication, full date (periodical), or date of creation or last update (electronic source) • Your access date for an electronic source (printed or written on your hard copy)	• Original date of publication for a literary work or classic
LOCATION OF INFORMATION	• Article's opening and concluding page numbers	• Paragraph, screen, or column numbers if supplied or section names
MEDIUM OF PUBLICATION	• Medium of publication or reception (for MLA)	

Article in a Magazine

Record this information in your notes about each source:

1 The complete name of the author

2 The title and any subtitle of the article

3 The title and any subtitle of the magazine

4 The full date of the issue

5 The article's page numbers

6 The periodical's volume number if available (for APA)

7 The medium of publication (for MLA)

JUMPING TO CONCLUSIONS

Can people be counted on to make sound judgments?

By Deanna Kuhn

A four-year-old watches as a monkey hand puppet approaches a vase containing a red and a blue plastic flower. The monkey sneezes. The monkey backs away, returns to sniff again, and again sneezes. An adult then removes the red flower and replaces it with a yellow one. The monkey comes up to smell the yellow and blue flowers twice and each time sneezes. The adult next replaces the blue flower with the red one. The monkey comes up to smell the red and yellow flowers and this time does not sneeze.

The child is then asked, "Can you give me the flower that makes Monkey sneeze?" When psychologists Laura E. Schulz and Alison Gopnik, both then at the University of California, Berkeley, did this experiment, 79 percent of four-year-olds correctly chose the blue flower. As their research makes clear, even very young children have begun to understand cause and effect. This process is critical to their ability to make sense of their world and to make their way in it.

With such powers of discernment already in place by age four, people should be highly skilled at identifying cause and effect—causal reasoning—by the time they are adults, shouldn't they? Indeed, a substantial body of contemporary research suggests that is the case, highlighting the nuanced judgments adults are capable of—such as making consistent estimates, across different circumstances, of the numerical probabilities that two events are causally related.

Here I present some evidence that gives a very different impression: the everyday causal reasoning of the average adult regarding familiar topics appears highly fallible. People connect two events as cause and effect based on little or no evidence, and they act on these judgments—they jump to conclusions. By learning more about precisely how they do so, researchers can develop ways to improve thinking. Such efforts could help educators in their mission to inspire solid, careful thinking in young minds.

A possible explanation for the discrepancy between our findings and much of the relevant literature is that researchers studying

Create a source entry out of the information you collect:

Source entry in MLA style

1 2
Kuhn, Deanna. "Jumping to Conclusions: Can People Be Counted on to Make

3   4   5   7
Sound Judgments?" *Scientific American Mind* Feb.-Mar. 2007: 44-51. Print.

Presents research on how reasoning mistakes can lead to bad decisions and explains how we can become better decision makers.

Source entry in APA style

1   4   2
Kuhn, D. (2007, February/March). Jumping to conclusions: Can people be counted

3   6 5
on to make sound judgments? *Scientific American Mind, 18,* 44-51.

Explores research on decision making, examining the factors behind poor decisions and possible alternatives for improving them.

607

Article in a Scholarly Journal from a Database

Record this information in your notes about each source:

1 The complete name of the author

2 The title and any subtitle of the article

3 The title and any subtitle of the journal

4 The journal volume and issue

5 The year of the issue

6 The printed article's original page numbers

7 The name of the database, subscriber service, or library service

8 The medium of publication (for MLA)

9 The access date when you used the source

10 The internet address (URL) or your search path

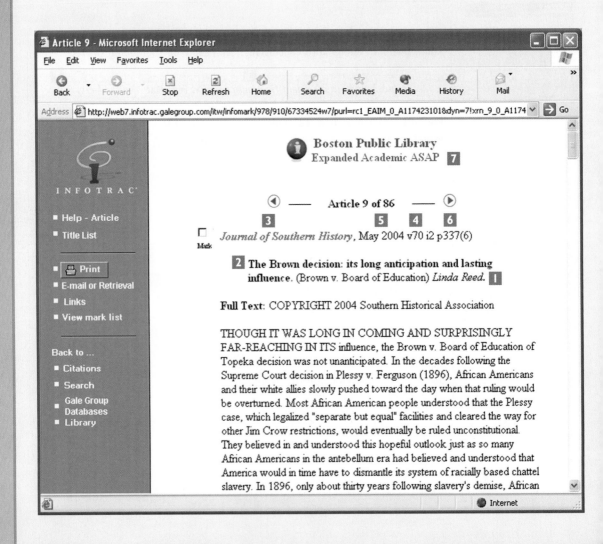

Create a source entry out of the information you collect:

Source entry in MLA style, e-mailed from database and recorded in a computer file

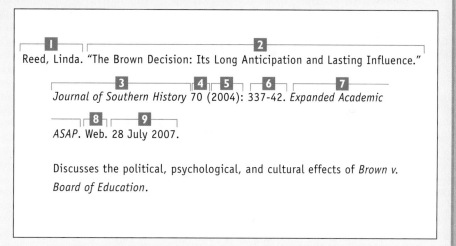

Reed, Linda. "The Brown Decision: Its Long Anticipation and Lasting Influence." *Journal of Southern History* 70 (2004): 337-42. *Expanded Academic ASAP*. Web. 28 July 2007.

Discusses the political, psychological, and cultural effects of *Brown v. Board of Education*.

Source entry in APA style, e-mailed from database and recorded in a computer file

Reed, L. (2004). The Brown decision: Its long anticipation and lasting influence. *Journal of Southern History, 70*(2), 337-342. Retrieved from http://infotrac.galegroup.com

Explores the social context and consequences of the *Brown* decision.

[If a digital object identifier (DOI) is specified, use this instead of the database home page URL.]

Book

Record this information in your notes about each source:

1 The complete name of the author

2 The title and any subtitle of the book

3 The place of publication, using the first city listed

4 The name of the publisher

5 The date of publication (from the front or back of the title page)

6 The medium of publication (for MLA)

7 The call number or library location (for your future use)

8 Keyword or author (for your filing system)

Title page

1 DAVID CALLAHAN

2 the **cheating** culture

Why More Americans Are
Doing Wrong to Get Ahead

4
3 HARCOURT, INC.

ORLANDO   AUSTIN   NEW YORK   SAN DIEGO   TORONTO   LONDON

Back of
title page

5
Copyright © 2004 by David Callahan

Create a source entry out of the information you collect:

MLA

Source entry in MLA style, recorded on a card

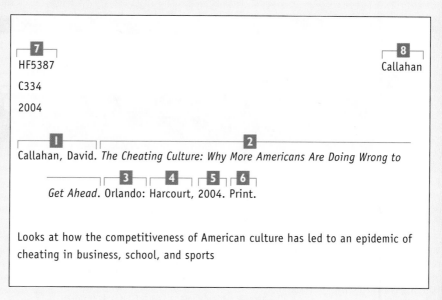

7
HF5387
C334
2004

8
Callahan

1 **2**
Callahan, David. *The Cheating Culture: Why More Americans Are Doing Wrong to*
3 **4** **5** **6**
Get Ahead. Orlando: Harcourt, 2004. Print.

Looks at how the competitiveness of American culture has led to an epidemic of cheating in business, school, and sports

APA

Source entry in APA style, recorded on a card

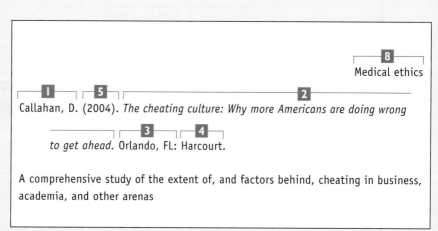

8
Medical ethics

1 **5** **2**
Callahan, D. (2004). *The cheating culture: Why more Americans are doing wrong*
3 **4**
to get ahead. Orlando, FL: Harcourt.

A comprehensive study of the extent of, and factors behind, cheating in business, academia, and other arenas

Source Navigator

Page from a Web Site

Record this information in your notes about each source:

1. The complete name of the author, if available, often from the beginning or end of the page
2. The title of the page
3. The name of the site
4. The name of any sponsoring organization

5. The date of the last update
6. The medium of publication (for MLA)
7. The access date when you used the source
8. The Internet address (URL) or search path (for APA)

Create a source entry out of the information you collect:

Source entry in MLA style, recorded in a computer file

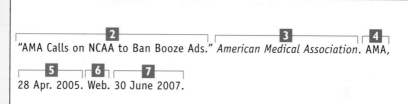

"AMA Calls on NCAA to Ban Booze Ads." *American Medical Association*. AMA,

28 Apr. 2005. Web. 30 June 2007.

Describes the AMA's appeal to ban beer commercials during college sporting and athletic events.

Source entry in APA style, recorded in a computer file

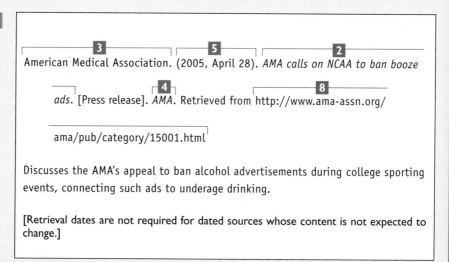

American Medical Association. (2005, April 28). *AMA calls on NCAA to ban booze*

ads. [Press release]. *AMA*. Retrieved from http://www.ama-assn.org/

ama/pub/category/15001.html

Discusses the AMA's appeal to ban alcohol advertisements during college sporting events, connecting such ads to underage drinking.

[Retrieval dates are not required for dated sources whose content is not expected to change.]

Notes for a Field Source

Record this information in your notes about each source:

1 The complete name of the person you interviewed or the setting you observed

2 A descriptive label, such as "Personal interview" or "E-mail interview"

3 The date you conducted the interview or observation

Create a source entry out of the information you collect:

MLA

Source entry in MLA style, recorded in a handheld electronic storage tool

> **1** **2** **3**
> Cardone, Amy. Personal interview. 20 Apr. 2007.
>
> Anecdotal evidence. Describes sports injuries in children she's treated.

APA

Source entry in APA style recorded in a handheld electronic storage tool

> **1** **2** **3**
> (A. Cardone, personal communication, April 20, 2007)
>   Reminder to me: Cite personal communications only in the text, not in the list of references.
>
> Cardone, a physical therapist, discusses sports injuries in children she's treated and the potential for long-term consequences of these injuries.

Capturing Information by Quoting, Paraphrasing, and Summarizing in Your Notes

Before you spend time taking source notes on outside material, read critically to decide what the source offers to you. If you cannot understand a source that requires specialized background, don't take notes or use it in your paper. On the other hand, if the evidence in a source seems accurate, logical, and relevant, consider exactly how you might want to record it and eventually add it to your paper.

Identify What's from Where.   Whatever your system of recording information, be certain that you clearly note the author of the source, a brief title if needed, and the page number (or other location) where a reader could find the information. To cite and list each source correctly, you will need the author (or title) to connect each source note to your corresponding bibliography entry. Adding a keyword at the top of each note also will help you cluster related material and select its place in your paper.

Besides grouping material and linking your notes with your sources, you also need a reliable system for identifying which ideas are yours and which are your source's. For example, you might mark your source notes with these labels:

"...": quotation marks to set off all the exact words of the source

para: your paraphrase, restatement, or translation of a passage from the source into your own words and sentences

sum: your overall summary of the source's main point

paste: your cut-and-paste, quoting an entire passage pulled from an electronic document

JN (your initials) or [ ]: your own ideas, connections, reactions, or conclusions

Not only will a system like this help you avoid confusing your paraphrase or cut-and-paste with your own ideas, it will help you to highlight and develop your own thinking as your paper evolves. Careful notes also help you to avoid accidental plagiarism, using another writer's words or ideas without appropriate credit.

■ For more on plagiarism, see pp. 663–66 and pp. 670–72.

Decide What You Need.   When it comes time to draft your paper, you will incorporate your source material in a variety of ways:

- Quoting: transcribing the author's exact words directly from the source

- Paraphrasing: fully rewording or translating the author's ideas into your own words

- Summarizing: reducing the author's main point to essentials

■ To practice quoting, paraphrasing, and summarizing, visit <bedfordstmartins.com/bedguide> and do a keyword search:

source practice

■ For more on recording notes, see pp. 600–01.

Your notes, too, should use these three forms—and the form you pick for each bit of information should represent your best guess as to the form you will use in the final paper. Weighing each source carefully and deciding how to use it—even as you are reading—is part of the dynamic process of research. You should always be thinking critically about how you will use your sources—otherwise, they'll end up using you.

■ For more examples, see pp. 214–21.

Sample Quotations, Paraphrase, and Summary (MLA Style)

Passage from Original Source
Obesity is a major issue because (1) vast numbers of people are affected; (2) the prevalence is growing; (3) rates are increasing in children; (4) the medical, psychological, and social effects are severe; (5) the behaviors that cause it (poor diet and inactivity) are themselves major contributors to ill health; and (6) treatment is expensive, rarely effective, and impractical to use on a large scale.

   Biology and environment conspire to promote obesity. Biology is an enabling factor, but the obesity epidemic, and the consequent human tragedy, is a function of the worsening food and physical activity environment. Governments and societies have come to this conclusion very late. There is much catching up to do.

Sample Quotations from Second Paragraph
Although human biology has contributed to the pudgy American society, everyone now faces the powerful challenge of a "worsening food and physical activity environment" (Brownell and Horgen 51). As Brownell and Horgen conclude, "There is much catching up to do" (51).

Sample Paraphrase of First Paragraph
The current concern with increasing American weight has developed for half a dozen reasons, according to Brownell and Horgen. They attribute the shift in awareness to the number of obese people and the increase in this number, especially among youngsters. In addition, excess weight carries harsh consequences for individual physical and mental health and for society's welfare. Lack of exercise and unhealthy food choices worsen the health consequences, especially because there's no cheap and easy cure for the effects of eating too much and exercising too little (51).

Sample Summary
After outlining six reasons why obesity is a critical issue, Brownell and Horgen urge Americans to eat less and become more active (51).

Works Cited Entry (MLA Style)
Brownell, Kelly D., and Katherine Battle Horgen. *Food Fight: The Inside Story of the Food Industry, America's Obesity Crisis, and What We Can Do about It.* Chicago: Contemporary-McGraw, 2004. Print.

QUOTING

If you intend to use a direct quotation, capture the quotation carefully, copying by hand or pasting electronically. Reproduce the words, spelling, order, and punctuation exactly, even if they're unusual. Put quotation marks around the material so that when you add it to your paper, you'll remember that it's a direct quotation. (See Figure 29.1 for an example of a note quoting a source.)

For more about quoting from sources, see pp. 214–15, 667–69, and D3 in the Quick Research Guide (the dark-red-edged pages).

RECORDING A GOOD QUOTATION

1. Quote sparingly, selecting only notable passages that might add support and authority to your assertions.
2. Mark the beginning and the ending with quotation marks.
3. Carefully write out or copy and paste each quotation. Check your copy — word by word — for accuracy.
4. Record the exact number of the page where the quotation appears in the source. If it falls on two pages, note both, marking where the page turns.

Sometimes it doesn't pay to copy a long quotation word for word. Parts may fail to serve your purpose, such as transitions, parenthetical remarks, and irrelevant information. If you take out one or more words, indicate the omission in your note by using an ellipsis mark (. . .). If you need to add wording, especially so that a selection makes sense, enclose your addition in brackets [like this].

For more on quotations and ellipsis marks, see C3 in the Quick Editing Guide (the dark-blue-edged pages).

PARAPHRASING

When paraphrasing, you restate an author's ideas in your own words. Simply try to express them fairly and accurately. Avoid judging, interpreting, or hovering so close to them that your paraphrase is merely an echo of the original. A good paraphrase retains the organization, emphasis, and often many of the details of the original, so it may not be much shorter. Even so, paraphrasing is useful when the language of another writer is not particularly memorable,

For more about paraphrasing sources, see pp. 218–19, 667–69, and D4 in the Quick Research Guide (the dark-red-edged pages).

Children and sports   Leonard 140

" . . . [in organized sports] children may be subject to intense emotional stress caused by fear and anxiety, concern about physical safety, and doubts about performances and outcomes. This anxiety may emerge if children are ignored, chastised, or made to feel that they are no good. Scanlan and Passer's study of preadolescent male soccer players showed that losing players evidenced more postgame anxiety than winning players. Children who experience anxiety in sport competition may try to avoid failure by shying away from active participation, by developing excuses, or by refusing to try new things." [Good quote!]

Figure 29.1
A sample source note cut and pasted into a computer file capturing a direct quotation from a source

but you want to walk your readers through the points made in the original source. (See Figure 29.2 for an example of a note paraphrasing a source.)

ORIGINAL	"In staging an ancient Greek tragedy today, most directors do not mask the actors."
TOO CLOSE TO THE ORIGINAL	Most directors, in staging an ancient Greek play today, do not mask the actors.
A GOOD PARAPHRASE	Few contemporary directors of Greek tragedy insist that their actors wear masks.

WRITING A GOOD PARAPHRASE

1. Read the entire passage through several times.
2. Divide the passage into its most important ideas or points, either in your mind or by highlighting or annotating the page. Noting three or four points for each paragraph will make the task manageable.
3. Look away from the original, and restate the first idea in your own words. Sum up the support for this idea. Review the section if necessary.
4. Go on to the next idea, and follow the same procedure. Continue in this way until you reach the last point.
5. Go back and reread the entire original passage one more time, making sure you've conveyed its ideas faithfully but without repeating its words or sentence structure. Revise your paraphrase if necessary.

SUMMARIZING

Sometimes a paraphrase will unnecessarily use up space or disrupt the flow of your own ideas. Often all you need is a summary that captures the main point of a source "in a nutshell." Summarizing alerts your readers to the most important ideas of a passage by restating them in your own words. This strategy can save a lot of space, distilling a page or more of detailed text

Paraphrase somewhat shorter than the original passage

Emphasis of original maintained with word choice and order reworked to avoid plagiarism

No interpretation or evaluation of original passage included

Children and sports   Leonard 140

Stress and anxiety on the playing field can result in children backing away from participating in sports because they fear rejection if they perform poorly. This anxiety and stress is a result of the child's fears of being hurt or not being good enough. Research by Scanlan and Passer confirms these findings, showing that boys who lose in soccer have more anxiety after a game than boys who win.

Figure 29.2
A sample source note paraphrasing the quotation from Leonard's book (Figure 29.1)

into one or two succinct sentences. Be careful, though, that in reducing a long passage you do not distort the original meaning or emphasis. (See p. 616 for an example summarizing a passage and Figure 29.3 on this page for an example summarizing an interview.)

WRITING A GOOD SUMMARY
1. Read the original passage several times.
2. Without looking back at the passage, state its central point or the main sense as you remember it.
3. Reread the original passage one more time, making sure you've conveyed its ideas faithfully. Revise your summary if necessary.

Learning to select appropriate quotations and to write useful paraphrases and summaries takes time and practice. Use the following questions to help you improve these research skills:

For more about summarizing, see p. 220, pp. 669–70, and D5 and D6 in the Quick Research Guide (the dark-red-edged pages). For an extended summary of a literary work, see pp. 257–58.

RESEARCH CHECKLIST

Taking Notes with Quotations, Paraphrases, and Summaries

—— For each source note, have you identified the source (by the author's last name or a key word from the title) and the exact page? Have you added a keyword heading to each note?

—— Have you made a companion source entry in your working bibliography for each new source discovered during your research?

—— Have you remained true to the meaning of the original source?

—— Have you quoted sparingly — selecting striking, short passages?

—— Have you quoted sources exactly? Do you use quotation marks around significant words, phrases, and passages from the original sources? Do you use ellipsis marks or brackets as needed to show where any words are omitted or added?

To practice quoting, paraphrasing, and summarizing, visit <bedfordstmartins.com/bedguide> and do a keyword search:

source practice

Reasons for moving to Las Animas	Aaron Sanchez Interview, 3-11-07

In 1974, my father Octavio and his family (father, mother, four brothers, three sisters) moved to Las Animas because they couldn't make enough money where they were living in New Mexico. The inheritance from his mother's father went to her brothers, and she got nothing. They moved to the Las Animas region, settling in a <u>colonia</u> (labor camp).

Subject heading
Identifier: person interviewed and date

Main points clearly broken out

Terse, even fragmentary, notes convey the gist of the interview

Figure 29.3
A sample source note handwritten on a card summarizing a source

___ Are most notes in your own words — paraphrasing or summarizing?

___ Have you avoided paraphrasing too close to the source?

■ Activity: Capturing Information from Sources

■ For more exercises
on incorporating
sources, visit
<bedfordstmartins.com/
bedguide> and do a key-
word search:

sources

Select one of the following passages, and study it until you understand it thoroughly. Use this passage as you respond to the first three activities that follow.

PASSAGE I

Within the next decades education will change more than it has changed since the modern school was created by the printed book over three hundred years ago. An economy in which knowledge is becoming the true capital and the premier wealth-producing resource makes new and stringent demands on the schools for educational performance and educational responsibility. A society dominated by knowledge workers makes even newer — and even more stringent — demands for social performance and social responsibility. Once again we will have to think through what an educated person is. At the same time, how we learn and how we teach are changing drastically and fast — the result, in part, of new theoretical understanding of the learning process, in part of new technology. Finally, many of the traditional disciplines of the schools are becoming sterile, if not obsolescent. We thus also face changes in what we learn and teach and, indeed, in what we mean by knowledge.

— Peter F. Drucker, *The New Realities*

PASSAGE 2

When I look to the future of humanity beyond the twenty-first century, I see on my list of things to come the extension of our inquisitiveness from the objective domain of science to the subjective domain of feeling and memory. Homo sapiens, the exploring animal, will not be content with merely physical exploration. Our curiosity will drive us to explore the dimensions of the mind as vigorously as we explore the dimensions of space and time. For every pioneer who explores a new asteroid or a new planet, there will be another pioneer who explores from the inside the minds of our fellow passengers on planet Earth. It is our nature to strive to explore everything, alive and dead, present and past and future. When once the technology exists to read and write memories from one mind into another, the age of mental exploration will begin in earnest. Instead of admiring the beauties of nature from the outside, we will look at nature directly through the eyes of the elephant, the eagle, and the whale. We will be able, through the magic of science, to feel in our own minds the pride of the peacock and the wrath of the lion. That magic is no greater than the magic that enables me to see the rocking horse through the eyes of the child who rode it sixty years ago.

— Freeman Dyson, *Infinite in All Directions*

1. Quoting
    Identify one notable quotation from the passage you selected. Write a brief paragraph justifying your selection. Explain why you find the quota-

tion notable and why you might want to use it in a paper. Share your selection and your justification paragraph with classmates who have worked
with the same passage. Did any of you select the same quotation? If you
did, in what ways were your reasons similar or different? If you selected
different quotations, what were your reasons for your choices?

2. Paraphrasing
Write a paraphrase of the passage you selected. Use your own language to
capture what the original passage says without parroting its wording or
sentence patterns. Compare and contrast your version with those of classmates who selected the same passage. With their help, evaluate your version. What are its strengths and weaknesses? Where might you want to reword or freshen the language?

3. Summarizing
In one or two sentences, write a summary of the passage you selected.
Concentrate on capturing the essence of the passage in your own words.
Compare and contrast your summary with those of classmates who have
worked on the same passage. With their help, evaluate your summary.
What are its strengths and weaknesses? Where might you want to simplify
or clarify it?

4. Reflecting and Exchanging
After completing 1, 2, and 3 above, decide which method of working with
a passage proved most challenging for you: quoting, paraphrasing, or
summarizing. Based on your experience, write out some specific tips for
yourself about how you might make that task easier, faster, and more successful in the future. Compare your tips with those of your classmates so
that you all gain fresh ideas about how to quote, paraphrase, and summarize effectively.

Developing an Annotated Bibliography

An annotated bibliography is a list of your sources — those read to date or
those credited in your final paper — that includes a short summary or an an-
notation for each source entry. Compiling an annotated bibliography is a
common assignment because it quickly informs a reader about the direction
and depth of your research. It also demonstrates your mastery of two major
college research skills: identifying a source and writing a summary. Sometimes you will hand in your annotated bibliography at intervals during the
research process to show how your investigation is proceeding. Often, the
final version will be due with your paper. An annotated bibliography also
may be assigned as a group project with each person preparing a section on
a subtopic or a portion of the entries.

When you develop an annotated bibliography, clarify two points from
the beginning. First, find out which format you are expected to use as you
identify the sources in your bibliography. Next, determine what your anno-
tation should do — summarize only, add evaluation, or meet a special

For more on the
MLA and APA formats,
see Ch. 34.

For more on summary, see p. 220, pp. 618–19, and pp. 669–70; for more on evaluation, see Ch. 11.

requirement (such as interpretation). A summary is a brief, neutral explanation in your own words of the thesis or main points covered in a source. In contrast, an evaluation is a judgment of the source, generally assessing its accuracy, reliability, or relevance to your research question. In all cases, your goal is to read critically and to convey clearly your understanding of the source.

Summary.   Alan Espenlaub prepared an annotated bibliography for his term paper, "Coming of Age under Sputnik: Teenage Male Anxiety and Uncertainty in 1958 America." The following example, in MLA style, briefly summarizes one of his sources.

Barson, Michael, and Stephen Heller. *Red Scared: The Commie Menace in Propaganda and Popular Culture*. San Francisco: Chronicle, 2001. Print.

Chapter 6 ("We Will Bury You!") documents the relationships among the post-WWII phase of the red scare in America, Sputnik's launch, the U.S. Vanguard missile failure, the space race, and popular-culture manifestations such as Cold War movies and board games that reflected the fears and anxieties of the time.

Summary with Evaluation.   As Stephanie Hawkins worked on the annotated bibliography for her APA-style paper "Japanese: Linguistic Diversity" for an independent study, she wanted to show her critical thinking about the topic. Besides briefly summarizing her sources, she also evaluated their contributions, relationships, or usefulness to her study.

Abe, H. N. (1995). From stereotype to context: The study of Japanese women's speech. *Feminist Studies 21*, 647–671. Retrieved September 27, 2006, from EB-SCOHost database.

Abe discusses the roots of Japanese women's language, beginning in ancient Japan and continuing into modern times. I was able to use this peer-reviewed source to expand on the format of women's language and the consequences of its use.

Kristof, N. (1995, September 24). On language: Too polite for words. *New York Times Magazine*, pp. SM22-SM23.

Kristof, a regular columnist for the *New York Times Magazine*, briefly describes the use of honorifics as an outlet for sarcasm and insults. Although the article discusses cultures other than Japanese, it provides insight into the polite vulgarity of the Japanese language.

Summary with Interpretation.   When Alan Espenlaub added a section on primary (original, not secondhand) sources to his annotated bibliography for "Coming of Age under Sputnik: Teenage Male Anxiety and Uncertainty in 1958 America," he included this summary and interpretation of a visual source.

The Edsel by Ford Motor Company. Advertisement. *Life* 28 Oct. 1957. Print.

> This double-page full-color advertisement shows a shopping-center parking lot full of shining new Edsel cars and happy shoppers. Palm trees in the background suggest that the southern California lifestyle goes along with the new Edsel lifestyle (1958 was the first year for the Edsel). In the center of the ad is a two-toned blue Edsel Citation two-door hardtop with a poodle in the front seat, even though the windows are rolled down. The ratio of male to female shoppers pictured at the center is one in ten. Many dyads appear to be mother and daughter. No boys are in the picture. Since the ad's target audience was most probably adult male providers, it is possible that including a teenage son in a picture of a new car would be a negative signal in the potential purchaser's mind. On the other hand, males would feel good about being able to provide a new car for "the little woman," Mrs. Consumer.

Chapter 30

Finding Sources in the Library, on the Internet, and in the Field

■ For more on managing your research project, see Ch. 28.

By now you have narrowed your research question, begun your research archive, and started your working bibliography. Consult your schedule so that you stay on track, and revise it if necessary. This chapter will help you continue your research by using efficient strategies for searching the library, the Internet, and the field for relevant material.

Searching the Online Library Catalog

Your college library is usually the best place to begin your search for reliable sources though you may do so from its computer terminals, your home, or your dorm room. Although much of the library's information is stored on printed pages, the way it has been for centuries, the tools for locating these pages and, increasingly, the information itself are taking electronic form. Today's researcher needs to navigate both the print and electronic worlds.

BECOMING A FLEXIBLE SEARCHER

From your library's home page, you can access a wide variety of resources — the online catalog, periodical databases, online reference material, guides to the Internet. The catalog itself provides information about the books, periodicals, videos, databases, and other materials available through the library. Typically, catalogs do not provide information about individual articles in periodicals. They do, however, provide you with the periodical's publication

Figure 30.1
Sample home page from the
Tuskegee University
Libraries

A. Overview of libraries and their purpose
B. Access to library holdings and resources
C. Information on specific campus libraries
D. Other research resources

information (title, date, publisher, and so on), call number, location, and in some cases availability.

Your library may also offer tours, online tutorials, or brochures explaining the library's organization and services. (See Figure 30.1 for a sample library home page.) Reference librarians are available to help you answer questions, from specifics such as "What is the GNP of Brazil?" to general queries such as "Where can I find out about the Brazilian economy?" Before you look for sources for your paper, it pays to do a little research on the library itself, starting with the following questions:

RESEARCH CHECKLIST

Investigating Your Library

___ Where can you find a Web site or pamphlet mapping locations of library holdings, describing library resources, and explaining services?

___ Where is the reference desk, and what hours is it open?

___ How do you access the library's catalog? Can you search it or other library databases from your home computer or the campus network?

___ Where are periodicals kept, and how are they arranged?

—— What kinds of indexes or computerized databases are available, and how can you access them? Where can you get advice about which ones to use for your project?

—— Can you use interlibrary loan to order material the library doesn't have?

—— How long is the check-out period for books? How do you request items, renew them, or use other circulation services?

For more about using your research question to identify keywords, see pp. 597–98.

Search Creatively.   When library catalogs were limited to printed file cards, they allowed searches only by author, title, or subject. Now, electronic catalogs may greatly expand these search options, as the following chart illustrates. Consult a librarian or follow the catalog prompts to find out which searches your library catalog allows. Try options that restrict a search

TYPE OF SEARCH	EXPLANATION	EXAMPLES	SEARCH TIPS
Keyword	Terms that identify topics discussed in the source, including works by or about an author, and may generate long lists of relevant and irrelevant sources	• workplace mental health • geriatric home health care • Creole cookbook • Jane Austen novels	Use a cluster of keywords to avoid broad terms (whale, nursing) or to reduce irrelevant topics using the same terms (people of color, color graphics)
Subject	Terms assigned by library catalogers, often following the *Library of Congress Subject Headings* (*LCSH*)	• motion pictures (not films) • developing countries (not third world) • cookery (not cookbooks)	Consult the *LCSH,* a set of large red books often shelved near the catalog terminals, to find the exact phrasing used
Author	Name of individual, organization, or group, leading to list of print (and possibly online) works by author	• Hawthorne, Nathaniel • Colorado School of Mines • North Atlantic Treaty Organization	Begin as directed with an individual's last name or first; for a group, first use a keyword search to identify its exact name
Title	Name of book, pamphlet, journal, magazine, newspaper, video, CD, or other material	• *Peace and Conflict Studies* • *Los Angeles Times* • *Nursing Outlook*	Look for a separate search option for titles of periodicals (journals, newspapers, magazines)
Identification Numbers	Library or consortium call numbers, publisher or government publication numbers	• MJ BASI, local call number for recordings by Count Basie	Use the call number of a useful source to find related items shelved nearby
Dates	Publication or other dates used to search (or limit searches) for current or historical materials	• Elizabeth 1558 (when she became queen of England) • science teaching 2008	Add dates to keyword or other searches to limit the topics or time of publication

by date, location, type of material, or other characteristics. Once you locate a relevant item, check its detailed record for alternative search terms that may help focus your search more productively.

Sort Your Search Results.   When your search produces a list of possible sources, click on the most promising individual items to learn more about them. See Figure 30.2 for a sample keyword search and Figure 30.3 for the sample online record for one source. In addition to the call number or shelf location, the record will identify the author, title, place of publication, and date. Often it will describe what the book contains, how long it is, and which subject headings define its scope. Though each library presents information slightly differently, the elements generally are the same. Use these clues to help you select and evaluate your options wisely.

Consult Catalogs at Other Libraries.   Most college and university library catalogs are available over the Internet or through regional, state, or other consolidated catalogs. Use these catalogs to find books or other materials that you can borrow through interlibrary loan or by visiting a nearby library. If you're not sure how to access such catalogs ask a librarian. You may be able to connect directly to them via the Internet or through your own library's catalog.

■ To practice using keywords, visit the Bedford Research Room Web site at <bedfordstmartins.com/ researchroom>.

▨ For more on evaluating sources, see Ch. 31.

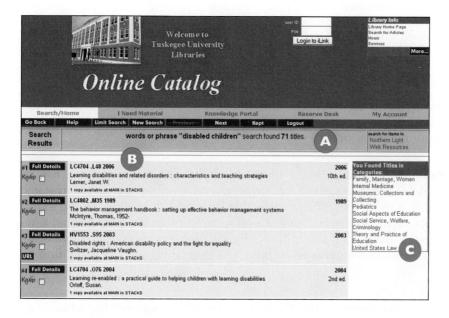

Figure 30.2
General results of a keyword search on "disabled children" using an online library catalog

A. Number of search results
B. Results screen (linked to full entries) with call numbers, titles, authors, and availability
C. Topic areas where results found

Figure 30.3
Specific record selected
from keyword search
results

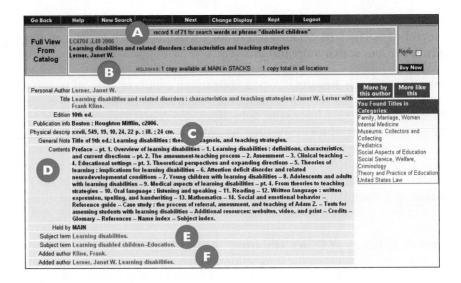

A. Call number, title, and author

B. Availability and location

C. Number of pages, illustrations, and height of book

D. Contents by part and chapter

E. Alternate subject heading (often hyperlinked)

F. Additional author

LOOKING FOR RESOURCES GROUPED BY FIELD

Some researchers investigate current popular topics, such as social or environmental issues. Others investigate questions of concern to a specific academic discipline or field.

Sample the Field.   Many libraries supply electronic or printed lists of available resources that are well-regarded starting points for research within a field. These lists are valuable shortcuts for quickly finding a cluster of useful resources. The chart on page 630 supplies only a small sampling of the specialized indexes, dictionaries, encyclopedias, handbooks, yearbooks, and other types of print and electronic resources you'll find on such lists.

Browse for Items on the Shelves.   A book's call number, like a building's address, tells where the book "resides." This number is carefully chosen so that books on the same subject end up as neighbors on the shelves. College libraries generally use the classification system devised by the Library of Congress. Its call letters and numbers direct you to items grouped by subject

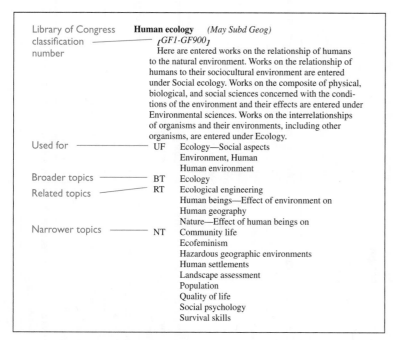

Figure 30.4
Entries from the Library of Congress
Subject Headings

(See Figure 30.4.) Other libraries use the older and more familiar Dewey decimal system, which assigns items to large categories by number. In either case, reserve some of your research time for browsing because you will almost certainly find interesting materials on the shelf next to the ones you found through the catalog. The two common classification systems are outlined here. Both have added newer fields, such as computer science, mass communications, and environmental studies, to related areas.

LIBRARY OF CONGRESS CLASSIFICATION SYSTEM

A   General Works
B   Philosophy, Psychology, Religion
C   Auxiliary Sciences of History
D   History: General and Old World
E   History: America
F   History: America
G   Geography, Anthropology, Recreation
H   Social Sciences
J   Political Science
K   Law
L   Education
M   Music and Books on Music
N   Fine Arts
P   Language and Literature
Q   Science
R   Medicine
S   Agriculture
T   Technology
U   Military Science
V   Naval Science
Z   Library Science

DEWEY DECIMAL CLASSIFICATION SYSTEM

000–009   General Works
100–199   Philosophy
200–299   Religion
300–399   Social Sciences, Government, Customs
400–499   Language
500–599   Natural Sciences
600–699   Applied Sciences
700–799   Fine and Decorative Arts
800–899   Literature
900–999   History, Travel, Biography

Field	SPECIALIZED INDEXES	REFERENCE WORKS	GOVERNMENT RESOURCES	INTERNET RESOURCES
HUMANITIES	Essay and General Literature Index	The Humanities: A Selective Guide to Information Sources	EDSITEment at <edsitement.neh.gov>	Voice of the Shuttle at <vos.ucsb.edu>
FILM AND THEATER	Film Literature Index	McGraw-Hill Encyclopedia of World Drama	Smithsonian: Film, Theater and TV at <www.si.edu/art_and_design/film_theater_and_tv/>	Theatre History Sites on the WWW at <www.win.net/kudzu/history.html>
HISTORY	Historical Abstracts	Dictionary of Concepts in History	The Library of Congress: American Memory at <memory.loc.gov/ammem/index.html>	WWW Virtual Library: History Central Catalogue at <www.vlib.iue.it/history/index.html>
LITERATURE	MLA International Bibliography	Encyclopedia of the Novel	National Endowment for the Humanities at <www.neh.gov>	American Studies Crossroads at <www.georgetown.edu/crossroads/asw/>
SOCIAL SCIENCES	Social Sciences Citation Index	International Encyclopedia of the Social and Behavioral Sciences	Fedstats at <www.fedstats.gov>	Intute: Social Sciences at <www.intute.ac.uk/socialsciences/>
EDUCATION	Education Index	International Encyclopedia of Education	National Center for Education Statistics at <nces.ed.gov>	ERIC: Education Resources Information Center at <eric.ed.gov>
POLITICAL SCIENCE	ABC Pol Sci: Bibliography of Current Contents: Political Science and Government	State Legislative Sourcebook: A Resource Guide to Legislative Information in the 50 States	Fedworld at <www.fedworld.gov/>	Political Resources on the Net at <www.politicalresources.net> National Security Archive at <www.gwu.edu/~nsarchiv>
WOMEN'S STUDIES	Women's Studies Abstracts	Women in World History: A Biographical Encyclopedia	U.S. Department of Labor Women's Bureau at <www.dol.gov/wb/welcome.html>	Institute for Women's Policy Research at <www.iwpr.org>
SCIENCE AND TECHNOLOGY	General Science Index	McGraw-Hill Encyclopedia of Science and Technology	National Science Foundation at <www.nsf.gov>	EurekAlert! at <www.eurekalert.org>
EARTH SCIENCES	Bibliography and Index of Geology	Facts on File Dictionary of Earth Science	USGS (U.S. Geological Survey): Science for a Changing World at <www.usgs.gov>	Center for International Earth Science Information Network at <www.ciesin.org>
ENVIRONMENTAL STUDIES	Environmental Abstracts	Encyclopedia of Environmental Science	EPA: U.S. Environmental Protection Agency at <www.epa.gov>	EnviroLink at <envirolink.org>
LIFE SCIENCES	Biological Abstracts	Encyclopedia of Human Biology	National Agricultural Library at <www.nal.usda.gov>	Health Web at <healthweb.org>

Searching Databases: Periodical Indexes and Bibliographies

Information on current topics often appears first in periodicals rather than books. Periodicals are journals, magazines, newspapers, and other publications issued daily, weekly, monthly, quarterly, or at other regular intervals. Many indexes — guides to material published within other works — exist to help you locate articles in periodicals. Bibliographies — lists of sources on a particular topic — also can lead you to relevant materials, often those you would never think to trace in a catalog.

For more on timeliness and other characteristics of periodicals and other sources, see the charts on pp. 658–61 and in B2 in the Quick Research Guide (the dark-red-edged pages).

If you have questions about which database to use or how to access it, ask a reference or subject-area librarian. Many library indexes and databases are not available free to the general public; your library selects these resources and subscribes to them so that you — and other campus researchers — can find the most current and reliable sources as quickly and easily as possible. Academic librarians, often expert research advisors, are specially trained to help you search efficiently in the most appropriate databases. They are available in person, generally at the reference desk, and often by e-mail, telephone, appointment, or live chat online.

To practice using databases, visit the Bedford Research Room Web site at <bedfordstmartins/researchroom.com>.

USING PERIODICAL INDEXES

In a periodical index, you'll find every article — listed by author, title, and subject — for the periodicals and time period covered by the index. The index also includes the source information you'll need to find each article in the library, usually the periodical title, date, volume or issue number, and page numbers.

Electronic indexes — often called periodical databases — are organized as a series of records or entries for an item, such as a newspaper or journal article. You can easily search for these records using author, title, subject, or keyword. Electronic indexes may include more information on each article than print indexes do, such as a short summary or abstract or even the full text of the article, which you can print or download for later use. Electronic indexes may complement, replace, or duplicate print indexes though some indexes are available in both forms.

Each periodical index includes entries only for its specific collection of periodicals, so finding the right article is largely a matter of finding the right index. Before you use a periodical index, ask these questions:

RESEARCH CHECKLIST

Finding the Right Index

___ Is your subject covered in this index? Does the index cover a broad field or a very specific subject in depth?

___ Does the index cover the period you're interested in? If the index is electronic, how far back does it go? How often is it updated?

___ Does the index cover scholarly journals written for an expert audience or popular magazines for a more general audience?

___ Does the index simply identify an article, add a summary or abstract, or supply a link to its full text?

___ Is the index an online subscription service available to students on a library terminal, campus network, or home computer? Is it a public index available on the Web and conveniently linked from the library's Web site?

___ Are older print or CD-ROM indexes, sometimes needed for historical research, available in the reference area or elsewhere in the library?

■ For more on types and characteristics of periodicals, see the charts on pp. 658–61 and B2 in the Quick Research Guide (the dark-red-edged pages).

General Indexes. Several indexes can help you if you're looking for magazine or newspaper articles addressed to the general population.

The *Readers' Guide to Periodical Literature* started publication in 1900, so you can use the current or retrospective indexes to locate popular press coverage of events at any time in the twentieth century or later — for example, articles published days after the bombing of Pearl Harbor in December 1941.

The *New York Times Index,* dating back to 1851, can help you track down that newspaper's current or historical coverage of events.

Academic Search Premier and *InfoTrac* include the full text of many articles written for a fairly general audience. (See Figure 30.5 for a sample entry.)

America's Newspapers (NewsBank), with daily updates, indexes over seven hundred local U.S. papers.

Lexis-Nexis Academic carries mainly full-text articles from newspapers, wire services, and other general-interest publications.

Figure 30.5
Search result from
InfoTrac *index*

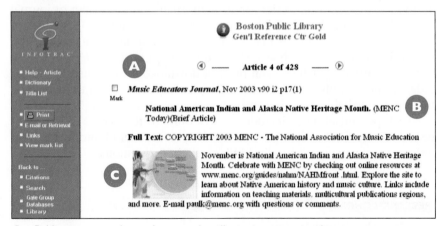

A. Publication name, date, volume number, illustrations, page number, total pages in article

B. Article title (and author, if available)

C. Text of short article

Specialized Indexes.   Discipline-specific indexes are more likely to analyze scholarly journals with peer-reviewed articles that have been critiqued
by other experts before being accepted for publication. Such articles are
aimed at a more specialized audience and provide more analysis than articles
in popular magazines. If you are looking for literary criticism, research on
social issues, or scientific or medical research only summarized or reported in
the popular press, turn to indexes such as these:

Humanities Index or *Humanities Abstracts*

Social Sciences Index or *Social Sciences Abstracts*

Business Periodicals Index

PAIS International (an index focusing on public affairs)

Follow your library's advice, and ask these questions as you use periodical indexes.

RESEARCH CHECKLIST

Selecting Sources from a Periodical Index

____ What does the title of the periodical suggest about its audience, interest
area, and popular or scholarly orientation? How likely are the articles in
that periodical to supply what you need to find?

____ Does the title or description of the article suggest that it will answer your research question? Or does the entry sound intriguing but irrelevant?

____ Does the date of the article fit your need for current, contemporary, eyewitness, or classic material?

____ Does the length of the article suggest that it is a short review, a concise
overview of a topic, or an exhaustive discussion? How much detail will you
need about its topic?

____ Is the periodical containing the article likely to be available on your library's
shelves, in its microform files, or among its online resources?

FINDING BIBLIOGRAPHIES

When you use a bibliography — a list of sources on a specific subject — you
take advantage of the research others have already done. Every time you find
a good book or article, look at the sources the author draws on; some of
these may be useful to you, too. Look for a section at the back of a book labeled "Bibliography" or perhaps "For Further Reading." If the author has
quoted or referred to other works, look for a list called "References" or
"Works Cited" at the end of the work. If the book or article uses footnotes or
endnotes, check those, too, for possible leads.

Sometimes you may locate a book-length bibliography on your subject,
compiled by a researcher and published so that other researchers (including

you) won't have to duplicate the work. Bibliographies cite a wide variety of materials—books, articles, and also films, manuscripts, letters, government documents, and pamphlets—and they can lead you to sources that you wouldn't otherwise find.

■ For more on keyword searches, see pp. 597–98 and pp. 626–27.

For example, *The Essential Shakespeare: An Annotated Bibliography of Major Modern Studies* lists the best books and articles published on each of Shakespeare's works, a wonderful shortcut when you're looking for worthwhile criticism. If you're lucky, adding the word *bibliography* to a subject or keyword search will turn up a list of sources with annotations that describe and evaluate each one.

Before turning to the wealth of other library and Web resources available, use the checklist below to assess where you are in your project. If you have a clear idea of what's left to accomplish, you will find it easier to stick to your research schedule and, in the final stage, to write your paper.

RESEARCH CHECKLIST

Managing Your Project

■ For downloadable sample schedules (and research checklists), visit <bedfordstmartins.com/bedguide> and do a keyword search:

schedules

___ Are you on schedule? Do you need to adjust your timetable to give yourself more or less time for any of the stages?

___ Are you using your research question to stay on track and avoid digressions?

___ Are you keeping your materials up-to-date—listing new sources in your working bibliography and labeling and storing new material in your archives?

___ Do you have a clear idea of where you are in the research process?

Using Other Library Resources

Many other library resources are available to you beyond what you can access from your library's home page. One of the most overlooked resources is library staff. Besides knowing the library better than anyone else, librarians are constantly working with its catalog, reference books, databases, and new additions to the collections. If you need help locating or using materials, consult a librarian.

CONSULTING REFERENCE MATERIALS

Because the library contains an amazing array of reference material, spending time in the library can save you hours and effort in the long run. Remember, the library and all of its resources—whether electronic or print—are specifically designed to help researchers like you to find information quickly and efficiently. Here you can familiarize yourself with a topic or fine-tune your research by filling in detailed definitions, dates, statistics, or facts.

General Encyclopedias.   These multivolume references, such as the *New Encyclopaedia Britannica* and *Encyclopedia Americana,* may be especially valuable when you first take an overview of a topic. Although they also can supply a missing fact here or there, they will serve you best by preparing you to move to specialized resources.

Specialized Encyclopedias.   These references cover a field in much greater depth than general encyclopedias do, as these sample titles suggest:

> *Dictionary of American History*
> *Encyclopedia of Human Biology*
> *Encyclopedia of Psychology*
> *Encyclopedia of Sociology*
> *Encyclopedia of World Cultures*
> *The Gale Encyclopedia of Science*
> *New Grove Dictionary of Music and Musicians*

Dictionaries.   Large and specialized dictionaries cover foreign languages, abbreviations, and slang as well as the terminology of a particular field as in *Black's Law Dictionary, Stedman's Medical Dictionary,* or the *Oxford Dictionary of Natural History.* Unabridged dictionaries, often available on dictionary stands, explain what the most obscure words mean as well as how they are pronounced.

Handbooks and Companions.   These concise surveys of terms and topics relating to a specific subject feature articles longer than dictionary entries but more concise than those in encyclopedias. Check with a reference librarian to see if specialized handbooks, such as the following, are available for your topic.

> *Blackwell Encyclopaedia of Political Thought*
> *Bloomsbury Guide to Women's Literature*
> *Dictionary of the Vietnam War*
> *Oxford Companion to English Literature*

Statistical Sources.   If numbers are a key type of evidence for your research, you can find sources for statistics in the library and on the Web.

- The *Statistical Abstract of the United States.* Perhaps the most useful single compilation of statistics, this resource contains hundreds of tables relating to population, social issues, economics, and so on.

- *Gallup Poll.* Good resources for public-opinion statistics, the surveys conducted by the Gallup Organization are published in annual volumes, in a monthly magazine, and on the Web.

- *<www.census.gov>.* The federal government collects an extraordinary amount of statistical data and releases much of it on the Web. Check also <www.fedworld.gov> and <www.fedstats.gov> for lists of other government statistics available on the Web.

Atlases.   If your research has a geographical angle, maps and atlases may be useful. Besides atlases of countries, regions, and the world, others cover history, natural resources, ethnic groups, and many other special topics.

Biographical Sources.   Useful directories list basic information — degrees, work history, honors, addresses — for prominent people. You can use tools such as *Biography Index* and the *Biography and Genealogy Master Index* to locate resources such as these:

> *American Men and Women of Science*
>
> *The Dictionary of American Biography*
>
> *The Dictionary of National Biography*
>
> *Who's Who in Politics*
>
> *Who's Who in the United States*

LOCATING SPECIAL MATERIALS

Your library is likely to have other collections of materials, especially on regional or specialized topics, but you may need to ask what's available.

Periodicals on Microform.   This technology puts a large amount of printed material — for example, two weeks of the *New York Times* — on a durable roll of film (microfilm) that fits into a small box or on a set of plastic sheets the size of index cards (microfiche). The machines used to read microforms often print out full-sized copies of pages.

Primary Materials on Microform.   Many libraries also have primary, or firsthand, material in microform. For example, the *American Culture Series* reproduces books and pamphlets (1493 to 1875) along with a good subject index, making it possible to view colonial religious tracts or nineteenth-century abolitionist pamphlets without traveling to a museum or rare books collection. The *American Women's Diaries* collection provides firsthand glimpses of the past through the words of New England and Southern women who traveled west as pioneers.

Primary Materials in Digitized Format.   Firsthand materials such as diaries, letters, speeches, and interviews are increasingly available in digitized databases that can be searched using keywords, authors, titles, or other means. Examples include *Black Thought and Culture, Oral History Online,* and *North American Immigrant Letters, Diaries, and Oral Histories* (1840 on).

Resources from Organizations.   Your library may collect pamphlets and reports distributed by companies, trade groups, or professional organizations. The *Encyclopedia of Associations,* organized by subject or group name, or the *United States Government Manual,* listing government agencies, can lead you to useful materials and contacts, especially for field research.

Government Documents.   The U.S. government is the most prolific publisher in the world and, in an effort to make information accessible to all citizens, makes an increasing number of documents available on the Web along with indexes like these:

- *Monthly Catalog of United States Government Publications,* which is the most complete index to federal documents available
- *CIS Index,* which specializes in congressional documents and includes a handy legislative history index
- *Congressional Record Index,* which indexes reports on what happens in Congress each day

Besides congressional hearings, presidential papers, and reports from federal agencies, the government has published something on practically any topic you can think of, as the following sampling suggests:

The Annual Homeless Assessment Report to Congress

Ozone Depletion, the Greenhouse Effect, and Climate Change

Small Business and the International Economy

Violence on Television

If you plan to use government documents, reports, or statistics in your research, don't be shy about asking a librarian for help. The documents can be difficult to locate both on the shelves and on the Web.

Using the Internet for Research

The Internet contains an enormous and ever-growing number of resources that vary greatly in quality and purpose. For example, a quick search for information about Yellowstone National Park turns up nearly anything you might want to find: contacts for cabin reservations, photographs of family trips, the Greater Yellowstone Coalition's spirited defense of the park's ecosystem, scientific studies of regrowth following the 1988 fire, the Old Faithful Webcam, and technical reports such as the official Yellowstone

Wildland Fire Management Plan. Unfortunately, because of the sheer bulk of this information, searching for relevant materials can be both too easy and too difficult. Finding information that is actually useful can be time consuming, but understanding a few basic principles can help a great deal.

FINDING RECOMMENDED INTERNET RESOURCES

For a checklist for finding recommended sources, see B1 in the Quick Research Guide (the dark-red-edged pages).

For more on evaluating sources, see Ch. 31.

Instead of beginning your Web research with a few keywords and your favorite search engine, go first to online resources recommended by your instructor, department, library, or other reliable source. Their well-chosen site recommendations save the time required to search and screen randomly chosen sites. More important, they can take you directly to respected resources prepared by experts (scholars or librarians), directed to academic researchers (like you), and used successfully by others on campus.

How can you locate recommended sources appropriate for your research question? Browse to find collections of links to resources such as these on your library or other campus Web site:

See the list of search sites on p. 642. See also the Online Reference Sites and other examples in the charts on p. 630, pp. 658–61, and in B2 in the Quick Research Guide (the dark-red-edged pages).

- Self-help guides or Internet databases organized by area (social sciences or business), topic (literary analysis), or type of information, such as the extensive Auraria Library *Statistics and Facts* guide at <http://library.auraria.edu/guides/subject/statistics/statistics.html>.

- Research Web sites sponsored by another library, academic institution, or consortium such as the Internet Public Library at <www.ipl.org>, the Librarians' Internet Index at <http://lii.org>, or the Michigan eLibrary at <http://mel.org>.

- Other research centers or major libraries with their own collections of links, such as the Library of Congress page "Newspaper & Current Periodical Reading Room" at <http://www.loc.gov/rr/news/lists.html>.

- Specialty search engines for government materials — <www.fedworld.gov>, <www.usa.gov>, or <www.google.com/ig/usgov> — along with advice about using them such as that on the California State University Northridge Web site at <http://library.csun.edu/Find_Resources/Government_Publications/index.html>.

- Specialty search engines for specific materials such as images at <www.ditto.com>.

- Collections of online sources such as those for the humanities at the Electronic Text Center at <http://etext.lib.virginia.edu>.

- Collections of e-books, including reference books and literary texts now out of copyright, such as *Bartleby.com* at <www.bartleby.com/> and *Project Gutenberg* at <www.gutenberg.org/>.

- Web databases with "unrestricted access" (not online subscription services restricted to campus users) as varied as the country-by-country data of *InfoNation* at <www.un.org/Pubs/CyberSchoolBus/res.html> and the extensive health resources of *MedlinePlus (Pub Med)* at <medlineplus.gov>.

- Community resources or organizations, often useful for local research and service learning reports.

SELECTING SEARCH ENGINES

Unlike a library, the Internet has no handy, systematic catalog. Search engines bring the vast resources of the Internet to your computer screen, but they are not unbiased, objective searchers. Each has its own system of locating material, categorizing it, and establishing the sequence for reporting results. One search site, patterned on a library catalog or index, might be selective, designed to advance the investigations of students, faculty, and professionals. Another might carry extensive advertising but separate it from search results, while a third organizes search results so that the sites that pay advertising fees ("sponsors") pop up first in the list, even though sites listed on later pages might better match the searcher's needs. Take a close look at the practices of your favorite search engine (which may be described on an "About" page), and consider trying some others to find those that most efficiently supply the reliable sources you need.

CONDUCTING ADVANCED ELECTRONIC SEARCHES

Search engines contain millions of records on Web sites, much as a database or library catalog contains records on books, periodicals, or other materials found in a library. Generally, search engines can be searched by broad categories such as *education* or *health* or by more specific keywords.

When you limit your search simply to keywords and broad categories, however, you may be overwhelmed with information not directly related to your research question. For example, Figure 30.6 illustrates a keyword search for sources on *foster care* on Google that produced more than 17 million entries. A keyword search may be ideal if you search for a highly specialized term or topic, such as training for distance runners. For a more general topic — such as *foster care* — you may turn up seemingly endless lists of results.

For more on keywords see pp. 597–98 and pp. 626–27.

Several techniques are available for more sophisticated searches of the Web, databases, and library catalogs. Some of these techniques can expand your search, but most researchers want to limit their searches in order to find more results relevant to their research. As Figure 30.7 shows, an advanced search produced fewer sources on one aspect of foster care — placing teenagers in foster care.

Use Wildcards.   Wildcards are symbols that tell the search engine to look for all possible endings to a word. For instance, if you search for the keyword *runner*, you'll get every entry containing that word but not entries containing

Figure 30.6
Results of a keyword
search for foster care
using Google, reporting
more than 17 million
entries

A. Search terms

B. Total number of entries located

C. Highlighted search terms found in entries

only *run, runs,* or *running.* Using a wildcard symbol such as run*, you can search for all words that begin with *run,* thus increasing the range of your results. The most common wildcard symbols are an asterisk (*) for multiple letters, numbers, or symbols and a question mark (?) for single characters. Check your search engine's symbols by clicking on search tips.

Combine Terms in Boolean Searches.   A Boolean search, named after the nineteenth-century mathematician George Boole, lets you specify the relationships between your keywords and phrases. Common Boolean search terms include *AND* (all terms must appear in a result), *OR* (one or more of the terms must appear), and *NOT* (one or more terms can appear, but another must not).

Search for: history AND California

Result: all entries containing both *history* and *California*

Search for: history OR California
Result: all entries containing *history* or *California* or both

Search for: history NOT California
Result: all entries containing *history* but not containing *California*

Figure 30.7
Advanced search results on
foster care + placing
teenagers *using Google,*
reporting 47 entries

A. Search terms
B. Total number of entries located
C. Highlighted search terms found in entries

Search for: history AND California NOT Los Angeles
Result: all entries containing *history* and *California* but not those containing *Los Angeles*

Select Limitations for Advanced Searches.   Many search engines will automatically combine terms for Boolean searches when you select the advanced search option. Google and Metacrawler, for example, allow you to limit searches to all, exactly, any, or none of the words you enter. Look for directions for limitations such as these:

- A phrase such as *elementary school safety,* requested as a unit (exactly these words) or enclosed in quotation marks to mark it as a unit

- A specific language (human or computer) such as English or Spanish

- A specific format or type of software such as a PDF file

- A date range (before, after, or between dates for creation, revision, or indexing)

- A domain such as .edu (educational institution), .gov (government), .org (organization), or .com (commercial site or company), which indicates the type of group sponsoring the site

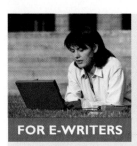

FOR E-WRITERS

Leading Internet Search Sites

The best search site is the one you learn to use well. In addition to following general search strategies, you should note each site's Search tips and Help instructions.

If you are uncertain about your topic, use a directory site like Web Crawler, at <www.webcrawler.com>, that begins searches with categories. Next, think of searching like a zoom lens. If you zoom into "no results" or "no pages found," then you can step back and add more information until you start to focus on sites you want to explore. By tinkering with your words, you can improve your searches and locate Web pages with titles and ideas closer to your research goals. This process is much easier than starting with a general prompt and finding thousands of potential sites.

SUBJECT CATALOGS, DIRECTORIES, AND GUIDES

Ask.com <www.ask.com>
Digital Librarian (Margaret Vail Anderson)
Encyclopaedia Britannica Online
Google Directory (Open Directory Project)
        <http://directory.google.com/>
Infomine: Scholarly Internet Resource Collections
        <http://infomine.ucr.edu>
Librarians' Internet Index <http://lii.org/>
Michigan ELibrary <http://mel.org/>
UC Berkeley electronic resources database
        <www.lib.berkeley.edu/find/types/electronic_resources.html>
Web Crawler <www.webcrawler.com>
Yahoo!

INDEXES WITH CONTENT GATHERED BY COMPUTER "SPIDERS" OR "ROBOTS"

AlltheWeb <www.alltheweb.com>
Alta Vista
Google
Google Scholar <http://scholar.google.com>

SITES THAT SEARCH MULTIPLE INDEXES AT ONE TIME

Dogpile
Ixquick
Metacrawler
MetaEureka
Search.com
SurfWax

- A part of the world, such as North America or Africa
- The location (such as the title, the URL, or the text) of the search term
- The audio or visual media enhancements
- The file size

FINDING SPECIALIZED ONLINE MATERIALS

You can locate a variety of material online, ranging from e-zines (electronic magazines) to conversations among people interested in your topic.

Look for Electronic Publications.   Wide public access to the Internet has given individuals and small interest groups an economical publication option. Although such texts must be used cautiously, you can locate a wide range through the Etext Archives at <www.etext.org/index.shtml>.

Browse the Blogs.   Globe of Blogs at <www.globeofblogs.com> indexes many blogs (short for Web logs), providing access to the personal, political, and topical observations and commentaries of individuals around the globe. Google features blog searches by topic at <blogsearch.google.com>. Given the rapid growth of blogs, you may want to use RSS (often expanded as "Real Simple Syndication") software to alert you to breaking news or to sample wide-ranging commentary on a current topic. Introductory versions of these feeds are available free at sites such as <newsgator.com> or <bloglines.com> (sponsored by Ask.com).

Keep Up with the News.   Try sites such as <http://news.google.com> for easy access to current national or international coverage of major stories by thousands of newspapers or news services. Click on "Personalize this page" if you want to rearrange the page to suit your interests, track a topic during the preceding month, or focus on a specific country or news source. RSS feeds are available for news as well as specialized topics, such as historical events on the current date from *Encyclopaedia Britannica Online,* as illustrated on the "On This Day" page at <http://newsletters.britannica.com/onthisday/otd_sample.html>.

Search Newsgroups and Mailing Lists.   Newsgroups and mailing lists, among the oldest forms of Internet communication, generate an enormous amount of text each day. Both types of exchange support the discussion of topics such as adult education or immigration among people with a shared interest. If you're working on a current issue, the archives of such groups will require cautious reading but may supply detailed analyses by interested members of the public or acknowledged experts. Google (at <groups.google.com>) allows you to search for mailing lists and newsgroups.

Find Chat Transcripts.   Major news organizations, such as ABC News, use chat to interview public figures or industry leaders in advertised sessions attended by hundreds or even thousands of participants. You can view transcripts of these sessions by visiting <http://abcnews.go.com> and searching under "chat." Similarly, major search sites, such as Yahoo!, host regular chat sessions on topics including entertainment and finance. Yahoo! also provides transcripts of past sessions.

Finding Sources in the Field

The goal of field research is the same as that of library and Internet research—to gather the information you need to answer your research question and then to marshal persuasive evidence to support your conclusions in your research paper. The only difference is where you conduct the research. Many rich, unprinted sources lie beyond the library and the Internet, providing opportunities to explore matters that few researchers have investigated.

When you interview, observe, or ask questions of people, you generate your own firsthand (or primary) evidence. Almost any paper will be enriched by authentic and persuasive field sources, and you'll almost certainly learn more about your topic by going into the field. In this section, we focus on field research techniques that have proven most useful for college students. Before you begin, however, be sure to find out from your instructor whether you need institutional approval for research involving other people ("human subjects approval").

INTERVIEWING

For more on preparing for an interview, see pp. 96–97.

Interviews — conversations with a purpose — may prove to be your main source of field material. Choose your interview subjects carefully, whenever possible interviewing an expert in the field or, if you are researching a group of people, someone representative or typical. Regardless of your interview subject, preparation is central to a good interview.

TIPS FOR INTERVIEWING
- Be sure your prospect is willing to be quoted in writing.
- Make an appointment for a day when the person will have enough time — an hour if possible — to have a thorough talk with you.
- Arrive promptly, with carefully thought-out questions to ask.
- Come ready to take notes. If you also want to tape-record the interview, ask permission of the interviewee.
- Really listen. Let the person open up.

- Be flexible, and allow the interview to move in unanticipated directions.

- If a question draws no response, don't persist; go on to the next one.

- At the end of the interview, thank your interviewee, and arrange for an opportunity to clarify comments and confirm direct quotations.

- Make additional notes right after the interview to preserve anything you didn't have time to record during the interview.

Take notes even if you use a tape recorder so that you can remember the interview accurately, distill its most important points, and reconstruct it in your paper. Besides recording key points and quotations, you should note any telling details that might prove useful later — the interviewee's appearance, the setting, the mood, any notable gestures.

For more on recording an interview, see pp. 97–98.

If you can't talk to an expert in person, your next best resource may be a telephone interview. Make a phone appointment for a time convenient for both you and your interviewee. A busy person may not be able to give you a half hour of conversation on the spur of a moment, and it is polite to ask for a time when you may call again. Have written questions in hand before you dial so you don't waste the person's time (and yours). Take notes.

Federal regulations, by the way, forbid recording a phone interview without notifying the person talking that you are recording his or her remarks.

OBSERVING

An observation may provide essential information about a setting such as a business or a school. If so, you will need to make an appointment and, as soon as you arrive, identify yourself and your purpose. Some receptionists will insist on identification. You might ask your instructor for a statement on college letterhead declaring that you are a bona fide student doing field research. Follow-up trips may be needed if you find gaps in your research or need to test new ideas by further observation.

For more on observing, see Ch. 5.

TIPS FOR OBSERVING

- Establish a clear purpose — exactly what you want to observe and why.

- Take notes so that you don't forget important details when you review your findings and incorporate them into your paper.

- Record facts, telling details, and sensory impressions. Notice the features of the place, the actions or relationships of the people who are there, or whatever relates to the purpose of your observation.

- Consider using a still or video camera if you have equipment available and can operate it without being distracted from the scene you are observing. Photographs can illustrate your paper and help you interpret your observations or remember details while you write. If you are in a private place, be sure to get written permission from the owner (or other authority) and from any people you film or photograph.

- Pause, look around the setting, and check over your notes before you leave the observation site. Fill in any missing details, and confirm that your notes accurately record what you have actually observed — even if it surprised you — rather than what you'd hoped or expected to see.

- Thank the person who has arranged or approved your observation so that you will be welcome again if you need to return.

USING QUESTIONNAIRES

Questionnaires are widely used to gather the responses of a number of people to a fixed set of questions. For example, a marketing department might want to find out how readers react to a magazine's new features, partisans of a ballot issue might wonder how women are likely to vote, and workplace experts might wish to learn how many applicants for jobs in a particular sector are likely to hold a college degree. To answer such questions, professional researchers may carefully design their questions and randomly select representative people to respond to them in order to reach reliable answers.

Because your survey will not be as extensive as a professional one, you should avoid generalizing about your findings as if they were unimpeachable facts. It's one thing to say that "many of the students" who filled out a questionnaire on reading habits hadn't read a newspaper in the past month; it's another to claim that this is true of 72 percent of the students at your school — especially when you gave questionnaires only to those who ate in the dining hall the day you were there and most of them just threw their forms into the trash.

A far more reliable way for you to use questionnaires is to treat them as group interviews: assume that the information you collect represents typical views, use it to build your overall knowledge of the subject, and cull the responses for interesting or persuasive details or quotations. Use a questionnaire when you want to concentrate on what a group thinks as a whole rather than on what a particular individual has to say or when you find an interview that would cover all your questions impractical. (See Figure 30.8 for an example of a student questionnaire.)

TIPS FOR USING A QUESTIONNAIRE

- Ask yourself what you want to discover with your questionnaire. Then thoughtfully invent questions to fulfill that purpose.

- State your questions clearly, and supply simple directions for easy responses. Test your questionnaire on classmates or friends before you distribute it to the group you want to study.

- Ask questions that call for checking alternative answers, marking yes or no, circling a number on a five-point scale, or writing a few words so that responses are easy to tally. Try to ask for just one piece of information per question.

Figure 30.8   *Questionnaire asking college students about Internet use*

QUESTIONNAIRE

Thank you for completing this questionnaire. All information you supply will be kept strictly confidential.

1. What is your age? _____
2. What is your class?
   _____ First year   _____ Junior
   _____ Sophomore   _____ Senior
3. How old were you when you first began using the Internet? _____
4. How do you currently access the Internet? Indicate which of the following statements is true for you.
   _____ With my own computer   _____ With computers at the library or campus lab
   _____ Someone I live with has a computer   _____ I never use a computer
         with Internet access
   _____ Other (please specify): _____
5. Approximately how many hours a week do you use the Internet? _____
6. What is your primary reason for using the Internet?
   _____ Personal   _____ School-related   _____ Work-related
7. Check all of the ways in which you use the Internet.
   _____ E-mailing
   _____ Recreational Web surfing
   _____ Recreational media use (listening to music, watching videos, playing games)
   _____ Conducting optional research for a class
   _____ Conducting mandatory research for a class
   _____ Conducting personal research (such as planning travel, evaluating
         products, or searching for a job)
   _____ Managing financial accounts
   _____ Visiting chat rooms
   _____ Posting résumés or job applications
   _____ Designing or posting Web sites
   Other: _____
8. For which of the activities above do you use the Internet most? _____
   _____
9. On a scale of 1 to 5, rate how comfortable you are using the Internet.
   (not very comfortable) 1 2 3 4 5 (very comfortable)
10. Do you feel that you could benefit from further instruction in using the Internet?
    _____ Yes   _____ No   _____ Maybe

- If you wish to consider differences based on age, gender, or other variables, include some demographic questions.

- Write unbiased questions that will solicit factual responses. Do not ask, "How religious are you?" Instead ask, "What is your religious affiliation?" and "How often do you attend religious services?" Based on responses to the last two questions, you could report actual numbers and draw logical inferences about the respondents.

- When appropriate, ask open-ended questions that call for short written responses. Although these will be difficult to tally and fewer people are likely to respond, the answers may supply worthwhile quotations or suggest important issues or factors when you mull over the findings.

- If possible, distribute your questionnaires at a set location or event, and collect them as soon as they are completed. If necessary, ask respondents to return them to your campus mailbox or some other secure location. The more immediate and convenient the return location, the higher your return rate is likely to be.

- Use a blank questionnaire or make an answer grid so that you can quickly and accurately mark and add up the answers selected for each question. Total the responses as well if you want to be able to say that a certain portion or percentage of the respondents selected a specific answer.

- For fill-in or short answers, an easy procedure is to type each respondent's answer into a computer file. (Identify each questionnaire with a code number, and note it along with the answer if you might want to return to the individual questionnaire.) You can rearrange the answers in the file, looking for logical groups, categories, or patterns that accurately reflect the responses and enrich your analysis.

CORRESPONDING

For advice on writing business letters and e-mail messages, see pp. 266–69 and 270–72.

Is there a person whose views you need but who lives too far away to interview? Do you need information that you might request from a group such as the American Red Cross or the National Wildlife Federation? Could an elected official provide what you need? Sending a traditional business letter or a formal e-mail request is another way to gather field material. In addition, you can check your library or the Internet for directories of professional organizations, businesses, government agencies, or special-interest groups that might supply expert information. If you visit an organization's Web site, look for an e-mail option for sending your request, a correspondence address, a FAQ page (that answers frequently asked questions), or downloadable PDF files of brochures or other materials.

TIPS FOR CORRESPONDING

- Plan ahead, and allow plenty of time for responses to your requests.
- Make your letter or e-mail message short and polite. Identify yourself, explain what you want to find out, and request what you need. Thank your correspondent for helping you.

- If you want specific information from an individual, send your questionnaire or a short list of pointed questions. If you e-mail your message, insert the questions from your questionnaire into the message.

- Enclose a stamped, self-addressed envelope for a reply by mail. If you are sending an e-mail message, include your e-mail address in the message.

ATTENDING PUBLIC AND ONLINE EVENTS

College organizations frequently bring interesting speakers to campus. Check the schedules of events on bulletin boards and in your campus newspaper. In addition, professionals and special-interest groups sometimes convene for a regional or national conference. These meetings can be fertile sources of fresh ideas for your research. Attending a lecture or conference can be an excellent way to begin to learn the language of a discipline.

TIPS FOR ATTENDING EVENTS

- Take notes on the lectures, which are usually given by experts in the field and supply firsthand opinions or research findings.

- Ask questions from the audience or corner a speaker or two later for an informal talk.

- Record who attended the event, how the audience reacted, or other background details that could prove useful in writing your paper.

- Depending on the nature of the gathering, a speaker might distribute copies of the paper presented or be willing to send a copy to you. Conferences often publish their proceedings — usually a set of all the lectures delivered — but publication generally takes months or even years after the conference. Try the library for proceedings of past conferences.

If you join an online discussion — such as the chat sessions sponsored by Web search engines like Yahoo! or Web sites like CNN Online — you can observe or perhaps even ask a question. Often, chat sponsors make transcripts available that you can save or print for your records.

For more about online discussions, see pp. 643–44.

Chapter 31
Evaluating Sources

For more on critical reading, see Ch. 2.

Locating and collecting information are only two of the many activities involved in writing a research paper. You also have to think critically about what you find. You need to evaluate — in other words, judge — your sources, exploring the ideas, opinions, facts, and beliefs they express.

- Which of your sources are reliable?
- Which of these sources are relevant to your topic?
- What evidence from these sources is most useful for your paper?

As you identify, select, and read sources, you'll use evaluation from start to finish. This extremely useful skill is one that you can apply both in college and beyond.

Evaluating Library and Internet Sources

For exercises on evaluating Web sources, visit <bedfordstmartins.com/bedguide> and do a keyword search:

evaluate

Not every source you locate will be equally reliable or equally useful to you. Sites recommended by your library will have been screened by professionals, but each will have its own point of view or approach, often a necessary bias to restrict its focus. Sources from the Web require sharp attention and special care. Like other firsthand materials, individual postings, Web logs ("blogs"), and Web sites will reflect the biases, interests, or information gaps of their writers or sponsors. Commercial and organizational sites may supply very useful material, but they'll provide only what supports their objectives — selling their products, serving their clients, enlisting new members, or persuading others to support their activities or views. See Figure 31.1 for a sample evaluation of a Web site that provides both informative and persuasive materials about its topic.

Even so, your selection of sources can itself simplify evaluation. For example, when you draw information from an article in a print or online peer-

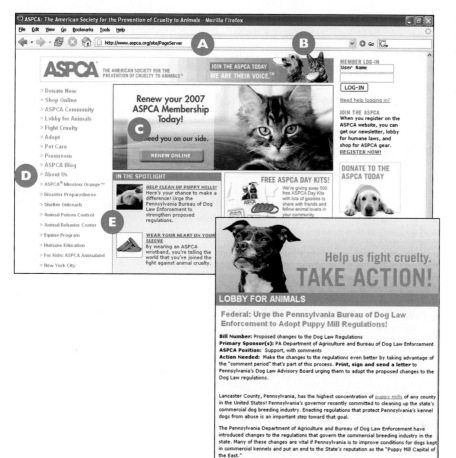

Figure 31.1
Evaluating the purpose,
audience, and bias of a
Web site offering informa-
tive and persuasive
materials

A. Identifies group as organization (.org), not school (.edu) or company (.com)
B. Uses engaging animal graphics
C. Appeals for support
D. Explains purpose of group and provides link to contact information
E. Links to information and recommends action about issues that concern animal lovers

reviewed journal, the process of evaluation for that article actually began when the editors of the journal first read the article and then asked expert reviewers to evaluate whether it merited publication. Similarly, a serious book from a major publishing company or university press probably has been submitted to knowledgeable reviewers. Such reviewers may be asked to assess whether the article or book is well reasoned, logically presented, and competently researched. However, such reviewers can't decide if the work is pertinent to your research question or contains evidence useful for your paper. For this reason, a key part of conducting research is thinking critically about sources so that you select the best evidence for your purposes.

▨ For more about the characteristics of various types of sources, see the charts on pp. 658–61 and B2 in the Quick Research Guide (the dark-red-edged pages).

How do you know what evidence is best? Do what experienced re-searchers do — ask a series of key questions in order to evaluate your sources. The following checklist suggests how you can use the time-tested journalist's questions — who, what, when, where, why, and how — to evalu-ate each print or electronic source that you consider using.

RESEARCH CHECKLIST

Evaluating Sources

Who?

For advice on evaluat-ing field sources, see pp. 657–61.

___ Who is the author of the source? What are the author's credentials and pro-fession? What might be the author's point of view?

___ Who is the intended audience of the source? Experts in the field? Profes-sionals? General readers? People with a special interest? In what ways does the source's tone or evidence appeal to this audience?

___ Who is the publisher of the source or the sponsor of the site? Is it a corpora-tion, a scholarly organization, a professional association, a government agency, or an issue-oriented group? Have you heard of this publisher or sponsor before? Is it well regarded? Does it seem reputable and responsible? Is it considered academic or popular?

___ Who has reviewed the source prior to publication? Only the author? Peer reviewers who are experts in the area? An editorial staff?

What?

___ What is the purpose of the publication or Web site? Is it to sell a product or service? To entertain? To supply information? To publish new research? To shape opinion about an issue or a cause?

___ What bias or point of view might affect the reliability of the source?

___ What kind of information does the source supply? Is it a primary source (a firsthand account) or a secondary source (an analysis of primary material)? If it is a secondary source, does it rely on sound evidence from primary sources?

___ What evidence does the source present? Does it seem trustworthy, sufficient, and relevant given what you know about the subject? Does its argument or analysis seem logical and complete, or does it leave many questions unan-swered? Does it identify and list its sources? If it is electronic, does it supply appropriate, active links?

When?

___ When was the source published or created? Is its information current?

___ When was it last revised or updated? Is its information up-to-date?

Where?

___ Where have you found the source? Is it a prescreened source available through your campus library? Is it a Web site that popped up during a gen-eral search?

—— Where has the source been recommended? On an instructor's syllabus or Web page? On a library list? In another reliable source? During a conference with an instructor or a librarian?

Why?

—— Why should you use this source rather than others?

—— Why is its information directly relevant to your research question?

How?

—— How does the selection of evidence in the source reflect the interests and expertise of its author, publisher or sponsor, and intended audience? How might you need to qualify its use in your paper?

—— How would its information add to your paper? How would it help answer your research question and provide compelling evidence to persuade your readers?

WHO IS THE AUTHOR?

Make every effort to learn about each author's credentials, affiliations with institutions or organizations, and reputation among peers. Try to make sure that any author who shapes or supports your ideas is reliable and trustworthy.

Print Credentials.   Check an article or a book for the author's background or biography, especially in any preface, introduction, or concluding note. National newsmagazines (for example, *Newsweek, Time,* and *U.S. News & World Report*) usually identify any expert authors before or next to their contributions. However, most of their articles are written by reporters who try to substantiate the facts and cover multiple points of view, perhaps compiling regional contributions. On the other hand, some other magazines select facts that mirror the opinions of their editors.

Internet Credentials.   If your source is a Web site, look for a link on its home page to information about the author and an e-mail address that you could use to contact the author about his or her background. If your source is a posting to a newsgroup or a mailing list, deduce what you can from the writer's e-mail address and any signature file. Try a Web search for the person's name, looking for associated sites or links to or from the author's site. If you can't find out anything about the author, it is best not to use the information in your paper, though it might provide useful background for you.

Field Credentials.   When you conduct field research, you may be able to select your sources. If you are investigating safety standards for infant car seats, for example, a personal interview with a local pediatrician will probably produce different information from an interview with the manufacturer's sales representative. You can also affect the results of your research by distributing a questionnaire to a certain group of people or by observing a particular setting. Delve deeply, widely, and fairly.

Reputation.   The best measure of someone's expertise is the regard of other experts. Do others cite the work of your source's author? Does your instructor or someone else on campus who knows the field recognize or recommend the author? Is the author listed in a biographical database?

Material with No Author Identified.   If no author is given, try to identify the sponsoring organization or publisher. On a Web site, check the home page or search for a disclaimer, contact information, or an "About This Site" page. If a print source doesn't list an author, consider the nature of the publication: Is the article published in a nationally respected newspaper like the *Wall Street Journal* or in a supermarket tabloid? Is the brochure published by a leading organization in its field?

WHO ELSE IS INVOLVED?

Intended Audience.   A source written for authorities in a field is likely to assume that readers already have plenty of background knowledge. For this reason, such sources typically skip general overviews and tailor their detailed discussions for experts. In contrast, sources written for general audiences usually define terms and supply background. For example, for your paper on current treatments for HIV, you locate an article in a well-known medical journal that discusses the most favorable chemical composition for an effective protease inhibitor drug. Instead of beginning with this article, written by a physician for other physicians, you might turn first to a source that defines *protease inhibitor* and discusses how it helps HIV patients. Considering the intended audience can help you identify sources appropriate for your project.

Publisher or Sponsor.   Experienced researchers know that the person, organization, government agency, or corporation that prints or electronically distributes a source also may shape its content. Like authors, publishers often hold a point of view. Businesses are likely to present their own products and services more favorably than those of competitors. Political sponsors, such as the major parties, or special-issue groups, such as the American Civil Liberties Union or the National Rifle Association, are likely to publish materials supporting policies they favor. To learn about a Web site sponsor, look for a disclaimer, a mission statement, or an "About" description (as shown in Figure 31.1).

As you evaluate a source, ask critical questions about what might motivate its publisher. Is a Web site created for commercial (.com) purposes, such as selling a product or service? Is it sponsored by an organization (.org, as in Figure 31.1) or a government agency (.gov)? Is it devoted to a specific cause? Is it the work of an individual with strong opinions but little expertise? Is a newsgroup or mailing list limited to a particular interest? Is a publisher noted for its works in a specific field or with a specific political agenda? Does a periodical have a predictable point of view? For example, a faith-based publication will take a different view from a news magazine, just as a conservative publication will differ from a liberal one. Because these questions can be difficult, even for experienced researchers, consult a librarian if you need help finding answers.

For an example showing how a URL identifies a publisher, see A on p. 651.

Reviewers before Publication.   Consider whether a publisher has an editorial staff, an expert editor, or an advisory board of experts. Does it rely on peer reviewers to critique articles or books under consideration? Does it expect research to meet professional standards? Does it outline such standards in its advice for prospective authors or its description of its purpose or mission? Does any sponsor have a solid reputation as a professional organization?

WHAT IS THE PURPOSE?

Understanding the purpose or intention of a source will help you decide whether it is likely to supply solid evidence for your project. A reference book in a library serves a different purpose from a newspaper editorial, a magazine advertisement, or a Web site that promotes a product or service. Asking critical questions is crucial: Is the purpose of this source to explain or inform? To report new research? To persuade? To offer another viewpoint? To sell a product? Does the source acknowledge its purpose in its preface, mission statement, or "About Us" or FAQ (Frequently Asked Questions) page?

Bias.   A *bias* is a preference for a particular side of an issue. Because most authors and most publishers have opinions on their topics, there's little point in asking whether they are biased. Instead, ask how that viewpoint affects the presentation of information and opinion. What are the author's or sponsor's allegiances? Does the source treat one side of an issue more favorably than another? Is that bias hidden or stated? Having a strong bias does not invalidate a source. However, if you recognize such bias early on, you may want to look for other viewpoints that will help you avoid lopsided analyses or arguments.

Primary or Secondary Information.   A *primary source* is a firsthand account written by an eyewitness or a participant. It contains raw data and immediate impressions. A *secondary source* is an analysis of the information contained in one or more primary sources. For example, primary sources for investigating the Korean War might include diaries or letters written by military personnel, accounts of civilian witnesses, articles by journalists who were on the scene, and official military reports. If a military historian used those accounts as background or evidence in a study of military strategy or if a peace activist used them in a book on consequences of warfare for civilians, these resulting works would be secondary sources.

Most research papers benefit from both primary and secondary sources. If you repeatedly cite a fact or an authority quoted in someone else's analysis, try to go to the primary source itself. For example, statistics can be used by those on both sides of an issue; often only the interpretation differs. After all, a bombing raid that spared 70 percent of a village also leveled 30 percent of it. Going to the original research or statistics (published as a primary source) can help you to learn where the facts end and the interpretation begins.

WHEN WAS THE SOURCE PUBLISHED?

For more about the characteristics and timeliness of various sources, see the charts on pp. 658–61 and in B2 in the Quick Research Guide (the dark-red-edged pages).

In general, you should try to rely on current sources. In most fields, new information and discoveries appear every year, so the evidence in a source needs to be up-to-date or at least still timely. New information may appear first in Web postings, media broadcasts, and periodicals such as newspapers and eventually magazines, though such sources may not allow the time needed to consider information thoughtfully. Later, as material is more fully developed or examined, it may be treated in scholarly journal articles and books. For this reason, older materials can supply a valuable historical, theoretical, or analytical focus.

WHERE DID YOU FIND THE SOURCE?

Is it recommended by your instructor? Is it located on the library's Web page or in its book collection? When instructors or academic units direct you to sources, you benefit from their experience teaching students as well as their subject-matter expertise. On the other hand, when you find a Web source while randomly browsing or pick up a magazine at the dentist's office, you'll need to do all the source evaluation yourself.

WHY WOULD YOU USE THIS SOURCE?

For more on selecting sources, see section B in the Quick Research Guide (the dark-red-edged pages).

For more on testing evidence, see pp. 39–40.

Why use one source rather than another? Is the information it contains useful for your purposes? Does it provide strong quotations or hard facts that would be effective in your paper? Does it tackle the topic in a relevant way? For one paper, you might appropriately rely on an article from a popular magazine; for another, you might need the findings published in the scholarly article on which the magazine article was based. As you look for the best possible sources for your purpose, always ask yourself not only "Will this do?" but also "Would something else be better?"

HOW WOULD THIS SOURCE CONTRIBUTE TO YOUR PAPER?

For more on evidence,

The evidence in a source—its ideas, information, facts, and expert or other opinions—can tell you a great deal about its reliability and usefulness for your research project. Is its evidence complete, up-to-date, and carefully assembled? Is its argument or analysis convincingly supported by the evidence? Is there enough evidence to support the claims being made? Does visual material enhance the source rather than distract from its argument or information? Does the source formally identify its own sources in citations and a bibliography? If the source leaves important questions unanswered, you might want to look elsewhere for your own evidence. Even if the source seems highly reliable, it needs to be relevant to your research question and your ideas about how to answer that question. An interesting fact or opinion could be just that — interesting. Instead, you need facts, expert opinions, information, and quotations that relate directly to the purpose and audience of your research paper.

The charts on pages 658–61 will help you choose solid sources whatever your purpose and needs.

Evaluating Field Sources

Although the general criteria for evaluating print and electronic sources may also apply to field resources, you might want to ask these questions as well:

RESEARCH CHECKLIST
Evaluating Field Sources

___ Does your source seem biased or prejudiced? If so, is this viewpoint so strong that you have to discount some of the source's information?

___ Does your source provide evidence to support or corroborate its claims? Have you compared different people's opinions, accounts, or evidence?

___ Is any of your evidence hearsay — one person telling you the thoughts of another or recounting actions that he or she hasn't witnessed? If so, can you check the information by turning to another source or to a different type of evidence?

___ Does your source seem to respond consistently, seriously, and honestly? If a respondent has told you about past events, has time possibly distorted his or her memory?

Each type of field research can also raise particular questions. For example, if you are observing an event or a setting, are people aware of being observed? Often, knowing that they are being observed can change people's behavior. If you have tried to question a random sampling of people, do you feel that they are truly representative? Or, if you have tried to question everyone in a group, have you been thorough enough?

Typical Features of Print Sources	LOCATION INFORMATION	TYPICAL AUDIENCE	AUTHORS AND CONTRIBUTORS	QUALITY CONTROLS
SCHOLARLY BOOK	Library online catalog or database	Specialists, researchers, students, professionals	Scholars, researchers, specialists, professionals	Peer reviews, editorial standards
POPULAR NON-FICTION BOOK	Library online catalog, public library, or bookstore	General readers interested in book's topic	Informed writers, journalists, specialists, professionals	Reviews for publisher, editorial standards
SCHOLARLY JOURNAL	Library periodical index (print or online)	Specialists, researchers, students, professionals	Scholars, researchers, specialists, professionals	Peer reviews, editorial standards
NEWS MAGAZINE	Library periodical index (print or online) or newsstand	General readers interested in current events	Freelance and staff journalists, editorial staff	Editorial and journalistic standards
POPULAR MAGAZINE	Library periodical index (print or online) or newsstand	General readers interested in magazine's focus	Freelance and staff writers, editorial staff, guest contributors	Editorial standards
NEWSPAPER	Library periodical index (print or online) or newsstand	General or local readers	Freelance and staff journalists, editorial staff, columnists	Editorial and journalistic standards
PAMPHLET OR BOOKLET	Library collection (such as government, business, historical, or civic material)	Specialists, professionals, students, general or local readers	Range from specialists and researchers to sponsoring groups or individuals	Editorial standards of sponsor
REFERENCE WORK	Library online catalog or database	Specialists, researchers, students, professionals	Scholars, specialists, staff experts	Selection of contributors, editorial standards

TYPICAL PUBLICATION TIME FRAME	SPONSOR OR PUBLISHER	POSSIBLE PURPOSES OF PUBLICATION	CONTENT FOR RESEARCHERS	USE OF SOURCE CITATIONS
...onths or years of ...eparation for publica-...on probably following ...ars of research and ...riting	Major or specialty publisher, or university press such as University of Chicago Press	Explore issues or topics in the field, advance knowledge, sell books	In-depth library or field research that meets academic standards	Yes—supplies in-text citations, notes, or bibliography
...onths or years of ...eparation for publica-...on possibly following ...onths or years of ...riting	Major or specialty publisher such as Simon & Schuster	Present popular issues, explore trends, provide advice, sell books	Substantial research, investigative journalism, or opinion based on experience	Maybe—possibly identifies sources in chapters, notes, or bibliography
...onths (or longer) for ...ceptance and publica-...on probably following ...onths or years of ...search and writing	Scholarly or professional organization or publisher such as Modern Language Association	Explore topics of concern to journal readers and specialists in the field	In-depth library or field research or professional critique that meets field's standards	Yes—supplies in-text citations, notes, and references following format used in the field
...ays or weeks for publi-...tion following current ... long-term investigation	Commercial or specialty publisher such as Time Warner	Cover news, promote magazine's viewpoint, sell advertising and magazines	News reports supported by facts, observation, and interviews; investigative journalism	Maybe—might name popular or expert sources mentioned or quoted but does not list sources
...ays, weeks, or months ...r publication following ...ng-term or immediate ...pic development	Commercial or specialty publisher such as National Geographic or Rodale	Cover popular topics and readers' interests, sell advertising and magazines	Current advice, expert views reduced to popular applications	Maybe—might name sources mentioned or quoted in article but does not list sources
...ays or weeks for publi-...tion following current ... long-term topic devel-...ment or investigation	Newspaper publisher or media group	Cover news, current events, and timely issues; sell advertising and newspapers	News reports supported by facts, observation, and interviews; investigative journalism	Maybe—might name popular or expert sources mentioned or quoted but does not list sources
...ays or months of prepa-...tion for publication ...llowing development of ...aterial	Government, civic, business, health, or other professional group	Supply timely and useful information in short form, promote sponsor or writer's specialty	Concise presentation of advice, information, opinion, or research findings	Maybe—might supply full, some, or no source citations, depending on purpose and sponsor
...onths or years of ...eparation for publica-...on probably following ...onths or years of re-...arch and writing	Major or specialty publisher	Present accurate information on topic, sell books	Concise and accurate presentation of facts, terms, and background for topic	Maybe—may or may not list standard sources or recommend other sources

Typical Features of Electronic Sources	LOCATION INFORMATION AND EXAMPLES	TYPICAL AUDIENCE	AUTHORS OR EXPERT CONTRIBUTORS	QUALITY CONTROLS
ONLINE REFERENCE SITE	Recommended sites such as *Pinakes: A Subject Launchpad* at <www.hw.ac.uk/ libwww/irn/pinakes/ pinakes.html>	Researchers, scholars, professionals, students	Librarians, information specialists	Site selection criteria and standards
GATEWAY SITE FOR A TOPIC OR FIELD	Recommended sites such as *Voice of the Shuttle* for the humanities at <http:// vos.ucsb.edu> or *Intute: Social Sciences* at <www.intute.ac.uk/ socialsciences>	Researchers, scholars, professionals, students	Librarians, information specialists in field	Site selection criteria and standards
ONLINE DOCUMENT COLLECTION	Specialized collections such as the historical documents at <http://thomas.loc.gov>	Researchers, scholars, professionals, students, general readers	Librarians, information specialists, topic specialists	Site selection criteria
PROFESSIONAL WEB SITE	Links to corporations, non-profits, and foundations on sites such as <www.apple.com> or the Foundation Center at <http://foundationcenter.org>	Professionals, business people, consumers, students, interested readers	Professionals, scholars, business people, organization staff	Site objectives; public or customer-service standar
ACADEMIC WEB SITE	Lists of Web pages such as those at <www.utexas .edu/world/univ/state> or at <www.utexas.edu/ world/comcol/state>	Students, graduates, faculty, staff, parents, visitors	Campus units, groups, Web staff	Campus criteria for inclusion
GOVERNMENT WEB SITE	Index to federal Web sites at <www.usa.gov> or Google's search engine at <www.google.com/ ig.usgov>	General public, other agencies, researchers, specialists	Agency information specialists, staff, consultants	Agency mission, research and editorial standards
ONLINE NEWSPAPER OR NEWS SERVICE	Collections of links such as *Onlinenewspapers* at <www.onlinenewspapers .com> and *Arts & Letters Daily* at <www.aldaily.com>	General or local readers, researchers, professionals, students	Journalists, editorial staff, columnists	Journalistic and editorial standards
INTEREST GROUP OR PERSONAL WEB SITE	Collections of links such as those of the American Academy of Pediatrics at <www.aap.org/ advocacy.html>	Issue-oriented visitors, students, researchers	Activists, concerned citizens, individuals	Individual or group objectives

TYPICAL PUBLICATION TIME FRAME	SPONSOR OR PUBLISHER	POSSIBLE PURPOSES OF PUBLICATION	CONTENT FOR RESEARCHERS	USE OF SOURCE CITATIONS
Immediate, daily, or regular updates	Library or information organization	Assist scholars, researchers, and students	In-depth academic, professional, or personal research	Yes (Web links) — lists sites and provides links, often grouped and annotated
Regular or irregular updates, depending on sponsor or Webmaster	Library or professional organization	Assist scholars, researchers, and students; encourage interest in specialty	In-depth academic and professional research in discipline	Yes (Web links) — lists sites and provides links, often grouped and annotated
Regular or irregular updates, depending on materials or Webmaster	Library or special-interest sponsor	Assist scholars, researchers, and students to access documents	Easy access to selected texts for researchers or readers	Yes (Web links) — identifies documents and may supply background for texts
Regular or irregular updates, depending on sponsor	Professional group, nonprofit agency, corporation, or corporate foundation	Promote interests of organization; attract and assist members, clients, professionals, or site visitors	Promotion of organization and its research, civic, economic, or other interests	Maybe — may present information, with or without sources, or may supply links
Regular or irregular updates, depending on academic unit maintaining page	College or university	Assist campus community, attract future students, promote family and public support	Promotion of campus programs and activities, including academic research	Maybe — may supply campus information without sources as well as academic texts and resource lists or links
Regular or irregular updates, depending on government agency	Federal, state, local, or foreign government division or agency	Fulfill agency objectives by providing public information and assistance	Authoritative information for citizens, policy makers, and agencies based on reliable research	Maybe — may present reports or texts with source citations as well as popular information without sources
Immediate updates as events occur along with archives of past coverage	Newspaper or media group	Cover news, current events, and timely issues; sell advertising	Accurate news reports supported by facts, observation, interviews, and visuals; investigative journalism	Maybe — might identify popular or expert sources mentioned or quoted but not other sources
Regular or irregular updates, depending on individual or group	Partisan group, special-interest group, or individual	Promote special interests of group or individual	Range from academic interests to partisan activism to individual interests	Maybe — may or may not identify sources of information or use reliable sources

Reconsidering Your Purpose and Your Thesis

As you evaluate your sources, you will critically examine each individual source, assessing its specific strengths, shortcomings, and possible contributions to your paper. Once you have gathered and evaluated a reasonable collection of sources, it's time to step back and consider them as a group — lifting your eyes from the maples, red oaks, and elms to the forest as a whole.

- Have you found enough relevant and credible sources to satisfy the requirements of your assignment? Have you found enough to suggest sound answers to your research question?

- Are your sources thought provoking? Can you tell which information is generally accepted, which is controversial, and which may be unreliable? Have your sources engaged and enlightened you while substantiating, refining, or changing your original ideas?

- Are your sources varied? Have they helped you achieve a reasonably complete view of your topic? Have they suggested other perspectives, approaches, alternatives, or interpretations that you will want to acknowledge? Have they deepened your understanding and helped you reach well-reasoned, balanced conclusions?

- Are your sources appropriate? Do they answer your question with evidence your readers will find persuasive? Do they have the range and depth necessary to achieve your purpose and satisfy your readers?

Use these questions to check in with yourself. Make sure that you have a clear direction for your research — whether it's the same direction you started with or a completely new one. Perhaps you are ready to answer your research question, refine your thesis, and begin to draft a paper that pulls together your own ideas and those of your sources. On the other hand, you may want to find additional sources that support or challenge your assumptions about the topic. Maybe you need to hunt for specific counterevidence that responds to strong evidence against your position — or change your working thesis to account for that evidence. On the other hand, you might want to pursue a new direction that seems more tantalizing than your original one.

Chapter 32

Integrating Sources

Once you have found, evaluated, and drawn valuable information from sources that respond to your research question, you are ready to work all that persuasive evidence into your paper. Your paper should project your own voice and showcase your ideas — your thesis and main points about your research question. It also should marshal compelling support for those ideas using the evidence that you have quoted, paraphrased, and summarized from your sources. You will need to add this support responsibly, identifying both the sources and the ideas or exact words captured from them.

■ For more on using sources in your writing, see Ch. 12 and D1–D6 in the Quick Research Guide (the dark-red-edged pages).

■ For more on planning, drafting, revising, and editing your paper, see Ch. 33.

Using Sources Ethically

Although research can be a complex, lively process, enriched by the exchange of ideas and findings, discussions of research ethics sometimes reduce that topic to one issue: plagiarism. Plagiarists intentionally present someone else's work as their own — whether they dishonestly submit as their own a paper purchased from the Web, pretend that passages copied from an article are their own writing, appropriate the ideas or theories of others without identifying their sources, or paste in someone else's graphics without acknowledgment or permission.

Plagiarism is viewed especially seriously in college because it shows a deep disrespect for the work of the academic world — analyzing, interpreting, creating, investigating, and assessing ideas. And it may have serious consequences — failing a paper, failing a course, or being dismissed from the institution.

Although college writers may not intend to plagiarize, campus policies are likely to look at the outcome, not the intent. Working carefully with sources and treating respectfully the ideas and expressions of others can help you build the skills necessary to avoid mistakes. Educating yourself about the standards of your institution, instructor, and profession (once you've moved from college to the workplace) also can protect you from ethical errors that may carry heavy consequences. The following chart illustrates how to avoid or remedy common situations that can generate ethical problems.

PLAGIARISM PROBLEM	REMEDY
You have scarcely started your paper, and it's due soon. Someone gives you the address for a Web site selling papers for $59.95. The visuals on the site show smiling students, but you aren't smiling because you know that this choice is wrong. In addition, the sample topics don't sound quite like your assignment, your instructor expects to receive both your annotated bibliography and your draft (not just a final paper), and you wonder whether the college uses a plagiarism-detection system that would easily catch you.	Don't buy a paper, but immediately throw yourself on the mercy of your instructor. Explain that you have fallen behind; ask for help and a time extension, even if it carries a penalty. Cancel all your social plans for the next week or so, and follow the advice in this book about finding recommended sources. Consider this one of your most valuable college experiences: you have saved the cost of a phony paper; you have not jeopardized your very expensive education; you won't need to explain to your family why you have failed a course or been suspended; and you have shown intellectual integrity and personal maturity.
You're investigating a serious research question about a problem that affects a family member. You started your research right away, taking lots of notes from sources. Now, however, your note file is getting long, and you're mixing up which ideas you quoted from sources, which you summed up, and which you thought up yourself. You're beginning to worry that your disorganization will lead to plagiarism because you won't be able to credit your sources accurately.	Stop where you are and get organized. Set up a linking system so that you can tell what comes from where. Record the author's last name or a brief source title and page number when you begin taking any notes from a source, add divider lines between notes from different sources, or move your existing notes to separate files, each clearly labeled as the only file for that source. Reread pp. 603–15 on keeping a working bibliography and recording source notes. Use any unidentified leftover notes as background, but don't add them to your paper if you can't credit your source.
You had an hour between classes and found a new book on reserve in the library. You had to write quickly to avoid being late to class. Here's part of what you found in your research notebook later that day: InDfCult, HUP, Cambridge, Carol Padden, Tom Humphries, 5 122 For Df voice/technol = issue Relates to cult def	Go back to the library. This time, record clear information (without potentially confusing abbreviations) about *Inside Deaf Culture,* written by Carol Padden and Tom Humphries and published in Cambridge, MA, by Harvard University Press in 2005. Then turn back to page 122. Decide what you want to do: quote these authors or sum up their view. Add quotation marks to identify their exact words. Otherwise, rewrite their ideas in your own words and sentences so you don't "parrot" your source (see pp. 218–20 and pp. 617–19).
You have never read a book as hard as the one you checked out of the campus library. You have no clue what words like *transmogrify* and *heuristic* mean. With the help of a dictionary, you tried to paraphrase the ideas in your own words, but you can't restate the big words (and the big ideas) because you don't understand them. You are afraid that your instructor will think you're a cheater who mostly copied from the book, not a hardworking student, but you're embarrassed to admit that the reading is just too hard.	Stop using a source that you don't understand. Look for others on the same topic — shelved nearby, listed under the same keywords, or suggested by your instructor or librarian. If you must use a difficult source, read and reread — passage by passage — to master it. Sum up each passage in turn; then rewrite your notes until they are your own. Carefully mark any words taken directly from the source with quotation marks, whether a short passage or a few words sprinkled here and there in your notes. Allow time for the practice necessary to boost your research and reading skills.

PLAGIARISM PROBLEM	REMEDY
You have worked hard to find reliable sources, but you're having trouble beginning your paper. You e-mail your friends and eat all the leftover pizza. The afternoon is nearly gone by the time you finally figure out how to get started. Soon you're busily writing a few sentences, then cutting and pasting in quotations and notes, then writing again. You suddenly wonder how you'll be able to figure out where it all came from when you have to add your source citations. What if your instructor thinks that you are plagiarizing if you don't identify a few sources or add the page numbers for quotations?	Backtrack as fast as you can. For each chunk you've pasted in, add obvious notes to yourself (using color, brackets, or your software's comment feature) so that you will know exactly where to add a formal source citation later. For yourself, note at least the basics — the author's name and the page number in the original. Put quotation marks around any words directly from the source — using color for them in your draft if you need a temporary reminder about the need to present these words accurately. See pages 672–73 on weaving source material into your paper.

Careful researchers acknowledge their intellectual obligations and their respect for the researchers, scholars, and writers who came before them. Careful researchers also respect readers who are likely to be curious about the discoveries, reasons, and evidence marshaled by others. Finally, careful researchers respect themselves. Instead of trying to evade the intellectual responsibilities and benefits of a college education, they try to figure out the practices that will give their writing credibility with academic readers. In short, they learn how to write solid research papers from the best teacher of all — experience.

Ask yourself the following questions as you consider how to meet college and professional research standards.

RESEARCH CHECKLIST

Learning How to Conduct Research Ethically

___ Have you accepted the responsibility of reviewing your campus standards for ethical academic conduct? Have you checked your syllabus or course handouts for any explanation about how those standards apply in your course?

___ Are you accurately and regularly recording source entries in your working bibliography?

___ Are you carefully distinguishing your own ideas from those of your sources when you record notes or gather material for your research archive?

___ Are you sticking to your research schedule so that you can avoid a deadline crisis?

___ Have you analyzed your typical paper-writing habits to identify any, such as procrastination, that might create ethical problems for you? How do you plan to change such habits to avoid problems?

___ Have you become aware of any research skills (such as quoting, paraphrasing, or summarizing) that you need to practice or polish? If so, have you used this book's index or table of contents to review the sections that explain those skills?

___ Have you found the section in this book that explains the documentation style you'll use in your paper?

___ Have you identified and followed campus procedures for conducting field research involving other people?

___ Have you recorded contact information so that you can request permission to include any visual materials from sources in your paper?

___ If your research is part of a group project, have you honored your agreements with your instructor and your peers, meeting your obligations in a timely manner?

___ If you feel ill prepared for your research assignment, have you sought help from your instructor or staff at the library, writing center, computer lab, or other campus facility?

___ Have you asked your instructor's advice about any other ethical issues that have arisen during your research project?

Capturing, Launching, and Citing Evidence from Sources

Sources alone do not make for an effective research paper. Instead, the ideas, explanations, and details from your sources need to be integrated — combined and mixed — with your own thoughts and conclusions about the question you have investigated. Together they eventually form a unified whole that conveys your perspective, along with the evidence that logically supports it, to your audience. To make sure that your voice isn't drowned out by your sources, keep your research question and your working thesis — maybe still evolving — in front of you as you work in information. On the other hand, make sure that you identify and credit your sources appropriately, treating them with the respect they deserve.

▨ For more on stating a thesis, see pp. 312–19.

▧ To practice quoting, paraphrasing, and summarizing, visit <bedfordstmartins.com/ bedguide> and do a keyword search:

▨ For more about how to quote, paraphrase, and summarize, see pp. 212–21 and 617–19.

Once you have recorded a source note, it's a great temptation to include it in your paper at all costs. Resist. Include only material that answers your research question and supports your thesis. A note dragged in by force always sticks out like a pig in the belly of a boa constrictor.

When material does fit, consider how to incorporate it effectively and ethically. Quoting reproduces an author's exact words. Paraphrasing restates an author's ideas in your own words and sentences. Summarizing extracts the essence of an author's meaning and states it "in a nutshell." Besides using these methods in your paper, you also need to launch captured material by introducing it to readers and to cite it by crediting its source.

• Quote	• Identify authority	• Credit the source
• Paraphrase	• Provide credentials for credibility	• Link the citation to your final list of sources
• Summarize	• Usher in the source	• Specify the location of the material used
• Synthesize	• Connect support to your points	

QUOTING AND PARAPHRASING ACCURATELY

To illustrate the art of capturing source material effectively, let's first look at a passage from historian Barbara W. Tuchman. In *The Distant Mirror: The Calamitous Fourteenth Century* (New York: Knopf, 1978), Tuchman sets forth the effects of the famous plague known as the Black Death. In her foreword, she admits that any historian dealing with the Middle Ages faces difficulties. For one, large gaps exist in the recorded information. Here is Tuchman's original wording:

ORIGINAL

    A greater hazard, built into the very nature of recorded history, is over- 1
load of the negative: the disproportionate survival of the bad side — of evil,
misery, contention, and harm. In history this is exactly the same as in the
daily newspaper. The normal does not make news. History is made by the
documents that survive, and these lean heavily on crisis and calamity, crime 5
and misbehavior, because such things are the subject matter of the documentary process — of lawsuits, treaties, moralists' denunciations, literary
satire, papal Bulls. No Pope ever issued a Bull to approve of something.
Negative overload can be seen at work in the religious reformer Nicolas de
Clamanges, who, in denouncing unfit and worldly prelates in 1401, said 10
that in his anxiety for reform he would not discuss the good clerics because
"they do not count beside the perverse men."
    Disaster is rarely as pervasive as it seems from recorded accounts. The
fact of being on the record makes it appear continuous and ubiquitous
whereas it is more likely to have been sporadic both in time and place. Be- 15
sides, persistence of the normal is usually greater than the effect of disturbance, as we know from our own times. After absorbing the news of today,
one expects to face a world consisting entirely of strikes, crimes, power failures, broken water mains, stalled trains, school shutdowns, muggers, drug
addicts, neo-Nazis, and rapists. The fact is that one can come home in the 20
evening — on a lucky day — without having encountered more than one or
two of these phenomena.

Although you might have copied or highlighted this entire passage when you read it and recorded your notes, it is too long to include in your paper. Quoting it directly would allow your source to overshadow your own voice. Instead, you might want to quote a striking line or so and paraphrase the rest by restating the details in your own words. In the following para-phrase of this passage, notice how the writer has put Tuchman's ideas into other words but retained her major points and given her credit for the ideas.

PARAPHRASE WITH QUOTATION

Tuchman points out that historians find some distortion of the truth hard to avoid, for more documentation exists for crimes, suffering, and calamities than for the events of ordinary life. As a result, history may overemphasize the negative. The author reminds us that we are familiar with this process from our contemporary news coverage, which plays up bad news as being of greater interest than good news. If we believed that news stories told all the truth, we would feel threatened at all times by technical failures, strikes, crime, and violence—but we are threatened only some of the time, and normal life goes on. The good, dull, ordinary parts of our lives do not make the front page, and praiseworthy things tend to be ignored. "No Pope," says Tuchman, "ever issued a Bull to approve of something." But in truth, social upheaval did not prevail as widely as we might think from the surviving documents of medieval life. Nor, the author observes, can we agree with a critic of the church, Nicolas de Clamanges, in whose view evildoers in the clergy mattered more than men of goodwill (xviii).

In this reasonably complete and accurate paraphrase, about three-quarters the length of the original, most of Tuchman's points have been preserved and spelled out fully. The writer doesn't interpret or evaluate Tuchman's ideas — she only passes them on. Paraphrasing enables her to emphasize ideas important to her research. It also makes readers more aware of them as support for her thesis than if the whole passage had been quoted directly. But notice that the writer has kept Tuchman's remark about papal Bulls as a direct quotation because that statement is short and memorable, and it would be hard to improve on her words.

Often you paraphrase to emphasize one essential point. Here is an orig-inal passage from Evelyn Underhill's classic study *Mysticism* (New York: Doubleday, 1990):

ORIGINAL

In the evidence given during the process for St. Teresa's beatification, Maria de San Francisco of Medina, one of her early nuns, stated that on entering the saint's cell whilst she was writing this same "Interior Castle" she found her [St. Teresa] so absorbed in contemplation as to be unaware of the external world. "If we made a noise close to her," said another, Maria del Nacimiento, "she neither ceased to write nor complained of being dis-turbed." Both these nuns, and also Ana de la Encarnacion, prioress of Granada, affirmed that she wrote with immense speed, never stopping to erase or to correct, being anxious, as she said, to write what the Lord had given her before she forgot it.

Suppose that the names of the witnesses do not matter to a researcher who wishes to emphasize, in fewer words, the renowned mystic's writing habits. That writer might paraphrase the passage (and quote it in part) like this:

PARAPHRASE WITH QUOTATION

Underhill has recalled the testimony of those who saw St. Teresa at work on *The Interior Castle*. Oblivious to noise, the celebrated mystic appeared to write in a state of complete absorption, driving her pen "with immense speed, never stopping to erase or to correct, being anxious, as she said, to write what the Lord had given her before she forgot it" (242).

SUMMARIZING CONCISELY

To illustrate how summarizing can serve you, here is an example showing how a writer might sum up the passage from Tuchman:

SUMMARY

Tuchman reminds us that history lays stress on misery and misdeeds because these negative events attracted notice in their time and so were reported in writing; just as in news stories today, bad news predominates. But we should remember that suffering and social upheaval didn't prevail everywhere all the time (xviii).

■ For Tuchman's original passage, see p. 667.

As you can see, this summary merely abstracts from the original. Not everything has been preserved — not Tuchman's thought about papal Bulls, not examples such as Nicolas de Clamanges or the modern neo-Nazis. But the gist — the summary of the main idea — echoes Tuchman faithfully.

Before you write a summary, an effective way to sense the gist of a passage is to pare away examples, details, modifiers, offhand remarks, and nonessential points. Following is the original quotation from Tuchman as one student marked it up on a photocopy, crossing out elements she decided to omit from her summary.

A greater hazard, built into the ~~very~~ nature of recorded history, is ~~over-load of the negative~~: the disproportionate survival of the bad side — ~~of evil, misery, contention, and harm. In history~~ this is exactly the same as in the daily newspaper. ~~The normal does not make news. History is made by the~~ documents that survive, ~~and these~~ lean heavily on crisis and calamity, crime and misbehavior, because such things are the subject matter of the documentary process — ~~of lawsuits, treaties, moralists' denunciations, literary satire, papal Bulls. No Pope ever issued a Bull to approve of something. Negative overload can be seen at work in the religious reformer Nicolas de Clamanges, who, in denouncing unfit and worldly prelates in 1401, said that in his anxiety for reform he would not discuss the good clerics because "they do not count beside the perverse men."~~

Disaster is rarely as pervasive as it seems from recorded accounts. ~~The fact of being on the record makes it appear continuous and ubiquitous~~

~~whereas~~ it is more likely to have been sporadic both in time and place. Besides, persistence of the normal is usually greater than the effect of disturbance, as we know from our own times. ~~After absorbing the news of today,
one expects to face a world consisting entirely of strikes, crimes, power failures, broken water mains, stalled trains, school shutdowns, muggers, drug
addicts, neo Nazis, and rapists. The fact is that one can come home in the
evening — on a lucky day — without having encountered more than one or
two of these phenomena.~~

Rewording what was left, she wrote the following condensed version:

SUMMARY

History, like a morning newspaper, reports more bad than good. Why? Because
the documents that have come down to us tend to deal with upheavals and dis-
turbances, which are seldom as extensive and long-lasting as history books
might lead us to believe (Tuchman xviii).

In writing her summary, the student couldn't simply omit the words she
had deleted. The result would have been less readable and still long. She
knew she couldn't use Tuchman's very words: that would be plagiarism. To
make a compact, honest summary that would fit smoothly into her paper,
she had to condense the passage into her own words.

AVOIDING PLAGIARISM

■ For more on avoiding
plagiarism and using ac-
cepted methods of adding
source material, see pp.
663–66 and D1 in the
Quick Research Guide
(the dark-red-edged
pages).

Here is a point we can't stress too strongly: never lift another writer's words
or ideas without giving that writer due credit and transforming them into
words of your own. If you do use words or ideas without giving credit, you
are plagiarizing. You have seen in this chapter examples of honest summarizing and paraphrasing. Introducing them into a paper, a writer would
clearly indicate that their ideas belong to the originator, Barbara Tuchman
or Evelyn Underhill. Now here are a few unacceptable examples — paraphrases of Tuchman's passage that lift, without thanks, her ideas and even
her very words. Finding such gross borrowings in a paper, an instructor
might hear the ringing of a burglar alarm. The first example lifts both
thoughts and words, highlighted here with their lines in the original noted
in the margin.

■ For Tuchman's original
passage, see p. 667.

PLAGIARIZED THOUGHTS AND WORDS

Quoted from line 2

Close to lines 5–6

Sometimes it's difficult for historians to learn the truth about the everyday lives
of people from past societies because of <u>the disproportionate survival of the
bad side of things.</u> Historical documents, like today's newspapers, tend to lean
rather heavily on <u>crisis, crime, and misbehavior.</u> Reading the newspaper could

lead one to expect a world consisting entirely of strikes, crimes, power failures, ——— Close to line 18

muggers, drug addicts, and rapists. In fact, though, disaster is rarely so perva- ——— Lists from lines 18–20

sive as recorded accounts can make it seem. ————————————————— Close to ¶ 2 opening

The student who attempted this paraphrase did not understand the passage well enough to put Tuchman's ideas in his or her own words. Students who allow enough time to read, to think, and to write are likely to handle sources more effectively than those who procrastinate or rush through the research process.

■ For more on managing a research project, see Ch. 28.

This next example is a more subtle theft, lifting thoughts but not words.

PLAGIARIZED THOUGHTS

It's not always easy to determine the truth about the everyday lives of people from past societies because bad news gets recorded a lot more frequently than good news does. Historical documents, like today's news channels, tend to pick up on malice and disaster and ignore flat normality. If I were to base my opinion of the world on what I see on the seven o'clock news, I would expect to see death and destruction around me all the time. Actually, though, I rarely come up against true disaster.

By using the first-person pronoun *I*, this student suggests that Tuchman's ideas are his own. That is just as dishonest as quoting without using quotation marks, as reprehensible as not citing the source of ideas.

The next example fails to make clear which ideas belong to the writer and which belong to Tuchman.

PLAGIARIZED WITH FAULTY CREDIT

Barbara Tuchman explains that it can be difficult for historians to learn about the everyday lives of people who lived a long time ago because historical documents tend to record only the bad news. Today's newspapers are like that, too: disaster, malice, and confusion take up a lot more room on the front page than happiness and serenity. Just as the ins and outs of our everyday lives go unreported, we can suspect that upheavals do not really play so important a part in the making of history as they seem to do.

■ For a tutorial on avoiding plagiarism, visit <bedfordstmartins.com/rewriting>.

After rightfully attributing the ideas in the first sentence to Tuchman, the writer makes a comparison to today's world in sentence 2. Then in sentence 3, she returns to Tuchman's ideas without giving Tuchman credit. The placement of the final sentence suggests that this last idea is the student's whereas it is really Tuchman's.

As you write your paper, use ideas and words from your sources carefully, and credit those sources. Supply introductory and transitional comments to launch and attribute quotations, paraphrases, and summaries to the original

■ For more on working with sources, see Chs. 12 and 29 as well as the Quick Research Guide (the dark-red-edged pages). For more on quotation marks, ellipses, and brackets, see C3 in the Quick Editing Guide (the dark-blue-edged pages).

source ("As Tuchman observes . . ."). Rely on quotation marks and other punctuation to show exactly which words come from your sources. Use the questions in the following checklist to help you avoid plagiarizing:

RESEARCH CHECKLIST

Avoiding Plagiarism

___ Have you identified the author of material you quote, paraphrase, or summarize? Have you credited the originator of facts and ideas you use?

___ Have you clearly indicated where another writer's ideas stop and yours begin?

___ Have you checked each paraphrase or summary against the original for accuracy? Do you use your own words? Do you avoid wording and sentence structure close to that in the original? Do you avoid misinterpreting or distorting the meaning of the original?

___ Have you checked each quotation against the original for accuracy? Have you used quotation marks for both passages and significant words taken directly from your source?

___ Have you used an ellipsis mark (. . .) to show where you have omitted something from the original? Have you used brackets ([ ]) to indicate your changes or additions in a quotation? Have you avoided distorting the meaning of the original?

LAUNCHING SOURCE MATERIAL

You need to identify the source of each detail and each idea — whether a quotation, summary, or paraphrase — drawn from your reading or field research in a launch statement. Whenever possible, help readers understand why you have selected your particular sources, why you find their evidence pertinent, or how they support your conclusions. Use your launch statements to show not only that you have read your sources but also that you have absorbed and applied what they say about your research question. The following strategies suggest ways of strengthening your launch statements.

- Identify the name of the author in the sentence that introduces the source:

  As Wood explains, the goal of American education continues to fluctuate between gaining knowledge and applying it (58).

- Add the author's name in the middle of the source material:

  In *Romeo and Juliet,* "That which we call a rose," Shakespeare claims, "By any other word would smell as sweet" (2.2.43–44).

- Note the professional title or affiliation of someone you've interviewed to add authority and increase the credibility of your source:

  According to Joan Lewis, an environmental attorney at Saunders and Gonzales, . . .

Briefly noting relevant background or experience can do the same:

Recalling events during a three-year tour of duty in Afghanistan, Sergeant Nelson indicated . . .

- Identify information from your own field research:

  When interviewed about the campus disaster plan, Natalie Chan, Director of Campus Services, confirmed . . .

- Name the author only in the source citation in parentheses if you want to keep your focus on the topic:

  A second march on Washington followed the first (Whitlock 83).

- Explain for the reader why you have selected and included the material:

  As Serrano's three-year investigation of tragic border incidents shows, the current policies carry high financial and human costs.

- Interpret what you see as the point or relevance of the material:

  Stein's argument focuses on stem-cell research, but his discussion of potential ethical implications (18) also applies to other kinds of medical investigation.

- Relate the source clearly to the paper's thesis or to the specific point it supports:

  Although Robinson analyzes workplace interactions, her conclusions (289–92) suggest the importance of examining these same issues in arenas such as schools.

- Compare or contrast the point of view or evidence of one source with that of another source:

  While Desmond emphasizes the European economic disputes, Lewis turns to the social stresses that also set the stage for World War II.

Often adding transitional expressions to guide readers can strengthen your launch statements by relating one source to another (*in addition, in contrast, more recently, in a more favorable view*) or particular evidence to your line of reasoning (*next, furthermore, in addition, despite, nevertheless, on the other hand*).

For more on transitions, see pp. 346–49.

Regardless of how you launch sources, you need to figure out how to integrate and synthesize your sources more effectively. Use the Draft Doctor (pp. 674–75) for this purpose. Skim down the left column to identify questions you might ask about problems in your draft. When you answer a question with "Yes" or "Maybe," move straight across the row to the Diagnose column next to that question. Use the diagnostic activities to identify gaps or weaknesses, and then move straight across the row again to the Treat column on the right. Use the advice that suits your problem as you revise.

To get online help from the Draft Doctor, visit <bedfordstmartins.com/bedguide>.

Draft Doctor: Integrating and Synthesizing Sources

If you sense a problem, ASK	If you answer *Yes/Maybe,* DIAGNOSE	If you diagnose a problem, TREAT
Sources Difficult to Understand? Am I relying on a group of sources that I don't understand very well?	• Use a different color to identify each source you are synthesizing in your draft. • Read through your explanation of the material from each source you've identified. Note any places where you've guessed at the meaning, quoted in self-defense (because you couldn't explain the source in your own words), or generalized.	• Master each source individually: reread, annotate, write a response, discuss with a classmate, or meet with your instructor. If a source is too advanced to master, drop it if you can. • Eliminate the fudging: pin down what you've guessed, summarize or paraphrase your quotations, and specify rather than generalize.
Weak Group of Sources? Are my reasons unclear for trying to synthesize a group of sources?	• List the sources you're trying to pull together. • Write out the principles you have used (or could use) for selecting and grouping them — for example, chronology to show change over time, theme to show aspects of a topic, comparison to show similarities and alternatives, or another system.	• Assess each source, writing down how each develops your principles. • Adjust your principles, or redefine your ideas about what each source shows as needed. • Revise your grouping. Drop or add sources; use some elsewhere if they don't fit together well. If a source fits at several places, pick the best spot or fill a potential gap.
Too Little Time to Think? Do I need to spend more time thinking about the ideas in my sources to understand and connect them?	• Schedule several blocks of time so that you can concentrate on your intellectual task. • Set priorities for using your time — several key sources to master, a weak passage to revise, or another task that requires focused thought.	• During your first block of time, work on your first-priority task. Tackle one item at a time. • Before your time ends, do something specific — summarize your difficult sources, revise your weak section, or record your working thoughts.

If you sense a problem, **ASK**	If you answer *Yes/Maybe,* **DIAGNOSE**	If you diagnose a problem, **TREAT**
Unclear Connections? Do I need to relate my sources more deeply and clearly to each other?	• First clarify the focus of each source: collect your notes, and print out your discussion of it in your draft. • Highlight connective statements or transitions already used in your draft to link the sources. • Mark all the spots where your draft jumps from source to source without explaining connections to your audience.	• Review your existing source notes, and weigh them against your written statements about their connections. • Brainstorm or make notes (see Ch. 16) to refine, restate, or expand connections. Use your notes to clarify and deepen connections as you revise.
No New Ideas? Do I need to deepen my synthesis so that it goes beyond the ideas from my sources to my own new ideas?	• Reread your synthesis. Mark any part that reads like a grocery list (bread, eggs, bananas or Smith, Jones, Chu). • Reread again. Mark places where you think a reader might find an evaluation or interpretation useful.	• Generate ideas (see Ch. 16) to build a cache of notes and ideas about how you want to connect your sources and what they collectively suggest. Be creative, allowing your original ideas to emerge. • Connect the listed sources, filling the gaps with your new ideas.
Lost Point? Do I need to reshape my synthesis so that it supports my thesis and makes my point?	• Highlight all of your comments, interpretations, and explanations for the sources you are synthesizing. • Place a check mark by any of these comments that do not clearly state a connection to your thesis. • Place a star by any of these comments that seem to repeat the point of the source instead of relating it to your point.	• Rework your checked comments, explaining how they relate to your thesis and support it. • Rework your starred points, connecting them to your point. • Return to your unchecked comments, expanding these as needed to clarify your assumptions and ideas for your audience.
Any Other Synthesis Improvements? After a final look at the synthesis of sources in my draft, should I do anything else to revise?	• Read your draft out loud to yourself, marking any weak or incomplete synthesis of sources. • Ask peer editors how you might more effectively and fully synthesize your sources.	• Return to each mark to strengthen your synthesis; add connections and deepen your conclusions. • Consider the useful advice of your peers. • Revise until your draft does what you want it to do.

CITING EACH SOURCE CLEARLY

For examples of citations see pp. 689–96) for MLA) or 719–24 (for APA).

Often your launch statement does double duty: naming your source as well as introducing the quotation, paraphrase, or summary from it. Naming, or citing, each source is important; then a reader can easily locate it in the list of sources at the end of your paper. In that list, you provide full publication information so that readers could find your original sources if they wished. To make this connection, identify each source by mentioning the author (or the title if the author is not identified) as you add information from the source to your paper. (In APA style, also add the date.) You can emphasize this identification by including it in your launch statement as you introduce your source, or you can tuck it into parentheses after the information. Then, supply the specific location of any quotation or paraphrase (usually the page number in the original) so that a reader could easily turn to the exact information you have used. Check your text citations against your concluding list of sources to be sure that the two correspond.

Synthesizing Ideas and Sources

For more on synthesizing, see p. 224. For a Draft Doctor on synthesizing, see pp. 674–75.

Integrating sources into your paper generally requires positioning materials in a sequence, fitting them in place, and reworking them so that they advance your case. Your source notes need your interpretation to convert them into effective evidence.

You'll also want to synthesize your sources and evidence, to weave them into a unified whole. Build your synthesis on your critical reading and thinking: pulling together what you read and think, relating ideas and information, and drawing conclusions that go beyond those of your separate sources. If you have a sure sense of your paper's direction, you may find this synthesis fairly easy. On the other hand, if your research question or working thesis has changed, perhaps because you have unearthed persuasive information at odds with your original direction, consider these questions:

- Taken as a whole, what does all this information mean?
- What does it actually tell you about the answer to your research question?
- What's the most important thing you've learned?
- What's the most important thing you can tell your readers?

Chapter 33

Writing Your Research Paper

Y ou may have your own tried-and-true system of moving from research notes to a rough draft. If so, feel free to stick to your own system. On the other hand, you may be worried about how to pull together your paper — perhaps the longest and most complex one you've ever written. In this case, try some of the suggestions here as you plan, draft, revise, and edit your paper.

Planning and Drafting

You began gathering material from library, Internet, and field sources with a question in mind. By now, if your research has been thorough and fruitful, you know your answer. The moment has come to draft your paper, weaving together the material you have gathered. We can vouch for two time-proven methods.

The Thesis Method. Decide what your research has led you to believe. What does it all mean? Sum up that view in a sentence. That sentence is your thesis, the one main idea your paper will demonstrate. You can then start planning and drafting, including only material that supports your thesis, concentrating from beginning to end on making that thesis clear.

For advice on stating and using a thesis, see pp. 312–19.

The Answer Method. Some writers have an easier time if they plunge in and start writing without first stating any thesis at all. If you try this method, recall your original research question. Start writing with the purpose of answering it, lining up evidence as you go and discovering what you want to say as you write. (Note that this method usually requires more revising than the thesis method.)

For revision strategies, see Ch. 20.

USING YOUR SOURCES TO SUPPORT YOUR IDEAS

For more on integrating sources, see Ch. 32.

If your source notes are to end up in a readable, unified whole, you need to put these nuggets into the proper setting, shaping and finely polishing them to fit into your first draft. Moving from nuggets of information to a smooth, persuasive analysis or argument is the most challenging part of the research process — and, ironically, the part on which we can give the least concrete advice. Every writer's habits of mind are different. Even so, you'll probably cycle again and again through four basic activities:

- Interpreting the material captured from your sources
- Refining your thesis
- Organizing your ideas
- Putting your thoughts into the form of a draft

For more on evidence, see pp. 37–42, 152–56, and section A in the Quick Research Guide (the dark-red-edged pages).

Interpret Your Sources.   On their own, your source notes are only pieces of information. They need your interpretation to transform them into effective evidence. As a researcher and writer, you have to think critically about each fact. What does it mean in the context of your paper? Is it strong enough to bear the weight of the claim you're going to base on it? Do you need more evidence to shore up an interesting but ambiguous fact? Keep your sources in their supporting role and your voice in the lead. Alternate statements and support to sustain this balance.

For more on stating and using a thesis, see pp. 312–19.

Refine Your Thesis.   A thesis is a clear, precise statement of the point you want to make in your paper. It will help you decide what to say and how to say it. When your thesis is clear to your readers, it will help them interpret what you present by letting them know in advance the scope of your paper and your general message.

If you've used a working thesis to guide your research, sharpen and refine it before you start drafting. Later you may need to change it even further, but a clear thesis will guide you in organizing and expressing your ideas. Explicitly stating your thesis as the first or last sentence in your opening paragraph is only one option. Sometimes you can craft your opening so that your readers know exactly what your thesis is even though you only imply it. (Check with your instructor if you're unsure whether an implicit thesis statement will be acceptable.)

In your thesis, try to be precise and concrete, and don't claim more than you can demonstrate in your paper. If your paper is argumentative — that is, if you take a stand, propose a solution, or evaluate something — then you should make your stand, solution, or appraisal clear.

TOPIC	Americans' attitudes toward sports
RESEARCH QUESTION	Is America obsessed with sports?
THESIS	The national obsession with sports must end.

Outlining and Organizing Your Draft

Check your word processor for an outline tool, often in the View menu. As you think critically about your organization, you can assign outline levels to your headings or to individual paragraphs, letting the word processor automatically fashion your sequence in outline form. You then can display headings by hiding text or manipulate text while you reorganize your thinking.

FOR E-WRITERS

You can also personalize a system of coding using bold, italics, underlining, color, or other highlighting. Some writers like to organize their ideas around italicized questions, while others prefer bold headings. Some use a color scheme to show pro and con thinking; others highlight their main pro and con points. These computer features can make your ideas more visual and easier to organize.

Organize Your Ideas.   In writing your paper, it isn't enough to describe your research steps or to string data together in chronological order. You aren't writing a memoir; you're reporting the significance of what you found out. Put your material together in various combinations until you arrive at an organization that fulfills your purpose.

For more on organizing and developing ideas, see Chs. 17 and 19.

If you began with a clear research question, select and organize your evidence to answer it. But don't be afraid to ditch an original question that no longer works and to reorganize around a newly formed question. If your material seems to resist taking shape, you might arrange your source notes or archive in an order that makes sense. Then this sequence becomes a plan you can follow as you write. Or you can write out an informal or formal outline on paper or on the computer.

For more on research questions, see pp. 590–92 and pp. 593–95.

For more on outlining, see pp. 319–33.

Begin to Draft.   An outline is only a skeleton until you flesh it out with details. Use your outline as a working plan, but change the subdivisions or the order of the parts if you discover a better way as you draft. Compare each section of your outline with the source notes you have on hand for it. If for a certain section you lack notes, reconsider your plan, or seek other sources to fill the gap in your research.

For more strategies for drafting, see Ch. 18.

Even if everything hasn't fallen into perfect order, get something down on paper so that you will have something to revise. Start at the beginning or wherever you feel most comfortable. Try also to connect the parts of your paper. For example, summarizing the previous section will remind your reader of what you have already said, especially in a long paper when readers' memories may need refreshing.

As you write, cultivate a certain detachment rather than swaggering in triumph over what you have discovered. Make no exorbitant claims for what you have discovered ("Thus I have shown that day-care centers deserve the trust of parents in the state of Washington"). You have probably not answered your research question for all time; you need not claim to be irrefutable.

LAUNCHING AND CITING YOUR SOURCES AS YOU DRAFT

■ For advice on integrating sources and avoiding plagiarism, see Ch. 32. For more on citing sources, see Ch. 34.

Citing your sources as you draft saves fuss when you're putting your paper into final form. And it prevents unintentional plagiarism. Right after every idea, fact, quotation, paraphrase, or summary captured from your reading or field research, you need to refer your readers to the exact source of your material. If you are following MLA style, note the name of the author and the page of the book or article you borrowed from. (In APA style, add the date.) If you are quoting a field source, include the name of the person speaking, if any.

■ For more on launching source material, see pp. 223–24 and D6 in the Quick Research Guide (the dark-red-edged pages).

When you include a direct quotation in your draft, you can just copy the passage from your computer file and paste it where you want it in your draft file, setting it off with quotation marks. If it is on a note card, you can just tape the whole card into a handwritten or printed draft. If your draft looks sloppy, who cares? Then, as you lay the quotation into place, add a few words to launch or introduce it. Even a brief transition can establish why you have quoted the source or what authority its author lends to your paper.

■ For more on transitions, see pp. 346–49.

If no transition occurs to you as you place a quotation or borrowed idea into your draft, don't sit around waiting for one. A series of slapped-in summaries and quotations makes rough reading, but you can write yourself a reminder in the margin or in brackets to add a transition. Keep writing while the spirit moves you; later, you can add connective tissue.

BEGINNING AND ENDING

Perhaps you will think of a good beginning and conclusion only after you have written the body of your paper. The head and tail of your paper might simply make clear your answer to your initial question. But that is not the only way to begin and end a research paper.

■ For exercises on opening and concluding writing, visit <bedfordstmartins.com/bedguide> and do a keyword search:

open_end

Build to Your Finish.   You might prefer to start out slowly by opening with a clear account of an event to draw your readers into the paper. You could then build up to a strong finish, saving your strongest argument until the end — after you have presented all the evidence to support your thesis. For example, if your paper argues that American children are being harmed by the national obsession with sports, you might organize like this:

- Begin with a factual account of a real event, putting you and your reader on the same footing.
- Explore that event's implications to prepare your reader for your view.
- State your thesis (main idea): for example, "The national obsession with sports must end."
- Support your thesis with evidence captured from well-chosen sources, moving to your strongest argument.
- Then end with a rousing call to action:

For the sake of our children and the future of our country, isn't it time that we put the brakes on America's sports mania? The youth of America have been sold a false and harmful bill of goods. We owe it to the children of America and to ourselves to stop such madness now.

Sum Up the Findings of Others.   Still another way to begin a research paper is to summarize the work of other scholars. One research biologist, Edgar F. Warner, has reduced this time-tested opening to a formula.

> First, in one or two paragraphs, you review everything that has been said about your topic, naming the most prominent earlier commentators. Next you declare why all of them are wrong. Then you set forth your own claim, and you spend the rest of your paper supporting it.

That pattern may seem cut and dried, but it is clear and useful because it places your research and ideas into a historical and conceptual framework. If you browse in specialized journals in many fields — literary criticism, social studies, sciences — you may be surprised to see how many articles begin this very way. Of course, one or two other writers may be enough to argue with. For example, a student writing on the American poet Charles Olson starts her research paper by disputing two views of him.

To Cid Corman, Charles Olson of Gloucester, Massachusetts, is "the one dynamic and original epic poet twentieth-century America has produced" (116). To Allen Tate, Olson is "a loquacious charlatan" (McFinnery 92). The truth lies between these two extremes, nearer to Corman's view.

Whether or not you fully stated your view at the beginning, you will certainly need to make it clear in your closing paragraph. A suggestion: before writing the last lines of your paper, read over what you have written. Then, without referring to your paper, try to put your view into writing.

For more strategies for opening and concluding, see pp. 340–44.

Revising and Editing

Looking over your draft, you may find your essay changing. Don't be afraid to develop a whole new interpretation, shift the organization, strengthen your evidence, drop a section, or add a new one. Answering these questions may help you see how to improve your draft:

For more revising and editing strategies, see Ch. 20.

REVISION CHECKLIST

____ Have you said something original, not just heaped up facts and statements by other writers? Does your voice interpret and unify your materials so that your ideas dominate, not those of your sources?

For more on using your own voice, see p. 210 and pp. 224–25.

___ Is your thesis (main idea) clear?

___ Do all your points support your main idea? Does all your evidence support your points?

___ Does each new idea or piece of information follow from the one before it? Can you see any stronger arrangement? Have you provided transitions to connect the parts?

___ Do you need more—or better—evidence to back up any point? If so, where might you find it?

___ Are the words that you quote truly memorable? Are your paraphrases and summaries accurate and clear? Have you launched (or introduced) everything from a source?

___ Is the source of every quotation, every fact, every idea you have borrowed made unmistakably clear?

After you have revised your research paper, edit and proofread it. Carefully check the grammar, word choice, punctuation, and mechanics—and then correct any problems you find. Check your documentation, too—how you identify sources and how you list the works you have cited in your paper. Here are some questions to get you started editing and proofreading your paper:

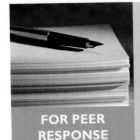

FOR PEER RESPONSE

For general questions for a peer editor, see p. 377.

Have a classmate or friend read your draft and suggest how you might make your paper more informative, tightly reasoned, and interesting. Ask your peer editor to answer questions such as these about writing from sources:

• What is your overall reaction to this paper?

• What is the research question? Does the writer answer that question?

• How effective is the opening? Does it draw you into the paper?

• How effective is the conclusion? Does it merely restate the introduction? Is it too abrupt or too hurried?

• Is the organization logical and easy to follow? Are there any places where the essay is hard to follow?

• Do you know which information is from the writer and which is from the research sources?

• Does the writer need all the quotations he or she has used?

• Do you have any questions about the writer's evidence or the conclusions drawn from the evidence? Point out any areas where the writer has not fully backed up his or her conclusions.

• If this were your paper, what is the one thing you would be sure to work on before handing it in?

Revising a Research Paper

To help you step back from a draft, begin by duplicating your file. (Use a command such as Save As or Versions from the File menu.) This step is important because it will let you experiment without losing your existing draft. Your software may also have a revision option such as Track Changes in the Tools menu. By using colors and cross-outs to highlight text and record comments, this resource allows you to see the changes you make in a text. It can even automatically compare documents so that you can see how much your revision has changed from the previous draft.

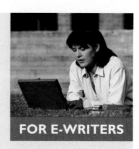
FOR E-WRITERS

EDITING CHECKLIST

____ Have you used commas correctly, especially in complicated sentences   C1
that quote or refer to sources?
____ Have you punctuated quotations correctly?   C3
____ Have you used capital letters correctly, especially in titles of sources?   D1
____ Have you used correct manuscript form?   D3
____ Have you used correct documentation style?

▨ For more help, turn to the dark-blue-edged pages, and find the Quick Editing Guide sections noted here.

▨ For more on documentation, see Ch. 34.

Documenting Sources

A research paper calls on you to follow special rules in documenting your sources — in citing them as you write and in listing them at the end of your paper. At first, these rules may seem fiendishly fussy, but research papers that follow the rules are easy to read and easy to set into type. The rules also ensure that any interested reader can use complete and accurate source information to look up the original materials.

In humanities courses and the social sciences, most writers of research papers follow the style of the Modern Language Association (MLA) or the American Psychological Association (APA). Your instructor will probably suggest which style to follow; if you are not told, use MLA. The first time you prepare a research paper according to MLA or APA rules, you'll need extra time to look up exactly what to do in each situation.

▨ For exercises on citing and listing sources, visit <bedfordstmartins.com/bedguide> and do a keyword search:

cite

▨ For more on using these styles, see pp. 689–707 (MLA) or pp. 718–33 (APA).

OTHER ASSIGNMENTS

Using library, Internet, and field sources, write a research paper on one of the following topics or another that your instructor approves. Proceed as if you had chosen to work on the main assignment described on page 590.

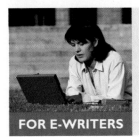

FOR E-WRITERS

Using Software to Document Sources

The Bedford Bibliographer can help you generate bibliographies in MLA, APA, and other styles. To access this tool, visit <bedfordstmartins.com/rewriting>. You can also go to <mla.org> or <apastyle.org/pubmanual.html> to get advice and style updates for the MLA and APA documentation styles.

1. Investigate career opportunities, workplace changes, or trends in a line of work that interests you. Include data from interviews with people in the field.
2. Write a paper discussing the progress being made in the prevention, control, or cure of a disease, including current data.
3. Discuss recent political or economic changes in another country.
4. Compare student achievement in schools with different characteristics — for example, those with limited or extensive computer access or those with low and high numbers of students who move.
5. Study the growth of telecommuting or another technological advance that has changed the relationship between work and home.
6. Write a portrait of life in your town or neighborhood as it was in the past, using sources such as local library archives, photographs or other visual evidence, articles in the local newspaper, and interviews with long-time residents or a local historian.
7. Write a short history of your immediate family, drawing on interviews, photographs, scrapbooks, old letters, and any other available sources.
8. Study the reasons students today give for going to college. Gather your information from interviews or surveys of a variety of students at your college.
9. Investigate a current trend you have noticed on television, collecting evidence by observing programs or commercials.
10. Write a survey of recent films of a certain kind (such as horror movies, martial arts films, comedies, or love stories), supporting your generalizations with evidence from your film watching.

Applying What You Learn: Some Uses of Research

In College Courses.   In many courses beyond your composition class, you will write papers incorporating library, Internet, and field research.

- Some courses require short papers using a few sources, but you'll still need to apply all your research skills — finding, evaluating, and documenting sources or conducting your own field research.

- The more deeply you move into specialized courses for your major, the more independent research you will do. Some colleges require a long research paper of all seniors.

- In some courses, you may prepare a review of the literature or an annotated bibliography on a topic or research question. To do so, you will need to locate, evaluate, and summarize major sources in the field.

For advice on annotated bibliographies, see pp. 621–23.

In the Workplace.   Many workplaces demand — and value — writing based on research that supports their products and services.

- If you took an entry-level job at corporate headquarters, you might be told, "We're opening a branch office in Sri Lanka, and the V.P. doesn't know a thing about the place. Can you write a report on it — customs, geography, climate, government, economy, political stability, religion, lifestyle, and all that?"

- If you start your own business, plan to spend time with print, electronic, and human resources to investigate market segments, growth trends, budgeting, strategic planning, and product development.

- At a large newspaper, reporters and feature writers conduct library and Internet research as well as field interviews and surveys. The newspaper's article archives on subjects covered in the past are in constant use.

In the Community.   Research often benefits you or your community by answering questions, solving problems, or satisfying your curiosity.

- If you oppose plans for a nearby factory that you think might be environmentally unsound, your research on zoning laws and environmental issues will strengthen your appeal to the local planning board.

- As a volunteer at the local women's shelter, you may want to persuade board members to open a second facility by researching other shelters, citing authoritative sources, and reporting your findings.

- Research can be a great help when you or an organization needs to write a grant proposal or to purchase something — be it a new kitchen for the community center or a new car for yourself.

Chapter 34
Documenting Sources

When you use information from other sources — written or spoken — you must document those sources.

- In the text of a paper, cite, or identify, the exact source (book or article, person interviewed, television program, Web site) for every fact or idea that you summarize, paraphrase, or quote from sources.

- At the end of a paper, list the sources that were cited.

The purpose of citing and listing sources is twofold: (1) to give proper credit to the original writer or speaker and (2) to enable any interested reader to look up a source for further information. The mechanics of documentation may seem fussy, but the obligation to cite and list sources keeps research writers truthful and responsible.

Writers of college research papers most often follow the rules for citing and listing sources from either of two style manuals — one compiled by the Modern Language Association (MLA) and the other by the American Psychological Association (APA). MLA style is frequently used in English composition, literature, history, foreign languages, and other humanities courses. APA style usually prevails in the social sciences and business. If your research takes you into scholarly or professional journals in these areas, you will probably find that the articles follow a recognizable style. Other disciplines follow other style manuals: *Scientific Style and Format: The CSE Manual for Authors, Editors, and Publishers,* Seventh Edition (2006), for instance, is used in the sciences and medicine.

You need not memorize any of the documentation styles. Instead, you should understand that you will use different styles in different disciplines, and you need to practice using at least one style to become accustomed to scholarly practices. For your composition course, more than likely your instructor will ask you to use the MLA style. The first part of this chapter illustrates how to cite and list sources in MLA style, and it includes a sample paper. The second part of the chapter shows APA source entries and sample pages from a paper in APA style. This chapter is here for handy reference. It provides a generous sample of print, online, and field examples to help you write your research paper.

Understanding MLA Style

The *MLA Handbook for Writers of Research Papers,* Seventh Edition (New York: MLA, 2009), supplies extensive recommendations for citing sources in your paper and then listing them at the end in a section titled "Works Cited." If you want more detailed advice than that given here, you can purchase a copy of the *MLA Handbook* or consult a copy in the reference room of your college library. Additional advice from MLA is available at <mla.org/style_faq>.

MLA style uses a two-part system to credit sources. First, you briefly cite or identify the source in your text, either by mentioning it directly in your discussion or by noting it in parentheses right after you use the information drawn from it. In most cases, the page number in the original source follows this identification. Second, you lead from this brief identification, usually the author's last name, to a full description of the source in your concluding list, called "Works Cited."

Use the Draft Doctor (pp. 690–91) to figure out how to improve the MLA style in your draft. Skim down the left column to identify questions you might ask about problems in your draft. When you answer a question with "Yes" or "Maybe," move straight across the row to the Diagnose column next to that question. Use the diagnostic activities to identify gaps or weaknesses, and then move straight across the row again to the Treat column on the right. Use the advice that suits your problem as you revise.

■ For a brief overview of MLA style, see E1–E2 in the Quick Research Guide (the dark-red-edged pages).

■ To review how to find details about sources, turn to the Source Navigators on pp. 606–14.

■ To get online help from the Draft Doctor, visit <bedfordstmartins.com/bedguide>.

Citing and Listing Sources in MLA Style

Skim the following directory to find sample entries to guide you as you cite and list your sources. Notice that the examples are organized according to questions you might ask and that comparable print and electronic sources are grouped together. Also see pages 707–17 for a sample paper that illustrates MLA style.

CITING SOURCES IN MLA STYLE

(continued)

Citing and Listing Sources in MLA Style (continued)

Citing Sources in MLA Style

The core of an MLA citation is the author of the source. That person's last name links your use of the source in your paper with its full description in your list of works cited. The most common addition to this name is a specific location, usually a page number, identifying where the material appears in the original source: (Valero 231). This basic form applies whatever the type of source — article, book, or Web page.

As you check your MLA style, keep in mind these three questions:

- Who wrote it?
- What type of source is it?
- How are you capturing the source material?

WHO WROTE IT?

INDIVIDUAL AUTHOR NOT NAMED IN SENTENCE

Placing the author's last name in parentheses, right after the source information, can keep readers focused on the sequence and content of your sentences.

One approach to the complex politics of Puerto Rican statehood is to return to the island's colonial history (Negrón-Mutaner 3).

INDIVIDUAL AUTHOR NAMED IN SENTENCE

Naming the author in your sentence, perhaps with pertinent credentials or experience, may allow you to capitalize on the persuasive value of the author's "expert" status.

The analysis of filmmaker and scholar Frances Negrón-Mutaner connects Puerto Rican history and politics with cultural influences (xvii).

TWO OR THREE AUTHORS

Include each author's last name either in your sentence or in parentheses.

As magazines and newspapers multiplied in eighteenth-century Europe, these publications supplied new knowledge while popularizing old folk traditions (Davies and de Blécourt 6).

FOUR AUTHORS OR MORE

Name all the authors, or follow the name of the first author with the abbreviation "et al." (Latin for "and others"). Identify the source the same way in your list of works cited.

See the listing on p. 697.

Between 1870 and 1900, the nation's cities grew at an astonishing rate (Roark et al. 671).

Draft Doctor: Citing and Listing Sources Accurately in MLA Style

If you sense a problem, ASK	If you answer *Yes/Maybe*, DIAGNOSE	If you diagnose a problem, TREAT
Missing Author or Title Citations? Do I need to add any source citations in my text?	• Highlight each reference to a source. Include all quotations, paraphrases, and summaries. • Check for any other information from an uncredited source.	• Mention the author's last name—or the first words of the title if the author is not identified—in your launch statement or in parentheses right after the source information: Smith explains ... or (Smith). • Add any missing author or title.
Missing Page Numbers or Other Locations? Do I need to add the exact location in the source where I found the information I quoted, paraphrased, or mentioned?	• Mark each quotation and paraphrase because you have drawn them from specific places in the source. • Mark any other material from a specific location in the source.	• Check each mark. Add any missing location as supplied in the source: page (Smith 14), screen (Smith, screen 4), paragraph (Smith, pars. 4-5), volume and page (Smith 3: 288), section (Smith, ch. 3). • Leave out the location for any unnumbered, one-page, or nonprint source or for an entire source: Smith suggests ... or (Smith).
Different Citations in Your Text and Your Works Cited Entries? Do any of my text citations differ from my works cited entries at the end of my paper — or vice versa?	• Check off each text citation that matches a works cited entry. • Check off each works cited entry that matches a text citation. • Circle any source not in both places.	• Add to your works cited any missing source. • Drop from your works cited any source not cited in your draft. (Or add it to your draft if it belongs there.) • Confirm that the names of authors are spelled the same in both places.
Incorrect Author Formats? Have I inconsistently or incorrectly presented any of the authors in my concluding list of works cited?	• Read only the author part of each entry. • Circle any spot in the author part of the entry where you need to check spelling, punctuation, or arrangement of the names.	• Make sure the first of several authors appears last name first and all the rest are first name first: Bradley, Jess, and Lyn Fuller. • Correct spelling or punctuation errors, such as a missing comma after the first name of the first of several authors, and conclude each author section with a period.

If you sense a problem, ASK	If you answer *Yes/Maybe*, DIAGNOSE	If you diagnose a problem, TREAT
Incorrect Source Title Formats? Have I inconsistently or incorrectly presented any source titles in my concluding list of works cited?	• Read only the title part of each entry, checking the format of each article, journal, book, Web site, or other title. • Circle any entry that you need to correct or look up by type.	• Use quotation marks for an article or a posting title; italicize a book, journal, or site title (see the MLA models beginning on p. 698.) • Correct the capitalization, spelling, or punctuation. • End each title with a period before a closing quotation mark or after underlining.
Missing or Incorrect Publication Details? Have I inconsistently or incorrectly presented any source details in my concluding list of works cited?	• Read through only the publication details for each entry, checking the format for the type of source. • Note in the margin each complicated entry (such as that for a work in an anthology). • Circle tricky details (such as a newspaper section).	• Look up a sample entry for each type of source you noted in the margin or for any circled topic, and follow its pattern in your entry. • Check punctuation and spacing in each entry. Improve consistency by working on similar entries, such as all the newspaper articles, at one time.
Unconventional Format for Works Cited Page? Do I need to revise the sequence or format of my list of works cited? (See the sample on pp. 716–17.)	• Check that the entries are in alphabetical order by author's last name or by title (if no author is identified). • Check the margins, spacing, and entry indentation.	• Rearrange entries as needed. • Use your software's Format-Paragraph menu to set a $1/2$-inch hanging indentation for the works cited page. Use the File-Page Setup menu to set 1-inch margins. • Replace any single spacing or extra lines between entries with double spacing.
Any Other Improvements in MLA Style? After a final look at my source citations and list of sources, should I do anything else to improve the MLA style?	• Read your draft out loud to yourself, marking missing, incomplete, or odd source credits. • Ask your peer editors if they spot any inaccurate source credits.	• Return to any marks to correct or complete a text citation or works cited entry. • Consider the useful advice of your peers. • Edit the details until your sources are credited as conventionally as possible.

ORGANIZATION AUTHOR

If a source is sponsored by a corporation, a professional society, or another group, name the sponsor as the author if no one else is specified.

Each year, the Kids Count program (Annie E. Casey Foundation) alerts children's advocates about the status of children in their state.

AUTHOR OF AN ESSAY FROM A READER OR COLLECTION

Cite the author of the essay, not the editor of the collection in which it appears. For example, suppose you consulted Amy Tan's essay "Mother Tongue," which appeared in a collection edited by Wendy Martin. You'd cite Tan as the author, not Martin, and also begin your works cited entry with her name (see p. 700).

Amy Tan explains the "Englishes" of her childhood and family (32).

UNIDENTIFIED AUTHOR

For a source with an unknown author, supply the complete title in your sentence or the first main word or two of the title in parentheses.

According to a recent study, drivers are 42% more likely to get into an accident if they are using a wireless phone while driving ("Driving Dangerously" 32).

SAME AUTHOR WITH MULTIPLE WORKS

If you are citing several of an author's works, the author's name alone won't identify which one you mean. To ensure clarity, add the title, or identify it with a few key words. For example, you would cite two books by Ann Charters, *Major Writers of Short Fiction* and *The Story and Its Writer*, as follows.

▧ Note that italics are used in MLA style for titles of books, periodicals, and Web sites. For more style conventions, see pp. 696–97.

One observer notes the flood of magazine fiction which carries with it "stories of real distinction" (Charters, *Major Writers* 1408). In fact, Charters believes that "the range and quality of the writer's mind are the only limitations on a story's shape" (*Story* 3).

DIFFERENT AUTHORS OF MULTIPLE WORKS

If you cite more than one source in parentheses, separate the works with a semicolon. To keep your paper easy to read, favor shorter, separate references, not long strings of sources.

Ray Charles and Quincy Jones worked together professionally for many years and maintained a strong friendship throughout Charles's life (Lydon 386; Jones 58-59).

WHAT TYPE OF SOURCE IS IT?

Because naming the author is the core of your citation, the basic form applies to any type of source. Even so, a few types of sources may present complications.

A MULTIVOLUME WORK

After the author's name, add the volume number, a colon, and then the specific page.

Malthus has long been credited with this conservative shift in population theory (Durant and Durant 11: 400-03).

INDIRECT SOURCE

If possible, locate and cite the original source. If you do not have access to that source, add "qtd. in" to indicate that the material was "quoted in" the source you cite.

Zill says that, psychologically, children in stepfamilies, even those living in a two-parent household, most resemble children in single-parent families (qtd. in Derber 119).

VISUAL MATERIAL

Many visuals, like other copyrighted materials, cannot be reproduced without the permission of the copyright holder. (Web sites often state their policies and supply contact information.) Ask your instructor for advice whenever you are uncertain about how to handle such material or about whether the "fair use" provision of the copyright law applies, allowing use of a small amount of copyrighted material for purposes such as research.

When you include a visual, help your reader connect it to your text. In your discussion, identify the artist or the artwork, and refer to its figure number.

Eastman Johnson's painting *Life in the South* is a sentimental depiction of American blacks after the Civil War (see fig. 1).

Below the visual, supply a figure number and title, including the source.

Fig. 1. Eastman Johnson, *Life in the South*, 1870, High Museum of Art, Atlanta.

HOW ARE YOU CAPTURING THE SOURCE MATERIAL?

The way you have captured source material—whether in your own words or in a short or long quotation—affects how you present and credit it. Always identify words taken directly from a source by setting them off with quotation marks or using the indented form for a long "block" quotation.

If the material, quoted or not, comes from a specific place in your source, add a page number or other location, such as a paragraph or screen

■ For more on capturing and integrating source materials, see pp. 214–20, pp. 617–19, and Ch. 32.

■ For a sample block quotation, see pp. 694–95.

■ For sample quotations from literature, see pp. 695–96.

number supplied in an electronic source or a chapter or line from a literary work. No page number is needed if the material is general (such as an over-all theme or concept), the source has only one page, or the source — such as a Web site, film, recording, or performance — lacks page numbers.

OVERALL SUMMARY OR IMPORTANT IDEA

Terrill's recent study *Malcolm X: Inventing Radical Judgment* takes a fresh look at the rhetorical power and strategies of Malcolm X's speeches.

SPECIFIC SUMMARY OR PARAPHRASE

One analysis of Malcolm X's 1964 speech "The Ballot or the Bullet" concludes that it exhorts listeners to the radical action of changing vantage point (Terrill 129-31).

Should you paraphrase from a one-page article, no page number is needed because it will be supplied in your list of works cited.

Vacuum-tube audio equipment is making a comeback, with aficionados praising the warmth and glow from the tubes, as well as the sound (Patton).

BLENDED PARAPHRASE AND QUOTATION

When your words are blended with those of your source, clearly distinguish the two. Use quotation marks to set apart the words of your source, and sup-ply the page number in the original.

Some less-than-perfect means have been used to measure television viewing habits, including a sensor that scans rooms for "hot bodies" (Larson 69).

BRIEF QUOTATION WITH FORMAL LAUNCH STATEMENT

Arthur Frank opens his essay with a powerful claim: "Suffering has always animated life writing" (174).

BRIEF QUOTATION INTEGRATED IN SENTENCE

Pain, illness, and disability all contribute to the heartache that "has always animated life writing" (Frank 174).

"Suffering," according to Arthur Frank, "has always animated life writing" (174).

In "Moral Non-fiction: Life Writing and Children's Disability," Frank observes, "Suffering has always animated life writing" (174).

LONG QUOTATION

When a quotation is longer than four typed lines, double-space and indent the entire quotation one inch, or ten spaces, instead of placing quotation marks around it. If the quotation is one paragraph or less, begin its first line without any extra paragraph indentation. Use ellipsis marks (. . .) to show where you omit anything from the middle of the quotation.

Cynthia Griffin Wolff comments on Emily Dickinson's incisive use of language:

> Language, of course, was a far subtler weapon than a hammer. Dickinson's verbal maneuvers would increasingly reveal immense skill in avoiding a frontal attack; she preferred the silent knife of irony to the strident battering of loud complaint. She had never suffered fools gladly. . . . Scarcely submissive, she had acquired the cool calculation of an assassin. (170-71)

QUOTATION FROM THE BIBLE

Instead of the page number, note the version, book, and chapter and verse numbers.

Once again, the author alludes to the same passage: "What He has seen and heard, of that He testifies" (*New American Bible*, John 3.32).

QUOTATION FROM A NOVEL OR SHORT STORY

Give the page number from your own copy first. If possible, include the section or chapter where the passage can be found in any edition.

In *A Tale of Two Cities*, Dickens describes the aptly named Stryver as "shouldering himself (morally and physically) into companies and conversations" (110; bk. 2, ch. 4).

QUOTATION FROM A PLAY

For a verse play, list the act, scene, and line numbers, separated by periods.

"Love," Iago says, "is merely a lust of the blood and a permission of the will" (*Oth.* 1.3.326).

QUOTATION FROM A POEM

Add a slash mark to show where each new line begins. Use the word "line" or "lines" in the first reference but only numbers in subsequent references, as in these examples from William Wordsworth's "The World Is Too Much with Us." The first reference:

"The world is too much with us; late and soon / Getting and spending, we lay waste our powers" (lines 1-2).

The subsequent reference:

"Or hear old Triton blow his wreathed horn" (14).

If a poem has multiple parts, include the part and line numbers, separated by a period, without the word "line."

In "Ode: Intimations of Immortality," Wordsworth ponders the truths of human existence, "Which we are toiling all our lives to find, / In darkness lost, the darkness of the grave" (8.116-17).

Use the following questions to make sure that you have cited sources correctly in MLA style:

RESEARCH CHECKLIST

Citing Sources in MLA Style

___ Have you double-checked to be sure that you have acknowledged all material from a source?

___ Have you placed your citation right after your quotation, paraphrase, summary, or other reference to the source?

___ Have you identified the author of each source in your text or in parentheses?

___ Have you used the first few words of the title to cite a work without an identified author?

___ Have you noted a page number or other specific location whenever needed and available?

___ Have you added any necessary extras, whether volume numbers or poetry lines?

___ Have you checked your final draft to be sure that every source cited in your text also appears in your list of works cited?

Listing Sources in MLA Style

■ For a sample works cited page, see pp. 716–17.

At the end of your paper, list the sources from which you have cited material. Center the title "Works Cited" at the top of a new page. Double-space the list, and alphabetize the entries by authors' last names or, for works with no author, by title. When an entry exceeds one line, indent the following lines one-half inch (or five spaces). (Use the menu in your software — Format-Paragraph-Indentation — to set up this special "hanging" indentation.) Include only sources actually cited in your paper.

To a great extent, listing sources correctly depends on following patterns and paying attention to details such as capitalization and punctuation. For example, the basic MLA pattern places a period after each of an entry's three main parts: (1) author, (2) title, and (3) publication details. In addition, MLA style simplifies the following details:

- Abbreviate months, state names, and scholarly terms.
- List only the first of several cities where a publisher has offices.

- List only the first name (without initials) of a publishing company.
- Drop "Inc.," "Co.," and "Press" from the company name, and abbreviate "University Press" as "UP".
- Use the most recent copyright date for a book, and abbreviate the month of publication for a periodical or Web site.

As you prepare your own entries, begin with the author: first things first. The various author formats apply no matter what your source — article, book, Web page, or other material. Then, from the following examples, select the format for the rest of the entry depending on the type of work you have used. Match your entry to the example, supplying the same information in the same order with the same punctuation and other features. As you work on your list, keep in mind these two key questions, which are used to organize the sample entries that follow:

Who wrote it?

What type of source is it?

WHO WROTE IT?

INDIVIDUAL AUTHOR

Hazzard, Shirley. *The Great Fire*. New York: Farrar, 2003. Print.

TWO OR THREE AUTHORS

Name the authors in the order in which they are listed on the title page.

Phelan, James R., and Lewis Chester. *The Money: The Battle for Howard Hughes's Billions*. New York: Random, 1997. Print.

FOUR AUTHORS OR MORE

Name all the authors, or follow the name of the first author with the abbreviation "et al." (Latin for "and others"). Identify the source in the same way you cite it in the text.

Roark, James L., et al. *The American Promise*. Boston: Bedford, 1998. Print.

See the citation on p. 689.

SAME AUTHOR WITH MULTIPLE WORKS

Arrange the author's works alphabetically by title. Use the author's name for the first entry only; for the other entries, replace the name with three hyphens.

Gould, Stephen Jay. *Full House: The Spread of Excellence from Plato to Darwin*. New York: Harmony, 1996. Print.

---. *Triumph and Tragedy in Mudville: A Lifelong Passion for Baseball*. New York:
    Norton, 2003. Print.

ORGANIZATION AUTHOR

Name the organization as author without its opening "the," "a," or "an."
(The name may reappear as the publisher.)

Student Conservation Association. *The Guide to Graduate Environmental Programs*.
    Washington: Island, 1997. Print.

AUTHOR AND EDITOR

If your paper focuses on the work or its author, cite the author first.

Marx, Karl, and Frederick Engels. *The Communist Manifesto*. 1848. Ed. John E. Toews.
    Boston: Bedford, 1999. Print.

If your paper focuses on the editor or the edition used, cite the editor first.

Toews, John E., ed. *The Communist Manifesto*. By Karl Marx and Frederick Engels.
    1848. Boston: Bedford, 1999. Print.

AUTHOR AND TRANSLATOR

Hoeg, Peter. *Tales of the Night*. Trans. Barbara Haveland. New York: Farrar, 1998. Print.

If your paper focuses on the translation, cite the translator first. Print.

Haveland, Barbara, trans. *Tales of the Night*. By Peter Hoeg. New York: Farrar, 1998.
    Print.

UNIDENTIFIED AUTHOR

"BlogWatch." *Newsweek*. Newsweek, 12 Mar. 2007. Web. 12 Mar. 2007.

WHAT TYPE OF SOURCE IS IT?

Once you have found the format that fits the author, look for the type of
source and the specific entry that best matches yours. Mix and match the
patterns illustrated as needed. For example, a two-volume printed book in
its second edition might send you to several examples until you have covered all of its elements.

Printed or Electronic Book

PRINTED BOOK

■ To see how to create
the listing for a book, turn
to pp. 610–11.

Volkan, Vamik. *Blind Trust: Large Groups and Their Leaders in Times of Crisis
    and Terror*. Charlottesville: Pitchstone, 2004. Print.

ONLINE BOOK

For an online book, supply what you would for a printed book. Then add the name of the site, the electronic publication date, your access date, and the address or URL (uniform resource locator).

Wharton, Edith. *The Age of Innocence*. New York: Appleton, 1920. N. pag.
    Bartleby.com: Great Books Online. Web. 8 Mar. 2007.

MULTIVOLUME WORK

To cite the full work, include the number of volumes ("vols.") after the title.

Who Built America? Working People and the Nation's Economy, Politics, Culture,
    and Society. 2 vols. New York: Worth, 2000. Print.

To cite only one volume, give its number after the title. If you wish, you then can add the total number of volumes after the date.

Who Built America? Working People and the Nation's Economy, Politics, Culture,
    and Society. Vol. 1. New York: Worth, 2000. Print. 2 vols.

REVISED EDITION

Volti, Rudi. *Society and Technological Change*. 5th ed. New York: Worth, 2006. Print.

BOOK PUBLISHED IN A SERIES

After the title, add the series name as it appears on the title page, followed by any series number.

Berlin, Jeffrey B., ed. *Approaches to Teaching Mann's* Death in Venice *and Other Short*
    Fiction. New York: MLA, 1992. Print. Approaches to Teaching World Lit. 43.

BOOK WITH COPUBLISHERS

If a book has more than one publisher, list them in the order given on the title page, separated by a semicolon. (If the publisher uses an imprint name for a line of books, simply identify both with the imprint first: AltaMira-Rowman.)

Hiatt, Alfred. *The Making of Medieval Forgeries: False Documents in Fifteenth-*
    Century England. London: British Library; Toronto: U of Toronto P, 2004. Print.

BOOK WITHOUT PUBLISHER, DATE, OR PAGE NUMBERS

Provide as much information as you can. Use brackets to identify anything that does not come from the source itself. Use "c." (meaning "around" from the Latin *circa*) to indicate an approximate date: c. 1995. Show uncertainty with a question mark: [1972?].

If the date is unknown, use "n.d." (no date). Use "n.p." for no publisher or no place, or simply omit the publisher's name if the work is pre-1900: New York, 1882. If pages are not numbered, use "n. pag." (no pagination), which will clarify why you have omitted page references.

Rosholt, Malcolm. *Days of the Ching Pao: A Photographic Record of the Flying Tigers-14th Air Force in China in World War II*. N.p.: n.p., 1978. Print.

Part of a Printed or an Electronic Book

When citing part of a book, give the author of that part first. Add the editor of the book after its title and the page numbers of the selection after the publication information. For an online book, add the name of the site, any electronic publication date, your access date, and the URL.

SELECTION FROM A PRINTED BOOK

Burke, Kenneth. "A Grammar of Motives." *The Rhetorical Tradition: Readings from Classical Times to the Present*. Ed. Patricia Bizzell and Bruce Herzberg. Boston: Bedford, 2001. 1298-324. Print.

SELECTION FROM AN ONLINE BOOK

Webster, Augusta. "Not Love." *A Book of Rhyme*. London, 1881. *Victorian Women Writers Project*. Web. 8 Mar. 2007.

PREFACE, INTRODUCTION, FOREWORD, OR AFTERWORD

Harjo, Joy. Introduction. *The Secret Powers of Naming*. By Sara Littlecrow-Russell. Tucson: U of Arizona P, 2006. ix-xi. Print.

ESSAY, SHORT STORY, OR POEM FROM AN EDITED COLLECTION

Rothman, Rodney. "My Fake Job." *The Best American Nonrequired Reading*. Ed. Dave Eggers. Boston: Houghton, 2002. 117-32. Print.

TWO OR MORE WORKS FROM THE SAME EDITED COLLECTION

If you list more than one selection from an anthology, you can prepare an entry for the collection (instead of repeating it for each selection) and refer to it from the entries for the readings.

Cisneros, Sandra. "Only Daughter." Martin 10-13.

Martin, Wendy, ed. *The Beacon Book of Essays by Contemporary American Women*. Boston: Beacon, 1996. Print.

Tan, Amy. "Mother Tongue." Martin 32-37.

ARTICLE FROM A PRINTED REFERENCE WORK

It is not necessary to supply the editor, publisher, or place of publication for well-known references such as *Webster's, The Random House Dictionary, World Book Encyclopedia,* and *Encyclopaedia Britannica.* No volume and page numbers are needed when a reference book is organized alphabetically. If an article's author is identified by initials, check the book's list of contributors, which should supply the full name.

Raymer, John D., and Margarita Nieto. "Octavio Paz." *Notable Latino Writers.*
    Pasadena: Salem, 2006. Print.

ARTICLE FROM AN ONLINE REFERENCE WORK

"Harlem Renaissance." *Encyclopaedia Britannica.* 2007. *Encyclopaedia Britannica.*
    Web. 26 July 2007.

Article in a Printed or an Electronic Periodical

ARTICLE FROM A JOURNAL PAGINATED BY VOLUME

For an article from a journal in which page numbers run continuously through all issues of a volume, give the volume number, issue number, year, page numbers, and medium.

Daly, Mary E. "Recent Writing on Modern Irish History: The Interaction between Past
    and Present." *Journal of Modern History* 69.3 (1997): 512-33. Print.

ARTICLE FROM A JOURNAL PAGINATED BY ISSUE

For an article from a journal that starts each issue with page 1, provide the same information as above: the volume number, issue number, year, page numbers, and medium.

McHaney, Pearl Amelia. "Eudora Welty (1909-2001)." *South Atlantic Review* 66.4
    (2001): 134-36. Print.

ARTICLE FROM AN ONLINE JOURNAL

Supply the same information that you would for a print article, using "n. pag." if the source does not provide page numbers; end with the medium and your access date.

Purdy, James P., and Joyce R. Walker. "Digital Breadcrumbs: Case Studies of Online
    Research." *Kairos* 11.2 (2007): n. pag. Web. 8 Mar. 2007.

ARTICLE ACCESSED ONLINE THROUGH A LIBRARY OR SUBSCRIPTION SERVICE

If you find a source through a library subscription service, include the name of the service, the medium, and your access date.

To see how to create the listing for a journal article from a database, turn to pp. 608–09.

Sataline, Suzanne. "Charter Schools Could Hit Ceiling." *Boston Globe* 31 Mar. 2004:
    B1. *America's Newspapers*. Web. 31 Aug. 2007.

If you use a personal subscription service such as *America Online*, give the same information as for a library subscription service.

"Echocardiography." *Merriam-Webster Medical Dictionary*. 4 Feb. 2003. *America
    Online*. Web. 14 Mar. 2007.

ARTICLE FROM A PRINTED MAGAZINE

To see how to create the listing for a magazine article, turn to pp. 606–07.

Give the month and year of the issue, or its specific date, after the title of the magazine.

Rushin, Steve. "Don't Mess with the Ballpoint Pen." *Sports Illustrated* 15 Mar.
    2004: 15. Print.

If the article's pages are not consecutive, add a + after its initial page.

"A User's Guide to the Brain." *Time* 29 Jan. 2007: 55+. Print.

ARTICLE FROM AN ONLINE MAGAZINE

Bowden, Mark. "Jihadists in Paradise." *Atlantic*. Atlantic Monthly Group, Mar. 2007.
    Web. 8 Mar. 2007.

ARTICLE FROM A PRINTED NEWSPAPER

If the newspaper has different editions, indicate after the date the one where the article can be found: natl. ed. If the pages for the article are not consecutive, add a + after its initial page.

Fahrenthold, David A. "What Would It Take to Clean Up the Bay by 2010?"
    Washington Post 29 Jan. 2007: A1+. Print.

ARTICLE FROM AN ONLINE NEWSPAPER

Austen, Ian. "The Internet: It's the New TV." *New York Times*. New York Times, 24
    Feb. 2005. Web. 8 Mar. 2007

EDITORIAL FROM A PRINTED PERIODICAL

Jacoby, Jeff. "When Jerusalem Was Divided." Editorial. *Boston Globe* 8 Jan.
    2001: A11. Print.

"Media Reform's Moment." Editorial. *Nation* 29 Jan. 2007: 4. Print.

EDITORIAL FROM AN ONLINE PERIODICAL

"Latin America's Turn." Editorial. *Washington Post*. Washington Post, 7 Mar. 2007.
    Web. 8 Mar. 2007.

LETTER TO THE EDITOR

Evans, Harold. Letter. *Atlantic Monthly* Jan.-Feb. 2007: 20. Print.

REVIEW

Include the words "Rev. of " before the title of the work reviewed.

Coukell, Allan. "The Cell That Wouldn't Die." Rev. of *Culturing Life: How Cells Became*
    Technologies, by Hannah Landecker. *Discover* Feb. 2007: 68. Print.

Other Printed or Electronic Document

PRINTED GOVERNMENT DOCUMENT

Generally, the "author" will be the name of the government and the government agency, separated by periods. If the document names an author or editor, that name may be provided either before the title or after it, if you identify the agency as author.

United States. Census Bureau. *Statistical Abstract of the United States, 2007:*
    The National Data Book. 126th ed. Washington: GPO, 2007. Print.

ONLINE GOVERNMENT DOCUMENT

United States. National Institutes of Health. National Institute of Child Health
    and Human Development. "Why Are the Tween and Teen Years So Critical?" *Milk*
    Matters. NICHD, 21 Aug. 2006. Web. 8 Mar. 2007.

ONLINE DOCUMENT

First identify the document; then supply the details about its electronic
location.

Carter, Jimmy. "Inaugural Address of Jimmy Carter." 20 Jan. 1977. *The Avalon*
    Project. Yale Law School, 1997. Web. 8 Mar. 2007.

PAMPHLET

Health Center at Auraria. *Healthy Moves: Health Education Programming Fall*
    2007/Spring 2008. Denver: Health Center at Auraria, 2007. Print.

DOCTORAL DISSERTATION OR MASTER'S THESIS

If the study is unpublished, place the title in quotation marks; if published,
underline the title. Follow the title with "Diss." (for a dissertation) or with
an apt master's abbreviation (such as "MA thesis").

Beilke, Debra J. "Cracking Up the South: Humor and Identity in Southern
    Renaissance Fiction." Diss. U of Wisconsin, Madison, 1997. Print.

Internet or Electronic Source

Helping a reader find the same material you cited and listed can be difficult with Internet materials. Some sources, such as Web sites, exist only in electronic form and may disappear or change at random. New electronic forms (such as blogs) can rapidly develop.

PERSONAL WEB PAGE

If no title is available, include an identification such as "Home page."

■ See the directory on pp. 687–88 for entries for other electronic sources, including books and articles.

Tannen, Deborah. Home page. Georgetown U and Deborah Tannen, 1997. Web. 8 Mar. 2007.

ORGANIZATION WEB PAGE

"Office for Research and Statistics." *American Library Association*. ALA, 2007. Web. 8 Mar. 2007.

HOME PAGE FOR A CAMPUS DEPARTMENT OR COURSE

UCLA Department of Sociology. UCLA, n.d. Web. 8 Mar. 2007.

BLOG OR BLOG ENTRY

■ To see how to create the listing for a Web page, turn to pp. 612–13.

To cite a blog entry, give the title of the entry in quotation marks. If a blog comment does not have a title, use a label such as "Blog comment."

Owazny, Kit. Blog comment. *Culture Monster*. Los Angeles Times, 31 May 2009. Web. 31 May 2009.

If there is no apparent sponsor of the blog you are citing, use "N.p" for no publisher.

Finnerty, Erin. *Verbs of Leisure*. N.p., 10 Feb. 2008. Web. 14 Feb. 2008.

PUBLICATION ON CD-ROM

Sheehy, Donald, ed. *Robert Frost: Poems, Life, Legacy*. New York: Holt, 1997. CD-ROM.

COMPUTER SOFTWARE

Electronic Supplements for Real Writing: 1. Interactive Writing Software. Vers. 1. Boston: Bedford, 2004. CD-ROM.

Visual or Audio Source

ADVERTISEMENT

Starbucks. Advertisement. *Vanity Fair* Apr. 2007: 205. Print.

COMIC OR CARTOON

Supply the cartoonist's name and identification as a comic strip or cartoon.

McDonnell, Patrick. "Mutts." Comic strip. *Atlanta Journal Constitution* 2 Feb. 2005: F5.
    Print.

PHOTOGRAPH

Supply the place (museum or gallery and city) where the photograph is
housed. If you are citing it from a publication, identify that source.

Stieglitz, Alfred. *Self-Portrait*. J. Paul Getty Museum, Los Angeles. *Stieglitz: A
    Beginning Light*. By Katherine Hoffman. New Haven: Yale UP, 2004. 251. Print.

Strand, Paul. *Fifth Avenue, New York*. 1915. Photograph. Museum of Modern Art, New
    York.

For a family or personal photograph, identify who took it and when.

Bay Street Food Pantry. Personal photograph by author. 6 Nov. 2007.

WORK OF ART

Botticelli, Sandro. *The Birth of Venus*. 1482–86. Tempera on canvas. Uffizi Gallery,
    Florence.

AUDIOTAPE OR RECORDING

Begin with the name of the artist, composer, speaker, writer, or other contributor, based on your interest in the recording. Include the medium using
a designation such as "Audiocassette," "CD," or "LP."

Byrne, Gabriel. *The James Joyce Collection*. Dove Audio, 1996. Audiocassette.

PROGRAM ON TELEVISION OR RADIO

Blue Man Group: Inside the Tube. PBS. WGBH, Boston. 10 Mar. 2007. Television.

"Marvel Comics Kills Off Captain America." *Morning Edition*. Natl. Public Radio. KPFR,
    Denver. 8 Mar. 2007. Radio

FILM

Start with the title unless you wish to emphasize the work of a person connected with the film.

Lord of the Rings: The Return of the King. Dir. Peter Jackson. New Line Cinema, 2003.
    Film.

Jackson, Peter, dir. *Lord of the Rings: The Return of the King*. New Line Cinema, 2003.
   Film.

LIVE PERFORMANCE

Rock 'n' Roll. By Tom Stoppard. Dir. Trevor Nunn. Perf. Nicole Ansari, Louise Bangay,
   Anthony Calf, and Martin Chamberlain. Royal Court Theatre, London. 5 June 2006.
   Performance.

Conversation or Field Artifact

PERSONAL, TELEPHONE, OR E-MAIL INTERVIEW

Indicate how you conducted the interview: in person, by telephone, or by
e-mail.

■ To see how to create
the listing for an inter-
view, turn to p. 614.

Boyd, Dierdre. Personal interview. 5 Feb. 2007.

BROADCAST INTERVIEW

Identify the source by the person interviewed; if you wish, you may also
identify the interviewer (Interview by X).

Raddatz, Martha. Interview. *Fresh Air*. Natl. Public Radio. WBUR, Boston. 3 Mar. 2007.
   Radio.

PUBLISHED INTERVIEW

Marshall, Chan. Interview. *Spin*. Dec. 2006: 72-75. Print.

SPEECH OR LECTURE

Wexel, Beth. Fall Convocation. Craig Hall, Wilton College. 29 Aug. 2007. Address.

PERSONAL LETTER

Use "MS" for a manuscript (a letter written by hand) or "TS" for a typescript
(a letter composed on a machine).

Finch, Katherine. Letter to the author. 1 Nov. 2007. TS.

E-MAIL

Moore, Jack. Message to the author. 11 Oct. 2007. E-mail.

ONLINE POSTING

Use the subject line as the title. Use the label "Online posting" if the posting
has no title.

Robinson, Meena. "Mansfield Park." *PBS Discussions*. PBS, 28 Jan. 2008. Web. 18 May
   2008.

Cite a posting received via an e-mail discussion group or forum just as you would an e-mail message.

Walsh, Karen. "Responsible Use of Technology." Message to the education technology discussion list. 28 May 2009. E-mail.

Use the following questions to make sure that you have listed sources correctly in MLA style:

Listing Sources in MLA Style

—— Have you begun each entry with the appropriate pattern for the author's name?

—— Have you figured out what type of source you have used? Have you followed the sample pattern for that type as exactly as possible?

—— Have you used quotation marks and underlining correctly for titles?

—— Have you used the conventional punctuation — periods, commas, colons, parentheses — in your entry?

—— Have you accurately recorded the name of the author, title, publisher, and so on?

—— Have you checked the accuracy of numbers such as pages, volumes, and dates?

—— Have you correctly identified the medium of publication or reception, using a label such as Print, Web, CD, DVD, Film, Lecture, Performance, Radio, Television, or E-mail?

—— Have you arranged your entries in alphabetical order?

—— Have you checked your final list against your text citations so that every source appears in both places?

—— Have you double-spaced your list, just like the rest of your paper? Have you allowed an inch margin on all sides?

—— Have you begun the first line of each entry at the left margin? Have you indented each additional line one-half inch (or five spaces)?

A Sample MLA Research Paper

In her paper "Higher Education: Pricey or Priceless?" Maegan Kinkelaar investigates why the costs of a college education are increasing and how schools and students are responding to the problem. Besides incorporating many features of effective research papers, this paper also illustrates the conventions for citing and listing sources in MLA style. Because an outline also was required, it precedes the paper.

*Writer's last name, fol-
lowed by page number in
small roman numerals, on
upper right corner of all
pages of outline*

*"Outline" centered, one
inch from top*

Main idea stated in thesis

*Double-spacing through-
out*

*Sentence outline providing
a skeleton of the research
paper*

■ For more sample stu-
dent research papers, visit
<bedfordstmartins.com/
bedguide> and do a key-
word search:

sample papers

Kinkelaar i

Outline

Higher Education: Pricey or Priceless?

Thesis: Although state and federal governments and individual
schools are taking steps to make higher education more
affordable, paying for college remains a challenge for many
students and their families.

   I. Give a three-year-old $5, and he will think he is rich.
       A. With tuition rising, he will need multitudes of those bills
           for college.
       B. Paying for college remains a challenge for many students
           and their families.
  II. No type of higher education is safe from the increases.
       A. Tuition rose at public two-year colleges, public four-year
           colleges, and private four-year institutions.
       B. Concern continues about the level of increases.
 III. The current financial situation of U.S. colleges began about
       ten years ago.
       A. A growing economy encouraged expansion.
       B. When the economy shifted, financial support was no
           longer available.
       C. The lack of funding has been worsened by recession and
           competing priorities.
  IV. Because the schools have received less money, they have had
       to come up with the funds somehow.
       A. The most common way has been to raise tuition and fees.
       B. Another way is to increase costs of student programs and
           services.
           1. One example is raising the price of football tickets.
           2. Another example is cutting financial aid.
           3. Other cuts reduce new library books and sports teams.
           4. More drastic cuts reduce the number of incoming
               freshmen and staff.
   V. States and colleges try to lessen the blow to students' and
       parents' bank accounts.

Kinkelaar ii

A. The Democratic Governors Association has proposed a refundable tax credit for families and block grants for states.

B. Grants have increased, but more students are asking for them.

C. Certain schools are going to great lengths to appeal to lower-income students.

   1. Some schools are offering free tuition.

   2. Others have gotten rid of loans for low-income students.

VI. Low-income students still need to pay any additional tuition and other expenses.

A. More and more students are turning to loans.

   1. The biggest problem is that loans have to be paid back with interest.

   2. Debt loads can be crushing.

   3. Loans take years to pay off.

B. Many students take jobs during school to avoid or lessen the need for loans.

   1. Of the large percentage with jobs, many work full time.

   2. Some take federal work-study jobs.

   3. Some find a second job or another job altogether.

VII. Paying for a college education is not easy for most students and their families.

Writer's last name and
page number ½" from top
of page

Writer's name
Instructor's name
Course
Date
Title, centered

*For more on beginning
a research paper, see
pp. 680–81.*

Double spacing throughout

*Thesis previewing paper's
development*
*For more on a thesis
for a research paper, see
pp. 677–78.*

*Electronic source without
page number cited only
by author*

*Title used in launch
statement for source
without an author*

*Page number locates
information in source*

*Evidence from Hebel
summarized*

History explored

*Launch statement names
article, publication, and
author*

1"

½"
Kinkelaar 1

Maegan Kinkelaar
Professor Waters
English Composition II
9 January 2007

½" indent
(or 5 spaces)   Higher Education: Pricey or Priceless?

Give a three-year-old $5, and he will think he is rich.
With that money in his hand, he will imagine that he can get
anything or go anywhere in the world. Give the same kid $5
when he is eighteen, and he will want to know why you
did not give him more. Now he has graduated from high
school and wants to go to college. How far will that $5 take
him toward getting an education at his chosen school? With
college tuition rising nationwide, he will need multitudes of
$5 bills. Although state and federal governments and individual
schools are taking steps to make higher education more
affordable, paying for college remains a challenge for many
students and their families.

No type of higher education is safe from the increases.
On average, for the 2005-2006 academic year, tuition rose by
3.2% at public two-year colleges, by 4.8% at public four-year
colleges, and by 3.7% at private four-year institutions, senior
reporter Sara Hebel writes in the *Chronicle of Higher Education*.
And the upward climb is continuing. The College Board's
Trends in College Pricing 2006 reports that for the 2006-2007
academic year, the increase was 4.1% at public two-year
colleges, 6.3% at public four-year colleges, and 5.9% at
private four-year institutions (4). Although growth in tuition is
slowing, observers of higher education remain concerned about
the level of increases students have seen—and will likely
continue to see (Hebel).

The current financial situation of U.S. colleges began
with the strong economy about ten years ago. In an article titled
"College Students Strain to Cover Rising Tuition at Public
Institutions," *Education Week* writer Sean Cavanagh reports,

1"

Kinkelaar 2

"When the economy is thriving, as in the late 1990s, states tend to spend generously on higher education. . . . States expand university programs with little regard for their long-term costs . . . while keeping tuition increases to a minimum." The colleges could afford the new programs and all their expenses while the economy was on the rise, Cavanagh writes; however, they failed to prepare for times when the economy was not as stable and money was not as accessible for colleges and students alike.

Experts say that a major reason for increased tuition for higher education has been a lack of state and federal funding for schools, worsened by an economic recession that took hold early in this decade. In 2003 William Trombley, senior editor at the National Center for Public Policy and Higher Education, reported on this trend and competing spending priorities, such as the war in Iraq, Medicaid, and education for students in kindergarten through twelfth grade. Because the schools have received less money, they have had to come up with the funds somehow. The most common way of making up for the shortfall has been to raise the tuition and fees for each college student. Although state finances have improved somewhat since the time of Trombley's article (Hebel), government funding for education remains a concern.

Another way colleges look to gain money is by increasing costs of student programs and services. In a 2004 article in the *Battalion*, the student newspaper at Texas A&M University, writer Sara Foley reports that, due to a tuition increase, the university's athletic department raised the price of football tickets. According to department chief of staff Penny King, roughly 420 of 650 student athletes at the school are on scholarship (Foley). When tuition increases, either the number of scholarships given out must decrease or the scholarship money available must increase to keep the same number of students on scholarship. The former development places yet another potential strain on the college students' bank accounts. *Education Week*'s Cavanagh explains that

Direct quotation selected to make critical point

Ellipses show where words are omitted

Paraphrase of original source
No page number needed for one-page article

■ For an explanation of the difference between paraphrasing and summa-rizing, see p. 617–19.

Launch statement names author and notes credentials

Author named in paren-theses; no page number for online source without page numbers

Transition leads into another way of obtaining funds

Kinkelaar 3

Ellipses show information omitted from original

No page number available in online source

Point from last paragraph used for transition to new point

Only one citation needed for material in sequence in a paragraph and clearly from the same source

For more on integrating sources, see Ch. 32.

For an explanation of statistics as evidence, see pp. 38–39.

Facts and statistics support main point

during prosperous economic times like those of the 1990s, schools put new programs into place. However, he writes, "when harder economic times come around . . . states end up cutting money for those same programs."

Aside from cuts in financial aid, Trombley points to other consequences of tuition increases and constrained funding for higher education, such as reduced budgets to buy new library books and cuts to sports teams. He reports that some schools are even going as far as to lower the number of incoming freshmen. With fewer freshmen, less staffing is needed. As he illustrates, some staff members take early retirement, while remaining personnel go without raises. The rising cost of higher education does not just hurt the pocketbooks of students and their parents; it affects many more.

Despite what one might think, states and colleges alike are trying to lessen the blow to students' and parents' bank accounts. In a 2006 *Education Week* article, "College Try," Alyson Klein reports that in an attempt to increase the number of college graduates by over one million and to make college more affordable, the Democratic Governors Association has proposed a refundable college-tuition tax credit of $3,000 for families and block grants for states. If these proposals are enacted, the school or university would get its money while tuition payers, whether students or their parents, would get a tax break on education expenses. Also, aid in the form of grants has increased, notes *Chronicle of Higher Education* senior reporter Elizabeth Farrell, pointing out that grant awards have increased at a higher rate than tuition prices over the past decade. Yet she adds that an 11% increase in the number of students awarded Pell Grants over this period was nearly offset by an increase in Pell Grant funding of just 15%. In other words, while the total amount of financial aid is growing, so is the number of students who are asking for it, and that's not good news for lower-income students.

Kinkelaar 4

Nevertheless, certain universities are going to great lengths to appeal to lower-income students who have difficulty paying for college. For instance, some schools are even offering free tuition, as journalist Emily Brandon reported recently in *U.S. News & World Report* (74-75). Brandon described the University of Virginia's AccessUV, a program which caps eligible students' loans at approximately 25% of the cost of in-state tuition over the course of their education (74). The school then gives grants for what is not covered by the loans. Basically, this means that a low-income student would have to pay only one year's worth of tuition while earning a four-year degree. Additionally, other institutions (Miami University in Ohio, Michigan State University, Rice University, the University of North Carolina-Chapel Hill, and the University of Pennsylvania) have gotten rid of loans for low-income students altogether. While these and other aid programs help many, low-income students still need to come up with any additional required tuition payments, as well as money for room and board, books, transportation, and other educational expenses—no small feat.

Loans and jobs are two common ways in which students pay for their education, and more and more students are turning to loans. Between the 2002-03 school year and the 2003-04 school year, the number of loans taken out from private lenders increased by 43% (Hoover). And between 1992-93 and 1999-2000, the percentage of bachelor's degree recipients who took out loans increased in every income category, for both dependent and independent students (see Fig. 1).

The biggest problem with loans is that, unlike grants, they have to be paid back and with interest. Because of interest expenses, borrowers end up paying considerably more for their education than those who did not have to take out loans. Even without factoring in interest payments, debt loads can be crushing. According to a recent report from the U.S. Department

Page numbers provided for print article

Key term, free tuition, *defined*

Specific examples noted

Additional statistics provided

Figure cited in text

Kinkelaar 5

Source presents and credits findings of another study

[1]Refers to 1992-93 or 1999-2000 status. Dependency status and income may have varied throughout students' undergraduate education.

Figure labeled in caption; source information provided

Fig 1. Percentage of 1992-93 and 1999-2000 Bachelor's Degree Recipients Who Borrowed for Their Undergraduate Education, by Family Income and Dependency Status, United States, Dept. of Educ., Natl. Center for Educ. Statistics, *Baccalaureate and Beyond Longitudinal Study, 1993-94 and 2000-01* (qtd. in Choy and Li).

of Education, *Action Plan for Higher Education: Improving Accessibility, Affordability, and Accountability*, between 1995 and 2005, students graduating from four-year institutions had median debt levels in the five digits: $15,500 for public colleges and $19,400 for private institutions. Although most loans do not have to be paid back as long as students remain in school, once they quit or graduate, they are expected to begin making payments. And loans take years to pay off. Many students take jobs during school to lessen the need for loans or to avoid taking out loans in the first place. Cavanagh gives the surprising statistic that approximately 75% of students at four-year institutions have jobs with 25% of these students working full-time.

Some students take federal work-study jobs offered by their college or university. *Peterson's College Money Handbook* explains the federal work-study program:

Kinkelaar 6

This program provides jobs for students who demonstrate

1" indent
(or 10 spaces)
need. Salaries are paid by funds from the federal
government as well as the college. You work on an
hourly basis on or off campus and must be paid at least
the federal minimum wage. You may earn only up to the
amount awarded in the financial aid package. (19)

Work-study can be a great way for students to gain experience in
their field of study. Also, since students are employed by the
school, the hours are usually flexible, and supervisors are
understanding about high-stress times such as finals week. While
some think that work-study is the ideal college job, others
disagree because of the limit in income a student can earn. Some
students find a second job or another job altogether. They, like all
employed students, have to balance school, work, family
responsibilities, and a social life. Is this tough? Yes, but somehow
students do it.

Paying for a college education is not easy for most students
and their families. Loans for a four-year degree could take more
than ten years to pay back. Students who choose to work full
time instead of taking out loans will probably take longer to
finish school because of their inability to focus fully on classes
and homework. If you are trying to decide whether college is right
for you, take a minute to ask yourself a couple of questions: How
do you plan to pay for college? Is college worth the price you
pay? When you figure out the answer to those questions, you will
know whether a higher education is just pricey or whether it is
priceless.

Direct quotation of longer than four lines set off from text without quotation marks, followed by page number in parentheses

For more on concluding a research paper, see pp. 680–81.

Conclusion emphasizes critical points and raises intriguing questions

List of works cited on a separate page

List alphabetized by names of authors or by titles (when no author is named)

First line of entry at left margin

Additional lines indented ¹/₂"

Kinkelaar 7

Works Cited

Brandon, Emily. "Better Yet, No Tuition." *U.S. News & World Report* 18 Sept. 2006: 74-75. Print.

Cavanagh, Sean. "College Students Strain to Cover Rising Tuition at Public Institutions." *Education Week* 21.38 (2002): 6. *Academic Search Premier*. Web. 5 Jan. 2007.

Choy, Susan P., and Xiaojie Li. "Debt Burden: A Comparison of 1992-93 and 1999-2000 Bachelor's Degree Recipients a Year After Graduating." *Education Statistics Quarterly* 7.1-2 (2006): n. pag. Web. 4 Jan. 2007.

Farrell, Elizabeth. "Public-College Tuition Rise Is Largest in Three Decades." *Chronicle of Higher Education* 31 Oct. 2003. *FirstSearch*. Web. 5 Jan. 2007.

Foley, Sara. "Ticket Price Increase Due to Rising Tuition." *Battalion*. Battalion Online, 26 Oct. 2004. Web. 27 Dec. 2006.

Hebel, Sara. "Tuition: Some Increases Slow Down, but Concerns Linger." *Chronicle of Higher Education* 6 Jan. 2006. *FirstSearch*. Web. 5 Jan. 2007.

Hoover, Eric. "Public Colleges See a Ten Percent Rise in Tuition for 2004-5." *Chronicle of Higher Education* 29 Oct. 2004. *FirstSearch*. Web. 4 Jan. 2007.

Klein, Alyson. "College Try." *Education Week* 25.43 (2006): 30. *Academic Search Premier*. Web. 5 Jan. 2007.

Peterson's College Money Handbook. Lawrenceville: Thomson/Peterson's, 2005. Print.

"Trends in College Pricing 2006." *College Board*. College Board, 2006. Web. 27 Dec. 2006.

Trombley, William. "The Rising Price of Higher Education." *College Affordability in Jeopardy: A Special Supplement to National Crosstalk*. National Center for Public Policy and Higher Education, Winter 2003. Web. 5 Jan. 2007.

United States. Dept. of Education. *Action Plan for Higher Education: Improving Accessibility, Affordability, and Accountability*. Sept. 2006. Web. 5 Jan. 2007.

■ For a brief overview of APA style, see E1–E2 in the Quick Research Guide (the dark-red-edged pages).

Understanding APA Style

The American Psychological Association (APA) details the style most commonly used in the social sciences in its *Publication Manual,* Fifth Edition (Washington, D.C.: APA, 2001), and its *Style Guide to Electronic References* (2007). For more advice and updates, visit <apastyle.apa.org>.

APA style uses a two-part system to credit sources. First, you briefly cite or identify the author and date of the source in your text, either by mentioning them in your discussion or by noting them in parentheses right after you refer to the information drawn from the source. In many cases, you also supply the page number or other location in the original source. Second, you lead from this brief identification, through the author's name, to a full description of the source in your concluding list, called "References."

Citing and Listing Sources in APA Style

Skim the following directory to find sample entries to guide you as you cite and list your sources. Notice that the examples are organized according to questions you might ask and that comparable print and electronic sources are grouped together. Also see pages 733–36 for selections from a sample paper that illustrates APA style.

(continued)

Citing and Listing Sources in APA Style (continued)

Citing Sources in APA Style

The core of an APA citation is the author of the source. That person's last name links your use of the source in your paper with its full description in your list of references. Next comes the date of the source, which often establishes its currency or its classic status for readers. (Within a paragraph, you don't need to repeat this date if you refer to the source again unless a reader might mix up the sources under discussion.) A common addition is a specific location, such as a page number (using "p." for "page" or "pp." for "pages"), that tells where the material appears in the original source. Unless the source does not have page numbers or other locators, this information is required for quotations and recommended for paraphrases and key concepts. When you supply these elements in parentheses, separate them with commas: (Westin, 2005, p. 48). This basic form applies whatever the type of source — article, book, or Web page.

As you check your APA style, keep in mind these three questions:

- Who wrote it?
- What type of source is it?
- How are you capturing the source material?

WHO WROTE IT?

INDIVIDUAL AUTHOR NOT NAMED IN SENTENCE

Some experts feel that adolescent boys who bully are depressed and acting out in an aggressive manner (Pollack, 2000).

INDIVIDUAL AUTHOR NAMED IN SENTENCE

Pollack (2000) contends that boys tend to contain their pain for fear of appearing vulnerable and inviting ridicule.

TWO AUTHORS

List the last names of coauthors in the order in which they appear in the source. Join the names with "and" if you mention them in your text and with an ampersand (&) if the citation is in parentheses.

A group's cultural development enhances its chance for survival, providing both physical and psychological protection (Anderson & Ross, 1998).

Anderson and Ross (1998) maintain that the development of a group's culture provides both physical and psychological protection.

THREE AUTHORS OR MORE

For three to five authors, include all the last names in your first reference. In any later references, identify only the first author and add "et al." (for "and others"), whether in the text or in parentheses. For six authors or more, simply use the name of the first author with "et al." for all citations.

The field of conservation biology has developed in response to the accelerating rate at which species are being lost (Purves, Orians, & Heller, 1999). Purves et al. specifically explore the consequences of human activities in relation to this acceleration.

ORGANIZATION AUTHOR

Important as nutrition is for healthy people, it is even more critical for cancer patients who may have specific dietary needs such as more protein (American Cancer Society, 2003, p. 7).

AUTHOR OF AN ESSAY FROM A READER OR COLLECTION

Cite the author of the essay; the editor of the collection is identified later in your reference list.

Although rapes occur each year in campus fraternity houses, research studies have yet to investigate why these locations are more likely venues for rape than other college gathering places (Martin & Hummer, 2003).

See the listing on p. 727.

UNIDENTIFIED AUTHOR

Identify the source with a short title, beginning with the first few words so that it is easy to locate in your alphabetical list of references.

Parents are encouraged to monitor their child's online activities ("Social Networking," 2006).

SAME AUTHOR WITH MULTIPLE WORKS

Three significant trends in parent-school relations evolved (Grimley, 2007) after the original multistate study (Grimley, 1987).

DIFFERENT AUTHORS WITH MULTIPLE WORKS

Within a single citation, list the authors of multiple works in alphabetical order (as in your reference list). Separate the works with semicolons.

Several studies have been designed to determine reasons for minority underperformance in educational attainment (Bowen & Bok, 1998; Charles, Dinwiddie, & Massey, 2004; Glazer, 1997).

WHAT TYPE OF SOURCE IS IT?

Naming the author is the core of the basic APA citation form, regardless of the type of source you have used. Even so, a few types of sources may present complications.

INDIRECT SOURCE

If possible, locate and cite the original source. Otherwise, begin your citation with "as cited in" and name your source.

According to Claude Fischer, the belief in individualism favors "the individual over the group or institution" (as cited in Hansen, 2005, p. 5).

GOVERNMENT OR ORGANIZATION DOCUMENT

If no specific author is identified, treat the sponsoring agency as the author, and give its full name in the first citation in your text. If the name is complicated or commonly shortened, you may add an abbreviation in brackets.

The *2005 National Gang Threat Assessment* (National Alliance of Gang Investigators Associations [NAGIA], 2005, pp. vii-viii) identified regional trends that may help to account for the city's recent gang violence.

In later citations, use just the abbreviation and the date:

(NAGIA, 2005)

WEB SITE OR OTHER ONLINE DOCUMENT

When possible, cite a Web resource or online article as you would any other source.

Breast cancer survival rates depend on early detection before the cancer has a chance to spread (Bruckheim, 1998).

If no author is named, supply the full title in your text or the first word or two in parentheses. When the date is unknown, use "n.d." ("no date"). When pages are not numbered in the original, give a location such as a paragraph number ("para. 3"), chapter number ("chap. 2"), or section heading that will help readers find the material.

> Note that italics, not underlining, are used in APA style for titles of books, periodicals, and Web sites. For more style conventions, see pp. 725–26.

Interval training encourages rotation between high-intensity spurts and "active recovery, which is typically a less-intense form of the original activity" (*Interval training*, n.d., para. 2).

A CLASSIC

If the date of a classic is unknown, use "n.d." ("no date"). If the original date is known, show it along with your edition's date: (Burton 1621/1977). For ancient texts, use the year of the translation: (Homer, trans. 1990). The corresponding entry in your reference list will identify the translator.

For a quotation from a classic, identify lines, sections, or other standard divisions instead of pages so that a passage could be located in any edition. For biblical references, you should specify the version in your initial citation but need not add it to your reference list.

Many cultures affirm the importance of religious covenant in accounts as varied as the biblical "Behold, I make a covenant" in Exodus 34:10 (King James Version) and *The Iliad* (Homer, trans. 1990), which opens with the cause of the Trojan War, "all because Agamemnon spurned Apollo's priest" (Book 1, line 12).

VISUAL MATERIAL

To refer to your own figure or table, mention its number in your sentence: "As Figure 2 shows, . . ." Clearly identify a visual cited from a source.

Teenagers who play video games with a high degree of violence are more likely to show aggressive behavior (Anderson & Bushman, 2001, Table 1).

To include or adopt a table or a visual from a source, you may need to request permission from the author or copyright holder. Many sources — from scholarly journals to Web sites — state their permissions policy in the issue or on the site. (Ask your instructor for advice if you are uncertain about how to proceed.) Credit such material in a "From" or "Adapted from" note below it. The journal in this example allows the use of a table but requires adding the concluding credit line.

Note. From "Inequality in Preschool Education and School Readiness," by K. A. Magnuson, M. K. Meyers, C. J. Ruhm, and J. Waldfogel, 2004, *American Educational Research Journal, 41,* p. 125. Copyright 2004 by the American Educational Research Association; reproduced with permission from the publisher.

PERSONAL COMMUNICATION

Personal communications — such as face-to-face interviews, letters, telephone conversations, memos, and e-mail — are not included in the reference list because your readers would not be able to find and use such sources. Simply name your source and the date of the communication in the text of your paper.

To see another example for an interview, turn to p. 614.

J. T. Moore (personal communication, October 10, 2007) has made specific suggestions for stimulating the local economy.

HOW ARE YOU CAPTURING THE SOURCE MATERIAL?

The way that you have captured source material — whether in your own words or in a quotation — affects how you present and credit it. Always identify words taken directly from a source by using quotation marks or the indented form for a long "block" quotation. Specify the page or other location of quoted words, unless the source lacks clear location information. If you present in your own words material from a specific place in your source, APA recommends that you add a page number or another location. A citation, but no location, is needed for general information, such as your summary of an overall finding.

For more on capturing and integrating source material, see pp. 214–20, 617–19, and Ch. 32.

The next four examples illustrate how Ross Rocketto varied his presentation of sources in his paper "Robin Hood: Prince of Thieves? An Analysis of Current School Finance Legislation in Texas."

OVERALL SUMMARY OR IMPORTANT IDEA

The resulting educational inequities have become particularly problematic because of technological changes that require higher levels of education for higher paying jobs (Wilson, 1996).

BLENDED PARAPHRASE AND QUOTATION

According to William Julius Wilson (1996), the economic restructuring of the 1970s created what he refers to as "new urban poverty"--"segregated neighborhoods in which a substantial majority of individual adults are either unemployed or have dropped out of the labor force altogether" (p. 19).

BRIEF QUOTATION INTEGRATED IN SENTENCE

According to Castells, the city is the "most efficient and convenient form of collective consumption" (as cited in Savage, 2003, p. 162), that is, the best means of providing public housing, transport, education, and so on.

LONG QUOTATION

If you quote forty words or more, indent the quotation one-half inch and double-space it instead of using quotation marks. After it, add your citation with no additional period, including whatever information you have not already mentioned in your launch statement.

This phenomenon is explained further by Hoxby (1998):

> First, districts that are good, efficient providers of schooling tend to be rewarded with larger budgets. This fiscal reward process works because a district's budget nearly always depends on property taxes, which in turn depend on home prices within the district, which in turn depend on how the marginal home buyers value the local schools. (p. 48)

Use the following questions to make sure that you have cited sources correctly in APA style:

RESEARCH CHECKLIST

Citing Sources in APA Style

___ Have you double-checked to be sure that you have acknowledged all material from a source?

___ Have you placed your citation right after your quotation or reference to the source?

___ Have you identified the author of each source in your text or in parentheses?

___ Have you used the first few words of the title to cite a work without an identified author?

___ Have you noted the date (or added "n.d." for "no date") for each source?

___ Have you added a page number or other location whenever needed?

___ Have you checked your final draft to be sure that every source cited in your text also appears in your list of references?

Listing Sources in APA Style

List your sources at the end of your paper. Begin a new page with the title "References" centered. Double-space your list, and organize it alphabetically by authors' last names (or by titles for works without an identified author). Arrange several works by the same author by date, moving from earliest to most recent. Should an author have written two works published in the same year, arrange these alphabetically, and add a letter after each date (2004a, 2004b) so that the date in your text citation leads to the correct entry. Format each entry with a "hanging indent" so that subsequent lines are indented one-half inch (about five to seven spaces), just as a paragraph is. (Use the menu in your software — Format-Paragraph-Indentation — to set up this hanging or special indentation.) Include only sources that you actually cite in your paper unless your instructor has requested otherwise.

For a sample reference page, see p. 736.

APA style simplifies the following details.

- Supply only initials (with a space between them) for an author's first and middle names.

- Use an ampersand (&), not "and," before the name of the last of a series of authors (even though you would write "and" in your paper except in a citation in parentheses). If the source has eight or more authors, give only the names of the first six authors, followed by three periods (. . .) and the name of the last author. Do not use an ampersand.

- Spell out names of months, but abbreviate terms common in academic writing (such as "p.m.," "Vol." for "Volume," or "No." for "Number").

- Capitalize only the first word, proper names, and the first word after a colon in the title of a book, article, or Web site. Capitalize all main words in the title of a journal or other periodical.

- Do not use quotation marks or italics for an article title in your reference list (even though you would use quotation marks if you mentioned it in your paper).

- Italicize a Web site, book, or periodical title (and its volume number).

- List only the first of several cities where a publisher has offices. Add a state abbreviation (or full country name, for sources published outside the United States) unless a university press's name includes the state. Omit place and publisher for online sources.

- Shorten the name of a publisher, but include "Press."

- Use "Author" instead of the publisher's name if the two are the same.

- For online articles, give volume, issue, and any digital object identifier (DOI) numbers. If no DOI is available, supply the subscription journal home page, database name, or URL.

- Include an access date only for online sources that might change.

- Omit a final period after the URL for an electronic source.

As you prepare your own entries, begin with the author. The various author formats apply whatever your source — article, book, Web page, or other material. Then, from the following examples, select the format for the rest of the entry depending on the type of source you have used. Follow its pattern in your entry, supplying the same information in the same order with the same punctuation and other features. Keep in mind these two key questions, which are used to organize the sample entries that follow:

Who wrote it?

What type of source is it?

WHO WROTE IT?

INDIVIDUAL AUTHOR

O'Reilly, B. (2006). *Culture warrior*. New York: Broadway Books.

TWO AUTHORS

Boggs, C., & Pollard, T. (2007). *The Hollywood war machine: U.S. militarism and popular culture*. Boulder, CO: Paradigm.

THREE AUTHORS OR MORE

Provide names for three to seven authors; for more seven, give only the names of the first six authors, followed by three periods (. . .) and the name of the last author.

Evans, B., Joas, M., Sundback, S., & Theobald, K. (2005). *Governing sustainable cities*. London: Earthscan.

SAME AUTHOR WITH MULTIPLE WORKS

Arrange the titles by date, the earliest first. If some share the same date, arrange them alphabetically and letter them after the date.

Gould, S. J. (1996). *Full house: The spread of excellence from Plato to Darwin*. New York: Harmony.

Gould, S. J. (2003a). *The hedgehog, the fox, and the magister's pox: Mending the gap between science and the humanities*. New York: Harmony.

Gould, S. J. (2003b). *Triumph and tragedy in Mudville: A lifelong passion for baseball*. New York: Norton.

ORGANIZATION AUTHOR

American Red Cross. (2004). *CPR/AED for the professional rescuer*. Washington, DC: Author.

AUTHOR OF EDITED WORK

Bolles, E. B. (Ed.). (1999). *Galileo's commandment: 2,500 years of great science writing*. New York: Freeman.

AUTHOR AND TRANSLATOR

Ishinomori, I. (1998). *Japan Inc.: Introduction to Japanese economics* (B. Schneiner,
    Trans.). Berkeley: University of California Press. (Original work published 1986)

UNIDENTIFIED AUTHOR

Environment awareness: No child left inside. (2007, February 10). *The Economist,*
    382, 32-33.

WHAT TYPE OF SOURCE IS IT?

Once you have found the appropriate author format, look for the type of
source and the specific entry that best matches yours. Mix and match the
patterns illustrated as needed. For example, the revised edition of an edited
collection of articles might send you to several examples until you have
identified all of its elements.

Printed or Electronic Book

PRINTED BOOK

Rosenthal, A. (2004). *Heavy lifting: The job of the American legislature.* Washington,
    DC: CQ Press.

To see how to create a listing for a book, turn to pp. 610–11.

ONLINE BOOK

Add the URL (uniform resource locator) but not a period after the address.
No retrieval date is needed for a stable text.

Oblinger, D. G., & Oblinger, J. L. (Eds.) (2005). *Educating the Net generation.*
    Retrieved from http://www.educause.edu/educatingthenetgen/

MULTIVOLUME WORK

Friedman, H. S. (Ed.). (1998). *Encyclopedia of mental health* (Vols. 1-3). San Diego,
    CA: Academic Press.

REVISED EDITION

Coleman, J. W. (2006). *The criminal elite: Understanding white-collar crime*
    (6th ed.). New York, NY: Worth.

BOOK WITHOUT A DATE

Reade, T. (n.d.). *American originals.* Wichita, KS: Midtown Press.

Part of a Printed or an Electronic Book

SELECTION FROM A PRINTED BOOK

Martin, P. V., & Hummer, R. A. (2003). Fraternities and rape on campus. In
    M. Silberman (Ed.), *Violence and society: A reader* (pp. 215-222). Upper Saddle
    River, NJ: Prentice Hall.

See the citation on p. 721.

SELECTION FROM AN ONLINE BOOK

Brown, M. (2005). Learning spaces. In D. G. Oblinger & J. L. Oblinger
(Eds.), *Educating the Net generation* (chap. 12). Retrieved from
http://www.educause.edu/educatingthenetgen/

PREFACE, INTRODUCTION, FOREWORD, OR AFTERWORD

Godwin, M. (1996). Foreword. In P. Ludlow (Ed.), *High noon on the electronic
frontier* (pp. xiii-xvi). Cambridge, MA: MIT Press.

ARTICLE FROM A REFERENCE WORK

Norman, C. E. (2003). Religion and food. In *Encyclopedia of food and culture*
(Vol. 3, pp. 171-176). New York, NY: Charles Scribner's Sons.

Article in a Printed or an Electronic Periodical

ARTICLE FROM A JOURNAL PAGINATED BY VOLUME

If the pages in all the issues for the year's volume are numbered consecutively, no issue number is needed. Italicize the volume number as well as the
title of the journal.

Kissam, E. (2005). The fulcrum for immigrant civic engagement. *Journal of
Latino-Latin American Studies, 1,* 191-205.

If you want to list a special issue about a topic as a whole, rather than sin-
gling out an article, begin with the issue editor or, if none, with the issue
title.

Latinos in rural America [Special issue]. (2005). *Journal of Latino-Latin American
Studies, 1.*

ARTICLE FROM A JOURNAL PAGINATED BY ISSUE

If each issue begins with page 1, or the source is online, add the issue number in parentheses with no space after the volume number.

Lipkin, S. N. (1999). Real emotional logic: Persuasive strategies in docudrama.
Cinema Journal, 38(4), 68-85.

ARTICLE FROM AN ONLINE JOURNAL

Give volume, issue, and digital object identifier (DOI) numbers, if available.
Otherwise, supply the subscription journal home page, database name, or
URL. No access date is needed for a published article.

Het, S., & Wolf, O. T. (2007). Mood changes in response to psychosocial stress in
healthy young women: Effects of pretreatment with cortisol. *Behavioral
Neuroscience, 121*(1), 11-20. doi:10.1037/0735-7044.121.1.11

Doherty, S. D., & Rosen, T. (2006). Shark skin laceration. *Dermatology Online Journal, 12*(6), 6. Retrieved from http://dermatology.cdlib.org/126/case_reports/shark/rosen.html

ARTICLE ACCESSED ONLINE THROUGH A LIBRARY OR SUBSCRIPTION SERVICE

If you access only an abstract for the article, add "Abstract" in brackets after the title. If there is a DOI, do not name the database home page.

Allison, S. (2004). On-screen smoking influences young viewers. *Youth Studies Australia, 23*(3), 6. Retrieved from http://www.gale.cengage.com/onefile.

ARTICLE FROM A PRINTED MAGAZINE

Neimark, J. (2007, April). Autism: It's not just in the head. *Discover, 28,* 32-36, 38, 75.

ARTICLE FROM AN ONLINE MAGAZINE

Chandler, K. (2005, June 18). Anger management. *Salon.com.* Retrieved from http://www.salon.com

ARTICLE FROM A NEWSLETTER

Anti-evolution teachings gain in U.S. schools. (2005, January). *Newsletter on Intellectual Freedom, 54*(3), 27-28.

ARTICLE FROM A PRINTED NEWSPAPER

Stein, R. (2004, March 11). Breast-cancer drug changes suggested. *The Boston Globe,* p. A4.

ARTICLE FROM AN ONLINE NEWSPAPER

Martin, A. (2007, March 7). Makers of sodas try a new pitch: They're healthy. *The New York Times.* Retrieved from http://www.nytimes.com

EDITORIAL

Rushed primaries. (2007, March 19). [Editorial]. *The Nation, 284,* 3.

LETTER TO THE EDITOR

Lardner, G. (2007, March 19). Impeach, impeach, impeach [Letter to the editor]. *The Nation, 284,* 24.

REVIEW

Rose, T. (1998, February 24). Blues sisters [Review of the book *Blues legacies and black feminism: Gertrude "Ma" Rainey, Bessie Smith, and Billie Holliday*]. *The Village Voice,* pp. 139-141.

■ To see how to create the listing for a journal article from a database, turn to pp. 608–09.

■ To see how to create the listing for a magazine article, turn to pp. 606–07.

Printed or Electronic Report or Other Document

Many research reports and similar documents are collaborative products, prepared under the auspices of government, academic, or other organizational sponsors. Start with the agency name if no specific author is identified. In parentheses, add any report number assigned by the agency right after the title, but add any number from a document service (such as ERIC, Educational Resources Information Center, or NTIS, National Technical Information Service) or your access date and the URL after the entire entry, without any period at the end.

PRINTED GOVERNMENT DOCUMENT

U.S. Census Bureau. (2006). *State and metropolitan area data book: 2006*. (126th ed.). Washington, DC: U.S. Government Printing Office.

ONLINE GOVERNMENT DOCUMENT

U.S. Federal Trade Commission. (2006). *Electronic banking*. Retrieved from http://www.ftc.gov/bcp/edu/pubs/consumer/credit/cre14.pdf

RESEARCH REPORT

Liu, J., Allspach, J. R., Feigenbaum, M., Oh, H.-J., & Burton, N. (2004). *A study of fatigue effects from the new SAT* (RR-04-46). Princeton, NJ: Educational Testing Service.

ONLINE RESEARCH REPORT

National Institute on Drug Abuse. (2005). *Inhalant abuse* (NIH Publication No. 00-3818). Retrieved from http://www.nida.nih.gov/PDF/RRInhalants.pdf

ONLINE RESEARCH REPORT FROM A DOCUMENT SERVICE

Ross, D. B., & Driscoll, R. (2006). *Test anxiety: Age appropriate interventions*. Retrieved from http://www.eric.ed.gov. (ERIC Document Reproduction Service No. ED493897)

REPORT FROM AN ACADEMIC INSTITUTION

Bunn, M., Wier, A., & Holdren, J. P. (2003). *Controlling nuclear warheads and materials: A report card and action plan*. Cambridge, MA: Harvard University, Belfer Center for Science and International Affairs.

PAMPHLET

Label the source in brackets as a brochure.

U.S. Department of the Interior. (2002). *Lewis and Clark Trail: National historic trail, Illinois to Oregon* [Brochure]. Washington, DC: Author.

DOCTORAL DISSERTATION

Richter, P. (2004). *Improving nursing in the age of managed care.* Unpublished
     doctoral dissertation, University of Wisconsin, Madison.

Internet or Electronic Source

Helping a reader find the same material you cited and listed can be complicated for Internet sources. Some sources, such as Web sites, are available only
in electronic form and may disappear or change at random. New electronic
forms (such as blogs) can rapidly evolve. Despite such complications, try to
cite a specific document (not a general home page), make sure each URL is
correct, and supply information to help a reader access the material.

See the directory on
pp. 718–19 for entries for
other electronic sources,
including books and
articles.

For any updates on
online formats, visit the
APA Web site at
<apastyle.apa.org>.

SECTION OR PAGE FROM A WEB DOCUMENT

Instead of referring to an entire Web site, whenever possible identify the specific material that you have used by supplying its section number or its own
URL.

Detweiler, L. (1993). What is the future of privacy on the Internet? In *Identity,*
     privacy, and anonymity on the Internet (sec. 2.12). Retrieved from
     http://eserver.org/internet/Identity-Privacy-Anonymity.txt

National Eating Disorders Association. (2006). *Anorexia, bulimia, & binge eating*
     disorder: What is an eating disorder? Retrieved from http://
     www.nationaleatingdisorders.org/p.asp?WebPage_ID=286&Profile_ID=41145

DOCUMENT FROM A CAMPUS WEB SITE

Identify the university and sponsoring program or department (if applicable) before giving the URL for the specific page or document.

To see how to create
the listing for a Web page,
turn to pp. 612–13.

Allin, C. (2007). *Common sense for college students: How to do better than*
     you thought possible. Retrieved March 23, 2007, from Cornell College,
     Department of Politics Web site: http://www.cornellcollege.edu/politics/
     common-sense_cwa.shtml

COMPUTER SOFTWARE

Microsoft Office Excel 2003 [Computer software]. (2003). Redmond, WA:
     Microsoft.

Visual or Audio Source

AUDIOTAPE OR RECORDING

Ellis, A. (Writer/Producer). (1995). *Helping students develop their IEPs*
     [Audiotape]. Washington, DC: National Dissemination Center for Children
     with Disabilities.

PROGRAM ON TELEVISION OR RADIO

Clark, L. (Writer/Director/Producer). (2004). Descent into the ice [Television series episode]. In P. Aspell (Executive Producer), *Nova*. Boston: WGBH.

FILM

Lustig, B., Molen, G., & Spielberg, S. (Producers). (1993). *Schindler's list* [Motion picture]. United States: Universal.

Conversation or Field Artifact

PERSONAL INTERVIEW

See the citation on p. 723.

Omit a personal interview from your reference list because it is not accessible to readers. Instead, mention it in your paper as a personal communication.

E-MAIL OR ELECTRONIC MAILING LIST MESSAGE

See the citation on p. 723.

Cite inaccessible messages as personal communications. Otherwise, supply author, date, title, and this pattern: Message posted to . . . [list name] electronic mailing list, archived at . . . [the archive's URL].

Use these questions to check your APA references.

RESEARCH CHECKLIST

Listing Sources in APA Style

___ Have you started each entry with the appropriate pattern for the author's name? Have you left spaces between the initials for each name?

___ Have you used "&," not "and," to add the last coauthor's name?

___ Have you included the date in each entry?

___ Have you followed the sample pattern for the type of source you have used?

___ Have you used capitals and italics correctly for the various titles in your entries?

___ Have you included the conventional punctuation — periods, commas, colons, parentheses — in your entry?

___ Have you accurately recorded the name of the author, title, publisher, and so on?

___ Have you checked the accuracy of dates, pages, and other numbers?

___ Have you correctly typed or pasted in the digital object identifier (DOI) or URL (address) of an electronic source? Have you split a long URL before a period or another punctuation mark or following a slash? Have you ended an entry without adding a final period after a DOI or URL?

___ Have you arranged your entries in alphabetical order?

___ Have you checked your final list of references against your text citations so that every source appears in both places?

— Have you double-spaced your reference list, like the rest of your paper? Have you allowed an inch margin on all sides?

— Have you begun the first line of each entry at the left margin? Have you indented each additional line one-half inch (or five to seven spaces)?

Selections from a Sample APA Research Paper

In "Crucial Choices: Who Will Save the Wetlands if Everyone Is at the Mall?" Linn Bourgeau explores the loss of the Illinois wetlands, including both consequences and possible remedies. The following selections from her paper illustrate APA paper format and the APA conventions for citing and listing sources.

Short title, 5 spaces, and page number

Crucial Choices   1

Keyword running head for cover page

Running head: CRUCIAL CHOICES: SAVE THE WETLANDS

Title

Crucial Choices: Who Will Save the
Wetlands if Everyone Is at the Mall?

Author

Linn Bourgeau

School

Roosevelt University

Crucial Choices   2

Heading, centered

Abstract

No paragraph indentation

Over the last three centuries, Illinois has lost its abundant
wetlands that once protected against flooding and cleaned the
water. Now federal regulations are needed to foster state laws and
educational requirements that will protect the remaining wetlands
and restore as many as possible of those that have been
destroyed or damaged. Because of the wide diversity of wetlands
and their functions, the federal definition should include all
varieties and emphasize the vital concept of interconnectedness,
now missing from wetland laws. If major changes in attitudes and
laws are not made soon, Illinois will waste more money on
flooding and water treatment than is necessary and, in the
meantime, destroy the natural beauty and natural benefits of
wetlands.

Double spaced

Main ideas summed up in no more than 120 words

▨ For sample outlines of this paper, see pp. 330–33.

Crucial Choices   3

Crucial Choices: Who Will Save the
Wetlands if Everyone Is at the Mall?

Title centered

Each person, as part of nature's ecosystem, has the choice to interact with nature in any way that individual chooses. Over the past 288 years, the people of Illinois have chosen to legislate and drain away 90% of the wetlands that were once abundant across this state (Illinois Chapter of the Sierra Club, 2003, p. 2). If the current trend of destroying wetlands continues, Illinois will have more flooding and poorer water quality. The complex ability of wetlands to stave off floods, to clean the water supply, and to add to the aquifers that store water is not understood or protected to the same degree that the wetlands protect and serve humankind.

Double spaced throughout

Source, date, and page cited

Flood Protection

First-level heading, centered and boldface

Floods are dramatic and visible consequences of not protecting wetlands, but wetlands are rarely mentioned in the same newspaper headline with flooding. The cost of flooding can be tallied, not only in dollars spent on post-flood reconstruction, but in lives. Thirteen people died in floods in the decade between 1988 and 1998. Since that time, flooding has consistently cost Illinois approximately $39 million in any given year (Illinois Chapter of the Sierra Club, 2003, p. 5). Moreover, Gaddie and Regens (2000) reported that the Great Midwestern Flood of 1993, which damaged land and property along the Mississippi and Missouri rivers, could have been avoided along with billions of dollars spent in reconstruction (p. 24). At that time Illinois was not only one of the states with the most devastation, but also one of six states with the largest loss of wetlands (p. 25). Construction of roads, buildings, and other infrastructure along these rivers had changed the natural flood-plain channels, preventing wetlands from doing their work of diverting and absorbing excess water. Understandably, then, the areas historically known as wetlands were also the areas with the worst destruction.

Specific pages noted

Paper goes on to discuss benefits of wetlands, threats to them, and proposals for protecting them.

'/₂" indent
(or 5 spaces)

Page numbering continues

Heading, centered

First line of entry at left margin; additional lines indented ½"

List alphabetized by names of authors

All author names begin with last name

No period after URL

First word in title and after colon and all proper nouns capitalized, source not dated, so retrieval date given

■ For more sample student research papers, visit <bedfordstmartins.com/ bedguide> and do a keyword search:

sample papers

References

Applied Ecological Services. (2004). *Biodiversity: Business guide for commercial, industrial and municipal development in the village of Schaumburg.* Retrieved from http:// www.schaumburg.il.us

Chicago Wilderness. (n.d.). *Biodiversity recovery plan.* Retrieved November 15, 2006, from http://www.chicagowilderness.org/ pubprod/brp/index.cfm

Citizens for Conservation. (2006). *Flint Creek Watershed Partnership* [Brochure]. Barrington, IL: Author.

Gaddie, R. K., & Regens, J. L. (2000). *Regulating wetlands protection.* Albany: State University of New York Press.

Illinois Chapter of the Sierra Club. (2003). *Isolated: Illinois wetlands at risk.* Retrieved from http:// www.illinois.sierraclub.org

Middleton, B. A. (1999). *Wetland restoration, flood pulsing, and disturbance.* New York: Wiley.

Mitsch, W. J., & Gosselink, J. G. (2000). *Wetlands.* New York, NY: Wiley.

Mitsch, W. J., & Wilson, R. F. (1996). Improving the success of wetland creation and restoration with know-how, time and self-design. *Ecological Applications, 6*(1), 77–83. doi:10.2307/2269554

National Wildlife Federation. (n.d.). *Weakening the Clean Water Act: What it means for Illinois.* Retrieved December 11, 2006, from http://www.nwf.org/wildlife/pdfs/ CleanWaterAct

Packard, S. (2006, Spring). Chicago wilderness, 2030: Visions for the future. *Chicago Wilderness Magazine.* Retrieved from http://www.chicagowildernessmag.org

Weiss, J. D., Hondzo, M., & Semmens, M. (1983). Storm water detention ponds: Modeling heavy metal removal by plant species and sediments. *Journal of Environmental Engineering, 132*(9), 1034-1042. doi:10.1061/(ASCE)0733- 9372(2006)132:9(1034)

A
Writer's
Handbook

A Writer's Handbook Contents

***Introduction: Grammar, or
The Way Words Work   H-3***

For a more detailed Guide to the Handbook and an Index to ESL
Guidelines, turn to the back of the book after the Index.

Introduction:
Grammar, or The Way Words Work

Every speaker of English, even a child, commands a grammatical system of tremendous complexity. Take the sentence "A bear is occupying a telephone booth while a tourist impatiently waits in line." In theory, there are nineteen billion different ways to state the idea in that sentence.[1] (Another is "A tourist fumes while he waits for a bear to finish yakking on a pay phone.") How do we understand a unique sentence like that one? For we do understand it, even though we have never heard it before — not in those very same words, not in the very same order.

To begin with, we recognize familiar words and we know their meanings. Just as significantly, we recognize grammatical structures. As we read or hear the sentence, we know that it contains a familiar pattern of *syntax*, or word order, that helps the sentence make sense to us. Ordinarily we aren't even conscious of such an order, but to notice it, all we need do is rearrange the words of our sentence:

> Telephone a impatiently line in waits tourist bear a occupying is a booth while.

The result is nonsense: it defies English grammar. The would-be sentence doesn't follow familiar patterns or meet our expectations of order.

Hundreds of times a day, with wonderful efficiency, we perform tasks of understanding and constructing complex sentences. Why, then, think about grammar in college? Isn't it entirely possible to write well without contemplating grammar at all? Yes. If your innate sense of grammar is reliable, you can write clearly and logically and forcefully without knowing a predicate nominative from a handsaw. Most successful writers, though, have practiced for many years to gain this sense. When you doubt a word or a construction, a glance in a handbook often can clear up your confusion and restore your confidence — just as referring to a dictionary can help your spelling.

The grammatical conventions you'll find in this handbook are not mechanical specification but accepted ways in which skilled writers and speakers put words together to convey meaning clearly. The amateur writer can learn by following their example, just as an amateur athlete, artist, or even auto mechanic can learn by watching the professionals.

---

[1] Richard Ohmann, "Grammar and Meaning," *American Heritage Dictionary* (Boston: Houghton, 1979), pp. xxxi–xxxii.

This handbook, divided into the following chapters, presents the important rules and conventions of standard written English. Exercises are provided so you can practice putting the information to use.

35. Grammatical Sentences   38. Punctuation
36. Effective Sentences   39. Mechanics
37. Word Choice

Following the handbook are convenient appendices.

QUICK RESEARCH GUIDE
Identified by the dark-red-edged pages, this concise guide introduces how to find, evaluate, and use sources in your writing. Look here also for the basics of the MLA and APA documentation styles.

QUICK EDITING GUIDE
Identified by the dark-blue-edged pages, this guide briefly discusses how to edit the common grammar, style, punctuation, mechanics, and format problems found in college writing. Check its useful tables, lists, and editing checklists as well.

A GLOSSARY OF TROUBLEMAKERS
This glossary lists words and phrases that often trouble writers. Turn here when you wonder which of two words to select (*affect* or *effect,* for example) or how to use a word correctly.

ANSWERS FOR LETTERED EXERCISES
Use these excellent tools to test yourself on a particular skill. Simply answer the lettered exercise sentences in the handbook, and then turn to the answers to see how you did.

Here are some easy ways to find information in *A Writer's Handbook*:

- Use the *table of contents* at the beginning of the handbook (p. H-2). If you needed help with quotation marks, for instance, you would first look under the chapter titled "Punctuation." By scanning the list of topics, you would quickly spot what you need: section 25, Quotation Marks, p. H-116.

- Turn to the alphabetically arranged *index* at the back of the book. Here you will find all of the key terms used in the handbook followed by the exact page that you should turn to.

- Skim the "Guide to the Handbook" located a few pages before the back cover. Pick out a specific topic to check, or select a section for review.

- For those of you who are multilingual or speak English as a second language, near the back of the book is an *ESL index* listing all the ESL boxes in the handbook.

Chapter 35
Grammatical Sentences

 ## *Sentence Fragments*

Unlike a complete sentence, a *fragment* is partial or incomplete. It may lack a subject (naming someone or something), a predicate (making an assertion about the subject), or both. A fragment also may otherwise fail to express a complete thought. Unless you add what's missing or reword what's incomplete, a fragment cannot stand alone as a sentence. Even so, we all use fragments in everyday speech, where their context and delivery make them understandable and therefore acceptable.

> That bicycle over there.
>
> Good job.
>
> Not if I can help it.

In writing, fragments like these fail to communicate complete, coherent ideas. Notice how much more effective they are as complete sentences.

sentence: A word group that includes both a subject and a predicate and can stand alone

> I'd like to buy that bicycle over there.
>
> You did a good job sanding the floor.
>
> Nobody will steal my seat if I can help it.

Some writers use fragments on purpose. For example, advertisers are fond of short, emphatic fragments that command attention, like a series of quick jabs to the head.

> For seafood lovers. Every Tuesday night. All you can eat.

Those who text-message or write quick, casual e-mails may compress what they write because time and character space may be limited. Instead of making complete statements, they rely on the recipient of the message to fill in the gaps.

> Thru with lab. CU @ 8. Pizza?

In college writing, though, it is good practice to express your ideas in complete sentences. Besides, complete sentences usually convey more information than fragments — a big advantage in essay writing.

For more on editing for fragments, see A1 in the Quick Editing Guide (the dark-blue-edged pages).

If you sometimes write fragments without recognizing them, learn to edit your work. Luckily, fragments are fairly easy to correct. Often you can attach a fragment to a neighboring sentence with a comma, a dash, or a colon. Sometimes you can combine two thoughts without adding any punctuation at all.

Ia If a fragment is a phrase, link it to an adjoining sentence, or make it a complete sentence.

phrase: Two or more related words that work together but may lack a subject (will have been), a verb (my uncle Zeke), or both (in the attic)

You have two choices for revising a fragment if it is a phrase: (1) link it to an adjoining sentence using punctuation such as a comma or a colon, or (2) add a subject or a verb to the phrase to make it a complete sentence.

FRAGMENT   Malcolm has two goals in life. *Wealth and power.* [Phrase without verb]

subject: The part of a sentence that names something—a person, an object, an idea, a situation—about which the verb in the predicate makes an assertion: The king lives.

FRAGMENT   Schmidt ended his stories as he mixed his martinis. *With a twist.* [Prepositional phrase without subject or verb]

FRAGMENT   *To stamp out the union.* That was the bosses' plan. [Infinitive phrase without main verb or subject]

FRAGMENT   The students taking the final exam in the auditorium. [Participial phrase without complete verb]

verb: A word that shows action (The cow jumped over the moon) or a state of being (The cow is brown)

You can make each of these phrases express a complete thought by linking it with a neighboring sentence or by adding the missing element.

REVISED   Malcolm has two goals in life: wealth and power. [A colon links *wealth and power* to *goals.*]

REVISED   Schmidt ended his stories as he mixed his martinis, with a twist. [The prepositional phrase *with a twist* is connected to the main clause with a comma.]

REVISED   To stamp out the union was the bosses' plan. [The infinitive phrase *To stamp out the union* becomes the subject of the sentence.]

REVISED   The students were taking the final exam in the auditorium. [The helping verb *were* completes the verb and thus makes a sentence.]

Ib If a fragment is a subordinate clause, link it to an adjoining sentence, or eliminate the subordinating conjunction.

subordinate clause: A group of words that contains a subject and a verb but cannot stand alone because it depends on a main clause to help it make sense: Pia, who plays the oboe, prefers solitude. (See 14d–14f.)

Some fragments are missing neither subject nor verb. Instead, they are subordinate clauses, unable to express complete thoughts unless linked with main clauses. When you find a subordinating conjunction at the start or in the middle of a word group that looks like a sentence, that word group may be a subordinate clause and not a sentence at all.

FRAGMENT   The new law will help create jobs. *If it passes.*

FRAGMENT   George loves winter in the mountains. *Because he is an avid skier.*

If you have treated a subordinate clause as a complete sentence, you can correct the problem in one of two ways: (1) you can combine the fragment with a main clause (a complete sentence) nearby, or (2) you can make the subordinate clause into a complete sentence by dropping the subordinating conjunction.

REVISED   The new law will help create jobs, if it passes.

REVISED   George loves winter in the mountains. He is an avid skier.

A sentence is not necessarily a fragment just because it opens with a subordinating conjunction. Perfectly legitimate sentences with both main and subordinate clauses have conjunctions up front instead of in the middle.

If you leave early, say good-bye.

Because it rained all afternoon, the game was canceled.

> **subordinating conjunction:** A word (such as *because, although, if, when*) used to make one clause dependent on, or subordinate to, another: *Unless* you have a key, we are locked out. (See 14d–14f.)

1c   If a fragment has a participle but no other verb, change the participle to a main verb, or link the fragment to an adjoining sentence.

A present participle (the *-ing* form of the verb) can serve as the main verb in a sentence only when it is accompanied by a form of *be* ("Sally *is working* harder than usual"). When a writer mistakenly uses a participle alone as a main verb, the result is a fragment.

FRAGMENT   Jon was used to the pressure of deadlines. *Having worked the night shift at the daily newspaper.*

One solution is to combine the fragment with an adjoining sentence.

REVISED   Jon was used to the pressure of deadlines, having worked the night shift at the daily newspaper.

Another solution is to turn the fragment into a complete sentence by choosing a form of the verb other than the participle.

REVISED   Jon was used to the pressure of deadlines. He *had worked* the night shift at the daily newspaper.

> **participle:** A form of a verb that cannot function alone as a main verb, including present participles ending in *-ing* (*dancing*) and past participles often ending in *-ed* or *-d* (*danced*)

1d   If a fragment is part of a compound predicate, link it with the complete sentence containing the subject and the rest of the predicate.

FRAGMENT   In spite of a pulled muscle, Jeremy ran the race. *And won.*

A fragment such as *And won* sounds satisfyingly punchy. Still, it cannot stand on its own as a sentence because it lacks a subject. Create a complete sentence by linking the two verbs in the compound predicate.

> **compound predicate:** A predicate consisting of two or more verbs linked by a conjunction: My sister *stopped and stared.*

REVISED   In spite of a pulled muscle, Jeremy *ran* the race *and won.*

For advice on punctu-
ating linked phrases and
clauses, see 14a.

If you want to emphasize the second verb, you can turn the fragment into a full clause by adding punctuation and another subject.

REVISED   In spite of a pulled muscle, Jeremy ran the race — and *he* won.

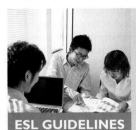

ESL GUIDELINES

participle: A form of a verb that cannot func-tion alone as a main verb, including present participles ending in *-ing* (*dancing*) and past participles often ending in *-ed* or *-d* (*danced*)
gerund: A form of a verb, ending in *-ing*, that functions as a noun: Lacey likes *playing* in the steel band.
infinitive: The base form of a verb, often pre-ceded by *to* (*to go, to play*)

Using Participles, Gerunds, and Infinitives

A *verbal* cannot function as the main verb in a sentence but can function as an adjective, an adverb, or a noun.

Using participles

When used as an adjective, the *-ing* form expresses cause, and the *-ed* and *-d* forms express effect or result.

The movie was *terrifying to the children.* [The movie caused terror.]

The children were *terrified by the movie.* [The movie resulted in terrified children.]

Using verbs with gerunds and infinitives

Some verbs are followed by gerunds; others are followed by infinitives. Still others can be followed by either.

- Verbs that are followed by gerunds

  appreciate, avoid, consider, deny, discuss, enjoy, finish, imagine, keep, miss, practice, recall, and *suggest,* among others

     My family enjoys *going* to the beach.

- Verbs that are followed by infinitives

  agree, decide, expect, pretend, refuse, and *want,* among others

     My mother decided *to eat* dinner at McDonald's.

- Verbs that can be followed by either a gerund or an infinitive

   continue, like, love, hate, remember, forget, start, and *stop,* among others

      I like *going* to the museum, but Nadine likes *to go* to the movies.

For practice, visit
<bedfordstmartins.com/
bedguide> and do a key-
word search:

ESL

NOTE: Some verbs, such as *stop, remember,* and *forget,* have significantly dif-ferent meanings when followed by a gerund or by an infinitive.

   I stopped *smoking.* [I don't smoke anymore.]

   I stopped *to smoke.* [I stopped so that I could smoke.]

- *Used to* (meaning "did in the past") is followed by the basic form of the verb. *Be used to* or *get used to* (meaning "be or become accustomed to") is followed by a gerund.

   I *used to live* in Rio, but now I live in Ohio. [I lived in Rio in the past.]

   I *am used to living* in Ohio. [I am accustomed to living in Ohio.]

   I *got used to living* in Ohio. [I became accustomed to living in Ohio.]

■ Exercise I–I

Eliminating Fragments

Find and eliminate any fragments in the following examples. Some sentences may be correct. Possible revisions for the lettered sentences appear in the back of the book. Example:

> Bryan hates parsnips. And loathes squash.
>
> Bryan hates parsnips *and* loathes squash.

■ For more practice, visit <bedfordstmartins.com/ bedguide> and do a key-word search:

fragments

a. Michael had a beautiful Southern accent. Having lived many years in Georgia.

b. Pat and Chris are determined to marry each other. Even if their families do not approve.

c. Jack seemed well qualified for a career in the air force. Except for his tendency to get airsick.

d. Lisa advocated sleeping no more than four hours a night. Until she started nodding through her classes.

e. They met. They talked. They fought. They reached agreement.

1. Being the first person in his family ever to attend college. Alex is determined to succeed.

2. Does our society rob children of their childhood? By making them aware too soon of adult ills?

3. Richard III supposedly had the young princes murdered. No one has ever found out what really happened to them.

4. For democracy to function, two elements are crucial. An educated populace and a collective belief in people's ability to chart their own course.

5. You must take his stories as others do. With a grain of salt.

■ Exercise I–2

Eliminating Fragments

Rewrite the following paragraph, eliminating all fragments. Explain why you made each change. Example:

> Many people exercise to change their body image. And may become obsessed with their looks. [The second word group is a fragment because it does not have a subject.]
>
> Many people exercise to change their body image *and* may become obsessed with their looks. [This revised sentence links the fragment to the rest of the sentence.]

   Some people assume that only women are overly concerned with body image. However, men often share this concern. While women tend to exercise vigorously to stay slender, men usually lift weights to "bulk up." Because of their desire to look masculine. Both are trying to achieve the "ideal" body form. The muscular male and the slim female. Sometimes working out begins to interfere with other aspects of life. Such as sleeping, eating regularly, or going to school or work. These are warning signs. Of too much emphasis on physical appearance. Preoccupation with body image may turn a healthy lifestyle into an unhealthy obsession. Many people believe that looking attractive will bring them happiness. Unfortunately, when they become compulsive. Beautiful people are not always happy.

2 Comma Splices and Fused Sentences

main clause: A group of words that has both a subject and a verb and can stand alone as a complete sentence: *My sister has a friend.*

■ For more on editing for comma splices and fused sentences, see A2 in the Quick Editing Guide (the dark-blue-edged pages).

Splice two ropes, or two strips of movie film, and you join them into one. Splice two main clauses by putting only a comma between them, however, and you get an ungainly construction called a *comma splice*. Here, for instance, are two perfectly good main clauses, each separate, each able to stand on its own as a sentence:

> The detective wriggled on his belly toward the campfire. The drunken smugglers didn't notice him.

Now let's splice those sentences with a comma.

> COMMA SPLICE The detective wriggled on his belly toward the campfire, the drunken smugglers didn't notice him.

The resulting comma splice makes for difficult reading.

Even more confusing than a comma splice is a *fused sentence*: two main clauses joined without any punctuation.

> FUSED SENTENCE The detective wriggled on his belly toward the campfire the drunken smugglers didn't notice him.

Lacking clues from the writer, a reader cannot tell where to pause. To understand the sentence, he or she must halt and reread.

The next two pages show five easy ways to eliminate both comma splices and fused sentences, also called **run-ons**. Your choice depends on the length and complexity of your main clauses and the effect you desire.

Sentence Parts at a Glance

The *subject* (S) of a sentence identifies some person, place, thing, situation, or idea.

The *predicate* (P) of a sentence includes a verb (expressing action or state of being) and makes an assertion about the subject.

An *object* (O) is the target or recipient of the action described by the verb.

A *complement* (C) renames or describes a subject or object.

　　　　　　S　　　P　　C　　　　　　　S　　　　P　　　O
The campus center is beautiful. The new sculpture draws crowds.

2a   Write separate complete sentences to correct a comma splice or a fused sentence.

sentence: A word group that includes both a subject and a predicate and can stand alone

COMMA SPLICE   Sigmund Freud has been called an enemy of sexual repression, the truth is that he is not a friend of free love.

FUSED SENTENCE   Sigmund Freud has been called an enemy of sexual repression the truth is that he is not a friend of free love.

Neither sentence yields its meaning without a struggle. To point readers in the right direction, separate the clauses.

REVISED   Sigmund Freud has been called an enemy of sexual repression. The truth is that he is not a friend of free love.

2b   Use a comma and a coordinating conjunction to correct a comma splice or a fused sentence.

coordinating conjunction: A one-syllable linking word (*and, but, for, or, nor, so, yet*) that joins elements with equal or near-equal importance: Jack *and* Jill, sink *or* swim

Is it always incorrect to join two main clauses with a comma? No. If both clauses are of roughly equal weight, you can use a comma to link them — as long as you add a coordinating conjunction after the comma.

COMMA SPLICE   Hurricane winds hit ninety miles an hour, they tore the roof from every house on Paradise Drive.

REVISED   Hurricane winds hit ninety miles an hour, *and* they tore the roof from every house on Paradise Drive.

▆ For advice on coordination, see 14a–14c.

2c   Use a semicolon or a colon to correct a comma splice or a fused sentence.

A semicolon can connect two closely related thoughts, giving full emphasis to each one.

COMMA SPLICE   Hurricane winds hit ninety miles an hour, they tore the roof from every house on Paradise Drive.

REVISED   Hurricane winds hit ninety miles an hour; they tore the roof from every house on Paradise Drive.

If the second thought clearly illustrates or explains the first, add it on with a colon.

REVISED   The hurricane caused extensive damage: it tore the roof from every house on Paradise Drive.

Remember that the only punctuation powerful enough to link two main clauses single-handedly is a semicolon, a colon, or a period. A lone comma won't do the job.

EXCEPTION: Certain very short, similar main clauses can be joined with a comma.

Jill runs by day, Tom walks by night.

I came, I saw, I conquered.

Commas are not obligatory with short, similar clauses. If you find this issue confusing, you can stick with semicolons to join all main clauses, short or long.

Jill runs by day; Tom walks by night.

I came; I saw; I conquered.

main clause: A group of words that has both a subject and a verb and can stand alone as a complete sentence: *My sister has a friend.*

subordinate clause: A group of words that contains a subject and a verb but cannot stand alone because it depends on a main clause to help it make sense: Pia, *who plays the oboe,* prefers solitude.

For advice on subordination, see 14d–14f. For a list of subordinating words, see p. H-74.

2d Use subordination to correct a comma splice or a fused sentence.

If one main clause is more important than the other, or if you want to give it more importance, you can make the less important one a subordinate clause. When you make one clause subordinate, you throw weight on the main clause. In effect, you show your reader how one idea relates to another: you decide which matters more.

FUSED SENTENCE   Hurricane winds hit ninety miles an hour they tore the roof from every house on Paradise Drive.

REVISED   *When hurricane winds hit ninety miles an hour,* they tore the roof from every house on Paradise Drive.

REVISED   Hurricane winds, *which tore the roof from every house on Paradise Drive,* hit ninety miles an hour.

2e Use a conjunctive adverb with a semicolon and a comma to correct a comma splice or a fused sentence.

conjunctive adverb: A linking word that can connect independent clauses and show a relationship between two ideas: Armando is a serious student; *therefore,* he studies every day. (See 14.)

For a list of conjunctive adverbs, see p. H-74.

If you want to cram more than one clause into a sentence, you may join two clauses with a *conjunctive adverb.* Conjunctive adverbs show relationships such as addition (*also, besides*), comparison (*likewise, similarly*), contrast (*instead, however*), emphasis (*namely, certainly*), cause and effect (*thus, therefore*), or time (*finally, subsequently*). These transitional words and phrases can be a useful way of linking clauses — but only with the right punctuation.

COMMA SPLICE   Sigmund Freud has been called an enemy of sexual repression, however the truth is that he is not a friend of free love.

A writer might consider a comma plus the conjunctive adverb *however* enough to combine the two main clauses, but that glue won't hold. Stronger binding — the semicolon along with a comma — is required.

REVISED   Sigmund Freud has been called an enemy of sexual repression; however, the truth is that he is not a friend of free love.

■ Exercise 2–1

Revising Comma Splices and Fused Sentences

In the following examples, correct each comma splice or fused sentence in two ways, and decide which way you believe works best. Be creative: don't correct every one in the same way. Some sentences may be correct as written. Possible revisions for the lettered sentences appear in the back of the book. Example:

■ For more practice, visit <bedfordstmartins.com/ bedguide> and do a key- word search:

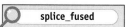

splice_fused

> The castle looked eerie from a distance, it filled us with nameless fear as we approached.

> The castle looked eerie from a *distance;* it filled us with nameless fear as we approached.

> *Or*

> The castle, *which looked eerie from a distance,* filled us with nameless fear as we approached.

a. We followed the scientist down a flight of wet stone steps at last he stopped before a huge oak door.

b. Dr. Frankenstein selected a heavy key, he twisted it in the lock.

c. The huge door gave a groan it swung open on a dimly lighted laboratory.

d. Before us on a dissecting table lay a form with closed eyes to behold it sent a quick chill down my spine.

e. The scientist strode to the table, he lifted a white-gloved hand.

1. Dr. Frankenstein flung a power switch, blue streamers of static electricity crackled about the table, the creature gave a grunt and opened smoldering eyes.

2. "I've won!" exclaimed the scientist in triumph he circled the room doing a demented Irish reel.

3. The creature's right hand strained, the heavy steel manacle imprisoning his wrist began to creak.

4. Like a staple wrenched from a document, the manacle yielded.

5. The creature sat upright and tugged at the shackles binding his ankles, Frankenstein uttered a piercing scream.

■ Exercise 2–2

Revising Comma Splices and Fused Sentences

Revise the following passage, using subordination, a conjunctive adverb, a semicolon, or a colon to correct each comma splice or fused sentence. You may also write separate complete sentences. Some sentences may be correct. Example:

> English can be difficult to learn, it is full of expressions that don't mean what they literally say.

> English can be difficult to learn *because* it is full of expressions that don't mean what they literally say.

Have you ever wondered why you drive on parkways and park on driveways, that's about as logical as your nose running while your feet smell! When you stop to think about it, these phrases don't make sense yet we tend to accept them without thinking about what they literally mean we simply take their intended meanings for granted. Think, however, how confusing they are for a person who is just learning the language. If, for example, you have just learned the verb *park*, you would logically assume that a parkway is where you should park your car, of course when most people see a parkway or a driveway they realize that braking on a parkway would be hazardous, while speeding through a driveway will not take them very far. However, our language is full of many idiomatic expressions that may be difficult for a person from another language background to understand. Fortunately, there are plenty of questions to keep us *all* confused, such as why Americans commonly refer to going to work as "punching the clock."

3   *Verbs*

For help editing verbs, see A3 in the Quick Editing Guide (the dark-blue-edged pages).

Most verbs are called ***action verbs*** because they show action (*swim, eat, sleep, win*). Some verbs are called ***linking verbs*** (*is, become, seem*) because they indicate a state of being by linking the subject of a sentence with a word that renames or describes it. A few verbs accompany a main verb to give more information about its action; they are called ***helping verbs*** or ***auxiliary verbs*** (*have, must, can*).

VERB FORMS

3a   Use a linking verb to connect the subject of a sentence with a subject complement.

linking verb: A verb (*is, become, seem, feel*) that shows a state of being by linking the sentence subject with a word that renames or describes the subject: The sky *is* blue.

subject complement: A noun, an adjective, or a group of words that follows a linking verb and renames or describes the subject: This plum tastes *ripe*.

transitive verb: An action verb that must have an object to complete its meaning: Alan *hit* the ball.

By indicating what the subject of a sentence *is* or is *like*, a linking verb (LV) creates a sort of equation, either positive or negative, between the subject and its complement. The subject complement (SC) can be a noun, a pronoun, or an adjective.

          LV   SC
Julia will *make* a good *doctor*. [Noun]

      LV   SC
Jorge *is* not the *one*. [Pronoun]

             LV SC
London weather *seems foggy*. [Adjective]

A verb may be a linking verb in some sentences and not in others. If you pay attention to what the verb means, you can usually tell how it is functioning.

I often *grow* sleepy after lunch. [Linking verb + subject complement *sleepy*]

I often *grow* tomatoes in my garden. [Transitive verb + direct object *tomatoes*]

Common Linking Verbs at a Glance

Some linking verbs tell what a noun is, was, or will be.

be, become, remain: I *remain* optimistic.

grow: The sky is *growing* dark.

make: One plus two *makes* three.

prove: His warning *proved* accurate.

turn: The weather *turned* cold.

Some linking verbs tell what a noun might be.

appear, seem, look: The child *looks* cold.

Most verbs of the senses can operate as linking verbs.

feel, smell, sound, taste: The smoothie *tastes* sweet.

3b Use helping verbs to add information about the main verb.

Adding a *helping* or *auxiliary verb* to a simple verb (*go, shoot, be*) allows you to express a wide variety of tenses and moods (*am going, did shoot, would have been*). (See 3g–3l and 3n–3p.)

The parts of this combination, called a *verb phrase*, need not appear together but may be separated by other words.

> I probably *am going* to France this summer.

> You *should* not *have shot* that pigeon.

> This change *may* well *have been* seriously *contemplated* before the election.

helping verb: A verb added to a main verb to show variations in its action (*do, can, have, will*)
main verb: The verb in a sentence that identifies the central action (*hit, stopped*)

Helping Verbs at a Glance

Of the twenty-three helping verbs in English, fourteen can also function as main verbs.

be, is, am, are, was, were, being, been

do, does, did

have, has, had

The other nine can function only as helping verbs, never as main verbs. As *modals*, they can show actions that are possible, doubtful, necessary, required, and so on.

can, could, should, would, may, might, must, shall, will

3c   Use the correct principal parts of the verb.

The *principal parts* are the forms the verb can take — alone or with helping verbs — to indicate the full range of times when an action or a state of being does, did, or will occur. Verbs have three principal parts: the base form or infinitive, the past tense, and the past participle.

For the principal parts of many irregular verbs, see A3 and A4 in the Quick Editing Guide (the dark-blue-edged pages).

- The *infinitive* is the simple, base, or dictionary form of the verb (*go, sing, laugh*), often preceded by *to* (*to go, to sing, to laugh*).
- The *past tense* signals that the verb's action is completed (*went, sang, laughed*).
- The *past participle* is combined with helping verbs to indicate action occurring at various times in the past or future (*have gone, had sung, will have laughed*). With forms of *be*, it makes the passive voice. (See 3m.)

In addition to the three principal parts, all verbs have a present participle, the *-ing* form of the verb (*going, singing, laughing*). This form is used to make the progressive tenses. (See 3k and 3l.) It also can modify nouns and pronouns ("the *leaking* bottle"); as a gerund, it can function as a noun ("*Sleeping all day* pleases me").

3d   Use *-d* or *-ed* to form the past tense and past participle of regular verbs.

Most verbs in English are *regular verbs*: they form the past tense and past participle in a standard, predictable way. Regular verbs that end in *-e* add *-d* to the infinitive; those that do not end in *-e* add *-ed*.

INFINITIVE	PAST TENSE	PAST PARTICIPLE
(to) smile	smiled	smiled
(to) act	acted	acted

3e   Use the correct forms for the past tense and past participle of irregular verbs.

For the forms of many irregular verbs, see A3 in the Quick Editing Guide (the dark-blue-edged pages). For the forms of *be* and *have*, see A4 in the Quick Editing Guide.

English has at least two hundred *irregular verbs*, which form the past tense and past participle in some other way than by adding *-d* or *-ed*. Most irregular verbs, familiar to native English speakers, pose no problem.

3f   Use the correct forms of *lie* and *lay* and *sit* and *set*.

intransitive verb: A verb that is complete in itself and needs no object: The surgeon *paused.*
transitive verb: A verb that must have an object to complete its meaning: Alan *hit* the ball.

Try taking two easy steps to eliminate confusion between *lie* and *lay*.

- First, memorize the principal parts and present participles of both verbs (see the chart on p. H-17).
- Second, fix in memory that *lie*, in all its forms, is intransitive and never takes a direct object: "The island *lies* due east." *Lay* is a transitive verb, so its forms always require an object: "*Lay* that pistol down."

Forms of *Lie* and *Lay*, *Sit* and *Set*

lie, lay, lain, lying: recline

PRESENT TENSE   PAST TENSE

I lie	we lie	I lay	we lay
you lie	you lie	you lay	you lay
he/she/it lies	they lie	he/she/it lay	they lay

PAST PARTICIPLE
lain   (We have *lain* in the sun long enough.)

PRESENT PARTICIPLE
lying   (At ten o'clock he was still *lying* in bed.)

lay, laid, laid, laying: put in place, deposit

PRESENT TENSE   PAST TENSE

I lay	we lay	I laid	we laid
you lay	you lay	you laid	you laid
he/she/it lays	they lay	he/she/it laid	they laid

PAST PARTICIPLE
laid   (Having *laid* his clothes on the bed, Mark jumped into the shower.)

PRESENT PARTICIPLE
laying   (*Laying* her cards on the table, Lola cried, "Gin!")

sit, sat, sat, sitting: be seated

PRESENT TENSE   PAST TENSE

I sit	we sit	I sat	we sat
you sit	you sit	you sat	you sat
he/she/it sits	they sit	he/she/it sat	they sat

PAST PARTICIPLE
sat   (I have *sat* here long enough.)

PRESENT PARTICIPLE
sitting (Why are you *sitting* on that rickety bench?)

set, set, set, setting: place

PRESENT TENSE   PAST TENSE

I set	we set	I set	we set
you set	you set	you set	you set
he/she/it sets	they set	he/she/it set	they set

PAST PARTICIPLE
set   (Paul has *set* the table for eight.)

PRESENT PARTICIPLE
setting (Chanh-Duy has been *setting* traps for the mice.)

The same distinction exists between *sit* and *set*. Usually, *sit* is intransitive: "He *sits* on the stairs." *Set*, on the other hand, almost always takes an object: "He *sets* the bottle on the counter." There are, however, a few easily memorized exceptions. The sun *sets*. A hen *sets*. Gelatin *sets*. You *sit* on a horse. You can *sit* yourself down at a table.

For more practice, visit <bedfordstmartins.com/bedguide> and do a keyword search:

verbs

■ Exercise 3–1

Using Irregular Verb Forms

Underline each incorrectly used irregular verb in the following sentences, and substitute the verb's correct form. Some sentences may be correct. Answers for the lettered sentences appear in the back of the book. Example:

> We have already <u>drove</u> eight hundred miles from campus.
>
> We have already *driven* eight hundred miles from campus.

a. In those days, Benjamin wrote all the music, and his sister sung all the songs.
b. After she had eaten her bagel, she drank a cup of coffee with milk.
c. When the bell rung, darkness had already fell.
d. Voters have chose some new senators, who won't take office until January.
e. Carol threw the ball into the water, and the dog swum after it.

1. He brought along two of the fish they had caught the day before.
2. By the time the sun set, the birds had all went away.
3. Teachers had spoke to his parents long before he stole the bicycle.
4. While the cat laid on the bed, the mouse ran beneath the door.
5. For the past three days the wind has blew hard from the south, but now the clouds have began to drift in.

TENSES

tense: The time when the action of a verb did, does, or will occur

For advice on consistent verb tense, see 9a.

With the *simple tenses* we can indicate whether the verb's action took place in the past, takes place in the present, or will take place in the future. The *perfect tenses* enable us to narrow the timing even further, specifying that the action was or will be completed by the time of some other action. With the *progressive tenses* we can indicate that the verb's action did, does, or will continue. Using this variety of verb forms can increase the precision of your writing.

3g **Use the simple present tense for actions that take place once, repeatedly, or continuously in the present.**

The simple present tense is the infinitive form of a regular verb plus *-s* or *-es* for the third-person singular (used with *he, she,* or *it*).

Selection of Verbs to Show the Past, Present, and Future

Picking the correct verb tense in English can be complicated. Besides considering when the action or state occurs, you may need to figure out its duration or its relationship to an action or event at some other time. After selecting a tense that will indicate the time you intend, turn to the appropriate section in this chapter to check its form. Examples of simple and perfect verbs are shown here and in 3g–3j; see 3k and 3l for progressive verbs.

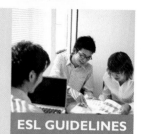

ESL GUIDELINES

TIME OF ACTION OR STATE + ITS DURATION OR TIME RELATIONSHIP	PAST TIME Yesterday, some time ago, long ago	PRESENT TIME Right now, today, or at this moment	FUTURE TIME Tomorrow, soon, or at some expected or possible moment
Action or state occurs once	The team *lost* the game last week. (past tense)	Everyone *is* now on the field. (present tense)	The bus *will leave* at noon on Friday. (future tense) The bus *leaves* after lunch. (present tense)
Action or state occurs repeatedly	The team *won* every home game. (past tense)	The team *wins* when everyone *concentrates* on the game. (present tense)	The bus *will leave* at noon on Fridays. (future tense) The bus *leaves* at noon on Fridays. (present tense)
Action or state occurs continuously	The team *defeated* each of its traditional rivals. (past tense)	The coach always *encourages* the players. (present tense)	The bus *will leave* at noon from now on. (future tense) The bus always *leaves* at noon. (present tense)
Action or state is a general or timeless fact		Coaching *is* a challenging job. (present tense)	
Action or state completed before the time of another action	The players *had practiced* for only two weeks in August before their games began. (past perfect tense)	The team *has played* every week this fall. (present perfect tense)	The team *will have played* at six other campuses before the season ends. (future perfect tense)
Action or state begun in the past but still going on		The players *have practiced* every day. (present perfect tense)	

Verb Tenses at a Glance

NOTE: The examples show first person only.

SIMPLE TENSES

Present	*Past*	*Future*
I cook	I cooked	I will cook
I see	I saw	I will see

PERFECT TENSES

Present perfect	*Past perfect*	*Future perfect*
I have cooked	I had cooked	I will have cooked
I have seen	I had seen	I will have seen

PROGRESSIVE TENSES

Present progressive	*Past progressive*	*Future progressive*
I am cooking	I was cooking	I will be cooking
I am seeing	I was seeing	I will be seeing
Present perfect progressive	*Past perfect progressive*	*Future perfect progressive*
I have been cooking	I had been cooking	I will have been cooking
I have been seeing	I had been seeing	I will have been seeing

I like, I watch	we like, we watch
you like, you watch	you like, you watch
he/she/it likes, he/she/it watches	they like, they watch

Some irregular verbs, such as *go*, form their simple present tense following the same rules as regular verbs (*go/goes*). Other irregular verbs, such as *be* and *have*, are special cases for which you should learn the correct forms.

I am, I have	we are, we have
you are, you have	you are, you have
he/she/it is, he/she/it has	they are, they have

You can use the simple present tense for an action happening right now ("I *welcome* this news"), happening repeatedly in the present ("Judy *goes* to church every Sunday"), or ongoing in the present ("Wesley *likes* ice cream"). In some cases, if you want to ask a question or intensify the action, use the helping verb *do* or *does* before the infinitive form of the main verb.

I *do think* you should take the job.

Does Christos *want* it?

You can use the simple present for future action: "Football season *starts* Wednesday." Use it also for a general truth, even if the rest of the sentence is in a different tense:

Columbus proved in 1492 that the world *is* round.

Mr. Hammond will argue that people *are* basically good.

The Simple Tenses

Present Tense: base form of the verb (+ *-s* or *-es* for *he, she, it*)

- Use the simple present tense to express general statements of fact or habitual activities or customs. Although it is called "present," this tense is really general or timeless.

    Zanetta *goes* to the movies every Sunday afternoon.

    You *make* wonderful coffee.

ESL GUIDELINES

- To form negatives and questions, use *do* or *does* + base form.

    Zanetta *does not* (*doesn't*) go to the movies during the week.

    Do you still *make* wonderful coffee?

Past Tense: base form + *-d* or *-ed* for regular verbs

- Use the simple past tense to express an action that occurred at a specific time in the past. The specific time may be stated or implied.

    The package *arrived* yesterday.

    They *went* to San Juan for spring break.

■ For the past forms of many irregular verbs, see A3 in the Quick Editing Guide (the dark-blue-edged pages).

- To form negatives and questions, use *did* + base form.

    They *did not* (*didn't*) go to Fort Lauderdale.

    Did the package *arrive* yesterday?

Future Tense: *will* or *be going to* + base form

- Use the simple future tense to express an action that will take place in the future. Also use *will* to imply promises and predictions.

    The students *will study* hard for their exam.

    The students *are going to study* hard for their exam.

    We *will help* you move. [Promise]

    Cosimo *will* soon *marry* his girlfriend. [Prediction]

■ For practice, visit <bedfordstmartins.com/bedguide> and do a keyword search:

ESL

- To form negatives and questions, use *will* + base form.

    José *will not* (*won't*) *graduate* this year.

    Will Cosimo *marry* his girlfriend?

NOTE: Use the simple present, not the future, to express future meaning in clauses beginning with *before*, *after*, or *when*.

    INCORRECT   When my mother *will get* home, we will make dinner.

    CORRECT   When my mother *gets* home, we will make dinner.

Use the simple present to show a future action when other words in the sentence make the future meaning clear.

    The bus *departs* in five minutes.

    We *leave* for Chicago in the morning and *return* next Wednesday.

3h Use the simple past tense for actions already completed.

For a chart of trouble-some irregular verbs, see A3 in the Quick Editing Guide (the dark-blue-edged pages).

Regular verbs form the past tense by adding *-d* or *-ed* to the infinitive; the past tense of irregular verbs must be memorized.

Jack *enjoyed* the party. [Regular verb]

Akira *went* home early. [Irregular verb]

Although speakers may not always pronounce the *-d* or *-ed* ending clearly, standard written English requires that you add the *-d* or *-ed* to all regular past tense verbs.

NONSTANDARD   I *use* to wear weird clothes when I was a child.

STANDARD   I *used* to wear weird clothes when I was a child.

In the past tense, you can use the helping verb *did* (past tense of *do*) to ask a question or intensify the action. Use *did* with the infinitive form of the main verb for both regular and irregular verbs.

I went.	I did go.	Why did I go?
You saw.	You did see.	What did you see?
She ran.	She did run.	Where did she run?

3i Use the simple future tense for actions that are expected to happen but have not happened yet.

Although the present tense can indicate future action ("We *go* on vacation next Monday"), most actions that have not yet taken place are expressed in the simple future tense.

George *will arrive* in time for dinner.

Will you please *show* him where to park?

To form the simple future tense, add *will* to the infinitive form of the verb.

I will go	we will go
you will go	you will go
he/she/it will go	they will go

You can also use *shall* to inject a tone of determination ("We *shall over-come!*") or in polite questions ("*Shall* we dance?").

3j Use the perfect tenses for actions completed at the time of another action.

The present perfect, past perfect, and future perfect tenses consist of a form of the helping verb *have* plus the past participle. The tense of *have* indicates the tense of the whole verb phrase.

The action of a ***present perfect*** verb was completed before the sentence is uttered. Its helping verb is in the present tense: *have* or *has*.

I *have* never *been* to Spain, but I *have been* to Oklahoma.

Mr. Grimaldi *has gone* home for the day.

Have you *seen* Johnny Depp's new film? I *have seen* that film.

You can use the present perfect tense for an action completed before some other action ("I *have washed* my hands of the whole affair, but I am watching from a distance") or for an action begun in the past and still going on ("Max *has worked* in this office for twelve years").

The Perfect Tenses

Present Perfect Tense: *has* or *have* + past participle (*-ed* or *-en* form)

- Use the present perfect tense when an action took place at some unspecified time in the past. The action may have occurred repeatedly.

  I *have traveled* to many countries.

  The dog *has bitten* my aunt twice.

- Use the present perfect tense with *for* and *since* to indicate that an action began in the past, is occurring now, and will probably continue.

  I *have gone* to school with Min and Paolo since fifth grade.

  Soo-Jung *has lived* next door to the Kramers for twelve years.

Past Perfect Tense: *had* + past participle

- Use the past perfect tense to indicate that an action was completed in the past before some other past action.

  Josef *had smoked* for many years before he decided to quit.

  We got rid of the dog because he *had bitten* my aunt twice.

- Particularly in speech or informal writing, the simple past may be used instead of the past perfect when the relationship between actions is made clear by a conjunction such as *when*, *before*, *after*, or *until*.

  Observers *saw* the plane catch fire before it landed.

Future Perfect Tense: *will* + *have* + past participle

- Use the future perfect tense when an action will take place before some time in the future.

  The package *will have* already *arrived* by the time we get home.

  By June, the students *will have studied* ten chapters.

ESL GUIDELINES

■ For more practice, visit <bedfordstmartins.com/ bedguide> and do a key-word search:

ESL

■ For the forms of many irregular verbs, see A3 in the Quick Editing Guide (the dark-blue-edged pages).

The action of a *past perfect* verb was completed before some other action in the past. Its helping verb is in the past tense: *had.*

The concert *had ended* by the time we found a parking space.

Until I met her, I *had* not *pictured* Jenna as a redhead.

Had you *wanted* to clean the house before your parents arrived?

The action of a *future perfect* verb will be completed by some point (specified or implied) in the future. Its helping verb is in the future tense: *will have.*

The builders *will have finished* the house by June.

When you get the Dutch Blue, *will* you *have collected* every stamp you need?

The store *will* not *have closed* by the time we get there.

3k Use the simple progressive tenses for actions in progress.

The present progressive, past progressive, and future progressive tenses consist of a form of the helping verb *be* plus the present participle (which is formed by adding *-ing* to the infinitive). The tense of *be* determines the tense of the whole verb phrase.

The *present progressive* expresses an action that is taking place now. Its helping verb is in the present tense: *am, is,* or *are.*

I *am thinking* of a word that starts with *R.*

Is Stefan *babysitting* while Marie *is visiting* her sister?

You can also express future action with the present progressive of *go* plus an infinitive phrase.

I *am going to read* Tolstoy's *War and Peace* someday.

Are you *going to sign up* for Professor Blaine's course on the sixties?

The *past progressive* expresses an action that took place continuously at some time in the past, whether or not that action is still going on. Its helping verb is in the past tense: *was* or *were.*

The old men *were sitting* on the porch when we passed.

Lucy *was planning* to take the weekend off.

The *future progressive* expresses an action that will take place continuously at some time in the future. Its helping verb is in the future tense: *will be.*

They *will be answering* the phones while she is gone.

Will we *be dining* out every night on our vacation?

The Simple Progressive Tenses

Present Progressive Tense: present tense of *be* + present participle (*-ing* form)

- Use the present progressive tense when an action began in the past, is happening now, and will end at some time in the future.

    The students *are studying* for their exam.

    My sister *is living* with us until she graduates from college.

- You can also use the present progressive tense to show a future action when other words in the sentence make the future meaning clear.

    Nili *is flying* to Pittsburgh on July 8.

NOTE: Linking verbs (such as *be, seem, look*), verbs that express an emotional or mental state (such as *trust, like, guess, realize*), and verbs without action (such as *belong, have, need*) are not generally used in the present progressive tense. For these verbs, use the present tense to express a continuous state.

INCORRECT   I *am liking* you very much.

CORRECT   I *like* you very much.

Past Progressive Tense: *was* or *were* + present participle

- Use the past progressive tense when an action began and continued at a specific time in the past.

    Maria *was watching* the news when I arrived.

    The students *were studying* for their exam all day.

Future Progressive Tense: *will be* + present participle or present tense of *be* + *going to be* + present participle

- Use the future progressive tense when an action will begin and will continue in the future.

    Hans *will be wearing* blue jeans to the party tonight.

    The students *are going to be studying* until midnight.

ESL GUIDELINES

■ For practice, visit <bedfordstmartins.com/ bedguide> and do a keyword search:

       ESL

---

31   **Use the perfect progressive tenses for continuing actions that began earlier.**

Use the present perfect progressive, the past perfect progressive, or the future perfect progressive tense for an action that began earlier and did, does, or will continue.

The *present perfect progressive* indicates an action that started in the past and is continuing in the present. Form it by adding the present perfect of *be* (*has been, have been*) to the present participle (*-ing* form) of the main verb.

All morning Fred *has been complaining* about his neighbor's wild parties.

Have you *been reading* Uma's postcards from England?

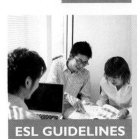

ESL GUIDELINES

■ For practice, visit
<bedfordstmartins.com/
bedguide> and do a
keyword search:

ESL

The Perfect Progressive Tenses

Present Perfect Progressive Tense: *have* or *has been* + present participle (*-ing* form)

- Use the present perfect progressive tense when an action began at some time in the past and has continued to the present. The words *for* and *since* are often used in sentences with this tense.

    She *has been answering* questions all day.

    The students *have been studying* for a long time.

Past Perfect Progressive Tense: *had been* + present participle

- Use the past perfect progressive tense when an action began and continued in the past and then was completed before some other past action.

    We *had been studying* for three hours before we took a break.

    Miguel *had been ringing* the doorbell for five minutes when we got home.

Future Perfect Progressive Tense: *will have been* + present participle

- Use the future perfect progressive tense when an action will continue in the future for a specific time and then end before or continue beyond another future action.

    The students *will have been studying* for twenty-four hours by the time they take the exam tomorrow.

    Jenn *will have been sailing* for a week when she reaches Jamaica.

    As of June, I *will have been playing* the drums for a year.

The *past perfect progressive* expresses a continuing action that was completed before another past action. Form it by adding the past perfect of *be* (*had been*) to the present participle of the main verb.

By the time Khalid finally arrived, I *had been waiting* for twenty minutes.

The *future perfect progressive* expresses an action that is expected to continue into the future for a specific time and then end before or continue beyond another future action. Form it by adding the future perfect of *be* (*will have been*) to the present participle of the main verb.

They *will have been driving* for three days by the time they get to Oregon.

By fall Joanne *will have been attending* school longer than anyone else I know.

■ For more practice, visit
<bedfordstmartins.com/
bedguide> and do a key-
word search:

verbs

■ Exercise 3–2

Identifying Verb Tenses

Underline each verb or verb phrase and identify its tense in the following sentences. Answers for the lettered sentences appear in the back of the book. Example:

John is living in Hinsdale, but he prefers Joliet.

John is living [present progressive] in Hinsdale, but he prefers [simple present] Joliet.

a. He has been living like a hunted animal ever since he hacked into the university computer lab in order to change all of his grades.

b. I have never appeared on a reality television show, and I will never appear on one unless my family gets selected.

c. James had been at the party for only fifteen minutes when his host suddenly pitched the caterer into the swimming pool.

d. As of next month, I will have been studying karate for six years, and I will be taking the test for my orange belt in July.

e. The dachshund was running at its fastest speed, but the squirrel strolled toward the tree without fear.

1. As of May 1, Ira and Sandy will have been going together for a year.
2. She will be working in her study if you need her.
3. Have you been hoping that Carlos will come to your party?
4. I know that he will not yet have returned from Chicago.
5. His parents had been expecting him home any day until they heard that he was still waiting for the bus.

VOICE

Intelligent students read challenging books.

Challenging books are read by intelligent students.

These two statements convey similar information, but their emphasis is different. In the first sentence, the subject (*students*) performs the verb's action (*read*); in the second sentence, the subject (*books*) receives the verb's action (*are read*). One sentence states its idea directly, the other indirectly. We say that the first sentence is in the *active voice* and the second is in the *passive voice*.

3m Use the active voice rather than the passive voice.

Verbs in the *active voice* consist of principal parts and helping verbs. Verbs in the *passive voice* consist of the past participle preceded by a form of *be* ("you *are given*," "I *was given*," "she *will be given*"). Most writers prefer the active to the passive voice because it is clearer and simpler, requires fewer words, and identifies the actor and the action more explicitly.

ACTIVE VOICE   *Sergeants give orders. Privates obey them.*

Normally the subject of a sentence is the focus of readers' attention. If that subject does not perform the verb's action but instead receives the

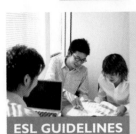

ESL GUIDELINES

■ For practice, visit
<bedfordstmartins.com/
bedguide> and do a key-
word search:

ESL

The Passive Voice

Passive Voice: form of *be* + past participle (*-ed* or *-en* form)

- In the passive voice, the subject of the sentence *receives* the action of the verb instead of performing it.

  ACTIVE   The university *awarded* Hamid a scholarship. [The subject (*university*) performs the action of *awarding*.]

  PASSIVE   Hamid *was awarded* a scholarship by the university. [The subject (*Hamid*) receives the action.]

- Often the identity of the action's performer is not important or is understood, and the *by* phrase is omitted.

  PASSIVE   Automobiles are built in Detroit. [It is understood that they are built *by people*.]

- When forming the passive, be careful to use the appropriate tenses of *be* to maintain the tense of the original active sentence.

  ACTIVE   Kip the clown *entertains* children. [Present tense]

  PASSIVE   Children *are entertained* by Kip the clown. [Present tense]

  ACTIVE   Kip the clown *entertained* the children. [Past tense]

  PASSIVE   The children *were entertained* by Kip the clown. [Past tense]

intransitive verb: A verb that is complete in itself and needs no object: The surgeon *paused.*

NOTE: Intransitive verbs are not used in the passive voice.

  INCORRECT   The plane *was arrived.*

  CORRECT   The plane *arrived.*

NOTE: The future progressive and future perfect progressive tenses are not used in the passive voice.

  INCORRECT   The novel *will be being read* by John.

  CORRECT   John *will be reading* the novel.

action, readers may wonder: What did the writer mean to emphasize? Just what is the point?

  PASSIVE VOICE   *Orders are given* by sergeants. *They are obeyed* by privates.

Other writers misuse the passive voice to try to lend pomp to a humble truth (or would-be truth): for example, "Slight technical difficulties are being experienced" may replace "The airplane needs repairs." Some even use the passive voice deliberately to obscure the truth.

You do not need to drop the passive voice entirely from your writing. Sometimes the performer of a verb's action is irrelevant, as in a lab report, which emphasizes the research, not the researcher. Other times the performer is unknown and simply omitted with a passive voice verb, as in "Many fortunes were lost in the stock market crash of 1929." It's a good idea, though, to substitute the active voice for the passive unless you have a good reason for using the passive.

■ Exercise 3–3

Using Active and Passive Voice Verbs

Revise the following passage, changing the passive voice to the active voice in each sentence, unless you can justify keeping the passive. Example:

> The Galápagos Islands were reached by many species of animals in ancient times.

> Many species of animals *reached* the Galápagos Islands in ancient times.

The unique creatures of the Galápagos Islands have been studied by many scientists. The islands were explored by Charles Darwin in 1835. His observations led to the theory of evolution, which he explained in his book *On the Origin of Species*. Thirteen species of finches on the islands were discovered by Darwin, all descended from a common stock; even today this great variety of species can be seen by visitors to the islands. Each island species has evolved by adapting to local conditions. A twig is used by the woodpecker finch to probe trees for grubs. Algae on the ocean floor is fed on by the marine iguana. Salt water can be drunk by the Galápagos cormorant, thanks to a salt-extracting gland. Because of the tameness of these animals, they can be studied by visitors at close range.

■ For more practice, visit <bedfordstmartins.com/bedguide> and do a keyword search:

    verbs

MOOD

Still another characteristic of every verb is its **mood**: *indicative, imperative,* or *subjunctive*. The indicative mood is the most common. The imperative and subjunctive moods add valuable versatility.

3n Use the indicative mood to state a fact, to ask a question, or to express an opinion.

Most verbs in English are in the indicative mood.

FACT   Danika *left* home two months ago.

QUESTION   *Will* she *find* happiness as a belly dancer?

OPINION   I *think* not.

3o Use the imperative mood to make a request or to give a command or direction.

The understood but usually unstated subject of a verb in the imperative mood is *you*. The verb's form is the base form or infinitive.

REQUEST   Please *be* there before noon. [*You* please be there. . . .]

COMMAND   *Hurry!* [*You* hurry!]

DIRECTION *Drive* east on State Street. [*You* drive east. . . .]

3p Use the subjunctive mood to express a wish, a requirement, a suggestion, or a condition contrary to fact.

subordinate clause: A group of words that contains a subject and a verb but cannot stand alone because it depends on a main clause to help it make sense: Pia, *who plays the oboe*, prefers solitude. (See 14d–14f.)

The subjunctive mood is used in a subordinate clause to suggest uncertainty: the action expressed by the verb may or may not actually take place as specified. In any clause opening with *that* and expressing a requirement, the verb is in the subjunctive mood and takes the base or infinitive form.

Professor Vogt requires that every student *deliver* his or her work promptly.

She asked that we *be* on time for all meetings.

When you use the subjunctive mood to describe a condition that is contrary to fact, use *were* if the verb is *be*; for other verbs, use the simple past tense. Wishes, whether present or past, follow the same rules.

If I *were* rich, I would be happy.

If I *had* a million dollars, I would be happy.

Elissa wishes that Ted *were* more goal oriented.

Elissa wished that Ted *knew* what he wanted to do.

For a condition that was contrary to fact at some point in the past, use the past perfect tense.

If I *had been* awake, I would have seen the meteor showers.

If Jessie *had known* you were coming, she would have cleaned her room.

infinitive: The base form of a verb, often preceded by *to* (*to go, to play*)

Although use of the subjunctive mood has grown scarcer over the years, it still sounds crude to write "If I *was* you. . . ." If you ever feel that the subjunctive mood makes a sentence sound stilted, you can rewrite it, substituting an infinitive phrase.

Professor Vogt requires every student *to deliver* his or her work promptly.

Conditionals

Conditional sentences usually contain an *if* clause, which states the condition, and a result clause.

- When the condition is true or possibly true in the present or future, use the present tense in the *if* clause and the present or future tense in the result clause. The future tense is not used in the *if* clause.

  If Jane *prepares* her essay early, she usually *writes* very well.

  If Maria *saves* enough money, she *will buy* a car.

- When the condition is not true in the present, for most verbs use the past tense in the *if* clause; for the verb *be*, use *were*. Use *would*, *could*, or *might* + infinitive form in the result clause.

  If Carlos *had* a computer, he *would need* a monitor, too.

  If Claudia *were* here, she *could do* it herself.

- When the condition was not true in the past, use the past perfect tense in the *if* clause. If the possible result was in the past, use *would have*, *could have*, or *might have* + past participle (*-ed* or *-en* form) in the result clause. If the possible result is in the present, use *would*, *could*, or *might* + infinitive form in the result clause.

  If Claudia *had saved* enough money last month, she *could have bought* a car. [Result in the past]

  If Annie *had finished* law school, she *might* be a successful lawyer now. [Result in the present]

ESL GUIDELINES

For practice, visit <bedfordstmartins.com/bedguide> and do a keyword search:

ESL

■ Exercise 3–4

Using the Correct Mood of Verbs

Find and correct any errors in mood in the following sentences. Identify the mood of the incorrect verb as well as its correct replacement. Some sentences may be correct. Answers for the lettered sentences appear in the back of the book. Example:

The law requires that each person files a tax return by April 15.

The law requires that each person *file* a tax return by April 15. [Incorrect: *files*, indicative; correct: *file*, subjunctive]

a. Dr. Belanger recommended that Juan flosses his teeth every day.
b. If I was you, I would have done the same thing.
c. Tradition demands that Daegun shows respect for his elders.
d. Please attends the training lesson if you plan to skydive later today.

1. If she was slightly older, she could stay home by herself.
2. If they have waited a little longer, they would have seen some amazing things.

For more practice, visit <bedfordstmartins.com/bedguide> and do a keyword search:

verbs

3. Emilia's contract stipulates that she works on Saturdays.

4. If James invested in the company ten years ago, he would have made a lot of money.

4   *Subject-Verb Agreement*

For more on editing for subject-verb agreement, see A4 in the Quick Editing Guide (the dark-blue-edged pages).

What does it mean for a subject and a verb to agree? Practically speaking, it means that their forms match: plural subjects take plural verbs, third-person subjects take third-person verbs, and so forth. When your subjects and verbs agree, you prevent a mismatch that could distract readers from your message.

4a   A verb agrees with its subject in person and number.

Subject and verb agree in person (first, second, or third):

I write my research papers on my laptop. [Subject and verb in first person]

Eamon writes his papers in the lab. [Subject and verb in third person]

Subject and verb agree in number (singular or plural):

Grace has enjoyed college. [Subject and verb singular]

She and Jim have enjoyed their vacation. [Subject and verb plural]

subject: The part of a sentence that names something—a person, an object, an idea, a situation—about which the predicate makes an assertion: The *king* lives.

verb: A word that shows action (The cow *jumped* over the moon) or a state of being (The cow *is* brown)

The present tense of most verbs is the infinitive form, with no added ending except in the third-person singular. (See 3g–3l.)

I enjoy	we enjoy
you enjoy	you enjoy
he/she/it enjoys	they enjoy

Forms of the verb *be* vary from this rule.

I am	we are
you are	you are
he/she/it is	they are

4b   A verb agrees with its subject, not with any words that intervene.

My *favorite* of O. Henry's short stories *is* "The Gift of the Magi."

Home sales, once driving the local economy, *have fallen* during the last year.

prepositional phrase: The preposition and its object (a noun or pronoun), plus any modifiers: *in the bar, under a rickety table*

A singular subject linked to another noun or pronoun by a prepositional phrase beginning with wording such as *along with, as well as,* or *in addition to* remains a singular subject and takes a singular verb.

My cousin *James* as well as his wife and son *plans* to vote for Levine.

4c Subjects joined by *and* usually take a plural verb.

In most cases, a compound subject takes a plural verb.

> *"Howl" and "Gerontion" are* Barry's favorite poems.
>
> *Sugar, salt, and fat* adversely *affect* people's health.

However, for phrases like *each man and woman* or *every dog and cat,* which consider the subjects individually, use a singular verb.

> *Each man and woman* in the room *has* a different story to tell.

Use a singular verb for two singular subjects that form or are one thing.

> *Lime juice and soda quenches* your thirst.

compound subject: A subject consisting of two or more nouns or pronouns linked by *and*: *My mother and my sister drove home.*

4d With subjects joined by *or* or *nor,* the verb agrees with the part of the subject nearest to it.

> Either they or *Max is* guilty.
>
> Neither Swaylhi nor *I am* willing to face the truth.

Subjects containing *not . . . but* follow this rule also.

> Not we but *George knows* the whole story.

You can remedy awkward constructions by rephrasing.

> Either they are guilty or Max is.
>
> Swaylhi and I are unwilling to face the truth.
>
> We do not know the whole story, but George does.

4e Most collective nouns take singular verbs.

When a collective noun refers to a group of people acting as one, use a singular verb.

> The *jury finds* the defendant guilty.

When the members act individually, use a plural verb.

> The *jury do* not yet *agree* on a verdict.

If you feel that using a plural verb results in an awkward sentence, reword the subject so that it refers to members of the group individually.

> The *jurors do* not yet *agree* on a verdict.

collective noun: A singular noun that represents a group of people or items, such as *committee, family, jury, trio*

■ For more on agreement with collective nouns, see 7e.

4f Most indefinite pronouns take a third-person singular verb.

indefinite pronoun: A pronoun standing for an unspecified person or thing, including singular forms (*each, everyone, no one*) and plural forms (*both, few*): *Everyone* is soaking wet.

The indefinite pronouns *each, one, either, neither, anyone, anybody, anything, everyone, everybody, everything, no one, nobody, nothing, someone, somebody,* and *something* are considered singular and take a third-person singular verb.

Someone is bothering me.

Even when one of these subjects is followed by a phrase containing a noun or pronoun of a different person or number, use a singular verb.

Each of you *is* here to stay.

One of the pandas *seems* dangerously ill.

■ For a list of indefinite pronouns, see A6 in the Quick Editing Guide (the dark-blue-edged pages).

4g The indefinite pronouns *all, any,* and *some* use a singular or plural verb, depending on their meaning.

I have no explanation. *Is any* needed?

Any of the changes considered critical *have* been made already.

All is lost.

All of the bananas *are gone.*

Some of the blame *is* mine.

Some of us *are* Democrats.

■ For more on agreement with indefinite pronouns, see 7d.

None — like *all, any,* and *some* — takes a singular or a plural verb, depending on the sense in which the pronoun is used.

None of you *is* exempt.

None of his wives *were* blond.

4h In a subordinate clause with a relative pronoun as the subject, the verb agrees with the antecedent.

subordinate clause: A group of words that contains a subject and a verb but cannot stand alone because it depends on a main clause to help it make sense: Pia, *who plays the oboe,* prefers solitude. (See 14d–14f.)

To determine the person and number of the verb in a subordinate clause whose subject is *who, which,* or *that,* look back at the word to which the pronoun refers. This word, known as an antecedent, is usually (but not always) the noun closest to the relative pronoun.

I have a roommate *who studies* day and night. [The antecedent of *who* is the third-person singular noun *roommate.* Therefore, the verb in the subordinate clause is third-person singular, *studies.*]

I bought one of the two hundred new cars *that have* defective upholstery. [The antecedent of *that* is *cars,* so the verb is third-person plural, *have.*]

This is the only one of the mayor's new ideas *that has* any worth. [Here *one,* not *ideas,* is the antecedent of *that.* Thus, the verb in the subordinate clause is third-person singular, *has,* not *have.*]

4i   A verb agrees with its subject even when the subject follows the verb.

In some sentences, introductory expressions such as *there* or *here* change the ordinary order so that the subject follows the verb. Remember that verbs agree with subjects and that *here* and *there* are never subjects.

Here *is* a *riddle* for you.

There *are* forty *people* in my law class.

Under the bridge *were* a broken-down *boat and* a worn *tire.*

4j   A linking verb agrees with its subject, not its subject complement.

When a form of the verb *be* is used to link two or more nouns, the subject is the noun that precedes the linking verb. Nouns that follow the linking verb are subject complements. Make a linking verb agree with the subject of the sentence, not with the subject complement.

Jim is a gentleman and a scholar.

Amy's *parents are* her most enthusiastic audience.

4k   When the subject is a title, use a singular verb.

When I was younger, *Harry Potter and the Sorcerer's Stone was* my favorite book.

"Memories" sung by Barbra Streisand *is* my aunt's favorite song.

4l   Singular nouns that end in -s take singular verbs.

Some nouns look plural even though they refer to a singular subject: *measles, logistics, mathematics, electronics.* Such nouns take singular verbs.

The *news is* that *economics has become* one of the most popular majors.

---

relative pronoun: A pronoun (*who, which, that, what, whom, whomever, whose*) that opens a subordinate clause, modifying a noun or pronoun in another clause: The gift *that* I received is very practical.

antecedent: The word to which a pronoun refers: *Lyn* plays golf, and *she* putts well.

linking verb: A verb (*is, become, seem, feel*) that shows a state of being by linking the sentence subject with a word that renames or describes the subject: The sky *is* blue. (See 3a.)

subject complement: A noun, an adjective, or a group of words that follows a linking verb and renames or describes the subject: This plum tastes *ripe.* (See 3a.)

■ Exercise 4–1

Making Subjects and Verbs Agree

■ For more practice, visit <bedfordstmartins.com/bedguide> and do a key-word search:

sv agreement

Find and correct any subject-verb agreement errors in the following sentences. Some sentences may be correct. Answers for the lettered sentences appear in the back of the book. Example:

> Addressing the audience tonight is the nominees for club president.
>
> Addressing the audience tonight *are* the nominees for club president.

a. For many college graduates, the process of looking for jobs are often long and stressful.

b. Not too long ago, searching the classifieds and inquiring in person was the primary methods of job hunting.

c. Today, however, everyone also seem to use the Internet to search for openings or to e-mail their résumés.

d. My classmates and my cousin sends most résumés over the Internet because it costs less than mailing them.

e. All of the résumés arrives quickly when they are sent electronically.

1. There are many people who thinks that interviewing is the most stressful part of the job search.

2. Sometimes only one person conducts an interview, while other times a whole committee conduct it.

3. Either the interviewer or the committee usually begin by asking simple questions about your background.

4. Making eye contact, dressing professionally, and appearing confident is some of the qualities an interviewer may consider important.

5. After an interview, most people sends a thank-you letter to the person who conducted it.

5   *Pronoun Case*

■ For advice on editing pronoun case, see A5 in the Quick Editing Guide (the dark-blue-edged pages).

As you know, pronouns come in distinctive forms. The first-person pronoun can be *I*, or it can be *me, my, mine, we, us, our,* or *ours*. Which form do you pick? It depends on what job you want the pronoun to do.

Depending on a pronoun's function in a sentence, we say that it is in the *subjective case*, the *objective case*, or the *possessive case*. Some pronouns change form when they change case, and some do not. The personal pronouns *I, he, she, we,* and *they* and the relative pronoun *who* have different forms in the subjective, objective, and possessive cases. Other pronouns, such as *you, it, that,* and *which,* have only two forms: the plain case (which serves as both subjective and objective) and the possessive case.

We can pin the labels *subjective, objective,* and *possessive* on nouns as well as on pronouns. Like the pronouns *you, it, that,* and *which,* nouns shift from plain form only in the possessive *(teacher's* pet, *Jonas's* poodle, her *parents'* home).

Beware, when you are not sure which case to choose, of the temptation to fall back on a reflexive pronoun *(myself, himself).* If you catch yourself writing, "You can return the form to John or *myself"* or "John and *myself* are in charge," replace the reflexive pronoun with one that is grammatically correct: "You can return the form to John or *me"*; "John and *I* are in charge."

5a   Use the subjective case for the subject of a sentence or clause.

Jed and *I* ate the granola.

Who cares?

Maya recalled that *she* played baseball.

Election officials are the people *who* count.

A pronoun serving as the subject for a verb is subjective even when the verb isn't written but is only implied:

Jed is hungrier than *I* [am].

Don't be fooled by a pronoun that appears immediately after a verb, looking as if it were a direct object but functioning as the subject of a clause. The pronoun's case is determined by its role, not by its position.

The judge didn't believe *I* hadn't been the driver.

We were happy to interview *whoever* was running. [Subject of *was running*]

5b   Use the subjective case for a subject complement.

When a pronoun functions as a subject complement, it plays essentially the same role as the subject and its case is subjective.

The phantom graffiti artist couldn't have been *he.* It was *I.*

5c   Use the subjective case for an appositive to a subject or subject complement.

A pronoun placed in apposition to a subject or subject complement is like an identical twin to the noun it stands beside. It has the same meaning and the same case.

The class *officers* — Ravi and *she* — announced a senior breakfast.

subject: The part of a sentence that names something — a person, an object, an idea, a situation — about which the predicate makes an assertion: The *king* lives.

direct object: The target of a verb that completes the action performed by the subject or asserted about the subject: I photographed *the sheriff.*

subject complement: A noun, an adjective, or a group of words that follows a linking verb *(is, become, feel, seem,* or another verb that shows a state of being) and that renames or describes the subject: This plum tastes *ripe.* (See 3a.)

appositive: A word or group of words that adds information about a subject or object by identifying it in a different way: my dog *Rover,* Hal's brother *Fred*

direct object: The target of a verb that completes the action performed by the subject or asserted about the subject: I photographed *the sheriff.*

indirect object: A person or thing affected by the subject's action, usually the recipient of the direct object, through the action indicated by a verb such as *bring, get, offer, promise, sell, show, tell,* and *write:* Charlene asked *you* a question.

object of a preposition: The noun or pronoun that follows the preposition (such as *in, on, at, of, from*) that connects it, along with any modifiers, to the rest of the sentence: She opened the door to the *garage.*

infinitive: The base form of a verb, often preceded by *to: to go, to play*

For a chart of possessive personal pronouns, see C2 in the Quick Editing Guide (the dark-blue-edged pages).

5d Use the objective case for a direct object, an indirect object, the object of a preposition, or a subject of an infinitive.

The custard pies hit *him* and *me.* [Direct object]

Mona threw *us* towels. [Indirect object]

Mona threw towels to *him* and *us.* [Object of a preposition]

We always expect *him* to win. [Subject of an infinitive]

5e Use the objective case for an appositive to a direct or indirect object or the object of a preposition.

Mona helped us *all* — Mrs. Van Dumont, *him,* and *me.* [*Him* and *me* are in apposition to the direct object *us.*]

Binks gave his favorite *students,* Tom and *her,* an approving nod. [*Her* is in apposition to the indirect object *students.*]

Yelling, the pie flingers ran after *us* — Mona, *him,* and *me.* [*Him* and *me* are in apposition to *us,* the object of the preposition *after.*]

5f Use the possessive case to show ownership.

Possessive pronouns can function as adjectives or as nouns. The pronouns *my, your, his, her, its, our,* and *their* function as adjectives by modifying nouns or pronouns.

My new bike is having *its* first road test today.

The possessive pronoun *its* does not contain an apostrophe. *It's* with an apostrophe is a contraction for *it is,* as in "*It's* a beautiful day for bike riding."

The possessive pronouns *mine, yours, his, hers, ours,* and *theirs* can discharge the whole range of noun duties, serving as subjects, subject complements, direct objects, indirect objects, or objects of prepositions.

Yours is the last vote we need. [Subject]

This day is *ours.* [Subject complement]

Don't take your car; take *mine.* [Direct object]

If we're honoring requests, give *hers* top priority. [Indirect object]

Give her request priority over *theirs.* [Object of a preposition]

5g Use the possessive case to modify a gerund.

gerund: A form of a verb, ending in *-ing,* that functions as a noun: Lacey likes *playing* in the steel band.

A possessive pronoun (or a possessive noun) is the appropriate escort for a gerund. As a noun, a gerund requires an adjective, not another noun, for a modifier.

Mary is tired of *his griping.* [The possessive pronoun *his* modifies the gerund *griping.*]

I can stand *their being* late every morning but not *his drinking* on the job. [The possessive pronoun *their* modifies the gerund *being;* the possessive pronoun *his* modifies the gerund *drinking.*]

Gerunds can cause confusion when you edit because they look exactly like present participles. Whereas a gerund functions as a noun, a participle often functions as an adjective modifying a noun or pronoun.

> **present participle:** A form of a verb ending in *-ing* that cannot function alone as a main verb but can act as an adjective: *Leading* the pack, Michael crossed the finish line.

Mary heard *him griping* about work. [The participle *griping* modifies the direct object *him.*]

If you are not sure whether to use a possessive or an objective pronoun with a word ending in *-ing,* look closely at your sentence. Which word — the pronoun or the *-ing* word — is the object of your main verb? That word functions as a noun; the other word modifies it.

Mr. Phipps remembered *them* smoking in the boys' room. [Mr. Phipps remembers *them,* those naughty students. *Them* is the object of the verb, so *smoking* is a participle modifying *them.*]

Mr. Phipps remembered *their* smoking in the boys' room. [Mr. Phipps remembers *smoking,* that nasty habit. The gerund *smoking* is the object of the verb, and the possessive pronoun *their* modifies it.]

In everyday speech, the rules about pronoun case apply less rigidly. Someone who correctly asks in conversation, "To whom are you referring?" is likely to sound pretentious. You are within your rights to reply, as did the comic-strip character Pogo Possum, "Youm, that's whom!" Say, if you like, "It's *me,*" but in formal situations write "It is *I.*" Say, if you wish, "*Who* did he ask to the party?" but write "*Whom* did he ask?"

■ Exercise 5–I

Using Pronouns Correctly

Replace any pronouns used incorrectly in the following sentences. (Consider all these examples as written — not spoken — English, so apply the rules strictly.) Explain why each pronoun was incorrect. Some sentences may be correct. Answers for the lettered sentences appear in the back of the book. Example:

> That is her, the new university president, at the podium.
>
> That is *she,* the new university president, at the podium. [*She* is a subject complement.]

■ For more practice, visit <bedfordstmartins.com/ bedguide> and do a keyword search:

case

a. I didn't appreciate you laughing at her and I.
b. Lee and me would be delighted to serenade whomever will listen.
c. The managers and us servers are highly trustworthy.
d. The neighbors were driven berserk by him singing.

e. Jerry and myself regard you and she as the very people who we wish to meet.

1. Have you guessed the identity of the person of who I am speaking?
2. It was him asking about the clock that started me suspecting him.
3. They — Jerry and her — are the troublemakers.
4. Mrs. Van Dumont awarded the prize to Mona and I.
5. The counterattack was launched by Dusty and myself.

6 *Pronoun Reference*

Look hard at just about any piece of writing — this discussion, if you like — and you'll find that practically every pronoun in it points to some noun. This is the main use of pronouns: to refer in a brief, convenient form to some *antecedent* that has already been named. A pronoun usually has a noun or another pronoun as its antecedent. Often the antecedent is the subject or object of the same clause in which the pronoun appears.

> Josie hit the *ball* after *its* first bounce.

> Smashing into *Greg*, the ball knocked off *his* glasses.

The antecedent also can appear in a different clause or even a different sentence from the pronoun.

> *Josie* hit the *ball* when *it* bounced back to *her*.

> The *ball* smashed into *Greg*. *It* knocked off *his* glasses.

A pronoun as well as a noun can be an antecedent.

> My *dog* hid in the closet when *she* had *her* puppies. [*Dog* is the antecedent of *she; she* is the antecedent of *her*.]

6a Name the pronoun's antecedent: don't just imply it.

antecedent: The word to which a pronoun refers: *Lyn* plays golf, and *she* putts well.

When editing, be sure you have identified clearly the antecedent of each pronoun. A writer who leaves a key idea unsaid is likely to confuse readers.

> VAGUE Ted wanted a Norwegian canoe because he'd heard that *they* produce the lightest canoes afloat.

What noun or pronoun does *they* refer to? Not to *Norwegian*, which is an adjective. We may guess that this writer has in mind Norwegian canoe builders, but no such noun has been mentioned. To make the sentence work, the writer must supply an antecedent for *they*.

> CLEAR Ted wanted a Norwegian canoe because he'd heard that Norway produces [*or* Norwegians produce] the lightest canoes afloat.

Watch out for possessive nouns. They won't work as antecedents.

VAGUE   On William's canoe, *he* painted a skull and bones. (For all we know, *he* might be some joker named Gustavo.)

CLEAR   On his canoe, William painted a skull and bones.

VAGUE   In Hemingway's story, he describes the powerful sea.

CLEAR   In the story, Hemingway describes the powerful sea.

Adjective Clauses and Relative Pronouns

ESL GUIDELINES

Be sure to use relative pronouns (*who, whose, which, that*) correctly in sentences with adjective clauses. Use *who,* not *which,* for a person. Select *that* to introduce necessary information that defines or specifies; reserve *which* for additional, but not defining, information.

- Do not omit the relative pronoun when it is the subject within the adjective clause.

INCORRECT   The woman *gave us directions to the museum* told us not to miss the Picasso exhibit.

CORRECT   The woman *who gave us directions to the museum* told us not to miss the Picasso exhibit. [*Who* is the subject of the adjective clause.]

■ For more on choosing *that* or *which,* see 21e.

- In speech and informal writing, you can imply (not state) a relative pronoun when it is the object of a verb or preposition within the adjective clause. In formal writing, you should use the relative pronoun.

FORMAL   Jamal forgot to return the book *that I gave him.* [*That* is the object of *gave.*]

INFORMAL   Jamal forgot to return the book *I gave him.* [The relative pronoun *that* is implied.]

FORMAL   This is the box *in which we found the jewelry.* [*Which* is the object of the preposition *in.*]

INFORMAL   This is the box *we found the jewelry in.* [The relative pronoun *which* is implied.]

■ For practice, visit <bedfordstmartins.com/bedguide> and do a keyword search:

ESL

NOTE: When the relative pronoun is omitted, the preposition moves to the end of the sentence but must not be left out.

- *Whose* is the only possessive form of a relative pronoun. It is used with persons, animals, and things.

INCORRECT   I sat on a chair *that its* legs were wobbly.

CORRECT   I sat on a chair *whose* legs were wobbly.

NOTE: If you are not sure how to use a relative pronoun, try rephrasing the sentence more simply.

   I sat on a chair *that had wobbly legs* [or *with wobbly legs*].

antecedent: The word to
which a pronoun refers:
Lyn plays golf, and *she*
putts well.

6b Give the pronoun *it, this, that,* or *which* a clear
antecedent.

Vagueness arises, thick as fog, whenever *it, this, that,* or *which* points to
something a writer assumes is said but indeed isn't. Often the best way out
of the fog is to substitute a specific noun or expression for the pronoun.

VAGUE   I was an only child, and *it* was hard.

CLEAR   I was an only child, and my solitary life was hard.

VAGUE   Judy could not get along with her younger brother. *This* is the rea-
         son she wanted to get her own apartment.

CLEAR   Because Judy could not get along with her younger brother, she
         wanted to get her own apartment.

6c Make the pronoun's antecedent clear.

Confusion strikes if a pronoun seems to point in two or more directions. In
such a puzzling situation, more than one antecedent looks possible. Baffled,
the reader wonders which the writer means.

CONFUSING   Hanwei shouted to Kenny to take off his burning sweater.

Whose sweater does *his* mean — Kenny's or Hanwei's? Simply changing
a pronoun won't clear up the confusion. The writer needs to revise enough
to move the two possible antecedents out of each other's way.

CLEAR   "Kenny!" shouted Hanwei. "Your sweater's on fire! Take it
         off!"

CLEAR   Flames were shooting from Kenny's sweater. Hanwei shouted
         to Kenny to take it off.

Pronouns referring to nouns of the same gender are particular offenders.

CONFUSING   Linda welcomed Lee-Ann's move into the apartment next
             door. Little did she dream that soon she would be secretly
             dating her husband.

Let meaning show you how to straighten out the grammatical tangle. If you
had written these sentences, you would know which person is the sneak.
One way to clarify the antecedents of *she* and *her* is to add information.

CLEAR   In welcoming Lee-Ann to the apartment next door, Linda
         didn't dream that soon her own husband would be secretly
         dating her former sorority sister.

6d **Place the pronoun close to its antecedent to keep the relationship clear.**

antecedent: The word to which a pronoun refers: *Lyn* plays golf, and *she* putts well.

Watch out for distractions that slip in between noun and pronoun. If your sentence contains two or more nouns that look like antecedents to a pronoun, your readers may become bewildered.

> CONFUSING Harper steered his dinghy alongside the cabin cruiser that the drug smugglers had left anchored under an overhanging willow in the tiny harbor and eased it to a stop.

What did Harper ease to a stop? By the time readers reach the end of the sentence, they are likely to have forgotten. To avoid confusion, keep the pronoun and its antecedent reasonably close together.

> CLEAR Harper steered his dinghy into the tiny harbor and eased it to a stop alongside the cabin cruiser that the drug smugglers had left anchored under an overhanging willow.

Never force your readers to stop and think, "What does that pronoun stand for?" You, the writer, have to do this thinking for them.

■ Exercise 6–1

Making Pronoun Reference Clear

Revise each sentence or group of sentences so that any pronoun needing an antecedent clearly points to one. Possible revisions for the lettered sentences appear in the back of the book. Example:

> I took the money out of the wallet and threw it in the trash.
>
> I took the money out of the wallet and threw *the wallet* in the trash.

a. I could see the moon and the faint shadow of the tree as it began to rise.

b. Katrina spent the summer in Paris and traveled throughout Europe, which broadened her awareness of cultural differences.

c. Most managers want employees to work as many hours as possible. They never consider the work they need to do at home.

d. I worked twelve hours a day and never got enough sleep, but it was worth it.

e. Kevin asked Mike to meet him for lunch but forgot that he had class at that time.

1. Bill's prank frightened Josh and made him wonder why he had done it.

2. Korean students study up to twenty subjects a year, including algebra, calculus, and engineering. Because they are required, they must study them year after year.

3. Pedro Martinez signed a baseball for Chad that he had used in a game.

■ For more practice, visit <bedfordstmartins.com/bedguide> and do a keyword search:

reference

4. When the bottle hit the windshield, it shattered.

5. My friends believe they are more mature than many of their peers because of the discipline enforced at their school. However, it can also lead to problems.

7   *Pronoun-Antecedent Agreement*

pronoun: A word that stands in place of a noun (*he, him,* or *his* for *Nate*)
antecedent: The word to which a pronoun refers: *Lyn* plays golf, and *she* putts well.

A pronoun's job is to fill in for a noun, much as an actor's double fills in for the actor. Pronouns are a short, convenient way for writers to avoid repeating the same noun over and over.

The sheriff drew a six-shooter; he fired twice.

In this action-packed sentence, first comes a noun (*sheriff*) and then a pronoun (*he*) that refers back to it. *Sheriff* is the antecedent of *he*.

Just as verbs need to agree with their subjects, pronouns need to agree with the nouns they stand for. A successful writer takes care not to shift number, person, or gender in midsentence ("The *sheriff* and the *outlaw* drew *their* six-shooters; *he* fired twice").

7a   Pronouns agree with their antecedents in person and number.

For more on editing for pronoun-antecedent agreement, see A6 in the Quick Editing Guide (the dark-blue-edged pages).

A pronoun matches its antecedent in person (first, second, or third) and in number (singular or plural), even when intervening words separate the pronoun and its antecedent.

FAULTY   All *campers* should bring *your* knapsacks.

Here, noun and pronoun disagree in person: *campers* is third person, but *your* is second person.

FAULTY   Every *camper* should bring *their* knapsack.

Here, noun and pronoun disagree in number: *camper* is singular, but *their* is plural.

REVISED   All *campers* should bring *their* knapsacks.

REVISED   Every *camper* should bring *his or her* knapsack. (See also 7f.)

7b   Most antecedents joined by *and* require a plural pronoun.

compound subject: A subject consisting of two or more nouns or pronouns linked by *and: My mother and my sister* drove home.

A *compound subject* is plural; use a plural pronoun to refer to it.

George, who has been here before, *and Jenn,* who hasn't, should bring *their* knapsacks.

If the nouns in a compound subject refer to the same person or thing, they make up a singular antecedent. Use a singular pronoun too.

> The *owner and founder* of this camp carries *his* own knapsack everywhere.

7c   A pronoun agrees with the closest part of an antecedent joined by *or* or *nor*.

If your subject is two or more nouns (or a combination of nouns and pronouns) connected by *or* or *nor*, look closely at the subject's parts. Are they all singular? If so, your pronoun should be singular.

> Neither *Joy nor Jean* remembered *her* knapsack last year.

> If *Sam, Arthur, or Dieter* shows up, tell *him* I'm looking for *him*.

If the part of the subject closest to the pronoun is plural, the pronoun should be plural.

> Neither *Joy nor her sisters* remembered *their* knapsacks last year.

> If you see *Sam, Arthur, or their friends,* tell *them* I'm looking for *them*.

7d   An antecedent that is an indefinite pronoun takes a singular pronoun.

Indefinite pronouns are usually singular in meaning, so a pronoun referring to one of them is also singular.

> *Either* of the boys can do it, as long as *he's* on time.

> Warn *anybody* who's still in *her* swimsuit that a uniform is required for dinner.

Sometimes the meaning of an indefinite pronoun is plural. To avoid awkwardness, avoid using such a pronoun as an antecedent.

> AWKWARD   Tell *everyone* in Cabin B that I'm looking for *him*.

This sentence works better if it is phrased differently.

> REVISED   Tell *all the campers* in Cabin B that I'm looking for *them*.

7e   Most collective nouns used as antecedents require singular pronouns.

When the members of such a group act as a unit, use a singular pronoun to refer to them.

> The *cast* for the play will be posted as soon as the director chooses *it*.

When the group members act individually, use a plural pronoun.

> The *cast* will go *their* separate ways when summer ends.

---

indefinite pronoun: A pronoun standing for an unspecified person or thing, including singular forms (*each, everyone, no one*) and plural forms (*both, few*): *Everyone is soaking wet.*

■ For a list of indefinite pronouns, see A6 in the Quick Editing Guide (the dark-blue-edged pages). For more on agreement with indefinite pronouns, see 4f and 7f.

collective noun: A singular noun that represents a group of people or items, such as *committee, family, jury, trio*

■ For more on agreement with collective nouns, see 4e.

7f **A pronoun agrees with its antecedent in gender.**

If *one of your parents* brings you to camp, invite *him* to stay for lunch.

For more on bias-free language, see 18.

While technically correct (the singular pronoun *he* refers to the singular antecedent *one*), this sentence overlooks the fact that some parents are male, some female. To make sure the pronoun covers both, a writer has two choices.

If *one of your parents* brings you to camp, invite *him or her* to stay for lunch.

If your *parents* bring you to camp, invite *them* to stay for lunch.

■ Exercise 7–1

For more practice, visit <bedfordstmartins.com/bedguide> and do a keyword search:

[🔍   pa agreement   ]

Making Pronouns and Antecedents Agree

If any nouns and pronouns disagree in number, person, or gender in the following sentences, substitute pronouns that agree with the nouns. If you prefer, strengthen any sentence by rewriting it. Some sentences may be correct. Possible revisions for the lettered sentences appear in the back of the book. Example:

A cat expects people to feed them often.

A *cat* expects people to feed *it* often. *Or*

Cats expect people to feed *them* often.

a. Many architects find work their greatest pleasure.
b. Neither Melissa nor James has received their application form yet.
c. He is the kind of man who gets their fun out of just sipping one's beer and watching his Saturday games on TV.
d. Many a mother has mourned the loss of their child.
e. When one enjoys one's work, it's easy to spend all your spare time thinking about it.

1. All students are urged to complete your registration on time.
2. When a baby doesn't know their own mother, they may have been born with some kind of vision deficiency.
3. Each member of the sorority has to make her own bed.
4. If you don't like the songs the choir sings, don't join them.
5. Young people should know how to protect oneself against AIDS.

adjective: A word or phrase that describes, or modifies, a noun or a pronoun: The *small brown* cow leaned against the *old* fence.

8 *Adjectives and Adverbs*

An adjective's job is to provide information about the person, place, object, or idea named by the noun or pronoun. The adjective typically answers the question Which? or What kind?

Karen bought a *small red* car.

The radios *on sale* are an *excellent* value.

An adverb typically answers the question How? or When? or Where? Sometimes it answers the question Why?

Karen bought her car *quickly.*

The MP3 players arrived *yesterday;* Denis put them *in the electronics department.*

Karen needed her new car *to commute to school.*

The common problems that writers have with adjectives and adverbs involve mixing them up: sending an adjective to do an adverb's job or vice versa.

8a   Use an adverb, not an adjective, to modify a verb, adjective, or another adverb.

FAULTY   Karen bought her car *quick.*

FAULTY   It's *awful* hot today.

Though an informal speaker might get away with these sentences, a writer cannot. *Quick* and *awful* are adjectives, so they can modify only nouns or pronouns. Adverbs are needed to modify the verb *bought* and the adjective *hot.*

REVISED   Karen bought her car *quickly.*

REVISED   It's *awfully* hot today.

8b   Use an adjective, not an adverb, as a subject complement or an object complement.

If we write, "Her old car looked awful," the adjective *awful* is a **subject complement**: it follows a linking verb and modifies the subject, *car.* An **object complement** completes the description of a direct object and can be an adjective or a noun, but never an adverb.

Adjectives and Adverbs at a Glance

ADJECTIVES
1. Typically answer the question Which? or What kind?
2. Modify nouns or pronouns

ADVERBS
3. Answer the question How? When? Where? or sometimes Why?
4. Modify verbs, adjectives, and other adverbs

For advice on nouns and articles, see pp. H-52–H-53.

adverb: A word or phrase that modifies a verb, an adjective, or another adverb: The cow bawled *loudly.*

For more on editing adjectives and adverbs, see A7 in the Quick Editing Guide (the dark-blue-edged pages).

subject complement: A noun, an adjective, or a group of words that follows a linking verb (*is, become, feel, seem* or another verb that shows a state of being) and renames or describes the subject: This plum tastes *ripe.* (See 3a.)

object complement: A noun, an adjective, or a group of words that renames or describes a direct object: The judges rated Hugo *the best skater.*

Early to bed and early to rise makes a man *healthy, wealthy,* and *wise.* [Adjectives modifying the direct object *man*]

When you are not sure whether you're dealing with an object complement or an adverb, look closely at the word's role in the sentence. If it modifies a noun, it is an object complement and therefore should be an adjective.

The coach called the referee *stupid* and *blind.* [*Stupid* and *blind* are adjectives modifying the direct object *referee.*]

If it modifies a verb, you want an adverb instead.

In fact, the ref had called the play *correctly.* [*Correctly* is an adverb modifying the verb *called.*]

8c Use *good* as an adjective and *well* as an adverb.

subject complement: A noun, an adjective, or a group of words that follows a linking verb and renames or describes the subject: This plum tastes *ripe.* (See 3a.)

linking verb: A verb (*is, become, seem, feel*) that shows a state of being by linking the sentence subject with a word that renames or describes the subject: The sky *is* blue. (See 3a.)

This sandwich tastes *good.* [The adjective *good* is a subject complement following the linking verb *tastes* and modifying the noun *sandwich.*]

Al's skin healed *well* after surgery. [The adverb *well* modifies the verb *healed.*]

Only if the verb is a linking verb can you safely follow it with *good.* Other kinds of verbs do not take subject complements. Instead, they need adverbs to modify them.

FAULTY   That painting came out *good.*

REVISED   That painting came out *well.*

Complications arise when we write or speak about health. It is perfectly correct to say *I feel good,* using the adjective *good* as a subject complement after the linking verb *feel.* However, generations of confusion have nudged the adverb *well* into the adjective category, too. A nurse may speak of "a well baby"; greeting cards urge patients to "get well"—meaning, "become healthy." Just as *healthy* is an adjective here, so is *well.*

What, then, is the best answer when someone asks, "How do you feel?" If you want to duck the issue, reply, "Fine!" Otherwise, in speech either *good* or *well* is acceptable; in writing, use *good.*

8d Form comparatives and superlatives of most adjectives with *-er* and *-est* and of most adverbs with *more* and *most.*

Comparatives and superlatives are special adjective and adverb forms that allow us to describe one thing in relation to another. Put most adjectives into comparative form (for two things) by adding *-er* and into superlative form (for three or more) by adding *-est.*

The budget deficit is *larger* than the trade deficit.

This year's trade deficit is the *largest* ever.

We usually form the comparative and superlative of potentially cumbersome long adjectives with *more* and *most* rather than with *-er* and *-est.*

> The lake is *more beautiful* than I'd imagined.

> The shoreline is the *most beautiful* in the region.

For short adverbs that do not end in *-ly,* usually add *-er* and *-est* in the comparative and superlative forms. With all other adverbs, use *more* and *most.* (Also see 8f.)

> The trade deficit grows *fastest* and *most uncontrollably* when exports are down and imports remain high.

For negative comparisons, use *less* and *least* for adjectives and adverbs.

> Michael's speech was *less dramatic* than Louie's.

> Paulette spoke *less dramatically* than Michael.

Comparative and superlative forms of irregular adjectives and adverbs (such as *bad* and *badly*) are also irregular and should be used with care.

> Tom's golf game is *bad,* but no *worse* than George's.

> Tom plays golf *badly,* but no *worse* than George does.

> ▨ For a chart of comparative forms of irregular adjectives and adverbs, see A7 in the Quick Editing Guide (the dark-blue-edged pages).

8e Omit *more* and *most* with an adjective or adverb that is already comparative or superlative.

Some words become comparative or superlative when we tack on *-er* or *-est.* Others, such as *top, favorite,* and *unique,* mark whatever they modify as one of a kind by definition. Neither category requires further assistance to make its point. To say "a *more worse* fate" or "my *most favorite* movie" is redundant: "a *worse* fate" or "my *favorite* movie" does the job.

> FAULTY   Lisa is *more uniquely* qualified for the job than any other candidate.

> REVISED   Lisa is *better* qualified for the job than any other candidate.

> REVISED   Lisa is *uniquely* qualified for the job.

8f Use the comparative form of an adjective or adverb to compare two people or things, the superlative form to compare more than two.

No matter how wonderful something is, we can call it the *best* only when we compare it with more than one other thing. Any comparison between two things uses the comparative form (*better*), not the superlative (*best*).

> FAULTY   Chocolate and vanilla are both good, but I like chocolate *best.*

> REVISED   Chocolate and vanilla are both good, but I like chocolate *better.*

ESL GUIDELINES

For advice on using commas with adjectives, see 21d.

For practice, visit <bedfordstmartins.com/bedguide> and do a keyword search:

ESL

Cumulative Adjectives

Cumulative adjectives are two or more adjectives used directly before a noun and not separated by commas or the word *and*.

> She is an *attractive older French* woman.
>
> His *expressive large brown* eyes moved me.

Cumulative adjectives usually follow a specific order of placement before a noun. Use this list as a guide, but keep in mind that the order can vary.

1. Articles or determiners
   a, an, the, some, this, these, his, my, two, several
2. Evaluative adjectives
   beautiful, wonderful, hard-working, distasteful
3. Size or dimension
   big, small, huge, obese, petite, six-foot
4. Length or shape
   long, short, round, square, oblong, oval
5. Age
   old, young, new, fresh, ancient
6. Color
   red, pink, aquamarine, orange
7. Nation or place of origin
   American, Japanese, European, Bostonian, Floridian
8. Religion
   Protestant, Muslim, Hindu, Buddhist, Catholic, Jewish
9. Matter or substance
   wood, gold, cotton, plastic, pine, metal
10. Noun used as an adjective
    car (as in *car mechanic*), *computer* (as in *computer software*)

For more practice, visit <bedfordstmartins.com/bedguide> and do a keyword search:

adj_adv

■ Exercise 8–1

Using Adjectives and Adverbs Correctly

Find and correct any improperly used adjectives and adverbs in the following sentences. Some sentences may be correct. Answers for the lettered sentences appear in the back of the book. Example:

> The deal worked out good for both of us.
>
> The deal worked out *well* for both of us.

a. Credit-card debt is becoming increasing common among college students, who have expenses but do not work full-time.

b. Nearly all credit-card companies try to convince students to apply by offering introductory rates that are enticingly low.

c. It then is easy for students to charge many items on different cards and make only the lower minimum payments each month.

d. Unfortunately, when juggling multiple credit cards, many students lose sight of how rapid the debt is accumulating.

e. It is a well idea to charge only as much as you can pay in full each month.

1. A popular trend in television today is voyeurism, or the act of secret watching people as they go about their daily lives.

2. In the late 1990s, the popularity of MTV's *The Real World* sparked increasingly interest in this concept.

3. Music videos and commercials also began to incorporate voyeuristic elements, although, of the two, videos used the technique most frequently.

4. With the millennium came a flood of new "reality" programs all trying to capitalize more distinctively on the current trend.

5. On the program *Survivor,* contestants are filmed living in challenging settings with limited supplies, while viewers at home watch breathless to see how the contestants will behave.

9 *Shifts*

Just as you can change position to view a scene from different vantage points, in your writing you can change the time or the actor to consider a subject in various ways. However, writers sometimes shift point of view unconsciously or unnecessarily within a passage, creating ambiguity and confusion for readers. Such shifts are evident in grammatical inconsistencies.

9a Maintain consistency in verb tense.

tense: The time when the action of a verb did, does, or will occur

When you write a paragraph or an essay, keep the verbs in the same tense unless the time changes.

INCONSISTENT   The driver *yelled* at us to get off the bus, so I *ask* him why, and he *tells* me it *is* none of my business.

CONSISTENT   The driver *yells* at us to get off the bus, so I *ask* him why, and he *tells* me it *is* none of my business. [All verbs are present tense.]

CONSISTENT   The driver *yelled* at us to get off the bus, so I *asked* him why, and he *told* me it *was* none of my business. [All verbs are past tense.]

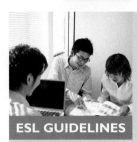

■ For practice, visit
<bedfordstmartins.com/
bedguide> and do a
keyword search:

ESL

Count Nouns and Articles

Nouns referring to items that can be counted are called *count* (or *countable*) nouns. Count nouns can be made plural.

> *table, chair, egg*   two *tables,* several *chairs,* a dozen *eggs*

Singular count nouns must be preceded by a *determiner*. The class of words called determiners includes *articles* (*a, an, the*), *possessives* (*John's, your, his, my,* and so on), *demonstratives* (*this, that, these, those*), *numbers* (*three, the third,* and so on), and *indefinite quantity words* (*no, some, many,* and so on).

> *a* dog, *the* football, *one* reason, *the first* page, *no* chance

Noncount Nouns and Articles

Nouns referring to items that cannot be counted are called *noncount* (or *uncountable*) nouns. Noncount nouns cannot be made plural.

INCORRECT   I need to learn more *grammars.*

CORRECT   I need to learn more *grammar.*

- Common categories of noncount nouns include types of *food* (*cheese, meat, bread*), *solids* (*dirt, salt, chalk*), *liquids* (*milk, juice, gasoline*), *gases* (*methane, hydrogen, air*), and *abstract ideas* including emotions (*democracy, gravity, love*).

- Another category of noncount nouns is *mass* nouns, which usually represent a large group of countable nouns (*furniture, mail, clothing*).

- The only way to count noncountable nouns is to use a countable noun with them, usually to indicate a quantity or a container.

  > one *piece* of furniture
  >
  > two *quarts* of water
  >
  > an *example* of jealousy

indefinite article: An article (*a* or *an*) that indicates any one of many possible items: I will make *a* cake or *a* pie.

- Noncount nouns are never preceded by an indefinite article; they are often preceded by *some*.

  INCORRECT   She gave us *a* good advice.

  CORRECT   She gave us good advice.

  CORRECT   She gave us *some* good advice.

definite article: An article (*the*) that indicates one particular item: I ordered *the* spaghetti, not *the* lasagna.

- When noncount nouns are *general* in meaning, no article is required, but when the context makes them specific (usually in a phrase or a clause after the noun), the definite article is used.

  GENERAL   Deliver us from *evil.*

  SPECIFIC   The *evil* that humans do lives after them.

The Definite Article (*the*)

- Use *the* with a specific count or noncount noun mentioned before or familiar to both the writer and the reader.

  She got a huge box in the mail. *The* box contained oranges from Florida. [*The* is used the second time the noun (*box*) is mentioned.]

  Did you feed *the* baby? [Both reader and writer know which baby.]

- Use *the* before specific count or noncount nouns when the reader is given enough information to identify what is being referred to.

  The furniture in my apartment is old and faded. [Specific furniture]

- Use *the* before a singular count noun to state a generality.

  The dog has been a companion for centuries. [*The dog* refers to all dogs.]

- Use *the* before some geographical names.

  Collective Nations: the United States, the United Kingdom

  Groups of Islands: the Bahamas, the Canary Islands

  Large Bodies of Water (except lakes): the Atlantic Ocean, the Dead Sea, the Monongahela River, the Gulf of Mexico

  Mountain Ranges: the Rockies, the Himalayas

- Use *the* or another determiner when plural count nouns name a definite or specific group; use no article when they name a general group.

  Hal is feeding *the horses* in the barn, and he has already fed *his cows*.

  Horses don't eat meat, and neither do *cows*.

ESL GUIDELINES

count noun: A noun with both singular and plural forms that refers to an item that can be counted: *apple, apples*

noncount noun: A noun that cannot be made plural because it refers to an item that cannot be counted: *cheese, salt, air*

The Indefinite Article (*a, an*)

- Use *a* or *an* with a nonspecific, singular count noun when it is not known to the reader or to the writer.

  Jay has *an* antique car. [The car's identity is unknown to the reader.]

  I saw *a* dog in my backyard this morning. [The dog's identity is unknown to the writer.]

- Use *a* or *an* when the noun is first used; use *the* when it is repeated.

  I saw *a* car that I would love to buy. *The* car was red with tan seats.

- Use *some* or no article with general noncount or plural nouns.

  INCORRECT   I am going to buy *a* furniture for my apartment.

  CORRECT   I am going to buy *some* furniture for my apartment.

  CORRECT   I am going to buy furniture for my apartment.

9b If the time changes, change the verb tense.

If you are writing about something that occurred in the past, use past tense verbs. If you are writing about something that occurs in the present, use present tense verbs. If the time shifts, change the verb tense.

> I *do* not *like* the new television programs this year. The situation comedies *are* too realistic to be amusing, the adventure shows *don't have* much action, and the law enforcement dramas *drag* on and on. Last year the television programs *were* different. The sitcoms *were* hilarious, the adventure shows *were* action packed, and the dramas *were* fast paced. I *prefer* last year's reruns to this year's new choices.

The time and the verb tense change appropriately from present (*do like, are, don't have, drag*) to past (*were, were, were, were*) back to present (*prefer*), contrasting this year's *present* programming with last year's *past* programming and ending with *present* opinion.

NOTE: When writing papers about literature, the accepted practice is to use present tense verbs to summarize what happens in a story, poem, or play. When discussing other aspects of a work, use present tense for present time, past tense for past, and future tense for future.

> John Steinbeck *wrote* "The Chrysanthemums" in 1937. [Past tense for past time]

> In "The Chrysanthemums," John Steinbeck *describes* the Salinas Valley as "a closed pot" cut off from the world by fog. [Present tense for story summary]

9c Maintain consistency in the voice of verbs.

■ For more on using active and passive voice, see 3m.

In most writing, active voice is preferable to passive voice. Shifting unnecessarily from active to passive voice may confuse readers.

INCONSISTENT   My roommates and I *sit* up late many nights talking about our problems. Grades, teachers, jobs, money, and dates *are discussed* at length.

CONSISTENT   My roommates and I *sit* up late many nights talking about our problems. We *discuss* grades, teachers, jobs, money, and dates at length.

9d Maintain consistency in person.

■ For more on pronoun forms, see 5 and also A5 in the Quick Editing Guide (the dark-blue-edged pages).

Person indicates your perspective as a writer. First person (*I, we*) establishes a personal, informal relationship with readers. Second person (*you*) is also informal and personal, bringing readers into the writing. Third person (*he, she, it, they*) is more formal and objective than the other two persons. In a formal scientific report, first and second person are seldom appropriate. In a

Negatives

You can make a sentence negative by using **not** or another negative adverb such as *seldom, rarely, never, hardly, hardly ever,* or *almost never.*

- With **not:** subject + helping verb + **not** + main verb

  Gina did *not* go to the concert.

  They will *not* call again.

- For questions: helping verb + *n't* (contraction for *not*) + subject + main verb

  Didn't [for *Did not*] Gina go to the concert?

  Won't [for *Will not*] they call again?

- With a negative adverb: subject + negative adverb + main verb **or** subject + helping verb + negative adverb + main verb

  My son *seldom* watches TV.

  Danh may *never* see them again.

- With a negative adverb at the beginning of a clause: negative adverb + helping verb + subject + verb

  Not only does Emma play tennis well, but she also excels in golf.

  Never before have I been so happy.

NOTE: If you pile up several negatives for intensity or emphasis in a sentence, your sentence will be faulty. Readers may consider double negatives such as *not never, not hardly,* or *wouldn't not* sloppy repetition or even decide that two negatives cancel each other out.

FAULTY	The students did *not never* arrive late.
REVISED	The students did *not* ever arrive late.
REVISED	The students *never* arrived late.

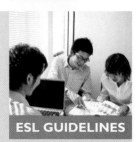

ESL GUIDELINES

For practice, visit <bedfordstmartins.com/bedguide> and do a keyword search:

ESL

personal essay, using *he, she,* or *one* to refer to yourself would sound stilted. Choose the person appropriate for your purpose, and stick to it.

INCONSISTENT	College *students* need transportation, but *you* need a job to pay for the insurance and the gasoline.
CONSISTENT	College *students* need transportation, but *they* need jobs to pay for the insurance and the gasoline.
INCONSISTENT	*Anyone* can go skydiving if *you* have the guts.
CONSISTENT	*Anyone* can go skydiving if *he or she* has the guts.
CONSISTENT	*You* can go skydiving if *you* have the guts.

9e Maintain consistency in the mood of verbs.

■ For examples of the three moods of verbs, see 3n–3p.

Closely related to shift in person is shift in the mood of the verb, usually from the indicative to the imperative.

INCONSISTENT   Counselors *advised* the students to register early. Also *pay* tuition on time to avoid being dropped from classes. [Shift from indicative to imperative]

CONSISTENT   Counselors *advised* the students to register early. They also *advised* them to pay their tuition on time to avoid being dropped from classes. [Both verbs in indicative]

9f Maintain consistency in level of language.

Attempting to impress readers, writers sometimes inflate their language or slip into slang or informal wording. The level of language should be appropriate to your purpose and your audience throughout an essay.

If you are writing a personal essay, use informal language.

INCONSISTENT   I felt like a typical tourist. I carried an expensive digital camera with lots of icons I didn't quite know how to decode. But I was in a quandary because there was such a plethora of picturesque tableaus to record for posterity.

Instead of suddenly shifting to formal language, the writer could end simply: *But with so much beautiful scenery all around, I just couldn't decide where to start.*

If you are writing an academic essay, use formal language.

INCONSISTENT   Puccini's final work *Turandot* is set in a China of legends, riddles, and fantasy. Brimming with beautiful melodies, this opera is music drama at its most spectacular. It rules!

Cutting the last sentence avoids an unnecessary shift in formality.

■ Exercise 9–1

■ For more practice, visit <bedfordstmartins.com/ bedguide> and do a keyword search:

Maintaining Grammatical Consistency

Revise the following sentences to eliminate shifts in verb tense, voice, mood, person, and level of language. Possible revisions for the lettered sentences appear in the back of the book. Example:

I needed the job at the restaurant, so I tried to tolerate the insults of my boss, but a person can take only so much.

I needed the job at the restaurant, so I tried to tolerate the insults of my boss, but *I could* take only so much.

a. Dr. Jamison is an erudite professor who cracks jokes in class.

b. The audience listened intently to the lecture, but the message was not understood.

c. Scientists can no longer evade the social, political, and ethical consequences of what they did in the laboratory.

d. To have good government, citizens must become informed on the issues.
Also, be sure to vote.

e. Good writing is essential to success in many professions, especially in
business, where ideas must be communicated in down-to-earth lingo.

1. Our legal system made it extremely difficult to prove a bribe. If the charges
are not proven to the satisfaction of a jury or a judge, then we jump to the
conclusion that the absence of a conviction demonstrates the innocence
of the subject.

2. Before Morris K. Udall, Democrat from Arizona, resigns his seat in the
U.S. House of Representatives, he helped preserve hundreds of acres of
wilderness.

3. Anyone can learn another language if you have the time and the patience.

4. The immigration officer asked how long we planned to stay, so I show
him my letter of acceptance from Tulane.

5. Archaeologists spent many months studying the site of the African city of
Zimbabwe, and many artifacts were uncovered.

Chapter 36
Effective Sentences

10 *Misplaced and Dangling Modifiers*

For more on editing for misplaced or dangling modifiers, see B1 in the Quick Editing Guide (the dark-blue-edged pages).

The purpose of a modifier is to give readers more information. To do so, the modifier must be linked clearly to whatever it is meant to modify. If you wrote, "We saw a stone wall around a house on a grassy hill, beautiful and distant," your readers would have to guess what was *beautiful* and *distant:* the wall, the house, or the hill. When you edit, double-check your modifiers — especially prepositional phrases and subordinate clauses — to make sure each one is in the right place.

10a Keep modifiers close to what they modify.

modifier: A word (such as an adjective or adverb), phrase, or clause that provides more information about other parts of a sentence: Plays *staged by the drama class* are *always successful.*

Misplaced modifiers — phrases and clauses that wander away from what they modify — produce results more likely to amuse readers than to inform them. Place your modifiers as close as possible to whatever they modify.

MISPLACED	She offered toys to all the children in colorful packages. [Does the phrase *in colorful packages* modify *toys* or *children?*]
CLEAR	She offered toys in colorful packages to all the children.
MISPLACED	We need to remove the dishes from the crates that got chipped. [Does the clause *that got chipped* modify *dishes* or *crates?*]
CLEAR	We need to remove from the crates the dishes that got chipped.

Sometimes when you move a misplaced modifier to a better place, you can make an additional change to clarify the sentence.

MISPLACED	Chuck offered cream and sugar to his guests in their coffee.
CLEAR	Chuck offered his guests cream and sugar in their coffee. [When *guests* is made an indirect object, *to* is cut.]

10b   Place each modifier so that it clearly modifies only one thing.

A *squinting modifier* is one that looks two ways, leaving the reader uncertain whether it modifies the word before it or the word after it. A good tactic to avoid ambiguity is to place your modifier close to the word or phrase it modifies and away from any others that might cause confusion.

SQUINTING   The book that appealed to Amy *tremendously* bored Marcus.

CLEAR   The book that *tremendously* appealed to Amy bored Marcus.

CLEAR   The book that appealed to Amy bored Marcus *tremendously*.

■ Exercise 10–1

Placing Modifiers

Revise the following sentences, which contain modifiers that are misplaced or squinting. Possible revisions for the lettered sentences appear in the back of the book. Example:

> Patti found the cat using a flashlight in the dark.
>
> *Using a flashlight in the dark,* Patti found the cat.

a. The bus got stuck in a ditch full of passengers.
b. He was daydreaming about fishing for trout in the middle of a staff meeting.
c. The boy threw the paper airplane through an open window with a smirk.
d. I reached for my sunglasses when the glare appeared from the glove compartment.
e. High above them, Sally and Glen watched the kites drift back and forth.

1. In her soup she found a fly at one of the best French restaurants in town.
2. Andy learned how to build kites from the pages of an old book.
3. Alex vowed to return to the island sometime soon on the day he left it.
4. The fish was carried in a suitcase wrapped in newspaper.
5. The reporters were informed of the crimes committed by a press release.

■ For more practice, visit <bedfordstmartins.com/ bedguide> and do a keyword search:

modifiers

10c   State something in the sentence for each modifier to modify.

Generally readers assume that a modifying phrase at the start of a sentence modifies the subject of the main clause to follow. If readers encounter a modifying phrase midway through a sentence, they assume that it modifies something just before or (less often) after it.

main clause: A group of words that has both a subject and a verb and can stand alone as a complete sentence: *My sister has a friend.*

Feeling tired after the long hike, Jason went to bed.

Alicia, while sympathetic, was not inclined to help.

Sometimes a writer slips up, allowing a modifying phrase to dangle. A **dangling modifier** is one that doesn't modify anything in its sentence.

DANGLING   *Noticing a pain behind his eyes,* an aspirin seemed like a good
            idea. [The opening phrase doesn't modify *aspirin* or, in fact,
            anything.]

To correct a dangling modifier, first figure out what noun, pronoun, or noun phrase the modifier is meant to modify. Then make that word or phrase the subject of the main clause.

CLEAR   *Noticing a pain behind his eyes, he* decided to take an aspirin.

Another way to correct a dangling modifier is to turn the dangler into a clause that includes the missing noun or pronoun.

DANGLING   *Her progress, although talented,* has been slowed by poor work
            habits.

CLEAR   *Although she is talented,* her progress has been slowed by poor
            work habits.

Sometimes rewriting will clarify what the modifier modifies and improve the sentence as well.

CLEAR   *Although talented,* she has been hampered by poor work habits.

■ Exercise 10–2

Revising Dangling Modifiers

■ For more practice, visit
<bedfordstmartins.com/
bedguide> and do a key-
word search:

Revise any sentences that contain dangling modifiers. Some sentences may be correct. Possible revisions for the lettered sentences appear in the back of the book. Example:

Angry at her poor showing, geology would never be Joan's favorite class.

Angry at her poor showing, Joan knew that geology would never be her favorite class.

a. Unpacking the suitcase, a horrible idea occurred to me.
b. After preparing breakfast that morning, the oven might still be left on at
   home.
c. Trying to reach my neighbor, her phone was busy.
d. Desperate to get information, my solution was to ask my mother to drive
   over to check the oven.
e. With enormous relief, my mother's call confirmed that everything was
   fine.

1. After working six hours, the job was done.
2. Further information can be obtained by calling the specified number.
3. To compete in the Olympics, talent, training, and dedication are needed.
4. Pressing hard on the brakes, the car spun into a hedge.
5. Showing a lack of design experience, the architect advised the student to take her model back to the drawing board.

11   *Incomplete Sentences*

A fragment fails to qualify as a sentence because it lacks a subject or a predicate (or both) or it fails to express a complete thought. However, a sentence with the essentials can still miss the mark. If it lacks a crucial word or phrase, the sentence may be *incomplete*. When you make comparisons and use elliptical constructions, be certain that you complete the thought you want to express.

▧ For advice on editing fragments, see 1 and also A1 in the Quick Editing Guide (the dark-blue-edged pages).

COMPARISONS

11a   Make your comparisons clear by stating fully what you are comparing with what.

INCOMPLETE   Roscoe loves spending time online more than Diane.

What is this writer trying to tell us? Does Roscoe prefer the company of a keyboard to the company of his friend? Or, of these two people, is Roscoe (and not Diane) the online addict? We can't be sure because the writer has not completed the comparison. Adding a word would solve the problem.

REVISED   Roscoe loves spending time online more than Diane *does.*

REVISED   Roscoe loves spending time online more than *with* Diane.

11b   When you start to draw a comparison, finish it.

The unfinished comparison is a favorite trick of advertisers — "Our product is better!" — because it dodges the question "Better than what?" A sharp writer (or shopper) knows that any item must be compared *with* something else.

INCOMPLETE   Scottish tweeds are warmer.

REVISED   Scottish tweeds are warmer *than any other fabric you can buy.*

11c   Be sure the things you compare are of the same kind.

A sentence that compares should reassure readers on two counts: the items involved are similar enough to compare, and the terms of the comparison are clear and logical.

INCOMPLETE   The engine of a Ford truck is heavier than a Piper Cub air-plane.

What is being compared? Truck engine and airplane? Or engine and engine? Because a truck engine is unlikely to outweigh an airplane, we can guess the writer meant to compare engines. Readers, however, should not have to make the effort to complete a writer's thought.

REVISED   The engine of a Ford truck is heavier than *that of* a Piper Cub airplane.

REVISED   A Ford truck's engine is heavier than a *Piper Cub's*.

■ For more on parallel structure, see 13.

In this last example, parallel structure (*Ford truck's* and *Piper Cub's*) helps to make the comparison concise as well as clear.

ll d To compare an item with others of its kind, use *any other*.

A comparison using *any* shows how something relates to a group without belonging to the group.

Alaska is larger than *any* country in Central America.

Bluefish has as much protein as *any* meat.

A comparison using *any other* shows how one member of a group relates to other members of the same group.

Death Valley is drier than *any other* place in the United States.

Bluefish has as distinctive a flavor as *any other* fish.

■ Exercise ll–l

Completing Comparisons

■ For more practice, visit <bedfordstmartins.com/bedguide> and do a key-word search:

incomplete

Revise the following sentences by adding needed words to any comparisons that are incomplete. (There may be more than one way to complete some comparisons.) Some sentences may be correct. Possible revisions for the let-tered sentences appear in the back of the book. Example:

I hate hot weather more than you.

I hate hot weather more than you *do. Or*

I hate hot weather more than *I hate* you.

a.   The movie version of *The Brady Bunch* was much more ironic.
b.   Taking care of a dog is often more demanding than a cat.
c.   I received more free calendars in the mail for 2008 than any year.
d.   The crime rate in the United States is higher than Canada.
e.   Liver contains more iron than any meat.

1. Driving a sports car means more to Jake than his professors.
2. People who go to college aren't necessarily smarter, but they will always have an advantage at job interviews.
3. I don't have as much trouble getting along with Michelle as Karen.
4. A hen lays fewer eggs than a turtle.
5. Singing is closer to prayer than a meal of Chicken McNuggets.

ELLIPTICAL CONSTRUCTIONS

Robert Frost begins his well-known poem "Fire and Ice" with these lines:

> Some say the world will end in fire, / Some say in ice.

When Frost wrote that opening, he avoided needless repetition by implying certain words rather than stating them. The result is more concise and more effective than a complete version of the same sentence would be:

> Some say the world will end in fire, some say the world will end in ice.

This common tactic produces an *elliptical construction* — one that leaves out (for conciseness) words that are unnecessary but clearly understood by readers. Elliptical constructions can be confusing, however, if a writer gives readers too little information to fill in those missing words accurately.

11e **When you eliminate repetition, keep all the words essential for clarity.**

An elliptical construction avoids repeating what a reader already knows, but it should omit only words that are stated elsewhere in the sentence. Otherwise, your reader may fill the gap incorrectly.

INCOMPLETE How can I date her, seeing that she is a senior, I a mere sophomore?

This elliptical construction won't work. A reader supplying the stated verb in the last part of the sentence would get "I *is* a mere sophomore."

REVISED How can I date her, seeing that she is a senior and I *am* a mere sophomore?

Be sure to state necessary prepositions as well.

INCOMPLETE The train neither goes nor returns from Middletown.

Readers are likely to fill in an extra *from* after *goes*. Write instead:

REVISED The train neither goes *to* nor returns from Middletown.

11f In a compound predicate, leave out only verb forms that have already been stated.

compound predicate: A predicate consisting of two or more verbs linked by a conjunction: My sister *stopped and stared.*

Compound predicates are prone to incomplete constructions, especially if the verbs are in different tenses. Be sure no necessary part is missing.

INCOMPLETE   The mayor never has and never will vote to raise taxes.

REVISED   The mayor never has *voted* and never will vote to raise taxes.

11g If you mix comparisons using *as* and *than,* include both words.

■ For more on comparative forms, see 8d–8f.

To contrast two things, we normally use the comparative form of an adjective followed by *than: better than, more than, fewer than.* To show a similarity between two things, we normally sandwich the simple form of an adjective between *as* and *as: as good as, as many as, as few as.* Often we can combine two *than* or two *as* comparisons into an elliptical construction.

The White House is smaller [than] and newer than Buckingham Palace.

Some elegant homes are as large [as] and as grand as the White House.

However, merging a *than* comparison with an *as* comparison won't work.

INCOMPLETE   The White House is smaller but just as beautiful as Buckingham Palace.

REVISED   The White House is smaller *than* but just *as* beautiful *as* Buckingham Palace.

INCOMPLETE   Some elegant homes are as large and no less grand than the White House.

REVISED   Some elegant homes are *as* large *as* and no less grand *than* the White House.

■ Exercise 11–2

Completing Sentences

■ For more practice, visit <bedfordstmartins.com/ bedguide> and do a keyword search:

incomplete

Revise the following sentences by adding needed words to any constructions that are incomplete. (There may be more than one way to complete some constructions.) Some sentences may be correct. Possible revisions for the lettered sentences appear in the back of the book. Example:

President Kennedy should have but didn't see the perils of invading Cuba.

President Kennedy should have *seen* but didn't see the perils of invading Cuba.

a. Eighteenth-century China was as civilized and in many respects more so-phisticated than the Western world.

b. Pembroke was never contacted, much less involved with, the election committee.

c. I haven't yet but soon will finish my research paper.

d. Ron likes his popcorn with butter, Linda with parmesan cheese.

e. George Washington always has been and will be regarded as the father of this country.

1. You have traveled to exotic Tahiti; Maureen to Asbury Park, New Jersey.

2. The mayor refuses to negotiate or even talk to the civic association.

3. Building a new sewage treatment plant would be no more costly and just as effective as modifying the existing one.

4. You'll be able to tell Jon from the rest of the team: Jon wears white Reeboks, the others black high-tops.

5. Erosion has and always will reshape the shoreline.

12 *Mixed Constructions and Faulty Predication*

Sometimes a sentence contains all the necessary ingredients but still doesn't make sense. The problem may be a discord between two or more of its parts: phrases or clauses that don't fit together (a *mixed construction*) or a verb and its subject, object, or modifier (*faulty predication*) that don't match.

12a Link phrases and clauses logically.

A *mixed construction* results when a writer connects phrases or clauses (or both) that don't work together as a sentence.

MIXED   In her efforts to solve the tax problem only caused the mayor additional difficulties.

The prepositional phrase *In her efforts to solve the tax problem* is a modifier; it can't act as the subject of a sentence. The writer, however, has used this phrase as a noun—the subject of the verb *caused*. To untangle this mixed construction, the writer has two choices: (1) rewrite the phrase so that it works as a noun, or (2) use the phrase as a modifier, not a subject.

REVISED   Her efforts to solve the tax problem only caused the mayor additional difficulties. [With *in* gone, *efforts* becomes the subject.]

REVISED   In her efforts to solve the tax problem, the mayor created additional difficulties. [The phrase now modifies the verb *created*.]

phrase: Two or more related words that work together but may lack a subject (as in *will have been*), a verb (*my uncle Zeke*), or both (*in the attic*)

clause: A group of related words that includes both a subject and a verb: *The sailboats raced until the sun set.*

preposition: A transitional word (such as *in, on, at, of, from*) that leads into a phrase such as *in the bar, under a rickety table*

conjunction: A linking word that connects words or groups of words through coordination (*and, but*) or subordination (*because, although, unless*)

To avoid mixed constructions, check the links that join your phrases and clauses — especially prepositions and conjunctions. A sentence, like a chain, is only as strong as its weakest link.

> MIXED   Jack, although he was picked up by the police, but was not charged with anything.

Using both *although* and *but* gives this sentence one link too many. The writer could unmix the construction in two ways.

> REVISED   Jack was picked up by the police but was not charged with anything.

> REVISED   Although he was picked up by the police, Jack was not charged with anything.

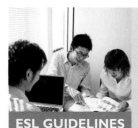

ESL GUIDELINES

 For more on coordination and subordination, see 14a–14c.

coordinating conjunction: A one-syllable linking word (*and, but, for, or, nor, so, yet*) that joins elements with equal or near-equal importance: Jack *and* Jill, sink *or* swim

subordinating conjunction: A word (such as *because, although, if, when*) used to make one clause dependent on, or subordinate to, another: *Unless* you have a key, we are locked out.

Mixed Constructions, Faulty Predication, and Subject Errors

Mixed constructions result when phrases or clauses are joined even though they do not logically go together. Combine clauses with either a coordinating conjunction or a subordinating conjunction, never both.

> INCORRECT   *Although* baseball is called "the national pastime" of the United States, *but* football is probably more popular.

> CORRECT   *Although* baseball is called "the national pastime" of the United States, football is probably more popular.

> CORRECT   Baseball is called "the national pastime" of the United States, *but* football is probably more popular.

Faulty predication results when a verb and its subject, object, or modifier do not match. Do not use a noun as both the subject of the sentence and the object of a preposition.

> INCORRECT   *In my neighborhood has* several good restaurants.

> CORRECT   *My neighborhood has* several good restaurants.

> CORRECT   *In my neighborhood, there are* several good restaurants.

Common *subject errors* include leaving out and repeating subjects of clauses.

- Do not omit *it* used as a subject. A subject is required in all English sentences except imperatives.

> INCORRECT   *Is* interesting to visit museums.

> CORRECT   *It is* interesting to visit museums.

- Do not repeat the subject of a sentence with a pronoun.

> INCORRECT   *My brother-in-law, he* is a successful investor.

> CORRECT   *My brother-in-law* is a successful investor.

12b   Relate the parts of a sentence logically.

Faulty predication refers to a skewed relationship between a verb and some other part of a sentence.

FAULTY   *The temperature of water freezes* at 32 degrees Fahrenheit.

At first glance, that sentence looks all right. It contains both subject and predicate. It expresses a complete thought. What is wrong with it? The writer has slipped into faulty predication by mismatching the subject and verb. The sentence tells us that *temperature freezes,* when science and common sense tell us it is *water* that freezes. To correct this error, the writer must select a subject and verb that fit each other.

REVISED   *Water freezes* at 32 degrees Fahrenheit.

Faulty predication also results from a mismatched verb and direct object.

FAULTY   Rising costs *diminish college* for many students.

Costs don't *diminish college.* To correct this error, the writer must change the sentence so that its direct object follows logically from its verb.

REVISED   Rising costs *diminish the number of students who can attend college.*

Subtler predication errors result when a writer uses a linking verb to forge a false connection between the subject and a subject complement.

FAULTY   *Industrial waste* has become *an important modern priority.*

Is it *waste* that has become a *priority*? Or is it *solving problems caused by careless disposal of industrial waste*? A writer who says all that, though, risks wordiness. Why not just replace *priority* with a closer match for *waste*?

REVISED   *Industrial waste* has become a *modern menace.*

Predication errors tend to plague writers who are too fond of the passive voice. Mismatches between a verb and another part of the sentence are easier to avoid when the verb is active rather than passive.

FAULTY   The idea of giving thanks for a good harvest *was not done* first by the Pilgrims.

REVISED   The idea of giving thanks for a good harvest *did not originate* with the Pilgrims.

12c   Avoid starting a definition with *when* or *where*.

A definition, like any other phrase or clause, needs to fit grammatically with the rest of the sentence.

FAULTY   Dyslexia is when you have a reading disorder.

REVISED   Dyslexia is a reading disorder.

---

verb: A word that shows action (The cow *jumped* over the moon) or a state of being (The cow *is* brown)

subject: The part of a sentence that names something—a person, an object, an idea, a situation—about which the predicate makes an assertion: The *king* lives.

predicate: The part of a sentence that makes an assertion about the subject involving an action (Birds *fly*), a relationship (Birds *have feathers*), or a state of being (Birds *are warm-blooded*)

direct object: The target of a verb that completes the action performed by or asserted about the subject: I photographed *the sheriff.*

linking verb: A verb (*is, become, seem, feel*) that shows a state of being by linking the sentence subject with a subject complement that renames or describes the subject: The sky *is* blue. (See 3a.)

■ For more on using active and passive voice, see 3m.

FAULTY   A lay-up is where a player dribbles close to the basket and then makes a one-handed, banked shot.

REVISED   To shoot a lay-up, a player dribbles in close to the basket and then makes a one-handed, banked shot.

12d Avoid using *the reason is because* . . .

Anytime you start an explanation with *the reason is,* what follows *is* should be a subject complement: an adjective, a noun, or a noun clause. *Because* is a conjunction; it cannot function as a noun or adjective.

FAULTY   *The reason* Gerard hesitates *is because* no one supported him two years ago.

REVISED   *The reason* Gerard hesitates *is that* no one supported him two years ago.

REVISED   Gerard hesitates *because* no one supported him two years ago.

REVISED   *The reason* Gerard hesitates *is simple*: no one supported him two years ago.

■ Exercise 12–1

Correcting Mixed Constructions and Faulty Predication

Correct any mixed constructions and faulty predication you find in the following sentences. Possible revisions for the lettered sentences appear in the back of the book. Example:

The storm damaged the beach erosion.

The storm worsened the beach erosion. *Or*

The storm damaged the beach.

a. The cost of health insurance protects people from big medical bills.
b. In his determination to prevail helped him finish the race.
c. The AIDS epidemic destroys the body's immune system.
d. The temperatures are too cold for the orange trees.
e. A recession is when economic growth is small or nonexistent and unemployment increases.

1. The opening of the new shopping mall should draw out-of-town shoppers for years to come.
2. The reason the referendum was defeated was because voters are tired of paying so much in taxes.
3. In the glacier's retreat created the valley.
4. A drop in prices could put farmers out of business.
5. The researchers' main goal is cancer.

■ For more practice, visit <bedfordstmartins.com/bedguide> and do a keyword search:

 mixed

13 *Parallel Structure*

You use *parallel structure,* or parallelism, when you create a series of words, phrases, clauses, or sentences with the same grammatical form. The pattern created by the series — its parallel structure — emphasizes the similarities or differences among the items, whether things, qualities, actions, or ideas.

> My favorite foods are roast beef, apple pie, and linguine with clam sauce.

> Louise is charming, witty, intelligent, and talented.

> Manuel likes to swim, ride, and run.

> Dave likes movies that scare him and books that make him laugh.

Each series is a perfect parallel construction, composed of equivalent words: nouns in the first example, adjectives in the second, verbs in the third, and adjective clauses in the fourth.

◼ For more on editing for parallel structure, see B2 in the Quick Editing Guide (the dark-blue-edged pages).

13a In a series linked by a coordinating conjunction, keep all elements in the same grammatical form.

A coordinating conjunction cues your readers to expect a parallel structure. Whether your series consists of single words, phrases, or clauses, its parts should balance one another.

AWKWARD   The puppies are *tiny, clumsily bumping* into each other, *and cute.*

Two elements in this series are parallel one-word adjectives (*tiny, cute*), but the third, the verb phrase *clumsily bumping,* is inconsistent.

PARALLEL   The puppies are *tiny, clumsy, and cute.*

Don't mix verb forms, such as gerunds and infinitives, in a series.

AWKWARD   Plan a winter vacation if you like *skiing and to skate.*

PARALLEL   Plan a winter vacation if you like *skiing and skating.*

PARALLEL   Plan a winter vacation if you like *to ski and to skate.*

In a series of phrases or clauses, be sure that all elements in the series are similar in form, even if they are not similar in length.

AWKWARD   The fight in the bar takes place *after the two lovers have their scene together* but *before the car chase.* [The clause starting with *after* is not parallel to the phrase starting with *before.*]

PARALLEL   The fight in the bar takes place *after the love scene* but *before the car chase.*

AWKWARD   You can take the key, or don't forget to leave it under the mat. [The declarative clause starting with *You can* is not parallel to the imperative clause starting with *don't forget.*]

PARALLEL   You can *take the key,* or you can *leave it* under the mat.

coordinating conjunction: A one-syllable linking word (*and, but, for, or, nor, so, yet*) that joins elements with equal or near-equal importance: Jack *and* Jill, sink *or* swim

◼ For more on coordination, see 14a–14c.

gerund: A form of a verb, ending in *-ing,* that functions as a noun: Lacey likes *playing* in the steel band.

infinitive: The base form of a verb, often preceded by *to* (*to go, to play*)

13b In a series linked by correlative conjunctions, keep all elements in the same grammatical form.

correlative conjunction:
A pair of linking words (such as *either/or, not only/but also*) that appear separately but work together to join elements of a sentence: *Neither* his friends *nor* hers like pizza.

When you use a correlative conjunction, follow each part with a similarly structured word, phrase, or clause.

AWKWARD   I'm looking forward *to either attending* Saturday's wrestling match *or to seeing* it on closed-circuit TV. [*To* precedes the first part of the correlative conjunction (*to either*) but follows the second part (*or to*).]

PARALLEL   I'm looking forward *either to attending* Saturday's wrestling match *or to seeing* it on closed-circuit television.

AWKWARD   Take my advice: try *neither to be first nor last* in the lunch line. [*To be* follows the first part of the correlative conjunction but not the second part.]

PARALLEL   Take my advice: try to be *neither first nor last* in the lunch line.

13c Make the elements in a comparison parallel in form.

For more on comparisons, see 11a–11d and 11g.

A comparative word such as *than* or *as* cues the reader to expect a parallel structure. This makes logical sense: to be compared, two things must resemble each other, and parallel structure emphasizes this resemblance.

AWKWARD   Philip likes *fishing* better than *to sail.*
PARALLEL   Philip likes *fishing* better than *sailing.*
PARALLEL   Philip likes *to fish* better than *to sail.*

AWKWARD   *Maintaining* railway lines is as important to the public transportation system as *to buy* new trains.
PARALLEL   *Maintaining* railway lines is as important to the public transportation system as *buying* new trains.

13d Reinforce parallel structure by repeating rather than mixing lead-in words.

Parallel structures are especially useful when a sentence contains a series of clauses or phrases. For example, try to precede potentially confusing clauses with *that, who, when, where,* or some other connective, repeating the same connective every time. To do so not only helps you to keep your thoughts in order but helps readers to follow them with ease.

No one in this country needs a government *that* aids big business at the expense of farmers and workers, *that* ravages the environment in the name of progress, or *that* slashes budgets for health and education.

Repeating an opening phrase can accomplish the same goal in a graceful series of parallel sentences.

The Russian dramatist is one who, walking through a cemetery, does not see the flowers on the graves. The American dramatist is one who, walking through a cemetery, does not see the graves under the flowers.

Sometimes the same lead-in word won't work for all elements in a series. In such cases you may be able to preserve a parallel structure by changing the order of the elements to minimize variation.

AWKWARD	The new school building is large but not very comfortable, and expensive but unattractive.
PARALLEL	The new school building is large and expensive, but uncomfortable and unattractive.

■ Exercise 13–1

Making Sentences Parallel

Revise the following sentences by substituting parallel structures for awkward ones. Possible revisions for the lettered sentences appear in the back of the book. Example:

In the Rio Grande Valley, the interests of conservationists, government officials, and those trying to immigrate collide.

In the Rio Grande Valley, the interests of conservationists, government officials, and immigrants collide.

a. The border separating Texas and Mexico marks not only the political boundary of two countries, but it also is the last frontier for some endangered wildlife.

b. In the Rio Grande Valley, both local residents and the people who happen to be tourists enjoy visiting the national wildlife refuges.

c. The tall grasses in this valley are the home of many insects, birds, and there are abundant small mammals.

d. Two endangered wildcats, the ocelot and another called the jaguarundi, also make the Rio Grande Valley their home.

e. Many people from Central America are desperate to immigrate to the United States by either legal or by illegal means.

1. Because the land along the Rio Grande has few human inhabitants and the fact that the river is often shallow, many illegal immigrants attempt to cross the border there.

2. To capture illegal immigrants more easily, the U.S. government has cut down tall grasses, put up fences, and the number of immigration patrols has been increased.

3. For illegal immigrants, crossing the border at night makes more sense than to enter the United States in broad daylight, so the U.S. government has recently installed bright lights along the border.

■ For more practice, visit <bedfordstmartins.com/ bedguide> and do a keyword search:

parallel

4. The ocelot and the jaguarundi need darkness, hiding places, and to have some solitude if they are to survive.

5. Neither the immigration officials nor have wildlife conservationists been able to find a solution that will protect both the U.S. border and these endangered wildcats.

14 *Coordination and Subordination*

conjunction: A linking word that connects words or groups of words through coordination (*and, but*) or subordination (*because, although, unless*)

Coordination and subordination can bring out the relationships between your ideas. Coordination connects thoughts of equal importance; subordination shows how one thought affects another. Often, conjunctions—words that link groups of words—specify these relationships. Together, coordination and subordination will help you produce sentences, paragraphs, and essays that function as a coherent whole.

14a Coordinate clauses or sentences that are related in theme and equal in importance.

The car skidded for a hundred yards. It crashed into a brick wall.

clause: A group of related words that includes both a subject and a verb: *The sailboats raced until the sun set.*

compound predicate: A predicate consisting of two or more verbs linked by a conjunction: *My sister stopped and stared.*

These two clauses make equally significant statements about the same subject, a car accident. Because the writer has indicated no link between the sentences, we can only guess that the crash followed from the skid; we cannot be sure. Suppose we join the two with a conjunction.

The car skidded for a hundred yards, and it crashed into a brick wall.

Now the sequence is clear: first the car skidded, then it crashed. That's coordination. To tighten the coordination, try combining the two clauses into a single sentence with a compound predicate.

The car skidded for a hundred yards and crashed into a brick wall.

Now the connection is so clear we can almost hear screeching brakes and crunching metal.

Once you decide to coordinate two clauses, there are three ways you can do it: with a conjunction, with a conjunctive adverb, or with punctuation.

1. Join two main clauses with a coordinating conjunction.

coordinating conjunction: A one-syllable linking word (*and, but, for, or, nor, so, yet*) that joins elements with equal or near-equal importance: Jack *and* Jill, sink *or* swim

UNCOORDINATED   Ari does not want to be placed on your mailing list. He does not want a salesperson to call him.

COORDINATED   Ari does not want to be placed on your mailing list, nor does he want a salesperson to call him.

COORDINATED   Ari does not want to be placed on your mailing list or called by a salesperson.

2. Join two main clauses with a semicolon and a conjunctive adverb. Conjunctive adverbs show relationships such as addition (*also, besides*), comparison (*likewise, similarly*), contrast (*instead, however*), emphasis (*namely, certainly*), cause and effect (*thus, therefore*), or time (*finally, subsequently*).

> UNCOORDINATED   The guerrillas did not observe the truce. They never intended to.
>
> COORDINATED   The guerrillas did not observe the truce; furthermore, they never intended to.

3. Join two main clauses with a semicolon or a colon.

> UNCOORDINATED   The government wants to negotiate. The guerrillas prefer to fight.
>
> COORDINATED   The government wants to negotiate; the guerrillas prefer to fight.
>
> UNCOORDINATED   The guerrillas have two advantages. They know the terrain, and the people support them.
>
> COORDINATED   The guerrillas have two advantages: they know the terrain, and the people support them.

conjunctive adverb: A linking word that can connect independent clauses and show a relationship between two ideas: Armando is a serious student; *therefore*, he studies every day.

■ For more on semicolons and colons, see 22 and 23.

14b Coordinate clauses only if they are clearly and logically related.

Whenever you hitch together two sentences, make sure they get along. Will the relationship between them be evident to your readers?

> FAULTY   The sportscasters were surprised by Easy Goer's failure to win the Kentucky Derby, but it rained on derby day.

The writer has not included enough information for the reader to see why these two clauses are connected.

> COORDINATED   The sportscasters were surprised by Easy Goer's failure to win the Kentucky Derby; *however, he runs poorly on a muddy track,* and it rained on derby day.

Have you chosen a coordinating conjunction, conjunctive adverb, or punctuation mark that accurately reflects this relationship?

> FAULTY   The sportscasters all expected Easy Goer to win the Kentucky Derby, and Sunday Silence beat him.

Because *and* implies that both clauses reflect the same assumptions, which is not the case, the writer should choose a conjunction that expresses difference.

> COORDINATED   The sportscasters all expected Easy Goer to win the Kentucky Derby, *but* Sunday Silence beat him.

■ For common types of sentences using coordination and subordination, see p. H-79.

Coordinating and Subordinating Words at a Glance

Coordinating Conjunctions

and, but, for, nor, or, so, yet

Correlative Conjunctions

as . . . as	just as . . . so	not only . . . but also
both . . . and	neither . . . nor	whether . . . or
either . . . or	not . . . but	

Common Conjunctive Adverbs

accordingly	finally	likewise	otherwise
also	furthermore	meanwhile	similarly
anyway	hence	moreover	still
as	however	nevertheless	then
besides	incidentally	next	therefore
certainly	indeed	nonetheless	thus
consequently	instead	now	undoubtedly

Common Subordinating Conjunctions

after	even if	since	when
although	even though	so	whenever
as	how	so that	where
as if	if	than	wherever
as soon as	in order that	that	while
as though	once	though	why
because	provided that	unless	
before	rather than	until	

Relative Pronouns

that	what	who	whom
which	whatever	whoever	whomever
whose			

14c Coordinate clauses only if they work together to make a coherent point.

When a writer strings together several clauses in a row, often the result is excessive coordination. Trying to pack too much information into a single sentence can make readers dizzy, unable to pick out which points really matter.

> EXCESSIVE   Easy Goer was the Kentucky Derby favorite, and all the sportscasters expected him to win, but he runs poorly on a muddy track, and it rained on derby day, so Sunday Silence beat him.

What are the main points in this passage? Each key idea deserves its own sentence so that readers will recognize it as important.

REVISED   Easy Goer was the Kentucky Derby favorite, and all the sports-
            casters expected him to win. However, he runs poorly on a
            muddy track, and it rained on derby day. Therefore, Sunday
            Silence beat him.

Excessive coordination also may result when a writer uses the same conjunction repeatedly.

EXCESSIVE Phil was out of the house all day, so he didn't know about the
            rain, so he went ahead and bet on Easy Goer, so he lost twenty
            bucks, so now he wants to borrow money from me.

REVISED   Phil was out of the house all day, so he didn't know about the
            rain. He went ahead and bet on Easy Goer, and he lost twenty
            bucks. Now he wants to borrow money from me.

One solution to excessive coordination is subordination: making one   For advice on subordi-
clause dependent on another instead of giving both clauses equal weight.   nation, see 14d.

■ Exercise 14–1

Using Coordination

Revise the following sentences, adding coordination where appropriate and re-   For more practice, visit
moving faulty or excessive coordination. Possible revisions for the lettered sen- <bedfordstmartins.com/
tences appear in the back of the book. Example: bedguide> and do a key-
                                                                                   word search:

> The wind was rising, and leaves tossed on the trees, and the air seemed to
> crackle with electricity, and we knew that a thunderstorm was on the way.

coord_subord

> The wind was rising, leaves tossed on the trees, and the air seemed to
> crackle with electricity. We knew that a thunderstorm was on the way.

a. Professional poker players try to win money and prizes in high-stakes
    tournaments. They may lose thousands of dollars.

b. Poker is not an easy way to make a living. Playing professional poker is
    not a good way to relax.

c. A good "poker face" reveals no emotions. Communicating too much in-
    formation puts a player at a disadvantage.

d. Hidden feelings may come out in unconscious movements. An expert
    poker player watches other players carefully.

e. Poker is different from most other casino gambling games, for it requires
    skill and it forces players to compete against each other, and other casino
    gambling pits players against the house, so they may win out of sheer
    luck, but skill has little to do with winning those games.

1. The rebels may take the capital in a week. They may not be able to hold it.

2. If you want to take Spanish this semester, you have only one choice. You
    must sign up for the 8 A.M. course.

3. Peterson's Market has raised its prices. Last week tuna fish cost $1.29 a
    can. Now it's up to $1.59.

4. Joe starts the morning with a cup of coffee, which wakes him up, and then at lunch he eats a chocolate bar, so that the sugar and caffeine will bring up his energy level.

5. The *Hindenburg* drifted peacefully over New York City. It exploded just before landing.

14d Subordinate less important ideas to more important ideas.

Subordination is one of the most useful of all writing strategies. By subordinating a less important clause to a more important one, you show your readers that one fact or idea follows from another or affects another. You stress what counts, thereby encouraging your readers to share your viewpoint.

When two sentences contain ideas that need connecting, you can subordinate one to the other in any of the following three ways.

1. Turn the less important idea into a subordinate clause by introducing it with a subordinating conjunction.

Jason has a keen sense of humor. He has an obnoxious, braying laugh.

From that pair of sentences, readers don't know what to feel about Jason. Is he likable or repellent? The writer needs to decide which trait matters more and to emphasize it.

Although Jason has a keen sense of humor, he has an obnoxious, braying laugh.

This revision makes Jason's sense of humor less important than his annoying hee-haw. The less important idea is stated as a subordinate clause opening with *Although;* the more important idea is stated as the main clause.

The writer could reverse the meaning by combining the two ideas the other way around:

Although Jason has an obnoxious, braying laugh, he has a keen sense of humor.

That version makes Jason sound fun to be with, despite his mannerism.

Which of Jason's traits to emphasize is up to the writer. What matters is that, in both combined versions, the writer takes a clear stand by making one sentence a main clause and the other a subordinate clause.

2. Turn the less important idea into a subordinate clause by introducing it with a relative pronoun such as *who, which,* or *that.*

Jason, *who has an obnoxious, braying laugh,* has a keen sense of humor.

Jason, *whose sense of humor is keen,* has an obnoxious, braying laugh.

3. Turn the less important idea into a phrase.

Jason, *a keen humorist,* has an obnoxious, braying laugh.

Despite his obnoxious, braying laugh, Jason has a keen sense of humor.

---

subordinating conjunction: A word (such as *because, although, if, when*) used to make one clause dependent on, or subordinate to, another: *Unless you have a key, we are locked out.*

■ For a list of subordinating words, see p. H-74.

main clause: A group of words that has both a subject and a verb and can stand alone as a complete sentence: *My sister has a friend.*

relative pronoun: A pronoun (*who, which, that, what, whom, whomever, whose*) that opens a subordinate clause, modifying a noun or pronoun in another clause: *The gift that* I received is very practical.

phrase: Two or more related words that work together but may lack a subject (as in *will have been*), a verb (*my uncle Zeke*), or both (*in the attic*)

14e Express the more important idea in the main clause.

Sometimes a writer accidentally subordinates a more important idea to a less important one and turns the sentence's meaning upside down.

FAULTY
SUBORDINATION   Although the heroism of the Allied troops on D-Day lives on in spirit, many of the World War II soldiers who invaded Normandy are dead now.

This sentence is accurate. Does the writer, however, want to stress death over life? This is the effect of putting *are dead now* in the main clause and *lives on* in the subordinate clause. Instead, the writer can reverse the two.

REVISED   Although many of the World War II soldiers who invaded Normandy are dead now, the heroism of the Allied troops on D-Day lives on in spirit.

14f Limit the number of subordinate clauses in a sentence.

Often the result of cramming too much information into one sentence, excessive subordination strings so many ideas together that readers may not be able to pick out what matters.

EXCESSIVE
SUBORDINATION   Debate over the Strategic Defense Initiative (SDI), which was originally proposed as a space-based defensive shield that would protect America from enemy attack, but which critics have suggested amounts to creating a first-strike capability in space, has to some extent focused on the wrong question.

> **subordinate clause:** A group of words that contains a subject and a verb but cannot stand alone because it depends on a main clause to help it make sense: Pia, *who plays the oboe*, prefers solitude.

In revising this sentence, the writer needs to decide which are the main points and turn each one into a main clause. Lesser points can remain as subordinate clauses, arranged so that each gets appropriate emphasis.

REVISED   Debate over the Strategic Defense Initiative (SDI) has to some extent focused on the wrong question. The plan was originally proposed as a space-based defensive shield that would protect America from enemy attack. Critics have suggested, however, that it amounts to creating a first-strike capability in space.

■ Exercise 14–2

Using Subordination

Revise the following sentences, adding subordination where appropriate and removing faulty or excessive subordination. Possible revisions for the lettered sentences appear in the back of the book. Example:

■ For more practice, visit <bedfordstmartins.com/bedguide> and do a keyword search:

coord_subord

Some playwrights like to work with performing theater companies. It is helpful to hear a script read aloud by actors.

Some playwrights like to work with performing theater companies *because* it is helpful to hear a script read aloud by actors.

a. Cape Cod is a peninsula in Massachusetts. It juts into the Atlantic Ocean south of Boston. The Cape marks the northern turning point of the Gulf Stream.

b. The developer had hoped the condominiums would sell quickly. Sales were sluggish.

c. Tourists love Italy. Italy has a wonderful climate, beautiful towns and cities, and a rich history.

d. At the end of Verdi's opera *La Traviata*, Alfredo has to see his beloved Violetta again. He knows she is dying and all he can say is good-bye.

e. I usually have more fun at a concert with Rico than with Morey. Rico loves music. Morey merely tolerates it.

1. Although we occasionally hear horror stories about fruits and vegetables being unsafe to eat because they were sprayed with toxic chemicals or were grown in contaminated soil, the fact remains that, given their high nutritional value, these fresh foods are generally much better for us than processed foods.

2. English has become an international language. Its grammar is filled with exceptions to the rules.

3. Some television cartoon shows have become cult classics. This has happened years after they went off the air. Examples include *Rocky and Bullwinkle* and *Speed Racer*.

4. Although investors have not fully regained confidence in the stock market, stock prices have gone up.

5. Violetta gives away her money. She bids adieu to her faithful servant. After that she dies in her lover's arms.

15 *Sentence Variety*

sentence: A word group that includes both a subject and a predicate and can stand alone

Most writers rely on some patterns more than others to express ideas directly and efficiently, but sometimes they combine sentence elements in unexpected ways to emphasize ideas and to surprise readers.

15a Normal Sentences

In a *normal sentence,* a writer puts the subject before the verb at the beginning of the main clause. This pattern is the most common in English because it expresses ideas in the most straightforward manner.

main clause: A group of words that has both a subject and a verb and can stand alone as a complete sentence: *My sister has a friend.*

Most college *students* today *want* interesting classes.

Types of Sentences at a Glance

Simple Sentences

Any sentence that contains only one main clause is a **simple sentence,** even if it includes modifiers, objects, complements, and phrases in addition to its subject and verb.

```
┌──────────────────── MAIN CLAUSE ────────────────────┐
```
Even amateur stargazers can easily locate the Big Dipper in the night sky.

A simple sentence may have a compound subject (*Fred and Sandy*) or a compound verb (*laughed and cried*). Sometimes the subject of a simple sentence is not stated but is clearly understood, as is *you* in the command "Run!"

Compound Sentences

A **compound sentence** consists of two or more main clauses joined by a coordinating conjunction such as *and, but,* or *for* or by a semicolon. Sometimes the semicolon is followed by a conjunctive adverb such as *however, nevertheless,* or *therefore.*

For lists of coordinating conjunctions, conjunctive adverbs, and subordinating words, see p. H-74.

```
┌──────── MAIN CLAUSE ────────┐   ┌ MAIN CLAUSE ┐
```
I would like to accompany you, but I can't.

```
┌── MAIN CLAUSE ──┐          ┌──── MAIN CLAUSE ────┐
```
My car broke down; therefore, I missed the first day of class.

Complex Sentences

A **complex sentence** consists of one main clause and one or more subordinate clauses.

```
        MAIN              SUBORDINATE
┌──── CLAUSE ────┐ ┌── CLAUSE ──┐
```
I will be at the airport when you arrive.

In some sentences, the relative pronoun linking the subordinate clause to the main clause is implied rather than stated.

```
MAIN        SUBORDINATE
CLAUSE  ┌── CLAUSE ──┐
```
I know [that] you saw us.

Compound-Complex Sentences

A **compound-complex sentence** shares the attributes of both a compound sentence (two or more main clauses) and a complex sentence (at least one subordinate clause).

```
    MAIN           SUBORDINATE    SUBORDINATE      MAIN
┌── CLAUSE ──┐ ┌── CLAUSE ────┐ ┌ CLAUSE ┐ ┌── CLAUSE ──┐
```
I'd gladly wait until you're ready; but if I do, I'll miss the boat.

15b Inverted Sentences

In an *inverted sentence,* a writer inverts or reverses the subject-verb order to emphasize an idea in the predicate.

NORMAL   *My peers are uninterested* in reading.

INVERTED   How *uninterested* in reading *are my peers*!

15c Cumulative Sentences

In a *cumulative sentence,* a writer piles details at the end of a sentence to help readers visualize a scene or understand an idea.

> They came walking out in heavily brocaded yellow and black costumes, the familiar "toreador" suit, heavy with gold embroidery, cape, jacket, shirt and collar, knee breeches, pink stockings, and low pumps.
> — Ernest Hemingway, "Bull Fighting a Tragedy"

15d Periodic Sentences

The positions of emphasis in a sentence are the beginning and the end. In a *periodic sentence*, a writer suspends the main clause for a climactic ending, emphasizing an idea by withholding it until the end.

> Leaning back in his chair, shaking his head slowly back and forth, frustrated over his inability to solve the quadratic equation, Franklin scowled.

■ Exercise 15–1

Increasing Sentence Variety

■ For more practice, visit <bedfordstmartins.com/bedguide> and do a key-word search:

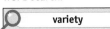

Revise the following passage, adding sentence variety to create interest, emphasize important ideas, and strengthen coherence.

We are terrified of death. We do not think of it, and we don't speak of death. We don't mourn in public. We don't know how to console a grieving friend. In fact, we have eliminated or suppressed all the traditional rituals surrounding death.

The Victorians coped with death differently. Their funerals were elaborate. The yards of black crepe around the hearse, hired professional mourners, and solemn procession leading to an ornate tomb are now only a distant memory. They wore mourning jewelry. They had a complicated dress code for the grieving process. It governed what mourners wore, and it governed how long they wore it. Many of these Victorian rituals may seem excessive or even morbid to us today. The rituals served a psychological purpose in helping the living deal with loss.

Chapter 37

Word Choice

16 *Appropriateness*

When you talk to people face to face, you can gauge their reactions to what you say. Often their responses guide your tone and your choice of words: if your listener chuckles at your humor, you go on being humorous; if your listener frowns, you cut the comedy and speak more seriously.

When you write, you cannot gauge your readers' reactions as easily because you cannot see them. Instead, you must imagine yourself in their place, focusing especially closely on their responses when you revise.

16a Choose a tone appropriate for your topic and audience.

Like a speaker, a writer may come across as friendly or aloof, furious or merely annoyed, playful or grimly serious. This attitude is the writer's *tone* and, like a speaker's tone, it strongly influences the audience's response. A tone that seems right to a reader conveys your concern for the reader's reaction. If you ignore your reader, then your tone may be inappropriate. For instance, taking a humorous approach to a disease such as cancer or AIDS probably would create an inappropriate tone. The reader, not finding the topic funny, would likely reject what you say.

To help you convey your tone, you may use sentence length, level of language, vocabulary, and other elements of style. You may choose formal or informal language, colorful or bland words, coolly objective words, or words loaded with emotional connotations ("You pig!" "You angel!").

16b Choose a level of formality appropriate for your tone.

Considering the tone you want to convey to your audience helps you choose words that are neither too formal nor too informal. By *formal* language, we mean the impersonal language of educated persons, usually written. In general, formal language is marked by relatively long and complex sentences and by a large, often esoteric, vocabulary. It doesn't use contractions (such as *doesn't*), and the writer's attitude toward the topic is serious.

Informal language more closely resembles ordinary conversation. Using relatively short and simple sentences, informal language is marked by common words and may include contractions, slang, and references to everyday objects and activities (cheeseburgers, T-shirts, CDs). It may address the reader as *you*, and the writer may use *I*.

The right language for most college essays lies somewhere between formal and informal. If your topic and tone are serious (say, for a research paper on terrorism), then your language may lean toward formality. If your topic is not weighty and your tone is light (say, for a humorous essay about giving your dog a bath), then your language may be informal.

■ For more practice, visit
<bedfordstmartins.com/
bedguide> and do a key-
word search:

appropriate

■ Exercise 16–1

Choosing an Appropriate Tone and Level of Formality

Revise the following passages to ensure that both the tone and the level of formality are appropriate for the topic and audience. Example:

> I'm sending you this letter because I want you to meet with me and give me some info about the job you do.

> I'm writing to inquire about the possibility of an informational interview about your profession.

1. Dear Senator Crowley:
   I think you've got to vote for the new environmental law, so I'm writing this letter. We're messing up forests and wetlands — maybe for good. Let's do something now for everybody who's born after us.
   Thanks,
   Glenn Turner

2. The United States Holocaust Memorial Museum in Washington, D.C., is a great museum dedicated to a real bad time in history. It's hard not to get bummed out by the stuff on show. Take it from me, it's an experience you won't forget.

3. Dear Elaine,
   I am so pleased that you plan on attending the homecoming dance with me on Friday. It promises to be a gala event, and I am confident that we will enjoy ourselves immensely. I understand a local recording act by the name of Electric Bunny will provide the musical entertainment. Please call me at your earliest convenience to inform me when to pick you up.
   Sincerely,
   Bill

16c   Choose common words instead of jargon.

Jargon is the term for the specialized vocabulary used by people in a certain field. Nearly every academic, professional, and even recreational field — music, carpentry, law, sports — has its own jargon. In baseball, retired pitcher Dennis Eckersley once said that when he faced a dangerous batter, he would think: "If I throw him *the heater*, maybe he *juices it out* on me" (emphasis added). Translation: "If I throw him a fastball, he might hit a home run."[1]

To a specialist addressing other specialists, jargon is convenient and necessary. Without technical terms, after all, two surgeons could hardly discuss a patient's anatomy. To an outsider, though, such terms may be incomprehensible. If your writing is meant (as it should be) to communicate information to your readers and not to make them feel excluded or confused, you should avoid unnecessary jargon.

Commonly, we apply the name *jargon* to any private, pretentious, or needlessly specialized language. Jargon can include not only words but ways of using words. Some politicians and bureaucrats like to make nouns into verbs by tacking on suffixes like *-ize*.

JARGON   The government intends to *privatize* federal land.

CLEAR   The government intends to *sell* federal land to *private buyers*.

Although *privatize* implies merely "convert to private ownership," usually its real meaning is "sell off" — as might occur were a national park to be auctioned to developers. *Privatize* thus also can be called a *euphemism*, a pleasant term that masks an unpleasant meaning (see 16d).

Besides confusing readers, jargon can mislead them. Recently, technology has made verbs of the familiar nouns *access*, *boot*, and *format* and has popularized *interface*, *x amount of*, *database*, and *parameters*. Such terms are useful to explain technical processes; when thoughtlessly applied to nontechnical ideas, they can obscure meaning.

JARGON   A democracy needs the electorate's *input*.

CLEAR   A democracy needs the electorate *to vote and to express its views to elected officials*.

Here's how to avoid needless jargon:

1. Beware of favoring a trendy word over a perfectly good old word.
2. Before using a word ending in *-ize*, *-wise*, or *-ism*, count to ten. This gives you time to think of a clearer alternative or to be sure that none exists.
3. Avoid the jargon of a special discipline — say, psychology or fly-fishing — unless you are writing of such matters for readers familiar with them. If you're writing for general readers about a field — such as hang gliding — in which you are an expert, define any specialized terms. Even when writing for fellow experts, use plain words and you'll rarely go wrong.

[1] Quoted by Mike Whiteford, *How to Talk Baseball* (New York: Dembner, 1983) 51.

■ For more practice, visit <bedfordstmartins.com/bedguide> and do a key-word search:

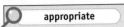
appropriate

■ Exercise 16–2

Avoiding Jargon

Revise the following sentences to eliminate the jargon. If necessary, revise extensively. If you can't tell what a sentence means, decide what it might mean, and rewrite it so that its meaning is clear. Possible revisions for the lettered sentences appear in the back of the book. Example:

> The proximity of Mr. Fitton's knife to Mr. Schering's arm produced a violation of the integrity of the skin.

> Mr. Fitton's knife cut Mr. Schering's arm.

a. Everyone at Boondoggle and Gall puts in face time at the holiday gatherings to maximize networking opportunities.

b. This year, in excess of fifty nonessential employees were negatively impacted by Boondoggle and Gall's decision to downsize effective September 1.

c. The layoffs made Jensen the sole point of responsibility for telephone interface in the customer-service department.

d. The numerical quotient of Jensen's telephonic exchanges increased by a factor of three post-downsizing, yet Jensen received no additional fiscal remuneration.

e. Jensen was not on the same page with management re her compensation, so she exercised the option to terminate her relationship with Boondoggle and Gall.

1. The driver-education course prepares the student for the skills of handling a vehicle on the highway transportation system.

2. We of the State Department have carefully contexted the riots in Lebanon intelligencewise and, after full and thorough database utilization, find them abnormalling rapidly.

3. In the heart area, Mr. Pitt is a prime candidate-elect for intervention of a multiple bypass nature.

4. Engaging in a conversational situation with God permits an individual to maximally interface with God.

5. The deer hunters number balance the ecological infrastructure by quietizing x amount of the deer populace.

16d   Use euphemisms sparingly.

Euphemisms are plain truths dressed attractively, sometimes hard facts stated gently. To say that someone *passed away* instead of *died* is a common euphemism—humane, perhaps, in breaking terrible news to an anxious family. In such shock-absorbing language, an army that *retreats* makes *a strategic withdrawal*, a person who is *underweight* turns *slim*, and an acne medication treats not *pimples* but *blemishes*. Even if you aren't prone to using euphemisms in your own writing, be aware of them when you read evidence from partisan sources and official spokespersons.

16e Avoid slang in formal writing.

Slang, especially when new, can be colorful ("She's not playing with a full deck"), playful ("He's wicked cute!"), and apt (*ice* for diamonds, a *stiff* for a corpse). The trouble with most slang, however, is that it quickly comes to seem as old and wrinkled as the Jazz Age's favorite exclamation of glee, *twenty-three skidoo!* To be understood in the classroom and out of it, your best bet is to stick to Standard English. Seek words that are usual but exact, not the latest thing, and your writing will stay young longer.

■ Exercise 16–3

Avoiding Euphemisms and Slang

Revise the following sentences to replace euphemisms with plainer words and slang with Standard English. Possible revisions for the lettered sentences appear in the back of the book. Example:

> Some dude ripped off my wallet, so I am currently experiencing a negative cash flow.
>
> *Someone stole* my wallet, so I am now *in debt.*

a. Our security forces have judiciously thinned an excessive number of political dissidents.

b. At three hundred bucks a month, the apartment is a steal.

c. The soldiers were victims of friendly fire during a strategic withdrawal.

d. Churchill was a wicked good politician.

e. The president's tax plan was toast; there was no way that Congress would approve it.

1. To bridge the projected shortfall between collections and expenditures in next year's budget, the governor advocates some form of revenue enhancement.

2. The course was a joke; the prof passed everyone and didn't even grade the stuff we turned in.

3. Saturday's weather forecast calls for extended periods of shower activity.

4. The caller to the talk-radio program sounded totally wigged out.

5. We anticipate a downturn in economic vitality.

■ For more practice, visit <bedfordstmartins.com/bedguide> and do a keyword search:

appropriate

17 *Exact Words*

What would you think if you read in a newspaper that a certain leading citizen is a *pillow of the community*? Good writing depends on knowing what words and phrases mean and using them precisely.

17a Choose words for their connotations as well as their denotations.

The *denotation* of a word is its basic meaning — its dictionary definition. *Excited, agitated,* and *exhilarated* all denote a similar state of physical and emotional arousal. When you look up a word in a dictionary or thesaurus, the synonyms you find have been selected for their shared denotation.

The *connotations* of a word are the shades of meaning that set it apart from its synonyms. You might be *agitated* by the prospect of final exams next week, but *exhilarated* by your plans for the long summer vacation afterward. When you choose one of several synonyms, you base your choice on connotation.

Paying attention to connotation helps a writer to say exactly what he or she intends, instead of almost but not quite.

IMPRECISE   Advertisers have given light beer a macho image by showing football players *sipping* the product with *enthusiasm.*

REVISED   Advertisers have given light beer a macho image by showing football players *guzzling* the product with *gusto.*

17b Avoid clichés.

A *cliché* is a trite expression, once vivid or figurative but now worn out from too much use. When a story begins, "It was a dark and stormy night," then its author is obviously using dull, predictable words. Many a strike is settled after a *marathon bargaining session* that *narrowly averts a walkout,* often *at the eleventh hour.* Fires customarily *race* and *gut.* And when everything is *fantastic* or *terrific,* a reader will suspect that it isn't. Clichés abound when writers and speakers try hard to sound vigorous and colorful but don't trouble themselves to invent anything vigorous, colorful, and new.

When editing your writing, you can often recognize any truly annoying cliché if you feel a sudden guilty desire to surround an expression with quotation marks, as if to apologize for it. You might also show your papers to friends, asking them to look for anything trite. As you go on in college, your awareness of clichés will grow with reading. The more you read, the easier it is to recognize a cliché, for you will have met it often before. If you find that a cliché turns up in your writing, replace it with something more vivid.

COMMON CLICHÉS

a skeleton in the closet	little did I dream
a sneaking suspicion	make a long story short
above and beyond the call of duty	neat as a pin
add insult to injury	nutty as a fruitcake
beyond a shadow of a doubt	old as the hills
burn one's bridges	on the brink of disaster
burn the midnight oil	pay through the nose
busy as a beaver (or a bee)	piece of cake
But that's another story.	point with pride
come hell or high water	pull the wool over someone's eyes
cool as a cucumber	sell like hotcakes
cream of the crop	since the dawn of time
dressed to kill	skating on thin ice
easy as taking candy from a baby	stab me in the back
feeling on top of the world	stick out like a sore thumb
few and far between	sweet as honey
golden years	That's the way the ball bounces.
greased lightning	The bottom line is ...
hands-on learning experience	through thick and thin
hard as a rock	tip of the iceberg
in my wildest dreams	too little and too late
last but not least	tried and true

17c Use idioms in their correct form.

Every language contains *idioms,* or *idiomatic expressions:* phrases that, through long use, have become standard even though their construction may defy logic or grammar. For example, although *fender bender* may suggest the outcome of a minor collision between two cars, someone unfamiliar with that expression might struggle to connect the literal words with the idiomatic meaning. In addition, many idiomatic expressions require us to choose the right preposition. To pause *for* a minute is not the same as to pause *in* a minute. We work *up* a sweat while working *out* in the gym. We argue *with* someone but *about* something, *for* or *against* it. And someone who decides to *set up* a meeting doesn't expect to be *upset*.

For some idioms we must know which article to use before a noun — or whether to use any article at all. We can be *in motion,* but we have to be *in the swim.* We're occasionally in *a tight spot* but never in *a trouble.* Certain idioms vary from country to country: in Britain, a patient has an operation *in hospital;* in America, *in the hospital.* Idioms can involve choosing the right verb with the right noun: we *seize* an opportunity, but we *catch* a plane.

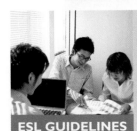

ESL GUIDELINES

preposition: A transitional word (such as *in, on, at, of, from*) that leads into a phrase such as *in the bar, under a rickety table*

■ For practice, visit <bedfordstmartins.com/bedguide> and do a keyword search:

ESL

In, On, At: Prepositions of Location and Time

Location Expressions

> Elaine lives *in* Manhattan *at* a swanky address *on* Fifth Avenue.

- *In* means "within" or "inside of" a place, including geographical areas, such as cities, states, countries, and continents.

    > I packed my books *in* my backpack and left to visit my cousins *in* Canada.

- Where *in* emphasizes *location* only, *at* is often used to refer to a place when a specific *activity* is implied: *at the store* (to shop), *at the office* (to work), *at the theater* (to see a play), and so on.

    > Angelo left his bicycle *in* the bike rack while he was *at* school.

- *On* means "on the surface of" or "on top of" something and is used with floors of buildings and planets. It is also used to indicate a location *beside* a lake, river, ocean, or other body of water.

    > The service department is *on* the fourth floor.

    > We have a cabin *on* Lake Michigan.

- *In, on,* and *at* can all be used in addresses. *In* is used to identify a general location, such as a city or neighborhood. *On* is used to identify a specific street. *At* is used to give an exact address.

    > We live *in* Boston *on* Medway Street.

    > We live *at* 20 Medway Street.

- *In* and *at* can both be used with the verb *arrive. In* indicates a large place, such as a city, state, country, or continent. *At* indicates a smaller place, such as a specific building or address. (*To* is never used with *arrive.*)

    > Alanya arrived *in* Alaska yesterday; Sanjei will arrive *at* the airport soon.

Time Expressions

- *In* indicates the span of time during which something occurs or a time in the future; it is also used in the expressions *in a minute* (meaning "shortly") and *in time* (meaning "soon enough" or "without a moment to spare"). *In* is also used with seasons, months, and periods of the day.

    > He needs to read this book *in* the next three days. [During the next three days]

    > I'll meet you *in* the morning *in* two weeks. [Two weeks from now]

- *On* is used with the days of the week, with the word *weekend,* and in the expression *on time* (meaning "punctually").

    > Let's have lunch *on* Friday.

- *At* is used in reference to a specific time on the clock as well as a specific time of the day (*at night, at dawn, at twilight*).

    > We'll meet again next Monday *at* 2:15 P.M.

To, For: Indirect Objects and Prepositions

These sentences mean the same thing:

> I sent the president a letter.
> I sent a letter to the president.

In the first sentence, *the president* is the **indirect object**: he or she receives the direct object (*a letter*), which was acted on (*sent*) by the subject of the sentence (*I*). In the second sentence, the same idea is expressed using a **prepositional phrase** beginning with *to*.

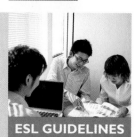
ESL GUIDELINES

indirect object: A person or thing affected by the subject's action, usually the recipient of the direct object, through the action indicated by a verb such as *bring, get, offer, promise, sell, show, tell,* and *write:* Charlene asked you a question.

preposition: A transitional word (such as *in, on, at, of, from*) that leads into a phrase such as *in the bar, under a rickety table*

- Some verbs can use either an indirect object or the preposition *to: give, send, lend, offer, owe, pay, sell, show, teach, tell.* Some verbs can use an indirect object or the preposition *for: bake, build, buy, cook, find, get, make.*

    I paid *the travel agent* one hundred dollars.

    I paid one hundred dollars *to the travel agent.*

    Margarita cooked *her family* some chicken.

    Margarita cooked some chicken *for her family.*

- Some verbs cannot have an indirect object; they must use a preposition. The following verbs must use the preposition *to: describe, demonstrate, explain, introduce,* and *suggest.*

    INCORRECT   Please explain me indirect objects.

    CORRECT   Please explain indirect objects *to me.*

- The following verbs must use the preposition *for: answer* and *prepare.*

    INCORRECT   He prepared me the punch.

    CORRECT   He prepared the punch *for me.*

- Some verbs must have an indirect object; they cannot use a preposition. The following verbs must have an indirect object: *ask* and *cost.*

    INCORRECT   Sasha asked a question to her.

    CORRECT   Sasha asked *her* a question.

Two-Word Verbs: Particles, Not Prepositions

Many two-word verbs end with a *particle*, a word that can be used as a preposition on its own but becomes part of a *phrasal verb*. Once the particle is added, the verb takes on a new idiomatic meaning that must be learned.

> break up: to separate; to end a romantic relationship; to laugh
>
> decide on: to select or to judge a person or thing
>
> eat at: to worry or disturb a person
>
> feel for [a person]: to sympathize with another's unhappiness
>
> see to: to take care of a person or situation
>
> take in [a person]: to house a person; to trick by gaining a person's trust

When you're at work on a paper, the dictionary can help you choose the appropriate idiom. Look up *agree* for instance, and you will probably find examples showing when to use *agree to, agree with,* or *agree that.* You can then pick the idiom that fits your sentence.

■ Exercise 17–1

Selecting Words

■ For more practice, visit <bedfordstmartins.com/ bedguide> and do a keyword search:

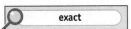

Revise the following passage to replace inappropriate connotations, clichés, and faulty idioms. Example:

> The Mayan city of Uxmal is a common tourist attraction. The ruins have stood alone in the jungle since time immemorial.

> The Mayan city of Uxmal is a *popular* tourist attraction. The ruins have stood alone in the jungle since *ancient times.*

We spent the first day of our holiday in Mexico arguing around what we wanted to see on our second day. We finally agreed to a day trip out to some Mayan ruins. The next day we arrived on the Mayan city of Uxmal, which is as old as the hills. It really is a sight for sore eyes, smack dab in a jungle stretching as far as the eye can see, with many buildings still covered in plants and iguanas moving quickly over the decayed buildings. The view from the top of the Soothsayer's Temple was good, although we noticed storm clouds gathering in the distance. The rain held up until we got off of the pyramid, but we drove back to the hotel in a lot of rain. After a day of sightseeing, we were so hungry that we could have eaten a horse, so we had a good meal before we turned in.

18 *Bias-Free Language*

The connotations of the words we use reveal our attitudes — our likes and dislikes, our preferences and prejudices. A *brat* is quite different from a *little angel,* a *sport utility vehicle* from a *limousine.*

Thoughtful writers try to avoid harmful bias in language. They respect their readers and don't want to insult them, anger them, or impede communication. You may not be able to eliminate discrimination from society, but you can eliminate discriminatory language in your writing. Be on the lookout for words that insult or stereotype individuals or groups by gender, age, race, ethnic origin, sexual preference, or religion.

18a To eliminate sexist language, use alternatives that make no reference to gender.

Among the prime targets of American feminists in the 1960s and 1970s was the male bias built into the English language. Why, they asked, do we talk about *prehistoric man, manpower,* and *the brotherhood of man,* when by *man* we mean the entire human race? Why do we focus attention on the gender of an accomplished woman by calling her a *poetess* or a *lady doctor*? Why does a letter to a corporation have to begin "Gentlemen:"?

Early efforts to find alternatives often led to awkward, even ungrammatical solutions. To substitute "Everyone prefers their own customs" for "Everyone prefers *his* own customs" is to replace sexism with bad grammar. How then can we as sensitive writers minimize the sexist constraints that the English language places in our path? Although there are no perfect solutions, we can try to steer around the potholes as smoothly as possible.

18b Avoid terms that include or imply *man.*

We all know that the obvious way to neuter *man* or a word starting with *man* is to substitute *human.* The result, however, is often clumsy.

SEXIST	Mankind remains obsessed with man's inhumanity to man.
NONSEXIST	*Humankind* remains obsessed with *humans'* inhumanity to *other humans.*

Adding *hu-* to *man* alleviates sexism but weighs down the sentence. Usually you can find a more graceful solution.

REVISED	*Human beings* remain obsessed with *people's* cruelty to one another.

Similarly, when you face a word that ends with *-man,* you need not simply replace that ending with *-person.* Take a different approach: think about what the word means and find a synonym that is truly neutral.

SEXIST	Did you leave a note for the mailman?
REVISED	Did you leave a note for the *mail carrier*?

The same tactic works for designations with a male and a female ending, such as *steward* and *stewardess.*

SEXIST	Ask your steward [or stewardess] for a pillow.
REVISED	Ask your *flight attendant* for a pillow.

18c Use plural instead of singular forms.

Another way to avoid sexist language is to use the plural rather than the singular (*they* and *their* rather than *he* and *his*). This strategy may also avoid the stereotype implied by a single individual standing for a diverse group.

SEXIST	Today's student values his education.
REVISED	Today's students value *their* education.
STEREOTYPE	The Englishman drives on the left-hand side of the road.
REVISED	*English drivers* use the left-hand side of the road.

18d   Where possible, omit words that denote gender.

You can make your language more bias-free by omitting pronouns and other words that needlessly indicate gender.

> SEXIST   For optimal results, there must be rapport between a stock-broker and his client, a teacher and her student, a doctor and his patient.
>
> REVISED   For optimal results, there must be rapport between stock-broker and *client*, teacher and *student*, doctor and *patient*.

Also treat men and women equally in terms of description or title.

> SEXIST   I now pronounce you man and wife.
>
> REVISED   I now pronounce you *husband* and wife.

> SEXIST   Please page Mr. Pease, Mr. Mankodi, and Susan Brillantes.
>
> REVISED   Please page Mr. Pease, Mr. Mankodi, and *Ms.* Brillantes.

18e   Avoid condescending labels.

A responsible writer does not call women *chicks, babes, woman drivers,* or any other names that imply that they are not to be taken seriously. Nor should an employee ever be called a *girl* or *boy*. Avoid terms that put down individuals or groups because of age (*old goat, the grannies*), race or ethnicity (*Indian giver, Chinaman's chance*), or disability (*amputee, handicapped*).

> CONDESCENDING   The girls in the office bought Mr. Baart a birthday cake.
>
> REVISED   The *administrative assistants* bought Mr. Baart a birthday cake.

> CONDESCENDING   My neighbor is just an old fogy.
>
> REVISED   My neighbor *has old-fashioned ideas*.

When describing any group, try to use the label or term that the members of that group prefer. While the preferred label is sometimes difficult to determine, the extra effort will be appreciated.

> POSSIBLY OFFENSIVE   Alice is interested in learning about Oriental culture.
>
> REVISED   Alice is interested in learning about *Asian* culture.

18f   Avoid implied stereotypes.

Sometimes a stereotype is linked to a title or designation indirectly. Aside from a few obvious exceptions such as *mothers* and *fathers,* never assume that all the members of a group are of the same gender.

> STEREOTYPE   Pilots have little time to spend with their wives and children.
>
> REVISED   Pilots have little time to spend with their *families*.

Sometimes we debase individuals or groups by assigning stereotypical descriptors to them. Be alert for such biases, whether negative or positive.

STEREOTYPE   Roberto isn't very good at paying his rent on time, which doesn't surprise me because he is from Mexico.

REVISED   Roberto isn't very good at paying his rent on time.

STEREOTYPE   I assume Ben will do very well in medical school because his parents are Jewish.

REVISED   I assume Ben will do very well in medical school.

18g Use *Ms.* for a woman with no other known title.

Ms. is now the preferred title of polite address for women because, like *Mr.* for men, it does not indicate marital status. Use *Miss* or *Mrs.* if you know that the woman being addressed prefers this form. If the woman holds a doctorate, a professional office, or some other position with a title, use that title rather than *Ms.*

Ms. Jane Doe, Editor   Dear Ms. Doe:
Professor Jane Doe, Department of English   Dear Professor Doe:
Senator Jane Doe, Washington, D.C.   Dear Senator Doe:

■ Exercise 18–1

Avoiding Bias

Revise the following sentences to eliminate bias. Possible revisions for the lettered sentences appear in the back of the book. Example:

A fireman needs to check his equipment regularly.

Firefighters need to check *their* equipment regularly.

■ For more practice, visit <bedfordstmartins.com/ bedguide> and do a keyword search:

bias-free

a. Our school's extensive athletic program will be of particular interest to black applicants.

b. The new physicians on our staff include Dr. Scalia, Anna Baniski, and Dr. Throckmorton.

c. A Native American, Joni believes in the healing properties of herbal remedies.

d. Philosophers have long pondered whether man is innately evil or innately good.

e. The diligent researcher will always find the sources he seeks.

1. Simon drinks like an Irishman.

2. The television crew conducted a series of man-on-the-street interviews about the new tax proposal.

3. Whether the president of the United States is a Democrat or a Republican, he will always be a symbol of the nation.

4. Like most Asian Americans, Soon Li excels at music and mathematics.
5. Dick drives a Porsche because he likes the way she handles on the road. He gets pretty upset at the little old ladies who slow down traffic.

19 *Wordiness*

For strategies for cutting extra words, see Ch. 20.

Conciseness takes more effort than wordiness, but it pays off in clarity. The following list includes common words and phrases that take up more room than they deserve. Each has a shorter substitute. This list can be useful for self-editing, particularly if you face a strict word limit.

WINDY WORDS AND PHRASES

WORDY	CONCISE
adequate enough	adequate
a period of a week	a week
approximately	about
area of, field of	[Omit.]
arrive at an agreement, conclude an agreement	agree
as a result of	because
at an earlier point in time	before, earlier
at a later moment	after, later
join together	join
kind of, sort of, type of	[Omit.]
large in size, large-sized	large
a large number of	many
lend assistance to	assist, aid, help
merge together	merge
numerous	many
on a daily basis	daily
other alternatives	alternatives
past experience, past history	experience, history
persons of the female gender	women
persons of the Methodist faith	Methodists
pertaining to	about, on
plan ahead for the future	plan
prior to	before
put an end to, terminate	end
refer back to	refer to
repeat again	repeat
resemble in appearance	look like
subsequent to	after
sufficient number (or amount) of	enough
true facts	facts, truth
until such time	until
utilize, make use of	use
very	[Omit unless you need it.]
whether or not, as to whether	whether

■ **Exercise 19–1**

Eliminating Wordiness

Revise the following passage to eliminate wordiness. Example:

> At this point in time, a debate pertaining to freedom of speech is raging across our campuses.

> A debate *about* freedom of speech is raging across our campuses.

■ For more practice, visit <bedfordstmartins.com/bedguide> and do a keyword search:

wordy

The media in recent times have become obsessed with the conflict on campuses across the nation between freedom of speech and the attempt to protect minorities from verbal abuse. Very innocent remarks or remarks of a humorous nature, sometimes taken out of context, have got a large number of students into trouble for the violation of college speech codes. Numerous students have become very vocal in attacking these "politically correct" speech codes and defending the right to free speech. But is the campaign against the politically correct really pertaining to freedom of speech, or is it itself a way in which to silence debate? Due to the fact that the phrase "politically correct" has become associated with liberal social causes and sensitivity to minority feelings, it now carries a very extraordinary stigma in the eyes of conservatives. It has become a kind of condemnation against which no defense is possible. To accuse someone of being politically correct is to refute their ideas before hearing their argument. The attempt to silence the members of the opposition is a dangerous sign of our times and suggests that we are indeed in the midst of a cultural war.

Chapter 38
Punctuation

20   *End Punctuation*

Three marks can signal the end of a sentence: the period, the exclamation point, and the question mark.

20a   Use a period to end a declarative sentence, a directive, or an indirect question.

Most English sentences are *declarative*, meaning simply that they make a statement. Whatever its topic, a declarative sentence ends with a period.

> Most people on earth are malnourished.

A period also follows a *directive*, a statement telling someone to do something.

> Please send a check or money order with your application.

Some readers are surprised to find a period, not a question mark, at the end of an *indirect question*. But an indirect question is really a kind of declarative sentence: it states that a question was asked or is being asked.

> The counselor asked Marcia why she rarely gets to class on time.
> I wonder why Roland didn't show up.

Written as *direct questions*, those sentences require a question mark.

> The counselor asked, "Marcia, why do you rarely get to class on time?"
> Why, I wonder, didn't Roland show up?

20b Use a period after some abbreviations.

A period within a sentence shows that what precedes it has been shortened.

> Dr. Robert A. Hooke's speech will be broadcast at 8:00 P.M.

The names of most organizations (YMCA, PTA), countries (USA, UK), and people (JFK, FDR) are abbreviated using all capitals without periods. Other abbreviations, such as those for designations of time, use periods. When an abbreviation ends a sentence, follow it with one period, not two.

▧ For more on abbreviating names, see 28e.

20c Use a question mark to end a direct question.

> How many angels can dance on the head of a pin?

The question mark comes at the end of the question even if the question is part of a longer declarative sentence.

> "What'll I do now?" Marjorie wailed.

You can also use a question mark to indicate doubt about the accuracy of a number or date.

> Aristophanes, born in 450(?) BC, became the master comic playwright of Greece's Golden Age.

Often the same purpose can be accomplished more gracefully in words:

> Aristophanes, born around 450 BC, became the master comic playwright of Greece's Golden Age.

In formal writing, avoid using a question mark to express irony or sarcasm: *her generous (?) gift.* If your doubts are worth including, state them directly: *her meager but highly publicized gift.*

▧ For advice on punctuating indirect quotations and questions, see 25a. For examples of indirect questions, see 20a.

20d Use an exclamation point to end an interjection or an urgent command.

An exclamation point signals strong, even violent, emotion. It can end any sentence that requires unusually strong emphasis.

> We've struck an iceberg! We're sinking! I can't believe it!

It may mark the short, emphatic structure known as an *interjection*.

> Oh, no! Fire!

Or it may indicate an urgent directive.

> Hurry up! Help me!

Because most essays appeal to readers' reason more than to their passions, you will rarely need this punctuation mark in college writing.

interjection: A word or expression (*oh, alas*) that inserts an outburst of feeling at the beginning, middle, or end of a sentence

■ Exercise 20–1

Using End Punctuation

■ For more practice, visit
<bedfordstmartins.com/
bedguide> and do a key-
word search:

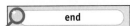

end

Where appropriate, correct the end punctuation in the following sentences. Give reasons for any changes you make. Some sentences may be correct. Answers for the lettered sentences appear in the back of the book. Example:

> Tom asked Cindy if she would be willing to coach him in tennis?
>
> Tom asked Cindy if she would be willing to coach him in tennis. [Not a direct question]

a. The question that still troubles the community after all these years is why federal agents did not act sooner?

b. We will ask him if he will help us build the canoe.

c. I wonder what he was thinking at the time?

d. One man, who suffered a broken leg, was rescued when he was heard screaming, "Help me. Help me."

e. If the suspect is convicted, will lawyers appeal the case?

1. What will Brad and Emilia do if they can't have their vacations at the same time.

2. When a tree falls in a forest, but no one hears it, does it make a sound.

3. If you have a chance to see the new Ang Lee film, you should do so. The acting is first-rate!

4. What will happen next is anyone's guess.

5. On what day does the fall term begin.

21 Commas

■ For more on comma
usage, see C1 in the
Quick Editing Guide (the
dark-blue-edged pages).

Speech without pauses would be difficult to listen to. Likewise, writing without commas would make hard reading. Like a split-second pause in conversation, a well-placed comma helps your readers to catch your train of thought. It keeps them, time and again, from stumbling over a solid block of words or drawing an inaccurate conclusion.

Consider the following sentence:

> Lyman paints fences and bowls.

From this statement, we can deduce that Lyman is a painter who works with both a large and a small brush. But add commas and the portrait changes:

> Lyman paints, fences, and bowls.

Now Lyman wields a paintbrush, a sword, and a bowling ball. What we learn about his activities depends on how the writer punctuates the sentence.

21a   Use a comma with a coordinating conjunction to join two main clauses.

Main clauses joined by a coordinating conjunction also need a comma. The comma comes after the first clause, right before the conjunction.

> The pie whooshed through the air, and it landed in Hal's face.

> The pie whooshed with deadly aim, but the agile Hal ducked.

If your clauses are short and parallel in form, you may omit the comma.

> Spring passed and summer came.

> They urged but I refused.

Or you may keep the comma. It can lend your words a speechlike ring, throwing a bit of emphasis on your second clause.

> Spring passed, and summer came.

> They urged, but I refused.

CAUTION: Don't use a comma with a coordinating conjunction that links two phrases or that links a phrase and a clause.

> FAULTY   The mustangs galloped, and cavorted across the plain.

> REVISED   The mustangs galloped and cavorted across the plain.

21b   Use a comma after an introductory clause, phrase, or word.

> *Weeping,* Lydia stumbled down the stairs.

> *Before that,* Arthur saw her reading an old love letter.

> *If he knew who the writer was,* he didn't tell.

Placed after any such opening word, phrase, or subordinate clause, a comma tells your reader, "Enough preliminaries: now the main clause starts."

EXCEPTION: You need not use a comma after a single introductory word or a short phrase or clause if there is no danger of misreading.

> *Sooner or later* Lydia will tell us the whole story.

■ Exercise 21–1

Using Commas

Add any necessary commas to the following sentences, and remove any commas that do not belong. Some sentences may be correct. Answers for the lettered sentences appear in the back of the book. Example:

> Your dog may have sharp teeth but my lawyer can bite harder.

---

main clause: A group of words that has both a subject and a verb and can stand alone as a complete sentence: *My sister has a friend.*

coordinating conjunction: A one-syllable linking word (*and, but, for, or, nor, so, yet*) that joins elements with equal or near-equal importance: Jack *and* Jill, sink *or* swim

phrase: Two or more related words that work together but may lack a subject (as in *will have been*), a verb (*my uncle Zeke*), or both (*in the attic*)

clause: A group of related words that includes both a subject and a verb: *The sailboats raced until the sun set.*

■ For more practice, visit <bedfordstmartins.com/ bedguide> and do a keyword search:

comma

Your dog may have sharp teeth, but my lawyer can bite harder.

a. Farmers around the world tend to rely on just a few breeds of livestock so some breeds are disappearing.

b. Older breeds of livestock are often less profitable, for they have not been genetically engineered to grow quickly.

c. For instance modern breeds of cattle usually grow larger, and produce more meat and milk than older breeds.

d. In both wild and domestic animals genetic diversity can make the animals resistant to disease, and parasites so older breeds can give scientists important information.

e. Until recently, small organic farmers were often the only ones interested in raising old-fashioned breeds but animal scientists now support this practice as well.

1. During the summer of the great soybean failure Larry took little interest in national affairs.

2. Unaware of the world he slept and grew within his mother's womb.

3. While across the nation farmers were begging for mortgages he swam without a care.

4. Neither the mounting agricultural crisis, nor any other current events, disturbed his tranquillity.

5. In fact you might have called him irresponsible.

21c   Use a comma between items in a series.

When you list three or more items, whether they are nouns, verbs, adjectives, adverbs, or entire phrases or clauses, separate them with commas.

Country ham, sweet corn, and potatoes weighted Grandma's table.

Joel prefers music that shakes, rattles, and rolls.

In one afternoon, we climbed the Matterhorn, voyaged beneath the sea, and flew on a rocket through space.

Notice that no comma *follows* the final item in the series.

NOTE: Some writers omit the comma *before* the final item in the series. This custom may throw off the rhythm of a sentence and, in some cases, obscure the writer's meaning. Using the comma in such a case is never wrong; omitting it can create confusion.

I was met at the station by my cousins, brother and sister.

Are these people a brother-and-sister pair who are the writer's cousins or a group consisting of the writer's cousins, her brother, and her sister? If they are in fact more than two people, a comma would clear up the confusion.

I was met at the station by my cousins, brother, and sister.

21d Use a comma between coordinate adjectives but not between cumulative adjectives.

Adjectives that function independently of each other, though they modify the same noun, are called *coordinate adjectives*. Set them off with commas.

> Ruth was a clear, vibrant, persuasive speaker.

> Life is nasty, brutish, and short.

CAUTION: Don't use a comma after the final adjective before a noun.

> FAULTY   My professor was a brilliant, caring, teacher.

> REVISED   My professor was a brilliant, caring teacher.

To check whether adjectives are coordinate, apply two tests. Can you rearrange the adjectives without distorting the meaning of the sentence? (*Ruth was a persuasive, vibrant, clear speaker.*) Can you insert *and* between them? (*Life is nasty and brutish and short.*)

If the answer to both questions is yes, the adjectives are coordinate. Removing any one of them would not greatly affect the others. Use commas between them to show that they are separate and equal.

NOTE: If you link coordinate adjectives with *and* or another conjunction, omit the commas except in a series (see 21c).

> New York City is huge and dirty and beautiful.

Cumulative adjectives work together to create a single unified picture of the noun they modify. Remove any one of them and you change the picture. No commas separate cumulative adjectives.

> Ruth has two small white poodles.

> Who's afraid of the big bad wolf?

If you rearrange cumulative adjectives or insert *and* between them, the effect is distorted (*two white small poodles; the big and bad wolf*).

conjunction: A linking word that connects words or groups of words through coordination (*and, but*) or subordination (*because, although, unless*)

For more on cumulative adjectives, see p. H-50.

■ Exercise 21–2

Using Commas

Add any necessary commas to the following sentences, remove any commas that do not belong, and change any punctuation that is incorrect. Some sentences may be correct. Answers for the lettered sentences appear in the back of the book. Example:

> Mel has been a faithful hard-working consistent band manager.

> Mel has been a faithful, hard-working, consistent band manager.

For more practice, visit <bedfordstmartins.com/bedguide> and do a keyword search:

comma

a. Mrs. Carver looks like a sweet, little, old lady, but she plays a wicked electric guitar.

b. Her bass player, her drummer and her keyboard player all live in the same retirement community.

c. They practice individually in the afternoon, rehearse together at night and play at the community's Saturday night dances.

d. The Rest Home Rebels have to rehearse quietly, and cautiously, to keep from disturbing the other residents.

e. Mrs. Carver has organized the group, scheduled their rehearsals, and acquired back-up instruments.

1. When she breaks a string, she doesn't want her elderly crew to have to grab the guitar change the string and hand it back to her, before the song ends.

2. The Rest Home Rebels' favorite bands are U2, Arcade Fire and Lester Lanin and his orchestra.

3. They watch a lot of MTV because it is fast-paced colorful exciting and informative and it has more variety than soap operas.

4. Just once, Mrs. Carver wants to play in a really, huge, sold-out, arena.

5. She hopes to borrow the community's big, white, van to take herself her band and their equipment to a major, professional, recording studio.

21e Use commas to set off a nonrestrictive phrase or clause.

modifier: A word (such as an adjective or adverb), phrase, or clause that provides more information about other parts of a sentence: *Plays staged by the drama class* are *always successful.*

A *nonrestrictive modifier* adds a fact that, while perhaps interesting and valuable, isn't essential. You could leave it out of the sentence and still make good sense. When a word in your sentence is modified by a nonrestrictive phrase or clause, set off the modifier with commas before and after it.

Potts Alley, *which runs north from Chestnut Street,* is too narrow for cars.

At the end of the alley, *where the fair was held last May,* a getaway car waited.

A *restrictive modifier* is essential. Omit it and you significantly change the meaning of the modified word and the sentence. Such a modifier is called *restrictive* because it limits what it modifies: it specifies this place, person, or action and no other. Because a restrictive modifier is part of the identity of whatever it modifies, no commas set it off from the rest of the sentence.

They picked the alley *that runs north from Chestnut Street* because it is close to the highway.

Anyone *who robs my house* will be disappointed.

Leave out the modifier in that last sentence — writing *Anyone will regret it* — and you change the meaning from potential robbers to all humankind.

NOTE: Use *that* to introduce (or to recognize) a restrictive phrase or clause. Use *which* to introduce (or to recognize) a nonrestrictive phrase or clause.

> The food *that I love best* is chocolate.

> Chocolate, *which I love,* is not on my diet.

21f   Use commas to set off nonrestrictive appositives.

Like the modifiers discussed in 21e, an **appositive** can be either restrictive or nonrestrictive. If it is nonrestrictive — if the sentence still makes sense when it is omitted or changed — then set it off with commas before and after.

> My third ex-husband, *Hugo,* will be glad to meet you.

> We are bringing dessert, *a blueberry pie,* to follow dinner.

If the appositive is restrictive — if you can't take it out or change it without changing your meaning — then include it without commas.

> Of all the men I've been married to, my ex-husband *Hugo* is the best cook.

appositive: A word or group of words that adds information about a subject or object by identifying it in a different way: my dog *Rover,* Hal's brother *Fred*

■ Exercise 21–3

Using Commas

Add any necessary commas to the following sentences, and remove any commas that do not belong. You may have to draw your own conclusions about what the writer meant to say. Some sentences may be correct. Possible revisions for the lettered sentences appear in the back of the book. Example:

> Jay and his wife the former Laura McCready were college sweethearts.

> Jay and his wife, the former Laura McCready, were college sweethearts.

a. We are bringing a dish vegetable lasagna, to the potluck supper.

b. I like to go to Central Bank, on this side of town, because this branch tends to have short lines.

c. The colony, that the English established at Roanoke disappeared mysteriously.

d. If the base commanders had checked their gun room where powder is stored, they would have found that several hundred pounds of gunpowder were missing.

e. Brazil's tropical rain forests which help produce the air we breathe all over the world, are being cut down at an alarming rate.

1. The aye-aye which is a member of the lemur family is threatened with extinction.

2. The party, a dismal occasion ended earlier than we had expected.

3. Secretary Stern warned that the concessions, that the West was prepared to make, would be withdrawn if not matched by the East.

■ For more practice, visit <bedfordstmartins.com/bedguide> and do a keyword search:

comma

4. Although both of Don's children are blond, his daughter Sharon has darker hair than his son Jake.

5. Herbal tea which has no caffeine makes a better after-dinner drink than coffee.

21g Use commas to set off conjunctive adverbs.

conjunctive adverb: A linking word that can connect independent clauses and show a relationship between two ideas: Armando is a serious student; *therefore,* he studies every day. (See 14.)

When you drop a conjunctive adverb into the middle of a clause, set it off with commas before and after it.

Using lead paint in homes has been illegal, *however,* since 1973.

Builders, *indeed,* gave it up some twenty years earlier.

21h Use commas to set off parenthetical expressions.

parenthetical expression: An aside to readers or a transitional expression such as *for example* or *in contrast*

Use a pair of commas around any parenthetical expression or any aside from you to your readers.

Home inspectors, *for this reason,* sometimes test for lead paint.

Cosmic Construction never used lead paint, *or so their spokesperson says,* even when it was legal.

21i Use commas to set off a phrase or clause expressing contrast.

It was Rudolph, *not Dasher,* who had a red nose.

EXCEPTION: Short contrasting phrases beginning with *but* need not be set off by commas.

It was not Dasher but Rudolph who had a red nose.

21j Use commas to set off an absolute phrase.

absolute phrase: An expression, usually a noun followed by a participle, that modifies an entire clause or sentence and can appear anywhere in the sentence: The stallion pawed the ground, *chestnut mane and tail swirling in the wind.*

The link between an absolute phrase and the rest of the sentence is a comma or two commas if the phrase falls in midsentence.

Our worst fears drawing us together, we huddled over the letter.

Luke, *his knife being the sharpest,* slit the envelope.

■ Exercise 21–4

Using Commas

Add any necessary commas to the following sentences, and change any punctuation that is incorrect. Answers for the lettered sentences appear in the back of the book. Example:

The officer a radar gun in his hand gauged the speed of the passing cars.

The officer, a radar gun in his hand, gauged the speed of the passing cars.

a. The university insisted however that the students were not accepted merely because of their parents' generous contributions.

b. This dispute in any case is an old one.

c. It was the young man's striking good looks not his acting ability that first attracted the Hollywood agents.

d. Gretchen learned moreover not to always accept as true what she had read in celebrity magazines.

e. The hikers most of them wearing ponchos or rain jackets headed out into the steady drizzle.

1. The lawsuit demanded furthermore that construction already under way be halted immediately.

2. It is the Supreme Court not Congress or the president that ultimately determines the legality of a law.

3. The judge complained that the case was being tried not by the court but by the media.

4. The actor kneeling recited the lines with great emotion.

5. Both sides' patience running thin workers and management carried the strike into its sixth week.

■ For more practice, visit <bedfordstmartins.com/ bedguide> and do a key-word search:

comma

21k Use commas to set off a direct quotation from your own words.

When you briefly quote someone, distinguish the source's words from yours with commas (and, of course, quotation marks). When you insert an explanation into a quotation (such as *he said*), set that off with commas.

Shakespeare wrote, "Some are born great, some achieve greatness, and some have greatness thrust upon them."

"The best thing that can come with success," commented the actress Liv Ullmann, "is the knowledge that it is nothing to long for."

The comma always comes *before* the quotation marks.

EXCEPTION: Do not use a comma with a very short quotation or one introduced by *that*.

Don't tell me "yes" if you mean "maybe."

Jules said that "Nothing ventured, nothing gained" is his motto.

Don't use a comma with any quotation run into your own sentence and read as part of it. Often such quotations are introduced by linking verbs.

For advice on using punctuation marks with quotations, see 25g–25i; for advice on using quotation marks, see 25a–25d and C3 in the Quick Editing Guide (the dark-blue-edged pages).

linking verb: A verb (*is, become, seem, feel*) that shows a state of being by linking the sentence subject with a word that renames or describes the subject: The sky *is* blue. (See 3a.)

Her favorite statement at age three was "I can do it myself."

Shakespeare originated the expression "my salad days, when I was green in judgment."

21l Use commas around *yes* and *no,* mild interjections, tag questions, and the name or title of someone directly addressed.

interjection: A word or expression (*oh, alas*) that inserts an outburst of feeling at the beginning, middle, or end of a sentence.

YES AND NO	*Yes,* I'd like a Rolls-Royce, but, *no,* I didn't order one.
INTERJECTION	*Well,* don't blame it on me.
TAG QUESTION	It would be fun to ride in a Silver Cloud, *wouldn't it?*
DIRECT ADDRESS	Drive us home, *James.*

21m Use commas to set off dates, states, countries, and addresses.

On June 6, 1979, Ned Shaw was born.

East Rutherford, New Jersey, seemed like Paris, France, to him.

His family moved to 11 Maple Street, Middletown, Ohio.

Do not add a comma between state and zip code: *Bedford, MA 01730.*

■ Exercise 21–5

Using Commas

■ For more practice, visit <bedfordstmartins.com/ bedguide> and do a keyword search:

comma

Add any necessary commas to the following sentences, remove any commas that do not belong, and change any punctuation that is incorrect. Some sentences may be correct. Answers for the lettered sentences appear in the back of the book. Example:

> When Alexander Graham Bell said "Mr. Watson come here, I want you" the telephone entered history.

> When Alexander Graham Bell said, "Mr. Watson, come here, I want you," the telephone entered history.

a. César Chávez was born on March 31 1927, on a farm in Yuma, Arizona.

b. Chávez, who spent years as a migrant farmworker, told other farm laborers "If you're outraged at conditions, then you can't possibly be free or happy until you devote all your time to changing them."

c. Chávez founded the United Farm Workers union and did indeed, devote all his time to changing conditions for farmworkers.

d. Robert F. Kennedy called Chávez, "one of the heroic figures of our time."

e. Chávez, who died on April 23, 1993, became the second Mexican American to receive the highest civilian honor in the United States, the Presidential Medal of Freedom.

1. Yes I was born on April 14 1983 in Bombay India.
2. Move downstage Gary, for Pete's sake or you'll run into Mrs. Clackett.
3. Vicki my precious, when you say, "great" or "terrific," look as though you mean it.
4. Perhaps you have forgotten darling that sometimes you make mistakes, too.
5. Well Dotty, it only makes sense that when you say, "Sardines!," you should go off to get the sardines.

21n Do not use a comma to separate a subject from its verb or a verb from its object.

FAULTY   The athlete driving the purple Jaguar, was Jim Fuld. [Subject separated from verb]

REVISED   The athlete driving the purple Jaguar was Jim Fuld.

FAULTY   The governor should not have given his campaign manager, such a prestigious appointment. [Verb separated from direct object]

REVISED   The governor should not have given his campaign manager such a prestigious appointment.

21o Do not use a comma between words or phrases joined by correlative or coordinating conjunctions.

Do not divide a compound subject or predicate unnecessarily with a comma.

FAULTY   Neither Peter Pan, nor the fairy Tinkerbell, saw the pirates sneaking toward their hideout. [Compound subject]

REVISED   Neither Peter Pan nor the fairy Tinkerbell saw the pirates sneaking toward their hideout.

FAULTY   The chickens clucked, and pecked, and flapped their wings. [Compound predicate]

REVISED   The chickens clucked and pecked and flapped their wings.

21p Do not use a comma before the first or after the last item in a series.

FAULTY   We had to see, my mother's doctor, my father's lawyer, and my dog's veterinarian, in one afternoon.

REVISED   We had to see my mother's doctor, my father's lawyer, and my dog's veterinarian in one afternoon.

---

subject: The part of a sentence that names something—a person, an object, an idea, a situation—about which the predicate makes an assertion: The *king* lives.

verb: A word that shows action (The cow *jumped* over the moon) or a state of being (The cow *is* brown)

direct object: The target of a verb that completes the action performed by the subject or asserted about the subject: I photographed *the sheriff.*

correlative conjunction: A pair of linking words (such as *either/or, not only/but also*) that appear separately but work together to join elements of a sentence: *Neither* his friends *nor* hers like pizza.

coordinating conjunction: A one-syllable linking word (*and, but, for, or, nor, so, yet*) that joins elements with equal or near-equal importance: Jack *and* Jill, sink *or* swim

21q Do not use a comma to set off a restrictive word, phrase, or clause.

For an explanation of restrictive modifiers, see 21e.

A restrictive modifier is essential to the definition or identification of whatever it modifies; a nonrestrictive modifier is not.

FAULTY　The fireworks, that I saw on Sunday, were the best I've ever seen.

REVISED　The fireworks that I saw on Sunday were the best I've ever seen.

21r Do not use commas to set off indirect quotations.

For more on quoting someone's exact words, see 25a–25c. For advice on quoting from sources, see D3 in the Quick Research Guide (the dark-red-edged pages).

When *that* introduces a quotation, the quotation is indirect and requires neither a comma nor quotation marks.

FAULTY　He told us that, we shouldn't have done it.

REVISED　He told us that we shouldn't have done it.

This sentence also would be correct if it were recast as a direct quotation, with a comma and quotation marks.

FAULTY　He told us that, "You shouldn't have done it."

REVISED　He told us, "You shouldn't have done it."

22 *Semicolons*

A semicolon is a sort of compromise between a comma and a period: it creates a stop without ending a sentence.

22a Use a semicolon to join two main clauses not joined by a coordinating conjunction.

coordinating conjunction: A one-syllable linking word (*and, but, for, or, nor, so, yet*) that joins elements with equal or near-equal importance: Jack *and* Jill, sink *or* swim

Suppose, having written one statement, you want to add another that is closely related in sense. You decide to keep them both in a single sentence.

Shooting clay pigeons was my mother's favorite sport; she would smash them for hours at a time.

A semicolon is a good substitute for a period when you don't want to bring your readers to a complete stop.

By the yard life is hard; by the inch it's a cinch.

NOTE: When you join a subordinate clause to a main one or join two statements with a coordinating conjunction, you can generally use just a comma. Reserve the semicolon to emphasize a close connection or to avoid confusion when long, complex clauses include internal punctuation.

22b Use a semicolon to join two main clauses that are linked by a conjunctive adverb.

You can use a conjunctive adverb to show a relationship between clauses such as addition (*also, besides*), comparison (*likewise, similarly*), contrast (*instead, however*), emphasis (*namely, certainly*), cause and effect (*thus, therefore*), or time (*finally, subsequently*). When a second statement begins with (or includes) a conjunctive adverb, you can join it to the first with a semicolon.

> Bert is a stand-out player; *indeed,* he's the one hope of our team.

> We yearned to attend the concert; tickets, *however,* were hard to come by.

Note in the second sentence that the conjunctive adverb falls within the second main clause. No matter where the conjunctive adverb appears, the semicolon is placed between the two clauses.

conjunctive adverb: A linking word that can connect independent clauses and show a relationship between two ideas: Armando is a serious student; *therefore,* he studies every day. (See 14.)

■ For punctuation with conjunctive adverbs within clauses, see 21g.

22c Use a semicolon to separate items in a series that contain internal punctuation or that are long and complex.

The semicolon is especially useful for setting off one group of items from another. More powerful than a comma, it divides a series of series.

> The auctioneer sold clocks, watches, and cameras; freezers of steaks and tons of bean sprouts; motorcycles, cars, speedboats, canoes, and cabin cruisers; and rare coins, curious stamps, and precious stones.

If the writer had used commas in place of semicolons in that sentence, the divisions would have been harder to notice.

Commas are not the only internal punctuation that warrants the extra force of semicolons between items.

> The auctioneer sold clocks and watches (with or without hands); freezers of steaks and tons of bean sprouts; trucks and motorcycles (some of which had working engines); and dozens of smaller items.

■ Exercise 22–1

Using Semicolons

Add any necessary semicolons to the following sentences, and change any that are incorrectly used. Some sentences may be correct. Answers for the lettered sentences appear in the back of the book. Example:

> They had used up all their money, they barely had enough left for the train trip home.

> They had used up all their money; they barely had enough left for the train trip home.

■ For more practice, visit <bedfordstmartins.com/bedguide> and do a keyword search:

semicolon

a. By the beginning of 2006, Shirley was eager to retire, nevertheless, she agreed to stay on for two more years.

b. In 1968 Lyndon Johnson abandoned his hopes for reelection; because of fierce opposition from within his own party.

c. The committee was asked to determine the extent of violent crime among teenagers, especially those between the ages of fourteen and sixteen, to act as a liaison between the city and schools and between churches and volunteer organizations, and to draw up a plan to reduce violence, both public and private, by the end of the century.

d. The leaves on the oak trees near the lake were tinged with red, swimmers no longer ventured into the water.

e. The football team has yet to win a game, however, the season is still young.

1. Although taking the subway is slow, it is still faster than driving to work.

2. When the harpist began to play; the bride and her father prepared to walk down the aisle.

3. The Mariners lost all three games to Milwaukee, worse yet, two star players were injured.

4. There was nothing the firefighters could do; the building already had been consumed by flames.

5. Chess is difficult to master; but even a child can learn the basic rules.

23 Colons

A colon introduces a further thought, one added to throw light on a first. In using it, a writer declares: "What follows will clarify what I've just said."

Some writers use a capital letter to start any complete sentence that follows a colon; others prefer a lowercase letter. Both habits are acceptable. Whichever you choose, be consistent. A phrase that follows a colon always begins with a lowercase letter.

phrase: Two or more related words that work together but may lack a subject (as in *will have been*), a verb (*my uncle Zeke*), or both (*in the attic*)

main clause: A group of words that has both a subject and a verb and can stand alone as a complete sentence: *My sister has a friend.*

23a Use a colon between two main clauses if the second exemplifies, explains, or summarizes the first.

Like a semicolon, a colon can join two sentences into one. The chief difference is this: a semicolon says merely that two main clauses are related; a colon, like an abbreviation for *that is* or *for example*, says that the second clause gives an example or explanation of the point in the first clause.

> She tried everything: she scoured the Internet, made dozens of phone calls, wrote e-mails, even consulted a lawyer.

23b Use a colon to introduce a list or a series.

A colon can introduce a word, a phrase, a series, or a second main clause, sometimes strengthened by *as follows* or *the following.*

> The dance steps are as follows: forward, back, turn, and glide.

> Engrave the following truth upon your memory: a colon is always constructed of two dots.

When a colon introduces a series of words or phrases, it often means *such as* or *for instance.* A list of examples after a colon need not include *and* before the last item unless all possible examples have been stated.

> On a Saturday night many kinds of people crowd our downtown area: drifters, bored senior citizens, college students out for a good time.

23c Use a colon to introduce an appositive.

A colon preceded by a main clause can introduce an appositive.

> I have discovered the key to the future: plastics.

appositive: A word or group of words that adds information about a subject or object by identifying it in a different way: my dog *Rover,* Hal's brother *Fred*

23d Use a colon to introduce a long or comma-filled quotation.

Sometimes you can't conveniently introduce a quoted passage with a comma. Perhaps the quotation is too long or heavily punctuated, or your prefatory remarks demand a longer pause. In either case, use a colon.

> God told Adam and Eve: "Be fruitful, and multiply, and replenish the earth, and subdue it."

23e Use a colon when convention calls for it.

AFTER A SALUTATION	Dear Professor James: Dear Account Representative:
BIBLICAL CITATIONS	Genesis 4:7 [The book of Genesis, chapter four, seventh verse]
BOOK TITLES AND SUBTITLES	*Convergences: Essays on Art and Literature* *In the Beginning: Creation Stories from around the World*
SOURCE REFERENCES	Welty, Eudora. *The Eye of the Story.* New York: Random, 1978.
TIME OF DAY	2:02 P.M.

main clause: A group of words that has both a subject and a verb and can stand alone as a complete sentence: *My sister has a friend.*

23f Use a colon only at the end of a main clause.

In a sentence, a colon always follows a clause, never a phrase. Avoid using a colon between a verb and its object, between a preposition and its object, and before a list introduced by *such as.* Any time you are in doubt about whether to use a colon, first make sure that the preceding statement is a complete sentence. Then you will not litter your writing with unnecessary colons.

FAULTY My mother and father are: Bella and Benjamin.

REVISED My mother and father are Bella and Benjamin.

FAULTY Many great inventors have changed our lives, such as: Edison, Marconi, and Glutz.

REVISED Many great inventors have changed our lives, such as Edison, Marconi, and Glutz.

REVISED Many great inventors have changed our lives: Edison, Marconi, Glutz.

Use either *such as* or a colon. You don't need both.

■ Exercise 23–I

Using Colons

■ For more practice, visit <bedfordstmartins.com/bedguide> and do a keyword search:

colon

Add, remove, or replace colons wherever appropriate in the following sentences. Where necessary, revise the sentences further to support your changes in punctuation. Some sentences may be correct. Possible revisions for the lettered sentences appear in the back of the book. Example:

Yum-Yum Burger has franchises in the following cities; New York, Chicago, Miami, San Francisco, and Seattle.

Yum-Yum Burger has franchises in the following cities: New York, Chicago, Miami, San Francisco, and Seattle.

a. The Continuing Education Program offers courses in: building and construction management, engineering, and design.

b. The interview ended with a test of skills, taking messages, operating the computer, typing a sample letter, and proofreading documents.

c. The sample letter began, "Dear Mr. Rasheed, Please accept our apologies for the late shipment."

d. If you go to the beach this summer, remember these three rules: wear plenty of sunscreen, drink water to replace lost fluids, and avoid exposure during the hottest hours of the day.

e. These are my dreams, to fly in a small plane, to gallop down a beach on horseback, and to cross the ocean in a sailboat.

1. In the case of *Bowers v. Hardwick,* the Supreme Court decided that: citizens had no right to sexual privacy.

2. He ended his speech with a quotation from Homer's *Iliad*, "Whoever obeys the gods, to him they particularly listen."

3. Professor Bligh's book is called *Management, A Networking Approach.*

4. George handed Cynthia a note, "Meet me after class under the big clock on Main Street."

5. Rosa expected to arrive at 4.10, but she didn't get there until 4.20.

24 Apostrophes

Use apostrophes for three purposes: to show possession, to indicate an omission, and to add an ending to a number, a letter, or an abbreviation.

■ For advice on editing for apostrophes, see C2 in the Quick Editing Guide (the dark-blue-edged pages).

24a To make a singular noun possessive, add -'s.

The *plumber's* wrench left grease stains on *Harry's* shirt.

Add -'s even when your singular noun ends with the sound of *s*.

Felix's roommate enjoys reading *Henry James's* novels.

Some writers find it awkward to add -'s to nouns that already end in an -s, especially those of two syllables or more. You may, if you wish, form such a possessive by adding only an apostrophe.

The Egyptian king *Cheops'* death occurred hundreds of years before *Socrates'.*

24b To make a plural noun ending in -s possessive, add an apostrophe.

A *stockbrokers'* meeting combines *foxes'* cunning with the noisy chaos of a *boys'* locker room.

Possessive Nouns and Plural Nouns at a Glance

Both plural nouns and possessive nouns often end with -*s*.

- *Plural* means more than one (two *dogs*, six *friends*), but *possessive* means ownership (the *dogs'* biscuits, my *friends'* cars).

- If you can substitute the word *of* for the -*s'* (the biscuits *of* the dogs, the cars *of* my friends), you need the plural possessive with an apostrophe after the -*s*.

- If you cannot substitute *of*, you need the simple plural with no apostrophe (the *dogs* are well fed, my *friends* have no money for gas).

24c To make a plural noun not ending in -*s* possessive, add -'*s*.

Nouns such as *men, mice, geese,* and *alumni* form the possessive case the same way as singular nouns: with -'*s*.

> What effect has the *women's* movement had on *children's* literature?

24d To show joint possession by two people or groups, add an apostrophe or -'*s* to the second noun of the pair.

> I left my *mother and father's* home with *friends and neighbors'* good wishes.

If the two members of a noun pair possess a set of things individually, add an apostrophe or -'*s* to each noun.

> *Men's* and *women's* marathon records are improving steadily.

24e To make a compound noun possessive, add an apostrophe or -'*s* to the last word in the compound.

For more on plurals of compound nouns, see p. H-143.

A compound noun consists of more than one word (*commander in chief, sons-in-law*); it may be either singular or plural.

> The *commander in chief's* duties will end on July 1.

> Esther does not approve of her *sons-in-law's* professions.

24f To make an indefinite pronoun possessive, add -'*s*.

Indefinite pronouns such as *anyone, nobody,* and *another* are usually singular in meaning. They form the possessive case the same way as singular nouns: with -'*s*. (See 24a.)

> What caused the accident is *anybody's* guess; but it appears to be *no one's* fault.

24g To indicate the possessive of a personal pronoun, use its possessive case.

personal pronoun: A pronoun (*I, me, you, it, he, we, them*) that stands for a noun that names a person or thing: Mark awoke slowly, but suddenly *he* bolted from the bed.

The personal pronouns are irregular; each has its own possessive form. No possessive personal pronoun contains an apostrophe. Resist the temptation to add an apostrophe or -'*s*.

NOTE: *Its* (no apostrophe) is always a possessive pronoun.

> I retreated when the Murphys' German shepherd bared *its* fangs.

It's (with an apostrophe) is always a contraction of *it is.*

> *It's* [It is] not our fault.

24h Use an apostrophe to indicate an omission in a contraction.

> *They're* [They are] too sophisticated for me.
>
> Pat *didn't* [did not] finish her assignment.
>
> Americans grow up admiring the Spirit of *'76* [1776].
>
> *It's* [It is] nearly eight *o'clock* [of the clock].

For a chart of posses-sive personal pronouns, see C2 in the Quick Edit-ing Guide (the dark-blue-edged pages).

24i Use an apostrophe to form the plural of a letter or word mentioned as a word.

LETTER	How many *n's* are there in *Cincinnati?*
WORD	Try replacing all the *should's* in that list with *could's.*

No apostrophes are needed for plural numbers and most abbreviations.

DECADE	The 1980s differed greatly from the 1970s.
NUMBER	Cut out two 3s to sew on Larry's shirt.
ABBREVIATION	Do we need IDs at YMCAs in other towns?

For advice on italicizing a letter, word, or number named as a word, see 31e.

■ Exercise 24–1

Using Apostrophes

Correct any errors in the use of the apostrophe in the following sentences. Some sentences may be correct. Answers for the lettered sentences appear in the back of the book. Example:

> Youd better put on you're new shoes.
>
> *You'd* better put on *your* new shoes.

a. Joe and Chucks' fathers were both in the class of 73.

b. They're going to finish their term papers as soon as the party ends.

c. It was a strange coincidence that all three womens' cars broke down after they had picked up their mother's-in-law.

d. Don't forget to dot you're *i*s and cross you're *t*s.

e. Mario and Shelley's son is marrying the editor's in chief's daughter.

1. The Hendersons' never change: their always whining about Mr. Scobee farming land thats rightfully their's.

For more practice, visit <bedfordstmartins.com/bedguide> and do a key-word search:

 apostrophe

2. Its hard to join a womens' basketball team because so few of them exist.

3. I had'nt expected to hear Janice' voice again.

4. Don't give the Murphy's dog it's biscuit until it's sitting up.

5. Isnt' it the mother and fathers' job to tell kid's to mind their *p*s and *q*s?

25   *Quotation Marks*

■ For more on editing quotation marks, see C3 in the Quick Editing Guide (the dark-blue-edged pages).

Quotation marks always come in pairs: one at the start and one at the finish of a quoted passage. In the United States, the double quotation mark (") is preferred over the single one (') for most uses. Use quotation marks to set off quoted or highlighted words from the rest of your text.

> "Injustice anywhere is a threat to justice everywhere," wrote Martin Luther King Jr.

■ For more on quoting, paraphrasing, and summarizing, see Ch. 12 and D3–D5 in the Quick Research Guide (the dark-red-edged pages).

25a Use quotation marks around direct quotations from another writer or speaker.

You can enrich the content, language, and authority of your writing by occasionally quoting a source whose ideas support your own. When you do this, you owe credit to the quoted person. If you use his or her exact words, enclose them in quotation marks.

■ For capitalization with quotation marks, see 29j.

> Anwar al-Sadat reflected the Arab concept of community when he said, "A man's village is his peace of mind."

■ For punctuation of direct and indirect quotations, see 21r.

In an indirect quotation, you report someone else's idea without using his or her exact words. Do not enclose an indirect quotation in quotation marks. Do name your source and accurately present what it said.

> Anwar al-Sadat asserted that a community provides a sense of well-being.

25b Use single quotation marks around a quotation inside another quotation.

Sometimes you may quote a source that quotes someone else or puts words in quotation marks. When that happens, use single quotation marks around the internal quotation (even if your source used double ones); put double quotation marks around the larger passage you are quoting.

> "My favorite advice from Socrates, 'Know thyself and fear all women,'" said Dr. Blatz, "has been getting me into trouble lately."

Direct and Indirect Quotations

When you quote directly, use the exact words of the original writer or speaker; set them off with double quotation marks. Avoid the problems that arise when a direct quotation is changed into an indirect quotation (someone else's idea reported without using his or her exact words). Be sure to rephrase an indirect quotation from a source to avoid repeating its original wording.

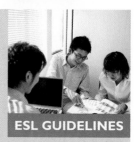

ESL GUIDELINES

- Be sure to change the punctuation and capitalization. You also may need to change the verb tense.

DIRECT QUOTATION   Pascal said, "The assignment is on Chinua Achebe, the Nigerian writer."

INDIRECT QUOTATION   Pascal said that the assignment was on Chinua Achebe, the Nigerian writer.

- If the direct quotation is a question, you must change the word order in the indirect quotation.

DIRECT QUOTATION   Jean asked, "How far is it to Boston?"

INDIRECT QUOTATION   Jean asked how far it was to Boston.

NOTE: Use a period, not a question mark, with questions in indirect quotations.

- Very often, you must change pronouns when using an indirect quotation.

DIRECT QUOTATION   Antonio said, "I think you are mistaken."

INDIRECT QUOTATION   Antonio said that he thought I was mistaken.

■ For practice, visit <bedfordstmartins.com/ bedguide> and do a keyword search:

ESL

According to the Organic Farming Research Foundation Web site at <http:// ofrf.org/resources/organicfaqs.html>, "All products sold as 'organic' must be certified."

25c   Instead of using quotation marks, indent longer quotations.

Suppose you are writing an essay about the value of a college education. You might include a paragraph like this:

In his 2004 commencement address at the College of William & Mary, comedian Jon Stewart advised students to look beyond academic definitions of success:

> College is something you complete. Life is something you experience. So don't worry about your grade, or the results or success. Success is defined in myriad ways, and you will find it, and people will no longer be grading

■ For more on quoting and paraphrasing, see Ch. 12 and D3 and D4 in the Quick Research Guide (the dark-red-edged pages).

> you, but it will come from your own internal sense of decency, which I
> imagine, after going through the program here, is quite strong . . .
> although I'm sure downloading illegal files . . . but, nah, that's a different
> story.

For more on the MLA and APA styles, see section E in the Quick Research Guide (the dark-red-edged pages).

Merely indenting the quoted passage shows that it is a direct quotation. You
need not frame it with quotation marks. In MLA style, typically used in English composition and other humanities courses, indent quotations of more
than four lines by one inch (or ten spaces). In APA style, typically used in
the social sciences and business, indent quotations of forty words or more
by one-half inch (or five to seven spaces). In both styles, double-space the
quoted lines, and add source information, if needed.

Follow the same practice if you quote more than three lines of a poem.

> Phillis Wheatley, the outstanding black poet of colonial America, often made emo-
> tional pleas in her poems:
>> Attend me, Virtue, thro' my youthful years
>>> O leave me not to the false joys of time!
>> But guide my steps to endless life and bliss.
>>> Greatness, or Goodness, say what I shall call thee,
>> To give me an higher appellation still,
>> Teach me a better strain, a nobler lay,
>> Oh thou, enthron'd with Cherubs in the realms of day (15-21).

For advice on capital-ization and quotations, see 29j.

Notice that not only the source's words but her punctuation, capitalization,
and line breaks are quoted exactly.

25d In dialogue, use quotation marks around a speaker's words, and mark each change of speaker with a new paragraph.

Randolph gazed at Ellen and sighed. "What extraordinary beauty."

"They are lovely," she replied, staring at the roses, "aren't they?"

25e Use quotation marks around the titles of a speech, an article in a newspaper or magazine, a short story, a poem shorter than book length, a chapter in a book, a song, and an episode of a television or radio program.

For advice on italicizing or underlining titles, see 31a and the chart on pp. H-136–H-137.

The article "An Updike Retrospective" praises "Solitaire" as the best story in
John Updike's collection *Museums and Women*.

In Chapter 5, "Expatriates," Schwartz discusses Eliot's famous poem "The
Love Song of J. Alfred Prufrock."

25f Avoid using quotation marks to indicate slang or to be witty or ironic.

INADVISABLE   By the time I finished all my chores, my "day off" was over.

REVISED   By the time I finished all my chores, my day off was over.

INADVISABLE   Liza looked like a born "loser," but Jerry was "hard up" for company.

REVISED   Liza looked like a born loser, but Jerry was hard up for company.

Stick your neck out. If you really want to use those words, just go ahead. Otherwise, reword the sentence.

No quotation marks are needed after *so-called* or similar words.

FAULTY   The meet included many so-called "champions."

REVISED   The meet included many so-called champions.

25g Put commas and periods inside quotation marks.

A comma or a period is always placed before quotation marks, even if it is not part of the quotation.

> We pleaded, "Keep off the grass," in hope of preserving the lawn.

> The sign warned pedestrians to "Keep off the grass."

■ For more on commas with quotations, see 21k.

25h Put semicolons and colons outside quotation marks.

> We said, "Keep off the grass"; they still tromped onward.

25i Put other punctuation inside or outside quotation marks depending on its function in the sentence.

Parentheses that are part of the quotation go inside the quotation marks. Parentheses that are your own, not part of the quotation, go outside the quotation marks.

> We said, "Keep off the grass (unless it's artificial turf)."

> They tromped onward (although we had said, "Keep off the grass").

If a question mark, exclamation point, or dash is part of the quotation, place it inside the quotation marks. Otherwise, place it after the closing quotation marks.

> She hollered, "Fire!"

> Who hollered "Fire"?

Don't close a sentence with two end punctuation marks, one inside and one outside the quotation marks. If the quoted passage ends with a dash, exclamation point, question mark, or period, you need not add any further end punctuation. If the quoted passage falls within a question asked by you, however, it should finish with a question mark, even if that means dropping other end punctuation (*Who hollered "Fire"?*).

■ For more practice, visit <bedfordstmartins.com/bedguide> and do a key-word search:

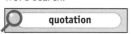
quotation

■ Exercise 25–1

Using Quotation Marks

Add quotation marks wherever they are needed in the following sentences, and correct any other errors. Answers for the lettered sentences appear in the back of the book. Example:

> Annie asked him, Do you believe in free will?
>
> Annie asked him, "Do you believe in free will?"

a. What we still need to figure out, the police chief said, is whether the victim was acquainted with his assailant.

b. A skillful orator, Patrick Henry is credited with the phrase Give me liberty or give me death.

c. I could hear the crowd chanting my name — Jones! Jones! — and that spurred me on, said Bruce Jones, the winner of the 5,000-meter race.

d. The video for the rock group Guns and Roses' epic song November Rain is based on a short story by Del James.

e. In response to a possible asteroid strike on Earth, former astronaut Rusty Schweickart says, Every country is at risk.

1. That day at school, the kids were as "high as kites."

2. Notice, the professor told the class, Cassius's choice of imagery when he asks, Upon what meat doth this our Caesar feed, / That he is grown so great?

3. "As I was rounding the bend," Peter explained, "I failed to see the sign that said Caution: Ice.

4. John Cheever's story The Swimmer begins with the line It was one of those midsummer Sundays when everyone sits around saying, I drank too much last night.

5. Who coined the saying Love is blind?

26 *Dashes*

A *dash* is a horizontal line used to separate parts of a sentence — a more dramatic substitute for a comma, semicolon, or colon. To type a dash, hit your hyphen key twice, and don't add any spaces.

26a Use a dash to indicate a sudden break in thought or shift in tone.

The dash signals that a surprise is in store: a shift in viewpoint, perhaps, or an unfinished statement.

> Ivan doesn't care which team wins — he bet on both.

> I didn't notice my parents' accented speech — at least not at home.

26b Use a dash to introduce an explanation, an illustration, or a series.

When you want a preparatory pause without the formality of a colon, try a dash.

> My advice to you is simple — stop complaining.

You can use a dash to introduce an appositive that needs drama or contains commas.

> Longfellow wrote about three young sisters — grave Alice, laughing Allegra, and Edith with golden hair — in "The Children's Hour."

appositive: A word or group of words that adds information about a subject or object by identifying it in a different way: my dog *Rover*, Hal's brother *Fred*

26c Use dashes to set off an emphatic aside or parenthetical expression from the rest of a sentence.

> It was as hot — and I mean *hot* — as the Fourth of July in Death Valley.

> If I went through anguish in botany and economics — for different reasons — sociology was even worse.

parenthetical expression: An aside to readers or a transitional expression such as *for example* or *in contrast*

26d Avoid overusing dashes.

Like a physical gesture of emphasis — a jab of a pointing finger — the dash becomes meaningless if used too often. Use it only when a comma, a colon, or parentheses don't seem strong enough.

▮ For more on dashes compared with commas, see 21, and with parentheses, see 27a–27b.

EXCESSIVE | Algy's grandmother — a sweet old lady — asked him to pick up some things at the store — milk, eggs, and cheese.

REVISED | Algy's grandmother, a sweet old lady, asked him to pick up some things at the store: milk, eggs, and cheese.

▪ Exercise 26–1

Using Dashes

Add, remove, or replace dashes wherever appropriate in the following sentences. Some sentences may be correct. Possible answers for the lettered sentences appear in the back of the book. Example:

▮ For more practice, visit <bedfordstmartins.com/ bedguide> and do a keyword search:

dash

Stanton had all the identifying marks, boating shoes, yellow slicker, sunblock, and an anchor, of a sailor.

Stanton had all the identifying marks — boating shoes, yellow slicker, sunblock, and an anchor — of a sailor.

a. I enjoy going hiking with my friend John — whom I've known for fifteen years.

b. Pedro's new boat is spectacular: a regular seagoing Ferrari.

c. The Thompsons devote their weekends to their favorite pastime, eating bags of potato chips and cookies beside the warm glow of the television.

1. The sport of fishing — or at least some people call it a sport — is boring, dirty — and tiring.

2. At that time, three states in the Sunbelt, Florida, California, and Arizona, were the fastest growing in the nation.

3. LuLu was ecstatic when she saw her grades, all A's!

27 *Parentheses, Brackets, and Ellipses*

Like quotation marks, parentheses (singular, *parenthesis*) work in pairs. So do brackets. Both sets of marks usually surround bits of information added to make a statement perfectly clear. An ellipsis mark is a trio of periods inserted to show that some information has been cut.

PARENTHESES

27a Use parentheses to set off interruptions that are useful but not essential.

FDR (as people called Franklin D. Roosevelt) won four presidential elections.

In fact, he occupied the White House for so many years (1933 to mid-1945) that babies became teenagers without having known any other president.

The material within the parentheses may be helpful, but it isn't essential. Without it, the sentences would still make good sense. Use parentheses when adding in midsentence a qualifying word or phrase, a helpful date, or a brief explanation — words that, in conversation, you might introduce in a changed tone of voice.

27b Use parentheses around letters or numbers indicating items in a series.

Archimedes asserted that, given (1) a lever long enough, (2) a fulcrum, and (3) a place to stand, he could move the earth.

You need not put parentheses around numbers or letters in a list that you set off from the text by indentation.

■ Exercise 27–1

Using Parentheses

Add, remove, or replace parentheses wherever appropriate in the following sentences. Some sentences may be correct. Possible answers for the lettered sentences appear in the back of the book. Example:

■ For more practice, visit <bedfordstmartins.com/bedguide> and do a keyword search:

> other punct

The Islamic fundamentalist Ayatollah Khomeini — 1903–1989 — was described as having led Iran forward into the fifteenth century.

The Islamic fundamentalist Ayatollah Khomeini (1903–1989) was described as having led Iran forward into the fifteenth century.

a. Our cafeteria serves the four basic food groups: white — milk, bread, and mashed potatoes — brown — mystery meat and gravy — green — overcooked vegetables and underwashed lettuce — and orange — squash, carrots, and tomato sauce.

b. The hijackers will release the hostages only if the government, 1, frees all political prisoners and, 2, allows the hijackers to leave the country unharmed.

c. When Phil said he works with whales (as well as other marine mammals) for the Whale Stranding Network, Lisa thought he meant that his group lures whales onto beaches.

1. The new pear-shaped bottles will hold 200 milliliters, 6.8 fluid ounces, of lotion.

2. World War I, or "The Great War," as it was once called, destroyed the old European order forever.

3. The Internet is a mine of fascinating, and sometimes useless, information.

BRACKETS

Brackets, those open-ended typographical boxes, work in pairs like parentheses. Their special purpose is to mark changes in quoted material.

27c Use brackets to add information or to make changes within a direct quotation.

For advice on quoting, paraphrasing, and summarizing, see Ch. 12 and D3–D5 in the Quick Research Guide (the dark-red-edged pages).

A quotation must be quoted exactly. If you add or alter a word or a phrase in a quotation from another writer, place brackets around your changes. Most often the need for such changes arises when you weave into your own prose a piece of someone else's.

Suppose you are writing about James McGuire's being named chairman of the board of directors of General Motors. In your source, the actual words are these: "A radio bulletin first brought the humble professor of philosophy the astounding news." But in your paper, you want readers to know the professor's identity. So you add that information, in brackets.

> "A radio bulletin first brought the humble professor of philosophy [James McGuire] the astounding news."

Be careful never to alter a quoted statement any more than you have to. Every time you consider an alteration, ask yourself: Do I really need this word-for-word quotation, or should I paraphrase?

27d Use brackets around *sic* to indicate an error in a direct quotation.

For more on brackets, see 27c.

When you faithfully quote a statement that contains an error, follow the error with a bracketed *sic* (Latin for "so" or "so the writer says").

> President George W. Bush once said, "We need an energy bill that encourages consumption [*sic*]."

Of course, such a statement might not be worth quoting. Usually you're better off paraphrasing an error-riddled passage than pointing out its weaknesses.

ELLIPSES

27e Use ellipses to signal that you have omitted part of a quotation.

Occasionally you will want to quote just the parts of a passage that relate to your topic. It's all right to make judicious cuts in a quotation, as long as you acknowledge them. To do this, use *ellipses*: three periods with a space between each one (. . .).

Say you are writing an essay, "Today's Children: Counselors on Marital Affairs." One of your sources, Marie Winn's book *Children without Childhood* (New York: Penguin, 1984), includes this passage:

Consider the demise of sexual innocence among children. We know that the casual integration of children into adult society in the Middle Ages included few sexual prohibitions. Today's nine- and ten-year-olds watch pornographic movies on cable TV, casually discourse about oral sex and sadomasochism, and not infrequently find themselves involved in their own parents' complicated sex lives, if not as actual observers or participants, at least as advisers, friendly commentators, and intermediaries.

You want to quote Winn's last sentence but omit some of its detail.

"Today's nine- and ten-year-olds . . . not infrequently find themselves involved in their own parents' complicated sex lives, . . . at least as advisers, friendly commentators, and intermediaries."

If ellipses conclude your sentence, precede them with a period placed directly after the end of the sentence.

"Consider the demise of sexual innocence. . . . Today's nine- and ten-year-olds [quotation continues as in preceding example]."

27f   Avoid using ellipses at the beginning or end of a quotation.

Even though the book *Children without Childhood* continues after the quoted passage, you don't need ellipses at the end of your quotation. Nor do you ever need to begin a quotation with three dots. Save the ellipses for words or sentences you omit *inside* whatever you quote.

Anytime you decide to alter a quotation, with ellipses or with brackets, ask yourself whether the quoted material is still necessary and still effective. If you plan to cut more than one or two sections from a quotation, think about paraphrasing instead.

For more on quoting, paraphrasing, and summarizing, see Ch. 12 and D3–D5 in the Quick Research Guide (the dark-red-edged pages).

■ Exercise 27–2

Using Brackets and Ellipses

The following are two hypothetical passages from original essays. Each one is followed by a set of quotations. Paraphrase or adapt each quotation, using brackets and ellipses, and splice it into the essay passage.

For more practice, visit <bedfordstmartins.com/ bedguide> and do a keyword search:

other punct

I. ESSAY PASSAGE

Most people are willing to work hard for a better life. Too often, however, Americans do not realize that the desire for more possessions leads them away from the happiness they hope to find. Many people work longer and longer hours to earn more money and as a result have less time to devote to family, friends, and activities that are truly important. When larger houses, sport-utility vehicles, and wide-screen TVs fail to bring them joy, they find even more things to buy and work even harder to pay for them. This cycle can grind down the most optimistic American. The only solution is to realize how few material possessions people absolutely need to have.

QUOTATIONS

a. Only when he has ceased to need things can a man truly be his own master and so really exist.

—Anwar al-Sadat

b. I like to walk amidst the beautiful things that adorn the world; but private wealth I should decline, or any sort of personal possessions, because they would take away my liberty.

—George Santayana

c. To live content with small means; to seek elegance rather than luxury, and refinement rather than fashion; to be worthy, not respectable and wealthy, not rich; to study hard, think quietly, talk gently, act frankly; to listen to stars and birds, to babes and sages, with open heart; to bear all cheerfully, do all bravely, await occasions, hurry never. In a word, to let the spiritual, unbidden and unconscious, grow up through the common. This is to be my symphony.

—William Henry Channing

2. ESSAY PASSAGE

Every human life is touched by the natural world. Before the modern industrial era, most people recognized the earth as the giver and supporter of existence. Nowadays, with the power of technology, we can (if we choose) destroy many of the complex balances of nature. With such power comes responsibility. We are no longer merely nature's children, but nature's parents as well.

QUOTATIONS

a. The overwhelming importance of the atmosphere means that there are no longer any frontiers to defend against pollution, attack, or propaganda. It means, further, that only by a deep patriotic devotion to one's country can there be a hope of the kind of protection of the whole planet, which is necessary for the survival of the people of other countries.

—Anthropologist Margaret Mead

b. The survival of our wildlife is a matter of grave concern to all of us in Africa. These wild creatures amid the wild places they inhabit are not only important as a source of wonder and inspiration but are an integral part of our natural resources and of our future livelihood and well-being.

—Former president of Tanzania Julius Nyerere

Chapter 39
Mechanics

28 *Abbreviations*

Abbreviations enable a writer to include necessary information in capsule form. Limit abbreviations to those common enough for readers to recognize, or add an explanation so that a reader does not wonder, "What does this mean?" If ever you're unsure about whether to abbreviate a word, remember: when in doubt, spell it out.

28a Use abbreviations for some titles with proper names.

Abbreviate the following titles:

Mr. and Mrs. Hubert Collins	Dr. Martin Luther King Jr.
Ms. Martha Reading	St. Matthew

For advice on punctuating abbreviations, see 20b.

Write out other titles in full, including titles that are unfamiliar to readers of English, such as *M.* (for the French *Monsieur*) or *Sr.* (for the Spanish *Señor*).

General Douglas MacArthur	Senator Dianne Feinstein
President George W. Bush	Professor Shirley Fixler

Spell out most titles that appear without proper names.

FAULTY   Tomás is studying to be a dr.

REVISED   Tomás is studying to be a doctor.

When an abbreviated title (such as an academic degree) follows a proper name, set it off with commas.

Alice Martin, CPA, is the accountant for Charlotte Cordera, PhD.

Lucy Chen, MD, and James Filbert, DDS, have moved to new offices.

An academic degree that appears without a proper name can be abbreviated, but it is not set off with commas.

My brother has a BA in economics.

Avoid repeating different forms of the same title before and after a proper name. You can properly refer to a doctor of dental surgery as either *Dr. Jane Doe* or *Jane Doe, DDS*, but not as *Dr. Jane Doe, DDS*.

28b Use *a.m., p.m., BC, AD,* and *$* with numbers.

9:05 a.m.   3:45 p.m.   2000 BC   AD 1066

The words for pinpointing years and times are so commonly abbreviated that many writers have forgotten what the letters stand for. In case you are curious: *a.m.* means *ante meridiem,* Latin for "before noon"; *p.m.* means *post meridiem,* "after noon." AD is *anno domini,* Latin for "in the year of the Lord" — that is, since the official year of Jesus' birth. BC stands for "before Christ" and BCE for "before the common era."

For exact prices that include cents and for amounts in the millions, use a dollar sign with figures (*$17.95, $10.52, $3.5 billion*).

Avoid using an abbreviation with wording that means the same thing: write *$1 million,* not *$1 million dollars*. Write *9:05 a.m.* or *9:05 in the morning,* not *9:05 a.m. in the morning*.

28c Avoid abbreviating names of months, days of the week, units of measurement, or parts of literary works.

Many references that can be abbreviated in source citations should be spelled out when they appear in the body of an essay.

NAMES OF MONTHS AND DAYS OF THE WEEK
FAULTY   After their session on 9/3, they did not meet until Fri., Dec. 12.

REVISED   After their session on September 3 [*or* the third of September], they did not meet until Friday, December 12.

UNITS OF MEASUREMENT
FAULTY   It would take 10,000 lbs. of concrete to build a causeway 25 ft. $\times$ 58 in. [*or* 25' $\times$ 58"].

REVISED   It would take 10,000 pounds of concrete to build a causeway 25 feet by 58 inches.

PARTS OF LITERARY WORKS
FAULTY   Von Bargen's reply appears in vol. 2, ch. 12, p. 187.

REVISED   Von Bargen's reply appears in volume 2, chapter 12, page 187.

FAULTY   Leona first speaks in act 1, sc. 2.

REVISED   Leona first speaks in act 1, scene 2 [*or* the second scene of act 1].

28d Use the full English version of most Latin abbreviations.

Unless you are writing for an audience of ancient Romans, translate most Latin abbreviations into English.

■ For the use of *sic* to identify an error, see 27d.

COMMON LATIN ABBREVIATIONS

ABBREVIATION	LATIN	ENGLISH
et al.	*et alia*	and others, and other people, and the others (people)
etc.	*et cetera*	and so forth, and others, and the rest (things)
i.e.	*id est*	that is
e.g.	*exempli gratia*	for example, such as

Latin abbreviations are acceptable, however, for source citations and for comments in parentheses and brackets. Follow the conventions of your citation style.

28e Use abbreviations for familiar organizations, corporations, and people.

Most sets of initials that are capitalized and read as letters do not require periods between the letters (CIA, JFK, UCLA). A set of initials that is pronounced as a word is called an *acronym* (NATO, AIDS, UNICEF) and never has periods between letters.

To avoid misunderstanding, write out an organization's full name the first time you mention it, followed by its initials in parentheses. Then, in later references, you can rely on initials alone. (For very familiar initials, such as FBI or CBS, you need not give the full name.)

28f Avoid abbreviations for countries.

When you mention the United States or another country in your text, give its full name unless the repetition would weigh down your paragraph.

The president will return to the United States [*not* US] on Tuesday from a trip to the United Kingdom [*not* UK].

EXCEPTION: Unlike *US* as a noun, the abbreviation, used consistently with traditional periods or without, is acceptable as an adjective: *US Senate, U.S. foreign policy.* For other countries, find an alternative: *British ambassador.* Follow the conventions of your citation style when you cite or list government documents.

■ For more practice, visit <bedfordstmartins.com/bedguide> and do a keyword search:

 abbreviate

■ Exercise 28–1

Using Abbreviations

Substitute abbreviations for words and vice versa wherever appropriate in the following sentences. Correct any incorrectly used abbreviations. Answers for the lettered sentences appear in the back of the book. Example:

> Please return this form to our office no later than noon on Wed., Apr. 7.

> Please return this form to our office no later than noon on *Wednesday, April 7.*

a. At 7:50 p.m. in the evening on election day, the media first awarded Florida to Al Gore, only to reverse that statement and declare George W. Bush the president a few hours later.

b. Biology lectures are only ninety mins. long because lab sessions immediately follow them.

c. Prof. James has office hours on Mon. and Tues., beginning at 10:00 a.m.

d. Emotional issues, e.g., abortion and capital punishment, cannot be settled easily by compromise.

e. The red peppers are selling for three dollars and twenty-five cents a lb.

1. Hamlet's famous soliloquy comes in act three, sc. one.

2. A.I.D.S. has affected people throughout U.S. society, not just gay men and IV-drug users.

3. Mister Robert Glendale, a C.P.A. accountant, is today's lucky winner of the daily double.

4. The end of the cold war between the U.S. and the Soviet Union complicated the role of the U.N. and drastically altered the purpose of N.A.T.O.

5. The salmon measured thirty-eight in. and weighed twenty-one lbs.

29 *Capital Letters*

■ For advice and a useful chart on capitalization, see D1 in the Quick Editing Guide (the dark-blue-edged pages).

■ For capitalization following a colon, see 23.

Use capital letters only with good reason. If you think a word will work in lowercase letters, you're probably right.

29a Capitalize proper names and adjectives made from proper names.

Proper names designate individuals, places, organizations, institutions, brand names, and certain other distinctive things.

Miles Standish	University of Iowa
Belgium	a Volkswagen
United Nations	a Xerox copier

Any proper name can have an adjective as well as a noun form. The adjective form is also capitalized.

Australian beer   a Renaissance man   Shakespearean comedy

29b Capitalize a title or rank before a proper name.

Now in her second term, Senator Wilimczyk serves on two committees.

In his lecture, Professor Jones analyzed fossil evidence.

Titles that do not come before proper names usually are not capitalized.

Ten senators voted against the stem-cell research appropriation.

Jones is the department's only full professor.

EXCEPTION: The abbreviation of an academic or professional degree is capitalized, whether or not it accompanies a proper name. The informal name of a degree is not capitalized.

Dora E. McLean, MD, also holds a BA in music.

Dora holds a bachelor's degree in music.

29c Capitalize a family relationship only when it is part of a proper name or when it substitutes for a proper name.

Do you know the song about Mother Machree?

I've invited Mother to visit next weekend.

I'd like you to meet my aunt, Emily Smith.

29d Capitalize the names of religions, their deities, and their followers.

Christianity	Muslims	Jehovah	Krishna
Islam	Methodists	Allah	the Holy Spirit

29e Capitalize proper names of places, regions, and geographic features.

Los Angeles	the Black Hills	the Atlantic Ocean
Death Valley	Big Sur	the Philippines

Do not capitalize *north, south, east,* or *west* unless it is part of a proper name (*West Virginia, South Orange*) or refers to formal geographic locations.

Drive south to Chicago and then east to Cleveland.

Jim, who has always lived in the South, likes to read about the Northeast.

A common noun such as *street, avenue, boulevard, park, lake,* or *hill* is capitalized when part of a proper name.

     Meinecke Avenue   Hamilton Park   Lake Michigan

29f Capitalize days of the week, months, and holidays, but not seasons or academic terms.

During spring term, by the Monday after Passover, I have to choose between the January study plan and junior year abroad.

29g Capitalize historical events, periods, and documents.

Black Monday	the Roaring Twenties
the Civil War [*but* a civil war]	Magna Carta
the Holocaust [*but* a holocaust]	Declaration of Independence
the Bronze Age	Atomic Energy Act

29h Capitalize the names of schools, colleges, departments, and courses.

West End School, Central High School [*but* elementary school, high school]

Reed College, Arizona State University [*but* the college, a university]

Department of History [*but* history department, department office]

Feminist Perspectives in Nineteenth-Century Literature [*but* literature course]

29i Capitalize the first, last, and main words in titles.

For advice on using quotation marks and italics for titles, see 25e and 31a.

When you write the title of a paper, book, article, work of art, television show, poem, or performance, capitalize the first and last words and all main words in between. Do not capitalize articles (*a, an, the*), coordinating conjunctions (*and, but, for, or, nor, so, yet*), or prepositions (such as *in, on, at, of, from*) unless they come first or last in the title or follow a colon.

ESSAY	"Once More to the Lake"
NOVEL	*Of Mice and Men*
VOLUME OF POETRY	*Poems after Martial*
POEM	"A Valediction: Of Weeping"
BALLET	*Swan Lake*

29j   Capitalize the first letter of a quoted sentence.

Oscar Wilde wrote, "The only way to get rid of a temptation is to yield to it."

For advice on punctuating quotations, see 25g–25i.

Only the first word of a quoted sentence is capitalized, even when you break the sentence with words of your own.

"The only way to get rid of a temptation," wrote Oscar Wilde, "is to yield to it."

If you quote more than one sentence, start each one with a capital letter.

"Art should never try to be popular," said Wilde. "The public should try to make itself artistic."

If the quoted passage blends in with your sentence, be sure to present every detail of your source accurately.

Oscar Wilde wrote that "The only way to get rid of a temptation is to yield to it."

■ Exercise 29–1

Using Capitalization

Correct any capitalization errors you find in the following sentences. Some sentences may be correct. Answers for the lettered sentences appear in the back of the book. Example:

For more practice, visit <bedfordstmartins.com/bedguide> and do a keyword search:

capitals

"The quality of mercy," says Portia in Shakespeare's *The Merchant Of Venice*, "Is not strained."

"The quality of mercy," says Portia in Shakespeare's *The Merchant of Venice*, "is not strained."

a. At our Family Reunion, I met my Cousin Sam for the first time, as well as my father's brother George.

b. I already knew from dad that his brother had moved to Australia years ago to explore the great barrier reef.

c. I had heard that uncle George was estranged from his Mother, a Roman catholic, after he married an Atheist.

d. She told George that God created many religions so that people would not become Atheists.

e. When my Uncle announced that he was moving to a Continent thousands of miles Southwest of the United States, his Mother gave him a bible to take along.

1. My Aunt, Linda McCallum, received her Doctorate from one of the State Universities in California.

2. After graduation she worked there as Registrar and lived in the San Fernando valley.

3. She has pursued her interest in Hispanic Studies by traveling to South America from her home in Northeastern Australia.

4. She uses her maiden name — Linda McCallum, PhD — for her nonprofit business, Hands across the Sea.

5. After dinner we all toasted grandmother's Ninetieth Birthday and sang "For She's A Jolly Good Fellow."

30　*Numbers*

When do you write out a number (*twenty-seven*) and when do you use figures for it (27)? Unless you are writing in a scientific field or your essay relies on statistics, you'll generally want to use words. Figures are most appropriate in contexts where readers are used to seeing them, such as times and dates (*11:05 p.m. on March 15*).

30a In general, write out a number that consists of one or two words, and use figures for longer numbers.

Short names of numbers are easily read (*ten, six hundred*); longer ones take more thought (*two thousand four hundred eighty-seven*). For numbers of more than a word or two, use figures.

> Two hundred fans paid twenty-five dollars apiece for that shirt.

> A frog's tongue has 970,580 taste buds; a human's has six times as many.

EXCEPTION: For multiples of a million or more, use a figure plus a word.

> The earth is 93 million miles from the sun.

30b Use figures for most addresses, dates, decimals, fractions, parts of literary works, percentages, exact prices, scores, statistics, and times.

■ For examples, see Figures at a Glance on p. H-135.

Using figures is mainly a matter of convenience. If you think words will be easier for your readers to follow, you can always write out a number.

30c Use words or figures consistently for numbers in the same category throughout a passage.

■ For more on the plurals of figures (6's, 1960s), see 24i.

Switching back and forth between words and figures for numbers can be distracting to readers. Choose whichever form suits like numbers in your passage, and use that form consistently for all numbers in the same category.

> Of the 276 representatives who voted, 97 supported a 25 percent raise, while 179 supported a 30 percent raise over five years.

Figures at a Glance

ADDRESSES	4 East 74th Street; also, One Copley Place, 5 Fifth Avenue
DATES	May 20, 2007; 450 bC; also, Fourth of July
DECIMALS	98.6° Fahrenheit; .57 acre
FRACTIONS	3½ years ago; 1¾ miles; also, half a loaf, three-fourths of voters surveyed
PARTS OF LITERARY WORKS	volume 2, chapter 5, page 37 act 1, scene 2 (*or* act I, scene ii)
PERCENTAGES	25 percent; 99.9 percent; also, 25%, 99.9%
EXACT PRICES	$1.99; $200,000; also, $5 million, ten cents, a dollar
SCORES	a 114–111 victory; a final score of 5 to 3
STATISTICS	men in the 25–30 age group; odds of 5 to 1 (*or* 5–1 odds); height 5'7"; also, three out of four doctors
TIMES	2:29 p.m.; 10:15 tomorrow morning; also, half past four, three o'clock (always with a number in words)

30d Write out a number that begins a sentence.

Readers recognize a new sentence by its initial capital; however, you can't capitalize a figure. When a number starts a sentence, either write it out or move it deeper into the sentence. If a number starting a sentence is followed by other numbers in the same category, write them out, too, unless doing so makes the sentence excessively awkward.

> Five percent of the frogs in our aquarium ate sixty-two percent of the flies.

> Ten thousand people packed an arena built for 8,550.

■ Exercise 30–I

Using Numbers

Correct any inappropriate uses of numbers in the following sentences. Some sentences may be correct. Answers for the lettered sentences appear in the back of the book. Example:

> As Feinberg notes on page 197, a delay of 3 minutes cost the researchers 5 years' worth of work.

> As Feinberg notes on page 197, a delay of *three* minutes cost the researchers *five* years' worth of work.

a. If the murder took place at approximately six-twenty p.m. and the suspect was ½ a mile away at the time, he could not possibly have committed the crime.

■ For more practice, visit <bedfordstmartins.com/ bedguide> and do a keyword search:

   numbers

b. A program to help save the sea otter transferred more than eighty animals to a new colony over the course of 2 years; however, all but 34 otters swam back home again.

c. 12 percent or so of the estimated fifteen billion plastic water bottles purchased annually in the United States is recycled.

d. The Reedville Rockets beat the Bolton Blasters ninety-four to four before a crowd of five hundred and fifty.

e. In act two, scene nine, of Shakespeare's *The Merchant of Venice,* Portia's 2nd suitor fails to guess which of 3 caskets contains her portrait.

1. *Fourscore* means 4 times 20; a *fortnight* means 2 weeks; and a *brace* is two of anything.

2. 50 years ago, traveling from New York City to San Francisco took approximately 15 hours by plane, 50 hours by train, and almost 100 hours by car.

3. The little cottage we bought for fifty-five thousand dollars in the nineteen-seventies may sell for $2,000,000 today.

4. At 7 o'clock this morning the temperature was already ninety-seven degrees Fahrenheit.

5. Angelica finished volume one of Proust's *Remembrance of Things Past,* but by the time she got to page forty of volume two, she had forgotten the beginning and had to start over.

31 *Italics*

Italic type — as in this line — slants to the right. In handwriting or typewriting, indicate italics by underlining. Slightly harder to read than perpendicular type, it is usually saved for emphasis or other special uses noted on page H-138.

31a Italicize the titles of magazines, newspapers, and long literary works (books, pamphlets, plays); the titles of films; the titles of paintings and other works of art; the titles of long musical works (operas, symphonies); the titles of CDs and record albums; and the names of television and radio programs.

We read the story "Araby" in James Joyce's book *Dubliners.*

The Broadway musical *My Fair Lady* was based on Shaw's play *Pygmalion.*

The names of the Bible (King James Version, Revised Standard Version), the books of the Bible (Genesis, Matthew), and other sacred books (the Koran, the Rig-Veda) are not italicized.

Italics at a Glance

TITLES

For titles that need to be placed in quotation marks, see 25e.

MAGAZINES, NEWSPAPERS, AND SCHOLARLY JOURNALS
Newsweek   the *London Times*   *Film & History*

LONG LITERARY WORKS
The Bluest Eye (a novel)   *The Less Deceived* (a collection of poems)

FILMS
Psycho   *Casablanca*

PAINTINGS AND OTHER WORKS OF ART
Four Dancers (a painting)   *The Thinker* (a sculpture)

LONG MUSICAL WORKS
Aïda   Handel's *Messiah*

CDS AND RECORD ALBUMS
Crash   *The Chronic*

TELEVISION AND RADIO PROGRAMS
Heroes   *All Things Considered*

OTHER WORDS AND PHRASES

NAMES OF AIRCRAFT, SPACECRAFT, SHIPS, AND TRAINS
the *Orient Express*   the *Challenger*

A WORD OR PHRASE FROM A FOREIGN LANGUAGE IF IT IS NOT IN EVERYDAY USE
The Finnish sauna ritual uses a *vihta,* a brush made of fresh birch branches.

A LETTER, NUMBER, WORD, OR PHRASE WHEN YOU DEFINE IT OR REFER TO IT AS A WORD
The neon *5* on the door identified the club's address.

What do you think *fiery* suggests in the second line?

When you give a synonym or translation — a definition of just a word or so — italicize the word and put its definition in quotation marks.

> The word *orthodoxy* means "conformity."
>
> *Trois, drei,* and *tres* are all words for "three."

31b   Italicize the names of ships, boats, trains, airplanes, and spacecraft.

The launching of the Venus probe *Magellan* was a heartening success after the *Challenger* disaster.

31c Italicize a word or phrase from a foreign language if it is not in everyday use.

Gandhi taught the principles of *satya* and *ahimsa:* truth and nonviolence.

Foreign words that are familiar to most American readers need not be italicized. (Check your dictionary to see which words are considered familiar.)

I prefer provolone to mozzarella.

31d Italicize a word when you define it.

The rhythmic motion of the walls of the alimentary canal is called *peristalsis.*

31e Italicize a letter, number, word, or phrase used as a word.

George Bernard Shaw pointed out that *fish* could be spelled *ghoti: gh* as in *tough, o* as in *women,* and *ti* as in *fiction.*

Watching the big red *8* on a basketball player's jersey, I recalled the scarlet letter *A* worn by Hester Prynne.

31f Use italics sparingly for emphasis.

When you absolutely *must* stress a point, use italics. In most cases, the structure of your sentence, not a typographical gimmick, should give emphasis where emphasis is due.

He suggested putting the package *under* the mailbox, not *into* the mailbox.

People living in affluent countries may not be aware that nearly *sixteen thousand children per day* die of starvation or malnutrition.

■ Exercise 31–1

Using Italics

■ For more practice, visit <bedfordstmartins.com/ bedguide> and do a keyword search:

Add or remove italics as needed in the following sentences. Some sentences may be correct. Answers for the lettered sentences appear in the back of the book. Example:

Hiram could not *believe* that his parents had seen *the Beatles'* legendary performance at Shea Stadium.

Hiram could not believe that his parents had seen the Beatles' legendary performance at Shea Stadium.

a. Does "avocado" mean "lawyer" in Spanish?

b. During this year's *First Night* celebrations, we heard Verdi's Requiem and Monteverdi's Orfeo.

c. You can pick out some of the best basketball players in the *NBA* by the 33 on their jerseys.

d. It was fun watching the passengers on the Europa trying to dance to *Blue Moon* in the midst of a storm.

e. In one episode of the sitcom "Seinfeld," Kramer gets a job as an underwear model.

1. *Eye* in French is *oeil*, while *eyes* is *yeux*.

2. "Deux yeux bleus" means "two blue eyes" in French.

3. Jan can never remember whether Cincinnati has three n's and one t or two n's and two t's.

4. My favorite comic bit in "The Pirates of Penzance" is Major General Stanley's confusion between "orphan" and "often."

5. In Tom Stoppard's play "The Real Thing," the character Henry accuses Bach of copying a *cantata* from a popular song by *Procol Harum*.

32   *Hyphens*

The hyphen, the transparent tape of punctuation, is used to join words and to connect parts of words.

32a   Use hyphens in compound words that require them.

Compound words in the English language take three forms:

1. Two or more words combined into one (*crossroads, salesperson*)
2. Two or more words that remain separate but function as one (*gas station, high school*)
3. Two or more words linked by hyphens (*sister-in-law, window-shop*)

Compound nouns and verbs fall into these categories more by custom than by rule. When you're not sure which way to write a compound, refer to a current dictionary. If the compound is not listed in your dictionary, write it as two words.

Use a hyphen in a compound word containing one or more elements beginning with a capital letter.

Bill says that, as a *neo-Marxist* living in an *A-frame* house, it would be politically incorrect for him to wear a Mickey Mouse *T-shirt*.

There are exceptions to this rule: unchristian, for one. If you think a compound word looks odd with a hyphen, check your dictionary.

32b **Use a hyphen in a compound adjective preceding, but not following, a noun.**

Jerome, a devotee of *twentieth-century* music, has no interest in the classic symphonies of the *eighteenth century.*

I'd like living in an *out-of-the-way* place better if it weren't so far *out of the way.*

In a series of hyphenated adjectives with the same second word, you can omit that word (but not the hyphen) in all but the last adjective of the series.

Julia is a lover of eighteenth-, nineteenth-, and twentieth-century music.

The adverb *well,* when coupled with an adjective, follows the same hyphenation rules as if it were an adjective.

It is *well known* that Tony has a *well-equipped* kitchen, although his is not as *well equipped* as the hotel's.

Do *not* use a hyphen to link an adverb ending in *-ly* with an adjective.

FAULTY   The sun hung like a newly-minted penny in a freshly-washed sky.

REVISED   The sun hung like a newly minted penny in a freshly washed sky.

32c **Use a hyphen after the prefixes *all-*, *ex-*, and *self-* and before the suffix *-elect.***

Lucille's *ex-husband* is studying *self-hypnosis.*

This *all-important* debate pits Senator Browning against the *president-elect.*

Note that these prefixes and suffixes also can function as parts of words that are not hyphenated (*exit, selfish*). Whenever you are unsure whether to use a hyphen, check a dictionary.

32d **Use a hyphen in most cases if an added prefix or suffix creates a double vowel, a triple consonant, or an ambiguous pronunciation.**

It is also acceptable to omit the hyphen in the case of a double *e: reeducate.*

The contractor's *pre-estimate* did not cover any *pre-existing* flaws in the house.

The recreation department favors the *re-creation* of a summer program.

32e **Use a hyphen in spelled-out fractions and compound whole numbers from twenty-one to ninety-nine.**

When her sister gave Leslie's age as six and *three-quarters,* Leslie corrected her: "I'm six and *five-sixths!*"

The fifth graders learned that *forty-four* rounds down to forty while *forty-five* rounds up to fifty.

32f Use a hyphen to indicate inclusive numbers.

The section covering the years 1975-1980 is found on pages 20-27.

32g Use a hyphen to break a word between syllables at the end of a line.

Although many readers will prefer that you turn off your word processor's automatic hyphenation function, using it will require that you check the word divisions it generates. Words are divided as they are pronounced, by syllables. Break a hyphenated compound at its hyphen and a nonhyphen-ated compound between the words that make it up. If you are not sure where to break a word, check your dictionary.

FAULTY   Bubba hates to be called an-
          ti-American.

REVISED   Bubba hates to be called anti-
          American.

Don't split a one-syllable word, even if keeping it intact makes your line come out a bit too short or too long.

FAULTY   I'm completely drench-
          ed.

REVISED   I'm completely drenched.

■ Exercise 32–1

Using Hyphens

Add necessary hyphens and remove incorrectly used hyphens in the following sentences. Some sentences may be correct. Answers for the lettered sentences appear in the back of the book. Example:

Her exhusband works part-time as a short order cook.

Her *ex-husband* works part-time as a *short-order* cook.

a. The strong smelling smoke alerted them to a potentially life threatening danger.

b. Burt's wildly-swinging opponent had tired himself out before the climactic third round.

c. Tony soaked his son's ketchup and mustard stained T shirt in a pail of water mixed with chlorine bleach.

■ For more practice, visit <bedfordstmartins.com/bedguide> and do a key-word search:

hyphen

    d. The badly damaged ship was in no condition to enter the wide-open waters beyond the bay.

    e. Tracy's brother in law lives with his family in a six room apartment.

1. Do you want salt-and-pepper on your roast beef sandwich?
2. Health insurance companies should not be allowed to exclude people on account of preexisting conditions.
3. Heat-seeking missiles are often employed in modern day air-to-air combat.
4. *The Piano* is a beautifully-crafted film with first-rate performances by Holly Hunter and Harvey Keitel.
5. Nearly three fourths of the money in the repair and maintenance account already has been spent.

33 *Spelling*

▣ For advice on spelling and for useful spelling lists, see D2 in the Quick Editing Guide (the dark-blue-edged pages).

English spelling so often defies the rules that many writers wonder if, indeed, there *are* rules. You probably learned to spell — as most of us did — mainly by memorizing. By now you remember that there's a *b* in *doubt* but not in *spout*. You know that the same sound can have several spellings, as in *here, ear, pier, sneer,* and *weird*. You are resigned to pronouncing *ou* differently in *four, round, ought,* and *double*. Still, like most people, you may have trouble spelling certain words.

How many times have you heard someone say "ath-uh-lete" for *athlete* or "gov-er-ment" for *government*? Get the pronunciation right and you realize that the spelling has to be *arctic* (not *artic*), *perform* (not *preform*), *surprise* (not *suprise*), and *similar* (not *similiar*). The trouble is that careful pronunciation is only sometimes a reliable guide to English spelling. Knowing how to pronounce *psychology, whistle, light, gauge,* and *rhythm* doesn't help you spell them. How, then, are you to cope? You can proofread carefully and use your spell checker. You can refer to lists of commonly misspelled words and of **homonyms,** words that sound the same, or almost the same, but are spelled differently. You can also follow the spelling rules and advice about spelling skills included in this section.

33a Follow spelling rules.

Fortunately, a few rules for spelling English words work most of the time. Learning them, and some of their exceptions, will give you a sturdy foundation on which to build.

EI or IE?   The best way to remember which words are spelled *ei* and which ones *ie* is to recall this familiar jingle:

I before *e* except after *c*,

Or when sounded like *a*, as in *neighbor* and *weigh*.

Niece, believe, field, receive, receipt, ceiling, beige, and *freight* are just a few of the words you'll be able to spell easily once you learn that rule. Then memorize a few of the exceptions:

counterfeit	foreign	kaleidoscope	protein	seize
either	forfeit	leisure	science	weird
financier	height	neither	seismograph	

Also among the rule breakers are words in which *cien* is pronounced "shen": *ancient, efficient, conscience, prescience.*

Plurals.   Here are six useful rules:

1. To form the plural of most common nouns, add *-s.* If a noun ends in *-ch, -sh, -s,* or *-x,* form its plural by adding *-es.*

   > **common noun:** A word that names a general class of person (*teacher*), place (*dormitory*), thing (*car*), or concept (*freedom*)

attack, attacks	umbrella, umbrellas
boss, bosses	zone, zones
sandwich, sandwiches	trellis, trellises
tax, taxes	crash, crashes

2. To form the plural of a common noun ending in *-o,* add *-s* if the *-o* follows a vowel and *-es* if it follows a consonant.

radio, radios	video, videos
hero, heroes	potato, potatoes

3. To form the plural of a common noun ending in *-y,* change the *y* to *i* and add *-es* if the *y* follows a consonant. Add only *-s* if the *y* follows a vowel.

baby, babies	sissy, sissies
toy, toys	day, days

4. To form the plural of a proper noun, add *-s* or *-es.* Proper nouns follow the same rules as common nouns, with one exception: a proper noun never changes its spelling in the plural form.

   > **proper noun:** A capitalized word that names a specific person (*Professor Graham*), place (*Milwaukee*), thing (*Cadillac*), or concept (*New Deal*)

Mary Jane, Mary Janes	Dr. Maddox, the Maddoxes
Professor Jones, the Joneses	Saturday, Saturdays

5. To form the plural of a compound noun, add *-s* or *-es* to the chief word or to the last word if all the words are equal in weight.

brother-in-law, brothers-in-law	actor-manager, actor-managers
aide-de-camp, aides-de-camp	tractor-trailer, tractor-trailers

6. Memorize the plural forms of nouns that diverge from these rules. Certain nouns have special plurals. Here are a few:

alumna, alumnae	half, halves	mouse, mice
alumnus, alumni	leaf, leaves	self, selves
child, children	man, men	tooth, teeth
goose, geese	medium, media	woman, women

Suffixes.   The *-s* added to a word to make it plural is one type of *suffix,* or tail section. Suffixes allow the same root word to do a variety of jobs, giving it different forms for different functions.

1. Drop a silent *e* before a suffix that begins with a vowel.

   move, mover, moved, moving   argue, arguer, argued, arguing

   EXCEPTION: If the *e* has an essential function, keep it before adding a suffix that begins with a vowel. In *singe,* for instance, the *e* changes the word's pronunciation from "sing" to "sinj." If you dropped the *e* in *singeing,* it would become *singing.*

   singe, singed, singeing   tiptoe, tiptoed, tiptoeing

2. Keep a silent *e* before a suffix that begins with a consonant.

   move, movement   hope, hopeless

   EXCEPTION: In a word ending in a silent *e* preceded by a vowel, sometimes (but not always) drop the *e.*

   argue, argument   true, truly

3. Change a final *y* to *i* before a suffix if the *y* follows a consonant but not if the *y* follows a vowel.

   cry, crier, cried   joy, joyous, joyful
   happy, happiest, happily   pray, prayed, prayer
   hurry, hurried

   EXCEPTION: Keep the *y* whenever the suffix is *-ing.*

   hurry, hurrying   pray, praying

   Drop a final *y* before the suffix *-ize.*

   deputy, deputize   memory, memorize

4. Double the final consonant of a one-syllable word before a suffix if (1) the suffix starts with a vowel *and* (2) the final consonant follows a single vowel.

   sit, sitter, sitting   rob, robbed, robbery

   Don't double the final consonant if it follows two vowels or another consonant.

   fail, failed, failure   stack, stacking, stackable

Don't double the final consonant if the suffix starts with a consonant.

>   top, topless   cap, capful

5. Double the final consonant of a word with two or more syllables if (1) the suffix starts with a vowel *and* (2) the final consonant follows a single vowel *and* (3) the last syllable of the stem is accented once the suffix is added.

>   commit, committed, committing   rebut, rebuttal
>   regret, regretted, regrettable

Don't double the final consonant if it follows more than one vowel —

>   avail, available   repeat, repeating

— or if it follows another consonant —

>   accent, accented   depend, dependence

— or the suffix starts with a consonant —

>   commit, commitment   jewel, jewelry

— or, when the suffix is added, the final syllable of the stem is unaccented.

>   confer, conference (*but* conferred)   travel, traveler

Prefixes.   The main point to remember when writing a word with a *prefix* (or nose section) is that the prefix usually does not alter the spelling of the root word it precedes.

> For advice on using a hyphen with a prefix, see 32c and 32d.

>   dis + appear = disappear   mis + understand = misunderstand
>   dis + satisfied = dissatisfied   with + hold = withhold
>   mis + step = misstep   un + necessary = unnecessary

33b Develop spelling skills.

Besides becoming familiar with the rules in this chapter, you can use several other tactics to teach yourself to be a better speller.

1. *Use mnemonic devices.* To make unusual spellings stick in your memory, invent associations. Using such mnemonic devices (tricks to aid memory) may help you with whatever troublesome spelling you are determined to remember. *Weird* behaves *weirdly.* Rise a*gain,* B*rit*ain! One *d* in *dish,* one in *radish.* Why isn't *mathe*matics like *athletics?* You write a *letter* on stationery. Any silly phrase or sentence will do, as long as it brings tricky spellings to mind.

2. *Keep a record of words you misspell.* Buy yourself a little notebook in which to enter words that invariably trip you up. Each time you proofread a paper you have written and each time you receive one back from your instruc-

tor, write down any words you have misspelled. Then practice pronouncing, writing, and spelling them out loud until you have mastered them.

3. *Check any questionable spelling by referring to your dictionary,* your good-as-gold best friend. Use it to check words as you come up with them and to double-check them as you proofread and edit. If you are multilingual and originally learned British English, a good dictionary will distinguish American and British spellings (*color, colour; terrorize, terrorise*).

4. *Learn commonly misspelled words.* To save you the trouble of looking up every spelling bugbear, the "Quick Editing Guide" has a list of words frequently misspelled (see D2). This list will serve to review our whole discussion of spelling, for it contains the trickiest words we've mentioned. Checkmark those that give you trouble—but don't stop there. Spend a few minutes each day going over them. Pronounce each one carefully or have a friend read the list to you. Spell every troublesome word out loud; write it ten times. Your spelling will improve rapidly.

■ Exercise 33–1

Spelling

■ For more practice, visit <bedfordstmartins.com/bedguide> and do a key-word search:

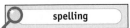

■ For helpful spelling lists, see D2 in the Quick Editing Guide (the dark-blue-edged pages).

Edit the following passage to correct misspelled words. Example:

> Exercize has several beneficial effects beyond improving strength and endureance.

> *Exercise* has several beneficial effects beyond improving strength and *endurance*.

You probly know about some of the benefits that exercisers recieve, but did you know that improved mental functioning might be one of them? A recent study found that human subjects who took up arobic exercise for three months grew new nerve cells—a fenomenon that earlyer studys suggested was impossible. It appears that physical activity improves the flow of blood and protiens known as growth factors to the brain, causing nerve cells to sprout and connect. This growth is limited to a part of the brain involved in learning and memry, but the affects can be significant. The arguement that exercise might help Alzheimer's patients remains controvershul. By the time people develope that disease, their brains may be too damaged, and quick fixs are unlikely to help. Reserchers advice that people get a checkup before comiting to an exercise program. Then, they should get close to an hour of moderit to strenuous exercise for most days of the weak. Couch potatos, you now have more good reasons than ever to get up and get moving.

Appendix
Quick Research Guide

When you begin college, you may feel awkward, uncertain about what to say and how to speak up. As you gain experience, you will join the intellectual exchange around you by reading, thinking, and writing with sources. For many college papers, you will be expected to turn to sources such as articles, books, and Web sites for the evidence needed to support your thesis and develop your ideas about it. This expectation reflects the academic view that knowledge advances through exchange: each writer reads and responds to the writing of others, building on earlier discussion while expanding the conversation.

This Quick Research Guide is designed to help you succeed in several common research situations. Conducting any research requires time to explore, to think, and to respond. However, efficient and purposeful research can produce greater success in less time than random searching or optimistic browsing.

Perhaps you are writing a paper based primarily on your own experience or observation, but you want to add a dash of supporting evidence from a source or two, using a simple research process. Maybe you want a warm-up to build your confidence before you tackle an extensive research project. Possibly you need good advice fast: you've procrastinated, you're overwhelmed by conflicting demands on your time, or you're uncertain about how to succeed as a college researcher.

■ For more on writing processes, see Ch. 1, any chapter (4–12) in Part Two, or Chs. 16–20.

To help you in such cases, this Quick Research Guide concentrates on five key steps: defining your quest, searching for recommended sources, evaluating those you find, adding evidence from them to your paper, and citing them correctly.

TURNING TO SOURCES FOR SUPPORTING EVIDENCE

DEFINE → **SEARCH** → **EVALUATE** → **ADD** → **CITE**

A   *Defining Your Quest*

Especially when your research goals are limited to finding pertinent evidence from only a few sources, you're more likely to be successful if you try to define the hunt in advance by considering questions such as these.

PURPOSE CHECKLIST

For more about stating and using a thesis, see pp. 312–19.

___ What is the thesis that you want to support, the point that you want to demonstrate, or the question you want to answer?

___ Does the assignment require or suggest any specific research focus — certain types of supporting evidence, sources, or presentations of material?

___ Which of your ideas do you want to support with good evidence?

___ Which of your ideas might you want to check, clarify, or change based on your research?

___ Which ideas or opinions of others do you want to verify or counter?

___ Do you want to analyze material yourself (for example, comparing different articles or Web sites) or to find someone else's analysis?

For more about types of evidence, see pp. 40–41.

___ What kinds of evidence do you want to use — facts, statistics, or expert testimony? Do you also want to add your own firsthand observation of the situation or scene?

A1   Consider the criteria of writers and readers.

Although supporting evidence can come from many sources — your experience, observation, imagination, or interaction with others — college instructors often expect you to turn to the writings of others. In those books, articles, and reports, you can find pertinent examples, illustrations, details, and expert testimony — in short, reliable information that will show that your claims and statements are sound. That evidence should satisfy you as a writer and also meet the criteria of your college readers — your instructors and possibly your classmates.

TWO VIEWS OF SUPPORTING EVIDENCE

COLLEGE WRITER	COLLEGE READER
• Does it answer my question and support my thesis?	• Is it relevant to the purpose and assignment?
• Does it seem accurate?	• Is it reliable, given academic standards?
• Is it recent enough?	• Is it current, given the standards of the field?
• Does it add enough depth?	• Is it of sufficient quantity, variety, and strength?
• Is it balanced enough?	• Is it typical, fair, and complex?
• Will it persuade my audience?	• Does the writer make a credible case?

For evidence check-lists, see p. 40 and p. A-6.

A2 Decide what supporting evidence you need.

When you need to add muscle to your college papers, the right resources can supply the facts, statistics, and expert testimony to back up your point. Sometimes you won't need comprehensive information about the topic, but you will want to hunt — quickly and efficiently — for exactly what you do need. Suppose, for example, that you are proposing solutions to your community's employment problem. Because you already have ideas based on your firsthand observations and the experiences of people you know, your research goals are limited. First, you want to add accurate facts and figures that will show why you believe a compelling problem exists. Next, you want to visit the Web sites of local educational institutions and possibly locate someone to interview about existing career development programs.

WORKING THESIS

Many residents of Aurora need more — and more innovative — post-secondary educational opportunities to improve their job skills and career alternatives.

Types of Evidence	DEFINITION	EXAMPLE	SOURCE
FACTS	Statements that can be verified objectively	When employment opportunities drop, college enrollments tend to go up because people are motivated to increase their skills.	Colorado Commission on Higher Education, "Governor's Task Force to Strengthen and Improve the Community College System: Final Report, April 5, 2004," page 16, at <www.state.co.us/cche>
STATISTICS	Facts stated in numbers	According to the U.S. Census Bureau, 85% of Aurora residents over age 25 have graduated from high school, 4.6% more than the national average. However, only 24.6% of this group have graduated from college, only 0.2% better than the 24.4% national average.	"Profile of Selected Social Characteristics: 2000" for Aurora, Colorado, and for United States, *U.S. Census Bureau Fact* at <http://factfinder.census.gov/home/saff/main.html?_lang=en>
EXPERT TESTIMONY	Information from a knowledgeable person who has studied or gained experience about the topic	According to information supplied by a representative of the Center for Workforce Development, students who join the Essential Skills certificate program gain computer and customer relations skills, earn college credits, and participate in an internship.	Center for Workforce Development Web page, <http://www.ccaurora.edu/industry/workforce_development.html>, and Essential Skills for the Workplace Certificates, <http://www.ccaurora.edu/programs/certificates/2006_2007/Essential%20Skills%20Cert%2006-07.pdf>
FIRSTHAND OBSERVATION	Your own unbiased, accurate eyewitness account	At the campus Web site and during my visit to the Community College of Aurora to interview a workforce specialist, I observed publicity for programs in computer systems, paramedic training, criminal justice, law enforcement, and early childhood education.	Your notes, your collection of campus materials, and your Web printouts

For more about these types of evidence, see pp. 40–41.

A3   Decide where you need supporting evidence.

Sometimes you will know exactly what your paper needs. In fact, as you plan or draft, you may tuck in notes to yourself—find this, look that up, add some numbers here. Other times, you may sense that your paper isn't as strong as you want it to be, but you may not know exactly what to add or where to add it. One way to determine where you need supporting evidence is to examine your draft, sentence by sentence.

- What does each sentence claim or promise to a reader?
- Where do you provide supporting evidence to demonstrate the claim or fulfill the promise?

The answers to these questions — your statements and your supporting evidence — often fall into a common alternating pattern:

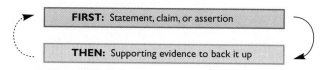

FIRST: Statement, claim, or assertion

THEN: Supporting evidence to back it up

When you spot a string of assertions without much support, you have found a place where you might need more evidence. Select your evidence carefully so that it substantiates the exact statement, claim, or assertion that precedes it. Likewise, if you spot a string of examples, details, facts, quotations, or other evidence, introduce or conclude it with an interpretive statement that explains the point the evidence supports. Make sure your general statement connects and pulls together all of the particular evidence.

When Carrie Williamson introduced the topic of her cause-and-effect paper, "Rain Forest Destruction," she made a general statement and then supported it by quoting facts from a source. Then she repeated this statement-support pattern, backing up her next statement in turn. By using this pattern from the very beginning, Carrie reassured her readers that she was a trustworthy writer who would try to supply convincing evidence throughout the rest of her paper.

■ For more about arguments based on claims of substantiation, evaluation, or policy, see pp. 152–54.

■ For more on inductive and deductive reasoning, see pp. 42–43.

■ For the source entries from Carrie Williamson's MLA list of works cited, see pp. A-22–A-24.

The tropical rain forests are among the most biologically diverse communities in the world. According to *Rainforestweb.org*, "More than 50 percent of the Earth's species live in tropical rainforests," and the "typical four-square-mile patch of tropical rainforest contains up to 1,500 species of flowering plants, 750 tree species, 125 mammal species, 400 bird species, 100 reptile species, 60 amphibian species, and 150 butterfly species" ("Rainforest Data"). These amazing communities that depend on each part being intact in order to function properly and successfully are being destroyed at an alarming rate. Each year "an area larger than Italy" (Soltani) is destroyed. Many rain forest conservationists debate what the leading cause of deforestation is. Regardless of which one is the major cause, the fact remains that both logging and slash-and-burn farming are destroying more and more acres of rain forests each year.

⅂– Statement

Supporting evidence: Statistics about species

├ Statement

Supporting evidence: Facts about destruction

Statement identifying cause-and-effect debate

Statement previewing points to come

Besides checking for the statement-support pattern, consider your paper's overall purpose, organization, and line of reasoning. The table on page A-6 shows some of the many ways this common statement-support pattern can be used to clarify and substantiate your ideas.

FIRST: STATEMENT, CLAIM, OR ASSERTION	THEN: POSSIBLE SUPPORTING EVIDENCE
Introduces a topic	Facts or statistics to justify the importance or significance of the topic
Describes a situation	Factual examples or illustrations to convey the reality or urgency of the situation
Introduces an event	Accurate firsthand observations to describe an event that you have witnessed
Presents a problem	Expert testimony or firsthand observation to establish the necessity or urgency of a solution
Explains an issue	Facts and details to clarify or justify the significance of the issue
States your point	Facts, statistics, or examples to support your viewpoint or position
Interprets and prepares readers for evidence that follows	Facts, examples, observations, or research findings to define and develop your case
Concludes with your recommendation or evaluation	Facts, examples, or expert testimony to persuade readers to accept your conclusion

Use the following checklist to help you decide whether — and where — you might need supporting evidence from sources.

EVIDENCE CHECKLIST

___ What does your thesis promise that you'll deliver? What additional evidence would ensure that you effectively demonstrate your thesis?

___ Are your statements, claims, and assertions backed up with supporting evidence? If not, what evidence might you add?

___ What evidence would most effectively persuade your readers?

___ What criteria for useful evidence are most important to your readers? What evidence would best meet these criteria?

___ Which parts of your paper sound weak or incomplete to you?

___ What facts or statistics would clarify your topic?

___ What examples or illustrations would make the background or the current circumstances clearer and more compelling for readers?

___ What does a reliable expert say about the situation your topic involves?

___ What firsthand observation would add authenticity?

___ Where have peer editors or your instructor suggested adding more evidence or stronger evidence?

B   *Searching for Recommended Sources*

Even researchers who need specific evidence from only a source or two may turn first to the nearly limitless Internet. However, random Web sites are likely to require you to do extra work — checking all the information presented as fact, looking for biases or financial motives, and searching for what's not stated rather than simply accepting what is. Such caution is required because anyone — expert or not — can build a Web site, write a blog, post a message in a public forum, or circulate an e-mail message. Repetition does not ensure the accuracy, reliability, or integrity of online information because the Internet as a whole has no quality controls.

On the other hand, when your college library buys books, subscribes to scholarly journals, and acquires reference materials, whether print or electronic, these publications are expected to follow accepted editorial practices. Well-regarded publishers and professional groups turn to peer reviewers — experts in the field — to assess articles or books before they are selected for publication. Their readers, in turn, count on these traditional quality controls to bring them material that meets academic or professional standards. When you need to conduct an efficient search, quick and focused, try to begin with reliable sources, already screened and recommended by professionals.

B1   Seek advice about reliable sources.

Although popular search engines can turn up sources on nearly any topic, you always need to ask whether those sources meet your criteria and your readers'. After all, your challenge is not simply to find any sources but to find solid sources with reliable evidence for a college paper. Very often your instructors will guide your search by specifying their requirements or general expectations. In addition, the following short-cuts can help you find solid sources fast — ideally already screened, selected, and organized for you.

RESOURCE CHECKLIST

___ Has your instructor suggested to the class where you might begin? Have you talked with your instructor after class, during office hours, or by e-mail to ask for specific advice about resources for your topic? Have you checked the assignment sheet, syllabus, handouts, or class Web site?

___ Have your classmates recommended useful academic databases, disciplinary Web sites, or similar resources?

___ Does the department offering the course have a Web site with lists of resources available at the library or links to sites well regarded in that field?

___ Does your textbook Web site provide links to additional resources?

—— Which library databases does the librarian at the reference desk recommend for your course level and your topic?

—— Which databases or links on your library's Web site lead to government (federal, state, or local) resources or articles in journals and newspapers?

—— Which resources are available on library terminals, in the new periodicals room, or in the reference area of your college library?

B2 Select reliable sources that meet your readers' criteria.

If you planned to investigate common Internet hoaxes for a paper about online practices, you might deliberately turn to sources that are, by definition, unreliable. However, in most cases, you want to turn right away to reliable sources. The charts on pages A-10–A-11 explain how to recognize different types of sources, gauge their currency, and select those appropriate for a given topic or assignment.

Each type of source analyzed in these charts might be credible and useful for a paper. For certain assignments, you might be expected to use sources as varied as reports from journalists, advice from practitioners in the field, accounts of historical eyewitnesses, or opposing opinions on civic policy. However, college instructors often expect you to turn not to popular sources but to scholarly ones — also identified as peer-reviewed or refereed sources — with characteristics such as these:

- in-depth investigation or interpretation of an academic topic or research problem

- discussion of previous studies, which are cited in the text and listed at the end for easy reference by readers

- use of research methods accepted in a discipline or several fields

- publication by a reputable company or sponsoring organization

- acceptance for publication based on reviews by experts (peer reviewers) who assess the quality of the study

- preparation for publication supervised by academic or expert editors or by authors and professional staff

Your instructors may be more confident of the quality controls of established publications, appearing in print or in simultaneous print and online versions, than of the procedures of newer or unfamiliar electronic sources. Your campus librarian can help you limit your searches to peer-reviewed journals or check the scholarly reputation of sources that you find.

C   *Evaluating Possible Sources*

You may dream that your research will instantly turn up the perfect source. Like the perfect wave, the perfect snowy slope, or the perfect day, such a source is likely to be hard to come by. After all, by what standards will you judge perfection? And what are the odds that you will find such perfection ever, much less during your limited research schedule? Instead of looking for perfect sources, most college researchers evaluate sources on the basis of their own practical needs, the standards of their readers, and the shared concern of writers and readers for reliable, appropriate evidence.

■ For exercises on evaluating Web sources in particular, visit <bedfordstmartins.com/bedguide> and do a keyword search:

evaluate

C1   Evaluate sources as a practical researcher.

Your situation as a writer may determine how long or how widely you can search for what you need or how deeply you can delve into the sources you find. For example, if you are worried about finishing your paper on time or about juggling several assignments at once, you will need to search efficiently, evaluating sources first in terms of your own practical criteria.

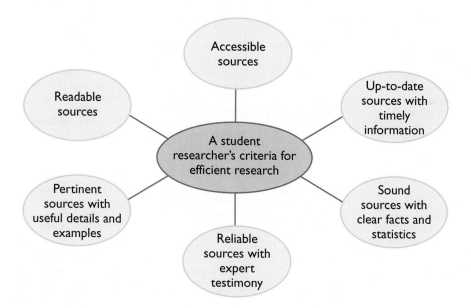

C2   Evaluate sources as your readers would.

You will want to consider what your readers expect of the sources you select and the way that you use them. If you are uncertain about college requirements, start with recommended sources that are easily accessible, readable, and

Understanding Print Sources and Their Applications	LIKELY APPEARANCE	TYPICAL PUBLICATION TIME FRAME	EXAMPLES	BEST FOR
SCHOLARLY BOOK	In-depth discussion, often hardbound with a plain cover, that presents research findings, references, and few, if any, illustrations to an academic audience	Months or years, probably following months or years for research and writing	*Improving Classroom Testing, The Information Society: A Skeptical View, The Psychology of Aggression, Theodore Roosevelt and His Times*	In-depth analysis and research into established academic topics
POPULAR NONFICTION BOOK	Trendy or topical hardbound or paperback publication, often with an eye-catching cover, that conveys information, advice, or instructions to general readers	Months or years, possibly following months or years for writing	*The World Is Flat, The Year of Magical Thinking, General Ike, A Short History of Nearly Everything*	Overview of current trends or issues, informative advice, personal experience, or life story
SCHOLARLY JOURNAL	Quarterly or monthly text-heavy publication, often sponsored by a scholarly group, with prominent table of contents listing long articles directed to specialists	Months (or longer), probably following months or years of research and writing	*American Economic Review, Journal of the American Medical Association (JAMA), PMLA (Publications of the Modern Language Association), Science and Technology Review*	In-depth, up-to-date research on discipline-specific topics
NEWS MAGAZINE	Weekly or monthly publication with color cover, photographs, and short articles (sometimes collaborative) on news stories, current events, and societal trends	Days or weeks, following current or long-term investigation	*Time, Newsweek, U.S. News & World Report*	The latest news on topics of regional, national, or international significance
POPULAR MAGAZINE	Colorful weekly, biweekly, or monthly publication with attention-grabbing cover, sidebars, photographs, and articles on its special interest	Days, weeks, or months, following immediate or long-term development	Range from *Atlantic Monthly, National Geographic, Psychology Today,* and *Smithsonian* to *People, Redbook,* and *US* (serious topics and in-depth stories to hobbies or celebrities)	Current information on popular issues or trends and subjects that interest readers
NEWSPAPER	Daily, weekly, or monthly publication with oversized pages, headlines, columns, photographs, graphics, and stories on current news and timely issues	Days or weeks, following current or long-term investigation	*New York Times, Washington Post, Wall Street Journal, Chronicle of Higher Education,* your local or regional newspaper	The latest news and opinions on topics of local, regional, state, national, or international significance
PAMPHLET OR BOOKLET	Brief paperbound publications, appearing irregularly, individually, or in a series, often sponsored by a scholarly, civic, business, government, or other group or agency	Days or months, following development of material	*GE Annual Report, The Unicorn Tapestries, Children of John and Sophia Walz, Medical History of Washington County with Some Personal Recollections*	In-depth coverage of specific topics, viewpoints, advice, or recollections of groups or individuals
REFERENCE WORK	Book or multivolume encyclopedia, handbook, dictionary, directory, almanac, atlas, fact book, or other informative guide, usually in the library's reference area	Months or years, probably following months or years for research and writing	*Encyclopedia of the Harlem Renaissance, Biographical Dictionary of Hispanic Americans, Oxford Dictionary of Literary Quotations, Facts on File, Atlas of World Cultures*	Concise background explanations, definitions, facts, statistics, biographies, and other specifics

Understanding Electronic Sources and Their Applications	LIKELY APPEARANCE	TYPICAL PUBLICATION TIME FRAME	EXAMPLES	BEST FOR
ONLINE REFERENCE SITE	Prominent search box, search options for fields or topics, links to specialized gateways or resources	Immediate, daily, or regular updates	*Infomine* at <http://infomine.ucr.edu>, *Internet Public Library* at <www.ipl.org>, *Librarians' Internet Index* at <www.lii.org>, *WWW Virtual Library* at <http://vlib.org>, *or Ask* at <www.ask.com>	Quick access to prescreened resources and links for researchers
GATEWAY SITE FOR A TOPIC OR FIELD	Prominent focus on discipline or topic with search or category options	Regular or irregular updates, depending on sponsor or Webmaster	*The American Civil-War Homepage* at <http://sunsite.utk.edu/civil-war>, *William Faulkner on the Web* at <www.mcsr.olemiss .edu/~egjbp/faulkner/ faulkner.html>	Quick access to prescreened resources and links on specific subjects
ONLINE DOCUMENT COLLECTION	List of available documents, groups of documents, or search options such as author or title	Regular or irregular updates, depending on materials or Webmaster	*Bartleby* at <http://bartleby.com>, *Project Gutenberg* at <http://gutenberg.org>, *American Memory* at <http://memory.loc.gov>	Easy access to large collections of texts and visuals
PROFESSIONAL WEB SITE	Conspicuous promotion of sponsor such as scholarly or field group, nonprofit agency, corporation, or foundation (.org, .net, or .com)	Regular or irregular updates, depending on sponsor	American Educational Research Association at <www.aera.net>, Better Business Bureau at <http://bbb.org>, MetLife Foundation, search at <www .metlife.com>	Resources or specialized materials related to sponsor's interests
ACADEMIC WEB SITE	Attractive presentation of institution (.edu) and its academic and other units	Regular or irregular updates, depending on academic or other unit maintaining page	College Web sites such as your campus site, library home page, or department or course page	Disciplinary and cross-disciplinary resources from campus units
GOVERNMENT WEB SITE	Prominent focus on federal, state, local, or other agencies (.gov), often with links and a search box	Regular or irregular updates, depending on government agency	Government gateways at <www.usa.gov>, agencies such as the Census Bureau at <http://factfinder .census.gov> or Environmental Protection Agency at <www.epa.gov>	Topic-specific statistics, reports, information about legislation and policies, consumer publications
ONLINE NEWSPAPER OR NEWS SERVICE	Banner headline of news organization with breaking news, section options, and archives	Immediate updates as events occur along with archives of past coverage	Online *New York Times, Washington Post, Wall Street Journal,* or local newspapers	The latest national or international news and views
INTEREST-GROUP OR PERSONAL WEB SITE	Logo or banner for partisan or special-interest group, discussion group, or individual pages or blogs (Web logs)	Regular or irregular updates, depending on individual or group	Democracy for America at <www .democracyforamerica .com>, Young Republicans at <www.yrnf.org>, ArtsJournal at <www.artsjournal.com>	Wide range of views, resources, opinions, and counterarguments which require evaluation of bias

up-to-date—and chock full of the reliable facts, statistics, research findings, case studies, observations, examples, illustrations, and expert testimony that will persuade your readers.

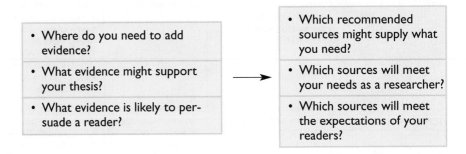

C3 Evaluate sources for reliable and appropriate evidence.

When you use evidence from sources to support your points, both you and your readers are likely to hold two simple expectations:

- that your sources are reliable so you can trust their information
- that the information you select from them is appropriate for your paper

After all, how could an unreliable source successfully support your ideas? And what could unsuitable or mismatched information contribute to your paper? The difficult task, of course, is learning how to judge what is reliable and appropriate. The following checklist suggests how you can use the time-tested journalist's questions—who, what, when, where, why, and how—to evaluate each print or electronic source that you consider using.

EVALUATION CHECKLIST

Who?

___ Who is the author of the source? What are the author's credentials and experience?

___ Who is the intended audience of the source?

___ Who publishes the source or sponsors the site? Is this publisher well regarded? Is the source aimed at an academic or a general audience?

___ Who has reviewed the source before publication? Only the author? Expert peer reviewers? An editorial staff?

What?

___ What is the purpose of the publication or Web site? Is it trying to sell, inform, report, or shape opinion?

—— What bias or point of view might affect the reliability of the source?

—— What evidence does the source present? Does the source seem trustworthy and logical? Does it identify its sources or supply active links?

When?

—— When was the source published or created?

—— When was it revised to stay up-to-date?

Where?

—— Where did you find the source?

—— Where is the source recommended? Has your library prescreened it?

Why?

—— Why would you use this source rather than others?

—— Why is its information relevant to your research question?

How?

—— How does the source reflect its author, publisher or sponsor, and audience? How might you need to qualify its use in your paper?

—— How would this source support your thesis and provide persuasive evidence?

D   *Capturing, Launching, and Citing Evidence Added from Sources*

Sometimes researchers concentrate so hard on hunting for reliable sources that they forget what comes next. The value of every source remains potential until you successfully capture its facts, statistics, expert testimony, examples, or other information in a form that you can incorporate into your paper. In addition, you need to launch — or introduce — the information in order to identify its source or its contribution to your paper. Finally, you must accurately cite, or credit, both in the text of your paper and in a final list of sources, each source whose words or ideas you use. (Follow the advice of the Modern Language Association, supplied here, or whatever other system your instructor requires.)

CAPTURE → **LAUNCH** → **CITE**

D1   Avoid plagiarism.

Be sure to allow enough time to add information from sources skillfully and correctly. Find out exactly how your instructor expects you to credit sources. Even if you do not intend to plagiarize—to use another writer's words or

■ For exercises on supporting a thesis statement, visit <bedfordstmartins.com/bedguide> and do a keyword search:

support

■ For examples in both MLA and APA style, see E1–E2.

■ For exercises on incorporating source material and avoiding plagiarism, visit <bedfordstmartins.com/bedguide> and do a keyword search:

sources

ideas without appropriately crediting them — a paper full of sloppy or careless short cuts can look just like a paper deliberately copied from unacknowledged sources. Instead, borrow carefully and honestly, fully acknowledging your debt to writers from whom you borrow anything.

Identify the source of information, an idea, a summary, a paraphrase, or a quotation right away, as soon as you write it in your notes. Carry that acknowledgment into your first draft and all that follow. You generally do not need to identify a source if you use what is called "common knowledge" — quotations, expressions, or information widely known and widely accepted. If you are uncertain about whether you need to cite a source, ask your instructor, or simply provide the citation.

The following chart reviews accepted methods of adding source material and identifies good research practices. These practices will help prevent common errors that may call into question your integrity or your attentiveness as a research writer.

D2 **Read your source critically.**

For more on critical reading, see Ch. 2.
For more on evaluating evidence, see pp. 39–40.
For more on logical fallacies, see pp. 162–63.

Before you pop any outside material into your paper, read critically to evaluate the reliability and suitability of the source. If you cannot understand a complicated source that requires specialized background, don't use it in your paper. If its ideas, facts, claims, or viewpoint seem unusual, incorporate only what

Accepted Methods of Adding and Crediting Source Material	OBJECTIVES OF METHOD	GOOD PRACTICES TO AVOID ERRORS
QUOTATION	Select and identify the exact words of a source in order to capture its vitality, authority, or incisiveness for your paper.	• Repeat the exact words of the source or properly indicate changes. • Use both opening and closing quotation marks. • Provide the page number or other location of the quotation in the source. • Supply complete identification of the source.
PARAPHRASE	Restate the detailed ideas of a source in your own words and sentences, with credit to the original source, in order to capture the content of a passage.	• Read carefully so that you can paraphrase accurately without distorting the source. • Use your own words and sentences to avoid following the pattern, sequence, or wording of the original. • Rephrase or add quotation marks to identify words from the source that slip into or add to your paraphrase.

Accepted Methods of Adding and Crediting Source Material	OBJECTIVES OF METHOD	GOOD PRACTICES TO AVOID ERRORS
PARAPHRASE (CONTINUED)		• Provide the page number or other location of the original passage in the source. • Clearly distinguish between the paraphrase and your own ideas to avoid confusing switches. • Supply complete identification of the source.
SUMMARY	Very briefly express the main point or key ideas of a source or passage in your own words, with credit to the original source, in order to capture its essential ideas or conclusion.	• Read carefully so that you can summarize accurately without distorting the source. • Rephrase or add quotation marks to identify words from the source that slip into your summary. • Give specific credit to the source for ideas that you include in your discussion. • Clearly distinguish between the summary and your own ideas to avoid confusing switches. • Supply complete identification of the source.
IN-TEXT CITATION	Credit each quotation, paraphrase, summary, or other reference to a source in short form by giving the author's last name in the text of the paper or with the page number in parentheses (MLA style).	• Supply consistent citations without forgetting or carelessly omitting sources. • Spell names of authors and titles correctly. • Provide accurate page references.
CONCLUDING LIST OF WORKS CITED	Credit each source cited in the text with a corresponding full entry in an alphabetical list at the end of the paper.	• Match each source citation in the text with an entry in the final list. • Provide consistent entries without forgetting or carelessly omitting sources. • Supply every detail expected in an entry, even if you must return to the library or go online to complete your source notes. • Follow the exact sequence, capitalization, punctuation, indentation pattern, and other details required by MLA or another style. • Check that each entry in your final list appears in alphabetical order.

you can substantiate in other unrelated sources. On the other hand, if its evidence seems accurate, logical, and relevant, consider exactly how you might want to add it to your paper — by quoting, paraphrasing, or summarizing.

D3   Quote accurately.

For advice about how to quote, see pp. 214–15; for more examples see E1.

For more on punctuating quotations and using ellipsis marks, see C3 in the Quick Editing Guide (the dark-blue-edged pages).

When you are taking notes from a source, record as many quotations as you want if that process helps you master the material. When you add quotations to your paper, however, be selective. Limit your direct quotations to compelling selections; after all, a quotation in itself is not necessarily effective evidence, and too many quotations will suggest that your writing is padded or lacks original thought. Be certain that you quote exactly, and credit your source using the format expected. Use the following questions to check the accuracy of your quotation.

QUOTATION CHECKLIST

___ Have you quoted only a notable passage that adds support and authority to your discussion?

___ Have you checked your quotation to be sure that it repeats your source word for word?

___ Have you marked the beginning and the ending of the quotation with quotation marks?

___ Have you used ellipses (. . .) to mark any spot where you have left out words in the original?

___ Have you identified the source of the quotation in a launch statement (see p. A-18) or in parentheses?

___ Have you specified in parentheses the page number where the quotation appears in the source?

D4   Paraphrase carefully.

For advice about how to paraphrase, see pp. 218–19.

While a quotation presents an idea in the exact and memorable words of a source, a paraphrase does the reverse. A paraphrase presents a passage from a source in your own words and sentences. It may include the same level of detail that the original does, but it should not slip into the wording of the original (unless you identify those snippets with quotation marks). Be sure to credit the original source when you paraphrase, just as you do when you quote. Use the following questions to help you keep your paraphrase fresh.

PARAPHRASE CHECKLIST

___ Have you read the passage critically to be sure that you fully understand it?

___ Have you paraphrased accurately, reflecting both the main points and the supporting details in the original?

—— Does your paraphrase use your own words without repeating or echoing the words or the sentence structure of the original?

—— Does your paraphrase stick to the ideas of the original without tucking in your own thoughts?

—— Have you reread and revised your paraphrase so that it reads smoothly and clearly?

—— Have you identified the source of the paraphrase in a launch statement (see p. A-18) or in parentheses?

—— Have you specified in parentheses the page number where the passage appears in the source?

D5   Summarize fairly.

Unlike a quotation or a paraphrase, a summary reduces the ideas of a source to their essence. Even though a summary uses your own words, you still must clearly identify the source. Your summary may boil a book, a chapter, an article, or a section down to a few sentences that accurately and clearly sum up the sense of the original. Use the following questions to help you assess the success of your summary.

For advice about how to summarize, see p. 220.

SUMMARY CHECKLIST

—— Have you fairly stated the author's thesis, or main point, in your own words in a sentence or two?

—— Have you briefly stated any supporting ideas that you wish to summarize?

—— Have you stuck to the overall point without getting bogged down in details or examples?

—— Has your summary remained respectful of the ideas and opinions of others, even if you disagree with them?

—— Have you reread and revised your summary so that it reads smoothly and clearly?

—— Have you identified the source of the summary in a launch statement (see D6) or in parentheses?

—— Have you specified in parentheses the page number where any specific passage appears in the source?

D6   Launch and cite each quotation, paraphrase, and summary.

Instead of dropping ideas from sources into your paper as if they had just arrived by flying saucer, weave them in so that they effectively support the point you want to make. As you integrate each idea from a source, take three steps.

1. Capture. Begin with the supporting evidence you have captured from your source in a quotation, paraphrase, or summary. Refine this material so that it will fit smoothly into your paper. Reduce your quotation to its most memorable words, freshen the wording of your paraphrase, or increase the precision of your summary. Position the evidence where it is needed to support your statements, claims, or assertions.

2. Launch. Launch, or introduce, the material captured from each source. Avoid tossing stand-alone quotations into your paper or stacking up a series of paraphrases and summaries. Instead, lead smoothly into your source information. As you write a launch statement, try to draw on the authority of the source, mention the author's credentials, or connect the material to other sources or your points. Let readers know why you have selected this evidence and what you think it contributes to your paper.

For more on launch statements, see pp. 223–24.

For more on punctuating quotations, see C3 in the Quick Editing Guide (the dark-blue-edged pages).

Dalton, long an advocate of "green" construction, recommends a five-year plan to . . . (18).

As a specialist in elder law, attorney Tamara Diaz suggests . . . .

Like Westin, regional director Neil urges that ". . ." (308). Brown, however, takes an innovative approach to local conservation practices and recommends . . . (108).

Another policy analyst, arguing from principles expressed in the Bill of Rights, maintains . . . (Frank 96).

While Congress pits secure borders against individual liberties, immigration analyst Smith proposes a third possibility that might . . . (42).

3. Cite. Identify each source briefly yet accurately.

For examples showing how to cite and list sources in your paper, see section E.

- Name the author in parentheses (unless already named in your launch statement).
- In APA style, add the date of the source.
- Add the page number to locate the original passage.
- If a source has no author, begin the citation with the first words of the title.
- Add a full entry for each source to a list at the end of your paper.

E   *Citing and Listing Sources in MLA or APA Style*

For exercises on citing and listing sources in MLA style, visit <bedfordstmartins.com/bedguide> and do a keyword search:

cite

MLA style is the format for crediting sources that is recommended by the Modern Language Association and often required in English classes. APA style is the format recommended by the American Psychological Association, often used in the social sciences, business, and some composition classes. These two styles are widely used in college papers, but your specialized courses may require other academic styles, depending on the field. Because instructors expect you to credit sources carefully, follow any directions or examples supplied, or refer to the style manual required. Although academic styles all credit sources, they have many detailed differences. Stick to the one expected.

In both the MLA and APA styles, your sources need to be identified twice in your paper: first, briefly, at the very moment you draw upon the source material and later, in full, at the end of your paper. The short reference includes the name of the author of the source (or a short form of the title if the source does not name an author), so it's easy for a reader to connect that short entry in your text with the related full entry in the final alphabetical list.

EI   Cite sources in your text.

MLA STYLE

Right in the text, at the moment you add a quotation, a paraphrase, or a summary, you need to identify the source. Your citation generally follows a simple pattern: name the author, and note the page in the original where the material is located.

(Last Name of Author ##)   (Talia 35)   (Smitt and Gilbert 152–53)

Place this citation immediately after a direct quotation or paraphrase.

> When "The Lottery" begins, the reader thinks of the "great pile of stones" (Jackson 191) as children's entertainment.

When the author is named in your launch statement, the citation can be even simpler.

> According to Hunt, the city faced "deficits and drought" (54) for ten more years.

For quotations from poems, plays, or novels, supply line, act and scene, or chapter numbers rather than page numbers.

> The speaker in Robinson's poem describes Richard Cory as "richer than a king" (line 9), an attractive man who "fluttered pulses when he said,/ 'Good-morning'" (7–8).

If you use only one source in your paper, identify it at the beginning of your essay. Then just give page or line numbers in parentheses after each quotation or paraphrase.

Use the following checklist to improve your source citations.

CITATION CHECKLIST

____ Have you placed your citation right after your quotation, paraphrase, or summary?

____ Have you enclosed your citation with a pair of parenthesis marks?

____ Have you provided the last name of the author either in your launch statement or in your citation?

____ Have you used the title for a work without an identified author?

—— Have you added the exact page, as numbered in the source, or another location number (such as a Web paragraph, poetry line, novel chapter, or play act and scene) to identify where the source material appears?

APA STYLE

After the author's last name, add the date. Use p. (for "page") or pp. (for "pages") before the page numbers.

> (Last Name of Author, Date, p. ##)   (Talia, 2007, p. 35)
> (Smith & Gilbert, 2004, pp. 152–153)

E2   List sources at the end.

At the end of your paper, add a list of your sources. For each source mentioned in the text, supply a corresponding full entry. Use this checklist to improve the accuracy of your entries.

WORKS CITED CHECKLIST

—— Have you figured out what type of source you have used? Have you followed the sample pattern for that type as exactly as possible?

—— Have you used quotation marks and underlining (MLA) or italics (APA) correctly for titles?

—— Have you used correct punctuation — periods, commas, colons, parentheses — in your entry?

—— Have you checked the accuracy of the numbers in your entry—pages, volume, and dates?

—— Have you accurately recorded the name of the author, title, publisher, and so on?

—— Have you correctly typed the address of an electronic source (or supplied a simpler address for the source's search page)?

—— Have you correctly arranged your entries in alphabetical order?

—— Have you checked your final list against your text citations so that every source appears in both places?

—— Have you double-spaced your list just like your paper, without any extra space between entries?

—— Have you begun the first line of each entry in your list at the left margin? Have you indented each additional line as you would indent a paragraph? (To do this automatically, use your software's "hanging" indentation option, possibly in the Format-Paragraph-Indentation-Special menu.)

The secret to figuring out what to include in a Works Cited entry generally comes down to this question about your source: What is it? Once you identify the type of source you have used, you can find a general pattern for it in this book or in your style guide. Then, using this pattern, you can examine the title page or other parts of your source to find the details needed to complete the pattern.

MLA STYLE

Call your list of sources Works Cited. Use the following examples as patterns for your entries. For each type of source, supply the same information in the same order using the same punctuation or other features.

BOOK

TEXT CITATION

(Rosenzweig 7)

WORKS CITED ENTRY

Author's name   Period   Title of book, italicized

Rosenzweig, Michael L. *Win-Win Ecology: How the Earth's Species Can Survive in the Midst of Human Enterprise*. New York: Oxford UP, 2003. Print.

Period   City of   Publisher   Year of   Period Medium of   Period
          publication   (shortened   publication   publication
                         name)

If you need to find formats for other types of sources, consult the current *MLA Handbook for Writers of Research Papers*, often available in the library, or check your research manual or research guide for more information.

ESSAY, STORY, OR POEM FROM A BOOK

TEXT CITATION

(Brady 498)

WORKS CITED ENTRY

Author of   Title of selection,   Title of book or
selection   in quotation marks   anthology, italicized

Brady, Judy. "I Want a Wife." *The Bedford Guide for College Writers*. 8th ed.
    Ed. X. J. Kennedy, Dorothy M. Kennedy, and Marcia F. Muth. ── Authors or editors of book
        Boston: Bedford, 2008. 497-99. Print. ── Period

City of   Publisher   Year of   Page numbers   Medium of
publication (shortened   publication   of the selection publication
             name)

See the title page of this book and the reading on page 497 to find the details needed for this entry.

POPULAR MAGAZINE ARTICLE

The author's name and the title generally appear at the beginning of an article. Typically, the magazine name, the date, and page numbers appear at the bottom of pages. Arrange the date in this order: 4 Oct. 2007.

See the *Utne Reader* and *Parenting* samples on p. 394.

TEXT CITATION

(Lobel 45)

WORKS CITED ENTRY

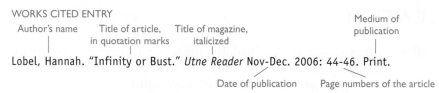

Author's name   Title of article,   Title of magazine,   Medium of
                 in quotation marks   italicized   publication

Lobel, Hannah. "Infinity or Bust." *Utne Reader* Nov-Dec. 2006: 44-46. Print.

                                    Date of publication   Page numbers of the article

If the author is not identified, simply begin with the title of the article.

"How We Celebrate July 4th." *Parenting* June-July 2003: 22-23. Print.

SCHOLARLY JOURNAL ARTICLE

Include the volume and issue numbers separated by a period: 98.5. Include only the year of publication in parentheses: (2007).

TEXT CITATION

(Baller 30)

WORKS CITED ENTRY

Author's name   Title of journal article in quotation marks

Baller, William. "Farm Families and the American Revolution." *Journal of Family History*

     31.1 (2006): 28-44. Print.   Title of journal,
                                                             italicized
     Volume   Year   Page numbers   Medium of
     and issue Colon of the article   publication
     numbers

ARTICLE FROM A LIBRARY DATABASE

For databases like *InfoTrac*, the full publication information for the print source often appears at the top of the online entry. A printout of the article usually will record this information as well as your date of access. Note that the first page number of the print source can be followed by a hyphen if the full page range is not known.

TEXT CITATION

See p. A-5 for the text reference from Carrie Williamson's paper.

The page number is not included because it is not available in the online version.

(Soltani)

WORKS CITED ENTRY

Author's   Pages of   Name of   Title of
name   Date   print version   Title of article   database   magazine

Soltani, Atossa. "Every Tree Killed Equals Another Life Lost." *Wood and Wood*

     Products 100.3 (1995): 86-. *Expanded Academic ASAP*. Web. 4 Apr. 2007.

     Volume and   Medium of   Date of
     issue numbers   publication   access

PAGE FROM A WEB SITE

The page title and site title often appear at the top of a given page. The date when a site was posted or last updated often appears at the bottom, as does the name of the sponsor. (However, sponsor information may appear as a link.) A print-out of the page will record this information as well as the date of access.

TEXT CITATION

The site is identified by title because it does not name an author. The page number is not included because it is not available for the Web page.

According to *Rainforestweb.org*, . . .

■ See p. A-5 for the text reference from Carrie Williamson's paper.

WORKS CITED ENTRY

| No author identified | Title of page, in quotation marks | | Title of site, italicized |

"Rainforest Data and Research." *Rainforestweb.org: World Rainforest Information Portal.*

   Rainforest Action Network, 2001. Web. 5 Apr. 2007.

| Name of sponsor | Date posted or updated | Medium of publication | Date of visit |

APA STYLE

Call your list of sources References. Use the following examples as patterns for your entries. For each type of source, supply the same information in the same order using the same punctuation or other features.

   If you need to find formats for other types of sources, consult the current *Publication Manual of the American Psychological Association,* often available in the library, or check your research manual or research guide for more information.

BOOK

TEXT CITATION

(Rosenzweig, 2003, p. 7)

REFERENCES ENTRY

Rosenzweig, M. L. (2003). *Win-win ecology: How the earth's species can survive in the midst of human enterprise.* Oxford, England: Oxford University Press.

WORK OR SECTION IN A BOOK

TEXT CITATION

(Brady, 1971/2008, p. 497)

■ Turn to the title page of this book and the reading selection on p. 497 to find the details needed for this entry.

REFERENCES ENTRY

Brady, J. (2008). I want a wife. In X. J. Kennedy, D. M. Kennedy, & M. F. Muth (Eds.), *The Bedford guide for college writers* (8th ed., pp. 497-499). Boston, MA: Bedford/St. Martin's. (Original work published 1971)

POPULAR MAGAZINE ARTICLE

Add any volume number (in italics) and a comma after the magazine title.

TEXT CITATION

("How We Celebrate," 2003, p. 22)

REFERENCES ENTRY

How we celebrate July 4th. (2003, June/July). *Parenting*, 22–23.

See the *Parenting* sample on p. 394.

SCHOLARLY JOURNAL ARTICLE

TEXT CITATION

(Niemi & Herrnson, 2003, p. 318)

REFERENCES ENTRY

Nieme, R. G., & Herrnson, P. S. (2003). Beyond the butterfly: The complexity of U.S. ballots. *Perspectives on Politics, 1*, 317-326.

ARTICLE FROM A LIBRARY DATABASE

IN-TEXT CITATION

Neither a page nor a paragraph number is available for the online article.

See p. A-5 for the text reference from Carrie Williamson's paper.

(Soltani, 1995)

REFERENCES ENTRY

Soltani, A. (1995). Every tree killed equals another life lost. *Wood and Wood Products, 100*(3), 86-87. Retrieved from Expanded Academic ASAP database.

PAGE FROM A WEB SITE

TEXT CITATION

The site is identified by title because it does not identify an author.

According to *Rainforestweb.org* ("Rainforest Data," 2001), . . .

REFERENCES ENTRY

Add your access date if the site may change.

Rainforest data and research. (2001). *Rainforestweb.org: World rainforest information portal*. Retrieved April 7, 2007, from http://www.rainforestweb.org/Rainforest_Information/Rainforest_Data_and_Research/

Appendix

Quick Editing Guide

Editing and proofreading are needed at the end of the writing process because writers — *all* writers — find it difficult to write error-free sentences the very first time they try. Sometimes as a writer you pay more attention to

Editing with a Computer

Computers can help you edit in several ways. Grammar checkers will catch some errors, but not others. For this reason, you always need to consider the grammar checker's suggestions carefully before accepting them.

FOR E-WRITERS

- A grammar checker cannot always correctly identify the subject or verb in a sentence; it may question whether a sentence is complete or whether its subject and verb agree, even when the sentence is correct.

- Grammar checkers are likely to miss certain problems such as misplaced modifiers, faulty parallelism, possessives without apostrophes, or incorrectly positioned commas.

- Most grammar checkers do a good job of spotting problems with adjectives and adverbs, such as confusing *good* and *well*.

You can also use your word processor to search for your own typical problems. Begin by keeping track of your mistakes so that you can develop an "error hit list." Then try to figure out how to use your software's Find and Replace capacity (probably in the Edit menu) to check quickly for some of these problems. For instance, you might search for all instances of *each* (always singular) or *few* (always plural) to see if all the verbs agree.

The computer can also help you read your draft more closely. For example, you can automatically isolate each sentence so that you are less likely to skip over sentence errors. First make a copy of your draft. Then select Replace in your software's Edit menu. Ask the software to find every period in the file and replace it with a period and two returns. This change will create a version with each sentence separated by several spaces so that you can easily check every one for fragments, comma splices, or other problems.

what you want to say than to how you say it. Sometimes you inaccurately remember spelling or grammar or punctuation. At other times you are distracted or simply make keyboarding errors. Once you are satisfied that you have expressed your ideas, you should make sure that each sentence and word is concise, clear, and correct.

For advice on writing more concisely, see pp. 379–81.

This Quick Editing Guide provides an overview of grammar, style, punctuation, and mechanics problems typical of college writing. Certain common errors in Standard Written English are like red flags to careful readers: they signal that the writer is either ignorant or careless. Use the editing checklist below to check your paper for these problems; then use the editing checklists in each section to help you correct specific errors. Concentrate on any problems likely to reappear in your writing.

For editing and proof-reading strategies, see pp. 384–87.

EDITING CHECKLIST

Common and Serious Problems in College Writing

Grammar Problems

___ Have you avoided writing sentence fragments?	**A1**
___ Have you avoided writing comma splices or fused sentences?	**A2**
___ Have you used the correct form for all verbs in the past tense?	**A3**
___ Do all verbs agree with their subjects?	**A4**
___ Have you used the correct case for all pronouns?	**A5**
___ Do all pronouns agree with their antecedents?	**A6**
___ Have you used adjectives and adverbs correctly?	**A7**

Sentence Problems

___ Does each modifier clearly modify the appropriate sentence element?	**B1**
___ Have you used parallel structure where needed?	**B2**

Punctuation Problems

___ Have you used commas correctly?	**C1**
___ Have you used apostrophes correctly?	**C2**
___ Have you punctuated quotations correctly?	**C3**

Mechanics and Format Problems

___ Have you used capital letters correctly?	**D1**
___ Have you spelled all words correctly?	**D2**
___ Have you used correct manuscript form?	**D3**

A *Editing for Common Grammar Problems*

A1 Check for any sentence fragments.

A complete sentence is one that has a subject, has a predicate, and can stand on its own. A *sentence fragment* lacks a subject, a predicate, or both, or for some other reason fails to convey a complete thought. It cannot stand on its own as a sentence.

Although they are common in advertising and fiction, fragments are usually ineffective in college writing because they do not communicate coherent thoughts. To edit for fragments, examine each sentence carefully to make sure that it has a subject and a verb and that it expresses a complete thought. To correct a fragment, you can make it into a complete sentence by adding a missing part, dropping an unnecessary subordinating conjunction, or joining it to a complete sentence nearby, if that would make more sense.

subject: The part of a sentence that names something—a person, an object, an idea, a situation—about which the predicate makes an assertion: The *king* lives.

predicate: The part of a sentence that makes an assertion about the subject involving an action (Birds *fly*), a relationship (Birds *have feathers*), or a state of being (Birds *are warm-blooded*)

subordinating conjunction: A word (such as *because, although, if, when*) used to make one clause dependent on, or subordinate to, another: *Unless* you have a key, we are locked out.

FRAGMENT	Roberto has two sisters. Maya and Leeza.
CORRECT	Roberto has two sisters, Maya and Leeza.
FRAGMENT	The children going to the zoo.
CORRECT	The children were going to the zoo.
CORRECT	The children going to the zoo were caught in a traffic jam.
FRAGMENT	Last night when we saw Cameron Diaz's most recent movie.
CORRECT	Last night we saw Cameron Diaz's most recent movie.

EDITING CHECKLIST

Fragments

___ Does the sentence have a subject?

___ Does the sentence have a complete verb?

___ If the sentence contains a subordinate clause, does it contain a clause that is a complete sentence too?

___ If you find a fragment, can you link it to an adjoining sentence, eliminate its subordinating conjunction, or add any missing element?

■ For exercises on fragments, visit <bedfordstmartins.com/bedguide> and do a keyword search:

fragments

A2 Check for any comma splices or fused sentences.

A complete sentence has a subject and a predicate and can stand on its own. When two sentences are joined together to form one sentence, each sentence within the larger one is called a *main clause*. However, there are rules for joining main clauses, and when writers fail to follow these rules, they create

main clause: A group of words that has both a subject and a verb and can stand alone as a complete sentence: *My sister has a friend.*

coordinating conjunction: A one-syllable linking word (*and, but, for, or, nor, so, yet*) that joins elements with equal or near-equal importance: Jack *and* Jill, sink *or* swim

subordinating conjunction: A word (such as *because, although, if, when*) used to make one clause dependent on, or subordinate to, another: *Unless* you have a key, we are locked out.

serious sentence errors — comma splices or fused sentences, also called run-on sentences. A *comma splice* is two main clauses joined with only a comma. A *fused sentence* is two main clauses joined with no punctuation at all.

COMMA SPLICE	I went to the mall, I bought a new coat.
FUSED SENTENCE	I went to the mall I bought a new coat.

To find comma splices and fused sentences, examine each sentence to be sure it is complete. If it has two main clauses, make sure they are joined correctly. If you find a comma splice or fused sentence, correct it in one of these four ways, depending on which makes the best sense:

ADD A PERIOD	I went to the mall. I bought a new coat.
ADD A COMMA AND A COORDINATING CONJUNCTION	I went to the mall, and I bought a new coat.
ADD A SEMICOLON	I went to the mall; I bought a new coat.
ADD A SUBORDINATING CONJUNCTION	I went to the mall where I bought a new coat.

■ For exercises on comma splices and fused sentences, visit <bedfordstmartins.com/bedguide> and do a key-word search:

🔍 splice_fused

EDITING CHECKLIST

Comma Splices and Fused Sentences

—— Can you make each main clause a separate sentence?
—— Can you link the two main clauses with a comma and a coordinating conjunction?
—— Can you link the two main clauses with a semicolon or, if appropriate, a colon?
—— Can you subordinate one clause to the other?

verb: A word that shows action (The cow *jumped* over the moon) or a state of being (The cow *is* brown)

A3　Check for correct past tense verb forms.

The *form* of a verb, the way it is spelled and pronounced, can change to show its *tense* — the time when its action did, does, or will occur (in the past, present, or future). A verb about something in the present will often be spelled and pronounced differently than a verb about something in the past.

PRESENT	Right now, I *watch* only a few minutes of television each day.
PAST	Last month, I *watched* television shows every evening.

Many writers fail to use the correct form for past tense verbs for two different reasons, depending on whether the verb is regular or irregular.

Regular verbs are verbs whose forms follow standard rules; they form the past tense by adding *-ed* or *-d* to the end of the present tense form: *watch/watched, look/looked, hope/hoped.* Check all regular verbs in the past tense to be sure you have used one of these endings.

FAULTY	I *ask* my brother for a loan yesterday.
CORRECT	I *asked* my brother for a loan yesterday.
FAULTY	Nicole *race* in the track meet last week.
CORRECT	Nicole *raced* in the track meet last week.

TIP: If you say the final *-d* sound when you talk, you may find it easier to add the final *-d* or *-ed* when you write past tense regular verbs.

Irregular verbs do not follow standard rules to make their forms. Their unpredictable past tense forms have to be memorized: *eat/ate, see/saw, get/got.* In addition, the past tense form may differ from the past participle: "She *ate* the whole pie; she *has eaten* two pies this week." The most troublesome irregular verbs are actually very common, so if you make the effort to learn the correct forms, you will quickly improve your writing.

▨ For a chart showing the forms of many irregular verbs, see pp. A-30–A-31.

FAULTY	My cat *laid* on the tile floor to take her nap.
CORRECT	My cat *lay* on the tile floor to take her nap.
FAULTY	I *have swam* twenty laps every day this month.
CORRECT	I *have swum* twenty laps every day this month.

participle: A form of a verb that cannot function alone as a main verb, including present participles ending in *-ing* (*dancing*) and past participles often ending in *-ed* or *-d* (*danced*)

TIP: In college papers, follow convention by using the present tense, not the past, to describe the work of an author or the events in a literary work.

FAULTY	In "The Lottery," Shirley Jackson *revealed* the power of tradition. As the story *opened*, the villagers *gathered* in the square.
CORRECT	In "The Lottery," Shirley Jackson *reveals* the power of tradition. As the story *opens*, the villagers *gather* in the square.

EDITING CHECKLIST

Past Tense Verb Forms

___ Have you identified the main verb in the sentence?

___ Is the sentence about the past, the present, or the future? Does the verb reflect this sense of time?

___ Is the verb regular or irregular?

___ Have you used the correct form to express your meaning?

▨ For exercises on verbs, visit <bedfordstmartins.com/bedguide> and do a keyword search:

verbs

Principal Parts of Common Irregular Verbs

INFINITIVE (BASE)	PAST TENSE	PAST PARTICIPLE
be	was	been
become	became	become
begin	began	begun
blow	blew	blown
break	broke	broken
bring	brought	brought
burst	burst	burst
catch	caught	caught
choose	chose	chosen
come	came	come
do	did	done
draw	drew	drawn
drink	drank	drunk
drive	drove	driven
eat	ate	eaten
fall	fell	fallen
fight	fought	fought
freeze	froze	frozen
get	got	got, gotten
give	gave	given
go	went	gone
grow	grew	grown
have	had	had
hear	heard	heard
hide	hid	hidden
know	knew	known
lay	laid	laid
lead	led	led
let	let	let
lie	lay	lain
make	made	made
raise	raised	raised
ride	rode	ridden
ring	rang	rung
rise	rose	risen
run	ran	run
say	said	said
see	saw	seen
set	set	set
sing	sang	sung
sit	sat	sat
slay	slew	slain
slide	slid	slid
speak	spoke	spoken

INFINITIVE (BASE)	PAST TENSE	PAST PARTICIPLE
spin	spun	spun
stand	stood	stood
steal	stole	stolen
swim	swam	swum
swing	swung	swung
teach	taught	taught
tear	tore	torn
think	thought	thought
throw	threw	thrown
wake	woke, waked	woken, waked
write	wrote	written

For the forms of irregular verbs not on this list, consult your dictionary. (Some dictionaries list principal parts for all verbs, some just for irregular verbs.)

A4   Check for correct subject-verb agreement.

The *form* of a verb, the way it is spelled and pronounced, can change to show *number*—whether the subject is singular (one) or plural (more than one). It can also show *person*—whether the subject is *you* or *she,* for example.

SINGULAR	Our instructor *grades* every paper carefully.
PLURAL	Most instructors *grade* tests using a standard scale.
SECOND PERSON	You *write* well-documented research papers.
THIRD PERSON	She *writes* good research papers, too.

A verb must match (or *agree with*) its subject in terms of number and person. Regular verbs (those that follow a standard rule to make the different forms) are problems only in the present tense, where they have two forms: one that ends in *-s* or *-es* and one that does not. Only the subjects *he, she, it,* and singular nouns use the verb form that ends in *-s* or *-es.*

I like	we like	Dan likes
you like	you like	the child likes
he/she/it likes	they like	the children like

The verbs *be* and *have* do not follow the *-s/no -s* pattern to form the present tense; they are irregular verbs, so their forms must be memorized. The verb *be* is also irregular in the past tense.

Problems in agreement often occur when the subject is difficult to find, is an indefinite pronoun, or is confusing for some other reason. In particular, make sure that you have not left off any *-s* or *-es* endings and that you have used the correct form for irregular verbs.

verb: A word that shows action (The cow *jumped* over the moon) or a state of being (The cow *is* brown)

subject: The part of a sentence that names something—a person, an object, an idea, a situation—about which the predicate makes an assertion: The *king* lives.

indefinite pronoun: A pronoun standing for an unspecified person or thing, including singular forms (*each, everyone, no one*) and plural forms (*both, few*): *Everyone* is soaking wet.

For a chart showing the forms of many irregular verbs, see pp. A-30–A-31.

Forms of *Be* and *Have* at a Glance

THE PRESENT TENSE OF *BE*

I am	we are
you are	you are
he/she/it is	they are

THE PAST TENSE OF *BE*

I was	we were
you were	you were
he/she/it was	they were

THE PRESENT TENSE OF *HAVE*

I have	we have
you have	you have
he/she/it has	they have

THE PAST TENSE OF *HAVE*

I had	we had
you had	you had
he/she/it had	they had

For exercises on subject-verb agreement, visit <bedfordstmartins.com/bedguide> and do a keyword search:

    sv agreement

FAULTY   Jim *write* at least fifty e-mails a day.
CORRECT   Jim *writes* at least fifty e-mails a day.

FAULTY   The students *has* difficulty with the assignment.
CORRECT   The students *have* difficulty with the assignment.

FAULTY   Every one of the cakes *were* sold at the fundraiser.
CORRECT   Every one of the cakes *was* sold at the fundraiser.

EDITING CHECKLIST

Subject-Verb Agreement

___ Have you correctly identified the subject and the verb in the sentence?
___ Is the subject singular or plural? Does the verb match?
___ Have you used the correct form of the verb?

pronoun: A word that stands in place of a noun (*he, him,* or *his* for *Nate*)
subject: The part of a sentence that names something—a person, an object, an idea, a situation—about which the predicate makes an assertion: The *king* lives.
subject complement: A noun, an adjective, or a group of words that follows a linking verb (*is, become, feel, seem,* or another verb that shows a state of being) and that renames or describes the subject: This plum tastes *ripe.*
object: The target or recipient of the action of a verb: Some geese bite *people.*

A5   Check for correct pronoun case.

Depending on the role a pronoun plays in a sentence, it is said to be in the *subjective case, objective case,* or *possessive case.* Use the subjective case if the pronoun is the subject of a sentence, the subject of a subordinate clause, or a subject complement (after a linking verb). Use the objective case if the pronoun is a direct or indirect object of a verb or the object of a preposition. Use the possessive case to show possession.

SUBJECTIVE   *I* will argue that our campus needs more parking.
OBJECTIVE   This issue is important to *me.*
POSSESSIVE   *My* argument will be quite persuasive.

There are many types of pronouns, but only some change form to show case. The personal pronouns *I, you, he, she, it, we,* and *they* and the relative pronoun *who* each have at least two forms.

Pronoun Cases at a Glance

SUBJECTIVE	OBJECTIVE	POSSESSIVE
I	me	my, mine
you	you	your, yours
he	him	his
she	her	hers
it	it	its
we	us	our, ours
they	them	their, theirs
who	whom	whose

There are two common errors in pronoun case. First, writers often use the subjective case when they should use the objective case—sometimes because they are trying to sound formal and correct. Instead, choose the correct form for a personal pronoun based on its function in the sentence. If the sentence pairs a noun and a pronoun, try the sentence with the pronoun alone.

FAULTY	My company gave my husband and *I* a trip to Hawaii.
PRONOUN ONLY	My company gave *I* a trip?
CORRECT	My company gave my husband and *me* a trip to Hawaii.
FAULTY	The argument occurred because my uncle and *me* had different expectations.
PRONOUN ONLY	*Me* had different expectations?
CORRECT	The argument occurred because my uncle and *I* had different expectations.
FAULTY	Jack ran faster than *me*.
PRONOUN ONLY	Jack ran faster than *me* ran?
CORRECT	Jack ran faster than *I*.

A second common error with pronoun case involves gerunds. Whenever you need a pronoun to modify a gerund, use the possessive case.

FAULTY	Our supervisor disapproves of *us* talking in the hallway.
CORRECT	Our supervisor disapproves of *our* talking in the hallway.

gerund: A form of a verb, ending in *-ing*, that functions as a noun: Lacey likes *playing* in the steel band.

EDITING CHECKLIST

Pronoun Case

___ Have you identified all the pronouns in the sentence?

___ Does each one function as a subject, an object, or a possessive?

___ Given the function of each, have you used the correct form?

■ For exercises on pronoun case, visit <bedfordstmartins.com/bedguide> and do a keyword search:

case

A6 Check for correct pronoun-antecedent agreement.

pronoun: A word that stands in place of a noun (*he, him,* or *his* for *Nate*)

The *form* of a pronoun, the way it is spelled and pronounced, changes depending on its use in a particular sentence. The form can change to show *number* — whether the subject is singular (one) or plural (more than one). It can change to show *gender* — masculine or feminine, for example — or *person*: first (*I, we*), second (*you*), or third (*he, she, it, they*).

SINGULAR	My brother took *his* coat and left.
PLURAL	My brothers took *their* coats and left.
MASCULINE	I talked to Steven before *he* had a chance to leave.
FEMININE	I talked to Stephanie before *she* had a chance to leave.

In most cases, a pronoun refers to a specific noun or pronoun mentioned nearby; that word is called the pronoun's **antecedent.** The connection between the pronoun and the antecedent must be clear so that readers know what the pronoun means in the sentence. One way to make this connection clear is to ensure that the pronoun and the antecedent match (or *agree*) in number and gender.

A common error in pronoun agreement is using a plural pronoun to refer to a singular antecedent. This error often crops up when the antecedent is difficult to find, when the antecedent is an indefinite pronoun, or when the antecedent is confusing for some other reason. When editing for pronoun-antecedent agreement, look carefully to find the correct antecedent, and make sure you know whether it is singular or plural. Then make the pronoun match its antecedent.

FAULTY	Each of the boys in the Classic Club has *their* own rebuilt car.
CORRECT	Each of the boys in the Classic Club has *his* own rebuilt car.

indefinite pronoun: A pronoun standing for an unspecified person or thing, including singular forms (*each, everyone, no one*) and plural forms (*both, few*): *Everyone* is soaking wet.

[The word *each*, not *boys*, is the antecedent. *Each* is an indefinite pronoun and is always singular, so any pronoun referring to it must be singular as well.]

FAULTY	Everyone in the meeting had *their* own cell phone.
CORRECT	Everyone in the meeting had *his or her* own cell phone.

[*Everyone* is an indefinite pronoun that is always singular, so any pronoun referring to it must be singular as well.]

Indefinite Pronouns at a Glance

ALWAYS SINGULAR			ALWAYS PLURAL
anybody	everyone	nothing	both
anyone	everything	one (of)	few
anything	much	somebody	many
each (of)	neither (of)	someone	several
either (of)	nobody	something	
everybody	no one		

FAULTY   Neither Luz nor Pam has received approval of *their* financial aid yet.

CORRECT   Neither Luz nor Pam has received approval of *her* financial aid yet.

[*Neither Luz nor Pam* is a compound subject joined by *nor*. Any pronoun referring to it must agree with only the nearer part of the compound. In other words, *her* needs to agree with *Pam*, which is singular.]

Indefinite pronouns as antecedents are troublesome when they are grammatically singular but create a plural image in the writer's mind. Fortunately, most indefinite pronouns are either always singular or always plural.

EDITING CHECKLIST

Pronoun-Antecedent Agreement

___ Have you identified the antecedent for each pronoun?

___ Is the antecedent singular or plural? Does the pronoun match?

___ Is the antecedent masculine, feminine, or neuter? Does the pronoun match?

___ Is the antecedent first, second, or third person? Does the pronoun match?

■ For exercises on pronoun-antecedent agreement, visit <bedfordstmartins.com/bedguide> and do a keyword search:

pa agreement

A7   Check for correct adjectives and adverbs.

Adjectives and *adverbs* describe or give more information about (*modify*) other words in a sentence. Many adverbs are formed by adding *-ly* to adjectives: *simple, simply; quiet, quietly*. Because adjectives and adverbs resemble one another, writers sometimes mistakenly use one instead of the other. To edit, find the word that the adjective or adverb modifies. If that word is a noun or pronoun, use an adjective. (An adjective typically describes which or what kind.) If that word is a verb, adjective, or another adverb, use an adverb. (An adverb typically describes how, when, where, or why.)

modifier: A word (such as an adjective or adverb), phrase, or clause that provides more information about other parts of a sentence: *Plays staged by the drama class are always successful.*

FAULTY   Kelly ran into the house *quick*.

CORRECT   Kelly ran into the house *quickly*.

Comparison of Irregular Adjectives and Adverbs

	POSITIVE	COMPARATIVE	SUPERLATIVE
ADJECTIVES	good	better	best
	bad	worse	worst
	little	less, littler	least, littlest
	many, some, much	more	most
ADVERBS	well	better	best
	badly	worse	worst
	little	less	least

FAULTY Gabriela looked *terribly* after her bout with the flu.

CORRECT Gabriela looked *terrible* after her bout with the flu.

Adjectives and adverbs that have similar comparative and superlative forms can also cause trouble. Always ask whether you need an adjective or an adverb in the sentence, and then use the correct word.

FAULTY His scar healed so *good* that it was barely visible.

CORRECT His scar healed so *well* that it was barely visible.

Good is an adjective; it describes a noun or pronoun. *Well* is an adverb; it modifies or adds to a verb (*heal*, in this case) or an adjective.

EDITING CHECKLIST

Adjectives and Adverbs

For exercises on adjectives and adverbs, visit <bedfordstmartins.com/bedguide> and do a keyword search:

 adj_adv

____ Have you identified which word the adjective or adverb modifies?

____ If the word modified is a noun or pronoun, have you used an adjective?

____ If the word modified is a verb, adjective, or adverb, have you used an adverb?

____ Have you used the correct comparative or superlative form?

Check your sentences to make sure that they are grammatically correct, especially that they are complete (see A1) with parts that agree (see A4). Use the Draft Doctor (pp. A-38–A-39) to help you figure out how to improve your problem sentences. Skim down the left column to identify questions you might ask about your draft. When you answer a question with "Yes" or "Maybe," move straight across the row to the Diagnose column next to that question. Use the diagnostic activities to identify gaps or weaknesses, and then move straight across the row again to the Treat column on the right. Use the advice that suits your problem, and review the relevant section in this guide.

B *Editing to Ensure Effective Sentences*

B1 Check for any misplaced or dangling modifiers.

modifier: A word (such as an adjective or adverb), phrase, or clause that provides more information about other parts of a sentence: Plays *staged by the drama class* are *always successful.*

For a sentence to be clear, the connection between a modifier and the thing it modifies must be obvious. Usually, a modifier should be placed right before or right after the sentence element it modifies. If the modifier is placed too close to some other sentence element, it is a *misplaced modifier*. If there is nothing in the sentence that the modifier can logically modify, it is a *dangling modifier*. Both of these errors cause confusion for readers — and they sometimes create unintentionally humorous images. As you edit, be sure that a modifier is placed directly before or after the word modified and that the connection between the two is clear.

MISPLACED	George found the leftovers when he visited in the refrigerator.
CORRECT	George found the leftovers in the refrigerator when he visited.

[In the faulty sentence, *in the refrigerator* seems to modify George's visit. Obviously the leftovers are in the refrigerator, not George.]

DANGLING	Looking out the window, the clouds were beautiful.
CORRECT	Looking out the window, I saw that the clouds were beautiful.
CORRECT	When I looked out the window, the clouds were beautiful.

[In the faulty sentence, *looking out the window* should modify *I*, but *I* is not in the sentence. The modifier is left without anything logical to modify—a dangling modifier. To correct this, the writer has to edit so that *I* is in the sentence.]

EDITING CHECKLIST

Misplaced and Dangling Modifiers

___ What is each modifier meant to modify? Is the modifier as close as possible to that sentence element? Is any misreading possible?

___ If a modifier is misplaced, can you move it to clarify the meaning?

___ What noun or pronoun is a dangling modifier meant to modify? Can you make that word or phrase the subject of the main clause? Or can you turn the dangling modifier into a clause that includes the missing noun or pronoun?

■ For exercises on misplaced and dangling modifiers, visit <bedfordstmartins.com/ bedguide> and do a keyword search:

modifiers

B2 Check for parallel structure.

A series of words, phrases, clauses, or sentences with the same grammatical form is said to be **parallel**. Using parallel form for elements that are parallel in meaning or function helps readers grasp the meaning of a sentence more easily. A lack of parallelism can distract, annoy, or even confuse readers.

To use parallelism, put nouns with nouns, verbs with verbs, and phrases with phrases. Parallelism is particularly important in a series, with correlative conjunctions, and in comparisons using *than* or *as*.

correlative conjunction: A pair of linking words (such as *either/or, not only/but also*) that appear separately but work together to join elements of a sentence: *Neither* his friends *nor* hers like pizza.

FAULTY	I like to go to Estes Park for skiing, ice skating, and to meet interesting people.
CORRECT	I like to go to Estes Park to ski, to ice skate, and to meet interesting people.
FAULTY	The proposal is neither practical, nor is it innovative.
CORRECT	The proposal is neither practical nor innovative.
FAULTY	A parent should have a few firm rules rather than having many flimsy ones.
CORRECT	A parent should have a few firm rules rather than many flimsy ones.

Draft Doctor: Correcting Major Sentence Errors

If you sense a problem, ASK	If you answer Yes/Maybe, DIAGNOSE	If you diagnose a problem, TREAT
Incomplete Sentences or Fragments? Have I written any sentences that actually might be incomplete?	• Check the parts of short or choppy sentences carefully. Put an * by any word group that does not state a verb. FRAGMENT (NO VERB): The fish in Trio Lake.* • Put an X by any word group that does not state a subject. FRAGMENT (NO SUBJECT): Suffer from illnesses and strange growth patterns. X • Underline any word group that begins with a subordinating word such as *because, although,* or *unless.* FRAGMENT: Unless state regulations change.	• Complete any sentence you have marked with an * or an X by adding the missing element (subject or verb) or by joining the incomplete part to a nearby complete sentence (see A1). COMPLETE (MISSING WORDS ADDED, IN ITALICS): The fish in Trio Lake *suffer from illnesses and strange growth patterns.* OR The fish in Trio Lake *are unhealthy. They* suffer from illnesses and strange growth patterns. • Connect any word group you have underlined to a nearby complete sentence, or drop the subordinating word and supply any missing words so that the word group can stand alone. COMPLETE: Unless state regulations change, *chemical run-off will continue to damage Trio Lake.* • Complete each sentence (see A1). Edit until it reads smoothly.
Sentences Fused or Spliced Together? Have I run together several sentences that might be incorrectly fused or spliced?	• Check any long sentences that might contain two or more complete sentences spliced together with a comma or simply fused together without any punctuation. • Underline or color code each separate sentence contained in the long sentence. • Mark any comma used to splice the sentences or any unpunctuated fusion. COMMA SPLICE: Organic crops are grown without chemical fertilizers or pesticides, farmers rely on traditional methods.	• Divide separate sentences with a period and a capital letter. DIVIDED: Organic crops are grown without chemical fertilizers or pesticides. Farmers rely on traditional methods. • Connect separate sentences in one of these ways: (1) with a comma and a coordinating conjunction (*and, but, for, or, nor, so, yet*), (2) with a colon or a semicolon, or (3) with a semicolon and a conjunctive adverb (such as *also, however, namely, therefore, finally*) (see A2). CONNECTED: Organic crops are grown without chemical fertilizers

If you sense a problem, ASK	If you answer *Yes/Maybe*, DIAGNOSE	If you diagnose a problem, TREAT
Sentences Fused or Spliced Together? (continued)		or pesticides, *and* farmers rely on traditional methods. • Connect the less important sentence with a subordinating word (for example, *because, despite, although, if, unless* or a relative pronoun such as *who, which, that*). CONNECTED: *Because* organic crops are grown without chemical fertilizers or pesticides, farmers rely on traditional methods. • Experiment and edit to find the version that presents what you mean (see A2).
Agreement Problems? Have I written any sentences whose parts do not match?	• Underline the subject, and note its form (first person *I*, second person *you*, or third person *he, she, it, they*). Double underline the verb, and see whether its form corresponds. • Underline the subject, and note its number (singular for one, plural for more). Double underline the verb or the related pronoun, and see whether it matches the subject. DRAFT: The <u>students</u> who filled out the survey form <u>agrees</u> strongly about the need to expand the studio.	• Correct any mismatched sentence by changing the subject to match the verb or by changing the verb to match the subject. • Watch for words between subject and verb that mislead you into picking the wrong form or number. • When the subject is a collective noun that refers to a group (such as *jury, committee, family*), treat the word as singular if the group acts as a single unit: The board <u>votes</u> <u>its</u> conscience today. Treat it as plural if the members act individually: The board <u>vote</u> as <u>their</u> consciences dictate. REVISED: The <u>students</u> who filled out the survey form <u>agree</u> strongly about the need to expand the studio. • Rewrite an awkward or misaligned sentence (see A4).
Any Other Sentence Errors? After a final look at the sentences in my draft, should I do anything else to correct them?	• Read your draft out loud to yourself, marking any other sentence errors. • Ask your peer editors whether they see other sentences you should correct.	• Return to each mark to complete, divide, connect, align, or otherwise correct any sentence errors. • Consider advice from your peers. • Edit until your sentences are correct and clear (see the Editing Checklist, p. A-26).

Take special care to reinforce parallel structures by repeating articles, conjunctions, prepositions, or lead-in words as needed.

AWKWARD   His dream was that he would never have to give up his routine but he would still find time to explore new frontiers.

PARALLEL   His dream was that he would never have to give up his routine but *that* he would still find time to explore new frontiers.

EDITING CHECKLIST

Parallel Structure

■ For exercises on parallel structure, visit <bedfordstmartins.com/bedguide> and do a keyword search:

parallel

___ Are all the elements in a series in the same grammatical form?
___ Are the elements in a comparison parallel in form?
___ Are the articles, conjunctions, or prepositions between elements repeated rather than mixed or omitted?
___ Are lead-in words repeated as needed?

Check your sentences to figure out how to construct or express them more effectively. Use the Draft Doctor (pp. A-41–A-43) to help you spot sentences with too much passive voice, faulty parallelism, or dull, repetitive, or wordy passages. Skim down the left column to identify questions you might ask about sentences in your draft. When you answer a question with "Yes" or "Maybe," move straight across the row to the Diagnose column next to that question. Use the diagnostic activities to identify gaps or weaknesses, and then move straight across the row again to the Treat column on the right. Use the advice that suits your problem, and review relevant sections of the book as needed.

C *Editing for Common Punctuation Problems*

C1 Check for correct use of commas.

The *comma* is a punctuation mark indicating a pause. By setting some words apart from others, commas help clarify relationships; they prevent the words on a page and the ideas they represent from becoming a jumble. Here are some of the most important conventional uses of commas.

1. Use a comma before a coordinating conjunction (*and, but, for, or, so, yet, nor*) joining two main clauses in a compound sentence.

   The discussion was brief, *so* the meeting was adjourned early.

2. Use a comma after an introductory word or word group unless it is short and cannot be misread.

   After the war, the North's economy developed rapidly.

3. Use commas to separate the items in a series of three or more items.

   The chief advantages will be *speed, durability,* and *longevity.*

4. Use commas to set off a modifying clause or phrase if it is nonrestrictive — that is, if it can be taken out of the sentence without significantly changing the essential meaning of the sentence.

   Good childcare, *which is difficult to find,* should be provided by the employer.

   Good childcare *that is reliable and inexpensive* is the right of every employee.

5. Use commas to set off a nonrestrictive appositive, an expression that comes directly after a noun or pronoun and renames it.

   Sheri, my sister, has a new job as an events coordinator.

6. Use commas to set off parenthetical expressions, conjunctive adverbs, and other interrupters.

   The proposal from the mayor's commission, however, is not feasible.

appositive: A word or group of words that adds information about a subject or object by identifying it in a different way: my dog *Rover,* Hal's brother *Fred*

parenthetical expression: An aside to readers or a transitional expression such as *for example* or *in contrast*

conjunctive adverb: A linking word that can connect independent clauses and show a relationship between two ideas: Armando is a serious student; *therefore,* he studies every day.

EDITING CHECKLIST

Commas

— Have you added a comma between two main clauses joined by a coordinating conjunction?

— Have you added commas needed after introductory words or word groups?

— Have you separated items in a series with commas?

— Have you avoided putting commas before the first item in a series or after the last?

— Have you used commas before and after each nonrestrictive word, phrase, or clause?

— Have you avoided using commas around a restrictive word, phrase, or clause?

— Have you used commas to set off appositives, parenthetical expressions, conjunctive adverbs, and other interrupters?

■ For exercises on commas, visit <bedfordstmartins.com/bedguide> and do a keyword search:

C2 **Check for correct use of apostrophes.**

An *apostrophe* is a punctuation mark that either shows possession (*Sylvia's*) or indicates that one or more letters have intentionally been left out to form a contraction (*didn't*). Because apostrophes are easy to overlook, writers often omit a necessary apostrophe, use one where it is not needed, or put one in the wrong place. An apostrophe is never used to create the possessive form of a pronoun; use the possessive pronoun form instead.

FAULTY   *Mikes* car was totaled in the accident.

CORRECT   *Mike's* car was totaled in the accident.

FAULTY   *Womens'* pay is often less than *mens'.*

CORRECT   *Women's* pay is often less than *men's.*

Draft Doctor: Improving Sentence Style

If you sense a problem, ASK	If you answer *Yes/Maybe*, DIAGNOSE	If you diagnose a problem, TREAT
Passive Voice? Have I relied on sentences in the passive voice instead of the active voice? Could I change a sentence like *The ball was thrown by John* (passive) to *John threw the ball* (active)?	• Reread your sentence. If its subject also performs the action, your sentence is in the active voice. (You might underline the performer and double underline the action.) • If the sentence subject does not perform the action, your sentence is in the passive voice. You have either not identified the performer of the action or tucked the performer into a *by* phrase.	• Consider changing passive voice to active. Make the performer of the action the sentence subject (which reduces extra words by dropping the *by* phrase). PASSIVE: The primate play area <u>was arranged</u> by the zookeeper. (nine words; emphasizes object of the action) ACTIVE: The zookeeper <u>arranged</u> the primate play area. (seven words; emphasizes zookeeper, who performed the action)
Faulty Parallelism? Have I missed opportunities to emphasize comparable ideas by stating them in comparable ways?	• Read your sentences, looking for lists or comparable items. • Underline items in a series to compare the ways you present them (see B2). DRAFT: Observing primates can reveal how they <u>cooperate</u>, <u>their tool use</u>, and <u>building</u> secure nests.	• Rework so that items in a series all follow the same grammatical pattern. • Select the common pattern based on the clarity and emphasis it adds to your sentence. PARALLEL: Observing primates can reveal how they <u>cooperate</u>, <u>use</u> tools, and <u>build</u> secure nests.
Repetitive Sentence Openings? Do I begin too many sentences the same way so that they all sound alike?	• Add a line break at the end of every sentence in a passage to compare your sentence openings. • Highlight any opening patterns that seem repetitive and dull.	• Rewrite for variety if you repeat opening expressions (*During, After, Then, And, Because*). • Rewrite for directness if you repeat indirect openings (*There are, There is, It is*).
Repetitive Sentence Patterns? Have I written sentences that are boring because they are the same length and follow the same pattern?	• Add a line break at the end of every sentence in a passage so you can easily compare their patterns. With software (or on your own), count the words in each sentence. • Search for variations such as colons (:) and semicolons (;) to see how often you use them.	• Vary sentence lengths if they are all about the same. Tuck in a few short, direct sentences. Combine short, choppy sentences. Add an occasional complicated sentence to elaborate on or build up to your point. • If you rarely use colons or semicolons, try adding some for variety.

If you sense a problem, ASK	If you answer *Yes/Maybe*, DIAGNOSE	If you diagnose a problem, TREAT
Dull Sentences? Have I written correct but boring sentences that will not motivate my audience to keep reading?	• Read the sentences in a passage, and highlight the key words or ideas you want to emphasize. • Read a dull passage, and circle the boring, uninteresting, or overused words.	• Rewrite so highlighted words play major roles as active subjects and lively verbs. Position them for emphasis — beginning or ending, not lost in the middle. • Replace circled words with concrete nouns, energetic verbs, or precise adjectives or adverbs.
Disconnected or Scattered Ideas? Have I tended to toss out my ideas without weighting or relating them?	• Highlight the transitional words (*First, second; for example; however*) in your sentences (see pp. 346–49). • Check all the sentences or sentence parts in a passage that seem to be of equal weight.	• Review passages with little highlighting; add more transitions to relate ideas. • In your checked sentences, introduce less significant parts with subordinating words (*because, although*). Use *and* or *but* to coordinate equal parts.
Wordy Sentences? Have I used more words than needed to say what I mean?	• Read your draft out loud. Check anything that sounds long-winded, repetitive, chatty, or clichéd. • Use past papers to help you list your favorite wordy expressions (such as *a large number of* for *many*) or extra words (such as *very* or *really*).	• At each check, rephrase with simpler expressions or more exact words (see pp. 379–81). • Search with your software for wordy expressions; replace or trim them. • Highlight a passage; use the Tools menu to count its words. See how many extra words you can drop.
Any Other Improvements in Sentence Style? After a final look at the sentences in my draft, should I do anything else to improve them?	• Read your draft out loud. Mark any sentences that sound awkward, confusing, or lifeless. • Ask your peer editors how you might make your sentences stronger and more stylish.	• Return to each mark to make weak sentences clear, emphatic, and lively. • Consider the useful suggestions of your peers. • Refer to Section B of this guide as you edit until your sentences express your ideas as you wish them to.

Possessive Personal Pronouns at a Glance

PERSONAL PRONOUN	POSSESSIVE CASE
I	my, mine
you	your, yours (*not* your's)
he	his
she	her, hers (*not* her's)
it	its (*not* it's)
we	our, ours (*not* our's)
they	their, theirs (*not* their's)
who	whose (*not* who's)

FAULTY   Che *did'nt* want to stay at home and study.

CORRECT   Che *didn't* want to stay at home and study.

FAULTY   The dog wagged *it's* tail happily.

CORRECT   The dog wagged *its* tail happily.

FAULTY   *Its* raining.

CORRECT   *It's* raining. [it's = it is]

EDITING CHECKLIST

For exercises on apostrophes, visit <bedfordstmartins.com/bedguide> and do a keyword search:

apostrophe

Apostrophes

___ Have you used an apostrophe when letters are left out in a contraction?

___ Have you used an apostrophe to create the possessive form of a noun?

___ Have you used the possessive case — rather than an apostrophe — to show that a pronoun is possessive?

___ Have you used *it's* correctly (to mean *it is*)?

C3 Check for correct punctuation of quotations.

When you quote the exact words of a person you have interviewed or a source you have read, be sure to enclose those words in quotation marks. Notice how student Betsy Buffo presents the words of her subject in this passage from her essay "Interview with an Artist":

> Derek is straightforward when asked about how his work is received in the local community: "My work is outside the mainstream. Because it's controversial, it's not easy for me to get exposure."

She might have expressed and punctuated this passage in other ways:

> Derek says that "it's not easy" for him to find an audience.

> Derek struggles for recognition because his art falls "outside the mainstream."

If your source is quoting someone else (a quotation within a quotation), put your subject's words in quotation marks and the words he or she is quoting in single quotation marks. Always put commas and periods inside the quotation marks; put semicolons and colons outside.

> As Betsy Buffo explains, "Derek struggles for recognition because his art falls 'outside the mainstream.'"

Substitute an ellipsis mark (. . .) — three spaced dots — for any words you have omitted from the middle of a direct quotation. If you are following MLA style, you may place the ellipses inside brackets ([. . .]) when necessary to avoid confusing your ellipsis marks with those of the original writer. If the ellipses come at the end of a sentence, add another period to conclude the sentence. You don't need an ellipsis mark to show the beginning or ending of a quotation that is clearly incomplete.

In this selection from "Playing Games with Women's Sports," student Kelly Grecian identifies both quotations and an omission:

> "The importance of what women athletes wear can't be underestimated," Rounds claims. "Beach volleyball, which is played . . . by bikini-clad women, rates network coverage" (44).

> For more about quotations from sources, see D3 in the Quick Research Guide (the dark-red-edged pages).

Common errors in punctuating quotations include leaving out necessary punctuation marks or putting them in the incorrect place or sequence.

EDITING CHECKLIST

Punctuation with Quotations

____ Are the exact words quoted from your source enclosed in quotation marks?

____ Are commas and periods placed inside closing quotation marks?

____ Are colons and semicolons placed outside closing quotation marks?

____ Have you used ellipses to show where any words are omitted from the middle of a quotation?

> For exercises on using and punctuating quotation marks, visit <bedfordstmartins.com/ bedguide> and do a keyword search:

quotation

D   *Editing for Common Mechanics and Format Problems*

D1   Check for correct use of capital letters.

Capital letters are used in three general situations: to begin a new sentence; to begin names of specific people, nationalities, places, dates, and things (proper nouns); and to begin main words in titles. Writers sometimes use capital letters where they are not needed, such as for emphasis, or fail to use them where they are needed.

FAULTY	During my Sophomore year in College, I took World Literature, Biology, History, Psychology, and French — courses required for a Humanities Major.
CORRECT	During my sophomore year in college, I took world literature, biology, history, psychology, and French — courses required for a humanities major.

EDITING CHECKLIST

■ For exercises on using capital letters, visit <bedfordstmartins.com/bedguide> and do a keyword search:

Capitalization

— Have you used a capital letter at the beginning of each complete sentence, including sentences that are quoted?
— Have you used capital letters for proper nouns and pronouns?

Capitalization at a Glance

Capitalize the following:

THE FIRST LETTER OF A SENTENCE, INCLUDING A QUOTED SENTENCE
She called out, "Come in! The water's warm."

PROPER NAMES AND ADJECTIVES MADE FROM THEM
Marie Curie   Cranberry Island
Smithsonian Institution   a Freudian reading

RANK OR TITLE BEFORE A PROPER NAME
Ms. Olson   Professor Santocolon

FAMILY RELATIONSHIP ONLY WHEN IT SUBSTITUTES FOR OR IS PART OF A PROPER NAME
Grandma Jones   Father Time

RELIGIONS, THEIR FOLLOWERS, AND DEITIES
Islam   Orthodox Jew   Buddha

PLACES, REGIONS, GEOGRAPHIC FEATURES, AND NATIONALITIES
Palo Alto   the Berkshire Mountains   Egyptians

DAYS OF THE WEEK, MONTHS, AND HOLIDAYS
Wednesday   July   Labor Day

HISTORICAL EVENTS, PERIODS, AND DOCUMENTS
the Boston Tea Party   the Middle Ages   the Constitution

SCHOOLS, COLLEGES, UNIVERSITIES, AND SPECIFIC COURSES
Temple University   Introduction to Clinical Psychology

FIRST, LAST, AND MAIN WORDS IN TITLES OF PAPERS, BOOKS, ARTICLES, WORKS OF ART, TELEVISION SHOWS, POEMS, AND PERFORMANCES
The Decline and Fall of the Roman Empire   "The Lottery"

—— Have you avoided using capital letters for emphasis?

—— Have you used a capital letter for each main word in a title, including the first word and the last word? (Prepositions, coordinating conjunctions, and articles are not considered main words.)

D2 Check spelling.

Misspelled words are difficult to spot in your own writing. You usually see what you think you wrote, and often pronunciation or faulty memory may interfere with correct spelling. When you proofread for spelling, check for words that sound alike but are spelled differently (*accept* and *except,* for example), words that are spelled differently than they are pronounced, words that do not follow the basic rules for spelling English words (*judgment,* for example), and words that you habitually confuse and misspell.

EDITING CHECKLIST

Spelling

—— Have you checked for the words you habitually misspell?

—— Have you checked for commonly confused or misspelled words?

—— Have you applied the standard spelling rules, including their exceptions?

—— Have you checked a dictionary for any words you are unsure about?

—— Have you run your spell checker? Have you read your paper carefully for errors that it would miss?

preposition: A transitional word (such as *in, on, at, of, from*) that leads into a phrase

coordinating conjunction: A one-syllable linking word (*and, but, for, or, nor, so, yet*) that joins elements with equal or near-equal importance

article: The word *a, an,* or *the*

▨ For a list of commonly confused words, see p. A-48. For a list of commonly misspelled words, see pp. A-49–A-51.

▨ For spelling exercises, visit <bedfordstmartins.com/ bedguide> and do a keyword search:

spelling

Checking Your Spelling

If you know the words you habitually misspell, you can use your software's Search or Find functions to locate all instances and check the spelling. Consider keeping track of misspelled words in your papers for a few weeks so you can take advantage of this feature to simplify your editing.

Spell checkers offer a handy alternative to the dictionary, but you need to be aware of their limitations. A spell checker compares the words in your text with the words listed in its dictionary, and it highlights words that do not appear there. (The size of computer spelling dictionaries varies greatly, but most contain fewer entries than a typical college-level dictionary in book form.) A spell checker cannot help you spell words that its dictionary does not contain, including most proper nouns. Spell checkers ignore one-letter words; for example, they will not flag a typographical error such as *s truck* for *a truck.* Nor will they highlight words that are misspelled as different words, such as *except* for *accept, to* for *too,* or *own* for *won.* Always check the spelling in your text by eye *after* you've used your spell checker.

Grammar checkers may note some commonly confused words, but they often do this even when you have used the correct form. Use a dictionary to decide whether to accept the grammar checker's suggestion.

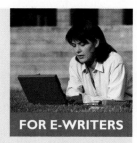

FOR E-WRITERS

COMMONLY CONFUSED HOMONYMS

accept (v., receive willingly); **except** (prep., other than)

Mimi could *accept* all of Lefty's gifts *except* his ring.

affect (v., influence); **effect** (n., result)

If the new rules *affect* us, what will be their *effect*?

allusion (n., reference); **illusion** (n., fantasy)

Any *allusion* to Norman's mother may revive his *illusion* that she is upstairs, alive, in her rocking chair.

capital (adj., uppercase; n., seat of government); **capitol** (n., government building)

The *Capitol* building in our nation's *capital* is spelled with a *capital C*.

cite (v., refer to); **sight** (n., vision or tourist attraction); **site** (n., place)

Did you *cite* Aunt Peg as your authority on which *sites* feature the most interesting *sights*?

complement (v., complete; n., counterpart); **compliment** (v. or n., praise)

For Lee to say that Sheila's beauty *complements* her intelligence may or may not be a *compliment*.

desert (v., abandon; n., hot, dry region); **dessert** (n., end-of-meal sweet)

Don't *desert* us by leaving for the *desert* before *dessert*.

elicit (v., bring out); **illicit** (adj., illegal)

By going undercover, Sonny should *elicit* some offers of *illicit* drugs.

formally (adv., officially); **formerly** (adv., in the past)

Jane and John Doe-Smith, *formerly* Jane Doe and John Smith, sent cards *formally* announcing their marriage.

led (v., past tense of *lead*); **lead** (n., a metal)

Gil's heart was heavy as *lead* when he *led* the mourners to the grave.

principal (n. or adj., chief); **principle** (n., rule or standard)

The *principal* problem is convincing the media that our school *principal* is a person of high *principles*.

stationary (adj., motionless); **stationery** (n., writing paper)

Hubert's *stationery* shop stood *stationary* until a flood swept it away.

their (pron., belonging to them); **there** (adv., in that place); **they're** (contraction of *they are*)

Sue said *they're* going over *there* to visit *their* aunt.

to (prep., toward); **too** (adv., also or excessively); **two** (n. or adj., numeral: one more than one)

Let's not take *two* cars *to* town — that's *too* many unless Hal comes *too*.

who's (contraction of *who is*); **whose** (pron., belonging to whom)

Who's going to tell me *whose* dog this is?

your (pron., belonging to you); **you're** (contraction of *you are*)

You're not getting *your* own way this time!

COMMONLY MISSPELLED WORDS

absence	believe	despair
academic	beneficial	desperate
acceptable	benefited	develop
accessible	breath (noun)	development
accidentally	breathe (verb)	device (noun)
accommodate	bureaucracy	devise (verb)
achievement	business	diary
acknowledgment	calendar	difference
acquaintance	careful	dilemma
acquire	casualties	dining
address	category	disappear
advertisement	cemetery	disappoint
advice	certain	disastrous
advise	changeable	discipline
aggravate	changing	discussion
aggressive	characteristic	disease
aging	chief	dissatisfied
allege	choose (present tense)	divide
all right	chose (past tense)	doesn't
all together (all in	climbed	dominant
one group)	column	don't
a lot	coming	drunkenness
already	commitment	efficiency
although	committed	eighth
altogether (entirely)	comparative	either
amateur	competition	embarrass
analysis	conceive	entirety
analyze	condemn	environment
answer	congratulate	equipped
anxiety	conscience	especially
appearance	conscientious	exaggerate
appetite	conscious	exceed
appreciate	consistent	excel
appropriate	controlled	excellence
arctic	criticism	exercise
argument	criticize	exhaust
ascent	curiosity	existence
assassinate	curious	experience
assistance	deceive	explanation
association	decision	extremely
athlete	defendant	familiar
athletics	deficient	fascinate
attendance	definite	February
audience	dependent	fiery
average	descendant	financial
awkward	describe	foreign
basically	description	foresee
beginning	desirable	forth

(continued)

COMMONLY MISSPELLED WORDS *(continued)*

forty	license	persistence
forward	lightning	personnel
fourth (number four)	literature	persuade
frantically	loneliness	physical
fraternities	loose (adjective)	playwright
friend	lose (verb)	possession
fulfill	lying	possibly
gaiety	magazine	practically
genealogy	maintenance	precede
generally	marriage	predominant
genuine	mathematics	preferred
government	medicine	prejudice
grammar	miniature	prevalent
grief	mischievous	privilege
guarantee	misspell	probably
guard	muscle	procedure
guidance	mysterious	proceed
harass	necessary	professor
height	neither	prominent
heroes	niece	pronounce
herring	ninety	pronunciation
humorous	ninth	pursue
illiterate	noticeable	quantity
illogical	notorious	quiet
imitation	nuclear	quite
immediately	nucleus	quizzes
incredible	numerous	realize
indefinite	obstacle	rebelled
independence	occasionally	recede
indispensable	occur	receipt
infinite	occurrence	receive
influential	official	recipe
intelligence	omission	recommend
intentionally	omitted	reference
interest	opinion	referring
interpret	opportunity	regrettable
interrupt	originally	relevance
irrelevant	outrageous	relief
irresistible	paid	relieve
irritable	pamphlet	religious
island	panicky	remembrance
its (possessive)	parallel	reminisce
it's (it is, it has)	particularly	reminiscence
jealousy	pastime	repetition
judgment	peaceable	representative
knowledge	perceive	resistance
laboratory	performance	restaurant
led (past tense of *lead*)	permanent	review
library	permissible	rhythm

ridiculous	supersede	unnoticed
roommate	suppress	until
sacrifice	surprise	useful
safety	suspicious	usually
scarcely	technical	valuable
schedule	technique	vengeance
secretary	temperature	vicious
seize	tendency	view
separate	therefore	villain
siege	thorough	warrant
similar	thoroughbred	weather
sincerely	though	Wednesday
sophomore	thought	weird
source	throughout	whether
specifically	tragedy	who's (who is)
sponsor	transferred	whose (possessive
strategy	traveling	of *who*)
strength	truly	withhold
stretch	twelfth	woman
succeed	tyranny	women
successful	unanimous	
suddenness	unnecessary	

D3   Check for correct manuscript form.

In case you have received no particular instructions for the form of your paper, here are some general, all-purpose specifications.

GENERAL MANUSCRIPT STYLE FOR COLLEGE ESSAYS, ARTICLES, AND REPORTS

    1. Pick a conventional, easy-to-read typeface such as Courier, Times New Roman, or Palatino. Make sure you have a fresh cartridge in your printer. If you handwrite your paper, keep your handwriting legible.

    2. Print in black ink. Use dark blue or black ink if you write by hand.

    3. Write or print on just one side of standard letter-size bond paper (8½ inches by 11 inches). If you handwrite your paper, use 8½-by-11-inch paper with smooth edges (not torn from a spiral-bound notebook).

    4. For a paper without a separate title page, place your name, your instructor's name, the number and section of the course, and the date in the upper left or right corner of the first page, each item on a new line. (Ask whether your instructor has a preference for which side.) Double-space and center your title. Don't underline the title, don't put it in quotation marks or use all capital letters, and don't put a period after it. Capitalize the first and last words, the first word after a colon or semicolon, and all other words except prepositions, coordinating conjunctions, and articles. Double-space between the title and the first line of your text. (Most instructors do not

■ For more on document design, see Ch. 21. For an example of MLA-style paper format, see p. 391.

preposition: A transitional word (such as *in, on, at, of, from*) that leads into a phrase

coordinating conjunction: A one-syllable linking word (*and, but, for, or, nor, so, yet*) that joins elements with equal or near-equal importance

article: The word *a, an,* or *the*

require a title page for short college papers. If your instructor requests one but doesn't give you any guidelines, see number 1 under Additional Suggestions for Research Papers, below.)

5. Number your pages consecutively, including the first. For a paper of two or more pages, use a running header to put your last name in the upper right corner of each sheet along with the page number. (Use the heading option under View or Edit.) Do not type the word *page* or the letter *p* before the number, and do not follow it with a period or parenthesis.

6. Leave ample margins — at least an inch — left, right, top, and bottom.

7. If you use a word processor, double-space your manuscript; if you handwrite, use wide-ruled paper or skip every other line.

8. Indent each new paragraph five spaces or one-half inch.

For more about citing sources, see D6 and E1 in the Quick Research Guide (the dark-red-edged pages).

9. Long quotations should be double-spaced like the rest of your paper but indented from the left margin — ten spaces (one inch) if you're following MLA (Modern Language Association) guidelines, five spaces (one-half inch) if you're using APA (American Psychological Association) guidelines. Put the source citation in parentheses immediately after the final punctuation mark of the block quotation.

10. Label all illustrations. Make sure any insertions are bound securely to the paper.

11. Staple the paper in the top left corner, or use a paper clip as MLA advises. Don't use any other method to secure the pages unless one is recommended by your instructor.

12. For safety's sake and peace of mind, make a copy of your paper, and back up your file.

ADDITIONAL SUGGESTIONS FOR RESEARCH PAPERS

For research papers, the format is the same as recommended in the previous section, with the following additional specifications.

1. The MLA guidelines do not recommend a title page. If your instructor wants one, type the title of your paper, centered and double-spaced, about a third of the way down the page. Go down two to four more lines and type your name, the instructor's name, the number and section of the course, and the date, each on a separate line and double-spaced.

For examples of MLA and APA documentation style, see E1 and E2 in the Quick Research Guide (the dark-red-edged pages).

2. Do not number your title page; number your outline, if you submit one with your paper, with small roman numerals (i, ii, iii, and so on). Number consecutively all subsequent pages in the essay, including your "Works Cited" or "References" pages, using arabic numerals (1, 2, 3, and so on) in the upper right corner of the page.

3. Double-space your list of works cited or references.

HOW TO MAKE A CORRECTION

Before you produce your final copy, make any large changes in your draft, edit and proofread carefully, and run your spell checker. When you give your paper a last once-over, however, don't be afraid to make small corrections in pen. In making such corrections, you may find it handy to use certain symbols used by printers and proofreaders.

A transposition mark (∩∪) reverses two words or two letters:

The nearby star Tau Ceti closely resmebles our sun.

Close-up marks (⊃) bring together the parts of a word accidentally split. A separation mark (|) inserts a space where one is needed:

The nearby star Tau Ceti closely re sembles our|sun.

To delete a letter or punctuation mark, draw a line with a curlicue through it:

The nearby star Tau Ceti closely ressembles our sun.

Use a caret (∧) to indicate where to insert a word or letter:

The nearby star Tau Ceti closely reembles our sun.

The symbol ¶ before a word or a line means "start a new paragraph":

Recently, astronomers have reduced their efforts to study dark nebulae. ¶ That other solar systems may also support life makes for another fascinating speculation.

To make a letter lowercase, draw a slanted line through it. To make a letter uppercase, put three short lines under it:

i read it for my History class.

You can always cross out a word neatly, with a single horizontal line, and write a better one over it.

closely
The nearby star Tau Ceti somewhat resembles our sun.

Finally, if a page has many corrections on it, print or write it over again.

See the back inside pages of this book for a list of correction symbols.

Appendix

A Glossary of Troublemakers

■ For advice on spelling, see D2 in the Quick Editing Guide (the dark-blue-edged pages). For advice on conciseness, see Ch. 20.

Usage refers to the way in which writers customarily use certain words and phrases, including matters of accepted practice or convention. This glossary lists words and phrases whose usage may trouble writers. Not every possible problem is listed — only some that frequently puzzle students. Refer to this brief list when needed, and follow its cross-references to *A Writer's Handbook.*

a, an   Use *an* only before a word beginning with a vowel sound. *"An* asp can eat *an* egg *an* hour." (Some words, such as *hour* and *honest,* open with a vowel sound even though spelled with an *h.*)

above   Using *above* or *below* to refer back or forward in an essay is awkward and may not be accurate. Instead, try "the *preceding* argument," "in the *following* discussion," "on the *next* page."

accept, except   *Accept* is a verb meaning "to receive willingly"; *except* is usually a preposition meaning "not including." "This childcare center *accepts* all children *except* those under two." Sometimes *except* is a verb, meaning "to exempt." "The entry fee *excepts* children under twelve."

advice, advise   *Advice* is a noun, *advise* a verb. When someone *advises* you, you receive *advice.*

affect, effect   Most of the time, the verb *affect* means "to act on" or "to influence." "Too much beer can *affect* your speech." *Affect* can also mean "to put on airs." "He *affected* a British accent." *Effect,* a noun, means "a result": "Too much beer has a numbing *effect.*" But *effect* is also a verb, meaning "to bring about." "Pride *effected* his downfall."

agree to, agree with, agree on   *Agree to* means "to consent to"; *agree with,* "to be in accord." "I *agreed to* attend the New Age lecture, but I didn't *agree with* the speaker's views." *Agree on* means "to come to or have an understanding about." "Chuck and I finally *agreed on* a compromise: the children would go to camp but not overnight."

ain't   Don't use *ain't* in writing; it is nonstandard English for *am not, is not* (*isn't*), and *are not* (*aren't*).

a lot   Many people mistakenly write the colloquial expression *a lot* as one word: *alot.* Use *a lot* if you must, but in writing *much* or *a large amount* is preferable. See also *lots, lots of, a lot of.*

already, all ready   *Already* means "by now"; *all ready* means "set to go." "At last our picnic was *all ready,* but *already* it was night."

altogether, all together   *Altogether* means "entirely." "He is *altogether* mistaken." *All together* means "in unison" or "assembled." "Now *all together* — heave!" "Inspector Trent gathered the suspects *all together* in the drawing room."

among, between   *Between* refers to two persons or things; *among,* to more than two. "Some disagreement *between* the two countries was inevitable. Still, there was general harmony *among* the five nations represented at the conference."

amount, number   Use *amount* to refer to quantities that cannot be counted or to bulk; use *number* to refer to countable, separate items. "The *number* of people you want to serve determines the *amount* of ice cream you'll need."

an, a   See *a, an.*

and/or   Usually use either *and* or *or* alone. "Tim *and* Elaine will come to the party." "Tim *or* Elaine will come to the party." For three options, write, "Tim *or* Elaine, *or both,* will come to the party, depending on whether they can find a babysitter."

A-54

ante-, anti-   The prefix *ante-* means "preceding." *Antebellum* means "before the Civil War." *Anti-* most often means "opposing": *antidepressant*. It needs a hyphen in front of *i* (*anti-inflationary*) or in front of a capital letter (*anti-Marxist*).

anybody, any body   When *anybody* is used as an indefinite pronoun, write it as one word: "*Anybody* in his or her right mind abhors murder." Because *anybody* is singular, do not write "Anybody in *their* right mind." (See 7d.) *Any body*, written as two words, is the adjective *any* modifying the noun *body*. "Name *any body* of water in Australia."

anyone, any one   *Anyone* is an indefinite pronoun written as one word. "Does *anyone* want dessert?" The phrase *any one* consists of the pronoun *one* modified by the adjective *any* and is used to single out something in a group: "Pick *any one* of the pies — they're all good."

anyplace   *Anyplace* is colloquial for *anywhere* and should not be used in formal writing.

anyways, anywheres   These nonstandard forms of *anyway* and *anywhere* should not be used in writing.

as   Sometimes using the subordinating conjunction *as* can make a sentence ambiguous. "*As* we were climbing the mountain, we put on heavy sweaters." Does *as* here mean "because" or "while"? Whenever using *as* would be confusing, use a more specific term instead, such as *because* or *while*.

as, like   Use *as, as if*, or *as though* rather than *like* to introduce clauses of comparison. "Dan's compositions are tuneful, *as* [not *like*] music ought to be." "Jeffrey behaves *as if* [not *like*] he were ill." *Like*, because it is a preposition, can introduce a phrase but not a clause. "My brother looks *like* me." "Henrietta runs *like* a duck."

as to   Usually this expression sounds stilted. Use *about* instead. "He complained *about* [not *as to*] the cockroaches."

at   See *where at, where to.*

bad, badly   *Bad* is an adjective; *badly* is an adverb. Following linking verbs (*be, appear, become, grow, seem, prove*) and verbs of the senses (*feel, look, smell, sound, taste*), use the adjective form. "I feel *bad* that we missed the plane." "The egg smells *bad*." (See 8a, 8b.) The adverb form is used to modify a verb or an adjective. "The Tartans played so *badly* they lost to the last-place team whose *badly* needed victory saved them from elimination."

being as, being that   Instead of "*being as* I was ignorant of the facts, I kept still," write "*Because* I was ignorant" or "*Not knowing* the facts."

beside, besides   *Beside* is a preposition meaning "next to." "Sheldon enjoyed sitting *beside* the guest of honor." *Besides* is an adverb meaning "in addition." "*Besides*, he has a sense of humor." *Besides* is also a preposition meaning "other than." "Something *besides* shyness caused his embarrassment."

between, among   See *among, between.*

between you and I   The preposition *between* always takes the objective case. "Between *you* and *me* [not *I*], Joe's story sounds suspicious." "Between *us* [not *we*], what's going on between Bob and *her* [not *she*] is unfathomable." (See 5a–5f.)

but that, but what   "I don't know *but what* [or *but that*] you're right" is a wordy, imprecise way of saying "Maybe you're right" or "I believe you're right."

can, may   Use *can* to show ability. "Jake *can* bench-press 650 pounds." *May* involves permission. "*May* I bench-press today?" "You *may*, if you *can*."

capital, capitol   A *capital* is a city that is the center of government for a state or country. *Capital* can also mean "wealth." A *capitol* is a building in which legislators meet. "Who knows what the *capital* of Finland is?" "The renovated *capitol* is a popular attraction."

center around   Say "Class discussion *centered on* [or *revolved around*] her paper." In this sense, the verb *center* means "to have one main concern" — the way a circle has a central point. (To say a discussion centers *around* anything is a murky metaphor.)

cite, sight, site   *Cite*, a verb, means "to quote from or refer to." *Sight* as a verb means "to see or glimpse"; as a noun it means "a view, a spectacle." "When the police officer *sighted* my terrier running across the playground, she *cited* the leash laws." *Site*, a noun, means "location." "Standing and weeping at the *site* of his childhood home, he was a pitiful *sight*."

climatic, climactic   *Climatic*, from *climate*, refers to meteorological conditions. Saying "climatic conditions," however, is wordy — you can usually substitute "the climate": "*Climatic* conditions are [or "The *climate* is"] changing because of the hole in the ozone layer." *Climactic*, from *climax*, refers to the culmination of a progression of events. "In the *climactic* scene the hero drives his car off the pier."

compare, contrast *Compare* has two main meanings. The first, "to liken or represent as similar," is followed by *to*. "She *compared* her room *to* a jail cell." The second, "to analyze for similarities and differences," is generally followed by *with*. "The speaker *compared* the American educational system *with* the Japanese system."

Contrast also has two main meanings. As a transitive verb, taking an object, it means "to analyze to emphasize differences" and is generally followed by *with*. "The speaker *contrasted* the social emphasis of the Japanese primary grades *with* the academic emphasis of ours." As an intransitive verb, *contrast* means "to exhibit differences when compared." "The sour taste of the milk *contrasted* sharply *with* its usual fresh flavor."

complement, compliment *Compliment* is a verb meaning "to praise" or a noun meaning "praise." "The professor *complimented* Sarah on her perceptiveness." *Complement* is a verb meaning "to complete or reinforce." "Jenn's experiences as an intern *complemented* what she learned in class."

could care less This is nonstandard English for *couldn't care less* and should not be used in writing. "The cat *couldn't* [not *could*] *care less* about which brand of cat food you buy."

could of *Could of* is colloquial for *could have* and should not be used in writing.

couple of Write "a *couple of* drinks" when you mean two. For more than two, say "a *few* [or *several*] drinks."

criteria, criterion *Criteria* is the plural of *criterion*, which means "a standard or requirement on which a judgment or decision is based." "The main *criteria* for this job are attention to detail and good computer skills."

data *Data* is a plural noun. Write "The data *are*" and "*these* data." The singular form of *data* is *datum* — rarely used because it sounds musty. Instead, use *fact, figure,* or *statistic*.

different from, different than *Different from* is usually the correct form to use. "How is good poetry *different from* prose?" Use *different than* when a whole clause follows. "Violin lessons with Mr. James were *different than* I had imagined."

don't, doesn't *Don't* is the contraction for *do not*, and *doesn't* is the contraction for *does not*. "They *don't* want to get dressed up for the ceremony." "The cat *doesn't* [not *don't*] like to be combed."

due to *Due* is an adjective and must modify a noun or pronoun; it can't modify a verb or an adjective. Begin a sentence with *due to* and you invite trouble: "*Due to* rain, the game was postponed." Write instead, "*Because of* rain." *Due to* works after the verb *be*. "His fall was *due to* a banana peel." There, *due* modifies the noun *fall*.

due to the fact that A windy expression for *because*.

effect, affect See *affect, effect*.

either Use *either* when referring to one of two things. "Both internships sound great; I'd be happy with *either*." When referring to one of three or more things, use *any one* or *any*. "*Any one* of our four counselors will be able to help you."

et cetera, etc. Sharpen your writing by replacing *et cetera* (or its abbreviation, *etc.*) with exact words. Even translating the Latin expression into English ("and other things") is an improvement, as in "high-jumping, shot-putting, and other field events."

everybody, every body When used as an indefinite pronoun, *everybody* is one word. "Why is *everybody* on the boys' team waving his arms?" Because *everybody* is singular, it is a mistake to write, "Why is *everybody* waving *their* arms?" (See 7d.) *Every body* written as two words refers to separate, individual bodies. "After the massacre, they buried *every body* in *its* [not *their*] own grave."

everyone, every one Used as an indefinite pronoun, *everyone* is one word. "*Everyone* has *his or her* own ideas." Because *everyone* is singular, it is incorrect to write, "*Everyone* has *their* own ideas." (See 7d.) *Every one* written as two words refers to individual, distinct items. "I studied *every one* of the chapters."

except, accept See *accept, except*.

expect In writing, avoid the informal use of *expect* to mean "suppose, assume, or think." "I *suppose* [not *expect*] you're going on the geology field trip."

fact that This is a wordy expression that, nearly always, you can do without. Instead of "*The fact that* he was puny went unnoticed," write, "That he was puny went unnoticed." "Because [not *Because of the fact that*] it snowed, the game was canceled."

farther, further In your writing, use *farther* to refer to literal distance. "Chicago is *farther* from Nome than from New York." When you mean additional degree, time, or quantity, use *further*: "Sally's idea requires *further* discussion."

fewer, less   *Less* refers to general quantity or bulk; *fewer* refers to separate, countable items. "Eat *less* pizza." "Salad has *fewer* calories."

field of   In a statement such as "He took courses in *the field of* economics," omit *the field of* to save words.

firstly   The recommended usage is *first* (and *second*, not *secondly; third,* not *thirdly;* and so on).

former, latter   *Former* means "first of two"; *latter,* "second of two." They are an acceptable but heavy-handed pair, often obliging your reader to back-track. Your writing generally will be clearer if you simply name again the persons or things you mean. Instead of "The *former* great artist is the master of the flowing line, while the *latter* is the master of color," write, "Picasso is the master of the flowing line, while Matisse is the master of color."

further, farther   See *farther, further.*

get, got   *Get* has many meanings, especially in slang and colloquial use. Some, such as the following, are not appropriate in formal writing:

To start, begin: "Let's start [not *get*] painting."

To stir the emotions: "His frequent interruptions finally started annoying [not *getting to*] me."

To harm, punish, or take revenge on: "She's going to take revenge on [not *get*] him." Or better, be even more specific: "She's going to spread rumors about him to ruin his reputation."

good, well   To modify a verb, use the adverb *well,* not the adjective *good.* "Jan dives *well* [not *good*]." Linking verbs (*be, appear, become, grow, seem, prove*) and verbs of the senses (such as *feel, look, smell, sound, taste*) call for the adjective *good.* "The paint job looks *good.*" *Well* is an adjective used only to refer to health. "She looks *well*" means that she seems to be in good health. "She looks *good*" means her appearance is attractive. (See 8b, 8c.)

hanged, hung   Both words are the past tense of the verb *hang. Hanged* refers to an execution. "The murderer was *hanged* at dawn." For all other situations, use *hung.* "Jim *hung* his wash on the line to dry."

have got to   In formal writing, avoid using the phrase *have got to* to mean "have to" or "must." "I *must* [not *have got to*] phone them right away."

he, she, he or she   Using *he* to refer to an indefinite person is considered sexist; so is using *she* with traditionally female occupations or pastimes.

However, the phrase *he or she* can seem wordy and awkward. For alternatives, see 18.

herself   See *-self, -selves.*

himself   See *-self, -selves.*

hopefully   *Hopefully* means "with hope." "The children turned *hopefully* toward the door, expecting Santa Claus." In writing, avoid *hopefully* when you mean "it is to be hoped" or "let us hope." "I hope [not *Hopefully*] the posse will arrive soon."

if, whether   Use *whether,* not *if,* in indirect questions and to introduce alternatives. "Father asked me *whether* [not *if*] I was planning to sleep all morning." "I'm so confused I don't know *whether* [not *if*] it's day or night."

imply, infer   *Imply* means "to suggest"; *infer* means "to draw a conclusion." "Maria *implied* that she was too busy to see Tom, but Tom *inferred* that Maria had lost interest in him."

in, into   *In* refers to a location or condition; *into* refers to the direction of movement or change. "The hero burst *into* the room and found the heroine *in* another man's arms."

infer, imply   See *imply, infer.*

in regards to   Write *in regard to, regarding,* or *about.*

inside of, outside of   As prepositions, *inside* and *outside* do not require *of.* "The students were more interested in events *outside* [not *outside of*] the building than those *inside* [not *inside of*] the classroom." In formal writing, do not use *inside of* to refer to time or *outside of* to mean "except." "I'll finish the assignment *within* [not *inside of*] two hours." "He told no one *except* [not *outside of*] a few friends."

irregardless   *Irregardless* is a double negative. Use *regardless.*

is because   See *reason is because,* reason . . . is.

is when, is where   Using these expressions results in errors in predication. "Obesity *is when* a person is greatly overweight." "Biology *is where* students dissect frogs." *When* refers to a point in time, but *obesity* is not a point in time; *where* refers to a place, but *biology* is not a place. Write instead, "Obesity is the condition of extreme overweight." "Biology is a laboratory course in which students dissect frogs." (See 12c.)

its, it's   *Its* is a possessive pronoun, never in need of an apostrophe. *It's* is a contraction for *it is.* "Every new experience has *its* bad moments. Still, *it's* exciting to explore the unknown." (See 24g.)

it's me, it is I   Although *it's me* is widely used in speech, don't use it in formal writing. Write "It is I," which is grammatically correct. The same applies to other personal pronouns. "It was *he* [not *him*] who started the mutiny." (See 5.)

kind of, sort of, type of   When you use *kind, sort,* or *type* — singular words — make sure that the sentence construction is singular. "That *type* of show *offends* me." "Those *types* of shows *offend* me." In speech, *kind of* and *sort of* are used as qualifiers. "He is *sort of* fat." Avoid them in writing. "He is *rather* [or *somewhat* or *slightly*] fat."

latter, former   See *former, latter.*

lay, lie   The verb *lay,* meaning "to put or place," takes an object. *"Lay* that pistol down." *Lie,* meaning "to rest or recline," does not. *"Lie* on the bed until your headache goes away." Their principal parts are *lay, laid, laid* and *lie, lay, lain.* (See 3f.)

less, fewer   See *fewer, less.*

liable, likely   Use *likely* to mean "plausible" or "having the potential." "Jake is *likely* [not *liable*] to win." Save *liable* for "legally obligated" or "susceptible." "A stunt man is *liable* to injury."

lie, lay   See *lay, lie.*

like, as   See *as, like.*

likely, liable   See *liable, likely.*

literally   Don't sling *literally* around for emphasis. Because it means "strictly according to the meaning of a word (or words)," it will wreck your credibility if you are speaking figuratively. "Professor Gray *literally* flew down the hall" means that Gray traveled on wings. Save *literally* to mean that you're reporting a fact. "Chemical wastes travel on the winds, and the skies *literally* rain poison."

loose, lose   *Loose,* an adjective, most commonly means "not fastened" or "poorly fastened." *Lose,* a verb, means "to misplace" or "to not win." "I have to be careful not to *lose* this button — it's so *loose.*"

lots, lots of, a lot of   Use these expressions only in informal speech. In formal writing, use *many* or *much.* See also *a lot.*

mankind   This term is considered sexist by many people. Use *humanity, humankind, the human race,* or *people* instead.

may, can   See *can, may.*

media, medium   *Media* is the plural of *medium* and most commonly refers to the various forms of public communication. "Some argue that, of all the *media,* television is the worst for children."

might of   *Might of* is colloquial for *might have* and should not be used in writing.

most   Do not use *most* when you mean "almost" or "nearly." *"Almost* [not *Most*] all of the students felt that Professor Crey should receive tenure."

must of   *Must of* is colloquial for *must have* and should not be used in writing.

myself   See *-self, -selves.*

not all that   *Not all that* is colloquial for *not very;* do not use it in formal writing. "The movie was *not very* [not *not all that*] exciting."

number, amount   See *amount, number.*

of   See *could of, might of, must of, should of.*

O.K., o.k., okay   In formal writing, do not use any of these expressions. *All right* and *I agree* are possible substitutes.

one   Like a balloon, *one,* meaning "a person," tends to inflate. One *one* can lead to another. "When *one* is in college, *one* learns to make up *one's* mind for *oneself.*" Avoid this pompous usage. Whenever possible, substitute *people* or a more specific plural noun. "When *students* are in college, *they* learn to make up their minds for *themselves.*"

ourselves   See *-self, -selves.*

outside of, inside of   See *inside of, outside of.*

percent, per cent, percentage   When you specify a number, write *percent* (also written *per cent*). "Nearly 40 *percent* of the listeners responded to the offer." The only time to use *percentage,* meaning "part," is with an adjective, when you mention no number. "A high *percentage* [or *a large percentage*] of listeners responded." *A large number* or *a large proportion* sounds better yet.

phenomenon, phenomena   *Phenomena* is the plural of *phenomenon,* which means "an observable fact or occurrence." "Of the many mysterious supernatural *phenomena,* clairvoyance is the strangest *phenomenon* of all."

precede, proceed   *Precede* means "to go before or ahead of"; *proceed* means "to go forward." "The fire drill *proceeded* smoothly; the children *preceded* the teachers onto the playground."

principal, principle *Principal* means "chief," whether used as an adjective or as a noun. "According to the *principal*, the school's *principal* goal will be teaching reading." Referring to money, *principal* means "capital." "Investors in high-risk companies may lose their *principal*." *Principle*, a noun, means *rule* or *standard*. "Let's apply the *principle* of equality in hiring."

proved, proven   Although both forms can be used as past participles, *proved* is recommended. Use *proven* as an adjective. "They had *proved* their skill in match after match." "Try this *proven* cough remedy."

quote, quotation   *Quote* is a verb meaning "to cite, to use the words of." *Quotation* is a noun meaning "something that is quoted." "The *quotation* [not *quote*] next to her photograph fits her perfectly."

raise, rise   *Raise*, meaning "to cause to move upward," is a transitive verb and takes an object. *Rise*, meaning "to move up (on its own)" is intransitive and does not take an object: "I *rose* from my seat and *raised* my arm."

rarely ever   *Rarely* by itself is strong enough. "George *rarely* [not *rarely ever*] eats dinner with his family."

real, really   *Real* is an adjective, *really* an adverb. Do not use *real* to modify a verb or another adjective, and avoid overusing either word. "The Ambassadors is a *really* [not *real*] fine novel." Even better: "The Ambassadors is a fine novel."

reason is because, reason . . . is   *Reason . . . is* requires a clause beginning with *that*. Using *because* is nonstandard. "The *reason* I can't come *is that* [not *is because*] I have the flu." It is simpler and more direct to write, "I can't come because I have the flu." (See 12d.)

rise   See *raise, rise.*

-self, -selves   Don't use a pronoun ending in -*self* or -*selves* in place of *her, him, me, them, us,* or *you.* "Nobody volunteered but Jim and *me* [not *myself*]." Use the -*self* pronouns to refer back to a noun or another pronoun and to lend emphasis. "We did it *ourselves*." "Sarah *herself* is a noted musician."

set, sit   *Set*, meaning "to put or place," is a transitive verb and takes an object. *Sit*, meaning "to be seated," is intransitive and does not take an

object. "We were asked to *set* our jewelry and metal objects on the counter and *sit* down." (See 3f.)

shall, will; should, would   The helping verb *shall* formerly was used with first-person pronouns. It is still used to express determination ("We *shall* overcome") or to ask consent ("*Shall* we march?"). Otherwise, *will* is commonly used with all three persons. "I *will* enter medical school in the fall." *Should* is a helping verb that expresses obligation; *would*, a helping verb that expresses a hypothetical condition. "I *should* wash the dishes before I watch TV." "He *would* learn to speak English if you *would* give him a chance."

she, he or she   See *he, she, he or she.*

should of   *Should of* is colloquial for *should have* and should not be used in writing.

sight   See *cite, sight, site.*

since   Sometimes using *since* can make a sentence ambiguous. "*Since* the babysitter left, the children have been watching television." Does *since* here mean "because" or "from the time that"? If using *since* might be confusing, use an unambiguous term (*because, ever since*).

sit   See *set, sit.*

site   See *cite, sight, site.*

sort of   See *kind of, sort of, type of.*

stationary, stationery   *Stationary*, an adjective, means "fixed, unmoving." "The fireplace remained *stationary* though the wind blew down the house." *Stationery* is paper for letter writing. To spell it right, remember that *letter* also contains -*er.*

suppose to   Write *supposed to.* "He was *supposed to* read a novel."

sure   *Sure* is an adjective, *surely* an adverb. Do not use *sure* to modify a verb or another adjective. If you mean "certainly," write *certainly* or *surely* instead. "He *surely* [not *sure*] makes the Civil War come alive."

than, then   *Than* is a conjunction used in comparisons; *then* is an adverb indicating time. "Marlene is brainier *than* her sister." "First crack six eggs; *then* beat them."

that, where   See *where, that.*

that, which   Which pronoun should open a clause —*that* or *which*? If the clause adds to its sentence an idea that, however interesting, could be left out, then the clause is nonrestrictive. It should begin with *which* and be separated from the rest of the sentence with commas. "The vampire, *which* hovered nearby, leaped for Sarah's throat."

If the clause is essential to your meaning, it is restrictive. It should begin with *that* and should not have commas around it. "The vampire *that* Mel brought from Transylvania leaped for Sarah's throat." The clause indicates not just any old vampire but one in particular. (See 21e.)

Don't use *which* to refer vaguely to an entire clause. Instead of "Jack was an expert drummer in high school, *which* won him a scholarship," write "Jack's skill as a drummer won him..." (See 6b.)

that, who, which, whose   See *who, which, that, whose.*

themselves   See *-self, -selves.*

then, than   See *than, then.*

there, their, they're   *There* is an adverb indicating place. *Their* is a possessive pronoun. *They're* is a contraction of *they are.* "After playing tennis *there* for three hours, Lamont and Laura went to change *their* clothes because *they're* going out to dinner."

to, too, two   *To* is a preposition. *Too* is an adverb meaning "also" or "in excess." *Two* is a number. "Janet wanted to go *too*, but she was *too* sick to travel for *two* days. Instead, she went *to* bed."

toward, towards   *Toward* is preferred in the United States, *towards* in Britain.

try and   Use *try to.* "I'll *try to* [not *try and*] attend the opening performance of your play."

type of   See *kind of, sort of, type of.*

unique   Nothing can be *more, less,* or *very unique. Unique* means "one of a kind." (See 8e.)

use to   Write *used to.* "Jeffrey *used to* have a beard, but now he is clean-shaven."

wait for, wait on   *Wait for* means "await"; *wait on* means "to serve." "While *waiting for* his friends, George decided to *wait on* one more customer."

well, good   See *good, well.*

where, that   Although speakers sometimes use *where* instead of *that,* you should not do so in writing. "I heard on the news *that* [not *where*] it got hot enough to fry eggs on car hoods."

where . . . at, where . . . to   The colloquial use of *at* or *to* after *where* is redundant. Write "*Where* were you?" not "*Where* were you *at?*" "I know *where* she was rushing [not *rushing to*]."

whether   See *if, whether.*

which, that   See *that, which.*

who, which, that, whose   *Who* refers to people, *which* to things and ideas. "Was it Pogo *who* said, 'We have met the enemy and he is us'?" "The blouse, *which* was green, accented her dark skin." *That* refers to things but can also be used for a class of people. "The team *that* increases sales the most will get a bonus." Because *of which* can be cumbersome, use *whose* even with things. "The mountain, *whose* snowy peaks were famous world over, was covered by fog." See also *that, which.*

who, whom   *Who* is used as a subject, *whom* as an object. In "*Whom* do I see?" *Whom* is the object of *see.* In "*Who* goes there?" *Who* is the subject of "goes." (See also 5a.)

who's, whose   *Who's* is a contraction for *who is* or *who has.* "*Who's* going with Phil?" *Whose* is a possessive pronoun. "Bill is a conservative politician *whose* ideas are unlikely to change."

whose, who, which, that   See *who, which, that, whose.*

will, shall   See *shall, will; should, would.*

would, should   See *shall, will; should, would.*

would of   *Would of* is colloquial for *would have* and should not be used in writing.

you   *You*, meaning "a person," occurs often in conversation. "When *you* go to college, *you* have to work hard." In writing, use *one* or a specific, preferably plural noun. "When *students* go to college, *they* have to work hard." See *one* and 18c.

your, you're   *Your* is a possessive pronoun; *you're* is the contraction for *you are.* "*You're* lying! It was *your* handwriting on the envelope."

yourself, yourselves   See *-self, -selves.*

Appendix
Answers for Lettered Exercises

EXERCISE 1–1   ELIMINATING FRAGMENTS, p. H-9

Suggested revisions:

a. Michael had a beautiful Southern accent, having lived many years in Georgia.
b. Pat and Chris are determined to marry each other, even if their families do not approve.
c. Jack seemed well qualified for a career in the air force, except for his tendency to get airsick.
d. Lisa advocated sleeping no more than four hours a night until she started nodding through her classes.
e. Complete sentences

EXERCISE 2–1   REVISING COMMA SPLICES AND FUSED SENTENCES, p. H-13

Suggested revisions:

a. We followed the scientist down a flight of wet stone steps. At last he stopped before a huge oak door.
We followed the scientist down a flight of wet stone steps until at last he stopped before a huge oak door.
b. Dr. Frankenstein selected a heavy key; he twisted it in the lock.
Dr. Frankenstein selected a heavy key, which he twisted in the lock.
c. The huge door gave a groan; it swung open on a dimly lighted laboratory.
The huge door gave a groan and swung open on a dimly lighted laboratory.
d. Before us on a dissecting table lay a form with closed eyes. To behold it sent a quick chill down my spine.
Before us on a dissecting table lay a form with closed eyes; beholding it sent a quick chill down my spine.
e. The scientist strode to the table and lifted a white-gloved hand.
The scientist strode to the table; he lifted a white-gloved hand.

EXERCISE 3–1   USING IRREGULAR VERB FORMS, p. H-18

a. In those days, Benjamin wrote all the music, and his sister *sang* all the songs.
b. Correct
c. When the bell *rang*, darkness had already *fallen*.
d. Voters have *chosen* some new senators, who won't take office until January.
e. Carol threw the ball into the water, and the dog *swam* after it.

EXERCISE 3–2   IDENTIFYING VERB TENSES, p. H-26

a. has been living: present perfect progressive; hacked: simple past; change: simple present   **b.** have never appeared: present perfect; will never appear: simple future; gets selected: simple present   **c.** had been: past perfect; pitched: simple past   **d.** will have been studying: future perfect progressive; will be taking: future progressive   **e.** was running: past progressive; strolled: simple past

EXERCISE 3–4   USING THE CORRECT MOOD OF VERBS, p. H-31

a. Dr. Belanger recommended that Juan *floss* his teeth every day. (Incorrect *flosses*, indicative; correct *floss*, subjunctive)
b. If I *were* you, I would have done the same thing. (Incorrect *was*, indicative; correct *were*, subjunctive)
c. Tradition demands that Daegun *show* respect for his elders. (Incorrect *shows*, indicative; correct *show*, subjunctive)
d. Please *attend* the training lesson if you plan to skydive later today. (Incorrect *attends*, indicative; correct *attend*, imperative)

EXERCISE 4–1   MAKING SUBJECTS AND VERBS AGREE, p. H-36

a. For many college graduates, the process of looking for jobs *is* often long and stressful.

b. Not too long ago, searching the classifieds and inquiring in person *were* the primary methods of job hunting.

c. Today, however, everyone also *seems* to use the Internet to search for openings or to e-mail *his or her* résumés.

d. My classmates and my cousin *send* most résumés over the Internet because it costs less than mailing them.

e. All of the résumés *arrive* quickly when they are sent electronically.

EXERCISE 5–1 USING PRONOUNS CORRECTLY, p. H-39

a. I didn't appreciate *your* laughing at her and *me*. (*Your* modifies the gerund *laughing; me* is an object of the preposition *at.*)

b. Lee and *I* would be delighted to serenade *whoever* will listen. (*I* is a subject of the verb phrase *would be delighted; whoever* is the subject of the clause *whoever will listen.*)

c. The managers and *we* servers are highly trustworthy. (*We* is a subject complement.)

d. The neighbors were driven berserk by *his* singing. (The gerund *singing* is the object of the verb *driven;* the possessive pronoun *his* modifies *singing.*) *Or*
Correct as is. (*Him* is the object of the verb *driven; singing* is a participle modifying *him.*)

e. Jerry and *I* regard you and *her* as the very people *whom* we wish to meet. (*I* is a subject of the verb *regard; her* is a direct object of the verb *regard; whom* is the object of the infinitive *to meet.*)

EXERCISE 6–1 MAKING PRONOUN REFERENCE CLEAR, p. H-43

Suggested revisions:

a. As the moon began to rise, I could see the faint shadow of the tree.

b. While she spent the summer in Paris, Katrina broadened her awareness of cultural differences by traveling throughout Europe.

c. Most managers want employees to work as many hours as possible. They never consider the work their employees need to do at home.

d. Working twelve hours a day and never getting enough sleep was worth it.

e. Kevin asked Mike to meet him for lunch but forgot that Mike had class at that time. *Or*
Kevin forgot that he had class at the time he asked Mike to meet him for lunch.

EXERCISE 7–1 MAKING PRONOUNS AND ANTECEDENTS AGREE, p. H-46

Suggested revisions:

a. Correct

b. Neither Melissa nor James has received an application form yet. *Or*

Melissa and James have not received their application forms yet.

c. He is the kind of man who gets his fun out of just sipping his beer and watching his Saturday games on TV.

d. Many a mother has mourned the loss of her child. *Or*
Many mothers have mourned the loss of their children.

e. When you enjoy your work, it's easy to spend all your spare time thinking about it. *Or*
When one enjoys one's work, it's easy to spend all one's spare time thinking about it.

EXERCISE 8–1 USING ADJECTIVES AND ADVERBS CORRECTLY, p. H-50

a. Change *increasing* to *increasingly.* b. Correct. c. Change *lower* to *lowest.* d. Change *rapid* to *rapidly.* e. Change *well* to *good.*

EXERCISE 9–1 MAINTAINING GRAMMATICAL CONSISTENCY, p. H-56

Suggested revisions:

a. Dr. Jamison is an erudite professor who tells amusing anecdotes in class. (Formal) *Or* Dr. Jamison is a funny teacher who cracks jokes in class. (Informal)

b. The audience listened intently to the lecture but did not understand the message.

c. Scientists can no longer evade the social, political, and ethical consequences of what they do in the laboratory.

d. To have good government, citizens must become informed on the issues. Also, they must vote.

e. Good writing is essential to success in many professions, especially in business, where ideas must be communicated clearly.

EXERCISE 10–1 PLACING MODIFIERS, p. H-59

Suggested revisions:

a. The bus full of passengers got stuck in a ditch.

b. In the middle of a staff meeting, he was daydreaming about fishing for trout.

c. With a smirk, the boy threw the paper airplane through an open window.

d. When the glare appeared, I reached for my sunglasses from the glove compartment.

e. Sally and Glen watched the kites high above them drift back and forth.

EXERCISE 10–2 REVISING DANGLING MODIFIERS, p. H-60

Suggested revisions:

a. As I was unpacking the suitcase, a horrible idea occurred to me.

b. After preparing breakfast that morning, I might have left the oven on at home.

c. Although I tried to reach my neighbor, her phone was busy.

d. Desperate to get information, I asked my mother to drive over to check the oven.

e. I felt enormous relief when my mother's call confirmed that everything was fine.

EXERCISE 11-1   COMPLETING COMPARISONS, p. H-62

Suggested revisions:

a. The movie version of *The Brady Bunch* was much more ironic *than the television show*.

b. Taking care of a dog is often more demanding than *taking care of* a cat.

c. I received more free calendars in the mail for the year 2008 than *I have for* any other year.

d. The crime rate in the United States is higher than *it is in* Canada.

e. Liver contains more iron than any *other* meat.

EXERCISE 11-2   COMPLETING SENTENCES, p. H-64

Suggested revisions:

a. Eighteenth-century China was as civilized *as* and in many respects more sophisticated than the Western world.

b. Pembroke was never contacted *by,* much less involved with, the election committee.

c. I haven't yet *finished* but soon will finish my research paper.

d. Ron likes his popcorn with butter; Linda *likes hers* with parmesan cheese.

e. Correct

EXERCISE 12-1   CORRECTING MIXED CONSTRUCTIONS AND FAULTY PREDICATION, p. H-68

Suggested revisions:

a. Health insurance protects people from big medical bills.

b. His determination to prevail helped him finish the race.

c. AIDS destroys the body's immune system.

d. The temperatures are too low for the orange trees.

e. In a recession, economic growth is small or nonexistent, and unemployment increases.

EXERCISE 13-1   MAKING SENTENCES PARALLEL, p. H-71

Suggested revisions:

a. The border separating Texas and Mexico marks not only the political boundary of two countries but also the last frontier for some endangered wildlife.

b. In the Rio Grande Valley, both local residents and tourists enjoy visiting the national wildlife refuges.

c. The tall grasses in this valley are the home of many insects, birds, and small mammals.

d. Two endangered wildcats, the ocelot and the jaguarundi, also make the Rio Grande Valley their home.

e. Many people from Central America are desperate to immigrate to the United States by either legal or illegal means.

EXERCISE 14-1   USING COORDINATION, p. H-75

Suggested revisions:

a. Professional poker players try to win money and prizes in high-stakes tournaments; however, they may lose thousands of dollars.

b. Poker is not an easy way to make a living, and playing professional poker is not a good way to relax.

c. A good "poker face" reveals no emotions, for communicating too much information puts a player at a disadvantage.

d. Hidden feelings may come out in unconscious movements, so an expert poker player watches other players carefully.

e. Poker is different from most other casino gambling games, for it requires skill and it forces players to compete against each other. Other casino gambling pits players against the house, so they may win out of sheer luck, but skill has little to do with winning those games.

EXERCISE 14-2   USING SUBORDINATION, p. H-77

Suggested revisions:

a. Cape Cod is a peninsula in Massachusetts that juts into the Atlantic Ocean south of Boston, marking the northern turning point of the Gulf Stream.

b. Although the developer had hoped the condominiums would sell quickly, sales were sluggish.

c. Tourists love Italy because it has a wonderful climate, beautiful towns and cities, and a rich history.

d. At the end of Verdi's opera *La Traviata*, Alfredo has to see his beloved Violetta again, even though he knows she is dying and all he can say is good-bye.

e. I usually have more fun at a concert with Rico than with Morey because Rico loves music while Morey merely tolerates it.

EXERCISE 16-2   AVOIDING JARGON, p. H-84

Suggested revisions:

a. Everyone at Boondoggle and Gall attends holiday gatherings in order to meet and socialize with potential business partners.

b. This year, more than fifty employees lost their jobs after Boondoggle and Gall's decision to reduce the number of employees by September 1.

c. The layoffs left Jensen in charge of all telephone calls in the customer-service department.

d. Jensen was responsible for handling three times as many telephone calls after the layoffs, yet she did not receive any extra pay.

e. Jensen and her managers could not agree on a fair compensation, so she decided to quit her job at Boondoggle and Gall.

EXERCISE 16–3 AVOIDING EUPHEMISMS AND SLANG, p. H-85

Suggested revisions:

a. Our security forces have arrested many political dissidents.

b. At three hundred dollars a month, the apartment is a bargain.

c. The soldiers were accidentally shot by members of their own troops while they were retreating.

d. Churchill was an excellent politician.

e. The president's tax plan was doomed; Congress would not approve it.

EXERCISE 18–1 AVOIDING BIAS, p. H-93

Suggested revisions:

a. Our school's extensive athletic program will be of interest to *many* applicants.

b. The new physicians on our staff include Dr. Scalia, *Dr.* Baniski, and Dr. Throckmorton.

c. Joni believes in the healing properties of herbal remedies.

d. Philosophers have long pondered whether *humans are* innately evil or innately good.

e. *Diligent researchers* will always find the sources *they* seek.

EXERCISE 20–1 USING END PUNCTUATION, p. H-98

a. The question that still troubles the community after all these years is why federal agents did not act sooner. [Not a direct question]

b. Correct

c. I wonder what he was thinking at the time. [Not a direct question]

d. One man, who suffered a broken leg, was rescued when he was heard screaming, "Help me! Help me!" [Urgent directive]

e. Correct

EXERCISE 21–1 USING COMMAS, p. H-99

a. Farmers around the world tend to rely on just a few breeds of livestock, so some breeds are disappearing.

b. Correct

c. For instance, modern breeds of cattle usually grow larger and produce more meat and milk than older breeds.

d. In both wild and domestic animals, genetic diversity can make the animals resistant to disease and parasites, so older breeds can give scientists important information.

e. Until recently, small organic farmers were often the only ones interested in raising old-fashioned breeds, but animal scientists now support this practice as well.

EXERCISE 21–2 USING COMMAS, p. H-101

a. Mrs. Carver looks like a sweet little old lady, but she plays a wicked electric guitar.

b. Her bass player, her drummer, and her keyboard player all live in the same retirement community.

c. They practice individually in the afternoon, rehearse together at night, and play at the community's Saturday night dances.

d. The Rest Home Rebels have to rehearse quietly and cautiously to keep from disturbing the other residents.

e. Correct

EXERCISE 21–3 USING COMMAS, p. H-103

Suggested revisions:

a. We are bringing a dish, vegetable lasagna, to the potluck supper.

b. I like to go to Central Bank on this side of town because this branch tends to have short lines.

c. The colony that the English established at Roanoke disappeared mysteriously.

d. If the base commanders had checked their gun room, where powder is stored, they would have found that several hundred pounds of gunpowder were missing.

e. Brazil's tropical rain forests, which help produce the air we breathe all over the world, are being cut down at an alarming rate.

EXERCISE 21–4 USING COMMAS, p. H-104

a. The university insisted, however, that the students were not accepted merely because of their parents' generous contributions.

b. This dispute, in any case, is an old one.

c. It was the young man's striking good looks, not his acting ability, that first attracted the Hollywood agents.

d. Gretchen learned, moreover, not to always accept as true what she had read in celebrity magazines.

e. The hikers, most of them wearing ponchos or rain jackets, headed out into the steady drizzle.

EXERCISE 21–5 USING COMMAS, p. H-106

a. César Chávez was born on March 31, 1927, on a farm in Yuma, Arizona.

b. Chávez, who spent years as a migrant farmworker, told other farm laborers, "If you're outraged at conditions, then you can't possibly be free or happy until you devote all your time to changing them."

c. Chávez founded the United Farm Workers union and did, indeed, devote all his time to changing conditions for farmworkers.

d. Robert F. Kennedy called Chávez "one of the heroic figures of our time."

e. Correct

EXERCISE 22–1 USING SEMICOLONS, p. H-109

a. By the beginning of 2006, Shirley was eager to retire; nevertheless, she agreed to stay on for two more years.

b. In 1968 Lyndon Johnson abandoned his hopes for reelection because of fierce opposition from within his own party.

c. The committee was asked to determine the extent of violent crime among teenagers, especially those between the ages of fourteen and sixteen; to act as a liaison between the city and schools and between churches and volunteer organizations; and to draw up a plan to reduce violence, both public and private, by the end of the century.

d. The leaves on the oak trees near the lake were tinged with red; swimmers no longer ventured into the water.

e. The football team has yet to win a game; however, the season is still young.

EXERCISE 23–1   USING COLONS, p. H-112

Suggested revisions:

a. The Continuing Education Program offers courses in building and construction management, engineering, and design.

b. The interview ended with a test of skills: taking messages, operating the computer, typing a sample letter, and proofreading documents.

c. The sample letter began, "Dear Mr. Rasheed: Please accept our apologies for the late shipment."

d. Correct

e. These are my dreams: to fly in a small plane, to gallop down a beach on horseback, and to cross the ocean in a sailboat.

EXERCISE 24–1   USING APOSTROPHES, p. H-115

a. Joe's and Chuck's fathers were both in the class of '73.

b. Correct

c. It was a strange coincidence that all three women's cars broke down after they had picked up their mothers-in-law.

d. Don't forget to dot your *i*'s and cross your *t*'s.

e. Mario and Shelley's son is marrying the editor in chief's daughter.

EXERCISE 25–1   USING QUOTATION MARKS, p. H-120

a. "What we still need to figure out," the police chief said, "is whether the victim was acquainted with his assailant."

b. A skillful orator, Patrick Henry is credited with the phrase "Give me liberty or give me death."

c. "I could hear the crowd chanting my name — 'Jones! Jones!' — and that spurred me on," said Bruce Jones, the winner of the 5,000-meter race.

d. The video for the rock group Guns and Roses' epic song "November Rain" is based on a short story by Del James.

e. In response to a possible asteroid strike on Earth, former astronaut Rusty Schweickart says, "Every country is at risk."

EXERCISE 26–1   USING DASHES, p. H-121

Suggested revisions:

a. I enjoy going hiking with my friend John, whom I've known for fifteen years.

b. Pedro's new boat is spectacular — a regular seagoing Ferrari.

c. The Thompsons devote their weekends to their favorite pastime — eating bags of potato chips and cookies beside the warm glow of the television.

EXERCISE 27–1   USING PARENTHESES, p. H-123

Suggested revisions:

a. Our cafeteria serves the four basic food groups: white (milk, bread, and mashed potatoes), brown (mystery meat and gravy), green (overcooked vegetables and underwashed lettuce), and orange (squash, carrots, and tomato sauce).

b. The hijackers will release the hostages only if the government (1) frees all political prisoners and (2) allows the hijackers to leave the country unharmed.

c. Correct

EXERCISE 28–1   USING ABBREVIATIONS, p. H-130

a. At 7:50 p.m. [*or* 7:50 in the evening] on election day, the media first awarded Florida to Al Gore, only to reverse that statement and declare George W. Bush the president a few hours later.

b. Biology lectures are only ninety *minutes* long because lab sessions immediately follow them.

c. *Professor* James has office hours on Monday and Tuesday, beginning at 10:00 a.m.

d. Emotional issues, *for example,* abortion and capital punishment, cannot be settled easily by compromise.

e. The red peppers are selling for *$3.25 a pound.*

EXERCISE 29–1   USING CAPITALIZATION, p. H-133

a. At our family reunion, I met my cousin Sam for the first time, as well as my father's brother George.

b. I already knew from Dad that his brother had moved to Australia years ago to explore the Great Barrier Reef.

c. I had heard that Uncle George was estranged from his mother, a Roman Catholic, after he married an atheist.

d. She told George that God created many religions so that people would not become atheists.

e. When my uncle announced that he was moving to a continent thousands of miles southwest of the United States, his mother gave him a Bible to take along.

EXERCISE 30–1   USING NUMBERS, p. H-135

a. If the murder took place at approximately 6:20 p.m. and the suspect was *half* a mile away at the time, he could not possibly have committed the crime.

b. A program to help save the sea otter transferred more than eighty animals to a new colony over the course of *two* years; however, all but *thirty-four* otters swam back home again.

c. *Twelve percent* or so of the estimated *15* billion plastic water bottles purchased annually in the United States is recycled.

d. The Reedville Rockets beat the Bolton Blasters *94–4* before a crowd of *550*.

e. In act II, scene ix, of Shakespeare's *The Merchant of Venice*, Portia's *second* suitor fails to guess which of *three* caskets contains her portrait.

EXERCISE 31–1   USING ITALICS, p. H-138

a. Does *avocado* mean "lawyer" in Spanish?

b. During this year's First Night celebrations, we heard Verdi's *Requiem* and Monteverdi's *Orfeo*.

c. You can pick out some of the best basketball players in the NBA by the *33* on their jerseys.

d. It was fun watching the passengers on the *Europa* trying to dance to "Blue Moon" in the midst of a storm.

e. In one episode of the sitcom *Seinfeld*, Kramer gets a job as an underwear model.

EXERCISE 32–1   USING HYPHENS, p. H-141

a. The strong-smelling smoke alerted them to a potentially life-threatening danger.

b. Burt's wildly swinging opponent had tired himself out before the climactic third round.

c. Tony soaked his son's ketchup- and mustard-stained T-shirt in a pail of water mixed with chlorine bleach.

d. Correct

e. Tracy's brother-in-law lives with his family in a six-room apartment.

ACKNOWLEDGMENTS (continued from p. iv)

Joe Brooks, excerpts from "How to Catch More Trout." First published in *Outdoor Life*, May 2006. Copyright © 2006 by Time4 Media, Inc. Reprinted with the permission of the publishers. All rights reserved. Reproduction in any medium is strictly prohibited without permission from Time4 Media, Inc. Such permission may be requested from *Outdoor Life* magazine.

Jonathan Burns, "The Hidden Truth: An Analysis of Shirley Jackson's 'The Lottery'" and "A Synopsis of 'The Lottery.'" Reprinted with the permission of the author.

David Callahan, "A Question of Character" from *The Cheating Culture: Why More Americans Are Doing Wrong to Get Ahead*. Copyright © 2004 by David Callahan. Reprinted with the permission of Harcourt, Inc., and the Stuart Agency. This material may not be reproduced in any form or by any means without the prior written permission of the publisher.

Tim Chabot, "Take Me Out to the Ballgame, but Which One?" Reprinted with the permission of the author.

Yun Yung Choi, "Invisible Women." Reprinted with the permission of the author.

Michael Coil, "Communications." Reprinted with the permission of the author.

Heather Colbenson, from "Missed Opportunities." Reprinted with the permission of the author.

Annie Dillard, from *An American Childhood* by Annie Dillard. Copyright © 1987 by Annie Dillard. Reprinted with the permission of HarperCollins Publishers, Inc.

Tamara Draut, "What's a Diploma Worth, Anyway?" First posted on <www.AlterNet.org>, September 7, 2006. Reprinted with the permission of the author.

Freeman Dyson, from *Infinite in All Directions* by Freeman Dyson. Copyright © 1988 by Freeman Dyson. Reprinted with the permission of HarperCollins Publishers, Inc.

David Edmonds and John Eidinow, from "Fear and Flight" in *Rousseau's Dog*. Copyright © 2006 by David Edmonds and John Eidinow. Reprinted with the permission of HarperCollins Publishers, Inc., and David Higham Associates, Ltd.

Barbara Ehrenreich, "Guys Just Want to Have Fun." First published in *Time*, July 31, 2006. Copyright © 2006 by Barbara Ehrenreich. Reprinted by permission of International Creative Management, Inc.

Alan Espenlaub, from "Coming of Age under Sputnik: Teenage Male Anxiety and Uncertainty in 1958 America." Reprinted with permission of the author.

Robert Frost, "Putting in the Seed" and "The Road Not Taken" from *The Poetry of Robert Frost*, edited by Edward Connery Lathem. Copyright 1916, 1969 by Henry Holt and Company. Reprinted with the permission of Henry Holt and Company, LLC.

David Gelernter, "Computers Cannot Teach Children Basic Skills" from "Unplugged" in the *New Republic*, September 19 and 25, 1994. Copyright © 1994. Reprinted by permission of the New Republic, LLC.

Nancy Gibbs, "Free the Children." Originally published in *Time*, July 14, 2003: 80. Copyright © 2003 by Time, Inc. Reprinted with permission.

Sarah E. Goers, from "Is Inclusion the Answer?" Reprinted with the permission of the author.

Terry Golway, "A Nation of Idol-Worshipers." First published in *America Magazine* 195.3, July 31, 2006: 9. Copyright © 2006. Reprinted with the permission of American Press, Inc. All rights reserved. For more information, visit <www.americamagazine.org>.

Suzan Shown Harjo. "Last Rites for Indian Dead." First published in the *Los Angeles Times*, September 16, 1989. Copyright © 1989 by Suzan Shown Harjo. Reprinted with the permission of the author.

Harvard Magazine, "Creating Community, Online and Off." First published in *Harvard Magazine*, January–February 2004. Copyright © 2004 by the President and Fellows of Harvard College. Reprinted with the permission of the publisher.

Stephanie Hawkins, from "Japanese: Linguistic Diversity." Reprinted with the permission of the author.

Shirley Jackson, "The Lottery" from *The Lottery and Other Stories* by Shirley Jackson. Copyright © 1948, 1949 by Shirley Jackson. Copyright renewed © 1976, 1977 by Laurence Hyman, Barry Hyman, Mrs. Sarah Webster, and Mrs. Joanne Schnurer. Reprinted with the permission of Farrar, Straus and Giroux, LLC.

Robert Jensen, "The High Cost of Manliness." Originally posted on <www.AlterNet.org>, September 8, 2006. Copyright © 2006 Independent Media Institute. Reprinted with permission. All rights reserved.

Stephen King, "Why We Crave Horror Movies." First published in *Playboy*, 1982. Copyright © by Stephen King. Reprinted with permission. All rights reserved.

Maegan Kinkelaar, "Higher Education: Pricey or Priceless?" Reprinted with the permission of the author.

Jeffrey Kluger, "The New Science of Siblings" from *Time*, July 10, 2006: 47-48. Copyright © 2006 by Time, Inc. Reprinted with permission.

Al Knight, "Perhaps We Should Move to Save Dogs from Their Owners" from the *Denver Post*, November 21, 2006. Reprinted with the permission of the author.

Susan Brady Konig, "They've Got to Be Carefully Taught" from *National Review*, September 15, 1997. Copyright © 1997 by National Review Inc. Reprinted with the permission of *National Review*, 215 Lexington Avenue, New York, NY 10016.

Alex Koppelman, "MySpace or OurSpace?" Posted on <www.Salon.com>, June 8, 2006. An online version remains in the Salon archives. Reprinted with permission.

Dawn Kortz, "Listen." Reprinted with the permission of the author.

William Severini Kowinski, "Kids in the Mall: Growing Up Controlled" from *The Malling of America: An Inside Look at the Great Consumer Paradise* by William Severini Kowinski. Published by New York: William Morrow, 1985. Copyright © 1985 by William Severini Kowinski. Reprinted with the permission of the author.

Ruth La Ferla, "Latino Style Is Cool. Oh, All Right: It's Hot" from the *New York Times*, April 15, 2001. Copyright © 2001 by the New York Times Company. Reprinted with permission.

Melissa Lamberth, "Overworked!" Reprinted with the permission of the author.

Jeffery M. Leving and Glenn Sacks, "Women Don't Want Men? Ha!" from the *Chicago Tribune*, January 21, 2007. Reprinted with the permission of the author.

Steven Levy, from *The Perfect Thing: How the iPod Shuffles Commerce, Culture, and Coolness* by Steven Levy. Copyright © 2006 by Steven Levy. Reprinted with the permission of Simon & Schuster Adult Publishing Group.

Eric Liu, "The Chinatown Idea" from *The Accidental Asian: Notes of a Native Speaker*. Copyright © 1998 by Eric Liu. Reprinted with the permission of Random House, Inc.

Charles C. Mann and Mark L. Plummer, "The Butterfly Problem." First published in the *Atlantic Monthly* 269, No. 1, January 1992. Copyright © 1992 by Charles C. Mann and Mark L. Plummer. Reprinted with the permission of the authors.

Index

Proofreading Symbols

Use these standard proofreading marks when making minor corrections in your final draft. If extensive revision is necessary, type or print out a clean copy.

∾	Transpose (reverse order)
≡	Capitalize
/	Lowercase
#	Add space
⌒	Close up space
ℯ	Delete
⎯	Stet (undo deletion)
∧	Insert
⊙	Insert period
⋏	Insert comma
;/	Insert semicolon
:/	Insert colon
∨	Insert apostrophe
⁇	Insert quotation marks
|=|	Insert hyphen
¶	New paragraph
no ¶	No new paragraph

Correction Symbols

Many instructors use these abbreviations and symbols to mark errors in student papers. Refer to this chart to find out what they mean.

Boldface numbers refer to sections of the handbook and the Quick Editing Guide.

abbr	faulty abbreviation **28**	⌃;	comma **21, C1**
ad	misuse of adverb or adjective **8, A7**	no ,	no comma **21n–r, C1**
agr	faulty agreement **4, 7, A4, A6**	;	semicolon **22**
appr	inappropriate language **9f, 16, 18**	:	colon **23**
awk	awkward	⌄,	apostrophe **24, C2**
cap	capital letter **29, D1**	" "	quotation marks **25, C3**
case	error in case **5, A5**	. ? !	period, question mark, exclamation point **20**
coord	faulty coordination **14a–c**	– ( ) [ ] . . .	dash, parentheses, brackets, ellipses **26–27**
cs	comma splice **2, A2**	par, ¶	new paragraph **D3**
dm	dangling modifier **10c, B1**	pass	ineffective passive **3m**
exact	inexact language **17**	ref	error in pronoun reference **6, A6**
frag	sentence fragment **1, A1**	rep	careless repetition **19**
fs	fused sentence **2, A2**	rev	revise
gl	see Glossary of Troublemakers	run-on	comma splice or fused sentence **2, A2**
gr	grammar **1–9, all of A**	sp	misspelled word **33, D2**
hyph	error in use of hyphen **32**	sub	faulty subordination **14d–f**
inc	incomplete construction **11**	t	error in verb tense **3g–l, 9a–b, A3**
irreg	error in irregular verb **3e–f, A3**	tense	error in verb tense **3g–l, 9a–b, A3**
ital	italics (underlining) **31**	v	voice **3m, 9c**
lc	use lowercase letter **29, D1**	vb	error in verb form **3a–f, A3**
mixed	mixed construction **12**	w	wordy **19**
mm	misplaced modifier **10a–b, B1**	//	faulty parallelism **13, B2**
mood	error in mood **3n–p, 9e**	⌃	insert **D3**
ms	manuscript form **D3**	x	obvious error
nonst	nonstandard usage **16, 17**	#	insert space
num	error in use of numbers **30**	⌣	close up space **D3**
om	omitted word **11**		
p	error in punctuation **20–27, C**		

Selected Features for College Writers

College writers need to develop the ability to read, to think, and to use information in ways that may be new to them. The special tasks of academic writing include

- Responding to a college audience
- Reading critically
- Thinking critically
- Supporting an argument or position
- Incorporating material from outside sources ethically
- Crediting sources correctly

This chart points to key places in *The Bedford Guide* where you can get help with these tasks.

Selected Visuals for Analysis—By Topic/Genre

Directory to MLA Documentation Models

Directory to APA Documentation Models

Index to ESL Guidelines

A Guide to the Handbook